Tolley's Capital Gains Tax

This edition gives the position as at 1 July 2024 for the tax year 2024/25 and covers all legislation, HMRC's published guidance and other relevant sources of information including the provisions of Finance Act 2024 and Finance (No 2) Act 2024.

Tolley's Capital Gains Tax 2024–25

by

Kevin Walton MA

Tolley®

LexisNexis® UK & Worldwide

United Kingdom	RELX (UK) Limited trading as LexisNexis®, 1–3 Strand, London WC2N 5JR
LNUK Global Partners	LexisNexis® encompasses authoritative legal publishing brands dating back to the 19th century including: Butterworths® in the United Kingdom, Canada and the Asia-Pacific region; Les Editions du Juris Classeur® in France; and Matthew Bender® worldwide. Details of LexisNexis® locations worldwide can be found at www.lexisnexis.com

Published by LexisNexis®
This is a Tolley® title

A CIP Catalogue record for this book is available from the British Library.

ISBN for this volume: 9780754559689

Printed and bound by CPI Group (UK) Ltd, Croydon, CR0 4YY

Visit LexisNexis® UK at www.lexisnexis.co.uk

About This Book

The text of this work includes full coverage of Finance Act 2024 and Finance (No 2) Act 2024 and all other relevant material to 1 July 2024 e.g. statutes, statutory instruments, court cases, Tribunal decisions, press releases, concessions, Statements of Practice, HMRC Briefs, and other publications.

We welcome all comments and suggestions for improvement to this work. Any technical queries will be passed on to the author.

Tolley's Capital Gains Tax 2024/25 sets out the position for 2024/25 and the four preceding years, i.e. for 2020/21 to 2023/24, but some references are still required to earlier years.

The approach which has been adopted to statutory references in this work is as follows.

(i) References to current legislation invariably quote the *TCGA 1992* reference in the familiar form, i.e. '*TCGA 1992, s XXX*' to identify a section and '*TCGA 1992, Sch XX*' to identify a Schedule. Where there has been no change in the legislation in the last four years, no statutory reference other than the current legislation is quoted.

(ii) Where the legislation has changed during the last four years, the earlier provisions continue to be described in the text, and the appropriate earlier statutory reference is quoted. Legislation current during those four years but now repealed is similarly dealt with. Where any part of the current legislation was introduced during those four years, the commencement date is quoted.

Contents

Abbreviations and References

Abbreviations

A-G	Attorney-General.
Art	Article.
BES	Business Expansion Scheme.
CA	Court of Appeal.
CAA	Capital Allowances Act.
CCA	Court of Criminal Appeal.
CCAB	Consultative Committee of Accountancy Bodies.
CES	Court of Exchequer (Scotland).
CGT	Capital Gains Tax.
CGTA	Capital Gains Tax Act.
CJEC	Court of Justice of the European Communities.
Ch D	Chancery Division.
CIR	Commissioners of Inland Revenue ('the Board' or 'the Revenue').
CRCA	Commissioners for Revenue and Customs Act.
CTA	Corporation Tax Act.
DC	Divisional Court.
EC	European Community.
ECHR	European Court of Human Rights.
EIS	Enterprise Investment Scheme.
ESC	HMRC Extra-Statutory Concession.
EU	European Union.
Ex D	Exchequer Division (now part of Chancery Division).
FA	Finance Act.
Fam D	Family Division.
FTT	First-tier Tribunal.

HC	House of Commons.
HL	House of Lords.
HMRC	Her Majesty's Revenue and Customs.
I	Ireland.
ICAEW	Institute of Chartered Accountants in England and Wales.
ICTA	Income and Corporation Taxes Act.
IHT	Inheritance Tax.
IHTA	Inheritance Tax Act.
ISA	Individual Savings Account.
ITA	Income Tax Act.
ITEPA	Income Tax (Earnings and Pensions) Act.
ITTOIA	Income Tax (Trading and Other Income) Act.
KB	King's Bench Division.
LLP	Limited Liability Partnership.
LLPA	Limited Liability Partnership Act.
NI	Northern Ireland.
OEIC	Open-ended Investment Company
PC	Privy Council.
PDA	Probate, Divorce and Admiralty Division (now Family Division).
QB	Queen's Bench Division.
QIS	Qualified Investor Scheme
R	Regina or Rex (i.e. The Crown).
Reg	Regulation.
RPI	Retail Prices Index.
s	Section.
SC	Supreme Court.
SC(I)	Supreme Court (Ireland).
SCS	Scottish Court of Session.
Sch	Schedule.
SE	*Societas Europaea* (European Company)
SI	Statutory Instrument.
SP	HMRC Statement of Practice.

Sp C	Special Commissioners.
TCEA	Tribunals, Courts and Enforcement Act.
TCGA	Taxation of Chargeable Gains Act.
TIOPA	Taxation (International and Other Provisions) Act.
TMA	Taxes Management Act.
UT	Upper Tribunal.

References

(*denotes a series accredited for citation in court).

All ER	*All England Law Reports (LexisNexis).
All ER(D)	All England Reporter Direct (LexisNexis).
AC	*Law Reports, Appeal Cases (Incorporated Council of Law Reporting for England and Wales).
ATC	*Annotated Tax Cases (publication discontinued).
Ch	*Law Reports, Chancery Division.
CMLR	Common Market Law Reports.
Ex D	Law Reports, Exchequer Division (1875–1880; see also below).
Fam D	*Law Reports, Family Division.
KB	*Law Reports, King's Bench Division (1900–1952).
IR	*Irish Reports (Incorporated Council of Law Reporting for Ireland).
ITC	*Irish Tax Cases.
LR Ex	*Law Reports, Exchequer Division (1865–1875; see also above).
NILR	Northern Ireland Law Reports.
QB	*Law Reports, Queen's Bench Division (1891–1901 and 1952 onwards).
QBD	Law Reports, Queen's Bench Division (1875–1890).
SFTD	*Simon's First-tier Tax Decisions (LexisNexis).
SLT	Scots Law Times.
Sp C	Special Commissioner's Decisions.

SSCD	Simon's Tax Cases—Special Commissioners' Decisions (LexisNexis).
STC	*Simon's Tax Cases (LexisNexis).
SWTI	Simon's Weekly Tax Intelligence (LexisNexis).
TC	*Official Reports of Tax Cases.
TR	Taxation Reports (publication discontinued).
WLR	*Weekly Law Reports (Incorporated Council of Law Reporting).

The first number in the citation refers to the volume, and the second to the page, so that [1978] 2 WLR 10 means that the report is to be found on page ten of the second volume of the Weekly Law Reports for 1978. Where no volume number is given, only one volume was produced in that year. Some series have continuous volume numbers.

Where legal decisions are very recent and in the lower courts, it must be remembered that they may be reversed on appeal. However, references to the official Tax Cases ('*TC*'), and to the Appeal Cases ('*AC*') may be taken as final.

In English cases, Scottish and Northern Irish decisions (unless there is a difference of law between the countries) are generally followed but are not binding, and Republic of Ireland decisions are considered (and vice versa).

1

Introduction to Capital Gains Tax

Basic principles of capital gains tax

[1.1] Capital gains tax is charged on chargeable gains made by individuals, personal representatives and trustees on the disposal of ASSETS (7.2). The tax is chargeable on the total gains on disposals in a 'tax year', after deductions, including LOSSES (38) and the annual exempt amount (see **2** ANNUAL RATES AND EXEMPTIONS). Every gain is a chargeable gain unless expressly excluded (see **23** EXEMPTIONS AND RELIEFS). For this purpose, a '*tax year*', otherwise known as a '*year of assessment*', is a year ending on 5 April. Thus, '2024/25' indicates the tax year ending on 5 April 2025 (and so on). [*TCGA 1992, s 288(1)(1ZA)*].

Companies and other corporate bodies within the scope of corporation tax do not pay capital gains tax as such but instead are chargeable to corporation tax on their chargeable gains. The computation of their gains is now significantly different from the computation principles applying for capital gains tax (see **14.2** COMPANIES). Companies pay corporation tax by reference to accounting periods rather than tax years.

For both capital gains tax and corporation tax purposes, a gain is computed by reference to the excess of the disposal consideration over the acquisition consideration, received and given, for an asset. In certain circumstances, the legislation deems a disposal or acquisition to take place where there is no actual disposal or acquisition. Certain types of expenditures are deductible in computing the gain. See **16** COMPUTATION OF GAINS AND LOSSES. For allowable expenditure incurred before December 2017, companies are given an allowance, known as the indexation allowance (see **32** INDEXATION), which for each gain adjusts for the effects of inflation. Indexation allowance is frozen at its December 2017 level. For CGT purposes, gains on certain business disposals may, subject to a lifetime limit, qualify for BUSINESS ASSET DISPOSAL RELIEF (**9**). Similarly, gains on certain disposals by individuals of shares in unlisted trading companies may, subject to a lifetime limit, qualify for INVESTORS' RELIEF (**34**). Business asset disposal relief and investors' relief do not apply for the purposes of corporation tax on chargeable gains.

Capital gains tax (CGT) was introduced by *FA 1965* and commenced on 6 April 1965. The legislation was consolidated by *CGTA 1979* and subsequently by *TCGA 1992*. Assets acquired before 7 April 1965 are within the charge if they are disposed of on or after that date, but there are special provisions dealing with the computation of gains on the disposal of such assets (see **8** ASSETS HELD ON 6 APRIL **1965**). *FA 1988* replaced the 1965 base date with 31 March 1982, subject to the detailed provisions of ASSETS HELD ON 31 MARCH **1982** (**8**). For CGT purposes, re-basing to 31 March 1982 applies to all assets held on that date without exception. Exceptions continue to apply for corporation tax purposes.

Both CGT and corporation tax are administered and paid under SELF-ASSESSMENT (**55**). A special compliance regime applies for CGT to all direct disposals of UK land where a residential property gain arises. A UK land disposal return must be made together with a payment on account of CGT on or before the 30th day following the day of the completion of the disposal. See **45.3** PAYMENT OF TAX and **52.22** RETURNS.

For individuals, gains are treated as if they were the top slice of the taxpayer's income. To the extent that gains fall within the basic rate band, they are taxable at 10% unless the gains are on disposals of residential property or carried interest, in which case, they are taxable at 18%. Where they exceed the basic rate band limit, gains are taxable at 20% or, for gains on disposals of residential property, 24%, or gains on carried interest, 28%. Trustees of settlements and personal representatives are chargeable to CGT at 20% or, for gains on disposals of residential property, 24% or for gains on carried interest, 28%. For 2023/24 and earlier years, the higher residential property gain rate is 28%. See **2** ANNUAL RATES AND EXEMPTIONS. For companies, chargeable gains form part of the taxable total profits and are accordingly taxable at the appropriate corporation tax rate. See **14** COMPANIES.

The charge to tax

[1.2] Subject to exceptions and special provisions, a person is chargeable to capital gains tax in respect of chargeable gains accruing to them in a tax year if they are resident in the UK during any part of the tax year. The charge applies to gains on assets situated both in the UK and overseas. In the case of personal representatives of a deceased person, the person in question is the deemed single and continuing body in **18.9** DEATH. In the case of the trustees of a settlement, the person in question is the deemed single person in **42.1** OFFSHORE SETTLEMENTS.

A person who is not resident in the UK during any part of a tax year is also chargeable to capital gains tax but only in respect of chargeable gains accruing in that year on the disposal of:

(i) UK-situated assets with a connection to the person's UK branch or agency (see **43.3** OVERSEAS MATTERS);
(ii) interests in UK land (see **35.23** LAND); and
(iii) assets deriving at least 75% of their value from UK land where the person has a substantial indirect interest in that land (see **35.24** LAND).

If the tax year is a split year for an individual under the statutory residence test (see **51.17** RESIDENCE AND DOMICILE), gains accruing in the overseas part of the year are only chargeable to capital gains tax if the assets disposed of are within (i)–(iii) above. This rule is subject to the charge on temporary non-residents (see **43.5** OVERSEAS MATTERS).

[*TCGA 1992, ss 1(1), 1A, 1G(2)*].

Companies are not chargeable to capital gains tax, but instead are chargeable to corporation tax in respect of their chargeable gains. [*TCGA 1992, s 1(2); FA 2019, Sch 1 para* 2]. UK-resident companies are chargeable to corporation tax on gains on assets situated in the UK or overseas. Non-resident companies are chargeable to corporation tax only on chargeable gains on the disposal of:

(a) UK-situated assets with a connection to the company's UK permanent establishment (see **43.3** OVERSEAS MATTERS);
(b) interests in UK land (see **35.23** LAND); and
(c) assets deriving at least 75% of their value from UK land where the company has a substantial indirect interest in that land (see **35.24** LAND).

[*TCGA 1992, s* 2].

See **14** COMPANIES and **51.28** RESIDENCE AND DOMICILE.

Special rules apply to persons not resident or individuals not domiciled in the UK, to temporary visitors to the UK and to persons becoming temporarily non-UK resident. See **43** OVERSEAS MATTERS, **44** PARTNERSHIPS, **49** REMITTANCE BASIS and **51** RESIDENCE AND DOMICILE.

Married persons and civil partners are taxed independently. Transfers between spouses or civil partners living together or in the process of separating are made on a 'no gain, no loss' basis. See **40** MARRIED PERSONS AND CIVIL PARTNERS.

Persons may be assessed in a representative capacity. See **6** ASSESSMENTS, **18** DEATH, **55** SELF-ASSESSMENT and **56** SETTLEMENTS.

There are special rules for UK resident shareholders of certain overseas resident companies. See **43.7** OVERSEAS MATTERS. See **42** OFFSHORE SETTLEMENTS for the provisions applying to trustees, settlors and beneficiaries of settlements which are or become overseas resident.

For unit and investment trusts, real estate investment trusts, open-ended investment companies and qualifying investor schemes, see **63** UNIT TRUSTS AND OTHER INVESTMENT VEHICLES. For venture capital trusts, see **64.6** VENTURE CAPITAL TRUSTS.

Brexit

[1.3] The UK left the European Union on 31 January 2020. An 11-month implementation period (or 'transition period') applied up to 31 December 2020 during which the UK continued to be subject to current EU laws, remaining a member of the Single Market and Customs Union.

On 24 December 2020, the European Commission and UK Government announced an agreement in principle on the legal terms of the future EU-UK relationship – the EU-UK Trade and Cooperation Agreement (TCA). The TCA was signed by UK and EU leaders and then approved by the UK Parliament on 30 December 2020 and applied provisionally until full ratification by the European Parliament with effect from 1 May 2021. The UK has enacted the *EU (Future Relationship) Act 2020*, which makes provision to implement the TCA in the UK.

The majority of key domestic tax changes associated with Brexit take effect from the end of the implementation period (specifically, 11pm (GMT) on 31 December 2020, referred to as 'IP completion day'), including the full repeal of the *European Communities Act 1972*, incorporation of retained EU law (see below) into the UK domestic legal regime, and the commencement of associated Brexit legislation and statutory instruments.

Retained EU law is a collective term given to the body of EU-derived laws preserved and converted into domestic UK law at IP completion day, when the repeal of the *European Communities Act 1972* took effect. As with other domestic law, it can be amended or repealed in the future. EU law that was not retained ceased to apply in relation to the UK following the end of the transition period. The initial post-Brexit application of EU law in the UK was further amended from 1 January 2024, as a result of the *Retained EU Law (Revocation and Reform) Act 2023*. In addition to revoking 587 pieces of EU-derived legislation, the Act abolished the supremacy of EU law and made clear that no general principle of EU law is part of domestic law. With effect from 1 January 2024, retained EU law is renamed as 'assimilated law'.

Before 1 January 2024, retained EU law fell into three categories:

(1) EU-derived domestic legislation – ie UK legislation which was enacted to give effect to EU legislation – for example, the mergers legislation (*TCGA 1992, s 140* onwards) which was introduced to implement the Mergers Directive. 130 items of secondary legislation are revoked with effect from 1 January 2024. Remaining EU-derived domestic legislation is assimilated law and continues to have effect in the UK from 1 January 2024;

(2) direct EU legislation – ie English language versions of EU regulations, EU decisions and EU tertiary legislation. 457 items of direct EU legislation are revoked with effect from 1 January 2024. Remaining direct EU legislation is assimilated law and continues to have effect in the UK from 1 January 2024. From that date, it must be read and given effect in a way which is compatible with UK legislation and is subject to UK legislation so far as it is compatible with it; and

(3) other rights, powers, etc. – these can include rights arising under Directives, but only if they are of a kind recognised by the Court of Justice in a case decided before IP completion day or by a UK court or tribunal in a case begun before IP completion day. This category is abolished with effect from 1 January 2024 and the rights, powers, etc. are not included in assimilated law (but they are mostly retained for VAT purposes).

[*EU(W)A 2018, ss 2, 3, 4; Retained EU Law (Revocation and Reform) Act 2023, s 2*].

Judgments of the CJEU made before IP completion day are binding on the First-tier Tribunal, the Upper Tribunal and the High Court, in relation to disputes about the validity, meaning or effect of retained EU law. There is an exception if the law has been modified since IP completion day and it would be inconsistent with the intention of the modifications for the court or tribunal to follow the EU judgment. The Supreme Court, and the UK's higher appeal courts including the Court of Appeal in England and Wales, the Court of Appeal in Northern Ireland and the Inner House of the Court of Session (in Scotland) are not bound by any judgments of the CJEU, whether made before or after IP completion day.

In deciding whether to depart from a pre-IP completion day EU judgment, these courts were initially required to apply the same test as the Supreme Court applies in deciding whether to depart from its own case law, namely, whether it appears right to do so. However, from 1 October 2024, the court is required to have regard to (amongst other things):

- the fact that decisions of a foreign court are not (unless otherwise provided) binding;
- any changes of circumstances which are relevant to the assimilated case law; and
- the extent to which the assimilated case law restricts the proper development of domestic law.

From 1 January 2024, lower courts and tribunals may also, at their discretion, refer a point of retained case law by which it is bound to a higher court to decide.

Judgments of the EU Court of Justice made after IP completion day are not binding on UK tribunals or courts, but they may 'have regard' to those judgments if they are relevant to the matter being litigated.

[*EU(W)A 2018, s 6; Retained EU Law (Revocation and Reform) Act 2023, s 6; SI 2020 No 1525; SI 2024 No 714*].

Key points on the charge to capital gains tax

[1.4] The simplest tax planning ideas can be very effective. Whenever advising on capital gains tax consider whether a potential gain can be:

- split over two tax years to utilise two annual exempt amounts/the remainder of the basic rate band;
- delayed in whole or part until after 6 April/next accounting period to provide a cash flow advantage in terms of payment of tax;
- split between spouses or civil partners to utilise two annual exempt amounts and the remainder of basic rate bands;
- offset by capital losses brought forward; always ask new clients and old accountants about any brought forward capital losses as they are often missed;
- offset by current year capital losses; consider any potential unrealised losses including assets held by any spouse, civil partner or connected companies;
- offset by any trade tax losses;
- made to qualify for business asset disposal relief, investors' relief or substantial shareholdings exemption;
- made to qualify in whole or part for deferral by reinvestment;

- potentially qualify for any other capital gains deduction or relief such as private residence relief, EIS, SEIS and double tax relief.

Other tax planning can centre on whether 'income' can be converted to a capital gain (taxable at 0%, 10%, 18%, 20%, 24% or 28%). For example, profits are rolled up in a limited company until the end of a venture, when the company is sold or wound up realising a capital gain. Assuming the gain qualifies for business asset disposal relief, it will be taxed at 10% up to the lifetime limit compared to profits being extracted via dividends liable to higher rates of income tax.

2

Annual Rates and Exemptions

Rates of tax

Rates of CGT for individuals

[2.1] For disposals on or after 6 April 2024, there are five rates of capital gains tax which may apply to gains: 10%, 18%, 20%, 24% and 28%. Previously, there were only four rates: 10%, 18%, 20% and 28%.

Where gains qualify for business asset disposal relief or investors' relief and a claim is made for relief, the rate of tax is **10%**. See **9.12** BUSINESS ASSET DISPOSAL RELIEF and **34.2** INVESTORS' RELIEF. In other cases, the rate depends on the type of asset disposed of and on the level of the individual's taxable income for the year. The applicable rates of tax are summarised in the table below:

	2024/25 onwards	**2023/24 and earlier**
Residential property gains		
– within unused part of the basic rate band	18%	18%
– otherwise	24%	28%
Carried interest gains		
– within unused part of the basic rate band	18%	18%
– otherwise	28%	28%
Gains to which business asset disposal relief applies	10%	10%
Gains to which investors' relief applies	10%	10%
All other chargeable gains		
– within unused part of the basic rate band	10%	10%

	2024/25 onwards	2023/24 and earlier
– otherwise	20%	20%

See below for the meaning of 'residential property gains'. '*Carried interest gains*' are:

- gains accruing under *TCGA 1992, s 103KA(2)(3)* (carried interest – see **44.19** PARTNERSHIPS);
- gains accruing to an individual as a result of carried interest arising to them where they perform investment management services directly or indirectly in respect of an investment scheme under arrangements not involving a partnership and the carried interest arises under the arrangements and does not constitute a 'co-investment' repayment or return (see **44.19** PARTNERSHIPS); and
- gains arising on deemed carried interest under an election for the accruals basis (see **44.20** PARTNERSHIPS).

The unused part of the basic rate band

An individual's '*unused part of the basic rate band*' is the amount by which the income tax basic rate limit (£37,700 for 2024/25) exceeds the taxable income for the year. The taxable income is defined for this purpose as the '*Step 3 income*', i.e. the net income less allowances deducted at Step 3 of the calculation in *ITA 2007, s 23* (calculation of income tax liability).

The basic rate limit for earlier years was as follows:

2023/24	£37,700
2022/23	£37,700
2021/22	£37,700
2020/21	£37,500

The basic rate limit is to remain at £37,700 for all years up to and including 2027/28.

An individual's taxable income for a tax year exceeds the basic rate limit if part of their income is taxable at the higher rate, default higher rate, savings higher rate or dividend upper rate – but see below for application to Scottish and Welsh taxpayers.

Residential property gains and carried interest gains only

The following applies for 2024/25 onwards, where the taxpayer's gains for the tax year consist entirely of residential property gains and/or carried interest gains or entirely of such gains and gains to which business asset disposal relief or investors' relief applies. Where the taxpayer's taxable income exceeds the basic rate limit, the rate of capital gains tax on the residential property gains is 24% and that on carried interest gains is 28%. In other cases, the rate is 18% on any part of the gains that does not exceed the unused part of the basic rate band for the year, and the 24% or 28% rates apply to any excess. The unused part of the basic rate band is set first against gains which are charged to tax at 10% as a result of a business asset disposal relief or investors' relief claim.

If the taxpayer has both residential property gains and carried interest gains, they may choose which gains are to be allocated to the unused part of the basic rate band (and therefore charged at the 18% rate), but only after allocating any gains charged to tax at 10% as a result of a business asset disposal relief or investors' relief claim. It will be most beneficial to allocate carried interest gains, giving an effective tax rate reduction of 10% as opposed to a 6% reduction for residential property gains.

For 2023/24 and earlier years, the rate of capital gains tax on residential property gains is 28% or 18% where the gain falls within the unused part of the basic rate band, and the above rules apply accordingly.

Other gains only

The following applies where the taxpayer's gains for the tax year consist entirely of gains other than residential property or carried interest gains or entirely of such gains and gains to which business asset disposal relief or investors' relief applies. Where the taxpayer's taxable income exceeds the basic rate limit, the rate of capital gains tax is 20%. In other cases, the rate is 10% on any part of the gains that does not exceed the unused part of the basic rate band for the year, and the 20% rate applies to any excess. The unused part of the basic rate band is set first against gains which are charged to tax at 10% as a result of a business asset disposal relief or investors' relief claim.

Residential property and carried interest gains and other gains accrued in same tax year

For 2024/25 onwards, where an individual makes residential property gains and/or carried interest gains and other gains in the same tax year and their taxable income exceeds the basic rate limit, the rate of tax is 24%, 28% or 20% as appropriate. In other cases, the rate is 18% or 10% on any part of the gains that does not exceed the unused part of the basic rate band for the year, and the 28%, 24% or 20% rates apply to any excess. The taxpayer may choose which gains are to be allocated to the unused part of the basic rate band (and therefore charged at the 10% or 18% rates), but only after allocating any gains charged to tax at 10% as a result of a business asset disposal relief or investors' relief claim. It will be most beneficial to allocate carried interest gains or other gains, giving an effective tax rate reduction of 10% as opposed to a 6% reduction for residential property gains.

For 2023/24 and earlier years, the rate of capital gains tax on residential property gains is 28% or 18% where the gain falls within the unused part of the basic rate band, and the above rules apply accordingly.

[*TCGA 1992, ss 1H(1)–(4)(9)–(11), 1I, 1J(1)(7); FA 2023, s 5(2); F(No 2)A 2023, s 42(3); F(No 2)A 2024, s 6*].

Devolution of income tax

For the purposes of the above provisions, an individual who is a Scottish taxpayer is treated as if they were not a Scottish taxpayer, i.e. the basic rate band for the rest of the UK (£37,700 for 2024/25) is used above when calculating capital gains tax and *not* the Scottish rate bands. This means, for example, that a Scottish taxpayer paying Scottish higher rate income tax on their non-savings income exceeding the Scottish intermediate rate band could still pay some capital gains tax at lower rates if they were within the basic rate band for the rest of the UK. See Tolley's Income Tax for details of the devolution of income tax. [*TCGA 1992, ss 1J(6), 4(10)(11)*].

Similarly, an individual who is a Welsh taxpayer is treated as if they were not a Welsh taxpayer. [*TCGA 1992, s 1J(6)*].

Special cases

Where:

(a) under *ITTOIA 2005, s 539* (gains from contracts for life insurance etc.), a person is entitled to relief by reference to the amount of a deficiency, or

(b) under *ITTOIA 2005, s 669(1)(2)* (reduction in residuary income: inheritance tax on accrued income) the residuary income of an estate is treated as reduced so as to reduce a person's income by any amount for the purposes of extra liability,

the person's Step 3 income for the year is treated (for the purpose only of computing the unused part of the basic rate band) as reduced by the amount of the deficiency or, as the case may be, the amount in (b) above. The Step 3 income cannot be reduced below zero (*Scott v HMRC* CA, [2020] STC 353).

Where under *ITTOIA 2005, s 465* (gains from contracts for life insurance etc.) a person's total income for the year is deemed to include any amount(s):

(i) in determining the unused part of the basic rate band, their Step 3 income is treated as including not the whole of the amount(s) concerned but only the annual equivalent within the meaning of *ITTOIA 2005, s 536(1)* or (as the case may be) the total annual equivalent within the meaning of *ITTOIA 2005, s 537*, and

(ii) if relief is given under *ITTOIA 2005, s 535* and the calculation under *s 536(1)* or *s 537* does not involve the higher rate of income tax, the capital gains tax rate is determined as if the person's taxable income does not exceed the basic rate limit as described above.

[*TCGA 1992, s 1J(2)–(5)(7)(8)*].

Deduction of losses and annual exempt amount

Losses may be used in the most beneficial way, and so may be deducted from a gain irrespective of the rate of tax which would otherwise apply. They can only be deducted from a gain so far as necessary to eliminate the gain. The taxpayer can also deduct the annual exempt amount (see **2.5** below) in the most beneficial way. This latter rule is, however, subject to any provision limiting the way in which losses can be deducted (for example, where a loss is made on a disposal to a connected person – see **38.7** LOSSES).

It will be most beneficial to set losses and the annual exempt amount against gains chargeable at 28% before those chargeable at 24%, against those chargeable at 24% before those chargeable at 20% and so on.

[*TCGA 1992, ss 1F(1)–(3), 1K(5)*].

Residential property gain

A '*residential property gain*' is so much of a chargeable gain on a 'disposal of residential property' as is attributable to that property. The proportion so attributable is equal to the number of days in the 'applicable period' on which the land consists of or includes a 'dwelling' divided by the total number of days in the applicable period. If there has been 'mixed use' of the land on one or more of the days in the applicable period, the proportion must be adjusted, on a just and reasonable basis, to take account of the mixed use.

The '*applicable period*' is the period beginning with the day on which the interest in land being disposed of was acquired (or 31 March 1982 if later) and ending the day before the day of the disposal. If the interest disposed of is in UK land and the person making the disposal is not UK-resident (or the disposal is made in the overseas part of a tax year which is split under the statutory residence test), the applicable period begins on 6 April 2015 if that date is later than the date on which the interest was acquired. There is 'mixed use' of land on any day on which it consists of both one or more dwellings and other land.

If the disposal is of an interest in land which subsists under a contract for an off-plan purchase, i.e. a contract for acquisition of land consisting of, or including, a building or part of a building that is to be constructed or adapted as a dwelling, the land is treated as consisting of, or including, a dwelling throughout the applicable period. Where the interest disposed of results from interests which have been acquired at different times, the date of acquisition of the first interest is taken as the date on which all the interests were acquired.

There is a '*disposal of residential property*' on a disposal of an 'interest in land' if the land consisted of or included a dwelling at any time in the applicable period; if the interest in land subsisted for the benefit of land consisting of or including a dwelling at any time in the applicable period or if the interest subsisted under a contract for an off-plan purchase. The grant of an option (defined as at 7.7 ASSETS) binding the grantor to sell an interest in land is treated for these purposes as the disposal of an interest in land.

An '*interest in land*' is an estate, interest, right or power in or over land, or the benefit of an obligation, restriction or condition affecting the value of such, but not including:

- any interest or right (other than a rentcharge or, in Scotland, a feu duty) held to secure payment of money or performance of any other obligation; or
- a licence to use or occupy land;
- in England, Wales or Northern Ireland, a tenancy at will or an advowson, franchise (i.e. a grant from the Crown, such as the right to hold a market or fair, or the right to take tolls) or manor; or
- any other interest or right specified in Treasury regulations.

In the case of non-UK land, the domestic legal concepts mentioned above must be read so as to produce the result most closely corresponding with that produced in relation to UK land.

A '*dwelling*' is a building (including a part of a building) which is used or suitable for use as a dwelling or is in the process of being constructed or adapted for such use. It includes gardens and grounds (and any building or structure in a garden or grounds). The following are excluded from being a dwelling:

- school residential accommodation;
- residential accommodation for members of the armed forces;
- homes or institutions providing residential accommodation for children;
- homes or institutions providing residential accommodation with personal care for the elderly, the disabled, persons with drug or alcohol dependency or a mental disorder;
- hospitals and hospices;
- prisons and similar establishments;
- hotels, inns and similar establishments;
- any other institution which is the sole or main residence of its residents; and
- buildings occupied by students managed or controlled by their educational establishments (within *Housing Act 2004, Sch 14 para 4* or corresponding Scottish or NI provision).

In addition, a building which includes at least 15 bedrooms, is purpose-built or converted for occupation by students other than school pupils and is occupied by them for at least 165 days in a tax year is not a dwelling for that year.

Buildings which become temporarily unsuitable for use as a dwelling are generally treated as continuing to be such, but there are some exceptions. A building is not considered suitable for use as a dwelling if the temporary unsuitability resulted from damage to the building which was accidental, or otherwise outside the control of the person making the disposal and the period of temporary unsuitability was at least 90 days (whether or not within the applicable period but ending before the disposal). If this is the case, any work done within that period is not treated as construction or adaptation of the building for use as a dwelling. Any damage occurring during alterations to, or partial demolition of, a building which involved, or could be expected to involve, the building being unsuitable for use as a dwelling for at least 30 days is not considered accidental or otherwise outside the control of the person making the disposal for these purposes.

A building which has been demolished either to ground level or, in accordance with planning permission or development consent, to a single facade (double if on a corner) is regarded as having ceased to exist. Where a person disposes of an interest in land which contains or contained a building which has been suitable for use as a dwelling and that building has undergone works which result in it ceasing to exist or becoming unsuitable as a dwelling before the 'completion' of disposal then the building is treated as being unsuitable as a dwelling throughout the period when the works were in progress, and any period ending immediately before that during which the building was, for reasons connected with the works, not used as a dwelling. This rule applies only if the works are '*qualifying works*', i.e. where any planning permission or development consent required for the works or any change or use with which they are associated has been granted (even if retrospectively after completion of the disposal) and the works were carried out in accordance with it. If, at any time when qualifying works were in progress, the building was undergoing any other work for which planning permission or development consent was required but not granted (unless given subsequently), or it was contravened, the building is not treated as being unsuitable as a dwelling during that time. If works are not qualifying works at the completion of the disposal, they do not affect the building's suitability as a dwelling at any time before the disposal.

'*Completion*' occurs either at the time of disposal or, where the contract is completed by conveyance, transfer or other instrument, when the instrument takes effect.

The Treasury may by regulations amend the definition of 'dwelling'.

[*TCGA 1992, Sch 1B*].

Example 1

Erica owns an established business and has taxable profits of £42,270 for her accounting year ended 5 April 2025. She has no other income for 2024/25 but she makes a chargeable gain (before deduction of the annual exempt amount) of £30,000. The gain is not a residential property or carried interest gain and does not qualify for business asset disposal relief. Her capital gains tax liability for 2024/25 is computed as follows:

		£
Trade profits		42,270
Deduct Personal allowance		12,570
Step 3 income		£29,700
Unused part of the basic rate band (£37,700 – £29,700)		£8,000
Chargeable gain		30,000
Deduct Annual exempt amount (see **2.5** below)		3,000
Taxable gain		£27,000
£		
8,000	@ 10%	800
19,000	@ 20%	3,800
£27,000		£4,600

Example 2

Felix owns an established business and has taxable profits of £42,500 for his accounting year ended 5 April 2025. He has no other income for 2024/25 but he makes two chargeable gains (before deducting the annual exempt amount) of £17,000 each. Neither gain is a residential property or carried interest gain, but one of them qualifies for business asset disposal relief. His capital gains tax liability for 2024/25 is computed as follows:

Disposal qualifying for business asset disposal relief

	£
Capital gains tax £17,000 × 10%	£1,700

Disposal not qualifying for business asset disposal relief	
Chargeable gain	17,000
Deduct Annual exempt amount (see **2.5** below)	3,000
Taxable gain	£14,000
Capital gains tax £14,000 × 20%	£2,800
Total capital gains tax for 2024/25 (£1,700 + £2,800)	£4,500

Notes to the example

(a) Gains qualifying for business asset disposal relief are treated as the lowest part of the gains for the year. The unused part of the basic rate band (£7,770) is set against the gain qualifying for business asset disposal relief even though it does not affect the rate of tax for that gain. The whole of the gain not qualifying for business asset disposal relief is therefore chargeable to tax at 20%.

(b) It is assumed that Felix sets his annual exempt amount against the gain chargeable at 20% as this achieves the greater tax saving.

Example 3

Marley owns an established business and has taxable profits of £42,770 for her accounting year ended 5 April 2025. She has no other income for 2024/25 but she makes two chargeable gains (before deducting the annual exempt amount) of £17,000 each. Neither gain qualifies for business asset disposal relief, but one of them is a residential property gain. Her capital gains tax liability for 2024/25 is computed as follows:

	£
Trade profits	42,770
Deduct Personal allowance	12,570
Step 3 income	£30,200
Unused part of the basic rate band (£37,700 – £30,200)	£7,500

Standard rate gain

£		£
7,500	@ 10%	750
9,500	@ 20%	1,900
£17,000		£2,650

Residential property gain	
Chargeable gain	17,000
Deduct Annual exempt amount (see **2.5** below)	3,000
Taxable gain	£14,000
Capital gains tax £14,000 × 24%	£3,360

Total capital gains tax for 2024/25 (£2,650 + £3,360)	£6,010

Notes to the example

(a) The taxpayer can choose to set the unused part of the basic rate band (£7,500) against either the residential property gain or the other gain. It is most beneficial to set it against the standard rate gain as there is a 10% reduction in the rate of CGT applicable to the gain falling within the unused part of the band, as opposed to a 6% reduction if the residential property gain were set against the unused part.

(b) It is assumed that Marley sets her annual exempt amount against the gain chargeable at 24% as this achieves the greater tax saving.

Rate of CGT for personal representatives

[2.2] Rates of tax are as shown in the table. [*TCGA 1992, ss 1H(5)(6), 4(3)*].

	2024/25 onwards	2023/24 and earlier
Residential property gains	24%	28%
Carried interest gains	28%	28%
All other chargeable gains	20%	20%

Where it is necessary to determine from which chargeable gains a loss may be deducted or which losses are to be deducted from a chargeable gain, the losses may be used in the most beneficial way. [*TCGA 1992, ss 1F(1), 4B*].

Rate of CGT for settlements

[2.3] See SETTLEMENTS (56.7).

Rate of tax on capital gains for companies

[2.4] Companies and other corporate bodies within the charge to corporation tax do not pay capital gains tax as such. Instead they are chargeable to corporation tax on their chargeable gains. The whole of a company's gains for an accounting period (net of allowable losses) are included in the profits chargeable to corporation tax.

Annual exempt amount

[2.5] For 2024/25, an individual who has chargeable gains for the year can deduct the annual exempt amount of £3,000 from those gains (but no further than is needed to reduce them to nil). (The annual exempt amount is sometimes referred to as the 'annual exemption'.)

The annual exempt amount for earlier years was as follows:

2023/24	£6,000
2022/23	£12,300
2021/22	£12,300
2020/21	£12,300

The annual exempt amount is deducted after deducting allowable losses of the same tax year, but before deducting any allowable losses brought forward from previous tax years or carried back from the tax year of death (see **18.7** DEATH). The taxpayer can deduct the annual exempt amount in the most beneficial way.

An individual who makes a claim under *ITA 2007, s 809B* for the remittance basis to apply for a tax year (see **49.2** REMITTANCE BASIS) is not entitled to the annual exempt amount for that year. The annual exempt amount cannot be deducted from foreign gains arising in one year and chargeable in a later tax year in which they are remitted to the UK.

The annual exempt amount is also available to personal representatives for the year of death and the following two tax years (see **18.9** DEATH).

[*TCGA 1992, ss 1K, 1L; FA 2021, s 40; FA 2023, s 8; SI 2020 No 333*].

Examples

For 2024/25, Pablo, who is resident in the UK, has chargeable gains of £14,500 and allowable losses of £1,200. He also has allowable losses of £17,000 brought forward.

	£
Net gains (£14,500 – £1,200)	13,300
Annual exempt amount	3,000
	10,300
Losses brought forward (part)	10,300
Taxable gains	Nil
Losses brought forward	17,000
Less utilised in 2024/25	10,300
Losses carried forward	£6,700

For 2024/25, Maria (who is also UK-resident) has the same gains and losses (including brought-forward losses) as Pablo above, but is also a beneficiary of an offshore trust. Trust gains of £12,600 are attributed to her for 2024/25 under *TCGA 1992, s 87*.

	£
Gains (£14,500 + £12,600)	27,100
Deduct current year loss	1,200
	25,900
Deduct Annual exempt amount	(3,000)

	£
	22,900
Deduct Losses brought forward (part)	(13,300)
Taxable gains*	£9,600
Losses brought forward	17,000
Less utilised in 2023/24	13,300
Losses carried forward	£3,700

* Attributed gains cannot be covered by personal losses. The annual exempt amount is therefore allocated to attributed gains in priority to personal gains as this results in the greatest reduction in taxable gains. £6,600 (£12,600 – £6,000) of the attributed gains remain taxable.

Key points on annual rates and exemptions

[2.6] Points to consider are as follows:

- At its lowest level, the annual exempt amount for 2024/25 is worth £300 (3,000 × 10%); at its highest, it is worth £840 (3,000 × 28%). Significant tax planning has revolved around trying to crystallise gains that will be covered by this relief (or multiple annual exempt amounts) and it is such planning that has triggered the government to lower the exempt amount significantly, with a further reduction to £3,000. These reductions obviously affect the benefits to be obtained from such planning, but some potential savings remain. For example, the overall tax rate may be reduced where a gain can be split between spouses or civil partners or over two tax years. Also, popular is partially breaking the terms for a relief, so a small gain arises (covered by the exemption) whilst the majority of the gain is rolled/held over. For example, adjust the consideration for the transfer such that a gain arises equal to the amount of the annual exempt amount. No tax is payable on the cash proceeds whilst the base cost is increased, reducing the potential gain on a future disposal.
- Business asset disposal relief and investors' relief reduce the rate of capital gains tax to 10% for gains on qualifying disposals of business assets. See **9** BUSINESS ASSET DISPOSAL RELIEF and **34** INVESTORS' RELIEF.
- Taxpayers can choose how the annual exempt amount and any allowable losses are allocated against gains. It is normally beneficial to offset these amounts against the gains taxable at the highest rates.
- A taxpayer's basic rate band is extended by qualifying pension contributions and gift aid donations (gross amounts). Certain gift aid donations can be carried back.

- If a taxpayer does not use the annual exempt amount for a tax year, it is wasted: the amount cannot be carried forward or transferred to a spouse or civil partner. Consideration should therefore be given to realising sufficient gains to maximise use of the exemption.
- Spouses and civil partners may consider transferring an asset to the other spouse or partner before disposal in order to benefit from a lower rate of capital gains tax or to utilise their annual exempt amount. However, care is required where the asset potentially qualifies for business asset disposal relief or investors' relief: will the other party also qualify?
- An individual who claims the remittance basis is not entitled to the annual exempt amount for that year.
- The higher rate for residential property has been cut to 24% for disposals on or after 6 April 2024. See **2.1**, **2.2** above and **56.7** SETTLEMENTS.

3

Alternative Finance Arrangements

Simon's Taxes. See **B5.6.**

Introduction to alternative finance arrangements

[3.1] Certain types of finance arrangements (known as '*alternative finance arrangements*') which are broadly equivalent to loans, deposits etc. but which do not involve the receipt or payment of interest are subject to special tax provisions designed to ensure that they are taxed no more nor less favourably than equivalent products which do involve interest. Such arrangements are usually aimed at those wishing to adhere to Shari'a law, which prohibits the receipt or payment of interest. The tax rules are not, however, restricted to Shari'a-compliant products, but apply to any arrangements falling within their terms.

This chapter describes the tax rules for alternative finance arrangements only to the extent of their effect on capital gains tax. See Tolley's Income Tax and Tolley's Corporation Tax for the detailed provisions.

For corporation tax purposes, the arrangements are loan relationships so that all profits and losses are dealt with as income: see **15.5** COMPANIES — CORPORATE FINANCE AND INTANGIBLES. For capital gains tax purposes, the return on the arrangement that is broadly equivalent to interest is excluded from the consideration for the purchase and sale of the asset purchased under the arrangements.

A further chargeable gains relief applies to certain investment bond arrangements involving land which are equivalent to a securitisation of the land.

The Treasury has the power by statutory instrument to amend the existing provisions, and to introduce new provisions, relating to alternative finance arrangements. [*CTA 2009, s 521; TIOPA 2010, s 366*].

Capital gains tax consequences of alternative finance arrangement

[3.2] Where, under any of three types of alternative finance arrangements, an asset is sold by one party to the arrangements to the other party, the 'alternative finance return' is excluded in determining for capital gains tax purposes the consideration for the sale and purchase of the asset. This does not affect the operation of any provision providing for the consideration to be treated as an amount other than the actual consideration.

This provision applies to the following types of arrangements: 'purchase and resale arrangements', 'diminishing shared ownership arrangements' and 'investment bond arrangements'. For each type of arrangement there is a particular definition of 'alternative finance return'.

Arrangements which are not at arm's length are not alternative finance arrangements for these purposes if the transfer pricing rules of *TIOPA 2010, s 147(3)(5)* require the alternative finance return to be recomputed on an arm's length basis and the party receiving the return is not subject to income tax, corporation tax or a corresponding foreign tax on the return.

[*TCGA 1992, ss 151O, 151X*].

Purchase and resale arrangements

For this purpose, '*purchase and resale arrangements*' are, broadly, arrangements entered into between two persons (A and B) under which:

(a) A purchases an asset and sells it to B;
(b) the amount payable by B in respect of the sale (the '*sale price*') is greater than the amount paid by A in respect of the purchase (the 'purchase price');
(c) all or part of the sale price does not have to be paid until a time after the sale; and
(d) the difference between the sale price and the purchase price equates, in substance, to the return on an investment of money at interest.

Either one or both of the parties must be a 'financial institution' (as defined) or, for arrangements entered into on or after 30 November 2021, the arrangements must be regulated electronic system facilitated arrangements (broadly arrangements facilitated by a Financial Conduct Authority-regulated peer-to-peer platform).

The sale of the asset in (a) above must take place immediately after the purchase unless A is a financial institution and the asset was purchased by A for the purpose of entering into the arrangements.

The '*alternative finance return*' is so much of the sale price as exceeds the purchase price. If, however, the purchase price is paid by instalments, the alternative finance return in each instalment is the amount of interest which would have been included in the instalment if the purchase price were a loan from A to B, the instalment were a part repayment of principal with interest and the loan were made on arm's length terms and accounted for under generally accepted accounting practice. If the alternative finance return is paid in a currency other than sterling, then if either A or B is not a company and the payment is not made for the purposes of a trade, profession, vocation or property business, the amount of the return is calculated in that currency and then translated into sterling at a spot rate for the day of payment.

[*TCGA 1992, ss 151J, 151P, 151Q; SI 2022 No 572, Regs 1, 6*].

Diminishing shared ownership arrangements

'*Diminishing shared ownership arrangements*' are, broadly, arrangements under which a 'first owner' and another person (the '*eventual owner*') both acquire a beneficial interest in an asset.

The '*first owner*' must be a financial institution or a regulated home purchase plan provider. Alternatively, the arrangements can be regulated electronic system facilitated arrangements (broadly, arrangements facilitated by a Financial Conduct Authority-regulated peer-to-peer platform). For arrangements entered into before 30 November 2021, the first owner must be a financial institution.

Under the arrangements, the eventual owner must:

(i) be required to make payments to the first owner amounting in aggregate to the consideration paid for the acquisition of its beneficial interest;
(ii) acquire (whether or not in stages) the first owner's beneficial interest as a result of those payments;
(iii) be required to make other payments to the first owner (whether under a lease forming part of the arrangements or otherwise);
(iv) have the exclusive right to occupy or otherwise use the asset; and
(v) be exclusively entitled to any income, profit or gain attributable to the asset (including any increase in its value).

The '*alternative finance return*' is equal to the payments made by the eventual owner under the arrangements other than payments within (ii) above and payments in respect of any arrangement fee or legal or other costs or expenses which the eventual owner is required to pay under the arrangements.

[*TCGA 1992, ss 151K, 151R; SI 2022 No 572, Regs 1, 3, 8*].

Investment bond arrangements

'*Investment bond arrangements*' are, broadly, arrangements which:

- provide for one person (the '*bond holder*') to pay a sum of money (the '*capital*') to another (the '*bond issuer*');
- identify assets or a class of assets which the bond issuer will acquire for the purpose of generating income or gains;
- specify a term at the end of which they cease to apply;
- include an undertaking by the bond issuer to dispose of any bond assets still in his possession at the end of the bond term;
- include an undertaking by the bond issuer to make a repayment of the capital to the bond holder during or at the end of the bond term (whether or not in instalments);
- include an undertaking by the bond issuer to make additional payments not exceeding a reasonable commercial return on a loan of the capital during or at the end of the bond term;
- include an undertaking by the bond issuer to arrange for the management of the bond assets with a view to generating sufficient income to pay the redemption payment and the additional payments;
- allow the bond holder to transfer the rights under the arrangements;

- are a listed security on a recognised stock exchange (see **57.27** SHARES AND SECURITIES) in the UK, EEA or Gibraltar or admitted to trading on a multilateral trading facility (as defined); and
- are wholly or partly treated in accordance with international accounting standards as a financial liability of the bond issuer (or would be if he applied them).

The '*alternative finance return*' is equal to the additional payments.

[*TCGA 1992, ss 151N, 151S(3); SI 2019 No 689, Regs 1, 6(13); European Union (Withdrawal Agreement) Act 2020, Sch 5 para 1(1)*].

Further consequences for diminishing shared ownership arrangements

[3.3] HMRC have published their view of the chargeable gains consequences arising where a person acquires an asset under a diminishing shared ownership arrangement. In their view, unless there are any special features leading to a different conclusion, the buyer is treated as acquiring each successive tranche of beneficial interest at the time they entered into the unconditional contracts with the seller and the financial institution. Where this is the case it follows that the date of acquisition of the asset for the purposes of indexation allowance (where available) is the date the diminishing shared ownership arrangements were entered into. (HMRC Brief 26/07).

A diminishing shared ownership arrangement is not a partnership for capital gains tax purposes. [*TCGA 1992, s 151Y*].

Further consequences for investment bond arrangements

[3.4] An alternative finance arrangement which is an investment bond arrangement is a security, but is neither an offshore fund nor a unit trust scheme, for capital gains purposes. [*TCGA 1992, ss 151V, 151W*].

Such an arrangement is also a qualifying corporate bond if certain conditions are met — see **48.3** QUALIFYING CORPORATE BONDS.

The bond holder is not treated as having a legal or beneficial interest in the bond assets and the bond issuer is not treated as a trustee of the assets. Gains accruing to the bond issuer in connection with the bond assets are gains of the bond issuer and not of the bond holder. Such gains do not accrue to the bond issuer in a fiduciary or representative capacity. Payments made by the bond issuer are not made in such a capacity. The bond holder is not entitled to relief for capital expenditure incurred in connection with the bond assets. [*TCGA 1992, s 151U*].

Investment bond arrangements where the underlying asset is land

[3.5] The following provisions (together with equivalent provisions relating to stamp duty land tax and capital allowances) are intended to ensure that the tax consequences of an alternative finance investment bond are the same as those for a conventional securitisation of land. The '*effective date*' of a land transaction is that date for the purposes of stamp duty land tax. Where a transaction is to be completed by conveyance, the effective date will in most cases be the date of completion. Where, however, 'substantial performance' of the contract takes place at an earlier date, that earlier date is the effective date. '*Substantial performance*' of a contract occurs when either the purchaser (or connected person) takes possession of substantially the whole of the interest or a substantial amount of the consideration is paid or provided. [*FA 2003, s 44; FA 2009, Sch 61 para 1(2)*]. See Tolley's Stamp Taxes for further details.

Relief for first transaction

Relief applies where:

(a) two persons ('P' and 'Q') enter into arrangements under which P transfers to Q a 'qualifying interest' in land (the '*first transaction*') and P and Q agree that when Q ceases to hold the interest as a 'bond asset' (see (b) below), Q will transfer the interest to P;

(b) Q, as 'bond issuer', enters into an alternative finance investment bond (see **3.2** above), either before or after making the arrangements in (a) above, and holds the interest in land as a bond asset; and

(c) to generate income or gains for the bond, Q and P enter into a leaseback agreement (i.e. Q grants a lease or sub-lease to P out of the interest transferred to Q by the first transaction).

For this purpose, '*bond asset*' and '*bond issuer*' have the same meaning as at **3.2** above. A '*qualifying interest*' in land is a major interest in land (within *FA 2003, s 117*), but leases with a term or period of less than 21 years are excluded. The Treasury can make regulations specifying an alternative to condition (c) above.

[*FA 2009, Sch 61 paras 1(1), 5(1)–(5)*].

If all of the above conditions are met within 30 days beginning with the effective date of the first transaction, that transaction is treated for chargeable gains purposes as being neither an acquisition by Q nor a disposal by Q. The granting of the lease or sub-lease under the leaseback agreement in (c) above is treated as neither an acquisition by P nor a disposal by Q. [*FA 2009, Sch 61 para 10*].

Withdrawal of relief

This relief is, however, withdrawn in certain circumstances. For this purpose, the following conditions are relevant.

(i) Within 120 days beginning with the effective date of the first transaction, Q must provide HMRC with evidence prescribed by HMRC in regulations that a satisfactory legal charge has been entered in the register of title kept under *Land Registration Act 2002, s 1* (or Scottish or NI equivalent). For this purpose, a charge is satisfactory if it is a first charge in favour of HMRC over the interest transferred by the first transaction for the amount of stamp duty land tax which would have been chargeable on the first transaction if it had been carried out at market value, together with any interest and penalties.

(ii) The total payments of 'capital' (see **3.2** above) made to Q before the termination of the bond must be not less than 60% of the value of the interest in land at the time of the first transaction.

(iii) (Subject to the substitution of asset rules below) Q must hold the interest in land as a bond asset until the termination of the bond.

(iv) Within 30 days beginning with the date on which the interest in land ceases to be held as a bond asset, it must be transferred by Q back to P (the '*second transaction*').

(v) The second transaction must be effected within ten years after the first transaction (or within a period specified by Treasury regulations).

The relief is withdrawn if:

(A) where the interest is in land in the UK, condition (i) above is not met;

(B) the interest in land is transferred by Q back to P without conditions (ii) and (iii) above having been met;

(C) the ten-year period in condition (v) above expires without conditions (ii) and (iii) above having been met; or

(D) it becomes apparent for any other reason at any time that any of conditions (ii) to (v) above cannot or will not be met.

If a chargeable gain or allowable loss arises as a result of the withdrawal of relief, it is treated as accruing:

- where (A) above applies, at the end of the 120-day period;
- where (B) above applies, immediately before the transfer from Q to P;
- where (C) above applies, at the end of the 10-year period; and
- where (D) above applies, at the time it becomes apparent that the conditions cannot or will not be met.

[*FA 2009, Sch 61 paras 5(6)–(12), 10, 11*].

Relief for second transaction

The second transaction (see (iv) above) is treated for chargeable gains purposes as being neither an acquisition by P nor a disposal by Q if (a) to (c) and (ii) to (v) above are satisfied and, where the land is in the UK, (i) above is satisfied. [*FA 2009, Sch 61 para 12*].

Substitution of asset

If the interest in land is transferred by Q back to P before the termination of the investment bond (so that condition (iii) above is not met), the above reliefs nevertheless continue to apply if conditions (iv) and (v) above are met and P and Q enter into further arrangements within (a) above relating to another interest in land. The value of the interest in the replacement land at the time it is transferred from P to Q must be equal to or greater than the value of the interest in the original land at the time of the first transaction.

In such circumstances, the reliefs in respect of the original land apply despite the fact that condition (iii) above has not been met, provided that (a)–(c) above and conditions (iii)–(v) above are met in relation to the replacement land.

In relation to the replacement land, condition (ii) above operates by reference to the value or the interest in the original land, and the ten-year limit in (v) above runs from the date of the first transaction relating to the original land.

These provisions also apply, with any necessary modifications where replacement land is itself replaced.

[*FA 2009, Sch 61 para 18*].

Anti-avoidance

The above reliefs are not available where control of the underlying asset is acquired by a bond holder (see **3.3** above) or a group of connected bond holders. This occurs where the rights of bond holders under a bond include the right of management and control of the bond assets and a bond holder or group acquires sufficient such rights to enable them to exercise that right to the exclusion of any other bond holders.

If the bond holder or group acquire such control before the end of the 30 days beginning with the effective date of the first transaction, no relief is available. If control is acquired at a later date, any relief already given is withdrawn as above.

This provision does not, however, prevent relief being given if either:

- at the time the rights were acquired, the bond holder or holders did not know and had no reason to suspect that the acquisition enabled the exercise of the right of management and control to the exclusion of other bond holders and as soon as reasonably practicable after becoming so aware they transfer sufficient rights for such management and control no longer to be possible; or
- the bond holder underwrites a public offer of rights under the bond and does not exercise the right of management and control of the bond assets.

For this purpose, a person underwrites an offer of rights if he agrees to make payments of capital under the bond in the event that others do not make the payments.

The above reliefs are also not available if the arrangements within (a) above are not made for genuine commercial reasons or form part of arrangements a main purpose of which is the avoidance of liability to income tax, corporation tax, capital gains tax, stamp duty or stamp duty land tax.

[*FA 2009, Sch 61 paras 20–22*].

4

Anti-Avoidance

Cross-references. See **14.6** COMPANIES for provisions relating to corporate losses; **17** CONNECTED PERSONS; **19** DISCLOSURE OF TAX AVOIDANCE SCHEMES; **20.8** DOUBLE TAX RELIEF for schemes and arrangements designed to increase such relief; **43** OVERSEAS MATTERS for provisions relating to overseas resident settlements; **43.9** OVERSEAS MATTERS for interests in controlled foreign companies and in offshore funds respectively; **44.16** PARTNERSHIPS; **56.16** SETTLEMENTS for restrictions on transfer of settlement losses to beneficiary becoming absolutely entitled to settled property; **56.20–56.22** SETTLEMENTS for further anti-avoidance provisions.

Introduction to anti-avoidance

[4.1] Anyone attempting to structure a transaction so as to avoid a liability to tax on chargeable gains arising or to mitigate such a liability must consider:

(a) whether the line of cases often referred to as the 'Ramsay principle' will operate to make the arrangements ineffective;
(b) whether the tax advantage under the arrangements is counteracted by the general anti-abuse rule;
(c) whether the arrangements give rise to a duty to disclose the details to HMRC under the provisions for DISCLOSURE OF TAX AVOIDANCE SCHEMES (**19**); and
(d) whether the arrangements fall foul of one of the many pieces of specific anti-avoidance legislation.

This chapter covers three of these considerations. For (c) above see **19** DISCLOSURE OF TAX AVOIDANCE SCHEMES.

The approach of the courts to avoidance cases is dealt with at **4.2** below. The general anti-abuse rule is described at **4.3–4.7** below. The next part of the chapter describes specific anti-avoidance provisions, many of which, it should be noted, apply where the particular conditions are satisfied whether or not there is any intention to avoid tax. Note that there are many anti-avoidance provisions which are dealt with outside this chapter where they relate to legislation described elsewhere in this work.

HMRC have powers, by way of a 'follower notice' to require a person using an avoidance scheme which is defeated in the courts in relation to another taxpayer to concede their position to reflect the court's decision. See **4.26** onwards below. HMRC also have the power to issue an 'accelerated payment notice' which requires a user of an avoidance scheme to pay tax upfront before the success or failure of the scheme has been finally determined. See **4.30** onwards below.

There is a regime of warnings and escalating sanctions for taxpayers ('serial avoiders') who persistently engage in tax avoidance schemes that are defeated by HMRC. See **4.33–4.41** below.

Approach of the Courts

[4.2] For the general approach of the courts to transactions entered into solely to avoid or reduce tax liability, leading cases are *Duke of Westminster v CIR HL 1935*, 19 TC 490; *W T Ramsay Ltd v CIR; Eilbeck v Rawling* HL 1981, 54 TC

101; *CIR v Burmah Oil Co Ltd* HL 1981, 54 TC 200; *Furniss v Dawson (and related appeals)* HL 1984, 55 TC 324; *Barclays Mercantile Business Finance Ltd v Mawson* HL 2004, [2005] STC 1; and *Hurstwood Properties (A) Ltd v Rossendale Borough Council* SC, [2021] UKSC 16. See also *Coates v Arndale Properties Ltd* HL 1984, 59 TC 516; *Reed v Nova Securities Ltd* HL 1985, 59 TC 516; *Magnavox Electronics Co Ltd (in liquidation) v Hall* CA 1986, 59 TC 610; *Commissioner of Inland Revenue v Challenge Corporation Ltd* PC, [1986] STC 548; *Craven v White; CIR v Bowater Property Developments Ltd; Baylis v Gregory* HL 1988, 62 TC 1; *Dunstan v Young Austen Young Ltd* CA 1988, 61 TC 448; *Shepherd v Lyntress Ltd; News International plc v Shepherd* Ch D 1989, 62 TC 495; *Ensign Tankers (Leasing) Ltd v Stokes* HL 1992, 64 TC 617; *Moodie v CIR and another (and related appeals)* HL 1993, 65 TC 610; *Countess Fitzwilliam and others v CIR (and related appeals)* HL 1993, 67 TC 614; *Pigott v Staines Investments Co Ltd* Ch D 1995, 68 TC 342; *CIR v McGuckian* HL 1997, 69 TC 1; *MacNiven v Westmoreland Investments Ltd* HL 2001, 73 TC 1; *CIR v Scottish Provident Institution* HL 2004, [2005] STC 15; and *HMRC v Tower Mcashback LLP1* SC, [2011] UKSC 19.

See also *DR Collins v HMRC* (Sp C 675), [2008] SSCD 718, *Trustees of the Eyretel Unapproved Pension Scheme v HMRC*, (Sp C 718), [2009] SSCD 17, *Mayes v HMRC* CA [2011] EWCA Civ 407; 2011 STI 1444, *Berry v HMRC* UT, [2011] STC 1057 and *Explainaway Ltd v HMRC* UT, [2012] STC 2525.

Classical interpretation

The classical interpretation of the constraints upon the courts in deciding cases involving tax avoidance schemes is summed up in Lord Tomlin's statement in the *Duke of Westminster* case that 'every man is entitled if he can to order his affairs so that the tax attaching . . . is less than it otherwise would be'. The judgment was concerned with the tax consequences of a single transaction, but in *Ramsay*, and subsequently in *Furniss v Dawson*, the House of Lords has set bounds on the ambit within which this principle can be applied in relation to modern sophisticated and increasingly artificial arrangements to avoid tax. In *CIR v McGuckian*, it was observed that while Lord Tomlin's words in the *Duke of Westminster* case 'still point to a material consideration, namely the general liberty of the citizen to arrange his financial affairs as he thinks fit, they have ceased to be canonical as to the tax consequences of a tax avoidance scheme'. It was further observed that the *Ramsay* approach was 'more natural and less extreme' than the majority decision in *Duke of Westminster*.

The 'Ramsay' approach

Ramsay concerned a complex 'circular' avoidance scheme at the end of which the financial position of the parties was little changed but it was claimed that a large capital gains tax loss had been created. It was held that where a preconceived series of transactions is entered into to avoid tax and with the clear intention to proceed through all stages to completion, once set in motion, the Duke of Westminster principle does not compel a consideration of the individual transactions and of the fiscal consequences of such transactions in isolation.

A series of subsequent cases have considered precisely what the *Ramsay* principle is and how it should be applied. The current consensus appears to be that stated by the House of Lords in *Barclays Mercantile (BMBF)*; tax legislation should be construed purposively not literally and, where appropriate (in the light of that purposive construction), the facts to which the legislation is applied should be viewed realistically.

The development of the case law on the *Ramsay* approach is summarised below.

The opinions of the House of Lords in *Furniss v Dawson* established, *inter alia*, that the *Ramsay* principle is not confined to 'circular' devices, and that if a series of transactions is 'preordained', a particular transaction within the series, accepted as genuine, may nevertheless be ignored if it was entered into solely for fiscal reasons and without any commercial purpose other than tax avoidance, even if the series of transactions as a whole has a legitimate commercial purpose.

However, in *Craven v White* the House of Lords indicated that for the *Ramsay* principle to apply all the transactions in a series have to be preordained with such a degree of certainty that, at the time of the earlier transactions, there is no practical likelihood that the transactions would not take place. It is not sufficient that the ultimate transaction is simply of a kind that was envisaged at the time of the earlier transactions. See, however, *CIR v Scottish Provident Institution* below. In the unanimous decision of the House of Lords in *Ensign Tankers (Leasing) Ltd v Stokes*, the lead judgment drew a clear distinction between 'tax avoidance' and 'tax mitigation', it being said that the *Duke of Westminster* principle is accurate as far as the latter is concerned but does not apply to the former.

Fitzwilliam involved five transactions entered into over a short period of time to avoid capital transfer tax on appointments from a will trust, the last four transactions being determined by the Revenue to form a preordained series of transactions subject to the *Ramsay* principle but which the taxpayers claimed should be viewed separately with the result that by reason of a number of available reliefs no liability to capital transfer tax arose. The House of Lords stated that the correct approach to a consideration of steps 2 to 5 was to ask whether realistically they constituted a single and indivisible whole in which one or more of the steps was simply an element without independent effect and whether it was intellectually possible so to treat them. It was held that both questions should be answered in the negative. The case put by the Revenue did not depend on disregarding for fiscal purposes any one or more of steps 2 to 5 as having been introduced for fiscal purposes only and as having no independent effect, nor on treating the whole of steps 2 to 5 as having no such effect. Each of the four steps had a fiscal effect of giving rise to an income tax charge on two of the taxpayers for a period of time, and there was a potential capital transfer tax charge should either have died whilst in enjoyment of the income associated with the transactions. Although steps 2 to 5 were 'preordained', in the sense that they formed part of a pre-planned tax avoidance scheme and that there was no reasonable possibility that they would not all be carried out, the fact of preordainment in that sense was not sufficient in itself to negative the application of an exemption from liability to tax which the series of transactions was intended to create, unless the series was capable of being construed in a manner inconsistent with the application of the exemption. In the particular circumstances of the case, the series of transactions could not be so construed. Two or more transactions in the series could not be run together, as in *Furniss v Dawson*, nor could any one or more of them be disregarded. There was no rational basis on which the four separate steps could be treated as effective for the purposes of one provision which created a charge to tax on a termination of an interest in possession but ineffective for the purposes of two other provisions which gave exemptions from that charge where the interest was disposed of for a consideration and where the interest reverted to the settlor. Accordingly, the case was one to which the *Ramsay* principle, as extended by *Furniss v Dawson*, did not apply.

In *MacNiven v Westmoreland Investments Ltd*, where the HL held that the *Ramsay* principle did not apply to a payment of interest, Lord Nicholls held that 'the very phrase "the *Ramsay* principle" is potentially misleading. In *Ramsay* the House did not enunciate any new legal principle. What the House did was to highlight that, confronted with new and sophisticated tax avoidance devices, the courts' duty is to determine the legal nature of the transactions in question and then relate them to the fiscal legislation'.

In *Mawson v Barclays Mercantile Business Finance Ltd*, the HL held that, in applying any statutory provision, it is necessary 'first, to decide, on a purposive construction, exactly what transaction will answer to the statutory description and secondly, whether the transaction in question does so'.

In *CIR v Scottish Provident Institution* the issue was whether the decision in *Craven v White* meant that a series of transactions could not be treated as a composite transaction under the *Ramsay* principle because there was a real commercial risk that the transactions would not take place. The HL held that 'it would destroy the value of the *Ramsay* principle . . . as referring to the effect of composite transactions if their composite effect had to be disregarded simply because the parties had deliberately included a commercially irrelevant contingency, creating an acceptable risk that the scheme might not work as planned'. Such a 'commercially irrelevant contingency' was found to be present in a purchased tax scheme involving options in *Schofield v HMRC* CA, [2012] STC 2019.

See also *Exors of Connell v HMRC* FTT, [2016] UKFTT 154 (TC); 2016 STI 1802 (market value of loan notes) and *Trustees of the Morrison 2002 Maintenance Trust v HMRC* CA, [2019] STC 400 (disposal of shares by trustees involving intermediate sale to non-resident trust).

Sham

In *Hitch and Others v Stone* CA, [2001] STC 214, the Revenue mounted a successful challenge to a complex and artificial tax avoidance scheme on the grounds that agreements on which it was based were shams. It was noted that 'sham' meant acts done or documents executed by the parties thereto which were intended by them to give to third parties or to the court the appearance of creating between the parties legal rights and obligations different from the actual legal rights and obligations (if any) which the parties intended to create. The law did not require that in every situation every party to the act or document should be a party to the sham, although a case where a document was properly held to be only in part a sham would be the exception rather than the rule and would occur only where the document reflected a transaction divisible into several parts.

Simon's Taxes. See **A1.120–A2.123.**

General anti-abuse rule

[4.3] The general anti-abuse rule ('GAAR') is intended to counteract the 'tax advantages' arising from 'tax arrangements' which are 'abusive'. Adjustments under the GAAR do not generally take effect until HMRC have referred the case to an independent GAAR Advisory Panel established by the Commissioners for HMRC. Before 22 July 2020, HMRC were generally required to refer the case to the Panel before making an adjustment, subject to the right to make a provisional counteraction before referral to the Panel where, for example, assessing time limits were about to expire. With effect from 22 July 2020, provisional counteraction is replaced with a system of protective GAAR notices. A GAAR Advisory Panel opinion allows HMRC to apply the GAAR to equivalent arrangements used by other taxpayers without further referral.

The GAAR applies to a range of taxes including income tax, corporation tax and capital gains tax.

[*FA 2013, s 206*].

HMRC do not give formal or informal clearances that the GAAR does not apply. As part of their engagement with large businesses and wealthy individuals, however, HMRC do discuss commercial arrangements and confirm where appropriate that they don't regard particular arrangements as tax avoidance. See www.gov.uk/government/collections/seeking-clearance-or-approval-for-a-transaction.

The GAAR Advisory Panel's published opinion notices are available at www.gov.uk/government/collections/tax-avoidance-general-anti-abuse-rule-gaar.

Definitions

Arrangements are '*tax arrangements*' if, having regard to all the circumstances, it would be reasonable to conclude that the obtaining of a tax advantage was the main purpose, or one of the main purposes, of the arrangements. For this purpose, '*arrangements*' include any agreement, understanding, scheme, transaction or series of transactions, whether or not legally enforceable.

Tax arrangements are '*abusive*' if entering into them or carrying them out cannot reasonably be regarded as a reasonable course of action in relation to the relevant tax provisions, having regard to all the circumstances. Those circumstances include:

- whether the substantive results of the arrangements are consistent with any express or implied principles on which the provisions are based and their policy objectives;

- whether the means of achieving the results of the arrangements involve one or more contrived or abnormal steps; and
- whether the arrangements are intended to exploit any shortcomings in the provisions.

Where the tax arrangements form part of other arrangements, regard must be had to those other arrangements.

The legislation gives the following non-exhaustive examples of what might indicate that tax arrangements are abusive.

- The arrangements result in taxable income, profits or gains significantly less than the economic amount.
- The arrangements result in a tax deduction or loss significantly greater than the economic amount.
- The arrangements result in a claim for repayment or crediting of tax, including foreign tax, that has not been, and is unlikely to be, paid.

The legislation also gives an example of what might indicate that arrangements are not abusive: the arrangements accord with established practice accepted by HMRC.

A '*tax advantage*' includes relief or increased relief from tax, repayment or increased repayment of tax, avoidance or reduction of a charge or assessment to tax, avoidance of a possible assessment to tax or of an obligation to deduct or account for tax, deferral of a payment of tax, and advancement of a repayment of tax.

[*FA 2013, ss 207, 208, 214(1)*].

Effect of the GAAR

The GAAR operates by counteracting the tax advantage under the tax arrangements by the making of adjustments that are just and reasonable, whether by HMRC or anyone else (the taxpayer or a responsible partner — see **4.7** below). Adjustments can be made by assessment, modification of an assessment, amendment or disallowance of a claim or otherwise. An adjustment can impose a tax liability where there would not otherwise be one or can increase an existing liability. Adjustments may be made in respect of the tax in question or any other tax to which the GAAR applies. Adjustments have effect for all tax purposes. The normal time limits for making assessments etc apply to the making of GAAR adjustments.

The effects of an adjustment under the GAAR are normally suspended until HMRC have followed the appropriate procedures at **4.4**, **4.6** or **4.7** below. Before 22 July 2020, HMRC had to follow the appropriate procedures *before* making an adjustment under the GAAR, subject to the right to make a provisional counteraction before referral to the Panel where, for example, assessing time limits were about to expire (see **4.5** below). With effect from 22 July 2020, provisional counteraction is replaced with a system of protective GAAR notices (see **4.5** below).

Where a matter is referred to the GAAR Advisory Panel (see **4.4**(4) or (6)), adjustments to counteract the tax advantage cannot be made in the '*closed period*' beginning with the 31st day after the end of the 45-day period for making representations (see **4.4**(2) and **4.7**(2) below) and ending immediately before the day on which notice is given of HMRC's final decision after considering the opinion of the Panel. Similarly, adjustments cannot be made in the closed period following the issue of a pooling notice or notice of binding (see **4.6** below). For this purpose, the 'closed period' is defined at **4.6** below.

[*FA 2013, s 209; FA 2020, Sch 14 paras 2, 10, 15; FA 2021, Sch 32 para 3*].

Consequential adjustments

Where the counteraction of a tax advantage is final and, if the counteraction was not made as a result of an HMRC final counteraction notice, the taxpayer or responsible partner (see **4.7** below) has notified HMRC of it, a person (not necessarily the taxpayer or responsible partner) has 12 months, beginning with the day the counteraction becomes final, to make a claim for one or more consequential adjustments to be made in respect of any tax to which the GAAR applies. For this purpose, counteraction of a tax advantage is final when the adjustments made and any amounts resulting from them can no longer be varied, on appeal or otherwise.

Consequential adjustments can be made for any period and may affect any person, whether or not a party to the tax arrangements. Adjustments are made on a just and reasonable basis but cannot increase a person's liability to any tax. HMRC must notify the person who made the claim of any adjustments made in writing. Consequential adjustments can be made by assessment, modification of an assessment, amendment of a claim or otherwise. There are no time limits for making such an adjustment.

The procedure for claims made outside a return in *TMA 1970, Sch 1A* (see **13.3** CLAIMS) applies to claims for consequential adjustments for income tax, capital gains tax and corporation tax purposes. See *FA 2013, s 210(6)* for the procedure rules for other taxes.

[*FA 2013, s 210; FA 2021, Sch 32 para 6*].

See **46.14** PENALTIES for the 60% penalty which applies to arrangements which are counteracted by the GAAR.

Court and tribunal proceedings

In any court or tribunal proceedings in connection with the GAAR, HMRC must show both that the tax arrangements are abusive and that the adjustments made to counteract the tax advantage are just and reasonable.

In making a decision in connection with the GAAR a court or tribunal must take into account any HMRC guidance on the GAAR which was approved by the GAAR Advisory Panel at the time the tax arrangements were entered into and also any relevant opinion of the sub-panel (see **4.4**(9) and **4.6** below).

[*FA 2013, s 211*].

Priority rule

The GAAR can override any priority rule in tax legislation, i.e. any rule to the effect that particular provisions have effect to the exclusion of, or otherwise in priority to, anything else. [*FA 2013, s 212*].

Procedure under the GAAR

[4.4] The normal procedure which HMRC must follow under the GAAR is set out below. See **4.5** below for alternative procedures where a protective GAAR notice is issued or, before 22 July 2020, a provisional counteraction notice was issued. See **4.6** below for alternative procedures in respect of equivalent arrangements. The normal procedure is modified for partnerships (see **4.7** below).

(1) An HMRC officer designated by the Commissioners for HMRC for the purpose of the GAAR must give the taxpayer a written notice specifying:
- the arrangements and the tax advantage;
- why the officer considers that a tax advantage has arisen from abusive tax arrangements;
- the counteraction which the officer considers should be taken;
- the period within which the taxpayer can make representations (see (2) below); and
- the effect of the rules in (3)–(5) below and of the PENALTIES (**46.14**) which may apply if the proposed counteraction takes effect.

The notice may set out steps that the taxpayer may take to avoid the application of the GAAR.

Where a notice is given on or after 22 July 2020, the adjustments specified in it have effect as if they were made under *FA 2013, s 209* (see **4.3** above under 'Effects of the GAAR'). This rule does not apply if a protective GAAR notice or a provisional counteraction notice have already been given in respect of the specified adjustments (see **4.5** below). The notice must normally be given within the normal time limits for assessments applicable to the proposed adjustments, but if the taxpayer's return is under enquiry and the adjustments relate to matters included in the return, the notice can be given at any time until the time the enquiry is completed.

If no appeal is made in respect of the adjustments or an appeal is withdrawn or determined by agreement, and no final counteraction notice is given under (10) below or the provisions at **4.6** below, the notice has effect as if it was a final counteraction notice (and therefore, as if the procedural requirements had been met). A penalty under *FA 2013, s 212A* (see **46.14** PENALTIES) cannot, however, be charged. In any other case, the specified adjustments have no effect unless they (or lesser adjustments) are subsequently specified in a final counteraction notice. The time limits for making the final counteraction notice are treated as met by the giving of the original notice.

(2) The taxpayer has 45 days starting with the day on which HMRC's notice is given to send written representations in response to the notice to the designated HMRC officer. The designated officer may extend the period if the taxpayer makes a written request.

(3) Where a person who has been given a notice under (1) takes 'corrective action' before the beginning of the closed period (see **4.3** above under 'Effect of the GAAR'), the matter is not referred to the GAAR Advisory Panel under (4) or (6) below. A person takes '*corrective action*' for this purpose only if he amends a return or claim to counteract the tax advantage or relinquishes the tax advantage by entering into a written

agreement with HMRC to do so. A person can amend a return or claim for this purpose during an enquiry even if the normal time limits have expired. No appeal may then be made against any enquiry closure notice (see **52.14** RETURNS) to the extent that it takes into account an amendment made as corrective action. The person must notify HMRC of the action taken and the additional tax amount which has or will become due. Where a person takes corrective action in this way no penalty can be charged under the provisions at **46.14** PENALTIES.

(4) If the taxpayer makes no representations and, where relevant, does not take corrective action, a designated HMRC officer must refer the matter to the GAAR Advisory Panel.
The officer must at the same time notify the taxpayer that the matter is being referred. The notice must inform the taxpayer of the period for making representations under (7) below and of the requirement to send any such representations to the officer. The officer must provide the Panel with a copy of the notice given to the taxpayer at step (1) above and the notice informing the taxpayer that the matter has been referred to the Panel.

(5) If the taxpayer does make representations but, where relevant, does not take corrective action, the representations must be considered by a designated HMRC officer.

(6) If the designated HMRC officer in (5) above still considers that the GAAR should apply, he must refer the matter to the GAAR Advisory Panel, together with a copy of the taxpayer's representations and any comments he has on those representations. The officer must notify the taxpayer of his decision on whether or not to refer the matter to the GAAR Advisory Panel as soon as is reasonably practicable.
The same requirements for the officer to notify the taxpayer and to provide information to the Panel apply as at step (4) above. The notice to the taxpayer must, however, also include a copy of any comments on the taxpayer's representations sent by the officer to the Panel.

(7) The taxpayer has 21 days to send written representations to the Panel and the designated HMRC officer about the notice given at step (1) above and any comments made by HMRC on the taxpayer's original representations. The Panel may extend the period for making representations if the taxpayer makes a written request.

(8) If the taxpayer makes representations at step (7) above but did not make representations at step (2) above, the designated HMRC officer may provide the Panel and the taxpayer with comments on the step (7) representations.

(9) A sub-panel of three members of the Panel will consider the matter in question. The sub-panel may invite the taxpayer or the designated HMRC officer to supply further information within a specified period. Information supplied to the sub-panel must also be sent to the other party.
The sub-panel must produce an opinion notice stating its collective opinion as to whether or not the entering into and carrying out of the tax arrangements was a reasonable course of action in relation to the relevant tax provisions, having regard to the circumstances outlined at **4.3** above. An opinion notice may indicate that the sub-panel considers

that it is not possible to reach a view on the information available. Alternatively, the sub-panel may produce two or three opinion notices which, taken together, state the opinions of all the members. An opinion notice must include the reasons for the opinion and is given to both the designated HMRC officer and the taxpayer.

(10) The designated HMRC officer must, having considered the sub-panel's opinion or opinions, give the taxpayer a written notice (a final counteraction notice) setting out whether or not the tax advantage under the arrangements is to be counteracted under the GAAR. It should be noted that HMRC are not bound by the decision of the sub-panel and may proceed with the application of the GAAR even if the sub-panel's opinion is that the GAAR ought not to apply.
If the GAAR is to apply, the final counteraction notice must specify the adjustments required and any steps that the taxpayer must take to give effect to them.

HMRC are not required to know for certain that a tax advantage has arisen before they embark on this procedure. A designated HMRC officer may carry out the above steps where they consider that a tax advantage might have arisen. Any notice they give may be expressed to be given on the assumption that a tax advantage arises.

[*FA 2013, ss 209AB, 209AC, Sch 43; FA 2020, Sch 14 paras 4, 12, 15; FA 2021, Sch 32 para 10*].

Protective GAAR notices

[4.5] With effect from 22 July 2020, regardless of when the tax arrangements were entered into, an HMRC officer may issue a protective GAAR notice, stating that a tax advantage might have arisen from abusive arrangements and that, if so, it ought to be counteracted under the GAAR. Such a notice will, for example, be issued to protect against loss of tax where an assessing time limit is about to expire. A notice must:

- specify the arrangements and tax advantage concerned; and
- specify the adjustments (as in **4.3** above) which, on the assumption that the advantage does arise from abusive tax arrangements, the officer proposes should be made.

A notice must normally be given within the normal time limits for assessments applicable to the proposed adjustments. If, however, the taxpayer's return is under enquiry and the return relates to the tax in respect of which the adjustments in the notice are to be made, the notice can be given at any time until the time the enquiry is completed.

A protective notice may not be given if a provisional counteraction notice was given before 22 July 2020 in respect of the same adjustments.

The adjustments specified in a protective notice have effect as if they were made under *FA 2013, s 209* (see **4.3** above under 'Effect of the GAAR').

An appeal can be made by notice against the specified adjustments but is stayed for a period of 12 months beginning with the day on which the protective notice was given. If a final counteraction notice under **4.4**(10) above or under the provisions at **4.6** below is given before the end of the 12-month period, the stay on the appeal ends when that notice is given.

If no appeal is made or an appeal is withdrawn or determined by agreement, and no final counteraction notice is given, the protective GAAR notice has effect as if it were a final counteraction notice (and therefore, that the procedural requirements in **4.4** above or **4.6** below had been met). A penalty under *FA 2013, s 212A* or *s 212B* (see **46.14** PENALTIES) cannot, however, be charged. In any other case, the specified adjustments have no effect unless they (or lesser adjustments) are subsequently specified in a final counteraction notice. The time limits for making the final counteraction notice are treated as met by the giving of the protective notice.

[*FA 2013, ss 209AA, 209AC; FA 2020, Sch 14 paras 3, 11, 15; FA 2021, Sch 32 para 5*].

Provisional counteraction notices before 22 July 2020

Before 22 July 2020, an HMRC officer could issue a provisional counteraction notice under the GAAR. Notices made before 22 July 2020 continue to operate on and after that date. A notice must:

- specify adjustments (as in **4.3** above) which the HMRC officer reasonably believes may be required to counteract a tax advantage that would (apart from the GAAR) arise to the recipient from tax arrangements;
- detail the arrangements and tax advantage concerned; and
- explain the appeals procedure and the circumstances in which the notice may be cancelled.

Adjustments specified in a notice which are made by HMRC are treated as effecting a valid counteraction of the tax advantage under the GAAR. The taxpayer may appeal against adjustments, stating the grounds of appeal, within the 30 days beginning with the date he receives the notice. If the taxpayer appeals the adjustments are treated as cancelled after 12 months from the date on which the provisional counteraction notice is given, unless, before that time (and whether before or after the issue of the provisional counteraction notice), an HMRC officer gives a notice to the taxpayer:

(1) cancelling the adjustments or withdrawing the notice (without cancelling the adjustments);
(2) issuing a notice within **4.4**(1) above in respect of the same arrangements and tax advantage and specifying the same or lesser adjustments as the counteraction which should be taken;
(3) issuing a pooling notice or a notice of binding (see **4.6** below) in respect of the same arrangements and tax advantage and specifying the same or lesser adjustments as the counteraction which should be taken; or
(4) issuing a generic referral notice (see **4.6** below) in respect of the same arrangements and tax advantage and specifying the same or lesser adjustments as the counteraction which should be taken.

Where a notice within (2)–(4) above specifies lesser adjustments, the provisional counteraction notice must be amended accordingly (unless it was issued after the notice in (2)–(4) above).

If a notice within (2) above is given and the matter is not referred to the GAAR Advisory Panel or if a notice within (2)–(4) above is given and subsequently the taxpayer is given a notice stating that the tax advantage is not to be counteracted under the GAAR, the adjustments in the provisional counteraction notice are treated as cancelled unless HMRC have the power to make the adjustments under provisions other than the GAAR and they state that the adjustments are therefore not cancelled. If a notice within (4) above is withdrawn, the adjustments in the provisional counteraction notice are likewise treated as cancelled, subject to the same exception.

Where a notice within (2)–(4) above is given and subsequently the taxpayer is given a notice stating that the tax advantage is to be counteracted, the adjustments in the provisional counteraction notice are confirmed so far as specified in the notice as adjustments required to give effect to the counteraction and are otherwise treated as cancelled.

[*FA 2013, ss 209A–209F; FA 2020, Sch 14 paras 6, 13, 15*].

Counteraction of equivalent arrangements

[4.6] There are provisions to enable the counteraction of 'equivalent' arrangements entered into by other taxpayers. The provisions enable HMRC to issue a 'pooling notice'

A designated HMRC officer may issue a '*pooling notice*' to a taxpayer (R), where:

(a) a person (P) has been given a notice under **4.4**(1) above in relation to tax arrangements ('*lead arrangements*');
(b) the 45-day period for representations in **4.4**(2) above has expired but no final counteraction notice under **4.4**(10) above or the generic referral provisions below has been given in respect of the matter;
(c) the officer considers that a tax advantage has arisen, or may have arisen, to R from tax arrangements which are abusive;
(d) the officer considers that those arrangements are equivalent to the lead arrangements; and
(e) the officer considers that the advantage should be counteracted.

The notice places R's arrangements in a pool comprising all the arrangements in relation to which pooling notices have been served in respect of the lead arrangements. A pooling notice may not be given if R has already been given a notice under **4.4**(1) above.

A designated HMRC officer may issue a '*notice of binding*' to a taxpayer (R), where:

(i) a person has been given a final counteraction notice under **4.4**(10) above or the generic referral provisions below in relation to tax arrangements ('*counteracted arrangements*') which are in a pool;

(ii) the officer considers that a tax advantage has arisen, or may have arisen, to R from tax arrangements which are abusive;
(iii) the officer considers that those arrangements are equivalent to the counteracted arrangements; and
(iv) the officer considers that the advantage should be counteracted.

A notice of binding may not be given if R has already been given a pooling notice or a notice under **4.4**(1) above.

A pooling notice or notice of binding must be given as soon as is reasonably practicable after HMRC become aware of the relevant facts. The notice must specify the tax arrangements and tax advantage concerned; explain why the officer considers them to be equivalent to the lead arrangements or the counteracted arrangements and why a tax advantage is considered to have arisen from abusive arrangements; set out the counteraction that the officer considers should be taken; and the effects of the notice. It may, but is not required to, set out steps which can be taken to avoid the proposed counteraction.

Where a pooling notice or notice of binding is given on or after 22 July 2020, the adjustments specified in it have effect as if they were made under *FA 2013, s 209* (see **4.3** above under 'Effects of the GAAR'). This rule does not apply if a protective GAAR notice or a provisional counteraction notice have already been given in respect of the specified adjustments (see **4.5** below). The notice must normally be given within the normal time limits for assessments applicable to the proposed adjustments but if the taxpayer's return is under enquiry and the adjustments relate to matters included in the return, the notice can be given at any time until the time the enquiry is completed.

If no appeal is made in respect of the adjustments or an appeal is withdrawn or determined by agreement, and no final counteraction notice (see below, **4.4**(10) above) is given, the notice has effect as if it were a final counteraction notice (and therefore as if the procedural requirements had been met). A penalty under *FA 2013, s 212A* or *212B* (see **46.14** PENALTIES) cannot, however, be charged. In any other case, the specified adjustments have no effect unless they (or lesser adjustments) are subsequently specified in a final counteraction notice. The time limits for making the final counteraction notice are treated as met by the giving of the pooling notice or notice of binding.

Arrangements are '*equivalent*' if they are substantially the same as one another, having regard to their results, the means of achieving those results, and the characteristics on the basis of which it could reasonably be argued in each case that the arrangements are abusive tax arrangements under which a tax advantage has arisen.

Where a person who has been given a pooling notice or a notice of binding takes 'corrective action' before the beginning of the 'closed period', he is treated as not having been given the notice and the arrangements are accordingly no longer in the pool. A person takes '*corrective action*' for this purpose only if he amends a return or claim to counteract the tax advantage or relinquishes the tax advantage by entering into an agreement with HMRC to determine an appeal. A person can amend a return or claim for this purpose during an enquiry even if the normal time limits have expired. No appeal may then be made against any enquiry closure notice (see **52.14** RETURNS) to the extent that it takes into account an amendment made as corrective action. The person must notify HMRC of the action taken and the additional tax amount which has or will become due. The '*closed period*' begins on the 31st day after the day on which the pooling notice or notice of binding was given. In the case of a pooling notice, the closed period ends immediately before the day on which notice is given of HMRC's final decision after considering the opinion of the GAAR Advisory Panel (see below). In the case of a notice of binding, the period is treated as ending at the same time as it begins. Where a person takes corrective action in this way, no penalty can be charged under the provisions at **46.14** PENALTIES.

Where, after a pooling notice has been issued to a person, the GAAR Advisory Panel issue an opinion notice (see **4.4**(9) above) in respect of another set of arrangements in the pool (the '*referred arrangements*'), the HMRC officer must give the person a '*pooled arrangements opinion notice*' setting out a report of the opinion and the person's right to make representations. Only one such notice may be given to a person about the same arrangements. The taxpayer has 30 days from the date of the notice to make representations that no tax advantage has arisen or that his arrangements are materially different from the referred arrangements.

The HMRC officer must consider any opinion of the GAAR Advisory Panel about the referred arrangements, together with any representations made, and issue a written notice with his decision as to whether the tax arrangements under consideration are to be counteracted under the GAAR. If so, the notice must set out the adjustments required to give effect to the counteraction and any steps that the taxpayer must take to give effect to it.

Where an HMRC officer gives a notice of binding, he must at the same time give a '*bound arrangements opinion notice*' setting out a report of any opinion of the GAAR Advisory Panel about the counteracted arrangements and the person's right to make representations. The taxpayer has 30 days from the date of the notice to make representations that no tax advantage has arisen to him or that his arrangements are materially different from the counteracted arrangements.

The HMRC officer must then consider any opinion of the GAAR Advisory Panel about the counteracted arrangements, together with any representations made, and issue a written notice (a final counteraction notice) with his decision as to whether the tax arrangements under consideration are to counteracted under the GAAR. If so, the notice must set out the adjustments required to give effect to the counteraction and any steps that the taxpayer must take to give effect to it.

See **4.7** below for modifications to these provisions which apply with effect from 10 June 2021 to counteract tax advantages included in partnership returns.

[*FA 2013, ss 209(9), 209AB, 209ABA, 209AC, Schs 43A, 43D para 12; FA 2020, Sch 14 paras 4, 8, 12, 15; FA 2021, Sch 32 paras 1, 3(4), 4, 5, 11*].

Generic referral of equivalent arrangements to the GAAR Advisory Panel

There are provisions for HMRC to make a generic referral to the GAAR Advisory Panel of arrangements in a pool.

The provisions apply where, further to pooling notices given as above, two or more sets of arrangements are in a pool relating to any lead arrangements, and P in (a) above took corrective action within the 75-day period beginning with the day on which the notice under **4.4**(1) was given (or within such longer period as P and HMRC may have agreed).

Provided none of the pooled arrangements have been referred to the GAAR Advisory Panel (see **4.4**(4), (6) above), a designated HMRC officer may give to each of the taxpayers whose arrangements are in the pool a notice of a proposal to make a generic referral to the Panel in respect of the arrangements in the pool. The notices must specify the arrangements and the tax advantage and the period within which the taxpayer can make a proposal (see below).

A person who has been given a notice has 30 days beginning with the day the notice was given to propose to HMRC that they should give him a notice under **4.4**(1) above and should not proceed with the generic referral.

If none of the notified taxpayers makes such a proposal within the 30-day period, the HMRC officer must make a referral (a '*generic referral*') to the GAAR Advisory Panel. If at least one of the recipients makes a proposal within the 30-day period, the officer must, after that period ends, decide whether to give one of the taxpayers a notice under **4.4**(1) above or to make a generic referral. The officer must make a generic referral if a taxpayer is duly given a notice under **4.4**(1) above but the matter is not referred to the GAAR Advisory Panel.

Where HMRC make a generic referral to the GAAR Advisory Panel, the designated HMRC officer must provide the Panel with a general statement of the material characteristics of the arrangements together with a declaration that this is applicable to *all* the arrangements and that nothing material to the panel's consideration has been omitted. The general statement must contain a factual description as well as HMRC's opinion, and a copy must be provided to the taxpayers.

A sub-panel of three members of the Panel will consider the referral. The sub-panel must produce an opinion notice stating its collective opinion as to whether or not the entering into and carrying out of the tax arrangements described in the general statement was a reasonable course of action in relation to the relevant tax provisions. An opinion notice may indicate that the sub-panel considers that it is not possible to reach a view on the information available. Alternatively, the sub-panel may produce two or three opinion notices which, taken together, state the opinions of all the members. An opinion notice must include the reasons for the opinion and is given to the designated HMRC officer.

The HMRC officer must then provide a copy of the opinion notice (or notices) to each taxpayer, any one of whom may then, within 30 days, make representations that:

- no tax advantage has arisen to him;
- he has already been given a bound arrangements opinion notice in relation to the arrangements concerned (see above); or
- a matter set out in HMRC's general statement is materially incorrect.

The officer must then, for each taxpayer, consider any opinion of the GAAR Advisory Panel, together with any representations made, and send a written notice (a final counteraction notice) with his decision as to whether the tax arrangements under consideration are to counteracted under the GAAR. If so, the notice must set out the adjustments required to give effect to the counteraction and the steps that the taxpayer must take to give effect to it.

[*FA 2013, s 214(3), Sch 43B; FA 2021, Sch 32 para 12*].

Application of the GAAR to partnerships

[4.7] *FA 2021* introduced provisions intended to enable the GAAR procedures to operate in the same way as that in which HMRC conduct enquiries into partnerships, allowing, for example, notices to be given via the representative partner, making amendments to the partnership return and feeding counteraction through to each partner's tax returns. The provisions apply with effect from 10 June 2021, regardless of when the tax arrangements were entered into and apply where a partnership return has been made under *TMA 1970, s 12AA* (see **52.18** RETURNS). They will also apply where a partnership return is made under the making tax digital provisions of *TMA 1970, Sch A1 para 10*. [*FA 2013, Sch 43D para 1; FA 2021, s 124, Sch 32 para 1*].

For the purposes of the provisions, the '*responsible partner*' is the person who delivered the partnership return or their successor (see **52.18** RETURNS for the appointment of a successor where a partner responsible for dealing with a return ceases to be available) or, in the case of a return under *TMA 1970, Sch A1*, the nominated partner. A partnership return is treated as made on the basis that a particular tax advantage arises to a partner from particular arrangements if it is made on the basis that an increase or decrease in any amounts included in the partnership statement (see **52.19** RETURNS) result from the arrangements and that increase or decrease results in a tax advantage for the partner. [*FA 2013, Sch 43D paras 2, 3; FA 2021, Sch 32 para 1*].

Specific legislation

[4.8] Specific anti-avoidance legislation is intended to counteract transactions designed to avoid tax, but genuine transactions may also sometimes be caught. Anti-avoidance provisions which are targeted at a specific area of legislation or a relief are included in the relevant chapter of this work; the remaining provisions are dealt with in this chapter.

Value shifting

[4.9] Without prejudice to the generality of *TCGA 1992*, any of the following transactions are to be treated as giving rise to a disposal of an asset for capital gains tax purposes and, if made gratuitously or at an undervalue, the consideration (or additional consideration) for the disposal which could have been obtained in an arm's length transaction is treated as having been actually received. The same disposal value is treated as the cost of acquisition to the person or persons acquiring value as a result of the transaction. [*TCGA 1992, s 29(1)*].

(a) If a person having control of a company exercises his control so that value passes out of shares in the company owned by him (or by CONNECTED PERSONS (17)) or out of rights over the company exercisable by him (or by connected persons) and passes into other shares in or rights over the company, a disposal is deemed to have been made out of those shares or rights. Losses arising from such a deemed disposal are not allowable. [*TCGA 1992, s 29(2)(3)*]. An omission to act may be treated as an exercise of control and 'person' includes the plural i.e. the provisions apply where two or more persons have control (*Floor v Davis* HL 1979, 52 TC 609).

(b) Where an owner of property enters into a transaction whereby he becomes the lessee of that property (e.g. a sale and lease-back) and there is a subsequent adjustment of the rights and liabilities under the lease (whether or not including the grant of a new lease) which is as a whole favourable to the lessor, such an adjustment is a disposal by the lessee of an interest in the property. [*TCGA 1992, s 29(4)*].

(c) If an asset is subject to any right or restriction, the extinction or abrogation, in whole or part, of that right etc. by the person entitled to enforce it is treated as a disposal thereof. [*TCGA 1992, s 29(5)*].

The aim of the legislation is to tax the amount of value passing *into* the transferee holdings, not (if different) the amount passing from the transferor. The disposal value is thus the value received by the transferee(s). (HMRC Capital Gains Manual CG58855). This will be of relevance where value passes from a majority shareholding into one or more minority holdings — see the *Example* at **4.10** below.

Example

[4.10]

Jak owns all the 1,000 £1 ordinary shares of K Ltd. The shares were acquired on subscription in 1978 and had a value of £65,250 on 31 March 1982. In December 2024, the trustees of Jak's family settlement subscribed at par for 250 £1 ordinary shares in K Ltd, thereby acquiring 20% of the voting power in the company. It is agreed that the value per share of Jak's holding immediately before the December 2024 share issue was £175 and immediately afterwards was £150. The value per share of the trust's holding, on issue, was £97 per share.

The proceeds of the deemed disposal are computed as follows

Value passing out of Jak's 1,000 shares is £25,000 (1,000 × £25 per share (£175 – £150)).

Value passing into the trust's 250 shares is £24,250 (250 × £97 per share) *less* the subscription price paid of £250 (250 × £1 per share) = £24,000.

The proceeds of the deemed disposal are equal to the value passing into the new shares, i.e. £24,000. (The trust's acquisition cost is £24,250, i.e. actual plus deemed consideration given).

The disposal is a part disposal (see **16.5** COMPUTATION OF GAINS AND LOSSES), the value of the part retained being £150,000 (1,000 × £150 per share).

Jak will have a capital gain for 2024/25 as follows:

		£
Proceeds of deemed disposal		24,000
	Allowable cost $\frac{24,000}{24,000 + 150,000} \times £65,250$	9,000
Chargeable gain		£15,000

Simon's Taxes. See **C2.115**.

Value shifting to give tax-free benefit

[4.11] The following provisions apply to the disposal of an asset (the *s 30* disposal) if a scheme has been effected or arrangements have been made (whether before or after the disposal) whereby the value of the asset has been materially reduced and a 'tax-free benefit' is conferred at any time on:

(a) the person making the disposal or a person connected with him (see **17** CONNECTED PERSONS); or
(b) any other person, except in a case where tax avoidance was not a main purpose of the scheme or arrangements.

Where the disposal of an asset precedes its acquisition, references to a reduction in value include references to an increase. See *Land Securities plc v HMRC* [2011] UKFTT 599 (TC), [2012] SFTD 215 and *Kerrison v HMRC* UT, [2019] STC 614 for the application of this rule to shares, etc. treated as acquired following disposal (see **58** SHARES AND SECURITIES — IDENTIFICATION RULES).

The provisions do not apply if the disposal of the asset is a disposal by a company of shares in, or securities (within *TCGA 1992, s 132* as in **23.5** EXEMPTIONS AND RELIEFS) of another company. Instead the provisions at **4.12** below apply.

Any allowable loss or chargeable gain accruing on the *s 30* disposal is to be calculated as if the consideration were increased by such amount as is 'just and reasonable' having regard to the scheme or arrangements and the tax-free benefit. Where such an increase of consideration has been made for one asset and the tax-free benefit was an increase in value of another asset, the consideration for the first subsequent disposal of that other asset is to be reduced by such amount as is 'just and reasonable' in the circumstances. (There is no provision for the acquirer's cost of the asset to be correspondingly increased or reduced.)

These provisions do not apply to disposals by personal representatives to legatees (see **18.14** DEATH), or between spouses living together (see **40.4** MARRIED PERSONS AND CIVIL PARTNERS) or between companies in a group (see **26.3** GROUPS OF COMPANIES).

[*TCGA 1992, s 30(1)(2)(4)–(7)(9)*].

A '*tax-free benefit*' arises to a person if he becomes entitled to money or money's worth or his interest in the value of any asset is increased or he is wholly or partly relieved from any liability to which he is subject *and* none of the foregoing benefits when conferred is otherwise liable to income tax, capital gains tax or corporation tax. [*TCGA 1992, s 30(3)*].

HMRC do not regard ordinary commercial group relief transactions (e.g. the purchase of group relief) as falling within *TCGA 1992, s 30*.

A lease of a farm at a rack-rent by a retiring farmer to his son, followed by a sale of the reversion at market value to an outside investor, would likewise be outside it (HMRC Statement of Practice D18).

Where a disposal within *TCGA 1992, s 30* would otherwise form the basis for a claim for loss relief against income under *ITA 2007, Pt 4 Ch 6* or *CTA 2010, Pt 4 Ch 5* these provisions apply if *any* benefit is conferred, whether tax-free or not. [*TCGA 1992, s 125A*]. See also **38.14** and **38.17** LOSSES.

Simon's Taxes. See **C2.116**.

Value shifting and certain disposals of shares by companies

[4.12] The following provision applies (and those at **4.11** above do not apply) for corporation tax purposes to the disposal by a company of shares in, or securities (within *TCGA 1992, s 132* as in **23.5** EXEMPTIONS AND RELIEFS) of, another company if:

(a) 'arrangements' have been made under which the value of the shares or securities, or any 'relevant asset' is materially reduced (or, where the disposal precedes the acquisition of the shares or securities, is materially increased);
(b) the main purpose, or one of the main purposes, of the arrangements is to avoid a liability to corporation tax on chargeable gains (of the disposing company or any other person); and
(c) the arrangements do not consist solely of the making of an 'exempt distribution'.

In calculating the chargeable gain or allowable loss on the disposal, the consideration is increased by an amount which is just and reasonable having regard to the arrangements and any charge to or relief from corporation tax that would have arisen from the disposal or arrangements but for this provision.

In (a) above, '*arrangements*' include any agreement, understanding, scheme, transaction or series of transactions, whether or not legally enforceable. An asset is a '*relevant asset*' if it is owned by a member of the disposing company's group (within *TCGA 1992, s 170* — see **26.2** GROUPS OF COMPANIES) at the time of the disposal. In (c) above, an '*exempt distribution*' is one within the exempt class under *CTA 2009, s 931H* or which would be within that class but for the recipient being a small company (within *CTA 2009, s 931S*).

The following applies where there are arrangements under which the value of shares or securities is materially reduced and the main purpose, or one of the main purposes of the arrangements, is to avoid a liability to corporation tax on chargeable gains (of the company carrying out the transaction concerned or any other person). If, but for the arrangements, a transaction would be treated as a disposal of shares by a company under *TCGA 1992, s 29(2)* (value passing out of shares in company — see **4.10**(a) above), the transaction is to be treated as such a disposal.

[*TCGA 1992, s 31*].

Transactions between connected persons

[4.13] **Simon's Taxes.** See **C2.110, C2.113.**

A transaction between CONNECTED PERSONS (**17**) is treated as having been made by way of a non-arm's length bargain so that acquisition and disposal are treated as being made at market value in most cases (see **39.1** MARKET VALUE). [*TCGA 1992, s 18(1)(2)*].

There are restrictions on losses in such circumstances. See **38.7** LOSSES.

Where the asset disposed of is subject to a right or restriction enforceable by the person making the disposal or a person connected with them, then if the acquisition consideration is treated as being the market value of the asset, that value is ascertained by deducting from the market value of the unencumbered asset either the market value of the right or restriction or, if less, the amount by which its extinction would enhance the value of the asset to its owner. Rights or restrictions the enforcement of which might effectively destroy or substantially impair the value of the asset without bringing any countervailing advantage either to the person making the disposal or to a person connected with them are disregarded, e.g. rights to extinguish incorporeal assets by way of forfeiture or merger (but see below). Options and other rights to acquire assets are also disregarded.

The valuation provisions outlined above do not apply to rights of forfeiture etc. exercisable on the breach of a covenant in a lease, nor to any right or restriction under a mortgage or other charge.

[*TCGA 1992, s 18(6)–(8)*].

Assets disposed of in a series of transactions

[4.14] **Simon's Taxes.** See **C2.114.**

Where by way of two or more 'material transactions' which are 'linked' (a '*series of linked transactions*')

(a) a person disposes of assets to another person with whom he is connected (or to two or more other persons with each of whom he is connected) (see **17** CONNECTED PERSONS); and
(b) the 'original market value' of the assets disposed of by any of the transactions in the series is less than the appropriate portion of the 'aggregate market value' of the assets disposed of by all the transactions in the series,

the disposal effected by the linked transaction in (b) is deemed to be for a consideration equal to the appropriate portion referred to in that paragraph. This rule does not apply to disposals between married persons or civil partners (see **40** MARRIED PERSONS AND CIVIL PARTNERS) treated as no gain/no loss transactions.

A '*material transaction*' is any transaction, whether by gift or otherwise (subject to the exception below as regards intra-group transfers). Two or more such transactions are '*linked*' if they occur within the period of **six years** ending on the date of the last of them.

The provisions apply *both* when a second material transaction causes a series of linked transactions to come into being *and* when an existing series is extended by a further material transaction (whether or not an earlier transaction ceases to form part of the series). Assessments and adjustments are made accordingly.

Original market value

If a transaction is the most recent in the series, the original market value of the assets disposed of by it is the market value which would otherwise be deemed to be the consideration for it under the general capital gains tax rules (e.g. MARKET VALUE (**39**)). In the case of any other transaction in the series, the original market value of the assets disposed of by it is the value which, prior to the occurrence of the most recent transaction in the series, was or would have been deemed to be the consideration, whether under the general capital gains tax rules or by the previous operation of these provisions.

Aggregate market value

Subject to further provisions below, aggregate market value is the amount which would have been the market value of all the transactions in the series under the general capital gains tax rules if, 'considering all the assets together', they had been disposed of by one disposal occurring at the time of the transaction concerned. The appropriate portion of the aggregate market value is that portion which it is reasonable to apportion to those of the assets which were actually disposed of by the transaction concerned.

'*Considering all the assets together*' refers not only to considering them as a group or holding or collection of assets retaining their separate identities but also (if it gives a higher market value) to considering them as brought together, physically or in law, so as to constitute either a single asset or a number of assets which are distinct from those which were comprised in each of the transactions concerned.

Groups of companies

Intra-group transfers of assets which are treated as taking place on a no gain/no loss basis (see **26.3** GROUPS OF COMPANIES) are not material transactions. In a case where:

(a) a company ('company A') disposes of an asset by way of a material transaction; and

(b) company A acquired the asset (after 19 March 1985) by way of an intra-group transfer as above; and

(c) the disposal by company A is to a person who is connected with another company ('company B') which at some time disposed of the asset by way of an intra-group transfer as above; and
(d) either the disposal by way of intra-group transfer which is referred to in (c) above was the occasion of the acquisition in (b) above or, between that disposal and acquisition, there has been no disposal of the asset which was not an intra-group transfer as above,

then, in determining whether the above provisions apply in relation to a series of linked transactions, the disposal by company A is treated as having been made by company B; but any increase in the consideration for that disposal resulting from the application of the new provisions has effect with respect to company A.

Disposal preceding acquisition

If any of the assets disposed of by all the transactions in a series of linked transactions were acquired after the time of the first of those transactions, then, in considering aggregate market value in relation to each of the transactions in the series, no account is taken of any assets which were acquired after the time of that transaction (unless they were acquired by way of an intra-group transfer). Further, the number of assets taken into account is limited to the maximum number held at any time in the period beginning immediately before the first transaction and ending immediately before the last; and in arriving at this figure any intra-group transfers prior to the first transaction are treated as taking place after that transaction. For identification purposes, fungible assets are treated as disposed of on a 'first in/first out' basis.

[*TCGA 1992, ss 19, 20*].

For further commentary and examples, see HMRC Capital Gains Manual CG14650–14740.

Example

L purchased a set of six antique chairs in June 1993 at a cost of £12,000. He gave two chairs to his daughter in February 2019, another pair to his son in November 2020 and sold the final pair to his brother for their market value in August 2024.

The market value of the chairs at the relevant dates were:

	2 chairs	4 chairs	6 chairs
	£	£	£
February 2019	6,000	14,000	26,000
November 2020	7,800	18,000	34,200
August 2024	10,400	24,000	46,200

The capital gains tax computations are as follows:

February 2019

Disposal to daughter

Deemed consideration	£6,000

February 2019

As the consideration does not exceed £6,000, the disposal is covered by the chattel exemption (see note (a)).

November 2020

(i) *2018/19 disposal to daughter recomputed*

Original market value (deemed disposal consideration at February 2019)	£6,000
Reasonable proportion of aggregate market value as at February 2019 of all assets disposed of to date:	
£14,000 × 2/4	£7,000

	£
Deemed consideration (greater of £6,000 and £7,000)	7,000
Cost $\frac{7,000}{7,000 + 14,000} \times £12,000$	4,000
Chargeable gain 2018/19	£3,000

(ii) *2020/21 disposal to son*

Original market value (deemed disposal consideration)	£7,800
Reasonable proportion of aggregate market value as at November 2020 of all assets disposed of to date:	
£18,000 × 2/4	£9,000

	£
Deemed consideration (greater of £7,800 and £9,000)	9,000
Cost $\frac{9,000}{9,000 + 7,800} \times (£12,000 - £4,000)$	4,286
Chargeable gain 2020/21	£4,714

August 2024

(i) *Gain on 2018/19 disposal to daughter recomputed*

Original market value (deemed consideration in recomputation at November 2020)	£7,000
Reasonable proportion of aggregate market value as at February 2019 of all assets disposed of to date:	
£26,000 × 2/6	£8,667

	£
Deemed consideration (greater of £7,000 and £8,667)	8,667
Cost $\frac{8,667}{8,667 + 14,000} \times £12,000$	4,588
Revised chargeable gain 2018/19	£4,079

(ii) *Gain on 2020/21 disposal to son recomputed*

Original market value (deemed consideration in computation at November 2020)	£9,000
Reasonable proportion of aggregate market value as at November 2020 of all assets disposed of to date:	
£34,200 × 2/6	£11,400

	£
Deemed consideration (greater of £9,000 and £11,400)	11,400
Cost $\frac{11,400}{11,400 + 7,800} \times (12,000 - 4,588)$	
	4,401
Revised chargeable gain 2020/21	£6,999

(iii) *Gain on 2024/25 disposal to brother*

	£
Original market value (actual consideration)	£10,400
Reasonable proportion of aggregate market value as at August 2024 of all assets disposed of to date:	
£46,200 × 2/6	£15,400

	£
Deemed consideration (greater of £10,400 and £15,400)	15,400
Cost (£12,000 – £4,588 – £4,401)	3,011
Chargeable gain 2024/25	£12,389

Notes to the example

(a) The disposal in February 2019 was at first covered by the chattel exemption (£6,000). As the second disposal in November 2020 is to a person connected with the recipient of the first disposal, the two must then be looked at together for the purposes of the chattel exemption, and, as the combined proceeds exceed the chattel exemption limit, the exemption is not available. [*TCGA 1992, s 262*].

(b) The three disposals are linked transactions within *TCGA 1992, s 19* as they are made by the same transferor to persons with whom he is connected, and take place within a six-year period.

(c) It is assumed in the above example that it is 'reasonable' to apportion the aggregate market value in proportion to the number of items. In other instances a different basis may be needed to give the 'reasonable' apportionment required by *TCGA 1992, s 20(4)*.

Close company transferring asset at undervalue

[4.15] Where, on or after 31 March 1982, a close company (within *CTA 2010, ss 439–454*) transfers (other than within a group of companies under *TCGA 1992, s 171(1)*, see **26.3** GROUPS OF COMPANIES) an asset to any person otherwise than at arm's length and for a consideration of an amount or value less than the market value of the asset, an amount equal to the difference is apportioned among the issued shares of the company. On a disposal of the shares by the person who owned them at the date of transfer, an amount equal to the amount so apportioned is not treated as allowable expenditure.

Where the owner of such shares is itself a close company, an amount equal to the amount apportioned to those shares is apportioned among the issued shares of that close company, the owners being treated as above, and so on through any number of close companies.

Where the gain or loss on disposal of shares held at 31 March 1982 falls to be computed *other than* by reference to their value at that date (see **8.2** ASSETS HELD ON 31 MARCH **1982**), any transfers of assets as above which were made before that date (but not before 6 April 1965) are also taken into account.

Where the asset is transferred to a settlement for the benefit of employees, etc. (see **23.84** EXEMPTIONS AND RELIEFS), the amount apportioned is the difference between the market value of the asset or the amount of the allowable expenditure attributable to the asset, whichever is the less, and the consideration. [*TCGA 1992, s 239(3)*].

The above provisions do not apply in two sets of circumstances. The first is where the transferee is a participator or an associate of a participator in the company and the undervalue amount is treated as a capital distribution within *TCGA 1992, s 122* (see **57.11** SHARES AND SECURITIES). The second is where the transferee is an employee of the company and the undervalue amount is charged to income tax as employment income (and is not exempt income).

[*TCGA 1992, s 125*].

Restrictions on company reconstructions

[4.16] *TCGA 1992, s 135* (share exchanges) applies to the takeover of one company by another wholly or partly for shares or debentures and provides that the original holding and the new holding are to be treated as the same asset. See **57.5** SHARES AND SECURITIES. *TCGA 1992, s 136* deals with company reconstructions where a company issues shares or debentures to another company's shareholders whose original holdings are either retained or cancelled. The original and new holdings are likewise treated as the same asset. See **57.7** SHARES AND SECURITIES.

Neither of these provisions applies, however, unless the exchange of securities or scheme of reconstruction is for 'bona fide commercial reasons', and not part of a scheme or arrangement for the main or only purpose of avoiding capital gains tax or corporation tax. This restriction does not apply where a recipient of the shares, etc. holds 5% or less of, or of any class of, the relevant shares, etc. (including holdings by connected persons) in the company being acquired etc., or where HMRC, on written application by either company, have given clearance before the issue is made. In determining whether a recipient holds 5% or less of the shares concerned for this purpose, any of its own shares that the company holds as treasury shares (see **57.19** SHARES AND SECURITIES) do not count (HMRC Capital Gains Manual CG52620).

The above provisions also apply to interests in a company without share capital (where relevant — see **57.5**, **57.7** SHARES AND SECURITIES) and certain quoted options.

Tax assessed on a person (the '*chargeable person*') by virtue of the above provisions and not paid within six months of the date when it is payable may be recovered, in whole or in part, from certain third parties, in the name of the chargeable person, within two years of that date. There is a right of recourse to the chargeable person for the tax so paid together with, in the case of corporation tax, interest paid in respect of that tax. The third parties are restricted to persons holding the shares, etc. issued to the chargeable person who acquired them as a result of one or more disposals within *TCGA 1992, s 58(1)* (spouses or civil partners living together) or *s 171(1)* (companies within same group) without any intervening disposals not within those provisions.

See *Snell v HMRC* Ch D, [2007] STC 1279 in which the above provisions were held to apply where the taxpayer became non-resident after exchanging his shareholding in a company for loan notes and before selling the loan notes. A similar decision was reached in *Coll and another v HMRC* UT, [2010] STC 1849.

In *Delinian Ltd v HMRC* CA, [2023] EWCA Civ 1281, [2023] STC 1862, the provisions were held not to apply even though one of the taxpayer's purposes was the avoidance of a tax liability. The CA held that the scheme or arrangements which had to be considered in applying the second limb of the anti-avoidance rule were the whole of the scheme or arrangements undertaken by the taxpayer, not a selected part of them. It was not necessary to sift through every permutation or combination of elements of a scheme to find one which has a main purpose of tax avoidance. It would not be a natural use of language to say that the entire exchange formed part of a scheme to replace part of the consideration originally intended to be received in cash with preference shares.

A similar decision was reached in *Wilkinson v HMRC* FTT 2023, [2024] SFTD 92.

Seeking to retain family control of a company may be a 'bona fide commercial reason', see *CIR v Brebner* HL 1967, 43 TC 705; *Clark v CIR* Ch D 1978, 52 TC 482 and *CIR v Goodwin* HL 1976, 50 TC 583, which dealt with the similar phrase in *ICTA 1988, s 703(1)*.

[*TCGA 1992, ss 137, 138*].

Clearance applications

Application for clearance must contain particulars of operations contemplated and HMRC may, within 30 days of receipt, call for further particulars (to be supplied within 30 days, or longer if HMRC allow). If the particulars are not supplied, the application lapses. Subject to this, HMRC must indicate their decision within a further 30 days. If not so notified, or if dissatisfied with the decision, the applicants may within a further 30 days require HMRC to refer the particulars to the Tribunal for its decision. All material facts and considerations must be disclosed; otherwise, any decision is void.

HMRC will not give clearance to arrangements which seek to avoid a criminal, civil or regulatory risk or liability because they consider that the 'bona fide commercial reasons' test expressly requires genuine, good faith, commercial reasons for undertaking the exchange or scheme of reconstruction (HMRC Capital Gains Manual CG52633).

Applications for clearance should be directed to BAI Clearance, HMRC BX9 1JL (if market-sensitive information is included, for the attention of the team leader). Applications may be emailed to reconstructions@hmrc.gov.uk. A hard copy need not then be sent. Only a single application need to be made as above for clearances under any one or more of: *CTA 2010, ss 1091, 1092* (demergers), *CTA 2010, ss 1044, 1045* (purchase of own shares), *ITA 2007, s 701* or *CTA 2010, s 748* (transactions in securities), *TCGA 1992, s 138(1)* (as above), *TCGA 1992, s 139(5)* (reconstructions involving the transfer of a business – see **14.12** COMPANIES), *TCGA 1992, s 140B* (transfer or division of a UK business between EU member states – **43.12** OVERSEAS MATTERS), *TCGA 1992, s 140D* (transfer or division of a non-UK business between EU member states – **43.13** OVERSEAS MATTERS) and *CTA 2009, s 831* (clearances under the corporation tax intangible assets regime). See www.gov.uk/guidance/seeking-clearance-or-approval-for-a-transaction.

Reconstructions and share exchanges involving non-UK incorporated close companies

[4.17] An anti-avoidance rule applies, subject to the detailed conditions below, where an individual with a degree of control over a UK-incorporated close company is issued shares or debentures in a non-UK-incorporated close company on or after 17 November 2022 as part of a share exchange to which *TCGA 1992, s 135* applies (see **57.5** SHARES AND SECURITIES) or a scheme of reconstruction to which *TCGA 1992, s 136* applies (see **57.7** SHARES AND SECURITIES). The rule does not disapply those provisions, but instead treats the new shares or debentures as located in the UK. (Under the principles at **7.3** ASSETS, the shares or debentures would otherwise generally be treated as located outside the UK.)

The intention of the rule is to prevent UK-resident but non-domiciled individuals from in effect converting UK-located assets into non-UK assets and then claiming remittance basis treatment for income and for any gain on disposal (see Treasury Explanatory Notes to the*Finance (No 2) Bill 2023*). There is no avoidance motive test in the provisions, however, so that they apply wherever the conditions are met, subject to the making of the election below.

The rule applies where:

- *TCGA 1992, s 135* or *s 136* apply to an issue of shares or debentures by a company (company B) to an individual (P) in exchange for, or in respect of, shares or debentures of another company (company A);
- immediately before the issue, company A is a 'close company' incorporated in the UK (whether or not UK-resident) and P is a participator with a 'material interest' in the company; and
- immediately after the issue, company B is a close company which is not incorporated in the UK (whether or not UK-resident) and P is a participator with a 'material interest' in the company.

A company is a '*close company*' for this purpose if it is a close company within the meaning of *CTA 2010, s 439*, or would be if it were UK-resident.

An individual (P) has a '*material interest*' in a company if P, an associate of P, or P or an associate together with one or more other associates, is the beneficial owner of, or able to control, more than 5% of the company's ordinary share capital (as defined at *CTA 2010, s 1119*). P also has a material interest in a company if P, an associate of P, or P or an associate together with one or more other associates, possesses or is entitled to acquire rights which would give an entitlement to receive more than 5% of the company's assets available for distribution on a winding-up or in other circumstances.

If the share exchange or reconstruction involves a company with no share capital, these conditions (and the provisions below) apply as if the interests of the company possessed by its members were shares or debentures and the total of all such interests were the company's ordinary share capital.

Effect of the anti-avoidance rule

Where the above conditions are met, the following are treated as located in the UK whilst they are held by P or P's spouse or civil partner (S):

(i) the exchanged shares or debentures (i.e. the shares or debentures in company B issued to P on the share exchange or reconstruction);
(ii) any other shares or debentures in company B acquired by P on or after the day the exchanged shares or debentures were issued;
(iii) where there is a repo of any shares or debentures treated as located in the UK under these provisions, any 'similar' shares or debentures transferred back to P under the repo (see **57.26** below);
(iv) where P transfers shares or debentures treated as located in the UK under these provisions to another person under a stock lending arrangement, shares or debentures of the 'same description' transferred back to P under the arrangement (see **57.25** below);
(v) shares or debentures of a company issued to P in exchange for, or in respect of, shares or debentures in company B treated as located in the UK under these provisions, in circumstances where *TCGA 1992, s 135* or *136* applies, provided that P has a material interest (as above) in that company;
(vi) any other shares or debentures of the company in (v) above acquired by P on or after the day of the issue of shares or debentures in (v) above.

This rule does not apply to shares or debentures held by S following a transfer by P, or by P following a transfer from S, if the transfer is not treated as a no gain/no loss transaction (see **40.4** MARRIED PERSONS AND CIVIL PARTNERS).

As indicated above, the rule continues to apply where P transfers shares or debentures to S and the transfer is at no gain/no loss. Following such a transfer, the references to P in (ii)–(vi) above are taken to be to P or S. This applies even if S no longer holds the shares or debentures.

It does not matter whether or not any consideration is given by P (or S) for the shares or debentures in (ii), (v) or (vi) above nor whether or not the shares or debentures are of a different class from the exchanged shares or debentures.

Income from shares or debentures treated as located in the UK under these provisions is not foreign income for income tax purposes (see *ITTOIA 2005, s 830(3A)*).

Election to disapply share exchange or reconstruction treatment

If the above rule would otherwise apply, P can make an election to disapply *TCGA 1992, s 135* or *136* (as applicable). Where the election is made, the above rule does not apply, but an immediate gain may be triggered in respect of company A's shares or debentures. An election must be made no later than 31 January following the tax year in which the shares or debentures are issued.

[*TCGA 1992, ss 138ZA–138ZC; F(No 2)A 2023, s 36*].

Schemes involving the transfer of a business owned by companies

[4.18] See **14.12** COMPANIES where a scheme of reconstruction involves the transfer of a UK resident company's business to another UK resident company for no consideration other than the assumption of liabilities of the business. [*TCGA 1992, s 139*].

Depreciatory transactions within groups of companies

[4.19] Simon's Taxes. See D2.350.

Where two or more members of a group of companies are parties to a 'disposal of assets' at other than market value which has the effect of materially reducing the value of the shares or 'securities' of one of those companies ('a depreciatory transaction'), any loss arising on the ultimate disposal of those shares or securities by a member or a former member of the group (having been a member when the transaction took place) is to be allowable only so far as is 'just and reasonable'. Account may be taken of any other post-30 March 1982 transaction which has:

(i) enhanced the value of the assets of the company the shares in which are being disposed of; and
(ii) depreciated the assets of any other group member.

Any depreciatory transactions occurring on or after 31 March 1982 are taken into account.

Where a loss has been wholly or partly disallowed as above, any chargeable gain accruing within six years of the depreciatory transaction on the disposal of shares or securities of another company which was a party to it is reduced as is just and reasonable (but not so as to exceed the reduction in the allowable loss). Regard is to be had to the effect of the depreciatory transaction on the value of the shares at the date of disposal. All adjustments, by discharge or repayment of tax, or otherwise, as are required to give effect to these provisions may be made at any time.

A '*depreciatory transaction*' also includes any other transaction where:

(a) the company, the shares or securities in which are the subject of the ultimate disposal, or any 75% subsidiary of that company, was party to that transaction; and
(b) the parties to the transaction were, or included, two or more companies which, when the transaction occurred, were in the same group.

A transaction is not depreciatory to the extent that it is a payment which is required to be, or has been, brought into account in computing a chargeable gain or allowable loss of the company making the ultimate disposal. Cancellation within *Companies Act 2006, s 641* of shares or securities of one member of a group which are owned by another is deemed to be a depreciatory transaction unless it falls within this exemption. The deemed disposal arising under a claim that shares or securities have become of negligible value (see **38.10** LOSSES) may constitute a depreciatory transaction.

References to '*disposal of assets*' include appropriation by one member of a group of the goodwill of another member.

'*Securities*' includes loan stock or similar securities whether secured or unsecured.

A group of companies, and related expressions, are construed for these purposes in accordance with **26.2** GROUPS OF COMPANIES.

[*TCGA 1992, s 176*].

Where a subsidiary company pays dividends to its parent out of post-acquisition profits, HMRC do not regard the payment as being a depreciatory transaction (HMRC Capital Gains Manual CG46540).

For consideration of these provisions, see HMRC Capital Gains Manual CG46500–46580.

Dividend stripping

[4.20] Simon's Taxes. See D2.352.

Where a company (the 'first company') holds 10% or more of a class of shares in another company (the 'second company') otherwise than as a dealing company, and a distribution is or has been made to the first company which materially reduces or has reduced the value of the holding, the distribution is to be treated as a depreciatory transaction under *TCGA 1992, s 176* (see **4.19** above) in relation to any disposal of the shares. This applies whether the disposal is by the first company or any other company to which the holding has been transferred under the provisions of *TCGA 1992, s 140A* (transfer or division of UK business between companies in different EC member states, see **43.12** OVERSEAS MATTERS) or *s 171* (transfers within a group, see **26.3** GROUPS OF COMPANIES). If the first and second companies are not members of the same group, they are deemed to be so.

For these purposes, a company's holding of different classes in another company are treated as separate holdings and holdings of the same class which differ in the entitlements or obligations they confer are treated as holdings of different classes. Subject to this, all of a company's holdings of the same class in another company must be treated as a single holding and other holdings of the same class held by connected persons are aggregated in determining whether the 10% test is satisfied. For the meaning of connected persons, see **17** CONNECTED PERSONS. For the above provisions only, the persons mentioned in **17.5** specifically include persons acting together to secure or acquire a holding in a company (and not just control).

A distribution need not be treated as a depreciatory transaction under these provisions to the extent that it consists of a payment which is required to be, or has been, brought into account in calculating a chargeable gain or allowable loss by the person making the ultimate disposal.

[*TCGA 1992, s 177*].

Abuse of concessions

[4.21] A statutory charge applies where a person (the '*original taxpayer*') has at any time obtained the benefit of a capital gains relief in reliance on a 'concession' and circumstances arise in a subsequent chargeable period which, if that benefit had been obtained under a statutory relief, would have resulted in the whole (or part) of the benefit falling to be recouped from any person (whether or not the original taxpayer). A chargeable gain equal to the full amount of that benefit is deemed to accrue to the latter person for the chargeable period in which the circumstances arise. The chargeable gain is not eligible for ROLLOVER RELIEF (53) (see HMRC Capital Gains Manual CG13659). The total recouped under these provisions cannot exceed the original benefit (which might otherwise have been the case where there are part disposals — see HMRC Capital Gains Manual CG13655).

The above provision does not, however, apply where the person to whom the deemed chargeable gain would otherwise accrue indicates in writing to HMRC that he accepts that the benefit obtained by the original taxpayer may be recouped from him. Such acceptance may be indicated simply by the making or amending of a self-assessment to include the deferred gain. Where, *following* an assessment under this provision:

- such indication of acceptance is given on or before the latest of the deadlines listed below; or
- it transpires that the original taxpayer did not, or was not entitled to, rely on the concession and *his* tax position for the earlier period is finally determined on that basis,

such adjustments are to be made to ensure that the chargeable person's liability is no greater than would have been the case had such an event occurred earlier such that no assessment would have been necessary. The above-mentioned deadlines are:

- twelve months after an assessment is made under the above provision;
- the latest date for amending the self-assessment tax return or company tax return for the period in which the gain accrues (see **52.9**, **52.21** RETURNS); and
- where a claim for further relief (for example, rollover relief) is possible against the gain and is made, the latest possible date for making that claim.

For the purpose of the above provision, '*concession*' means any concession which:

- was first published by the Revenue before 9 March 1999 or replaces a concession so published and having similar effect;

- was available generally to any person falling within its terms at the time it was relied upon by the original taxpayer,

and which has the effect of:

- applying (with or without modifications) the provisions of any enactment to a case to which they would not otherwise have applied; or
- treating, without applying a specific enactment:
  - (i) any asset as the same as any other asset and acquired as the other asset was acquired;
  - (ii) any two or more assets as a single asset; or
  - (iii) any disposal as having been a disposal on which neither a gain nor a loss accrued.

For these purposes, the term 'concession' is not restricted to those listed at www.gov.uk/government/publications/extra-statutory-concessions-ex-inland-revenue but includes any practice, interpretation or other statement in the nature of a concession and within the above definition.

[*TCGA 1992, ss 284A, 284B*].

The following extra-statutory concessions are *examples* of concessions at which the above provisions are aimed.

- D16 (which extends rollover relief on business assets where the proceeds from the disposal of an asset are reinvested in the repurchase of the same asset — see **53.2** ROLLOVER RELIEF).
- D22 (which extends rollover relief on business assets where the proceeds from the disposal of an asset are used to enhance the value of another asset — see **53.2** ROLLOVER RELIEF).
- D39 (which treats a lease of property which is surrendered before its expiry date as the same asset as a new lease to replace it — see **35.13** LAND).

(Treasury Explanatory Notes to the Finance Bill 1999). For further commentary and examples, see HMRC Capital Gains Manual CG13650–13662.

Factoring of income receipts

[4.22] Anti-avoidance provisions apply to counter schemes (defined in the legislation as any of three types of structured finance arrangement) involving the factoring of income receipts. The schemes involve the transfer of an asset on which there is a predictable income stream or a transfer of the right to such an income stream, in return for a lump sum. The income stream acquired by the transferee is then sufficient to repay both the lump sum and interest. The transferor then claims that the income or receipts arising during the period of the arrangement are not taxable on him and that the lump sum is either a capital receipt giving rise to a chargeable gain only or is not taxable at all. Broadly, the provisions operate by deeming the intended effects of the arrangements not to have effect for tax purposes. See *ITA 2007, ss 809BZA–809BZS*, *CTA 2010, ss 758–776* and Tolley's Income Tax and Corporation Tax for full details.

For capital gains purposes, where:

(a) *ITA 2007, ss 809BZB* or *809BZC* or *CTA 2010, ss 759* or *760* apply to a 'type 1 finance arrangement';

(b) the 'borrower' or a person connected with him (other than the 'lender') makes a disposal at any time of any 'security' under the arrangement to or for the benefit of the lender or a person connected with him (other than the borrower); and

(c) either:
  - the person making the disposal, and no-one else, has the right or obligation under the arrangement (whether or not subject to conditions) to acquire the asset disposed of at any subsequent time; or
  - the asset will subsequently cease to exist and it is intended that the asset will be held by the lender or connected person from the time of the disposal until it ceases to exist,

then the disposal of the security in (b) above and (except where there has been a deemed disposal as below) any subsequent re-acquisition of the asset are disregarded.

If it becomes apparent at any time after the disposal that the person making the disposal will not subsequently acquire the asset disposed of or that the asset will not be held by the lender or connected person from the time of the disposal until it ceases to exist, then the person making the disposal is treated as disposing of the asset at that time at market value.

An 'arrangement' is a '*type 1 finance arrangement*' in relation to a person (the '*borrower*') for these purposes if:

(i) under the arrangement the borrower receives from another person (the '*lender*') any money or other asset (the '*advance*') in any period;

(ii) the accounts of the borrower for that period record a financial liability in respect of the advance in accordance with generally accepted accounting practice (or would so record a financial liability if accounts were drawn up in accordance with generally accepted accounting practice);

(iii) the borrower or a person connected with him (other than the lender) makes a disposal (including anything which would constitute a disposal for capital gains purposes) under the arrangement of an asset (the '*security*') to or for the benefit of the lender or a person connected with him (other than the borrower);

(iv) the lender or a person connected with him (other than the borrower) is entitled to 'payments' in respect of the security under the arrangements; and

(v) those payments reduce the amount of the financial liability in respect of the advance recorded in the accounts of the borrower in accordance with generally accepted accounting practice (or would so reduce the amount if accounts were drawn up in accordance with generally accepted accounting practice).

The circumstances in which the borrower is treated for the purposes of (i) above as receiving an asset include the borrower's obtaining directly or indirectly the value of the asset or otherwise deriving directly or indirectly any benefit from it and the discharge, in whole or part, of any liability of the borrower. Similarly, the circumstances in which the lender or other person is treated as entitled to payments in respect of the security for the purposes of (iv) above include the person's obtaining directly or indirectly the value of the security or otherwise deriving directly or indirectly any benefit from it and payments in respect of any other asset substituted for the security under the arrangement. Where the borrower is a partnership, references above to the accounts of the borrower include the accounts of any member of the partnership.

For the purposes of (iv) above it does not matter if the entitlement to payments is subject to any condition.

Where the borrower is a company, references to the accounts of the borrower include the consolidated group accounts of any group of companies of which it is a member. An '*arrangement*' includes any agreement or understanding, whether or not legally enforceable.

[*TCGA 1992, s 263E; ITA 2007, ss 809BZA, 809BZQ–809BZS; CTA 2010, ss 758, 774–776*].

Transfer of income stream

[4.23] Anti-avoidance provisions apply to ensure that where a person sells or otherwise disposes of a right to receive income and does not sell the underlaying asset from which the income derives, the lump sum obtained is taxed as income and not as a chargeable gain.

The provisions apply where a taxpayer 'transfers' a right to any income which would otherwise be chargeable to income tax or corporation tax as income of the taxpayer or brought into account in calculating the taxpayer's profits for tax purposes. The transfer must not be a consequence of the transfer of an asset (other than a transfer under a sale and repurchase agreement) from which the right to the income arises. This condition does not apply if the transfer of the right is a consequence of a transfer of all rights under an agreement for annual payments.

A transfer consisting of the reduction of the transferor's share in the profits or losses of a partnership is regarded for this purpose as a consequence of the transfer of an asset from which the right to income arose. The grant or surrender of a lease of land is regarded for the purposes of the above provisions, as a transfer of the land, and the disposal of an interest in an oil licence is treated as a transfer of the licence. Where the transferor is a company, the grant or disposal of an interest in intellectual property excluded from the intangible fixed assets regime by its commencement provisions (see **15.13** COMPANIES — CORPORATE FINANCE AND INTANGIBLES) is treated as a transfer of that property. The Treasury can, by order, added other transactions which are to be treated as the transfer of an asset.

The provisions do not apply to the extent that the income is charged to tax as income of the transferor, or brought into account as income in calculating the transferor's profits, under other provisions. They also do not apply if the income is brought into account for capital allowances purposes, if the consideration for the transfer is the advance under a structured finance arrangement within the provisions mentioned at **4.22** above or if the right is to annual payments under certain annuities.

A '*transfer*' includes a sale, exchange, gift, assignment or any other arrangement equating in substance to a transfer. Also included are transfers to or by a partnership of which the transferor or transferee is a member and transfers to the trustees of a trust of which the transferee is a beneficiary.

Effect of provisions

Where the provisions apply, the consideration for the transfer of the right to income is treated as income of the transferor chargeable to income tax or corporation tax in the same way and to the same extent as the income would have been chargeable but for the transfer. Where there is no consideration or the consideration is less than the market value of the right, the market value of the right is so treated as income of the transferor. If the transferee is a company, the consideration for the transfer is treated as a loan relationship.

[*ITA 2007, ss 809AZA–809AZF; CTA 2009, ss 486F, 486G; CTA 2010, ss 752–757*].

Disposal of income stream through partnership

[4.24] Anti-avoidance legislation applies to ensure that where a person sells or otherwise disposes of a right to receive income by or through a partnership, the consideration obtained is taxed as income and not as a chargeable gain.

The provisions apply where, directly or indirectly in consequence of, or otherwise in connection with, 'arrangements' involving a person within the charge to income tax or corporation tax (the 'transferor') and another person (the 'transferee'):

(a) there is, or is in substance, a disposal of a right to receive any income which would otherwise be chargeable to income tax or corporation tax as income of the transferor (directly or as a partner) or brought into account in calculating the taxpayer's profits (directly or as a partner) for tax purposes;
(b) the disposal is effected wholly or partly by or through a partnership, including a limited liability partnership;
(c) at any time the transferor is a member of the partnership or an associated partnership and the transferee is a member of the partnership or an associated partnership (and for this purpose it does not matter if the transferor and transferee are not members of such a partnership at the same time); and
(d) the main purpose, or one of the main purposes, of one or more steps taken in effecting the disposal is the obtaining of a tax advantage (within *CTA 2010, s 1139*) for any person.

The provisions do not apply if the transferor is the spouse or civil partner of the transferee and they are living together or if the transferor is a brother, sister, ancestor or lineal descendant of the transferee.

In (a) above, 'disposal' of a right includes anything constituting a disposal of such a right for capital gains purposes. For the purposes of (b) above, it is specifically stated that the disposal might, in particular, be effected by an acquisition or disposal of, or an increase or decrease in, an interest in the partnership (including a share of the profits or assets of the partnership or an interest in such a share). In (c) above, the references to the transferor and transferor include a connected person. A partnership is associated with the partnership through which the disposal is effected if it is a member of that partnership or it is a member of a partnership which is itself a member of that associated partnership (and so on). '*Arrangements*' include any agreement, understanding, scheme, transaction or series of transactions (whether or not legally enforceable).

Effect of provisions

Where the provisions apply, the consideration for the disposal of the right to income is treated as income of the transferor chargeable to income tax or corporation tax in the same way and to the same extent as the income would have been chargeable but for the disposal. Where there is no consideration or the consideration is less than the market value of the right, the market value of the right is so treated as income of the transferor.

Priority rule

Where these provisions and those at **4.25** below would otherwise both apply to a disposal, only the provisions which give the greater amount of income chargeable to tax apply.

[*ITA 2007, ss 809AAZA, 809AAZB; CTA 2010, ss 757A, 757B*].

Disposal of asset through partnership

[4.25] Anti-avoidance legislation applies to ensure that where a person disposes of an asset by or through a partnership and the consideration would have been chargeable to tax as income had the disposal been made directly to the transferee, the consideration is taxed as income and not as a chargeable gain. The provisions apply where both condition A and condition B below are met.

Condition A is that directly or indirectly in consequence of, or otherwise in connection with, 'arrangements' involving a person within the charge to income tax or corporation tax (the 'transferor') and another person (the 'transferee'):

(a) there is, or is in substance, a disposal of an asset by the transferor to the transferee;
(b) the disposal is effected wholly or partly by or through a partnership, including a limited liability partnership;
(c) at any time the transferor is a member of the partnership or an associated partnership and the transferee is a member of the partnership or an associated partnership (and for this purpose it does not matter if the transferor and transferee are not members of such a partnership at the same time); and
(d) the main purpose, or one of the main purposes, of one or more steps taken in effecting the disposal is the obtaining of a tax advantage (within *CTA 2010, s 1139*) for any person.

Condition A is not met if the transferor is the spouse or civil partner of the transferee and they are living together or if the transferor is a brother, sister, ancestor or lineal descendant of the transferee.

In (a) above, 'disposal' of a right includes anything constituting a disposal of such a right for capital gains purposes. For the purposes of (b) above, it is specifically stated that the disposal might, in particular, be effected by an acquisition or disposal of, or an increase or decrease in, an interest in the partnership (including a share of the profits or assets of the partnership or an interest in such a share). In (c) above, the references to the transferor and transferor include a connected person. A partnership is associated with the partnership through which the disposal is effected if it is a member of that partnership or it is a member of a partnership which is itself a member of that associated partnership (and so on). '*Arrangements*' include any agreement, understanding, scheme, transaction or series of transactions (whether or not legally enforceable).

Condition B is that it is reasonable to assume that, had the transferred asset been disposed of directly by the transferor to the transferee, the consideration received by the transferor would have been chargeable to income tax or corporation tax as income or would have been brought into account as income in calculating profits for income tax or corporation tax purposes. If the transferor receives no consideration or consideration which is substantially less than the asset's market value he is treated for this purpose as receiving consideration equal to the market value.

Effect of provisions

Where the provisions apply, the consideration received by the transferor for the disposal of the asset (or its market value) is treated as income of the transferor chargeable to income tax or corporation tax in the same way and to the same extent as it would have been chargeable had the asset been transferred directly from the transferor to the transferee.

Priority rule

Where these provisions and those at **4.24** above would otherwise both apply to a disposal, only the provisions which give the greater amount of income chargeable to tax apply.

[*ITA 2007, ss 809DZA, 809DZB; CTA 2010, ss 779A, 779B*].

Follower notices

[4.26] Users of avoidance schemes which have been defeated in a Tribunal or court hearing in another taxpayer's case can be required to concede their position to reflect the Tribunal's or court's decision. HMRC can issue a follower notice requiring such users for whom there is an open enquiry or appeal to amend their tax return or agree to resolve their appeal in accordance with the decision.

The taxes covered by the provisions are income tax, capital gains tax, corporation tax (including amounts chargeable as if they were corporation tax or treated as if they were corporation tax), inheritance tax, stamp duty land tax and annual tax on enveloped dwellings. The Treasury may extend the provisions to other taxes by order. [*FA 2014, ss 200, 232*]. The provisions are described below only to the extent that they relate to income tax, capital gains tax and corporation tax.

An application for judicial review of follower notices was unsuccessful in *R (oao Broomfield) v HMRC* QB, [2018] STC 1790.

For HMRC guidance see www.gov.uk/government/publications/follower-notices-and-accelerated-payments/follower-notices-and-accelerated-payments.

Simon's Taxes. See **A7.247**.

Definitions

Arrangements are '*tax arrangements*' if, having regard to all the circumstances, it would be reasonable to conclude that the obtaining of a 'tax advantage' was their main purpose or one of the main purposes of them. '*Arrangements*' include any agreement, understanding, scheme, transaction or series of transactions, whether or not legally enforceable.

A '*tax advantage*' includes relief or increased relief from tax, repayment or increased repayment of tax, avoidance or reduction of a charge or assessment to tax, avoidance of a possible assessment to tax, deferral of a payment, or advancement of a repayment, of tax and avoidance of an obligation to deduct or account for tax.

An '*enquiry*' means an enquiry under *TMA 1970, ss 9A* or *12AC* (see **52.11**, **52.20** RETURNS), *TMA 1970, Sch 1A para 5* (see **13.3** CLAIMS) or *FA 1998, Sch 18 para 24* (see **52.21** RETURNS). An enquiry is '*in progress*' in the period beginning with the day on which the notice of enquiry is given and ending on the day on which the enquiry is completed.

An '*appeal*' means an appeal or further appeal against an assessment, amendment of a self-assessment, closure notice, amendment of a partnership return or a counteraction notice under *ITA 2007, s 705* or *CTA 2010, s 750* (transactions in securities).

A '*judicial ruling*' means a ruling of a court or tribunal on one or more issues. Such a ruling is relevant to particular tax arrangements if it relates to tax arrangements, it is a 'final ruling' and the principles laid down, or reasoning given, in it would, if applied to the arrangements in question, deny the asserted tax advantage or part of it. A judicial ruling is a '*final ruling*' if it is a decision of the Supreme Court, if no further appeal can be made (including where a time limit for further action by the appellant has expired) or if a further appeal was abandoned or otherwise disposed of before it was determined. If a ruling becomes final because of the passing of a time limit or because a further appeal is abandoned or otherwise disposed of before being determined, the ruling is treated as made at the time when the time limit expired or the appeal was abandoned or disposed of.

[*FA 2014, ss 201–203, 205*].

Giving of follower notices

[4.27] HMRC may give a follower notice to a person if:

(a) an enquiry into a return or claim made by that person is in progress or that person has made an appeal which has not been finally determined, abandoned or otherwise disposed of;

(b) the return, claim or appeal is made on the basis that a particular tax advantage results from particular tax arrangements;
(c) HMRC are of the opinion that there is a judicial ruling which is relevant to those arrangements; and
(d) no previous follower notice has been given to the same person (and not withdrawn) by reference to the same tax advantage, tax arrangements, judicial ruling and tax year or accounting period.

A follower notice must identify the judicial ruling, explain why HMRC consider that the ruling is relevant to the tax arrangements and explain the effects of the notice. A notice may not be given after the end of the 12-month period beginning with the later of the date of the judicial ruling and the date the return or claim was received by HMRC or the appeal was made.

The recipient of a follower notice has 90 days beginning with the date the notice is given to send written representations to HMRC objecting to the notice on the grounds that any of (a), (b) or (d) above are not satisfied, that the judicial ruling is not relevant to the arrangements or that the notice was not given within the time limit. Having considered the representations, HMRC will notify the recipient of whether they have decided to confirm the notice or withdraw it.

The Supreme Court has ruled that, to issue a valid notice, HMRC must be of the opinion that the principles applied to the defeated scheme would also apply to the taxpayer, i.e. that there was no scope for a reasonable person to disagree that they would do so (*R (on the application of Haworth) v HMRC* SC, [2021] STC 1329). The court found that HMRC had misdirected themselves as to the statutory test, by proceeding on the basis that a *likelihood* that the principles would also apply to the taxpayer was sufficient for a follower notice to be issued.

An application for judicial review of a follower notice was also successful in *R (on the application of Locke) v HMRC* CA, [2019] STC 2543. The taxpayer was a partner in an Eclipse Film Partnership, Eclipse 10, and HMRC had contended that his circumstances were the same as those in *Eclipse Film Partners No 35 LLP v HMRC* CA, [2015] STC 1429. The court held, however, that the decision in that case was focused on whether the partnership carried on a trade, which was not relevant to Mr Locke's case.

In *Pitt v HMRC* UT, [2024] UKUT 21 (TCC) (an appeal against a penalty for failure to take corrective action), the taxpayer (P) argued that the decision on which HMRC relied to issue the follower notice (*Audley v HMRC* FTT, [2011] UKFTT 219 (TC)) was not a relevant judicial ruling. Before the UT, P argued that *Audley* was heavily fact-dependent and that the FTT had failed to distinguish between primary facts and 'reconstituted' or evaluative' facts arising through the application of the purposive *Ramsay* approach, i.e. facts found realistically in the light of the purpose of the legislation. 'Reconstituted facts' included findings that there was a single composite transaction and that the issue of the loan notes had no commercial or purpose. P argued that the FTT should have made a straightforward comparison of whether the primary facts were the same as those in *Audley*. These were sufficiently different that the principles and reasoning in *Audley* would not apply to P. The UT held that the legislation required the extraction of the principles and reasoning in *Audley* and seeing whether those would, if applied to the taxpayer, similarly deny the tax advantage sought. It made no sense to apply that reasoning only to the primary facts because it was inherent in the reasoning that the facts should be looked at realistically in the light of the purpose of the legislation. There was, moreover, no real distinction between facts and facts found realistically; such reconstituted facts were no less facts. The UT therefore concluded that 'the whole premise' of the appeal was flawed. There was no error in the FTT's approach and so the UT dismissed the appeal.

Partnerships

A follower notice may be given to a partnership in respect of a partnership return (see **52.18** RETURNS) or an appeal relating to such a return. The notice is given to the representative partner (i.e. the partner responsible for dealing with the return) or to the successor of that partner (see **52.18** RETURNS). For the purposes of (b) above, a return or appeal is made on the basis that a particular tax advantage results from particular tax arrangements if the arrangements increase or reduce any of the items required to be included in the return and they result in a tax advantage for at least one of the partners. Where a partnership follower notice is given to a person as representative partner or to the successor of that partner, (d) above does not prevent a follower notice from being given to that person in another capacity. All notices given to the representative partner and any successor, in that capacity, are treated as given to the same person for the purposes of (d) above.

[*FA 2014, ss 204, 206, 207, 217, Sch 31 paras 2, 3*].

Action required following giving of follower notice

[4.28] Where a person is given a follower notice and it is not withdrawn, he (or, in the case of a partnership notice given to a representative partner who is no longer available, his successor) must take the following corrective action before the time specified below. Where an enquiry is in progress, the person must amend the return or claim to counteract the tax advantage denied by principles laid down, or reasoning given, in the judicial ruling. If an appeal is open, the person must take all necessary action to enter into a written agreement with HMRC for the purpose of relinquishing the denied advantage. After carrying out the necessary action the person must, before the specified time, notify HMRC that he has done so, including details of the denied advantage and (except in the case of a partnership follower notice) any additional amount of tax that has or will become due and payable.

If no representations were made following the giving of the notice, the specified time is the end of the period of 90 days beginning with the day on which the notice was given. If representations were made and the notice confirmed, the specified time is the later of the end of that 90-day period and the end of the period of 30 days beginning with the day on which the person is notified of HMRC's decision to confirm the notice.

No appeal may be brought against an amendment made by an enquiry closure notice to the extent that it takes into account an amendment to a return or claim resulting from corrective action under the above provision. Where the corrective action requires an amendment to a return or claim, such an amendment is not prevented by any time limit.

Where a person fails to take the necessary corrective action before the specified time, a penalty arises. See **46.1** PENALTIES.

[*FA 2014, s 208, Sch 31 para 4*].

Late appeal against a judicial ruling

[4.29] Where a final judicial ruling is reopened because a court or Tribunal grants leave to appeal out of time, and a follower notice has been given based on that ruling, the notice is suspended until HMRC notify the taxpayer that the appeal has resulted in a final judicial ruling or has been abandoned or otherwise disposed of. HMRC must notify the taxpayer that the follower notice has been suspended. No new follower notice may be issued in respect of the original ruling unless the new appeal is abandoned or disposed of without being determined by a court or Tribunal, but this does not prevent a follower notice from being issued in respect of a new final ruling resulting from the appeal. Where the appeal is abandoned or so disposed of, the period beginning when leave to appeal out of time was granted and ending when the appeal is disposed of does not count towards the twelve-month time limit for issuing follower notices in respect of the original ruling (see **4.27** above).

If a new final ruling results from the appeal and it is not relevant to the tax arrangements in question, a suspended follower notice ceases to have effect. In any other case it continues to have effect after the suspension ends and, if there is a new final ruling, the notice is treated as if it were in respect of that ruling. HMRC's notification to the taxpayer that the suspension has ended must indicate which of these outcomes applies. If there is a new final ruling, the notification must also make any amendments to the follower notice needed to reflect the new ruling.

The period during which a follower notice is suspended does not count in determining the specified time by which corrective action must be taken (see **4.28** above).

[*FA 2014, s 216*].

Accelerated payment notices

[4.30] Users of avoidance schemes may be required to pay tax upfront before the success or failure of the scheme has been finally determined. HMRC may issue an 'accelerated payment notice' in certain cases which may override any postponement of tax pending an appeal or, where there is no appeal, require the payment of disputed tax within a specified time. There are special provisions for partnerships. The provisions also prevent the surrender as group relief of corporation tax losses etc. arising from an avoidance scheme.

The taxes covered by the provisions are income tax, capital gains tax, corporation tax (including amounts chargeable as if they were corporation tax or treated as if they were corporation tax), inheritance tax, stamp duty land tax and annual tax on enveloped dwellings. The Treasury may extend the provisions to other taxes by order. [*FA 2014, ss 200, 232*]. The provisions are described below only to the extent that they relate to income tax, capital gains tax and corporation tax (except that the extension of the provisions to surrenders of group relief are not covered).

Where relevant, the definitions at **4.26** above apply for the purposes of these provisions.

HMRC have published a list of disclosed avoidance schemes likely to be subject to accelerated payment notices. See gov.uk/government/publications/tax-avoidance-schemes-on-which-accelerated-payments-may-be-charged-by-hmrc.

For HMRC guidance generally see www.gov.uk/government/publications/follower-notices-and-accelerated-payments/follower-notices-and-accelerated-payments.

Simon's Taxes. See **A7.248–A7.248D.**

Attempts to have the giving of an accelerated payment notice declared unlawful were unsuccessful in *R (on the application of Walapu) v HMRC* QB, [2016] STC 1682 and *R (on the application of Graham) v HMRC* QB, [2017] STC 1. Judicial review applications were unsuccessful in *Sword Services Ltd v HMRC* QB, [2016] EWHC 1473 (Admin) and *R (on the application of Dickinson) v HMRC* CA, [2019] STC 319, *R (on the application of Rowe) v HMRC* CA 2017, [2018] STC 462 and *R (on the application of Carlton) v HMRC* QB, [2018] STC 589.

In *Beadle v HMRC* CA, [2020] STC 1058, the CA confirmed that the FTT has no jurisdiction to consider a challenge to the validity of a notice on appeal against a penalty for late payment of the tax charged by the notice.

Giving of accelerated payment notice

[4.31] HMRC may give an accelerated payment notice to a person if:

(a) an enquiry into a return or claim made by that person is in progress or that person has made an appeal which has not been finally determined, abandoned or otherwise disposed of;

(b) the return, claim or appeal is made on the basis that a particular tax advantage results from particular arrangements;

(c) either HMRC have given a follower notice (see **4.26** above) in relation to the same return, claim or appeal by reason of the same tax advantage and the arrangements, the arrangements are 'DOTAS arrangements' or a final counteraction notice under the general anti-abuse rule (see **4.4** and **4.6** above) has been given for the tax advantage (or part of it) and the arrangements in circumstances in which at least two members of the sub-panel of the GAAR Advisory Panel which considered the case concluded that entering into the tax arrangements (or the equivalent arrangements the Panel considered) was not a reasonable course of action (see **4.4**(9) and **4.6** above).

In (c) above, '*DOTAS arrangements*' are arrangements to which HMRC have allocated a reference number under the provisions for DISCLOSURE OF TAX AVOIDANCE SCHEMES (see **19.2** onwards), arrangements implementing a proposal where HMRC have allocated a reference number to the proposed arrangements or arrangements in respect of which a person must provide prescribed information by reason of the arrangements being substantially the same as such arrangements. Arrangements are excluded if HMRC have given notice that the reference number need not be notified to clients.

A notice must specify which of the requirements in (c) above applies and must explain its effects. If the notice is given whilst an enquiry is in progress, it must specify the accelerated payment required; if an appeal is open it must state the amount of the disputed tax (see **4.32** below).

The recipient of an accelerated payment notice has 90 days beginning with the date the notice is given to send written representations to HMRC objecting to the notice on the grounds that any of (a)–(c) above are not satisfied or objecting to the amount specified. Having considered the representations, HMRC will notify the recipient of whether they have decided to confirm the notice, to withdraw it or to amend the amount specified in it. In *R (on the application of Archer) v HMRC* CA, [2019] EWCA Civ 1021, the court held that representations must be made before having resort to judicial review.

[*FA 2014, ss 219, 220(2), 221(2), 222; FA 2021, Sch 31 para 43(2)*].

Partnerships

Where a partnership return (see **52.18** RETURNS) has been made, no accelerated payment notice may be given to the representative partner (i.e. the partner responsible for dealing with the return) or to the successor of that partner (see **52.18** RETURNS) if an enquiry is in progress into that return or an appeal has been made against an amendment of that return or, following an enquiry into that return, a conclusion stated in a closure notice. Instead, a '*partner payment notice*' may be given to each person who was a partner at any time in the period to which the return relates if:

(1) the return or appeal is made on the basis that a particular advantage results from particular tax arrangements;
(2) either HMRC have given a follower notice (see **4.26** above) to the representative partner or successor in relation to the same return or appeal by reason of the same tax advantage and the arrangements, the tax arrangements are DOTAS arrangements or the partner in question has been given a final counteraction notice under the general anti-abuse rule (see **4.4** and **4.6** above) for the tax advantage (or part of it) and the arrangements in circumstances in which at least two members of the sub-panel of the GAAR Advisory Panel which considered the case concluded that entering into the tax arrangements (or the equivalent arrangements the Panel considered) was not a reasonable course of action (see **4.4**(8) above).

For the purposes of (1) above, a return or appeal is made on the basis that a particular tax advantage results from particular tax arrangements if the arrangements increase or reduce any of the items required to be included in the return and they result in a tax advantage for at least one of the partners.

There are provisions as to the contents of a notice and as to representations by the recipient which are similar to those applicable to accelerated payment notices (see above).

[*FA 2014, Sch 32 paras 1–3, 4(1), 5*].

Withdrawal, modification or suspension

HMRC may withdraw a notice at any time and if they do so the notice is treated as never having had effect and any accelerated payments (and penalties) paid must be repaid. If a notice is given as a result of more than one of the requirements in (c) or (2) above, they may at any time withdraw it to the extent that it is given by one of those requirements (leaving it effective to the extent it was given by virtue of the remaining requirements). HMRC may also reduce the amount of the accelerated or partner payment required or the disputed tax specified in the notice (and, where an accelerated payment has already been made in excess of the reduced amount, that excess must be repaid).

An accelerated or partner payment notice given by virtue of a follower notice must be withdrawn if the follower notice is withdrawn (to the extent that it is given by virtue of the follower notice). If a follower notice is suspended following a late appeal against a judicial ruling (see **4.29** above), the accelerated or partner payment notice is similarly suspended and the period of suspension does not count towards the 30-day and 90-day periods in **4.32** below. A notice is not so suspended if it was also given (and not withdrawn) by virtue of either of the other requirements in (c) or (2) above. If a follower notice is amended following such a late appeal, HMRC may by notice make consequential amendments to the accelerated payment notice.

HMRC must withdraw a notice to the extent that it is given by virtue of DOTAS arrangements if they withdraw the scheme reference number or they give notice under *FA 2004, s 312(6)* or *s 312ZA(4)* with the result that notification to clients of the reference number is no longer required (see **19.4** DISCLOSURE OF TAX AVOIDANCE SCHEMES). Before 10 June 2021, HMRC were only required to withdraw the notice if they gave notice under *FA 2004, s 312(6)* that promoters were no longer required to notify clients of the reference number.

Where a notice is given by virtue of more than one of the requirements in (c) or (2) above and is withdrawn to the extent that it was given by virtue of one of those requirements and that requirement was the one stated in the notice to apply to determine the accelerated payment required or disputed tax (see **4.32** below), HMRC must modify the notice to specify one of the remaining requirements as the one which applies for that purpose (and to reduce the payment or tax where necessary). This rule also applies where a a follower notice by virtue of which the accelerated payment notice was given is suspended as if the follower notice were withdrawn, but any change made only applies during the period of suspension.

Where a partnership return to which a notice relates is amended under *TMA 1970, s 12ABZB* (amendment following tribunal determination of partners' shares — see **52.19** RETURNS), HMRC may (by notice) make consequential amendments to the notice. If the amount payable under the notice is increased, the amount of the increase must be paid within the 30 days beginning with the day on which the notice of the amendments was given (if that is later than the normal due date within **4.32** below). If the amount payable is decreased, HMRC must repay any excess amount paid.

[*FA 2014, s 227, Sch 32 para 8; FA 2021, Sch 31 paras 43(3), 44*].

Effects of accelerated payment notice

[4.32] If an accelerated payment notice is given whilst an enquiry is in progress or a partner payment notice is given, the recipient of the notice must make the payment specified in it. If no representations were made following the giving of the notice, the payment must be made within the period of 90 days beginning with the day on which the notice was given. If representations were made and the notice confirmed or amended, the payment must be made by the later of the end of that 90-day period and the end of the period of 30 days beginning with the day on which the person is notified of HMRC's decision to confirm or amend the notice.

The amount of the payment required is (subject to any representations) the amount which a designated HMRC officer determines, to the best of his information and belief as the 'understated tax' (disregarding any partnership dispute referred to the tribunal under *TMA 1970, s 12ABZB* (determination by tribunal of partners' shares — see **52.19** RETURNS), but not yet determined).

(1) Where the notice is given as a result of a follower notice, the '*understated tax*' is the additional amount that would be due and payable if the necessary corrective action under the follower notice were taken in respect of what the designated HMRC officer determines, to the best of his information and belief, as the tax advantage denied by the judicial ruling (see **4.28** above).

(2) Where the notice is given because the tax arrangements are DOTAS arrangements, the '*understated tax*' is the additional amount that would be due and payable if adjustments were made to counteract what the designated HMRC officer determines, to the best of his information and belief, as so much of the asserted tax advantage as is not a tax advantage which results from the arrangements or otherwise.

(3) Where the notice is given as a result of a GAAR counteraction notice, the '*understated tax*' is the additional amount that would be due and payable if the adjustments set out in that notice which counteract the asserted tax advantage were made.

Where more than one of (1)–(3) above would apply, the notice must stipulate which of them applies and the payment required must be determined accordingly. Where any of the tax included in the accelerated payment required under the notice has already been paid, the payment required is treated as having been paid at the time of the earlier payment. HMRC's recovery powers apply to the required payment as they apply to payments of tax (see **45** PAYMENT OF TAX).

If an accelerated payment notice is given (and not withdrawn) whilst an appeal is open, the understated tax or understated partner tax or the disputed tax (see below) cannot be postponed (see **45.18** PAYMENT OF TAX) pending the outcome of the appeal. Any additional tax arising from the amendment of an accelerated payment notice as a result of the amendment of a partnership return under *TMA 1970, s 12ABZB* (amendment following tribunal determination of partners' shares — see **52.19** RETURNS) also cannot be postponed. If an amount of disputed tax is postponed immediately before the giving of an accelerated payment notice, it ceases to be postponed at that time and becomes due and payable on or before the last day of the 90-day period beginning with the day the notice is given. If representations are made against the notice (see **4.31** above), the tax becomes due and payable on or before the later of the end of that 90-day period and the last day of the 30-day period beginning on the day on which HMRC notify their decision about the representations. If additional tax arising from the amendment of an accelerated payment notice following amendment of a partnership return under *TMA 1970, s 12ABZB* is postponed immediately before the giving of the notice amending the accelerated payment notice, it ceases to be postponed at that time. The additional tax becomes due and payable on or before the last day of the 30-day period beginning with the day the notice is given or, if later, the last day on which it would have been payable had it been disputed tax included in the accelerated payment notice as originally issued.

The '*disputed tax*' is so much of the tax which is the subject of the appeal as the designated HMRC officer determines, to the best of his information and belief, as the amount required to counteract what that officer so determines to be the tax advantage in dispute (calculated in the same way as the understated tax in (1)–(3) above). Where more than one of (1)–(3) above would apply, the notice must stipulate which of them applies and the tax advantage in dispute must be determined accordingly.

Where an accelerated payment notice is in force in relation to an open appeal and a court or Tribunal decides against HMRC but they seek permission to appeal against the decision, they may apply to the court or Tribunal from which they are seeking permission to appeal to disapply the rule requiring repayment of tax in accordance with the decision (see **45.19** PAYMENT OF TAX). If the court or Tribunal considers it necessary for the protection of the revenue, it may give permission to withhold the affected repayment or to require the provision of adequate security before repayment is made.

[*TMA 1970, ss 55(8B)–(8E), 56(4)–(6); FA 2014, ss 220(3)–(7), 221(3)–(5), 223, 224(1), 225(1), Sch 32 paras 4(2)–(5), 6*].

See **49.29** PENALTIES for the penalties chargeable for failure to make an accelerated payment.

Serial avoiders regime

[4.33] A regime of warnings and escalating sanctions applies to taxpayers who persistently engage in tax avoidance schemes that are successfully counteracted ('*defeated*') by HMRC. Following the first defeat of a scheme, HMRC will place the taxpayer on a warning (see **4.34**, **4.35** below). The taxpayer has to annually provide HMRC with information during a five-year warning period (see **4.36** below). If the taxpayer uses any such avoidance scheme while under warning, penalties of up to 60% of the understated tax will be charged (see **46.24** PENALTIES) if the scheme is defeated. If three avoidance schemes which exploit reliefs are used while under warning and are defeated, the taxpayer is denied further benefit of reliefs until the warning period expires (see **4.37**). If HMRC defeat three avoidance schemes while the taxpayer is on warning, the taxpayer's details can be published (see **4.41**). See **4.38** for the application of the regime to partnerships.

The regime applies to a number of direct and indirect taxes and also national insurance contributions (see *FA 2016, Sch 18 para 4* for the full list). It is described below in terms of its application to capital gains tax and corporation tax on chargeable gains, but it should be noted that the regime does not operate independently for each type of tax but embraces all avoidance schemes that a person uses which cover any tax on the list.

In relation to taxes other than VAT, '*tax advantage*' is defined widely by *FA 2016, Sch 18 para 7* for the purposes of these provisions.

Simon's Taxes. See A7.330–A7.335.

For HMRC guidance, see www.gov.uk/government/collections/serial-tax-avoidance-regime.

Warning notices

[4.34] Where a person has incurred a 'relevant defeat' (see **4.35** below) in relation to any arrangements (as widely defined), HMRC must give that person a written notice (a '*warning notice*') within the 90 days beginning with the day on which the defeat is incurred. The warning notice must specify the defeat in question, state when the 'warning period' begins and ends and explain the statutory consequences of the notice. The '*warning period*' is the five years following the day on which the warning notice is given. If a person incurs a relevant defeat during a warning period, that period is extended to the end of the five years following the day on which the defeat occurs. [*FA 2016, Sch 18 paras 2, 3*].

Associated persons

Where a person (P) incurs a relevant defeat in relation to any arrangements, any person who is 'associated' with P at the time when P is given the warning notice is also treated for the above purposes as having incurred that relevant defeat, unless both persons are companies in the same group. However, a warning notice thus given to an associated person is disregarded for the purposes of **4.37** below (restriction of relief notices) and see **46.24** PENALTIES. For these purposes, two persons are '*associated*' with one another only if one of them is a body corporate which is controlled (as defined) by the other or if they are bodies corporate under common control (as defined). [*FA 2016, Sch 18 paras 47, 48*].

Meaning of 'relevant defeat'

[4.35] For the purposes of taxes other than VAT, a person (P) incurs a '*relevant defeat*' in relation to arrangements if any of conditions A to C below is met in relation to P and the arrangements. The relevant defeat is incurred when the condition in question is first met.

- Condition A is that a tax advantage has arisen to P from the arrangements and this has been counteracted as in **4.3** above (the GAAR), with the counteraction having become final.
- Condition B is that (in a case not falling within Condition A) a follower notice (see **4.26** above) has been given to P by reference to the arrangements (and not withdrawn) and either the necessary corrective action

has been taken (see **4.28** above) or the denied tax advantage has been otherwise counteracted, with the counteraction having become final (determined in the same manner as under **4.3** above).

- Condition C is that (in a case not falling within Condition A or B) the arrangements are 'DOTAS arrangements' (see below) on which P has relied, and the arrangements have been counteracted, with the counteraction having become final. The time at which it falls to be determined whether or not the arrangements are DOTAS arrangements is when the counteraction becomes final.

Condition B applies also where the follower notice is a partnership follower notice in connection with a partnership return and is given to a partnership in which P was a partner in the period covered by the return.

For the purposes of Condition C, P relies on the arrangements if he makes a return, claim or election, or a partnership return is made, on the basis that a 'relevant tax advantage' arises, or if P fails to discharge a 'relevant obligation' and there is reason to believe that the failure is connected with the arrangements. A '*relevant tax advantage*' is one which the arrangements might be expected to enable P to obtain. An obligation is a '*relevant obligation*' if the arrangements might be expected to have the result that the obligation does not arise.

Arrangements are counteracted for the purposes of Condition C if P's tax position is adjusted (other than at his own behest), or an HMRC assessment is made on P, or any other action is taken by HMRC, on the basis that the whole or part of the relevant tax advantage does not arise or that the relevant obligation does arise. Contract settlements (see **6.8** ASSESSMENTS) are treated as assessments for this purpose. P's tax position is adjusted at his own behest if he makes the adjustment at a time when he had no reason to believe that an HMRC enquiry was in the offing (regarding the tax in question) or if HMRC make the adjustment as a result of a full and explicit disclosure by P which is made at such a time.

A counteraction is final for the purposes of Condition C when the assessment, adjustments or action in question, and any amounts thereby arising, can no longer be varied on appeal or otherwise.

[*FA 2016, Sch 18 paras 11–14, 54*].

Meaning of 'DOTAS arrangements'

For the purposes of the serial avoiders regime, arrangements are '*DOTAS arrangements*' at any time if they are 'notifiable arrangements' at that time and a person has provided information in relation to them under *FA 2004, s 308(3)* (obligation of promoter in relation to notifiable arrangements), *s 309* (obligation of person dealing with non-UK promoter) or *s 310* (obligation of parties to notifiable arrangements not involving a promoter) or has failed to comply with any of those provisions in relation to the arrangements. They do not include arrangements in respect of which HMRC have given notice that promoters are not under a duty to notify clients of the reference number. However, they do include arrangements which are excepted from the notification requirement for the reason only that they either had been notified as proposed arrangements or are substantially the same as arrangements already notified.

For the meaning of 'notifiable arrangements' and more on the above-mentioned *FA 2004* provisions, see **19.3** DISCLOSURE OF TAX AVOIDANCE SCHEMES. For the above purposes, a person fails to comply with any of those provisions if (and only if) the Tribunal has determined this to be the case (or has determined against a reasonable excuse), and their determination can no longer be appealed, or the person has made a written admission of such failure to HMRC.

[*FA 2016, Sch 18 paras 8, 10*].

Requirement of annual information notices

[4.36] A person (P) who has been given a warning notice (as in **4.34** above) must give HMRC a written notice (an '*information notice*') in respect of each 'reporting period' within the warning period. The information notice must be given within 30 days after the end of the reporting period to which it relates. Groups of companies may give a combined information notice. The first '*reporting period*' begins with the first day of the warning period and ends with a day specified by HMRC. The remainder of the warning period is divided into further reporting periods of 12 months duration, though the final reporting period ends at the same time as the warning period, even if that results in a reporting period of less than 12 months.

An information notice must state whether, in the reporting period, P:

(a) has made a return, claim or election on the basis that a 'relevant tax advantage' arises (and this includes a return made on that basis since the reporting period ended if the return was due in the reporting period); or
(b) has failed to take action which he would be required to take under, or by virtue of, any tax enactment if it were not for particular DOTAS arrangements (see **4.35** above) or 'disclosable VAT arrangements' (within *FA 2016, Sch 18 para 9*) to which he is a party; or
(c) has become a party to arrangements relating to a supplier's VAT position which might be expected to enable P to obtain a relevant tax advantage in connection with the supplies,

and whether or not P has failed to make any return that he was required to make by a date falling in the reporting period.

A '*relevant tax advantage*' is a tax advantage which particular DOTAS arrangements or disclosable VAT arrangements enable, or might be expected to enable, P to obtain. If (a) above is in point, P must include in the information notice an explanation of how the tax advantage arises and its amount. If (b) is in point, P must similarly explain how the arrangements result in there being no requirement to take the action in question and state the amount of any resulting tax advantage. If (c) is in point, P must state whether it is his view that the relevant tax advantage arises to him and, if so, he must explain how the arrangements enable him to obtain the advantage and state its amount.

If the due date for a return falls within the reporting period and P fails to make the return in that period, HMRC may require from P a supplementary information notice setting out any matters which he would have been required to include in the original information notice if it had not been for that failure. Any such HMRC requirement must be notified in writing and must state the period allowed for compliance.

If P fails to provide a notice (whether an information notice or a supplementary information notice) or provides a notice that is defective, HMRC may by written notice extend the warning period to the end of the five years beginning with the day by which the notice should have been given, or the day on which the defective notice was given. The warning period cannot thus be extended by more than five years from what would otherwise have been its expiry date.

[*FA 2016, Sch 18 para 17*].

Restriction of reliefs

[4.37] HMRC must give a person a written notice (a '*restriction of relief notice*') if:

- the person incurs a relevant defeat (see **4.35** above) in relation to arrangements which he has used whilst in a warning period (see **4.34** above);
- he has been given at least two warning notices in respect of other relevant defeats of arrangements used in that same warning period;
- all the relevant defeats are by virtue of Condition A, B or C in **4.35** (as opposed to conditions relating to VAT that are not reproduced here);
- all the relevant defeats relate to the misuse of a relief; and
- in the case of each of the relevant defeats, either the counteraction was made on the basis that a particular 'avoidance-related rule' applied in relation to a person's affairs or the misused relief in question was a relief for losses under *ITA 2007, Pt 4* or *CTA 2010, Pts 4, 5*.

If a person has been given a single warning notice in relation to two or more relevant defeats, he is treated for the above purposes as having been given a separate warning notice in relation to each defeat. The time at which, for the purposes of the serial avoiders regime, a person has 'used' arrangements is determined by *FA 2016, Sch 18 para 55* in terms of the filing date for returns (meaning the earlier of the actual filing date and the due date), the dates on which claims and elections are made and the date of any failure to comply with an obligation (meaning the date on which the person is first in breach of the obligation).

A relevant defeat relates to the misuse of a relief if the tax advantage in question (or part of it), results from a relief (or an increased relief) or it is reasonable to conclude that the making of a particular claim for relief, or the use of a particular relief, is a significant component of the arrangements in question. A relief means any relief from tax (however described) which must be claimed; management expenses of a company's investment business; any relief for losses under *ITA 2007, Pt 4* or *CTA 2010, Pts 4, 5*; or any other relief listed in *ITA 2007, s 24* (reliefs deductible at Step 2 of the calculation of income tax liability).

'*Avoidance-related rule*' is defined by *FA 2016, Sch 18 para 25*, which also includes an example of such a rule. A statutory rule to the effect that the avoidance of tax must not be a main object or an expected benefit of a transaction or arrangements, or that an action must be carried out for commercial reasons, would be an avoidance-related rule.

The restricted period

A restriction of relief notice must explain its effect (see below) and state when the 'restricted period' begins and ends. The '*restricted period*' is the three years beginning with the day on which the restriction of relief notice is given. If during the restricted period the person to whom a restriction of relief notice has been given incurs a further relevant defeat, HMRC must give him a written notice (a '*restricted period extension notice*'); this extends the restricted period to the end of the three years beginning with the day on which the further defeat occurs. A further defeat is taken into account for this purpose only if it is incurred by virtue of Condition A, B or C in relation to arrangements which the person used in the warning period and relates to the misuse of a relief. If a person to whom a restriction of relief notice has been given incurs a further defeat after the restricted period has ended but during a warning period which at some time ran concurrently with the restricted period, HMRC must give that person a restriction of relief notice.

Effect of restriction of relief notice

A person to whom a restriction of relief notice has been given may not, in the restricted period, make any claim for relief. (For the purposes of the serial avoiders regime, 'claim for relief' includes any election or similar action which is in substance a claim for relief.) Reliefs for charitable giving and contributions to a registered pension scheme are excluded from this restriction, as are claims for relief under a double tax treaty. No losses may be deducted in calculating the total amount of chargeable gains, or the total amount of ATED-related gains or NRCGT gains, for any tax year the first day of which is in the restricted period. Further restrictions are listed in *FA 2016, Sch 18 para 20*.

Mitigation, reasonable excuse and appeals

The Commissioners for HMRC may mitigate, in any way they think appropriate, the effect of a restriction of relief notice insofar as it appears to them that there are exceptional circumstances such that it would otherwise have an unduly serious impact with respect to the tax affairs of the taxpayer concerned or another person.

If a person (P) who has incurred a relevant defeat satisfies HMRC or, on appeal, the Tribunal that he had a reasonable excuse for the matters to which the defeat relates, he is treated for the purposes of the restriction of relief provisions as not having incurred that defeat, and any warning notice given to him in relation to that defeat is treated as not having been given. Reasonable excuse does not include insufficiency of funds (unless attributable to events outside P's control), reliance on another person to do anything (unless P took reasonable care to avoid the failure or inaccuracy in question) or reliance on advice if that advice is addressed to, or was given to, a person other than P or takes no account of P's individual circumstances. A person with a reasonable excuse is treated as having continued to have it if the failure or inaccuracy in question was remedied without unreasonable delay after the excuse ceased.

A person may appeal against a restriction of relief notice or a restricted period extension notice within 30 days beginning with the day on which the notice is given. The appeal is to be treated in the same way as an appeal against an income tax assessment. The Tribunal, on an appeal brought before it, may cancel or affirm HMRC's decision to issue the notice. It may also mitigate the effect of a notice to the same extent as HMRC (see above) or to a different extent, but in the latter case only if the Tribunal regards HMRC's decision on mitigation as flawed.

[*FA 2016, Sch 18 paras 19–29, 55*].

Partnerships

[4.38] The consequences described below apply in relation to a partnership tax return under *TMA 1970, s 12AA* if:

- the return has been made on the basis that a tax advantage arises to a partner from any arrangements and that partner has incurred, in relation to that tax advantage and those arrangements, a relevant defeat by virtue of Condition A or Condition C in **4.35** above; or
- a person has incurred a relevant defeat by virtue of Condition B in **4.35** above and the follower notice in question is a partnership follower notice.

A partnership return is regarded as made on the basis that a particular tax advantage arises to a partner from particular arrangements if it is made on the basis that an increase or reduction in any of the items to be included in the partnership statement (see **52.19** RETURNS) results from those arrangements and that increase or reduction results in that tax advantage for the partner. Limited liability partnerships are within these rules in the same way as other partnerships. For the above purposes a relevant defeat does not include one which an associated person is treated as having incurred (see **4.34** above).

Each 'relevant partner' is treated for the purposes of the serial avoiders regime as having also incurred the relevant defeat in question. A '*relevant partner*' is any person who was a member of the partnership at any time during the period covered by the partnership return.

The appropriate partner (meaning a partner nominated by HMRC for this purpose) must give HMRC a written notice (a '*partnership information notice*') in respect of each sub-period in the 'information period'. The '*information period*' is the five years following the day of the relevant defeat. If a new information period (relating to another partnership return) begins during an existing information period, those periods are treated as a single period. An information period ends if the partnership ceases. The partnership information notice must be given within 30 days after the end of the sub-period to which it relates. The first sub-period begins with the first day of the information period and ends with a day specified by HMRC. The remainder of the information period is divided into further sub-periods of 12 months duration, though the final sub-period ends at the same time as the information period, even if that results in a sub-period of less than 12 months. A partnership information notice must state (i) whether or not any partnership return which was, or was required to be, delivered in the sub-period has been made on the basis that a 'relevant tax advantage' arises; and (ii) whether or not there has been a failure to deliver a partnership return in the sub-period. A '*relevant tax advantage*' is a tax advantage which particular DOTAS arrangements (see **4.35** above) enable, or might be expected to enable, a member of the partnership to obtain. Where relevant, the information notice must go on to explain how the DOTAS arrangements enable the tax advantage to be obtained and describe any variation in the amounts required to be stated in the partnership statement included in the return. There is similar provision to require supplementary information notices as in **4.36** above, and similar consequences for failure to provide an accurate information notice.

There is provision to the effect that if a partnership return is amended, whether by the partnership itself or by HMRC following an unprompted disclosure, then, for the purpose of applying Condition C in **4.35** above, each affected partner is treated as having simultaneously amended his own return so as to give effect to the amendment of the partnership return.

[*FA 2016, Sch 18 paras 49–53, 58(1)(4)*].

Groups of companies

[4.39] Where HMRC have a duty to give a warning notice (see **4.34** above) to a company (C) which is a member of a 'group', that duty has effect as a duty to give such a notice to every other company which is then a member of the group. HMRC may fulfil that duty by delivering the notice to C (and if it does so may combine warning notices in a single notice). Any warning notice previously given to a current group member is treated as having been given to each current group member.

Where a group company incurs a relevant defeat, however, the provisions for restriction of relief notices (see **4.37** above) and penalties (see **4.40** below) apply by reference only to warning periods of the company which would be warning periods if the above provisions did not apply.

Any warning notice which applies to a company only as a result of the above provisions ceases to apply to it when it leaves the group.

Two companies are members of the same group for this purpose if one is a 75% subsidiary (within *CTA 2010, s 1154*) of the other or both are 75% subsidiaries of a third company.

The warning period rules at **4.35** above apply as if successive representative members of a VAT group were a single person, but the serial avoiders regime applies in general to any company as if the company acting in its capacity as representative member were a different person from the company acting in any other capacity.

[*FA 2016, Sch 18 paras 45, 46*].

Penalties

[4.40] See **46.24** PENALTIES which apply where a person incurs a relevant defeat in relation to any arrangements used during a warning period.

Publishing taxpayer's details

[4.41] The Commissioners for HMRC may publish information about a person if he incurs a relevant defeat (see **4.35** above) in relation to arrangements which he has used in a warning period and has been given at least two warning notices (see **4.34** above) in respect of other defeats of arrangements which were used in the same warning period. If a person has been given a single warning notice in relation to two or more relevant defeats, he is treated for these purposes as having been given a separate warning notice in relation to each of those defeats.

The Commissioners can publish the person's name (including trading name, previous name or pseudonym), address or registered office, the nature of any business carried on, information about the fiscal effect of relevant defeated arrangements (had they not been defeated), e.g. the amount of tax understated, the amount of any penalty, the periods in which or times when relevant defeated arrangements were used, and any other information which they consider appropriate in order to make the person's identity clear. In the case of a person carrying on a trade or business in partnership, the information which may be published includes any trading name of the partnership and the names and addresses of the partners. In the case of a company which is a member of a group, the information which may be published includes any trading name of the group and the name, address or registered office and nature of business of any other group member. Defeated arrangements are relevant if the person used them in the said warning period and has been given a warning notice in respect of them. The information may be published in any manner the Commissioners consider appropriate. It can only be first published in the period of one year beginning with the giving of the most recent of the warning notices in question, and information cannot continue to be published for more than a year. Before publishing the information, the Commissioners must inform the person that they are doing so and provide a reasonable opportunity to make representations about whether it should be published.

[*FA 2016, Sch 18 para 18*].

Key points on anti-avoidance

[4.42] Points to consider are as follows.

- If you are considering a complex tax mitigation scheme, be sure that the intended result at each stage reflects the documentation. If the intention is to do something different, and the scheme is found to be a sham, then you have not only failed in your objective but you have almost certainly wasted a great deal of time and money along the way.
- Correct implementation is also crucial. Many schemes have failed because the documents were not signed in the right order, directors were not in the country when board meeting purportedly took place, etc. These practical issues matter — HMRC will happily negate the effect of a piece of tax planning because it was not correctly implemented.
- In cases of incorrect implementation, HMRC also consider that it can charge penalties for the submission of incorrect returns.

- The experience of recent years suggests that the Tribunals and courts are more likely to find for the taxpayer where there is some commercial motivation behind the transactions carried out. So it is important to consider commercial reasons in advance and to keep a record of them. HMRC enquiries can last a long time and, by the time evidence of a commercial rationale is required, the people who know why things were done may no longer be with the organisation.
- For similar reasons, a full set of all documents and supporting evidence should be collected together immediately after the transactions are complete. If one set is kept by the client and another by the adviser, there is a good chance that at least one will be accessible when HMRC's enquiries commence.
- *TCGA 1992, s 3* applies to attribute gains to corporate shareholders as well as individuals. This point is often forgotten by advisers. See **4.8**.
- It is not clear whether there is an implicit motive test in *TCGA 1992, s 29*; this may depend on the meaning attributed to the words 'so that'. But a subscription by a third party on arm's length terms should not give rise to a value shifting charge, if the subscription turns out on later analysis as having been at less than market value. See **4.9**.
- A transfer of assets (or cash) by a close company, on less than arm's-length terms, may also be a chargeable transfer for the purposes of inheritance tax (*IHTA 1984, s 94*). See **4.15**.
- It is important to note that an HMRC clearance only states that HMRC are satisfied that the transactions are being entered into for bona fide commercial reasons and not for the avoidance of corporation tax. The clearance does not confirm that HMRC agree that the transaction amounts to a reorganisation or a scheme of reconstruction.
- The depreciatory transactions rules will not generally be applied to dividend strips where the dividends were paid out of post-acquisition profits, i.e. profits that arose after the shares were acquired by the shareholder. The rationale is that it would not be just or reasonable to apply an adjustment when a shareholder is merely exercising their rights to access profits that accrued during their period of ownership. See **4.20**.
- Plans should also consider the general anti-abuse rule.

5

Appeals

Cross-references. See **6** ASSESSMENTS; **13.3** CLAIMS for appeals in connection with claims and elections made outside the annual tax return; **29** HMRC INVESTIGATORY POWERS; **36.2** LATE PAYMENT INTEREST AND PENALTIES as regards interest on tax becoming due where an appeal is made or determined; **45.19** PAYMENT OF TAX for postponement provisions; **49.29, 46.30** PENALTIES.

Simon's Taxes. See **A5.3, A5.5, A5.6.**

Introduction to appeals

[5.1] A taxpayer who disagrees with an assessment or other decision made by HMRC can appeal against it. This is done by giving notice in writing to HMRC, stating the grounds of appeal. The notice must normally be given within 30 days after the date of issue of the assessment or decision, although late appeals can be made in some circumstances (see **5.3** below).

After a taxpayer appeals there are three main options:

- a different HMRC officer can carry out a review of the decision;
- the taxpayer can ask the Tribunal to decide the matter in dispute;
- the appeal can be settled by agreement at any time.

Taxpayers can also apply to use alternative dispute resolution to settle the dispute. See **5.10** below.

Reviews are not compulsory, and where HMRC carry out a review but the taxpayer still disagrees with the decision, they can ask the Tribunal to decide the issue (or continue negotiations with HMRC in order to settle the appeal by agreement).

For HMRC reviews, see **5.6** below and for settlement by agreement, see **5.9** below.

Where the taxpayer asks the Tribunal to decide the appeal, the case is usually dealt with by the First-tier Tribunal. The appeal is allocated to one of four categories, default paper, basic, standard or complex, and the process differs according to the category. Basic, standard and complex cases are normally decided at a hearing at which the taxpayer (or their representative) and HMRC are able to present their cases.

Default paper cases can also be decided at a hearing where one of the parties requests a hearing. Complex cases can be transferred for hearing by the Upper Tribunal, although this is rare in practice.

For the First-tier Tribunal process, see **5.12–5.24** below.

If either the taxpayer or HMRC disagree with a decision of the First-tier Tribunal, there is a further right of appeal to the Upper Tribunal, but only on a point of law. Permission to appeal must be obtained from the First-tier Tribunal, or where it refuses permission, from the Upper Tribunal.

For the Upper Tribunal process, see **5.25–5.33** below. Where either party disagrees with an Upper Tribunal decision, there is a similar right of appeal to the Court of Appeal. See **5.34** below.

Where there is no right of appeal or a taxpayer is dissatisfied with the exercise by HMRC or the Tribunal of administrative powers, they may in certain circumstances seek a remedy by way of application for judicial review. See **5.35** below.

Costs can be awarded to or against a taxpayer in cases dealt with by either tribunal or by the courts. See **5.24**, **5.33** and **5.36** below.

See generally HMRC Appeals, Reviews and Tribunals Guide.

Coronavirus (COVID-19)

A number of temporary changes were made to the provisions in this chapter as a result of the coronavirus pandemic. The changes included a temporary stay on proceedings, extension of time limits and the introduction of remote hearings. For details, see the 2023/24 edition of this work.

Right of appeal

[5.2] A taxpayer can appeal against:

(a) any assessment other than a self-assessment;
(b) any conclusion stated, or amendment made, by a final or partial closure notice on completion or part completion of an enquiry into a personal, trustees' or partnership tax return (see **52.14** RETURNS);
(c) any HMRC amendment made by a final or partial closure notice on completion or part completion of an enquiry into a company tax return;
(d) any HMRC amendment (of a self-assessment) made, during an enquiry, to prevent potential loss of tax (see **52.15** RETURNS);
(e) any amendment of a partnership return where loss of tax is 'discovered' (see **6.11** ASSESSMENTS);
(f) any discovery determination (i.e. a determination by HMRC of an amount included in a company tax return which affects the tax payable for another accounting period or by another company).

The right of appeal in (a) above includes a right of appeal against a 'simple assessment', but an appeal can be made only after the person assessed has raised a query about the assessment and has been given a final response to that query. See **6.9** ASSESSMENTS.

An appeal within (d) above while an enquiry is in progress in relation to any matter affected by the amendment cannot be taken forward until a partial closure notice is issued in relation to the matter or, if no such notice is issued, a final closure notice is issued (see **52.14** RETURNS).

[*TMA 1970, s 31(1)(2)(3A); FA 1998, Sch 18 paras 30(3), 34(3), 48(1), 49*].

An appeal against an assessment to corporation tax is an appeal against the total amount of profits charged to tax in the assessment (*Owton Fens Properties Ltd v Redden* Ch D 1984, 58 TC 218).

In partnership cases, the right of appeal is not restricted to the nominated partner (*Phillips v HMRC* FTT, [2010] SFTD 332). See, however, **46.30** PENALTIES for the restriction of the right of appeal against a penalty under *FA 2009, Sch 55* to the nominated partner (which restriction was upheld in *Dyson v HMRC* FTT, [2015] SFTD 529, despite the Tribunal holding that the provision contravened the European Convention on Human Rights).

Specific rights of appeal against HMRC decisions, notices or determinations are also included in a number of other provisions and, where relevant, such rights are referred to at the appropriate place in this work. Appeals in connection with claims and elections, where made outside the tax return, are dealt with at **13.3** CLAIMS.

There is no right of appeal against a determination of liability made by HMRC in the event of non-submission of a tax return (see **52.17** RETURNS).

Unless otherwise stated or required by context, the remainder of this chapter applies to all appeals and all matters treated as appeals, and not only to appeals within (a)–(f) above. [*TMA 1970, s 48*].

Making an appeal

[5.3] An appeal is made by giving notice in writing to the HMRC officer concerned and specifying the grounds of appeal. Notice must normally be given within 30 days after the date of issue of the assessment or determination, the closure notice or the notice of amendment. In the case of a 'simple assessment' (see **6.9** ASSESSMENTS) notice of appeal must be given within 30 days after the date on which the person assessed is given notice by HMRC of their final response to his query about the assessment. [*TMA 1970, s 31A(1)–(5); FA 1998, Sch 18 paras 30(3)(4), 34(3)(4), 48(2), 92(2)*].

See **5.1** above for the extension of the time limit in certain cases for taxpayers affected by the coronavirus.

Late appeals

If a taxpayer fails to make an appeal within the normal time limit, an appeal can still be made if HMRC agree or, where HMRC do not agree, the Tribunal gives permission.

HMRC must agree to a written request for a late appeal if they are satisfied that there was a reasonable excuse for not making the appeal within the time limit and that the request was made without unreasonable delay after the reasonable excuse ceased.

[*TMA 1970, s 49*].

In the event of refusal to accept a late appeal, the decision is not subject to further appeal (*R v Special Commrs (ex p. Magill)* QB (NI) 1979, 53 TC 135), but is subject to judicial review (see *R v Hastings and Bexhill General Commrs and CIR (ex p. Goodacre)* QB 1994, 67 TC 126, in which a refusal was quashed and the matter remitted to a different body of Appeal Commissioners).

The leading decision on the approach which the Tribunal will take in deciding whether to allow a late appeal is an excise duty case, *Martland v HMRC* UT, [2018] UKUT 178 (TCC). This requires the tribunal to apply a three-step process, as follows:

(1) establish the length of the delay in making the application;
(2) establish the reason(s) for that delay;
(3) evaluate all the circumstances of the case.

The balancing exercise at stage three will assess the merits of the reasons for the delay and the prejudice which would be caused to both parties by granting or refusing permission. That balancing exercise will take into account the particular importance of the need for litigation to be conducted efficiently and at proportionate cost, and for statutory time limits to be respected. Aspects like the strength of the case, the reason for the delay and the impact on the appellant if permission is refused, can be included in the stage three exercise.

Withdrawing an appeal

An appeal once made cannot, strictly, be withdrawn unilaterally (see *R v Special Commissioners (ex p. Elmhirst)* CA 1935, 20 TC 381 and *Beach v Willesden General Commissioners* Ch D 1981, 55 TC 663). If, however, a taxpayer or his agent gives HMRC oral or written notice of his desire not to proceed with an appeal, the appeal is treated as if settled by agreement, so that the provisions at **5.9** below apply (and the appeal is settled without any variation). Agreement is effective from the date of the taxpayer's notification. This does not apply if HMRC give written notice of objection within 30 days of the taxpayer's notice. [*TMA 1970, s 54(4)(5)*].

Payment of tax

For postponement of tax pending appeal and for payment of tax on determination of the appeal, see respectively **45.19** PAYMENT OF TAX.

Special regulations for capital gains tax appeals

[5.4] *The Capital Gains Tax Regulations 1967 (SI 1967 No 149)* make special provisions in relation to CGT appeals and are summarised below. In particular, they lay down procedures under which a question of market value or apportionment which affects the liability of two or more persons (e.g. a donor and donee, or a vendor and purchaser in a transaction not at arm's length) can be settled.

Joinder of third parties in appeals

Where the market value of an asset on a particular date or the apportionment of any amount or value is a material question in an appeal, any person whose liability to CGT for any period may be affected by that market value may apply to be joined in the appeal. Application is in writing to HMRC and should state, *inter alia*, how the applicant's liability may be affected and his contention in relation to the matters under appeal. A copy of the application is sent by HMRC to the appellant and any other party to the appeal. If the application is received before the appeal has been notified to the tribunal (or, before 1 April 2009, more than 30 days before the date of the appeal hearing, or before that date is set), then if HMRC are satisfied with the propriety of the applicant's case, the applicant will be joined as a third party and appropriate notice given to the other parties. Otherwise, HMRC will refer the application to the Tribunal who may allow or refuse the application at its discretion. Insofar as his interest is being considered, the third party has the same rights as the appellant. [*SI 1967 No 149, Reg 8*].

Applications for determination of market value

Where the market value of an asset or the apportionment of any amount or value may affect the liability to CGT of two or more persons, either or any of them may apply to the Tribunal for a ruling if the point is not, nor has been, a material question in an appeal brought by any of them. HMRC are a party to such proceedings. [*SI 1967 No 149, Reg 9*].

Conclusive effect of determination on appeal

The values as determined are conclusive between HMRC, the parties to the appeal and any third party who was given notice of the appeal in reasonable time unless that person's application (made without undue delay) to be joined as a party to the appeal was refused. [*SI 1967 No 149, Reg 11*].

Agreements in writing

There can be no binding agreement on the value of an asset between HMRC and the taxpayer unless the agreement is joined by any proper third party to the appeal. A written agreement will be effective against the taxpayer's personal representatives, trustee in bankruptcy etc. An agreement conclusive against trustees of a settlement will be effective against any person becoming absolutely entitled to the settled property. [*SI 1967 No 149, Regs 12, 13*].

The appeal process

[5.5] When an appeal to HMRC is made, there are four options for the appeal to proceed:

(a) the appellant can require HMRC to review the matter in question;
(b) HMRC can offer to review the matter in question;
(c) the appellant can notify the appeal to the Tribunal for it to decide the matter in question; or
(d) the appeal can be settled by agreement between HMRC and the appellant (including by way of alternative dispute resolution).

Where the appellant requires an HMRC review, they can still notify the appeal to the Tribunal if they disagree with the review's conclusions or HMRC fail to complete a review within the required time. If HMRC offer a review and the appellant does not accept the offer, they can likewise notify the appeal to the Tribunal. Taking any of options (a) to (c) above does not prevent the appeal from being settled by agreement at any time.

[*TMA 1970, s 49A*].

For details of the review process, see **5.6** below; for notifying an appeal to the tribunal, see **5.8** below; and for settlement of appeals by agreement, see **5.9** below.

Notices

All notices given under the appeal provisions must be made in writing. Notifications by the appellant can be made by a person acting on their behalf, but all HMRC notifications must be made directly to the appellant (although copies can be sent to their agent). [*TMA 1970, s 49I*].

HMRC review

[5.6] Where an appellant notifies HMRC that they require them to review the matter in question, HMRC must first notify them of their view of the matter. They must do this within the 30 days beginning with the day on which they receive the notification from the appellant, or within such longer period as is reasonable. They must then carry out a review of the matter in question, as described at 5.7 below.

The appellant cannot request a second review of the matter in question and neither can they request a review if they have already notified the appeal to the tribunal.

If it is HMRC who offer to review the matter in question, they must, when they notify the appellant of the offer, also notify the appellant of their view of the matter. The appellant then has 30 days beginning with the date of the document notifying the offer to notify HMRC of acceptance of it. If the appellant does so, HMRC must then carry out a review of the matter in question, as described at **5.7** below. Alternatively, the appellant can, within the same 30-day period, notify the appeal to the Tribunal for it to decide the matter in question.

If the appellant does not either accept the offer of review or notify the appeal to the tribunal within the 30-day period, then HMRC's view of the matter in question is treated as if it were contained in a written agreement for the settlement of the appeal, so that the provisions at **5.9** below apply (and the appeal is settled on the basis of HMRC's view). The appellant's normal right to withdraw from such agreements does not apply to the deemed agreement. The tribunal may, however, give permission for the appellant to notify the appeal to it after the 30-day period has ended.

HMRC cannot make a second offer of a review or make an offer if the appellant has already required a review or has notified the appeal to the tribunal.

[*TMA 1970, ss 49B, 49C, 49H*].

Conduct of the review

[5.7] The nature and extent of HMRC's review will be determined by them as seems appropriate in the circumstances, but they must take into account the steps taken before the start of the review both by them in deciding the matter in question and by anyone else seeking to resolve the disagreement. They must also take into account representations made by the appellant, provided that these are made at a stage which gives HMRC a reasonable opportunity to consider them.

The review must be completed and HMRC's conclusions notified to the appellant in writing within 45 days beginning with:

- where the appellant required the review, the day HMRC notified him of their view of the matter in question; or
- where HMRC offered the review, the day HMRC received notification of the appellant's acceptance of the offer.

HMRC and the appellant can, however, agree any other period for completion of the review.

If HMRC fail to notify the appellant of their conclusions within the required period, the review is treated as if the conclusion was that HMRC's original view of the matter in question were upheld. HMRC must notify the appellant in writing accordingly.

[*TMA 1970, s 49E; FA 2021, Sch 27 para 4*].

In the case of an appeal against a points-based late filing penalty under *FA 2021, Sch 24* (see **46.8** PENALTIES), HMRC's review may also conclude that the appellant's liability to any of the penalty points by virtue of which the appellant was liable to the penalty should be upheld or, as the case may be, cancelled. This applies in relation to a penalty point even if the time limit for appealing against it expired before notice of appeal against the penalty was given. It does not apply if it was concluded in an earlier review that the appellant was liable to the penalty point in question or if liability to the penalty point has been affirmed on appeal. [*TMA 1970, s 49EA; FA 2021, Sch 27 para 5*].

Effect of conclusions

HMRC's notice stating the conclusions to the review is treated as a written agreement for the settlement of the appeal, so that the provisions at **5.9** below apply (and the appeal is settled on the basis of those conclusions). The appellant's normal right to withdraw from such agreements does not apply to the deemed agreement.

The appellant does, however, have a further opportunity to notify the appeal to the tribunal for them to determine the matter in question. This must normally be done within the period of 30 days beginning with the date of the document notifying the conclusions of the review. Where, however, HMRC have failed to notify the conclusions within the required period, the time limit is extended to 30 days after the date of the document notifying the appellant that the review is to be treated as if concluded on the basis of HMRC's original opinion. The tribunal may give permission for an appeal to be notified to them after the time limits have expired.

[*TMA 1970, ss 49F, 49G*].

Where, in a review of a points-based late filing penalty under *FA 2021, Sch 24* (see **46.8** PENALTIES), both a penalty and one or more penalty points are cancelled, similar consequences ensue as in **46.30** PENALTIES where the decision to cancel is made by the Tribunal. [*TMA 1970, s 49; FA 2021, Sch 27 para 6*].

Reviews are carried out by HMRC officers who have experience of the subject matter of the appeal but are independent of the decision maker and the decision maker's line management (HMRC Appeals, Reviews and Tribunals Guide, ARTG4310).

See further HMRC Appeals, Reviews and Tribunals Guide, ARTG4000–4860.

Appeal to the Tribunal

[5.8] A taxpayer who has appealed to HMRC can notify the appeal to the Tribunal without requesting an HMRC review first. If they do so, HMRC cannot then make an offer of a review. [*TMA 1970, s 49D*].

An appellant can also notify an appeal to the Tribunal if they do not wish to accept an HMRC offer of a review or if they disagree with the conclusions of a review. In both cases, there are short time limits within which notification must be made, although the Tribunal can give permission for notification to be made outside those limits: see **5.6** and **5.7** above.

There is no provision for HMRC to notify an appeal to the tribunal.

Notice of appeal must include the appellant's details, details of the decision etc. appealed against, the result the appellant is seeking and the grounds of appeal. The notice must be accompanied by a copy of any written record of the decision and the reasons for it that the appellant has or can reasonably obtain. If the notice is made late it must also include a request for extension of time and the reason for lateness. [*SI 2009 No 273, Rule 20*].

Appeals should be notified to the Tribunal online at www.gov.uk/tax-tribunal/appeal-to-tribunal or by post to the HM Courts and Tribunals Service, First-tier Tribunal (Tax Chamber), PO Box 16972, Birmingham B16 6TZ. A Notice of Appeal form (T240) can be downloaded from www.gov.uk/government/publications/notice-of-appeal-ask-a-tax-judge-to-examine-a-dispute-form-t240 or obtained from the Tribunals Service by phoning 0300 123 1024.

See **5.11** onwards below for the process by which an appeal notified to the tribunal is decided.

Settlement by agreement

[5.9] At any time before an appeal is determined by the tribunal, it may be settled by agreement between HMRC and the appellant or his agent. Where such an agreement is reached, in writing or otherwise, the assessment or decision as upheld, varied, discharged, or cancelled by that agreement, is treated as if it had been determined on appeal. Oral agreements are, however, effective only if confirmed in writing by either side (the date of such confirmation then being the effective date of agreement).

The taxpayer may withdraw from the agreement by giving written notice within 30 days of making it.
[*TMA 1970, s 54(1)–(3)(5)*].

The agreement must specify the figure for assessment or a precise formula for ascertaining it (*Delbourgo v Field* CA 1978, 52 TC 225).

The agreement only covers the assessments (or decisions) which are the subject of the appeal, and does not bind HMRC for subsequent years, for example where relievable amounts are purported to be carried forward from the year in question (*MacNiven v Westmoreland Investments Ltd* HL 2001, 73 TC 1 and see also *Tod v South Essex Motors (Basildon)* Ltd Ch D 1987, 60 TC 598).

The issue of an amended notice of assessment cannot in itself constitute an offer for the purposes of a *s 54* agreement; nor can a lack of response by the taxpayer constitute acceptance of an offer (*Schuldenfrei v Hilton* CA 1999, 72 TC 167).

An agreement based on a mutual mistake of fact was as a result invalid, so that the taxpayer could proceed with his appeal (*Fox v Rothwell* (Sp C 50), [1995] SSCD 336).

See *Gibson v General Commissioners for Stroud* Ch D 1989, 61 TC 645 for a case where there was held not to have been a determination and *R v Inspector of Taxes, ex p. Bass Holdings Ltd; Richart v Bass Holdings Ltd* QB 1992, 65 TC 495 for one where rectification of an agreement was ordered where a relief had been deducted twice contrary to the intention of Revenue and taxpayer.

See *CIR v West* CA 1991, 64 TC 196 for a case where the taxpayer was unsuccessful in seeking leave to defend a Crown action for payment of tax on the ground that the accountant who had entered into an agreement had no authority to do so given him by the taxpayer.

In *Foulser v HMRC* FTT, [2014] UKFTT 483 (TC); 2014 STI 2764 the taxpayer argued that he had sent a cheque to HMRC with a covering letter indicating that it was 'in full and final settlement' of his liability, and that since HMRC had cashed the cheque, this should be treated as a settlement by agreement of the appeal. The FTT rejected this contention.

The 30-day period for withdrawal from an agreement cannot be extended on the grounds of reasonable excuse (*Bull v HMRC* FTT, [2019] SFTD 911).

Alternative dispute resolution

[5.10] Taxpayers can apply to HMRC to use alternative dispute resolution (ADR) to seek to settle tax disputes, whether or not an appealable tax decision or assessment has been made by HMRC. Entering into the ADR process does not affect the taxpayer's existing review and appeal rights.

ADR involves an independent person from HMRC (known as a 'facilitator'), who has not previously been involved in the dispute, working with both the taxpayer and the HMRC case owner to try to broker an agreement between them. The process does not guarantee resolution of the dispute. See www.gov.uk/guidance/tax-disputes-alternative-dispute-resolution-adr.

Taxpayers can apply to use ADR by following the link from the above web page and completing the online form.

HMRC have published an Alternative Dispute Resolution Guidance Manual containing detailed guidance on the process. See, in particular, ADRG02700 for the types of cases which HMRC consider to be suitable for ADR.

With effect from 15 June 2020, the FTT will allow a stay on proceedings of 150 days to allow for ADR if the hearing has not yet been listed. If the hearing has been listed, the FTT will only stay on proceedings if both taxpayer and HMRC confirm that they can go ahead on the hearing date if ADR fails. (First-tier Tribunal (Tax Chamber) Practice Statement 15 June 2020.) Previously, once an appeal had notified to the FTT and HMRC's statement of case had been served, the FTT would only allow ADR in exceptional circumstances.

The Tribunal

[5.11] Under the unified tribunal system established by the *Tribunals, Courts and Enforcement Act 2007*, there are two tribunals; the First-tier Tribunal and the Upper Tribunal. The Tribunals are presided over by a Senior President of Tribunals. [*TCEA 2007, s 3*].

The First-tier Tribunal

Tax appeals notified to the Tribunal are in most cases initially heard and decided by the First-tier Tribunal. [*TMA 1970, s 47C*].

The First-tier Tribunal is organised into separate chambers each with responsibility for different areas of the law and with its own Chamber President. With certain exceptions, the Tax Chamber is responsible for all appeals, applications, references or other proceedings in respect of the functions of HMRC. It is also responsible for appeals etc. in respect of the exercise of Revenue functions by the National Crime Agency (see **27.10** HMRC — ADMINISTRATION) and for appeals relating to certain other non-tax matters. The exceptions relate to certain tax credit and national insurance matters and to matters for which the Upper Tribunal is responsible. [*TCEA 2007, s 7; SI 2008 No 2684, Arts 2, 5A; SI 2009 No 196, Arts 3, 5; SI 2010 No 2655, Art* 2].

The Upper Tribunal

The Upper Tribunal is a superior court of record, so that its decisions create legally binding precedents. [*TCEA 2007, s 3(5)*].

It is similarly divided into chambers, including the Tax and Chancery Chamber. In relation to tax matters, the Chamber is responsible for:

(a) further appeals against decisions by the First-tier Tribunal Tax Chamber (see **5.27** below);
(b) applications by HMRC for a tax-related penalty under *FA 2008, Sch 36 para 50* in respect of failure to comply with an information notice or obstruction of an inspection (see **46.19** PENALTIES);
(c) complex appeals, applications or references transferred from the First-tier Tribunal (see **5.29** below); and
(d) matters referred to the Upper Tribunal following a decision by the First-tier Tribunal Tax Chamber to set aside its own original decision (see **5.29** below); and
(e) applications for judicial review (see **5.35** below).

[*SI 2008 No 2684, Arts 6, 8; SI 2009 No 196, Arts 6, 8; SI 2009 No 1590, Art 8; SI 2010 No 2655, Arts 9, 13*].

Overriding objective

The Tribunal Procedure Rules which govern the operation of the Tribunals include an explicit statement of their overriding objective, which is to deal with cases fairly and justly. The Tribunals are required to deal with each case in ways proportionate to its importance, its complexity and the anticipated costs and resources of the parties to the appeal etc. They must avoid unnecessary formality and delay and seek flexibility in the proceedings. They must ensure that the parties are able to participate fully in the proceedings.

The parties to the appeal etc. are in turn required to help the Tribunal to further the overriding objective and to co-operate with the Tribunal generally.

[*SI 2008 No 2698, Rule 2; SI 2009 No 273, Rule* 2].

Alternative dispute resolution

The Tribunals also have an explicit duty to point out to the parties the availability of any alternative procedure for resolving the dispute and to facilitate the use of the procedure if the parties wish. [*SI 2008 No 2698, Rule 3; SI 2009 No 273, Rule* 3]. See **5.10** above for HMRC's alternative dispute resolution process.

Composition of tribunals

Both the First-tier and Upper Tribunals consist of judges who have particular legal qualifications or experience and other members who are not legally qualified but meet specified selection criteria.

First-tier Tribunal procedure

Case management

[5.12] The Tribunal has wide powers to regulate its own procedures and to give directions about the conduct or disposal of cases. In particular it can, by direction:

- consolidate or hear two or more cases together or treat a case as a lead case (see *SI 2009 No 273, Rule 18*);
- permit or require a party to the case or another person to provide documents, information or submissions to the tribunal or another party;
- hold a hearing to consider any matter, including a case management hearing;
- decide the form of any hearing;
- require a party to produce a bundle of documents for a hearing.

The Tribunal can also substitute a party to a case where necessary or add a person to the case as a respondent. A person who is not party to the case can apply to the Tribunal to be added as a party.

Either party to a case can apply for the Tribunal to make a direction, either in writing or orally at a hearing, or the Tribunal can make a direction on its own initiative. Applications for a direction must include the reason for making it. Directions can be challenged by applying for a further direction.

Any action required to be done in relation to a case on or by a particular day must be done before 5pm on that day (or, if that day is not a working day, by 5pm on the next working day).

[*SI 2009 No 273, Rules 5, 6, 9, 12*].

Administration of cases referred to the Tribunal, including the categorisation of cases (see **5.14** below), is carried out by the Courts and Tribunals Service.

Starting proceedings

See **5.8** above for how to notify an appeal to the Tribunal. There are also rules for proceedings to be determined without notice to a respondent (*Rule 19*), and for proceedings started by originating application or reference (*Rule 21*).

Representation

A party to a case can appoint a representative to represent them in the proceedings. The representative does not need to be a lawyer. The party has to notify the Tribunal and the other parties of the appointment of a representative and they will then treat the representative as authorised until notified otherwise.

Where no such person has been appointed, a party can, with the Tribunal's permission, nevertheless be accompanied at a hearing by another person who can act as a representative or assist in presenting the case.

[*SI 2009 No 273, Rule 11; SI 2010 No 40, Rule 16*].

Withdrawal from a case

Subject to any legislation relating to withdrawal from or settlement of particular proceedings, a party can notify the Tribunal of the withdrawal of its case, or part of it. This can be done in writing before a hearing or orally at a hearing. If the case is to be settled without a hearing, written notice must be given before the Tribunal disposes of the case.

A party who has withdrawn its case can, however, apply (in writing) to the Tribunal to reinstate it. The application must be received by the Tribunal within 28 days after it received the withdrawal notice or the date of the hearing.

[*SI 2009 No 273, Rule 17; SI 2013 No 477, Rules 1, 39*].

Failure to comply with rules

[5.13] An irregularity resulting from any failure to comply with the Tribunal Procedure Rules, a practice direction or a direction by the Tribunal does not in itself make the proceedings void.

Where a party fails to comply with the Rules etc. the Tribunal can take such action as it considers just. This could be to require compliance or waive the requirement, to strike the case out (see below) or, in certain cases, to refer the failure to the Upper Tribunal.

The Tribunal can refer to the Upper Tribunal any failure to:

- attend a hearing, or otherwise be available, to give evidence;
- to swear an oath in connection with giving evidence;
- to give evidence as a witness;
- to produce a document; or
- to facilitate the inspection of a document or other thing (including premises).

The Upper Tribunal then has the same powers as the High Court to deal with the failure (which may include financial penalties).

[*TCEA 2007, s 25; SI 2009 No 273, Rule 7*].

Striking out a case

A case will automatically be struck out if the appellant fails to comply with a direction which states that failure to comply will lead to striking out.

The Tribunal can also strike out a case if the appellant fails to comply with a direction which states that failure to comply may lead to striking out, if the appellant has failed to co-operate with the Tribunal to such an extent that the case cannot be dealt with fairly and justly, or if the Tribunal considers that there is no reasonable prospect of the appellant's case succeeding. In the last two cases, however, the Tribunal must first give the appellant an opportunity to make representations.

If the case is struck out because of the appellant's failure to comply with a direction, the appellant can apply for the case to be reinstated. This must be done in writing within 28 days after the date the Tribunal sent the notification of the striking out.

The above rules also apply to respondents except that, instead of the case being struck out, the respondent is barred from taking any further part in the case.

[*SI 2009 No 273, Rule 8*].

A struck-out appeal was reinstated in *Nowroozi v HMRC* FTT, [2019] UKFTT 533 (TC). The taxpayer had relied on his accountants to deal with directions of the Tribunal at a time when he had been diagnosed with stage four cancer.

An attempt to have HMRC barred from taking any part in a case was unsuccessful in *Ritchie v HMRC* FTT, [2016] UKFTT 509 (TC).

Categorisation of cases

[5.14] When an appeal, application or reference is notified to the Tribunal, the Tribunals Service allocates it to one of four categories of case: default paper, basic, standard or complex.

Cases may be re-categorised by the Tribunal at any time either on the application of one of the parties or on the Tribunal's own initiative.

[*SI 2009 No 273, Rule 23(1)–(3); SI 2013 No 477, Rules 1, 34, 41*].

The process by which the appeal etc. will be decided varies according to the category to which the case is allocated as described below.

Default paper cases

[5.15] The following types of cases are normally categorised as default paper cases:

(a) appeals against fixed penalties of not more than £500 (£2,000 before 1 June 2022) for late self-assessment tax returns (see **46.4–46.6** PENALTIES) and certain other late returns or notifications;
(b) appeals against penalties of not more than £500 (£2,000 before 1 June 2022) for late payment of tax (see **36.6** LATE PAYMENT INTEREST AND PENALTIES).

Cases can be allocated to a different category if the Tribunal considers it appropriate to do so.

(Practice Direction for the First-tier Tribunal Tax Chamber, 12 May 2022; Tribunals Practice Statement, 29 April 2013).

The limit for allocation to the default paper category was temporarily increased to £20,000 during the coronavirus pandemic until 30 June 2021.

In a default paper case, the respondent (i.e., in an appeal, HMRC) must provide a statement of case to the Tribunal, the appellant and any other respondents to be received within 42 days after the Tribunal sends it notice of the proceedings (or by such time as the Tribunal directs). The statement must state the legislation under which the decision in question was made and set out the respondent's position. If the statement is late it must also include a request for a time extension and give the reason for lateness.

The statement can also contain a request for the case to be dealt with either at or without a hearing.

Once such a statement has been given to the appellant, they may send a written reply to the Tribunal. The reply must be received within 30 days after the date on which the respondent sent its statement to the appellant and must be sent also to each respondent. The reply may include the appellant's response to the respondent's statement of case, provide any further relevant information and contain a request for the case to be dealt with at a hearing. If the reply is late, it must also include a request for a time extension and give the reason for lateness.

The Tribunal must hold a hearing before determining a case if any party has requested one in writing. Otherwise, on receipt of the appellant's reply or the expiry of the time limit for such a reply, the Tribunal will determine the case without a hearing, unless it directs otherwise.

[*SI 2009 No 273, Rules 25, 26*].

Default paper cases are decided by one judge or other member of the First-tier Tribunal. (Tribunals Practice Statement, 10 March 2009).

Basic cases

[5.16] The following types of cases are normally allocated as basic cases (unless they are allocated as default paper cases):

(a) appeals against penalties for late filing and late payment, including daily penalties;
(b) appeals against penalties under *FA 2007, Sch 24* (errors in documents and failure to notify HMRC of errors in assessments — see **46.11–46.13** PENALTIES) except where the penalties are for deliberate action or an appeal is also brought against the assessment to which the penalty relates;
(c) appeals seeking the mitigation or reduction of penalties and those in which reasonable excuse is asserted;
(d) appeals against information notices (including those at **29.4** and **32.11**(d) HMRC INVESTIGATORY POWERS and **52.13** RETURNS) and penalties for non-compliance;
(e) applications for permission to make a late appeal (see **5.3** above);
(f) applications for the postponement of tax pending an appeal (see **45.18** PAYMENT OF TAX); and
(g) applications for a direction that HMRC close an enquiry (see **52.14** RETURNS).

Cases can be allocated to a different category if the Tribunal considers it appropriate to do so.

(Practice Direction for the First-tier Tribunal Tax Chamber, 12 May 2022; Tribunals Practice Direction, 10 March 2009).

Basic cases normally proceed directly to a hearing, without the need for the respondent to produce a statement of case. Where, however, the respondent intends to raise grounds at the hearing of which the appellant has not been informed, the appellant must be notified of those grounds as soon as is reasonably practicable. The respondent must include sufficient detail to enable the appellant to respond to the grounds at the hearing. [*SI 2009 No 273, Rule 24*].

Standard cases

[5.17] In a standard case, the respondent (i.e., in an appeal, HMRC) must provide a statement of case to the tribunal, the appellant and any other respondents to be received within 60 days after the Tribunal sends it notice of the proceedings (or by such time as the Tribunal directs). The statement must state the legislation under which the decision in question was made and set out the respondent's position. If the statement is late it must also include a request for a time extension and give the reason for lateness.

The statement can also contain a request for the case to be dealt with either at or without a hearing.

Within 42 days after the date on which the respondent sent the statement of case, each party to the case must send to the Tribunal and each other party a list of documents of which that party has possession (or the right to take possession or make copies) and on which the party intends to rely or to produce in the proceedings. The other parties must then be allowed to inspect or copy those documents, except for any which are privileged.

The case will then normally proceed to a hearing (see **5.19** below).

[*SI 2009 No 273, Rules 25, 27*].

In *Addo v HMRC* FTT 2018, [2019] SFTD 168, the Tribunal held that the obligation to disclose documents was subject to the duty of all parties to help the Tribunal to further the overriding objective to deal with cases fairly and justly. If the level of disclosure, whilst abiding by the strict terms of the rules, fell short of the level that would be required to further the overriding objective, further disclosure could be required by the making of orders or directions by the Tribunal.

Complex cases

[5.18] A case can be classified as a complex case only if the Tribunal considers that it will require lengthy or complex evidence or a lengthy hearing, involves a complex or important principle or issue, or involves a large financial sum. [*SI 2009 No 273, Rule 23(4)*].

A financial sum is generally considered to be large for this purposes if the amount in dispute is £750,000 or more (Practice Direction for the First-tier Tribunal Tax Chamber, 12 May 2022).

The criteria for categorising a case as complex are considered in *Capital Air Services Ltd v HMRC* UT, [2010] STC 2726.

The procedures in a complex case are the same as those described at **5.17** above for standard cases. The same rules regarding the membership of the Tribunal also apply.

Transfer to Upper Tribunal

The Tribunal can, with the consent of the parties, refer a complex case or a preliminary issue to the Chamber President with a request for transfer to the Upper Tribunal. The Chamber President can then, with the agreement of the President of the Tax and Chancery Chamber of the Upper Tribunal, direct that the case be so transferred. [*SI 2009 No 273, Rule 28*].

Costs

See **5.24** below for the taxpayer's option to request that a complex case be excluded from potential liability for costs.

The hearing

[5.19] Basic, standard and complex cases normally require a hearing before they are decided (and see **5.15** above for hearings in default paper cases).

This does not apply, however, if all of the parties consent to a decision without a hearing and the Tribunal considers that it is able to make a decision without a hearing. Hearings are also not required for the correction, setting aside, review or appeal of a tribunal decision (see **5.20–5.22** below) or where the Tribunal strikes out a party's case (see **5.13** above).

Each party to the proceedings is normally entitled to attend the hearing and the Tribunal must give reasonable notice of its time and place. Where the hearing is to consider disposal of the proceedings, at least 14 days' notice must be given except in urgent or exceptional circumstances or with the consent of the parties.

A hearing may be held in person or held remotely by telephone or video link or as a 'hybrid' hearing, where some participants are in a physical hearing room and others are attending remotely.

Hearings are normally held in public and there are provisions to enable third parties to attend remote hearings. The public interest generally requires the precise facts relevant to the decision to be a matter of public record, and not to be veiled by a process of anonymisation or redaction (*HMRC v Banerjee* [2009] EWHC 1229 (Ch), [2009] 3 All ER 930n, [2009] STC 1930), and see *Mr D v HMRC* [2017] UKFTT 850 (TC). The Tribunal may, however, direct that a hearing should be private if it considers that restricting access is justified in the interests of public order or national security, to protect a person's right to respect for their private and family life, to maintain the confidentiality of sensitive information, to avoid serious harm to the public interest or because not to do so would prejudice the interest of justice. An application for an appeal by a well-known broadcaster to be heard in private, and for any published decision to be anonymised, was refused in *A v HMRC* FTT, [2012] SFTD 1257. The Tribunal ruled that the fact that a taxpayer was rich, or that he was in the public eye, did not dictate a different approach to other cases. The hearing of the appeal of such a person in private would give rise to the suspicion that riches or fame could buy anonymity and protection from scrutiny which others could not avoid. It would not be in the public interest to release a decision which, by concealing the appellant's personal characteristics, made it impossible for the reader to reach a full understanding of why the appeal had been determined as it had (*Clunes v HMRC* FTT (TC 5692), [2017] UKFTT 204 (TC)).

A decision was anonymised due to concerns about human rights in the taxpayer's home country in *Foreign National v HMRC* FTT, [2023] UKFTT (TC), [2023] UKFTT 475 (TC). The Tribunal upheld an application for a decision to be anonymised on health grounds in *L v HMRC* FTT, [2024] UKFTT 401 (TC).

[*SI 2009 No 273, Rules 29–32*].

Failure to attend hearing

If a party fails to attend a hearing, the Tribunal can nevertheless proceed with the hearing if it considers that it is in the interests of justice to do so. The Tribunal must be satisfied that the party was notified of the hearing or that reasonable steps were taken to notify the party. [*SI 2009 No 273, Rule 33*].

Evidence and submissions

The Tribunal has wide powers to make directions as to issues on which it requires evidence or submissions, including the nature of such evidence or submissions, the way in which and time at which it must be provided and the need for expert evidence. It may also limit the number of witnesses whose evidence a party can put forward.

The Tribunal can accept evidence whether or not it would be admissible in a civil trial and can exclude evidence provided late or not in accordance with a direction.

[*SI 2009 No 273, Rule 15(1)(2)*].

In *HMRC v Tower MCashback LLP1* SC, [2011] UKSC 19 it was held that HMRC were entitled to rely on grounds to defend an enquiry closure notice other than the grounds which had been stated in that notice.

HMRC were prohibited by the First-tier Tribunal from citing an unpublished Special Commissioners' decision in *Ardmore Construction Ltd v HMRC* FTT, [2014] UKFTT 453 (TC); 2014 STI 2585.

Giving evidence from abroad

Witnesses cannot give evidence by video or telephone from an overseas location (i.e. from outside the UK, the Crown Dependencies or the British Overseas Territories) unless the FCDO Taking of Evidence Unit has confirmed that the foreign state in which the witness is located does not object to the giving of evidence in tax appeals. The FTT published guidance to this effect following the decision in an asylum case in *Secretary of State for the Home Department v Agbabiaka* UT, [2021] UKUT 286 (IAC), [2022] INLR 304, [2021] All ER (D) 77 (Nov).

The FCDO set up the Taking of Evidence Unit in 2021. It checks whether overseas governments object to the taking of oral evidence from an individual within their territory. The response of the unit about the stance of a particular overseas government is treated as determinative.

Any party wishing to rely on oral evidence given overseas must notify the FTT as soon as it is aware that such evidence may be needed and at least eight weeks before the hearing is due to take place, and send a copy of the notification to the other party. The FTT will be responsible for contacting the Taking of Evidence Unit. For the information which should be included when notifying the FTT, and full details of the process, see www.judiciary.uk/guidance-and-resources/first-tier-tribunal-tax-chamber-guidance-oral-evidence-from-abroad/.

Witnesses

The Tribunal, on the application of any party to the proceedings or its own initiative, can issue a summons (in Scotland, a citation) requiring any person either to attend the hearing of those proceedings to give evidence or to produce any relevant document in his possession or control. A witness required to attend a hearing must be given 14 days' notice or a shorter period if the Tribunal so directs and, if the witness is not a party, the summons or citations must make provision for necessary expenses of attendance and state who is to pay them. If, before the summons or citation was issued, the witness did not have an opportunity to object, he may apply to the Tribunal for the summons to be varied or set aside. The application must be made as soon as reasonably practicable after the summons or citation is received.

A witness cannot be compelled to give evidence or produce documents which he could not be compelled to give or produce in an action in a court of law.

[*SI 2009 No 273, Rule 16*].

The Tribunal has issued guidance on its practice in relation to witness statements and the production of documents (Practice Statement for the First-tier Tribunal (Tax Chamber), 15 June 2022).

The Tribunal's decision

[5.20] In an appeal case, if the Tribunal decides:

(a) that the appellant is overcharged or undercharged by a self-assessment;
(b) that any amounts in a partnership statement (see **52.19** RETURNS) are excessive or insufficient; or
(c) that the appellant is overcharged or undercharged by an assessment other than a self-assessment,

the assessment or amounts are reduced or increased accordingly, but otherwise the assessment or statement stands good. The Tribunal is given the power to vary the extent to which a claim or election included in a tax return is disallowed following an enquiry. (Separate rules apply to claims and elections made outside returns, for which see **13.3** CLAIMS.) In a case within (c) above, the Tribunal can normally only reduce or increase the amount assessed, and this determines the appeal; the Tribunal is not obliged to determine the revised tax payable. In a case within (b) above, HMRC must amend the partners' own tax returns to give effect to the reductions or increases made.

The Tribunal's decision is final and conclusive, subject to:

(i) the correction of clerical mistakes etc. (see **5.21** below);

(ii) the setting aside of a decision (see **5.21** below); and
(iii) a further appeal against the decision (see **5.22** below).

[*TMA 1970, s 50(6)–(11); SI 2009 No 56, Art 31*].

See **46.4** PENALTIES for the Tribunal's options in an appeal against a late filing penalty, which turns on the question of whether the appellant had a 'reasonable excuse' for his non-compliance.

The Tribunal can give its decision orally at a hearing or in writing. In either case it will give each party a decision notice in writing within 28 days after making a decision which finally disposes of all the issues in the case or as soon as practicable. The notice will also inform the party of any further right of appeal.

Unless each party agrees otherwise the notice should also include a summary of the findings of fact and the reason for the decision. If it does not, any party to the case can apply for full written findings and reasons, and must do so before applying for permission to appeal (see **5.22** below). The application must be made in writing so that the Tribunal receives it within 28 days after the date it sent the decision notice.

[*SI 2009 No 273, Rule 35; SI 2013 No 477, Rules 1, 42*].

Burden of proof

It is clear from *TMA 1970, s 50(6)* (see above) that the onus is on the appellant to displace an assessment. The burden of proving that the conditions for making an assessment are met lies, however, with HMRC. See, for example, *Burgess v HMRC* UT, [2015] UKUT 578 (TCC), where the Upper Tribunal found that HMRC had failed to discharge the burden of proving that the conditions for a discovery assessment were satisfied. Once HMRC have met their burden of showing that an assessment is validly made, the burden of proof on the substantive issue of whether or not the tax liability actually arises, reverts to the taxpayer.

In an appeal against a penalty assessment, the initial burden lies on HMRC to establish that the assessment is validly made and that events have occurred as a result of which a penalty is, prima facie, due (*Perrin v HMRC* UT, [2018] UKUT 156 (TCC)). Once this burden is met, it will then be for the taxpayer to show that any inaccuracy did not result from deliberate or careless behaviour or that they had a reasonable excuse for any failure.

For the standard of proof required in evidence, see *Les Croupiers Casino Club v Pattinson* CA 1987, 60 TC 196.

Consent orders

The case can also be settled by the Tribunal making a consent order where the parties have reached agreement. Such an order is made at the request of the parties but only if the Tribunal considers it appropriate to do so. No hearing is necessary if such an order is made. [*SI 2009 No 273, Rule 34*].

Correction of mistakes in a decision

[5.21] The Tribunal can correct any clerical mistake or other accidental slip or omission in a decision at any time by notifying the parties of the amended decision. This rule applies also to directions and any other document produced by the Tribunal. [*SI 2009 No 273, Rule 37*].

Setting aside a decision

The Tribunal can set aside a decision disposing of a case and re-make the decision if it considers that to do is in the interests of justice and one of the following applies:

- a relevant document was not sent to, or was not received at an appropriate time by, a party or his representative;
- a relevant document was not sent to the Tribunal at a relevant time;
- there was some other procedural irregularity; or
- a party or representative was not present at a hearing.

A party to a case can apply for a decision to be set aside. The application must be in writing and must be received by the Tribunal within 28 days after the date on which the Tribunal sent the decision notice.

[*SI 2009 No 273, Rule 38*].

An application for a decision to be set aside was successful in *Wright v HMRC (No 3)* FTT, [2009] UKFTT 227 (TC); 2009 STI 2813. In *SRI International v HMRC* FTT, [2010] SFTD 873 the taxpayer's application was unsuccessful as it sought to introduce new evidence which had been available to it before the appeal was heard and could have been brought forward even before the hearing.

Appeal against the Tribunal's decision

[5.22] A further appeal to the Upper Tribunal can be made against the First-tier Tribunal's decision. The appeal can be made only on a point of law. No appeal can be made against a decision on whether or not to review a decision (see below), to set aside a decision (see **5.21** above) or to refer a matter to the Upper Tribunal.

A person wishing to appeal must make a written application to the First-tier Tribunal for permission to appeal. Such an application must be received by the Tribunal no later than 56-days after the date the Tribunal sent full reasons for the decision to that person. Where a decision has been amended or corrected following a review (see below) or an application (other than a late application) for a decision to be struck out has been unsuccessful (see **5.21** above), the 56 day limit runs from the date on which the Tribunal sent the notification of amended reasons or correction of the decision or of the failure of the striking out application. The Tribunal can direct that the 56 days within which a party may apply for permission to appeal against a decision that disposes of a preliminary issue shall run from the date of the decision that disposes of all issues in the proceedings.

The application must identify the alleged errors in the decision and state the result sought. Late applications must include a request for extension of time and the reason for lateness.

On receiving an application, the Tribunal will first consider whether to review the decision. It can do so only if satisfied that there was an error in law in the decision. Unless it decides to take no action following the review, the Tribunal will notify the parties of the outcome and must give them an opportunity to make representations before taking any action.

If the Tribunal decides not to review the decision or, following a review, decides to take no action, it will then consider whether to give permission to appeal to the Upper Tribunal. It will send a record of its decision to the parties as soon as practicable together with, where it decides not to give permission, a statements of its reasons for refusal and details of the right to apply directly to the Upper Tribunal for permission to appeal (see **5.27** below). The Tribunal's permission can be in respect of part only of the decision or on limited grounds.

[*TCEA 2007, s 11; SI 2009 No 273, Rules 39–41; SI 2013 No 477, Rules 1, 43*].

Payment of tax pending further appeal

[5.23] Tax is payable or repayable in accordance with the decision of the Tribunal even if a party appeals to the Upper Tribunal. If the amount charged in the assessment concerned is subsequently altered by the Upper Tribunal, any amount undercharged is due and payable at the end of the 30 days beginning with the date on which HMRC issue the appellant a notice of the amount payable in accordance with the Upper Tribunal's decision. Any amount overpaid will be refunded along with such interest as may be allowed by the decision. See **4.32** ANTI-AVOIDANCE for applications to the court or Tribunal by HMRC to disapply the requirement to repay tax where an accelerated payment notice is in force.

This provision applies equally to any further appeal from a decision of the Upper Tribunal to the Courts.

[*TMA 1970, s 56*].

Award of costs

[5.24] The Tribunal can make an order awarding costs (or, in Scotland, expenses):

(a) under *TCEA 2007, s 29(4)* ('wasted costs') and costs incurred in applying for such costs;
(b) where it considers that a party or representative has acted unreasonably in bringing, defending or conducting the case; and
(c) in a complex case (see **5.18** above), where the taxpayer has not sent a written request that the case be excluded from potential liability for costs or expenses.

A request within (c) above must be sent within 28 days of the taxpayer receiving notice that the case has been allocated as a complex case.

'*Wasted costs*' are any costs incurred by a party because of an improper, unreasonable or negligent act or omission by any representative or employee of a representative, which the Tribunal considers it unreasonable for the party to pay.

Before making an order for costs, the Tribunal must give the person who will have to pay them the chance to make representations. If the payer is an individual, it must consider his financial means.

The Tribunal can make an order on its own initiative or on an application from one of the parties. Such an application must be sent both to the Tribunal and to the person from whom costs are sought, together with a schedule of the costs claimed. An application must be made no later than 28 days after the date on which the Tribunal sends a notice recording the decision which finally disposes of all the issues or notice of a withdrawal which ends the case.

The amount of costs will be decided either by agreement of the parties, by summary assessment by the Tribunal or, if not agreed, by assessment. Where the amount is to be decided by assessment, either the payer or the person to whom the costs are to be paid can apply to a county court, the High Court or the Costs Office of the Supreme Court for a detailed assessment of the costs on the standard basis or, where the tribunal's order so specifies, the indemnity basis. Upon making an order for the assessment of costs, the Tribunal may order an amount to be paid on account before the costs are assessed.

[*TCEA 2007, s 29(4); SI 2009 No 273, Rule 10; SI 2013 No 477, Rules 1, 35–38*].

For the award of costs where HMRC successfully applied to admit late evidence, see *Earthshine Ltd v HMRC* FTT, [2010] UKFTT 314 (TC), 2010 STI 2621. An application for costs arising from an application to have a case recategorised as complex was unsuccessful in *Capital Air Services Ltd v HMRC* UT, [2011] STC 617. Partially successful appellants were ordered to pay two-thirds of HMRC's costs in *Bastionspark LLP v HMRC* UT, [2016] STC 2549. An application for costs where HMRC had withdrawn their case during the hearing was unsuccessful in *Elliott Knight Ltd v HMRC* FTT, [2018] SFTD 818. The appellant's dishonest evidence resulted in a substantial reduction in the costs awarded in *Ulster Metal Refiners Ltd v HMRC* UT, [2024] UKUT 184 (TCC).

An application for costs to be awarded on the indemnity basis rather than the standard basis was unsuccessful in *Gigabiz Ltd v HMRC* FTT, [2023] UKFTT 693 (TC). Even though HMRC had conceded only on the last day of the hearing, their conduct was not unreasonable to the necessary serious degree in the context of the dispute.

The power of the Tribunal to award costs does not include a power to direct, before the conclusion of an appeal, that the costs of complying with a direction should be borne by one party rather than the other, or by both (*Eclipse Film Partners No. 35 LLP v HMRC* SC, [6] STC 1385).

Upper Tribunal procedure

Case management

[5.25] The powers of the Upper Tribunal to regulate its own proceedings are broadly the same as the powers of the First-tier Tribunal. See *SI 2008 No 2698, Rules 5, 6, 9, 12* and **5.12** above.

Representation

The same rights to representation in a case before the Upper Tribunal apply as in a case before the First-tier Tribunal. See *SI 2008 No 2698, Rule 11* and **5.12** above.

Withdrawal from a case

A party can notify the Upper Tribunal of the withdrawal of its case, or part of it. This can be done in writing before a hearing or orally at a hearing. If the case is to be settled without a hearing, written notice must be given before the Tribunal disposes of the case.

The withdrawal only takes effect, however, if the Tribunal consents (but this requirement does not apply to the withdrawal of an application for permission to appeal).

A party who has withdrawn its case can, however, apply (in writing) to the Tribunal to reinstate it. The application must be received by the Tribunal within one month after it received the withdrawal notice or the date of the hearing.

[*SI 2008 No 2698, Rule 17; SI 2013 No 477, Rules 1, 54*].

Failure to comply with rules

[5.26] An irregularity resulting from any failure to comply with the Tribunal Procedure Rules, a practice direction or a direction by the Upper Tribunal does not in itself make the proceedings void.

Where a party fails to comply with the Rules etc. the Upper Tribunal can take such action as it considers just. This could be to require compliance or waive the requirement, to strike the case out (see below) or to restrict a party's participation in the case.

The Upper Tribunal has the same powers as the High Court to deal with the failure (which may include financial penalties).

[*TCEA 2007, s 25; SI 2008 No 2698, Rule 7*].

Striking out a case

The Upper Tribunal has similar powers to strike out a case as the First-tier Tribunal. See *SI 2008 No 2698, Rule 8* and **5.13** above. Note, however, that the Upper Tribunal cannot strike out an appeal from the decision of another tribunal or judicial review proceedings on the grounds that there is no reasonable prospect of the appellant's case succeeding.

Appeal against decisions of the First-tier Tribunal

Application for permission to appeal

[5.27] A party to a case who disagrees with a decision of the First-tier Tribunal can apply for permission to appeal against it. Applications must first be made to the First-tier Tribunal (see **5.22** above), but if that Tribunal refuses permission a further application can be made to the Upper Tribunal.

Applications to the Upper Tribunal must be in writing and must be received no later than one month after the date on which the First-tier Tribunal sent the notice refusing permission to appeal. An application must include the grounds for appeal and state whether the appellant wants the application to be dealt with at a hearing. It must be accompanied by copies of any written record of the decision being challenged, any statement of reasons for that decision, and the notice of the First-tier Tribunal's refusal of permission to appeal. Late applications must include a request for extension of time and the reason for lateness.

If the application to the First-tier Tribunal for permission to appeal was refused because it was made out of time, the application to the Upper Tribunal must include the reason for the lateness of the first application. The Upper Tribunal can then admit the application only if it considers that it is in the interests of justice to do so.

If the Tribunal refuses permission to appeal, it will notify the appellant of its decision and its reasons. If the refusal is made without a hearing, the appellant can apply in writing for the decision to be reconsidered at a hearing. The application must be received by the Tribunal within 14 days after the date that written notice of its decision was sent. This rule applies also where the Tribunal gives permission on limited grounds or subject to conditions without a hearing. With effect from 6 April 2022, no application for a hearing can be made if the Tribunal's decision on the permission to appeal application indicated that it considered that the application was totally without merit.

If the Tribunal grants permission, the application for permission is then normally treated as a notice of appeal, and the case will proceed accordingly. If all the parties agree, the appeal can be determined without obtaining any further response.

[*SI 2008 No 2698, Rules 21, 22; SI 2009 No 274, Rule 14; SI 2009 No 1975, Rules 15, 16; SI 2022 No 312, Rules 1, 3*].

See the Tribunals Service leaflet 'Appealing to the Upper Tribunal (Tax and Chancery Chamber)' at www.gov.uk/government/publications/upper-tribunal-appeals-tax-and-chancery-additional-guidance-t399.

Notice of appeal

[5.28] If the First-tier Tribunal gives permission to appeal to the Upper Tribunal (or the Upper Tribunal gives permission but directs that the application for permission should not be treated as a notice of appeal) an appellant can appeal to the Upper Tribunal by providing a notice of appeal. This must be received by the tribunal within one month after the notice giving permission to appeal was sent.

The notice must include the grounds for appeal and state whether the appellant wants the application to be dealt with at a hearing. If the First-tier Tribunal gave permission to appeal, the notice must be accompanied by copies of any written record of the decision being challenged, any statement of reasons for that decision and the notice of permission to appeal. Late applications must include a request for extension of time and the reason for lateness.

A copy of the notice and the documents provided will then be sent by the Upper Tribunal to the respondents who can provide a written response. Any response must be received by the Tribunal not later than one month after the copy of the notice of appeal was sent. (Where an application for permission to appeal stands as the notice of appeal (see 5.27 above), the response must be received not later than one month after the Tribunal sent to the respondent notice that it had granted permission to appeal.)

With effect from 6 April 2022, the respondents **must** provide a written response if they wish the Upper Tribunal to uphold the decision on different grounds or if they intend to rely on grounds which did not succeed before the FTT. To the extent that the respondents require any permission (including permission to cross-appeal), the response must include an application for that permission.

Any response must indicate whether the respondent opposes the appeal, and if so, the grounds for opposition (including grounds to uphold the decision for reasons other than those given by the FTT or which were unsuccessful before the FTT) and whether the respondent wants the case to be dealt with at a hearing. Late responses must include a request for extension of time and the reason for lateness.

A copy of the response and any documents provided will then be sent by the Tribunal to the appellant and any other parties to the case who can, in turn, provide a written reply. The reply must be received by the Tribunal within one month of the date the tribunal sent the copy of the respondent's response.

[*SI 2008 No 2698, Rules 23–25; SI 2009 No 1975, Rules 17, 18; SI 2022 No 312, Rules 1, 3*].

An application by HMRC for the Tribunal to accept a late notice of appeal was rejected in *HMRC v McCarthy and Stone (Developments) Ltd* UT, [2014] STC 973.

Other cases before the Upper Tribunal

[5.29] Where a case has been transferred or referred to the Upper Tribunal from the First-tier Tribunal (see **5.18** above) or where a case is started by direct application to the Upper Tribunal, the Upper Tribunal will determine by direction the procedure for considering and disposing of the case. [*SI 2008 No 2698, Rule 26A; SI 2009 No 274, Rule 16; SI 2009 No 1975, Rule 19*].

The hearing

[5.30] The Upper Tribunal can make any decision with or without a hearing, but in deciding whether to hold a hearing, it must have regard to any view expressed by any party to the case.

See **5.1** above for the temporary power for the Tribunal to direct that a case be determined on the papers despite the objections of any party during the coronavirus pandemic.

Each party is normally entitled to attend the hearing and the Upper Tribunal must give reasonable notice of its time and place. At least 14 days' notice must normally be given except in urgent or exceptional circumstances or with the consent of the parties. In application for permission to bring judicial review cases, the notice period must normally be at least two days.

Hearings are normally held in public, but the Tribunal can direct that a hearing, or part of it, should be held in private.

[*SI 2008 No 2698, Rules 34–37; SI 2009 No 274, Rule 19; SI 2009 No 1975, Rule 29*].

Failure to attend hearing

If a party fails to attend a hearing, the Upper Tribunal can nevertheless proceed with the hearing if it considers that it is in the interests of justice to do so. The Tribunal must be satisfied that the party was notified of the hearing or that reasonable steps were taken to notify the party. [*SI 2008 No 2698, Rule 38*].

Evidence and witnesses

Similar rules apply in relation to evidence, submission and witnesses as apply to the First-tier Tribunal. See *SI 2008 No 2698, Rules 15, 16* and **5.19** above.

The Upper Tribunal's decision

[5.31] If the Upper Tribunal decides that the First-tier Tribunal's decision involved an error on a point of law it can set aside that decision and either remit the case back to the First-tier Tribunal or remake the decision itself.

If it remits the case to the First-tier Tribunal, the Upper Tribunal can direct that the case is reheard by different members.

If it decides to remake the decision itself, the Upper Tribunal is free to make any decision that the First-tier Tribunal could make if it were rehearing the case (see **5.20** above) and can make such findings of fact as it considers appropriate.

[*TCEA 2007, s 12*].

The Upper Tribunal can give its decision orally at a hearing or in writing. In either case it will give each party a decision notice in writing as soon as practicable. The notice will include written reasons for the decision unless the decision was made with the consent of the parties or the parties have consented to the tribunal not giving written reasons. The notice will also inform the party of any further right of appeal. [*SI 2008 No 2698, Rule 40; SI 2009 No 274, Rule 21; SI 2009 No 1975, Rule 21; SI 2013 No 477, Rules 1, 56*].

Consent orders

The case can also be settled by the Upper Tribunal making a consent order where the parties have reached agreement. Such an order is made at the request of the parties but only if the Tribunal considers it appropriate to do so. No hearing is necessary if such an order is made. [*SI 2008 No 2698, Rule 39; SI 2009 No 274, Rule 20*].

Correction of mistakes in a decision

Identical provisions to those applicable to decisions by the First-tier Tribunal apply to decisions of the Upper Tribunal. See *SI 2008 No 2698, Rule 42* and **5.21** above.

Setting aside a decision

Virtually identical provisions to those applicable to decisions by the First-tier Tribunal apply to decisions of the Upper Tribunal. An application for a decision to be set aside must be received by the Upper Tribunal no later than one month after the date on which the Tribunal sent the decision notice. See *SI 2008 No 2698, Rule 43* and **5.21** above.

Appeal against the Tribunal's decision

[5.32] A further appeal to the Court of Appeal (in Scotland, the Court of Session) can be made against the Upper Tribunal's decision. The appeal can be made only on a point of law and the Tribunal will give permission to appeal only if the appeal would raise some important point of principle or practice or there is some other compelling reason for the Court to hear it.

A person wishing to appeal must make a written application to the Tribunal for permission to appeal. Such an application must be received by the Tribunal within one-month after the date the Tribunal sent written reasons for the decision to that person. Where a decision has been amended or corrected following a review (see below) or an application (other than a late application) for a decision to be struck out has been unsuccessful (see **5.26** above), the one month limit runs from the date on which the tribunal sent the notification of amended reasons or correction of the decision or of the failure of the striking out application.

The application must identify the alleged errors of law in the decision and state the result sought. Late applications must include a request for extension of time and the reason for lateness.

On receiving an application, the Upper Tribunal will first consider whether to review the decision. It can do so only if either it overlooked a legislative provision or binding authority which could have affected the decision or if a court has subsequently made a decision which is binding on the Upper Tribunal and could have affected the decision.

The Tribunal will notify the parties of the outcome of a review. If it decides to take any action following a review without first giving every party an opportunity to make representations, the notice must state that any party not given such an opportunity can apply for the action to be set aside and for the decision to be reviewed again.

If the Tribunal decides not to review the decision or, following a review, decides to take no action, it will then consider whether to give permission to appeal. It will send a record of its decision to the parties as soon as practicable together with, where it decides not to give permission, a statements of its reasons for refusal and details of the right to apply directly to the court for permission to appeal (see **5.34** below). The Tribunal's permission can be in respect of part only of the decision or on limited grounds.

[*TCEA 2007, s 13; SI 2008 No 2698, Rules 44–46; SI 2008 No 2834*].

See **5.23** above for the payment of tax pending an appeal from a decision of the Upper Tribunal.

Award of costs

[5.33] The Upper Tribunal can make an order awarding costs (or, in Scotland, expenses):

(a) in proceedings on appeal from the Tax Chamber of the First-tier Tribunal;

(b) in judicial review cases (see 5.35 below);
(c) in cases transferred from the Tax Chamber of the First-tier Tribunal;
(d) under *TCEA 2007, s 29(4)* (wasted costs — see **5.24** above) and costs incurred in applying for such costs; or
(e) where the Tribunal considers that a party or representative has acted unreasonably in bringing, defending or conducting the case.

Before making an order for costs, the Tribunal must give the person who will have to pay them the chance to make representations. If the payer is an individual, it must consider his financial means.

The Tribunal can make an order on its own initiative or on an application from one of the parties. Such an application must be sent both to the tribunal and to the person from whom costs are sought, together with a schedule of the costs claimed. An application must be made no later than one month after the date on which the Tribunal sends the notice recording the decision which finally disposes of all the issues in the case.

The amount of costs will be decided either by agreement of the parties, by summary assessment by the Tribunal or, if not agreed, by assessment. Where the amount is to be decided by assessment, either the payer or the person to whom the costs are to be paid can apply to a county court, the High Court or the Costs Office of the Supreme Court for a detailed assessment of the costs on the standard basis or, where the Tribunal's order so specifies, the indemnity basis. Upon making an order for the assessment of costs, the Tribunal may order an amount to be paid on account before the costs are assessed.

[*SI 2008 No 2698, Rule 1*].

Appeal to the Court of Appeal

[5.34] As noted at 5.32 above a party who disagrees with a decision of the Upper Tribunal can ask the Tribunal for permission to appeal to the Court of Appeal (in Scotland, the Court of Session). The appeal can be made only on a point of law.

If the Tribunal refuses permission, the party can seek permission to appeal directly from the Court. The Court will give permission only if the appeal would raise some important point of principle or practice or there is some other compelling reason for the Court to hear it.

[*TCEA 2007, s 13; SI 2008 No 2834*].

There are no tax-specific rules governing the making of applications for permission to appeal or for notifying appeals where permission has been given by the Court or Upper Tribunal. The *Civil Procedure Rules 1998, SI 1998 No 3132* therefore apply.

The Court's decision

If the Court finds that the decision of the Upper Tribunal involved an error on a point of law it can set aside the decision. It must then either remake the decision itself or remit the case back to either the Upper Tribunal or the First-tier Tribunal, with directions for its reconsideration. Those directions can include a direction that the case is to be re-heard by different tribunal members.

Where the case is remitted to the Upper Tribunal, it can itself decide to remit the case to the First-tier Tribunal.

If the Court decides to remake the decision itself, it can make any decision that the Upper Tribunal or first-tier Tribunal could have made, and can make such findings of fact as it considers appropriate.

[*TCEA 2007, s 14*].

Appeal restricted to point of law

Many court decisions turn on whether the Tribunal's decision was one of fact supported by the evidence and hence final. The courts will not disturb a finding of fact if there is reasonable evidence for it, notwithstanding that the evidence might support a different conclusion of fact. The leading case is *Edwards v Bairstow & Harrison* HL 1955, 36 TC 207, in which the issue was whether there had been an adventure in the nature of trade. The Commissioners' decision was reversed on the ground that the only reasonable conclusion from the evidence was that there had been such an adventure.

A new question of law may be raised in the courts on giving due notice to the other parties (*Muir v CIR* CA 1966, 43 TC 367) but the courts will neither admit evidence not in the stated case (*Watson v Samson Bros* Ch D 1959, 38 TC 346; *Cannon Industries Ltd v Edwards* Ch D 1965, 42 TC 625; *Frowd v Whalley* Ch D 1965, 42 TC 599, and see *R v Great Yarmouth Commrs (ex p. Amis)* QB 1960, 39 TC 143) nor consider contentions of which evidence in support was not produced before the Commissioners (*Denekamp v Pearce* Ch D 1998, 71 TC 213).

For the circumstances in which the court may permit a new ground of appeal, see *Altrad Services Ltd v HMRC* [2023] EWCA Civ 474, CA, [2023] STC 931. In that case, permission to appeal on the new ground was granted to HMRC on the basis that any prejudice to the taxpayers of not having called evidence from witnesses would be mitigated by the court making certain assumptions in their favour.

Use of Parliamentary material

Following the decision in *Pepper v Hart* HL 1992, 65 TC 421, the courts are prepared to consider the parliamentary history of legislation, or the official reports of debates in Hansard, where all of the following conditions are met.

- Legislation is ambiguous or obscure, or leads to an absurdity.
- The material relied upon consists of one or more statements by a Minister or other promoter of the Bill together if necessary with such other parliamentary material as is necessary to understand such statements and their effect.
- The statements relied upon are clear.

Status of decision

A court decision is a binding precedent for itself or an inferior court except that the Supreme Court, while treating its former decisions as normally binding, may depart from a previous decision should it appear right to do so. For this, see

Fitzleet Estates Ltd v Cherry HL 1977, 51 TC 708. Scottish decisions are not binding on the High Court but are normally followed. Decisions of the Privy Council and of the Irish Courts turning on comparable legislation are treated with respect. A court decision does not affect other assessments already final and conclusive (see **6.5** ASSESSMENTS) but may be followed, if relevant, in the determination of any open appeals against assessments and in assessments made subsequently irrespective of the years of assessment or taxpayers concerned (*Re Waring decd* Ch D, [1948] 1 All ER 257; *Gwyther v Boslymon Quarries Ltd* KB 1950, 29 ATC 1; *Bolands Ltd v CIR* SC(I) 1925, 4 ATC 526). Further, a court decision does not prevent the Crown from proceeding on a different basis for other years (*Hood Barrs v CIR (No 3)* CA 1960, 39 TC 209).

Judicial review

[5.35] A taxpayer who is dissatisfied with the exercise of administrative powers may, in certain circumstances, seek a remedy in a mandatory or prohibiting order or a quashing order. This is done by way of an application for judicial review to the High Court under *Supreme Court Act 1981, s 31* and *Part 54 of the Civil Procedure Rules*. The High Court can, in certain cases, transfer an application for judicial review or for leave to apply for judicial review to the Upper Tribunal (see *Supreme Court Act 1981, s 31A*).

Grounds for judicial review are procedural impropriety, illegality, irrationality and legitimate expectation (*R (on the application of Realreed Ltd) v HMRC* KB, [2023] EWHC 1572 (Admin); and *R (on the application of Gallaher Group Ltd) v Competition and Markets Authority* SC, [2018] UKSC 25).

With effect from 14 July 2022 judicial review proceedings cannot, subject to certain exceptions, be brought against a decision of the Upper Tribunal to refuse permission to appeal. See *Judicial Review and Courts Act 2022, s 2*.

Application for leave to apply for judicial review is made ex parte to a single judge who will usually determine the application without a hearing. The court will not grant leave unless the applicant has a sufficient interest in the matter to which the application relates. See *CIR v National Federation of Self-Employed and Small Businesses Ltd* HL 1981, 55 TC 133 for what is meant by 'sufficient interest'.

The issue on an application for leave to apply for judicial review is whether there is an arguable case (*R v CIR (ex p. Howmet Corporation and another)* QB, [1994] STC 413). The procedure is generally used where no other, adequate, remedy, such as a right of appeal, is available. See *R v Special Commr (ex p. Stipplechoice Ltd) (No 1)* CA, [1985] STC 248 and *(No 3)* QB 1988, 61 TC 391, *R v HMIT (ex p. Kissane and Another)* QB, [1986] STC 152, *R v CIR (ex p. Goldberg)* QB 1988, 61 TC 403 and *R v Dickinson (ex p. McGuckian)* CA(NI) 1999, 72 TC 343.

There is a very long line of cases in which the courts have consistently refused applications where a matter should have been pursued through the ordinary channels as described earlier in this chapter. See, for example, *R v Special Commrs (ex p. Morey)* CA 1972, 49 TC 71; *R v North London General Commrs (ex p. Nii-Amaa)* QB 1999, 72 TC 634; and *R (on the application of Derrin Brothers Properties Ltd) v HMRC (and related applications)* CA, [2016] STC 1081.

Simon's Taxes. See **A5.302–A5.310.**

Time limit

Applications must be made **within three months** of the date when the grounds for application arose. The Court has discretion to extend this time limit where there is good reason, subject to conditions, but is generally very reluctant to do so. Grant of leave for review does not amount to a ruling that application is made in good time (*R v Tavistock Commrs (ex p. Worth)* QB 1985, 59 TC 116).

Costs of appeals to the Court of Appeal etc.

[5.36] Costs may be awarded by the courts in the usual way. In suitable cases, e.g. 'test cases', HMRC may undertake to pay the taxpayer's costs. See **5.24** and **5.33** for the award of costs by the First-tier and Upper Tribunals.

Law costs of appeals are not allowable for tax purposes generally (*Allen v Farquharson* KB 1932, 17 TC 59; *Smith's Potato Estates Ltd v Bolland* HL 1948, 30 TC 267; *Rushden Heel Co v Keene* HL 1948, 30 TC 298; *Spofforth & Prince v Golder* KB 1945, 26 TC 310); and see **16.12** COMPUTATION OF GAINS AND LOSSES.

Key points on appeals

[5.37] Points to consider are as follows.

- HMRC provide the option of internally reviewing decisions made by its officers. A finite timeframe is given for providing the independent review decision. The benefits of an internal review are that an independent officer reviews the decision and how it was made, the quantum (where appropriate) and the risk to HMRC of losing the appeal. There is no material cost to the client in the majority of cases in opting for internal review.
- Any appeal or referral for internal review must accurately and clearly state the grounds for the appeal, as these are normally the points considered by the Tribunal. To avoid disputes over 'not at arms length' transactions it is essential a professional valuation is obtained at the time of the transfer.
- HMRC also operate an alternative dispute resolution process to settle disputes. This allows a facilitator (from HMRC) to mediate between the two parties. See **5.10** above.
- The Courts and Tribunals Service manages the appeal and the system is formal and structured so it is essential that the adviser is disciplined and organised to avoid damaging their client's case. If they are not happy with the categorisation of the appeal, they can ask for the appeal to be moved to another category, if they believe this will be beneficial.
- HMRC will often appoint Counsel to represent them so the adviser needs to consider seriously whether to appoint Counsel where a hearing is scheduled.

- In the majority of cases, the burden of proof rests with the taxpayer.
- Use the additional information 'white space' in the tax return to explain and provide information on transactions, estimated or provisional figures and other relevant information. If HMRC are made aware of these issues it restricts the chances HMRC can make a 'discovery' assessment.
- HMRC are guided by its Litigation and Settlement Strategy. If the dispute is over a point of law then it is not normally possible to negotiate a settlement for a proportion of the disputed figure.
- Taking matters before the Tribunal is costly in terms of time and money so the client needs to be made fully aware of these two factors when deciding whether to take an appeal before the Tribunal. What are the chances of success? Is the client prepared to pay the tax on top of the professional costs and to suffer the disruption the process will cause?

6

Assessments

Cross-references. See **5** APPEALS; **13.5** CLAIMS; **43.3** OVERSEAS MATTERS as regards UK representatives of non-residents; **44.2** PARTNERSHIPS; **52.17** RETURNS for HMRC determinations of tax liability in the event of the non-filing of a self-assessment tax return; **55** SELF-SSESSMENT.

Introduction to assessments

[6.1] Although both capital gains tax and corporation tax operate under a system of SELF-ASSESSMENT (**55**) so that taxpayers must self-assess their own tax liability, HMRC retain the power to make assessments where necessary. In particular, HMRC can make a 'discovery' assessment where they discover that any amount which ought to have been assessed to tax has not been assessed, that an existing assessment is insufficient or that any relief already given is excessive. The power to make an assessment is separate from HMRC's power to make a determination of tax liability in the event of the non-filing of a self-assessment tax return – see **52.17** RETURNS.

The power to make an assessment is, however, restricted by the operation of time limits within which it must be made. Normally an assessment for a tax year or accounting period must be made not more than four years after the end of the year or period. This time limit is extended in certain circumstances and in particular where a loss of tax involves an offshore matter or offshore transfer or has been brought about carelessly or deliberately by the taxpayer. In the case of a loss involving an offshore matter, or offshore transfer, the time limit is 12 years after the end of the tax year. In the case of a loss brought about carelessly the time limit is six years after the end of the year or period; for a loss brought about deliberately the time limit is twenty years.

HMRC can make a 'simple assessment' of an individual's or trustee's income tax or capital gains tax liability without the taxpayer first being required to complete a self-assessment tax return. The simple assessment will be made on the basis of information already held by HMRC. See **6.9** below.

Assessments in general

[6.2] Income tax assessments and CGT assessments on individuals (including individual members of partnerships), trustees and personal representatives are made for years of assessment (tax years). Corporation tax assessments on companies are made for accounting periods.

An assessment is made by an HMRC officer by the giving of a notice of assessment. The notice must be served on the person assessed (normally by post) and must state its date of issue and the time limit for giving notice of appeal (**5.3** APPEALS). All income tax falling to be charged by such an assessment, even if chargeable under more than one Part or Chapter of *ITTOIA 2005*, may be included in one assessment, but there is no provision for income tax and CGT to be charged in the same assessment.

Where any statutory provision gives the Commissioners for HMRC the power to make an assessment, the assessment is nevertheless to be made by an officer as described above.

[*TMA 1970, s 30A(1)–(3)(5); FA 1998, Sch 18 para 47(1)*].

See **27.3** HMRC—ADMINISTRATION for the exercise of functions of an HMRC officer by automated process.

An assessment must include a statement of the tax actually payable (*Hallamshire Industrial Finance Trust Ltd v CIR* Ch D 1978, 53 TC 631). An assessment defective in form or containing errors may be validated by *TMA 1970, s 114(1)*. However, *s 114(1)* does *not* extend to integral fundamental parts of the assessment such as an error in the year of assessment for which it is made (*Baylis v Gregory* HL 1988, 62 TC 1).

A taxpayer may authorise HMRC (on form 64-8) to automatically provide their agent with a copy of any assessment made on them. If an assessment is not dealt with promptly, interest (or additional interest) may arise on unpaid tax, and any appeal may be out of time.

See **52.17** RETURNS for HMRC's power to make a determination of the tax liability in a case where an annual self-assessment tax return has been issued but not filed. Tax is payable as if the determination were a self-assessment, with no right of appeal, and the determination can only be displaced by the filing of a return and the making of a self-assessment based on it.

See **14.16** COMPANIES regarding the application of the corporation tax provisions where a company ceases to be UK-resident in the course of the formation of an SE or where an SE becomes non-UK resident.

Construction of references to assessments etc.

[6.3] References to a person being assessed to tax, or being charged to tax by an assessment, are to be construed as including a reference to their being so assessed, or being so charged, by a self-assessment or by a determination under *TMA 1970, s 28C* or *FA 1998, Sch 18, paras 36, 37* (see **52.17, 52.21** RETURNS) which has not been superseded by a self-assessment. [*FA 1994, s 197; FA 1998, Sch 18 para 97*].

Double assessment

[6.4] Where there has been 'double assessment' for the same cause and for the same chargeable period, a claim may be made to the Commissioners for HMRC for the assessment reflecting the overcharge to be vacated. An appeal against a refusal of a claim may be made by giving notice to the HMRC officer concerned in writing within 30 days after the day on which notice of the refusal is given. [*TMA 1970, s 32*]. See **13.7** CLAIMS for claims for the recovery of tax charged in an assessment which the taxpayer believes not to be due and **33.1** INTERACTION WITH OTHER TAXES as regards alternative income tax and CGT assessments.

Finality of assessments

[6.5] An assessment cannot be altered after the notice has been served except in accordance with the express provisions of the *Taxes Acts* (for example, where the taxpayer appeals – see **5** APPEALS). [*TMA 1970, s 30A(4); FA 1998, Sch 18 para 47(2)*]. See **13.7** CLAIMS for claims for the recovery of tax charged in an assessment which the taxpayer believes not to be due. An assessment as determined on appeal, or not appealed against, is final and conclusive.

Trustees and personal representatives

[6.6] CGT due from trustees or personal representatives may be assessed and charged on and in the name of any one or more of the 'relevant trustees' or, as the case may be, 'relevant personal representatives'. In relation to chargeable gains, the '*relevant trustees*' means the trustees in the tax year in which the gains accrue and any subsequent trustees of the settlement, and '*relevant personal representatives*' has a corresponding meaning. See **42.2** OFFSHORE SETTLEMENTS for the modification of this rule in relation to the 'exit charge' under *TCGA 1992, s 80* on trustees ceasing to be resident in the UK.

Unless the assets are held by the trustees or personal representatives as nominees or bare trustees for another person absolutely (see **56.3** SETTLEMENTS), chargeable gains accruing to, and CGT chargeable on, the trustees or personal representatives are not to be regarded as accruing to, or chargeable on, any other person. No trustee or personal representative is to be regarded as an individual for the purposes of *TCGA 1992*.

[*TCGA 1992, s 65(1)(2)(4)*].

See also **56.6, 56.11** SETTLEMENTS.

Non-corporate bodies, personal representatives and receivers

[6.7] Assessments may be made on the treasurer etc. of bodies which are not corporations; on personal representatives in respect of disposals made *by the deceased person*; and receivers appointed by a court. [*TMA 1970, ss 71, 74, 75, 77*]. As regards receivers, however, see *CIR v Piacentini and others* QB 2003, 75 TC 288.

Contract settlements

[6.8] In cases where penalties are chargeable, the taxpayer may be invited to offer a sum in settlement of liability of tax, interest and penalties (a 'contract settlement') and such offers are often accepted by HMRC without assessment of all the tax. A binding agreement so made cannot be repudiated afterwards by the taxpayer or their executors. Where the liability is agreed and the tax etc. paid, this cannot afterwards be set aside, notwithstanding any alleged over-charge and no formal assessment (see cases at **46.26** PENALTIES and *CIR v Nuttall* CA 1989, 63 TC 148 and *CIR v Woollen* CA 1992, 65 TC 229). See, however, *R (oao HMRC) v Berkshire General Commissioners* Ch D 2007, [2008] STC 1494, in which a contract settlement included a provision allowing HMRC to make further inquiries in relation to a partnership in which certain of the parties to the settlement were partners.

Simple assessments

[6.9] HMRC can make a 'simple assessment' of an individual's or trustee's income tax or capital gains tax liability without the taxpayer first being required to complete a self-assessment tax return. The simple assessment will be made on the basis of information already held by HMRC, whether it was received from the taxpayer or a third party. HMRC can withdraw a simple assessment by notice to the taxpayer, and it is then taken as never having had any effect.

The notice of assessment must include particulars of the income and gains, and any relief or allowance, taken into account in the assessment, and must state the amount payable, net of any income tax deducted at source, and the due date for payment (see **45.2** PAYMENT OF TAX). In the case of a trust, the notice of assessment can be given to any one or more of the relevant trustees (see **56.11** SETTLEMENTS). HMRC can make more than one simple assessment on a person for any tax year. A simple assessment cannot be made if the taxpayer has already made a return or if he has been given notice to do so and that notice has not been withdrawn.

[*TMA 1970, ss 28H–28J*].

See **52.4** RETURNS for the real-time capital gains service which is underpinned by the simple assessment legislative framework.

Querying a simple assessment

An appeal can be made against a simple assessment (see **5.2** APPEALS) but only after the person assessed has raised a query about the assessment and has been given a final response to that query. The person may query the simple assessment by notifying HMRC of their belief that the assessment is, or may be, incorrect and stating the reasons for that belief. They must do so within 60 days after the date the notice of assessment was issued or such longer period as HMRC may allow in a particular case. They can withdraw their query at any time.

HMRC must consider a query and give a final response. If they need more time or information, they can postpone the simple assessment in whole or part (according to how much of it is being queried) and notify the taxpayer accordingly. If the simple assessment is postponed in part, HMRC must state the amount that remains payable. The taxpayer is under no obligation to pay a postponed amount. After considering the query, HMRC's final response must be to confirm, amend or withdraw the assessment, and in each case to notify the taxpayer in writing. An amended simple assessment given as a final response to a query cannot itself be queried.

[*TMA 1970, s 31AA*].

Discovery assessments

[6.10] If HMRC 'discover', as regards any person (the taxpayer) and a year of assessment, that:

(a) any amount of income tax or capital gains tax which ought to have been assessed to tax has not been assessed, or
(b) an assessment is or has become insufficient, or
(c) any relief given is or has become excessive,

then with the exceptions below, an assessment (a discovery assessment) may be made to make good to the Crown the apparent loss of tax. For assessments for 2020/21 and earlier years, the condition in (a) above is that any profits (i.e. income or chargeable gains) which ought to have been assessed to tax have not been assessed. The revised condition also applies retrospectively to 2020/21 and earlier years, however, in certain cases involving stand-alone income tax charges, for details of which see Tolley's Income Tax.

Similar rules apply for corporation tax purposes. A discovery assessment may be made (with the same exceptions) if HMRC discover as regards an accounting period of a company that:

(i) any amounts which ought to have been assessed to tax have not been assessed, or
(ii) an assessment is or has become insufficient, or
(iii) any relief given is or has become excessive.

The assessment must generally be made by the HMRC officer making the discovery. In *Brown v HMRC* FTT, [2024] UKFTT 245 (TC), it was accepted that the officer who had made the discovery had not made the assessment. Although it was possible for another officer to make the discovery again and then issue an assessment, there was no evidence of whether that had happened or of which officer made the assessment. The onus of proof fell on HMRC to demonstrate that all the requirements were met and they had failed to do so.

In a case where a return under *TMA 1970, s 8* or *s 8A* (see **52.5** RETURNS), or a company tax return (see **52.21** RETURNS), has been filed in respect of a chargeable period (i.e. for income tax and CGT purposes, a year of assessment or for corporation tax, an accounting period),

(1) no discovery assessment may be made in respect of that chargeable period if it would be attributable to an error or mistake in the return as to the basis on which the liability ought to have been computed and the return was, in fact, made on the basis, or in accordance with the practice, generally prevailing at the time when it was made;

(2) no discovery assessment may be made in respect of that chargeable period unless either:
  (i) the loss of tax is brought about carelessly or deliberately by the taxpayer or a person acting on his behalf, or
  (ii) at the time when an HMRC officer either ceased to be entitled to enquire (see **52.11** RETURNS) into the return or, where an enquiry has been opened, has issued a closure notice, he could not have been reasonably expected, on the basis of the information so far made available to him, to be aware of the loss of tax. The reference here to a closure notice is to a final closure notice or to a partial closure notice in respect of a matter to which the discovery relates (see **52.14** RETURNS).

See **6.14** and the case law below for the meaning of 'carelessly' and 'deliberately'.

For the purposes of (2)(ii) above, information is regarded as having been made available to HMRC if it has been included in:

(A) the return (or accompanying accounts, statements or documents) for the chargeable period concerned or for either of the two immediately preceding it, or

(B) a partnership return (see **52.18** RETURNS), where applicable, in respect of the chargeable period concerned or either of the two immediately preceding it, or

(C) (for disposals before 6 April 2019) an NRCGT return containing an advance self-assessment in respect of the tax year concerned or either of the two chargeable periods immediately preceding it, or

(D) any claim or any application under *ICTA 1988, s 751A* (reduction in profits of controlled foreign company for certain activities of EEA business establishments) for the chargeable period concerned, or

(E) documents, etc. produced for the purposes of any enquiries into such a return or claim,

or is information the existence and relevance of which could reasonably be expected to be inferred from the above-mentioned information or are notified in writing to HMRC. See also below.

The requirement for either of the conditions in (i) or (ii) in (2) above to be met does not apply in respect of chargeable gains (and income) in relation to which the taxpayer has been given, after the completion of any enquiries, a notice under *TCGA 1992, s 184G* or *s 184H* (avoidance utilising losses — see **14.7** COMPANIES).

An objection to a discovery assessment on the grounds that neither (i) nor (ii) in (2) above applies can be made only on an appeal against the assessment. (See **5.2** APPEALS for right of appeal.)

For the purposes of the above provisions, a UK land disposal return (see **52.22** RETURNS) is treated as if it were an assessment required to be included as part of the taxpayer's ordinary self-assessment tax return (whether or not an ordinary return is actually required). References above to a return include a UK land disposal return.

[*TMA 1970, s 29; FA 1998, s 117, Sch 18 paras 41–45; FA 2008, s 118, Sch 36 para 71; FA 2019, Sch 2 para 23; FA 2022, s 97*].

See **45.2** PAYMENT OF TAX as regards due date of payment of income tax and CGT under these provisions. For time limits for making assessments, see **6.12** onwards below.

A change of HMRC opinion on information previously made available to them is not grounds for a discovery assessment. See **52.6** RETURNS for the use of discovery assessments in amending provisional figures in a self-assessment.

See **13.5** CLAIMS for extended time limits for claims where a discovery assessment is made in a case where no careless of deliberate conduct is involved.

HMRC guidance on discovery

Particularly in large or complex cases, the standard accounts information details and other information included in the personal tax return may not provide a means of disclosure adequate to avoid falling within (2)(ii) above. The submission of further information, including perhaps accounts, may be considered appropriate but will not necessarily provide protection against a discovery assessment beyond that arising from submission of the return alone. The 'reasonably expectated' test (see (2)(ii) above) must be satisfied. Where voluminous information beyond the accounts and computations is sent with the return, HMRC do not accept that the test is satisfied if the information is so extensive that an officer could not reasonably be expected to be aware of the significance of particular information and the officer's attention has not been drawn to it by the taxpayer.

Where an entry in a return depends on the valuation of an asset, HMRC consider that most taxpayers who state in the additional information space at the end of the return that a valuation has been used, by whom it has been carried out, and that it was carried out by a named independent and suitably qualified valuer if that was the case, on the appropriate basis, will be able to rely on protection from a later discovery assessment after the enquiry period, provided those statements are true. Alternatively, in capital gains cases, completion of the entry in the capital gains pages indicating that a valuation has been made and inclusion of a copy of the valuation with the return will be sufficient to provide protection if the copy of the valuation includes all the information mentioned above. In some circumstances, provision of the above information will not protect against a discovery assessment, particularly where other parties to the same transaction subsequently include a (different) valuation of the asset in their return.

Where a properly advised taxpayer adopts a different view of the law from that published as HMRC's view, to protect against a discovery assessment after the enquiry period, HMRC consider that the return would have to indicate that a different view had been adopted. This might be done by an entry in the additional information space to the effect that HMRC guidance has not been followed on the issue or that no adjustment has been made to take account of it. In HMRC's view, it is not necessary for the taxpayer to provide with the return enough information for the HMRC officer to be able to quantify any resulting under assessment of tax.

(HMRC Statement of Practice SP 1/06).

Simon's Taxes. See **A6.7.**

Case law on discovery

The conditions in (2) above are objective tests which, once an assessment has been made, can be tested on appeal (*Hankinson v HMRC* CA 2011, [2011] EWCA Civ 1566, [2012] 1 WLR 2322, [2012] STC 485). The conditions are not concerned with the subjective view of the assessing HMRC officer.

Carelessly or deliberately (TMA 1970, s 29(4); FA 1998, Sch 18 para 43)

In *Hancock v CIR* (Sp C 213), [1999] SSCD 287, it was held that a taxpayer who had made errors in his tax return had exhibited standards of competence beneath those to be reasonably expected, that his conduct thus amounted to negligence (under the legislation then applicable — see now (2)(i) above), and that the Revenue did therefore have the power to make a discovery assessment.

In *McEwan v Martin* Ch D, [2005] STC 993, a capital gains tax computation prepared by a professional adviser was held to constitute negligent conduct on the taxpayer's behalf, so that a discovery assessment could be made. The Revenue were entitled to assume that a professionally prepared tax computation was prepared properly, and the fact that they accepted a negligent computation at face value did not mean that it somehow ceased to be prepared negligently.

In *Anderson v HMRC* FTT, [2017] SFTD 100, the appellant had relied on a valuation of shares by the corporate finance department of a leading firm of accountants. The Tribunal held that he had not been careless in doing so. His appeal against a discovery assessment charging CGT on the disposal of the shares was therefore upheld.

The SC held that a discovery assessment which relied on the extended time limits for 'deliberate conduct' was invalid because the taxpayer's conduct had not been deliberate in *Tooth v HMRC* SC, [2021] STC 1049. The court held that a deliberate inaccuracy means a statement which, when made, was deliberately inaccurate, and not a deliberate statement which is (in fact) inaccurate. The accuracy of a statement should be determined in the light of the whole tax return.

Carelessness by a person 'acting on behalf of' the taxpayer was considered In *HMRC v Hicks* UT, [2020] STC 254. The taxpayer's accountant (B) had advised him in relation to entering an avoidance scheme and had prepared his tax returns. The accountant had not been suitably qualified to form an independent opinion on the workings of the scheme. Having taken on the role of a tax adviser, however, B's advice would nevertheless be judged against the standard expected of a reasonably competent tax adviser giving advice to a taxpayer on the matter in question. B's advice had not met that standard and the Tribunal therefore found that the insufficiency in the assessments had been brought about carelessly by a person acting on behalf of the taxpayer. The discovery assessment was therefore validly made.

In *McCumiskey v HMRC* FTT, [2022] UKFTT 128 (TC), M was the victim of a fraud in which a fictitious tax return was submitted on his behalf. HMRC made a tax refund arising from a fraudulent claim to SEIS relief but made it direct to an account nominated by the fraudsters. HMRC raised a discovery assessment on M to collect the tax over-repaid. The FTT held that neither of the conditions in (2) above were met and allowed M's appeal. M had appointed an agent (A) and had given A all necessary information to enable a return to be filed. The purported return had been filed by someone else (B). It was held that there was no authority given by M for A to appoint B as a sub-agent, and M had not ratified any such appointment. B could not be regarded as acting on behalf of M. Neither had M been careless himself, having engaged a professional tax agent. The FTT also did not accept that there was insufficient information available to the HMRC officer to doubt the validity of a claim for relief on a £15,000 SEIS investment, by its very nature a high-risk investment, by a person of modest income.

Available information (TMA 1970, s 29(5); FA 1998, Sch 18 para 44)

The test in (2)(ii) above was considered in *Veltema v Langham* CA, [2004] STC 544. A company director (V) was liable to income tax on the value of a house, and in his tax return he submitted a valuation of £100,000. After the deadline for making an enquiry into the return (see **52.11** RETURNS) had passed, the Revenue formed the opinion that the value of the house had been more than £100,000, and they subsequently issued a further assessment on the basis that the true value had been £145,000. V appealed, contending that the issue of a further assessment was not authorised by *TMA 1970, s 29*. The CA rejected this contention and upheld the assessment, holding that the assessment was not prohibited by *TMA 1970, s 29(5)* (i.e. (2)(ii) above). Prior to the enquiry deadline, the Revenue 'could not have been reasonably expected' to be aware that the valuation was inadequate. The CA observed that 'it would frustrate the aims of the self-assessment scheme, namely simplicity and early finality of assessment to tax, to interpret *s 29(5)* so as to introduce an obligation on tax inspectors to conduct an immediate and possibly time consuming scrutiny of self-assessment returns . . . when they do not disclose insufficiency, but only circumstances further investigation of which might or might not show it'. Furthermore, the definition of 'information made available' to the Revenue given above was exhaustive for the purpose of (2)(ii) above. The key to the scheme was that the inspector was precluded from making a discovery assessment under *s 29* only when the taxpayer or his representatives, in making an honest and accurate return, had clearly alerted him to the insufficiency of the assessment. He was not precluded from making an assessment where he might be able to obtain some other information, not normally part of his checks, that might put the sufficiency of the assessment in question.

Following the decision in this case, HMRC issued Statement of Practice SP 1/06 (see above).

In *Corbally-Stourton v HMRC* (Sp C 692), [2008] SSCD 907 the taxpayer (C) entered into a marketed scheme as a result of which on her tax return she declared that she had made a substantial capital loss. The return included a description of the scheme in the 'white space'. HMRC subsequently reached the conclusion that the scheme did not work and that the loss was not allowable and made a discovery assessment under *TMA 1970, s 29*. C appealed, contending that the assessment was prohibited by *s 29(5)*. The Special Commissioner rejected this contention and dismissed the appeal. The fact that C had claimed a large 'round sum' loss in her tax return meant that 'an inspector could have been expected to have been aware that it was possible that there was an insufficiency but could not have been reasonably expected to conclude that it was probable that there was an insufficiency'. Accordingly the conditions of *s 29(5)* were satisfied and the assessment was not prohibited. This decision was followed in *R (oao Pattullo) v HMRC* CS, [2010] STC 107 and a similar decision was reached in *Sanderson v HMRC* CA, [2016] STC 638.

In *Anderson v HMRC* FTT, [2009] UKFTT 258 (TC); [2009] SWTI 2938, the taxpayer incorrectly treated a chargeable event gain on an offshore investment bond as if it were from an onshore gain and claimed a tax credit to which she was not entitled. The provision to HMRC of a chargeable event certificate by the insurance company which issued the bond was disregarded in determining whether HMRC could make a discovery assessment to disallow the tax credit. Similarly, information in a trust return was disregarded in determining whether HMRC could make a discovery assessment in respect of income from the trust omitted from an individual's return in *Trustees of the Bessie Taube Discretionary Settlement Trust v HMRC* FTT 2010, [2011] SFTD 153.

An appeal against an assessment succeeded in *HMRC v Landsdowne Partners Ltd Partnership* CA 2011, [2012] STC 544, on the basis that the condition in (2)(ii) above applied.

Information provided with the taxpayer's return was sufficient to show that 'no officer could have missed the point that an artificial tax avoidance scheme had been implemented' in *Charlton v HMRC* UT, [2013] STC 866. 'On the basis of the information made available to him before the closure of the enquiry window, an officer would have been reasonably expected to have been aware of the insufficiency of tax such as to justify an assessment'; therefore, no discovery assessment was possible. It was not necessary that a hypothetical officer should have been able to comprehend all the workings of the scheme, or the legal and factual arguments that might arise, or be able to form a reasoned view of those matters. Discovery assessments in cases involving avoidance schemes were, however, upheld in *Smith v HMRC* FTT, [2013] UKFTT 368 (TC) and *Pattullo v HMRC (No 2)* UT, [2016] STC 2043.

Timing of the assessment

HMRC cannot raise a discovery assessment relying on the condition in (2)(ii) above where the enquiry window is still open (see **52.11** RETURNS). See *Norton v HMRC* UT, [2023] UKUT 48 (TCC). There is, however, nothing to stop HMRC raising a discovery assessment relying on the condition in (2)(i) above (or recognising the potential for doing so in setting the amount of a contract settlement – see **6.8** above) where the enquiry window is still open. See HMRC Enquiry Manual EM3250 for examples of where HMRC will or will not make a discovery assessment.

In *Tooth v HMRC* SC, [2021] STC 1036, the court ruled that there was no concept of 'staleness' in the statutory scheme for raising discovery assessments. This concept had been used in a number of cases to rule that a discovery assessment was invalid. In *Beagles v HMRC* UT, [2019] STC 54, for example, there was a two and a half year gap between HMRC making a discovery and issuing an assessment. There was no ongoing litigation at the time of the discovery. The Upper Tribunal held that the discovery had become 'stale' and had lost its quality of newness before the assessment was made, and that the assessment was therefore invalid. The SC has now ruled that staleness cannot prevent HMRC from raising a valid assessment. An attempt to argue that the SC's comments on staleness were merely *obiter dicta* and so not binding failed in *Harrison v HMRC* UT, [2023] STC 580. The SC had provided 'clear and comprehensive general guidance' which could not be ignored.

Discovery assessment following appeal settled by agreement

In *Easinghall Ltd v HMRC* UT, [2016] STC 1476, an additional discovery assessment made following an agreement under *TMA 1970, s 54* (see **5.9** APPEALS) was held to be invalid. Such an assessment could only be made if it was founded on a point other than the particular matter which had been the subject of the agreement.

Estimates in discovery assessments

In *Cussens v HMRC* FTT, [2019] UKFTT 542 (TC); 2019 SWTI 1555, discovery assessments were held not to be valid because they had not been made using best judgement. HMRC had made assessments on an uncooperative taxpayer by taking an estimate of sales and deducting 50% for expenses. The Tribunal found that it was 'unthinkable' that such a high net profit could be achieved and there was no evidence that HMRC had undertaken any research into the margins achieved by similar businesses.

Amendment of partnership return on discovery

[6.11] Provisions broadly similar to those in **6.10** above apply to an understatement of profits or excessive claim for relief or allowances in a partnership statement (see **52.19** RETURNS), although HMRC's remedy in this case is to amend the partnership return, with consequent amendment of partners' own returns. [*TMA 1970, s 30B*].

Time limits

[6.12] The normal time limit for the making of an assessment to income tax, capital gains tax and corporation tax is four years after the end of the tax year or accounting period in question. An 'assessment' for this purpose includes a determination under *TMA 1970, s 29A* (see **6.12** above).

The time limit normally applies by reference to the tax year or accounting period in which the disposal takes place. Where an asset is disposed of and acquired under a contract, this is the year or period in which the contract is made or, if the contract is conditional, the year or period in which the conditions are met (see **16.4** COMPUTATION OF GAINS AND LOSSES).

For contracts entered into on or after 6 April 2023 (1 April 2023 for corporation tax), the time limit is extended in certain cases where the asset is not conveyed or transferred until a later tax year or accounting period. For capital gains tax purposes, this applies where the asset is not conveyed or transferred until after 5 October following the tax year in which the contract is made. The time limit for making an assessment runs from the end of the tax year of the conveyance or transfer. For corporation tax purposes, the extension applies where the asset is not conveyed or transferred until more than twelve months after the end of the accounting period in which the contract is made. The time limit for making an assessment then runs from the end of the accounting period of conveyance or transfer.

[*TMA 1970, s 34(1)(1A); TCGA 1992, s 28A; FA 1998, s 117, Sch 18 para 46(1); F(No 2)A 2023, s 40*].

The latest time for assessing the personal representatives of a deceased person in respect of gains accruing before his death is four years after the end of the tax year of death. [*TMA 1970, s 40(1)(3)*].

In certain cases, specific provisions also extend the normal time limits (see, for example, **13.5** CLAIMS, **45.26** PAYMENT OF TAX). For extended time limits in cases of a loss of tax involving an offshore matter or offshore transfer, see **6.13** below and for extended time limits in cases of a loss of tax brought about carelessly or deliberately, see **6.14** below.

An objection to the making of any assessment on the grounds that it is out of time can only be made on an appeal against the assessment. [*TMA 1970, s 34(2); FA 1998, s 117, Sch 18 para 46(3)*].

Self-assessments

The above time limits do not apply to self-assessments (see *R (oao Higgs) v HMRC* UT [2015] STC 1600). [*TMA 1970, s 34(3)*]. See **52.8** RETURNS for the time limits which apply to the making of a self-assessment contained in a return.

Extended time limit where loss of tax involves offshore matter or offshore transfer

[6.13] An assessment in a case involving a loss of income tax or capital gains tax where the lost tax involves either an 'offshore transfer' which makes the tax significantly harder to identify or an 'offshore matter' may be made at any time not more than 12 years after the end of the tax year to which the tax relates. This rule applies generally to assessments for 2015/16 onwards. Where, however, the loss of tax is brought about carelessly by the taxpayer (see **6.14** below) or someone acting on his behalf, the extended time limit applies also to assessments for 2013/14 and 2014/15.

If the taxpayer so requires, the assessment may give effect to reliefs or allowances to which he would have been entitled had he made the necessary claims within the relevant time limits (with some exceptions for income tax).

An assessment cannot be made under this provision if, before the time limit that would otherwise apply, HMRC received information from an overseas authority (under EU law or any international agreement) on the basis of which they could reasonably have been expected to become aware of the lost tax and to have made the assessment within that time limit.

The extended time limit also does not apply to transfer pricing adjustments under *TIOPA 2010, Pt 4*.

Lost tax involves an '*offshore transfer*' if it does not involve an offshore matter and the income or disposal proceeds by reference to which it is charged are transferred to a territory outside the UK before the date on which the taxpayer delivers his tax return for the tax year or, if no return is made, before 31 January following the tax year. The transfer of assets derived from or representing such income or proceeds is, for this purpose, treated as a transfer of the income or proceeds. The circumstances in which a transfer makes the lost tax significantly harder to identify include cases where the transfer makes it significantly less likely for HMRC to become aware of the lost tax or makes it likely for HMRC to become aware of the lost tax at a significantly later time.

Lost tax involves an '*offshore matter*' if it is charge on or by reference to income arising from a source in a foreign territory, assets situated or held in a foreign territory, income or assets received in a foreign territory, activities carried on wholly or mainly in a foreign territory, or anything having effect as if it were such income, assets or activities.

'*Assets*' for these purposes are defined as for capital gains purposes, but also include sterling.

The time limit under these provisions does not prevent an assessment from being made at a later time under any other provision which allows for a longer period (such as the 20-year period at **6.14** below).

[*TMA 1970, s 36A*].

Extended time limits where loss or tax brought about carelessly or deliberately

[6.14] An assessment in a case involving a loss of income tax, capital gains tax or corporation tax brought about carelessly by the taxpayer (or by a person acting on their behalf or, where the taxpayer is a company, a partner of the company) may be made at any time not more than six years after the end of the tax year or accounting period to which it relates.

Where the loss of tax is brought about deliberately (by the taxpayer, a person acting on his behalf or a partner of a company), an assessment may be made at any time not more than 20 years after the end of the tax year or accounting period to which it relates. This time limit applies also where a loss of tax is attributable to:

(a) a failure to notify chargeability under *TMA 1970, s 7* or *FA 1998, Sch 18 para 2* (see **46.3** PENALTIES);
(b) avoidance arrangements in respect of which the taxpayer failed to make a disclosure under *FA 2004, ss 309, 310* or *313* (see **19.2** DISCLOSURE OF TAX AVOIDANCE SCHEMES); or
(c) arrangements which were expected to result in a tax advantage in respect of which the taxpayer was under an obligation to notify HMRC of a monitored promoter's reference number under the high-risk promoters of avoidance schemes provisions but failed to do so,

but, where the tax year involved is 2008/09 or an earlier year, only where the assessment is for the purposes of making good to the Crown a loss of tax attributable to the taxpayer's negligent conduct or such conduct by a person acting on his behalf.

The above time limits normally apply by reference to the tax year or accounting period in which the disposal takes place. Where an asset is disposed of and acquired under a contract, this is the year or period in which the contract is made or, if the contract is conditional, the year or period in which the conditions are met (see **16.4** COMPUTATION OF GAINS AND LOSSES).

Where the taxpayer has a reasonable excuse (see **46.2** PENALTIES) for a failure to notify chargeability, the extended time limit provided for in (a) does not apply (*Hextall v HMRC* FTT, [2023] SFTD 1053).

For contracts entered into on or after 6 April 2023 (1 April 2023 for corporation tax), the time limit is extended in certain cases where the asset is not conveyed or transferred until a later tax year or accounting period. For capital gains tax purposes, this applies where the asset is not conveyed or transferred until after 5 October following the tax year in which the contract is made. The time limit for making an assessment runs from the end of the tax year of the conveyance or transfer. For corporation tax purposes, the extension applies where the asset is not conveyed or transferred until more than twelve months after the end of the accounting period in which the contract is made. The time limit for making an assessment then runs from the end of the accounting period of conveyance or transfer.

If the taxpayer so requires, the assessment may give effect to reliefs or allowances to which he would have been entitled had he made the necessary claims within the relevant time limits (with some exceptions for income tax).

[*TMA 1970, s 36(1)–(1B)(3)(3A); TCGA 1992, s 28A; FA 1998, Sch 18 paras 46(2)–(2B), 65; F(No 2)A 2023, s 40*].

For the purposes of the above provisions, a loss of tax is brought about carelessly by a person if they fail to take reasonable care to avoid bringing about that loss. Where information is given to HMRC and the person providing it (or on whose behalf it is given) later discovers it was inaccurate and fails to take reasonable steps to inform HMRC, any loss of tax brought about by the inaccuracy is treated as having been brought about carelessly. A loss of tax brought about deliberately includes a loss brought about as a result of a deliberate inaccuracy in a document given to HMRC. [*TMA 1970, s 118(5)*]. For HMRC's view of what constitutes 'reasonable care' see **46.11** PENALTIES.

If HMRC has met its burden of proof under the provisions at **6.10** above to show that there is an undercharge to tax brought about carelessly or deliberately, it has no further burden in relation to the time limits provisions other than to show that it has in fact made the assessment in time (*Mullens v HMRC* UT, [2023] UKUT 244 (TCC), [2023] STC 1716).

An objection to the making of any assessment on the grounds that it is out of time can only be made on an appeal against the assessment. [*TMA 1970, s 34(2); FA 1998, s 117, Sch 18 para 46(3)*].

Deceased persons

[6.15] In the case of a loss of tax brought about carelessly or deliberately by a deceased person (or by a person acting on the deceased's behalf before his death), assessments on his chargeable gains accrued before death must be made on the personal representatives no later than four years after the end of the tax year in which death occurred, for any year of assessment ending *not earlier* than six years before the death. [*TMA 1970, s 40(2)(3)*].

7

Assets

Cross-references. See 8 ASSETS HELD ON 6 APRIL 1965; 8 ASSETS HELD ON 31 MARCH 1982; 23 EXEMPTIONS AND RELIEFS for assets exempt from capital gains tax; 24 FURNISHED HOLIDAY ACCOMMODATION; 28 GOVERNMENT SECURITIES; 37 LAND; 38.10 LOSSES for assets of negligible value; 47 PRIVATE RESIDENCES; 48 QUALIFYING CORPORATE BONDS; 57 SHARES AND SECURITIES; 63 UNIT TRUSTS AND OTHER INVESTMENT VEHICLES; 65 WASTING ASSETS.

Introduction to assets

[7.1] Capital gains tax is charged in respect of chargeable gains accruing to a person on the disposal of 'assets'. [*TCGA 1992, s 1(1)*]. By implication, this applies also to corporation tax on chargeable gains. The definition of 'assets' is very widely drawn to include almost all forms of property and is discussed further at 7.2 below.

Specific provisions apply to particular types of assets and these are described in this chapter and in dedicated chapters throughout this work as follows.

Type of asset	Location
Assets held under alternative finance arrangements	3 ALTERNATIVE FINANCE ARRANGEMENTS
Derivative contracts of companies	15.8–15.12 COMPANIES — CORPORATE FINANCE AND INTANGIBLES
Basic payment scheme for farmers	7.12
Bookmakers' pitches	7.9
Business assets	30.2 HOLD-OVER RELIEFS; 53 ROLLOVER RELIEF

Type of asset	Location
Cryptoassets	7.10
Exempt assets	23.2–23.17 EXEMPTIONS AND RELIEFS
Furnished holiday accommodation	24 FURNISHED HOLIDAY ACCOMMODATION
Futures contracts	7.8
Government securities	28 GOVERNMENT SECURITIES
Image rights	7.11
Intangible fixed assets of companies	15.13, 15.14 COMPANIES — CORPORATE FINANCE AND INTANGIBLES
Know-how	7.4
Life insurance policies etc.	37 LIFE INSURANCE POLICIES AND DEFERRED ANNUITIES
Land	35 LAND
Loan relationships of companies	15.2–15.7 COMPANIES — CORPORATE FINANCE AND INTANGIBLES
Options	7.7
Patents	7.5
Plant or machinery used for long funding lease	7.6
Private residences	47 PRIVATE RESIDENCES
Qualifying corporate bonds	48 QUALIFYING CORPORATE BONDS
Shares and securities	21 EMPLOYEE SHARE SCHEMES; 57 SHARES AND SECURITIES; 58 SHARES AND SECURITIES — IDENTIFICATION RULES; 60 SUBSTANTIAL SHAREHOLDINGS OF COMPANIES
Wasting assets	65 WASTING ASSETS

Meaning of 'assets'

[7.2] '*Assets*' comprise all forms of property, wherever situated, including incorporeal property (goodwill, options, debts, etc.), currency other than sterling, and any form of property created by the disposer, or otherwise coming to be owned without being acquired. [*TCGA 1992, s 21(1)*]. Sovereigns minted after 1837 are still sterling currency and as such are not within this definition.

The restating in euros of a holding of a participating EU currency on or after 1 January 1999 is not treated as involving the disposal of the original currency or the acquisition of a new holding of euros. The original currency and the new holding are treated as the same asset, acquired as the original currency was acquired. [*SI 1998 No 3177, Reg 36*].

For the treatment of currency other than sterling when disposed of by a 'qualifying company' in certain circumstances, see **23.5** and **23.8** EXEMPTIONS AND RELIEFS.

There is no general principle that assets must have a market value or that they must be transferable or assignable (*O'Brien v Benson's Hosiery (Holdings) Ltd* HL 1979, 53 TC 241). A right to share in a statutory fund for compensation to owners of expropriated foreign property is a form of property and therefore an asset (*Davenport v Chilver* Ch D 1983, 57 TC 661). (To a great extent this decision is superseded by *TCGA 1992, s 268B* (see **10.2** CAPITAL SUMS DERIVED FROM ASSETS).) Tax is only chargeable in relation to an asset which existed at the time of disposal and not to an asset coming into existence only on a disposal which created it. 'Property' has the meaning of that which is capable of being owned in a normal legal sense and thus does not extend to include the right of freedom to trade and compete in the market place, but such a right must be distinguished from the goodwill in respect of the trade in question and which is an asset for capital gains tax purposes (*Kirby v Thorn EMI plc* CA 1987, 60 TC 519). The right to unquantified and contingent future consideration on the disposal of an asset is itself an asset (*Marren v Ingles* HL 1980, 54 TC 76).

The right to bring an action to enforce a genuine claim, and which can be turned to account by negotiating a compromise yielding a capital sum, constitutes an asset. Such a right is acquired otherwise than by way of a bargain made at arm's length and at the time when the cause of action arises. Any capital sum received derives only from the right and not from other assets which may have been associated with the existence of the right (*Zim Properties Ltd v Proctor* Ch D 1984, 58 TC 371). However, in similar cases not involving contractual or statutory rights of action (see HMRC Capital Gains Manual CG13020) by concession, HMRC treat damages and compensation payments as derived from any underlying asset (and therefore exempt or taxable like that asset). If there is no underlying asset, HMRC treat damages and compensation as exempt up to a limit of £500,000 for any amount awarded in a single set of legal proceedings. Where compensation exceeds the limit, HMRC will consider a claim for further relief on a case-by-case basis. Entitlement to other reliefs is also determined on the same basis, and HMRC are prepared to consider extending time limits for claims where there has been a delay in obtaining compensation. (HMRC Extra-Statutory Concession D33).

See also **10.2** CAPITAL SUMS DERIVED FROM ASSETS.

Location of assets ('situs')

[7.3] Where liability depends on where the assets are actually situated (e.g. a non-resident trading in the UK or individuals not domiciled here, see **43** OVERSEAS MATTERS) the following provisions apply to determine the location of assets.

(a) The situation of rights or interests (otherwise than by way of security) in or over *immovable property* is that of the immovable property.
(b) Subject to the following provisions, the situation of rights or interests (otherwise than by way of security) in or over *tangible movable property* is that of the tangible movable property.
(c) Subject to the following provisions, *a debt*, secured or unsecured, is situated in the UK if, and only if, the creditor is resident in the UK.
(d) *Shares or debentures issued by any municipal or governmental authority*, or by any body created by such an authority, are situated in the country of that authority.
(e) Subject to paragraph (d) above, *shares in or debentures of a company incorporated in the UK* are situated in the UK.

(f) Subject to paragraphs (d) and (e) above, *registered shares or debentures* are situated where they are registered and, if registered in more than one register, where the principal register is situated.

(g) A *ship or aircraft* is situated in the UK if, and only if, the owner is then resident in the UK, and an interest or right in or over a ship or aircraft is situated in the UK if, and only if, the person entitled to the interest or right is resident in the UK.

(h) The situation of *goodwill* as a trade, business or professional asset is at the place where the trade, business or profession is carried on.

(i) *Patents, trade-marks and registered designs* are situated where they are registered, and if registered in more than one register, where each register is situated, and rights and licences in respect of a patent, trade-mark or registered design are situated in the UK if they, or any rights derived from them, are exercisable in the UK. This provision applies equally to rights under the law of a country or territory outside the UK which correspond or are similar to rights under patents, trade-marks or registered designs.

(j) *Copyright, design right and franchises*, and rights or licences in respect of any copyright work or design in which design right subsists, are situated in the UK if they or any right derived from them are exercisable in the UK. This provision applies equally to rights under the law of a country or territory outside the UK which correspond or are similar to copyright, design right or franchises.

(k) A *judgment debt* is situated where the judgment is recorded.

(l) A *non-sterling debt owed by a bank* and represented by a sum standing to the credit of an individual not domiciled (nor deemed domiciled) in the UK is situated in the UK if, and only if, that individual is resident in the UK and the branch or other place of business of the bank where the account is maintained is itself situated in the UK.

See **4.17** ANTI-AVOIDANCE for the treatment of shares or securities of a company incorporated outside the UK as located in the UK in certain cases following a share exchange or reconstruction.

In relation to a company that has no share capital, references in paragraphs (d), (e) and (f) above to shares or debentures include any interests in the company possessed by members of the company. References to 'debentures' in (d) and (f) above include, in relation to a person other than a company, securities.

[*TCGA 1992, s 275*].

Under the general law, *bearer shares and securities* transferable by delivery are situated where the certificate, etc. is kept (*Winans v A-G (No 2)* HL, [1910] AC 27).

See also *Standard Chartered Bank Ltd v CIR* Ch D, [1978] STC 272 where share certificates lodged in the UK by a person who was resident and domiciled abroad were held to be situated abroad, being registered in South Africa and effectively transferable only in that country. Renounceable letters of allotment of registered shares in a company are documents evidencing rights against the company and are only enforceable (and thus situated) where the register is kept (*Young and Another v Phillips* Ch D 1984, 58 TC 232).

Securities issued by designated European Communities or international organisations (e.g. The Asian Development Bank, The African Development Bank, The European and International Banks for Reconstruction and Development and the Caribbean Development Bank) or the European Investment Bank are taken for capital gains purposes to be situated outside the UK. Organisations are designated by Treasury order. [*TCGA 1992, s 265*]. A similar treatment applies to securities issued by the Inter-American Development Bank [*TCGA 1992, s 266*] and by the OECD Support Fund [*OECD Support Fund Act 1975, s 4*].

Other intangible assets

Where the situation of an 'intangible asset' is not otherwise determined (under the above provisions or any other provision of *TCGA 1992*), the asset is taken at all times to be situated in the UK if it is 'subject to UK law' at the time it is created. For this purpose, an '*intangible asset*' is intangible or incorporeal property including a thing in action or anything which corresponds to or is similar to intangible or incorporeal property or a thing in action under the law of a country or territory outside the UK. An asset is '*subject to UK law*' at a particular time if any right or interest which comprises or forms part of it is at that time governed by or otherwise subject to, or enforceable under, the law of any part of the UK.

Non-UK futures and options

Special rules apply in the case of an intangible asset ('*asset A*') which is a 'future' or 'option' which is not subject to UK law at the time it is created. Broadly, whether asset A is treated as situated in the UK will depend on its 'underlying subject matter' (as defined). If the underlying subject matter consists of or includes a future or option, asset A is treated as situated in the UK at all times if that future or option is subject to UK law at the time it is created and, on the assumption that there were no rights in or over that contract, its situation would not be otherwise determined. Where there is a nested sequence of futures or options, in which the underlying subject matter of each contract in the sequence consists of or includes the next contract in the sequence, asset A is taken to be situated in the UK at all times if any contract in the sequence meets those conditions. Asset A is also treated as situated in the UK at any time at which its underlying subject matter either consists of or includes shares or debentures of a company incorporated in the UK which had not been issued at the time the contract was created or is otherwise treated for capital gains purposes as being situated in the UK. Again, where there is a nested sequence of futures or options, asset A is taken to be situated in the UK if any contract in the sequence meets those conditions. For these purposes, '*future*' and '*option*' have the same meaning as for the derivative contract provisions (see **15.9** COMPANIES — CORPORATE FINANCE AND INTANGIBLES).

[*TCGA 1992, ss 275A, 275B*].

Interests of co-owners

In determining the situation of any asset, the situation of an 'interest' in an asset is taken to be the same as the situation of the asset, determined on the assumption that the asset is wholly-owned by the person holding the interest in it. An '*interest*' in an asset for this purpose means an interest as a co-owner of the asset, whether the asset is owned jointly or in common, and whether or not the interests of the co-owners are equal. [*TCGA 1992, s 275C*].

Simon's Taxes. See **C1.604–C1.604B**.

Treatment of particular assets

Know-how

[7.4] For corporation tax purposes, 'know-how' is generally within the definition of an intangible fixed asset for the purposes of the intangible assets regime (see **15.13** COMPANIES — CORPORATE FINANCE AND INTANGIBLES). Broadly, know-how created after 31 March 2002, acquired by a company from an unrelated party after that date or acquired from anyone on or after 1 July 2020 falls within that regime (and see **15.13** COMPANIES — CORPORATE FINANCE AND INTANGIBLES for the detailed transitional provisions).

The following provisions apply for capital gains tax purposes and for corporation tax purposes where know-how does not fall within that regime.

Consideration for a disposal of know-how used in a trade which continues to be carried on by the disposer after the disposal is treated, for all purposes, as a trading receipt unless:

(i) the consideration is brought into account as a disposal value for the purposes of *CAA 2001, s 462* or is otherwise chargeable as a revenue or income receipt; or
(ii) the buyer is a body of persons (this term, here and in (iii) and (iv) below, includes a partnership), exercising control over the seller; or
(iii) the seller is a body of persons exercising control over the buyer; or
(iv) the buyer and seller are bodies of persons together controlled by a third person.

Where a person disposes of know-how in connection with the disposal of part or the whole of the trade in which it was used, any consideration for the know-how is treated as a capital payment for goodwill. This provision does not apply to:

(a) both parties where a written joint election is made within two years of the disposal; or
(b) the acquirer only where the trade concerned was, before the acquisition, carried on wholly outside the UK.

If the consideration is, under (a) or (b), not regarded as a payment for goodwill, the acquirer is treated, for the purpose of claiming writing-down allowances, as if he had acquired the know-how for use in a trade previously carried on by him. However, the exclusion at (a) or (b) does not apply where any of (ii)–(iv) above applies.

Where consideration for the disposal of know-how is not taxed as a deemed trading receipt, or otherwise as an income or revenue receipt, or as a payment for goodwill, it is charged to income tax under *ITTOIA 2005, s 583* or to corporation tax under *CTA 2009, s 908* unless any one of (ii)–(iv) above applies. The consideration received is subject to the deduction of expenditure wholly and exclusively incurred in the acquisition or disposal of the know-how concerned.

For the above purposes, '*know-how*' is defined as any industrial information and techniques likely to assist in the manufacture or processing of goods or materials, in the working of a mine, oil-well or other source of mineral deposits (including the searching for, discovery or testing of deposits or the winning of access thereto), or in the carrying out of any agricultural, forestry or fishing operations.

[*TCGA 1992, s 261A; ITTOIA 2005, ss 192–195, 583–586; CTA 2009, ss 176–179, 908–910*].

Patents

[7.5] Except where the corporation tax intangible assets regime applies (see 15.13 COMPANIES — CORPORATE FINANCE AND INTANGIBLES and Tolley's Corporation Tax under Intangible Assets), capital sums received from the sale of patent rights are specifically taxable as income (see Tolley's Income Tax under Intellectual Property). In either case, the consideration for the sale is not therefore taxable as a chargeable gain.

Plant or machinery used for long funding lease

[7.6] Where plant or machinery is used for the purpose of leasing under a 'long funding lease', the 'lessor' is treated for chargeable gains purposes as disposing of and immediately reacquiring the plant or machinery at the 'commencement' of the 'term' of the lease for an amount equal to:

(a) where the lease is a 'long funding finance lease', the greater of the market value of the plant or machinery at the commencement of the term of the lease or the 'qualifying lease payments';
(b) where the lease is a 'long funding operating lease', the market value of the plant or machinery at the commencement of the term of the lease.

In (a) above, the '*qualifying lease payments*' are the minimum payments under the lease, including any initial payment, but excluding any amount which would fall under generally accepted accounting practice to be treated as the gross return on investment in the lease, any amount representing charges for services and any amount representing UK or foreign tax (other than income tax, corporation tax of foreign equivalent) to be paid by the lessor.

On 'termination' of the lease, the lessor is treated as having disposed of and immediately reacquired the asset for a consideration equal to the 'termination amount'.

For the purposes of these provisions, a '*long funding lease*' is, broadly (and subject to further exclusions), a lease of plant or machinery with a term of more than five years (seven years in certain cases) which at its inception meets one or more of the following tests:

- the lease would fall, under generally accepted accounting practice, to be treated as a finance lease or a loan;
- the present value of the minimum lease payments equals 80% or more of the fair value of the leased plant or machinery; or
- the term of the lease is more than 65% of the remaining useful economic life of the leased plant or machinery.

The expressions '*lessor*', '*commencement*', '*term*', '*long funding finance lease*', '*long funding operating lease*', '*termination*' and '*termination amount*' are defined as in *CAA 2001, Pt 2 Ch 6A*. See Tolley's Income Tax or Tolley's Corporation Tax.

[*TCGA 1992, s 25A; CAA 2001, ss 70G–70U, 70YI(2)*].

For the restriction of a loss arising on the disposal of an asset which includes plant or machinery which is a fixture and which has been used for leasing under a long funding lease, see **16.14** COMPUTATION OF GAINS AND LOSSES.

Options

[7.7] The tax treatment of an option is different for companies and capital gains tax payers.

Companies

As regards companies, see **15.8–15.12** COMPANIES — CORPORATE FINANCE AND INTANGIBLES for a summary of the rules on **derivative contracts.** An option is a derivative contract unless falling within one of the exclusions. See Tolley's Corporation Tax for full details.

Employee share options

See **21** EMPLOYEE SHARE SCHEMES.

Grant of option

The grant of an option is the disposal of an asset (i.e. the option). This applies in particular to the grant of an option under which the grantor binds himself to sell what he does not own, and because the option is abandoned, never has occasion to own, and the grant of an option under which the grantor binds himself to buy that which he does not acquire because the option is abandoned. This treatment is without prejudice to *TCGA 1992, s 21* (see **7.2** ASSETS and **16.5** COMPUTATION OF GAINS AND LOSSES) and is subject to the provisions below as to treating the grant of an option as part of a larger transaction. [*TCGA 1992, s 144(1)*]. A grant of an option is not a part disposal of an asset that was the subject of the option even though the grantor possessed that asset at the time of the grant (*Strange v Openshaw* Ch D 1983, 57 TC 544).

Any reference to an 'option' includes a reference to an option binding the grantor to grant a lease for a premium, or enter into any other transaction that is not a sale, so that references to 'buying' and 'selling' under an option are construed accordingly. [*TCGA 1992, s 144(6)*]. Arrangements which are in substance loans can fall outside the definition of options for capital gains purposes (*Krishnamohan v HMRC* FTT, [2024] UKFTT 346 (TC)).

Exercise of option

Subject to the treatment of cash-settled options below, if an option is exercised, the grant of the option and the transaction entered into by the grantor in fulfilment of his obligations under the option are treated as a single transaction, so if a sale by the grantor can be called for under the option (a call option), the option consideration is part of the consideration for the sale, and if the grantor can be called on to buy (a put option), the option consideration is deducted from the acquisition cost incurred by him in buying in accordance with his option obligations. The exercise of an option by the grantee is not a disposal, but in that event, the acquisition of the option (whether directly from the grantor or not) and the transaction entered into by the grantee (or his assignee, etc.) on the exercise are treated as a single transaction. Therefore, if a sale by the grantor can be called for under the option, the option cost is part of the cost of acquiring what is sold, and if the grantor can be called on to buy, the option cost is treated as an incidental cost of disposal of what is bought by the grantor. [*TCGA 1992, s 144(2)(3)*]. The time of the 'single transaction' is taken to be the time the option is exercised. [*TCGA 1992, s 28(2)*].

As a consequence of the option being exercised, any tax paid on the gain arising on the grant of the option should be set off or repaid (HMRC Capital Gains Manual CG12317).

Example

On 1 February 2021, F granted an option to G for £10,000 to acquire freehold land bought by F for £50,000 in September 2004. The option is for a period of five years, and the option price is £100,000 plus 1% thereof for each month since the option was granted. On 1 February 2023, G sold the option to H for £20,000. On 30 June 2024, H exercises the option and pays F £141,000 for the land. Neither G nor H intended to use the land for the purposes of a trade.

2021 Grant of option by F

	£
Disposal proceeds	10,000
Allowable cost	—
Chargeable gain	£10,000

2023 Disposal of option by G

	£	£
Disposal proceeds		20,000
Allowable cost	10,000	
Less: Wasted – $^2/_5$ × £10,000	4,000	
		6,000
Chargeable gain		£14,000

2024 Exercise of option

	£
(i) Earlier charge on F vacated	
(ii) Aggregate disposal proceeds	
(£10,000 + £141,000)	151,000
Allowable cost of land	50,000
Chargeable gain (on F)	£101,000

H's allowable expenditure is

	£
Cost of option	20,000
Cost of land	141,000
	£161,000

Options binding buyer to sell and buy

If an option binds the grantor both to sell and to buy, it is treated for the purposes of the above provisions (and for the purposes of *TCGA 1992, ss 144ZA–144ZD* below) as two separate options with half the consideration attributable to each. [*TCGA 1992, s 144(5)*]. Any reference to an 'option' includes a reference to an option binding the grantor to grant a lease for a premium, or enter into any other transaction that is not a sale, so that references to 'buying' and 'selling' under an option are construed accordingly. [*TCGA 1992, s 144(6)*].

Application of market value rule

A special rule applies where an option is exercised (so that the grant and exercise are treated as a single transaction) and any of the grant or acquisition of the option or its exercise would otherwise be treated as for consideration equal to market value (see **39.1** MARKET VALUE).

Where the option binds the grantor to sell, the market value rule does not apply for determining the consideration for the sale, except to the extent (if any) that it applies for determining the option consideration (which forms part of the sale consideration as indicated above). Likewise, the rule does not apply for determining the acquisition cost of the person exercising the option, except to the extent (if any) that it applies for determining the cost of acquiring the option.

Where the option binds the grantor to buy, the market value rule does not apply for determining the acquisition cost of the grantor, except to the extent (if any) that it applies for determining the option consideration. Likewise, it does not apply for determining the disposal consideration, but without prejudice to its application for determining the cost of the option.

To the extent that the market value rule is disapplied in determining an amount or value by the above provisions, the amount or value to be taken into account as consideration is the 'exercise price' (subject to the inclusion of any amount by virtue of *TCGA 1992, s 119A* — see **21.6**, **21.8**, **21.13**, **21.14** and **21.21** EMPLOYEE SHARE SCHEMES).

The '*exercise price*' for this purpose is the amount of value of the consideration which, under the terms of the option, is receivable (where the option binds the grantor to buy) or payable (if it binds the grantor to sell) as a result of the exercise of the option, but does not include the amount or value of any consideration for the acquisition of the option.

[*TCGA 1992, s 144ZA*].

The reason that only the grant of the option is under the market value rule, and not the exercise of the option and the transfer of the underlying asset, is that the market value of the option will take into account the consideration payable when the option is exercised. For example, an option allowing the holder to acquire an asset for a sum considerably below the current value of the asset would be expected to have a higher market value than an option allowing the acquisition at a sum similar to current market value (HMRC Capital Gains Manual CG12395).

In *Davies v HMRC* UT [2018] STC 1258, it was held that *TCGA 1992, s 144ZA* applied in a case where the option allowed the grantor to deliver cash in lieu of all or any portion of the shares otherwise deliverable.

An attempt to exploit *TCGA 1992, s 144ZA* as part of an avoidance scheme failed in *Trustees of the Morrison 2002 Maintenance Trust v HMRC* CA, [2019] STC 400.

Non-commercial options

The above special rule does not apply to options which are exercised 'non-commercially'. In such cases, the single transaction rule in *TCGA 1992, s 144(2)(3)* above is also applied in modified form. An option is exercised '*non-commercially*' if, in the case of an option which binds the grantor to buy, the exercise price (see below) is less than the open market price of what is bought. In the case of an option binding the grantor to sell, the option is exercised non-commercially if the exercise price is greater than the open market price of what is sold.

The 'single transaction' rule continues to apply, but if the option binds the grantor to buy, his cost of acquisition in buying, and the disposal consideration for what he buys are deemed for chargeable gains purposes to be the market value of what is bought at the time of exercise. If the option binds the grantor to sell, the consideration for the sale and the cost to the person exercising the option are deemed to be the market value of what is sold at the time of exercise.

If the whole or any part of the 'underlying subject matter' (i.e. the asset to be bought or sold under the option) is subject to any right or restriction which is enforceable by the person disposing of it or a connected person, the market value of the underlying subject matter is determined as if the right or restriction did not exist and *TCGA 1992, s 18(6)(7)* (disposal to connected person of asset subject to right or restriction — see **4.13** ANTI-AVOIDANCE) is disapplied.

This provision does not apply if the option is a 'share option' to which the income tax provisions at **21.6** EMPLOYEE SHARE SCHEMES apply. It also does not apply if:

- at the time the option is exercised the 'open market price' of the underlying subject matter differs from its open market price at the time the option was granted;
- some or all of that change in open market value results, directly or indirectly, from 'relevant arrangements';
- the exercise of the option would not be non-commercial if there were to be disregarded so much of that change in open market value as results to any extent, directly or indirectly, from the relevant arrangements; and
- the grantor and the person exercising the option would otherwise obtain, or might be expected to obtain, a tax advantage (as defined) directly or indirectly in consequence of, or otherwise in connection with, the exercise of the option.

For these purposes, the '*open market price*' of the underlying subject matter of an option is the price which that subject matter might reasonably be expected to fetch on a sale in the open market at the time of exercise, with no allowance made for any reduction arising out of the whole of the assets being placed on the market at one and the same time. Where the underlying subject matter includes unquoted shares or securities, the open market price is determined on the assumption that all information is available which a prudent prospective purchaser might reasonably require before purchase by private treaty at arm's length from a willing vendor. If any part of the underlying subject matter is subject to a right or restriction enforceable by the person disposing of it or a connected person, the open market price is determined as if the right or restriction did not exist.

'*Relevant arrangements*' are arrangements (including any agreement, understanding, scheme, transaction or series of transactions, whether or not legally enforceable) to which, or which include one or more transactions to which, a '*relevant person*' (i.e. the grantor, any person holding the option at any time, or any person connected with either of them) is or has been a party.

[*TCGA 1992, ss 144ZB–144ZD*].

TCGA 1992, s 144ZA above was introduced to reverse the effect of the decision in *Mansworth v Jelley* CA 2002, 75 TC 1.

Cash-settled options

Alternative provisions to those in *TCGA 1992, s 144(2)(3)* above apply to a 'cash-settled' option, i.e. an option which is exercised where the nature of the option (or its exercise) is such that the grantor is liable to make, and the grantee is entitled to receive, a payment in full settlement (for partial settlement, see below) of all obligations under the option. [*TCGA 1992, s 144A(1)*].

Under the alternative provisions, the grantor of a cash-settled option is treated as having disposed of an asset consisting of the liability to make the payment and the payment is treated as an incidental cost of making the disposal. Here, the grant of the option and the disposal are treated as a single transaction and the consideration for the option is treated as the consideration for the disposal. The grantee of the cash-settled option is treated as having disposed of an asset consisting of the entitlement to receive the payment and the payment received is treated as the consideration for the disposal. In this case, the acquisition of the option and the disposal are treated as a single transaction and the cost of acquiring the option and related expenses is treated as allowable expenditure deductible under *TCGA 1992, s 38(1)(a)* (acquisition and incidental costs; see **16.12** COMPUTATION OF GAINS AND LOSSES). [*TCGA 1992, s 144A(2)(3)(a)(b)*].

Where a payment is only in partial settlement of obligations under a cash-settled option, the alternative provisions apply only to so much of option as relates to the making and receipt of the payment. The consideration for, or the cost of or of acquiring, the option is apportioned on a just and reasonable basis. [*TCGA 1992, s 144A(4)(5)*].

Other matters

The above provisions apply generally but the further treatment of options depends on the circumstances as follows.

(a) **Options to acquire assets for trading use.** An option to acquire an asset exercisable by a person intending to use it, if acquired, for the purpose of a trade carried on by him, is not a wasting asset, and abandonment of such an option constitutes a disposal of it (such that an allowable loss may accrue). [*TCGA 1992, ss 144(4)(c), 146(1)(c)*].

(b) **Traded options.** A 'traded option', i.e. an option listed on a 'recognised stock exchange', or on a 'recognised futures exchange', is not a wasting asset, and an abandonment of such an option constitutes a disposal of it (so that an allowable loss may accrue). [*TCGA 1992, ss 144(4)(b), (8)(b), 146(1)(b), (4)(a)*].

'*Recognised stock exchange*' has the meaning given at **57.27** SHARES AND SECURITIES.

'*Recognised futures exchange*' means the London International Financial Futures and Options Exchange and any other UK or non-UK futures exchange designated by order. [*TCGA 1992, s 288(6)(7)*]. A list of recognised futures exchanges appears in **Whillans Tax Tables.**

Gains arising in the course of dealing in traded options, which, but for the exemption in *CTA 2009, s 981* or *ITTOIA 2005, s 779*, would have been chargeable to tax as income under *CTA 2009, Pt 10, Ch 8* or under *ITTOIA 2005, Pt 5, Ch 8* (the miscellaneous income 'sweep up' charge) are instead within the scope of capital gains tax. Losses are treated similarly. [*TCGA 1992, s 143(1)(2)(b)*]. See also **7.8** below.

Where a person ('the grantor') who has granted a traded option ('the original option') closes it out by acquiring a traded option of the same description ('the second option'), any disposal by the grantor involved in closing out the original option is disregarded for the purposes of capital gains tax. The allowable expenditure attributable to the incidental costs to the grantor of making the disposal constituted by the original option is treated as increased by the aggregate of the amount or value of the consideration, in money or money's worth, given by him or on his behalf wholly and exclusively for the acquisition of the second option and the incidental costs of that acquisition. [*TCGA 1992, s 148*].

(c) **Quoted options to subscribe for shares (share warrants).** An option to *subscribe* for shares in a company, which option is itself listed on a recognised stock exchange (see (b) above), is not a wasting asset and an abandonment of such an option constitutes a disposal of it (such that an allowable loss may accrue). [*TCGA 1992, ss 144(4)(a), (8)(a), 146(1)(a), (4)(a)*].

(d) **Financial options.** 'Financial options' are treated in the same way as traded options in (b) above, except that *TCGA 1992, s 148* does not apply to financial options. A '*financial option*' is an option, other than a traded option, which:

(i) relates to currency, shares, securities or an interest rate and is granted (otherwise than as agent) by a member of a recognised stock exchange, an 'authorised person' (defined by reference to *Financial Services and Markets Act 2000, s 31* and *SI 2001 No 544*); or

(ii) relates to shares or securities which are quoted on a recognised stock exchange (see (b) above) and is granted by a member of such an exchange, acting as agent; or

(iii) relates to currency, shares, securities or an interest rate and is granted to an authorised person and concurrently and in association with an option falling within (i) above which is granted by the authorised person concerned to the grantor of the first-mentioned option; or

(iv) relates to shares or securities which are quoted on a recognised stock exchange and is granted to a member of such an exchange, including such a member acting as agent; or

(v) is of a description specified in a Treasury order.

[*TCGA 1992, ss 144(4)(b), (8)(c), (9), 146(1)(b), (4)(a)*].

Two options, purchased by the taxpayer company from the same fellow group company, intended to have effect together, and undoubtedly financial options within (i) above when considered separately, could not be re-characterised as a loan (*Griffin v Citibank Investments Ltd* Ch D 2000, 73 TC 352).

(e) **Options to acquire or dispose of gilt-edged securities and qualifying corporate bonds.** Disposals of any such options are exempt. [*TCGA 1992, s 115(1)(b)*].

(f) **Options not within** (a)–(e) **above.** Such options are WASTING ASSETS (65) and the abandonment of such an option is not a disposal. Options (other than those in (b), (c) or (d) above) to buy or sell quoted shares and securities (being shares or securities which are listed on a recognised stock exchange in the UK or elsewhere — see **57.27** SHARES AND SECURITIES) are regarded as wasting assets, the life of which end when the right to exercise the option ends, or when the option becomes valueless, whichever is the earlier. [*TCGA 1992, ss 144(4), 146(2)(3)(4)(b)*].

A sum paid to a person to relinquish his rights under an option to call on another person to buy property from him is a capital sum derived from an asset (the option) and can bring about a chargeable gain, although such a transaction is not able to give rise to an allowable loss. Properly construed, the provision above that an abandonment of an option is not to be treated as a disposal is a specific exception to the general rule that the extinction of an asset constitutes a disposal of it (see **10.2** CAPITAL SUMS DERIVED FROM ASSETS) for the purpose of allowable losses. However, the provision does not exempt a gain made from such a transaction (*Golding v Kaufman* Ch D 1984, 58 TC 296; *Powlson v Welbeck Securities Ltd* CA 1987, 60 TC 269).

The consideration to be taken into account in respect of the receipt of a contingently repayable sum in return for the grant of an option to purchase land is valued subject to the contingency, provided the contingency is not within **16.14**(f) and (g) COMPUTATION OF GAINS AND LOSSES (*Randall v Plumb* Ch D 1974, 50 TC 392). If, however, a contingency is related to matters which do not directly bear upon the value of the consideration, it does not necessarily have to be taken into account (*Garner v Pounds Shipowners & Shipbreakers Ltd (and related appeal)* HL 2000, 72 TC 561).

If, under *Building Societies Act 1986*, the whole of a building society's business is transferred to a successor company, and in connection therewith rights are conferred on members to acquire shares in priority to other persons, at a discount or for no payment, the rights are treated as options within *TCGA 1992, s 144* having no value and granted for no consideration. [*TCGA 1992, ss 216(1), 217(1)(6)*]. Similar provisions apply where a building society confers on its members or former members (or any class of them) similar acquisition rights after 24 July 1991 over 'qualifying shares' in the society (meaning, generally, permanent interest bearing shares (PIBS) — see **48.3** QUALIFYING CORPORATE BONDS for full definition). [*TCGA 1992, s 149*].

Statement of Practice SP 3/02 sets out HMRC's views, with examples, on the tax treatment of transactions in financial options (and futures) otherwise within *TCGA 1992, s 143* (see (b) and (d) above and **7.8** below) and relating to shares, securities, foreign currency or other financial instruments, with particular reference to whether or not such transactions are to be regarded as profits or losses of a trade (in which case *s 143* is of no application) or taxed under the chargeable gains rules. The principles they set out are of relevance to UK residents, such as unauthorised unit trusts, charities and others (including companies) and non-resident collective investment vehicles, pension funds and others (including companies) which either do not trade or whose principal trade is outside the financial area.

As regards companies, the principles do not apply to derivative contracts within **15.8–15.12** COMPANIES — CORPORATE FINANCE AND INTANGIBLES.

Whilst each case must be judged on its merits, HMRC consider that an *individual* is unlikely to be regarded as trading as a result of purely speculative transactions in financial futures or options, whereas transactions in financial futures or options by a company may be either trading or capital in nature. In *all* cases where the transaction is clearly ancillary to another transaction, the question of whether it is trading or capital will depend on the nature of the other transaction. The Statement lists factors to be considered in determining whether an ancillary relationship exists between the financial futures or options transaction and another transaction. In particular, such a relationship exists if the intention is to eliminate or reduce risk, or to reduce transaction costs, in respect of the other transaction, and the financial futures or options transaction is 'economically appropriate' (as defined) to such elimination or reduction. Even if the other transaction is abandoned, these principles will normally be applied, although it is politic to close out the financial futures or options transaction as soon thereafter as is practicable.

See **23.56** EXEMPTIONS AND RELIEFS for options contracts entered into by pension schemes.

See **57.9** SHARES AND SECURITIES and **21** EMPLOYEE SHARE SCHEMES for quoted options granted following a reorganisation and options granted to employees respectively.

See **32.8** INDEXATION for indexation allowance provisions relating to options generally.

Derivatives over assets which are the subject of euroconversion

The following applies where: (A) a 'derivative' represents rights or obligations in respect of an asset, liability or other amount; (B) there is a 'euroconversion' of the underlying asset; (C) a transaction is entered into that would otherwise result in a disposal of the original derivative and the acquisition of a new derivative; (D) the terms of the new derivative differ from those of the original only to the extent necessary to reflect the euroconversion; *and* (E) no party to the transaction receives any consideration other than the new derivative. The transaction is not treated as involving a disposal or acquisition for CGT purposes. Instead, the original derivative and the new derivative are treated as the same asset, acquired as the original derivative was acquired. '*Derivative*' means any commodity or financial futures or an option. A '*euroconversion*', in relation to an asset, liability, contract or instrument, is the redenomination into euros of that asset etc. where it was previously expressed in the currency of an EU member state participating in the European single currency. [*SI 1998 No 3177, Regs 2, 3, 38*].

Futures contracts

[7.8] The tax treatment of a futures contract differs for companies and capital gains tax payers.

Companies

See **15.8–15.12** COMPANIES — CORPORATE FINANCE AND INTANGIBLES for a summary of the special rules on **derivative contracts**. A future (as defined) is a derivative contract unless falling within one of the exclusions. See Tolley's Corporation Tax for full details.

Commodity and financial futures

Gains arising in the course of dealing in commodity or financial futures dealt in on a 'recognised futures exchange' (as in 7.7(b) above)) which would otherwise (apart from the exemption in *CTA 2009, s 981* or *ITTOIA 2005, s 779*) have been chargeable to tax as income under *CTA 2009, Pt 10, Ch 8* or under *ITTOIA 2005, Pt 5, Ch 8* (the miscellaneous income 'sweep up' charge) are instead brought within the scope of tax on chargeable gains. Losses are treated similarly. This treatment applies also to the following transactions except in so far as any gain or loss arises in the course of a trade.

(a) A transaction under which an 'authorised person' (as defined by reference to *Financial Services and Markets Act 2000, s 31* and *SI 2001 No 544*) enters into a commodity or financial futures contract with another person.
(b) A transaction under which the outstanding obligations under a commodity or financial futures contract to which an authorised person is a party are brought to an end by a further contract between the parties to the futures contract.

[*TCGA 1992, s 143(1)(2)(a), (3)(8)*].

For the purposes of *TCGA 1992*, where, in the course of dealing in commodity or financial futures (whether or not dealt in on a recognised futures exchange), a person who has entered into a futures contract closes out that contract by entering into another futures contract with reciprocal obligations to those of the first contract, the transaction is regarded as the disposal of an asset consisting of the outstanding obligations under the first contract. Any money received or paid on the transaction is treated, respectively, as consideration for the disposal or as incidental costs of the disposal. [*TCGA 1992, s 143(5)*].

In any case where, in the course of dealing in commodity or financial futures (whether or not dealt in on a recognised futures exchange), a person has entered into a futures contract and has not closed out that contract as above, and he becomes entitled to receive, or liable to make, a payment, whether under the contract or otherwise, in full or partial settlement of any obligations under the contract, he is treated for the purposes of *TCGA 1992* as having disposed of an asset consisting of that entitlement or liability. The payment received or made is treated, respectively, as consideration for, or as incidental costs of, the disposal. [*TCGA 1992, s 143(6)*].

TCGA 1992, s 46 (**65** WASTING ASSETS) does not apply to obligations under a commodity or financial futures contract which is entered into by a person in the course of dealing in such futures on a recognised futures exchange, or a commodity or financial futures contract to which an authorised person is a party. [*TCGA 1992, s 143(7)(8)*].

See **7.7** above as regards SP 3/02 setting out HMRC's views on whether isolated transactions in financial futures are to be regarded as trading or taxed under the chargeable gains rules.

See **23.56** EXEMPTIONS AND RELIEFS for futures contracts entered into by pension schemes.

Gilt-edged securities and qualifying corporate bonds

The disposal of the outstanding obligation under any contract to acquire or dispose of such securities and bonds is exempt. Without prejudice to the provisions within *TCGA 1992, s 143(5)* above regarding the closing out of futures contracts generally, where a person closes out a contract for gilts or bonds as above by entering into another, reciprocal, contract, that transaction is treated as a disposal of the outstanding obligation under the first-mentioned contract. [*TCGA 1992, s 115(1)(b), (2)(3)*].

Derivatives over assets which are the subject of euroconversion

See 7.7 above.

Bookmakers' pitches

[7.9] A bookmaker's pitch is a specified position at a racecourse on which the bookmaker may erect a stand and take bets. HMRC take the view that the right to occupy a particular pitch at a particular racecourse is an asset for capital gains tax purposes. A disposal of such a right by way of auction is therefore a disposal of a chargeable asset. The date of disposal is the date on which the purchaser's bid is accepted. Where a pitch has not previously changed hands by way of auction or inheritance, it will normally have no acquisition cost (and no 31 March 1982 value).

A pitch does not fall within any of the classes of asset qualifying for ROLLOVER RELIEF (**53.4**).

(Revenue Tax Bulletin October 1999 pp 699, 700).

Cryptoassets

[7.10] HMRC have published guidance on the potential tax liabilities for individuals in respect of cryptoassets, which has now been incorporated into a Cryptoassets Manual. Broadly, cryptoassets are cryptographically secured digital representations of value or contractual rights which can be transferred, stored and traded electronically. All cryptoassets use some form of distributed ledger technology (blockchain) but there are different types which work in different ways. The main types include:

- exchange tokens (intended as a method of payment, but also becoming popular as an investment, for example cryptocurrencies such as bitcoin);
- utility tokens (which provide access to particular goods or services on a platform);
- security tokens (which provide the holder with particular interests in a business);
- stablecoins (which minimise volatility as they may be pegged to a stable asset such as a fiat currency or precious metal) (HMRC Cryptoassets Manual CRYPTO10100).

HMRC consider that cryptoassets are not money or currency and do not normally consider the buying and selling of cryptoassets to be the same as gambling (CRYPTO10100, 10450). Cryptoassets are chargeable assets for capital gains tax purposes if they are both capable of being owned and have a value that can be realised (CRYPTO22050). Cryptoassets held by companies may, however, fall within the intangible fixed assets rules if they are intangible assets for accounting purposes and meet the definition of an intangible fixed asset (which requires them to have been created or acquired for use on a continuing basis) (CRYPTO41150). The acquisition of exchange tokens does not generally involve entering into a loan relationship (CRYPTO41100).

In some cases, an individual may be carrying on a business of financial trading in cryptoassets, so that profits are chargeable to income tax, but where cryptoassets are held as investments, a disposal will trigger a chargeable gain or allowable loss (CRYPTO22050). Mining of cryptoassets (i.e. generating new cryptoassets as a reward for verifying additions to the blockchain) is likely either to amount to trading or to give rise to miscellaneous income. Costs of mining activities, such as computer equipment and electricity, are not allowable deductions for capital gains purposes (but may be allowable in computing profits of the mining activity) (CRYPTO22150).

A disposal of a cryptoasset may occur where the asset is sold for money, where it is exchanged for another cryptoasset, where it is used to pay for goods or services or where it is given to another person. Using a mixer, tumbler or similar service so that the taxpayer receives the same type of tokens they put into the transaction is not a disposal (CRYPTO22100). Where cryptoassets are fungible, the share identification rules at 58 SHARES AND SECURITIES—IDENTIFICATION RULES apply to them, so that assets of the same type are pooled (subject to the same-day and 30-day rules). For example, where a person owns bitcoin, ether and litecoin, he would have three separate pools. See CRYPTO22251–22257 for examples. Difficulties may arise where there is a 'hard fork' in the blockchain for a cryptoasset which results in new tokens coming into existence. Where as a result of a fork an individual holds both original assets and new assets, the two must be held in separate pools and the allowable costs for the old assets split between them on a just and reasonable basis (CRYPTO22300).

There is no disposal of a cryptoasset if an individual loses their private key so that they cannot access the asset. If, however, it can be shown that there is no prospect of recovering the key or accessing the assets, a negligible value claim can be made (CRYPTO22400).

The UK government intends to implement the OECD Cryptoasset Reporting Framework (CARF) and is consulting on its incorporation into UK law. The CARF is the international tax transparency regime for the automatic exchange of information on cryptoassets. The consultation also covers the possible extension of CARF to domestic reporting (i.e. UK service providers reporting on UK resident taxpayers). See www.gov.uk/government/publications/spring-budget-2024-overview-of-tax-legislation-and-rates-ootlar/spring-budget-2024-overview-of-tax-legislation-and-rates-ootlar, paras 2.13 and 2.14.

Image rights

[7.11] For a discussion of the legal status and capital gains tax treatment of 'image rights' see HMRC Capital Gains Manual CG68405-68450.

Basic payment scheme for farmers

[7.12] The basic payment scheme is the scheme of income support for farmers created under *European Parliament and Council Regulation 2013 (SI 2013 No 1307)* and is administered by the UK government in England and the devolved administrations in Scotland, Wales and Northern Ireland. Following Brexit, the basic payment scheme has continued, but the four governments can develop their own schemes. *Agriculture Act 2020* sets out a legislative framework for a new subsidy regime in England. One element of the regime is the replacement of basic payment scheme payments with 'delinked payments' in 2024. See www.gov.uk/guidance/delinked-payments-replacing-the-basic-payment-scheme.

Rollover relief

Basic payment scheme entitlement is a qualifying asset for rollover relief (see 53.4 ROLLOVER RELIEF).

Lump sum exit scheme

The lump sum exit scheme was introduced in 2022 and was open to farmers in England who were within the basic payment scheme and wished to leave or retire from farming. The scheme provided for eligible farmers to receive a lump sum in lieu of future basic payment scheme payments and delinked payments. For details of the scheme, see www.gov.uk/government/publications/apply-for-a-lump-sum-payment-to-leave-or-retire-from-farming/how-to-apply-for-a-lump-sum-payment-to-leave-or-retire-from-farming. Applications had to be submitted no later than 30 September 2022.

An amount paid under the lump sum exit scheme is treated as capital in nature if the recipient met the eligibility conditions when the payment was made. The chargeable gain is equal to the amount of the payment.

If the recipient did not meet the eligibility conditions at the time the payment was made, the lump sum is treated as revenue in nature.

If a person who applies for a lump sum receives a payment under the basic payment scheme in the period 26 March 2022 to 31 May 2024 (the interim period), that payment is treated as capital if the person meets the eligibility conditions for the lump sum exit scheme at any time in the interim period. The chargeable gain is equal to the amount of the payment. If the recipient does not meet the eligibility conditions at any time in the interim period, the payment is treated as revenue in nature.

[*F(No 2)A 2023, s 39; SI 2022 No 390*].

8

Assets Held on 31 March 1982

Cross-references. See **58.5** SHARES AND SECURITIES — IDENTIFICATION RULES for identification of certain share pools held by companies at 31 March 1982; **44.7** PARTNERSHIPS for partnership transactions involving assets held on 31 March 1982.

Simon's Taxes. See C2.6.

Introduction to assets held on 31 March 1982

[8.1] Subject to certain exceptions, disposals of assets which were held on 31 March 1982 by the person making the disposal are 're-based' by reference to the market value of the assets on that date; see **8.2** below. Where indexation allowance is applicable (see below), re-basing applies to both the unindexed gain and the indexation allowance.

Capital gains tax

For capital gains tax purposes, re-basing applies automatically and with no exceptions. For disposals before 6 April 2008, the same exceptions applied as for corporation tax (see below) and the same irrevocable election for indexation to apply to all assets regardless of the exceptions could be made. The 50% reduction mentioned below for certain deferred gains also applied for disposals before 6 April 2008.

Corporation tax

For corporation tax purposes, re-basing applies subject to exceptions where its application would result in a larger gain or loss. The company may irrevocably elect (with one exception mentioned in **8.3** below) for such re-basing to apply to all assets held on 31 March 1982, regardless of the exceptions; see **8.3** below. See **8.12** below, where re-basing does not apply and the asset was held by the company on 6 April 1965 (when tax on capital gains was introduced).

A 50% reduction is made in taxing certain deferred gains (except, in certain cases, where the deferred gain is never deemed to accrue at all) where such gains are wholly or partly attributable to an increase in value of an asset before 31 March 1982; see **8.11** below.

General re-basing rule

[8.2] The general re-basing rule is that on a disposal of an asset held on 31 March 1982, it is to be assumed that the asset was sold on that date by the person making the disposal and immediately reacquired by them at its market value on that date.

For capital gains tax purposes (i.e. in relation to disposals by individuals, trustees and personal representatives), the general rule applies without any exceptions (see **8.1** above). The exceptions below apply for the purposes of corporation tax on chargeable gains.

[*TCGA 1992, s 35(1)–(2A)*].

Indexation allowance

Indexation allowance on the disposal of an asset held on 31 March 1982 is calculated, without need for a claim, on the assumption that the asset was sold on that date by the person making the disposal and immediately reacquired by them at its market value on that date. [*TCGA 1992, s 55(1)*]. Except where an irrevocable election as in **8.3** below has effect, neither this provision nor the general rebasing rule of *TCGA 1992, s 35(1)(2)* above applies for the purposes of calculating indexation allowance in a case where that allowance would be greater if they did not apply. [*TCGA 1992, s 55(2)*]. Note that indexation allowance is only available for the purposes of corporation tax on chargeable gains (having been abolished for capital gains tax purposes for disposals on or after 6 April 2008) and has been frozen at December 2017. See **32.1** INDEXATION.

Exceptions to general rule ('kink test')

For corporation tax purposes, the following exceptions to the general rule apply. They are, however, subject to the irrevocable election in **8.3** below.

The exceptions (often referred to as the 'kink test') are where:

(a) a gain would accrue on the disposal if the general rule applied, and either a smaller gain or a loss would accrue if it did not; or
(b) a loss would accrue if the general rule applied, and either a smaller loss or a gain would accrue if it did not; or
(c) either on the facts of the case or by virtue of the provisions for assets held on 6 April 1965 (see **8.12** below) in *TCGA 1992, Sch 2*, neither a gain nor a loss would accrue if the general rule did not apply; or
(d) where, under *TCGA 1992, ss 195B, 195C* or *195E* (oil licence swaps) the disposal gives rise to neither a gain nor a loss; or

(e) the disposal is one within the 'no gain/no loss provisions' as in **8.6** below.

[*TCGA 1992, s 35(3)*].

Where the effect of the general re-basing rule would be to substitute a loss for a gain or a gain for a loss, but under (a)–(e) the application of that rule is excluded, it is to be assumed in relation to the disposal that the asset was acquired for a consideration such that, on the disposal, neither a gain nor a loss accrues. [*TCGA 1992, s 35(4)*].

Valuations

Shares etc.

Where, for the purposes of the re-basing and indexation provisions above, it is necessary to determine the market value of shares or securities of the same class in any company on 31 March 1982, all the shares or securities held at that date will be valued as a single holding whether they were acquired on or before 6 April 1965 or after that date. If the shares or securities in the disposal concerned represent some but not all of those valued at 31 March 1982 then the allowable cost or indexation allowance as appropriate will be based on the proportion that the shares or securities disposed of bears to the total holding at 31 March 1982 (HMRC Extra-Statutory Concession D34). See also **8.6** below for HMRC's practice as to the valuation of shares deemed held on 31 March 1982 by reason of 'no gain/no loss disposals' since that date.

Land and buildings

To reduce the compliance burden of valuation work where there are a considerable number of transactions in land in a tax year or an accounting period, the Land Portfolio Valuation Unit (LPVU) of the Valuation Office Agency operates a Multiple Land Valuation Scheme. The scheme may be applied to a taxpayer (or a group of companies) if more than 30 properties need to be valued and computations are presented in a way which will enable HMRC to identify the properties to be valued. LPVU refer a proportion of the valuations to the Valuation Office Agency, and if those are satisfactory, all the valuations will be accepted. (HMRC Capital Gains Manual CG74050).

Example 1

Robbie sells an asset on 25 April 2024 for £200,000. He had purchased the asset in 1979 for £50,000, and its value at 31 March 1982 was £42,000. The chargeable gain on the asset is computed as follows:

	£
Sale proceeds	200,000
31.3.1982 value	42,000
Chargeable gain	£158,000

Note

(a) As, for capital gains tax purposes, re-basing applies without any exceptions, the 31 March 1982 value is used in the computation even though it is less than the original cost.

Example 2

An asset (which is neither tangible movable property nor otherwise exempt) was acquired by a company for £900 in 1980 and, after having been held continuously by the same company, is disposed of in July 2024. The indexation factor for March 1982 to December 2017 is 2.501. The disposal proceeds are £4,300. The corporation tax consequences, for differing 31 March 1982 values, are as follows. 'N/A' means that indexation allowance is not applicable and 'NGNL' means that the disposal is treated as giving rise to neither a gain nor a loss.

Example 2A

	(1)	(2)
	£	£
Sale proceeds	4,300	4,300
(1) Cost; (2) 31.3.1982 value	900	1,000
Unindexed gain	3,400	3,300
Indexation allowance		
at 2.501 × £1,000 (higher of (1) and (2))	2,501	2,501
Gain arising	£899	£799
Chargeable gain		£799

Example 2B

	(1)	(2)
	£	£
Sale proceeds	4,300	4,300
(1) Cost; (2) 31.3.1982 value	900	1,300
Unindexed gain	3,400	3,000
Indexation allowance		
at 2.501 × £1,300 (higher of (1) and (2))	3,251	N/A
Gain/NGNL arising	£149	£NGNL

The disposal is treated as giving rise to neither a gain nor a loss. The corresponding acquisition is unaffected by this treatment.

Example 2C

	(1)	(2)
	£	£
Sale proceeds	4,300	4,300
(1) Cost; (2) 31.3.1982 value	900	800
Unindexed gain	3,400	3,500

	(1)	(2)
	£	£
Indexation allowance		
at 2.501 × £3,500 (higher of (1) and (2))	2,251	2,251
Gain arising	£1,149	£1,249
Chargeable gain	£1,149	

Example 2D

	(1)	(2)
	£	£
Sale proceeds	3,900	3,900
(1) Cost; (2) 31.3.1982 value	900	5,000
Unindexed gain/(Loss)	3,000	(1,100)
Indexation allowance		
at 2.501 of higher of (1) and (2)	N/A	N/A
NGNL/(Loss) arising	NGNL	£(1,100)

The disposal is treated as giving rise to neither a gain nor a loss. The corresponding acquisition is unaffected by this treatment.

Example 3

An asset (which is neither tangible movable property, land with development value, quoted securities nor otherwise exempt) was acquired by a company in 1960 for £400. After having been held continuously by the company, the asset is completely destroyed in July 2024. The asset was underinsured and, later in the month of disposal, £4,752 only was recovered from the insurers. The company elects for valuation at 6 April 1965, which value is later agreed with HMRC to be £4,800. The value at 31 March 1982 was similarly agreed at £1,700.

	(1)	(2)
	£	£
Insurance proceeds	4,752	4,752
(1) Cost; (2) 6.4.1965 value	400	4,800
	4,352	(48)
Indexation allowance		
at 2.501 × 31.3.1982 value (£1,700) for (1) only	4,252	N/A
Gain/(Loss) arising	£100	£(48)

Re-basing at 31 March 1982 does not apply since, under *TCGA 1992, Sch 2 para 17(2)* (see **8.12** below), the disposal is deemed to have given rise to neither a gain nor a loss. The corresponding acquisition is unaffected by this treatment.

Note to the examples

For corporation tax purposes, indexation allowance is frozen at its December 2017 level. No indexation allowance is available in respect of expenditure incurred after 31 December 2017, and for expenditure incurred on or before that date and falling to be deducted on a disposal after that date, indexation allowance is computed up to and including December 2017 only. See **32.2** INDEXATION.

Election for universal re-basing at 31 March 1982

[8.3] If a company so elects, disposals made by it (including any made by it before the election) after 5 April 1988 of assets which it held on 31 March 1982 will all have the general re-basing rule of *TCGA 1992, s 35(1)(2)* in **8.2** above applied to them regardless of the exclusion of that rule that might otherwise apply under *TCGA 1992, s 35(3)*.

Similarly in such a case, indexation allowance will always be calculated under the equivalent provision of *TCGA 1992, s 55(1)* as in **8.2** above regardless of the exclusion of that provision that might otherwise apply under *TCGA 1992, s 55(2)*.

[*TCGA 1992, s 35(5), s 55(2)*].

An election is irrevocable and must be made by notice in writing to HMRC at any time before 6 April 1990 or at any time during the period beginning with the time of the first disposal after 5 April 1988 of an asset held on 31 March 1982 or treated (see **8.6** below) as so held ('*the first relevant disposal*') and ending within two years after the end of the accounting period in which the disposal is made or such later period as HMRC may allow. An election made by a company in one capacity does not cover disposals made by it in another capacity. Adjustments as required may be made, whether by way of discharge or repayment of tax, the making of assessments or otherwise, to give effect to an election. [*TCGA 1992, s 35(6)–(8)*].

Time limit for elections — HMRC practice

HMRC will always exercise their discretion to extend the time limit for an election to at least the date on which the statutory time limit would expire if certain disposals did not count as a first relevant disposal. The disposals in question are those on which gains would not be chargeable by virtue of particular statutory provisions and excluded disposals within **8.4** below. As sterling is not an asset for capital gains purposes (see **7.2** ASSETS), a disposal of it cannot be a first relevant disposal.

Where a company holds assets in more than one capacity (for example, as trustee, partner or member of a UK or European Economic Interest Grouping), there will be a first relevant disposal and a separate time limit for each group of assets which the company holds in a different capacity. See also **44** PARTNERSHIPS.

Where a company which is non-UK resident on 6 April 1988 makes a disposal which would otherwise count as a first relevant disposal between that date and the date on which it first becomes UK resident, HMRC will give sympathetic consideration to extending the time limit to the end of the second accounting period after that in which the first disposal is made *after becoming UK resident*. In other words, the disposal made while non-resident may be disregarded at the discretion of HMRC.

There are a variety of other circumstances where, having regard to the facts of each case, HMRC will or may exercise their discretion to extend the statutory time limit.

(HMRC Statement of Practice SP 4/92).

In circumstances other than those covered by SP 4/92, HMRC may accept a late election by exercising its collection and management powers. In exercising those powers, HMRC adopt the same principles as they apply to late claims — see **61.1** TIME LIMITS — FIXED DATES. (HMRC Capital Gains Manual CG13800, 16780).

HMRC point out that in special cases, elections need to be made by a person other than the person assessed. In the case of an assessment under *TCGA 1992, s 3* (charge on UK resident shareholder of an overseas resident company – see **43.7** OVERSEAS MATTERS), the election needs to be made by the overseas resident company. (HMRC Capital Gains Manual CG16760).

Excluded disposals

[8.4] An election does not cover a disposal of (or of an interest in):

- plant or machinery;
- an asset which the person making the disposal held at any time for the purposes of or in connection with a trade or part of a trade involving the working of a 'source of mineral deposits' (within *CAA 2001, s 394*);
- a licence under *Petroleum Act 1998, Pt I* (or earlier corresponding legislation) or *Petroleum (Production) Act (Northern Ireland) 1964*; or
- 'shares' which, on 31 March 1982, were 'unquoted' and derived their value, or the greater part thereof, directly or indirectly from 'oil exploration or exploitation assets' situated in the UK or a 'designated area' or from such assets and 'oil exploration or exploitation rights' taken together (the quoted terms having the meanings given by the legislation).

However, disposals within the first two of these four categories are not excluded unless a capital allowance in respect of any expenditure attributable to the asset has been made to the person making the disposal or would have been made to it had it made a claim. Where that person acquired the asset on a 'no gain/no loss disposal' (see **8.6** below), references in the foregoing to the person making the disposal are references to that person, the person who last acquired the asset other than on a no gain/no loss disposal or any person who subsequently acquired the asset on such a disposal.

[*TCGA 1992, Sch 3 para* 7].

For capital gains tax purposes the general re-basing rule at **8.2** above applies to the above assets automatically and without exceptions.

Effect of election on transfers within groups of companies

[8.5] Where a member of a group of companies disposes of an asset acquired by it from another group member after 5 April 1988 and the no gain/no loss basis of *TCGA 1992, s 171* applied to the acquisition (see **26.3** GROUPS OF

COMPANIES and **8.6** below), an election made by the transferee company does not apply to the disposal, and, whether or not an election is made by that company, the making of such an election by the transferor company applies to the ultimate disposal made by the transferee company. Where the transferor company also acquired the asset after 5 April 1988 and *TCGA 1992, s 171* applied to that acquisition, an election made by it does not have effect on the ultimate disposal, but an election made by the last company by which the asset was acquired after 5 April 1988 otherwise than on an acquisition to which *TCGA 1992, s 171* applied or, if there is no such company, the company which held the asset on 5 April 1988, does have effect on the ultimate disposal. [*TCGA 1992, Sch 3 para 2*].

Election by principal company

Only a company which is the 'principal company' of a 'group' (for both of which see **26.2** GROUPS OF COMPANIES) may make an election unless the company did not become a group member until after the 'relevant time'. For this purpose the time limit for the making of an election (see **8.3** above) applies with the modification that a reference to 'the first relevant disposal' is a reference to the first disposal after 5 April 1988 of an asset held on 31 March 1982 by a company which is *either* a group member but not an 'outgoing company' in relation to the group *or* an 'incoming company' in relation to the group.

An election made by the principal company also has effect as one made by any other company which is a group member at the relevant time. This treatment does not, however, extend to a company which, in some period after 5 April 1988 and before the relevant time, is not a member of the group if during that period the company makes a disposal of an asset which it held on 31 March 1982 and the time limit for the making of an election expires without an election having been made. However, the effect of an election continues to extend to a company notwithstanding that it ceases to be a group member after the relevant time except where it is an outgoing company in relation to the group and the election relating to the group is made after it ceases to be a group member. [*TCGA 1992, Sch 3 para 8, para 9(3)*].

'*The relevant time*', in relation to a group, is the earliest of: the first time when any company which is then a group member, and is not an outgoing member in relation to the group, makes a disposal after 5 April 1988 of an asset which it held on 31 March 1982; the time immediately following the first occasion when a company which is an incoming company in relation to the group becomes a group member; and the time when an election is made by the principal company. [*TCGA 1992, Sch 3 para 9(1)*].

'*Incoming company*', in relation to a group, means a company which makes its first disposal after 5 April 1988 of an asset which it held on 31 March 1982 at a time when it is not a group member, and which becomes a group member before the expiry of the time limit for the making of an election which would apply to it and at a time when no such election has been made.

'*Outgoing company*', in relation to a group, means a company which ceases to be a group member before the expiry of the time limit for the making of an election which would apply to it and at a time when no such election has been made. [*TCGA 1992, Sch 3 para 9(2)*].

See HMRC Capital Gains Manual CG46330–46395 for consideration of the above provisions (including extension of time limits in certain cases).

Previous no gain/no loss disposals

[8.6] For corporation tax purposes, where:

(a) a company makes a disposal, other than one within the 'no gain/no loss provisions', of an asset which it acquired after 31 March 1982, and
(b) the disposal by which it acquired the asset and any previous disposal of the asset after 31 March 1982 was a no gain/no loss disposal,

it is treated for the purposes of the re-basing provisions of *TCGA 1992, s 35* and the equivalent provisions for indexation allowance of *TCGA 1992, s 55(1)* in **8.2** and **8.3** above as having held the asset on 31 March 1982. [*TCGA 1992, ss 52A, 55(5)(6)(a), Sch 3 para 1*].

HMRC have confirmed that where a company is treated as having held an asset on 31 March 1982 under these provisions, enhancement expenditure on the asset incurred after 31 March 1982 by a previous owner may be taken into account for indexation and re-basing purposes on a disposal by the current owner (HMRC Capital Gains Manual CG16880).

Capital gains tax – previous no gain no loss transfer before 6 April 2008

For capital gains tax purposes (but not corporation tax purposes), in relation to disposals on or after 6 April 2008, where:

- a person makes a disposal (including a no gain/no loss disposal) of an asset which they acquired after 31 March 1982 and before 6 April 2008,
- the disposal by which they acquired the asset and any previous disposal of the asset after 31 March 1982 was a disposal on which, under any enactment, neither a gain nor a loss accrued to the person making the disposal, and
- the re-basing provisions of *TCGA 1992, s 35* did not apply to the disposal by which they acquired the asset,

it is assumed that the re-basing provisions did apply to that disposal and that *TCGA 1992, s 56(2)* (deemed consideration on no gain/no loss disposal — see **32.4** INDEXATION) applied accordingly. [*TCGA 1992, s 35A*]. The effect of this provision is that, in computing the gain or loss on the post-5 April 2008 disposal, the allowable expenditure includes the value of the asset at 31 March 1982 and the indexation allowance due for the period from that date to the date on which the person making the post-5 April 2008 disposal acquired the asset (or April 1998 if earlier). The provision does not affect the position of the person from whom the person making the post-5 April 2008 disposal acquired the asset.

No gain/no loss provisions

The '*no gain/no loss provisions*' are the following enactments (being enactments by virtue of which neither a gain nor a loss accrues).

(i) *TCGA 1992, s 58* (transfers between spouses or civil partners, see **40.4** MARRIED PERSONS AND CIVIL PARTNERS), *s 73* (reversion of settled property to settlor on death of person entitled to life interest, see **56.18** SETTLEMENTS), *s 139* (company reconstructions, see **14.12** COMPANIES), *s 140A* (transfer or division of UK business between companies in different EC member states, see **43.12** OVERSEAS MATTERS), *s 140E* (European cross-border merger: assets left within UK tax charge, see **43.14** OVERSEAS MATTERS), *s 171* (intra-group disposals of assets, see **26.3** GROUPS OF COMPANIES), *s 172* (transfer of UK branch or agency before 1 April 2000, see **43.3** OVERSEAS MATTERS), *s 211* (insurance business transfer schemes), *s 215* (amalgamation of building societies, see **14.12** COMPANIES), *s 216* (transfer of building society's business to company, see **14.12** COMPANIES), *s 217A* (transfer of assets on incorporation of registered friendly society, see **23.49** EXEMPTIONS AND RELIEFS), *s 271D* (disposal of assets on union, amalgamation or transfer of engagements of registered societies etc., see **14.12** COMPANIES), *ss 218–220* (housing associations, see **23.51** EXEMPTIONS AND RELIEFS), *s 221* (transfers before 1 April 2013 under harbour reorganisation schemes), *s 257(3)* (gifts to charities etc. out of settlements, see **11.6** CHARITIES), *s 258(4)* (gifts of national heritage property, see **23.79** EXEMPTIONS AND RELIEFS), *s 264* (transfers between constituency associations, see **23.67** EXEMPTIONS AND RELIEFS) and *s 267(2)* (sharing of transmission facilities, see **14.12** COMPANIES);

(ii) *CGTA 1979, s 148* (assets transferred to maintenance funds for historic buildings);
(iii) *FA 1982, s 148* (transfers by Hops Marketing Board, see **25.74** EXEMPTIONS AND RELIEFS);
(iv) *Trustee Savings Banks Act 1985, Sch 2 para 2* (see **14.12** COMPANIES);
(v) *Transport Act 1985, s 130(3)* (see **14.12** COMPANIES);
(vi) *ICTA 1988, s 486(8)* (amalgamation of industrial and provident societies before enactment of *CTA 2010*, see **14.12** COMPANIES);
(vii) *FA 1990, Sch 12 para 2(1)* (broadcasting undertakings, see **14.12** COMPANIES);
(viii) *F(No 2)A 1992, Sch 17 para 5(3)* (privatisation of Northern Ireland Electricity, see **14.12** COMPANIES);
(ix) *FA 1994, Sch 24 para 2(1), para 7(2), para 11(3)(4), para 25(2)* (provisions relating to *Railways Act 1993*, see **14.12** COMPANIES);
(x) *FA 1994, Sch 25 para 4(2)* (Northern Ireland Airports Ltd, see **14.12** COMPANIES);
(xi) *Coal Industry Act 1994, Sch 4 para 2(1)*;
(xii) *Broadcasting Act 1996, Sch 7 para 2(1)*;
(xiii) *Transport Act 2000, Sch 7 para 2(1)*;
(xiv) *Transport Act 2000, Sch 26 paras 3, 9*;
(xv) *Energy Act 2004, Sch 9 paras 3, 18, 29, 32*;
(xvi) *Railways Act 2005, Sch 10 paras 5, 16*;
(xvii) *Consumers, Estate Agents and Redress Act 2007, Sch 9 para 4*;
(xviii) *Housing and Regeneration Act 2008, Sch 7*;
(xix) *SI 2009 No 3227, Reg 3(1)*;
(xx) *Localism Act 2011, Sch 24 para 6(1)*;
(xxi) *SI 2012 No 1709, Art 5(1)*; and
(xxii) *SI 2015 No 1540, Reg 6(1)*.

[*TCGA 1992, ss 35(3)(d), 288(3A); Localism Act 2011, Sch 24 para 6(3); FA 2012, Sch 39 para 17; SI 2008 No 3002, Sch 1 para 43; SI 2009 No 3227, Reg 3; SI 2012 No 1709, Art 5; SI 2015 No 1540, Reg 6*].

Neither *TCGA 1992, s 257(2)* (gifts to charities etc., see **11.5** CHARITIES), nor *s 259(2)* (gifts to housing associations, see **23.51** EXEMPTIONS AND RELIEFS), is included as a no gain/no loss provision. They are, however, included for the equivalent provisions for indexation allowance under *TCGA 1992, s 55(1)*. However, both provisions deem (for the purposes of *TCGA 1992*) the original acquisition by the transferor making the disposal to which the provision concerned applies to be the acquisition of the transferee on the occasion of the transferee making a subsequent disposal. Consequently it seems that in practice both provisions are no gain/no loss provisions for the purposes of re-basing under *TCGA 1992, s 35*. Special rules apply to disposals giving rise to neither gain nor loss under *TCGA 1992, ss 195B, 195C* or *195E* (oil licence swaps).

Certain disposals of a share in partnership assets may be treated as if they were no gain/no loss disposals. See **44.7** PARTNERSHIPS.

Where a company to which an election under *CTA 2009, s 18A* exemption for foreign permanent establishments) applies makes a no gain/no loss disposal, the amount of the deemed consideration which results in that no gain/no loss, is to be arrived at after taking account of any adjustments under those provisions—see **43.8** OVERSEAS MATTERS.

Indexation allowance

Where *TCGA 1992, s 55(5)* (see above) applies on the disposal of an asset (so that, as stated above, the person making the disposal is treated for the purposes of computing the indexation allowance on the disposal as having held the asset on 31 March 1982 (*TCGA 1992, s 55(6)(a)*)), then for the purpose of determining any gain or loss on the disposal, the consideration which otherwise that person would be treated as having given for the asset is reduced by the amount of indexation allowance brought into account under *TCGA 1992, s 56(2)* (consideration on disposal treated as giving rise to neither a gain nor a loss to be computed on assumption that on the disposal an unindexed gain accrues equal to the indexation allowance on the disposal; see **32.4** INDEXATION) on any disposal falling within (b) above. [*TCGA 1992, s 55(6)(b)*].

Further rules as below apply (after the application of the computation of any indexation allowance under *TCGA 1992, s 53* (see **32.2** INDEXATION) but before the application of the provisions of *TCGA 1992, s 35(3)* or *(4)* (which disapply or amend the general re-basing rule of *TCGA 1992, s 35(1)(2)* in certain cases; see **8.2** above) in relation to disposals on or after 30 November 1993. The rules apply where *TCGA 1992, s 55(5)* above applies to the disposal ('*the disposal in question*') of an asset by any person ('*the transferor*') and, but for *TCGA 1992, s 55(6)(b)* above, the consideration the transferor would be treated as having given for the asset would include an amount or amounts of indexation allowance brought into account under *TCGA 1992, s 56(2)* on any disposal made before 30 November 1993. [*TCGA 1992, s 55(7)*]. The rules are that:

(A) where otherwise there would be a loss, an amount equal to the 'rolled-up indexation' is added to it so as to increase it,

(B) where otherwise the unindexed gain or loss would be nil, a loss is deemed to accrue equal to the rolled-up indexation, and

(C) where otherwise there would be an unindexed gain and the gain or loss would be nil but the amount of the indexation allowance used to extinguish the gain would be less than the rolled-up indexation, the difference is deemed to constitute a loss.

[*TCGA 1992, s 55(8)*].

For the purposes of the above, the '*rolled-up indexation*' means, subject to *TCGA 1992, s 55(10)* and *(11)* below (which provisions, as well as applying on the disposal in question, are also treated as having applied on any previous part disposal by the transferor), the amount or, as the case may be, the aggregate of the amounts of indexation allowance which, but for *TCGA 1992, s 55(6)(b)* above, would be brought into account under *TCGA 1992, s 56(2)* on any disposal made before 30 November 1993. [*TCGA 1992, s 55(9)*].

Where, for the purposes of any disposal of the asset made by the transferor on or after 30 November 1993, any amount, amounts or combination of amounts within *TCGA 1992, s 38(1)(a)–(c)* (acquisition consideration etc., enhancement expenditure etc. and incidental disposal costs respectively; see **16.12** COMPUTATION OF GAINS AND LOSSES) is required to be excluded, reduced or written down, the amount or amounts constituting the rolled-up indexation (or so much of it as remains after the application of this provision and *TCGA 1992, s 55(11)* below on a previous part disposal) are reduced in proportion to any reduction made in the amount falling within one or any combination of *TCGA 1992, s 38(1)(a)–(c)*. [*TCGA 1992, s 55(10)*].

Where the transferor makes a part disposal of the asset at any time on or after 30 November 1993, then, for the purposes of that and any subsequent part disposal, the amount or amounts constituting the rolled-up indexation (or so much of it as remains after the application of this provision and *TCGA 1992, s 55(10)* above on a previous part disposal by him or after the application of *TCGA 1992, s 55(10)* on the part disposal) is apportioned between the property disposed of and the property which remains in the same proportions as the amounts within *TCGA 1992, s 38(1)(a)* and *(b)*. [*TCGA 1992, s 55(11)*].

Note that indexation allowance is now available only for the purposes of corporation tax on chargeable gains and is frozen at its December 2017 level. See **32.1** INDEXATION.

Example

X Ltd, Y Ltd and Z Ltd are all members of the same group within *TCGA 1992, s 170* (see **26.2** GROUPS OF COMPANIES), all three companies having joined the group before 1 April 1987 and making up annual accounts for calendar years. No election under *TCGA 1992, s 35(5)* (universal re-basing — see **8.3** and **8.5** above) is in force. An asset was acquired by X Ltd from outside the group for £90,000 in 1980 and at 31 March 1982, the value of the asset was £100,000. The asset was transferred to Y Ltd in October 1985, such that the no gain/no loss basis of *TCGA 1992, s 171* (see **26.3** GROUPS OF COMPANIES) applied. X Ltd made the appropriate election under *FA 1985, s 68(4)(5)* (indexation allowance to be calculated by reference to value at 31 March 1982 rather than original cost — see **9.12** below). In January 1995, Y Ltd transferred the asset to Z Ltd such that *TCGA 1992, s 171* again applied. Z Ltd sells the asset outside the group in March 2025 for £80,000. The relevant retail price indices are:

March 1982	79.44	January 1995	146.00
October 1985	95.59		

	£
Original cost of asset to X Ltd in 1980	90,000
Indexation allowance: March 1982–October 1985 on 31 March 1982 value under *FA 1985, s 68(4)(5)*	
$\frac{95.59 - 79.44}{79.44} \times £100{,}000$ (indexation factor 0.203)	20,300
Deemed consideration under *TCGA 1992, s 56(2)*	£110,300

	£
Deemed cost of asset to Y Ltd in October 1985	110,300
Indexation allowance: October 1985–January 1995	
$\frac{146.0 - 95.59}{95.59} \times £110{,}300$ (indexation factor 0.527)	58,128
Deemed consideration under *TCGA 1992, s 56(2)*	£168,428

Under *TCGA 1992, ss 35(10), 55(6)(a), Sch 3 para 1*, Z Ltd is treated as having held the asset on 31 March 1982 for the purposes of re-basing under *TCGA 1992, s 35* and calculating indexation allowance.

	Cost	Re-base
	£	£
Proceeds received by Z Ltd	80,000	80,000
Deemed consideration under *TCGA 1992, s 55(6)(b)* (£168,428 – £58,128 – £20,300)	90,000	
Market value at 31 March 1982		100,000
Loss before *TCGA 1992, s 55(8)* adjustment	10,000	20,000
Rolled-up indexation under *TCGA 1992, s 55(9)*	20,300	20,300
Loss after *TCGA 1992, s 55(8)* adjustment	£30,300	£40,300

TCGA 1992, s 35(3) applies, so the allowable loss arising is £30,300.

Note to the example

(1) It should be noted that the effect of the legislation in force for disposals before 30 November 1993 meant that Z Ltd would not have been prejudiced on the ultimate disposal outside the group if X Ltd had not made a valid claim under *FA 1985, s 68(4)(5)* within the time limit in respect of the transfer of the asset to Y Ltd in October 1985. However, the legislation in force for disposals on or after 30 November 1993 means that, in the

absence of such an election in respect of that disposal, the rolled-up indexation in the above example would have to be computed by reference to the original cost to X Ltd (i.e. 0.203 × £90,000 = £18,270). The allowable loss would then be £28,270 (i.e. £18,270 + £10,000).

Shares and securities

Shares or securities of the same class in any company which are *treated* as above as held on 31 March 1982 by a person will be treated as a single holding with any shares or securities of the same class in the same company *actually* held by that person in determining the market value for re-basing purposes of the shares or securities. If the shares or securities in the relevant disposal represent some but not all of those valued at 31 March 1982, then the allowable cost or indexation allowance as appropriate will be based on the proportion that the shares or securities disposed of bears to the total holding (HMRC Statement of Practice SP 5/89). See also **8.2** above regarding the concessional valuation of a holding of shares or securities at 31 March 1982 where part of the holding was held on 6 April 1965.

Valuation

The following treatment applies where a company disposes of shares or securities of the same class in a company and some or all of the shares or securities were held by another company on 31 March 1982 but are treated as above both as having been held by the company on 31 March 1982 and as constituting or forming part of a single holding held by the company on that date. Both the disposal by which the company acquired the shares or securities, and any previous disposal of them after 31 March 1982, must have been by way of no gain/no loss transfer under *TCGA 1992, s 171* (intra-group disposals). Where the company makes a claim, the market value at 31 March 1982 of the shares or securities disposed of is regarded as the appropriate proportion of the value of any larger holding of shares or securities of the same class which included some or all of those disposed of and which was held by the other company at that date. If some of the shares or securities disposed of in fact formed part of two or more larger holdings held by two different companies on 31 March 1982, the apportionment is made by reference to the largest such holding. A claim for this treatment must be made within two years (or such further time as HMRC may allow) of the end of the accounting period in which the disposal is made.

[TCGA 1992, s 55(6)(aa), Sch 3 para 1A].

Supplementary provisions

Capital allowances

[8.7] If, under either the re-basing provisions of *TCGA 1992, s 35* or the equivalent provisions for indexation allowance of *TCGA 1992, s 55(1)* (see **8.2** and **8.3** above), it is to be assumed that any asset was on 31 March 1982 sold by the person making the disposal and immediately reacquired by them, *TCGA*

1992, s 41 (restriction of losses by reference to capital allowances, see **16.14**(i) COMPUTATION OF GAINS AND LOSSES) and *s 47* (wasting assets qualifying for capital allowances, see **65.2** WASTING ASSETS) apply with suitable modifications on the assumed reacquisition at 31 March 1982. [*TCGA 1992, s 55(3)*].

Part disposals etc.

[8.8] Where, on a disposal to which the general re-basing rule of *TCGA 1992, s 35(1)(2)* in **8.2** above applies, *TCGA 1992, s 42* (allowable expenditure on a part disposal, see **16.5** COMPUTATION OF GAINS AND LOSSES) has effect by reason of an earlier disposal made after 31 March 1982 and before 6 April 1988, the sums to be apportioned under that provision on the later disposal are to take the general re-basing rule into account. [*TCGA 1992, Sch 3 para 4(1)*].

If in relation to disposals after 5 April 1989 the general re-basing rule of *TCGA 1992, s 35(1)(2)* applies, and if that rule did not apply expenditure would under specified enactments not be allowable in computing a gain arising on the disposal, and the disallowance would be attributable to the reduction of the amount of the consideration for a disposal made after 31 March 1982 but before 6 April 1988, the amount otherwise allowable as a deduction on the disposal is reduced by the amount of the disallowance that would have been made if the general re-basing rule had not applied. The enactments specified are:

(i) *TCGA 1992, s 23(2)* (disallowance of allowable expenditure where allowance already given against receipts of compensation or insurance money, see **10.3** CAPITAL SUMS DERIVED FROM ASSETS);
(ii) *TCGA 1992, s 122(4)* (disallowance where allowance already given against capital distribution, see **57.11** SHARES AND SECURITIES);
(iii) *TCGA 1992, s 133(4)* (disallowance where allowance already given against premium on conversion of securities, see **57.8** SHARES AND SECURITIES); and
(iv) *TCGA 1992, s 244* (disallowance where allowance already given against gain from small part disposal of land, see **35.7** and **35.9** LAND).

[*TCGA 1992, Sch 3 para 4(2)*].

Assets derived from other assets

[8.9] The re-basing provisions of *TCGA 1992, s 35* in **8.2** and **8.3** above apply with the necessary modifications in relation to a disposal of an asset which was not held on 31 March 1982, if its value is derived from another asset which is taken into account under *TCGA 1992, s 43* (assets derived from other assets, see **16.5** COMPUTATION OF GAINS AND LOSSES). [*TCGA 1992, Sch 3 para 5*]. For indexation allowance purposes, where, after 31 March 1982, an asset which was held on that date has been merged or divided or has changed its nature or rights in or over the asset have been created, then *TCGA 1992, s 55(1)(2)* (re-basing for indexation allowance purposes) in **8.2** above has effect to determine for the purposes of *TCGA 1992, s 43* the amount of the consideration for the acquisition of the asset which was so held. [*TCGA 1992, s 55(4)*]. Note that indexation allowance is available only for the purposes of corporation tax on chargeable gains. See **32.1** INDEXATION.

Time apportionment of pre-6 April 1965 gains and losses

[8.10] If *TCGA 1992, Sch 2 para 16* (time apportionment of gains and losses accruing on assets held on 6 April 1965, see **8.12** below) applies so that only part of a gain or loss is a chargeable gain or an allowable loss, the exclusion of the general re-basing rule of *TCGA 1992, s 35(1)(2)* under **8.2**(a) and (b) above has effect as if the amount of the gain or loss that would accrue if the general re-basing rule did not apply were equal to that part. [*TCGA 1992, Sch 3 para 6*]. (*Schedule 2 para 16* does not apply for capital gains tax purposes, as re-basing to 31 March 1982 applies without exceptions for such disposals.)

Deferred charges on gains before 31 March 1982

[8.11] The following relief applies for the purposes of corporation tax on chargeable gains (and, for disposals before 6 April 2008 only, capital gains tax). [*TCGA 1992, s 36, Sch 4 para A1*].

Subject to the above, the relief applies where, before 6 April 1988, a gain was deferred in respect of one or more disposals which related in whole or in part to an asset acquired before 31 March 1982, and the deferred gain is brought into charge on a disposal or other occasion after 5 April 1988. The deferred gain is, subject to conditions and on a claim, halved (except, in certain cases, where the deferred gain is never deemed to accrue at all) when the charge to tax is computed in respect of it.

The provisions under which a gain can be deferred effectively fall into two groups for this purpose. In the first group (*TCGA 1992, Sch 4 para 2*), which includes the hold-over provisions for gifts made before 14 March 1989 and rollover relief on the replacement of business assets, the deferred gain is deducted from the expenditure allowable in computing the gain on a later disposal. In the second group (*TCGA 1992, Sch 4 paras 3, 4*), the deferred gain is brought into charge on the occurrence of a subsequent event. For both groups, the deferred gain will be half of what it would otherwise be. [*TCGA 1992, s 36, Sch 4 para 1*].

Group 1

As regards the first group of provisions, both of the following circumstances must be fulfilled in order to bring about the halving of the deferred gain.

(a) There is a disposal, other than one within the 'no gain/no loss provisions' (see **8.6** above), after 5 April 1988 of an asset acquired after 31 March 1982 by the person making the disposal.

(b) A deduction from allowable expenditure falls to be made under any of the first group of provisions in computing the gain on that disposal and is attributable directly or indirectly, in whole or in part, to a chargeable gain accruing on the disposal before 6 April 1988 of an asset acquired before 31 March 1982 by the person making that disposal.

No relief is given under *TCGA 1992, Sch 4* where, by reason of the previous operation of it, the amount of the deduction in (b) is less than it otherwise would be. Where the disposal takes place after 18 March 1991, no relief under *TCGA*

1992, Sch 4 is available if the amount of the deduction would have been less had relief by virtue of a previous application of it been duly claimed. (In effect, for disposals after 18 March 1991, the relief for the first group of provisions (*TCGA 1992, Sch 4 para* 2) cannot be claimed twice for the same gain and must be claimed in respect of the earliest possible occasion. For disposals after 5 April 1988 and before 19 March 1991, it was possible to claim other than on the earliest possible occasion. See below as regards time limits for claims affected by this change.) [*TCGA 1992, Sch 4 para 2(1)–(3)*].

Where the asset was acquired after 18 March 1991, the deduction is partly attributable to a claim under *TCGA 1992, s 154(4)* (rollover into non-depreciating asset instead of into depreciating asset, see **53.9** ROLLOVER RELIEF), and the claim applies to the asset, no relief under *TCGA 1992, Sch 4* is available by virtue of its application in respect of the first group of provisions below (*TCGA 1992, Sch 4 para* 2) (but see below as regards the relief available in respect of the second group of provisions). [*TCGA 1992, Sch 4 para 2(4)*].

In the case of rollover relief on the replacement of business assets and subject to the usual time limits, the disposal of the old asset may be before 31 March 1982, and the replacement asset may be acquired afterwards (Revenue Press Release 8 July 1988).

For the circumstances in which HMRC will require a valuation of the asset transferred where a hold-over relief claim is made, see **30.2** HOLD-OVER RELIEFS.

The first group of provisions mentioned above is as follows.

(i) *TCGA 1992, s 23(4)(5)* (rollover where replacement asset acquired after receipt of compensation or insurance money, see **10.4** CAPITAL SUMS DERIVED FROM ASSETS);
(ii) *TCGA 1992, s 152* (rollover where replacement asset acquired on disposal of business asset, see **53** ROLLOVER RELIEF);
(iii) *TCGA 1992, s 247* (rollover where replacement land acquired on compulsory acquisition of other land, see **35.10** LAND).

[*TCGA 1992, Sch 4 para 2(5)*].

Where deferral has been claimed under one of the first group of provisions and there is a subsequent no gain/no loss disposal (or continuous series of such disposals) as in **8.6** above, relief is available (subject to the conditions in (a) and (b) above) in computing the gain on the first later disposal which is not within the no gain/no loss provisions. [*TCGA 1992, Sch 4 paras 6, 7*].

Group 2

As regards the second group of provisions and subject to the exception below, both of the following circumstances must be fulfilled in order to bring about the halving of the deferred gain.

(A) Under any of the second group of provisions a gain is treated as accruing in consequence of an event occurring after 5 April 1988.
(B) The gain is attributable directly or indirectly, in whole or in part, to the disposal before 6 April 1988 of an asset acquired before 31 March 1982 by the person making that disposal.

[*TCGA 1992, Sch 4 para 4(1)*].

Where a gain is treated as accruing in consequence of an event after 18 March 1991, relief under *TCGA 1992, Sch 4* does not apply if the gain is attributable directly or indirectly, in whole or in part, to the disposal of an asset after 5 April 1988, or the amount of the gain would have been less had relief by virtue of a previous application of *TCGA 1992, Sch 4* been duly claimed. [*TCGA 1992, Sch 4 para 4(4)*]. (In effect, for events after 18 March 1991, the relief for the second group of provisions (*TCGA 1992, Sch 4 paras 3, 4*, and see below as regards *TCGA 1992, Sch 4 para 3*) cannot be claimed twice for the same gain and must be claimed in respect of the earliest possible occasion. For events after 5 April 1988 and before 19 March 1991, it was possible to claim other than on the earliest possible occasion and more than once. See below as regards time limits for claims affected by this change.)

The second group of provisions mentioned above is as follows (and see also below).

(I) *TCGA 1992, s 116(10)(11)* (postponement of charge on reorganisation etc. involving acquisition of qualifying corporate bonds, see **48.4** QUALIFYING CORPORATE BONDS).

(II) *TCGA 1992, s 134* (postponement of charge where gilts acquired on compulsory acquisition of shares, see **57.8** SHARES AND SECURITIES);

(III) *TCGA 1992, s 140* (postponement of charge where securities acquired in exchange for business acquired by overseas resident company until transferor company disposes of securities as mentioned in *s 140(4)* or transferee company within six years of exchange disposes of assets acquired on exchange as mentioned in *s 140(5)*, see **43.10** OVERSEAS MATTERS);

(IV) *TCGA 1992, s 154(2)* (postponement of charge where depreciating asset acquired as replacement for business asset, see **53.9** ROLLOVER RELIEF) (and see below as regards *TCGA 1992, Sch 4 para 3*);

(V) *TCGA 1992, s 179(3)* (or earlier equivalent) (charge on company leaving group of companies in respect of asset acquired from another member of same group within previous six years, see **26.7** GROUPS OF COMPANIES, but only if the asset was acquired by the chargeable company before 6 April 1988, so no longer relevant);

(VI) *TCGA 1992, s 248(3)* (postponement of charge where depreciating asset acquired on compulsory acquisition of land, see **35.10** LAND).

[*TCGA 1992, Sch 4 para 4(2)(3)*].

Where relief under *TCGA 1992, Sch 4* would have applied on a disposal but for the effect of *TCGA 1992, Sch 4 para 2(4)* (exclusion of relief under *TCGA 1992, Sch 4 para* 2 where deduction partly attributable to claim under *TCGA 1992, s 154(4)*) above, then such relief (on the same lines as for the second group of provisions above) is available (under *TCGA 1992, Sch 4 para* 3) if the relief for the second group of provisions (*TCGA 1992, Sch 4 para* 4) would have applied had *TCGA 1992, s 154(2)* (see (IV) above) continued to apply to the gain carried forward as a result of the claim under *TCGA 1992, s 154(4)*, and the time of disposal been the time when that gain was treated as accruing by virtue of *TCGA 1992, s 154(2)*. [*TCGA 1992, Sch 4 para 3*].

There is an exception to the bringing about of the halving of the deferred gain in respect of certain provisions contained in the second group. Neither *TCGA 1992, s 134, s 140(4), s 154(2)* nor *s 248(3)* (see (II)–(IV) and (VI) above) is to apply in consequence of an event occurring after 5 April 1988 if its application would be *directly* attributable to the disposal of an asset before 1 April 1982. [*TCGA 1992, Sch 4 para 4(5)*]. In effect the deferred gain is in such circumstances never deemed to accrue. See also below regarding views expressed by HMRC.

It is understood that HMRC accept that the crystallisation under *TCGA 1992, s 67(4)(5)* of a gain deferred by *FA 1980, s 79* (as extended by *FA 1981, s 78* and *FA 1982, s 82*) (clawback of deferred gain on death of life tenant, see **30.8** and **30.12** HOLD-OVER RELIEFS) can by concession be treated as if it were amongst the second group of provisions in (I)–(VI) above. In addition, a gain deferred on a transfer into settlement occurring before 1 April 1982 and which would otherwise crystallise on the death after 5 April 1988 of a life tenant will by concession be deemed never to accrue (and so treated in the same way as for the exception given by *TCGA 1992, Sch 4 para 4(5)* above).

Asset not held on 31 March 1982

Relief is available as regards both groups of provisions where a person makes a disposal of an asset which he acquired after 30 March 1982 where the disposal by which he acquired it and any previous disposal of it after that date was within the 'no gain/no loss provisions' (see **8.6** above). In such a case, the person is treated for the purposes of (b) and (B) above as having acquired the asset before 31 March 1982. [*TCGA 1992, Sch 4 paras 5, 7*].

Relief is available as regards both groups of provisions for an asset which was not acquired before 31 March 1982 if its value was derived from another asset which was so acquired and which is taken into account under *TCGA 1992, s 43* (see **16.5** COMPUTATION OF GAINS AND LOSSES). [*TCGA 1992, Sch 4 para 8*].

Claims

No relief is available under *TCGA 1992, Sch 4* unless a claim is made:

(a) in respect of gains accruing to a person chargeable to corporation tax within two years of the end of the accounting period, and
(b) on or before such later date as HMRC may allow,

in which, for the first group of provisions, the disposal to which the claim relates is made, or for the second group of provisions, the deferred gain is treated as accruing (except where (V) above applied where the claim had to be made within two years of the end of the accounting period in which the chargeable company ceased to be a member of the group). A claim must be supported by any particulars the inspector may require for establishing the validity and quantum of any relief. [*TCGA 1992, Sch 4 para 9*]. HMRC may accept a late claim by exercising its collection and management powers — see **61.1** TIME LIMITS — FIXED DATES. (HMRC Capital Gains Manual CG13800, 17010).

Assets held by a company on 6 April 1965

[8.12] Assets held by a company on 6 April 1965 (the original base date for the purposes of capital gains tax) are subject to special provisions contained in *TCGA 1992, Sch 2* and described in this chapter. The provisions do not apply for capital gains tax because, for such purposes, the general re-basing rule for assets held on 31 March 1982 applies automatically without exception.

In practice, the provisions will only apply in exceptional cases, because re-basing to 31 March 1982 will generally apply, either because the March 1982 value is higher than the cost or value at 6 April 1965 or because the company has made an election for universal re-basing.

The provisions apply to three categories of assets:

(i) quoted securities;
(ii) land reflecting development value; and
(iii) other assets.

For disposals of assets in categories (i) or (ii), generally the gain or loss is calculated taking into account the original cost as well as the 6 April 1965 and 31 March 1982 values. The lowest gain is brought into charge or the lowest loss is allowable.

For other assets, the gain or loss is generally calculated either by reference to the 31 March 1982 value or by time apportionment of the cost between the periods of ownership up to and after 5 April 1965.

There are provisions that allowed for an election to use the April 1965 market value. Such an election is irrevocable and binds a company where the assets were transferred under the no gain/no loss provisions. Such an election can be superseded by an election for universal re-basing to 31 March 1982.

[*TCGA 1992, Sch 2*].

For the detailed provisions, see the 2023/24 edition of this work or **Simon's Taxes C2.610–C2.613**. See also Example 3 at **8.2** above.

Groups of companies

The special provisions apply to the disposal of an asset by a company which is or has been a member of a group of companies (within **26.2** GROUPS OF COMPANIES) and which acquired the asset from another member of the group at a time when both were members of the group, as if all members of the group for the time being were the same person, and as if the acquisition or provision of the asset by the group, taken as a single person, had been the acquisition or provision of it by the member disposing of it. This does not apply where the disposing company is an investment trust or acquired the asset after 31 March 1980, from an investment trust. [*TCGA 1992, s 174(4)(5)*].

Capital allowances

Where the gain on the disposal of an asset is calculated by reference to its value on 6 April 1965, the restriction of relief given for losses accruing on assets which have qualified for capital allowances (*TCGA 1992, s 41*, see **16.14**(i)

COMPUTATION OF GAINS AND LOSSES) and the provisions relating to wasting assets qualifying for capital allowances (*TCGA 1992, s 47*, see **65.2** WASTING ASSETS) apply as if the capital allowances for 1965/66 and subsequent years were allowances in respect of expenditure incurred on the asset on 6 April 1965. [*TCGA 1992, Sch 2 para 20*].

Assets transferred to close companies

Where, at any time, a person who has 'control' of a 'close company', or a person 'connected' with him, transfers an asset to the company, and subsequently the first person (or any person with a 'substantial holding' of shares in the company) disposes of shares in circumstances, such that the chargeable gain is to be determined by time apportionment, to the extent that the gain accruing on the disposal is attributable to a profit on the asset transferred, the shares are deemed to have been acquired at the date when the asset was transferred. The provisions do not apply where a loss accrues on the disposal. [*TCGA 1992, Sch 2 para 21*].

'*Control*' is as given by *CTA 2010, ss 450, 451*. '*Close company*' has the meaning given by *CTA 2010, ss 439–454*. '*Connected*' is as given at **17** CONNECTED PERSONS. '*Substantial holding*' is not defined.

9

Business Asset Disposal Relief

Cross-references. See **16** COMPUTATION OF GAINS AND LOSSES; **34** INVESTORS' RELIEF.

Simon's Taxes. See **C3.1301–C3.1314.**

Introduction to business asset disposal relief

[9.1] Business asset disposal relief ('BADR') provides for a reduced rate of capital gains tax of 10% for gains made in respect of qualifying business disposals. For 2019/20 and earlier years, the relief was known as 'entrepreneurs' relief'. The relief applies for capital gains tax purposes only and is not available to companies.

A disposal by an **individual** qualifies for the relief if it is a disposal of:

- the whole or part of a business;
- business assets when the business ceases;
- shares in a trading company of which the individual is an employee and meets a minimum shareholding requirement;
- shares in a trading company of which the individual is an employee which were acquired by the exercise of an option under the enterprise management incentives scheme; or

- an asset used by a partnership or company if the disposal (an 'associated disposal') is associated with a disposal of an interest in the assets of the partnership or shares in the company which itself qualifies for business asset disposal relief.

BADR is also available to an individual who carries on a business as a member of a partnership. The legislation treats the partnership business as owned, at any time, by each individual who is a partner at that time.

A disposal by the **trustees** of a settlement qualifies for relief if it is a disposal of shares in a company and the company meets requirements in relation to a beneficiary which are similar to those for individuals or if it is a disposal of assets used in a business carried on by a beneficiary which has ceased.

See **9.2–9.9** below for the full conditions. See also **9.11** below for assets which qualify for relief and restrictions on relief for disposals of goodwill.

The relief is given by deducting the aggregate losses arising on the disposal from the aggregate gains and treating the resulting amount as a single chargeable gain taxable at a rate of **10%**. See **9.12** below.

The relief is subject to a lifetime limit, which is currently £1 million — see **9.12** below. This means that the maximum relief is £100,000 (i.e. a 10% reduction in the CGT rate on the assumption that the rate would otherwise be 20%). Before 11 March 2020, the relief was much more generous — the lifetime limit was £10 million. Disposals before 6 April 2008 do not affect the lifetime limit except in the case of deferred gains on which business asset disposal relief is claimed under the transitional rules at **9.16–9.17** below.

Further restrictions on the amount of relief available are described at **9.13** and **9.14** below, and for the application of the relief to deferred gains or where there is a reorganisation of share capital, see **9.16, 9.17** below.

Individuals can make an election allowing business asset disposal relief in certain cases where relief would otherwise become unavailable as a result of a company ceasing to be the individual's personal company. The provisions apply where the company ceases to be the individual's personal company as a result of the company issuing shares on or after 6 April 2019. The individual can elect to be treated as having made that disposal at that time and immediately reacquiring the shares or securities, thus crystallising a gain on which business asset disposal relief may be claimed. A further election can be made to defer the gain arising as a result of the first election until such time as a subsequent actual disposal of shares or securities is made. See **9.15** below.

See also HMRC Capital Gains Manual CG63950–64173, and Chartered Institute of Taxation Notice 13 February 2012 for HMRC's responses to various technical questions concerning the relief.

Qualifying business disposals

[9.2] BADR can be claimed in respect of a '*qualifying business disposal*', which is any of the following:

(a) a 'material disposal of business assets' by an individual (see **9.4** below);

(b) a 'disposal of trust business assets' by the trustees of a settlement (see **9.8** below); or

(c) a disposal by an individual associated with a material disposal of either their interest in a partnership or shares or securities in a company (usually referred to as an 'associated disposal') (see **9.9** below).

Meaning of 'business'

Throughout this chapter, a '*business*' means a 'trade', profession or vocation which is conducted on a commercial basis and with a view to the realisation of profits. Preparing to carry on a trade is not a business (*Wardle v HMRC* FTT, [2021] UKFTT 124 (TC)), but note that preparing to carry on a trade is a trading activity for the purposes of the definition of a 'trading company' (see **9.7** below). In a subsequent case involving the same taxpayer but a different business (*Wardle v HMRC* FTT, [2024] UKFTT 543 (TC)), the tribunal applied the tests in *Mansell v HMRC* [2006] SSCD 605 to determine that the trade had commenced before the start of the two-year period needed for BADR to be available. A '*trade*' includes a venture in the nature of trade. Prior to April 2025, any property business which consists of, or so far as it consists of, the commercial letting of FURNISHED HOLIDAY ACCOMMODATION (**24**) is treated as a trade. The government announced at Spring Budget 2024 that this treatment is to be abolished with effect from April 2025 (and an anti-forestalling rule to prevent the use of unconditional contracts to access beneficial capital gains tax treatment will apply retrospectively from 6 March 2024). See **24.1** FURNISHED HOLIDAY ACCOMMODATION.

[*TCGA 1992, ss 169H(2), 169S(1), 241(3)(3A)*].

Partnerships and BADR

[9.3] BADR is available to an individual who carries on a business as a member of a partnership. The legislation treats the partnership business as owned, at any time, by each individual who is a partner at that time. A disposal by an individual of the whole or part of their interest in the assets of a partnership is treated as a disposal of the whole or part of the partnership business.

This means that an individual partner may be able to claim BADR on any of the following

- a disposal by the individual of the whole or part of their interest in the partnership (by treating it as the disposal of the whole or part of a business) (see **9.4** below);
- a disposal by the partnership of the whole or part of the partnership business (by treating the business as owned by each individual partner);
- a disposal by the partnership of shares; a disposal of partnership assets within the three years following the cessation of the partnership business; or
- an associated disposal (HMRC Capital Gains Manual CG63975).

In addition, where an individual carrying on a business as a sole trader enters into a partnership which is to carry on the business and, on entering into the partnership, they dispose of, or dispose of an interest in, assets used for the purposes of the business, they are treated as disposing of part of a business.

[*TCGA 1992, ss 169I, 169S(2)–(5); CTA 2010, s 158*].

Material disposal of business assets

[9.4] A '*material disposal of business assets*' is a disposal by an individual of one of the following:

(a) A disposal of the **whole or part of a business** owned by the individual throughout the two-year period ending with the date of disposal. See further **9.5** below.

(b) A disposal of, or a disposal of an interest in, one or more assets in use, at the time at which a **business ceases to be carried on**, for the purposes of the business, where the business was owned by the individual throughout the two-year period ending with the cessation of the business. The disposal must be made within the three-year period beginning with the date of cessation.
HMRC consider that, where the effect of *TCGA 1992, s 28* (disposal deemed to occur on date contract made: see **16.4** COMPUTATION OF GAINS AND LOSSES) is that the disposal of an asset precedes the cessation of the business, business asset disposal relief will nevertheless be available, provided that there is a genuine business disposal linked to a genuine business cessation (Chartered Institute of Taxation Notice 13 February 2012).

(c) A disposal of, or a disposal of an interest in, shares or 'securities' of a company where:
- the company is the individual's 'personal company' (see **9.6** below);
- the company is either a 'trading company' or the 'holding company' of a 'trading group' (see **9.7** below); and
- the individual is an officer or employee of the company or, where the company is a member of a trading group, of one or more companies which are members of the group.

These conditions must be met throughout either:
(i) the two-year period ending with the date of disposal; or
(ii) the two-year period ending with the date on which the company ceases to be a trading company without continuing to be or becoming a member of a trading group or ceases to be a member of a trading group without continuing to be or becoming a trading company.

Where (ii) above applies, the disposal must be made within the three-year period beginning with the date of cessation.
Where any of the shares were issued to the individual wholly or partly in exchange for the transfer of a business as a going concern together with all of the business's assets (or all of the assets other than cash), the above conditions are treated as met in any period ending immediately before the transfer throughout which the individual owned the business. The latter period can therefore count towards the two-year periods in (i) and (ii) above.

A disposal of an interest in shares includes a deemed disposal of an interest in shares under *TCGA 1992, s 122* (capital distributions — see **57.11** SHARES AND SECURITIES). '*Securities*' include debentures deemed to be securities under *TCGA 1992, s 251(6)* (see **23.5** EXEMPTIONS AND RELIEFS). Where a company has genuine doubt or difficulty as to its trading status it can seek an opinion from HMRC using the non-statutory clearance service (see **27.4** HMRC — ADMINISTRATION), provided that the uncertainty is over HMRC's interpretation of the legislation rather than a question of fact (HMRC Capital Gains Manual CG64100).

The meanings of 'officer' and 'employee' were considered in *Hirst v HMRC* FTT, [2014] UKFTT 924 (TC), 2015 STI 135.

HMRC accept in principle that, where there has been a share exchange to which *TCGA 1992, s 127* applied, the two-year period requirement can be satisfied by reference to both the old and the new holding of shares. Both holdings must satisfy the other conditions for business asset disposal relief (and there must have been no election in relation to the exchange under the provisions at **9.17** below). (Chartered Institute of Taxation Technical Note, 27 May 2010).

(d) A disposal of 'relevant EMI shares' in a company where:

- the company is either a 'trading company' or the 'holding company' of a 'trading group' (see **9.7** below); and
- the individual is an officer or employee of the company or, where the company is a member of a trading group, of one or more companies which are members of the group.

There is no requirement for the company to be the individual's personal company.

These conditions must be met throughout either:

(i) the two-year period ending with the date of disposal; or

(ii) the two-year period ending with the date on which the company ceases to be a trading company without continuing to be or becoming a member of a trading group or ceases to be a member of a trading group without continuing to be or becoming a trading company. If the shares disposed of (or, where there has been a reorganisation or share exchange (see below), the original shares) were acquired after a disqualifying event under the enterprise management incentives (EMI) rules within *ITEPA 2003, s 534(1)(c)* (company ceasing to meet the trading activities requirement) but the option was exercised within 90 days after the event occurred, the two-year period is that ending with the first day of the 90-day period if that day is later than the cessation date.

Where (ii) above applies, the disposal must be made within the three-year period beginning with the date of cessation and the shares must be acquired before that date. Where the shareholding is a new holding following a reorganisation of share capital (see further below), the question of whether the shares were acquired before the cessation date is determined by reference to the date of acquisition of the original relevant EMI shares.

It is a further condition that the 'option grant date' must be on or before the first day of the two-year period ending on the date of disposal (or where (ii) above applies, the cessation date). If the shares disposed of (or, where there has been a reorganisation or share exchange, the original shares) were acquired after a disqualifying event under the EMI rules (within *ITEPA 2003, s 533*) but the option was exercised within 90 days after the event occurred, the option grant date must be on or before the first day of the two-year period ending on the date of the disqualifying event rather than the date of disposal.

The '*option grant date*' is the date on which the qualifying option was granted or, where the option is a replacement option, the date on which the old option was granted (or, where the old option was itself a replacement option, the date on which the earlier old option was granted, and so on). During the currency of an old option, the trading company/group and employee/officer conditions above must be considered by reference to the company whose shares were subject to that option.

See **58.2** SHARES AND SECURITIES — IDENTIFICATION RULES for special identification rules for relevant EMI shares.

Meaning of 'relevant EMI shares'

Shares are '*relevant EMI shares*' if they are acquired by an individual on or after 6 April 2013 as a result of the exercise of an enterprise management incentives qualifying option (within *ITEPA 2003, s 527(4)* — see **21.21** EMPLOYEE SHARE SCHEMES) within ten years of its grant (or, where the option is a 'replacement option' (within *ITEPA 2003, Sch 5 para 41*), within ten years of the grant of the original qualifying option). Shares are excluded if a disqualifying event occurred before the exercise of the option and the option was not exercised within 90 days after the event occurred.

Shares acquired in 2012/13 are also 'relevant EMI shares' if they would have met the above definition if they had been acquired on or after 6 April 2013 and the individual made no disposals during 2012/13 of any shares of the same class.

Shares are also '*relevant EMI shares*' if they are the new holding following a reorganisation of share capital within *TCGA 1992, s 126* (see **57.2** SHARES AND SECURITIES) or a share exchange within *TCGA 1992, s 135* (see **57.5** SHARES AND SECURITIES) and the original shares were themselves relevant EMI shares. In the case of a share exchange, there are additional conditions that the exchange must be a qualifying exchange of shares within *ITEPA 2003, Sch 5 para 40* and that, when the exchange occurs, the EMI independence and trading requirements (within *ITEPA 2003, Sch 5 paras 9, 13, 14*) are met by the new company. Where shares are relevant EMI shares under this rule, the trading company/group and employee/officer conditions above must be considered at any time by reference to the company in which the individual held the shares at that time.

Disposal of the whole or part of a business

[9.5] As explained at **9.4** above, BADR is available on the disposal by an individual of the whole or part of a business owned by the individual throughout the two-year period ending with the date of disposal.

There must be a disposal of part of a business rather than a mere sale of an asset used in the business. In *M Gilbert v HMRC* FTT, [2011] UKFTT 705 (TC), a trader had carried on a business of selling food on commission, representing nine different suppliers. He received £285,000 from one of the suppliers under an agreement whereby he agreed to have no further contact with the supplier's customers. He claimed entrepreneurs' relief, as business asset disposal relief was then known, on the gain. The FTT concluded that the taxpayer had sold part of his business as a going concern. Judge Radford held that 'what characterises a sale as a going concern is a sale of goodwill where it exists'. The taxpayer had sold the goodwill and had 'also sold his customer database, a crucial asset in distinguishing a sale of a going concern from a mere sale of assets'.

The rules for BADR are broadly based on those for a previous CGT relief, retirement relief, which was abolished in 2003. Although retirement relief cases are not binding precedent for BADR purposes, HMRC consider that the courts are likely to consider them persuasive (HMRC Capital Gains Manual CG64010). Accordingly, the following retirement relief cases are thought to be relevant to BADR.

What constitutes the disposal of 'part of a business' was considered in a number of retirement relief cases, particularly relating to farming. In *McGregor v Adcock* Ch D 1977, 51 TC 692, a farmer sold part of his land for which outline planning permission had been obtained and was refused retirement relief. This decision was followed in *Atkinson v Dancer and Mannion v Johnston* Ch D 1988, 61 TC 598. In *Jarmin v Rawlings* Ch D 1994, 67 TC 130, in which retirement relief was allowed, it was held that the taxpayer had disposed of a dairy farming business, which was 'a separate and distinguishable part' of his business. In *Barrett v Powell* Ch D 1998, 70 TC 432, it was held that a disposal of a tenancy to farm land which the taxpayer then continued to farm under a temporary licence did not qualify for retirement relief; the taxpayer had continued to carry on exactly the same business as before, albeit more precariously; see also *Purves v Harrison* Ch D 2000, 73 TC 390.

A disposal of Lloyd's syndicate capacity was held not to be the disposal of the whole or part of a business for BADR purposes (and did not fall within **9.4**(b) above as a disposal of business assets following cessation) in *Carver v HMRC* FTT, [2015] SFTD 573.

In unusual circumstances, the tribunal found that relief was available on the disposal by a partner in an accountancy firm of its business premises (*Thomson v HMRC* FTT, 2021, [2022] SFTD 314). Even though the disposal of a single asset would not normally qualify, on the facts of this case, the disposal of partnership premises was part of a wider disposal to enable the taxpayer to exit the business, notwithstanding that the wider disposal had been going on for 22 years. The taxpayer had been one of two partners in the firm since 1970. In 1996, he started to consider retirement and succession. He identified two accountants working in the practice (the 'new partners') as suitable successors and made an unwritten agreement with them. Under the agreement, the new partners would pay an annual amount to the taxpayer for the firm's work in progress until he was left with a token 1%; the taxpayer would gradually transfer clients to the new partners, and accordingly, his share of the profits and working hours would gradually reduce. The transfer took longer than anticipated, due to complications with existing clients, and the taxpayer handed over his last personal client in 2021. There was no specific agreement about the firm's premises, in which the taxpayer had a 99% interest, but it was understood that some arrangement would be needed. In 2017, the premises were sold to the taxpayer's pension scheme and leased back to the firm. The FTT held that the disposal of the premises was 'part and parcel' of the wider disposal of the taxpayer's share of the partnership assets. It was not the disposal of a single asset. The taxpayer had been trying to transfer ownership of the practice to the new partners since 1996, a process which was still ongoing in 2017. The disposal therefore satisfied the requirements of *TCGA 1992, s 169I* and qualified for business asset disposal relief.

For HMRC's views on the disposal of part of a business and discussion of the case law, see HMRC Capital Gains Manual CG64015–64040.

Meaning of 'personal company'

[9.6] As explained at **9.4** above, an individual can claim BADR in respect of a disposal of shares or securities in their 'personal company' (provided the other conditions mentioned at **9.4** above are met).

An individual's '*personal company*' is a company in which they hold at least 5% of the ordinary share capital (within *ITA 2007, s 989*) and in which, by virtue of that holding:

- they are able to exercise at least 5% of the voting rights by virtue of that holding; and
- either:
  - (a) by virtue of that holding, they are beneficially entitled to at least 5% of the profits available for distribution to the 'equity holders' of the company and would be beneficially entitled, on a winding up, to at least 5% of the assets of the company available for distribution to the equity holders; or
  - (b) in the event of a disposal of the whole of the company's ordinary share capital, they would be beneficially entitled to at least 5% of the proceeds.

For this purpose, where an individual holds any shares in the company jointly or in common with one or more others, each is treated as the sole holder of so many of the shares as is proportionate to the value of their share.

'*Equity holder*' is defined as for the purposes of corporation tax group relief, but with the modifications required by *TCGA 1992, s 169S(3E)*. Broadly (and subject to further provisions), an equity holder of a company is a holder of its 'ordinary shares' (as defined in *CTA 2010, s 160*) or a loan creditor of the company in respect of a loan other than a 'normal commercial loan' (as defined in *CTA 2010, s 162*). A person is a loan creditor of the company if they are a creditor in respect of redeemable loan capital issued by the company or in respect of a debt incurred by the company for any money borrowed or capital assets acquired by the company, for any right of the company to receive income or for consideration, the value to the creditor company of which was, at the time the debt was incurred, substantially less than the amount of the debt (including any debt premium). A bank is not a loan creditor of a company in respect of any loan capital or debt for money lent in the ordinary course of its business.

In determining whether the condition in (b) above applies at any time in a particular period, it must be assumed that the disposal takes place at that time at the market value of the shares on the final day of the period, and that the taxpayer is entitled to the proceeds which it would be reasonable to expect them to be entitled to, with regard to all the circumstances at that time. The effect of any avoidance arrangements (i.e. arrangements with a main purpose to secure that any business asset disposal relief provision does or does not apply) is ignored for this purpose.

Deferred shares which carried no voting or income rights were held to be ordinary share capital in *Castledine v HMRC* FTT, [2016] SFTD 484. In *McQuillan v HMRC* UT, [2017] STC 2192, the UT held that redeemable shares which carried no right to a dividend were ordinary share capital. The tribunal observed that the definition of ordinary share capital was not susceptible to analysis by reference to economic risk and reward and that the classification of the redeemable shares as debt, as opposed to equity, in the accounts did not prevent them from being ordinary shares for the purpose of *ITA 2007, s 989*. In *HMRC v Warshaw* UT, 2020, [2021] STC 247, cumulative preference shares were held to be ordinary share capital.

In *Tenconi v HMRC* FTT, [2021] UKFTT 107 (TC), 'guarantee rights' in a company were not shares and so a disposal of the beneficial interest in them did not qualify for relief. The company was limited both by share capital and guarantee rights. Its articles of association provided for two classes of members: shareholder members and investor members. Shareholder members held shares which carried no voting rights but were entitled to dividends up to the lower of the profits and £2,000 (apportioned according to total shares). Investor members held 'distribution rights' each of which cost £100 and carried general voting rights and an entitlement to share in the profits available for distribution in excess of £2,000. Ownership of shares could be transferred but there was no provision for the transfer of distribution rights. (Note that this issue was not considered by the UT on appeal by the taxpayer (see [2024] UKUT 110 (TCC)).)

The 5% limits above are strict ones. A holding of 4.997% did not meet the conditions in *Kavanagh v HMRC* FTT, [2022] UKFTT 173 (TC). The taxpayer argued that the remaining fraction required to bring his holding up to 5% was held for him on trust, but he failed to establish this on the facts.

In *Cooke v HMRC* FTT, [2024] UKFTT 272 (TC), however, a holding of 4.99998% was held to meet the requirement. It was intended that the taxpayer should have acquired a 5% holding, but due to a rounding error in a spreadsheet used to calculate the acquisition from two existing shareholders, he was one share short of 5%. The FTT considered that, in the particular circumstances of the case, the High Court would have ordered the rectification of the purchase agreement to include the extra share. The FTT therefore proceeded as if rectification had been ordered and allowed the taxpayer's appeal.

The 5% of ordinary share capital test applies by reference to the nominal value of the shares and not the number of shares (*Hunt v HMRC* FTT, [2019] SFTD 784). In that case, the taxpayer held 5.94% of the issued shares of a company, giving him 5.94% of the voting rights. The FTT held, however, that he did not hold 5% of the ordinary share capital of the company as his holding was only 4.16% of the nominal value of the ordinary share capital.

Meaning of 'trading company', 'holding company' and 'trading group'

[9.7] As explained at **9.4** above, an individual can claim BADR in respect of a disposal of shares or securities in a 'trading company' or the 'holding company' of a 'trading group' if the other conditions mentioned at **9.4** above are met. BADR can also be claimed by trustees of a settlement on a disposal of shares or securities in such a company (again subject to further conditions, see **9.8** below).

The BADR legislation applies the same definitions of 'trading company', holding company' and 'trading group' as apply for the purposes of hold-over relief for gifts of business assets (see **30.3** HOLD-OVER RELIEFS). For the purposes of determining whether the conditions for relief at **9.4**(c) and (d) and **9.8**(i) below are met, however, the definitions are subject to the modifications for joint venture companies and companies in a partnership below. For all other BADR purposes, those modifications do not apply and 'trading company' and 'trading group' have the same meaning as for the purposes of hold-over relief for gifts of business assets, except that the provisions relating to joint venture companies in *TCGA 1992, s 165A(7)(12)* do not apply.

The meaning of 'trading company' was considered in *Potter v HMRC* FTT, 2019, [2020] SFTD 82. Mr and Mrs P were the directors and equal shareholders of G Ltd. The company was involved in the London Metal Exchange ('LME') where Mr P was an 'introducing broker' and a 'dealer'. As a result of the 2008 crash, the volume of trades declined dramatically and G Ltd issued its last invoice in March 2009. Also in 2009, Mr P continued to seek trades despite having lost the support of the company's bank. Negotiations eventually started to 'come through' in 2011, but Mr P suffered 'severe medical issues and personal misfortunes'. G Ltd was eventually put in voluntary liquidation in 2015/16 and the P's claimed BADR on the CGT liability triggered by the deemed disposal. They submitted that G Ltd had continued to be a trading company until June 2014, less than three years before its liquidation. The FTT accepted Mr P's account of his activities after 2009 and found that the company had been carrying on trading activities with a view to reviving its old trade. The FTT noted, however, that the asset and income position of the company pointed away from a finding that the company was trading, given that during the relevant period, it had derived all of its income from bonds. But the tribunal also observed that 'once the company had put its money into the bonds it did not, and indeed could not, do anything else in relation to them for six years until they matured'. It was therefore not carrying on investment activities and its activities were entirely directed at reviving its trade. The company had continued to be a trading company for many years after the issue of its last invoice, so that its directors were entitled to BADR on its liquidation.

In *Stolkin v HMRC* FTT, [2024] UKFTT 160 (TC), business asset disposal relief was denied because the company, which had acquired a single parcel of land, initially as an investment, was held not to be a trading company even though it had changed its plans for the site and had appropriated it to trading stock.

Joint venture companies

The modification to the holdover relief definitions of 'trading company' and 'trading group' for joint venture companies mentioned above is as follows. Activities of a joint venture company are attributed to a company under *TCGA 1992, s 165A(7)(12)*, only if the individual (P) making the disposal passes both the shareholding test and the voting rights test below in relation to the joint venture company.

In the case of a disposal by trustees, the tests are applied to each of the 'relevant beneficiaries' and the resulting percentages are aggregated to determine whether the tests are passed by those beneficiaries, considered as a single body. References to P in the following paragraphs should be interpreted accordingly. The '*relevant beneficiaries*' are the qualifying beneficiary and any other beneficiaries with an interest in possession as in **9.13** below.

The shareholding test

P passes the shareholding test if, throughout the 'relevant period', the sum of the following percentages is at least 5%:

- the percentage of the ordinary share capital of the joint venture company owned directly by P; and
- the percentage of the ordinary share capital of the joint venture company owned indirectly by P through '*investing companies*' (i.e. the company whose shares are the subject of the business asset disposal relief claim and any other company of which P owns part of the ordinary share capital).

The percentage of the ordinary share capital of the joint venture company owned indirectly by P through a particular investing company is:

$R \times S \times 100$

where R is the fraction of the investing company's ordinary share capital owned by P; and S is the fraction of the joint venture company's ordinary share capital owned by the investing company (whether directly, indirectly or both).

In computing amount S for a particular investing company, the fraction of the joint venture company's ordinary share capital owned indirectly by the investing company is calculated by applying *CTA 2010, ss 1155–1157* using the following assumptions. Where the investing company directly owns more than 50% of the ordinary share capital of a company, it is taken to own the whole of the ordinary share capital. Where a company other than the investing company (company B) directly owns more than 50% of the ordinary share capital of another company (company C) which is a member of the same group as the investing company, company B is taken to own the whole of the ordinary share capital of company C.

The '*relevant period*' is the two-year period ending with the date of disposal or with the date on which the company ceases to be a trading company without continuing to be or becoming a member of a trading group or ceases to be a member of a trading group without continuing to be or becoming a trading company, as appropriate. In the case of a disposal by trustees, it is a two-year period ending no earlier than three years before the date of the disposal.

The voting rights test

P passes the voting rights test if, throughout the relevant period, the sum of the following percentages is at least 5%:

- the percentage of the voting rights of the joint venture company held directly by P; and
- the percentage of the voting rights of the joint venture company held indirectly by P through investing companies.

The percentage of the voting rights of the joint venture company held indirectly by P through a particular investing company is calculated in the same way as the percentage of ordinary share capital. A person who has the ability to control the exercise of voting rights by another person is treated for this purpose as holding those rights.

Company in a partnership

The modification to the holdover relief definitions of 'trading company' and 'trading group' for companies which are a member of a partnership mentioned above is as follows. Activities carried on by a company as a member of a partnership are treated as not being trading activities of the company within *TCGA 1992, s 165A(4)(9)* if P (defined as above for joint venture companies) fails either the profits and assets test or the voting rights test below. Activities are also treated as not being trading activities of the company if the company is not a member of the partnership throughout the relevant period. The relevant period for this purpose also has the same meaning as for the joint venture companies modification above.

Assets held by a Scottish partnership or any other partnership under the law of another territory where assets of a partnership are treated as held by the partnership as such are treated for the purposes of the two tests as held by the partners in the proportions in which they are entitled to share in the partnership's capital profits.

The profits and assets test

P passes the profits and assets test if, throughout the relevant period, the sum of the following percentages is at least 5%:

(1) the percentage which is P's direct interest in the partnership's assets;
(2) the percentage which is P's share of the partnership through investing companies which are partnership members; and
(3) the percentage which is P's share of the partnership through investing companies and 'relevant corporate partners' in the partnership.

A company is a '*relevant corporate partner*' in relation to P and a partnership if an investing company owns some portion of its ordinary share capital directly or indirectly (or both), it is a member of the same group as the investing company and is a member of the partnership.

The percentage in (2) above which is P's share of the partnership through a particular investing company which is a partnership member is:

R × V × 100

where R is the fraction of the investing company's ordinary share capital owned by P; and V is the lower of the fraction of the partnership's profits or the fraction of the partnership's assets in which the investing company has an interest.

The percentage in (3) above which is P's share of the partnership through a particular investing company and a particular relevant corporate partner is:

R × V × W × 100

where R is the fraction of the investing company's ordinary share capital owned by P; V is the lower of the fraction of the partnership's profits or the fraction of the partnership's assets in which the relevant corporate partner has an interest; and W is the fraction of the relevant corporate partner's ordinary share capital that is owned by the investing company directly or indirectly (or both).

In computing amount W, the fraction of a company's ordinary share capital owned indirectly by the investing company is calculated by applying *CTA 2010, ss 1155–1157* using the following assumptions. Where the investing company directly owns more than 50% of the ordinary share capital of a company, it is taken to own the whole of the ordinary share capital. Where a company other than the investing company (company B) directly owns more than 50% of the ordinary share capital of another company (company C) which is a member of the same group as the investing company, company B is taken to own the whole of the ordinary share capital of company C.

The voting rights test

P passes the voting rights test if, throughout the relevant period, the sum of the following percentages is at least 5%:

- the sum of the percentages of voting rights held directly by P in investing companies which are members of the partnership; and
- the sum of the percentages which are P's indirect holdings of voting rights in relevant corporate partners in the partnership through investing companies.

The percentage which is P's indirect holding of voting rights in a particular relevant corporate partner in the partnership through a particular investing company is:

T × X × 100

where T is the fraction of the voting rights in the investing company held by P; and X is the fraction of the voting rights in the relevant corporate partner that is held by the investing company directly or indirectly (or both).

In computing amount X, the fraction of a company's voting rights held indirectly by the investing company is calculated by applying *CTA 2010, ss 1155–1157* using the following assumptions. Where the investing company directly holds more than 50% of the voting rights in a company, it is taken to all the voting rights. Where a company other than the investing company (company B) directly holds more than 50% of the voting rights in another company (company C) which is a member of the same group as the investing company, company B is taken to hold all of the voting rights in company C. A person who has the ability to control the exercise of voting rights by another person is treated for this purpose as holding those rights.

[*TCGA 1992, ss 169S(5), 169SA, Sch 7ZA*].

Disposal of trust business assets

[9.8] BADR can be claimed in respect of a '*disposal of trust business assets*', i.e. a disposal, by the trustees of a settlement, of settled property of one of the following types:

(a) shares in, or 'securities' of, a company, or an interest in such shares or securities; or
(b) assets or interests in assets used or previously used for the purposes of a business.

An individual (a '*qualifying beneficiary*') must, under the settlement, have an interest in possession (excluding one for a fixed term) in either the whole of the settled property or a part of it which includes the assets disposed of and the following conditions must be met.

Disposal of shares etc.

Where the disposal is of assets within (a) above, the conditions are that:

- the company is the qualifying beneficiary's 'personal company' (see **9.6** above);
- the company is either a 'trading company' or the 'holding company' of a 'trading group' (see **9.7** above); and
- the qualifying beneficiary is an officer or employee of the company or, where the company is a member of a trading group, of one or more companies which are members of the group.

These conditions must be met throughout a two-year period ending not earlier than three years before the date of disposal.

A disposal of an interest in shares includes a deemed disposal of an interest in shares under *TCGA 1992, s 122* (capital distributions — see **57.11** SHARES AND SECURITIES).

In *Trustees of the Peter Buckley Settlement v HMRC* FTT, [2024] UKFTT 29 (TC), the trustees sold the single share in a trading company. Relief was denied because the qualifying beneficiary did not hold 5% of the shares in his personal capacity (so that the company was not his personal company), but only in his capacity as trustee.

Assets used for the purposes of a business

Where the disposal is of assets within (b) above, conditions are that the assets must be used for the purposes of a business carried on by the qualifying beneficiary throughout a two-year period ending not earlier than three years before the date of the disposal, and the qualifying beneficiary must cease to carry on the business on the date of the disposal or within the three years before that date.

Alternatively, the assets must be used for the purposes of a business carried on by a partnership of which the qualifying beneficiary is a member throughout a two-year period ending not earlier than three years before the date of the disposal, and the qualifying beneficiary must cease to be a member of the partnership, or the partnership must cease to carry on the business, on the date of the disposal or within the three years before that date.

[*TCGA 1992, ss 169J, 169S(2)–(5)*].

In *HMRC v Quentin Skinner 2005 Settlement L* CA, [2022] STC 1795, the CA considered whether an individual had only to be a qualifying beneficiary at the time of disposal (as the FTT had held) or had to have been a qualifying beneficiary throughout the one-year (now two-year) qualifying period (as the UT had held). The CA restored the FTT decision, allowing the taxpayers' appeals. It held that both the 'logical structure and drafting technique' of *TCGA 1992, s 169J* required the reader to consider in turn whether the three ingredients of a qualifying disposal of trust business assets were present. The first ingredient, whether there was a disposal of business assets, was not in dispute. The second was the identification of a qualifying beneficiary. The definition simply required the beneficiary to have an interest in possession at the time of the disposal; there was no requirement in the definition for the interest to have been held for a minimum period. The final ingredient was whether the other conditions were met throughout the one-year period. It was not part of these conditions that the qualifying beneficiary should have had the interest in possession throughout that period. It would have been wholly foreign to the statutory scheme to extract a further condition from the third ingredient that was 'nowhere expressly articulated' and which was 'conspicuously absent' from the definition of a qualifying beneficiary. References to the qualifying beneficiary in the other conditions (and elsewhere in the business asset disposal relief provisions) were simply to the individual who had been identified as such.

Associated disposals

[9.9] Subject to the additional requirements below, where an individual makes a material disposal of business assets (see **9.4** above) which is a disposal of either all or part of their interest in the assets of a partnership or shares in or securities of a company (or an interest in such shares or securities), they may claim BADR in respect of any disposal which is associated with the material disposal (an 'associated disposal'). An individual makes an associated disposal if:

(a) the disposal is made as part of their withdrawal from participation in the business of the partnership or company (or, where the company is a member of a trading group, the business of a member of the trading group); and

(b) the assets which are disposed of (or the assets an interest in which are disposed of) are in use for the purposes of the business throughout the two-year period ending with the earlier of the date of the material disposal of business assets and the cessation of the business of the partnership or company; and

(c) for disposals of assets acquired on or after 13 June 2016, the disposal is of an asset or assets which the individual has owned throughout the three years ending with the date of disposal.

As the disposal must be associated with the material disposal, HMRC consider that there should normally be no significant interval between the disposals. They accept, however, that this will not always be the case, particularly where the business of the partnership or company ceases. They will therefore accept that a disposal of an asset is associated with the material disposal if it takes place:

- within one year of the cessation of a business;
- within three years of the cessation of a business if the asset has not been leased or used for any other purpose at any time after the business ceased; or
- where the business has not ceased, within three years of the material disposal provided the asset has not been used for any purpose other than that of the business.

Where these conditions are not met, the disposal will be considered on its particular facts. If the asset has been used for any other purpose for a significant period, it is unlikely that HMRC will accept that the conditions for relief are satisfied.

(HMRC Capital Gains Manual CG63998).

The following further requirements also apply, depending on the nature of the material disposal of business assets.

Disposal of interest in partnership assets

Where the material disposal consists of the disposal of all or part of the individual's interest in the assets of a partnership, either:

- the disposed of interest must be at least a 5% interest in the partnership's assets and there must be no 'partnership purchase arrangements' at the date of the disposal; or
- if the disposed of interest is an interest of less than 5%, the disposal must be of the whole of the individual's interest, the individual must have held at least a 5% interest in the partnership's assets for a continuous period of at least three years in the eight years ending on the date of the disposal and there must be no partnership purchase arrangements at the date of the disposal.

For this purpose, '*partnership purchase arrangements*' are arrangements (other than the material disposal) under which the individual or a connected person is entitled to acquire an interest in, or an increased interest in, the partnership (including a share of its profits or assets or an interest in such a share). Arrangements are not, however, partnership purchase arrangements if they were made before both the material disposal and the associated disposal and without regard to either of them.

'*Arrangements*' include any agreement, understanding, scheme, transaction or series of transactions (whether or not legally enforceable). A person is considered entitled to acquire anything they are entitled to acquire in the future or will be entitled to acquire at a future date.

The assets of a Scottish partnership or a non-UK partnership, the assets of which are regarded as held by the partnership as such are treated as held by the partners in the proportions in which they are entitled to share in the capital profits.

Disposal of shares

Where the material disposal consists of the disposal of shares in a company (or an interest in such shares), all or some of which are ordinary shares, the ordinary shares disposed of must constitute at least 5% of the company's ordinary share capital and be shares in the individual's 'personal company'.

'*Personal company*' has the same meaning as at **9.6** above. In determining whether the condition at **9.6**(b) above (entitlement to at least 5% of proceeds on disposal of the whole of the ordinary share capital) applies for this purpose, the reference to the final day of the period is taken to be a reference to the date of the disposal.

In addition, there must be no 'share purchase arrangements' at the date of the disposal. For this purpose, '*share purchase arrangements*' are arrangements (other than the material disposal) under which the individual or a connected person is entitled to acquire shares or securities in the company or a company which is a member of the same trading group. Arrangements are not, however, share purchase arrangements if they were made before both the material disposal and the associated disposal and without regard to either of them. Two companies are treated as members of the same trading group if, at the date of the disposal, arrangements exist which it is reasonable to assume will result in them becoming such members.

This requirement is not met if the disposal of shares is a deemed disposal in consideration of a capital distribution within *TCGA 1992, s 122* (see **57.11** SHARES AND SECURITIES) other than one made in the course of dissolving or winding up the company.

Disposal of securities

Where the material disposal consists of the disposal of securities in a company (or an interest in such securities), the securities disposed of must constitute at least 5% of the value of the company's securities and there must be no share purchase arrangements (as above) at the date of the disposal.

Withdrawal from participation

A disposal is not treated as part of an individual's withdrawal from participation within (a) above if there are any partnership purchase arrangements or, as appropriate, share purchase arrangements on the date of disposal.

HMRC consider that it is not necessary that the individual reduce the amount of work that he does for the partnership or company; only that the disposal be related to the required reduction of their interest in the partnership or holding of shares in the company (HMRC Capital Gains Manual CG63998).

[*TCGA 1992, s 169K*].

Claims for business asset disposal relief

[9.10] BADR must be claimed on or before the first anniversary of the 31 January following the tax year in which the qualifying business disposal is made. In the case of a disposal of trust business assets (see **9.8** above), the claim must be made jointly by the trustees and the qualifying beneficiary. [*TCGA 1992, s 169M(1)–(3)*]. Where the taxpayer is temporarily non-resident or claims the remittance basis, so that it is not immediately clear whether or not a chargeable gain will arise in respect of the qualifying business disposal, a protective claim can be made within the time limit (Chartered Institute of Taxation Notice 13 February 2012).

Assets qualifying for business asset disposal relief

[9.11] Except where the qualifying business disposal is of shares or securities or an interest in shares or securities, BADR is given only in respect of the disposal of the following assets, or of interests in the following assets, comprised in a qualifying business disposal.

(a) In the case of a material disposal of business assets (see **9.4** above); assets used for the purposes of a business carried on by the individual or a partnership of which the individual is a member.

(b) In the case of a disposal of trust business assets (see **9.8** above); assets used for the purposes of a business carried on by the qualifying beneficiary or a partnership of which he is a member.

(c) In the case of an associated disposal (see **9.9** above); assets used for the purposes of a business carried on by the partnership or company.

Shares and securities, and other assets held as investments, are excluded from (a)–(c) above.

Goodwill

Goodwill is included in the assets within (a)–(c) above except where a person (P) disposes of goodwill to a close company (or a non-UK resident company which would be a close company if it were UK-resident) and, immediately after the disposal:

(i) P and any 'relevant connected person' together own 5% or more of the ordinary share capital of the company or of any company in the same group; or

(ii) P and any relevant connected person together hold 5% of the voting rights in the company or in any company in the same group; or

(iii) either:

   (A) P and any relevant connected person together are beneficially entitled to at least 5% of the profits available for distribution to the 'equity holders' (see **9.6** above) of the company and would be beneficially entitled, on a winding up, to at least 5% of the assets of the company available for distribution to the equity holders; or

(B) in the event of a disposal of the whole of the company's ordinary share capital, P and any relevant connected person together would be beneficially entitled to at least 5% of the proceeds.

In determining whether (B) above applies, it must be assumed that the disposal takes place at the market value of the shares immediately after the disposal by P and that P and any relevant connected persons are entitled to the proceeds which it would be reasonable to expect them to be entitled to, with regard to all the circumstances at that time. The effect of any avoidance arrangements (i.e. arrangements with a main purpose to secure that any business asset disposal relief provision does or does not apply) is ignored for this purpose.

The exclusion does not, however, apply if P and any relevant connected person dispose of the close company's share capital to another company (company A) so that neither P nor any relevant connected person own any of the ordinary share capital immediately before the end of the period of 28 days beginning with the date of the qualifying business disposal (or such longer period as HMRC allow). If company A is itself a close company (or a non-UK resident company which would be a close company if it were UK-resident), P and any relevant connected person must, immediately before the end of that period, together own less than 5% of the ordinary share capital or voting rights of company A or of any company in the same group. A '*relevant connected person*' means a company connected with P or trustees connected with P.

The exclusion of goodwill from (a)–(c) above also applies to a disposal of goodwill if the person making the disposal is a party to arrangements one of the main purposes of which is to secure that the above exclusion does not apply to the goodwill.

'*Arrangements*' include any agreement, understanding, scheme, transaction or series of transactions (whether or not legally enforceable). '*Associate*', '*control*', '*major interest*' and '*participator*' are as defined at *CTA 2009, ss 836, 837* and *841*.

[*TCGA 1992, ss 169L, 169LA*].

Amount of business asset disposal relief

Basic computation

[9.12] Subject to the application of the lifetime limit and the restrictions on relief at **9.13** and **9.14** below, the amount to which BADR applies is computed by deducting the aggregate 'relevant losses' from the aggregate 'relevant gains'. If the resulting amount is positive, it is then treated as a single chargeable gain accruing at the time of the disposal to the individual or trustees by whom the claim is made, chargeable at a rate of **10%**. The relevant gains and losses taken into account in computing the relief are treated as not themselves being chargeable gains or allowable losses. If the result is negative, no claim to BADR will be appropriate and the relevant gains and losses will be dealt with in the normal way.

For this purpose, '*relevant gains*' are, where the qualifying business disposal is of shares or securities or of interests in shares or securities, the gains on the disposal (computed under normal capital gains tax principles). In any other case, the relevant gains are the gains on the disposal of any assets qualifying for relief (as above) comprised in the qualifying business disposal (again, computed under normal capital gains tax principles). '*Relevant losses*' are losses made in circumstances in which a gain would be a relevant gain, computed under normal capital gains tax principles on the assumption that notice has been given under *TCGA 1992, s 16(2A)* (notification of capital loss — see **38.5** LOSSES) in respect of them.

Gains to which BADR applies are taxed in priority to other gains. This means that any unused part of the basic rate limit is set against gains taxed at 10% as a result of BADR (or an investors' relief claim) before any other gains. The annual exempt amount can, however, be allocated against gains as the taxpayer chooses. See **2.1** ANNUAL RATES AND EXEMPTIONS.

Application of lifetime limit

Business asset disposal relief is subject to a lifetime limit of £1 million, which applies as follows.

The amount to which relief would otherwise apply in respect of a qualifying business disposal is added to any amounts to which relief applied in respect of earlier qualifying business disposals. Where the total exceeds the limit, only so much (if any) of the amount to which relief would otherwise apply in respect of the current disposal as, together with the earlier amounts, does not exceed the limit qualifies for the relief. Any part of the deemed gain excluded by the application of this rule is chargeable at the normal rates of CGT.

The earlier qualifying business disposals to be taken into account are:

- where the current qualifying business disposal is made by an individual, earlier qualifying business disposals made by them and earlier disposals of trust business assets (see **9.8** above) in respect of which they are the qualifying beneficiary; and
- where the current qualifying business disposal is a disposal of trust business assets in respect of which an individual is the qualifying beneficiary, earlier disposals of trust business assets in respect of which that individual is the qualifying beneficiary and earlier qualifying business disposals made by that individual.

Where there is a disposal of trust business assets in respect of which an individual is the qualifying beneficiary and a qualifying business disposal by that individual on the same day, then, in applying the lifetime limit, the disposal of trust business assets is treated as the later event.

Disposals before 6 April 2008 do not affect the lifetime limit except in the case of deferred gains on which business asset disposal relief is claimed under the transitional rules at **9.16–9.17** below.

It is the taxpayer's responsibility to keep records of claims to enable the application of the lifetime limit. Where BADR is claimed by a remittance basis user, it is HMRC's view that the lifetime limit to apply in respect of remittance basis gains is the limit in force when the gains arise (HMRC Capital Gains Manual CG63956).

Changes in the lifetime limit

The lifetime limit for BADR has changed several times since its introduction in 2008. For disposals before 11 March 2020, it was £10 million; £5 million for disposals before 6 April 2011; £2 million for disposals before 23 June 2010; £1 million for disposals before 6 April 2010. The first reduction in the limit therefore took effect for disposals on or after 11 March 2020 and anti-forestalling rules applied to prevent taxpayers from circumventing the reduction. See the 2023/24 and earlier editions of this work.

Where a lifetime limit was exceeded on disposals made before an increase to the limit, no further relief could be obtained for those disposals following the increase. Relief could, however, be obtained for qualifying business disposals on or after the date of increase up to the appropriate new limit. Relief on disposals before 11 March 2020 is not withdrawn as a result of the reduction in the lifetime limit.

Where BADR is claimed by a remittance basis user, it is HMRC's view that the lifetime limit to apply in respect of remittance basis gains is the limit in force when the gains arise (HMRC Capital Gains Manual CG63956).

[*TCGA 1992, ss 169M(4), 169N; FA 2020, s 23, Sch 3 paras 1, 2*].

Example 1

In May 2024, Mr Henry sells his business, Joe's Toys, which he has owned since 1998, to an unrelated party, realising the following chargeable gains and allowable losses.

	Gain/(loss)
	£
Goodwill	700,000
Freehold shop 1	200,000
Freehold shop 2	200,000
Freehold shop 3	(150,000)

Mr Henry claims business asset disposal relief in respect of the sale of the business. He has made no previous claim to business asset disposal relief. He makes no other disposals in 2024/25.

Mr Henry's capital gains tax liability for 2024/25 is calculated as follows.

	£
Gains qualifying for business asset disposal relief	
Goodwill	700,000
Freehold shop 1	200,000
Freehold shop 2	200,000
	1,100,000
Less Loss on freehold shop 3	150,000
Deemed chargeable gain qualifying for business asset disposal relief	950,000
Annual exempt amount	3,000
Gain chargeable to tax	£947,000

Capital gains tax payable (£947,000 × 10%)	£94,700

Mr Henry has used £950,000 of his lifetime limit of £1 million. Any subsequent BADR claim will therefore be restricted to gains of £50,000.

Example 2

In August 2024, Mr Robertson sells his entire shareholding in Robbie Ltd, realising a gain of £1,050,000, which qualifies for BADR. Mr Robertson makes no other disposals in 2024/25 and has made no previous disposals qualifying for business asset disposal relief. He is an additional rate income taxpayer for 2024/25.

Mr Robertson's capital gains tax liability for 2024/25 is calculated as follows.

	£
Deemed chargeable gain qualifying for business asset disposal relief (subject to lifetime limit £1,000,000)	1,050,000
Annual exempt amount	3,000
Gain chargeable to tax	£1,047,000
Capital gains tax payable	
£1,000,000 × 10%	100,000
£47,000 × 20%	9,400
	£109,400

Note to the example

(a) The annual exempt amount of £3,000 is allocated against the part of the gain chargeable to tax at 20% as this gives the greater tax saving.

Example 3

In May 2024, Mr Helm sells his entire shareholding in Levon Ltd for £400,000. He had acquired the shares in March 2018 for £150,000 and has been a director of the company since that time. Levon Ltd is a trading company and qualifies as Mr Helm's personal company. He makes no other disposals in 2024/25 and has made no previous claims to BADR. He claims BADR in respect of the gain on the shares. Mr Helm made another gain on the disposal of an investment asset during 2024/25 which used the annual exempt amount.

Mr Helm's capital gains tax liability for 2024/25 on the sale of the shares is calculated as follows.

	£
Sale proceeds	400,000
Cost	150,000
Chargeable gain qualifying for business asset disposal relief	250,000
Capital gains tax payable (£250,000 × 10%)	£25,000

Following the disposal of his shares in Levon Ltd, Mr Helm buys a 25% shareholding in Amy Ltd, another trading company, for £200,000, and starts work as a director of the company. He continues as a director of the company until May 2027, when he sells his entire shareholding for £1,100,000. He claims business asset disposal relief in respect of the disposal. He makes no other disposals in 2027/28, but pays income tax at the additional rate. It is assumed for the purpose of this example only that the annual exempt amount for 2027/28 is £3,000 and the rates of tax remain as for 2024/25.

Mr Helm's capital gains tax liability for 2027/28 is calculated as follows.

	£
Sale proceeds	1,100,000
Cost	200,000
Chargeable gain qualifying for BADR (subject to lifetime limit £1,000,000)	900,000
Annual exempt amount	3,000
Gain chargeable to tax	£897,000
Capital gains tax payable	
£750,000 × 10%	75,000
£147,000 × 20%	29,400
	£104,400

Notes to the example

(a) The lifetime limit applies to restrict the amount of the gain in 2027/28 which qualifies for BADR as follows. Of the limit of £1,000,000, £250,000 was used in 2024/25 leaving (£1,000,000 – £250,000) = £750,000 unused. As the otherwise qualifying gain for 2027/28 is greater than the unused part of the limit, BADR is restricted so that the 10% rate applies to £750,000.

(b) The annual exempt amount of £3,000 is allocated against the part of the gain chargeable to tax at 20% as this gives the greater tax saving.

Restriction on business asset disposal relief for trust disposals

[9.13] BADR on a disposal of trust business assets (see 9.8 above) is restricted where there is, in addition to the qualifying beneficiary, at least one other beneficiary who, at the 'material time', has an interest in possession in either the whole of the settled property or a part of it which includes the assets, or interests in the assets, disposed of.

In such circumstances, relief applies only to a proportion of the amount to which it would otherwise apply. The remainder of that amount is treated as a chargeable gain to which the normal rate of CGT applies.

The proportion is the same as the proportion which, at the material time, the qualifying beneficiary's interest in the income of the part of the settled property comprising the assets, or interests in the assets, disposed of bears to the interests in that income of all the beneficiaries, including the qualifying beneficiary, who then have interests in possession in that part of the settled property.

For this purpose, the '*material time*' is the end of the latest two-year period ending not earlier than three years before the date of the disposal throughout which:

- in the case of a disposal of shares or securities or interests in shares or securities, the conditions at **9.8** above for such disposals are satisfied; or
- in the case of a disposal of assets, or interests in assets, used or previously used for the purposes of a business, the business is carried on by the qualifying beneficiary.

In calculating the proportion above, only the interest by virtue of which the qualifying beneficiary is the qualifying beneficiary is taken into account in calculating his interest in the income of the part of the settled property concerned (and not any other interest they may have).

[*TCGA 1992, s 169O*].

Restriction on business asset disposal relief for associated disposals

[9.14] BADR on an associated disposal (see **9.9** above) is also restricted where:

(a) the assets which are disposed of (or interests in which are disposed of) are in use for the purposes of the business only for part of the period in which they are owned by the individual;
(b) only part of those assets are in use for the purposes of the business for that period;
(c) the individual is concerned in the carrying on of the business (personally, in partnership or as an officer or employee of his personal company) for only part of the period in which the assets are in use for the purposes of the business; or
(d) for any part of the period for which the assets are in use for the purposes of the business, their availability is dependent on the payment of rent (which term includes any form of consideration given for the use of an asset). Any part of the period falling before 6 April 2008 is ignored for this purpose.

Where any of the above apply, relief applies only to such part of the amount to which business asset disposal relief would otherwise apply as is just and reasonable. The remainder of that amount is treated as a chargeable gain to which the normal CGT rates apply. In applying the 'just and reasonable' test, regard is to be had to the following:

(i) where (a) above applies, the length of the period for which the assets are in use for the purposes of the business;
(ii) where (b) above applies, the part of the assets that are in use for the purposes of the business;
(iii) where (c) above applies, the length of the period for which the individual is concerned in the carrying on of the business; and
(iv) where (d) above applies, the extent to which the rent paid is less than the rent which would be payable in the open market.

[*TCGA 1992, ss 169P, 169S(5)*].

For HMRC's approach to the restriction, including worked examples, see HMRC Capital Gains Manual CG64145.

Business asset disposal relief where shareholding in personal company diluted by share issue

[9.15] Special rules apply where BADR would otherwise become unavailable because a company ceases to be an individual's personal company as a result of the company issuing additional shares (so that the 5% ownership threshold is no longer met (see **9.4**(c) above)). The individual can make either one or two elections to retain the benefit of BADR.

References below to shares or securities include interests in shares or securities.

[*TCGA 1992, ss 169SB, 169SC(7)*].

Election for deemed disposal of shares or securities

An individual can make an election where, as a result of an issue of shares by a company for consideration wholly in cash, the company ceases to be their personal company. The shares must be subscribed and issued for genuine commercial reasons and not as part of arrangements to secure a tax advantage (as defined) for any person.

An election can only be made if a disposal of all the individual's shares and/or securities in the company immediately before the share issue at their 'relevant value' would have been a material disposal of business assets resulting in a single chargeable gain (see **9.12** above) qualifying for business asset disposal relief (the '*notional gain*').

Where such an election is made, the individual is treated for CGT purposes as having disposed of all of their shares or securities in the company immediately before the share issue and having reacquired them immediately afterwards at their relevant value. The effect of the election is therefore to trigger a chargeable gain, equal to the notional gain, which qualifies for BADR.

For a deemed disposal of shares, the '*relevant value*' is the amount that would be apportioned to the shares on a sale of the entire issued share capital at market value immediately before the share issue. Otherwise, the relevant value is the market value of the asset at the time of the share issue.

[*TCGA 1992, s 169SC*].

Supplementary election to defer deemed gains until subsequent disposal

Where an individual makes an election for a deemed disposal of shares or securities, an additional election may be made so that no chargeable gain or allowable loss is treated as arising on the deemed disposal but instead all or part of the notional gain is deferred. All or part of the gain is then treated as arising when the individual subsequently disposes of any of the shares or securities. The gain is in addition to any actual gain or loss arising on the disposal.

Where not all of the shares and/or securities are disposed of, the amount of the notional gain brought into charge is calculated by taking the following steps.

Step 1. The notional gain is attributed to each of the classes of shares in or securities of the company which are the subject of the deemed disposal. The attribution is made by reference to the deemed relevant gain on each class (see **9.12** above).

Step 2. The amounts identified in Step 1 are apportioned to the shares or securities of each class which are actually disposed of. This is done by reference to the nominal value of the shares or securities of that class.

Step 3. The amount of the notional gain to be brought into charge is the total of the amounts apportioned in Step 2. For each class, however, the amount included cannot exceed the amount attributed to the class in Step 1 less any amount already taken into account under these provisions in respect of any previous disposals.

Where the subsequent disposal is a capital distribution (under *TCGA 1992, s 122* – see **57.11** SHARES AND SECURITIES), the apportionment in Step 2 is made as if all of the shares of the class in question that were included in the deemed disposal were actually disposed of.

[*TCGA 1992, s 169SD*].

Reorganisations

Where, following the making of the above elections, there is a reorganisation of share capital to which *TCGA 1992, ss 127–130* (see **57.2** SHARES AND SECURITIES) apply, on a subsequent disposal of all or part of the 'new holding', any necessary apportionment of the notional gain between shares or securities forming part of the new holding must be made in the same proportions as those in which the costs of acquisition of the original shares were apportioned under the reorganisation provisions. If the taxpayer received consideration other than the new holding on the reorganisation, they are treated for the purposes of the above provisions as having disposed of an interest in the original shares at the time of the reorganisation. [*TCGA 1992, s 169SF*].

Where, following the making of the above elections, there is a reorganisation of share capital involving the acquisition of QUALIFYING CORPORATE BONDS (**48.4**), a gain must be calculated under the above provisions as if the reorganisation had been a disposal of the shares in question. The gain is not immediately charged, however, but is deferred until there is a subsequent disposal of some or all of the qualifying corporate bonds. The whole or a corresponding part of the gain is then treated as a chargeable gain at that time, in addition to any actual gain or loss on the disposal and any gain deemed to arise under *TCGA 1992, s 116* (see **48.4** QUALIFYING CORPORATE BONDS). [*TCGA 1992, s 169SE*].

Making of elections and claims

Both of the above elections are irrevocable.

An election for a deemed disposal of shares or securities must be made on or before the first anniversary of 31 January following the tax year in which the deemed disposal is made. An election to defer the gain until the shares or securities are disposed of must be made within four years of the end of that tax year.

If an individual makes both elections and a tax return would not otherwise be required for the tax year in which the deemed disposal is made, they can make the elections by giving notice to HMRC on or before the first anniversary of 31 January following that tax year.

Where an election to defer the deemed gain has been made, the taxpayer must make a claim for business asset disposal relief on or before the first anniversary of 31 January following the first tax year in which the gain is brought into charge. Relief is then given as if the gain arises from a qualifying business disposal made when the gain is brought into charge. Where only a part of the gain is brought back into charge, relief for subsequent gains is similarly given as if they arose from a qualifying business disposal made when they are brought back into charge. In either case, the company is deemed to be the taxpayer's personal company throughout the two years ending with the time the gain is brought into charge.

[*TCGA 1992, ss 169SG, 169SH*].

Business asset disposal relief and deferred gains

[9.16] Where a chargeable gain (the '*first eventual gain*') arises as result of a chargeable event under either of the ENTERPRISE INVESTMENT SCHEME (**22.16**) or SOCIAL INVESTMENT RELIEF (**59.14**) deferral reliefs, the gain will qualify for BADR if:

(a) the original disposal took place on or after 3 December 2014;
(b) the original gain would, but for its deferral, have arisen from a material disposal of business assets (within **9.4** above) or an associated disposal (within **9.9** above); and
(c) the first eventual gain is the first gain brought into charge in respect of the deferred original gain (so that if a previous chargeable event had resulted in a gain in respect of part of the original gain becoming chargeable and no claim to BADR was made, no such claim may be made on a subsequent chargeable event).

Where a gain has been deferred more than once, the conditions in (a) and (b) above must be satisfied by the first gain to be deferred. For the purposes of (b) above, whether a disposal would have been a material disposal of business assets or a disposal associated with such a disposal is determined according to the law applicable at the time of that disposal.

A claim for relief must be made on or before the first anniversary of 31 January following the tax year in which the first eventual gain arises. Where such a claim is made, the first eventual gain is treated as if it were an amount resulting from a basic computation within **9.12** above in respect of a qualifying business disposal made when that gain arose. The gain is then ignored for any other chargeable gains purposes. If the first eventual gain does not represent the whole of the deferred gain, any remaining part of the gain brought into charge on a subsequent chargeable event is treated in the same way (but the qualifying business disposal is treated as occurring at the time of the later gain). No further claim is required.

If the disposal in (b) above would have been an associated disposal, the relief for the deemed qualifying business disposal is subject to the restriction in **9.14** above (applied by reference to the disposal in (b) above).

[*TCGA 1992, ss 169T–169V*].

Transitional relief for enterprise investment scheme and venture capital trust deferral reliefs

Business asset disposal relief can be claimed where a chargeable gain (the '*original gain*') which would have accrued before the introduction of the relief (i.e. before 6 April 2008) has been deferred under either the enterprise investment scheme (see **22.16** ENTERPRISE INVESTMENT SCHEME) or venture capital trusts scheme (see **64.8** VENTURE CAPITAL TRUSTS) and there is a chargeable event on or after that date in relation to any of the 'relevant shares' still held by the original investor immediately before the first such chargeable event. For this purpose, the '*relevant shares*' are the shares acquired in making the investment by virtue of which EIS or VCT deferral relief applies to the original gain and, in a case where the original gain accrued at a time after the making of the investment, still held at that time.

For BADR to apply in such circumstances, the 'relevant disposal' must have been such that, had the provisions of this chapter then applied, it would have been a material disposal of business assets (see **9.4** above). The '*relevant disposal*' is normally the disposal on which the original gain would have accrued but for the deferral. Where, however, the original gain itself arose on the occurrence of a chargeable event under the EIS or VCT deferral provisions or to give effect to a withdrawal under *TCGA 1992, s 164F* or *164FA* of general reinvestment relief (see **23.80** EXEMPTIONS AND RELIEFS), the relevant disposal is the disposal (not being a deemed disposal on the occurrence of a chargeable event) by virtue of which the deferral provisions first had effect.

Where BADR is claimed, the amount treated under the EIS or VCT deferral relief provisions as accruing on the chargeable event in respect of the original gain is the amount that would be arrived at under the rules at **9.12** above if the chargeable event were a qualifying business disposal and the amount to which relief applies were the proportion of the postponed gain equal to the proportion of the relevant shares held by the investor immediately before the first chargeable event on or after 6 April 2008. Where the chargeable event in question is a chargeable event in relation only to a proportion of the relevant shares held by the investor immediately before the first chargeable event on or after 6 April 2008, however, only a corresponding proportion of that amount is taken to be the amount accruing under the deferral provisions.

A claim for business asset disposal relief to apply in the above circumstances must be made on or before the first anniversary of the 31 January following the tax year in which the first chargeable event on or after 6 April 2008 occurs.

[*FA 2008, Sch 3 para 8*].

Business asset disposal relief and reorganisations

[9.17] Where a reorganisation of share capital (within *TCGA 1992, s 126* — see **57.2** SHARES AND SECURITIES) takes place and *TCGA 1992, s 127* would otherwise apply to treat the 'original shares' and the 'new holding' (as defined for the purposes of that section — see **57.2**) as the same asset, an election can be made to disapply that section so that BADR can be claimed in respect of the disposal of the original shares. (Note that the disapplication of *s 127* takes effect only where a claim to BADR is made; without such a claim, the election has no effect.)

The election must be made on or before the first anniversary of the 31 January following the tax year in which the reorganisation takes place (which date is also the time limit for making the claim for relief — see **9.10** above). If the reorganisation would, if treated as a disposal, involve a disposal of trust business assets (see **9.8** above), the election must be made jointly by the trustees and the qualifying beneficiary.

The above provision applies also to exchanges of securities within *TCGA 1992, s 135* (see **57.5** SHARES AND SECURITIES) and to schemes of reconstruction within *TCGA 1992, s 136* (see **57.7** SHARES AND SECURITIES) to which *TCGA 1992, s 127* applies.

[*TCGA 1992, s 169Q*].

Reorganisations involving acquisition of qualifying corporate bonds

Where there is a reorganisation of share capital involving the acquisition of qualifying corporate bonds and the calculation required as a result by *TCGA 1992, s 116(10)(a)* produces a (deferred) chargeable gain for an individual (see **48.4**(a) QUALIFYING CORPORATE BONDS), the provisions of this chapter apply as follows.

An election can be made so that a claim for BADR can in turn be made on the basis that the reorganisation involved a disposal of the 'old asset'. Where such a claim is made, *TCGA 1992, s 116(10)* is disapplied so that a gain on the old asset will arise at the time of the reorganisation and can qualify for BADR (if all the conditions are satisfied).

The election must be made on or before the first anniversary of the 31 January following the tax year in which the reorganisation takes place (which date is also the time limit for making the claim for relief — see **9.10** above). If the reorganisation would, if treated as a disposal, involve a disposal of trust business assets (see **9.8** above), the election must be made jointly by the trustees and the qualifying beneficiary.

If no election is made and the gain on the old asset is therefore deferred, it is likely that, in almost all cases, the gain will not qualify for BADR when it comes into charge at a later date.

Definitions

'Old asset' and 'new asset' are defined for this purpose as at **48.4** QUALIFYING CORPORATE BONDS.

[*TCGA 1992, s 169R*].

Transitional relief for reorganisations involving acquisition of qualifying corporate bonds before 6 April 2008

Relief can be available where a chargeable gain is deemed to accrue to an individual on a disposal after the introduction of BADR (i.e. on or after 6 April 2008) (a '*relevant disposal*') under *TCGA 1992, s 116(10)(b)* (see **48.4**(b)

QUALIFYING CORPORATE BONDS) by reason of a reorganisation to which that individual was a party and which took place before that date. In such circumstances, BADR can be claimed (provided that the other conditions are satisfied) as if the reorganisation were a disposal of the 'old asset' by the individual, even though the deemed disposal was made before 6 April 2008.

The amount to which BADR applies is (subject to the lifetime limit (see **9.12** above)) the amount of the deferred chargeable gain calculated under *TCGA 1992, s 116(10)(a)* (see **48.4**(a) QUALIFYING CORPORATE BONDS) less any part of it deemed to accrue before 6 April 2008.

'Old asset' and 'new asset' are defined for this purpose as at **48.4** QUALIFYING CORPORATE BONDS.

Where the above provisions apply, a claim must be made on or before the first anniversary of the 31 January following the tax year in which the first disposal on or after 6 April 2008 of the whole or part of the new asset is made.

[*FA 2008, Sch 3 para 7*].

Key points concerning business asset disposal relief

[9.18] Points to consider are as follows.

- BADR is subject to a lifetime limit, so it is necessary to obtain details of any previous qualifying disposals since its introduction in 2008/09. The lifetime limit has also changed four times since its introduction. The current limit is £1 million for disposals on or after 11 March 2020. Qualifying gains are taxed at 10%. Assuming that the gains would otherwise be taxed at 20%, the lifetime tax saving is therefore £100,000.
- The relief is aimed at gains arising on the disposal of a business (or part of a business) and can include gains arising on the disposal of shares in an individual's personal company (broadly a trading company where the individual owns at least 5%) and shares acquired under the enterprise management incentives scheme. The relief can be available to trustees in certain circumstances.
- Special rules apply where relief would otherwise become unavailable because a company ceases to be an individual's personal company as a result of the company issuing additional shares (so that the 5% ownership threshold is no longer met). The individual can make either one or two elections to retain the benefit of business asset disposal relief up to the date of issue.
- Capital gains tax planning can seek to maximise relief. However, it is complex and easy to fall foul of the various conditions. Some common areas to watch:
  - Giving shares to a spouse or civil partner. This can originally occur for a number of reasons, such as to utilise their basic rate bands. However, it is worth ensuring the spouse meets the requirements to potentially qualify for BADR in their

own right. For example, sufficient length of ownership (24 months) qualifies as personal company (5%) and officer or employee (role of company secretary often popular). A spouse or civil partner does not inherit their partner's entitlement to BADR and must qualify in their own right.

- Commercial property owned outside the company, e.g. business premises. When commercial property is owned outside a company, it can still qualify for BADR as an associated disposal (in relation to a material disposal of shares or securities in the company) provided the asset was used for business purposes for the relevant period and has been owned for at least three years. However, relief is restricted where rent is paid. This can create problems, especially where the purchase of the property has been funded by a mortgage (the individual needs to fund the loan repayments). It may therefore be worth comparing individual ownership to corporate ownership or, where possible, ownership by a self-invested pension plan (SIPP).
- Does the company/group qualify as 'trading'? If investment activity is significant can the position be improved with corporate restructuring?
- Business property relief for IHT. Although a disposal may potentially qualify for BADR, is it advantageous and possible for the taxpayer to retain assets qualifying for BPR, as on death, there may be no charge to IHT and uplift to market value for capital gains tax?
- Is the sale of 'part of a business' or merely a disposal of business assets? The relief applies to the disposal of part of a business, but not assets, unless trading has ceased. HMRC believe the 'part' sold should be separately identifiable in its own right. This is a complex area giving rise to case law such as *M Gilbert v HMRC* FTT, [2011] UKFTT 705 (TC).
- Shares and securities can qualify for BADR even though they do not count towards the 'personal company' requirement. For example, non-voting shares can qualify provided the individual meets the 'personal company' condition via other shares they hold.
- A shareholder can, in theory, make several disposals of shares over a number of years in the same company and claim BADR on all gains provided they can meet the personal company, trading, ownership period and employment tests for each disposal.
- The conditions for BADR generally need to be satisfied for at least two years up to the date of disposal or cessation of the business. Where possible, consideration should be given to whether the conditions are met well in advance of a contemplated disposal so that remedial action can be taken to ensure that BADR will be available.

The relief needs to be claimed — it is not automatic.

10

Capital Sums Derived from Assets

Cross-references. See 7 ASSETS; 33.1 INTERACTION WITH OTHER TAXES; 35.7 and 35.9 LAND for small part disposals of land.

Simon's Taxes. See C1.319.

Introduction to capital sums derived from assets

[10.1] There is a disposal of an asset by its owner where any capital sum is derived from it, even though an asset may not be acquired by the person paying the sum. Accordingly, a chargeable gain or allowable loss will normally result from the receipt of such a sum. Circumstances where this rule applies may include, for example, the receipt of compensation for damage or loss or payment for use of an asset. This rule can be disapplied in certain cases where the capital sum is applied in restoring the asset or where the sum is small as compared with the value of the asset. Where an asset has been lost or destroyed and the capital sum received in compensation is used to acquire a replacement asset, the gain on the deemed disposal under the above provisions can be deferred by treating the disposal as giving rise to neither a gain nor a loss (and reducing the acquisition cost of the new asset accordingly). Partial relief is also available.

General rule for capital sums derived from assets

[10.2] Subject to 10.3, 10.4 and the exception below, there is a disposal of assets by their owner where any 'capital sum' is *derived from* them, 'notwithstanding that no asset is acquired by the person paying the capital sum' (which means 'whether or not an asset is acquired', see *Marren v Ingles* HL 1980, 54 TC 76). See also *Kirby v Thorn EMI plc* CA 1987, 60 TC 519.

For general consideration of what constitutes an 'asset' for tax purposes, see 7.2 ASSETS.

'*Capital sum*' means any money or money's worth which is not otherwise excluded from the computation of chargeable gains.

The provisions apply in particular to capital sums received as follows (other than those brought into charge to income tax).

(a) By way of compensation for any kind of damage or injury to assets or for the loss, destruction or dissipation of assets or for any depreciation or risk of depreciation of an asset.
Following *Stoke-on-Trent City Council v Wood Mitchell & Co Ltd* CA 1978, [1979] STC 197, any element of compensation paid for the acquisition of business property by an authority possessing powers of compulsory acquisition which relates to temporary loss of profits is treated as a trading receipt. Compensation for losses on trading stock and to reimburse revenue expenditure, such as removal expenses and interest, are similarly treated. (HMRC Statement of Practice SP 8/79). See also *Lang v Rice* CA (NI) 1983, 57 TC 80 and **33.1** INTERACTION WITH OTHER TAXES.
In *Pennine Raceway Ltd v Kirklees Metropolitan Borough Council* CA, 1988, [1989] STC 122, to which the Revenue was not a party, the company held a licence to conduct motor racing in accordance with existing planning permission. Compensation under *Town and Country Planning Act 1971* paid by the local authority for revoking the planning permission was held to be derived from the licence, the value of which had been depreciated.

(b) Under a policy of insurance of the risk of any kind of damage or injury to, or the loss or depreciation of, assets.

(c) In return for the forfeiture or surrender of rights or for refraining from exercising rights.
Statutory compensation payable to agricultural tenants under *Agricultural Holdings Act 1986, ss 60, 64* or under *Agricultural Tenancies Act 1995, s 16* and to business tenants under *Landlord and Tenant Act 1954, s 37* is not chargeable to capital gains tax. This follows the decision in *Davis v Powell* Ch D 1976, 51 TC 492 where a tenant quit the holding in consequence of a notice to quit.
Following the decisions in *Davis v Henderson* (Sp C 46), [1995] SSCD 308 and *Pritchard v Purves* (Sp C 47), [1995] SSCD 316, where a tenant is issued with a notice to quit and quits before the expiry of the notice period in return for payments made by his landlord under a surrender agreement, HMRC does not consider that the part of the landlord's payment that represents statutory compensation is chargeable to capital gains tax. (Revenue Tax Bulletin April 1996 pp 303, 304). (Grants for giving up agricultural land may be specifically exempt.) Compensation under *Landlord and Tenant Act 1954, Pt II* to a tenant giving up possession is similarly excluded (*Drummond v Austin Brown* CA 1984, 58 TC 67).

(d) As consideration for use or exploitation of assets.

Time of disposal under (a) to (d) above is when the capital sum is received.

The above provision does not apply where a company receives, or becomes entitled to receive, a capital distribution (within *TCGA 1992, s 122* — see **57.11** SHARES AND SECURITIES) or a distribution to which a charge under *CTA 2009, Pt 9A* applies or would apply were the distribution not exempt.

[*TCGA 1992, s 22*].

HMRC consider that *TCGA 1992, s 22* does not change the normal meaning of the word 'owner' so all that the provision needs for it to apply is that the person receiving the capital sum has, or had, beneficial ownership of the asset, and the receipt of a capital sum derived from that ownership. They cite the case of an asset being damaged prior to its sale where a claim for compensation results in compensation being received after the time of sale. Unless the owner has assigned their rights to compensation, the receipt of compensation will be chargeable within the provision. (HMRC Capital Gains Manual CG12975).

See *British Telecommunications plc v HMRC* (Sp C 535), [2006] SSCD 347 where a payment received (in unusual circumstances) on the termination of a merger agreement was held not to constitute a capital sum derived from an asset.

A right to unquantified and contingent future consideration on the disposal of an asset is itself an asset and the future consideration, if received, is a capital sum derived from that asset (*Marren v Ingles* above and *Marson v Marriage* Ch D 1979, 54 TC 59), but see **57.6** SHARES AND SECURITIES for mitigation of this principle in the case of 'earn-outs'.

Entire loss, destruction etc. of asset

The *entire* loss, destruction, dissipation or extinction of an asset (whether or not any capital sum is received as above) constitutes a disposal of that asset (with certain exceptions for options as in **7.7** ASSETS). (The fact that the asset may be a capital asset employed in a business makes no difference to this tax treatment — see Revenue Tax Bulletin December 1997 pp 490, 491.)

For this purpose, land and buildings may be regarded as separate assets so that where there is a deemed disposal of a building, the land comprising the site of the building (including any land occupied for purposes ancillary to the use of that building) is treated as if it were sold and immediately reacquired at its then market value. Where, however, the asset is a leasehold interest in a building or structure by reference to which a person is entitled to a structures and buildings allowance under *CAA 2001, Pt 2A*, this rule is disapplied. The land and building or structure are still treated as separate assets but there is no deemed disposal of the land. An irrevocable election can be made to disapply the special treatment (so that there is a deemed disposal of the land). Such an election must be made by the person deemed to dispose of the building or structure by notice to HMRC by the first anniversary of 31 January following the tax year of the deemed disposal (or, for corporation tax purposes, within two years of the end of the accounting period of the deemed disposal).

[*TCGA 1992, s 24(1)(3)–(3F)*].

Where a person (P) makes a deemed disposal under *TCGA 1992, s 24(1)* of an interest in a building or structure which is either an interest in UK land (within the meaning of *TCGA 1992, s 1C*) or an equivalent interest in land outside the UK and another person (the contributor) has received a capital allowance under *CAA 2001, s 538A* (contribution allowances) in relation to the building or structure, the contributor may claim an allowable loss equal to the 'unclaimed allowance amount'. This applies only if the contributor does not have an interest in the building or structure which is an interest in UK land (within *s 1C*). A claim must identify the building or structure and quantify the unclaimed allowance amount.

The '*unclaimed allowance amount*' is the difference between the amount in respect of which the contribution allowance was originally available (so far as not allowable as a deduction in computing the gain on the deemed disposal by P) and the total contribution allowances to which the contributor was entitled before the deemed disposal (on the assumption that the allowance was available at all times since an entitlement to the allowance first arose).

[*TCGA 1992, s 24A*].

See also the treatment under *TCGA 1992, s 23(4)(5)* in **10.3** below. For relief where the value of an asset becomes *negligible*, see **38.10** LOSSES.

Compensation for deprivation of foreign assets

Subject to the conditions below, a capital sum is not treated as giving rise to a chargeable gain on the person entitled to receive it, where it is received as compensation for the loss or deprivation of property then situated outside the UK. The payment of the compensation must be:

(i) under a statutory order under *Foreign Compensation Act 1950* or under equivalent arrangements set up by foreign governments; or
(ii) in consequence of a recommendation of the Spoliation Advisory Panel (set up by the Government to consider claims for the return of cultural items looted during the Nazi era (1933–1945)) or of any non-UK equivalent body; or
(iii) in settlement of legal claims to the effect that the deprivation was unlawful or in accordance with a judgment to that effect.

Deprivation of property includes its sale under duress for less than market value. Payment of a capital sum includes a payment as a result of the abandonment or extinguishment of rights in respect of the deprivation or the return of the asset itself.

The provision applies only where no form of legal redress was available to the owner at the time the property was confiscated, expropriated or destroyed and where a claim is made.

If the capital sum is paid to a person other than the person who owned the asset at the time of the deprivation, the provision can still apply provided that no consideration has been given (whether by that person or another) for the right to receive the compensation. Any consideration given for a no gain/no loss transfer of the right between spouses or group companies is, however, ignored for this purpose.

If an allowable capital loss has been established in consequence of the loss or deprivation, the provision does not apply to so much of the gain as is equal to the allowable loss claimed.

Where this provision applies to a capital sum paid by means of a transfer of an asset or the foreign asset is returned, that asset is treated as acquired for its market value at the time of the transfer or return.

This provision does not apply to a gain to which *TCGA 1992, s 268A* (exemption for gain on disposal of right to receive interest on deposit of victim of Nazi persecution — see **23.14** EXEMPTIONS AND RELIEFS) applies.

[*TCGA 1992, s 268B*].

Capital sums applied in restoring assets and small capital sums

[10.3] Where a capital sum within **10.2**(a)–(d) above is derived from an asset which is not lost or destroyed, the recipient may claim under *TCGA 1992, s 23(1)* that the asset is not treated as disposed of, provided the capital sum is:

(a) wholly applied in restoring the asset; or
(b) (subject to the following) applied in restoring the asset (not being a wasting asset) except for a part which is not reasonably required for the purpose and which is 'small' compared with the whole capital sum; or
(c) (subject to the following) 'small' as compared with the value of the asset (not being a wasting asset).

'*Small*' for the purposes of (b) and (c) above is normally taken by HMRC to mean the greater of an amount not exceeding 5% and £3,000 (HMRC Capital Gains Manual CG15703). Additionally, for small part disposals of land, see **35.7** and **35.9** LAND.

If the receipt is not treated as a disposal, the capital sum is deducted from the allowable expenditure on a subsequent disposal. [*TCGA 1992, s 23(1)(6)(8)(a)*].

Where the allowable expenditure relating to the asset (not being a wasting asset) immediately prior to the receipt of the capital sum (including the cost of any restoration work before receipt) is less than the capital sum (or is nil), (b) and (c) above do not apply, but the recipient may elect under *TCGA 1992, s 23(2)* to reduce the capital sum by the amount of any allowable expenditure. The balance of the capital sum is treated as a part disposal. The capital sum so utilised cannot be deducted again either on the part disposal or any subsequent disposal of the asset by the recipient. [*TCGA 1992, s 23(2)(6)(8)(a)*]. Where the capital sum received is subsequently wholly applied in restoring the asset, the recipient may alternatively make a claim as under (a) above for the asset not to be disposed of.

If part only of the capital sum within **10.2**(a) or (b) derived from an asset is applied in restoring the asset (but not sufficient so as to fall within (b) above) the recipient may claim under *TCGA 1992, s 23(3)* to have the part so applied deducted from any allowable expenditure on a subsequent disposal. The balance of the capital sum is treated as a part disposal of the asset. [*TCGA 1992, s 23(3)(6)(8)*]. In the part disposal computation, HMRC take the market value after any restoration work.

Where *TCGA 1992, s 23(1)* or *(3)* above applies in the case of a wasting asset, the amount of the allowable expenditure from which the appropriate deduction is made is the amount that would have been allowable if the asset had been disposed of immediately after the application of the capital sum. [*TCGA 1992, s 23(8)(b)*].

Examples

An Old Master painting belonging to X and worth £100,000 (in its undamaged state) is damaged in June 2024. Subsequently, X successfully claims £20,000 from his insurance company. The picture cost X £40,000 in 1996 and in its damaged state in 2024 is valued at £60,000. The following possibilities arise, the capital gains tax calculations being as shown.

(i) X retains the insurance moneys and does nothing to restore the picture. He is treated as having made a part disposal, and the gain is computed according to the formula for part-disposals (see **16.5** COMPUTATION OF GAINS AND LOSSES). The allowable expenditure apportioned to the disposal is thus £10,000.

(ii) X subsequently expends the whole of the sum on restoration of the picture, but *does not* make a claim under (a) above. He will be treated as having made a part disposal as in (i) above, and his allowable expenditure on a future disposal is computed as follows.

	£
Original allowable expenditure	40,000
Deduct: apportioned allowable expenditure	10,000
	30,000
Add: Expenditure on restoration	20,000
Revised allowable expenditure	£50,000

(iii) X expends the whole of the sum on restoration of the asset *and* makes a claim under (a) above. The position is as follows

	£
Original allowable expenditure	40,000
Deduct: compensation moneys received	20,000
	20,000
Add: Expenditure incurred on the asset after compensation received	20,000
Revised allowable expenditure	£40,000

(iv) X expends £19,000 on restoration of the asset and makes a claim under (b) above. The shortfall of £1,000 is small in relation to the compensation moneys received, and will effectively be treated as a deferred capital gain.

	£
Original allowable expenditure	40,000
Deduct: compensation	20,000
	20,000
Add: Expenditure out of compensation	19,000
Revised allowable expenditure	£39,000

(v) X manages to have the asset restored for £15,000. The shortfall is not small in relation to the compensation moneys received. X makes a claim under *TCGA 1992, s 23(3)*. The market value of the restored asset is £95,000.

	£
Consideration deemed to have been received for the part disposal (£20,000 – £15,000)	5,000
Deduct: Allowable expenditure on that disposal	
$\frac{5,000}{(5,000+95,000)} \times £(40,000+15,000)$	2,750
Gain	£2,250

The allowable expenditure on a future disposal is as follows

	£
Allowable expenditure after part disposal £(40,000 + 15,000 – 2,750)	52,250
Deduct: Compensation expended on asset	15,000
Revised allowable expenditure	£37,250

Assets lost and replaced out of compensation

[10.4] Where an asset is lost or destroyed and a capital sum is received in compensation, there is a disposal of the asset under *TCGA 1992, s 22(1)* as in **10.2** above. A form of rollover relief is available, however, where within one year of receipt (or such longer period as HMRC allow) the whole capital sum is applied in acquiring a replacement asset. HMRC indicate that they will interpret 'replacement' reasonably (HMRC Capital Gains Manual CG15740).

HMRC may allow two years from receipt for the acquisition of the replacement asset where the delay can reasonably be regarded as unavoidable (HMRC Capital Gains Manual CG15740).

In these circumstances, the owner may claim under *TCGA 1992, s 23(4)* to have the disposal of the old asset (if otherwise greater) treated as made at a consideration giving rise to neither a gain nor a loss. The consideration for the acquisition of the new asset is then reduced by the amount of the excess of the capital sum received plus any residual or scrap value of the old asset over the amount of the deemed consideration.

[*TCGA 1992, s 23(4)(6)(8)*].

Where (for corporation tax purposes only) all of the gain on the disposal of the old asset is not chargeable as it was acquired before 6 April 1965, the amount of the reduction in the acquisition cost of the new asset is the amount of the chargeable gain and not the whole amount of the gain. [*TCGA 1992, Sch 2 para 23*].

Partial relief

If part only of the capital sum received in respect of the old asset is applied in acquiring the new asset, the relief above cannot be claimed. However, provided that the amount not applied is less than the gain (whether chargeable or not) accruing on the disposal of the old asset, the owner can claim under *TCGA 1992, s 23(5)* to reduce the gain arising to the amount not applied (and if not all chargeable, with a proportionate reduction in the amount of the chargeable gain). The amount of the consideration for the acquisition of the new asset is reduced by the same amount as the original gain. [*TCGA 1992, s 23(5)(6)(8)*].

Where (for corporation tax purposes only) all of the gain on the disposal of the old asset is not chargeable as it was acquired before 6 April 1965, the amount of the reduction in acquisition cost is the amount by which the chargeable gain is reduced and not the amount by which the original gain is reduced. [*TCGA 1992, Sch 2 para 23*].

Buildings

If a building (including a structure in the nature of a building) is destroyed or irreparably damaged, and all or part of any capital sum received is applied by the recipient in constructing or otherwise acquiring a replacement building (but excluding the land on which the building stands) situated elsewhere, then for the purposes of a claim under *TCGA 1992, s 23(4)* or *(5)* above each of the old building and the new building are regarded as an asset separate from the land on which it was or is situated and the old building treated as lost or destroyed. Just and reasonable apportionments of expenditure, compensation or consideration are made for this purpose. [*TCGA 1992, s 23(6)(7)*]. Cf. the treatment under *TCGA 1992, s 24(1)(3)* in **16.6** COMPUTATION OF GAINS AND LOSSES.

Examples

(a) A Ltd bought an asset for £50,000 in September 2011. It is subsequently destroyed by fire in October 2024 and A Ltd receives £90,000 compensation later in that month. A Ltd buys a new asset six months later for £100,000 and makes a claim under *TCGA 1992, s 23(4)*. The indexation factor for the period September 2011 to December 2017 is 0.169.

	£
Cost of destroyed asset	50,000
Indexation allowance £50,000 × 0.169	8,450
Deemed consideration	£58,450
Compensation received	90,000
Deemed consideration	58,450
Excess (i.e. the gain otherwise accruing)	£31,550
Consideration for acquisition of new asset	100,000
Excess as above	31,550
Reduced allowable expenditure on new asset	£68,450

(b) Facts as in *Example* (a) above except that A Ltd buys another asset to replace the old at a cost of £80,000 and makes a claim under *TCGA 1992, s 23(5)*.

	£	£
Gain on disposal (see above)		£31,550
Compensation moneys received	90,000	
Compensation moneys expended	80,000	
Excess (being less than the gain of £31,550)	£10,000	
The chargeable gain is treated as reduced to the balance arrived at as above and is		£10,000
Amount by which the gain otherwise chargeable is reduced (£31,550 – £10,000)		£21,550

The allowable expenditure on the new asset is reduced as follows

	£
Actual expenditure	80,000
Amount by which chargeable gain is reduced	21,550
Total allowable expenditure	£58,450

11

Charities

Simon's Taxes. See **B1.440, B5.801–B5.823, B5.840, C1.220, C3.1902, E1.811.**

Introduction to charities

[11.1] A gain made by a charity is exempt from tax on chargeable gains provided that the gain is 'applicable and applied for charitable purposes only'.

This exemption is, however, restricted, together with similar income tax and corporation tax exemptions, where a charity incurs non-charitable expenditure. The expression 'non-charitable expenditure' is widely defined to include losses in, and payments in connection with, non-exempt businesses carried on by the charity, as well as non-approved investments and loans.

Relief from tax on chargeable gains is also available to donors. Where a person gives an asset to a charity (or sells it to the charity for no more than its cost) the disposal is treated as one giving rise to neither a gain nor a loss. Where an asset is sold to a charity for more than its acquisition cost but the sale is not at arm's length, the normal rule treating the disposal as made at market value is disapplied.

Relief for donations of money by individuals under Gift Aid is also covered in this chapter, as capital gains tax paid can be used to cover any liability for the income tax treated as deducted from such donations.

Anti-avoidance provisions apply to donations which are tainted by arrangements for the donor to obtain a financial advantage.

For the meaning of 'charity', see *FA 2010, Sch 6, Pt 1*. The treatment of sports clubs which are registered as community amateur sports clubs as charities for the purposes of the various reliefs is described at **11.10** below.

Exemption from tax on chargeable gains

[11.2] Subject to the restrictions in **11.3** below, a gain accruing to a charity is not a chargeable gain provided it is 'applicable and applied for charitable purposes only'. [*TCGA 1992, s 256(1)*]. For the scope of 'applicable and applied for charitable purposes only', see *Lawrence v CIR* KB 1940, 23 TC 333, *Slater (Helen) Charitable Trust Ltd* CA 1981, 55 TC 230 and *Guild and others v CIR* CS 1993, 66 TC 1.

Where a UK charity is a beneficiary of an offshore trust and receives a capital payment, such that a gain would otherwise be treated as accruing to the charity under *TCGA 1992, s 87* (see **42.13** OFFSHORE SETTLEMENTS), the above exemption is available to the extent that the capital payment is applicable and applied for charitable purposes. (Revenue Tax Bulletin August 1998 pp 573, 574).

Where property held on charitable trusts ceases to be subject to those trusts, the trustees are deemed to have disposed of, and immediately reacquired, the property at its market value at that time. Any gain arising is not treated as accruing to a charity. Furthermore, insofar as the property represents, directly or indirectly, the consideration for the disposal of assets by the trustees, any gain accruing on that earlier disposal (and previously exempt) is treated as not having accrued to a charity and capital gains tax is chargeable as if the exemption had never applied. A cumulative liability may therefore arise and an assessment may be made within three years of the end of the year of assessment in which the property ceases to be subject to charitable trusts. [*TCGA 1992, s 256(2)*]. Such an assessment seems to be able to be made even where the gain arising on an earlier disposal is outside the normal time limit for assessment.

Restriction of exemption

[11.3] If, in any 'chargeable period' (i.e. tax year or accounting period), a charity incurs (or is treated as incurring) 'non-charitable expenditure', the amount of relief given under the following exemptions is reduced by an amount equal to that expenditure (or, if less, the total otherwise exempt income and gains). The exemptions are those under:

- *TCGA 1992, s 256* (see **11.2** above);
- *ITA 2007, ss 524–537* (income tax exemptions for charitable trusts);
- *CTA 2010, ss 478–489* (corporation tax exemptions for charitable companies);
- *ICTA 1988, s 56(3)(c); CTA 2010, Sch 2 para 70* (exemption for certain income of charitable companies from certificates of deposit in existence before 1 April 1996); and
- *SI 2009 No 3001, Reg 31* (exemption for offshore income gains of charitable companies).

The charity may by notice in writing to HMRC specify against which items of income or gains the reduction is to be treated as made. If, within 30 days of a request to do so, the charity does not give such notice, HMRC determine the attribution.

If the charity's non-charitable expenditure for a chargeable period exceeds the aggregate for the period of:

- income and gains which, but for the application of these provisions, would qualify for any of the above exemptions;
- other income and gains chargeable to tax; and
- donations, legacies and other similar receipts that are not chargeable to tax,

the excess is treated as non-charitable expenditure of previous chargeable periods ending not more than six years before the end of the chargeable period in which the expenditure was actually incurred. Attributions are made to later periods in priority to earlier periods. Adjustments by way of assessment or otherwise are made in consequence of an attribution to a previous period.

Non-charitable expenditure

A charity's '*non-charitable expenditure*' for a tax year or accounting period is:

(a) any loss made in the year or period (i.e., for income tax purposes, any loss made in the basis period for the year) in a trade other than a trade within one of the charitable exemptions;

(b) (for charitable trusts only) any payment made in the year in connection with a trade where post-cessation expenditure relief within *ITA 2007, s 96* is available unless the trade was within one of the charitable exemptions at *ITA 2007, ss 526, 529* or *530* at cessation;

(c) any loss made in the year or period in a trade, UK or overseas property business where the loss relates to land and any profits generated from the land for the year would not have been within the exemption at *ITA 2007, s 531* or *CTA 2010, s 485*;

(d) (for charitable trusts only) any payment made in the year in connection with a trade or UK or overseas property business where post-cessation expenditure relief within *ITA 2007, ss 96* or *125* is available where the payment relates to land and any profits generated from the land immediately before cessation would not be within the exemption at *ITA 2007, s 531*;

(e) any loss made in the year or period in a 'miscellaneous transaction' entered into otherwise than in the course of carrying on a charitable purpose;

(f) any 'expenditure' incurred in the year or period not within (b) or (d) above which is not incurred solely for charitable purposes and is not required to be taken into account in calculating the profits or losses of any trade or property business or miscellaneous transaction;

(g) any amounts for the year or period treated as non-charitable expenditure under the substantial donor provisions at **11.5** below;

(h) the amount of any funds invested in the year in any investment which is not an 'approved charitable investment'; and

(i) any amount lent in the year by the trust, if the loan is neither an investment nor an 'approved charitable loan'.

Any amount falling within more than one of the above categories is treated as non-charitable expenditure only once.

For the purposes of (e) and (f) above, a '*miscellaneous transaction*' is a transaction any income or gains from which would have been chargeable to income tax or corporation tax under any of the provisions listed in *ITA 2007, s 1016* or *CTA 2010, s 1173* but for the miscellaneous income and gains exemption at *ITA 2007, s 527* and *CTA 2010, s 481*.

For the purposes of (f) above, '*expenditure*' includes capital expenditure but does not include the investment of any of the charity's funds, the making of a loan by the trust or the repayment by the charity of the whole or part of a loan. Expenditure which is referable to commitments (contractual or otherwise) entered into before or during a particular tax year or accounting period is treated as incurred in that year or period if, had accounts been drawn up in accordance with UK generally accepted accounting practice for the year or period, it would have had to be taken into account in preparing those accounts.

The further provisions at (i) and (iii) above apply also for the purposes of the above definition.

The following are '*approved charitable investments*'.

(A) An investment in securities (including shares, stocks and debentures (as defined)):
- issued or guaranteed by the government of the UK or an EU member state or the government or a governmental body of any territory or part of a territory;
- issued by an international entity listed in the Annex to Council Directive 2003/48/EC;
- issued by an entity meeting the four criteria set out at the end of that Annex;
- issued by a building society;
- issued by a credit institution operating on mutual principles which is authorised by an appropriate governmental body in the territory of issue;
- issued by an open-ended investment company (within *CTA 2010, ss 613, 615*);
- issued by a company and listed on a recognised stock exchange (within *ITA 2007, s 1005*); or
- issued by a company and not listed on a recognised stock exchange.

Further conditions (see *ITA 2007, s 560* and *CTA 2010, s 513*) must be met in the case of certain of the above securities.

(B) An investment in a common investment fund established under *Charities Act 1960, s 22* (or NI equivalent) or *Charities Act 1993, s 24*.

(C) An investment in a common deposit fund established under *Charities Act 1960, s 22A* or *Charities Act 1993, s 25*.

(D) An investment in a fund which is similar to those in (B) or (C) above which is established for the exclusive benefit of charities by or under legislation relating to any particular charities or class of charities.

(E) An interest in land other than an interest held as security for a debt.

(F) Any bills, certificates of tax deposit, savings certificates or tax reserve certificates issued in the UK by the Government.

(G) Northern Ireland Treasury bills.

(H) Units in a unit trust scheme within *Financial Services and Markets Act 2000, s 237(1)* or in a recognised scheme within *Financial Services and Markets Act 2000, s 237(3)*.

(I) A deposit with a bank (within *ITA 2007, s 991*) in respect of which interest is payable at a commercial rate, but excluding a deposit made as part of an arrangement under which the bank makes a loan to a third party.

(J) A deposit with the National Savings Bank, a building society or a credit institution operating on mutual principles which is authorised by an appropriate governmental body in the territory in which the deposit is taken.

(K) Certificates of deposit within *ITTOIA 2005, s 552(2)*, including uncertificated eligible debt security units as defined in *ITA 2007, s 986(3)*.

(L) Any loan or other investment as to which HMRC are satisfied, on a claim, that it is made for the benefit of the charity and not for the avoidance of tax (whether by the charity or any other person). Loans secured by mortgage etc. over land are within this heading.

As regards swap contracts, e.g. interest rate or currency swaps, see Revenue Tax Bulletin August 2003 p 1056.

The following are '*approved charitable loans*' if they are not made by way of investment.

(1) A loan made to another charity for charitable purposes only.

(2) A loan to a beneficiary of the charity which is made in the course of carrying out the purposes of the charity.

(3) Money placed on a current account with a bank (within *ITA 2007, s 991*), but excluding a loan made as part of an arrangement under which the bank makes a loan to a third party.

(4) A loan, not within (1)–(3) above, as to which HMRC are satisfied, on a claim, that the loan is made for the benefit of the charity and not for tax avoidance purposes (whether by the charity or by a third party).

[*ITA 2007, ss 539–548, 558–564; CTA 2010, ss 492–501, 511–517, Sch 2 para 77; TCGA 1992, ss 256(3)–(8), 256A–256D; SI 2019 No 689, Regs 15(6), 17(7)*].

Reliefs for donations to charities

[11.4] Relief from tax is available to donors to charities. Reliefs which are relevant to tax on chargeable gains are for gifts of assets and gifts by individuals of cash. Those reliefs are covered at **11.5** to **11.8** below. Anti-avoidance provisions apply to donations which are tainted by arrangements for the donor to obtain a financial advantage — see **11.9** below.

Gifts of assets to charities

[11.5] Where a disposal of an asset is made otherwise than under a bargain at arm's length to a charity, the normal MARKET VALUE (**39**) provisions (which deem the acquisition and disposal as being made at market value) do not apply. See **11.9** below for the anti-avoidance provision for tainted donations which disapplies this rule in certain cases.

If the disposal is by way of gift (including a gift into settlement) or for a consideration not exceeding the allowable expenditure which would be available on a disposal of the asset (see **16.12** COMPUTATION OF GAINS AND LOSSES) the transaction is treated as made for a consideration producing neither a gain nor a loss. Where the asset is subsequently disposed of by the charity, its acquisition by the person making the original disposal is treated as the acquisition of the asset by the charity. See **8.6** ASSETS HELD ON 31 MARCH **1982** and **32.4** INDEXATION for consequential re-basing and indexation provisions. Where the asset is a qualifying investment for the purposes of *ITA 2007, ss 431–446* or *CTA 2010, ss 203–217* (gifts of shares, securities and real property to charities) and the disposal qualifies for income tax or corporation tax relief under those sections (see Tolley's Income Tax and Tolley's Corporation Tax under Charities), the amount treated as the charity's acquisition cost is reduced by the amount on which income tax or corporation tax relief is given or, if this would otherwise produce a negative figure, is reduced to nil.

If the disposal to the charity is for a consideration exceeding the allowable expenditure, the market value is not substituted for the actual consideration.

These provisions apply also to gifts made to a registered community amateur sports club (see **11.10** below).

See **48.4** QUALIFYING CORPORATE BONDS as regards making a gift of such a bond received on a reorganisation of share capital.

These provisions do not apply to disposals in relation to which venture capital trust relief is available (see **64** VENTURE CAPITAL TRUSTS).

The above provisions do apply to disposals made otherwise than under a bargain at arm's length to any of the bodies mentioned in *IHTA 1984, Sch 3*.

[*TCGA 1992, s 257(1)(2)–(2C)(4)(5)*].

The bodies listed in *IHTA 1984, Sch 3* comprise:

- The National Gallery.
- The British Museum.
- The National Museum of Scotland.
- The National Museum of Wales.
- The Ulster Museum.
- Any other similar national institution which exists wholly or mainly for the purpose of preserving for the public benefit a collection of scientific, historic or artistic interest and which is approved for this purpose by the Treasury (see list at HMRC Capital Gains Manual Appendix 4).
- Any museum or art gallery in the UK which exists wholly or mainly for that purpose and is maintained by a local authority or university in the UK.
- Any library the main function of which is to serve the needs of teaching and research at a university in the UK.
- The Historic Buildings and Monuments Commission for England.
- The National Trust for Places of Historic Interest or Natural Beauty.
- The National Trust for Scotland for Places of Historic Interest or Natural Beauty.
- The National Art Collections Fund.

- The Trustees of the National Heritage Memorial Fund.
- The Friends of the National Libraries.
- The Historic Churches Preservation Trust.
- Nature Conservancy Council for England.
- Natural England.
- Scottish National Heritage.
- Countryside Council for Wales.
- The Marine Management Organisation.
- Any local authority.
- Any Government department (including the National Debt Commissioners).
- Any university or university college in the UK.
- A health service body within *CTA 2010, s 986*.

Gifts of assets out of settlements

[11.6] Where a charity becomes absolutely entitled to any assets (or part thereof) which were previously settled property and those assets are deemed to be disposed of and reacquired by the trustees on that occasion (under *TCGA 1992, s 71* — see **56.16** SETTLEMENTS) then, if no consideration is received by any person for or in connection with the transaction, the disposal is deemed to take place on a no gain, no loss basis. This does *not* apply where the charity becomes absolutely entitled to the assets on the termination of a life interest (within the meaning of *TCGA 1992, s 72*, see **56.4** SETTLEMENTS) by the death of the person entitled to it. These provisions also apply to a gift to a registered community amateur sports club (see **11.10** below) or any of the bodies mentioned in *IHTA 1984, Sch 3* (gifts for national purposes). See **11.5** above. See also **11.9** below for anti-avoidance provisions. [*TCGA 1992, s 257(3)*].

In *Prest v Bettinson* Ch D 1980, 53 TC 437, the residue of an estate was held on trust for five institutions, four of which were charities, subject to the payment of annuities to six individuals. No specific fund was set aside, but distributions of capital and income were made annually to the five institutions, the income of the residuary fund being more than sufficient to pay the annuities. The trustee failed in his claim that four-fifths of any capital gain arising was exempt as accruing for charitable purposes. Since no fund had been set aside to pay the annuities, the trustee retained full control of the trust property until the distribution of the proceeds of sale, and any gain from a disposal thereof had accrued to him as trustee and not to the charities.

Gifts of pre-eminent property to the nation

[11.7] An individual or company making a 'qualifying gift' of 'pre-eminent property' to be held for the benefit of the public or the nation qualifies for a reduction in tax liability equal to a percentage of the value of the property. A gain accruing on a qualifying gift is not a chargeable gain (and a loss is not an allowable loss). [*TCGA 1992, s 258(1A)*].

It is explicitly provided that nothing in the following provisions gives rise to any right or expectation that an offer to make a qualifying gift will be accepted. [*FA 2012, Sch 14 para 25*].

Qualifying gift

A person makes a '*qualifying gift*' if:

(a) they offer to give pre-eminent property to be held for the benefit of the public or nation;
(b) they are legally and beneficially entitled to the property and the property is not owned jointly or in common with others;
(c) the offer is in accordance with a scheme set up for this purpose by the Secretary of State;
(d) the offer is registered in accordance with the scheme;
(e) the offer, or part of it, is accepted in accordance with the scheme; and
(f) the gift is made pursuant to the offer, or part, accepted.

In the following paragraphs, the '*agreed terms*' means the terms on which acceptance of the offer is agreed, as recorded in the way required by the scheme, and the '*offer registration date*' means the date the offer was registered under (d) above.

[*FA 2012, Sch 14 para 1*].

Pre-eminent property

'*Pre-eminent property*' means:

(1) any picture, print, book, manuscript, work of art, scientific object or other thing that the relevant Minister (i.e. the Secretary of State and/or Scottish, Welsh or Northern Irish equivalent as applicable — see *FA 2012, Sch 14 para 23*) is satisfied is pre-eminent for its national, scientific, historic or artistic interest;
(2) any collection or group of pictures, prints, books, manuscripts, works of art, scientific objects or other things if the relevant Minister is satisfied that the collection or group taken as a whole is pre-eminent for its national, scientific, historic or artistic interest; or
(3) any object that is or has been kept in a significant building (within *IHTA 1984, s 230(3)(a)–(d)*) if it appears to the relevant Minister desirable for the object to remain associated with the building.

For this purpose, '*national interest*' includes interest within any part of the UK. In determining whether an object or collection or group of objects is pre-eminent, regard must be had to any significant association which they have with a particular place.

[*FA 2012, Sch 14 paras 22, 23*].

Relief for individuals

Relief is given by way of a total reduction of the individual's liability to income tax and capital gains tax equal to 30% of the value set out in the agreed terms as the agreed value of the property. The reduction can be spread across any or all of the tax year in which the offer registration date occurs and the four following tax years. The taxpayer is free to allocate the total reduction to those tax years as he wishes, but the allocations must form part of the agreed terms.

Where all or part of the total tax reduction is allocated to a tax year, a portion of the taxpayer's income tax and capital gains tax liability for that year is treated as satisfied, as if he had paid that portion when it became due (or on the offer registration date, if the portion became due before that date). The portion so treated as satisfied is the smaller of:

(i) the part of the tax reduction allocated to the tax year; and
(ii) the taxpayer's income tax and capital gains tax liability for the year, less any amount allocated to the year in respect of a previous qualifying gift.

Where the amount allocated to the year is less than the amount in (ii) above, the tax reduction is allocated between income tax and capital gains tax liabilities in the order specified in the agreed terms or, if no order is specified, against the income tax liability before the capital gains tax liability. If the taxpayer's tax liability is revised at any time, the relief given under these provisions must be recalculated (but revision of the agreed terms is not permitted).

Relief is not available to an individual in the capacity of trustee or personal representative.

[*FA 2012, Sch 14 paras 2–5, 7*].

If a qualifying gift is set aside or declared void, the tax reduction is withdrawn and the taxpayer is required to pay the portions of his liabilities no longer treated as satisfied under the above provisions, together with any late payment interest and penalties in respect of them by the later of the end of the period of 30 days beginning with the day on which the gift was set aside or declared void and the date by which he would have been required to pay those amounts but for the relief. [*FA 2012, Sch 14 para 8*].

Effect on interest and penalties

Any liability to pay late payment interest or late payment penalties (and interest on such penalties) arising in the period beginning with the offer registration date and ending with the date the qualifying gift is made ceases when the gift is made, and is treated as if it had never arisen, to the extent that the tax concerned is treated as satisfied under the above provisions. In determining whether or to what extent interest or a penalty is attributable to that tax, any attribution or apportionment is to be done so as to minimise the interest and penalties payable by the taxpayer. This provision does not affect any interest that accrued, or penalty to which the taxpayer became liable, before the offer registration date. [*FA 2012, Sch 14 para 6*].

The effect of this provision is negated if the qualifying gift is set aside or declared void. [*FA 2012, Sch 14 para 8(b)*].

Suspension of tax pending negotiations

Where an individual makes an offer within (a) above and:

(A) the offer is registered in accordance with the scheme;
(B) the offer includes a proposal of what should be the agreed terms;
(C) the individual will be required to pay an amount of, or on account of, income tax or capital gains tax for a tax year for which a tax reduction is proposed by a certain date; and

(D) the negotiation of the terms is not expected to conclude before that date,

he may make a request that the obligation to pay the amount by the due date be suspended until the negotiations conclude. Such a request must be made in writing to HMRC at least 45 days before the due date concerned, and must be accompanied by a copy of the donor's proposal within (B) above and such other information as HMRC may reasonably require. The running total of amounts for which suspension can be requested in respect of the same offer and the same tax year must not exceed the proposed tax reduction figure for that year. For these purposes, negotiations conclude when the qualifying gift is made or when the offer is withdrawn or rejected.

Suspension of an amount stops the donor from becoming liable to late payment penalties for failing to pay that amount but does not stop late payment interest from accruing.

In considering whether or to what extent to agree to a request, HMRC must have regard to all the circumstances of the case (including the creditworthiness of the potential donor, and they may impose conditions on their agreement to the suspension. HMRC may by notice in writing to the potential donor, withdraw its agreement to a suspension with effect from the date specified in the notice. If they do so, the potential donor must pay the suspended amount, together with any late payment interest, by the end of the period of 30 days beginning with the specified date. The last day of that period is then treated for the purposes of late payment penalties as the date on or before which the amount must be paid.

When the negotiations conclude, then, if the offer is withdrawn or rejected, the potential donor must pay the amount suspended, together with any late payment interest, within 30 days. The last day of the 30-day period is treated for the purposes of late payment penalties as the date on or before which the amount must be paid. If the negotiations conclude because a qualifying gift is made, the potential donor is only required to pay so much as is not treated as satisfied under the above provisions. If the negotiations conclude in relation only to part of the offer, these provisions take effect as far as reasonably practicable in relation to that part and, on receipt of a revised copy of the donor's proposal, HMRC may agree to a further suspension in relation to the part still under negotiation.

[*FA 2012, Sch 14 paras 9–11*].

Relief for companies

Relief is given by way of a reduction of the company's corporation tax liability for the accounting period in which the offer registration date falls. A portion of the liability is treated as satisfied, as if the company had paid that portion when it became due (or on the offer registration date, if the portion became due before that date). The portion so treated as satisfied is the smaller of:

- 20% of the value set out in the agreed terms as the agreed value of the property (or such lower figure as may be specified in the agreed terms); and
- the company's corporation tax liability for the accounting period, less any amount treated as satisfied in respect of a previous qualifying gift.

If the company's corporation tax liability is revised at any time, the relief given must be recalculated (but revision of the agreed terms is not permitted).

Provisions similar to those applying to individuals relating to a qualifying gift being set aside or declared void, interest and penalties and suspension of tax pending negotiations apply for corporation tax purposes.

[*FA 2012, Sch 14 paras 12–20*].

Gift aid donations by individuals

[11.8] Gifts of money made by individuals to charities which are 'qualifying donations' attract relief under the Gift Aid provisions described below. The provisions are subject to the anti-avoidance rules at **11.9** below. For the Gift Aid provisions applicable to companies, see the corresponding chapter of Tolley's Corporation Tax.

For the purposes of these provisions, '*charity*' has the same meaning as in **12.2** above, but also includes the Trustees of the National Heritage Memorial Fund, the historic Buildings and Monuments Commission for England and the National Endowment for Science, Technology and the Arts. The provisions have effect as if a registered community amateur sports club (see **11.10** below) were a charity, but club membership fees are not gifts for the purposes of these provisions. [*ITA 2007, s 430*].

The donor

Where a qualifying donation is made by an individual ('*the donor*') in a tax year, then, for that year, he is treated for the purposes of income tax and CGT as if:

(a) the gift had been made after deduction of income tax at the basic rate; and
(b) the basic rate limit and the higher rate limit (and, for Scottish taxpayers, the upper limit for the Scottish basic rate and the limits for any Scottish rates above that rate) were increased by an amount equal to the 'grossed up amount of the gift' (i.e. the amount which, after deducting income tax at the basic rate for the tax year in which the gift is made, leaves the amount of the gift).

As the basic rate limit is used in determining the CGT liability of a higher rate taxpayer, the increase mentioned in (b) above gives potential CGT relief for those years in a case where *income* is insufficient to fully obtain higher rate relief on the amount of the gift. For this purpose, higher rate relief means relief for the excess of tax at the higher rate over tax at the basic rate for which relief is effectively given at source. The increase in the basic rate limit does not apply for the purposes of computing top-slicing relief on life assurance policy gains chargeable to income tax.

To the extent, if any, necessary to ensure that the amount of income tax and capital gains tax to which the donor is charged for a tax year in which one or more gifts is made is an amount at least equal to the tax treated under (a) above as deducted from the gift or gifts, the donor is *not* entitled to the following reliefs for that year:

- the personal allowance;
- the blind person's allowance;
- the married couple's allowance; and
- the miscellaneous life assurance-related reliefs at *ITA 2007, ss 457, 458* (payments to trade unions and police organisations) and *ITA 2007, s 459* (payments for benefit of family members).

The restriction does not adversely affect the donor's ability to transfer unused married couple's allowance to a spouse or civil partner.

Where the tax treated as deducted exceeds the amount of income tax and capital gains tax to which the donor is charged for the year (or, for capital gains tax, the amount to which the donor would be charged but for double tax relief) after taking into account the above restriction of reliefs, the donor is liable to an income tax charge for the year, the tax chargeable being equal to the excess.

The amount of income tax to which the donor is charged for a tax year for these purposes is calculated according to the steps at *ITA 2007, s 23* (see Tolley's Income Tax under Allowances and Tax Rates), but with the following modifications.

(i) At Step 6 (tax reductions), the following tax reductions are ignored:
   - relief for qualifying maintenance payments within *ITA 2007, s 453*; and
   - any double tax relief (whether given under a double tax agreement or unilaterally).

(ii) Step 7 is ignored.

(iii) The following amounts are then deducted:
   - any notional tax treated as having been paid under *ITTOIA 2005, s 399* or *s 400* (distributions without a tax credit), *ITTOIA 2005, s 414* (stock dividends), *ITTOIA 2005, s 421* (release of loan to participator in close company), *ITTOIA 2005 s 530* (life assurance gains), or *ITTOIA 2005, s 685A* (payments from settlor-interested settlements); and
   - any tax treated as deducted from estate income under *ITTOIA 2005, s 656(3) or s 657(4)*, to the extent that it is treated as paid out of sums within *ITTOIA 2005, s 680(3)(b)* or *(4)*.

There are provisions to deal with any differences between the UK, Scottish and Welsh basic rates, but currently, these are all the same (20%).

[*ITA 2007, ss 414, 414A, 415, 423–425*].

Carry-back of relief

A person making a qualifying donation can elect for it to be treated, for the purposes of the above provisions, as if it were a qualifying donation made in the previous tax year, provided that the condition below is satisfied.

The condition is that the donor's 'charged amount' for that previous tax year must be at least equal to the 'increased total of gifts'. For this purpose, the donor's '*charged amount*' for a tax year is the sum of his 'modified net income' (as defined at *ITA 2007, s 1025*) and the amount on which he is chargeable to capital gains tax for the year. The '*increased total of gifts*' is the aggregate of the sum of the grossed up amounts of all the gifts made in the current year which are to be, or have already been (by an earlier election), carried back to the previous year and the sum of the grossed up amounts of any qualifying donations actually made in the previous year (and not themselves carried back). All the grossed up amounts are calculated for this purpose as if the gifts were made in the previous year.

The election must be made by notice in writing to an officer of HMRC on or before the date on which the donor delivers his tax return for the previous tax year, and not later than 31 January in the tax year in which the gift is actually made. An election cannot be made by way of amendment to a return (*Cameron v HMRC* FTT, [2010] UKFTT 104 (TC), 2010 STI 1726).

The carry-back facility is *not* available in respect of gifts made through the self-assessment return as below.

[*ITA 2007, ss 426, 427*].

The charity

The receipt by a charity of a qualifying donation is treated as the receipt, under deduction of income tax at the basic rate for the tax year in which the gift is made, of an amount equal to the 'grossed up amount of the gift' (see (a) above). [*ITA 2007, s 520; CTA 2010, ss 471, 661D*]. An election by the donor to treat a qualifying donation as being made in the previous tax year does not affect the position of the charity; the donation is grossed up by reference to the basic rate for the tax year in which payment is *actually* made.

Qualifying donations

A '*qualifying donation*' is a gift to a charity by the donor which meets the following conditions:

(I) it takes the form of a payment of a sum of money;
(II) it is not subject to a condition as to repayment;
(III) it is not deductible under the payroll deduction scheme — see Tolley's Income Tax under Charities);
(IV) it is not deductible in calculating the donor's income from any source;
(V) it is not conditional on or associated with, or part of an arrangement involving, the acquisition of property by the charity, otherwise than by way of gift, from the donor or a person connected with him;
(VI) neither the donor nor any person connected with him (see **17** CONNECTED PERSONS) receives any benefit, in consequence of making it, in excess of specified limits (see below); and
(VII) the donor or an 'intermediary' representing the donor gives the charity or, for donations on or after the same date, an intermediary representing the charity, a 'gift aid declaration' in relation to it.

A gift to charity is also a '*qualifying donation*' if it meets the conditions above and the payment is by way of a waiver by the individual of entitlement to sums (whether principal or interest) due to him from the charity in respect of an amount advanced to the charity on which social investment income tax relief has been obtained (see **59** SOCIAL INVESTMENT RELIEF).

A '*gift aid declaration*' for the purposes of (VII) above is a declaration which is given in the manner prescribed by regulations. It may be made in writing, by fax, over the internet or orally (e.g. by telephone). It must contain the donor's name and address, the name of the charity, a description of the gift(s) to which it relates and a statement that the gift(s) is (are) to be treated as qualifying donations for these purposes. In order for the declaration to have effect, it must have been explained to the donor that he must pay sufficient income tax or capital gains tax to cover the tax deemed to be deducted at source from the donation. No signature is required. Charities and intermediaries must maintain a satisfactory auditable (by HMRC) record of declarations given to them. A donor may still cancel the donation of his own volition. An '*intermediary*' is a person authorised by the donor to give a declaration on his behalf to the charity; a person authorised by a charity to receive a declaration on its behalf; or a person authorised to perform both of those roles. Penalties may be imposed on charities and intermediaries who fail to comply with the regulations.

[*ITA 2007, ss 416, 417, 422, 428; SI 2000 No 2074; SI 2016 No 1195*].

As regards (VI) above, the benefit does not have to be received from the charity to be taken into account (see *St Dunstan's v Major* (Sp C 127), [1997] SSCD 212, in which the saving of inheritance tax by personal representatives as a result of the variation of a will to provide for a donation which would otherwise qualify under these provisions constituted a benefit).

The release of a loan not for consideration and not under seal cannot amount to a gift of money (see *Battle Baptist Church v CIR and Woodham* (Sp C 23), [1995] SSCD 176).

Limits on donor benefits

Where the donor or a person connected with him receives a benefit or benefits in consequence of making the gift, the gift will not be a qualifying donation if either:

(1) the aggregate value of the benefits received exceeds:
- where the gift is £100 or less, 25% of the amount of the gift;
- where the gift is greater than £100, £25 plus 5% of the excess over £100; or

(2) the aggregate of the value of the benefits received in relation to the gift and the value of any benefits received in relation to any qualifying donations previously made to the charity by the donor in the same tax year exceeds £2,500.

The operation of (1) above is modified where a benefit:

(A) consists of the right to receive benefits at intervals over a period of less than twelve months;
(B) relates to a period of less than twelve months;
(C) is one of a series of benefits received at intervals in consequence of making a series of gifts at intervals of less than twelve months; or
(D) is not one of a series of benefits but the gift is one of a series of gifts made at intervals of less then twelve months.

Where (A), (B) or (C) above apply, the value of the benefit and the amount of the gift are 'annualised' for the purposes of (1) above. Where (D) above applies, the amount of the gift (but not the value of the benefit) is likewise annualised. For these purposes a gift or benefit is '*annualised*' by multiplying the amount or value by 365 and dividing the result by the number of days in the period of less than twelve months or the average number of days in the intervals of less than twelve months as appropriate.

In applying the above limits, the benefit of a 'right of admission' is disregarded provided that:

- the opportunity to make a gift and to receive the right of admission in consequence is available to the public;
- the right of admission is a right granted by the charity for the purpose of viewing property preserved, maintained, kept or created by a charity in pursuance of its charitable purposes, including buildings, grounds or other land, plants, animals, works of art (but not performances), artefacts and property of a scientific nature; and
- either:
  - a member of the public could purchase the same right of admission (i.e. a right relating to the same property, classes of person and period of time) and the amount of the gift is at least 10% greater than the amount payable for that right, or
  - the right of admission applies, for a period of at least one year, at all times at which the public can obtain admission other than certain days specified by the charity as an 'event day' (i.e. a day on which an event is to take place on the premises concerned). Where the right is for a period of one year, there must be no more than five specified days in the period. Where the right is for a period of more than one year, there must be no more than five specified days in each calendar year during all or part of which the right applies.

For this purpose, a '*right of admission*' is a right of free or reduced-price admission for the donor (or for the donor and one or more family members, whether or not the right must be exercised by all those persons at the same time) to premises or property to which the public are admitted on payment of an admission fee.

[*ITA 2007, ss 417–421*].

Anti-avoidance: tainted donations

[11.9] There are anti-avoidance provisions which remove entitlement to tax reliefs and counteract tax advantages where a person makes a relievable charitable donation which is a 'tainted donation' (see below, but broadly a donation linked to arrangements for the donor to obtain a financial advantage). The provisions apply equally to donations to community amateur sports clubs (see **11.10** below).

The following reliefs can be denied under the provisions:

(a) gifts of chargeable assets (*TCGA 1992, s 257* — see **11.5**, **11.6** above);
(b) gifts of plant and machinery (*CAA 2001, s 63(2)*);
(c) payroll giving (*ITEPA 2003, Pt 12*);
(d) gifts of trading stock (*ITTOIA 2005, s 108; CTA 2009, s 105*);
(e) gift aid donations by individuals (*ITA 2007, Pt 8 Ch 2* — see **11.8** above);

(f) gifts of shares and real property (*ITA 2007, Pt 8 Ch 3; CTA 2010, Pt 6 Ch 3*);
(g) cash gifts by companies (*CTA 2010, Pt 6 Ch 2*); and
(h) any other gift or disposal in respect of which a charity is entitled to claim a repayment of tax.

An amount of income arising under a UK settlement (within *ITTOIA 2005, s 628*) to which a charity is entitled under the settlement's terms is treated for these purposes as an amount gifted to the charity by the trustees.

[*ITA 2007, ss 809ZH, 809ZI, 809ZR(1); CTA 2010, ss 939A, 939B, 939I(1)*].

Tainted donations

A donation is a '*tainted donation*' if each of the following three conditions is satisfied.

(1) The donor or a person connected with him (a '*linked person*') enters into 'arrangements' (before or after the donation is made) and it is reasonable to assume from the likely effects of the donation and the arrangements or of the circumstances in which they are made that neither would have been made independently of one another. Where it is a connected person who enters into the arrangements, he must be connected (see below) with the donor at a time in the period beginning with the earliest, and ending with the latest, of the time the arrangements are made, the time the donation is made, and the time when the arrangements are first materially implemented.
(2) The main purpose, or one of the main purposes, of the linked person entering into the arrangements is to obtain a financial advantage directly or indirectly from the charity or a connected charity for one or more linked persons.
(3) The donor is neither a 'qualifying charity-owned company' nor a 'housing provider' linked with the charity. A housing provider is linked with a charity if one is wholly owned or subject to control by the other or both are wholly owned or subject to control by the same person.

For the above purposes, '*arrangements*' include any scheme, arrangement or understanding of any kind, whether or not legally enforceable, involving a transaction or transactions. *ITA 2007, s 993* and *CTA 2010, s 1122* apply to determine whether two persons are '*connected*', but in addition, a beneficiary is treated as connected with a person in the capacity as trustee and with the settlor. In applying those sections for the purposes of these provisions, persons living together as husband and wife or as if they were civil partners are treated as if they were in fact husband and wife or civil partners of each other and 'close company' includes a company which would be close if it were UK-resident. Two charities are connected for the purposes of (2) above if they are connected in a matter relating to the structure, administration or control of either of them.

A '*qualifying charity-owned company*' is a company which:

(i) is wholly owned by one or more charities (within *CTA 2010, s 200*), at least one of which is the charity to whom the donation is made or a connected charity; and

(ii) has not previously been under the control of, and does not carry on a trade previously carried on by, any of the linked persons potentially financially advantaged by the arrangements or any person (other than a charity) connected with such a linked person at any time in the four years ending on the day on which (i) above was first satisfied.

A '*housing provider*' is a body which is a non-profit provider of social housing or is entered on a register maintained under *Housing Act 1996, s 1, Housing (Scotland) Act 2001, s 57, Housing (Scotland) Act 2010, s 20* or NI equivalent.

[*ITA 2007, ss 809ZJ, 809ZP, 809ZQ, 809ZR(1); CTA 2010, ss 939C, 939G, 939H, 939I(1)*].

Financial advantage

The following applies where the arrangements involve a 'transaction' to which the linked person entering into them or any other linked person ('X') and another person ('Y') are parties. X is treated as obtaining a financial advantage within (2) above if the terms of the transaction are less beneficial to Y or more beneficial to X (or both) than those reasonably to be expected in a transaction at arm's length or if the transaction is not of a kind which a person acting at arm's length and in Y's place might reasonably be expected to make. This rule is not, however, intended to limit the circumstances in which a person is treated as obtaining a financial advantage. '*Transaction*' includes, for example, the sale, letting or exchange of property, the provision of services or of a loan, or other form of financial assistance, and investment in a business.

A financial advantage is ignored for the purposes of the above provisions in the following circumstances:

- where the advantage is applied by the person obtaining it for charitable purposes only;
- where the advantage is a benefit associated with a gift aid donation (within *ITA 2007, s 417* — see **11.8** above) or with a payment within (g) above;
- where the donation is within (f) above and the advantage is a benefit of value which would be taken into account in determining the relievable amount for the purposes of the reliefs in (f) above; and
- where the donation is within (d) above and the advantage would be brought into account under *ITTOIA 2005, s 109* or *CTA 2009, s 108* (receipt of benefits by donor or connected person).

[*ITA 2007, ss 809ZK, 809ZL; CTA 2010, ss 939D, 939E*].

Effect of provisions

Where the provisions apply, any relief that would otherwise have been available in respect of the tainted donation or an 'associated donation' under (a) to (h) above is not available. For the purposes of tax on chargeable gains, *TCGA 1992, s 257* (disapplication of market value rule for gifts of assets to charities — see **11.5** above) does not apply to the tainted donation or any associated donation.

An '*associated donation*' is an otherwise relievable donation made under the arrangements by a person other than a company which is a qualifying charity-owned company (see above) in relation to the donation or a housing provider (see above) linked with the charity to which the donation is made.

A gift aid donation for which relief is not available is nevertheless treated as a qualifying donation in the hands of the charity (see **11.8** above under 'The charity') and a similar rule applies where the donation is made under the payroll giving scheme.

[*TCGA 1992, s 257A; ITA 2007, s 809ZM; CTA 2010, s 939F*].

Where a tainted donation is made and it or an associated donation would otherwise be a qualifying donation for gift aid purposes, an income tax charge will apply on an amount equal to the repayment which the charity is entitled to claim. The liability falls jointly and severally on the donor of the gift aid donation, the donor of the tainted donation (if different), any linked person potentially advantaged under the arrangement and the charity receiving the gift aid donation or the tainted donation (if different) and certain connected charities. See *ITA 2007, s 809ZN*. See also *ITA 2007, s 809ZO* for a similar provision applying to donations made through a settlement.

Community amateur sports clubs

[11.10] An exemption for certain gains can be claimed by sports clubs which are registered with HMRC as community amateur sports clubs ('*registered clubs*').

For a club to be eligible to register, it must, and its constitution must require it to:

- be 'open to the whole community';
- be 'organised on an amateur basis'; and
- have as its main purpose the provision of facilities for, and promotion of participation in, one or more 'eligible sports'.

The club must also meet the location condition, the management condition and the income condition.

For the above purposes, a club is '*open to the whole community*' if membership is open to all, and the club facilities are available to members, without discrimination (leaving aside necessary differentiation on grounds of age, gender or disability relative to a particular sport). Additionally, fees must be set at a level which does not pose a significant obstacle to membership, use of the facilities or full participation in club activities. Costs are deemed to represent a significant obstacle if the total of the membership fees and sporting activity costs exceed £520 per year and the club has not made arrangements to ensure that the costs do not represent an obstacle to membership. A club is not eligible to register if it receives membership fees exceeding £1,612 in respect of any member for any year. For the meaning of 'membership fees', 'sporting activity costs' and for the increase or decrease of the limits for periods of more than or less than a year see *SI 2015 No 725, Regs 7–9*.

A club is not prevented from being open to the whole community simply because it charges different fees for different descriptions of persons.

A club is '*organised on an amateur basis*' if it meets the following four conditions.

(a) The club must be non-profit making, i.e. its constitution must require surplus income or gains to be reinvested in the club and must not permit the distribution of club assets (whether in cash or in kind) to members or third parties. However, donations by a club to charities or other registered clubs are allowed.

(b) It must provide only the following benefits for members and their guests:
   - provision of sporting facilities and suitably qualified coaches;
   - reasonable provision and maintenance of club-owned sports equipment;
   - provision of, or reimbursement of the costs of, coaching courses;
   - provision of insurance cover and medical treatment;
   - reimbursement of reasonable and necessary travel or subsistence expenses incurred by players, match officials, coaches, first aiders and accompanying individuals travelling to away matches;
   - reasonable provision of post-match refreshments for players and match officials; and
   - sale or supply of food or drink as a social adjunct to the sporting purposes of the club.

(c) It does not exceed the limit on paid players. The limit is, broadly, £10,000 per year. For the detailed rules see *SI 2015 No 725, Regs 11–13*.

(d) The club's constitution must provide for any net assets on the dissolution of the club to be applied for the purposes of:
   - a charity;
   - another registered club; or
   - the governing body of an eligible sport for the purposes of which the club existed, for use in related community sport,

   as approved by the members of the club in general meeting or by its governing body.

An '*eligible sport*' is one designated as such by Treasury order for the purposes of these provisions. See now *SI 2002 No 1966* which designates for these purposes sports appearing on the National Sports Councils list of activities recognised by them.

A club is not regarded as a community amateur sports club if the number of social members within the club exceeds 50% of the total members. For these purposes a social member is defined as a member who either does not participate or only occasionally participates in the sports activities of the club. For the meaning of 'participation' and 'occasional participation' and for the method of calculating the percentage of social members see *SI 2015 No 725, Regs 16–19*.

A club meets the location condition if it is established in the UK and its facilities for eligible sports are all in the UK.

For accounting periods beginning before 1 April 2024, a club can also meet the location condition if it is established in an EU member state or a territory specified in HMRC regulations (Iceland, Norway or Liechtenstein) and its facilities for eligible sports are all in one such State or territory. If, however, the club has not asserted its status as a community amateur sports club before 15 March 2023, it cannot meet the condition in relation to accounting periods beginning on or after that date.

For this purpose, a club has asserted its status as a community amateur sports club if, immediately before 15 March 2023, it is registered as such a club or it has applied for registration.

For these purposes, accounting periods which straddle 1 April 2024 or, where relevant, 15 March 2023 are treated as two separate accounting purposes, the first ending on 31 March 2024 or 14 March 2023 as appropriate.

A club meets the management condition if its managers are fit and proper persons. For this purpose, the managers are the persons with the general control and management of the administration of the club. If this condition is not met for a period of time it is nevertheless treated as met throughout that period if HMRC consider either that the failure has not prejudiced the purposes of the club or that it is just and reasonable for the condition to be treated as met. The expression 'fit and proper' is not defined and so takes its natural meaning. HMRC consider that the fit and proper person test is the same as that for charities (see **12.2** above).

A club meets the income condition if the total of its trading receipts and property receipts does not exceed £100,000 for an accounting period. The limit is reduced proportionately where the accounting period is less than 12 months. The receipts taken into account are those that would be included in computing the club's trading income and property income for corporation tax if the exemptions for such income did not apply.

[*CTA 2010, ss 658(1)–(1C), 659–661CA; FA 2013, Sch 21 para 8; F(No 2)A 2023, s 345; SI 2010 No 1904; SI 2015 No 725*].

For HMRC guidance on eligibility conditions see www.gov.uk/government/publications/community-amateur-sports-clubs-detailed-guidance-notes/community-amateur-sports-clubs-detailed-guidance-notes.

Registration

Applications for registration are made to HMRC. Registration may be backdated (possibly to before the date of the application).

HMRC may terminate a club's registration (possibly with retrospective effect) if it appears to them that the club is not, or is no longer, entitled to be registered.

HMRC must notify a club of a decision to register it, to refuse its application or to terminate its registration. The club may appeal against any such decision by notice in writing to HMRC within 30 days of the date of the notification. The notice of appeal must specify the grounds of appeal. The provisions of *TMA 1970* relating to 5 APPEALS apply to such an appeal. If not dismissing the appeal, the Tribunal may either remit the matter to HMRC for reconsideration, or, as applicable, direct that the club be registered from a particular date, rescind a termination of registration, or direct that a termination take effect on a particular date.

HMRC publishes the names and addresses of registered clubs. This enables potential donors to confirm that they are donating to a registered club (and, therefore, that the donation may qualify for gift aid relief — see below). For a list of the names of registered clubs see www.gov.uk/government/publications/community-amateur-sports-clubs-casc-registered-with-hmrc--2.

[*CTA 2010, ss 658(2)–(5), 670, 671*].

Tax exemptions

Subject to the restriction noted below, a gain accruing to a registered club is not a chargeable gain if it is wholly applied for 'qualifying purposes' and the club makes a claim to that effect. '*Qualifying purposes*' means purposes of providing facilities for, and promoting participation in, one or more eligible sports (and in the following paragraphs, '*non-qualifying purposes*' are to be construed accordingly). [*CTA 2010, ss 661(3), 665*].

In addition to the exemption for gains, registered clubs also enjoy tax exemptions relating to trading income, interest and gift aid income and property income. For full details, see Tolley's Corporation Tax under Voluntary Associations.

Restriction of exemption

The above exemptions are restricted where a registered club incurs any expenditure for non-qualifying purposes in an accounting period and any of the club's income or gains for that period are exempted from tax (or would be but for the restriction).

The restriction operates by comparing the amount of the expenditure incurred in the accounting period for non-qualifying purposes ('*the non-qualifying expenditure*') with the aggregate of the club's income (whether or not taxable, and before deducting expenses) and gains (whether chargeable gains or gains exempted as above) for the accounting period ('*the total income and gains*'), as follows.

(1) Where the non-qualifying expenditure is less than the total income and gains, the amount of exempt income and gains is restricted in the proportion that the non-qualifying expenditure bears to the total income and gains.

(2) Where the non-qualifying expenditure equals the total income and gains, the amount of exempt income and gains is reduced to nil.

(3) Where the non-qualifying expenditure exceeds the total income and gains, the amount of exempt income and gains is reduced to nil, and the 'surplus amount' is carried back to previous accounting periods (latest first) ending not more than six years before the end of the current period, and deducted from income and gains exempted for those periods. To the extent that the amount exempted for an accounting period has already been reduced under this provision or (1) or (2) above, it cannot be reduced again by reference to expenditure of a later accounting period. The '*surplus amount*' is the excess of:

    (i) an amount equal to the proportion of the originally exempt income and gains that the non-qualifying expenditure bears to the total income and gains, over;

(ii) the amount of the originally exempt income and gains.

Where, as a consequence of this restriction, a registered club has an amount of income and gains for which exemption is not available, the club may, by notice to HMRC, specify which items of income and gains are, in whole or part, to be attributed to that amount. If no such notice is given by the club within 30 days of being required to do so by HMRC, it falls to HMRC to make the attribution.

[*CTA 2010, ss 666–668*].

Property ceasing to be held for qualifying purposes

Where a club holds property and, without disposing of it, ceases at any time to be a registered club or to hold the property for 'qualifying purposes' (see under 'Tax Exemptions' above), it is treated for the purposes of *TCGA 1992* as having disposed of, and immediately reacquired, the property at that time at its then market value. Any gain resulting from the deemed disposal does not attract the above exemption. Additionally, to the extent that any of the property represents, directly or indirectly, the consideration for the disposal of assets by the club, any gain that accrued on that disposal does not attract the exemption. Assessments in respect of resulting chargeable gains can be made at any time not later than three years after the end of the accounting period in which falls the event giving rise to this treatment. [*CTA 2010, s 669*].

Reliefs for donations

Gifts to registered clubs by individuals can qualify for relief under the gift aid provisions (see **11.8** above) and gifts of assets can qualify for relief under *TCGA 1992, s 257* (gifts of assets to charities — see **11.5**, **11.6** above).

12

Children

Cross-references. See **23.24** EXEMPTIONS AND RELIEFS for Child Trust Funds; **51.29** RESIDENCE AND DOMICILE for domicile of children.

General matters relating to children

[12.1] There is no general bar to the chargeable gains made by a child (i.e. an individual under 18 years of age) being assessed and charged on the child personally (see *R v Newmarket Commissioners (ex p. Huxley)* CA 1916, 7 TC 49 and *FA 2012, s 222(3)*). HMRC must, therefore, resort directly to the child, subject to the general legal framework for appointing people to assist those who lack capacity.

A child is entitled to the same capital gains tax reliefs and exemptions as an adult (subject to specific exclusions).

Nominees and bare trustees

[12.2] Where property is held by a person as nominee or as trustee for any person who would be absolutely entitled against that person but for being a child, the provisions of *TCGA 1992* apply as if the acts of the nominee or trustee are the acts of the child. Acquisitions from or to the trustee or nominee to or from the child are accordingly disregarded. References in *TCGA 1992* to a person being absolutely entitled against the trustee mean that the person has the exclusive right (subject only to satisfying any outstanding charge, lien or other right of the trustee to resort to the relevant property for payment of duty, taxes, costs or other outgoings) to direct how the property shall be dealt with. [*TCGA 1992, s 60*]. For the wider implications of nominees and bare trustees generally, see **56.3** SETTLEMENTS.

13

Claims

Cross-reference. See 38.5 LOSSES for requirement to notify capital losses.

Introduction to claims

[13.1] This chapter outlines the procedures and time limits for making claims and elections for reliefs, allowances and tax repayments for both capital gains tax and corporation tax purposes.

Claims are personal matters and (except in the case of trustees for persons under disability etc.) can be made only by the person entitled to the relief (cf. *Fulford v Hyslop* Ch D 1929, 8 ATC 588). See **52.6** RETURNS for the signing of claims by an attorney.

Also covered in this chapter are two specific types of claim:

(a) claims for recovery of overpaid tax; and
(b) claims through the courts for the restitution of payments made under a mistake of law.

Capital gains tax claims and elections

[13.2] A formal procedure applies to the making of capital gains tax (and income tax) claims, elections and notices. A claim for a relief, allowance or tax repayment must be for an amount quantified at the time of the claim. Where notice has been given by HMRC requiring the delivery of a return (see **52.5**, **52.18** RETURNS), a claim etc. can only be made at any time by inclusion in such a return (or by virtue of an amendment to a return) *unless it could not be so included* either at that time or subsequently (but see below for claims involving two or more years). These provisions do not apply to claims to be given effect by a PAYE coding adjustment, to claims by charities for specified exemptions and repayments of income tax, or to claims for consequential adjustments after the counteraction of a tax advantage under the GAAR (see **4.3** ANTI-AVOIDANCE).

In the case of a partnership business, a claim under any of numerous provisions specified in *TMA 1970, s 42(7)* must be made by a partner nominated by the partnership if it cannot be included in a partnership return (or amendment to such a return). See **13.3** below for provisions applying where a claim etc. is made otherwise than by inclusion in a return.

Where a claimant discovers that an error or mistake has been made in a claim (whether or not made in a return), they may make a supplementary claim within the time allowed for making the original claim.

[*TMA 1970, s 42; FA 2024, Sch 10 para 36*].

Claims for relief involving two or more years

A claim for a loss incurred or payment made in one tax year to be carried back to an earlier year or years need not be made in a return, is treated as a claim for the year of loss or payment (the later year), must be for an amount equal to what would otherwise have been the tax saving for the earlier year, and is given effect *in relation to the later year* by repayment, set-off etc. or by treating the said amount as a tax payment made on account under SELF-ASSESSMENT (**55.2**). The tax position for the earlier year is not adjusted. [*TMA 1970, Sch 1B para 2*]. See Tolley's Income Tax for more details. The non-reopening of the earlier year's self-assessment does not prevent the making or revising of other claims for that earlier year that are consequential to the carry-back (Revenue Tax Bulletin August 2000 pp 774, 775). In relation to the carry-back claim, repayment interest may be due as in **50.2** REPAYMENT INTEREST, though only from 31 January following the *later year* (as above). An example of a capital gains provision affected by these rules is the potential three-year carry-back of capital losses incurred by an individual in the tax year in which they die — see **18.7** DEATH.

Claims etc. not included in returns

[13.3] Subject to any specific provision requiring a claim, etc. to be made to the Commissioners for HMRC, an income tax or capital gains tax claim or election made otherwise than in a return (see **13.2** above) must be made to an HMRC officer. The claim, etc. must include a declaration by the claimant that all particulars are correctly stated to the best of their information or belief. No claim requiring a tax repayment can be made unless the claimant has documentary proof that the tax has been paid or deducted. The claim must be made in a form determined by HMRC and may require, inter alia, a statement of the amount of tax to be discharged or repaid and supporting information and documentation. In the case of a claim by or on behalf of a person who is not resident in the UK, HMRC may require a statement or declaration in support of the claim to be made by affidavit.

A person who may wish to make a claim must keep all such records as may be requisite for the purpose and must preserve them until such time as HMRC may no longer enquire into the claim (see below) or any such enquiry is completed. HMRC have the power to make regulations specifying records which are required to be kept. There is a maximum penalty of £3,000 for non-compliance in relation to any claim actually made. Similar provisions and exceptions apply as in **52.10** RETURNS as to the preservation of copies of documents instead of originals.

Provisions similar to those in **52.9** RETURNS (amendments of self-assessments) apply to enable a claimant (within 12 months of the claim) or HMRC officer (within nine months of the claim) to amend a claim, etc. HMRC has powers of enquiry into a claim, etc. (or amendment) similar to that in **52.11** RETURNS (enquiries into returns). Notice of intention to enquire must be given by the first anniversary of 31 January following the tax year (or where the claim relates to a period other than a tax year, the first anniversary of the end of that period) or, if later, the quarter day (meaning 31 January, 30 April, etc.) next following the first anniversary of the date of claim, etc. See also **29.3–29.10** HMRC INVESTIGATORY POWERS. Where an enquiry is in progress, an HMRC officer may give provisional effect to the claim, etc. (or amendment to a claim) to such extent as they think fit. Provisions similar to those in **52.14–52.15** RETURNS apply as regards completion of enquiries and amendments of claims upon completion (except there is no provision for issuing *partial* closure notices). HMRC must give effect (by assessment, discharge or repayment) to an amendment arising out of an enquiry within 30 days after the date of issue of the closure notice. An appeal may be made against any conclusion stated, or amendment made, by a closure notice by giving written notice to the relevant officer within 30 days after the date of issue of the closure notice, extended to three months where certain specified issues concerning residence are involved. If an amendment is varied on appeal, HMRC must give effect to the variation within 30 days.

Where a claim etc. does not give rise to a discharge or repayment of tax, there are provisions for disallowance of the claim on completion of enquiry, with appeal procedures similar to those above.

[*TMA 1970, s 42(11), Sch 1A*].

In *Cotter v HMRC* SC, [2013] STC 2480, a claim for the carry-back of an income tax loss which was included in a tax return form was held to be made outside the return and therefore subject to the enquiry provisions above. For the purposes of the enquiry provisions, a tax return referred to the information in the return form which was submitted for the purpose of establishing the amounts in which a person was chargeable to tax for the relevant tax year. In this case, the claim had no effect on the tax chargeable for the year concerned and so did not form part of the tax return.

The decision in *Cotter* was distinguished, however, in *Cumming-Bruce v HMRC* UT, [2022] STC 1669 which was concerned with a capital loss notified in an amendment to a return. The taxpayer had made a number of gains and losses, but as the losses included in the original return already exceeded the gains, the amendment did not change the outcome that no CGT was payable. The UT rejected the taxpayer's argument that, because the loss claimed did not change the taxpayer's CGT liability or tax payable, it was not in the return. The UT concluded that as a matter of law all allowable losses are taken into account in determining the CGT payable for a tax year, and all allowable losses arising in a tax year must be included in the return for that year. HMRC had therefore correctly enquired into the losses under the provisions at **52.14** RETURNS rather than under the provisions above.

Corporation tax claims

[13.4] Under corporation tax self-assessment, provisions having broadly similar effect as those in **13.2** above (other than those of *TMA 1970, Sch 1B*) apply to companies. Subject to any express provision to the contrary and certain exceptions for charitable companies, claims and elections made after notice has been given requiring the delivery of a company tax return must be made in the return, or by amendment of the return, if they can be so made (see **52.21** RETURNS) and must be quantified. A claim etc. made by a company which could have been made by amending the return is treated for this purpose as an amendment of the return. Otherwise, *TMA 1970, Sch 1A* (see **13.3** above) provides the procedure for claims etc. A supplementary claim (where there was an error or mistake in the original claim) may be made within the time limit for the original claim. A group relief or capital allowances claim *must* be made in a return or by amendment of a return. [*FA 1998, Sch 18 paras 9, 10, 54, 56–60*].

Time limits for claims

[13.5] See **61** TIME LIMITS — FIXED DATES and **62** TIME LIMITS — MISCELLANEOUS for check-lists of claims and elections.

Where no specific time limit is prescribed, a claim must be made within **four years** of the end of the tax year or accounting period to which it relates.

Where an asset is disposed of and acquired under a contract, the gain or loss arises at the time the contract is made (see **16.4** COMPUTATION OF GAINS AND LOSSES) or, if the contract is conditional, at the time when the conditions are satisfied. The time limit for making a claim relating to the gain or loss therefore normally runs from the end of the tax year or accounting period in which that time falls.

For contracts entered into on or after 6 April 2023 (1 April 2023 for corporation tax), the time limit is extended in certain cases where the asset is not conveyed or transferred until a later tax year or accounting period. For capital gains tax purposes, this applies where the asset is not conveyed or transferred until after 5 October following the tax year in which the contract is made. The time limit for making a claim runs from the end of the tax year of the conveyance or transfer. For corporation tax purposes, the extension applies where the asset is not conveyed or transferred until more than 12 months after the end of the accounting period in which the contract is made. The time limit for making a claim then runs from the end of the accounting period of conveyance or transfer.

[*TMA 1970, s 43(1); TCGA 1992, s 28A; FA 1998, s 117, Sch 18 para 55; F(No 2)A 2023, s 40*].

By concession, where an overpayment of tax arises because of an error by HMRC or another Government department and where there is no dispute as to the facts, claims to repayment of the tax overpaid made outside of the statutory period will be allowed (HMRC Extra-Statutory Concession B41).

A claim (including a supplementary claim) which could not have been allowed but for the making of an assessment to capital gains tax after the tax year to which it relates, may be made at any time before the end of the tax year following that in which the assessment was made. [*TMA 1970, s 43(2)*].

If an assessment is made under the extended time limits at **6.14** ASSESSMENTS, the person assessed can require effect to be given to reliefs or allowances to which they would have been entitled had they made the necessary claims within the relevant time limits. [*TMA 1970, s 36(3); FA 1998, s 117, Sch 18 para 65*].

Where HMRC issue an amendment to a return as part of an enquiry closure notice (see **52.14** RETURNS), the above extended time limits apply in relation to the amendment as they apply in relation to assessments. [*TMA 1970, s 43C(1)–(3)*].

Discovery etc.

In the case of a 'discovery' assessment (see **6.10** ASSESSMENTS), which is *not* for making good loss of tax brought about carelessly or deliberately,

(a) any 'relevant' claim, election, application or notice which could have been made or given within the normal time limits may be made or given within a year of the end of the chargeable period in which the assessment is made, and
(b) any 'relevant' claim, etc. previously made or given, except an irrevocable one, can, with the consent of the person(s) by whom it was made or given (or their personal representatives), be revoked or varied in the manner in which it was made or given.

A claim, etc. is '*relevant*' to an assessment for a chargeable period if:

(i) it relates to, or to an event occurring in, the chargeable period, and
(ii) it, or its revocation or variation, reduces, or could reduce,
  (A) the increased tax liability resulting from the assessment, or
  (B) any other liability of the person for that chargeable period or a later one ending not more than one year after the period in which the assessment is made.

A claim in respect of overpaid tax within **13.7** below is also 'relevant' to an assessment for a tax year if it relates to that year.

These extended time limits cannot be used for the purpose of making an election for universal re-basing under *TCGA 1992, s 35(5)* (see **8.3** ASSETS HELD ON 31 MARCH **1982**).

The normal APPEALS (**5**) provisions apply, with any necessary modifications.

If the making, etc. of a claim, etc. would alter another person's tax liability, the consent of that person (or his personal representatives) is needed. If such alteration is an increase, the other person cannot make, etc. a claim, etc. under the foregoing provisions.

If the reduction in tax liability resulting from one or more claims etc. would exceed the additional tax assessed, relief is not available for the excess. If the reduction involves more than one period, or more than one person, HMRC will specify by notice in writing how it is to be apportioned; but within 30 days of the notice being given, or the last notice being given if there is more than one person, the person (or persons jointly) can specify the apportionment by notice in writing to HMRC.

[*TMA 1970, ss 43A, 43B*].

Where HMRC issue an amendment to a return as part of an enquiry closure notice (see **52.14** RETURNS), these provisions apply to the amendment as they apply to assessments. [*TMA 1970, s 43C(2)(3)*].

The provisions broadly apply to companies under corporation tax self-assessment. [*FA 1998, s 117, Sch 18 paras 61–64*].

Extended time limits for assessment

Where it is necessary to make an assessment on any person to give effect to, or as a result of allowing, a claim, supplementary claim, election, application or notice given or made under the extended time limits of *TMA 1970, ss 36(3), 43(3), 43A* or *43C* above, the assessment is not out of time if made within one year of the final determination of the claim etc. For this purpose a claim etc. is finally determined when it can no longer be varied, on appeal or otherwise. [*TMA 1970, s 43C(4)(5)*].

Appeals in respect of claims

[13.6] See 13.3 above and 5.2 APPEALS.

Claim for recovery of overpaid tax

[13.7] Where a taxpayer has paid an amount of capital gains tax (or income tax) or corporation tax and believes that the tax is not due, he can make a claim to HMRC for repayment of the tax. Where a taxpayer has been assessed as liable to pay an amount of tax, or there has been a determination or direction to that effect, he can likewise make a claim for the amount to be discharged if he believes that the tax is not due. For these purposes, tax paid by one person on behalf of another is treated as paid by the other person.

HMRC will not give effect to such a claim in the following circumstances:

(a) the amount is excessive because of a mistake in a claim or a mistake consisting of making, or failing to make, an election claim or notice (or because of certain mistakes relating to capital allowances);
(b) the claimant can seek relief by taking other steps under tax legislation;
(c) the claimant could have sought relief by taking such steps within a period which has expired by the time the claim is made, if he knew, or ought reasonably to have known, before the end of that period that such relief was available;
(d) the claim is made on grounds that have been put to a court or tribunal in the course of an appeal relating to the amount or grounds that have been put to HMRC in the course of such an appeal settled by agreement;
(e) the claimant knew, or ought reasonably to have known, of the grounds for the claim before the latest of: the date an appeal relating to the amount was determined by a court or tribunal, the date on which such an appeal was withdrawn by the claimant, and the end of the period in which the claimant could have appealed;
(f) the amount was due as a result of proceedings by HMRC against the claimant, or under an agreement between the claimant and HMRC settling such proceedings; and

(g) the amount is excessive because of a mistake in calculating the claimant's liability where the liability was calculated in accordance with the practice generally prevailing at the time (and for this purpose special rules apply in relation to PAYE).

The exclusion in (g) above does not apply where a claim to relief relates to tax charged contrary to EU law. For this purpose, an amount is charged contrary to EU law if it is contrary to the provisions of the Treaty on the Functioning of the European Union relating to the free movement of goods, persons, services or capital (or replacement provisions under any subsequent treaty).

[*TMA 1970, s 33, Sch 1AB paras 1, 2; FA 1998, Sch 18 paras 51, 51A*].

Where a claim can be made under these provisions, it is not open to the taxpayer to, instead, make a claim under the common law as at **13.8** below. See *Wallace v HMRC* Ch D, [2018] STC 790 in which the time limit for making a claim under these provisions had expired.

Making a claim

For capital gains tax (and income tax) purposes, a claim must be made within four years after the end of the tax year concerned. Where the claim relates to tax overpaid, that year is the year in respect of which the payment was made or, where the amount paid is excessive due to a mistake in a tax return or returns, the year to which the return (or if more than one, the first return) relates. Where the claim relates to an assessment, determination or direction, the year concerned is the year to which that assessment etc. relates or, where the amount due is excessive due to a mistake in a tax return or returns, the year to which the return (or if more than one, the first return) relates.

For corporation tax purposes, a claim must be made within four years after the end of the accounting period concerned. Where the claim relates to tax overpaid, that accounting period is the period in respect of which the payment was made or, where the amount paid is excessive due to a mistake in a tax return or returns, the period to which the return (or if more than one, the first return) relates. Where the claim relates to an assessment, determination or direction, the accounting period concerned is that to which that assessment etc. relates or, where the amount due is excessive due to a mistake in a tax return or returns, the period to which the return (or if more than one, the first return) relates.

In *Raftopoulou v HMRC* CA, [2018] STC 988, the provisions of *TMA 1970, s 118(2)* (see **46.2** PENALTIES) were held not to apply to a late claim under these provisions. A late claim cannot be treated as made within the time limits by virtue of there being a reasonable excuse for the failure to make the claim on time.

A claim cannot be made in a tax return.

Where, under PAYE, the construction industry scheme or other tax legislation, one person (P) is accountable to HMRC for capital gains tax (or income tax) or corporation tax payable by another person or for any other amount that has been or is to be set off against another person's liability, a claim in respect of the amount can only be made by that other person. If, however, P has paid such an amount but was not in fact accountable to HMRC for it, P, and only P, can make a claim in respect of that amount. Effect will not be given to such a claim by P to the extent that the amount has been repaid to, or set against amounts payable by, the other person.

Partnerships

A claim in respect of an amount paid or due by one or more partners in accordance with a self-assessment which is excessive because of a mistake in a partnership return must be made by a nominated partner (or his personal representative). The partner must have been a partner at some time in the period for which the return was made.

[*TMA 1970, Sch 1AB paras 3–5; FA 1998, Sch 18 paras 51B–51D*].

Discovery assessment etc. following claim

Where the grounds for a claim also provide grounds for HMRC to make a discovery assessment or determination (see **6.10** ASSESSMENTS) for any period and such an assessment or determination could not otherwise be made as a result of one of the restrictions noted below, those restrictions are disregarded and an assessment or determination is not out of time if made before the final determination of the claim (i.e. before the time at which the claim can no longer be varied). The restrictions concerned are those at **6.10**(2) ASSESSMENTS and the expiry of a time limit for making a discovery assessment or determination (see **6.12**, **6.14** ASSESSMENTS).

Similar provisions apply in relation to amendments of partnership returns.

[*TMA 1970, Sch 1AB paras 6, 7; FA 1998, Sch 18 paras 51E, 51F*].

Contract settlements

The above provisions apply also to amounts paid under a contract settlement (see **6.8** ASSESSMENTS). If the person who paid the amounts due under the settlement (the '*payer*') was not the person from whom the tax concerned was due (the '*taxpayer*'), then the provisions are modified accordingly. If an amount is repayable to the payer as a result of a claim, HMRC can set the amount repayable against any amount payable by the taxpayer under any discovery assessment or determination made as a result of the claim.

[*TMA 1970, Sch 1AB para 8; FA 1998, Sch 18 para 51G*].

Special relief

A claim can be made for discharge or repayment of tax charged in an HMRC determination (under *TMA 1970, s 28C* or *FA 1998, Sch 18 paras 36, 37* — see **52.17**, **52.21** RETURNS) if the following apply:

(1) the claimant believes the tax is not due or, if already paid, was not due;
(2) relief under the above provisions would have been available but for (c) above or because the tax is due as a result of proceedings by HMRC against the claimant (see (f) above) or because more than four years have passed since the end of the tax year or accounting period; and

(3) where the claim would fail because the tax is due as a result of proceedings by HMRC, the claimant was neither present nor legally represented during the proceedings.

HMRC will not give effect to the claim unless:

(i) in HMRC's opinion it would be unconscionable to seek to recover the tax or withhold repayment of it;
(ii) the taxpayer's affairs (in matters concerning HMRC) are otherwise up to date or satisfactory arrangements have been put in place to bring them up to date as far as possible; and
(iii) either the taxpayer has not previously made a claim for relief or relief under HMRC's equitable liability practice or, where such a claim has been made, the exceptional circumstances of the case mean that the present claim should be allowed.

For the purposes of (iii) above, it does not matter whether the previous claim succeeded. A claim must include information and documentation which is reasonably required to determine whether (i)–(iii) above apply.

The jurisdiction of the Tribunal in determining whether (i) above applies is limited to deciding whether the opinion of HMRC was 'unreasonable' in the judicial review sense. The Tribunal cannot consider afresh whether it would be unconscionable to seek to recover the tax or withhold repayment. See *Currie v HMRC* FTT 2014, [2015] SFTD 51. An appeal against HMRC's refusal to allow relief was successful in *Clark v HMRC* FTT, [2015] UKFTT 324 (TC), [2015] STI 2660. HMRC had failed to take into account the taxpayer's learning difficulties and other personal problems. An appeal was also successful in *Scott v HMRC* FTT, [2015] UKFTT 420 (TC); HMRC had failed to consider the disparity between the tax due as per the determinations made by HMRC and the tax due as per the appellant's late self-assessments.

[*TMA 1970, Sch 1AB para 3A; FA 1998, Sch 18 para 51BA*].

Claim for restitution of payment made under mistake of law

[13.8] It was confirmed in *R v CIR (ex p. Woolwich Equitable Building Society)*, HL 1990, 63 TC 589 that a claim can be made through the courts, under common law, for restitution of tax payments made to HMRC under an unlawful statutory demand and that interest is payable from the dates of the payments. In *Deutsche Morgan Grenfell Group plc v CIR* HL 2006, [2007] STC 1, the company successfully sought to obtain this remedy in respect of tax paid under a mistake of law. In making its claim, the company contended that under *Limitation Act 1980, s 32(1)(c)*, it could make the claim for restitution within six years of the time it discovered the mistake (or could with reasonable diligence have discovered it), rather than within the normal time limit of six years from the time of payment under *Limitation Act 1980, s 5*. In upholding the company's claim, the House of Lords held that the effect of *Limitation Act 1980, s 32(1)(c)* was that the limitation period had not begun until 8 March 2001 (the date of the CJEC decision in *Metalgesellschaft Ltd & Others v CIR* CJEC 2001, [2001] STC 452). The Supreme Court overruled this part of the decision, however, in *Test Claimants in the FII Litigation and Others v HMRC* SC, [2020] STC 2387. It held that the correct approach was that time begins to run under *Limitation Act 1980, s 32(1)(c)* when the claimant discovers, or could with reasonable diligence discover, his mistake 'in the sense of recognising that a worthwhile claim arises' with sufficient confidence to justify obtaining legal advice and collecting evidence with a view to commencing a claim.

Following the High Court decision in *Deutsche Morgan Grenfell*, provisions were included in *FA 2004* to prevent the application of the extended time limit of *Limitation Act 1980, s 32(1)(c)* to taxation matters. Accordingly, *s 32(1)(c)* (and the NI equivalent) does not apply in relation to any action or claim for relief from the consequences of a mistake of law relating to a taxation matter under the care and management of HMRC brought after 7 September 2003, whether the action or claim is expressed to be brought on the grounds of mistake or on some other ground (such as unlawful demand or *ultra vires*). [*FA 2004, s 320(1)(6)*]. The effect of this provision is that court actions for restitution based on mistake of law must generally be brought within six years of the tax having been paid.

The above provisions take legal effect only on 22 July 2004 (the date of Royal Assent to *FA 2004*). *FA 2004, s 320(3)* therefore deems an action begun before that date but after 7 September 2003, or a claim to amend an existing action made before 22 July 2004 but after 19 November 2003 to be discontinued on 22 July 2004 and provides for the recovery (with interest) of any amount paid out by the Revenue in relation to such an action or amendment.

These provisions are extended by *FA 2007, s 107* to prevent the application of *Limitation Act 1980, s 32(1)(c)* in relation to actions brought before 8 September 2003 as well as those brought on or after that date. This is subject to the following exceptions:

(a) where the action, or cause of action, has been the subject of a House of Lords judgment or order before 6 December 2006 as to the application of *s 32(1)(c)*;
(b) where the parties to the action are bound, under a group litigation order, by a House of Lords judgment or order before 6 December 2006 in another action as to the application of *s 32(1)(c)*; and
(c) where the action, or cause of action, relates to the charging of tax contrary to European Union law.

The extended provisions take legal effect only on 19 July 2007 (the date of Royal Assent to *FA 2007*). Any court judgment or order given or made before that date but after 5 December 2006 is therefore deemed to have been what it would have been had the extended provisions been in force at all times since the action was brought and any available defence of limitation had been raised. Any payment made under the judgment that is accordingly taken not to have been imposed is repayable with interest.

In *Test Claimants in the FII Group Litigation v HMRC* CJEU, [2014] STC 638 *FA 2007, s 107* above was held to breach European Community law because it does not incorporate any transitional provisions. The exception in (c) above was introduced by *FA 2014, s 299* to amend *FA 2007, s 107* to comply with that decision. Although the exception takes legal effect on 17 July 2014 (the date of

Royal Assent to *FA 2014*), it applies to actions brought, and causes of action arising, before, on or after that date. See also *United Kingdom v European Commission* CJEU, (C-640/13); 2015 STI 52, which confirmed that *FA 2007, s 107* breached EU law (but note that the decision did not consider the changes made by *FA 2014*).

In *Wallace v HMRC* Ch D, [2018] STC 790, it was held that a common law claim for restitution cannot be made where a claim for recovery of overpaid tax under **13.7** above can be made.

Key points concerning claims

[13.9] Points to consider are as follows.

- For capital gains tax claims, the time limit is four years after the end of a tax year. Care needs to be taken to ensure time limits are not missed. The same time limits also apply to the notification of a capital loss. In certain cases, the time limit runs from the end of the tax year of conveyance or transfer.
- Where the taxpayer has received notice to file a tax return the claim must be included in the tax return unless it could not be included or the claim involves two or more years.
- Claims can be made for recovery of overpaid tax where the taxpayer believes that the tax is not due. This procedure cannot be used where there is a mistake in a claim or as a result of omitting to make a claim. Where there is an error in a claim this can only be revised within the time periods for making the claim.

14

Companies

Cross-references. See **4.15** ANTI-AVOIDANCE where a close company transfers an asset otherwise than at arm's length for a consideration less than market value; **15** COMPANIES — CORPORATE FINANCE AND INTANGIBLES; **26** GROUPS OF COMPANIES; **51.28** RESIDENCE AND DOMICILE for company residence; **57** SHARES AND SECURITIES; **60** SUBSTANTIAL SHAREHOLDINGS OF COMPANIES; **63** UNIT TRUSTS ETC.; **64** VENTURE CAPITAL TRUSTS.

Simon's Taxes. See **D1.9**, **D6.450**.

Introduction to companies

[14.1] Companies do not pay capital gains tax. Instead they pay corporation tax on their chargeable gains. Gains are included in a company's profits liable to corporation tax and taxed at the applicable rate.

Chargeable gains and allowable losses are nevertheless computed according to capital gains tax principles, although there are many important differences in the computational rules. The main differences are listed at **14.2** below.

This chapter also covers a number of additional issues specific to companies. Provisions relating to capital losses, including anti-avoidance provisions and the corporate capital loss restriction, are detailed at **14.6–14.11** below. Reliefs for reconstructions etc. of companies are at **14.13** below. Overseas matters are noted at **14.14–14.17** below, including provisions relating to the formation and residence of European Companies and European Co-operatives.

Senior accounting officers of certain large companies are required to take steps to ensure that the company maintains adequate tax accounting arrangements to enable the company's tax liabilities to be calculated accurately. See **14.19** below.

Large companies (and partnerships) must publish an annual tax strategy online, outlining their approach to tax risk, tax planning and dealing with HMRC (see **14.20** below). If they have a history of unco-operative behaviour they may become subject to a special measures regime (see **14.21** below).

Liability of companies to corporation tax on their chargeable gains

[14.2] Companies are liable to corporation tax on their chargeable gains. These gains are included in their profits liable to corporation tax as described in **14.3** below.

UK-resident companies are chargeable to corporation tax on gains on assets situated in the UK or overseas. Non-resident companies are chargeable to corporation tax only on chargeable gains on the disposal of:

(a) UK-situated assets with a connection to the company's UK permanent establishment (see **43.3** OVERSEAS MATTERS);
(b) (for disposals on or after 6 April 2019) interests in UK land (see **35.23** LAND); and
(c) (for disposals on or after 6 April 2019) assets deriving at least 75% of their value from UK land where the company has a substantial indirect interest in that land (see **35.24** LAND).

Companies accordingly do not pay 'capital gains tax' as such, but for disposals before 6 April 2019, there were two exceptions to this rule. The exceptions were for the capital gains tax charges on high value disposals of dwellings and non-resident disposals of UK residential property interests (see **35.31** LAND). For later disposals, the charge on high value disposals of dwellings is abolished and the charge on UK residential property interests is replaced by the corporation tax charge in (b) above.

[*TCGA 1992, ss 1(2), 2B; CTA 2009, ss 4, 19*].

Chargeable gains and allowable losses are nevertheless computed in accordance with provisions relating to capital gains tax, except that:

(i) computations are made by reference to accounting periods instead of tax years [*TCGA 1992, s 2D*];
(ii) provisions in the legislation confined to individuals do not apply to companies [*TCGA 1992, ss 2E, 2F*];
(iii) re-basing to market value at 31 March 1982 applies to companies subject to certain exceptions (see **8** ASSETS HELD ON 31 MARCH **1982**);

(iv) special provisions apply to tax as income gains and losses in respect of loan relationships, derivative contracts and intangible assets (see **15** COMPANIES — CORPORATE FINANCE AND INTANGIBLES);
(v) BUSINESS ASSET DISPOSAL RELIEF (**9**) applies to qualifying business disposals by individuals, etc., but not by companies;
(vi) INVESTORS' RELIEF (**34**) applies to disposals of qualifying shares by individuals and trustees but not by companies;
(vii) indexation allowance is available to companies, but has been frozen at its December 2017 level (see **32.1** INDEXATION);
(viii) the rules for matching shares and securities sold with those acquired are not the same for corporation tax as for capital gains tax (see **58.1** SHARES AND SECURITIES — IDENTIFICATION RULES);
(ix) certain provisions, as contained in this chapter, apply only to companies.

See also **6** ASSESSMENTS; **36** LATE PAYMENT INTEREST AND PENALTIES; **45** PAYMENT OF TAX; **46** PENALTIES; **50** REPAYMENT INTEREST; and **52** RETURNS for matters applicable to companies generally.

The definition of 'company' includes any body corporate or unincorporated association but does not include a partnership. [*TCGA 1992, s 288(1)*]. References to 'persons' in the capital gains tax legislation generally include unincorporated associations (*CIR v Worthing Rugby Football Club Trustees* CA 1987, 60 TC 482).

Rate of corporation tax in respect of chargeable gains

[14.3] The whole of the chargeable gains (net of allowable losses under **14.6** below) of a company is included in the taxable total profits, chargeable to corporation tax. For financial years 2023, 2024 and 2025, the main rate is 25% and the small profits rate is 19%. If the company's accounting period straddles different financial years with different rates, chargeable profits are apportioned on a time basis between the years. For all financial years 2020–22, there is a single rate of 19%. [*CTA 2009, s 8; TCGA 1992, s 2A(1); FA 2020, ss 5, 6; FA 2021, ss 6, 7; F(No 2)A 2023, ss 5, 6; F(No 2)A 2024, ss 12, 13*].

Alternative rules apply as in **63** UNIT TRUSTS AND OTHER INVESTMENT VEHICLES and **64.6** VENTURE CAPITAL TRUSTS.

Liquidation

[14.4] The vesting of a company's assets in a liquidator is disregarded for chargeable gains purposes (i.e. the assets are not treated as disposed of). All the acts of the liquidator in relation to such assets are treated as acts of the company. [*TCGA 1992, s 2G*].

See also **57.11**, **57.12** and **57.13** SHARES AND SECURITIES.

Interest charged to capital

[14.5] For interest paid in accounting periods beginning after 31 March 1981, interest on money borrowed by a company for the construction of any building, structure or works, and referable to a time before disposal of it, may be added to the expenditure allowable as a deduction under *TCGA 1992, s 38* in computing the gain on the disposal of the building etc. by the company, provided the expenditure on the construction was itself so allowable. No such relief is given for interest referable to any accounting period ending after 31 March 1996 (in consequence of the loan relationship provisions at **15.2** COMPANIES — CORPORATE FINANCE AND INTANGIBLES) or for interest treated as a charge on income under *ICTA 1988, s 338*. This restriction also applies to any amount which is allowable as a deduction in computing income, profits, gains or losses for corporation tax purposes (or would be so but for an insufficiency of profits or gains) or which would be allowable if the building etc. was held as a fixed asset of a trade. The practical effect of these restrictions is that a payment of interest is unlikely to qualify as allowable expenditure in computing a chargeable gain.

For interest paid in accounting periods ending before 1 April 1981, the provisions and comment made in the last two sentences above do not apply. Instead, interest had to be charged to capital in order to qualify as allowable expenditure, which treatment prevented it being treated as a charge on income by virtue of *ICTA 1970, s 248(5)(a) as originally enacted.*

[*TCGA 1992, s 40*].

Capital losses

[14.6] The amount of chargeable gains to be taken into account for an accounting period is the amount of the chargeable gains accruing to the company in that period less the aggregate amount of the allowable losses in that period and allowable losses and allowable NRCGT losses (in respect of non-resident CGT disposals of UK residential property interests before 6 April 2019 — see **35.31** LAND) brought forward from any previous period. Allowable losses include short-term losses accruing under *Schedule D, Case VII* for years before 1971/72 which remain unrelieved.

A special rule applies where a company has two or more accounting periods falling wholly within the same financial year, is chargeable to corporation tax for each period only because of a chargeable gain (or allowable loss) arising on the disposal of an asset, and during any gaps between those periods is not chargeable to corporation tax. So far as not otherwise deducted, losses arising in one of the periods can be deducted from gains arising in any of the other periods. The effect is that a loss arising in a later period can be carried back to an earlier period and a loss in an earlier period can be carried forward. To the extent that the loss is carried forward to an accounting period falling wholly within the same financial year, it can be deducted without the application of the corporate loss restriction rules at **14.11** below. The restriction will apply to its deduction in any later accounting period. This provision will be relevant in particular to non-UK resident companies making direct or indirect disposals of UK land (see **35.23** LAND).

[*TCGA 1992, s 2A(1), Sch 11 para 12; FA 2020, Sch 4 para 39*].

For corporation tax on chargeable gains purposes, an allowable loss does not include any loss which, if it had been a gain, would have been exempt from corporation tax in the hands of the company (and see also the anti-avoidance provisions mentioned below). [*TCGA 1992, s 2A(2)*].

Corporate allowable losses cannot normally be offset against trading profits or other income but see **38.17** LOSSES. Since chargeable gains are included in total profits which are liable to corporation tax as in **14.2** above, claims under *CTA 2010, s 37* to set trading losses against such profits mean that trading losses can be set against chargeable gains arising in the same accounting period and, to the extent permitted by that *section*, preceding accounting periods. Trading losses arising on or after 1 April 2017 may also be carried forward and set against the total profits (including gains) of future periods, subject to certain restrictions. See Tolley's Corporation Tax under Losses for the detailed provisions. [*CTA 2010, s 37*].

Management expenses of a company with investment business may be offset against chargeable gains within the same or succeeding accounting periods. [*CTA 2009, ss 1219, 1223*].

Anti-avoidance

There are a number of anti-avoidance provisions relating specifically to corporate capital losses. In particular, there are three targeted provisions attacking arrangements entered into which have as a main purpose the obtaining of a tax advantage. For details of the provisions, see **14.7–14.9** below (avoidance utilising losses), **26.16, 26.17** GROUPS OF COMPANIES (gain buying and loss buying) and **38.8** LOSSES (losses accruing from arrangements to secure tax advantage).

See also **26.18** GROUPS OF COMPANIES for the restriction, where the provisions at **26.16, 26.17** GROUPS OF COMPANIES do not apply, on set-off of pre-entry losses where a company joins a group.

Corporate capital loss restriction

See **14.11** below for restrictions on the use of brought forward capital losses by companies to 50% of annual capital gains.

Avoidance utilising capital losses

[14.7] The following provisions are intended to ensure that capital losses cannot be used against income profits. HMRC have indicated that the provisions are intended to affect only companies that deliberately and knowingly enter into arrangements to avoid tax (HMRC Guidance 'Avoidance through the creation and use of capital losses by companies', 22 March 2006).

Two strategies to utilise capital losses are targeted by the provisions. The first is to turn an income receipt into capital (see **14.8** below). The second is to generate a deduction from income as part of arrangements to crystallise a capital gain (see **14.9** below). The effect is to restrict the use of capital losses. In both cases, the provisions apply only where HMRC issue a notice to the company concerned (see below).

Both sets of provisions require that there be 'arrangements' the main purpose, or one of the main purposes, of which is to secure a 'tax advantage' (although each contains a qualification of the definition of tax advantage given below — see **14.8** and **14.9** below). [*TCGA 1992, ss 184G(2)(5), 184H(2)(4)*].

'*Arrangements*' for this purpose include any agreement, understanding, scheme, transaction or series of transactions, whether or not legally enforceable. A '*tax advantage*' means obtaining or increasing relief from, or repayment of, corporation tax, the avoidance or reduction of a corporation tax charge or assessment or the avoidance of a possible assessment to corporation tax. [*TCGA 1992, ss 184D, 184G(10), 184H(10)*].

For HMRC's view on the application of the terms 'arrangements', 'tax advantage' and 'main purpose', see **38.8** LOSSES and HMRC Capital Gains Manual CG44102–44106.

HMRC notices

As noted above, the application of the provisions is contingent upon the issue of a notice to the company by HMRC. Such a notice may be issued if HMRC have reasonable grounds for considering that the statutory conditions triggering the legislation are present. It must specify the arrangements in question, the accounting period (or periods) involved and the effect of the anti-avoidance provisions.

If the company has not yet made a return for the accounting period it may, if it makes a return within the 90-day period beginning with the day on which the notice is given, make the return disregarding the notice and make any necessary amendment later within the same 90-day period.

If the company has already made a return for the accounting period, HMRC may only issue a notice if a notice of enquiry (see **52.21** RETURNS) has been given in respect of that return. The company may amend its return in light of the notice at any time within the 90-day period beginning with the day on which the notice is given. A closure notice in respect of the enquiry may not be issued before the earlier of the company amending its return or the end of the 90-day period. This does not apply to a partial closure notice which does not relate to any matter to which the notice here relates.

If enquiries into the return have been completed in relation to any matters, the power enjoyed by HMRC to issue a notice relating to those matters is subject to two requirements, both of which must be met. The first is that at the time those enquiries were completed HMRC could not, on the basis of information made available to them (within *FA 1998, Sch 18 para 44(2)(3)* — see **6.10** ASSESSMENTS) before that time, reasonably have been aware of circumstances indicating that a notice could have been issued. The second is that a request for information was made during the enquiry relating to the matters in question which, if duly complied with, would have resulted in a reasonable expectation that HMRC would issue a notice. If a notice is issued in these circumstances, no discovery assessment may be made before the earlier of the company amending its return or the end of the 90-day period beginning with the day on which the notice is given. However, the normal restrictions on making discovery assessments in *FA 1998, Sch 18 paras 43, 44* do not apply (see **6.10** ASSESSMENTS).

On receiving a notice containing HMRC's view of the position, it is up to the company to decide if it needs to amend its self-assessment. If it fails to make an amendment which ought to have been made its return will be incorrect (with all the resulting implications for penalties, etc.).

[*TCGA 1992, ss 184G(6)(8)(9), 184H(6)(8)(9), 184I*].

Clearances

HMRC operate an informal clearance procedure and will give advice on actual or proposed transactions. Applications for clearance should be sent to reconstr uctions@hmrc.gov.uk or by post to BAI Clearance, HM Revenue & Customs, BX9 1JL. A clearance will state the terms on which it has been given and HMRC will regard itself bound by a clearance provided that all relevant facts are accurately given and (where the clearance is sought in advance) the transaction is executed in accordance with the proposals set out in the clearance application. Where a clearance cannot be given HMRC will state the reasons, but taxpayers are not bound by their decision. For details of the information required by HMRC in clearance applications, see HMRC Capital Gains Manual CG44156. (HMRC Capital Gains Manual CG44150–44156).

Schemes converting income into capital

[14.8] HMRC may issue a notice (see **14.7** above) invoking anti-avoidance measures where it has reasonable grounds for considering that the following four conditions are, or may be, satisfied:

(a) a receipt or other amount arises to a company directly or indirectly in consequence of, or otherwise in connection with, any arrangements (see **14.7** above);
(b) that amount is taken into account in calculating a chargeable gain (the '*relevant gain*') accruing to a company (the '*relevant company*') and losses arise (or have arisen) to that company, whether before or after or as part of the arrangements;
(c) but for the arrangements an amount would have been taken into account wholly or partly instead of the amount in (a) above as income of the relevant company (or as the income of a company in the same capital gains tax group (see **26.2** GROUPS OF COMPANIES) at any time in the period beginning with the time at which the arrangements were made and ending when the matters, other than the tax advantage, intended to be secured by the arrangements are secured); and
(d) the main purpose, or one of the main purposes, of the arrangements was the obtaining of a tax advantage (see **14.7** above) involving the deduction of the capital losses from the relevant gain.

If all these conditions are satisfied when the HMRC notice is given, the relevant company may not deduct any loss from the relevant gain.

[*TCGA 1992, s 184G(1)–(5)(7)(10)*].

Schemes securing deductions

[14.9] HMRC may issue a notice (see **14.7** above) invoking anti-avoidance measures where it has reasonable grounds for considering that the following four conditions are, or may be, satisfied:

(a) a chargeable gain (the '*relevant gain*') accrues to a company (the '*relevant company*') directly or indirectly in consequence of, or otherwise in connection with, any arrangements (see **14.7** above) and that company has capital losses available;

(b) the relevant company, or a company connected with it, becomes entitled to an 'income deduction' directly or indirectly in consequence of, or otherwise in connection with, the arrangements;

(c) the main purpose, or one of the main purposes, of the arrangements was the obtaining of a tax advantage (see **14.7** above) involving both the income deduction and the deduction of losses from the relevant gain; and

(d) the arrangements are not 'excluded arrangements' (see below).

It does not matter whether the tax advantage is secured for the relevant company or any other company.

'*Excluded arrangements*' are certain arm's length sale and leaseback transactions involving land where there is no connection between the lessor and the lessee. An '*income deduction*' means a deduction in calculating income for corporation tax purposes or a deduction from total profits.

If all the above conditions are satisfied when the HMRC notice is given, the relevant company may not deduct any loss from the relevant gain.

[*TCGA 1992, s 184H(1)–(5)(7)(10)(11)*].

Avoidance involving corporation tax losses generally

[14.10] There are provisions which counteract 'loss-related' tax advantages arising from 'tax arrangements'. Originally, the provisions applied only to income losses, but as noted below, they have now been extended to capital losses.

'*Tax arrangements*' are arrangements (as widely defined) with a main purpose of obtaining a loss-related tax advantage if it is reasonable to regard them as circumventing the intended limits of relief under the provisions in question or otherwise exploiting shortcomings in those provisions. All relevant circumstances must be taken into account, including whether there are any steps which are contrived or abnormal or lack a genuine commercial purpose.

A tax advantage (within *CTA 2010, s 1139*) is '*loss-related*' if it arises as a result of a deduction (or increased deduction) in respect of trade losses, non-trading loan relationship deficits, non-trading losses on intangible assets, management expenses, UK property business losses, group relief, group relief for carried-forward losses or allowable capital losses.

Counteraction is made by the making of just and reasonable adjustments (by HMRC or the company) by way of an assessment, the modification of an assessment, amendment or disallowance of a claim or otherwise.

[*F(No 2)A 2017, s 19; FA 2020, Sch 4 para 23*].

Corporate capital loss restriction

[14.11] There are provisions which restrict the deduction of carried-forward losses, including capital losses (*CTA 2010, ss 269ZA–269ZZB*). Broadly, the restriction limits the amount of profits against which any carried-forward losses

can be relieved to 50% of profits over an annual 'deductions allowance' of £5 million. A single £5 million limit is shared between all of the members of a group, but can be allocated to each company as the group sees fit.

The provisions operate by separating carried-forward losses between those which can be set off against total profits, profits of the same trade, non-trading income profits or chargeable gains and applying a maximum deduction in each case. A company can choose how to allocate its deductions allowance to each category by specifying the amount of a trading profits deductions allowance, a chargeable gains deductions allowance and so on.

The commentary below covers the restriction only so far as it applies to capital losses. For full coverage of the provisions, see Tolley's Corporation Tax under Losses.

Deductions from chargeable gains

In calculating a company's taxable total profits, the total deductions for allowable capital losses brought forward for set-off against chargeable gains are restricted to the sum of:

- 50% of the company's 'relevant chargeable gains' (see further below) for the period; and
- the company's 'chargeable gains deductions allowance' for the period, i.e. so much of its overall deductions allowance as is specified in the company tax return for the period (and therefore nil if no such amount is specified).

The amount specified as the chargeable gains deductions allowance may not be greater than the difference between the overall deductions allowance and the total of any parts of the allowance allocated in the return to trading profits and non-trading income profits.

This restriction does not apply if the company's modified total profits (see **44.14** below) are not greater than nil.

[*CTA 2010, s 269ZBA; FA 2020, Sch 4 paras 2, 42*].

Pre-entry losses are not treated as brought forward losses for these purposes, but see **26.20** GROUPS OF COMPANIES for the effect of these provisions for such losses. See also **14.6** above for the exclusion of certain losses carried forward to an accounting period falling wholly within the same financial year as that in which they arose and **38.7** LOSSES for a claim which can be made to mitigate the effect of the restriction in relation to clogged losses.

Relevant chargeable gains

A company's *relevant chargeable gains*' are the 'qualifying chargeable gains' less the chargeable gains deductions allowance for the period. A negative amount is taken to be nil. The '*qualifying chargeable gains*' are calculated by applying five steps which also determine equivalent amounts in respect of the different categories of income to which the restriction applies ('qualifying trading profits' and 'qualifying non-trading income profits'). The steps are as follows.

(1) Calculate the company's 'modified total profits' for the period. If the modified total profits are not greater than nil, then both the qualifying trading profits, qualifying non-trading income profits and qualifying chargeable gains are taken to be nil. The '*modified total profits*' are the total profits for the period modified by:

- ignoring income consisting of distributions;
- making no deductions for trade losses brought forward for deduction against profits of the same trade (other than certain deductions that would be ignored for the purposes of the restriction by reason of the creative industries reliefs or the provisions for UK and EEA furnished holiday lettings);
- making no deductions for non-trading loan relationship deficits carried forward for set-off against non-trading profits; and
- making no deductions for allowable capital losses brought forward.

(2) Calculate the sum of any amounts which could be relieved against the company's total profits (as modified in (1) above) of the period, ignoring any 'excluded deductions'. If the amount in (1) above does not exceed the amount given by this step, then the qualifying trading profits, qualifying non-trading income profits and qualifying chargeable gains are each taken to be nil. The following are '*excluded deductions*':

- non-trading loan relationship deficits carried forward against total profits (*CTA 2009, s 463G*);
- non-trading losses on intangible fixed assets (*CTA 2009, s 753*);
- management expenses carried forward and treated as management expenses of the accounting period (*CTA 2009, s 1219*);
- UK property business losses carried forward and treated as management expenses of the accounting period (*CTA 2009, s 1219*);
- trade losses arising to a production company under one of the creative industries reliefs (for films, TV, theatrical productions etc.) carried forward and treated as a loss of a later period for set-off against profits of that or earlier periods;
- trade losses carried forward for set-off against total profits (*CTA 2010, s 45A*);
- UK property business losses carried forward and treated as a loss of the period (*CTA 2010, s 62(3)*);
- group relief in respect of a loss surrendered by a production company under one of the creative industries reliefs in respect of brought forward treated as losses of a later period;
- group relief for carried-forward losses (*CTA 2010, Pt 5A*);
- trade losses carried back from a later accounting period (*CTA 2010, s 37*);
- a terminal loss for carried-forward losses (*CTA 2010, s 45F*);
- excess special leasing capital allowances carried back (*CAA 2001, s 260(3)*); and
- non-trading loan relationship deficit carried back from a later accounting period (*CTA 2009, s 463E*).

(3) Divide the modified total profits into trade profits (i.e. the profits of a trade of the company), non-trade income profits (the remaining profits other than any chargeable gains) and chargeable gains.
(4) Allocate the whole of the amount found in (2) above to one or more of the amounts found in (3) above and reduce each of those amounts by the amount so allocated. The company can allocate the reliefs within (2) above to the amounts in (3) above as it wishes but the trade profits, non-trade income profits and chargeable gains cannot be reduced below nil.
(5) The amounts found in (4) above are the company's qualifying trading profits, qualifying non-trading income profits and qualifying chargeable gains.

[*CTA 2010, s 269ZF; FA 2020, Sch 4 paras 5–7, 29, 42–46*].

Deductions allowance

Subject to the claim for an alternative calculation available to companies without a source of chargeable income (see below), the '*deductions allowance*' for a company which is not a member of a group for an accounting period is £5 million. If the period is less than 12 months long, the deductions allowance is proportionately reduced.

Where a company is a member of a group (and at least one other member is within the charge to corporation tax), its deduction allowance is the part of the 'group deductions allowance' allocated to it. Where the company joins or leaves the group during an accounting period, it is also entitled to a proportionate part of the £5 million limit for any part of the period for which it is not a member of a group. The company's overall deductions allowance cannot exceed £5 million (reduced proportionately for a period of less than 12 months).

Where two or more members of a group are within the charge to corporation tax, all of them need jointly to nominate one of their number to be responsible for allocating the group deductions allowance. The '*group deductions allowance*' is £5 million for each accounting period of the nominated company throughout which the group allowance nomination has effect (reduced proportionately for periods of less than 12 months). If a nomination takes effect, or ceases to take effect part way through an accounting period, the two parts must be dealt with separately — the nominated company can only allocate a proportionate part of the allowance for the whole period.

The amount of a company's deductions allowance is increased in certain circumstances where a credit or other income is brought into account in connection with an onerous lease in calculating the company's modified total profits for the accounting period. The allowance is increased by the amount of the credit or income (or, if lower, the amount of the modified total profits). The credit or income must be a credit in respect of the reversal of an onerous lease provision or right of use asset impairment loss, a credit in respect of the remeasurement of the lease liability or a credit or other income resulting from a change in lease payments payable before 30 June 2022 as a result of the COVID-19 pandemic and accounted for by means of variable lease payments.

A company's deductions allowance is increased where it is in insolvent liquidation (i.e. where its assets are insufficient to pay its debts, liabilities and the expenses of the winding-up). For each accounting period during the winding-up, the deductions allowance is increased by the lower of the chargeable gains arising the period after deducting allowable losses arising in the period and the total allowable losses brought forward to that period. For this purpose, gains (but not losses) are ignored if the asset was acquired by the company by intra-group transfer during the winding-up and the transfer was treated as no gain/no loss (under *TCGA 1992, s 171* — see **26.3** GROUPS OF COMPANIES), provided that the transferor was not itself in insolvent liquidation at the time of the transfer. Gains (but not losses) are also ignored if they were transferred to the company by way of a *TCGA 1992, s 171A* election (see **26.13** GROUPS OF COMPANIES) during the winding-up from a company which was not itself in insolvent liquidation at the time the election was made.

If a company makes any of the deductions which may be restricted by these provisions for an accounting period, it must state the amount of its deductions allowance for the period in its company tax return. If the allowance is increased because of the reversal of an onerous lease provision or because the company is in insolvent liquidation, it must also state what the allowance would have been without the increase. If a company's tax return specifies an excessive amount as its deductions allowance, its trading profits deduction allowance, its chargeable gains deductions allowance or its non-trading income profits deductions allowance (previously its non-trading profits deduction allowance), it must amend the return so that the amounts are not excessive. If an HMRC officer considers that an undue amount of relief has been given because of the inclusion of an excessive amount, he may make an assessment in the amount which in his opinion ought to be charged. If the amount became excessive because of a change in the amount of group deductions allowance allocated to the company and the company fails, or is unable to amend its return accordingly, an HMRC assessment is not out of time if made within 12 months of the date on which the change took place.

[*CTA 2010, ss 269ZDA, 269ZR, 269ZS(1)–(4), 269ZW–269ZY, 269ZZ–269ZZA; FA 2020, Sch 4 paras 8, 9, 28, 32–35, 42–46; FA 2022, s 30*].

Companies without a source of chargeable income

Where a company has no source of chargeable income throughout a financial year, it can make a claim for its deductions allowance to be calculated in a different way for accounting periods falling wholly within that year if it is chargeable to corporation tax for the period only because of a chargeable gain arising on the disposal of an asset.

The company must, at all times in the financial year, either be outside the charge to corporation tax or be chargeable to corporation tax only because of a chargeable gain arising on the disposal of an asset. If the company is a member of a group, every other group member must also satisfy this requirement.

A claim is made for a specific accounting period, but a company may have more than one accounting period falling wholly within a financial year. A period for which a claim is made is referred to below as a 'claim AP'. An accounting period falling wholly within the same financial year as a claim AP but for which no claim is made is an 'alternative AP'.

A company's deductions allowance for a claim AP is the lower of:

- the 'available deductions allowance amount';
- the total allowable capital losses carried forward to the period; or
- the chargeable gains arising in the period.

A company's deductions amount for an alternative AP is the lower of the deductions amount that would be found using the normal rules and the available deductions allowance amount.

The '*available deductions allowance amount*' for an accounting period is £5 million less the total of any deductions allowances already claimed by the company (or any other group member) for any claim APs and alternative APs falling wholly within the financial year. For this purpose, the deductions allowance already claimed in respect of an alternative AP is taken to be the amount specified in the company's return for the period as its chargeable gains deduction allowance. Deductions allowances are treated as claimed in the order shown in the following table.

Case	Rule
1. There is a claim AP and another claim AP starting on the same or a different day.	The order in which the claims are made.
2. There is an alternative AP (AP1) and another alternative AP (AP2) starting on a later day.	AP1 before AP2.
3. There is an alternative AP and another alternative AP starting on the same day.	The order in which the tax returns for the alternative APs are delivered.
4. There is a claim AP and an alternative AP starting on the same day, earlier day or a later day.	The claim AP before the alternative AP.

A claim must be made within two years after the end of the accounting period but cannot be made before the end of the financial year. If a company files its tax return for an accounting period before the end of the financial year, it can, however, include a declaration that the requirements for a claim are met and that it intends to make a claim. If it does so, it is treated as if it had made a claim until either the declaration is withdrawn or an actual claim is made. A declaration also ceases to have effect if the company, or a group member, comes within the charge to corporation tax before the end of the financial year otherwise than as a result of a chargeable gain arising on the disposal of an asset. If it has not otherwise ceased to have effect, a declaration ceases to have effect two years after the end of the accounting period. Any adjustments to returns, assessments etc. required when a determination ceases to have effect can be made regardless of any time limits.

[*CTA 2010, ss 269ZYA, 269ZYB; FA 2020, Sch 4 paras 10, 42–46*].

See also **14.6** above for losses arising in different accounting periods within the same financial year to a company within the charge to corporation tax only because of chargeable gains.

Group allowance nomination

A group allowance nomination must be signed by an appropriate representative of each member which is within the charge to corporation tax and must state the date on which it takes effect (which may be before the nomination is actually made). A nomination ceases to have effect when a new nomination is made, when an appropriate representative of one of the companies notifies HMRC in writing to that effect or when the nominated company ceases to be a member of the group or within the charge to corporation tax.

The nominated company must submit a group allowance allocation statement to HMRC for each accounting period before the first anniversary of the filing date for the company tax return for the period, or by such later time as HMRC allow. If a new nomination takes effect before the statement for an accounting period is submitted, it is the new nominated company which must make the submission. This rule does not, however, affect the validity of a statement submitted before the new nomination is made. A statement must be signed by an appropriate representative of the nominated company and must allocate amounts of the group deductions allowance to one or more group members. For each amount allocated, it must specify the accounting period of the member company to which it is allocated. Where a company's accounting period does not coincide exactly with that of the nominated company, only part of the group deductions allowance can be allocated to that accounting period, proportionate to the part of the period which overlaps with the nominated company's accounting period. The total allocations must not exceed the group deductions allowance. If the allocations exceed the maximum for a particular company or the overall maximum, the nominated company must submit a revised statement within 30 days of the original submission or within such period as HMRC allow. If the allocations in a statement subsequently become excessive, a revised statement must be submitted within 30 days of the date the allocations became excessive or within such period as HMRC allow. If a company fails to submit a revised statement, HMRC may amend the original statement as they think fit by notice in writing to the company (and must send a copy of the amended statement to each company to which an allocation is made). The normal time limits for amending company tax returns are disapplied to amendments made as a result of the submission of a statement.

A nominated company may submit a revised statement at any time before the latest of: the first anniversary of the filing date for the company's accounting period; 30 days after the completion of an enquiry into a return of any of the group companies to which an allocation was, or could have been, made in the original return; 30 days after an HMRC amendment to such a return following an enquiry; 30 days after any appeal against such an amendment is finally determined and any later time allowed by HMRC.

HMRC have the power to make regulations relating to administrative requirements for nominations and group allowance allocation statements.

[*CTA 2010, ss 269ZS(5)–(10), 269ZT–269ZV*].

Meaning of 'group'

A '*group*' consists of two or more companies, one of which is the 'ultimate parent' of the others but is not the ultimate parent of any other companies. A company is the '*ultimate parent*' of another company if it is the parent of the other company and no company is the parent of both of them. A company (A) is the parent of another company (B) if B is a 75% subsidiary of A, if A is beneficially entitled to at least 75% of any profits available for distribution to equity holders of B or A would be so entitled to at least 75% of any assets of B available to equity holders on a winding up. '75% subsidiary' and 'equity holder' are defined as for group relief (see *CTA 2010, ss 157–182*) but extended to apply to companies without ordinary share capital, unincorporated associations, and to ownership through entities other than companies, trusts or other arrangements.

An offshore collective investment vehicle (see **35.26** LAND) which is neither a company nor a partnership is treated for these purposes as if it were a company and as if the rights of the participants were shares in that company.

[*CTA 2010, s 269ZZB; FA 2020, Sch 4 paras 11, 42–46*].

Example

ABC Ltd, which is not a member of a group, has a 31 March year end. At 1 April 2024, it has an allowable capital loss brought forward of £8 million. Its profits for the year ended 31 March 2025 are as follows:

	£'000
Trading profits	3,000
Chargeable gains	6,000
Total	£9,000

ABC Ltd's taxable total profits for the year ended 31 March 2025 will be as follows:

	£'000
Trading profits	3,000
Capital gains	6,000
Less loss brought forward from y/e 31.3.24 (restricted)	(5,500)
TTP	3,500

The restriction on the set-off of the carried-forward loss against profits for the year ending 31 March 2025 is calculated as follows.

	£'000
Qualifying chargeable gains	6,000
Less deductions allowance	(5,000)
Relevant chargeable gains	£1,000
Relevant chargeable gains × 50%	500

Add deductions allowance	5,000
Maximum set-off	£5,500

Losses Summary:

	£'000
Capital losses b/fwd	8,000
Current year setoff	(5,500)
Capital losses c/fwd	£2,500

Company reconstructions

Reconstructions involving transfer of business

[14.12] See also 57.5 and 57.7 SHARES AND SECURITIES.

If the conditions below are satisfied, where a 'scheme of reconstruction' involves the transfer of a company's business to another company for no consideration (other than the assumption of liabilities of the business), capital assets (not used as trading stock by either company) are regarded as being transferred at a 'no gain/no loss' disposal value and the acquiring company takes over the disposing company's acquisition date for the purposes of ASSETS HELD ON 6 APRIL 1965 (8).

For this purpose, '*scheme of reconstruction*' is as defined by *TCGA 1992, s 136, Sch 5AA* (see 57.7 SHARES AND SECURITIES). For practical illustrations of schemes of reconstruction, see HMRC Capital Gains Manual CG52720–52728.

The conditions that must be satisfied are:

- that *either* the transferee company is UK-resident at the time of acquisition *or* the assets are 'chargeable assets'; *and*
- that *either* the transferor company is UK-resident at that time *or* the assets are 'chargeable assets'.

For these purposes, an asset is a '*chargeable asset*' in relation to a company at a particular time if, on a disposal by that company at that time, any gain would be a chargeable gain chargeable to corporation tax (see **14.2**(a)–(c) above).

[*TCGA 1992, s 139(1)(1A)(1AA)(2)(9)*].

See **45.10** PAYMENT OF TAX for CT payment plans for transactions with EEA resident group members which allow for payment by instalments where *TCGA 1992, s 139* is disapplied.

Anti-avoidance, disapplication of relief and advance clearance

TCGA 1992, s 139 will not apply to any transfer unless either the scheme is for bona fide commercial reasons and not to avoid corporation tax, capital gains tax or income tax, or HMRC, on written application by the acquiring company, has notified its satisfaction with the scheme before the transfer is made. HMRC may, within 30 days of receipt, call for further particulars to be supplied within 30 days, or longer if HMRC allows; if the information is not supplied, the application lapses. Subject to this, HMRC must notify its decision within a further 30 days. If not so notified, or if dissatisfied with the decision, the applicant may within a further 30 days require HMRC to refer the application to the Tribunal for its decision. All material facts and considerations must be disclosed, otherwise any decision is void. [*TCGA 1992, ss 138(2)–(5), 139(5); SI 2009 No 56, Sch 1 para 179*].

Applications for clearance should be directed to BAI Clearance, HMRC BX9 1JL (if market-sensitive information is included, for the attention of the team leader). Applications may be emailed to reconstructions@hmrc.gov.uk. A hard copy need not then be sent. Only a single application need be made for clearances under any one or more of: *CTA 2010, ss 1091, 1092* (demergers), *CTA 2010, ss 1044, 1045* (purchase of own shares), *ITA 2007, s 701* or *CTA 2010, s 748* (transactions in securities), *TCGA 1992, s 138(1)* (share exchanges — see **4.16** ANTI-AVOIDANCE), *TCGA 1992, s 139(5)* (as above), *TCGA 1992, s 140B* (transfer or division of a UK business between EU member states — **43.12** OVERSEAS MATTERS), *TCGA 1992, s 140D* (transfer or division of a non-UK business between EU member states — **43.13** OVERSEAS MATTERS) and *CTA 2009, s 831* (various clearances under the corporation tax intangible assets regime). See www.gov.uk/guidance/seeking-clearance-or-approval-for-a-transaction.

Where, if the disposing company had not been wound up, tax could have been assessed on it because of the effect of *TCGA 1992, s 139(5)* above, that tax can be assessed and charged (in the name of the disposing company) on the acquiring company. Subject to this, tax assessed on either company which is unpaid six months after the date when it is payable, may be similarly assessed and charged on certain third parties. The third parties are restricted to any person holding all or any part of the assets in respect of which the tax is charged and who either is the acquiring company or subsequently acquired them as a result of one or more disposals within *TCGA 1992, s 139* or *s 171(1)* (companies within same group) without any intervening disposals not within those provisions. Tax assessed on the third party is restricted to the proportion held of the assets in respect of which the tax was originally charged and may be recovered from the company originally assessed, along with any interest which the third party has paid on the outstanding tax. The assessment on the third party must be made within two years after the later of the date the tax became due and payable by the company and the date the assessment was made on the company. [*TCGA 1992, s 139(6)–(8); SI 1992 No 3066*].

Unit, investment and venture capital trusts

The provisions of *TCGA 1992, s 139* do not apply in the case of a transfer of the whole or part of a company's business to a unit trust scheme (including an umbrella scheme), within *TCGA 1992, s 100(2)* or which is an authorised unit trust, to an investment trust or to a venture capital trust (see **63** UNIT TRUSTS AND OTHER INVESTMENT VEHICLES and **64** VENTURE CAPITAL TRUSTS). [*TCGA 1992, ss 99A(3), 139(4)*].

Where *TCGA 1992, s 139* has applied in relation to a transfer to a company which was not then an investment trust but which subsequently becomes one for an accounting period, then any assets transferred and still owned by the company at the beginning of that accounting period are deemed to have been sold and immediately reacquired by the transferee company, immediately after the transfer, at their market value at that time. The resulting chargeable gain or allowable loss arising is deemed to accrue to the transferee company not at the time of the deemed disposal but at the end of the accounting period preceding the accounting period in which the company becomes an investment trust. Notwithstanding normal time limits, a corporation tax assessment in respect of any resulting liability can be made within six years after the end of the last-mentioned accounting period.

Similar provisions apply where, after a transfer to which *TCGA 1992, s 139* applied, the transferee company becomes a venture capital trust (see **64** VENTURE CAPITAL TRUSTS). They apply by reference to the time at which HMRC's approval of the company as a VCT comes into effect, and the resulting gain or loss is deemed to accrue immediately before that time rather than at the time of the deemed disposal. In a case in which HMRC's approval has effect as from the beginning of an accounting period, any consequential corporation tax assessment can be made, notwithstanding normal time limits, within six years after the end of that accounting period. These provisions do not apply if those above relating to investment trusts have already applied (in relation to the same transfer of assets) and *vice versa*.

[*TCGA 1992, ss 101, 101B*].

Building society's business etc. transferred to a company or other building society

Similar provisions apply where there is a transfer of the whole of a building society's business to a successor company in accordance with the relevant provisions of *Building Societies Act 1986* [*TCGA 1992, s 216*] and where there is a disposal by one society to another as part of an amalgamation etc. of societies. [*TCGA 1992, s 215*]. Similar provisions also apply to transfers of assets as part of the transfer by a building society of the whole of its business to a subsidiary of a mutual society. [*SI 2009 No 2971, Regs 3, 5–7*].

Co-operative and community benefit societies etc.

Similar provisions apply where there is a union or amalgamation of two or more registered societies within *Co-operative and Community Benefit Societies Act 2014* or NI equivalent or a transfer of engagements from one society to another. This treatment also applies to certain co-operative associations established and resident in the UK, the primary purposes of which are to assist members in carrying on husbandry in the UK or fishery operations. [*TCGA 1992, s 217D*]. Similar provisions also apply where a society converts into a company, amalgamates with a company, or transfers the whole of its business to a company. [*SI 2009 No 2971, Regs 3, 16–18*].

Demergers

[14.13] The provisions of *CTA 2010, ss 1073–1099* have effect for facilitating certain transactions whereby trading activities carried on by a single company or 'group' are divided so as to be carried on by two or more companies not belonging to the same group or by two or more independent groups. '*Group*' means a company and all of its 75% subsidiaries (with the effect of direct and indirect ownership of shares held as trading stock being ignored in deciding whether one company is a 75% subsidiary of another).

An exempt distribution within *CTA 2010, s 1076* (transfer by company of shares in one or more 75% subsidiaries) is not a capital distribution within *TCGA 1992, s 122* (see **57.11** SHARES AND SECURITIES). *TCGA 1992, ss 126–130* (see generally **57.2** SHARES AND SECURITIES) are applied as if that company and the subsidiary whose shares are transferred were the same company and the distribution were a reorganisation of share capital.

A charge under *TCGA 1992, s 179* (see **26.7** GROUPS OF COMPANIES) on a company ceasing to be a member of a group does not apply where the cessation is by reason only of an exempt distribution. However, this exemption does not apply if there is a chargeable payment (within *CTA 2010, s 1088*: payment not made for genuine commercial reasons or made for tax avoidance purposes) within five years of the exempt distribution, and such a payment will result in the *TCGA 1992, s 179* charge being able to be the subject of an assessment made within three years of the chargeable payment.

[*TCGA 1992, s 192*].

For full details of the provisions see Tolley's Corporation Tax under Distributions. For the treatment of distributions arising from demergers in the hands of trustees, see HMRC Capital Gains Manual CG33900.

See also **43.12**, **43.13** OVERSEAS MATTERS for division of a business between companies in the UK and different EU member states.

Overseas matters

[14.14] Where a UK resident company transfers all or part of a trade carried on by it outside the UK to a company not resident in the UK in exchange, wholly or partly, for shares, see **43.10** OVERSEAS MATTERS. Where the transferee company is resident in an EC member state, see **43.13** OVERSEAS MATTERS. Where a UK company's business is carried on in the UK and is transferred to a company resident in another EC member state, see **43.12** OVERSEAS MATTERS. For European cross-border mergers, see **43.14** OVERSEAS MATTERS.

There are 'exit charges' and provisions for the recovery of unpaid tax where a company ceases to be UK resident etc., is a dual resident company or is not resident in the UK. See **43.16** and **43.17** OVERSEAS MATTERS.

See also **14.16** below as regards European Companies (SEs) and **14.17** below as regards European Co-operatives (SCEs).

Use of non-sterling currencies

[14.15] There are provisions (see now *CTA 2010, ss 5–17*) under which a currency other than sterling is used to determine profits and losses of a company for corporation tax purposes. For full details see Tolley's Corporation Tax.

Chargeable gains and allowable capital losses are generally excluded from the provisions (but see further below). Such gains and losses must be calculated and expressed in sterling. [*CTA 2010, s 5(1)*]. They are translated into sterling using the rules at **16.12**(a) COMPUTATION OF GAINS AND LOSSES, subject to the exception there noted.

Special rules apply where a company disposes of a ship, aircraft, stocks or shares or an interest in stocks or shares if at any time in the company's period of ownership of the asset its 'relevant currency' is not sterling. If the company incurs allowable expenditure within **16.12** COMPUTATION OF GAINS AND LOSSES before it acquires the asset, the period of ownership is treated for this purpose as beginning at the time the first such expenditure was incurred.

For this purpose '*ship*' and '*aircraft*' include the benefit of a finance lease or hire purchase contract to which *CAA 2001, s 67* applies and which relates to plant or machinery which is a ship or aircraft.

A company's '*relevant currency*' at any time is its 'functional currency' at that time or, where the company is a UK resident investment company which has made an election under *CTA 2010, s 9A*, the currency designated in the election. A company's '*functional currency*' is the currency of the primary economic environment in which it operates.

If the company's relevant currency when it disposes of the ship etc. is not sterling, the gain or loss is calculated in the relevant currency at the time of the disposal and then translated into sterling by reference to the spot rate of exchange on the day of the disposal.

In all cases where the special rules apply (whether or not the relevant currency is sterling at the date of disposal), the following computational rules must be followed.

(a) Where any allowable expenditure within **16.12** COMPUTATION OF GAINS AND LOSSES is incurred in a currency other than the company's then relevant currency, it must be translated into the relevant currency using the spot rate of exchange for the day on which it is incurred.
(b) Where there is a change in the company's relevant currency before the asset is disposed of, allowable expenditure incurred before the change must be translated into the new relevant currency using the spot rate for the day of the change.
(c) Any disposal consideration given in a currency other than the company's relevant currency must be translated into the relevant currency using the spot rate for the day of the disposal.

Any translation of expenditure under (a) above must be done before any translation of the expenditure under (b) above. If there is more than one change in a company's relevant currency, (b) above must be applied to each change in order, earliest first. If the acquisition of the asset was treated either as a no gain/no loss transaction or was treated as made at market value, the deemed expenditure is treated for these purposes as incurred at the time of the acquisition.

[*CTA 2010, ss 9C, 17(4)*].

European Company (Societas Europaea)

[14.16] *Council Regulation (EC) No 2157/2001* provides for the formation of a company as a European Company or *Societas Europaea* ('SE'). It permits the formation of new SEs and also allows for the 'transformation' of existing companies into SEs and for the merger between two (or more) companies in different member states into an SE. For most tax purposes, an SE based in the UK is treated like a UK-resident plc, but special provisions are required to deal with, among other matters, the formation of SEs by cross-border merger. The provisions are intended to be broadly tax-neutral. (Revenue Technical Note, 'Implementation of the European Company Statute', January 2005).

From Brexit IP completion day (11pm on 31 December 2020), no new SEs can be formed in the UK. From IP completion day, every SE that is registered in the UK immediately before that day is automatically converted into a 'UK Societas'.

Formation of SE by merger

See **43.14** OVERSEAS MATTERS.

Residence

For the residence for tax purposes of an SE transferring its registered office to the UK, see **51.28** RESIDENCE AND DOMICILE.

Continuity on ceasing to be UK resident

If at any time a company ceases to be resident in the UK in the course of the formation of an SE by merger (whether or not the company continues to exist following the merger), *FA 1998, Sch 18* (company RETURNS (**52.21**), ASSESSMENTS (**6**), APPEALS (**5**), etc.) applies after that time in relation to liabilities accruing and other matters arising before that time as if the company were still UK-resident and, if the company has ceased to exist, as if the SE were the company.

Where an SE transfers its registered office outside the UK and ceases to be UK-resident, *FA 1998, Sch 18* applies after that time in relation to liabilities accruing and other matters arising before that time as if the SE were still UK-resident.

[*FA 1998, Sch 18 paras 87A–87C*].

Groups of companies

See **26.2** GROUPS OF COMPANIES.

European Co-operative (Societas Co-operative Europaea)

[14.17] *Council Regulation (EC) No 1435/2003* provides for the formation of a co-operative as a European Co-operative or *Societas Co-operative Europaea* ('SCE'). It permits the formation of new SCEs and also allows for the 'transformation' of existing co-operatives into SEs and for the merger between two (or more) co-operatives in different member states into an SCE. For most tax purposes, an SCE based in the UK is treated like a registered society within *Co-operative and Community Benefit Societies Act 2014*, but special provisions are required to deal with, among other matters, the formation of SCEs by cross-border merger.

From Brexit IP completion day (11pm on 31 December 2020), no new SCEs can be formed in the UK.

[*SI 2019 No 710, Reg 25*].

Formation of SCE by merger

See **43.14** OVERSEAS MATTERS.

Residence

For the residence for tax purposes of an SE transferring its registered office to the UK, see **51.28** RESIDENCE AND DOMICILE.

Assets subject to EU exit charge

[14.18] The following applies where an asset becomes a chargeable asset of a company because either the company becomes resident in the UK or the asset begins to be held for the purposes of a trade carried on by the company in the UK through a permanent establishment. If, at the time the asset becomes a chargeable asset, it is also subject to an 'EU exit charge', it is treated for chargeable gains purposes as if the company had acquired it for its market value at that time.

For this purpose, an asset is a chargeable asset of a company if its disposal would give rise to a UK chargeable gain or allowable loss. An 'EU exit charge' is a charge to tax under the law of a member state in accordance with the EU Anti Tax Avoidance Directive (*Directive (EU) 2016/1194, Art 5(1)*).

[*TCGA 1992, s 184J*].

This provision relieves any potential double taxation at the time of the disposal of the asset by exempting from UK tax any gain or loss arising before the asset came within the scope of UK tax on chargeable gains.

Tax accounting arrangements of large companies

[14.19] The 'senior accounting officer' of a 'qualifying company' has a statutory duty to take reasonable steps to ensure that the company establishes and maintains 'appropriate tax accounting arrangements'. In particular, the officer must take reasonable steps to monitor the accounting arrangements of the company and to identify any respects in which they are not appropriate tax accounting arrangements. Failure to comply with this obligation will result in the officer becoming liable to a penalty of £5,000 for each financial year involved.

For this purpose, '*appropriate tax accounting arrangements*' are accounting arrangements, including arrangements for keeping accounting records, which enable the company's relevant tax liabilities (including corporation tax on chargeable gains) to be calculated accurately in all material respects. Subject to the Treasury's power to make regulations excluding certain companies, a '*qualifying company*' is, broadly a company with a turnover of more than

£200 million and/or a balance sheet total of more than £2 billion. Where the company is a member of a group, the requirements relate to the aggregate amounts for the group. A company's 'senior accounting officer' is the director or officer or group director or officer with overall responsibility for the company's financial accounting arrangements. A person can be the senior accounting officer of more than one company.

The officer must also provide HMRC with a certificate for every financial year, stating whether the company had appropriate arrangements throughout the year and, if not, explaining the ways in which the arrangements were deficient. The certificate must be given to HMRC not later than the end of the *Companies Act 2006, s 442* period for filing the accounts (or such later time as HMRC allow) and can relate to more than one qualifying company. If the officer fails to provide the certificate, or provides a certificate containing a careless or deliberate error, he will be liable to a penalty of £5,000. An error that is neither careless nor deliberate is treated for this purpose as careless if the officer later discovered it and did not take reasonable steps to inform HMRC. A penalty cannot be charged for a financial year if the officer has already been assessed to a penalty under this provision in respect of another company in the same group for a year ending in the same financial year.

To facilitate the operation of these provisions, a qualifying company must ensure HMRC are notified of the name of each person who was its senior accounting officer at any time during a financial year. Notification must be given not later than the end of the *Companies Act 2006, s 442* period for filing the accounts (or such later time as HMRC have allowed for providing the certificate for the year). A single notification can be made for more than one company. Failure to notify will result in the company being liable to a penalty of £5,000. A penalty cannot, however, be charged for a financial year if another company in the same group has already been assessed to a penalty under this provision for a year ending in the same financial year.

A company or officer can appeal against the above penalties within 30 days of the date of the HMRC notification of the penalty. No penalty will be due if HMRC or, on appeal, the Tribunal, are satisfied that there was a reasonable excuse for the failure. Insufficiency of funds or reliance on another person to do anything are not normally reasonable excuses, and where a reasonable excuse ceases, the failure must be rectified without unreasonable delay. A reasonable excuse for failure to comply includes any circumstance where the failure is attributable to any matter outside the person's control or any matter of which a person could not reasonably be expected to be aware. Where the identity of the senior accounting officer changes during a financial year, there are provisions to ensure that only one person is liable to any of the penalties (and to determine which of the officers it will be).

In *Castlelaw (No 628) Ltd v HMRC* FTT, [2020] SFTD 491, a penalty was charged in respect of a dormant company whose details were omitted from a notification by a 100 company group. The Tribunal upheld the penalty, holding that the SAO of the company had no reasonable excuse.

[*FA 2009, s 93, Sch 46*].

HMRC have published guidance on the above provisions in their Senior Accounting Officer Guidance Manual.

Publication of tax strategies by large businesses

[14.20] Certain large businesses must publish their tax strategy each year. The strategy must be published on the internet before the end of the financial year to which it relates. If the business was required to publish its tax strategy for the previous financial year, the current year's strategy must be published no more than 15 months after the previous strategy was published. The strategy must be freely available to public view free of charge and must remain so until the next year's strategy is published or, if no such strategy need be published, for at least one year. The strategy may be published either as a separate document or as a self-contained part of a wider document.

The requirement to publish a tax strategy applies to the following entities.

(1) The 'head' of a 'UK group' which is a 'qualifying group' for the financial year. A '*UK group*' is a 'group' whose head is a body corporate incorporated in the UK. A '*group*' is either an 'MNE group' (as defined in the OECD Model Legislation in the OECD Country-by-Country Reporting Implementation Package) or a 'group other than an MNE group' (as defined by reference to 51% subsidiaries and including at least two UK companies or UK permanent establishments). The '*head*' of a group is the member of the group which is not a 51% subsidiary of another member of the group.
A group other than an MNE group is a '*qualifying group*' for a financial year if either the aggregate turnover of its UK companies and UK permanent establishments for the preceding year was more than £200 million or the aggregate balance sheet total assets for those companies and permanent establishments for that year exceeded £2 billion. An MNE group is a 'qualifying group' for a financial year if there was a mandatory country-by-country reporting requirement under *FA 2015, s 122* for the previous financial year or there would have been if the head of the group were UK-resident for tax purposes.

(2) The 'head' of a 'UK sub-group' of a 'foreign' group' where the foreign group is a qualifying group for the financial year. A '*foreign group*' is a group whose head is a body corporate incorporated outside the UK. A '*UK sub-group*' consists of two or more bodies corporate that would be a UK group but for the fact that they are members of a larger foreign group. The '*head*' of a UK sub-group is the member of the sub-group which is not a 51% subsidiary of another member of the sub-group.

(3) A UK company which is a 'qualifying company' for the financial year. A company is a '*qualifying company*' for a financial year if at the end of the previous financial year it was not a member of a UK group or a UK sub-group and for that year its turnover exceeded £200 million or its balance sheet total assets exceeded £2 billion. If the company was a member of a foreign group at the end of the previous year, the turnover and balance sheet thresholds apply as in (1) above. The requirement to

publish the company's tax strategy for a financial year applies even if the company becomes a member of a group or UK sub-group during the year.

A UK permanent establishment of a foreign body corporate is treated as if it were a company for these purposes and, if the foreign body corporate is a member of a group or a UK sub-group, as a member of that group or sub-group.

(4) A 'UK partnership' which is a 'qualifying partnership' for the financial year. A '*UK partnership*' is a UK partnership, limited partnership or limited liability partnership which is carrying on a trade, business or profession with a view to profit. A UK partnership is a 'qualifying partnership' if, for the previous financial year, its turnover exceeded £200 million or its balance sheet total assets exceeded £2 billion.

In relation to a partnership, a '*financial year*' means any period of account for which its representative partner is required to provide a partnership statement in a return (see **52.19** RETURNS).

A tax strategy must set out the following:

- the approach of the group, sub-group, company, permanent establishment or partnership to risk management and governance in relation to UK taxation;
- the attitude of the group etc. towards tax planning affecting UK taxation;
- the level of risk in relation to UK taxation that the group etc. is prepared to accept; and
- the approach of the group etc. towards its dealings with HMRC.

It may include other information relating to taxation (UK or otherwise). In the case of a group or sub-group, the tax strategy may set out the required information by reference to the group or sub-group as a whole or to individual members (or both). Information about activities consisting of the provision of tax advice or related professional services to other persons does not have to be included in the tax strategy. The strategy must make it clear that the group etc. regards its publication as complying with the above requirements. The Treasury may be regulations require group tax strategies to include a country-by-country report (as defined).

For HMRC guidance see www.gov.uk/guidance/large-businesses-publish-your-tax-strategy.

Penalty for failure to comply

See **46.1** PENALTIES.

[*FA 2016, s 161(2), Sch 19 paras 1–17, 19, 20, 22, 23, 25*].

Special measures regime for unco-operative large businesses

[14.21] A special measures regime applies to large businesses which engage in what HMRC consider to be aggressive tax planning or which do not engage with HMRC in an 'open and collaborative manner' (see HM Treasury Explanatory Notes to the 2016 Finance Bill). The regime operates by HMRC first issuing a warning notice which provides the taxpayer with an opportunity to make representations about whether the regime should apply. A warning notice may be followed by a special measures notice, the effect of which is that any inaccuracies in a document given to HMRC are deemed to be at least careless (and therefore subject to a penalty). If a special measures notice is confirmed by a confirmation notice, then HMRC may publicly identify the taxpayer as subject to the regime.

The regime is described in the following paragraphs as it applies to UK groups. See below for its application to other types of taxpayer.

Warning notice

An HMRC officer who has been designated for the purpose may give a notice (a '*warning notice*') to the 'head' of a 'UK group' if he considers that the group is a 'qualifying group' that meets the following conditions. The conditions are that:

(1) the group has 'persistently' engaged in 'unco-operative behaviour';
(2) some or all of that behaviour has caused or contributed to two or more 'significant tax issues' in respect of the group or members of it which are unresolved; and
(3) there is a reasonable likelihood of further instances of unco-operative behaviour causing or contributing to significant tax issues in respect of the group or its members.

For this purpose a UK group has engaged in '*unco-operative behaviour*' if a member of the group or two or more members taken together satisfy either or both of the behaviour condition or the arrangements condition. A group has '*persistently*' engaged in such behaviour if a member of the group or two or more members taken together have done so on a sufficient number of occasions for it to be clear that it represents a pattern of behaviour.

A group member, or two or more members taken together, satisfy the behaviour condition if they behave in a way which has delayed or otherwise hindered HMRC in the exercise of their functions in connection with determining the UK tax liability of the group or a member. The extent to which HMRC have used statutory powers to obtain information, the reasons why those powers have been used, the number and seriousness of inaccuracies in and omissions from documents given to HMRC and the extent to which group members (or their agents) have relief on interpretations of UK tax legislation which are 'speculative' are all actors indicative of such behaviour. An interpretation is '*speculative*' for this purpose if it is likely that a court or tribunal would disagree with it.

A member of a UK group satisfies the arrangements condition if it is a party to a '*tax avoidance scheme*': i.e. arrangements in respect of which a final counter-action notice under the general anti-abuse rule (see **4.3** ANTI-AVOIDANCE), arrangements which are notifiable arrangements under the provisions for DISCLOSURE OF TAX AVOIDANCE SCHEMES (**19.4**) other than any arrangements for which the promoter has been notified that clients need no longer be provided with the scheme number) or arrangements notifiable under equivalent VAT provisions.

There is a 'significant tax issue' in respect of a UK group or a group member if there is a disagreement (or reasonable likelihood of a disagreement) between HMRC and a group member about an issue affecting the amount of the UK tax liability of the group or member which has been, or could be, referred to a court or tribunal to determine. The tax at stake must be, or be likely to be, at least £2 million.

'UK group', 'qualifying group' and the 'head' of a UK group are all as defined at **14.20**(1) above. References above to things done by a group member include acts or omissions of former members when they were still members of the group but do not include acts or omissions of current members before they joined.

The warning notice must set out the reasons why the officer considers that the above conditions are met and may be withdrawn at any time by giving a further notice to that effect. If the notice has not been withdrawn it expires after 15 months. Once a warning notice has been given, the notice, and any subsequent special measures notice (see below), continue to have effect even if the group ceases to be a qualifying group, changes its membership or becomes a UK sub-group of a foreign group (see **14.20**(2) above).

If, while the warning notice is in effect, the head of the group becomes a member of a group headed by another body corporate (H), the warning notice is treated as having been given to H on the day it was actually given to the original head of the group. A notice deemed to be given in this way is valid even if H is not the head of a qualifying UK group to which the conditions at (1)–(3) above apply.

Special measures notice

A designated HMRC officer may give the head of a UK group a '*special measures notice*' if:

(a) a warning notice has been given to the head and not withdrawn;
(b) twelve months have passed since the day on which the warning notice was given;
(c) the 15 months beginning with the day on which the warning notice was given have not elapsed; and
(d) the officer considers that the UK group meets the conditions at (1)–(3) above. The officer may take into account any behaviour for this purpose, whether or not mentioned in the warning notice and must consider any representations made by any group member before the end of the twelve months beginning with the day the warning notice was given.

The special measures notice must set out the reasons why the officer considers that the above conditions are met and may be withdrawn at any time by giving a further notice to that effect. If the notice has not been withdrawn it expires after 27 months beginning with the later of the day it was given and the day on which it was last confirmed (see below).

A designated HMRC officer may also give the head of a UK group a special measures notice if:

(A) a warning notice or special measures notice has been given to the head and has expired;

(B) it appears to the officer that in the period of six months since the notice expired the group has engaged in unco-operative behaviour and there is a reasonable likelihood that, if the behaviour had occurred before the notice expired a special measures notice or confirmation notice could have been given;

(C) during the seven months beginning with the day on which the notice expired HMRC have notified the head of the group that a special measures notice may be given; and

(D) no more than nine months have elapsed since the notice expired.

In deciding whether to give such a notice the officer must consider any representations made by any group member within eight months from the day the original notice expired.

If, while a special measures notice is in effect, the head of the group becomes a member of a group headed by another body corporate (H), the notice is treated as having been given to H on the day it was actually given to the original head of the group. A notice deemed to be given in this way is valid even if H is not the head of a qualifying UK group to which the conditions at (1)–(3) above apply.

Confirmation notice

A designated HMRC officer may give the head of a UK group a notice (a '*confirmation notice*') confirming a special measures notice if:

(i) a special measures notice has been given to the head and not withdrawn;

(ii) 24 months have passed since the later of the day on which the special measures notice was given and the day on which it was last confirmed;

(iii) the 27 months beginning with the later of the day the notice was given and the day on which it was last confirmed have not elapsed; and

(iv) the officer considers that the UK group meets the conditions at (1)–(3) above. The officer may take into account any behaviour for this purpose, whether or not mentioned in the warning notice, special measures notice or a previous confirmation notice and must consider any representations made by any group member before the end of the period in (ii) above.

The confirmation notice must set out the reasons why the officer considers that the above conditions are met and may be withdrawn at any time by giving a further notice to that effect. If the notice has not been withdrawn it expires after 27 months beginning with the day on which it was given.

If, while a confirmation notice is in effect, the head of the group becomes a member of a group headed by another body corporate (H), the notice is treated as having been given to H on the day it was actually given to the original head of the group. A notice deemed to be given in this way is valid even if H is not the head of a qualifying UK group to which the conditions at (1)–(3) above apply.

Sanctions

Penalties

For the purposes of the penalty provisions at **46.11** PENALTIES, an inaccuracy in a document given to HMRC by or on behalf of a member of a group whilst the group is subject to a special measures notice is treated as being due to failure by the member to take reasonable care if either:

- the inaccuracy relates to a tax avoidance scheme which was entered into whilst the group member at a time when it was a member of a group and the group was subject to a special measures notice; or
- the inaccuracy is attributable, wholly or in part, to an interpretation of UK tax law which, at the time the document was given, was speculative.

This rule does not, however, apply to treat a deliberate inaccuracy as merely careless. It also does not apply where, during the currency of a special measures notice, the head of the group becomes a member of a group headed by another body corporate (H), and the inaccuracy is in a document given to HMRC by a member of H's group at a time before the head of the group to which the notice was originally given became a member of H's group.

Publication of information

The Commissioners for HMRC may publish certain information about a UK group if a special measures notice given to the head of the group is in force and the notice has been confirmed by a confirmation notice. They may also publish information if a special measures notice confirmed by a confirmation notice has expired but a further special measures notice has been given to the head of the group as a result of the conditions in (A)–(D) above and is in force.

The information which may be published is the name of the group and its address or registered office, the fact that it is subject to a confirmed special measures notice and any other information HMRC consider it appropriate to publish in order to identify the group. When the group ceases to be subject to a special measures notice HMRC must publish a notice stating that it is no longer subject to the notice within the 30 days beginning with that on which the notice is withdrawn or expires.

Before publishing information the Commissioners must inform the head of the group of their intention to do so and allow the head a reasonable opportunity to make representations about whether publication should go ahead.

Application of regime to UK sub-groups, companies and partnerships

The special measures regime applies to UK sub-groups of overseas groups which are qualifying groups (see **14.20**(2) above), qualifying companies (see **14.20**(3) above) and qualifying partnerships (see **14.20**(4) above), the above provisions being modified as necessary. In particular, in the case of a UK sub-group, once a warning notice has been given, the notice, and any subsequent special measures notice, continue to have effect even if the group ceases to be a qualifying group, the sub-group changes its membership or becomes a UK sub-group of another foreign group. In the case of a partnership, references to the head of a UK group should be read as references to the representative partner of the partnership, and references to a member of a group as references to a partner in a partnership acting in his capacity as partner.

[*FA 2016, Sch 19 paras 35–53*].

Key points concerning companies

[**14.22**] Points to consider are as follows.

- If a company enters administration or liquidation, an accounting period is ended and a new one begins. The timing of the process may therefore be crucial in deciding what rate of corporation tax is applicable to the pre- and post-insolvency periods. See **14.4.**
- Similarly, since the ranking of pre- and post-liquidation tax debts is different, it may be appropriate for creditors to give some thought to the timing of the appointment of a liquidator, to maximise the return to business creditors. See **14.4.**
- Capital losses are often carried forward for many years before they are used. It is therefore essential that companies have reliable long-term record keeping processes in place, so that the availability of an agreed loss can be demonstrated at the point of use. See **14.6.**
- One often overlooked impact of the substantial shareholdings exemption is that there is no relief for losses arising on qualifying shares, because the sale of those shares at a profit would have been exempt. See **14.6.**
- There is a targeted anti-avoidance rule at *TCGA 1992, s 16A* which denies companies the benefit of capital losses that arise in disqualifying circumstances, i.e. the loss arises from arrangements designed to generate a tax advantage. Losses arising in disqualifying circumstances are just lost and can never be used. See **14.7.**
- Where there are schemes to turn income into capital or to secure a deduction, the company should self-assess on the basis of the arrangements entered into. It is implicit in the fact that HMRC must issue a notice to counteract these schemes that there is no requirement to consider the anti-avoidance legislation when preparing the company's self-assessment. See **14.7–14.9.**
- Further helpful guidance about clearances can be found on the gov.uk website at www.gov.uk/government/collections/seeking-clearance-or-approval-for-a-transaction. See **14.12.**
- It is important to note that an HMRC clearance under *TCGA 1992, s 138* or *s 139* only states that HMRC is satisfied that the transactions are being entered into for bona fide commercial reasons and not for the avoidance of corporation tax. The clearance does not confirm that HMRC agrees that the transaction amounts to a reorganisation or a scheme of reconstruction. See **14.12.**
- A clearance for a demerger will necessarily confirm that HMRC agrees that the detailed technical requirements of the legislation are satisfied. As such, these clearances are quite comprehensive, in comparison to clearances under *TCGA 1992, s 138* or *s 139* (see **4.16, 14.12**). See **14.13.**
- HMRC have a toolkit 'chargeable gains for companies' that considers the perceived risk areas such as access to historical data, date of disposal, valuations, qualifying expenditure and reliefs. Using the toolkit or an alternative checklist may help show that reasonable care has been taken. Showing reasonable care is important if the computation of the gain is subsequently challenged and found to be incorrect as it affects the penalty that can be charged.

- Large companies (and partnerships) must publish an annual tax strategy online, outlining their approach to tax risk, tax planning and dealing with HMRC (see **14.20** above). If they have a history of unco-operative behaviour they may become subject to a special measures regime (see **14.21** above).

15

Companies — Corporate Finance and Intangibles

Introduction to companies: corporate finance and intangibles

[15.1] There are three sets of special corporation tax rules which seek to apply accepted accounting principles to particular types of profits and gains. Broadly (and with certain exceptions), under each of the regimes all profits are treated for corporation tax purposes as income and all losses as income losses, including those which would ordinarily be capital. The regimes concerned are those which cover:

- loan relationships (see **15.2–15.7** below);
- derivative contracts (see **15.8–15.12** below); and
- intangible fixed assets (see **15.13, 15.15** below).

This chapter describes these regimes in detail only insofar as they interact with chargeable gains provisions. For full coverage see Tolley's Corporation Tax.

See also **45.9** PAYMENT OF TAX for exit charge payment plans which companies may enter into with HMRC where they incur certain exit charges, including those under the three regimes discussed in this chapter.

Loan relationships

[15.2] The intention of the loan relationship provisions is for the corporate taxation of income and expenditure from corporate and government debt to equate with its accepted accounting treatment. This is brought about by first establishing the existence of a 'loan relationship' and secondly, by treating all company profits and losses from such relationships as income and not capital, regardless of whether the company is borrower or lender.

See also 28 GOVERNMENT SECURITIES, 48 QUALIFYING CORPORATE BONDS and HMRC Corporate Finance Manual CFM30000 onwards.

Summary of provisions

[15.3] As the underlying criteria is for the tax treatment of each loan relationship to follow generally accepted accounting practice, the terms *debit* and *credit* are used to describe the method of accounting for individual items of income and expenditure. The debits and credits will include all profits, gains and losses, including those of a capital nature, interest payments, charges and expenses appertaining to the company's loan relationship or its attributed rights and liabilities. Charges and expenses appertaining to loan relationships include only those incurred directly:

(i) in bringing any of the loan relationships into existence;
in entering into or giving effect to any of the related transactions;
in making payments under any of the relationships or in pursuance of any of the related transactions; or

(ii) in taking steps for ensuring the receipt of payments under any of the relationships or in accordance with any of the related transactions.

[*CTA 2009, ss 306A, 307*].

Interest on money debts which are not themselves loan relationships is also brought into account as debits and credits under the provisions. Profits from disposals of interest and from discounts are also brought into account. [*CTA 2009, ss 478–486*].

Return on arrangements which is 'economically equivalent to interest' (defined broadly as for the provisions treating shares as creditor relationships — see **15.6** below) is also treated as a profit from a loan relationship. [*CTA 2009, ss 486A–486E*].

For the calculation of credits and debits, see *CTA 2009, ss 306–327*.

Debits and credits arising from loan relationships to which a company is party are brought into account according to the purposes for which the company is party to it. Where the loan relationship is one to which the company is party for trading purposes, credits and debits are treated as receipts and expenses to be brought into account in computing the profits of the trade. Credits and debits in respect of non-trading loan relationships are aggregated and, where the aggregate credits exceed the aggregate debits, that excess is taxable as income. Relief is available for deficits. If only part of a loan relates to trading purposes the debits and credits should be apportioned accordingly. [*CTA 2009, ss 295–301*].

However, a general corporate interest restriction places a limit on the amount of interest expense and certain other finance costs that companies with high interest costs can deduct when calculating profits subject to corporation tax. For details of the corporate interest restriction, see Tolley's Corporation Tax. [*F(No 2)A 2017, s 20, Sch 5*].

Foreign exchange gains and losses

The reference above to profits, gains and losses to be included in debits and credits includes, subject to certain exceptions, foreign exchange gains and losses arising to a company in relation to any asset or liability representing a loan relationship of the company.

Hedging instruments

Special rules apply where a loan relationship is a hedging instrument matched with another foreign currency asset. Broadly (and subject to anti-avoidance provisions), exchange gains or losses on such relationships are initially disregarded and are then brought back into charge when the matched asset is disposed of (otherwise than on a no gain/no loss disposal).

If the matched asset is itself a loan relationship, a ship or an aircraft, the exchange gains and losses are brought back into charge as loan relationship debits and credits. In most other cases, the exchange gains and losses are brought back into charge under the chargeable gains rules. Any net exchange gain (i.e. gains less losses) is added to the consideration for the disposal. Any net loss is deducted from the consideration, and where the loss exceeds the consideration, the excess is added to the acquisition cost. The exchange gains or losses are not brought back in to charge if the disposal of the asset is within the exemption for SUBSTANTIAL SHAREHOLDINGS OF COMPANIES (**60**) or if the asset is an asset of a foreign branch (other than shares not held on trading account).

[*TCGA 1992, s 151E; CTA 2009, ss 328–328H, 475A; SI 2002 No 1970; SI 2004 No 3256; SI 2014 No 3325*].

Loan relationships with embedded derivatives

[15.4] Special provisions apply to loan relationships with 'embedded derivatives'. This is where a company in accordance with generally accepted accounting practice splits the rights and liabilities under the loan relationship into those under the loan relationship (the '*host contract*') and '*embedded derivatives*', which are those under one or more derivative financial instruments or equity instruments (as defined). In this case, the host contract will fall, for corporation tax purposes, within the loan relationship rules and the embedded derivative within the derivative contracts rules (see **15.8** below) which provide, in certain cases, for the embedded derivative to be taxed on a chargeable gains basis. The embedded derivative is treated as having the character (be it an option, a future or a contract for differences) which the rights and liabilities would have if contained in a separate contract. [*CTA 2009, s 415*].

Simon's Taxes. See **D1.723.**

Definition of 'loan relationship'

[15.5] A '*loan relationship*' exists whenever a company is in the position of debtor or creditor to a 'money debt' which arises from the lending of money. [*CTA 2009, s 302(1)*].

A '*money debt*' is defined as a debt which is, or at any time has been, one that falls (or that may at the option of the debtor or of the creditor fall) to be settled:

(a) by the payment of money;
(b) by the transfer of a right to settlement under a debt which is itself a money debt; or
(c) by the issue or transfer of shares in any company;

disregarding any other option exercisable by either party.

[*CTA 2009, s 303*].

The legislation does not define a *debtor* or *creditor* and therefore the accepted meaning is understood to apply.

Examples of loan relationships are: bank overdrafts, bank borrowings and third party borrowings plus corporate bonds and gilt-edged securities.

However, normal debtor/creditor relationships are not included as these do not arise from the lending of money and a debt arising from shareholders' rights is specifically excluded. Thus, ordinary shares and preference shares are not loan relationships. However, all building society shares, including permanent interest bearing shares, are within the loan relationships rules.

[*CTA 2009, ss 303(4), 305*].

Alternative finance arrangements within *CTA 2009, ss 503–507* are also loan relationships. [*CTA 2009, s 501*].

Certain 'investment life insurance contracts' (broadly, life insurance policies which have a surrender value, contracts for a purchased life annuity and capital redemption policies) held by a company which is not a life insurance company are treated as creditor relationships of the company. See *CTA 2009, ss 560–569*.

An advance under a repo or quasi-repo within the regime for sale and repurchase of securities (see **57.26** SHARES AND SECURITIES) is treated as a money debt for the above purposes — see *CTA 2009, ss 546(2), 551(2)*.

A '*creditor relationship*', in relation to a company, is a loan relationship of that company where it stands in the position of a creditor as respects the debt in question. A '*debtor relationship*' has a corresponding meaning. '*Fair value*' has the meaning it has for accounting purposes. [*CTA 2009, ss 302(5)(6), 313(6), 476(1)*].

Corporate holdings in authorised unit trusts, open-ended insurance companies, and offshore funds

Holdings of rights under a unit trust scheme, shares in an open-ended investment company or interests in an offshore fund which fail to satisfy the 'qualifying investments test' at any time in an accounting period, are treated for that period as rights under creditor relationships, in relation to which a fair value basis of accounting must be used.

The '*qualifying investments test*' requires that not more than 60% of the market value of scheme or fund investments is represented by 'qualifying investments' (as defined, and including money placed at interest, securities, derivative contracts etc.).

Where the above provisions start or cease to apply to a holding without the company disposing of it, that event is treated as if it resulted from a reorganisation within *TCGA 1992, s 116* (see **48.4** QUALIFYING CORPORATE BONDS). The holding immediately before the end of the accounting period at the end of which the above provisions started or ceased to apply is the 'old asset' for the purposes of *section 116* and the holding immediately afterwards is the 'new asset'.

[*CTA 2009, ss 487–497; TCGA 1992, s 116A; TIOPA 2010, Sch 8 para 172; SI 2006 No 964, Regs 90, 95, 96A; SI 2006 No 981; SI 2009 No 3001, Reg 131*].

Simon's Taxes. See **D1.703, D1.788.**

Shares treated as creditor relationships

[15.6] There are provisions which treat certain shares held by companies as rights under creditor relationships.

The provisions apply in relation to times in a company's accounting period when the company (the '*investing company*') holds a share in another company (the '*issuing company*') and:

(i) the share would, in accordance with generally accepted accounting practice, be accounted for by the issuing company as a liability;
(ii) the share produces for the investing company a return in relation to any amount which is 'economically equivalent to interest';
(iii) the issuing and investing companies are not connected companies (within *CTA 2009, s 466*);
(iv) the share is not treated as rights under a creditor relationship under *CTA 2009, s 490* (holdings in open-ended investment companies, unit trusts and offshore funds);
(v) the share is not an 'excepted share'; and
(vi) the investing company holds the share for an 'unallowable purpose'.

For this purpose, a return is '*economically equivalent to interest*' in relation to an amount only if it is reasonable to assume that it is a return by reference to the time value of the amount and it is at a rate reasonably comparable to a commercial rate of interest. At the time the company first holds the share (or, if later, when the share begins to produce a return) there must be no practical likelihood that the return will cease to be produced unless the payer is prevented from paying it.

A share is an '*excepted share*' if it was issued as part of an issue to persons not connected with the issuer provided that less than 10% of the shares in that issue are held by the investing company or persons connected with it. A share is also an excepted share if it mirrors a public issue (as defined).

A company holds a share for an '*unallowable purpose*' if one of the main purposes for which it holds the share is to obtain a tax advantage (as defined) in relation to the return on the share.

Where these provisions would not otherwise apply because condition (vi) above is not satisfied, the investing company can make an election for them to apply. Such an election is irrevocable and must normally be made no later then the time the company first holds the share or, if later, when the share begins to produce a return.

At any time at which the above conditions apply, the share is treated as if it were rights under a creditor relationship of the investing company. No debits are to be brought into account by the investing company (other than any debits in respect of exchange gains or losses). If a share begins or cease to be within the provisions the investing company is treated for loan relationship purposes as having disposed of it and immediately reacquired it for consideration equal to what would have been its tax-adjusted carrying value (as defined) if accounts had been drawn up at that time.

[*CTA 2009, ss 521A–521F*].

Chargeable gains

Where the above provisions begin to apply in the case of any shares, the investing company is deemed for chargeable gains purposes to have disposed of the share immediately before that time, and to have immediately reacquired it. The consideration for the deemed disposal and acquisition is the amount that would be the share's carrying value if accounts were drawn up on that date.

Where at any time, the above provisions cease to apply to a share, the investing company is deemed for chargeable gains purposes to have disposed of the share immediately before that time, and to have immediately reacquired it. The consideration for the deemed disposal and acquisition is the amount that would be the share's carrying value if accounts were drawn up on that date.

[*TCGA 1992, s 116B*].

Chargeable gains

[15.7] No chargeable gain will arise on the disposal of any loan relationship because every asset representing a loan relationship of a company is a QUALIFYING CORPORATE BOND (see **48.3**).

Derivative contracts

[15.8] Subject to the special rules below for certain contracts which are taxed on a chargeable gains basis, under the derivative contracts regime, all profits/and losses arising to a company from its derivative contracts are taxed as/(relieved against) income, using credits and debits under rules analogous to those for taxing loan relationships (see **15.3** above). Non-trading credits and debits are, in fact, taken into account under the loan relationships rules themselves. Such profits/(losses) are thus outside the charge to corporation tax on chargeable gains. [*CTA 2009, ss 571, 572, 574*]. The same treatment is applied to certain foreign exchange gains and losses arising to a company from its derivative contracts, and there are 'matching' rules similar to those referred to at **15.3** above. There are anti-avoidance and other special computational provisions (see *CTA 2009, ss 624–638, 674–698D*).

Special provisions apply to certain contracts whose value derives essentially from land or tangible movable property and certain 'embedded derivatives'. Non-trading profits, gains and losses on such derivative contracts are treated as capital gains and allowable losses (see **15.10** below). [*SI 2004 No 2201, Art 1*].

See Tolley's Corporation Tax under Derivative Contracts for detailed coverage.

Simon's Taxes. See **D1.8.**

Definition of 'derivative contract'

[15.9] For the purposes of **15.8** above, a company's '*derivative contracts*' are 'relevant contracts' entered into or acquired by it which are not excluded under the accounting conditions referred to below or by virtue of their underlying subject matter (see below). A '*relevant contract*' is any of the following:

- an option (including a warrant (as defined)); or
- a future, i.e. a contract for the sale of property under which delivery is to be made at a date and price agreed (as defined) when the contract is made; or
- a contract for differences, i.e. a contract the purpose or pretended purpose of which is to make a profit or avoid a loss by reference to fluctuations in the value or price of property described in the contract or fluctuations in an index or other factor designated in the contract. A contract within *Energy Act 2013, s 6(2)* or *Sch 2 para 1(1)* is also a contract for differences. None of the following is a contract for differences: an option, a future, a contract of insurance, a capital redemption policy (as defined), a contract of indemnity, a guarantee, a warranty or a loan relationship.

A contract which can only be cash settled, and which does not provide for the delivery of any property, is excluded from being an option or a future but not from being a contract for differences. This does not apply if the underlying subject matter (see below) of the contract is currency.

Embedded and hybrid derivatives

A company is also treated as party to a relevant contract in the following circumstances.

(I) Where a company, in accordance with generally accepted accounting practice, treats rights and liabilities under a loan relationship to which it is party, as divided between rights and liabilities under a loan relationship and rights and liabilities under one or more derivative financial instruments or equity instruments ('embedded derivatives'). The company is treated for the purposes of these provisions as party to a relevant contract (or contracts) whose rights and liabilities consist only of those of the derivative or derivatives. The embedded derivative is treated as having the character (be it an option, a future or a contract for differences) which the rights and liabilities would have if contained in a separate contract. See also **15.4** above.

(II) Where a company, in accordance with generally accepted accounting practice, treats rights and liabilities under a contract to which it is party and which is neither a loan relationship nor within (III) below, as divided between rights and liabilities under one or more derivatives and the remaining rights and liabilities (the 'host contract'). The company is treated for the purposes of these provisions as party to a relevant contract (or contracts) whose rights and liabilities consist only of those of the derivative or derivatives (referred to as 'embedded derivatives'). The embedded derivative is treated as having the character (be it an option, a future or a contract for differences) which the rights and liabilities would have if contained in a separate contract.

(III) Where a company, in accordance with generally accepted accounting practice, treats rights and liabilities under a relevant contract within (2), (3) or (4) below to which it is party as divided between rights and liabilities under one or more derivatives ('embedded derivatives') and the remaining rights and liabilities (the 'host contract') and a contract consisting only of those remaining rights and liabilities would be a relevant contract. The company is treated for the purposes of these provisions as party to a relevant contract (or contracts) whose rights and liabilities consist only of those of the embedded derivative or derivatives and to a relevant contract whose rights and liabilities are those of the host contract. Each relevant contract is treated as having the character (be it an option, a future or a contract for differences) which the rights and liabilities would have if contained in a separate contract.

A contract which is a relevant contract other than by virtue of (I) to (III) above is referred to as a '*plain vanilla contract*'.

[*CTA 2009, ss 576–578, 580–582, 584–586*].

Accounting condition

A relevant contract is a derivative contract for the purposes of these provisions for an accounting period if it meets the accounting condition.

The accounting condition is that the relevant contract is treated as a derivative for the purposes of the relevant accounting standard for the accounting period in question or would be so treated for accounting purposes were the relevant accounting standard used.

The '*relevant accounting standard*' is:

- FRS 25 issued in December 2004 (now superseded); or
- for any accounting period for which it is required or permitted to be used, any subsequent accounting standard dealing with transactions which are derivatives.

[*CTA 2009, s 579(1)(a), (3), (5)*].

As IAS39, IFRS9, FRS26 and FRS102 all define derivative in essentially the same way, a contract that is a derivative within one of those standards will satisfy the accounting test (HMRC Corporate Finance Manual CFM50220).

A relevant contract which did not satisfy the accounting test solely because it failed to satisfy the requirements of FRS 26, para 9(b) (essentially, this prevented prepaid or substantially prepaid contracts from falling within the definition of a derivative for the purposes of FRS 26) was brought within the derivative contracts legislation. The profits and losses arising on the derivative contract for the purposes of the derivative contracts legislation have to be determined using a fair value basis of accounting.

[*CTA 2009, ss 579(1)(b), (4), 600*].

Where a relevant contract does not satisfy the accounting condition, it is nevertheless brought within the derivative contracts legislation if:

(a) the 'underlying subject matter' of the contract (see below) is commodities; or
(b) the contract is a contract for differences whose underlying subject matter is: land; tangible movable property other than commodities which are tangible assets; intangible fixed assets; weather conditions; or creditworthiness.

[*CTA 2009, s 579(2)*].

Contracts excluded by virtue of their underlying subject matter

Subject to the qualifications below, a relevant contract is *not* a derivative contract for the purposes of these provisions if its underlying subject matter consists wholly of one or more types of 'excluded property'.

The following are '*excluded property*':

(A) intangible fixed assets (see **15.13** below) (but these are not excluded if the relevant contract is a contract for differences);
(B) shares in a company (as defined);
(C) rights of a unit holder under a unit trust scheme.

Exclusions (B) and (C) above apply only where certain further conditions are met, including where the contract is entered into for non-trading purposes or by a life assurance company or mutual trading company or where the contract is part of a hedging relationship or where the contract is designed to produce a return equating in substance to the return on an investment of money at a commercial rate of interest.

The underlying subject matter of a relevant contract is *treated* as consisting wholly of one or more of the above in certain circumstances if it consists partly of such property and partly of other property, where the latter is subordinate to the former or of small value compared with the whole. See also **15.12** below for the splitting of a contract into two notional contracts (applicable only to futures and options).

The '*underlying subject matter*' of a relevant contract is:

- (in the case of an option) the property which would fall to be delivered if the option were exercised; or, where such property is itself a derivative contract, the underlying subject matter of that contract;
- (in the case of a future) the property which, if the future were to run to delivery, would fall to be delivered at the date and price agreed when the contract is made; or, where such property is itself a derivative contract, the underlying subject matter of that contract;
- (in the case of a contract for differences), where the contract relates to fluctuations in the value or price of property described in the contract, the property so described; or, where the contract designates an index or

factor, the matter by reference to which the index or factor is determined (and in particular, underlying subject matter may include interest rates, weather conditions or creditworthiness, but the use of interest rates to establish the amount of a payment whose due date may vary does not make those rates the underlying subject matter of the contract).

Where the underlying subject matter of a relevant contract consists of or includes income from shares in a company or rights of a unit trust holder or unit trust scheme, the underlying subject matter is not to be treated, by reason only of that income, as being such shares or right.

[*CTA 2009, ss 583, 589–592*].

Derivative contracts taxed on a chargeable gains basis

[15.10] Non-trading debits and credits in respect of certain types of derivative contract are not brought into account under the loan relationship rules as outlined at **15.8** above. Instead, where such credits of a company for an accounting period exceed the debits for that period, a chargeable gain is deemed to accrue to the company in that period. Where the debits exceed the credits an allowable loss arises. See below for the carry back of allowable losses arising under these provisions.

This treatment applies to the following types of contract where the contract is not one to which the company is party at any time in the accounting period concerned for the purposes of a trade carried on by it (other than life assurance business or mutual trading):

(a) contracts where the underlying subject matter relates to land (wherever situated) or tangible movable property other than commodities which are tangible assets;
(b) certain 'embedded derivatives' which are options or exactly tracking contracts for differences (see further below);
(c) contracts which are 'property-based total return swaps'.

In addition, for (a) and (c) above, no two or more of the parties to the derivative contract can be connected parties.

Chargeable gains treatment does not apply where the company is an authorised unit trust, an investment trust, an open-ended investment company or a venture capital trust. As regards (a) above, where the underlying subject matter includes income, this is ignored in determining the underlying subject matter of the contract, where it is subordinate to the land or property in question, or small in value in comparison with the underlying subject matter of the contract as a whole.

[*CTA 2009, ss 639–641, 643–650*].

Embedded derivatives

Chargeable gains treatment as above applies to two types of embedded derivative within **15.9**(I) above where the loan relationship in which the derivative is embedded is a creditor relationship of the company. Subject to further conditions and exclusions, these are:

(i) options whose underlying subject matter is 'qualifying ordinary shares' or 'mandatorily convertible preference shares' (both as defined); and
(ii) contracts for differences whose subject matter is land or qualifying ordinary shares and which are 'exactly tracking contracts' (as defined).

Chargeable gains treatment does not apply in the case of (i) above, where the SUBSTANTIAL SHAREHOLDING EXEMPTION (60.4) would apply to a gain arising on the disposal at the end of the accounting period in question of the option if it were contained in a separate contract.

Where chargeable gains treatment applies to embedded derivatives within (i) or (ii) above, the loan relationship in which they are embedded are not QUALIFYING CORPORATE BONDS (48).

[*CTA 2009, ss 642, 645–649*].

See *CTA 2009, s 592* for the tax treatment of host contracts and embedded derivatives whose underlying subject matter is shares or rights of a unit trust holder in a unit trust scheme.

Property-based total return swaps

A '*property-based total return swap*' is a contract for differences in which one or more indices is designated where at least one of the indices is an index of changes in the value of land (wherever situated) and the underlying subject matter of the contract also includes interest rates. Special rules apply to determine the debits and credits to be taken into account in computing the chargeable gains and allowable losses under the above provisions. [*CTA 2009, ss 650, 659(3)–(6)*].

Carry back of losses

Where there is a 'net loss' under the above provisions in an accounting period and, in a previous accounting period falling wholly or partly within 24 months immediately preceding the start of the loss period, there is a 'net gain' under the above provisions, a claim can be made for the loss to be wholly or partly carried back and set against part or all of the gain (but not so as to reduce either the loss or the gain below nil). The claim must be made within two years of the end of the period in which the net loss arose. Losses must be set against gains of a later period before those of an earlier period. Where a gain period falls partly before the 24-month period mentioned above, the loss can be only offset against the proportion of the gain falling within the 24-month period (time-apportioned based on the number of days).

A '*net loss*' in this case is the sum of any allowable losses arising under the above provisions ('*section 641 losses*') in a period less the sum of any chargeable gains arising under the above provisions ('*section 641 gains*') in the same period, in both cases in respect of the company's derivative contracts. A '*net gain*' is the excess of *section 641* gains over *section 641* losses, further reduced by any 'non-section 641 allowable losses' (i.e. allowable losses arising other than under the above provisions). Any non-*section 641* allowable losses must be set against any non-section 641 gains before the remainder is deducted from section 641 gains.

[*CTA 2009, ss 663, 664*].

Terminal exercise of options

There are provisions dealing with the chargeable gains consequences of the exercise or disposal of rights to acquire shares comprised in a derivative contract which is, or is treated as, an option.

Where the contract is an embedded derivative within (i) above, the following applies.

(A) In computing any chargeable gain accruing on a disposal of the asset representing the original creditor relationship associated with the embedded derivative, the acquisition cost is increased by the amount by which G (see below) exceeds L or, where L exceeds G, is reduced by the excess.

(B) In computing any chargeable gain accruing on a disposal of all the shares acquired in exercising the rights where the acquisition was in circumstances such that no disposal was deemed to arise by virtue of *TCGA 1992, s 127* (reorganisation of share capital — see **57.2** SHARES AND SECURITIES), the acquisition cost is increased by the amount by which G (see below) exceeds L or, where L exceeds G, is reduced by the excess. In the case of a part disposal of the shares, the part disposal apportionment rule at **16.5** COMPUTATION OF GAINS AND LOSSES applies accordingly.

In either case, where L exceeds G and the excess is greater than the acquisition cost, any remaining amount is added to the disposal consideration.

TCGA 1992, s 37 (exclusion from consideration of amounts charged to tax as income — see **33.1** INTERACTION WITH OTHER TAXES) and *TCGA 1992, s 39* (exclusion from allowable expenditure of amounts deductible in computing profits or losses for income tax purposes — see **33.1** INTERACTION WITH OTHER TAXES) do not apply to any of the disposals mentioned above.

For these purposes, G is the sum of CV and any chargeable gains accruing under the above provisions in respect of the contract for the accounting period in which the disposal is made and any previous accounting periods so far as they are referable, on a just and reasonable apportionment, to the shares. L is the sum of any allowable losses accruing for those accounting periods so far as they are so referable. CV is the amount by which the tax-adjusted carrying value of the host contract at the date on which the option is exercised exceeds the tax-adjusted carrying value of that contract at the date on which the company became party to the loan relationship or, if later, the date that the derivative contract came within (i) above.

[*CTA 2009, ss 670, 671*].

Where the contract is a plain vanilla contract (i.e. it is not an embedded derivative), in computing any chargeable gain accruing on a disposal of all the shares acquired in exercising the rights, the acquisition cost is increased by the amount by which X (see below) exceeds Y or, where Y exceeds X, is reduced by the excess and, in the case of a part disposal of the shares, the part disposal apportionment rule at **16.5** COMPUTATION OF GAINS AND LOSSES applies accordingly. Where Y exceeds X and the excess is greater than the acquisition cost, any remaining amount is added to the disposal consideration.

For this purpose, X is the sum of any credits brought into account as trading receipts in respect of the derivative contract for the accounting period in which the disposal is made and any previous accounting periods so far as they are referable, on a just and reasonable apportionment, to the shares. Y is the sum of any debits so brought into account for those accounting periods so far as they are so referable.

This provision applies also where delivery is taken of shares in accordance with the terms of a plain vanilla contract which is a future.

[*CTA 2009, ss 667–669*].

Disposal of embedded exactly tracking contracts for differences

There are provisions dealing with the chargeable gains consequences of the disposal of an asset representing a creditor relationship in which a derivative contract within (ii) above is embedded.

In computing any chargeable gain accruing on the disposal, the acquisition cost is increased by the amount by which G exceeds L or, where L exceeds G, is reduced by the excess. Where L exceeds G and the excess is greater than the acquisition cost, any remaining amount is added to the disposal consideration. For these purposes, G is the sum of CV and any chargeable gains accruing under the above provisions in respect of the contract for the accounting period in which the disposal is made and any previous accounting periods. L is the sum of any allowable losses accruing for those accounting periods. CV is the amount by which the tax-adjusted carrying value of the host contract at the date of the disposal exceeds the tax-adjusted carrying value of that contract at the date on which the company became party to the loan relationship.

TCGA 1992, s 37 (exclusion from consideration of amounts charged to tax as income — see **33.1** INTERACTION WITH OTHER TAXES) and *TCGA 1992, s 39* (exclusion from allowable expenditure of amounts deductible in computing profits or losses for income tax purposes — see **33.1** INTERACTION WITH OTHER TAXES) do not apply to the disposal.

[*CTA 2009, ss 672, 673*].

Issuers of securities with embedded derivatives

[15.11] There are also provisions dealing with certain embedded derivatives within **15.9**(I) above on a chargeable gains basis where the loan relationship in which the derivative is embedded is a *debtor* relationship of the company.

Deemed options

Subject to further conditions, the following provisions apply to embedded derivatives which are deemed to be options and whose underlying subject matter is shares.

Where the provisions apply, non-trading and trading debits and credits are not brought into account under the loan relationship rules as outlined at **15.8** above. Instead, the following applies.

(a) Where the option is exercised and shares are issued or transferred in fulfilment of the obligations under the option (the '*relevant disposal*'), *TCGA 1992, s 144(2)* (see **7.7** ASSETS) applies to the relevant disposal as if the tax-adjusted carrying value of the option at the time the company became party to the loan relationship was the consideration for the grant of the option. The market value rule at *TCGA 1992, s 17(1)* (see **39.1** MARKET VALUE) is disapplied.

(b) Where the option is exercised, there is no relevant disposal and an amount is paid in fulfilment of the obligations under the option, a chargeable gain is treated as accruing to the company equal to the amount by which E exceeds F. If F exceeds E, an allowable loss equal to the excess is treated as accruing. For this purpose, E is the tax-adjusted carrying value of the option at the time the company became party to the loan relationship. F is the amount paid by the debtor in fulfilment of the obligations under the debtor relationship reduced, but not below nil, by the fair value of the host contract at the date on which the option is exercised.

(c) Where the debtor relationship comes to an end without the option having been exercised, the company is treated for the purposes of corporation tax on chargeable gains as having disposed of an asset for an amount equal to the tax-adjusted carrying value of the option at the time the company became party to the loan relationship. The company is treated as having acquired the asset for a consideration equal, where the company ceases to be party to the relationship on the redemption or repayment of the liability, to the amount paid by the company or in any other case, the consideration given by the company on the relationship coming to an end less, in either case, the fair value of the host contract at the date the relationship comes to an end.

[*CTA 2009, ss 652–655*].

Equity instruments

Subject to further conditions, the following applies where a debtor relationship is divided under the embedded derivatives provisions between the loan relationship and an equity instrument of the company, such that the equity instrument is a relevant contract treated as an option. Where the company pays an amount to the person who is party to the loan relationship as creditor in discharge of any obligations under the relationship, an allowable loss is treated as accruing to the extent that RA exceeds E. RA is the amount so paid reduced (but not below nil) by the fair value of the host contract at the time the payment is made. E is the amount treated as the tax-adjusted carrying value of the relevant contract at the time the company became party to the loan relationship. [*CTA 2009, ss 665, 666*].

Deemed contracts for difference

Subject to further conditions, the following applies where a debtor relationship is divided under the embedded derivatives provisions such that the relevant contract to which the company is treated as being party is a derivative contract whose underlying subject matter is shares and which is a contract for differences (other than one falling within *CTA 2009, s 652* above). The contract must be an exactly tracking contract (as defined).

Debits and credits are not brought into account under the loan relationship rules as outlined at **15.8** above. Where the debtor relationship comes to an end and an amount is paid to discharge all of the company's obligations (the '*discharge amount*'), a chargeable gain or allowable loss is treated as accruing, calculated on the assumption that the derivative contract is an asset of the company, that there is a disposal of that asset at the time the relationship comes to an end, and that the cost of the asset is the discharge amount. The consideration for the disposal is deemed to be equal to the amount of the proceeds of issue of the security representing the relationship, except where the company became party to the loan relationship after its creation, in which case the consideration is equal to the amount of the tax-adjusted carrying value of the host contract at the time of its creation.

[*CTA 2009, ss 656–658*].

Miscellaneous rules with potential chargeable gains consequences

[15.12] The following provisions potentially give rise to chargeable gains consequences.

Contracts which become or cease to be derivative contracts

The following provision applies where a company is a party to a relevant contract which, having not been a derivative contract, becomes a derivative contract if, immediately before the change, the contract was a chargeable asset (i.e. an asset on a disposal of which any gain would be a chargeable gain, including any obligation under a futures contract which would be regarded as a chargeable asset by virtue of *TCGA 1992, s 143* (see **7.8** ASSETS)). When the company ceases to be a party to the relevant contract it must bring into account (for the accounting period in which it so ceases) a chargeable gain or allowable loss calculated on the basis that the company had disposed of the contract immediately before the time it became a derivative contract for a consideration equal to the 'notional carrying value' at that time. For this purpose, the '*notional carrying value*' of a contract at any time is the amount which would have been the tax-adjusted carrying value had an accounting period ended immediately before that time. [*CTA 2009, ss 622(4), 661, 703*].

Where a company is party to a relevant contract which ceases to be a derivative contract, the company is treated:

- for the purposes of the derivative contracts provisions, as if it had disposed of the contract at the time it ceased to be a derivative contract for consideration equal to the notional carrying value of the contract at that time, and
- for the purposes of *TCGA 1992*, as if it had acquired the contract immediately after that time for the same consideration.

[*CTA 2009, s 662*].

Contracts treated as two separate contracts

Where a relevant contract is an option or a future and its underlying subject matter consists partly of excluded property (as in **15.9** above) and partly of non-excluded property, it is treated, for all corporation tax purposes (including those of corporation tax on chargeable gains), as split (on a just and reasonable basis) into two separate notional contracts. This treatment does not apply if the contract is excluded under the accounting tests etc. referred to above or if the non-excluded property meets the 'subordinate' or 'small value' tests referred to immediately following **15.9**(f) above (in which case it is merely disregarded rather than dealt with separately). [*CTA 2009, s 593*].

Intangible fixed assets

[15.13] A special corporation tax regime applies to expenditure and receipts in respect of 'intangible fixed assets' (see **15.14** below). Such assets are therefore removed from the charge to corporation tax on chargeable gains, subject to the commencement provisions described below. For full details of the regime, see Tolley's Corporation Tax under Intangible Assets.

In summary, the regime encompasses expenditure on the creation, acquisition and enhancement of intangibles (including abortive expenditure) as well as on their preservation and maintenance, and also applies to payments for the use of such assets, e.g. royalties. Profits on disposal of such assets are taxed as income. Losses on disposal and payments are relievable against income. The tax treatment of amortisation normally follows the accounts treatment, but for assets with an indefinite or longer life, a company can elect for a fixed allowance of 4% per annum. A form of rollover relief (similar to, but not to be confused with, capital gains tax rollover relief) is available where realisation proceeds of intangibles are reinvested in new intangibles. The relief is available even on the disposal of an intangible asset excluded from the regime by the commencement provisions, and in such a case, it may reduce or eliminate a chargeable gain (and reduce the tax-recognised cost of the new intangible asset for the purposes of the regime). See also **31.4** INCORPORATION AND DISINCORPORATION RELIEFS and **53.3–53.4** ROLLOVER RELIEF.

Simon's Taxes. See D1.6.

Commencement

The regime applies only to intangible fixed assets of a company that are:

- (a) created by the company after 31 March 2002; or
- (b) acquired by the company after 31 March 2002 and before 1 July 2020 from a person who is not a 'related party' (as defined at **39.2** MARKET VALUE; and see further below); or
- (c) acquired by the company after 31 March 2002 and before 1 July 2020 from a related party in the following cases:
  - (i) where the asset is acquired from a company in whose hands the asset fell within the intangible assets regime;
  - (ii) where the asset is acquired from an intermediary who acquired the asset after 31 March 2002 from a third party which was not a related party of the intermediary (at the time of the intermediary's acquisition of the asset) or of the company (at the time of the company's acquisition); or
  - (iii) where the asset was created by any person after 31 March 2002;

(d) acquired by the company on or after 1 July 2020;
(e) held by the company immediately before 1 July 2020 where at that time, the company is not within the charge to corporation tax in respect of the asset.

Assets within (d) or (e) above are within the regime only for accounting periods beginning on or after 1 July 2020, and for this purpose, an accounting period straddling that date is treated as two separate accounting periods, the second of which begins on that date. Assets within (d) above are subject to special rules restricting debits where they are 'restricted assets' (as defined; broadly assets acquired by a company on or after 1 July 2020 directly or indirectly from a related party which were previously excluded from the regime by the commencement rules).

In (b) above, the circumstances in which persons are treated as related parties include where the transfer pricing 'participation condition' (see *TIOPA 2010, s 147*) is met between them.

The condition in (e) above is not met if, at any time in the period 19 March 2020 to 30 June 2020 inclusive, the asset is excluded from the regime by the commencement rules in the hands of any company that is within the charge to corporation tax in respect of it unless after that time, but during that period, the asset is acquired by any other company from a person who at the time of acquisition is not a related party of that other company.

Anti-avoidance provisions apply, broadly, to treat an asset created after commencement and acquired by a company before 1 July 2020 from a related party as excluded from the regime by the above provisions where either the asset is derived from assets themselves so excluded, or the acquisition is directly or indirectly in consequence of, or in connection with, the disposal of an excluded asset.

For the above purposes and subject to the exceptions below, an asset is treated as acquired or created after 31 March 2002 to the extent that expenditure on its acquisition or creation is incurred after that date. Similar rules apply to determine whether assets are treated as acquired on or after 1 July 2020, between 1 April 2002 and 30 June 2020 or between 19 March 2020 and 30 June 2020. Where as a result of these rules, the asset would fall within the regime only to a limited extent, the asset is treated as two separate assets, one falling within the regime and one not; expenditure on the asset is apportioned between the two notional assets on a just and reasonable basis. In general, expenditure is regarded as incurred for this purpose when it is recognised for 'accounting purposes' (see **15.14** below). In certain cases, however, either the capital gains rule (see **16.4** COMPUTATION OF GAINS AND LOSSES), or the capital allowances rule governing the date expenditure is treated as incurred is applied.

Goodwill is treated as created before 1 April 2002 if the business in question was carried on at any time before that date by the company concerned or a 'related party' (as defined at **39.2** MARKET VALUE) and is treated as created on or after that date in any other case. There is therefore no division of goodwill created before 1 April 2002 into two notional assets, and on disposal it will remain within the charge to corporation tax on chargeable gains.

A similar rule applies in the case of an asset, other than goodwill, which represents expenditure which would not be qualifying expenditure for capital allowances purposes under the law applicable prior to the introduction of the intangible assets regime. Such an asset is treated as created before 1 April 2002 if it was held at any time before that date by the company concerned or a related party, and in any other case is treated as created on or after that date. Where part of the expenditure on such an asset would have qualified for capital allowances, the asset is treated as two separate assets, one qualifying for capital allowances and one not. The notional asset which would have qualified for capital allowances is then treated as created or acquired at the time given by the general provisions above (but using the capital allowances rule to determine the date the expenditure is deemed to have been incurred). Necessary apportionments are made for this purpose on a just and reasonable basis. This provision previously applied to internally-generated assets, subject to the same commencement provisions as apply to the goodwill provisions above.

Assets acquired by means of certain no gain/no loss transfers made after 27 June 2002 are excluded from the intangible assets regime in the hands of the transferee company if they fell outside the regime in the hands of the transferor company. The transfers in question are those within *TCGA 1992, s 139* (company reconstructions involving transfer of business — see **14.12** COMPANIES), *TCGA 1992, s 140A* (transfer of UK business between companies resident in different EC member states — see **43.12** OVERSEAS MATTERS), *TCGA 1992, s 140E* (European cross-border merger: assets left within UK tax charge — see **43.14** OVERSEAS MATTERS) or, where the transfer is on or after 1 July 2020, *TCGA 1992, s 171* (transfers within a group — see **26.3** GROUPS OF COMPANIES).

Special commencement provisions apply in the case of assets consisting of licences or other rights within *FA 2000, Sch 23* (certain telecommunications rights) and Lloyd's syndicate capacity. The intangible assets regime applies to such assets in respect of any amounts to be brought into account for tax purposes in accounting periods ending after 31 March 2002.

Special commencement provisions also apply in the case of fungible assets. For the purpose of the intangible assets regime, fungible assets of the same kind held by the same person in the same capacity are generally pooled and treated as indistinguishable parts of a single asset. For this purpose, however, assets which do not fall within the regime ('pre-FA 2002 assets'), assets which are restricted assets (see above) and other assets which fall within the regime (standard intangible fixed assets) are treated as assets of different kinds. Each type of asset is allocated to a separate pool which is regarded as a single asset of a type determined in accordance with the assets allocated to it (so that the pool to which restricted assets are allocated is treated as a single restricted asset, and so on). Realisations of assets are treated as diminishing the pre-FA 2002 pool first, then the restricted assets pool, and finally the standard intangible fixed assets pool. Assets acquired are allocated to the pre-FA 2002 pool or the restricted assets pool to the extent that they can be identified with assets realised by the company from the pre-FA 2002 or restricted assets pool in accordance with the following rules. The rules are that acquisitions are to be identified with pre-FA 2002 assets or restricted assets realised within the period beginning 30 days before and ending 30 days after the acquisition; assets realised earlier fall to be identified before those realised later, and acquisitions are considered in the date order in which they take place.

Royalties from intangible fixed assets which are recognised for accounting purposes after 31 March 2002 fall within the intangible assets regime regardless of whether or not the asset in respect of which they are payable does so. Transitional provisions apply to prevent royalties being taken into account for tax purposes more than once.

[*CTA 2009, ss 858, 880–900O; FA 2020, s 31*].

Definition of 'intangible fixed asset'

[15.14] The term '*intangible asset*' has the same meaning for the purposes of the intangible assets regime as it has for '*accounting purposes*' (i.e. for the purposes of accounts drawn up in accordance with generally accepted accounting practice). The definition includes also any '*intellectual property*', being:

- any patent, trade mark, registered design, copyright or design right, plant breeders' rights or rights under *Plant Varieties Act 1997, s 7*; or
- any corresponding non-UK right; or
- any information or technique not protected by any of the rights above but having industrial, commercial or other economic value; or
- any licence or other right in respect of any of the above rights, information or techniques.

An '*intangible fixed asset*' is an intangible asset acquired or created by a company for use on a continuing basis in the course of the company's activities, and includes options or other rights to acquire or dispose of an intangible fixed asset. An intangible asset is an intangible fixed asset if it falls within this definition, whether or not it is capitalised in the company's accounts.

'Goodwill' (defined as for accounting purposes — see above) is specifically included within the intangible assets regime.

It is specifically enacted that intangible assets include internally-generated intangible assets, that goodwill includes internally-generated goodwill, and that goodwill is treated as created in the course of carrying on the business in question.

[*CTA 2009, ss 712, 713, 715*].

Assets excluded

The following types of intangible fixed asset (and options or other rights to acquire or dispose of such assets) are excluded from the intangible assets regime:

(a) assets representing rights enjoyed by virtue of an estate, interest or right in or over land;

(b) assets representing rights in relation to tangible movable property (see **23.4** EXEMPTIONS AND RELIEFS);

(c) an oil licence (as defined) or an interest in an oil licence (including all goodwill, and any other intangible asset, relating to, deriving from or connected with such a licence or interest);

(d) financial assets (as defined for accounting purposes (see above) and including loan relationships (see **15.2** above), derivative contracts (see **15.8** above), contracts or policies of insurance or capital redemption policies and assets derived from or referable to such policies, and rights under a collective investment scheme within the meaning of *Financial Services and Markets Act 2000*);
(e) an asset representing shares or other rights in relation to the profits, governance or winding up of a company;
(f) an asset representing rights under a trust (other than rights that for accounting purposes fall to be treated as representing an interest in trust property that is an intangible fixed asset within the regime);
(g) an asset representing the interest of a partner in a partnership (other than an interest that for accounting purposes falls to be treated as representing an interest in partnership property that is an intangible fixed asset within the regime);
(h) assets held for a purpose that is not a business or commercial purpose;
(i) assets held for the purpose of activities of a company in respect of which the company is outside the charge to corporation tax (otherwise than as a result of an election to exempt profits of a foreign permanent establishment — see **43.8** OVERSEAS MATTERS);
(j) an asset held by a company treated as carrying on a separate trade under the regimes for production of films, TV programmes, video games, orchestral concerts and museum and gallery exhibitions, so far as the asset represents expenditure of the separate trade;
(k) (except in relation to royalties) an asset (other than computer software) held for the purposes of a life assurance business;
(l) (except in relation to royalties) an asset held for the purposes of a mutual trade or business;
(m) (except in relation to royalties) an asset representing expenditure on the production of, or on the acquisition before 31 March 2008 of, the original master version (as defined) of a film to which *FA 2006, Sch 4* does not apply;
(n) (except in relation to royalties) an asset representing expenditure on the production or acquisition of the master version of a sound recording;
(o) (except in relation to royalties) an asset which represents expenditure on computer software that is to be treated for accounting purposes as part of the cost of the related hardware; and
(p) assets previously treated as tangible assets in accounts of the company concerned and in respect of which capital allowances have been made to the company under *CAA 2001, Pt 2* (plant and machinery).

Where an asset does not wholly fall within one of the above categories, it is treated as if it were two separate assets, one falling within the intangible assets regime and one not so falling; any necessary apportionment is to be made on a just and reasonable basis. Assets representing expenditure on research and development or (by election) computer software are excluded from the regime to a limited extent, but proceeds from a disposal of such an asset do fall within the regime to the extent that they are not brought into account for capital allowances purposes.

[*CTA 2009, ss 800–816; FA 2004, Sch 2 para 5*].

Subject to the commencement rules above (as modified for this purpose), the intangible assets regime is applied (with exceptions and modifications), in relation to corporate finance lessors, to any intangible asset that is the subject of a finance lease (notwithstanding that the asset may be accounted for by the finance lessor as a financial asset — see exclusions above). [*SI 2002 No 1967*].

Assets excluded from the intangible assets regime are not excluded from the charge to corporation tax on chargeable gains as a result of the introduction of the regime (although assets within a number of the above categories are not within the charge in any event).

Key points concerning companies: corporate finance and intangibles

[15.15] Points to consider are as follows.

- Since a loan relationship can only arise from the lending of money, there is no loan relationship between the parties where an amount of consideration in a transaction is merely left outstanding for a period. But it is vital to properly document the position at the time. See **15.5**.
- An amount left outstanding can then be converted into a loan relationship by agreement between the parties. But, again, proper and contemporaneous documentation is essential. See **15.5**.
- Where intangibles are disposed of, the gain cannot be rolled over into chargeable assets under *TCGA 1992, s 152*, they can only be rolled over into the acquisition of new intangible fixed assets. This applies even to intangibles excluded from the intangibles regime by the commencement rules. See **15.13**.
- There is a further rollover relief where the acquisition is of a company holding chargeable intangible assets: the gain on the disposal of the old intangible fixed asset can be rolled over into those underlying chargeable intangible assets, reducing their tax cost in respect of any further realisation. See **15.13**.

16

Computation of Gains and Losses

Cross-references. See 2.5 ANNUAL RATES AND EXEMPTIONS; 7.7 ASSETS for options; 8 ASSETS HELD ON 6 APRIL 1965; 8 ASSETS HELD ON 31 MARCH 1982; 10 CAPITAL SUMS DERIVED FROM ASSETS; 32 INDEXATION; 33 INTERACTION WITH OTHER TAXES; 35 LAND for disposals of land and leases; 38 LOSSES; 39 MARKET VALUE; 58 SHARES AND SECURITIES — IDENTIFICATION RULES; 65 WASTING ASSETS.

Simon's Taxes. See C1.105, Part C2.

Introduction to computation of gains and losses

[16.1] Gains and losses on disposals of assets are initially computed by deducting allowable expenditure (broadly, the acquisition cost, incidental costs of acquisition and disposal and the costs of any improvements) from the amount realised on the disposal. There are, however, a number of issues which make this apparently straightforward exercise more complicated. Allowances, reliefs and special computational rules can all operate to affect the computation, often with different rules applying depending on whether the gain or loss is within the scope of capital gains tax or corporation tax on chargeable gains. These complexities are summarised at **16.2** below and covered in this chapter and throughout this work.

The circumstances in which there is a disposal of an asset include where it is sold or given away but there are also a number of situations in which a disposal is deemed to occur even though there is no actual disposal. Special computational provisions apply to apportion the acquisition cost where only part of the asset is disposed of.

In certain circumstances, the actual amount received for the disposal is not used in computing the gain or loss. Instead a deemed consideration is taken, which may be the amount which leads to there being neither a gain nor a loss or the market value of the asset. In some cases, certain amounts are excluded from the consideration.

Basic computation

[16.2] Gains and losses accruing on disposals (see **16.3** below) of assets are computed by deducting allowable expenditure (see **16.12–16.14** below) from the amount realised or deemed to be realised on the disposal (i.e. the actual or deemed consideration — see **16.8** below). [*TCGA 1992, ss 15, 38*].

There are special computational provisions in respect of certain types of assets. See the list at **7.1** ASSETS.

No deduction is allowable more than once from any sum or from more than one sum. [*TCGA 1992, s 52(1)*].

See **16.4** below for date of disposal. See **16.5** below for part disposals.

For the use by certain companies of foreign currencies in computing chargeable gains on ships, aircraft and shares see **14.15** COMPANIES.

Bundles of assets

Where a bundle of assets is sold together, it is necessary to consider each disposal separately, in the light of the rules which apply to that asset (*Aberdeen Construction Group Ltd v CIR* HL 1978, 52 TC 281). See also *Fullarton and ors v CIR* Sp C, [2004] SSCD 207. See also HMRC's Practice Note at www.gov.uk/government/publications/practice-note-apportioning-the-price-paid-for-a-business-transferred-as-a-going-concern which describes HMRC's approach to the apportionment of sale proceeds of a business as a going concern where the assets sold include a 'trade related property' such as a public house, hotel, petrol station, restaurant or care home.

Indexation

For corporation tax purposes the gain (if any) arrived at as above is termed the '*unindexed gain*' and indexation allowance (if due) is deducted from it to give the gain for the purposes of *TCGA 1992* unless otherwise provided. If the allowance equals or exceeds the unindexed gain, no gain or loss arises. If a loss arises as above, no indexation allowance is available. See **32.1, 32.2** INDEXATION.

Losses

See **38** LOSSES for the deduction of allowable losses from chargeable gains.

Business asset disposal relief

Business asset disposal relief applies (on a claim) to certain gains realised on business disposals by individuals and trustees. The relief is subject to a lifetime limit of gains, currently £1 million. Where the relief is claimed, qualifying gains are taxed at a rate of 10%. See **9** BUSINESS ASSET DISPOSAL RELIEF.

Investors' relief

Investors' relief applies (on a claim) to certain gains on disposals by individuals of shares in unlisted trading companies. The relief is subject to a lifetime limit of gains, currently £10 million, and operates by taxing the gains at a rate of 10%. See **34** INVESTORS' RELIEF.

Annual exempt amount

Individuals are exempt from capital gains tax in respect of so much of their taxable gains for a tax year as do not exceed the annual exempt amount. Where the gains exceed that amount, only the excess is taxable. Personal representatives (for a limited period) and trustees of settlements are also entitled to an annual exempt amount, but companies are not. See **2.5** ANNUAL RATES AND EXEMPTIONS.

Assets held on 6 April 1965

For corporation tax purposes, there are special computational provisions for assets held on 6 April 1965, the broad purpose of which is to exclude from tax that part of the eventual gain on disposal which accrued before that date. See **8.12** ASSETS HELD ON 31 MARCH **1982**. For most disposals on or after 6 April 1988, the provisions are displaced by the rebasing provisions for assets held on 31 March 1982 (see below), but they still apply in certain cases.

Assets held on 31 March 1982

Special provisions also apply to the disposal after 5 April 1988 of assets held on 31 March 1982. Broadly, on the disposal of such an asset, the acquisition cost for tax purposes is re-based to its market value on 31 March 1982. For corporation tax purposes this only applies where it results in a smaller gain or loss than would be the case using the actual acquisition cost (or applying the rules for assets held on 6 April 1965) in the computation. For capital gains tax purposes re-basing applies automatically to all assets held on 31 March 1982. Companies are able to make a universal rebasing election for re-basing to apply to all of their assets held on 31 March 1982 and so avoid the need for comparative computations on each disposal. See **8** ASSETS HELD ON 31 MARCH **1982**.

Assets held on 5 April 2017: deemed domicile

Special provisions apply to disposals of foreign assets held on 5 April 2017 by certain non-UK domiciled individuals, who are deemed domiciled in the UK from 2017/18 due to long-term residence (see **51.29** RESIDENCE AND DOMICILE). The acquisition cost of such an asset is re-based to its market value on 5 April 2017, provided qualifying conditions are met in respect of the individual and the asset (see **51.29** RESIDENCE AND DOMICILE).

Examples

(1) Ray acquired an asset in November 1987 for £28,000. He sells the asset on 11 June 2024 for £99,000. Ray incurs allowable sale costs of £5,000. Ray makes no other disposals in 2024/25 and his taxable gains for the year are as follows.

	£
Sale consideration	99,000
Less costs of sale	5,000
Cost of asset	28,000
Chargeable gain	66,000
Annual exempt amount	3,000
Taxable gain	£63,000

(2) The facts are as in (1) above except that the taxpayer is a company and its accounting date is 30 June. The indexation factor for the period November 1987 to December 2017 is 1.690. The company's taxable gain for the accounting period ended 30 June 2024 is as follows.

	£
Sale consideration	99,000
Less costs of sale	5,000
Cost of asset	28,000
Unindexed gain	66,000
Less indexation allowance £28,000 × 1.690	47,320
Chargeable (and taxable) gain	£18,680

Disposal

[16.3] Simon's Taxes. See **C1.104, C1.307.**

'*Disposal*' is not defined in the legislation. The term includes a part disposal (see **16.5** below) and there are numerous circumstances in which the legislation deems there to be a disposal for tax purposes even though there has been no actual disposal. See in particular **10** CAPITAL SUMS DERIVED FROM ASSETS, **16.4** below for assets lost or destroyed and **38.10** LOSSES for assets becoming of negligible value.

A conveyance or transfer of an asset or of a right therein *by way of security* (e.g. a mortgage) is not a disposal, but if the creditor or any person appointed as receiver, manager, etc. deals with the asset in order to enforce the security, his activities are imputed to the giver of the security. The existence of a security is ignored for both acquisition and disposal of an asset save that the amount of liability assumed forms part of the acquisition and disposal consideration in addition to any other consideration. [*TCGA 1992, s 26*]. Relief is available if there has been a sale of an asset at arm's length in circumstances such that the vendor granted the purchaser a mortgage (in full or in part) in order for the purchaser to buy and where there has later been a default on the mortgage loan. If, as a result, the vendor regains beneficial ownership of the asset he has contracted to sell he may elect that the gain realised by him on that sale be taken as limited to the net proceeds (after incidental costs of disposal) retained by him and for the loan to be treated as never coming into existence (although interest on the loan would be subject to income tax in the usual way). On any subsequent disposal of the asset concerned, the computation will be by reference to the original date and costs of acquisition etc. (HMRC Extra-Statutory Concession D18).

A taxpayer who, in consideration of a loan, promised his parents 60% of the net proceeds of any sale of his shares in his personal company, whilst retaining beneficial ownership of the shares in the meantime, was held liable to capital gains tax in respect of the total proceeds of the eventual sale (*Burca v Parkinson* Ch D 2001, 74 TC 125).

An argument that a transfer of properties to a company never took place because the transfer was rescinded was unsuccessful in *Mahmood v HMRC* FTT, [2024] UKFTT 114 (TC). The taxpayer had mistakenly believed that the transfer would be free of CGT and, when he discovered otherwise, arranged for the properties to be transferred back to him. The FTT said that the taxpayer was relying on the common law doctrine of 'common mistake' under which a transaction may be void if the parties enter into the transaction on the basis of a mistaken belief which is sufficiently fundamental. However, the judge said this was not the case here. Had the transaction been only partly executed so that one or both parties still had outstanding obligations to perform, rescission may have been possible. But the transaction was 'fully executed' and it was therefore 'questionable' whether it was possible to rescind, as opposed to reverse, the transaction. Further, even if the transaction had been validly rescinded, this did not mean that the transfer of the properties could be ignored. It 'simply' put an end to any further obligations yet to be performed. The tribunal concluded that even though the transaction had been reversed, the transfer of the properties to the company could not be treated as if it had never taken place. There was a disposal of properties by the taxpayer which gave rise to a CGT liability.

See also *Underwood v HMRC* CA 2008, [2009] STC 239.

Date of disposal

[16.4] **Simon's Taxes. See C1.322.**

Contracts

Where an asset is disposed of and acquired under a contract, the disposal and acquisition are made at the time the contract is made (and not, if different, the time at which the asset is conveyed or transferred, e.g. on a contract for the sale of land). This rule applies even if the contract is unenforceable, provided that the disposal is actually completed (*Thompson v Salah* Ch D 1971, 47 TC 559). However, this case is no longer valid in the case of a contract in respect of UK land because the general law requires that contracts must be made in writing (as is required under *Law of Property (Miscellaneous Provisions) Act 1989* and which applies in England and Wales although a similar requirement applies in Scotland (HMRC Capital Gains Manual CG14262, 70280)).) If the contract is conditional (and, in particular, if it is conditional on the exercise of an option), the disposal and acquisition are made at the time the condition is satisfied. [*TCGA 1992, s 28*].

See *Eastham v Leigh London & Provincial Properties Ltd* 1971, 46 TC 687; *Johnson v Edwards* Ch D 1981, 54 TC 488; *Burt v HMRC* (Sp C 684), [2008] SSCD 814.

In *Jerome v Kelly* HL, [2004] STC 887; [2004] All ER(D) 168(May), in which there was an intermediate disposal of part of the asset to a Bermudan trust between contract and completion, the taxpayer was held not to be liable to CGT on the original disposal of the part of the asset covered by the intermediate disposal. Lord Hoffmann observed that the draftsman responsible for what is now *TCGA 1992, s 28(1)* 'did not think about what should happen in the situation which has arisen in this case'. He held that it would be wrong 'to attribute to Parliament an intention to impose a liability to tax upon a person who would not be treated as having made a disposal under the carefully constructed scheme for taxing the disposals of assets held on trust'. *TCGA 1992, s 28(1)* should be treated as 'concerned solely with fixing the time of disposal by a person whose identity is to be ascertained by other means'.

A question of whether the buyer and seller under a conditional contract are connected (see, for example **38.7** LOSSES) is determined as of the time the contract becomes unconditional — see *Kellogg Brown and Root Holdings (UK) Ltd v HMRC* CA, [2010] EWCA Civ 118, 2010 STI 558.

See also under hire purchase below.

For the extension of certain time limits where a disposal and acquisition is made under a contract but the conveyance or transfer does not take place until a later tax year or accounting period, see **6.12**, **6.14** ASSESSMENTS, **13.5** CLAIMS and **46.3** PENALTIES.

Gifts

A gift is treated as having been made when the donor has done everything within his power to transfer the property to the donee (*Re Rose, Rose and ors v CIR* CA, [1952] 1 All ER 1217).

Hire purchase

A transaction under which the assets may pass to the hirer at the end of the hire is treated as a disposal of the whole asset at the beginning of that period, with subsequent adjustments if the agreement terminates without the hirer acquiring the asset. [*TCGA 1992, s 27*]. For consideration of hire-purchase and conditional contracts (see above), see *Lyon v Pettigrew* Ch D 1985, 58 TC 452.

Capital sums

Deemed disposals covered by **10** CAPITAL SUMS DERIVED FROM ASSETS take place on the receipt of the capital sum. [*TCGA 1992, s 22(2)*]. See *Chaloner v Pellipar Investments Ltd* Ch D 1996, 68 TC 238 in which it was held, by reference to the particular facts of the case, that a capital sum received by the taxpayer in 'money's worth' fell outside *s 22* and that the date of disposal had thus to be determined by reference to the contract date as above.

Options

See 7.7 ASSETS.

Assets lost or destroyed

Such assets are deemed to be disposed of at the time of loss etc. [*TCGA 1992, s 24(1)*]. It seems that this provision does not override *TCGA 1992, s 22(2)* above where an actual capital sum is received subsequent to the loss etc. (see comments by Hoffmann J in the Ch D in *Powlson v Welbeck Securities Ltd* CA 1987, 60 TC 269).

Assets becoming of negligible value

See 38.10 LOSSES.

Land compulsorily acquired

See 35.8 LAND for acquisition of land by an authority possessing any power of compulsory purchase.

Rollover relief

See 53.1 ROLLOVER RELIEF.

Part disposals

[16.5] Simon's Taxes. See C2.4.

References to a disposal for the purposes of the chargeable gains legislation include, unless otherwise required, references to a part disposal. There is a part disposal of an asset where an interest or right in or over the asset is created by the disposal, as well as where it subsists before the disposal, and generally, there is a part disposal of an asset where, on a person making a disposal, any description of property derived from the asset remains undisposed of. [*TCGA 1992, s 21(2)*].

Where a disposal is partial, those deductions which are not wholly attributable either to the part retained or to the part disposed of are apportioned over the total value of the asset, including the part retained, and only the portion relative to the part disposed of is deductible from the consideration received for it. The apportioned allowable expenditure is calculated by reference to the formula:

$$\frac{A}{A + B}$$

where:

A is the consideration received or deemed to have been received; and

B is the market value of the part retained.

For corporation tax, this apportionment also applies for indexation allowance purposes.

Any such apportionment is to be made before applying the following provisions.

(a) *TCGA 1992, s 41* (restriction of losses by reference to capital allowances, see **16.14**(i) below). (If after the part disposal there is a subsequent disposal of the asset, the capital allowances to be taken into account on that subsequent disposal are those referable to the expenditure incurred under **16.12**(a)–(c) below whether before or after the part disposal, but those allowances are reduced by the amount, if any, by which the loss on the earlier disposal was restricted under *TCGA 1992, s 41*.)

(b) *TCGA 1992, s 58(1)* (transfers between spouses or civil partners, see **40.4** MARRIED PERSONS AND CIVIL PARTNERS).

(c) *TCGA 1992, ss 152–158* (replacement of business assets, see **53** ROLL-OVER RELIEF).

(d) *TCGA 1992, s 171(1)* (transfers within GROUPS OF COMPANIES (**26.3**)).

(e) Any other provision making an adjustment to secure that neither a gain nor a loss occurs on disposal.

(f) The computation of any indexation allowance. [*TCGA 1992, s 56(1)*].

[*TCGA 1992, s 42*].

Similar apportionments of allowable deductions are made where assets have been merged or divided, have changed their nature, or have had interests created out of them, etc. [*TCGA 1992, s 43*].

See **8** ASSETS HELD ON **31** MARCH **1982** for further applications of *TCGA 1992, s 42* and *s 43*.

Any other necessary apportionment is to be made as may be 'just and reasonable'. [*TCGA 1992, s 52(4), Sch 11 para 11*]. HMRC cite the case of *EV Booth (Holdings) Ltd v Buckwell* Ch D 1980, 53 TC 425 as authority for their view that it is not open to either of the parties to a contract to seek to alter an apportionment contained in the contract for capital gains tax purposes. HMRC also consider that they can apply *TCGA 1992, s 52(4)* only where no apportionment is provided or where the apportionment provided is unreasonable on the facts of the case (HMRC Capital Gains Manual CG14773).

Example

X buys a piece of land in 1989 for £182,000. He subsequently sells half of it to Y in May 2024 for £150,000. The remainder of the land, because of its better position, is estimated to be then worth £200,000.

X's chargeable gain is computed as follows

A = £150,000

B = £200,000

Allowable expenditure attributable to the part disposed of

$$\frac{150,000}{(150,000+200,000)} \times £182,000 = £78,000$$

Chargeable gain: £150,000 – £78,000 = £72,000

The allowable expenditure on a disposal of the remaining land will be £104,000, i.e. £182,000 less £78,000.

In *Anders Utkilens Rederi A/S v O/Y Lovisa Stevedoring Co A/B and anor* Ch D 1984, [1985] STC 301, a plaintiff had initially obtained judgment for a liquidated sum against a defendant, but the action was then compromised by an agreement for the defendant's property to be sold and the proceeds divided between the parties. It was held that there had been a part disposal of an interest in the property by the defendant to the plaintiff followed by a disposal by each party of his interest then held to the final purchaser.

See **35.6** LAND for relief for certain part disposals of land and **35.15** where part of the premium received for a lease is liable to income tax.

Simon's Taxes. See C2.4.

Forfeited deposit of purchase money

[16.6] A forfeited deposit of purchase money or other consideration money for a prospective purchase or other transaction which is abandoned is treated in the same way as consideration given for an option to purchase which is not exercised. [*TCGA 1992, s 144(7)*]. There is no disposal for capital gains tax purposes by the person who abandons his deposit and no loss relief is available (except in the case of a forfeited deposit on an asset intended to be used, if acquired, for the purposes of a trade carried on by the forfeiter (see 7.7(a) ASSETS)). There is, however, a disposal of an asset to which no allowable expenditure attaches by the person receiving the forfeited deposit the amount of which is treated as the consideration received. See **7.7** ASSETS.

In *Hardy v HMRC* UT, [2016] UKUT 332 (TCC), [2016] STI 2590, the rescinding of two contracts for the purchase of land was held not to constitute the disposal of assets. The loss of the deposits paid by the intended buyer was not a loss capable of being allowed against chargeable gains.

Transfer of dormant assets

[16.7] Under the *Dormant Bank and Building Society Accounts Act 2008*, a bank or building society can transfer the funds in a dormant account (broadly, an account in respect of which no transactions have been carried out for 15 years) to an authorised reclaim fund for use for the benefit of good causes. In the case of building societies and certain smaller banks, part of the balance can be transferred directly to a charity. Where such a transfer is carried out, the account holder ceases to have any rights against the bank or building society for payment of the balance, but acquires equivalent rights against the reclaim fund.

The *Dormant Assets Act 2022* extends the dormant assets scheme to certain other financial assets: proceeds of a long-term insurance contract; benefits under a personal pension scheme; certain amounts owing in respect of shares in an open-ended investment company or units in an authorised unit trust or authorised contractual scheme; client money held by a financial institution; and distributions and other proceeds arising from shares in a traded public company.

A transfer under the above provisions is not treated for capital gains purposes as involving any disposal or acquisition of an asset. The account holder's rights against the reclaim fund are treated as the same asset as the original rights against the bank, building society or institution, acquired as those rights were acquired and having the same characteristics as those rights. The extension of this rule to assets under the *Dormant Assets Act 2022* applies from a date to be appointed by statutory instrument. [*TCGA 1992, s 26A; FA 2022, s 31, Sch 6 para 1*].

Where an amount is paid out of an authorised reclaim fund in respect of a dormant asset on or after the appointed date, it is exempt from capital gains tax (and income tax) if the amount originally transferred to the fund was from an ISA. [*FA 2022, Sch 6 paras 4, 6*].

Consideration

[16.8] The consideration for the disposal or acquisition of an asset which is to be used in computing a gain or loss is, in the most straightforward cases, the agreed sale or purchase price. This applies regardless of how the price is to be applied (*Spectros International plc v Madden* Ch D 1996, 70 TC 349, *McEnroe v HMRC* UT, [2023] UKUT 255 (TCC)). See also *Crusader v HMRC* Sp C 2007 (Sp C 640), [2008] SSCD 281, where an amount paid to a charity by the purchaser of a company was held to form part of the consideration for the sale of the company. See also *Collins v HMRC* [2009] STC 1077, in which a payment to a company under the terms of an agreement for the sale by the taxpayer of the shares in the company was held to form part of the consideration for the sale of the shares.

Where a bundle of assets is sold together (see **16.2** above) it may be necessary to apportion the consideration between the assets. Any necessary apportionment is to be made as may be 'just and reasonable'. [*TCGA 1992, s 52(4), Sch 11 para 11*]. HMRC cite the case of *EV Booth (Holdings) Ltd v Buckwell* Ch D 1980, 53 TC 425 as authority for their view that it is not open to either of the parties to a contract to seek to alter an apportionment contained in the contract for capital gains tax purposes. HMRC also consider that they can apply *TCGA 1992, s 52(4)* only where no apportionment is provided or where the apportionment provided is unreasonable on the facts of the case (HMRC Capital Gains Manual CG14773).

In certain circumstances a disposal (and/or acquisition) may be deemed by the legislation to be made at MARKET VALUE (see **39.1**) or on a no gain/no loss basis (see, in particular, **26.3** GROUPS OF COMPANIES, **40.4** MARRIED PERSONS AND CIVIL PARTNERS and the list of no gain/no loss provisions at **8.6** ASSETS HELD ON 31 MARCH 1982).

There are also a number of circumstances where certain amounts are excluded from the consideration. See **33.1** INTERACTION WITH OTHER TAXES for the exclusion of amounts charged to income tax; **63.11** UNIT TRUSTS AND OTHER INVESTMENT VEHICLES for the deduction from consideration of the amount of an income gain under the FINROF rules; and **3** ALTERNATIVE FINANCE ARRANGEMENTS for the exclusion of the return on such arrangements that is broadly equivalent to interest from the consideration for the purchase and sale of the asset involved.

Appropriations to and from trading stock

[16.9] Where an asset acquired by a person otherwise than as trading stock is appropriated by them for the purposes of their trade as trading stock (whether on the commencement of the trade or otherwise) and a chargeable gain or allowable loss would have accrued to them if they had then sold the asset for its market value, they are treated as having then disposed of the asset at its then market value. Where the asset is appropriated for the purposes of a trade carried on wholly or partly in the UK and chargeable to income tax or corporation tax and a chargeable gain would otherwise arise, the person may alternatively elect (under *TCGA 1992, s 161(3)*) that, in computing the assessable profits of the trade, the market value of the asset is reduced by the amount of the chargeable gain that would otherwise arise (i.e. they may treat the gain as subject to tax as income rather than as a capital gain). A partner must have the agreement of all their co-partners to make the election effective.

For CGT purposes the election must be made on or before the first anniversary of 31 January following the tax year in which ends the period of account in which the asset is appropriated. For corporation tax purposes it must be made within two years after the end of the accounting period in which the asset is appropriated.

[*TCGA 1992, ss 161(1)(3)(3A)(4), 288(1)*].

If any gain (or loss) on a sale of the asset would have been exempt (or non-allowable) under the provisions of *TCGA 1992, Sch 7AC* (see **60** SUBSTANTIAL SHAREHOLDING EXEMPTION), the appropriation is still treated as a disposal at market value. [*TCGA 1992, Sch 7AC para 36*].

Where an asset forming part of a person's trading stock is:

(a) appropriated by them for any other purpose, or
(b) retained by them on their ceasing to carry on the trade,

they are treated as having acquired it at the time for a consideration equal to the amount brought into the accounts of the trade for tax purposes. [*TCGA 1992, s 161(2)*]. For the valuation of trading stock in such circumstances, see Tolley's Income Tax under Trading Income.

See **26.4** GROUPS OF COMPANIES for intra-group transfers of assets which are trading stock of one of the companies but not of the other and for acquisition 'as trading stock' generally.

See **35.4** LAND for deemed appropriation as trading stock on certain transactions in land.

Finance leases

[16.10] There are anti-avoidance provisions which apply to finance leases for both corporation tax and income tax purposes. The provisions are intended to ensure that the tax treatment of such leases is aligned with the commercial accounting treatment in two situations. The first situation is arrangements by finance lessors to turn some of the lease rental income into capital receipts and the provisions ensure that any part of the capital receipt which is recognised as return on investment under generally accepted accounting practice is brought into account for tax purposes as income. See *ITA 2007, ss 614B–614BY* and *CTA 2010, ss 899–924*. The second situation is arrangements under which rentals are concentrated towards the end of the lease term: see *ITA 2007, ss 614C–614CD* and *CTA 2010, ss 925–929*. See Tolley's Income Tax and Tolley's Corporation Tax for the detailed provisions.

Where a lessor under a lease within the provisions (or a connected person) disposes of his interest in the lease, the leased asset or an asset representing the leased asset, the consideration for the disposal is reduced by setting against it any 'cumulative accountancy rental excess' which relates to the lease for the period of account of the disposal.

Broadly, the '*cumulative accountancy rental excess*' represents the amount by which the taxable rental income of the lessor (or connected person) under the above provisions exceeds the actual rental income over the period for which he was the lessor. See *ITA 2007, s 614BH, CTA 2010, s 907* for the detailed definition.

Where the disposal concerned is a part disposal, the cumulative accountancy rental excess must be apportioned using the formula at **16.5** above. If two or more disposals which trigger an adjustment to the consideration take place at the same time, the cumulative accountancy rental excess must be apportioned between the disposals on a just and reasonable basis.

Where an adjustment to the disposal consideration is made under these provisions, no further adjustment is made under *TCGA 1992, s 37* (see **33.1** INTERACTION WITH OTHER TAXES).

[*TCGA 1992, s 37A*].

Structures and buildings allowance

[16.11] Under the capital allowances code for structures and buildings (SBAs; see *CAA 2001, Pt 2A*), there are no balancing adjustments. Instead, an adjustment is made for capital gains purposes where a person disposes of an interest in a building or structure which is either an interest in UK land (within the meaning of *TCGA 1992, s 1C*) or an equivalent interest in land outside the UK and by reference to which they have obtained an allowance (including a contribution allowance). If the expenditure by reference to which the allowance has been made is allowable as a deduction in computing the gain or loss on disposal, the consideration for the disposal is treated as increased by the amount of the allowance given to the seller. The adjustment is made after any other capital gains provisions which apply to determine the amount of the consideration. (See **16.14** (a), (b), (j) below for the deductibility of expenditure by reference to which an SBA has been given.)

If the consideration is subject to apportionment under *TCGA 1992, s 45(3)* or *s 47(2)* (see **23.4** EXEMPTIONS AND RELIEFS or **65.2** WASTING ASSETS, the allowance is added to the part of the consideration apportioned in the same proportion as the expenditure qualifying for capital allowances. If the asset disposed of is a leasehold interest subject to *CAA 2001, s 270DD* (leases granted for 35 years or more) and it is a wasting asset, the amount of the allowance to be added is reduced in the same way as allowable expenditure on a lease which is a wasting asset is reduced, in accordance with the table in *TCGA 1992, Sch 8 para 1* (see **35.13** LAND).

Where either the disposal is a no gain/no loss disposal, incorporation relief under *TCGA 1992, s 162* applies or the disposal is a deemed disposal under *CTA 2010, s 579(4)* (cessation of real estate investment trust), the buyer is treated on a subsequent disposal as if the allowance given to the seller had been made to him.

[*TCGA 1992, s 37B*].

Allowable and non-allowable expenditure

General provisions

[16.12] Simon's Taxes. See C2.2.

Except as otherwise expressly provided, the sums allowable as a deduction from the consideration in the computation of any gain accruing to a person on the disposal of an asset are restricted to the following.

(a) **The amount or value of the consideration, in money or money's worth, given wholly and exclusively for the acquisition of the asset** (plus 'incidental costs') or expenditure incurred wholly and exclusively in providing the asset. [*TCGA 1992, s 38(1)(a)*].
See also *Cleveleys Investment Trust Co v CIR (No 2)* CS 1975, 51 TC 26; *Allison v Murray* Ch D 1975, 51 TC 57; *Garner v Pounds Shipowners & Shipbreakers Ltd (and related appeal)* HL 2000, 72 TC 561.
'*Incidental costs*' of acquisition are (strictly) limited to expenditure wholly and exclusively incurred for the purposes of the acquisition, being:
   (i) fees, commission or remuneration for the professional services of a surveyor, valuer, auctioneer, accountant, agent or legal adviser;
   (ii) transfer/conveyancing charges (including stamp duty); and
   (iii) advertising to find a seller.
[*TCGA 1992, s 38(2)*].
Where the purchaser is a company, and the purchase price is satisfied by the issue of fully paid-up shares in the company, the consideration is the shares and their value is normally that placed on them by the parties, i.e. the purchase price satisfied by the issue. 'Value' in *TCGA 1992, s 38(1)(a)* (see above) does not mean 'market value' (*Stanton v Drayton Commercial Investment Co Ltd* HL 1982, 55 TC 286). Disposals which are deemed to take place at market value will, generally speaking, give rise to an equivalent base cost in the acquirer's hands (but see **39.1** MARKET VALUE). No allowance is given for notional costs of disposal or reacquisition, where there is a deemed disposal and reacquisition. [*TCGA 1992, ss 17, 38(4)*].
See (b) below for capital contributions by shareholders.

A company with an annual turnover of not less than £5 million may round incidental costs of acquisition to the nearest £1,000 subject to certain conditions and exceptions (HMRC Statement of Practice SP 15/93).

Foreign currency. Where the cost (or deemed cost) of an asset is in foreign currency, it is converted into sterling at the exchange rate ruling at the time of acquisition. Similarly, consideration is converted at the date of disposal. (*Bentley v Pike* Ch D 1981, 53 TC 590; *Capcount Trading v Evans* CA 1992, 65 TC 545). HMRC does not prescribe what reference point should be used to establish an exchange rate, but expects that a reasonable and consistent method is used (HMRC Capital Gains Manual CG78310). For the use by certain companies of foreign currencies in computing chargeable gains on ships, aircraft and shares, see **14.15** COMPANIES.

See also **15.3** COMPANIES — CORPORATE FINANCE AND INTANGIBLES for matching of exchange differences on chargeable assets generally with those on borrowings.

(b) **Expenditure wholly and exclusively incurred for the purpose of enhancing the value of the asset being expenditure reflected in the state or nature of the asset at the time of disposal.** [*TCGA 1992, s 38(1)(b)*].

Expenditure on initial repairs (including decoration) to a property, undertaken to put it into a fit state for letting, and not allowable in computing taxable property business profits, is regarded as allowable expenditure under this heading (HMRC Statement of Practice SP D24).

HMRC consider that capital contributions made to a company by shareholders are not normally allowable expenditure under this heading except where made at the time of issue of the shares as part of the terms of the issue of the shares (HMRC Capital Gains Manual CG43500–43502). This view was upheld in *Trustees of the FD Fenston Will Trusts v HMRC*, (Sp C 589), [2007] SSCD 316. See also **16.14**(a) below.

In *Blackwell v HMRC* CA, [2017] EWCA Civ 232 it was held that this provision applied to the bundle of rights and obligations which would be acquired by the purchaser at the time of the disposal, not the asset as it operated in the vendor's hands.

'*Expenditure*' does not include the value of personal labour and skill (*Oram v Johnson* Ch D 1980, 53 TC 319). However, it may be in the form of providing money's worth and may be first reflected in the state or nature of the asset before completion even if this is after the time of disposal (*Chaney v Watkis* Ch D 1985, 58 TC 707).

No deduction was allowed on the grant of a lease for the value of the taxpayer having released the previous tenant from an obligation to reinstate the land on the surrender of its lease in *The Wakelyn Trust v HMRC* FTT, [2022] UKFTT 23 (TC).

(c) **Expenditure wholly and exclusively incurred in establishing, preserving or defending title to, or to a right over, the asset.** [*TCGA 1992, s 38(1)(b)*]. This includes resealing Scottish confirmation and other probate etc. expenses incurred to establish the title of the personal representatives (*Richards' Executors* HL 1971, 46 TC 626 and see **18.10** DEATH) and see **56.16** SETTLEMENTS.

In *Lee v Jewitt* (Sp C 257), [2000] SSCD 517, legal costs incurred by a partner in defending an action by fellow partners resulting in dissolution of the partnership were held to have been incurred under this heading.

(d) **Incidental costs of disposal.** [*TCGA 1992, s 38(1)(c)*]. Strictly, such costs are limited to expenditure wholly and exclusively incurred for the purposes of the disposal, being:

(i) fees, commission or remuneration for the professional services of a surveyor, valuer, auctioneer, accountant, agent or legal adviser;
(ii) transfer/conveyancing charges (including stamp duty);
(iii) advertising to find a buyer; and
(iv) any other costs reasonably incurred in making any valuation or apportionment for capital gains tax purposes, including, in particular, expenses reasonably incurred in ascertaining market value where this is required under *TCGA 1992*.

[*TCGA 1992, s 38(2)*].

Expenses of terminating a settlement incurred to bring about a chargeable occasion within *TCGA 1992, s 71* are allowable (*Chubb's Trustee* CS 1971, 47 TC 353).

Costs within (iv) above extend only to costs reasonably incurred in making the valuation or apportionment, and not to any subsequent costs incurred in negotiating a value with HMRC or in litigation with them concerning the value (Revenue Tax Bulletin February 1994 p 116) and see *Caton's Administrators v Couch* CA 1997, 70 TC 10. The same principle applies where the costs are incurred in relation to a post-transaction valuation check (see **52.7** RETURNS) (HMRC Capital Gains Manual CG15260, 16615).

In *O'Donnell v HMRC* FTT (TC 5821), [2017] UKFTT 347 (TC) O was unable to repay loans, secured on properties he owned, when called for immediate repayment by the bank. The properties were conveyed to O's uncle and charged to his lender. When calculating the gain realised by O on sale to his uncle, the First-tier Tribunal rejected mortgage broker fees incurred by O as 'incidental costs of disposal' as those fees had been incurred for the purpose of retaining rather than disposing of the properties. The First-tier Tribunal also rejected the notion that an allowable loss arose on the mortgage loan which should be offset against any gain as *TCGA 1992* is concerned with losses on assets, not liabilities.

Expenditure within (a)–(c) includes expenditure incurred on behalf of the person making the disposal. This requires the person incurring the expenditure to be acting as the agent of the taxpayer (*Lowe v HMRC* UT, [2022] STC 805).

A company with an annual turnover of not less than £5 million may round incidental costs of disposal to the nearest £1,000 subject to certain conditions and exceptions (HMRC Statement of Practice 15/93).

Example

Mr Hopkins bought a second home in August 1978 for £15,000. Mr Hopkins' neighbour, Mr Douglas, claimed that part of the garden of the house belonged to him. Mr Hopkins won the court case resulting, but incurred legal fees of £5,000 in September 1985.

In 2001 Mr Hopkins had a tennis court built for £5,000, but this was demolished in 2008.

Mr Hopkins sold the house in November 2024 for £126,000. It was agreed that the value of the house at 31 March 1982 was £25,000. The house has never been treated as Mr Hopkins' main residence.

The chargeable gain is as follows.

	£
Sale consideration	126,000
Less 31 March 1982 value	25,000
Legal fees re boundary dispute	5,000
Chargeable gain	£96,000

Note to the example

(a) The expenditure on the tennis court in 2001 is not allowable as it is not reflected in the state or nature of the asset at the time of disposal in November 2022. The demolition of the tennis court is not within *TCGA 1992, s 24(1)* as it is not the 'entire loss, destruction, dissipation or extinction' of an asset because the court is not an 'asset': it is only part of an asset, the land (see HMRC Capital Gains Manual CG15190).

Special cases

[16.13] In addition to the general provisions relating to allowable expenditure in **16.12** above, specific items of expenditure are allowed as follows.

(a) **Interest in certain (now very rare) circumstances** on money borrowed by a *company* for financing allowable expenditure on the construction of a building, structure, or work. There is no such provision for individuals, trustees, etc. See **14.5** COMPANIES.

(b) **Income tax paid by a close company participator** on income which has been apportioned to him (broadly in relation only to accounting periods ending before 1 April 1989) but which remains undistributed is an allowable deduction. [*TCGA 1992, s 124*]. See also **4.15** ANTI-AVOIDANCE regarding *TCGA 1992, s 125* (close company transferring assets at undervalue).

(c) **Foreign tax** borne by the disposer on the disposal is deductible. See **20.4** DOUBLE TAX RELIEF.

(d) **Inheritance tax** is a deduction in some circumstances. See **33.2** INTERACTION WITH OTHER TAXES.

(e) **Acquisitions from persons neither resident nor ordinarily resident in the UK.** Where, *after 9 March 1981 and before 6 April 1983*:

(i) a person acquired an asset for no valuable consideration, or for a consideration lower than the asset's market value, and no other amount or value was imputed to the consideration by operation of *CGTA 1979* (e.g. under the MARKET VALUE (**39**) rules); and
(ii) there was a corresponding disposal of the asset by a person neither resident nor ordinarily resident in the UK; and
(iii) a charge to income tax, corporation tax or capital gains tax arose in respect of the acquisition in (i) above,

a deduction is given on the subsequent disposal of the asset by the acquirer, equal to the amount in respect of which the charge in (iii) above arises. The condition in (iii) above was taken to be satisfied where, under *FA 1981, s 80(3)* (see now *TCGA 1992, s 87* at **42.13** OFFSHORE SETTLEMENTS), in any year of assessment, gains were attributed to a beneficiary of a non-resident settlement, by reason of that beneficiary's acquisition of an asset in that or an earlier fiscal year. In such circumstances, the deduction is the amount of the gains attributed to the beneficiary because of the acquisition of the said asset.

After 5 April 1983, the market value rules were amended so that, subject to the election below, an acquisition under the circumstances in (i) to (iii) is treated as being made at market value and the above provisions do not apply. Where, however, the corresponding disposal under (ii) is made *after 5 April 1983 and before 6 April 1985* the persons acquiring and disposing of the asset could jointly elect that both the acquisition and disposal were excepted from the amended market value rules in which case the above provisions still apply. [*CGTA 1979, s 32(5)(6); FA 1981, s 90(2); FA 1984, s 66(3)*]. See **39.1** MARKET VALUE for further details.

(f) **Stock dividends.** The 'appropriate amount in cash' relating to a stock dividend is deductible. See **57.10** SHARES AND SECURITIES.

(g) **Offshore funds.** Certain sums charged to income tax on the disposal of interests in offshore funds. See **43.9–43.12** OVERSEAS MATTERS.

(h) **Shares acquired by employees.** See **21** EMPLOYEE SHARE SCHEMES.

(i) **Legatees and beneficiaries.** Where a person disposes of an asset held by a personal representative or trustee to which he became absolutely entitled as legatee or as against the trustee, any incidental expenditure incurred by that person, the personal representative or the trustee in relation to the transfer of the asset to him, is allowable. [*TCGA 1992, s 64(1)*]. See **18.14** DEATH and **56.16** SETTLEMENTS.

(j) **Devaluation of sterling in November 1967.** In computing gains on the disposal of foreign securities purchased out of foreign currency borrowed before 19 November 1967 for that purpose (by permission given, subject to specified conditions, under *Exchange Control Act 1947*) the deduction under **16.12**(a) above is increased by one-sixth. A similar increase applies to disposals after 18 November 1967 of foreign securities which at that date formed part of a trust fund established abroad by a Lloyd's underwriter, etc., or a company engaged in marine protection or indemnity assurance on a mutual basis, which consists of premiums received and used mainly for meeting business liabilities arising in the country in which the fund is set up. [*TCGA 1992, Sch 11 paras 13, 14*].

(k) **Betterment levy.** Betterment levy paid in respect of certain development land is deductible as expenditure wholly and exclusively incurred in enhancing the value of the asset in the CGT computation arising on the disposal or part disposal of that land. [*TCGA 1992, Sch 11 para 17*].

Non-allowable expenditure

[16.14] In no case is allowance given for the following.

(a) Expenditure which is deductible in computing profits or losses for income tax purposes [*TCGA 1992, s 39(1)*] or would be so deductible if the asset were held as a fixed asset of a trade [*TCGA 1992, s 39(2)*]. See *Emmerson v Computer Time International Ltd* CA 1977, 50 TC 628. However, when calculating a gain, deductions are allowable for expenditure on which capital allowances are made or for capital expenditure deducted when calculating profits under the cash basis for small businesses or unincorporated property businesses, but see (i) below in respect of losses. [*TCGA 1992, s 41(1)(4)(9); F(No 2)A 2017, Sch 2 paras 45, 64(1); FA 2024, Sch 10 para 37*].
It is specifically provided that *s 39* does not exclude any expenditure in respect of which a structures and buildings allowance has been made. [*TCGA 1992, s 39(3B); SI 2019 No 1087, Reg 4(5)*]. See, however, (b) below for special rules for certain lessors where a lessee has received an allowance.

(b) Where a person who is, or has been, the lessor under a lease of a building or structure by reference to which a capital allowance under *CAA 2001, Pt 2A* (structures and buildings allowance) has been made, and the lease is, or has been, subject to *CAA 2001, s 270DD* (leases granted for 35 years or more), disposes of the building or structure or an interest in it to a connected person, any expenditure by reference to which an allowance has been made to the lessee is not an allowable deduction in computing the gain or loss on disposal. [*TCGA 1992, s 39A*].

(c) Premiums paid to cover the risk of damage to, or loss or depreciation of, the asset. [*TCGA 1992, s 205*].

(d) Any expenditure recoverable from any government or public or local authority in the UK or elsewhere. Where such a grant is subsequently repaid, the consideration on disposal of the asset may be treated, by concession, as reduced by the amount repaid. (HMRC Extra-Statutory Concession D53). [*TCGA 1992, s 50*]. This provision has no effect on the quantum of rollover relief available under *TCGA 1992, s 152* (see **53.1** ROLLOVER RELIEF) where the asset attracting the grant is the new asset for the purposes of that relief (*Wardhaugh v Penrith Rugby Union Football Club* Ch D 2002, 74 TC 499).

(e) Interest, except as under **16.13**(a) above. [*TCGA 1992, s 38(3)*].

(f) Income tax chargeable on shares acquired under certain employee schemes. See **21** EMPLOYEE SHARE SCHEMES.

(g) Liabilities remaining with, or assumed by, the disposer contingent upon the default of the assignee of a lease, or upon the breach of covenants in a conveyance or lease of land, or of warranties, or representations made on the sale or lease of other property. If the contingent liability subsequently becomes enforceable and is enforced, relief is given by way of discharge, repayment or other adjustment. [*TCGA 1992, s 49*]. An amount received under a warranty or indemnity is normally deductible from the purchaser's acquisition cost (HMRC Extra-Statutory Concession D33). See further **35.22** LAND. A payment made by the chairman of a company to settle legal proceedings alleging fraudulent misrepresentation in relation to the takeover of the company and associated legal costs were held to fall within *s 49* in *HMRC v Morrison* SCS, [2015] STC 659.

(h) Any discount for postponement of receipt of the consideration and, in the first instance, for any risk of non-recovery, or for any contingency in the right to receive any part of the consideration. If, however, any part of the consideration subsequently proves to be irrecoverable, on a claim to that effect the tax liability will be adjusted accordingly which may result in a discharge or repayment of tax. This provision does not apply to so much of any consideration as consists of rights under a creditor relationship (see **15.5** COMPANIES — CORPORATE FINANCE AND INTANGIBLES) to which a company becomes a party as a result of the disposal. Instead, the amount to be brought into account in respect of that consideration is the 'fair value' (within *CTA 2009, s 313(6)*) of the creditor relationship. [*TCGA 1992, s 48*]. (See *Marson v Marriage* Ch D 1979, 54 TC 59.) See also **10.2** CAPITAL SUMS DERIVED FROM ASSETS and **45.5** PAYMENT OF TAX for the possibility of payment by instalments.

Where consideration for a disposal is fixed in a foreign currency, any subsequent loss on exchange is not irrecoverable consideration for the purposes of a claim under *TCGA 1992, s 48*. See *Goodbrand v Loffland Bros North Sea Inc* CA 1998, 71 TC 57.

A subsequent payment, by the vendor of an option to a third party, to release restrictive covenants did not alter the consideration received for the option and was not allowable expenditure in computing the gain (*Garner v Pounds Shipowners & Shipbreakers Ltd (and related appeal)* HL 2000, 72 TC 561).

(i) Notional expenses on deemed disposals and acquisitions. [*TCGA 1992, s 38(4)*].

(j) Where a 'loss' would otherwise be shown, expenditure otherwise allowable as a deduction is reduced to the extent that capital allowances have been made in respect of it. The capital allowances taken into account are those granted (less any balancing charge) to the disposer. Where the asset was treated for capital allowance purposes as acquired at written-down value, allowances granted to any former owner which were not taken into account in restricting his loss are also deducted from allowable expenditure.

'Capital allowance' for the purpose of this restriction includes any deduction allowable for capital expenditure when calculating profits on the cash basis for small businesses or unincorporated property businesses. Structures and buildings allowances are, however, excluded from the definition of capital allowances for this purpose.

Where the loss-making disposal is of plant or machinery in relation to expenditure on which allowances or charges have been made for capital allowance purposes (but not where this includes an allowable deduction under the cash basis) and which has been used solely for trade purposes and has not attracted partial depreciation subsidies which would deny capital allowances, the capital allowances (if any) are deemed to be the difference between the qualifying expenditure incurred (or treated as incurred) by the disposer, and the disposal value. Where the allowances *do* include an allowable deduction under the cash basis, the capital allowances to be taken into account are deemed to equal the total amount of expenditure which has qualified for capital allowances less any balancing charge to which the disposer is liable. [*TCGA 1992, ss 41(1)–(10), 53(3)*]. See also **8.11** ASSETS held on 6 April 1965, **8.7** and ASSETS 31 March 1982.

In *HMRC v Smallwood* CA, [2007] STC 1237, *TCGA 1992, s 41* was held not to restrict a loss on units in an enterprise zone unit trust where the trustees of the unit trust had used the funds subscribed for the units to acquire land and buildings, in respect of which the taxpayer had been credited with capital allowances. The Court upheld the Special Commissioner's decision that capital allowances had not been made in respect of the taxpayer's expenditure in subscribing for the units. It was the trustees' expenditure that had resulted in capital allowances for the taxpayer.

(k) Where a loss would otherwise be shown on the disposal of an asset which includes plant or machinery which is a fixture for the purposes of *CAA 2001, Pt 2 Ch 6A* (long funding leases: interpretation) and which has been used by the person making the disposal for the purpose of leasing under one or more 'long funding leases', expenditure otherwise allowable as a deduction is reduced by an amount equal to the fall in value of the plant or machinery during the period of that lease (or, where there was more than one such lease, the periods of those leases). For this purpose, the fall in value of plant or machinery during the period of a lease is equal to the excess of the 'market value' of the plant or machinery at the 'commencement' of the 'term' of the lease over its market value at the 'termination' of the lease.

For the meaning of '*long funding lease*' see **7.6** ASSETS. '*Market value*' is determined on the assumption of a disposal by an absolute owner free from all leases and other encumbrances. The expressions '*commencement*', '*term*', and '*termination*' are defined as in *CAA 2001, Pt 2 Ch 6A*. See Tolley's Income Tax or Tolley's Corporation Tax.

[*TCGA 1992, s 41A*].

Key points concerning computation of gains and losses

[16.15] Points to consider are as follows.

- Where property is owned jointly between two (or more) persons, each person is able to set their annual exempt amount against their share of the gain. Consider whether each joint owner has the full annual exempt amount available in the tax year of disposal or whether a delay in the disposal date may be beneficial. The successive reductions in the annual exempt amount for 2023/24 and 2024/25 have reduced any tax savings which can be achieved.

- Transfers between spouses or civil partners are free from capital gains tax and it may be tax efficient to consider a transfer prior to disposal. Although watch entitlement to any reliefs such as business asset disposal relief and whether both parties will still qualify.
- Market value must be used in place of any actual proceeds in the computation of a chargeable gain on the disposal of an asset otherwise than at arm's length (e.g. a gift or disposal to a connected person). Professional valuation may be needed to ensure that the figure will be agreed by HMRC.
- Consider the timing of the disposal and potentially spreading the disposal across two tax years where part disposals are a possibility. Two part disposals on either side of the tax year end will each be eligible for a full year's annual exempt amount (assuming that it is fully available), which may give a beneficial result in terms of tax payable.
- Remember to offset all deductible items against acquisition costs and costs of disposal, including accountancy fees for the transaction itself such as determining market value.

17

Connected Persons

[*ITA 2007, s 993; CTA 2010, s 1122; TCGA 1992, s 286*].

Cross-references. See **4.13**, **4.14** ANTI-AVOIDANCE for certain disposals between connected persons; **38.7** LOSSES for losses on disposals to connected persons; **44.4** PARTNERSHIPS for transactions between partners; and **56.14** SETTLEMENTS for settlors and trustees being connected persons.

Meaning of 'connected'

Individuals

[17.1] An individual is connected with his spouse or civil partner, any 'relative' of himself or of his spouse or civil partner, and with the spouse or civil partner of any such relative. It appears that a widow or widower is no longer a spouse (*Vestey's Exors and Vestey v CIR* HL 1949, 31 TC 1). Spouses divorced by conditional order (formerly decree nisi) remain connected persons until the divorce is made final (*Aspden v Hildesley* Ch D 1981, 55 TC 609).

Trustees of a settlement

[17.2] A 'trustee' of a 'settlement', in their capacity as such, is connected with:

(a) the 'settlor' (if an individual),
(b) any person connected with the settlor,
(c) a 'body corporate connected with the settlement',
(d) if the settlement is the principal settlement in relation to one or more sub-fund settlements (see **56.12** SETTLEMENTS), the trustees of those settlements, and
(e) if the settlement is a sub-fund settlement, the trustees of any other sub-fund settlements of its principal settlement.

Partners

[17.3] Partners are connected with each other and with each other's spouses (see **17.1** above), civil partners and relatives (see **17.6** below), except in connection with acquisitions and disposals of partnership assets made pursuant to *bona fide* commercial arrangements. See also **17.5** below.

Companies

[17.4] A company is connected with another company if:

(a) the same person 'controls' both, or
(b) one is controlled by a person who has control of the other in conjunction with persons connected with them, or
(c) a person controls one company and persons connected with them control the other, or
(d) the same group of persons controls both, or
(e) the companies are controlled by separate groups which can be regarded as the same by interchanging connected persons.

For consideration of (d) above, see *Kellogg Brown and Root Holdings (UK) Ltd v HMRC* CA, [2010] STC 925.

Person controlling company

[17.5] A company is connected with another person who (either alone or with persons connected with them) has control of it.

Persons acting together to secure or exercise control of a company are treated in relation to that company as connected with each other and with any other person acting on the direction of any of them to secure or exercise such control (see *Steele v EVC International NV* CA 1996, 69 TC 88). Control may be 'exercised' passively. See *Floor v Davis* HL 1979, 52 TC 609. See **4.20** ANTI-AVOIDANCE for an extension of this provision in connection with dividend stripping.

Meaning of expressions used to define 'connected persons'

[17.6] '*Company*' includes any body corporate, unincorporated association or unit trust scheme but does not include a partnership.

'*Control*' is as defined in *CTA 2010, ss 450, 451*. [*TCGA 1992, s 288(1)*]. See Tolley's Corporation Tax under Close Companies.

'*Relative*' means brother, sister, ancestor or lineal descendant. [*TCGA 1992, s 286(8)*].

'*Settlement*' includes any disposition, trust, covenant, agreement, arrangement or transfer of assets. [*ITTOIA 2005, s 620(1)*]. It must contain an element of bounty. It does not include a transfer of assets for full consideration (*CIR v*

Plummer HL 1979, 54 TC 1). '*Trustee*' specifically includes, where otherwise a settlement would have no trustees, any person in whom the settled property or its management is vested. [*TCGA 1992, s 286(3ZA)*].

'*A body corporate connected with the settlement*' is a close company (or one which would be so if resident in the UK) the participators in which include the trustees of the settlement, or a company controlled by such a close company. Control for these purposes is as under *CTA 2010, s 1124*: namely, the power of a person by shareholding or voting power (whether directly or through another company), or under Articles of Association, to secure that the company's affairs are conducted according to his wishes.

'*Settlor*' is as at **56.5** SETTLEMENTS. [*ITTOIA 2005, s 620(2)(3)*]. See *Countess Fitzwilliam and ors v CIR (and related appeals)* HL 1993, 67 TC 614.

18

Death

Cross-references. See **33.2** INTERACTION WITH OTHER TAXES for inheritance tax; **36.5** LATE PAYMENT INTEREST AND PENALTIES for relief given if probate is delayed; **39** MARKET VALUE; **52.5** RETURNS for simplified procedures for small deceased estates; **56.3** SETTLEMENTS for death of a bankrupt etc. and **56.16–56.18** for termination of a life interest by the death of the person entitled thereto; **57.20** SHARES AND SECURITIES.

Simon's Taxes. See **C1.206–C1.206C, I4.5.**

Introduction to death

[18.1] This chapter examines the capital gains tax consequences of a person's death from the perspective of the deceased, the personal representatives and the legatees. In summary, the consequences are as follows. No liability to capital gains tax arises on death. The personal representatives are treated as having acquired the deceased's assets at market value at the time of death and are liable to capital gains tax on disposals of assets made by them. They are entitled to the same annual exempt amount as individuals for the year of death and the following two years. No liability to capital gains tax arises on the transfer of assets from the personal representatives to a legatee. The legatee is then treated as having acquired the asset at market value at the time of death.

In addition, a special relief applies to allowable losses incurred by the deceased in the tax year of death (on disposals made before death). Where the losses exceed the deceased's chargeable gains for the tax year, the excess can be carried back and set off against chargeable gains in the three preceding tax years.

General provisions applying on death of taxpayer

[18.2] All 'assets of which a deceased person was competent to dispose' are deemed to have been acquired on their death by their personal representatives (or other person on whom they devolve) for a consideration equal to their market value at the date of death. However, they are not deemed to be disposed of by the deceased on their death (whether or not they were the subject of a testamentary disposition). The effect of these provisions is that no chargeable gain or allowable loss arises on death and any gain or loss arising on the disposal of the asset by the personal representatives, etc. after the death is calculated by reference to the market value of the asset at the date of death (subject to the further provisions in this chapter).

'*Assets of which the deceased was competent to dispose*' are those assets which (otherwise than in right of a power of appointment or of the testamentary power conferred by statute to dispose of entailed interests) the deceased could, if of full age and capacity, have disposed of by their will, assuming that all the assets were situated in England and, if they were not domiciled in the United Kingdom, that they were domiciled in England, and include references to their severable share in any assets to which, immediately before their death, they were beneficially entitled as joint tenant.

[*TCGA 1992, s 62(1)(10)*].

Scotland

[18.3] So far as the provisions in *TCGA 1992* relate to the consequences of the death of a proper liferenter of any property, then, on the death of any such liferenter, the person (if any) who, on the death of the liferenter, becomes entitled to possession of the property as heir, is deemed to have acquired all the assets forming part of the property at the date of the deceased's death for a consideration equal to their market value at that date. [*TCGA 1992, s 63*].

Northern Ireland

[18.4] So far as the provisions in *TCGA 1992* relate to the consequences of the death of a person to whom property in Northern Ireland stands limited for life, a person who acquires property in fee simple absolute or fee tail in possession as a consequence of the deceased's death, is deemed to have acquired all the assets forming part of the property at the date of death for a consideration equal to their market value at that date. [*TCGA 1992, s 63A*].

Valuation

[18.5] Where on the death of any person, inheritance tax is chargeable on the value of their estate immediately before their death and the value of an asset forming part of their estate has been ascertained for the purposes of the application of that tax to the estate, that value is taken to be the market value at the date of death for capital gains tax purposes. [*TCGA 1992, s 274*].

Therefore, where the inheritance tax valuation for quoted shares and securities (see **39.3** MARKET VALUE) has been used to determine inheritance tax on death, those shares are valued in the same way for capital gains tax. In the case of land

and quoted shares and securities, proceeds of certain post-death sales within a specified period may be substituted for values at date of death for inheritance tax purposes. The value of related property (as defined for inheritance tax purposes) may also be revised in the event of a post-death sale. If such substitutions/revisions are made for inheritance tax purposes, they must be made for CGT purposes also (but see *Stonor and Another (Executors of Dickinson deceased) v CIR* (Sp C 288), [2001] SSCD 199 in which the executors failed in an attempt to use this rule to upgrade values of freehold properties for CGT purposes where there was no inheritance tax liability). See Tolley's Inheritance Tax for details.

Following the decision in *Gray v CIR* CA, [1994] STC 360, the Revenue published its view that two or more different assets comprised in an estate can be treated as a single unit of property if disposal as one unit was the course that a prudent hypothetical vendor would have adopted in order to obtain the most favourable price without undue expenditure of time and effort.

This principle will apply for capital gains tax purposes in the following cases:

(a) An acquisition by personal representatives or legatees under *TCGA 1992, s 62* of assets which a deceased person was competent to dispose.
(b) An acquisition of settled property under *TCGA 1992, s 71(1)* on the occasion of a person becoming absolutely entitled to that settled property.

There are certain situations when a single valuation will still apply, such as:

(i) the disposal of an asset for consideration deemed to be equal to its market value under *TCGA 1992, s 17*;
(ii) when a valuation of an asset is required for the purpose of re-basing to 31 March 1992 under *TCGA 1992, s 35*.

The single asset valuation for *TCGA 1992, s 17* is modified by *TCGA 1992, s 19* where there is a series of linked transactions between connected persons. Each disposal in the series may be treated as being made for consideration equal to a proportion of the aggregate value of all the assets in the series.

(Revenue Tax Bulletin August 1996, p 337).

Donatio mortis causa

[18.6] No chargeable gain arises on the making of a disposal by way of '*donatio mortis causa*' i.e. a gift of personal property made in 'contemplation of the conceived approach of death' (see *Duffield v Elwes* Ch D 1827, 1 Bligh's Reports (New Series) 497), and the recipient is treated as a legatee acquiring the property at the date of death. [*TCGA 1992, ss 62(5), 64(2)*].

Carry-back of losses

[18.7] Allowable losses in excess of chargeable gains incurred by the deceased in the tax year in which death occurs can be carried back and set off against chargeable gains in the three preceding tax years. See **2.5**, ANNUAL RATES AND

EXEMPTIONS for the interaction between losses carried back and the annual exempt amount. Subject to this, chargeable gains accruing in a later year must be relieved before those of an earlier year. Losses carried back cannot be set against gains treated under *TCGA 1992, ss 87, 87K, 87L* or *89(2)* as accruing to the individual in respect of a non-UK resident settlement (see **42.13–42.20** OFFSHORE SETTLEMENTS) or against 'non-resident gains'. For this purpose, '*non-resident gains*' are gains on direct or indirect disposals of UK land by non-residents (see **35.23, 35.24** LAND) or, for disposals before 6 April 2019, NRCGT gains (i.e. gains on non-resident disposals of UK residential property interests (see **35.31** LAND)).

[*TCGA 1992, s 62(2)(2A)(11)*].

Similarly, 'non-resident losses' which cannot be relieved against gains incurred by the deceased in the tax year in which death occurs can be carried back and set off against non-resident gains in the three preceding tax years (taking gains accruing in a later year first). '*Non-resident losses*' are allowable losses arising on disposals which, had a gain arisen, would have given rise to a non-resident gain. [*TCGA 1992, s 62(2AA)(11)*].

Any remaining unused losses *cannot* be carried forward and set off against gains made by the personal representatives or legatees.

A carry-back of a loss is within the scope of *TMA 1970, Sch 1B* (claims for relief involving two or more years). This provision is fully covered in Tolley's Income Tax (and see also **13.2** CLAIMS) and its effect is that whilst the resulting tax saving/repayment is computed by reference to the facts for the tax year(s) to which the loss is carried back (the earlier year), it is then treated as a reduction or repayment of tax for the tax year in which the loss is incurred (the later year). The tax position for the earlier year is not adjusted. The general requirement that claims be made in a self-assessment tax return (see **13.2** CLAIMS) does not apply to a carry-back under *section 62(2)*. [*TMA 1970, Sch 1B para 2*]. Repayment interest may be due as in **50.2** REPAYMENT INTEREST, though only from 31 January following the *later year* (as above).

Example

On 1 June 2024, Paul sells an asset, realising an allowable loss of £15,000. On 30 June 2024, he dies. Paul has no chargeable gains for 2024/25 but in 2023/24 and 2022/23, he made chargeable gains (before the annual exempt amount) of £14,700 and £22,300 respectively.

The 2024/25 allowable loss is carried back and set off against the gains for 2023/24 and 2022/23 as follows.

2023/24	
	£
Adjusted net gains	14,700
Loss carried back (part)	8,700
	12,300
Annual exempt amount	6,000
Taxable gains	Nil

Losses brought back	15,000
Less utilised in 2023/4	8,700
Losses carried back	£6,300
2022/23	
	£
Adjusted net gains	22,300
Loss carried back	6,300
	16,000
Annual exempt amount	12,300
Taxable gains	£3,700
Losses brought back	6,300
Less utilised in 2022/23	6,300
Losses carried back	£Nil

Deeds of family arrangement etc.

[18.8] Variations or disclaimers of the dispositions (whether effected by will, under the intestacy rules or otherwise) of the 'property of which the deceased was competent to dispose' (see **18.2** above) which are made by deed of family arrangement (or similar instrument in writing) within two years of death do not constitute disposals but are related back to the date of death so that a variation is treated as having been effected by the deceased and a disclaimed benefit is treated as never having been conferred. Such treatment does not apply in respect of variations or disclaimers made for any consideration in money or money's worth other than consideration consisting of the making of a variation or disclaimer in respect of another of the dispositions.

In the case of a variation (as opposed to a disclaimer), the above treatment applies only if the instrument contains a statement by the persons making the instrument to the effect that they intend the treatment to apply. It is necessary to send HMRC a copy of the instrument only if it has immediate tax consequences or if it is requested as part of an enquiry (see Revenue Tax Bulletin August 2002 pp 957–959).

The above provisions apply whether or not the administration of the estate is complete or the property has been distributed in accordance with the original dispositions.

[*TCGA 1992, s 62(6)–(9)*].

In a case based upon the original *FA 1965* legislation, it was held that the equivalent provisions to *TCGA 1992, s 62(6)* above and *s 62(4)* (see **18.14** below), although deeming provisions, were to be given their normal and natural meaning. But, where such construction would lead to an injustice or absurdity, the application of the statutory fiction should be limited to the extent needed to avoid such injustice or absurdity. Thus, nothing in *TCGA 1992, s 62(6)* requires one to assume something which is inconsistent with the legatee under an original will, who then varies dispositions under *TCGA 1992, s 62(6)* to a third party, as having been the actual settlor of the arrangement. The deeming provisions apply only to assets of which the testator was competent to dispose at their death. However, the property settled by the legatee comprised, not the assets in the deceased's estate which eventually came to be vested in the third party, but a separate chose in action, i.e. the right to due administration of the estate, and this could only have been settled by the legatee and not by the deceased. (*Marshall v Kerr* HL 1994, 67 TC 56). Where, in the rare event, the administration of an estate has been completed before a deed of variation is made, a different analysis may follow.

For HMRC's comments on the provisions affecting the variation of the devolution of a deceased estate, see HMRC Capital Gains Manual CG31400–32080. For cases bearing on the effectiveness of similar deeds used for inheritance tax purposes, see Tolley's Inheritance Tax under Deeds Varying Dispositions on Death.

Personal representatives

[18.9] Personal representatives are treated as a single and continuing body (distinct from persons who may from time to time be the personal representatives) which has the deceased's residence and domicile at the date of death. [*TCGA 1992, s 62(3)*].

They are liable to capital gains tax on disposals of assets made by them by reference to the disposal proceeds and the market value at the date of death (but see **18.10** below). They may be chargeable in respect of disposals made by the deceased prior to death as well as in respect of their own disposals. See **6.6, 6.12** ASSESSMENTS.

For the tax year in which death occurs and the following two tax years, the personal representatives are entitled to the same annual exempt amount as individuals, with the same general provisions applying. [*TCGA 1992, s 1K(7)*]. See **2.5** ANNUAL RATES AND EXEMPTIONS.

See **2.2** ANNUAL RATES AND EXEMPTIONS for the rates of capital gains tax applicable to personal representatives.

Losses made by personal representatives during the administration period cannot be passed on to the legatees. The position should be compared with that for losses made by trustees as in **56.16** SETTLEMENTS.

CGT due from personal representatives may be assessed and charged on and in the name of any one or more of the 'relevant personal representatives'. In relation to chargeable gains, the '*relevant personal representatives*' means the personal representatives in the tax year in which the gains accrue and any subsequent personal representatives of the deceased. [*TCGA 1992, s 65(1)((4)*].

Allowable expenditure

[18.10] The decision in *Richards' Executors* HL 1971, 46 TC 626 enables personal representatives, in computing chargeable gains on the disposal of assets, to add to the cost of acquiring the assets from the testator (i.e. the market value at the date of death) those legal and accountancy costs that are involved in preparing the inheritance tax or capital transfer tax account and obtaining the grant of probate etc. See also 16.12 COMPUTATION OF GAINS AND LOSSES.

Because of the practical difficulty of identifying the costs applicable to individual assets comprised in the estate, HMRC have agreed expenditure based on the following scales (HMRC Statement of Practice 2/04).

Personal representatives

[18.11] Deaths after 5 April 2004

	Gross value of estate	*Allowable expenditure*
A	Up to £50,000	1.8% of the probate value of the assets sold by the personal representatives.
B	Between £50,001 and £90,000	A fixed amount of £900, to be divided between all the assets in the estate in proportion to the probate values, and allowed in those proportions on assets sold by the personal representatives.
C	Between £90,001 and £400,000	1% of the probate value of the assets sold.
D	Between £400,001 and £500,000	A fixed amount of £4,000, to be divided as at B above.
E	Between £500,001 and £1,000,000	0.8% of the probate value of the assets sold.
F	Between £1,000,001 and £5,000,000	A fixed amount of £8,000, to be divided as at B above
G	Over £5,000,000	0.16% of the probate value of the assets sold, subject to a maximum of £10,000

In practice, HMRC will accept computations based either on these scales or on the actual expenditure incurred.

Corporate trustees

[18.12] HMRC have also agreed the following scales of allowable expenditure for expenses incurred by corporate trustees in the administration of estates and trusts. They will accept computations based either on these scales or on the actual allowable expenditure incurred.

Acquisitions and disposals, or deemed disposals, after 5 April 2004

[18.13]

(a) Transfers of assets to beneficiaries etc.

(1)	Publicly marketed shares and securities	
	(A) One beneficiary	£25 per holding transferred.
	(B) More than one beneficiary between whom a holding must be divided	As (A), to be divided in equal shares between the beneficiaries.
(2)	Other shares and securities	As (1) above, with the addition of any exceptional expenditure.
(3)	Other assets	As (1) above, with the addition of any exceptional expenditure.

Shares and securities are regarded as marketed to the general public for this purpose if buying and selling prices are regularly published in the financial pages of a national or regional newspaper, magazine or journal.

(b)	Actual disposals and acquisitions	
(1)	Publicly marketed shares and securities	The investment fee as charged by the trustees.
(2)	Other shares and securities	As (1) above, plus actual valuation costs.
(3)	Other assets	The investment fee as charged by the trustees, subject to a maximum of £75, plus actual valuation costs.

Where a comprehensive annual management fee is charged, covering both the cost of administering the trust and the expenses of actual disposals and acquisitions, the investment fee for (1)–(3) above will be taken to be £0.25 per £100 on the sale or purchase moneys.

(c)	Deemed disposals by trustees	
(1)	Publicly marketed shares and securities	£8 per holding disposed of.
(2)	Other shares and securities	Actual valuation costs.
(3)	Other assets	Actual valuation costs.

Legatees

[18.14] A '*legatee*' includes any person taking under a testamentary disposition or an intestacy or partial intestacy, whether they take beneficially or as trustee. [*TCGA 1992, s 64(2)*].

On a 'person acquiring any asset as legatee', no chargeable gain accrues to the personal representatives, and the legatee is treated as if the personal representatives' acquisition of the asset had been their acquisition of it. The Treasury may make regulations to apply in place of this rule in respect of assets formerly held in an individual savings account. [*TCGA 1992, s 62(4)(4A)*]. The consequences of this are that the asset is taken as acquired at either the market value at the date of death or, if the asset was acquired subsequent to death, the allowable expenditure incurred by the personal representatives in providing etc. the asset. See also **18.8** above.

For the purposes of the meaning of '*legatee*' and '*person acquiring an asset as legatee*', property taken under a testamentary disposition or on an intestacy or partial intestacy includes any asset appropriated by the personal representative in or towards satisfaction of a pecuniary legacy or any other interest or share in the property devolving. [*TCGA 1992, s 64(3)*].

Where a person disposes of an asset held by a personal representative to which they became absolutely entitled as legatee, any incidental expenditure incurred by that person or the personal representative in relation to the transfer of the asset to them is allowable as a deduction in the computation of the gain arising on the disposal. [*TCGA 1992, s 64(1)*].

Key points concerning death

[18.15] Points to consider are as follows.

- Deeds of variation are deemed to take effect from the date of death for CGT and inheritance tax, but not for income tax.
- Personal representatives do not need to claim for the capital gains tax free uplift on death — this is given automatically.
- When disposing of assets from the estate, the capital gain is calculated by subtracting the probate value of the asset from the sale proceeds. Note that, for inheritance tax purposes, the sale proceeds may be substituted for the probate value, which will have a knock-on effect on the capital gains tax due.
- Where the personal representatives wish to sell property realising a gain it can be advantageous to transfer the assets to the legatees prior to the sale and use the legatees' annual exempt amounts and CGT rates. Specific calculations are required to reflect the actual circumstances. In general a higher potential benefit may exist where:
  - there is a high number of legatees (more annual exempt amounts); and or
  - some legatees are not liable to UK CGT (eg non resident or UK charities); and or
  - legatees' personal incomes are low and hence the gain will be partly taxable at 10%/18%.
- Death cannot normally be predicted although it should always be considered in significant transactions where assets qualify for IHT business property relief. For example, Albert, 60 sells his shares in the family company to his sons for £1 million cash. Two days later he goes into hospital for planned major surgery and dies. His estate has a liability for capital gains tax on the sale (at 10%, assuming that business asset disposal relief applies) and includes the balance of the cash proceeds which are potentially liable to IHT (at 40%).

If he had held the shares at death they would have qualified for IHT relief and received uplift to market value for capital gains tax; therefore avoiding both of the above tax liabilities.

19

Disclosure of Tax Avoidance Schemes

Introduction to disclosure of tax avoidance schemes

[19.1] There are provisions requiring 'promoters' of, and, in some cases, taxpayers making use of, tax avoidance schemes to disclose details to HMRC. The provisions (often referred to as 'DOTAS') apply to schemes which have the features of one or more prescribed 'hallmarks'. See **19.2** onwards below.

There are also provisions which require disclosure to HMRC of information about certain offshore tax arrangements. UK-only provisions have been introduced with effect from 28 March 2023, replacing the previous rules which were based on the EU's sixth Directive on Administrative Co-operation in the field of taxation (EU Directive 2018/822/EU (amending Directive 2011/16/EU)) (DAC 6).

A special compliance regime (often referred to as 'POTAS') applies to certain high-risk promoters of tax avoidance schemes. See **19.9** below.

See **49.37** PENALTIES for application by HMRC for a freezing order where they have commenced, or are about to commence, proceedings before the First-tier Tribunal in respect of a penalty under the DOTAS or POTAS provisions.

Simon's Taxes. See **A6.1204A, A6.1204B, A7.2, A7.301–A7.313.**

Disclosure regime

[19.2] 'Promoters' of tax avoidance schemes and, in some cases, taxpayers making use of such schemes are required to disclose details to HMRC. The disclosure provisions cover a number of taxes including income tax, capital gains tax and corporation tax and are triggered where arrangements feature one of a number of hallmarks. There are compliance powers specific to the disclosure regime.

Disclosure can be made online via the GOV.UK website (www.gov.uk/guidance/forms-to-disclose-tax-avoidance-schemes), or alternatively, forms for making disclosures can be completed and printed from the same location.

Legal professional privilege

The provisions do not require the disclosure of any information with respect to which a claim to legal professional privilege (or, in Scotland, to confidentiality of communications) could be maintained in legal proceedings. [*FA 2004, s 314*].

Note, however, that where a person who would otherwise be a promoter is not required to make a disclosure as a result of this provision, they are treated as not being a promoter, and the obligation to disclose the arrangements will (if there is no other person who is a promoter) fall on the taxpayer making use of the scheme (as the scheme will be one with no promoter). See further below.

Arrangements requiring disclosure

'*Notifiable arrangements*' requiring disclosure under the provisions are 'arrangements' which:

- fall within any description prescribed by Treasury regulations (see below);
- enable, or might be expected to enable, any person to obtain an 'advantage' in relation to any tax (which may include capital gains tax and corporation tax) that is so prescribed in relation to arrangements of that description; and
- are such that the main benefit, or one of the main benefits, that might be expected to arise from the arrangements is the obtaining of that advantage.

The provisions also require disclosure of '*notifiable proposals*', i.e. proposals for arrangements which would be notifiable arrangements if entered into, whether the proposal relates to a particular person or to any person who may seek to take advantage of it.

For these purposes, '*arrangements*' include any scheme, transaction or series of transactions. An '*advantage*', in relation to any tax, means:

- relief or increased relief from, or repayment or increased repayment of, that tax;
- the avoidance or reduction of a charge or assessment to that tax;
- the avoidance of a possible assessment to that tax;
- the deferral of any payment of tax;
- the advancement of any repayment of tax; or
- the avoidance of any obligation to deduct or account for any tax.

[*FA 2004, ss 306, 318(1)*].

Prescribed arrangements

Any arrangements which fall within any of the descriptions (or '*hallmarks*') listed below are prescribed by the Treasury for the purposes of these provisions. The taxes covered are income tax, capital gains tax and corporation tax. The hallmarks are as follows.

(1) **Confidentiality in cases involving a promoter.** Arrangements fall within this hallmark if it might be reasonably expected that a promoter would wish the way in which the arrangements secure a tax advantage (or might secure a tax advantage) to be kept confidential from any other promoter at any time following the event which triggers the disclosure. Arrangements also fall within this hallmark if:

- it might reasonably be expected that a promoter would, but for these provisions, wish to keep the way in which the arrangements secure or might secure) a tax advantage confidential from HMRC for some or all of that period, and a reason for doing so is to facilitate repeated or continued use of the element of the arrangements which secure the advantage or of substantially the same element; or
- where there is no promoter by virtue only of the provision relating to legal professional privilege in **19.3**(C) below, or the promoter is not UK resident, it might reasonably be expected that the user of the arrangements would wish to keep confidential from HMRC the way that the arrangements secure a tax advantage for some or all of that period.

(2) **Confidentiality in cases not involving a promoter.** Arrangements fall within this hallmark if there is no promoter and:

(a) the intended user of the arrangements is a business (as defined) which is not a '*small or medium-sized enterprise*' (broadly, a micro, small or medium-sized enterprise as defined in the EU Commission Recommendation of 6 May 2003);

(b) it might reasonably be expected that the user would wish the way in which the arrangements secure a tax advantage to be kept confidential from HMRC at any time following the event triggering the disclosure; and

(c) a reason for doing so is to facilitate repeated or continued use of the element of the arrangements which secure the advantage or of substantially the same element or to reduce the risk of HMRC opening an enquiry into a return or account.

Arrangements also fall within this hallmark if there is no promoter and (a) above applies and, if there had been a promoter, it might reasonably be expected that they would wish to have kept the way in which the arrangements secure a tax advantage to be kept confidential from HMRC at any time following the event triggering the disclosure and a reason for doing so would be to facilitate repeated or continued use of the element of the arrangements which secure the advantage or of substantially the same element.

(3) **Premium fee.** Arrangements fall within this hallmark if they are such that it might reasonably be expected that a promoter or a person connected with a promoter of arrangements that are the same as, or substantially similar to, the arrangements in question, would, but for these provisions, be able to obtain a 'premium fee' from a person experienced in receiving services of the type being provided. Arrangements where there is no promoter or where the tax advantage is intended to be obtained by an individual, or business that is a small or medium-sized enterprise, are excluded. A '*premium fee*' for this purpose is one chargeable by virtue of

any element of the arrangements from which the tax advantage is expected to arise and which is to a significant extent attributable to, or to any extent contingent on the obtaining of, that advantage. The premium fee must be so attributable on the obtaining of the tax advantage as a matter of law (rather than upon other factors such as the take up of an employment scheme by a certain number of employees).

(4) **Standardised tax products.** Arrangements fall within this hallmark if they are made available by a promoter for implementation by more than one person and an informed observer who had studied the arrangements could reasonably be expected to conclude that:

- the arrangements have substantially standardised documentation to enable implementation, the form of that documentation is determined by the promoter and the substance of the documentation does not need to be tailored to any material extent;
- a person implementing the arrangements must enter into a specific transaction or series of transactions;
- the transaction or series of transactions are substantially standardised in form; and
- either the main purpose of the arrangements is to enable a person to obtain a tax advantage or the arrangements would be unlikely to be entered into but for the expectation of obtaining a tax advantage.

Arrangements consisting solely of one or more plant or machinery leases (see (6) below) are excluded, as are an ENTERPRISE INVESTMENT SCHEME (**22**) or ISA, arrangements using the CORPORATE VENTURING SCHEME (**19**) or VENTURE CAPITAL TRUSTS (**64**), arrangements qualifying for community investment tax relief, specified EMPLOYEE SHARE SCHEMES (**21**), certain pension schemes; schemes to which *ITTOIA 2005, s 731* (periodical payments of personal injury damages) applies and arrangements which would fall within (8) below but for the exclusions from that hallmark.

(5) **Loss schemes.** Arrangements are within this hallmark if the promoter expects more than one individual to implement them or to implement arrangements which are substantially the same and an informed observer, having studied them, could reasonably be expected to conclude that:

(a) the main benefit or one of the main benefits of the arrangements for some or all of the participants is the provision of losses;
(b) the arrangements (including the way they are structured) contain an element or elements unlikely to have been entered into but for the provision of those losses; and
(c) the participants would be expected to use the losses to reduce their liability to income tax or capital gains tax.

(6) **Leasing arrangements.** This hallmark covers certain arrangements which include high-value plant or machinery leases. See Tolley's Corporation Tax for further details.

(7) **Employment income provided through third parties.** See Tolley's Income Tax for further details.

(8) **Financial products.** Arrangements are within the hallmark if they include at least one 'specified financial product' and it would be reasonable to expect an informed observer (having studied the arrangements and having regard to all relevant circumstances) to conclude that:

(a) one of the main benefits of including a specified financial product in the arrangements is to give rise to a tax advantage; and

(b) either:

(i) a specified financial product included in the arrangements contains at least one term unlikely to have been entered into were it not for the tax advantage; or

(ii) the arrangements involve one or more contrived or abnormal steps (other than certain specified steps which are deemed not to be contrived or abnormal) without which the tax advantage could not be obtained.

The condition at (b)(i) is treated as not met if it would otherwise be met only because the specified financial product includes a term requiring that it be held for a minimum period before it is redeemed and *TCGA 1992, s 135* (exchange of securities — see **57.5** SHARES AND SECURITIES) or *s 136* (schemes of reconstruction — see **57.7** SHARES AND SECURITIES) applies to it. The condition is also treated as not met if it would otherwise be met only because the specified financial product includes a term under which the issuing company can secure that the redemption date falls before the end of the 'permitted period' and but for that term, the specified financial product would be an 'equity note'. 'Permitted period' and 'equity note' are defined for this purpose by *CTA 2010, s 1016*. Both of the conditions at (b) above are treated as not met if they would otherwise both be met only because the specified financial product includes a term providing for conversion into, or redemption in, a currency other than sterling.

The '*specified financial products*' are loans, shares, derivative contracts, certain repos and quasi-repos, stock lending arrangements, alternative finance arrangements and contracts which, whether alone or in combination with other contracts, are required under generally accepted accounting practice to be treated as a loan, deposit or other financial asset or obligation or would be if the person entering into the arrangements were a company. Financial products held in an individual savings account are excluded.

Arrangements are excluded from the hallmark if a promoter is a participating entity or part of a participating group in the Code of Practice on Taxation for Banks and HMRC had confirmed or could reasonably be expected to confirm to the promoter that the arrangements are acceptable transactions under the Code.

For the purpose only of determining whether arrangements are prescribed by (1)–(3) or (6) above, **19.3**(C) below is disregarded.

[*SI 2006 No 1543*].

Hallmarks (3), (4) and (5) were considered in *HMRC v Redbox Tax Associates LLP* FTT 2021, [2022] SFTD 1. Hallmarks (3) and (4) were considered in *HMRC v AML Tax (UK) Ltd* FTT, [2022] UKFTT 174 (TC).

Persons required to make disclosure

[19.3] The following persons are required to make disclosures of avoidance schemes in particular circumstances.

Disclosure by promoter

A 'promoter' must provide HMRC with specified information on any notifiable proposal within five business days of the '*relevant date*' (i.e. the earliest of: the date he first makes a firm approach to another person; the date on which he makes the proposal available for implementation by any person; and the date he first becomes aware of any transaction forming part of arrangements implementing the proposal).

There is a separate requirement for a promoter to provide HMRC with specified information relating to notifiable arrangements and to do so within five business days of the date on which he first becomes aware of any transaction forming part of those arrangements; but this does not apply if the arrangements implement a proposal which has been notified as above.

The disclosure under these provisions must provide sufficient information as might be reasonably expected to enable an HMRC officer to comprehend the manner in which the proposal or arrangements are intended to operate, including the details specified in *SI 2012 No 1836, Reg 4*.

Where a promoter has complied with the above requirements and another person is a promoter in relation to the same proposal or arrangements or to a proposal or arrangements that are substantially the same (whether they relate to the same or different parties), the notification obligation of that other promoter is discharged if:

- the promoter who made the disclosure has notified the identity and address of the other promoter to HMRC or the other promoter holds the reference number allocated to the arrangements; and
- the other promoter holds the information included in the disclosure.

If a promoter has discharged his obligations in relation to a proposal or arrangements, he is not required to notify proposals or arrangements which are substantially the same as those already notified (whether or not they relate to the same parties).

[*FA 2004, s 308; SI 2012 No 1836, Regs 4(1), 5(1)(4)(5)*].

Details of clients

A further disclosure requirement applies where a promoter of notifiable arrangements provides services to any client in connection with the arrangements and either the promoter is subject to the requirement to provide the client with the reference number allocated under **19.4**(a) below or would be subject to that requirement if he had not failed to make the necessary disclosure of the proposal or arrangements. The requirement also applies to a provider of services who is subject to the requirement to provide a client with specified information relating to a reference number under **19.4**(b) below. Unless HMRC have withdrawn the obligation to notify the reference number to the client, the promoter or provider must provide HMRC with specified information about the client within 30 days of the end of each calendar quarter (i.e. 31 March etc.) during which the promoter or provider is subject to the requirement in question. The specified information is the scheme reference number (if there is one), the name, address, unique taxpayer reference number and national insurance number of the client, the promoter or provider's name and address and the end date of the quarter in relation to which the information is provided. In certain circumstances, the 30-day limit is extended to 60 days to the extent that the specified information consists of the client's unique taxpayer reference number and national insurance number.

HMRC have a further power which applies where a promoter or provider has provided HMRC with the specified information but HMRC suspect that a person other than the client to whom the information relates is or is likely to be a party to the arrangements. HMRC may, by written notice, require the promoter or provider to provide specified information about any person they might reasonably be expected to know is or is likely to be a party to the arrangements. The promoter or provider must comply with the requirement within ten days of receiving the notice or such longer period as HMRC direct. The specified information is the name and address of, and any identification number allocated by HMRC to, any person other than the client who is or is likely to be a party to the arrangements (but only those who will, or are likely to, either sell the arrangements to another person or achieve a tax advantage by implementing the arrangements), together with sufficient information as might be reasonably expected to enable HMRC to comprehend how such a person is involved in the arrangements. Only information held by the promoter or provider at the time of receipt of the notice can be required.

[*FA 2004, ss 313ZA, 313ZB; FA 2021, Sch 31 paras 11, 12; SI 2012 No 1836, Regs 13, 13A, 18; SI 2021 No 980, Regs 10, 11*].

Duty to provide updated information

Where, in compliance with the main obligations above, information has been provided to HMRC about notifiable arrangements, or proposed notifiable arrangements, and a reference number has been allocated to the arrangements (see **19.4** below), the promoter must inform HMRC of:

(i) any change in the name by which the notifiable arrangements are known; and
(ii) any change in the name or address of any person who is a promoter in relation to the notifiable arrangements or the notifiable proposal.

The promoter must give HMRC the updated information (on the prescribed form) within 30 days after the change occurs. If there is more than one promoter, the obligation to inform HMRC of a change within (ii) above falls on the promoter whose details have changed. Once a promoter has informed HMRC of a change within (i) or (ii), the duty of any other promoter to inform HMRC of that change is discharged.

[*FA 2004, ss 310C, 316; FA 2021, Sch 31 para 14*].

Meaning of promoter

A '*promoter*' is a person who conducts a 'relevant business' and who in the course of that business:

(a) in relation to a notifiable proposal:
  (i) is to any extent responsible for the design of the proposed arrangements; or
  (ii) makes a 'firm approach' to another person with a view to making the proposal available for implementation by that person or any other person; or
  (iii) makes a notifiable proposal available for implementation by another person; or
(b) in relation to notifiable arrangements:
  (i) is a promoter by virtue of (a)(ii) or (iii) above in relation to a notifiable proposal which is implemented by the arrangements;
  (ii) is to any extent responsible for the design of the arrangements; or
  (iii) is to any extent responsible for the organisation or management of the arrangements.

A '*relevant business*' for this purpose is a trade, profession or business which involves the provision to other persons of services relating to taxation or which is carried on by a bank (within *CTA 2010, s 1120*) or securities house (within *CTA 2010, s 1009(3)*). Anything done by a company which is a member of the same 51% group (as defined) as a bank or securities house is taken to be done in the course of a relevant business if it is done for the purposes of the trade etc. of the bank or securities house.

For the purposes of (a)(ii) above, a person makes a '*firm approach*' to another person if he makes a 'marketing contact' with that person when the proposed arrangements have been 'substantially designed'. A promoter makes a '*marketing contact*' with another person if he provides information about the proposal, including an explanation of the tax advantage to be obtained, with a view to that person or any other person entering into transactions forming part of the proposed arrangements. Arrangements have been '*substantially designed*' when it would be reasonable to believe that a person wishing to obtain the tax advantage might use the scheme or a scheme which is not substantially different.

The following exclusions apply.

(A) A company providing services within (a) or (b) above to a company which is a member of the same group (as defined) is not a promoter.
(B) Neither is an employee of (or of a person connected (within **17** CONNECTED PERSONS) with) either a promoter or a person entering into any transaction forming part of the proposed arrangements. The exclusion of employees is disapplied in cases where a non-UK resident promoter fails to disclose.
(C) A person is not treated as a promoter where his involvement in the proposal or arrangements is such that he is not required to provide all of the required information because of the legal professional privilege rules above.
(D) A person is not treated as a promoter by virtue of (a)(i) or (b)(ii) above where:

- in the course of providing tax advice, he is not responsible for the design of any element of the proposed arrangements or arrangements from which the tax advantage expected to be obtained arises;
- his relevant business is the provision of tax services but he does not provide tax advice in the course of carrying out his responsibilities in relation to the proposed arrangements or arrangements; or
- he is not responsible for the design of all the elements of the proposed arrangements or arrangements from which the tax advantage is expected to be obtained arises and could not reasonably be expected to have sufficient information to comply with the disclosure requirements or to know whether a disclosure is required.

[*FA 2004, s 307; FA 2021, Sch 31 para 3; SI 2004 No 1865*].

Disclosure by introducer

Where HMRC suspect that a person (P) is an 'introducer' of a proposal which may be notifiable, they can by notice require P to provide them with the name and address of each person who has provided him with information about the proposal (usually a promoter or another introducer). HMRC may also, or alternatively, require P to provide them with specified information in relation to each person with whom P has made a 'marketing contact' (see above under 'Meaning of promoter') in relation to the proposal. The notice must be in writing and must specify the proposal concerned. P must comply with the notice within ten days or such longer time as HMRC direct.

A person is an '*introducer*' of a notifiable proposal if he makes a marketing contact with another person about the proposal. A person is not, however, an introducer by reason of anything done in circumstances prescribed in regulations.

[*FA 2004, ss 307, 313C; SI 2012 No 1836, Reg 15*].

Disclosure by person dealing with non-UK promoter

A person who enters into any transaction forming part of notifiable arrangements in relation to which there is a non-UK resident promoter (and no UK resident promoter) must himself provide HMRC with specified information relating to those arrangements. He must do so within five business days after entering into the first such transaction. The information to be supplied to HMRC is similar to that which promoters must provide (see above). This obligation is discharged if a promoter makes disclosure of the notifiable arrangements in question.

[*FA 2004, ss 309, 319(4); SI 2012 No 1836, Regs 4(2)(4), 5(6)*].

Disclosure by parties to arrangements not involving a promoter

A person who enters into any transaction forming part of notifiable arrangements in respect of which neither he nor any other person in the UK has a disclosure obligation under the above provisions must himself provide HMRC with specified information relating to those arrangements. Such disclosure must normally be made within 30 days beginning with the day after the day in which he enters into the first transaction forming part of the arrangements. Where, however, there is no promoter only because the person who would otherwise be the promoter is not required to make a disclosure because of the legal professional privilege rules above, the disclosure by the client must be made within five days after the day on which he enters into the first transaction. The information to be supplied to HMRC is similar to that which promoters must provide (see above).

[*FA 2004, ss 310, 319(4); SI 2012 No 1836, Regs 4(3)(4), 5(7)(8)*].

Further information requested by HMRC

Where a person has provided the required information about notifiable proposals or arrangements in accordance with *FA 2004, ss 308, 309* or *310* above or has provided information in purported compliance with *FA 2004, ss 309* or *310* but HMRC believe that not all of the required information has been provided, HMRC may require that person to provide further specified information about the proposals or arrangements (in addition to that required under *FA 2004, ss 308, 309* or *310*) and documents relating to the proposals or arrangements. The information or documents must be provided within the ten working days (as defined) beginning with the day on which HMRC imposed the requirement or within such longer period as HMRC direct. Where HMRC believe that a person has failed to provide the required information or documents they may apply to the Tribunal for an order requiring them to be provided. The Tribunal may make such an order only if satisfied that HMRC have reasonable grounds for suspecting that the information or documents will assist them in considering the proposals or arrangements. If the Tribunal make an order, the information or documents must be provided within the ten working days (as defined) beginning with the day on which the order is made or within such longer period as HMRC direct. [*FA 2004, ss 310A, 310B*].

Duty of client to provide employee details

The following applies if a promoter of notifiable arrangements or a notifiable proposal or another person provides services to any client in connection with the arrangements or proposal and the following conditions are met:

(I) the client receives from the promoter or provider the reference number allocated to the arrangements (or proposed arrangements) as in **19.4** below; and

(II) the client is an employer, and, as a result of the arrangements (or proposed arrangements):
   - (i) one or more of the client's employees receive, or might reasonably be expected to receive, in relation to their employment, an advantage in relation to any tax covered by the DOTAS regime; or
   - (ii) the client receives, or might reasonably be expected to receive, any such advantage in relation to the employment of one or more of the client's employees.

Where an employee is within subsection (II)(i) above, or is an employee within (II)(ii), the client must provide HMRC with prescribed information relating to the employee within 14 days after the end of the final PAYE tax month or quarter of the tax year in which any person first enters into a transaction forming part of the arrangements and on the same date in each subsequent year until an advantage ceases to apply to either employee or employer. For this purpose, 'employee' includes an office holder and a former employee. Regulations may exempt a client from complying with this duty in prescribed circumstances.

The information is the name, address and reference number of the employer; the name and any NI number of the employee; the scheme reference number; the tax year in which the employee obtains or expects to obtain the tax advantage (or confirmation it is nil); and the name and address of the promoter or provider and the name of the arrangements. The information must be provided in the prescribed form and manner or the duty will not be regarded as complied with. If, as in **19.4** below, HMRC have given notice, in relation to specified arrangements, that promoters no longer have to pass on reference numbers, or that parties do not have to report such numbers to HMRC, the client is discharged from the above obligation in relation to those arrangements.

[*FA 2004, ss 313ZC, 316; FA 2021, Sch 31 paras 13, 14; SI 2012 No 1836, Reg 13B; SI 2021 No 980, Reg 12*].

Reference numbers allocated to arrangements

[19.4] HMRC may allocate a reference number (sometimes referred to as a 'scheme reference number' or SRN) to arrangements or proposed arrangements in the following circumstances:

(a) *Disclosure made*. Where a person has made a disclosure as above, HMRC may allocate a reference number to the arrangements in question within 90 days after the disclosure. HMRC may allocate a reference number even if the disclosure is incomplete or defective.

(b) *Notice of potential allocation not complied with*. HMRC may also allocate a reference number to arrangements or proposed arrangements where:
   (i) they become aware that, on or after 10 June 2021, a transaction forming part of the arrangements has been entered into, a firm approach has been made with a view to making a proposal for arrangements available for implementation or a proposal has been so made available;
   (ii) HMRC have issued a notice explaining that, unless the recipient can satisfy them, before the end of the 'notice period', that the arrangements or proposal are not notifiable, they may allocate a reference number to them;
   (iii) the recipient has failed to satisfy HMRC before the expiry of the notice period.

   In this case, HMRC may allocate the reference number within the year beginning the day after the end of the notice period. The '*notice period*' is the 30 days beginning with the day on which the notice in (ii) above is issued, or a longer period if HMRC so direct.

HMRC must issue a notice to anyone they reasonably suspect to be a promoter of the arrangements or proposal. They may, but are not required to, issue a notice to any other person they reasonably suspect to be involved in the supply of the arrangements or proposed arrangements. A notice cannot be issued until 15 days after HMRC become aware that a condition within (i) has been met.

HMRC may withdraw a reference number allocated under this provision at any time.

The allocation of a reference number does not in itself indicate that HMRC accept that the arrangements could as a matter of law result in the obtaining by any person of a tax advantage.

Where a reference number is allocated under (a) above, HMRC must then notify the number to the person making the disclosure and to any co-promoter whose identity and address has been notified to HMRC by that person. Where a reference number is allocated under (b) above, HMRC must notify the number to any person they reasonably suspect to be a promoter or involved in the supply of the arrangements or proposed arrangements (whether or not the notice in (b)(ii) above was given to that person).

Appeal against allocation of number

A person who has been notified, as above, of a reference number allocated under (b) above, may appeal to the Tribunal against HMRC's decision to allocate it. Notice of appeal must be given to the Tribunal in writing within the 30 days beginning with the day of notification, stating the grounds of appeal. The Tribunal may, however, accept a late appeal. An appeal can be brought on the grounds that HMRC did not act in accordance with the requirements in (b) above or that the arrangements or proposal are not notifiable.

If the Tribunal cancels HMRC's decision, HMRC must withdraw the number. Making an appeal does not, however, prevent the powers and duties deriving from the allocation of the number from applying during the appeal process.

Further information requested by HMRC

Where HMRC have allocated a reference number under (b) above, they may require any person they reasonably suspect to be, or to have been, a promoter of, or otherwise involved in the supply of, the arrangements or proposed arrangements to provide specified information or documents. HMRC must have reasonable grounds for suspecting that the information or documents will assist them in considering the arrangements or proposed arrangements. The information or documents must be provided to HMRC within the ten working days beginning with the day on which HMRC imposed the requirement (or by a later date if HMRC so direct).

Duty to provide number to clients and other parties

A promoter who is providing services to a client in connection with notifiable arrangements must pass on to the client any reference number allocated under (a) above for those arrangements or for arrangements which are substantially the same as those arrangements. He must do so within 30 days after the date he first becomes aware of any transaction forming part of the arrangements or, if later, the date on which the reference number is notified to him (by HMRC or a co-promoter).

The duty of a promoter to notify the reference number to the client is discharged where he has provided the client with prescribed information relating to the reference number allocated to a notifiable proposal for the arrangements, provided that the proposal and the arrangements are substantially the same.

Where a reference number is allocated under (b) above, a person (a '*provider*') who provides services on or after 10 June 2021 to a client in connection with the arrangements or proposed arrangements must provide prescribed information relating to the number to the client. The provider must do so within 30 days beginning with the date of notification of the number (whether the notification was by HMRC or another person).

HMRC may, by notice, withdraw the obligation to provide information to clients.

A client who has been notified of a reference number or prescribed information must notify the reference number or information to any other person that he might reasonably be expected to know is, or is likely to be, a party to the arrangements and who might reasonably be expected to gain a tax advantage under the arrangements. He must do so within 30 days beginning with the date he first becomes aware of any transaction forming part of the arrangements or, if later, the date on which the reference number is notified to him.

Where client is an employer

Where the client is an employer and receives, or might reasonably be expected to receive, by reason of the notifiable arrangements, a tax advantage covered by the regime in relation to the employment of any of the client's employees, the client must, within 30 days, provide (on the prescribed form) the reference number to each of the employees in question. For this purpose, 'employee' includes an office holder and a former employee. Regulations may exempt a client from complying with this duty in prescribed circumstances.

HMRC may give notice that, in relation to notifiable arrangements or a notifiable proposal specified in that notice, clients do not have to pass on reference numbers after the date specified in the notice.

Duty to report number to HMRC

A party to any arrangements giving rise to an income tax or capital gains tax advantage must quote the allocated reference number in his personal tax return for the year in which the person first enters into a transaction forming part of the arrangements and in all subsequent returns until the advantage ceases to apply to him. He must also quote the tax year in which, or the date on which, the advantage is expected to arise. Comparable provisions apply for corporation tax. For arrangements connected with employment, see **19.3** above. Persons not required to file a tax return must instead provide HMRC (on form AAG4) with specified information no later than what would have been the filing date for such a return. If the notifiable arrangements give rise to a claim (made outside a tax return) to relieve a trading loss, the claimant must provide HMRC (on form AAG4) with specified information at the time the claim is made. These duties are disapplied for employees in cases where an employer has a duty under **19.3** above to provide HMRC with information relating to those employees.

HMRC may give notice that, in relation to arrangements specified in that notice, the above obligation does not apply after the date specified in the notice. To this end, a list of withdrawn scheme reference numbers is now published at www.gov.uk/government/publications/tax-avoidance-withdrawn-scheme-reference-numbers. Clients and other parties who have received any of these reference numbers no longer have a duty to notify them to HMRC on their tax returns or on form AAG4 from the date shown on the list.

Duty of client to provide information

Where a promoter or other person has provided the reference number to a client under the above provisions, the client must provide that person with specified information. The client must provide the information within the ten days beginning with the later of the date the client receives the reference number and the date the client first enters into a transaction forming part of the notifiable arrangements. The information required is the client's unique tax reference number or national insurance number or confirmation that he does not have such a number.

Duty to provide additional information to clients or other parties

Where, as above, a promoter or provider is required to pass on to the client the reference number for arrangements, or a client is required to pass on the reference number to other parties, HMRC may specify additional information which must be simultaneously passed on in each case. This is confined to information supplied by HMRC relating to proposals or arrangements in general. HMRC may specify the form and manner in which such additional information is to be provided.

[*FA 2004, ss 310D–313, 316, 316A; FA 2021, Sch 31 paras 4–10, 14, 15, 44, 45(1); SI 2012 No 1836, Regs 8A–12; SI 2021 No 980, Regs 5–9*].

Compliance

[19.5] The following compliance powers apply.

Pre-disclosure enquiries

If HMRC suspects that a person is the introducer of a proposal, or the promoter of a proposal or arrangements, which may be notifiable under the above provisions, they may, by written notice, require that person to state whether in his opinion notification is required, and if not, the reasons for his opinion. In giving those reasons, it is not sufficient to indicate that a lawyer or other professional has given an opinion. The recipient of a notice must comply with it within the ten days beginning on the day after that on which the notice is issued. HMRC may also, or alternatively, require a person that they suspect is an introducer of a proposal to provide them with specified information in relation to each person with whom the person has made a marketing contact in relation to the proposal.

If HMRC receive a statement (whether or not in response to a notice) giving reasons why a proposal or arrangements are not notifiable, they may apply to the Tribunal for an order requiring specified further information or documents to be provided in support of the reasons. The information or documents must be provided within the 14 days beginning on the day after that on which the order is made.

[*FA 2004, ss 313A, 313B; SI 2012 No 1836, Reg 14*].

Order to disclose

HMRC can apply to the Tribunal for an order that a proposal or arrangements are notifiable under the above provisions. The application must specify both the proposal or arrangements concerned and the promoter. [*FA 2004, s 314A*].

They can also apply to the Tribunal for an order that a proposal or arrangements be treated as notifiable. Again, the application must specify both the proposal or arrangements concerned and the promoter. Before making such an order, the Tribunal must be satisfied that HMRC have taken all reasonable steps (which need not include making use of the pre-disclosure enquiry provisions above) to establish whether the proposal or arrangements are notifiable and have reasonable grounds for suspecting that they may be notifiable. Grounds for suspicion may include an attempt by the promoter to avoid or delay providing information or documents under the pre-disclosure enquiry provisions and failure to comply with a requirement under those provisions in relation to other proposals or arrangements. The disclosure required as a result of an order under this provision must be made within the ten days beginning on the day after that on which the order is made. [*FA 2004, s 306A*].

Supplementary information

Where HMRC believe that a disclosure by a promoter has not included all the information required to be disclosed they can apply to the Tribunal for an order requiring the promoter to provide specified information or documents. Before making an order, the Tribunal must be satisfied that HMRC have reasonable grounds for suspecting that the information or documents form part of, or will support or explain, the required information. Information or documents required by an order under this provision must be provided within the ten days beginning on the day after that on which the order is made. [*FA 2004, s 308A*].

Penalties

See **46.1** PENALTIES for the penalties applicable for failure to fulfil the above requirements.

Voluntary disclosure of information to HMRC

No duty of confidentiality or other restriction on disclosure (however imposed) prevents the voluntary disclosure by any person to HMRC of information or documents which the person has reasonable grounds for suspecting will assist HMRC in determining whether there has been a breach of any requirement imposed as above under the DOTAS regime. [*FA 2004, s 316B*].

A disclosure by an independent financial advisor of information relating to tax avoidance schemes was held to meet these requirements in *R (oao Emblin) v HMRC* QB [2018] STC 934.

Publication of information by HMRC

[19.6] HMRC may publish specified information about arrangements (or proposed arrangements) to which a reference number is allocated (see **19.4** above), any person who is a promoter in relation to them and, where the number is allocated under **19.4**(b) above, any person otherwise involved, on or after 10 June 2021, in their supply. This can include information identifying a person as a promoter or other person involved in the supply of the arrangements, but in this case, HMRC must first inform him that they are considering publishing that information and give him reasonable opportunity to make representations about whether it should be published. No information can be published that identifies a person who enters into a transaction forming part of the arrangements (unless he is identified as a promoter or other person involved in the supply of the arrangements). No information may be published about a person involved in the supply of the arrangements if there are reasonable grounds for believing that their involvement is limited to activities subject to legal professional privilege.

Where the reference number is allocated under **19.4**(b) above, information identifying a promoter or other person involved in the supply of the arrangements can only be published for the first time within one year of the day on which the number is allocated. The information may not continue to be published for more than one year after its first publication. In determining the one-year periods, no account is taken of any period during which HMRC are prohibited from publishing the information because of court or tribunal proceedings.

Once any such information has been published about arrangements, HMRC must also publish information about any ruling of a court or tribunal that is made in relation to arrangements intended to secure a tax advantage if, in HMRC's opinion, the ruling is relevant to the arrangements in question. A ruling is relevant to the arrangements if it is final and if the principles laid down, or reasoning given, in the ruling would, if applied to the arrangements, allow the purported tax advantage arising from those arrangements.

[*FA 2004, ss 316C, 316D; FA 2021, Sch 31 paras 16, 17, 44, 45(3)*].

Mandatory disclosure of offshore arrangements

[19.7] There are requirements for taxpayers, promoters and advisers to disclose to HMRC details of certain offshore avoidance arrangements under the Mandatory Disclosure Rules (MDR). This might include simple transactions such as the transfer of funds between bank accounts in different countries, or settling funds in an offshore trust. The MDR apply with effect from 28 March 2023. They replace the DAC 6 regime (see **19.8** below) which was introduced when the UK was a member of the EU. The UK MDR derive from the OECD's M odel Mandatory Disclosure Rules for Common Reporting Standard Avoidance Arrangements and Opaque Offshore Structures, published in 2018.

MDR disclosure needs to be made in respect of any:

- CRS Avoidance Arrangement. These are arrangements for which it is reasonable to conclude that they are designed to circumvent the Common Reporting Standard.
- Opaque Offshore Structure. This is an offshore vehicle without any substantive economic activity which is held through an opaque structure used to obscure beneficial ownership.

[*SI 2023 No 38*].

For commentary on the provisions, see **Simon's Taxes, A6.1204B.**

EU disclosure rules for cross-border tax arrangements (DAC 6)

[19.8] Requirements for intermediaries and taxpayers to disclose to HMRC information about certain cross-border tax arrangements to give effect to international rules applied broadly from 1 July 2000 (subject to a delay due to the coronavirus pandemic) to 27 March 2023. The requirements have now been replaced by the Mandatory Disclosure Rules at **19.7** above. The provisions were introduced in response to the EU's sixth Directive on Administrative Co-operation in the field of taxation (EU Directive 2018/822/EU (amending Directive 2011/16/EU)) (DAC 6).

An arrangement will be reportable if it meets at least one of five hallmarks. Only hallmarks within (D) below apply with effect from IP completion day (11pm on 31 December 2020).

The hallmarks are listed in Annex IV to DAC 6 (see https://eur-lex.europa.eu/legal-content/EN/TXT/PDF/?uri=CELEX:32018L0822&from=EN) and are described as presenting an indication of a potential risk of tax avoidance, although there is no requirement for a tax avoidance motive. All of the generic hallmarks, and some of the specific hallmarks, are taken into account for the purposes of DAC 6 only if they fulfil the main benefit test. The main benefit test is fulfilled if the main benefit which, having regard to all relevant facts and circumstances, that a person may reasonably expect to derive from an arrangement is the obtaining of a tax advantage.

The hallmarks are as follows:

(A) Generic hallmarks linked to the main benefit test: arrangements that give rise to performance fees or which involve mass-marketed schemes.

(B) Specific hallmarks linked to the main benefit test: this includes certain tax planning features, such as buying a loss-making company to exploit its losses in order to reduce tax liability. Another example would involve arrangements aimed at converting income into capital in order to obtain a tax benefit.

(C) Specific hallmarks related to cross-border transactions; some of these hallmarks are subject to the main benefit test: for example, deductible cross-border payments between associated enterprises where the recipient is essentially subject to no tax, zero or almost zero tax. Another hallmark is about deductions for the same depreciation on an asset claimed in more than one jurisdiction.

(D) Specific hallmarks concerning the automatic exchange of information and beneficial ownership: an arrangement is reportable if it has the effect of undermining the rules on anti-money laundering, transparency of beneficial ownership or the automatic exchange of financial account information.

(E) Specific hallmarks concerning transfer pricing: these include the use of unilateral safe harbours; the transfer of hard-to-value intangible assets when no reliable comparables exist and the projection of future cash flows or income are highly uncertain.

[*SI 2020 No 25; SI 2020 No 1649; SI 2023 No 38, Reg 21*].

For detailed commentary on the provisions, see **Simon's Taxes, A6.1204A.**

High-risk promoters of avoidance schemes (POTAS)

[19.9] A special compliance regime (sometimes referred to as the 'POTAS' regime) applies to certain promoters of tax avoidance schemes. With effect from 10 June 2021, HMRC can issue a 'stop notice' requiring a promoter to stop marketing a particular scheme if it satisfies certain conditions. This power can apply even if the scheme in question has not been defeated before a Tribunal or court. Names and other details of promoters subject to such a notice may be published. HMRC's other powers under the regime are aimed at promoters who satisfy one or more 'threshold conditions' relating to previous behaviour or who promote a series of avoidance schemes which are defeated. HMRC can issue a 'conduct notice' requiring the recipient to comply with specified conditions as to the information they provide to clients, compliance with any disclosure requirements under the DOTAS provisions and not promoting schemes which rely on contrived or abnormal steps to produce a tax advantage. Promoters who fail to comply with a conduct notice may be issued with a monitoring notice. Names of promoters subject to such a notice may be published by HMRC, including details of how the conduct notice was breached, and promoters are required to notify their monitored status to clients. Information powers and penalties apply to promoters subject to a stop notice or conduct notice and to promoters subject to a monitoring notice and their clients and intermediaries. With effect from 24 February 2022, HMRC have the power to apply for the winding-up of a body (including a partnership) which is itself a high-risk promoter or is connected with a body which is a high-risk promoter.

The taxes covered by the provisions are income tax, capital gains tax, corporation tax, petroleum revenue tax, inheritance tax, stamp duty land tax, stamp duty reserve tax and annual tax on enveloped dwellings. The provisions applicable to promoters who promote a series of avoidance schemes which are defeated also apply to VAT.

Clients of promoters subject to a monitoring notice must notify HMRC of the promoter's reference number. Clients who fail to comply with this duty are subject to extended time limits for assessment (see **6.14** ASSESSMENTS).

[*FA 2014, ss 234–283, Schs 33A–36; FA 2022, ss 85, 86; SI 2015 Nos 130, 131, 549*].

For detailed commentary, see **Simon's Taxes, A7.3.**

Key points on disclosure of tax avoidance schemes

[19.10] Points to consider are as follows.

- A key point about the disclosure of tax avoidance schemes rules is that it is the promoter that has initial responsibility for deciding whether to disclose a piece of planning. While counsel's opinion can be helpful, HMRC will not accept this as an excuse for a failure to disclose. That said, in the case of *HMRC v Mercury Tax Group* (Sp C 737), 2009 STI 628, the Special Commissioner decided that the fact that the company had gone 'to the trouble and expense of taking counsel's opinion' meant that no penalty should be charged for a failure to disclose. But another Tribunal judge on another day might take a different view.
- While lawyers are able to avoid disclosure on the basis of legal professional privilege, there is no such protection for accountants, even if the advice is given in contemplation of litigation (see *R (on the application of Prudential plc and another) v Special Commissioner of Income Tax and another* QB 2009, [2010] STC 161).
- It is important to remember that any one hallmark is sufficient to trigger a disclosure requirement. So, for example, even if a piece of planning is well known within the tax profession and even to HMRC, if a promoter is able to obtain a premium fee (as defined), a disclosure is required.
- The hallmark for standardised tax products does not apply just because a particular type of transaction always uses the same documents. For example, settling funds into a trust isn't necessarily disclosable tax planning, just because the lawyers always use a standard trust deed.
- You are not a promoter of a scheme if your client merely asks you to review it and say if it works. But you may become a promoter if you were to suggest improvements or to assist the promoter in fitting the scheme to your client's circumstances.

20

Double Tax Relief

(See also HMRC Guidance RDR1 and Capital Gains Manual CG14380.)

Cross-references. See **42** OFFSHORE SETTLEMENTS; **43** OVERSEAS MATTERS; **44.2** PARTNERSHIPS; **49** REMITTANCE BASIS; and **51** RESIDENCE AND DOMICILE.

Simon's Taxes. See **E6.438**.

Introduction to double tax relief

[20.1] Double tax relief operates to mitigate the effect of a single source of income, chargeable gain etc. being chargeable to tax in both the UK and another country. This chapter describes the reliefs available insofar as they apply to UK taxpayers in respect of UK capital gains tax and corporation tax on chargeable gains. Broadly, where the same gain is liable to be taxed in both the UK and another country, relief may be available as follows.

(a) Under the specific terms of a double tax agreement between the UK and that other country. In most cases, such agreements provide for credit against UK tax for foreign taxes on gains arising to UK residents. In some cases, however, agreements provide for exemption from taxes on gains in the country where they arise for UK residents.
(b) Under the unilateral double tax relief provisions contained in UK tax legislation. The provisions provide for credit against UK tax for foreign taxes on gains arising to UK residents.
(c) By deduction. Where no relief can be obtained under (a) or (b) above, relief may be given by deducting foreign tax paid in computing the chargeable gain for UK tax purposes.

There are anti-avoidance provisions which operate to defeat schemes designed to increase credit relief for foreign tax.

Relief under double tax agreements

[20.2] The UK has made, and continues to make, bilateral agreements, usually known as double tax agreements, with other countries for the avoidance of double taxation. Under these agreements, exemption from taxes in the country where they arise may be granted for gains realised by UK residents, whether individuals or companies. More usually, however, agreements provide for overseas tax to be allowed as a credit against UK tax on the gain in respect of which the overseas tax was computed. For the way in which such credit relief is given see **20.5** below. Reciprocal relief under agreements is given to overseas residents from UK capital gains tax and corporation tax. See **20.5** below as regards claims.

[*TIOPA 2010, ss 2–7, 26; TCGA 1992, s 277*].

For a list of the UK's current double tax agreements, see *Whillans Tax Tables*, T9.103.

The specific provisions of the particular agreement concerned must be examined carefully. For relevant court decisions, see Tolley's Tax Cases. Where tax on overseas gains is not relieved, or is only partly relieved, under an agreement, unilateral relief (see **20.3** below) will normally apply.

Where double tax relief by credit applies under an agreement, no deduction for foreign tax is allowed in computing the foreign gains. If a taxpayer chooses not to take relief by way of credit, any foreign tax paid is treated as allowable expenditure for the purposes of the UK tax charge. See **20.4** below.

For further details of how relief by credit is given, see **20.5** below.

The OECD's Multilateral Convention to Implement Tax Treaty Related Measures to Prevent Base Erosion and Profit Shifting, brought into effect in the UK by *SI 2018 No 630*, modifies existing double tax agreements between signatory jurisdictions which have agreed to apply it. It includes arbitration provisions to help resolve disputes.

Unilateral relief by UK

[20.3] Tax on chargeable gains payable under the law of any territory outside the UK and computed by reference to gains arising in that territory is allowed as a credit against UK tax paid on those gains by UK residents (and certain non-residents — see below).

The above relief (known as '*unilateral relief*') is not available where relief or credit for foreign tax is available under a double tax agreement.

The foreign taxes must be charged on gains and correspond to capital gains tax or corporation tax in the UK but may include similar taxes payable under the law of a province, state or part of a country, or a municipality or other local body. See *Yates v GCA International Ltd (and cross-appeal)* Ch D 1991, 64 TC 37. HMRC examine foreign taxes to determine whether, in their own legislative context, they serve the same function as UK taxes, and are thus eligible for unilateral relief. (HMRC Statement of Practice SP 7/91). The overseas taxes which the HMRC consider admissible or inadmissible for relief are listed country by country in the HMRC Double Taxation Relief Manual at DT2100 onwards.

The requirement for the claimant to be UK resident does not apply in the following cases.

(a) Unilateral relief is available for foreign tax paid in respect of the chargeable gains of a UK branch or agency of a non-UK resident person or UK permanent establishment of a non-UK resident company. The relief does not extend to taxes of the non-resident's home state, and it is limited to that which would have been available if the branch or agency or permanent establishment had been a UK-resident person to whom such gains had accrued.

(b) Credit for Channel Islands or Isle of Man tax if the claimant is resident for the particular year of assessment or accounting period either in the UK or the Channel Islands or Isle of Man. The restriction to tax on '*income arising in the territory*' does not apply in the case of the Channel Islands or the Isle of Man.

In relation to double tax agreements made after 20 March 2000, unilateral relief will not be given in particular circumstances if the agreement expressly precludes relief by credit under the agreement in those circumstances.

[*TIOPA 2010, ss 8, 9, 11, 26, 28, 30, Sch 9 para 13; TCGA 1992, s 277*].

For further details of how unilateral relief by credit is given, see **20.5** below.

Relief by deduction

[20.4] Foreign tax on the disposal of an asset which is borne by the disposer is an *allowable deduction* in computing UK chargeable gains, to the extent that no relief is allowed by way of credit under a double tax agreement or as unilateral relief.

Where the amount of any deduction allowed is rendered excessive or insufficient by an adjustment of any tax payable either in the UK or under the law of any other territory, the time limit for revising the UK liability accordingly is extended to six years after the time when all material determinations (i.e. assessments etc.) have been made to give effect to the adjustment.

In a case where a deduction is rendered excessive because of an adjustment of a foreign tax charge, the taxpayer must give HMRC written notification of the adjustment within one year of its being made. The maximum penalty for non-compliance is equal to the additional tax payable for the tax year or company accounting period in question.

[*TIOPA 2010, ss 31(2), 113–115; TCGA 1992, s 278*].

Credit relief — further provisions

[20.5] Relief by way of credit under double tax arrangements or as unilateral relief must be claimed and is given effect by reducing the capital gains tax or corporation tax chargeable in respect of the gain by the amount of the credit. No credit is available for tax paid by a company in respect of profits subject to an election under *CTA 2009, s 18A* (exemption for company foreign permanent establishments — see **43.8** OVERSEAS MATTERS). [*TIOPA 2010, s 18; TCGA 1992, s 277(1)*]. See *George Wimpey International Ltd v Rolfe* Ch D 1989, 62 TC 597 and *Yates v GCA International Ltd (and cross-appeal)* Ch D 1991, 64 TC 37.

Computation of gain where credit allowable

Remittance basis

Where credit for foreign tax is allowable in respect of a gain which is chargeable on the remittance basis, the amount received in the UK and so chargeable is treated as increased by the foreign tax on that gain. [*TIOPA 2010, s 32; TCGA 1992, s 277(1)–(1C)*].

Arising basis

Where the remittance basis does not apply and credit for foreign tax is to be allowed in respect of a gain, no deduction may be made in the computation of the gain for foreign tax on that, or any other gain. [*TIOPA 2010, s 31; TCGA 1992, s 277(1)*].

Limits of relief

For capital gains tax purposes, credit relief is limited to the difference between the capital gains tax (before double tax relief) which would be payable by the claimant:

(i) if he were charged on his total capital gains, and
(ii) if he were charged on those gains excluding the gain in respect of which the credit is to be allowed.

Where double tax relief is due from more than one gain, this limitation is applied successively to each gain, but so that on each successive application, (i) above applies to the total capital gains exclusive of the capital gains to which the limitation has already been applied.

[*TIOPA 2010, s 40*].

Where the above provision applies to restrict the set-off of an amount of credit, the taxpayer's chargeable gains are treated as reduced by the amount of the disallowed credit. This applies only so far as the disallowed credit does not exceed any loss attributable to the gain in respect of which the foreign tax was paid. In calculating any such loss for this purpose, the payment of the foreign tax is taken into account. [*TIOPA 2010, s 35*].

In no case may a person's total credits in respect of income and chargeable gains exceed the total capital gains tax payable by the claimant for the tax year. [*TIOPA 2010, s 41*].

For corporation tax purposes, credit cannot exceed the amount of the gain multiplied by the company's tax rate (before deduction of any credit). [*TIOPA 2010, s 42*].

HMRC accept that if the UK chargeable gain (before deducting any losses) is less than the sterling equivalent of the gain chargeable in the overseas territory, the whole of the foreign tax will nevertheless be allowable up to the amount of the UK tax on the gain, provided that the gain charged in both countries relates to the same disposal. (HMRC Brief 17/10).

Minimisation of foreign tax

Credit relief is restricted to the foreign tax that would have been payable had all reasonable steps been taken, under the law of the territory concerned and under any double tax agreement, and on the assumption that no double tax relief were available, to minimise the liability. Such steps include the claiming of available reliefs and allowances and the making of available elections. [*TIOPA 2010, s 33*]. For a case in which HMRC sought unsuccessfully to include in these provisions steps which could have been taken before the transaction concerned, see *Hill Samuel Investments Ltd v HMRC* (Sp C 738), [2009] SSCD 315.

Payment received by reference to foreign tax

Where credit for foreign tax is to be allowed and a payment is made by a tax authority by reference to that foreign tax, either to the taxpayer, a person connected with him (within *CTA 2010, s 1122*) or to some other person directly or indirectly under a 'scheme' that has been entered into, the amount of the credit is reduced by the amount of the payment. A '*scheme*' includes any scheme, arrangement or understanding of any kind, whether or not legally enforceable, involving one or more transactions. [*TIOPA 2010, s 34*].

Example

Lyra, a higher rate income tax payer, has the following chargeable gains for 2024/25.

UK gain	£31,000	
Foreign gain	16,000	(Foreign tax £6,400)

Neither of the gains are upper rate gains. Lyra claims credit relief for the foreign tax paid. Her capital gains tax liability for 2024/25 is as follows.

	UK gain	Foreign gain
	£	£
Chargeable gain	31,000	16,000
Less annual exempt amount	3,000	—
Gain chargeable to tax	28,000	16,000
Capital gains tax: £25,000/£16,000 × 20%	5,600	3,200
Less credit for foreign tax	—	3,200
Tax payable	£5,600	Nil

Notes to the example

(a) No relief is available for the excess of the foreign tax over the CGT liability in respect of the foreign gain (£6,400 – £3,200 = £3,200).

(b) The annual exempt amount is allocated against the UK gain as this maximises the double tax relief available.

Claims

[20.6] The normal time limit for claims for credit relief is not more than four years after the end of the tax year or accounting period for which the gain is chargeable.

The claim deadline is extended to 31 January following the tax year in which the foreign tax is paid or one year after the end of the company accounting period in which the foreign tax is paid, where this is later than the deadline given above.

[*TIOPA 2010, s 19; TCGA 1992, s 277*].

Written notice must be given to HMRC where any credit allowed for foreign tax has become excessive by reason of a reduction in credit because of a payment in respect of the foreign tax (see **20.5** above) or an adjustment of the amount of any foreign tax payable. The notice must be given within one year after the making of the reduction or adjustment. The maximum penalty for failure to comply is the amount by which the credit was rendered excessive by the reduction or adjustment. [*TIOPA 2010, s 80*].

HMRC practice

[20.7] The standard credit article in double tax agreements provides for overseas tax to be allowed as a credit against UK tax on the gain in respect of which the overseas tax was computed. Unilateral relief operates similarly. There is no requirement for the two liabilities to arise at the same time or on the same persons; and therefore HMRC consider that relief is available in the following situations.

(a) A capital gain is taxed overseas as income.
(b) Tax is charged overseas on a no gain/no loss transfer within a group of companies, and a UK liability arises on a subsequent disposal (see **26.3**, **26.7** GROUPS OF COMPANIES).
(c) An overseas trade carried on through a branch or agency is transferred to a local subsidiary, with an immediate overseas tax charge; and a UK tax charge arises on a subsequent disposal of the securities or on a disposal of the assets by the subsidiary within six years (see **43.10** OVERSEAS MATTERS).
(d) UK liability arises on a disposal of assets after overseas tax has become payable by reference to an increase in value without a disposal.

This relief is not available where a gain is rolled over in the UK (see **53** ROLLOVER RELIEF); but the overseas tax can be deducted from the gain (see **20.4** above).

(HMRC Statement of Practice SP6/88).

Anti-avoidance — schemes and arrangements designed to increase relief

[20.8] There are anti-avoidance provisions which are intended to defeat schemes designed to increase credit relief for 'foreign tax'. The provisions apply where the following conditions are satisfied.

(a) In relation to any chargeable gains (or income) taken or to be taken into account for the purposes of determining a person's liability to tax in a chargeable period there is an amount of foreign tax for which, under any arrangements, credit is allowable against UK tax for that period.

(b) There is a scheme or arrangement the main purpose, or one of the main purposes, of which is to cause an amount of foreign tax to be taken into account in the case of that person for that chargeable period.

(c) The scheme or arrangement is a 'prescribed scheme or arrangement' within (1) to (6) below.

(d) The aggregate of the amount of the claims for credit made by the person for that chargeable period and the amount of claims for credit made by all the persons connected to that person for an overlapping chargeable period is more than a minimal amount. For this purpose, a chargeable period of one person overlaps with a chargeable period of another if they have at least one day in common.

Where the conditions are satisfied, the provisions apply automatically and operate by requiring the making of any adjustments (by the taxpayer or, if the taxpayer fails to make the adjustments, by HMRC) necessary to counteract the effects of the scheme or arrangement. The adjustments may be made by way of assessment, modification of an assessment, amendment or disallowance of a claim or otherwise.

'*Foreign tax*' includes any tax which is treated under *TIOPA 2010, s 63(5)* (dividends paid between related companies) as payable under the law of a territory outside the UK.

[*TIOPA 2010, ss 81, 82*].

Prescribed scheme or arrangement

The above provisions apply to schemes or arrangements falling within one or more of the following types.

(1) A scheme or arrangement which enables a person who is party to it or concerned in it to pay, in respect of a chargeable gain (or source of income), an amount of foreign tax all or part of which is properly attributable to one or more other gains (or sources of income).

(2) A scheme or arrangement under which a person (the '*claimant*') has claimed, or is in a position to claim, for a chargeable period, any credit that under any double tax arrangements is allowable for the payment of an amount of foreign tax if, when the claimant entered into the scheme, it could reasonably be expected that the effect on the 'foreign tax total' of the amount being paid or payable would be to increase it by less than the amount allowable as a credit in respect of the payment.
For these purposes, the '*foreign tax total*' is the amount found by aggregating the amounts paid or payable in respect of the transactions forming part of the scheme or arrangement by persons party to it or concerned in it and taking into account any reliefs, deductions, reductions or allowances against or in respect of any tax that arise to those persons (including any such reliefs etc. arising as a consequence of the amount of foreign tax being paid or payable).

(3) A scheme or arrangement under which, in relation to a claimant, an amount ('*amount X*') is treated under the Tax Acts as if it were an amount of foreign tax paid or payable in respect of a source of income or a chargeable gain and it could reasonably be expected by the claimant, at the time he entered the scheme, either that no real foreign tax would be paid or payable by a participant or that such an amount would be paid or payable but would increase the foreign tax total (as in (2) above) by less than the amount allowable to the claimant for amount X.

(4) A scheme or arrangement where a step is taken by a person who is party to it or concerned in it or a step that could have been taken by such a person is not taken where that action or omission has the effect of increasing a claim made by such a person for an allowance by way of credit or of giving rise to such a claim. The steps concerned are those that may be made under the law of any territory or under double tax arrangements made in relation to any territory and include claiming or otherwise securing the benefit of reliefs, deductions, reductions or allowances, and making elections for tax purposes. Steps taken or not taken before the scheme or arrangement was made are taken into account and the reason for taking or not taking a step is irrelevant if it has the requisite effect.

(5) A scheme or arrangement under which 'amount A' is less than 'amount B' in relation to a person who has claimed, or is in a position to claim, for a chargeable period an allowance by way of credit for foreign tax. For this purpose, '*amount A*' is the total amount of UK tax payable by the person and any connected persons (within *CTA 2010, s 1122*) in respect of income and chargeable gains arising in the chargeable period and '*amount B*' is the total amount of UK tax that would be payable by the person and any connected persons in respect of income and chargeable gains for the period if, in determining that amount, the transactions forming part of the scheme or arrangement were disregarded.

(6) A scheme or arrangement which includes the making by a person (A) of a 'relevant payment' or payments and the giving, for that payment or payments, of consideration, all or part of which consists of a payment or payments made to A, or a person connected (within *CTA 2010, s 1122*) with A, which is chargeable to tax under the law of a territory outside the UK. For this purpose, a '*relevant payment*' is a payment by A all or part of which may be brought into account in computing A's income for UK tax purposes. A '*payment*' includes the transfer of money's worth.

[*TIOPA 2010, ss 83–88*].

Double tax dispute resolution in the EU

[20.9] Before Brexit, the UK was subject to Council Directive (EU) 2017/1852 on tax dispute resolution mechanisms in the EU which applies a framework for resolving double tax disputes between member states. It features a binding procedure for resolving disputes within two years, with a framework for further time-limited arbitration proceedings. Taxpayers faced with tax treaty disputes can initiate a procedure whereby the member states in question must try to resolve the dispute amicably within two years. If at the end of this period, no solution has been found, the member states must set up an Advisory Commission to arbitrate. If member states fail to do this, the taxpayer can bring an action before the national court (in the UK, the Upper Tribunal) to do so. The Advisory Commission will be comprised of three independent members and representatives of the competent authorities in question. It will have six months to deliver an opinion leading to a final, binding decision. This decision will be immediately enforceable and must resolve the dispute.

The UK legislation which implemented the Directive, *SI 2020 No 51*, applied to questions in dispute relating to income or capital earned in a tax period commencing on or after 1 January 2018. The UK legislation is revoked with effect from IP completion day (11pm GMT on 31 December 2020) by *SI 2020 No 1383*.

Secrecy requirements under any enactment do not prevent HMRC or certain other persons from disclosing information required to be disclosed under any instrument, agreement or arrangement covered by the regulations. [*TIOPA 2010, s 128C*].

Key points concerning double tax relief

[20.10] Points to consider are as follows.

- Relief is available against UK tax where overseas tax is paid on a gain chargeable to tax in another country.
- Where there is no double tax treaty in place the relief is given in accordance with UK legislation (unilateral relief) which provides for a credit for overseas tax paid or where relief is not available as a credit it can be treated as an allowable deduction.
- If there is a double tax agreement in place the relief is available under the specific terms of the agreement. In some double tax agreements there may be an exemption from tax on gains in the overseas country where they arise to UK residents.
- The starting point in applying double tax relief is to look at what the domestic position is i.e. is there a taxable gain. If there is and overseas tax has been paid the next step is to check if there is a double tax agreement in place, if so it should be applied. If there is no double tax agreement in place the UK relieving provisions will apply.
- If relief is not available as a credit the foreign tax paid can be treated as a deductible expense in calculating the gain.
- New and amended treaties are regularly added to the list of treaties.
- See **43.8** OVERSEAS MATTERS for the exemption regime for profits of foreign permanent establishments of UK resident companies (which includes chargeable gains).

21

Employee Share Schemes

Cross-reference. See **23.84** EXEMPTIONS AND RELIEFS re employee trusts.

Introduction to employee share schemes

[21.1] Income tax and capital gains tax (CGT) legislation applies where there are arrangements to allow employees (which term includes for these purposes directors) to acquire shares in their employing companies. Tax reliefs and exemptions apply where such arrangements take the form of one or more of the various statutory schemes and have been granted HMRC approval.

This chapter is concerned with the CGT consequences of both tax-advantaged schemes and other schemes (and for these purposes the term 'scheme' encompasses any such arrangements as mentioned above). The expression 'shares' is used in its broadest sense. For the application of the chapter to stocks and securities, as well as shares, see **21.2** below. For context, the coverage includes in most cases a brief note of the income tax position, but for the full provisions (and, as regards approved schemes, the conditions for approval), see Tolley's Income Tax under Share Related Employment Income and Exemptions. For the general income tax liability in respect of shares given to employees as part of their earnings, see Tolley's Income Tax under Employment Income. See HMRC Capital Gains Manual CG56300–56550 for HMRC's own notes on the CGT provisions, and see generally **Simon's Taxes.** See **C2.810A–C2.816, C3.1919, E4.5**.

See **58.2, 58.4** SHARES AND SECURITIES — IDENTIFICATION RULES for special rules where shares are acquired as an employee and are subject to restricted disposal rights.

See also **7.7** ASSETS and **65** WASTING ASSETS for CGT treatment of options generally.

Extended meaning of 'shares'

[21.2] For the purposes of **21.6, 21.8–21.14** below, the meaning of 'shares' is extended to embrace a broader range of financial products, including, for example, government and local authority stocks. All of the following are 'shares' for these purposes:

- shares (including stock) in any body corporate, wherever incorporated, or in any unincorporated body constituted under the law of a foreign country;
- rights under 'contracts of insurance' other than 'excluded contracts' (but see further below);
- debentures, debenture stock, loan stock, bonds, certificates of deposit and other instruments creating or acknowledging indebtedness (other than contracts of insurance);
- warrants and other instruments entitling the holders to subscribe for securities;
- certificates and other instruments conferring rights in respect of securities held by persons other than the persons on whom the rights are conferred and which may be transferred without the consent of those persons;
- units in a collective investment scheme (as defined by *ITEPA 2003, s 420(2)*);
- futures (as defined by *ITEPA 2003, s 420(3)*) and options (other than 'share options' — see below);
- rights under contracts for differences (or under similar contracts — as defined by *ITEPA 2003, s 420(4)*), other than contracts of insurance;
- options;
- alternative finance arrangements which are investment bond arrangements (see **3.3** ALTERNATIVE FINANCE ARRANGEMENTS).

However, none of the following are 'shares' for these purposes: cheques, bills of exchange, bankers' drafts and letters of credit (other than bills of exchange accepted by a banker), money and statements showing balances on a current, deposit or savings account, leases and other dispositions of property, heritable securities and share options (within the meaning given at **21.6** below).

A contract of insurance is an '*excluded contract*' if it is:

- a contract for an annuity which is, or will be, pension income within *ITEPA 2003, Pt 9*;
- a 'contract of long-term insurance', other than an annuity contract, which does not have, and cannot acquire (whether on conversion or otherwise), a surrender value; or
- a 'contract of general insurance' other than one falling in accordance with generally accepted accounting practice (as defined in *FA 2004, s 50*) to be accounted for as a financial asset or liability.

For the above purposes, 'contract of insurance', 'contract of long-term insurance' and 'contract of general insurance' all have the same meaning as in *Financial Services and Markets Act 2000 (Regulated Activities) Order 2001 SI 2001 No 544*.

It is important to note that the above extended meaning of 'shares' does *not* apply for the purposes of the tax-advantaged schemes at **21.16** *et seq.* below. For the purposes of **21.21** below, 'shares' includes stock but not securities, and there are specific rules restricting the types of shares eligible under the other schemes. For details see Tolley's Income Tax under Share-Related Employment Income and Exemptions.

An '*interest in shares*', for the purposes of **21.6, 21.8–21.14** below, means an interest which is less than full beneficial ownership. It includes an interest in their sale proceeds but not a right to acquire them.

[*ITEPA 2003, ss 420, 516(4), 521(4), 548(1), Sch 5 para 58; TCGA 1992, ss 119A(7), 120(1)(7)(8); ITA 2007, s 564T; SI 2007 No 2130*].

For the purposes of this chapter, '*employment-related shares*' are shares or an interest in shares (as above) acquired by a person by virtue of a right or opportunity made available by reason of the employment (past, present or prospective) of that or any other person. For this purpose, shares are deemed to be acquired when the beneficial entitlement to them is acquired and not, if different, at the time of conveyance or transfer. Any right or opportunity made available by a person's employer, or by a person connected (within *ITA 2007, s 993*) with a person's employer, is treated as made available by reason of the employment of that person, other than in the case of an individual conferring a right or opportunity in the normal course of his domestic, family or personal relationships. There are rules dealing with company reorganisations (such as conversions, scrip issues and rights issues); these treat replacement shares or additional shares acquired on such a reorganisation as acquired by virtue of the same right or opportunity as the original interest and treat any consequent reduction in the market value of the original shares as consideration given or a payment made for the replacement shares or additional shares. [*ITEPA 2003, ss 421B, 421D*].

Consideration for grant of share option

[21.3] Where a 'share option' to which the income tax provisions at **21.6** below apply is granted, *TCGA 1992, s 17(1)* (see **39.1** MARKET VALUE) is disapplied (where it would otherwise apply), so that, for CGT purposes, the amount or value of the consideration for the grant, as regards both the company and employee, is the actual value or consideration passing (if any). However, in computing actual value for this purpose, any value put on the employee's services, past or present, is ignored. [*TCGA 1992, s 149A*].

Release and replacement of options

[21.4] The following applies where an option to acquire shares in a company ('*the old option*') which was obtained by an individual by reason of their office or employment as director or other employee of that or any other company is released in whole or in part for a consideration which consists of or includes the grant to them of another option ('*the new option*') to acquire shares in that or any other company. The new option is not regarded for CGT purposes as consideration received by the individual for the release of the old option. Any consideration given by the individual for the old option is taken to be the consideration given for the new option and any additional expenditure paid by them for the acquisition of the new option is treated as allowable expenditure. The release of the old option is disregarded in determining the consideration received for the new option by the grantor company. [*TCGA 1992, s 237A*].

Employee share schemes which are not tax-advantaged

[21.5] Where an employee (including a director) receives shares by reason of his employment and otherwise than under a tax-advantaged scheme (see **21.16–21.25** below), he is generally treated by virtue of *TCGA 1992, s 17* (see **39.1** MARKET VALUE) as acquiring them at their market value at the time of acquisition. Likewise, any disposal by the employer is treated as made at market value. As regards certain shares subject to risk of forfeiture, *s 17* is disapplied as regards the employee only.

See also, at **39.1** MARKET VALUE, the **exception to the market value rule** where an asset is acquired for nil consideration or at less than its market value *and* there is no corresponding disposal. This would apply, for example, where *new* shares are *issued* by a company to an employee (as opposed to existing shares being transferred), as an issue of shares is not a disposal by a company for the purposes of corporation tax on chargeable gains; in such a case, the employee's CGT acquisition cost of the shares is restricted to the actual consideration given (if any).

A transfer of shares to a director or other employee for nil consideration or at less than market value normally gives rise to a charge to income tax if regarded as part of general earnings. The amount so charged does not form part of the acquisition cost of the shares for CGT purposes (see also **21.6** below re shares acquired on the exercise of an option).

See **21.26** below for disapplication of market value rules where employees receive priority allocations in public share offers.

See **21.6** below where shares are acquired as a result of the *exercise* of an option.

Exercise of share option which is not tax-advantaged

[21.6] An income tax charge may arise on the exercise of a share option which is not tax-advantaged. The provisions apply to a 'share option' (an '*employment-related share option*') acquired by a person where the right or opportunity to acquire it is available by reason of the employment (past, present or prospective) of that person or any other person.

A '*share option*' is a right to acquire 'shares'. A right to acquire shares which is acquired pursuant to a right or opportunity made available under arrangements the main purpose, or one of the main purposes, of which is the avoidance of tax or national insurance contributions is not a share option. See the extended meaning of '*shares*' in **21.2** above.

Subject to exclusions, the acquisition of shares on the exercise of the option by an employee results in the chargeable amount being taxed as employment income of the employee for the tax year in which the exercise occurs under *ITEPA 2003, s 476*. The chargeable amount is the difference between the open market value of the acquired shares at the time of exercise and the aggregate of the consideration given for the shares and any given for the option. Certain other amounts may be deducted in arriving at the chargeable amount, including any amount charged on *grant* of the option. Relief is given by deduction from the chargeable amount in respect of any liability to secondary Class 1 national insurance contributions (i.e. employer contributions) in respect of the exercise of the option borne by the employee under a voluntary agreement or a joint election under *Social Security Contributions and Benefits Act 1992, Sch 1 para 3A* or *para 3B* (or NI equivalent). Consideration given for an option does not include any value placed on the performance of duties in connection with the employment. (In specified circumstances, a person is likewise chargeable even though the gain in question is realised by another person.)

[*ITEPA 2003, ss 419, 420(8), 421–421B, 421D, 471–484, ss 718, 721(1)*].

For shares in research institution spin-out companies, see **21.15** below.

Capital gains tax

Employment-related share options to which the above provisions apply are treated as options for capital gains tax purposes, whether or not they would ordinarily be regarded as such. The acquisition of shares pursuant to such an option is accordingly treated as the exercise of an option. [*TCGA 1992, s 288(1A)*].

The acquisition of an option and the transaction entered into by the grantee on the exercise of the option, being in this case an acquisition of shares, are treated for CGT purposes as a single transaction taking place at the time the option is exercised (see also **7.7** ASSETS).

Any sum charged to income tax as employment income under the above provisions forms part of the cost of acquisition of the shares for CGT purposes (within *TCGA 1992, s 38(1)(a)* — see **16.12**(a) COMPUTATION OF GAINS AND

LOSSES). For this purpose only, however, any deduction made in arriving at the amount chargeable to income tax in respect of any tax charged on *grant* of the option (see above) is added back and no account is taken of any relief given for national insurance contributions met by the employee. Where the shares would otherwise have ceased to be 'employment-related shares' (see **21.2** above) by virtue of *ITEPA 2003, s 421B(6)* (death of employee) or *s 421B(7)* (shares ceasing to be employment-related shares seven years after employee leaves), they are treated as continuing to be employment-related shares until they are next disposed of (so that on that disposal, any amounts counting as employment income under the above provisions can be added to the acquisition cost).

The amount counting as employment income for this purpose is reduced to the extent that it is unchargeable foreign securities income for the purposes of *ITEPA 2003, s 41F* (share income of internationally mobile employees; see *ITEPA 2003, s 41H*) or chargeable foreign securities income which has not been remitted to the UK by the end of the tax year in which the disposal occurs. Where, however, unremitted chargeable foreign securities income is subsequently remitted to the UK, the taxpayer can make a claim for the remittance to be treated as having occurred in the tax year of disposal.

[*TCGA 1992, ss 119A, 119B, 120(2)(4)(9), 144(3)*].

Where *TCGA 1992, s 144ZA* (see **7.7** ASSETS) applies, the cost of acquisition will therefore consist of the aggregate of:

- the amount counting as employment income (with the adjustments indicated above),
- the consideration given for the shares acquired on the exercise of the option, and
- any consideration given for the option.

Other charges in respect of share options which are not tax-advantaged

[21.7] An income tax charge under *ITEPA 2003, s 476* also arises on the happening of certain other events in relation to share options which are not tax-advantaged. The events are the assignment, release (including the cancellation or surrender), abandonment of the option or receipt of a benefit in connection with the option.

The assignment or release of an option is a CGT disposal, and the amount charged to income tax is excluded by *TCGA 1992, s 37* (see **33.1** INTERACTION WITH OTHER TAXES) from the proceeds to be taken into account for CGT purposes (HMRC Capital Gains Manual CG56384). See **21.4** above re the release of an option in return for a replacement option. By virtue of *TCGA 1992, s 144(4)* (see **7.7**(f) ASSETS), the abandonment (i.e. the lapse) of an employee share option is not a disposal for CGT purposes, so no capital loss may be claimed in respect of any consideration given for the option. Any amount charged to income tax in respect of a benefit in connection with an option is *not* added to the acquisition cost of the option or shares for CGT purposes.

Shares acquired for less than market value

[21.8] A charge to income tax may apply where an employee obtains shares for less than their market value. The provisions operate by creating the fiction of a notional interest-free loan on the amount of the under-value. See **21.2** above for the meaning of 'shares' for the purposes of these provisions.

Subject to the anti-avoidance provisions of *ITEPA 2003, s 446UA*, the provisions apply where, at the time of acquisition of the shares, either no payment is (or has been) made for them or a payment below market value is (or has been) made for them. The employee is regarded as having the benefit of an interest-free loan, which attracts a charge under the employment income benefits code. The amount of the notional loan is the market value less any payment made for the shares and any amounts treated as earnings (other than exempt income) or counting as employment income under other provisions (see in particular **21.5**, **21.6** above). The notional loan terminates on the happening of specified chargeable events, viz. (i) the making good of the loan by payments or further payments for the shares, (ii) any obligation to make further payment ceasing to bind the employee (or connected person), (iii) the disposal of the shares, (iv) the doing of something which affects the shares as part of a scheme or arrangement the main purpose, or one of the main purposes, of which is the avoidance of tax or National Insurance contributions, or (v) the death of the employee. Subject to further conditions, where the notional loan terminates as a result of any of (ii), (iii) or (iv), then the amount of the loan thus deemed to be written off is treated as employment income.

[*ITEPA 2003, ss 192–197, 419, 421, 421B–421D, 421E(2)–(5), 421F–421H, 446Q–446W*].

These provisions are most likely to be applied where shares are issued partly-paid, where payment is due in instalments or on the exercise of an option where the employment is outside the scope of *ITEPA 2003, s 476* in **21.6** above. See Tolley's Income Tax under Employment Income for further detail.

For shares in research institution spin-out companies, see **21.15** below.

Capital gains tax

Where a chargeable event is also a disposal of the shares for CGT purposes, and in any other case on the first disposal after a chargeable event, the aggregate of any amount counting as employment income in respect of that chargeable event and any other chargeable events occurring after the last disposal to which this provision applied, is added to the cost of acquisition (within *TCGA 1992, s 38(1)(a)* — see **16.12**(a) COMPUTATION OF GAINS AND LOSSES) of the person making the disposal. Where shares would otherwise cease to be employment-related shares by virtue of *ITEPA 2003, s 421B(6)* (death of employee) or *s 421B(7)* (shares ceasing to be employment-related shares seven years after employee leaves the employer, the company which issued the shares or connected person), they are treated as continuing to be employment-related shares until they are next disposed of (so that on that disposal, any amounts counting as employment income in respect of chargeable events can be added to the acquisition cost). The amount counting as employment income for this purpose is reduced to the extent that it is unchargeable foreign securities income for the purposes of

ITEPA 2003, s 41F (share income of internationally mobile employees; see *ITEPA 2003, s 41H*) or chargeable foreign securities income which has not been remitted to the UK by the end of the tax year in which the disposal occurs. Where, however, unremitted chargeable foreign securities income is subsequently remitted to the UK, the taxpayer can make a claim for the remittance to be treated as having occurred in the tax year of disposal. [*TCGA 1992, ss 119A, 119B, 120(2)(3)*].

Shares disposed of for more than market value

[21.9] A charge to income tax may apply where shares are disposed of for more than their market value. See **21.2** above for the meaning of 'shares' for the purposes of these provisions.

Where shares within these provisions are disposed of (such that no associated person any longer has a beneficial interest) at more than their market value at the time of disposal, the excess over market value is chargeable to income tax as employment income. Any expenses incurred in connection with the disposal are also deductible in arriving at the chargeable amount.

[*ITEPA 2003, ss 198–200, 419, 421, 421, 421A–421D, 421E(2)–(5), 421F–421H, 446X–446Z*].

The amount charged to income tax is excluded by *TCGA 1992, s 37* (see **33.1** INTERACTION WITH OTHER TAXES) from the proceeds to be taken into account for CGT purposes.

Anti-avoidance — shares with artificially depressed market value

[21.10] There are provisions 'designed to ensure that if the value of employment-related securities is depressed by means of non-commercial transaction(s), then that reduction in value is taxed on the employee.' (Treasury Explanatory Notes to Finance Bill 2003). Subject to exclusions, the provisions apply in certain cases where the market value of 'employment-related shares' (see **21.2** above) (or, where relevant, other shares or interests in shares) is reduced by things done otherwise than for genuine commercial purposes; this specifically includes anything done as part of a scheme or arrangement a main purpose of which is to avoid tax or national insurance contributions and any transaction (other than a payment for corporation tax group relief) between members of a 51% group of companies otherwise than on arm's length terms. See **21.2** above for the extended meaning of 'shares', in relation to these provisions.

If anything done otherwise than for genuine commercial purposes within the seven years ending with the acquisition reduces the market value of employment-related shares at acquisition by at least 10%, there is a charge to income tax on the employee for the tax year in which the acquisition occurs; the amount chargeable counts as employment income for tax purposes. The provisions may also modify the operation of those at **21.9** above and **21.12**, **21.13**, and **21.14** below, broadly with the effect of replacing, in computing various amounts, the artificially reduced market value with what would have been the market value if it were not for the reduction.

[*ITEPA 2003, ss 419, 421, 421A–421D, 421E(2)–(5), 421F–421I, 446A–446J*].

See Tolley's Income Tax under Share-Related Employment Income and Exemptions for the detailed provisions.

Amounts charged to income tax under these provisions on the acquisition of shares are *not* added to the acquisition cost of the shares for CGT purposes.

Anti-avoidance — shares with artificially enhanced market value

[21.11] There are provisions 'designed to ensure that if the value of employment-related securities is enhanced by means of non-commercial transaction(s) during any tax year, then that appreciation in value is taxed on the employee at the earlier of the disposal of the employment-related securities or 5 April.' (Treasury Explanatory Notes to Finance Bill 2003). Subject to exclusions, the provisions apply in certain cases where the market value of 'employment-related shares' (see **21.2** above) is increased by things done otherwise than for genuine commercial purposes (a '*non-commercial increase*'); this specifically includes anything done as part of a scheme or arrangement a main purpose of which is to avoid tax *or national insurance contributions* and any transaction (other than a payment for corporation tax group relief) between members of a 51% group of companies otherwise than on arm's length terms. See **21.2** above for the extended meaning of 'shares', in relation to these provisions.

Where, on the 'valuation date' for a 'relevant period', the market value of employment-related shares is at least 10% greater than it would be if any 'non-commercial increases' (see above) during the relevant period were disregarded, the whole of the excess is taxed as employment income of the employee for tax purposes for the tax year in which the valuation date falls. For these purposes:

- the '*valuation date*' is the last day of the 'relevant period'; and
- the '*relevant period*' means any tax year, except that the first such period runs from date of acquisition to the following 5 April and the last runs from 6 April to the date in the tax year on which the provisions cease to apply. If the provisions cease to apply to an interest in the shares, the relevant period ends at that time in relation to that interest, but these provisions apply separately to that interest and to what remains.

[*ITEPA 2003, ss 419, 421, 421B–421D, 421E(2)–(5), 421F–421H, 446K–446P*].

See Tolley's Income Tax under Share-Related Employment Income and Exemptions for the detailed provisions.

Amounts charged to income tax under these provisions are *not* added to the acquisition cost of the shares for CGT purposes.

For shares in research institution spin-out companies, see **21.15** below.

Post-acquisition benefits

[21.12] Subject to exclusions, the following provisions apply if an 'associated person' (as defined) receives a benefit in connection with 'employment-related shares' (see **21.2** above). The amount or market value (determined as for capital gains tax purposes) of the benefit is taxed as employment income of the employee for the tax year in which the benefit is received. [*ITEPA 2003, ss 421, 421B–421D, 421E(1)(1A)(1B)(3)–(5), 421F–421H, 447–450*].

For shares in research institution spin-out companies, see **21.15** below.

Capital gains tax

On a disposal of employment-related shares, where that disposal is the first following the receipt of a benefit within the above provisions which is an increase in the market value of the shares, the aggregate of any amount counting as employment income in respect of that benefit and any other such benefits occurring after the last disposal to which this provision applied, is added to the cost of acquisition of the person making the disposal. Where shares would otherwise cease to be employment-related shares by virtue of *ITEPA 2003, s 421B(6)* (death of employee) or *s 421B(7)* (shares ceasing to be employment-related shares seven years after employee leaves the employer, the company which issued the shares or connected person), they are treated as continuing to be employment-related shares until they are next disposed of (so that on that disposal, any amounts counting as employment income in respect of chargeable events can be added to the acquisition cost). The amount counting as employment income for this purpose is reduced to the extent that it is unchargeable foreign securities income for the purposes of *ITEPA 2003, s 41F* (share income of internationally mobile employees; see *ITEPA 2003, s 41H*) or chargeable foreign securities income which has not been remitted to the UK by the end of the tax year in which the disposal occurs. Where, however, unremitted chargeable foreign securities income is subsequently remitted to the UK, the taxpayer can make a claim for the remittance to be treated as having occurred in the tax year of disposal. [*TCGA 1992, ss 119A, 119B*].

Where the above does not apply, amounts charged to income tax under these provisions are *not* added to the acquisition costs of the shares for CGT purposes.

Restricted shares

[21.13] The following provisions apply, subject to exclusions, to 'employment-related shares' (see **21.2** above) if, at the time of acquisition, they are 'restricted shares' (or a 'restricted interest in shares'). Employment-related shares are '*restricted shares*' (or a '*restricted interest in shares*') if there is a contract, agreement, arrangement or condition that imposes any of three types of restriction *and* the market value of the shares or interest (determined as for capital gains purposes) is less than it otherwise would have been. The types of restriction covered are: any provision for the transfer, reversion or forfeiture of the shares; any restriction on the freedom of the holder to dispose of the shares (or to retain the proceeds if they are sold) or on his right to retain the shares or proceeds; or any right conferred by the shares themselves; and any provision whereby the disposal or retention of the shares, or the exercise of a right conferred by them, may result in a disadvantage to the holder or (if different) the employee or a connected person.

No liability to income tax under the general provisions at **21.5** above arises on the acquisition of employment-related shares if the shares are subject to transfer, reversion or forfeiture and will cease to be so within five years after the acquisition. If a 'chargeable event' occurs in relation to restricted shares, there is a charge to tax on the employee for the tax year in which it occurs, the amount chargeable (which is calculated by applying a complex formula) counting as employment income for tax purposes. Relief is given by deduction from the chargeable amount in respect of any liability to secondary Class 1 national insurance contributions (i.e. employer contributions) in respect of that amount which is borne by the employee under a voluntary agreement or a joint election under *Social Security Contributions and Benefits Act 1992, Sch 1 para 3A* or *para 3B* (or NI equivalent).

Broadly, a chargeable event occurs when the shares cease to be restricted shares or a restriction is varied or removed, or the shares are disposed of for consideration by an 'associated person' (as defined) at a time when they are still restricted shares. Various elections can be made jointly by the employer and employee to disapply or moderate these provisions.

[*ITEPA 2003, ss 419, 421, 421A–421D, 421E(1)(1A)(1B)(3)–(5), 421F–421I, 422–425, 432, 718*].

See Tolley's Income Tax under Share-Related Employment Income and Exemptions for full details of the provisions.

For shares in research institution spin-out companies, see **21.15** below.

Capital gains tax

Where an individual acquires employment-related shares which are restricted shares (or a restricted interest in shares), the consideration for the acquisition of the shares is taken as the aggregate of:

(i) the actual amount or value given for the restricted shares (or restricted interest in shares), and
(ii) any amount that constituted earnings for income tax purposes in relation to the acquisition.

This does not affect the calculation of the consideration received by the person from whom the acquisition is made.

Amounts of exempt income (within *ITEPA 2003, s 8*) and amounts which would have been exempt income if the taxpayer had been subject to income tax at the appropriate time are specifically excluded from the amount in (ii) above.

On a disposal of employment-related shares where that disposal constitutes a chargeable event under the restricted share provisions or is the first disposal of the shares following a chargeable event not involving disposal, the aggregate of any amount counting as employment income in respect of that chargeable event and any other chargeable events occurring after the last disposal to which this provision applied, is added to the cost of acquisition of the person making the disposal. In determining amounts counting as employment income for this purpose, no account is taken of any relief given for national insurance contributions borne by the employee (see above). Where shares would otherwise cease to be employment-related shares by virtue of *ITEPA 2003, s 421B(6)* (death of employee) or *s 421B(7)* (shares ceasing to be employment-related shares seven years after employee leaves the employer, the company which issued the shares or connected person), they are treated as continuing to be employment-related shares until they are next disposed of (so that on that disposal, any amounts counting as employment income in respect of chargeable events can be added to the acquisition cost). The amount counting as employment income for this purpose is reduced to the extent that it is unchargeable foreign securities income for the purposes of *ITEPA 2003, s 41F* (share income of internationally mobile employees; see *ITEPA 2003, s 41H*) or chargeable foreign securities income which has not been remitted to the UK by the end of the tax year in which the disposal occurs. Where, however, unremitted chargeable foreign securities income is subsequently remitted to the UK, the taxpayer can make a claim for the remittance to be treated as having occurred in the tax year of disposal.

[*TCGA 1992, ss 119A, 119B, 149AA*].

Example 1

Nick is given some shares in Lowe Ltd, the company that he works for on 1 July 2024. Nick is not allowed to sell the shares for three years. The shares have an unrestricted market value of £10,000 when received, but a restricted value (taking account of the fact that they cannot be sold for three years) of only £8,000. The value of the shares on 1 July 2027 when the restriction is lifted is £14,000. No elections in relation to the shares are made by Nick and Lowe Ltd. Nick sells the shares on 2 July 2027 for £14,000.

Nick is chargeable to income tax and capital gains tax as follows.

Income tax

When Nick receives the shares in Lowe Ltd, he is charged to income tax and NICs under the restricted shares provisions on the lower restricted value, i.e. £8,000. The uncharged proportion of the unrestricted original value is 20%. On 1 July 2027, when the restriction is lifted, there is a chargeable event. Nick is charged to income tax and NICs on 20% of the market value on that date, i.e. 20% × £14,000 = £2,800. Overall, therefore, Nick is charged to income tax on £10,800.

Capital gains tax

		£
Consideration for disposal of shares		14,000
Less	Acquisition cost	—
	Amount charged to income tax	10,800
Chargeable gain 2027/28		£3,200

Example 2

The facts are as in Example 1 above except that Nick and Lowe Ltd elect (before 15 July 2024) for the restriction on the shares to be disregarded. The tax consequences are as follows.

Income tax

When Nick receives the shares in Lowe Ltd, he will be charged to income tax and NICs on the unrestricted market value, i.e. £10,000. No income tax charge arises on the lifting of the restriction on 1 July 2027. Overall, therefore, Nick is charged to income tax on £10,000.

Capital gains tax

		£
Consideration for disposal of shares		14,000
Less	Acquisition cost	—
	Amount charged to income tax	10,000
Chargeable gain 2027/28		£4,000

Convertible shares

[21.14] The following provisions apply, subject to exclusions, to 'employment-related shares' (see **21.2** above) which are, at the time of acquisition, 'convertible shares' (or an interest in 'convertible shares'). For the extended meaning of 'shares', in relation to these provisions, see **21.2** above. Employment-related shares are '*convertible shares*' if they confer on the holder any entitlement to convert them into shares of a different description, or a contract, agreement, arrangement or condition authorises or requires the grant of such an entitlement to the holder if certain circumstances arise, or do not arise, or makes provision for the conversion of the shares (otherwise than by the holder) into shares of a different description.

For the purposes of any liability to income tax in respect of the acquisition of shares (under the general charging rules at **21.5** above, under **21.6** above (unapproved share options) or under **21.8** above (acquisition for less than market value)), the market value of the employment-related shares is to be determined as if they were not convertible shares or an interest in convertible shares. This does not apply if the shares are acquired as part of an arrangement to avoid tax or NICs. Instead, in such cases the market value is computed as if there were an immediate and unfettered right to convert (if this is greater than the value without the right to convert).

If a chargeable event occurs in relation to convertible shares, there is a charge to tax on the employee for the tax year in which it occurs, the amount chargeable counting as employment income for tax purposes. Broadly, the conversion of the employment-related shares (or the shares in which they are an interest) into shares of a different description, the disposal for consideration of the shares (or any interest in them), the release, for consideration, of the conversion right and the receipt by an 'associated person' (as defined) of a benefit in money or money's worth in connection with the conversion right are chargeable events.

The chargeable amount is found by computing the gain (if any) realised on the occurrence of the chargeable event and deducting from it any consideration given for the conversion right and any expenses incurred by the shareholder in connection with the conversion, disposal, release or receipt (whichever is applicable). An adjustment is made where the market value on acquisition was computed under the alternative rules for avoidance cases above. Relief is given by deduction from the chargeable amount in respect of any liability to secondary Class 1 national insurance contributions (i.e. employer contributions) in respect of that amount which is borne by the employee under a voluntary agreement or a joint election under *Social Security Contributions and Benefits Act 1992, Sch 1 para 3A* or *para 3B* (or NI equivalent).

[*ITEPA 2003, ss 419, 421, 421A–421D, 421E(1)(3)–(5), 421F–421I, 435–437, 444*].

See Tolley's Income Tax under Share-Related Employment Income and Exemptions for full details of the provisions.

For shares in research institution spin-out companies, see **21.15** below.

Capital gains tax

Where an individual acquires employment-related shares which are convertible shares (or an interest in convertible shares), the consideration for the acquisition of the shares is taken as the aggregate of:

(i) the actual amount or value given for the convertible shares (or interest in convertible shares), and
(ii) any amount that constituted earnings for income tax purposes in relation to the acquisition.

This does not affect the calculation of the consideration received by the person from whom the acquisition is made.

It is explicitly provided that amounts of exempt income (within *ITEPA 2003, s 8*) and amounts which would have been exempt income if the taxpayer had been subject to the charge to income tax at the appropriate time are excluded from the amount in (ii) above.

On a disposal of employment-related shares which constitutes a chargeable event under the convertible share provisions or is the first disposal of the shares following a chargeable event not involving disposal, the aggregate of any amount counting as employment income in respect of that chargeable event and any other chargeable events occurring after the last disposal to which this provision applied, is added to the cost of acquisition of the person making the disposal. In determining amounts counting as employment income for this purpose, no account is taken of any relief given for national insurance contributions borne by the employee (see above). Where shares would otherwise cease to be employment-related shares by virtue of *ITEPA 2003, s 421B(6)* (death of employee) or *s 421B(7)* (shares ceasing to be employment-related shares seven years after employee leaves the employer, the company which issued the shares or connected person), they are treated as continuing to be employment-related shares until they are next disposed of (so that on that disposal, any amounts counting as employment income in respect of chargeable events can be added to the acquisition cost). The amount counting as employment income for this purpose is reduced to the extent that it is unchargeable foreign securities income for the purposes of *ITEPA 2003, s 41F* (share income of internationally mobile employees; see *ITEPA 2003, s 41H*) or chargeable foreign securities income which has not been remitted to the UK by the end of the tax year in which the disposal occurs. Where, however, unremitted chargeable foreign securities income is subsequently remitted to the UK, the taxpayer can make a claim for the remittance to be treated as having occurred in the tax year of disposal.

[*TCGA 1992, ss 119A, 119B, 149AA*].

Research institution spin-out companies

[21.15] There are provisions which ensure, broadly, that no income tax charge arises on an increase in the value of academics' shares in 'spin-out companies' due to the transfer of intellectual property from a research institution or a company controlled by it. The provisions apply where:

- an agreement is made for one or more transfers of intellectual property from one or more research institutions to a company (a '*spin-out company*');
- a person acquires shares in the spin-out company either before the making of the agreement or within 183 days beginning with the date of the agreement;
- the right or opportunity to acquire the shares was available by reason of employment by any of the research institutions or the company; and
- the person is involved in research in relation to any of the intellectual property which is the subject of the agreement.

The provisions do not apply if the avoidance of tax or national insurance is one of the main purposes of the arrangements under which the shares are acquired.

Where the provisions apply, the following income tax consequences follow.

(a) On acquisition, the market value of the shares is calculated disregarding the effect of both the transfer agreement and the transfer itself.

(b) If the shares are acquired before the agreement is made or before any transfer, the taxable amount under the provisions at **21.12** above in respect of any benefit received by the employee deriving from the agreement or transfer in connection with the shares is treated as nil.

(c) If the shares are restricted shares, the employer and employee are (subject to a right to make an irrevocable agreement to the contrary) deemed to make an election disapplying the provisions at **21.13** above.

(d) For the purposes of **21.11** above, neither the transfer agreement nor any transfer pursuant to it are treated as things done otherwise than for genuine commercial purposes.

For the purposes of these provisions, the extended meaning of shares at **21.2** above does not apply, but '*shares*' includes stock and an interest in shares.

[*ITEPA 2003, ss 451–460*].

Capital gains tax

Where an individual acquires shares (or an interest in shares) in circumstances such that (a) above applies, the consideration for the acquisition is taken as the aggregate of:

- the actual amount or value given for the shares or interest, and
- any amount charged to income tax as earnings in relation to the acquisition.

This does not affect the calculation of the consideration received by the person from whom the acquisition is made.

Where shares would otherwise cease to be employment-related shares by virtue of *ITEPA 2003, s 421B(6)* (death of employee) or *s 421B(7)* (shares ceasing to be employment-related shares seven years after employee leaves the employer, the company which issued the shares or connected person), they are treated as continuing to be employment-related shares until they are next disposed of (so that on that disposal, any amounts counting as employment income in respect of chargeable events can be added to the acquisition cost). The amount counting as employment income for this purpose is reduced to the extent that it is unchargeable foreign securities income for the purposes of *ITEPA 2003, s 41F* (share income of internationally mobile employees; see *ITEPA 2003, s 41H*) or chargeable foreign securities income which has not been remitted to the UK by the end of the tax year in which the disposal occurs. Where, however, unremitted chargeable foreign securities income is subsequently remitted to the UK, the taxpayer can make a claim for the remittance to be treated as having applied in the tax year of disposal.

[*TCGA 1992, ss 119A, 119B, 149AB*].

Share incentive plans

[21.16] A company may set up a Share Incentive Plan (SIP), which is a tax-advantaged all-employee share plan of which the main features are as follows.

- A company which establishes a SIP must notify HMRC and make a declaration that the SIP meets the relevant conditions. Annual returns are also required by companies operating SIPs.
- A plan is operated by trustees, who buy or subscribe for shares with funds provided by the company (or, in the case of partnership shares, the employees) and appropriate them to the participating employees.
- With limited exceptions, the plan must be open to all employees (other than those with a material interest where the company is a close company), but may incorporate performance-related awards within certain parameters.
- An employer can appropriate to an employee free shares in the company valued at up to £3,600 per tax year without any charge to income tax at that time (‘*free share plans*’).

- An employee can buy shares in the company out of amounts deducted from his salary up to a limit of £1,800 in any tax year or, if less, 10% of salary (or such lower limits as the employer's particular plan may specify), these being allowable deductions for income tax (*'partnership share plans'*).
- In respect of each partnership share an employee buys, the employer may appropriate to him up to two free *'matching shares'*, again without any charge to income tax at that time.
- Free and matching shares must normally be kept in the plan for a specified period which must be not less than three years nor more than five (the *'holding period'*) — no such restriction applies to partnership shares. The employer's plan may provide that free and/or matching shares be forfeited in certain circumstances (see further below under Capital gains tax).
- An employee who keeps shares in the plan for at least five years after they are awarded to him receives them free of income tax. With some exceptions (e.g. on death, disability, normal retirement or redundancy), an employee who withdraws shares from the plan within three to five years pays income tax on the lower of their value at the time of award (or, for partnership shares, their cost) and their value at withdrawal. With similar exceptions, an employee who withdraws shares from the plan within three years of appropriation pays income tax on their value at withdrawal.
- An employer's plan may provide for reinvestment of up to £1,500 worth of dividends on plan shares per tax year, in which case such dividends are tax-free. Shares acquired by such reinvestment are known as *'dividend shares'*.
- The employer's costs of setting up and running the scheme are tax deductible as is the market value at acquisition of free and matching shares awarded to employees under the plan.

[*ITEPA 2003, ss 488–515, Sch 2; ITTOIA 2005, ss 392–396, 405–408, 770; CTA 2009, ss 983–998*].

For detailed coverage of the above, see Tolley's Income Tax under Share Related Employment Income and Exemptions.

Capital gains tax

Notwithstanding anything in the plan or the trust instrument, an employee (a *'participant'*) is treated for CGT purposes as absolutely entitled as against the plan trustees to any shares awarded to him under a SIP. [*TCGA 1992, s 238A, Sch 7D para 3*]. Shares are awarded to a participant when free or matching shares are appropriated to him or when partnership shares are acquired on his behalf. [*ITEPA 2003, Sch 2 para 5(1)*]. For the purpose of applying **58.2** SHARES AND SECURITIES — IDENTIFICATION RULES, plan shares (including free, matching, partnership and dividend shares) are treated as of a different class from any shares (otherwise of the same class) held by the participant outside the plan. [*TCGA 1992, Sch 7D para 4(1)*]. A company reconstruction is not normally treated as a disposal of plan shares (see Tolley's Income Tax for details and for a note on rights issues).

Shares cease to be subject to a plan when either the shares are withdrawn from the plan, or the participant ceases to be in relevant employment, or in certain circumstances the trustees dispose of shares in order to meet PAYE obligations. See Tolley's Income Tax for full details. Shares are withdrawn from the plan when on the direction of the participant (or, after his death, of his personal representatives) the plan trustees either transfer them (whether to the participant etc. or to another person) or dispose of them and similarly account for the proceeds, or when the participant etc. assigns, charges or otherwise disposes of his beneficial interest in them. [*ITEPA 2003, Sch 2 para 96*]. Shares which cease to be subject to a plan at any time are deemed to have been disposed of and immediately reacquired by the participant at their then market value, but no chargeable gain (or allowable loss) arises on the deemed disposal. [*TCGA 1992, Sch 7D para 5*].

Shares (but not securities or other rights) which have ceased to be subject to the plan but remain in the participant's beneficial ownership may be transferred without CGT consequences to an Individual Savings Account (see **23.30** EXEMPTIONS AND RELIEFS), subject to the annual subscription limits for such an Account (applied by reference to market value transferred) and provided the transfer is made within 90 days after the shares ceased to be subject to the plan.

Plan trustees

A gain (or loss) accruing in respect of shares to the trustees of a SIP is not a chargeable gain (or an allowable loss) if the shares:

- satisfy the requirements of *ITEPA 2003, Sch 2 Pt 4* as to the type of share that may be used in a plan (see Tolley's Income Tax); and
- are awarded to employees (see above), or acquired on their behalf as dividend shares, in accordance with the plan within the 'relevant period'; for these purposes, shares of a particular class acquired by the trustees are deemed to be awarded on a first in/first out basis (subject to special rules for shares acquired by qualifying transfer from an employee share ownership trust).

The '*relevant period*' depends on whether or not any of the shares in the company are 'readily convertible assets' within *ITEPA 2003, ss 701, 702* — broadly, whether or not they are capable of being readily converted into cash (see Tolley's Income Tax under Pay As You Earn). In determining whether shares are readily convertible assets, one may disregard any market for the shares which is created by virtue of the trustees acquiring shares for the plan and exists solely for the purposes of the plan. If any of the shares in the company are readily convertible assets at the time of acquisition by the trustees, the relevant period is the two years beginning with that time. If none of them are, the relevant period is extended to five years, but if within that period any of the shares in the company become readily convertible assets the relevant period ends no later than two years beginning with the date on which they did so.

A payment made by the employer company to the trustees sufficient to enable them to acquire a significant block of shares (at least 10% of the company's ordinary share capital) attracts an 'up-front' corporation tax deduction under *CTA 2009, s 989* (i.e. the deduction will not, as normal, be deferred until the shares are awarded to employees). The deduction will, however, be clawed back unless at least 30% of those shares are awarded within five years of acquisition by the trustees and all of the shares are awarded within ten years. As a consequence, the 'relevant period' above is extended to ten years in relation to shares acquired by virtue of such a payment.

[*TCGA 1992, Sch 7D para 2*].

If the plan trustees acquire shares from the trustees of an approved profit sharing scheme, the disposal by the scheme trustees and acquisition by the plan trustees are deemed to be made for such consideration as to secure that neither a gain nor a loss accrues on the disposal. For the purpose *only* of determining the relevant period as above, the shares are deemed to have been acquired by the plan trustees at the time they were acquired by the trustees of the profit sharing scheme. [*ITEPA 2003, Sch 7 para 86*].

A SIP *may* provide for free or matching shares to be forfeited in certain circumstances, i.e. if, other than for a permitted reason, the participant leaves the relevant employment within a specified forfeiture period of up to three years or withdraws the shares, or any related partnership shares, from the plan within that period. [*ITEPA 2003, Sch 2 para 32*]. Forfeited shares are deemed to have been disposed of by the participant and acquired by the plan trustees at their market value at the date of forfeiture, but no chargeable gain (or allowable loss) arises on the deemed disposal. [*TCGA 1992, Sch 7D para 7*].

Subject to their duty to act in accordance with the participant's directions, the plan trustees may dispose of some of the rights under a rights issue in respect of a participant's plan shares in order to raise funds to take up other rights under the issue. [*ITEPA 2003, Sch 2 para 77*]. Provided similar rights are conferred in respect of all ordinary shares in the company, the gain (or loss) arising on such a disposal is not a chargeable gain (or an allowable loss). [*TCGA 1992, Sch 7D para 8*].

For the purpose of applying **58.2** SHARES AND SECURITIES — IDENTIFICATION RULES,

- any shares transferred to the plan trustees by way of qualifying transfer from an employee share ownership trust (see Tolley's Income Tax) are treated as of a different class from any other shares (otherwise of the same class) held by the trustees; and
- any shares acquired by the trustees by virtue of a payment by the employer attracting an up-front corporation tax deduction under *CTA 2009, s 989* are treated as of a different class from any other shares (otherwise of the same class) held by the trustees.

[*TCGA 1992, Sch 7D para 4(2)–(6)*].

Rollover relief on disposals of shares to a SIP

[21.17] A form of capital gains rollover relief is available, as described below, on a disposal of shares, or an interest in shares, to the trustees of an approved share incentive plan and the reinvestment of the proceeds into a chargeable asset. The relief is not available where the person making the disposal is a company. [*TCGA 1992, s 236A, Sch 7C*].

Requirements for relief

The relief (see **21.18** below) applies only where all the following requirements are met.

(a) The person making the disposal (the claimant) obtains consideration for the disposal and, at any time in the '*acquisition period*' (the period of 6 months beginning with the date of disposal or, if later, the date on which the requirement at (d) below is first met) or under an unconditional contract made within that period, he either
   (i) applies the whole of the consideration in acquiring 'replacement assets', or
   (ii) applies part of the consideration as in (i) above, and the part *not* so applied is less than the gain on the disposal (whether all chargeable gain or not).

   A '*replacement asset*' is one which, immediately after the acquisition, is a 'chargeable asset' in relation to the claimant. The term includes an interest in an asset but does not include shares in, or debentures of, the company whose shares are the subject of the disposal or a company which, at the time of the acquisition, is in the same CGT group (see **26.2** GROUPS OF COMPANIES) as that company. A '*chargeable asset*' is broadly an asset the immediate disposal of which would give rise to a chargeable gain which would not be outside the charge to CGT as a result of the claimant's residence status or the terms of a double tax agreement.

(b) The plan must be a SIP at the time of the disposal.

(c) The shares disposed of
   – are not of a class listed on a recognised stock exchange (within *ITA 2007, s 1005* — see **57.27** SHARES AND SECURITIES),
   – are not shares in a company which is under the control (within *ITA 2007, s 995*) of a company (other than a close company or non-resident equivalent) whose shares are so listed,

   but otherwise meet the requirements of *ITEPA 2003, Sch 2 paras 25–33* (see Tolley's Income Tax) as to the types of share that may be awarded under a SIP. (This appears to be what the draftsman intended, and is confirmed by HMRC Capital Gains Manual CG61973, though the wording of the legislation is ambiguous.)

(d) At some time in the '*entitlement period*' (the period of 12 months beginning with the date of disposal), the plan trustees hold (for the beneficiaries) shares in the company concerned that constitute at least 10% of ordinary share capital and carry rights to at least 10% of distributable profits and of distributable assets on a winding-up. Shares appropriated under the plan, or acquired on a beneficiary's behalf, but still subject to the plan count towards this requirement.

(e) At no time in the '*proscribed period*' (the period beginning with the date of disposal and ending with the date of acquisition of the replacement asset or, if later, the date on which the requirement at (d) above is first met) are there any unauthorised arrangements under which the claimant (or a person connected with him — see **17** CONNECTED PERSONS) may be entitled to acquire (directly or indirectly) from the plan trustees any shares (or an interest in or right deriving from any shares). For this purpose, all arrangements are unauthorised unless they only allow shares to be appropriated to or acquired on behalf of an individual under the plan.

[*TCGA 1992, Sch 7C paras 1–4, 8*].

Form of relief

[21.18] Where the requirements at **21.17** are met, the person making the disposal may make a claim for rollover relief under these provisions, such claim to be made within the two years beginning with the acquisition.

Where the whole of the consideration was reinvested (as in **21.17**(a)(i) above), the effect of the claim is that for CGT purposes the disposal is deemed to have been made for such consideration (if it would otherwise be greater) as would result in no gain and no loss. The acquisition cost of the replacement asset is reduced by the excess of the actual consideration over the deemed consideration.

Where part only of the consideration was reinvested (as in **21.17**(a)(ii) above), the effect of the claim is that for CGT purposes the gain on the disposal is reduced to the amount of consideration not reinvested. The acquisition cost of the replacement asset is reduced by the amount by which the gain is reduced.

The other parties to the disposal and acquisition are not affected by a claim for relief. Any provision of *TCGA 1992* fixing deemed consideration for a disposal or acquisition is applied before the above adjustments are made.

[*TCGA 1992, Sch 7C para 5*].

Where a claim relates to more than one replacement asset, the relief is to be allocated between them on a just and reasonable basis (HMRC Capital Gains Manual CG61978).

Special rules where replacement asset is a dwelling-house

[21.19] Special rules may apply where:

- a rollover relief claim is made under **21.18** above,
- any replacement asset (as in **21.17**(a) above) is a dwelling-house, part of a dwelling-house or land, and,
- as is required, that asset was a chargeable asset in relation to the claimant immediately after the acquisition.

The said rules apply where the property later comes within the private residence exemption (see **47** PRIVATE RESIDENCES) (or would do if it were disposed of) by reference to the claimant or the claimant's spouse or civil partner (whether as an individual taxpayer or as a person entitled to occupy the property under the terms of a settlement).

If there is a time after the acquisition and *before* the making of the rollover relief claim when the dwelling-house etc. would fall within the private residence exemption, it is treated as if it had not been a chargeable asset in relation to the claimant immediately after the acquisition, with the result that the rollover relief claim fails. If, instead, there is a time *after* the making of the rollover relief claim when the dwelling-house etc. would fall within the private residence exemption, it is similarly treated, but in this case the gain rolled over is treated as not having accrued until that time (or until the earliest of such times if there is more than one).

Similar rules apply where the replacement asset is an option to acquire (or to acquire an interest in) a dwelling-house etc., and the option is exercised.

[*TCGA 1992, Sch 7C para 6*].

Special rules where replacement asset is EIS shares

[21.20] Special rules apply where:

- a rollover relief claim is made under **21.18** above;
- any replacement asset (as in **21.17**(a) above) is shares;
- that asset was a chargeable asset in relation to the claimant immediately after the acquisition; and
- the claimant makes a claim for Enterprise Investment Scheme (EIS) income tax relief in respect of the shares (see **22.3** ENTERPRISE INVESTMENT SCHEME).

Regardless of whether the EIS relief claim is made before or after the rollover relief claim, the shares are treated if they had not been a chargeable asset in relation to the claimant immediately after the acquisition, with the result that the rollover relief claim fails (and any relief already given is treated as if never due).

[*TCGA 1992, Sch 7C para 7*].

Enterprise management incentives

[21.21] 'Small higher risk' trading companies are able to grant options over shares worth (at time of grant) up to £250,000 to eligible employees without income tax consequences (except to the extent that the option is to acquire shares at less than their market value at time of grant). The total value of shares in respect of which unexercised options exist must not exceed £3 million. The company may be quoted or unquoted but must be an independent company trading or preparing to trade and whose gross assets do not exceed £30 million. The company must have a permanent establishment in the UK (or be the parent company of a company with such a permanent establishment). The company (or, where the company is a parent company, it and its subsidiaries) must have no more than the equivalent of 250 full-time employees. A company carrying on certain specified activities deemed to be lower risk activities does not qualify.

Broadly, employees are eligible if they are employed by the company for at least 25 hours per week or, if less, at least 75% of their total working time, and they control no more than 30% of the company's ordinary share capital. Certain permitted periods of absence from work do not result in an employee becoming ineligible. These include illness, reasonable holidays and any time in the period

19 March 2020 to 5 April 2022 inclusive during which the employee is not required to work for reasons connected with coronavirus (COVID-19) (for example, where the employee is furloughed). Companies must give notification to HMRC on or before 6 July following the tax year in which the option is granted. For options granted before 6 April 2024, the company had to notify HMRC within 92 days after an option was granted.

[*ITEPA 2003, ss 527–541, Sch 5; FA 2020, s 107; FA 2021, s 24; F(No 2)A 2023, s 17; FA 2024, s 13; SI 2001 No 3799*]. For full details, see Tolley's Income Tax under Share-Related Employment Income and Exemptions.

The enterprise management incentive scheme was subject to EU state aid approval. The original approval expired on 6 April 2018 and there was a delay before the European Commission issued a new approval. The new approval was issued on 15 May 2018 and applied until the end of the Brexit implementation period (European Commission Press Release 15 May 2018).

Capital gains tax

On a disposal of shares acquired under an option satisfying the requirements of the enterprise management incentives (EMI) scheme (hereafter referred to as a '*qualifying option*'), where *TCGA 1992, s 144ZA* (see **7.7** ASSETS) applies, the cost of acquisition of the shares for CGT purposes (within *TCGA 1992, s 38(1)(a)* — see **16.12**(a) COMPUTATION OF GAINS AND LOSSES) consists of the aggregate of:

- (by virtue of *TCGA 1992, ss 119A, 120(2)(4)* — see **21.6** above) any amount counting as employment income under *ITEPA 2003, s 476* after the deductions mentioned at **21.6** above, which might be the case if the option was to acquire shares at less than their market value at the time of grant or if a disqualifying event (see below) occurred while the option remained unexercised,
- the consideration given for the shares acquired on the exercise of the option, and
- any consideration given for the option.

The provisions at **21.7** above (as regards release of options) and **21.9** above apply to options under an EMI scheme and to shares acquired under such options. Those at **21.8** above are disapplied (see Tolley's Income Tax).

Chargeable gains arising on EMI shares are eligible for business asset disposal relief (formerly entrepreneurs' relief) — see **9.10**.

Rights issues

If there is a rights issue affecting qualifying shares, the share reorganisation rules of *TCGA 1992, ss 127–130* (see **57.2** SHARES AND SECURITIES) are disapplied, with the result that the rights shares are treated as a separate acquisition and are not qualifying shares.

[*TCGA 1992, Sch 7D paras 14, 16*].

Identification rules

For an election to modify the normal rules in a case where EMI scheme shares are acquired on the same day as other shares in the same company, see 58.2 SHARES AND SECURITIES — IDENTIFICATION RULES.

Other tax-advantaged share option schemes

[21.22] The following apply generally to other tax-advantaged share option schemes (see 21.23 onwards below).

Assignment, release or abandonment of tax-advantaged employee share option

The same comments apply as for unapproved options at 21.7 above.

Identification rules

For an election to modify the normal rules in a case where approved share option scheme shares are acquired on the same day as other shares in the same company, see 58.2 SHARES AND SECURITIES — IDENTIFICATION RULES.

Save as you earn (SAYE) share option schemes

[21.23] Under a SAYE share option scheme, a company grants to an employee of itself or its group an option to acquire ordinary shares in the company at a specified price (the option price) at a specified future date. No income tax charge arises on either the grant of the option or, on exercise of the option, on any excess of the then value of the shares over the option price. The option price must not be less than 80% of the market value of shares of the same class at the time the option is granted. The scheme is linked to an approved certified contractual savings (CCS) scheme with a bank, building society or other authorised provider, to which the employee makes regular contributions by deduction from salary and to which a tax-free bonus is added at maturity (the bonus date), the funds then being used to purchase the agreed number of shares at the option price (though the funds may alternatively be repaid to the employee if he so chooses, the option being allowed to lapse). Savings contracts of between three years and five years are available. Aggregate monthly contributions to all such schemes to which an employee contributes at any one time cannot exceed £500, and the minimum monthly contribution set for any scheme must not exceed £10 (although monthly contributions as low as £5 are permitted).

Other than in specified circumstances, the option cannot be exercised before the bonus date, nor can it be exercised, except in the case of death (for which special rules apply), more than six months after that date. The circumstances under which early exercise may be permitted include *inter alia* (i) the takeover of the company whose shares are scheme shares, (ii) where the eligible employment is in a subsidiary company, the company which established the scheme ceasing to have control of that subsidiary, and (iii) the transfer (to a person other than a subsidiary or associated company) of the business (or part thereof) to which the employment relates. In each case, the option can be exercised within six months of the change but if, in any of these three instances, the option is thus exercised within three years of its being granted, the income tax exemption on exercise is lost and a charge may arise under *ITEPA 2003, s 476* (see **21.6** above); the income tax exemption on the *grant* of the option does, however, continue to apply.

The scheme *must* be available on similar terms (subject to any variations by reference to salary level, period of service etc.) to all employees and full-time directors within *ITEPA 2003, s 15* and with a stipulated minimum period of service, which cannot be more than five years. It *may* be made available to other employees and directors.

[*ITEPA 2003, ss 516–520, Sch 3*].

See Tolley's Income Tax for the full provisions and conditions.

Capital gains tax

Other than where early exercise of the option results in the loss of the income tax exemption as mentioned above (in which case see **21.6** above), the provisions of *TCGA 1992, s 17* (see **39.1** MARKET VALUE) are specifically disapplied both in calculating the CGT acquisition cost of the shares to the employee and for the purposes of any corresponding disposal to him. Those provisions are likewise disapplied where an option is exercised following the death of the employee in accordance with a rule included in the scheme by virtue of *ITEPA 2003, Sch 3 para 32*. [*TCGA 1992, Sch 7D para 10*].

On a disposal of the shares by the employee, his allowable expenditure consists of the actual consideration given on the exercise of the option, i.e. the amount saved plus the tax-free bonus (plus, if applicable, any consideration given for the option itself — see **21.3** above). The date of acquisition of the shares for CGT purposes is the date the option is exercised.

Shares acquired through an approved SAYE share option scheme may be transferred without CGT consequences to an Individual Savings Account (see **23.30** EXEMPTIONS AND RELIEFS), subject to the annual subscription limits (applied by reference to market value transferred) and provided the transfer is made within 90 days after the option is exercised.

Company share option plan (CSOP) schemes

[21.24] Unlike SAYE share option schemes and profit sharing schemes, company share option plans are not required to be open to all employees, and are more likely to be used to reward directors and key employees.

Under a CSOP scheme, a company grants to an employee of itself or its group an option to acquire ordinary shares in the company at a specified price (the option price) at a specified future date. The option price should not be less than the market value of the shares at the time of the grant. Normally, no income tax charge arises on either the grant of the option or, on exercise of the option, on any excess of the then value of the shares over the option price. In the exceptional case where the aggregate of the option price and any amount paid for the option itself is less than the market value of the shares at the time of the grant, the amount of the difference counts as employment income for the tax year in which the option is granted. The normal tax exemption on *exercise* of the option does not apply if the scheme is no longer a tax-advantaged scheme at the time of exercise or if the option is exercised less than three years or more than ten years after it was granted. There is an exception for options exercised within three years of grant but no later than six months after the individual ceases to be a qualifying employee of the scheme organiser (or of a constituent company in a group scheme) because of injury, disability, redundancy or retirement. Special rules apply in cases of death.

Only full-time directors (generally taken to mean those working at least 25 hours per week) are eligible. Part-time employees (other than directors) may be included. Where the company is a close company, employees and directors with material interests are excluded.

It is a condition of approval that the aggregate market value (at the time of grant) of shares over which an individual may hold unexercised rights under the scheme (and any other CSOP scheme established by the company or an associated company) must at no time exceed £60,000 (£30,000 for share options granted before 6 April 2023).

[*ITEPA 2003, ss 521–526, Sch 4; F(No 2)A 2023, s 16*].

See Tolley's Income Tax for the full provisions and conditions.

Capital gains tax

Where the income tax exemption on exercise of the option applies (see above), the provisions of *TCGA 1992, s 17* (see **39.1** MARKET VALUE) are specifically disapplied both in calculating the CGT acquisition cost of the shares to the employee and for the purposes of any corresponding disposal to him. Those provisions are likewise disapplied where an option is exercised following the death of the employee in accordance with a rule included in the scheme by virtue of *ITEPA 2003, Sch 4 para 25*. [*TCGA 1992, Sch 7D para 13*].

Where, exceptionally, an income tax liability arises on the grant of the option (due to the option price being discounted — see above), the amount counted as employment income is included in the cost of acquisition of the shares for CGT purposes. This applies whether or not the exercise is in accordance with the provisions of the scheme and whether or not the scheme is still tax-advantaged at the time of the exercise. [*TCGA 1992, s 120(2)(6)(c), Sch 7D para 12*].

Thus, on a disposal of the shares by the employee, his allowable expenditure within *TCGA 1992, s 38(1)(a)* (see **16.12**(a) COMPUTATION OF GAINS AND LOSSES) consists of:

- the actual consideration given on the exercise of the option,
- any consideration given for the option itself, and
- the amount, if any, counting as employment income.

The date of acquisition of the shares for CGT purposes is the date the option is exercised. Any deemed expenditure corresponding to an amount chargeable to income tax is also deemed to have been incurred on that date.

Employee shareholder shares

[21.25] A special employment status, known as 'employee shareholder' status, was introduced by *Growth and Infrastructure Act 2013, s 31*. Employee shareholders are issued or allotted at least £2,000 worth of shares in consideration of an employee shareholder agreement. Subject to conditions, an income tax relief and capital gains tax exemption apply to the shares, as described below, but only to shares received through the adoption of employee shareholder status on or after 1 September 2013 but before December 2016 (see below). [*FA 2013, Sch 23 para 38; SI 2013 No 1755; FA 2017, ss 12–14*].

After only being in effect for just over three years, the income tax and capital gains tax reliefs in relation to employee shareholder status were withdrawn.

Agreements entered into before 1 December 2016, or before 2 December 2016 where independent advice was received on 23 November 2016 before 1:30 pm, retain their tax benefits, which are described below.

Charge to income tax — shares acquired prior to December 2016

The following income tax treatment applies to shares acquired before 1 December 2016 (or before 2 December 2016 where independent advice was received by the employee on 23 November 2016 before 1:30 pm). For employee shareholder shares issued after that date, an amount equal to the market value of shares is treated as earnings i.e. there is no deemed payment (see below).

When shares ('*employee shareholder shares*') with a market value of at least £2,000 are acquired by an employee in consideration of an 'employee shareholder agreement', an amount is treated as earnings from the employment, in respect of the acquisition of the shares, for the tax year in which they are acquired. The amount is found by applying a formula, MV – P where:

MV = the market value of the shares (see below) on the day on which they are acquired; and
P = the payment (if any) that the employee is treated as having made for the shares as set out below.

If P exceeds MV, the amount is nil.

Where the above applies, no other sums can constitute earnings from the employment in respect of the acquisition of the employee shareholder shares.

Market value is determined as for capital gains purposes.

An '*employee shareholder agreement*' means an agreement by virtue of which an employee is an employee shareholder (see *Employment Rights Act 1996, s 205A(1)(a)–(d)*). Shares are acquired by an employee for these purposes if the employee becomes beneficially entitled to them; they are acquired at the time when the employee becomes so entitled.

Deemed payment for the shares

Provided that, as above, shares with a market value of at least £2,000 are acquired by an employee in consideration of an employee shareholder agreement, the employee is treated, for income tax purposes, as having made a payment for those shares as follows. Where all the shares acquired in consideration of the agreement are acquired on the same day, the employee is treated as having made on that day a payment of £2,000 for those shares. Where shares are acquired by the employee in consideration of the agreement on more than one day, with shares with a market value of at least £2,000 acquired on the first of those days, the employee is treated as having made, on the first of those days, a payment of £2,000 for the shares acquired on that day. Where shares with a value in excess of £2,000 are acquired, the payment which the employee is treated as having made for each share is determined on a pro rata basis.

Except as provided above, the employee is to be treated for income tax purposes as having given no consideration for shares acquired in consideration of the employee shareholder agreement.

See Tolley's Income Tax for the full provisions and conditions.

[*ITEPA 2003, ss 226A–226D; FA 2017, s 12*].

Capital gains tax — shares acquired prior to December 2016

The capital gains tax exemption described below applies only to shares acquired before 1 December 2016 (or before 2 December 2016 where independent advice was received by the employee on 23 November 2016 before 1:30 pm).

Subject to the lifetime limit below, gains on 'exempt' employee shareholder shares are not chargeable gains when the shares are disposed of by the person who acquired them under the employee shareholder agreement. An employee shareholder share acquired in consideration of an employee shareholder agreement is '*exempt*' if, immediately after its acquisition, the total value of employee shareholder shares, in the employer company or an 'associated company', which have been acquired by the employee does not exceed £50,000. For these purposes, the value of a share at any time is its unrestricted market value at the time when it was acquired by the employee. Where shares acquired on a particular day take an employee over the £50,000 limit, an apportionment is made to treat the appropriate proportion up to the limit (rounded down to the nearest share) as acquired before the remainder (and so as exempt shares).

For these purposes, a company is an associated company of another if one has control of the other or both are under the control of the same person(s). 'Control' is construed in accordance with *CTA 2010, ss 450, 451*. If a company controls another when an employee shareholder agreement is entered into with an employee, this is treated as continuing to be the case when any subsequent employee shareholder agreement is entered into with that same employee. However, this does not apply if:

- one of the two companies has been dissolved;
- two years have passed since the date of dissolution; and
- the employee has not, at any time in that two-year period, been engaged in any office or employment (including engagement under a contract for services) with any company which is an associated company of the dissolved company.

An employee shareholder share is not exempt if:

- on the date on which the share is acquired or at any time in the twelve months ending on that date, the employee has (or has had) a 'material interest' in the employer company or a parent undertaking (within *Companies Act 2006, s 1162*) of the employer company; or
- on the date on which the share is acquired, the employee is connected (within **17** CONNECTED PERSONS) with an individual who has a material interest in the employer company or a parent undertaking or who has had such an interest at any time in the twelve months ending on that date.

For these purposes, an individual (A) has a '*material interest*' in a company if at least 25% of the voting rights are exercisable by A, or by persons connected with A, or by A and persons connected with A together. If the company is a close company, or would be but for being a non-UK resident company or a quoted company, A has a material interest in it if A, or persons connected with A, or A and persons connected with A together, are entitled to at least 25% of the assets available for distribution among the participators in a winding-up or in any other circumstances. A is *treated* as having a material interest in a company at any time if A, or persons connected with A, or A and persons connected with A together, have an entitlement to acquire such rights as would (together with any existing rights) give A a material interest in the company. Any arrangements in place (as widely defined and to which the employer company or a parent undertaking is also party) to acquire such rights must also be taken into account.

Where an individual has acquired shares in consideration of entering into an employee shareholder agreement, he is not regarded as disposing of an asset by reason of ceasing to have, or not acquiring, the rights mentioned in *Employment Rights Act 1996, s 205A* as a result of entering into the agreement.

The above exemption does not apply to gains arising on or after 6 April 2016 where the proceeds of the disposal constitute a disguised investment management fee within *ITA 2007, s 809EZA(3)* or carried interest within *ITA 2007, s 809EZC* (see **44.21** PARTNERSHIPS).

Lifetime limit

A lifetime limit of gains of £100,000 applies to disposals of exempt employee shareholder shares acquired under employee shareholder agreements entered into on or after 17 March 2016. Gains falling partly within the limit are exempt to the extent that they do not exceed the unused balance of the limit. Gains on disposals of shares acquired under agreements entered into before that date do not count in applying the limit.

See **40.4** MARRIED PERSONS AND CIVIL PARTNERS for transfers of exempt employee shareholder shares between spouses or civil partners and the effect of the lifetime limit.

Identification rules

The normal identification rules (see **58.2** SHARES AND SECURITIES — IDENTIFICATION RULES) are each disapplied as regards exempt employee shareholder shares. Where an employee holds shares of the same class in a company and only some of those shares are exempt employee shareholder shares, on a disposal of a part of that holding the employee may choose what proportion of the shares disposed of are to be treated as exempt employee shareholder shares (up to the number of such shares in the holding) and the consideration received is apportioned accordingly.

Reorganisations etc.

TCGA 1992, s 127 (reorganisations — see **57.2** SHARES AND SECURITIES) does not apply to exempt employee shareholder shares (including that section as applied by *TCGA 1992, ss 135, 136* (share exchanges and reconstructions — see **57.5**, **57.7** SHARES AND SECURITIES)). Where, however, there is a disposal of exempt employee shareholder shares on a reorganisation on or after 17 March 2016, the taxpayer is treated as disposing of the shares for a consideration calculated as follows.

(1) If the whole of the '*notional gain*' (i.e. the gain that would arise on the disposal if the shares were disposed of at market value) would be a chargeable gain because the taxpayer's lifetime limit has been used against previous disposals, the deemed consideration is the amount that would give rise to neither a gain nor a loss.

(2) If part (but not all) of the notional gain would be a chargeable gain as a result of the lifetime limit, the deemed consideration is the maximum amount (not exceeding market value) that would secure that no chargeable gain arises.

(3) If none of the notional gain would be a chargeable gain, the deemed consideration is the market value.

(4) If there would be no notional gain, the deemed consideration is the amount that would give rise to neither a gain nor a loss.

[*TCGA 1992, ss 236B–236G; FA 2016, s 88(2)(3)–(6)(10), s 89; FA 2017, s 13; SI 2013 No 1755*].

Example

On 15 May 2016, Sarah acquires 1,000 shares with a market value of £5,000 by way of an Employee Shareholder Agreement. The shares qualify as employee shareholder shares.

An amount of £3,000 (£5,000 less £2,000 deemed payment) is treated as earnings on the day on which she acquires them.

Sarah disposes of the shares when the market value is £10,000. There is no chargeable gain arising on the shares.

If Sarah had another 1,000 shares in the company and she disposed of these shares together with her qualifying employee shareholder shares for £30,000, then the proceeds could reasonably be divided as £15,000 for each of the employee shareholder shares and Sarah's other non-qualifying shareholding.

Priority allocations in public share offers

[21.26] If a benefit derived by an employee from a priority allocation of shares in a public offer is exempted from income tax by *ITEPA 2003, ss 542* or *544* (see Tolley's Income Tax under Employment Income), the usual MARKET VALUE (**39**) rules do not apply and the allowable expenditure for CGT on a disposal of the shares is the consideration given. [*TCGA 1992, s 149C*].

Key points concerning employee share schemes

[21.27] Points to consider are as follows.

- Generally, where employees receive remuneration from employment by means of shares or share options the value received is taxable as income deriving from that employment and is usually subject to national insurance as well.
- The meaning of 'shares' is quite wide and includes securities.
- Where the receipt of shares has been subjected to income tax, the amount of tax is generally taken into account in calculating the base cost for capital gains tax purposes.
- There are a number of tax-advantaged schemes which do not attract an income tax charge. As a result shares acquired under such arrangements will have a lower base cost.
- For capital gains tax purposes shares acquired on the same day are treated as a single acquisition, but, where some of the shares are acquired under an approved scheme and others are not, an election can be made to treat those shares as a separate acquisition. This enables shares disposed of to be identified first with those with a higher base cost.
- In some circumstances shares acquired by employees have restrictions attached to them which depress the market value and hence the income tax charge. If those restrictions are subsequently lifted and the value of the shares is increased, the proportionate increase in value can be applied to the gain on disposal and that proportion can be chargeable to income tax and national insurance rather than capital gains tax.
- However, it is possible to avoid this by making an election to be taxed on the unrestricted value when the shares are acquired. The election is made jointly with the employer and must be made within 14 days of acquiring the shares, although the election is not submitted to HMRC.

22

Enterprise Investment Scheme

Cross-references. See 21.20 EMPLOYEE SHARE SCHEMES for restriction on rollover relief arising from disposal of shares to an approved share incentive plan where replacement asset is shares and a claim for EIS income tax relief is made; 54 SEED ENTERPRISE INVESTMENT SCHEME; 57 SHARES AND SECURITIES; 64 VENTURE CAPITAL TRUSTS.

Simon's Taxes. See E3.185–E3.1123.

Introduction to the enterprise investment scheme

[22.1] The Enterprise Investment Scheme (EIS) offers income tax relief to a qualifying individual to whom shares in a qualifying company (see 22.7 below) have been issued by subscription. The company concerned must use the money raised within the specified time limit for a qualifying business activity (see 22.10 below).

For more detailed coverage of the income tax provisions, see Tolley's Income Tax under Enterprise Investment Scheme. As regards both income tax and CGT, see also HMRC Venture Capital Schemes Manual VCM10010 onwards.

Gains on disposal of shares on which EIS income tax relief has been given are not chargeable gains if the disposal is made after the end of a specified period. The capital gains tax exemption is described at **22.15** below. See **22.16** below for capital gains deferral relief.

State aid information

Before Brexit, the EIS fell within the EU's State aid rules. With effect from 1 January 2021, those rules are disapplied in the UK (subject to limited exceptions under the Northern Ireland Protocol). HMRC could give a company, in respect of whose shares EIS income tax relief had been given or could be given in future, a notice requiring it to provide specified information for the purpose of complying with the UK's EU State aid obligations. See *FA 2016, ss 180–182, Sch 24.*

Knowledge-intensive funds

[22.2] EIS relief is also available where shares are subscribed for by a nominee for the individual claiming relief, including the managers of an investment fund approved by HMRC for this purpose (an '*approved fund*'). The fund must be a knowledge-intensive fund, i.e. one established for the purpose of investing wholly, or substantially wholly, in knowledge-intensive companies (see **22.5** below under 'The maximum risk finance investment at the issue date requirement').

With regard to an approved fund closed for the acceptance of further investments, the provisions at **22.12** below (dealing with the form and attribution of relief) apply as if the eligible shares were issued at the time at which the fund was closed. This extends to an individual claiming relief as if some or all of the shares were issued in the tax year preceding that in which the fund is closed.

The amount subscribed on behalf of the individual for eligible shares must be not less than 50% of the individual's investment in the fund within 12 months after the closure of the fund and not less than 90% within 24 months. Within that 24-month period, at least 80% of the individual's investment in the fund must be represented by shares in companies which are knowledge-intensive companies at the time the shares are issued. The managers must also have fulfilled the reporting conditions required by HMRC.

[*ITA 2007, ss 250(1), 251(1)–(2A); FA 2020, s 36*].

Conditions for income tax relief

[22.3] An individual investor is eligible for EIS income tax relief in respect of an amount invested by him on his own behalf for an issue of shares in a company if:

(a) the risk-to-capital condition is met (see **22.4** below);
(b) the shares are issued to the investor;
(c) the general requirements at **22.5** below are met in respect of the shares;
(d) the investor is a 'qualifying investor' (see **22.6** below) in relation to the shares; and

(e) the company issuing the shares is a 'qualifying company' (see **22.7** below) in relation to the shares.

The EIS applies to shares issued before 6 April 2035 but this date may be amended by the Treasury via statutory instrument.

[*ITA 2007, s 157(1)(1A); FA 2024, s 11*].

Bare trustees and nominees

Relief is available where shares which satisfy the requirement at **22.5**(i) below are held on a bare trust for two or more beneficiaries as if each beneficiary had subscribed as an individual for all of those shares, and as if the amount subscribed by each was the total subscribed divided by the number of beneficiaries. [*ITA 2007, s 250(2)(3)*]. See **22.2** above as regards nominees, including approved funds.

The risk-to-capital condition

[22.4] The risk-to-capital condition mentioned at **22.3** above is an overarching condition which is met if, having regard to all existing circumstances at the time of issue of the EIS shares, it would be reasonable to conclude that:

- the issuing company has objectives to grow and develop its trade in the long term; and
- there is a significant risk of loss of capital of an amount greater than the net investment return, i.e. the net return to investors (whether by way of income or capital growth) taking into account the value of EIS relief. The risk and the return is to be determined with reference to the investors in general, and a loss of capital means a loss of at least part of the amounts subscribed for the shares by the investors.

[*ITA 2007, s 157A*].

The intention is to prevent tax-relieved investment in companies whose activities are geared towards preservation of investors' capital rather than the company's long-term growth and development. *ITA 2007, s 157A(3)* provides an illustrative, non-exhaustive list of the types of circumstance that may be taken into account in reaching any conclusion. For guidance on the condition, with examples, see HMRC Venture Capital Schemes Manual VCM8500–8560.

The risk-to-capital condition (under the EIS or SEIS scheme) was held to be satisfied in *Inferno Films Ltd v HMRC* FTT, [2022] UKFTT 141 (TC) and *Cry Me a River Ltd v HMRC* FTT, [2022] UKFTT 182 (TC) in which funds were raised to make, develop and sell films. The condition was also satisfied in *Coconut Animated Island Ltd v HMRC* FTT, [2022] UKFTT 303 (TC) and *Hoopla Animation Ltd (formerly known as Daisy Boo and Monkey Too Ltd) v HMRC* FTT, [2023] UKFTT 24 (TC) but the companies' appeals against HMRC's decision not to issue compliance certificates were dismissed because there were 'disqualifying arrangements' (see **22.5** below).

The condition was held not to be met in *Valyrian Bloodstock Ltd v HMRC* FTT, [2022] UKFTT 306 (TC). The company was established to carry on a business of buying racehorses at six to twelve months old and selling at three years plus (known as 'pinhooking'). The only contemporaneous evidence (the company's website) indicated that there was no intention to grow and develop the business, but instead, the company was a one-off investment for a three-year term which would be wound up after the last horse was sold.

General requirements

[22.5] The general requirements mentioned at **22.3**(c) above are as follows.

The shares requirement

The shares must:

(i) be ordinary shares which do not, at any time during 'period B', carry (subject to below) any present or future preferential right to dividends or to assets on a winding-up or any present or future right to be redeemed; and
(ii) unless they are 'bonus shares', be subscribed for wholly in cash and be fully paid up at the time of issue.

Shares are, however, permitted to carry a preferential right to dividends provided the amount and timing of the dividends do not depend on a decision of the company, the shareholder or any other person and provided the dividends are not cumulative. Shares with a preferential right to dividends were held not to qualify for this exemption in *Foojit Ltd v HMRC* UT, [2021] STC 262.

For the purposes of (i) above, '*period B*' is the three years beginning with the date of issue. If the company satisfied the purpose of the issue requirement below by virtue of (a) or (c) below and the trade had not yet commenced on the issue date, period B is the period from date of issue to immediately before the third anniversary of commencement. (In determining for this purpose the time at which a qualifying trade begins to be carried on by any 'qualifying 90% subsidiary' (see **22.9** below) of a company, any carrying on of the trade etc. by it before it became such a subsidiary is disregarded.)

For the purposes of (ii) above, '*bonus shares*' are shares issued otherwise than for payment (whether in cash or otherwise). Shares are not fully paid up if there is any undertaking to pay cash to any person at a later date in respect of the acquisition.

[*ITA 2007, ss 159(3), 173, 256, 257(1)*].

In *Flix Innovations Ltd v HMRC* UT, [2016] STC 2206, ordinary shares which carried small preferential rights to a return of capital on a winding-up were held not to qualify for relief.

Shares are not issued until the company's register of members has been completed (*National Westminster Bank plc v CIR; Barclays Bank plc v CIR* HL 1994, 67 TC 1.

The maximum amount raised annually through risk finance investments requirement

The total amount of 'relevant investments' (see below) made in the issuing company in the 12 months ending with the date of issue must not exceed:

(1) if the company is a knowledge-intensive company at that date, £10 million; and
(2) in any other case, £5 million.

See below for meaning of knowledge-intensive company, and note the special rule there for companies that have traded for less than three years before issuing the EIS shares.

Prior to the above taking effect the limit is £5 million in all cases.

The following also count towards this limit:

(a) any relevant investment in a 51% subsidiary (within *CTA 2010, Pt 24 Ch 3*) of the issuing company (including any made before it became a 51% subsidiary but not any made after it last ceased to be one);
(b) any relevant investment made in any company to the extent that the money raised by the investment has been employed for the purposes of a trade (as widely defined) carried on by another company that has at any time in the said 12-month period been a 51% subsidiary of the issuing company (disregarding any money so employed after it last ceased to be such a subsidiary); and
(c) any other relevant investment made in any company to the extent that the money raised has been employed for the purposes of a trade (as widely defined), and within that 12-month period, but after the investment was made, the trade (or a part of it) was transferred to the issuing company, a 51% subsidiary or a partnership of which the issuing company or a 51% subsidiary is a member (but disregarding trades transferred after a 51% subsidiary in question last ceased to be such a subsidiary).

[*ITA 2007, s 173A(1)–(2B)(6)(7)*].

Relevant investment

For the purposes of the EIS requirements, '*relevant investments*' comprise:

(I) investments (of any kind) made by a VENTURE CAPITAL TRUST (VCT) (**64**);
(II) money subscribed for shares issued under the EIS or the SEED ENTERPRISE INVESTMENT SCHEME (SEIS) (**54**);
(III) investments made under the SOCIAL INVESTMENT RELIEF (**59**) scheme; and
(IV) any other investment made which is aid received by the company pursuant to a measure approved by the EC before Brexit IP completion day (11pm on 31 December 2020) as compatible with Article 107 of the Treaty on the Functioning of the European Union in accordance with the principles laid down in the European Commission's Guidelines on State aid (as they had effect immediately before 11pm on 31 December 2020 (IP completion day)) to promote risk finance investment.

As regards (II) above, shares are treated as having been issued under the EIS or SEIS if at any time the investee company provides an EIS compliance statement (see **22.13** below) or SEIS equivalent in respect of those shares; an investment is regarded as made when the shares are issued. As regards (III) above, an investment is treated as made under the social investment relief scheme if at any time the investee company provides a compliance statement as in **59.4** SOCIAL INVESTMENT RELIEF; *ITA 2007, s 257KB* (see **59.1** SOCIAL INVESTMENT RELIEF) applies in determining when such an investment is made.

[*ITA 2007, s 173A(3)–(5); SI 2020 No 1499*].

The maximum risk finance investments at the issue date requirement

The total amount of 'relevant investments' (see above) made in the issuing company on or before the date the EIS shares are issued must not exceed £12 million or, if the company is a 'knowledge-intensive company' (see below) at the time the shares are issued, £20 million. Relevant investments of the kind in (a)–(c) above also count towards these limits, but disregarding references there to a 12-month period and instead taking into account all times before the issue date. [*ITA 2007, s 173AA*].

Knowledge-intensive companies

A '*knowledge-intensive company*' is broadly a company whose costs of research and development or innovation are at least 15% of its operating costs in at least one of the years comprising the 'relevant three-year period' or at least 10% of its operating costs in each of those years, and which meets at least one of the two conditions below. The '*relevant three-year period*' is normally the three years ending immediately before the beginning of the last accounts filing period. However, if the last accounts filing period ends more than 12 months before the issue date of the EIS shares in question, the relevant three-year period is the three years ending 12 months before the issue date. A company's operating costs are defined by reference to the items recognised as expenses in its profit and loss account. The conditions to be met are that:

- the company has created, is creating or is intending to create, intellectual property (the '*innovation condition*'); or
- the company's full-time employees with a relevant Masters or higher degree who are engaged in research and development or innovation comprise at least 20% of the total of its full-time employees (the '*skilled employee condition*'). The skilled employee condition must continue to be met throughout period B (subject to a let-out for companies entering administration or receivership).

In order to meet the innovation condition, the issuing company must be engaged in intellectual property creation at the time the EIS shares are issued, and it must be reasonable to assume that, within ten years after the issue, the exploitation of its intellectual property, or business which results from new or improved products, processes or services utilising its intellectual property, will form the greater part of its business. A company is engaged in intellectual property creation if intellectual property is being created by the company, or has been created by it within the previous three years; or the company is taking (or preparing to take) steps in order that intellectual property will be created by it; or the company demonstrates via an independent expert's report that it is reasonable to assume it will create intellectual property in the foreseeable future. Intellectual property is taken into account only if the whole or greater part (in terms of value) of it is created by the company and it is created in circumstances in which the right to exploit it vests in the company (whether alone or jointly with others).

If the issuing company is a parent company, the above rules are appropriately modified to also take account of its 'qualifying subsidiaries' (see **22.8** below).

[*ITA 2007, s 252A*].

Companies that have traded for less than three years

If the issuing company commenced trading less than three years before the date the EIS shares are issued, the above definition is modified for the purposes of **22.12**(i)–(iii) below (annual maximum on which an individual may obtain relief) and (1) and (2) above ('maximum amount raised annually through risk finance investments' requirement). The '*relevant three-year period*' is for those purposes the three years *beginning* on the date of issue of the shares. If the issuing company is a parent company, operating costs of a qualifying subsidiary (at time of issue) are not taken into account for any of those three years during any part of which it is not a qualifying subsidiary. [*ITA 2007, ss 158(6)(7), 173A(5A); FA 2018, Sch 4 paras 1(6), 2(3), 10*].

The 'maximum risk finance investments during period B' requirement

There is a requirement which is tested only during period B and only if the issuing company effectively acquires a company or trade after it receives the EIS investment in question. The requirement is that at any time in period B the total of the relevant investments (see above) so far made must not exceed £12 million or, if the company is a 'knowledge-intensive company' (see above) at the time the EIS shares are issued, £20 million. Without this requirement, the investment limits above could be sidestepped where the acquired company or trade had already benefited from earlier relevant investments. Relevant investments of the kind in (a)–(c) above also count towards these limits, but disregarding references there to a 12-month period and instead taking into account all times before the time in period B when the requirement is being tested. The requirement applies where:

- a company becomes a 51% subsidiary of the issuing company at a time during period B (other than as a result of an exchange of shares within *ITA 2007, s 247*);
- all or part of the money raised by the issue of the EIS shares in question is employed for the purposes of a qualifying business activity (see **22.10** below) consisting (wholly or partly) of a trade (as widely defined) carried on by that company; and
- the trade (or a part of it) was carried on by that company before that time.

The requirement also applies where all or part of the money raised by the issue of the EIS shares is employed for the purposes of a qualifying business activity consisting (wholly or partly) of a trade (as widely defined) which, during period B, is transferred as in (c) above.

[*ITA 2007, ss 173AB, 247(3A)*].

The purpose of the issue requirement

The shares, other than any which are bonus shares, must be issued to raise money (i.e. cash, see *Thompson v Hart* Ch D 2000, 72 TC 543) for the purpose of a 'qualifying business activity' (see **22.10** below). The issuing company must use the money for this purpose so as to promote the growth and development of the company or, where the company is a parent company, the group. [*ITA 2007, s 174*].

This requirement may be satisfied where money is raised to acquire shares in a company carrying on a 'qualifying trade' (see **22.11** below), provided the target company has no non-trading assets and the hive up of the trade is not unnecessarily delayed. Money used to meet the expenses of issuing the shares should be regarded as employed in the same way as the remainder of the money raised. Where the company obtains a listing, for example on the Alternative Investment Market, at the same time as it issues the shares, the use of money to meet the expenses of flotation is normally acceptable. (HMRC Venture Capital Schemes Manual VCM12060).

The requirement was held to be satisfied where the money raised was loaned to overseas subsidiaries for the purpose of enabling them to supply information and analysis for the purposes of the issuing company's business (*4Cast Ltd v Mitchell* (Sp C 455), [2005] SSCD 287).

The requirement is *not* satisfied if the money raised by the issue is used partly to pay dividends to investors (*Forthright (Wales) Ltd v A L Davies* Ch D 2004, 76 TC 138). The requirement was not satisfied where a company issued convertible loan notes which it subsequently converted into shares; the issue of the shares was not then for the purpose of raising money (*Optos plc v HMRC* (Sp C 560), 2006 STI 2236).

The use of money raised requirement

The 'money raised' must be employed wholly (disregarding insignificant amounts) for the purpose of the qualifying business activity for which it was raised by the end of the two years following the issue or, if the only qualifying business activity falls within **22.10**(a) or (c) below, and if later, by the end of the two years starting when the company (or, where applicable, a subsidiary) began to carry on the qualifying trade.

For this purpose, the '*money raised*' means the money raised by the issue of the shares in question (other than any of them which are bonus shares) and any other shares in the company of the same class (as defined) which are within (i) above and which are issued on the same day. In determining the time at which a qualifying trade begins to be carried on by a 'qualifying 90% subsidiary' of a company, any carrying on of the trade etc. by it before it became such a subsidiary is disregarded.

Employing money on the acquisition of shares in a company does not of itself amount to employing it for the purposes of a qualifying business activity. Additionally, employing money on the acquisition of any of the following does not amount to employing it for the purposes of a qualifying business activity: an interest in another company such that a company becomes a 51% subsidiary of the issuing company; a further interest in a 51% subsidiary of the issuing company; a trade (as widely defined); and goodwill or other intangible assets employed for the purposes of a trade.

[*ITA 2007, ss 175, 257(5)*].

See *Richards and another v HMRC* UT 2011, [2012] STC 174 in which money which was held to have been employed to supplement trading receipts in order to cover losses was held not to satisfy this requirement.

In *GC Trading Ltd v HMRC* Sp C 2007 (Sp C 630), [2008] SSCD 178, this condition was held to be satisfied even though the money raised was loaned to another company before being used to purchase a qualifying trade. On the evidence, the loans were the equivalent of a bank deposit and were simply the means used to preserve the money needed to acquire the trade.

In *Skye Inns Ltd v HMRC* FTT, [2009] UKFTT 266 (TC), 2010 STI 799 this requirement was held not to be satisfied where the company's purchase of a pub fell through at the last minute so that the funds raised were not used within the required period, even though the directors continued to look for new acquistions.

This requirement is *not* satisfied if the money raised by the issue is used partly to pay dividends to investors (*Forthright (Wales) Ltd v A L Davies* Ch D 2004, 76 TC 138).

The permitted maximum age requirement

If the EIS shares in question are issued after the 'initial investing period', one of three conditions must be met. These are that:

(A) a 'relevant investment' (see above) was made in the issuing company before the end of the initial investing period, and some or all of the money raised by that investment was employed for the purposes of the same qualifying business activity (see **22.10** below) as that for which the money raised by the current issue is employed;

(B) the total amount of relevant investments made in the issuing company in a period of 30 consecutive days which includes the date of issue of the shares is at least 50% of the annual turnover of the company averaged over five years (see *ITA 2007, s 175A(7)–(8)*), and the money raised by those investments is employed for the purpose of 'entering a new product or geographical market' (as defined in the General Block Exemption Regulation (Commission Regulation (EU) No 651/2014) as it had effect immediately before 11pm on 31 December 2020 (Brexit IP completion day)); or

(C) the condition in (B) or the equivalent condition for VCT approval (see **64** VENTURE CAPITAL TRUSTS) was previously met in relation to one or more relevant investments in the issuing company, and some or all of the money raised by those investments was employed for the purposes of the same qualifying business activity as that for which the money raised by the current issue is employed.

The '*initial investing period*' is seven years, beginning with the 'relevant first commercial sale' (ten years where the issuing company is a 'knowledge-intensive company' (see above) when the EIS shares are issued). '*First commercial sale*' has the same meaning as in the EC's Guidelines on State aid to promote risk finance investments as they had effect immediately before 11pm on 31 December 2020 (Brexit IP completion day)). The '*relevant first commercial sale*' is defined in *ITA 2007, s 175A(6)* by reference to the earliest date of any commercial sale made by (broadly) the company or a 51% subsidiary or any other person who has carried on any trade which is carried on by the company or a subsidiary.

An issuing company which is a knowledge-intensive company may elect to alter its initial investing period by substituting, for the date of the relevant first commercial sale, the date by reference to which it is treated as reaching an annual turnover of £200,000. That date is normally the last day of the accounting period in which annual turnover first reaches £200,000 or more (with modifications for accounting periods exceeding 12 months). Turnover of other companies in the group (where relevant) must also be taken into account. Any necessary apportionments must be made on a time basis, i.e. in the case of short or long accounting periods or companies joining or leaving the group part way through an accounting period.

[*ITA 2007, ss 175A, 247(3A), 252A; SI 2020 No 1499*].

The minimum period requirement

The trade or research and development within **22.10**(a), (b) below must have been carried on for a period of at least four months ending at or after the time of the share issue by no person other than the qualifying company or a 'qualifying 90% subsidiary' (see **22.9** below) of that company.

A period shorter than four months is permitted if this is by reason only of the winding-up or dissolution of any company or anything done as a consequence of a company being in administration or receivership, provided the winding-up etc. is for genuine commercial reasons and not part of a tax avoidance scheme or arrangements.

[*ITA 2007, s 176*].

The no pre-arranged exits requirement

The arrangements (as broadly defined) under which the shares are issued to the investor (or arrangements preceding the issue but in relation or in connection to it) must not:

- provide for the eventual disposal by the investor of the shares in question or other shares or securities of the company; or
- provide for the eventual cessation of a trade of the company or of a person connected with it; or
- provide for the eventual disposal of all, or a substantial amount (in terms of value) of, the assets of the company or of a person connected with it; or

- provide (by means of any insurance, indemnity, guarantee or otherwise) complete or partial protection for investors against the normal risks attaching to EIS investment (but excluding arrangements which merely protect the company and/or its subsidiaries against normal business risks).

Arrangements with a view to the company becoming a wholly-owned subsidiary of a new holding company within the terms of *ITA 2007, s 247(1)* (see **22.7** below) are excluded from (a) above. Arrangements with a view to shares in the company being exchanged for, or converted into, shares of a different class in that company, are also excluded from (a) above. Arrangements applicable only on an unanticipated winding-up of the company for genuine commercial reasons are excluded from (b) and (c) above.

[*ITA 2007, ss 177, 257(1)*].

The no tax avoidance requirement

The shares must be issued for genuine commercial reasons and not as part of a scheme or arrangement a main purpose of which is the avoidance of tax.

[*ITA 2007, s 178*].

The no disqualifying arrangements requirement

The shares must not be issued, nor any money raised by the issue spent, in consequence or anticipation of, or otherwise in connection with, 'disqualifying arrangements'. Arrangements (as broadly defined) are '*disqualifying arrangements*' if they are entered into with the purpose of ensuring that any of the 'relevant tax reliefs' (see below) are available in respect of the issuing company's business and either or both of conditions A and B below are met. It is immaterial whether the issuing company is a party to the arrangements.

Condition A is that, as a result of the money raised by the issue of the shares being employed as required by the use of the money raised requirement above, an amount representing the whole or most of the amount raised is, in the course of the arrangements, paid to (or for the benefit of) one or more parties to the arrangements or a person or persons connected with such a party (within **17** CONNECTED PERSONS). Condition B is that, in the absence of the arrangements, it would have been reasonable to expect that the whole or greater part of the component activities (as defined) of the qualifying business activity for which the issue of the shares raised money would have been carried on as part of another business by one or more parties to the arrangements or a person or persons connected with such a party.

The '*relevant tax reliefs*' comprise:

- EIS income tax and CGT reliefs (as in **22.12**, **22.15** and **22.16** below);
- SEIS income tax and CGT reliefs (see **54.33**, **54.44** and **54.46** SEED ENTERPRISE INVESTMENT SCHEME);
- qualification as an investee company for VCT purposes;
- share loss relief (see **38.14** LOSSES) and
- SOCIAL INVESTMENT RELIEF (**59**).

[*ITA 2007, ss 178A, 257(1)*].

Disqualifying arrangements were found to exist in *Coconut Animated Island Ltd v HMRC* UT, [2024] STC 880 (a SEIS case) and *Hoopla Animation Ltd (formerly known as Daisy Boo and Monkey Too Ltd) v HMRC* FTT, [2023] UKFTT 24 (TC). Both companies were formed by a group to exploit the rights to a cartoon concept for children. In both cases, the FTT found that a substantial proportion of the money raised by the share issues was paid to or for the benefit of one of the parties to the arrangements; in this case, another group member which had carried out development and production work.

Qualifying investor

[22.6] An individual is a '*qualifying investor*' in relation to shares if the following requirements are met.

The no connection with the issuing company requirement

The investor must not (except as below) be at any time in the period specified below 'connected with' the issuing company (whether before or after its incorporation) (i.e. there must be no such connection at any time in that period, see *Wild v Cannavan* CA 1997, 70 TC 554). The specified period is the period beginning two years before the issue of the shares and ending immediately before the third anniversary of the issue date or, if later and where relevant, the third anniversary of the date of commencement of the intended trade referred to in **22.10**(a) below.

In determining the time at which a qualifying trade begins to be carried on by any 'qualifying 90% subsidiary' (see **22.9** below) of a company, any carrying on of the trade by it before it became such a subsidiary is disregarded.

[*ITA 2007, ss 163, 256*].

An investor is '*connected with*' the issuing company if he, or an 'associate' of his, is either:

(a) an employee, partner, or director of, or an employee or director of a partner of, the issuing company or any 'subsidiary'; or
(b) an individual who directly or indirectly possesses or is entitled to acquire (whether he is so entitled at a future date or will at a future date be so entitled):
    (I) more than 30% of the voting power, the ordinary share capital or the issued share capital of the issuing company or any 'subsidiary'; or
    (II) such rights as would entitle him to more than 30% of the assets of the issuing company or any 'subsidiary' available for distribution to the company's equity holders (as defined); or
(c) an individual who has control (as defined by *ITA 2007, s 995*) of the issuing company or any 'subsidiary'; or
(d) an individual who subscribes for shares in the issuing company as part of an arrangement providing for another person to subscribe for shares in another company with which, were that other company an issuing company, the individual (or any other individual party to the arrangement) would be connected as above.

Rights or powers of associates are taken into account as regards (b) and (c) above (see *Cook v Billings CA*, [2001] STC 16 on the similar wording under the earlier BES provisions). An '*associate*' of any person is any 'relative' (i.e. spouse, civil partner, ancestor or linear descendant) of that person, the trustee(s) of any settlement in relation to which that person or any relative (living or dead) is or was a settlor and, where that person has an interest in any shares of obligations of a company which are subject to any trust or are part of a deceased estate, the trustee(s) of the settlement or the personal representatives of the deceased. For this purpose, 'settlor' is defined as in *ITA 2007, ss 467–473*.

As regards (b)(I) above, an individual is not connected with the company by virtue only of the fact that he or an associate is a shareholder if at that time the company has issued no shares other than subscriber shares and has neither commenced business nor made preparations for doing so.

A '*subsidiary*' for these purposes is a company more than 50% of whose ordinary share capital is at any time in 'period A' owned by the issuing company, regardless of whether or not that condition is fulfilled while the individual falls within (a)–(d) above in respect of it.

'*Period A*' for this purpose is the period beginning with the incorporation of the company or, if later, two years before the date of issue of the shares and ending immediately before the third anniversary of the issue date or, if later and where relevant, the third anniversary of the date of commencement of the intended trade referred to in **22.10**(a) below.

(In determining for this purpose the time at which a qualifying trade begins to be carried on by any 'qualifying 90% subsidiary' (see **22.9** below) of a company, any carrying on of the trade by it before it became such a subsidiary is disregarded.)

[*ITA 2007, ss 159(2), 166–167(1)(2), 170, 171, 253, 256*].

As regards (a) above, directorships are taken into account only where the individual or an associate (or a partnership of which either of them is a member) receives or is entitled to receive, during the period specified at (i)–(iii) above, a payment (whether directly or indirectly or to his order or for his benefit) from the issuing company or a 'related person' other than by way of:

(A) payment or reimbursement of allowable expenditure against employment income;
(B) interest at no more than a commercial rate on money lent;
(C) dividends etc. representing no more than a normal return on investment;
(D) payment for supply of goods at no more than market value;
(E) rent at no more than a reasonable and commercial rent for property occupied; or
(F) any reasonable and necessary remuneration for services rendered (other than secretarial or managerial services, or those rendered by the payer) which is taken into account in computing the recipient's trading profits.

A '*related person*' is any company of which the individual or an associate is a director and which is a subsidiary or partner of the issuing company, or a partner of the issuing company or a subsidiary, or any person connected (within

ITA 2007, s 993 — see **17** CONNECTED PERSONS) with such a company; 'subsidiary' for this purpose requiring ownership of more than 50% of ordinary share capital at some time in the specified period.

For these purposes (and those below), in the case of a person who is both a director and an employee of a company, references to him in his capacity as a director include him in his capacity as an employee, but otherwise he is not treated as an employee.

An individual who is connected with the issuing company may nevertheless qualify for relief if he is so connected only by reason of his (or his associate's) being a director of (or a partner of) the issuing company or any subsidiary receiving, or entitled to receive, remuneration (including any benefit or facility) as such, provided that:

(I) the remuneration (leaving out any within (F) above) is reasonable remuneration for services rendered to the company as a director;

(II) he subscribed for shares in the company meeting the requirement at **22.3**(i) above at a time when he had never been either:
  - (i) connected with the issuing company; or
  - (ii) involved (as sole trader, employee, partner or director) in carrying on its (or its subsidiary's) trade, business or profession (or any part thereof).

Where these conditions are satisfied in relation to an issue of shares, subsequent issues are treated as fulfilling (II) where they would not otherwise do so, provided that they are made within three years of the date of the last issue which did fulfil (II). Where relevant, the said three-year period is replaced by a longer period beginning with the date of the last such issue and ending with the date of commencement of the intended trade referred to in **22.10**(a) below. (In determining for these purposes the time at which a qualifying trade begins to be carried on by any 'qualifying 90% subsidiary' (see **22.9** below) of a company, any carrying on of the trade by it before it became such a subsidiary is disregarded.)

[*ITA 2007, ss 167(3), 168, 169, 256*].

The no linked loans requirement

No loan may be made to the investor or to an associate (see above) at any time in period A (see above) if it would not have been made, or would not have been made on the same terms, if the investor had not subscribed, or had not been proposing to subscribe, for the shares. The giving of credit to, or the assignment of a debt due from, the investor or associate is counted as a loan for these purposes. [*ITA 2007, s 164*].

For HMRC's views on loan-linked investments, see HMRC Statement of Practice SP 6/98.

The 'existing shareholdings' requirement

Shares subscribed for by an individual in a company in which he already holds shares are not eligible for EIS relief unless those other shares are a 'risk-finance investment'. The same applies if the pre-existing shareholding is in a qualifying subsidiary of the company (see **22.8** below). There is a let-out in certain cases where the pre-existing shares are subscriber shares. Shares are a '*risk-finance investment*' if they were issued by the company to the individual under the EIS, SEED ENTERPRISE INVESTMENT SCHEME (54) or SOCIAL INVESTMENT RELIEF (59) scheme. [*ITA 2007, s 164A*].

The no tax avoidance requirement

The shares must be subscribed for by the investor for genuine commercial reasons and not as part of a scheme or arrangement a main purpose of which is the avoidance of tax. [*ITA 2007, s 165*].

Qualifying company

[22.7] The issuing company is a '*qualifying company*' in relation to the shares if the following requirements are met. The company may be resident in the UK or elsewhere.

The UK permanent establishment requirement

The issuing company must have a 'permanent establishment' in the UK throughout 'period B'.

For this purpose, a company has a '*permanent establishment*' in the UK if, and only if, either:

- it has a 'fixed place of business' there through which its business is wholly or partly carried on; or
- an agent (other than one of independent status acting in the ordinary course of his business) acting on its behalf has, and habitually exercises there, authority to enter into contracts on the company's behalf,

unless the activities carried on in the UK are of a 'preparatory or auxiliary character'. The Treasury can amend this definition by regulations.

A '*fixed place of business*' includes a place of management, a branch, office, factory or workshop, a mine, oil or gas well, quarry or other place of natural resource extraction and a building site, construction or installation project. Activities of a '*preparatory or auxiliary character*' include the use of facilities for the purpose of storage, display or delivery of goods or merchandise belonging to the company; the maintenance of a stock of goods or merchandise belonging to the company for the purpose of storage, display, delivery or processing by another person; or purchasing goods or merchandise, or collecting information, for the company.

A company is not treated as having a permanent establishment in the UK by reason of its controlling a company resident there or a company carrying on business there (whether or not through a permanent establishment).

'*Period B*' is the period beginning with the date of issue of the shares and ending either three years after that date or, where **22.10**(a) below applies and the company (or subsidiary) was not carrying on the qualifying trade on that date, three years after the date on which it begins to carry on the trade. In determining for these purposes the time at which a qualifying trade begins to be carried on by any 'qualifying 90% subsidiary' (see **22.9** below) of a company, any carrying on of the trade by it before it became such a subsidiary is disregarded.

[*ITA 2007, ss 159(3), 180A, 191A*].

The financial health requirement

The company must not be 'in difficulty' at the beginning of period B (as above). For this purpose, a company is 'in difficulty' if it is reasonable to assume that it would be so regarded under the Community Guidelines on State Aid for Rescuing and Restructuring Firms in Difficulty (2004/C244/02). Following Brexit, the definition applies by reference to the Guidelines as they had effect immediately before 11pm on 31 December 2020 (IP completion day).

[*ITA 2007, s 180B; SI 2020 No 1499*].

The trading requirement

The company must, throughout period B (as above), either:

(a) exist wholly for the purpose of carrying on one or more 'qualifying trades' (see **22.11** below) (disregarding purposes having no significant effect on the extent of its activities); or
(b) be a '*parent company*' (i.e. a company that has one or more 'qualifying subsidiaries' (see **22.8** below)) and the business of the '*group*' (i.e. the company and its qualifying subsidiaries) must not consist wholly or as to a substantial part (i.e. broadly 20% — see HMRC Venture Capital Schemes Manual VCM3010) in the carrying on of 'non-qualifying activities'.

Where the company intends that one or more other companies should become its qualifying subsidiaries with a view to their carrying on one or more qualifying trades, then, until any time after which the intention is abandoned, the company is treated as a parent company and those other companies are included in the group for the purposes of (b) above.

For the purpose of (b) above, the business of the group means what would be the business of the group if the activities of the group companies taken together were regarded as one business. Activities are for this purpose disregarded to the extent that they consist in:

(i) holding shares in or securities of any of the company's subsidiaries;
(ii) making loans to another group company;
(iii) holding and managing property used by a group company for the purposes of a qualifying trade or trades carried on by any group company; or
(iv) holding and managing property used by a group company for the purposes of research and development from which it is intended either that a qualifying trade to be carried on by a group company will be derived or a qualifying trade carried on or to be carried on by a group company will benefit.

References in (iv) above to a group company include references to any existing or future company which will be a group company at any future time.

Activities are similarly disregarded to the extent that they consist, in the case of a subsidiary whose main purpose is the carrying on of qualifying trade(s) and whose other purposes have no significant effect on the extent of its activities (other than in relation to incidental matters), in activities not in pursuance of its main purpose.

'*Non-qualifying activities*' are:

(I) excluded activities within **22.11** below; and
(II) non-trading activities (not including research and development (see **22.10** below)).

[*ITA 2007, ss 181, 257(1)*].

For the ascertainment of the purposes for which a company exists, see HMRC Venture Capital Schemes Manual VCM13050.

Although a winding-up or dissolution in period B generally prevents a company meeting the above conditions, they are deemed met if the winding-up or dissolution is for genuine commercial reasons and not part of a scheme a main purpose of which is tax avoidance. A company does not cease to meet the above conditions by reason of anything done as a consequence of its being in administration or receivership (both as defined by *ITA 2007, s 252*), provided everything so done and the making of the relevant order are for genuine commercial (and not tax avoidance) reasons. These provisions apply also to the winding-up, dissolution, administration or receivership of any of the company's subsidiaries. [*ITA 2007, s 182*].

The issuing company to carry on the qualifying business activity requirement

At no time in period B (as above) must any of the following be carried on by a person other than the 'issuing company' or a 'qualifying 90% subsidiary' (see **22.9** below) of that company:

- the '*relevant qualifying trade*', i.e. the 'qualifying trade' which is the subject of the 'qualifying business activity' referred to under the purpose of the issue requirement at **22.5** above;
- '*relevant preparation work*', i.e. preparations to carry on a 'qualifying trade' where such preparations are the subject of that qualifying business activity (see **22.10**(c) below);
- research and development which is the subject of that qualifying business activity (see **22.10**(d) below); and
- any other preparations for the carrying on of the qualifying trade.

Where relevant preparation work is carried on by the issuing company or a qualifying 90% subsidiary, the carrying on of the 'relevant qualifying trade' by a company other than the issuing company or one of its subsidiaries is disregarded for these purposes if it occurs before the issuing company or a qualifying 90% subsidiary carries on that trade.

This requirement is not regarded as failing to be met if, by reason only of a company being wound up or dissolved or being in administration or receivership (both as defined by *ITA 2007, s 252*), the relevant qualifying trade ceases to be carried on in period B by the issuing company or any qualifying 90% subsidiary and is subsequently carried on by a person who is not connected (within *ITA 2007, s 993* — see **17** CONNECTED PERSONS) with the company at any time in 'period C'. This let-out applies only if the winding-up, dissolution or entry into administration or receivership (and everything done as a consequence of the company being in administration or receivership) is for genuine commercial reasons and not part of a tax avoidance scheme or arrangements.

'*Period C*' is the period beginning one year before the issue of eligible shares and ending immediately before the third anniversary of the issue date or, if later and where relevant, the third anniversary of the date of commencement of the intended trade referred to in **22.10**(a) or (c) below. In determining for these purposes the time at which a qualifying trade begins to be carried on by any qualifying 90% subsidiary (see **22.9** below) of a company, any carrying on of the trade by it before it became such a subsidiary is disregarded.

HMRC consider that where the relevant trade, preparation work or research and development, is carried on by the company in partnership or by a limited liability partnership of which the company is a member the above requirement is not satisfied. (HMRC Brief 77/09). HMRC also consider that the above requirement is not satisfied in the case of a film or television co-production (HMRC Guidance Note 12 March 2014).

Although a winding-up or dissolution in period B generally prevents a company meeting this requirement, it is deemed to be met if the winding-up or dissolution is for *bona fide* commercial reasons and is not part of a scheme a main purpose of which is tax avoidance. A company does not cease to meet the requirement by reason of anything done as a consequence of its being in administration or receivership (both as defined by *ITA 2007, s 252*), provided everything so done and the making of the relevant order are for *bona fide* commercial (and not tax avoidance) reasons.

[*ITA 2007, ss 159(4), 183*].

The unquoted status requirement

The issuing company must be 'unquoted' when the shares are issued and no arrangements must then exist for it to cease to be unquoted. If, at the time of issue, arrangements exist for the company to become a wholly-owned subsidiary of a new holding company by means of a share exchange within *ITA 2007, ss 247–249* (see below), no arrangements must exist for the new company to cease to be unquoted. A company is '*unquoted*' if none of its shares etc. are listed on a recognised stock exchange or on a foreign exchange designated for the purpose, or dealt in outside the UK by such means as may be designated for the purpose. Securities on the Alternative Investment Market ('AIM') or PLUS Markets (other than PLUS-listed) are treated as unquoted for these purposes. (HMRC Venture Capital Schemes Manual VCM13090).

[*ITA 2007, s 184*].

The control and independence requirement

The issuing company must not at any time in period B either:

(1) control another company other than a qualifying subsidiary (see **22.8** below), 'control' being construed in accordance with *CTA 2010, ss 450, 451* and being considered with or without connected persons within *ITA 2007, s 993*, or
(2) be a 51% subsidiary of another company or otherwise under the control of another company, 'control' being construed in accordance with *ITA 2007, s 995* and again being considered with or without connected persons, or
(3) be capable of falling within (1) or (2) by virtue of any arrangements (as broadly defined).

[*ITA 2007, ss 185, 257(1)(3)*].

The above is subject to provisions in *ITA 2007, ss 247–249* which enable an EIS company to become a wholly-owned subsidiary of a new holding company in certain circumstances. The investors receive shares in the new company in exchange for their original shares and the new shares then stand in the shoes of the old for the purposes of EIS income tax relief. See Tolley's Income Tax for details.

The gross assets requirement

The value of the issuing company's gross assets must not exceed £15 million immediately before the issue of EIS shares and must not exceed £16 million immediately afterwards.

If the issuing company is a parent company, the gross assets test applies by reference to the aggregate gross assets of the company and all its qualifying subsidiaries (disregarding certain assets held by any such company which correspond to liabilities of another). [*ITA 2007, s 186*].

For HMRC's approach to the gross assets requirement, see Statement of Practice SP 2/06.

The number of employees requirement

The 'full-time equivalent employee number' for the company must be less than 250 at the time the shares are issued. The limit of 250 is doubled to 500 if the issuing company is a 'knowledge-intensive company' (see **22.5** above) at the time the shares are issued. If the company is a parent company, the sum of the full-time equivalent employee numbers for it and each of its qualifying subsidiaries must be less than 250 (or 50) at the time the shares are issued.

A company's '*full-time equivalent employee number*' is the number of its full-time employees plus, for each employee who is not full-time, a just and reasonable fraction. Directors count as employees for this purpose, but employees on maternity or paternity leave and students on vocational training are excluded.

[*ITA 2007, s 186A*].

HMRC consider that a full-time employee is one whose standard working week (excluding lunch breaks and overtime) is at least 35 hours (HMRC Venture Capital Schemes Manual VCM13120).

The qualifying subsidiaries requirement

At any time in period B (as above) any subsidiary of the issuing company must be a 'qualifying subsidiary' (see **22.8** below). [*ITA 2007, s 187*].

The property managing subsidiaries requirement

The company must not at any time in period B (as above) have a 'property managing subsidiary' which is not a 'qualifying 90% subsidiary' (see **22.9** below) of the company. A '*property managing subsidiary*' is a subsidiary whose business consists wholly or mainly in the holding or managing of land or any 'property deriving its value from land'. For this purpose, '*property deriving its value from land*' includes any shareholding in a company, any partnership interest or interest in settled property, which derives its value directly or indirectly from land and any option, consent or embargo affecting the disposition of land. [*ITA 2007, s 188*].

Advance assurance

A company may apply to HMRC for assurance, in advance of a share issue, that it will meet the qualifying conditions of the EIS. Application can be made using the online form at www.gov.uk/guidance/venture-capital-schemes-apply-for-advance-assurance. HMRC will not provide advance assurances for investments that, taking into account all the facts that HMRC have available, will fail, or appear likely to fail, the risk-to-capital condition at **22.4** above. (HMRC Venture Capital Schemes Manual VCM8550).

Qualifying subsidiary

[22.8] The meaning of '*qualifying subsidiary*' is given below.

The subsidiary must be a '51% subsidiary' of the qualifying company (within *CTA 2010, Pt 24 Ch 3*) and no person other than the qualifying company or another of its subsidiaries may have control (within *ITA 2007, s 995*) of the subsidiary. Furthermore, no arrangements (as broadly defined) may exist by virtue of which either of these conditions would cease to be satisfied.

However, the above conditions are not regarded as ceasing to be satisfied by reason only of the subsidiary or any other company being wound up or dissolved or by reason only of anything done as a consequence of any such company being in administration or receivership (both as defined by *ITA 2007, s 252*), provided the winding-up, dissolution, entry into administration or receivership or anything done as a consequence of its being in administration or receivership is for genuine commercial reasons and is not part of a tax avoidance scheme or arrangements. Also, the above conditions are not regarded as ceasing to be satisfied by reason only of arrangements being in existence for the disposal of the interest in the subsidiary held by the qualifying company (or, as the case may be, by another of its subsidiaries) if the disposal is to be for genuine commercial reasons and is not to be part of a tax avoidance scheme or arrangements.

The above conditions must continue to be satisfied until the end of period B, except that the winding-up or dissolution, during that period, of the subsidiary or of the qualifying company does not prevent those conditions being satisfied, provided that the winding-up etc. meets the conditions applied in relation to qualifying companies (see the trading requirement at **22.7** above). The conditions are also not regarded as ceasing to be satisfied by reason only of the disposal of the interest in the subsidiary within the relevant period if it can be shown to be for genuine commercial reasons and not part of a tax avoidance scheme.

[*ITA 2007, ss 191, 257(1), 989*].

In *Hunters Property plc v HMRC* FTT, [2018] SFTD 910, a company which was limited by guarantee and which had no share capital was held not to be a qualifying subsidiary (although it was a subsidiary). As the company had no share capital, it could not be a '51% subsidiary'.

Qualifying 90% subsidiary

[22.9] A company (the subsidiary) is a '*qualifying 90% subsidiary*' of another company (the relevant company) if:

(a) the relevant company possesses at least **90%** of both the issued share capital of, and the voting power in, the subsidiary;
(b) the relevant company would be beneficially entitled to at least **90%** of the assets of the subsidiary available for distribution to equity holders on a winding-up or in any other circumstances;
(c) the relevant company is beneficially entitled to at least **90%** of any profits of the subsidiary available for distribution to equity holders;
(d) no person other than the relevant company has control (within *ITA 2007, s 995* — see **17** CONNECTED PERSONS) of the subsidiary; and
(e) no arrangements (as broadly defined) exist by virtue of which any of the above conditions would cease to be met.

For the above purposes, *CTA 2010, Pt 5 Ch 6* applies, with appropriate modifications, to determine the persons who are equity holders and the percentage of assets available to them.

The above conditions are not regarded as ceasing to be satisfied by reason only of the subsidiary or any other company being wound up or dissolved or by reason only of anything done as a consequence of any such company being in administration or receivership (both as defined by *ITA 2007, s 252*), provided the winding-up, dissolution, entry into administration or receivership or anything done as a consequence of its being in administration or receivership is for genuine commercial reasons and is not part of a tax avoidance scheme or arrangements. Also, the above conditions are not regarded as ceasing to be satisfied by reason only of arrangements being in existence for the disposal of the relevant company's interest in the subsidiary if the disposal is to be for genuine commercial reasons and is not to be part of a tax avoidance scheme or arrangements.

A company (company A) is also a qualifying 90% subsidiary of another company (company C) if:

- company A is a qualifying 90% subsidiary of another company (company B) and company B is a 'qualifying 100% subsidiary' of company C; or

- company A is a qualifying 100% subsidiary of company B and company B is a qualifying 90% subsidiary of company C.

No account is taken for this purpose of any control company C may have of company A. The definition of a qualifying 90% subsidiary is used to define a '*qualifying 100% subsidiary*' by replacing the references in that definition to 'at least 90%' with references to '100%'.

[*ITA 2007, ss 190, 257(1)*].

Qualifying business activity

[22.10] Either of the following is a '*qualifying business activity*' in relation to the issuing company.

(a) The issuing company or any 'qualifying 90% subsidiary' (see **22.9** above) (i) carrying on a 'qualifying trade' which, on the date of issue of the shares, the company or any such subsidiary is carrying on, or (ii) preparing to carry on such a trade which, on the date of issue of the shares, is intended to be carried on by the company or any such subsidiary and which is begun to be so carried on within two years after that date, or (iii) actually carrying on the trade mentioned in (ii) above.

(b) The issuing company or any 'qualifying 90% subsidiary' (see **22.9** above) carrying on research and development which, on the date of issue of the shares, the company or any such subsidiary is carrying on or which company or any such subsidiary begins to carry on immediately afterwards, and from which it is intended on that date that a 'qualifying trade' which the company or any such subsidiary will carry on will benefit.

In determining for the purposes of (a) and (b) above the time at which a qualifying trade or research and development begins to be carried on by a qualifying 90% subsidiary of the issuing company, any carrying on of the trade etc. by it before it became such a subsidiary is disregarded. References to a qualifying 90% subsidiary include, in cases where the qualifying trade is not carried on at the time of issue of the shares, references to any existing or future company which will be such a subsidiary at any future time.

[*ITA 2007, ss 179, 257(1)*].

As regards (a) above, 'preparing' to carry on a trade covers both the setting up of a new trade and the acquisition of an existing trade from its present owner. It does not cover preliminary activities such as market research aimed at discovering whether a trade would be likely to succeed or raising capital or research and development. (HMRC Venture Capital Schemes Manual VCM12110).

For HMRC's views as to whether a trade is carried on '*wholly or mainly in the UK*', see Statement of Practice 3/00.

For the manner in which the scheme operates where a company wishes to raise money by a single issue of shares either partly for preparing to carry on a trade and partly for the subsequent carrying on of that trade, or for more than one qualifying business activity (e.g. for a trade carried on by one subsidiary and for research and development carried on by another), see Revenue Tax Bulletin April 1996 pp 305, 306.

Qualifying trade

[22.11] A trade is a '*qualifying trade*' if it is conducted on a commercial basis with a view to the realisation of profits and it does not, at any time in period B (as defined in **22.7** above), consist to a substantial extent in the carrying on of 'excluded activities'. For these purposes, 'trade' (except in relation to the trade mentioned in (t) below) does not include a venture in the nature of trade.

A company was held not to be conducting a trade on a commercial basis as it had failed to show that there was a genuine subjective view to profit because the forecasts and figures produced were 'spectacularly optimistic' and 'wholly unrealistic' (*CHF Pip! plc v HMRC* FTT, [2021] UKFTT 383 (TC)).

Excluded activities

'*Excluded activities*' are:

(a) dealing in land, commodities or futures, or in shares, securities or other financial instruments;
(b) dealing in goods otherwise than in an ordinary trade of wholesale or retail distribution (see below);
(c) banking, insurance or any other financial activities;
(d) leasing or letting or receiving royalties or licence fees;
(e) providing legal or accountancy services;
(f) 'property development';
(g) farming or market gardening (in the UK or overseas);
(h) holding, managing or occupying woodlands, any other forestry activities or timber production;
(i) shipbuilding (defined by reference to relevant EU State aid rules);
(j) producing coal or steel (both defined by reference to relevant EU State aid rules and including the extraction of coal);
(k) operating or managing hotels or comparable establishments (i.e. guest houses, hostels and other establishments whose main purpose is to offer overnight accommodation with or without catering) or property used as such;
(l) operating or managing nursing homes or residential care homes (both as defined) or property used as such;
(m) generating or exporting electricity or making electricity generating capacity available;
(n) generating heat;
(o) generating any form of energy not within (m) or (n);
(p) producing gas or fuel; and
(q) providing services or facilities for any business consisting of activities within any of (a) to (p) and carried on by another person (other than a parent company), where one person has a 'controlling interest' in both that business and the business carried on by the provider.

As regards (e) above, the provision of the services of accountancy personnel is the provision of accountancy services (*Castleton Management Services Ltd v Kirkwood* (Sp C 276), [2001] SSCD 95).

Exclusions (l) and (m) apply only if the person carrying on the activity in question has an estate or interest (e.g. a lease) in the property concerned or occupies that property.

HMRC regard as 'substantial' for the above purposes a part of a trade which consists of more than 20% of total activities, judged by any reasonable measure (for instance turnover or capital employed). (HMRC Venture Capital Schemes Manual VCM3010). As regards (a) above, dealing in land includes cases where steps are taken, before selling the land, to make it more attractive to a purchaser; such steps might include the refurbishment of existing buildings. (HMRC Venture Capital Schemes Manual VCM3020).

As regards (b) above, a trade of wholesale distribution is a trade consisting of the offer of goods for sale either to persons for resale (or processing and resale) (which resale must be to members of the general public for their use or consumption) by them. A trade of retail distribution is a trade in which goods are offered or exposed for sale and sold to members of the general public for their use or consumption. A trade is not an ordinary wholesale or retail trade if it consists to a substantial extent of dealing in goods collected or held as an investment (or of that and any other activity within (a)–(q) above), and a substantial proportion of such goods is held for a significantly longer period than would reasonably be expected for a vendor trying to dispose of them at market value. Whether such trades are 'ordinary' is to be judged having regard to the following features, those under (A) supporting the categorisation as 'ordinary', those under (B) being indicative to the contrary.

(A)

- (i) The breaking of bulk.
- (ii) The purchase and sale of goods in different markets.
- (iii) The employment of staff and incurring of trade expenses other than the cost of goods or of remuneration of persons connected (within *ITA 2007, s 993*) with a company carrying on such a trade.

(B)

- (i) The purchase or sale of goods from or to persons connected (within *ITA 2007, s 993*) with the trader.
- (ii) The matching of purchases with sales.
- (iii) The holding of goods for longer than would normally be expected.
- (iv) The carrying on of the trade at a place not commonly used for wholesale or retail trading.
- (v) The absence of physical possession of the goods by the trader.

As regards the application of (d) above, a trade is not excluded from being a qualifying trade solely because at some time in period B it consists to a substantial extent in the receiving of royalties or licence fees substantially attributable (in terms of value) to the exploitation of 'relevant intangible assets'.

A '*relevant intangible asset*' is an 'intangible asset' the whole or greater part of which (by value) has been created by the issuing company or by a company which was a qualifying subsidiary (within **22.8** above) of the issuing company throughout the period during which it created the whole or greater part (by value) of the asset. For this purpose only, '*issuing company*' includes a company all of whose shares were acquired by the issuing company at a time when the only shares issued in the issuing company were subscriber shares and the consideration for the acquisition consisted wholly in the issue of shares in the issuing company.

Where the asset is 'intellectual property', it is treated as created by a company only if the right to exploit it vests in that company (alone or with others). The term '*intellectual property*' incorporates patents, trade marks, copyrights, design rights etc. and foreign equivalents. An '*intangible asset*' is an asset falling to be treated as such under generally accepted accounting practice, including all intellectual property and also industrial information and techniques (see HMRC Venture Capital Schemes Manual VCM3060).

Also as regards (d) above, a trade will not be excluded by reason only of its consisting of letting ships, other than offshore installations (previously oil rigs) or pleasure craft (as defined), on charter, provided that:

- (i) the company beneficially owns all the ships it so lets,
- (ii) every ship beneficially owned by the company is UK-registered,
- (iii) throughout period B, the company is solely responsible for arranging the marketing of the services of its ships, and
- (iv) in relation to every letting on charter, certain conditions as to length and terms of charter, and the arm's length character of the transaction, are fulfilled,

and if any of (i)–(iv) above is not fulfilled in relation to certain lettings, the trade is not thereby excluded if those lettings and any other excluded activities taken together do not amount to a substantial part of the trade.

For HMRC's views on the scope of the exclusions in relation to (e) above, see Revenue Tax Bulletin August 2001 pp 877, 878.

'*Property development*' in (f) above means the development of land by a company, which has (or has had at any time) an 'interest in the land' (as defined), with the sole or main object of realising a gain from the disposal of an interest in the developed land.

As regards (q) above, a person has a '*controlling interest*' in a business carried on by a company if he controls (within *CTA 2010, ss 450, 451*) the company; or if the company is a close company and he or an 'associate' is a director of the company and the owner of, or able to control, more than 30% of its ordinary share capital; or if at least half of its ordinary share capital is directly or indirectly owned by him. In any other case it is obtained by his being entitled to at least half of the assets used for, or income arising from, the business. In either case, the rights and powers of a person's 'associates' are attributed to him. An '*associate*' of any person is any 'relative' (i.e. spouse, civil partner, ancestor or linear descendant) of that person, the trustee(s) of any settlement in relation to which that person or any relative (living or dead) is or was a settlor and, where that person has an interest in any shares or obligations of a company which are subject to any trust or are part of a deceased estate, the trustee(s) of the settlement or the personal representatives of the deceased and, if that person is a company, any other company which has an interest in those shares or obligations. For this purpose, 'settlor' is defined as in *ITA 2007, ss 467–473*.

[*ITA 2007, ss 189, 192–199, 253, 257(3), 996(7); SI 2020 No 1499*].

Form of income tax relief

[22.12] Relief is (except as below) given for the tax year in which the shares were issued, by a reduction in what would otherwise be the individual's income tax liability (a '*tax reduction*') equal to tax at the 'EIS rate' (currently 30%) on the amount (or aggregate amounts) subscribed for shares in respect of which he is eligible for and claims EIS relief (subject to the maximum limits below). Investors may restrict a claim to EIS relief in respect of a single issue of shares so that relief is given only in respect of some of the shares.

For the order in which tax reductions are given against an individual's tax liability, see Tolley's Income Tax under Allowances and Tax Rates. A tax reduction must be restricted to the extent (if any) that it would otherwise exceed the individual's remaining income tax liability after making all prior reductions.

The individual may claim relief as if so many of the shares as he specifies had been issued in the preceding tax year.

[*ITA 2007, s 158*].

Attribution of relief to shares

Subject to any reduction or withdrawal of relief (see **26.9** onwards), where an individual's income tax liability is reduced for a tax year as above by reason of an issue or issues of shares made (or treated as made) in that year, the tax reduction is attributed to that issue or those issues (being apportioned in the latter case according to the amounts claimed for each issue). Issues of shares of the same class by a company to an individual on the same day are treated as a single issue for this purpose. A proportionate amount of the reduction attributed to an issue is attributed to each share in the issue in respect of which the claim was made and is adjusted correspondingly for any subsequent bonus issue of shares of the same class and carrying the same rights.

An issue to an individual part of which is treated as having been made in the preceding tax year (as above) is treated as two separate issues, one made on a day in the previous year.

Where relief attributable to an issue of shares falls to be withdrawn or reduced, the relief attributable to each of the shares in question is reduced to nil (if relief is withdrawn) or proportionately reduced (where relief is reduced).

[*ITA 2007, ss 201, 255*].

Annual maximum

There is an upper limit on the amount in respect of which an individual may obtain relief for a tax year (regardless of whether the shares were issued in that year or in the following year). The limit operates as follows:

(i) if the shares do not include any 'KIC shares', the limit is £1 million;
(ii) if the total amount subscribed for KIC shares is £1 million or more, the limit is £2 million; and
(iii) in any other case, the limit is £1 million plus total amount subscribed for KIC shares.

'*KIC shares*' are shares in any company which is a knowledge-intensive company at the time the shares are issued. See **22.5** above for meaning of knowledge-intensive company, and note the special rule there for companies that have traded for less than three years before issuing the EIS shares.

[*ITA 2007, s 158(2)(2ZA)(2ZB)*].

Claims for relief

[22.13] A claim for relief must be made not earlier than the end of the four-month minimum period referred to at **22.5** above, and not later than the fifth anniversary of 31 January following the tax year for which relief is claimed. A claim cannot be made until, with the authority of HMRC, the company has furnished the individual with a compliance certificate to the effect that, from its point of view, the conditions for the relief are satisfied. [*ITA 2007, ss 202, 203*].

Restriction or withdrawal of income tax relief

[22.14] EIS income tax relief is restricted or withdrawn in the circumstances described below. References to a reduction of relief include its reduction to nil, and references to the withdrawal of relief in respect of any shares are to the withdrawal of the relief attributable to those shares (see **22.12** above). Where no relief has yet been given, a reduction applies to reduce the amount which apart from the provision in question would be the relief, and a withdrawal means ceasing to be eligible for relief in respect of the shares in question. [*ITA 2007, s 257(4)*]. For the purposes of the following provisions, the '*EIS original rate*' means the EIS rate for the tax year for which income tax relief was obtained. [*ITA 2007, s 256A*].

An assessment to income tax withdrawing or reducing relief is made for the tax year for which the relief was given.

Disposal of shares

Where the investor disposes of shares (or an interest or right in or over shares) to which relief is attributable (see **22.12** above) or grants an option the exercise of which would bind him to sell the shares before the end of 'period A' (see **22.6** above):

(a) if the disposal is at arm's length, relief attributable to those shares (see **22.12** above) is withdrawn or, if that relief exceeds an amount equal to tax at the EIS original rate (see above) on the disposal consideration, reduced by that amount;
(b) otherwise, the relief is withdrawn.

Where the relief attributable to the shares was less than the tax at the EIS original rate on the amount subscribed for the issue, the amount referred to in (a) above is correspondingly reduced. For this purpose, shares are treated as having been issued in an earlier year where relief was carried back as in **22.10** above. Where the relief attributable to the shares has been reduced (otherwise than as a result of an issue of bonus shares (see **22.12** above)) before the relief was obtained, in calculating the amount referred to in (a) above, the gross relief attributable to the shares before that reduction is used.

Relief is also withdrawn where, during period A, an option is granted to the investor, the exercise of which would bind the grantor to purchase shares. There are provisions for identifying the shares to which an option relates, where these form part of a larger holding.

These provisions do not apply on a transfer to the investor's spouse or civil partner made at a time they are living together; the transferee stands in the shoes of the transferor as regards any subsequent disposal. The provisions also do not apply to a disposal of shares occurring as a result of the investor's death.

Disposals are identified with shares of the same class issued earlier before shares issued later (i.e. first in/first out (FIFO)). Further rules apply as to the order in which shares acquired on the same day are deemed to be disposed of where only some of those shares have attracted income tax relief and/or CGT deferral relief (see **22.16** below). These rules are the same as those described at **22.15** below (under 'Identification rules') for CGT purposes. A share exchange is treated as a disposal for these purposes unless it is within *ITA 2007, ss 247–249* (see **22.7** above).

[*ITA 2007, ss 209–212, 245, 246, 254*].

Value received by investor

Where, during a specified period, an investor receives value (other than insignificant value) from the company, any EIS income tax relief attributable to those shares (see **22.12** above) and not previously reduced in respect of the value received is withdrawn or, if that relief exceeds an amount equal to tax at the EIS original rate (see above) on the 'value received' reduced by that amount.

The provisions apply equally to value received from a person who is connected (within *ITA 2007, s 993* — see **17** CONNECTED PERSONS) with the issuing company.

If an individual to whom shares in a company have been issued enters into a convertible loan agreement with the company under the Future Fund on or after 20 May 2020, and subsequently receives value from the company under the terms of that agreement, the value received is ignored in relation to any EIS relief attributable to shares issued before the individual entered into the agreement. This is to ensure that investors in a company who also support the company using a Future Fund convertible loan note will not lose relief on any previous EIS investments when that loan is redeemed or converted into shares. The Future Fund was set up as part of government support to companies impacted by the 2020 COVID-19 (coronavirus) pandemic.

[*ITA 2007, ss 213–223; FA 2020, s 110*].

For full details of the provisions, see Tolley's Income Tax.

Value received other than by investor

Relief is similarly restricted or withdrawn where, within the same specified period, the company or any 51% subsidiary (as defined) of the company repays, redeems or repurchases any of its share capital belonging to a member other than:

- the individual; or
- another individual whose relief is thereby withdrawn or reduced (as above) or who thereby suffers a qualifying chargeable event under the capital gains deferral provisions (see **22.16** below); or
- another individual whose relief under the SEED ENTERPRISE INVESTMENT SCHEME (**54**) is thereby withdrawn or reduced; or
- a company whose investment relief under the CORPORATE VENTURING SCHEME (**19**) is thereby withdrawn or reduced,

or makes any payment to any such member for giving up rights on the cancellation or extinguishment of any of the share capital of the company or subsidiary. There is an exception for insignificant repayments etc.

[*ITA 2007, ss 224–230*].

For full details of the provisions, see Tolley's Income Tax.

Acquisition of a trade or trading assets

Relief is withdrawn if, at any time in period A (see **22.6** above), the company or any qualifying subsidiary (see **22.8** above), begins to carry on as its trade, business or profession (or part) a trade etc. (or part) previously carried on at any time in that period otherwise than by the company or a qualifying subsidiary, or acquires the whole or the greater part of the assets used for a trade etc. previously so carried on, and the individual is a person who, or one of a group of persons who together, either:

- owned more than a half share in the trade etc. previously carried on (ownership and, if appropriate, respective shares being determined by applying *CTA 2010, s 941(6)* and by treating an interest in a trade belonging to a company in accordance with the options in *CTA 2010, s 942*) at any time in period A, and also own or owned at any such time such a share in the trade etc. carried on by the company; or
- control (within *CTA 2010, ss 450, 451*), or at any time in period A have controlled, the company, and also, at any such time, controlled another company which previously carried on the trade etc.

For these purposes, interests etc. of 'associates' (see **22.6** above) are taken into account. There are special rules relating to shares held by certain directors of, or of a partner of, the issuing company or any subsidiary.

[*ITA 2007, ss 232, 257(3)*].

Acquisition of share capital

Relief is also withdrawn if the company, at any time in period A (see **22.6** above), comes to acquire all the issued share capital of another company, and where the individual is a person who, or one of a group of persons who together, control (within *CTA 2010, ss 450, 451*) or have, at any such time, controlled the company and who also, at any such time, controlled the other company. There are special rules relating to shares held by certain directors of, or a partner of, the issuing company or any subsidiary. [*ITA 2007, s 233*].

Relief subsequently found not to have been due

Relief is withdrawn if it is subsequently found not to have been due. Relief can be withdrawn on the ground that the issuing company is not a qualifying company (see **22.7** above) or that the purpose of the issue or use of money raised requirements at **22.5** are not met only if:

- the issuing company has given notice to that effect under *ITA 2007, s 241* or *TCGA 1992, Sch 5B para 16*; or
- an HMRC officer has given notice to the issuing company of his opinion that the whole or part of the relief was not due because of the ground in question.

The issuing company may appeal against an HMRC notice as though it were refusal of a claim by the company. The determination of an appeal against an HMRC notice under the capital gains deferral provisions is conclusive for the purposes of any income tax relief appeal.

[*ITA 2007, ss 234, 236*].

Capital gains tax

[22.15] See also **22.16** below re EIS deferral relief.

Gains

Gains arising on the disposal by the investor, after the end of 'period A' (see below), of shares on which EIS income tax relief has been given are not chargeable gains. (There is no such exemption for shares disposed of before the end of period A, and any EIS income tax relief given will be withdrawn — see **22.14** above.)

Where EIS income tax relief was not given on the full amount subscribed for the shares (other than by reason of the income tax liability being insufficient to support the relief), the capital gains tax exemption is restricted to a proportion of the gain. Where this arises, it will usually be because the investor's EIS subscriptions exceeded the annual maximum on which relief is available (see **22.3** above). The exempt gain is the proportion of the gain (after any indexation allowance available) found by applying the multiple A/B where:

A = the actual income tax relief given (expressed in terms of the reduction in the tax liability); and
B = tax at the 'EIS original rate' (i.e. the EIS rate for the tax year for which income tax relief was obtained) on the amount subscribed for the issue.

'*Period A*' for these purposes is the period beginning with the incorporation of the company or, if later, two years before the date of issue of the shares and ending immediately before the third anniversary of the issue date or, if later and where relevant, the third anniversary of the date of commencement of the intended trade referred to in **22.10**(a) or (c) above.

(In determining for this purpose the time at which a qualifying trade begins to be carried on by any 'qualifying 90% subsidiary' (see **22.9** above) of a company, any carrying on of the trade by it before it became such a subsidiary is disregarded.)

[*TCGA 1992, s 150A(2)(3); ITA 2007, ss 159(2), 256*].

See *Example 1* below.

In *Ames v HMRC* UT, [2018] STC 1704, it was held that the exemption did not apply in a case where the taxpayer had not claimed EIS income tax relief because he had had no taxable income in the year in which the shares were issued. However, the Upper Tribunal considered that HMRC had wrongly fettered their discretion to consider the taxpayer's late claim for EIS income tax relief and remitted the case to HMRC for reconsideration.

Losses

If a disposal of shares on which EIS income tax relief has been given results in a capital loss, the loss is allowable *regardless* of whether the disposal occurs within or without 'period A' (see above). However, in calculating the loss, or in ascertaining whether a loss has indeed arisen, the cost of the shares for CGT purposes is reduced by the amount of EIS income tax relief attributable to the shares disposed of (expressed in terms of the reduction in the tax liability) to the extent that this has not been, or does not fall to be, withdrawn. See *Examples 2 & 3* below. The loss qualifies for relief against income, if claimed, under the provisions for losses on shares in unlisted trading companies — see **38.14** LOSSES.

[*TCGA 1992, s 150A(1)(2A)*].

Example 1

On 8 November 2024, P subscribes £1,350,000 for 900,000 shares in the EIS company, S Ltd, which is not a knowledge-intensive company, and obtains the maximum EIS income tax relief of £300,000 (£1,000,000 × 30%) for 2024/25. On 3 April 2029, he sells the entire holding for £2,790,000.

The chargeable gain arising is calculated as follows:

	£
Disposal proceeds	2,790,000
Cost	1,350,000
Gain	1,440,000
Less TCGA 1992, s 150A(3) exemption	
£1,440,000 × (£300,000(A)/£405,000(B))	1,066,666
Chargeable gain	£373,334
Note:	
A = relief given (£1,000,000 × 30%)	£300,000
B = £1,350,000 × 30%	£405,000

Example 2

Assuming the facts are as in *Example 1* above except that the shares are sold for £1,000,000 on 3 April 2029.

The allowable loss arising is calculated as follows:

	£	£
Disposal proceeds		1,000,000

	£	£
Less Cost	1,350,000	
Less income tax relief given (and not withdrawn)	300,000	1,050,000
Allowable loss		£50,000

Example 3

Assuming the facts are as in *Example 1* above except that the shares are sold on 3 April 2026 for £1,100,000. Income tax relief of £1,100,000 × 30% × (300,000/405,000) = £244,444 is withdrawn (see below). The balance of £55,556 is not withdrawn and is attributable to the shares sold.

	£	£
Disposal proceeds		1,100,000
Less Cost	1,350,000	
Less income tax relief given (and not withdrawn)	55,556	1,294,444
Allowable loss		£194,444

In calculating the EIS withdrawal, as not all the subscriber shares qualified for EIS income tax relief, the consideration must be reduced by applying the formula A/B, to the amount of the consideration received. [*ITA 2007, s 210*]. For this purpose, A is the actual income tax reduction and B is the tax at the EIS rate on the amount subscribed for the issue, i.e. £1,100,000 × (300,000/405,000) = £814,814. The EIS relief withdrawn is then calculated on this result, i.e. £814,814 × 30% = £244,444.

See HMRC Venture Capital Schemes Manual VCM20120 for an example involving a part disposal.

Identification rules

The normal identification rules (see **58.2** SHARES AND SECURITIES — IDENTIFICATION RULES) are each disapplied as regards EIS shares. Instead, the rules described below apply to match disposals with acquisitions of shares of the same class in the same company, and they apply where at least some of those shares have attracted EIS income tax relief. Shares are not treated as being of the same class unless they would be so treated if dealt with on a recognised stock exchange.

Disposals are identified with acquisitions on different days on a first in/first out (FIFO) basis. Shares transferred between spouses or civil partners living together are treated as if they were acquired by the transferee on the day they were issued. Shares comprised in a 'new holding' following a reorganisation to which *TCGA 1992, s 127* applies (including a case where it applies by virtue of any other chargeable gains enactment — see, for example, **57.2, 57.5, 57.7, 57.8** SHARES AND SECURITIES) are treated as having been acquired when the original shares were acquired. Where shares within two or more of the categories listed below were acquired on the same day, any of those shares disposed of (applying the FIFO basis) are treated as disposed of in the order in which they are listed, as follows:

- shares to which no EIS income tax relief, EIS capital gains deferral relief (see **22.16** below) or SEIS relief (see **54** SEED ENTERPRISE INVESTMENT SCHEME) is attributable;
- shares to which SEIS income tax relief is attributable;
- shares to which EIS deferral relief, but not EIS income tax relief, is attributable;
- shares to which EIS income tax relief, but not EIS deferral relief, is attributable;
- shares to which both EIS income tax relief and EIS deferral relief are attributable.

Any shares within either of the last two categories which are treated as issued on an earlier day by virtue of the carry-back provisions at **22.12** above are to be treated as disposed of before any other shares within the same category.

[*TCGA 1992, s 150A(4)(5); ITA 2007, ss 246, 257(5)*].

The above rules are appropriately modified where an individual makes the election described at **58.2** SHARES AND SECURITIES — IDENTIFICATION RULES for alternative treatment of same-day acquisitions and the shares covered by the election include EIS shares. [*TCGA 1992, s 105A(4)(7)—(9)*].

Reorganisations of share capital

Where EIS income tax relief has been given on some shares in a particular company but not others and there is a reorganisation (including a bonus issue) within the meaning of *TCGA 1992, s 126*, then *TCGA 1992, s 127* (see **57.2** SHARES AND SECURITIES) applies separately as regards the shares attracting and not attracting relief so that, in each case, the new shares will stand in the place of the old shares. A distinction is also made, as regards shares attracting income tax relief, between those (if any) to which EIS deferral relief (see **22.16** below) is attributable and those to which it is not, and the separate treatment described above also applies to each of those two categories. A further distinction is made to provide for separate treatment as regards shares attracting SEIS income tax relief (see **54** SEED ENTERPRISE INVESTMENT SCHEME).

Rights issues

If, immediately following a rights issue, EIS relief is attributable either to the original holding or the rights shares, the share reorganisation rules of *TCGA 1992, ss 127–130* (see **57.2** SHARES AND SECURITIES) are disapplied, with the result that the rights shares are treated as a separate acquisition.

[*TCGA 1992, s 150A(6)(6A)(7)*].

Company reconstructions

If as part of a reconstruction, shares or debentures in another company are issued to an EIS shareholder in exchange for EIS shares to which income tax relief remains attributable, then the shares in the new company are not generally deemed to stand in the place of shares in the old company under *TCGA 1992, s 135* or *s 136* (see **57.5**, **57.7** SHARES AND SECURITIES) and there is thus a disposal of the shares in the old company. However, *s 135* or *136* does apply in the normal way if:

- the new holding consists of new ordinary shares issued after the end of 'period A' (as defined above under Gains and applied by reference to the original shares and the company which issued them) and carrying no present or future preferential rights to dividends or assets or right to redemption; and
- the company issuing the new shares has previously issued shares under the EIS and has issued the appropriate compliance certificate (see **22.13** above) enabling investors to obtain relief on that earlier issue.

In addition, *TCGA 1992, s 135* is not disapplied in a case to which *ITA 2007, s 247* applies. That provision enables an EIS company to become a wholly-owned subsidiary of a new holding company in certain circumstances. The investors receive shares in the new company in exchange for their original shares, and the new shares then stand in the shoes of the old for the purposes of EIS income tax relief. This treatment is generally applied for CGT purposes also. See Tolley's Income Tax for details.

[*TCGA 1992, s 150A(8)(8A)–(8D)*].

Reduction of relief where value received etc.

Where a gain on disposal of EIS shares would otherwise be exempt due to their having been held until after the end of the 'relevant period' (see above), a special rule applies if EIS income tax relief has been, or falls to be, reduced (though not fully withdrawn) as a result of either or both of the following events occurring before the disposal:

- the investor receives value from the company within the meaning of *ITA 2007, s 213* (see **22.14** above);
- there is a repayment, redemption, repurchase or payment in circumstances within *ITA 2007, s 224* (see **22.14** above).

The CGT exemption applies only to so much of the gain as remains after deducting so much of it as is represented by the fraction $^{X}/_{Y}$ where

X = the reduction(s) made, as mentioned above, to the income tax relief given, and
Y = the income tax relief given before applying such reductions.

Where the CGT exemption has already been restricted because EIS income tax relief was not given on the full amount subscribed for the shares (see above), the fraction is applied to the part of the gain otherwise exempt and the deduction made from that part.

[*TCGA 1992, s 150B*].

Example 4

On 9 November 2024, Q subscribed for 20,000 EIS £1 shares at par in H Ltd, which is not a knowledge-intensive company. The EIS relief given was £6,000. On 2 January 2026, he received £2,000 from the company, as a result of which EIS relief of £2,000 @ 30% = £600 is withdrawn under *ITA 2007, s 213*. In June 2029, the shares were sold for £60,000.

The CGT computation is as follows:

		£
Disposal consideration		60,000
Less Cost		20,000
Gain		£40,000
Chargeable gain		
$£40,000 \times \frac{600}{6,000}$ (TCGA 1992, s150B)		£4,000
Exempt gain (balance)		£36,000

If only £3,000 EIS relief were given (say because the investor was also given £297,000 EIS relief on another investment in 2024/25 in a company which is not a knowledge-intensive company, the maximum relief for that year being £300,000), the relief withdrawn would be (3,000/6,000) × £2,000 × 30% = £300.

The chargeable gain restriction would be calculated in two stages:

Gain as above		£40,000
Stage 1 (*TCGA 1992, s 150A(3)* restriction)		
Gain exempt:		
$£40,000 \times \frac{3,000}{6,000}$		£20,000
Gain chargeable (balance)		£20,000
Stage 2 (*TCGA 1992, s 150B* restriction)		
	Exempt	Chargeable
	£	£
Gain chargeable as above		20,000
Gain otherwise exempt	20,000	
Reduced by value received		
$£20,000 \times \frac{300}{3,000}$	(2,000)	2,000
Total chargeable gain		£22,000
Exempt gain	£18,000	

Capital gains deferral relief

[22.16] A specific deferral relief can be claimed whereby any chargeable gain can be deferred to the extent that it can be matched with an investment in EIS shares.

In relation to EIS shares issued after 5 April 1998, significant changes were made to the relief. In particular, it is not a requirement that the shares qualify for income tax relief nor that the individual be unconnected with the company. The provisions also extend to trustees. There is no limit on the amount of the gain that can be deferred but the gross assets test at **22.7** above does limit the amount that may be invested in any one EIS company (or group).

The main provisions of the EIS deferral relief are described at **22.17** below, with further provisions at **22.19** below. Their application to trustees is covered at **22.18** below. The provisions as they related to shares issued before 6 April 1998 are described briefly at **22.20** below.

Deferral relief is attributable to any EIS shares if expenditure on them has been used to defer the whole or part of any gain and there has been no chargeable event (see **22.17** and **22.20** below) in relation to those shares resulting in the deferred gain being brought back into charge. [*TCGA 1992, Sch 5B para 19(2)*].

Reinvestment into EIS shares issued after 5 April 1998

[22.17] Deferral relief applies where:

- a chargeable gain would otherwise accrue to an individual:
  - on the disposal by him of any asset; or
  - on the occurrence of a chargeable event under these provisions or the provisions governing reinvestment into VCT shares (see **64.8** VENTURE CAPITAL TRUSTS); or
  - to give effect to a withdrawal under *TCGA 1992, s 164F* or *s 164FA* of general reinvestment relief (see **23.80** EXEMPTIONS AND RELIEFS);
- the individual makes a 'qualifying investment'; and
- the individual is UK resident both when the chargeable gain accrues to him and when he makes the qualifying investment, and is not, at the time he makes the investment, regarded as resident outside the UK for the purposes of any double taxation arrangements the effect of which would be that he would not be liable to tax on a gain arising on a disposal, immediately after their acquisition, of the shares comprising the qualifying investment, disregarding any exemption available under *TCGA 1992, s 150A* (see **22.15** above).

See **22.18** below re the application of these provisions to trustees.

Subject to the further conditions below, a '*qualifying investment*' is a subscription for eligible shares (i.e. shares meeting the requirement at **22.5**(i) above) in a company which are issued within the one year immediately preceding or the three years immediately following the time the chargeable gain in question accrues. These time limits may be extended by HMRC in individual cases. If the shares are issued *before* the gain accrues, they must still be held at the time it accrues. For these purposes, shares are not treated as issued merely by being comprised in a letter of allotment or similar instrument. The further conditions are as follows:

(a) the shares (other than any of them which are 'bonus shares') must be subscribed for wholly in cash;
(b) the company must be a qualifying company (within **22.7** above) in relation to the shares;

(c) the shares must be fully paid up (see below) at time of issue (other than any of them which are bonus shares);
(d) the shares must be subscribed for and issued for *bona fide* commercial purposes and not as part of tax avoidance arrangements;
(e) the total amount of the 'relevant investments' (defined as for the purposes of the maximum amount raised annually through risk capital schemes requirement at **22.5** above) in the company and its subsidiaries in the year ending with the issue of the shares must not exceed £5 million;
(f) the issuing company to carry on the qualifying business activity requirement at **22.7** above must be satisfied in relation to the company;
(g) the shares (other than any of them which are bonus shares) must be issued to raise money for the purpose of a qualifying business activity (see **22.10** above); and
(h) the money raised by the issue of the shares and all other eligible shares in the company of the same class issued on the same day must be employed wholly (disregarding insignificant amounts) for that purpose by the end of the two years following the issue or, if the only qualifying business activity falls within **22.10**(a) above, and if later, by the end of the two years starting when the company (or subsidiary) began to carry on the qualifying trade (see **22.11** above).

These conditions draw on those applicable to income tax relief (see **22.3** onwards above). However, there is no requirement that any income tax relief be attributable to the shares, and, in contrast to the position for income tax relief, the individual does not have to be unconnected with the company. '*Bonus shares*' are shares issued otherwise than for payment, whether in cash or otherwise.

Shares are not fully paid up for the purposes of (c) above if there is any undertaking to pay cash to any person in respect of the acquisition of the shares at a future date.

Investments in subsidiaries count towards the limit in (e) above if the company concerned was a subsidiary of the issuing company at any time in the year and whether or not it was a subsidiary at the time of the investment.

In determining for the purposes of (h) above when a qualifying trade is begun to be carried on by a subsidiary, any carrying on of the trade by it before it became a qualifying 90% subsidiary (see **22.9** above) is disregarded.

In *R (oao Devine) v CIR* QB 2003, TL 3713, the taxpayer unsuccessfully applied for judicial review of the Revenue's decision not to extend the reinvestment time limits noted above.

In *GC Trading Ltd v HMRC* (Sp C 630), 2007 STI 2231, the condition in (h) above was held to be satisfied even though the money raised was loaned to another company before being used to purchase a qualifying trade. On the evidence, the loans were the equivalent of a bank deposit and were simply the means used to preserve the money needed to acquire the trade. In *Harvey's Jersey Cream Ltd v HMRC* FTT 2013, [2014] SFTD 599 the condition in (h) above was held not to be satisfied where a company which was a partner in a trading partnership raised money by issuing shares and increased its interest in the partnership (the money effectively being paid out to the other partners). Judge Hellier held that 'the monies raised were not employed in the activities of the qualifying trade', as 'there was no evidence that they were used for anything other than to pay for changing the partners' interests in the partnership'. Furthermore, 'there was no evidence that the monies were raised with the intention that the money would be employed in the activities of the trade' and 'all the evidence showed that the monies were intended to be employed in giving the money to the other partners'.

In *East Allenheads Estate Ltd v HMRC* FTT, [2015] SFTD 908, an investor was held to be ineligible for deferral relief because the company existed in part for the purpose of conferring a personal benefit on the investor.

See also *Blackburn and another v HMRC* CA 2009, [2009] STC 188 and *Domain Dynamics (Holdings) Ltd v HMRC* (Sp C 701), [2008] SSCD 1136.

Postponement of the original gain

Where a chargeable gain would otherwise accrue to an individual ('the investor'), and he acquires a qualifying investment, a claim can be made by him to defer the whole or part of that gain against his investment up to an amount specified in the claim (limited to the amount of the gain or, where applicable, the amount of the gain not already relieved under either these provisions or those at **54.46** SEED ENTERPRISE INVESTMENT SCHEME). The amount of investment available to be matched with gains in this way is limited to the amount of the qualifying investment (to the extent that it has not already been so matched). The gain eligible for deferral is the gain after any mandatory deductions and reliefs which have to be claimed (HMRC Venture Capital Schemes Manual VCM23010).

Claims

Subject to what is said at **13.2** CLAIMS re claims being included in a self-assessment tax return if possible, there is no statutory form in which a claim *must* be made (though the claim form attached to form EIS 3 – see below – *may* be used, with or without a tax return). The provisions for income tax relief claims (see **22.13** above) are applied, with modifications, to deferral relief claims. Thus, a deferral relief claim cannot be made earlier than the end of the four-month minimum period referred to at **22.5** above and cannot be made later than the fifth anniversary of 31 January following the tax year in which the shares were issued. A claim cannot be made until, with the authority of HMRC, the company has furnished the individual with a compliance certificate (on form EIS 3) to the effect that, from its point of view, the conditions for deferral relief are satisfied. For more details relating to the issue of the certificate, see Tolley's Income Tax.

Deferred gain becoming chargeable

The deferred gain will become chargeable upon the occurrence of, *and at the time of*, any of the chargeable events listed below. The amount of the gain accruing at the time of the chargeable event is equal to so much of the deferred gain as is attributable to the EIS shares in relation to which the chargeable event occurs. For these purposes, a proportionate part of the net deferred gain (i.e. the deferred gain less any amount brought into charge on an earlier part disposal) is attributed to each of the 'relevant shares' held, immediately before the chargeable event, by the investor or by a person who acquired them from the investor on a transfer between spouses or civil partners within *TCGA 1992, s 58*. The '*relevant shares*' are the shares acquired in making the qualifying investment and, in a case where the original gain accrued at a later time than the making of the qualifying investment, still held at that time. They also include any bonus shares issued in respect of the relevant shares and of the same class and carrying the same rights. The said chargeable events are as follows.

(i) The investor disposes of the EIS shares otherwise than by way of a transfer between spouses or civil partners to which *TCGA 1992, s 58* applies.

(ii) Subsequent to a transfer within *TCGA 1992, s 58*, the shares are disposed of by the investor's spouse or civil partner (otherwise than by way of transfer back to the investor).

(iii) Within the 'relevant period', the investor becomes not resident in the UK.

(iv) Within the relevant period, the investor's spouse or civil partner, having acquired the shares by way of transfer within *TCGA 1992, s 58*, becomes not resident in the UK.

(v) The shares cease to be eligible shares or are treated as so ceasing (see below).

For these purposes, the '*relevant period*' is the period ending immediately before the third anniversary of the date of issue of the shares or, if later and where relevant, the third anniversary of the date of commencement of the intended trade referred to in **22.10**(a) above.

In the case of (iii) or (iv) above (non-residence), the deferred gain does not become chargeable where the investor (or, where applicable, spouse or civil partner) becomes not resident through temporary working outside the UK and again becomes resident within three years of that event, without having disposed of any of the relevant shares in the meantime in circumstances such that a chargeable event would have occurred had he been UK resident. No assessment is to be made until it is clear that the person concerned will not regain UK resident status within the three-year period.

EIS shares are *treated* as ceasing to be eligible shares (in which case a chargeable event occurs under (v) above) in any of the following circumstances (and see also the further provisions in **22.19** below).

(1) The condition at (b) above (qualifying company) ceases to be satisfied in consequence of an event occurring after the issue of the shares: the shares cease to be eligible shares at the time of that event. HMRC have confirmed that the company is required to retain its qualifying status only for the duration of 'period B' (as defined in **22.7** above), so no chargeable event can occur under this heading by reason of anything happening beyond the end of that period (*Taxation 18 February 1999 p 486*).

(2) The condition at (e) above (relevant investments) ceases to be satisfied in consequence of an event occurring after the issue of the shares: the shares cease to be eligible shares at the time of that event.

(3) The condition at (f) above (compliance with the issuing company to carry on the qualifying business activity requirement) ceases to be satisfied in consequence of an event occurring after the issue of the shares: the shares cease to be eligible shares at the time of that event.

(4) The condition at (h) above (money raised to be used for purpose of qualifying business activity within a specified time period) is not satisfied and the deferral claim was made before the end of the time period of twelve months or two years (whichever is relevant): the shares cease to be eligible shares at the end of that time period. (If the deferral claim has not been made by then, or if the condition at (f) above is not satisfied at all, the shares are treated as never having been eligible shares.)

Death

The deferred gain does not become chargeable on the death of the investor (or, where applicable, spouse or civil partner) or on the occurrence after death of any event which would otherwise have been a chargeable event.

Identification rules

In determining whether any shares disposed of are shares to which deferral relief is attributable (see **22.16** above), the normal identification rules (see **58.2** SHARES AND SECURITIES — IDENTIFICATION RULES) are disapplied and, instead, the same rules as in **22.15** above apply (broadly, first in/first out but with special rules where shares acquired on the same day fall into different specified categories — see examples at HMRC Venture Capital Schemes Manual VCM23170).

Where at the time of the chargeable event, any of the relevant shares are regarded under capital gains tax legislation as represented by assets which consist of or include assets other than such shares, the deferred gain attributable to those shares is to be apportioned between those assets on a just and reasonable basis. As between different assets regarded as representing the same shares, the identification of those assets follows the same identification rules as for shares.

Persons chargeable

The chargeable gain is treated as accruing, depending on which type of chargeable event occurs, to:

- the individual who makes the disposal;
- the individual who becomes non-resident;
- the individual who holds the shares in question when they cease (or are treated as ceasing) to be eligible shares.

Where the last category applies and some of the shares are held by the investor and some by a person who acquired them from the investor by way of transfer between spouses or civil partners within *TCGA 1992, s 58*, the gain is computed separately as regards each individual without reference to the shares held by the other.

[*TCGA 1992, ss 105A(4)(7)–(9), 150C, Sch 5B paras 1–6, 19*].

See the further provisions at **22.19** below.

Example

Frank realises a chargeable gain of £270,000 in May 2024 on the disposal of an asset he had acquired in August 2009. He makes no other disposals in 2024/25. On 1 March 2025, he subscribes £234,000 for 60% of the issued ordinary share capital in a new company, ABC Ltd. The investment is a qualifying investment for the purposes of EIS deferral relief. Frank makes a claim to defer the maximum £234,000 of the May 2024 gain against the qualifying investment.

The CGT position for 2024/25 is as follows:

	£
Gain	270,000
Less deferred under EIS provisions	234,000
	36,000
Less annual exempt amount	3,000
Taxable gain 2024/25	£33,000

On 1 August 2030, he sells 40% of his holding of ABC Ltd shares for £213,600. The disposal does not qualify for BUSINESS ASSET DISPOSAL RELIEF (**9**). He makes no other disposals in 2030/31. His CGT position for that year is as follows:

	£
Gain on ABC Ltd shares	
Disposal proceeds	213,600
Less cost (£234,000 × 40%)	93,600
Gain	£120,000
Deferred gain brought into charge	
Total gain deferred	£234,000
Clawback restricted to expenditure to which disposal relates	£93,600
Taxable gains 2030/31 (subject to annual exempt amount) (£120,000 + £93,600)	£213,600
Gain remaining deferred until any future chargeable event (£234,000 – £93,600)	£140,400

Notes to the example

(a) Frank's subscription for ABC Ltd shares cannot qualify for EIS income tax relief. He is connected with the company by virtue of his shareholding being greater than 30%. (In practice, the holdings of his associates, e.g. wife and children, need to be taken into account as well.) See **22.6** above.

(b) As the ABC Ltd shares do not qualify for income tax relief, there is no exemption as in **22.15** above for the gain arising on part disposal, despite the shares having been held for over three years.

Reinvestment into EIS shares issued after 5 April 1998 — application to trustees

[22.18] The deferral provisions for individuals at **22.17** above (and the further provisions at **22.19** below) also apply to trustees of a settlement where, in a case where the gain to be deferred accrues to them on the disposal of an asset, that asset (the '*trust asset*') is comprised in settled property of the kind mentioned in either (a) or (b) below.

(a) Settled property on discretionary trusts (i.e. settlements where the beneficiaries' interests are not interests in possession, an interest in possession for this purpose excluding an interest for a fixed term; and see generally **56.4** SETTLEMENTS) where all of the beneficiaries are either individuals or charities.
(b) Settled property on non-discretionary trusts (i.e. settlements where the beneficiaries' interests are interests in possession as in (a) above) where any of the beneficiaries is an individual or a charity.

Where there is at least one beneficiary holding a non-discretionary interest and at least one beneficiary holding a discretionary interest (i.e. a mixed settlement), all of the discretionary interests are treated for these purposes as if they were a single interest in possession, and as if that interest were held, where all the discretionary beneficiaries are individuals or charities, by an individual or charity, and, in any other case, by a person who is not an individual or charity.

If, at the time of the disposal of the trust asset, the settled property comprising that asset is within (b) above but not all of the beneficiaries are individuals or charities, then only the 'relevant proportion' of the gain on the disposal is taken into account for the purposes of deferral relief. The '*relevant proportion*' at any time is the proportion which the aggregate amount of the income of the settled property interests in which are held by individuals or charities bears to the total amount of all of the income of the settled property.

If the settled property qualifies under (a) above at the time of the disposal of the trust asset, deferral relief is available only if, immediately after the acquisition of the EIS shares, the settled property comprising the EIS shares also qualifies under (a) above. This also applies with necessary modifications to settled property qualifying under (b) above but, if not all the beneficiaries are individuals or charities, with the additional condition that the relevant proportion immediately after the acquisition of the EIS shares must be not less than the relevant proportion at the time of the disposal of the trust asset.

[*TCGA 1992, Sch 5B para 17*].

Note that neither EIS income tax relief nor the CGT disposal relief at **22.15** above applies to trustees.

Reinvestment into EIS shares issued after 5 April 1998 — further provisions

[22.19] Some further provisions are as follows:

(1) **Reorganisations.** Provisions identical to those of *TCGA 1992, s 150A(6)(6A)(7)* (see **22.15** above under 'Reorganisations of share capital') apply in relation to shares to which deferral relief is attributable (see **22.16** above).

Acquisition of share capital by new company. Provisions similar to those of *ITA 2007, ss 247–249* (which enables an EIS company to become a wholly-owned subsidiary of a new holding company in certain circumstances — see **22.15** above under 'Company reconstructions' and also Tolley's Income Tax) apply for the purposes of deferral relief. Provided all the conditions are satisfied, deferral relief attributable to shares in the original EIS company is regarded as being attributable to the shares in the new company for which the original shares are exchanged.

Other reconstructions. Where *TCGA 1992, s 135* (exchange of securities — see **57.5** SHARES AND SECURITIES) or *s 136* (scheme of reconstruction involving issue of securities — see **57.7** SHARES AND SECURITIES) apply to shares to which deferral relief, but not income tax relief, is attributable, those sections are treated as not applying for the purpose of the provisions at **22.17** above under which a deferred gain becomes chargeable. There will therefore be a disposal of the shares for the purpose only of those provisions, giving rise to a chargeable event (see **22.17**(i) above). This does not apply where the acquisition of share capital by a new company provisions above apply or where:

- the new holding consists of new ordinary shares issued after the end of 'period A' (as defined at **22.15** above under Gains and applied by reference to the original shares and the company which issued them) and carrying no present or future preferential rights to dividends or assets or right to redemption; and
- the company issuing the new shares has previously issued shares under the EIS and has issued the appropriate compliance certificate (see **22.13** above) enabling investors to obtain relief on that earlier issue.

[*TCGA 1992, Sch 5B paras 7–9, 19*].

(2) **Anti-avoidance provisions.**

Reinvestment in same company etc. If an individual realises a gain on disposal of shares in or securities of a company (Company A), he cannot defer that gain by virtue of a subscription for shares in an EIS company which is either Company A itself or is, either at the time of the disposal or the time of the issue of the EIS shares, a member of the same 'group' as Company A. A '*group*' is defined for this purpose as consisting of a company which has one or more 51% subsidiaries (within *CTA 2010, Pt 24 Ch 3*) and those subsidiaries.

Further provisions apply where an individual defers a gain by subscribing for EIS shares, disposes of any of those shares and makes a further subscription for shares in the same company (or member of the same group); no deferral relief is allowed in respect of the second subscription. This also applies where there has been no disposal of the original EIS shares but the further subscription is for shares in a company a disposal of shares in which resulted in the initial deferral (or a member of the same group as that company). The definition of a group given above applies for these purposes.

Investment-linked loans. Provisions analogous to the no linked loans requirement at **22.6** above apply where an investment-linked loan etc. is made to the investor or his associate in 'period A' (as in **22.6** above). For deferral relief purposes, the EIS shares are treated as never having been eligible shares (with the result that no such relief is available) if the loan is made on or before the date of their issue and as otherwise ceasing to be eligible shares (with the result that a chargeable event occurs in respect of deferral relief claimed — see **22.17**(v) above) on the date the loan is made.

Where the shares are subscribed for by trustees, and relief claimed by virtue of **22.18** above, the above applies to loans made not only to the trustees but to any individual (or associate) or charity (or connected person) by virtue of whose interest (at the time the shares are issued and/or at the time the loan is made) deferral relief is available in respect of the settled property.

Pre-arranged exits. Provisions identical to the no pre-arranged exit requirement at **22.6** above apply to prevent EIS shares from being eligible shares for deferral relief purposes where certain exit arrangements are made in relation to their issue.

Disqualifying arrangements. Provisions identical to the no disqualifying arrangements requirement at **22.6** above apply (subject to the same commencement rule) to prevent EIS shares from being eligible shares for deferral relief purposes where such arrangements are made in relation to their issue.

Put and call options. The granting of a put option or call option prevents the EIS shares to which it relates from being eligible shares for deferral relief purposes if the option is granted on or before the date of issue of the shares, or otherwise causes them to be treated as ceasing to be eligible shares (with the result that a chargeable event occurs in respect of deferral relief claimed — see **22.17**(v) above) at the time the option is granted. The provisions apply where an individual subscribes for EIS shares (or acquires them on a no gain/no loss transfer from a subscriber spouse or civil partner) and, during 'period A' (defined as in **22.6** above), either:

- an option for the grantor to purchase such shares (a '*put option*') is granted to the individual, or
- an option for the individual to sell such shares (a '*call option*') is granted by the individual.

Comparable provisions apply for the purposes of EIS income tax relief.

Value received by the investor from the EIS company. Where the EIS investor (or his associate — within **22.6** above) receives any value from the company during the 'period of restriction' (see below), the shares are treated as never having been eligible shares for deferral relief purposes if the value is received on or before the date of the share issue or as otherwise ceasing to be eligible shares (with the result that a chargeable event occurs in respect of deferral relief claimed — see **22.17**(v) above) at the time value is received. Note that the full amount of the deferred gain falls to be clawed back even if the investor receives back only a proportion of the value of his investment (see *Segesta Ltd v HMRC* UT, [2012] STC 1847). The provisions of *TCGA 1992, Sch 5B para 13* which determine whether value is received from a company are based on the EIS income tax relief withdrawal provisions (now *ITA 2007, ss 213–223*). They are fairly widely drawn but *not* so as to catch, for example, reasonable remuneration (or reimbursement of expenses) to the individual as an officer or employee of the company, interest at a commercial rate on a loan made to the company or dividends which represent no more than a normal return on investment in that company. The provisions *do* include, for example, any repayment, redemption or repurchase by the company of any of its share capital or securities which belong to the individual, any loan or advance by the company to the individual which is not repaid before the EIS shares are issued, and the provision of a benefit or facility for the individual. Value received from a connected person of the company (within *TCGA 1992, s 286* — see **17** CONNECTED PERSONS) falls within the provisions if it would have done so had it been received from the EIS company itself.

Value received is disregarded if its amount is *insignificant*, i.e. if it does not exceed £1,000 or, in any other case, if it is insignificant in relation to that part of the amount expended on subscribing for the shares that has been used as in **22.17** above to defer chargeable gains. In applying this let-out, multiple receipts of value must be aggregated (see examples at HMRC Venture Capital Schemes Manual VCM23390), and the let-out is disapplied in certain cases where value received is pre-arranged. Value received is also disregarded if the person from whom the value was obtained receives at least equivalent *replacement value* from the original recipient, though certain types of payment are treated as not giving rise to a receipt of replacement value.

If an individual to whom shares in a company have been issued entered into a convertible loan agreement with the company under the Future Fund on or after 20 May 2020, and subsequently receives value from the company under the terms of that agreement, the value received is ignored in applying the above rules to shares issued before the individual entered into the agreement. This is to ensure that investors in a company who also support the company using a Future Fund convertible loan note will not lose relief on any previous EIS investments when that loan is redeemed or converted into shares. The Future Fund was set up as part of government support to companies impacted by the 2020 COVID-19 (coronavirus) pandemic.

Where the shares are subscribed for by trustees, and relief claimed by virtue of **22.18** above, the above provisions apply to value received not only by the trustees but by any individual (or associate) or charity (or connected person) by virtue of whose interest (at the time the shares are issued and/or at the time the value is received) deferral relief is available in respect of the settled property.

For these purposes, the '*period of restriction*' is the period beginning one year before the issue of the shares and ending immediately before the third anniversary of the issue date or, if later and where relevant, the third anniversary of the date of commencement of the intended trade referred to in **22.10**(a) above.

Where the trade is begun to be carried on by a subsidiary after the date of issue of the shares, in determining when the trade commenced, any carrying on of the trade by the subsidiary before it became a 'qualifying 90% subsidiary' (see **22.9** above) is disregarded.

See the corresponding chapter of Tolley's Income Tax for detailed coverage of the broadly equivalent income tax provisions.

See also *Blackburn and another v HMRC* CA 2008, [2009] STC 188 and *Segesta Ltd v HMRC* FTT, [2010] SFTD 962.

Value received by other persons from the EIS company. Provisions based on the EIS income tax relief withdrawal provisions (now *ITA 2007, ss 224–231*) apply where, at any time in the period of restriction (as defined immediately above), the EIS company (or one which is a 51% subsidiary at some time in 'period A' — defined as in **22.6** above) repays, redeems or repurchases any of its share capital from a member (other than the EIS investor in question) who does not thereby lose EIS income tax relief or deferral relief or corporate venturing scheme investment relief. They apply equally where the company or such subsidiary makes any payment to any such member for the giving up of rights to share capital on its cancellation or extinguishment. The shares are treated as never having been eligible shares for deferral relief purposes if such an event occurs on or before the date of the share issue or as otherwise ceasing to be eligible shares (with the result that a chargeable event occurs in respect of deferral relief claimed — see **22.17**(v) above) at the time such event occurs.

The absence of any loss of EIS income tax relief etc., as referred to above, is disregarded if it is due only to the amount received being of insignificant value. A repayment etc. is itself disregarded if the amount received by the member in question is insignificant in relation to the market value immediately after the event of the remaining issued share capital of the company or, as the case may be, 51% subsidiary. The assumption is made that the shares in question are cancelled at the time of the event. In applying the test, the market value, immediately before the event, of the shares to which the event relates is substituted for the amount received if this would give a greater amount. This let-out is disapplied in certain cases where a repayment etc. is pre-arranged. 'Insignificant' is taken by HMRC to mean 'trifling or completely unimportant' (HMRC Venture Capital Schemes Manual VCM23460).

[*TCGA 1992, Sch 5B paras 10–15, 18, 19; FA 2020, s 110*].

(3) **Information.** Certain chargeable events and failures of conditions must be notified to HMRC, generally within 60 days, by either the investor, the EIS company or any person connected with the EIS company having knowledge of the matter. HMRC may require such notice where they have reason to believe it should have been made, and are given broad powers to require information generally.

[*TCGA 1992, Sch 5B para 16*].

Reinvestment into EIS shares issued before 6 April 1998

[22.20] Deferral relief was available to an individual where:

(a) a chargeable gain would otherwise have accrued to him on the disposal by him of any asset (or on the occurrence of a chargeable event either under these provisions or the similar provisions governing reinvestment into VCT shares (see **64.8** VENTURE CAPITAL TRUSTS)); and

(b) he subscribed for shares to which any EIS income tax relief was attributable within the one year before ant the three years after the time the chargeable gain in (a) above accrued.

Deferred gain becoming chargeable

The deferred gain would become chargeable upon the occurrence of, and at the time of, any of a number of specified chargeable events. The only remaining circumstances in which a deferred gain can become chargeable are as follows.

(i) The investor disposes of the EIS shares otherwise than by way of a transfer to which *TCGA 1992, s 58* (see **40.4** MARRIED PERSONS AND CIVIL PARTNERS) applies. As regards part disposals, HMRC interpret the law as requiring a proportionate part of the deferred gain to be brought into account.

(ii) Subsequent to a transfer within *TCGA 1992, s 58*, the shares are disposed of by the investor's spouse (otherwise than by way of transfer back to the investor).

The deferred gain is treated as accruing to the individual making the disposal. [*TCGA 1992, s 150C, Sch 5B as originally enacted*].

Key points concerning enterprise investment scheme

[22.21] Points to consider are as follows.

- An investment in shares under the EIS provides for three types of tax relief: income tax relief; exemption from capital gains; and deferral of some other capital gain.
- CGT exemption is linked to income tax relief and relief for one is not possible without the other and is not available if the investor is connected with the company.
- CGT deferral can be obtained without income tax relief.
- EIS relief should not be claimed until a form EIS 3 has been issued by the company to the investor. It can be claimed via the Self Assessment Tax Return or separately. If the EIS 3 is available early enough relief can be included in a PAYE code.
- There is a maximum of up to £2,000,000 per year and an investment in one year can be carried back to the previous year subject to the maximum in that earlier year. If the shares acquired do not include any shares in knowledge-intensive companies ('KIC shares'), the limit is £1 million. If the total amount subscribed for KIC shares is £1 million or more, the limit is £2 million. In any other case, the limit is £1 million plus total amount subscribed for KIC shares.

- EIS relief is only available where funds are 'employed' by the EIS company within the qualifying period. Once an investment has been made there is a need to monitor that the company uses the correct portion of the funds raised for qualifying purposes within the time allowed. This can often cause problems, for example, when market conditions change or investments fall through following due diligence.
- EIS deferral relief operates by reducing the allowable cost of the shares. A claim should be restricted, if necessary in order to utilise the annual capital gains tax exempt amount.
- Where income tax relief is withdrawn or reduced it is done by means of an assessment issued by HMRC. It cannot be recovered through the Self Assessment Tax Return although the liability will be added to the Statement of Account.
- Where shares are disposed of or relief withdrawn any gain deferred, as a result of EIS deferral relief, will be revived as though it was a gain arising at the date of disposal of the EIS shares or the date of the event giving rise to the withdrawal of the relief.
- Where gains have been deferred in the past the rate of tax at the time may have been less than the current rates. If a gain is to be revived, it may be worth checking whether it is still within the time limit to revoke the deferral relief claim as the tax at a lower rate plus interest may be less than the tax due at current rates.
- Where the shares are disposed of at a loss (including negligible value claims), the loss is allowable even though any gain would have been exempt. If income tax relief is not withdrawn then the cost of the shares is reduced by the income tax relief obtained when calculating the loss. It should be possible to claim relief for the loss against income.
- A deferred gain does not become chargeable on the death of the investor.

23

Exemptions and Reliefs

Cross-references. See 8 ASSETS HELD ON 6 APRIL 1965; 8 ASSETS HELD ON 31 MARCH 1982; 9 BUSINESS ASSET DISPOSAL RELIEF; 11 CHARITIES; 19 CORPORATE VENTURING SCHEME; 18 DEATH; 20 DOUBLE TAX RELIEF; 22 ENTERPRISE INVESTMENT SCHEME; 28 GOVERNMENT SECURITIES; 30 HOLD-OVER RELIEFS; 32 INDEXATION; 38 LOSSES; 43 OVERSEAS MATTERS; 47 PRIVATE RESIDENCES; 48 QUALIFYING CORPORATE BONDS; 51 RESIDENCE AND DOMICILE; 53 ROLLOVER RELIEF — REPLACEMENT OF BUSINESS ASSETS; 57 SHARES AND SECURITIES; 60 SUBSTANTIAL SHAREHOLDINGS OF COMPANIES; 63 UNIT TRUSTS AND OTHER INVESTMENT VEHICLES; 64 VENTURE CAPITAL TRUSTS.

Introduction to exemptions and reliefs

[23.1] A person is chargeable to capital gains tax on chargeable gains accruing to them on the disposal of assets in any tax year during any part of which they are resident in the UK. All forms of property except sterling are regarded as assets for these purposes and every gain, except as otherwise expressly provided, is a chargeable gain. There are, however, a number of exemptions and reliefs. These may broadly be classified as follows.

(a) Exempt assets (see **23.2–23.17** below).
(b) Exempt gains and transactions (see **23.19–23.39** below).
(c) Exempt organisations and individuals (see **23.40–23.61** below).

In addition, a number of reliefs are available to reduce or defer the amount of capital gains tax payable. See **23.62–23.88** and certain provisions in **23.51** and **23.58** below.

Exempt assets

[23.2] Gains accruing on the disposal of certain assets are exempt from capital gains tax. The exemption (total or partial) of the various types of asset is examined in **23.3–23.17** below. Losses arising from such disposals are similarly not allowable unless expressly provided otherwise. [*TCGA 1992, s 16(2)*].

Annuities and annual payments

[23.3] A gain accruing on the disposal of a right to or to any part of an allowance, annuity, or capital sum from a *superannuation fund* or annual payments receivable under a 'covenant' not secured on property, is exempt. [*TCGA 1992, s 237(a)(c)*]. '*Covenant*' means a gratuitous promise enforceable solely due to the form in which it is evidenced (i.e., in England, in a document under seal). It does not include contracts enforceable as such (*Rank Xerox Ltd v Lane* HL 1979, 53 TC 185).

A gain accruing on the disposal of, or of an 'interest' in, rights under a contract for a 'non-deferred annuity' or an annuity granted (or deemed to be granted) under *Government Annuities Act 1929* is also exempt. For this purpose, a '*non-deferred annuity*' is an annuity (including an annuity which includes instalments of capital) which is not granted under a contract for a deferred annuity and which is granted in the ordinary course of a business granting annuities on the life of any person. An '*interest*' in rights means an interest as co-owner of the rights, and it is immaterial whether the rights are owned jointly or in common or whether or not the interests of the co-owners are equal. [*TCGA 1992, ss 204(5)(7)–(9), 237(b)*].

Chattels

[23.4] A tangible movable asset (other than a commodity disposed of by or through a dealer on a terminal market) is entirely exempt, provided that the asset is not 'currency of any description' and that the disposal is for a consideration of £6,000 or less.

If the consideration exceeds £6,000, the chargeable gain is limited to five-thirds of the excess.

[*TCGA 1992, s 262(1)(2)(6)*].

Examples

(i) A chattel which cost £5,000 in May 2016 is disposed of in May 2024 for £8,000. Assume expenses of disposal of £300. The chargeable gain is ascertained as follows.

Excess of consideration over £6,000	£2,000
£2,000 × $^5/_3$	£3,333
Actual gain is £2,700 which is less than £3,333	
Chargeable gain	£2,700

(ii) A chattel which cost £2,000 in May 2016 is disposed of in May 2024 for £8,000. Assume expenses of disposal of £280.

Excess of consideration over £6,000	£2,000
£2,000 × $^5/_3$	£3,333
Actual gain is £5,720 which is more than £3,333	
Chargeable gain	£3,333

Part disposal

Where the disposal is of a right or interest in or over a tangible movable asset, and the sum of the consideration received plus the value of what remains exceeds £6,000, a similar limitation of the chargeable gain applies but the excess for this purpose is computed as follows.

$$(\text{consideration received} + \text{value of remainder} - £6{,}000) \times \frac{\text{considerationreceived}}{\text{total value}}$$

[*TCGA 1992, s 262(5)*].

Losses

For the purposes of loss relief, a disposal of a tangible movable asset for a consideration of less than £6,000 is deemed to be made for a consideration of £6,000. In the case of a partial disposal of an asset the total value of which is less than £6,000, the deemed consideration for loss relief purposes is computed as follows.

$$(\text{£}6{,}000 - \text{total value}) \times \left(\frac{\text{consideration received}}{\text{total value}}\right) + \text{consideration received}$$

Simplified, this becomes (£6,000 × consideration/total value).

[*TCGA 1992, s 262(3)*].

Assets forming a set

Where these are owned by the same disposer they are to be treated as a single asset where they are disposed of, whether on the same or on different occasions, to the same person or to persons acting in concert, or to CONNECTED PERSONS (**17**). [*TCGA 1992, s 262(4)*]. For HMRC's views on the circumstances in which a number of bottles of wine may constitute a set, see Revenue Tax Bulletin August 1999 p 686. For an article on pairs of shotguns, see Revenue Tax Bulletin February 2000 pp 726, 727.

Wasting assets

Subject to the following exceptions, tangible movable assets which are WASTING ASSETS (**65**) are exempt whatever the consideration received. This exemption is restricted or eliminated to the extent that the asset, by reason of its having been used in trade or otherwise, has been or could have been the subject of a capital allowance.

The exemption is also eliminated where the asset has become plant as a result of its use for the purposes of a trade, profession or vocation carried on by a person other than the owner and it would not otherwise have been a wasting asset. This does not, however, apply if the asset is plant under a long funding lease and the disposal takes place during the term of the lease or it is a deemed disposal on termination of the lease (see **7.6** ASSETS).

The exemption is also not applicable to a disposal of commodities on a terminal market.

[*TCGA 1992, s 45*].

Where capital allowances were initially granted in respect of qualifying expenditure on movable machinery but were later withdrawn because the machinery was sold without it having been brought into use by the taxpayer, it was held that the taxpayer should be treated as if the allowance had never been made, with the result that the disposal on sale was exempt (*Burman v Westminster Press Ltd* Ch D 1987, 60 TC 418). If a restriction by reference to capital allowances would otherwise arise, relief as under *TCGA 1992, s 262* above may be available.

HMRC accept that any of the following is machinery and is thus a tangible movable wasting asset (see **65.2** WASTING ASSETS) which will be exempt where owned privately and not used in a business: antique clocks and watches; motor vehicles which are not normal private passenger vehicles and are thus outside the exemption at **23.11** below, e.g. taxi cabs, vans, motor cycles etc.; trawlers, fishing vessels, tankers and other vessels propelled by engines (and see below re boats generally). (HMRC Capital Gains Manual CG76904–CG76909). They 'generally accept' that all types of gun are within the general description of machinery (HMRC Capital Gains Manual CG76905).

For HMRC's views on the circumstances in which bottled wine may qualify as a wasting asset and thus an exempt chattel, see HMRC Capital Gains Manual CG76901.

Boats

Boats 'will generally be tangible movable wasting assets' and thus exempt (except where qualifying for capital allowances). This will not always apply to yachts, barges or boats used as a residence, as these may have a longer useful life. A houseboat which is permanently located on a site and connected to all mains services may in some circumstances be regarded as a dwelling house. (HMRC Capital Gains Manual CG64325 and see also above).

Debts

[23.5] A debt, other than a 'debt on a security' (see below), disposed of by the original creditor or their personal representative or legatee is exempt. The disposal of a debt includes, for this purpose, the disposal of an interest in a debt (and references below to the amount of a debt are, in such a case, references to the amount of the interest).

Where the trustees of a settlement are the original creditor, a person becoming absolutely entitled to the debt is treated as a personal representative or legatee as is his own personal representative or legatee.

[*TCGA 1992, s 251(1)(5)(5A)*].

A right possibly to receive an unidentifiable sum at an unascertainable date is not a 'debt' (*Marren v Ingles* HL 1980, 54 TC 76; *Marson v Marriage* Ch D 1979, 54 TC 59).

Subject to the above, the satisfaction of a debt (including a debt on a security) or part of it is treated as a disposal of the debt by the creditor made at the time when the debt is satisfied. Where a debt on a security is involved this rule is subject to the provisions in *TCGA 1992, ss 132, 135, 136* covering reorganisations of share capital (see **57.5**, **57.7** and **57.8** SHARES AND SECURITIES). [*TCGA 1992, s 251(2)*].

Where property is acquired by a creditor in satisfaction of a debt then, subject to any reorganisation of share capital as above, the property is not treated as disposed of by the debtor or acquired by the creditor for a consideration greater than its market value at the time of the creditor's acquisition of it. But if no chargeable gain accrues as regards the debt either because the creditor is the original creditor or under the share capital reorganisation rules *and* a chargeable gain accrues to the creditor on a disposal by him of the property, then any resulting chargeable gain is reduced so as not to exceed the chargeable gain that would have accrued if he had acquired the property for a consideration equal to the amount of the debt. [*TCGA 1992, s 251(3)*].

Loss relief

Where the original creditor and a subsequent creditor are CONNECTED PERSONS (**17**), a loss incurred by the subsequent creditor on the disposal of a debt is not an allowable loss. See **38.7** LOSSES.

Loss relief is available to the maker of a 'qualifying loan' or a guarantor of a qualifying loan. See **38.11** LOSSES. See **38.12** LOSSES for a corresponding relief where the borrower's debt is a debt on a security which is a qualifying corporate bond.

Foreign currency bank accounts

The exemption does not apply to the disposal of a bank balance in a foreign currency unless it is made by an individual, the trustees of a settlement or the personal representatives of a deceased person. [*TCGA 1992, s 252*].

Simon's Taxes. See **C1.608.**

Redenomination into euros

The redenomination into euros of a debt, other than a debt on a security, from the currency of a State participating in the European single currency on or after 1 January 1999 is not treated as involving the disposal of that debt or the acquisition of a new debt. The original debt and the new debt are treated as the same asset, acquired as the original debt was acquired. [*SI 1998 No 3177, Reg 37*]. Accordingly the disposal of the new debt by the original creditor retains its exemption.

Meaning of 'debt on a security'

A '*debt on a security*' is defined by reference to *TCGA 1992, s 132(3)(b),* so that '*security*' includes any loan stock or similar security of any government or public or local authority in the UK or elsewhere, or of any company, and whether secured or unsecured. The existence of a document may be indicative of a 'debt on a security', but it cannot be concluded from the absence of a document that the debt is not 'on a security' (*Aberdeen Construction Group Ltd v CIR* HL 1978, 52 TC 281; *W T Ramsay Ltd v CIR* HL 1981, 54 TC 101; *Cleveleys Investment Trust Co v CIR (No 1)* CS 1971, 47 TC 300). An intra-group loan secured on a promissory note was held not to be a marketable security in any realistic sense and was not a 'debt on a security' (*Taylor Clark International Ltd v Lewis* CA 1998, 71 TC 226). For further discussion of the meaning of 'security' see the income tax case of *Williams v Singer and Others* HL 1920, 7 TC 387, and for 'debt on security' see *Tarmac Roadstone Holdings Ltd v Williams* (Sp C 95), [1996] SSCD 409.

HMRC's view, based principally on the HL judgments of Lords Wilberforce and Fraser in *Ramsay*, is set out in HMRC Capital Gains Manual CG53420–53436. This guidance states that for a debt to be a debt on a security it should be capable of being *both*:

- held as an investment, and
- realised at a profit.

The position is to be judged by reference to circumstances prevailing at the time the debt is created, though these may include anticipated changes in market interest rates. For a debt to be capable of being held as an investment it should carry a commercial rate of interest, or offer an equivalent return by virtue of its being repayable at a premium or issued at a discount. It should also be marketable. Whether it can be realised at a profit depends not only on the rate of interest, premium etc. but also on whether the debt will last long enough to cover the costs of acquisition and obtain a worthwhile return. HMRC will accept that any loan which cannot be terminated by the borrower within a year of commencement will be outstanding long enough to have the required 'structure of permanence'. But a debt will not have a structure of permanence merely because the borrower is not in a position to repay it in the foreseeable future. A debt can, however, be capable of being realised at a profit if the terms require the lender to be adequately compensated in the event of early repayment. Standard clauses requiring early repayment on the happening of events such as the default or liquidation of the borrower, should not be seen as displacing any stated terms for repayment. The existence of a formal document constituting or evidencing the debt is not an *essential* feature of a debt on a security. Neither realised, nor potential, foreign exchange gains or losses should be taken into account in deciding whether a debt is a debt on a security.

A debenture issued by any company after 15 March 1993 is deemed to be a security within *TCGA 1992, s 132(3)(b)* above if:

(1) it is issued on a reorganisation or reduction of a company's share capital or in pursuance of its allotment on any such reorganisation or reduction;

(2) it is issued in exchange for shares in or debentures of another company and in a case to which *TCGA 1992, s 135* (see **57.5** SHARES AND SECURITIES) applies and which is unaffected by *TCGA 1992, s 137(1)* (restriction on application of share reorganisation rules in *TCGA 1992, ss 135, 136* — see **4.16** ANTI-AVOIDANCE);

(3) it is issued under any such arrangements as are mentioned in *TCGA 1992, s 136(1)(a)* (arrangement between company and share or debenture holders in connection with a scheme of reconstruction) and in a case unaffected by *TCGA 1992, s 137* where *s 136* requires shares or debentures in another company to be treated as exchanged for, or for anything that includes, that debenture; or

(4) it is issued in pursuance of rights attached to any debenture issued after 15 March 1993 and falling within (1), (2) or (3) above.

Any debenture resulting from a conversion of securities (within *TCGA 1992, s 132* — see **57.8** SHARES AND SECURITIES — and whether occurring before or after that date), or which is issued in pursuance of rights attaching to such a debenture, is similarly deemed to be a security.

[*TCGA 1992, s 251(6)*].

For the purposes of the above definition, the following instruments are deemed to be 'securities' where this would not otherwise be the case, but this fiction does not apply for the purposes of determining what is or is not an allowable loss in any case.

(i) Any instrument falling to be treated as an asset representing a company loan relationship if it were not for the exclusions at **15.7** COMPANIES — CORPORATE FINANCE AND INTANGIBLES.

(ii) Any instrument which, even apart from the exclusions mentioned in (i) above, is not a loan relationship of a company but which would be a deeply discounted security if it were not an 'excluded indexed security' (see **57.21** SHARES AND SECURITIES).

[*TCGA 1992, s 251(7)(8)*].

See also **48.3** QUALIFYING CORPORATE BONDS for a provision corresponding to *TCGA 1992, s 251(6)* and regarding the definition of 'corporate bond', so that combined the two provisions prevent, in the circumstances stated, the issue of a debenture which neither represents a debt on a security nor is a qualifying corporate bond.

Decorations

[23.6] A decoration for valour or gallantry (unless acquired by the vendor for money or money's worth) is exempt. [*TCGA 1992, s 268*].

Dwelling-houses

[23.7] A gain accruing to an individual on the disposal of (or of an interest in) a dwelling-house which has been their only or main residence during their period of ownership is exempt (or partly exempt). See **47** PRIVATE RESIDENCES for this exemption which is also extended, in certain circumstances, to trustees and personal representatives.

Foreign currency

[23.8] Foreign currency acquired for an individual's (or their dependant's) personal expenditure outside the UK (including the provision or maintenance of their residence outside the UK) is exempt. [*TCGA 1992, s 269*].

Exchange gains and losses of companies (FOREX) are dealt with under the loan relationships regime — see **15.3** COMPANIES — CORPORATE FINANCE AND INTANGIBLES.

See also **23.5** above.

Government securities

[23.9] Gains on disposals of specified UK government and public corporation stocks ('gilts') are not chargeable gains and losses are not allowable. [*TCGA 1992, s 115(1)(a)*].

The same applies to disposals of options or contracts to acquire or dispose of such gilts. See **7.7** and **7.8** ASSETS.

Gains and losses on disposals by companies of such assets are within the company loan relationship provisions described in **15.2–15.7** COMPANIES — CORPORATE FINANCE AND INTANGIBLES. They are thus treated for corporation tax purposes as *income* (and not capital) gains and losses, and are chargeable/allowable accordingly.

Those securities specified as exempt are listed in *TCGA 1992, Sch 9 Pt II* as supplemented by regular statutory instruments. In practice, all UK government securities charged on the National Loans Fund are so specified. A list of the exempt securities is been made available on the gov.uk website (www.gov.uk/gilt-edged-securities-exempt-from-capital-gains-tax).

Any security which is a strip (within *FA 1942, s 47*) of a security which is a gilt-specified as exempt is also itself a gilt-specified for the purposes of the exemption.

[*TCGA 1992, Sch 9*].

See **57.8** SHARES AND SECURITIES regarding government stock issued as compensation for shares compulsorily acquired.

Insurance policies

[23.10] A gain on the disposal of, or of an 'interest' in, the rights conferred by a 'non-life insurance policy' is exempt. Where the policy is for damage to, or loss or depreciation of, assets, the exemption applies only so far as the rights do not relate to assets which on disposal could give rise to a chargeable gain. (This does not prevent sums received under such policies for loss, damage, etc. to assets from being chargeable; see **10** CAPITAL SUMS DERIVED FROM ASSETS.)

For this purpose, a '*non-life insurance policy*' is a contract made in the course of a capital redemption business within *FA 2012, s 56(3)* (i.e. a capital redemption policy) or any policy of insurance which is not a policy of insurance on the life of any person. An '*interest*' in rights means an interest as co-owner of the rights, and it is immaterial whether the rights are owned jointly or in common or whether or not the interests of the co-owners are equal.

[*TCGA 1992, s 204(1)–(4)(7)(8)(10)*].

See also **37** LIFE INSURANCE POLICIES AND DEFERRED ANNUITIES.

Motor cars etc.

[23.11] A mechanically propelled road vehicle constructed or adapted for the carriage of passengers, except for a vehicle of a type not commonly used as a private vehicle and unsuitable to be so used, is not a chargeable asset, and thus no chargeable gain or allowable loss accrues on its disposal. [*TCGA 1992, s 263*].

This exemption applies regardless of whether or not the vehicle was eligible for capital allowances (see **23.4** above). For the interpretation of 'commonly used as a private vehicle' in relation to capital allowances, see cases mentioned in Tolley's Capital Allowances. Vehicles outside this exemption include taxi cabs, racing cars, single seat sports cars, vans, lorries, other commercial vehicles, motor cycles, scooters and motor cycle/sidecar combinations. Such motor vehicles, if privately owned and not used in a business, are exempt as tangible movable wasting assets (see **23.4** above). (HMRC Capital Gains Manual CG76906).

Personalised car number plates are not covered by either exemption. The value of the number plate itself is usually negligible, and the plate is regarded as part of the car when sold attached to it. However, the disposal of the inherent intangible right to use a specific combination of letters or numbers when registering a vehicle is neither a disposal of a motor car as above nor of a chattel as in 23.4 above, and any gain arising will be a chargeable gain. (HMRC Capital Gains Manual CG76923).

Qualifying corporate bonds

[23.12] Qualifying corporate bonds are exempt whatever the period of ownership. This also applies to options or contracts to acquire or dispose of such bonds. See **48** QUALIFYING CORPORATE BONDS, and see **7.7** and **7.8** ASSETS as regards options and contracts. For loans to traders evidenced by qualifying corporate bonds, see **38.12** LOSSES.

Renewables obligation certificates

[23.13] A gain on the disposal by an individual of a 'renewables obligation certificate' is exempt if:

- the individual acquired the certificate in connection with the generation of electricity by a microgeneration system (as defined);
- the system is installed at or near premises occupied by the individual and used wholly or mainly as a separate private dwelling; and
- the individual intends that the amount of electricity generated will not significantly exceed the amount of electricity consumed on those premises.

For this purpose, a '*renewables obligation certificate*' is a certificate issued under *Electricity Act 1989, s 32B* (or NI equivalent).

[*TCGA 1992, s 263AZA*].

Right to receive interest on deposit of victim of National-Socialist persecution

[23.14] A gain on the disposal of a right, or an 'interest' in a right, to receive the whole or any part of a payment of interest eligible for income tax exemption under *ITTOIA 2005, s 756A* is not a chargeable gain. That section provides, broadly, for income tax exemption for interest paid under certain compensation schemes for deposits made on or before 5 June 1945 by, or on behalf of, victims of National-Socialist persecution. See Tolley's Income Tax for further details.

An '*interest*' in a right is for this purpose an interest as a co-owner of the right and it is immaterial whether the right is owned jointly or in common, or whether or not the interests of the co-owners are equal.

This exemption was introduced in *FA 2006* and applies with retrospective effect to disposals on or after 6 April 1996. No loss accruing on a disposal before 6 April 2006 is, however, to cease to be an allowable loss as a consequence.

[*TCGA 1992, s 268A*].

See also **23.27** below for compensation from foreign governments for assets confiscated, destroyed etc.

Savings certificates, savings schemes and savings accounts etc.

[23.15] Savings certificates, and non-marketable securities issued under the *National Loans Acts 1939* and *1968* and corresponding NI enactments are not 'chargeable assets' and accordingly no chargeable gain accrues on their disposal. Interest resulting from certified SAYE savings arrangements and tax-exempt special savings accounts are ignored for capital gains tax purposes. [*TCGA 1992, ss 121, 271(4)*].

Settlements

[23.16] With certain exceptions, no chargeable gain accrues on the disposal of an interest created by or arising under a settlement by the original beneficiary or any other person (other than one who acquired, or derives his title from one who acquired, his interest for money or money's worth). See **56.15** SETTLEMENTS.

Ships and other assets within the tonnage tax regime

[23.17] Under this ring-fenced regime, a shipping company or group may elect to have its taxable profits computed by reference to the net tonnage of each of the qualifying ships it operates. Qualifying companies must normally make an election within 12 months of first qualifying, but an opportunity is available for companies which have not made an election within the time limit to do so at any time in the period 1 June 2023 to 30 November 2024. Ship managers which are not operators of ships can elect to join the regime from 1 April 2024. An election is normally expected to remain in force for at least eight years (ten years for elections made before 1 April 2022), although an opportunity to withdraw from an election may be provided for by Treasury order. Qualifying ships must be seagoing, of at least 100 tons gross tonnage and be engaged in qualifying activities, e.g. the transportation of goods or passengers by sea. Certain vessels are excluded, e.g. fishing and factory support vessels, harbour and river ferries, oil rigs, pleasure craft, floating restaurants etc. The strategic and commercial management of ships within the regime must be undertaken from the UK. Previously, new ships entering tonnage tax had to be registered in the EU, but this rule was disapplied for certain financial years by the Treasury and has been abolished with effect from 1 April 2022.

Capital gains accruing during the currency of the election are not chargeable gains (and losses are not allowable losses) to the extent that the assets disposed of were used exclusively for the qualifying shipping activity. In the event of a company leaving the regime for certain specified reasons, anti-avoidance provisions apply to bring into charge a previously exempt gain arising in the last six years.

[*FA 2000, s 82, Sch 22; FA 2022, s 25; FA 2024, s 9, Sch 8; SI 2023 No 508*].

HMRC have published guidance on the practical operation of the regime (see HMRC Statement of Practice SP 4/00 — in particular, para 131 on exemptions from exit charges).

Windrush and other compensation schemes

[23.18] An exemption from capital gains tax applies to the disposal of a right to receive payments under the Windrush Compensation Scheme and certain other compensations schemes administered by or on behalf of the UK governments, other foreign governments or local authorities etc.

A gain is exempt (i.e. it is not a chargeable gain) if it arises on:

- a disposal resulting from the forfeiture or surrender of rights, or as a result of refraining from exercising rights, in return for a 'qualifying payment';
- a disposal of the right to receive all or part of a qualifying payment; or
- a disposal of an interest (as co-owner) in such a right.

A '*qualifying payment*' is:

- a payment under the Windrush Compensation Scheme;
- a payment made to a person who made a claim under the Windrush Compensation Scheme (and was eligible to do so) which is made in connection with the same circumstances as gave rise to that eligibility and which is paid by the UK government, the government of part of the UK or a UK local or other public authority;
- a payment under the Troubles Permanent Disablement Payment Scheme (*SI 2020 No 103*);
- a payment under the Victims of Overseas Terrorism Compensation Scheme (*SI 2024 No 182*);
- (for disposals on or after 20 October 2021) a compensation payment under the LCF Compensation Scheme (*SI 2021 No 1385*);
- (for disposals on or after 22 July 2021) a compensation payment for an overturned historical conviction under the Post Office Horizon Compensation Scheme (*SI 2023 No 184*);
- (for disposals on or after 1 August 2022) a compensation payment by the Department for Business, Energy and Industrial Strategy under the Post Office Horizon Group Litigation Order Scheme or Group Litigation Order Nominated Individual Scheme (*SI 2023 No 184* and *SI 2024 No 182*);
- (for disposals on or after 28 October 2022) a compensation payment under the Infected Blood Scheme (under *SI 2023 No 184*);
- (for disposals on or after 6 April 2023) a public service pension schemes remedy compensation payment under *Public Service Pension and Judicial Offences Act 2022, Pt 1* (*SI 2023 No 113*);
- (for disposals on or after 1 August 2023) a top-up payment under the Post Office Horizon Shortfall Scheme (*SI 2023 No 772*);
- (for disposals on or after 8 November 2023) payments under the Post Office Horizon Process Review Scheme of Suspension Remuneration Review Scheme (*SI 2024 No 182*);
- (whenever the disposal is made) an onward payment of exempt Horizon compensation paid to a company (see below), whenever received (under *FA 2020, Sch 15, Pt 2, para 10(2)*);

- (for disposals on or after the date specified in the relevant regulations) a compensation payment of a description specified in regulations made by the Treasury and paid by or on behalf of the UK government, the government of part of the UK, a foreign government or a UK or foreign local or other public authority.

The exemption also applies in respect of certain onward payments (whenever made) of compensation received by a company. The onward payment must either be made to an individual who is or was an employee or director or to an individual as a distribution.

The compensation payment to the company must be made under one of the following schemes relating to the Post Office Horizon scandal: the GLO Compensation Scheme, the Horizon Shortfall Scheme, the Suspension Remuneration Review or the Post Office Process Review. In the case of the Horizon Shortfall Scheme and the Suspension Remuneration Review, the exemption applies only to payments made to top up the amount of compensation to account for sums lost to tax. The Treasury can add payments under further schemes by statutory instrument.

Compensation payments received by a company under any of the above Post Office Horizon schemes are exempt from corporation tax, whenever received. The receipt and any onward payment is ignored for all corporation tax purposes.

[*FA 2020, s 102, Sch 15 paras 1, 2, 4, 7–10; FA 2024, s 12*].

Note that equivalent exemptions from income tax and inheritance tax also apply.

Exempt gains and transactions

[23.19] The gains or transactions detailed in 23.20–23.39 below do not give rise to a liability to capital gains tax.

Assets used for the purposes of a trade etc. taxed on the cash basis

[23.20] There is an exemption from capital gains tax for disposals of certain assets used for the purposes of a trade charged to income tax on the cash basis for small businesses. The exemption also applies to disposals of certain assets used in an unincorporated property business charged to income tax on the cash basis.

The exemption applies to certain disposals whether the disposer is using the cash basis at the time of the disposal or has previously used the cash basis, provided the three conditions below are met.

- The asset is not land.
- The asset has been used at any time during the period of ownership by the person making the disposal for the purposes of a trade, profession, vocation, or property business.

- Disposal proceeds (as defined) are brought into account as a receipt (whether or not on the cash basis) when calculating the profits of the trading etc. business or property business (under *ITTOIA 2005 s 96A(3)* or *ITTOIA 2005, s 307E(12)* respectively) under, or after leaving, the cash basis.

Where an asset has been used partly for the purposes of the trade etc. and partly for other purposes or has been used for the purposes of the trade etc. for only part of the period of ownership, or where only part of the expenditure on the asset has qualified for capital allowances, an apportionment must be made. The disposal consideration and any acquisition or enhancement expenditure must be apportioned by reference to the extent that the expenditure qualified for capital allowances. Separate gains are then calculated using the apportioned parts of the consideration and expenditure, and the exemption applied accordingly.

[*TCGA 1992, ss 47A, 47B*].

See Tolley's Income Tax for detailed commentary on the cash basis for small businesses and for unincorporated property businesses.

Betting, lottery etc.

[23.21] Winnings from betting, including pool betting, or lotteries or games with prizes are not chargeable gains, and no chargeable gain or allowable loss accrues on the disposal of rights to such winnings obtained by participating. [*TCGA 1992, s 51(1)*].

Where prize winnings take the form of an asset, the recipient is regarded as having acquired the asset at its market value at the time of acquisition (HMRC Capital Gains Manual CG12602).

Business expansion scheme (BES)

[23.22] Any gain accruing to an individual, to whom BES income tax relief has been given, on the disposal of eligible shares issued after 18 March 1986 and before 1 January 1994 (when the scheme was abolished) is exempt from CGT provided the income tax relief has not been withdrawn. Similarly, any loss is not allowable. [*TCGA 1992, s 150(2)*].

If the BES shares have been disposed of to a spouse or civil partner and the inter-spouse/civil partner exemption applies under *TCGA 1992, s 58*, the BES exemption for capital gains will still apply to disposals by the recipient spouse or partner to third parties (see **40.4** MARRIED PERSONS AND CIVIL PARTNERS).

There are special identification rules and rules regarding reorganisations and reconstructions for BES shares. See *TCGA 1992, s 150.*

Cashbacks

[23.23] A cashback is a lump sum received by a customer as an inducement for entering into a transaction for the purchase of goods, investments or services and received as a direct consequence of having entered into that transaction. An example of such a transaction is the taking out of a mortgage. The payer may be either the provider of the goods etc. or an interested third party. The term 'cashback' does not include a cash payment by a building society to its members on a takeover or conversion, or by other mutual organisations such as insurance companies or friendly societies to their policy holders on demutualisation.

A cashback does not derive from a chargeable asset for CGT purposes. No chargeable gain therefore arises on its receipt. (An ordinary retail customer purchasing goods etc. at arm's length will not be liable to income tax on a cashback either.)

(HMRC Statement of Practice SP 4/97).

Child Trust Funds

[23.24] The Child Trust Fund scheme is a government assisted savings scheme for any child born after 31 August 2002 and before 3 January 2011 where, broadly, there is an entitlement to child benefit (an '*eligible child*'). The scheme provides for HMRC to make an initial contribution in the form of a voucher (initially worth £250, or £500 for children in lower income families), which is then used to open an account. Anyone, including the child, may then pay money into the account up to a yearly limit of £9,000 (£4,368 before 6 April 2020; £4,260 before 6 April 2019; £4,128 before 6 April 2018; £4,080 before 6 April 2017). For children born before 3 August 2010 HMRC made a further contribution when the child reached the age of seven. For 2010/11 a further government contribution was made to the accounts of disabled children. Government contributions of all kinds have, however, been phased out. For children born in the period 4 August 2010 to 2 January 2011 the initial contribution was £50 or £100. Disabled contributions ceased for 2011/12 onwards. Children born from 3 January 2011 onwards do not qualify for a child trust fund. Existing funds, however, continue to maturity and non-government contributions continue to be permitted. It is possible to transfer a child trust fund to a junior ISA.

The account provider, acting on the instructions of a nominated responsible person (the '*registered contact*'), or the child if over 16, invests the funds in a limited range of qualifying investments. Normally no withdrawals are permitted before the fund matures when the child reaches 18.

On the child's 18th birthday, the account provider must transfer the investments in the fund either to a 'matured CTF account' or an ISA to be held subject to the regulations applicable to such accounts and otherwise on the same terms and conditions which applied immediately before the transfer. No further contributions may be made to a matured CTF account, although amounts arising from the investments are credited to it. If the transfer is to an ISA, the investments are held separately and the same rules apply as to a matured CTF account. Alternatively, the child can give the account provider instructions as to what is to be done with the account investments either on their 18th birthday or subsequently in respect of a matured CTF account. The instructions can be to transfer the assets or, in the case of non-cash assets, either to transfer them or to realise them and transfer the proceeds. The transfer can be to the child directly or to an ISA (which in this case is not subject to the matured CTF account rules).

Where the investments from a fund are transferred to an ISA (either on instruction or automatically at maturity or on a subsequent instruction in relation to a matured CTF account), the transfer does not count towards the overall subscription limit, but, if the transfer is to a Lifetime ISA, it does count towards the Lifetime ISA subscription limit.

For further details see Tolley's Income Tax.

Tax treatment

No tax is chargeable in respect of interest, dividends, distributions, gains, alternative financial arrangement return or building society bonus on account investments. Capital losses on account investments are disregarded. Any income from account investments is not to be regarded as income for any income tax purposes. For capital gains tax purposes, any assets held as account investments are regarded as held by the child concerned in a separate capacity from that in which he holds any other assets of the same description. The child is treated as having sold all the account investments, and as having reacquired them in his personal capacity, for their market value immediately before attaining the age of 18. The tax reliefs continue to apply to a matured CTF account.

It is up to the account provider to make tax claims, conduct appeals, and agree liabilities and reliefs on behalf of the child or registered contact. It is unlikely therefore that the child or registered contact will have to deal with any tax matters arising from the account. However, there is power for HMRC to make an assessment as an alternative to the account provider in order to withdraw relief or recover tax.

[*Child Trust Funds Act 2004, s 13; SI 2004 No 1450, Regs 24–38; SI 2020 No 29*].

Damages and compensation

[23.25] Sums received by way of compensation or damages for any wrong or injury suffered by an individual 'in his person' or in his profession or vocation are not chargeable gains. [*TCGA 1992, s 51(2)*].

The words 'in his person' are distinct from 'in his finances', but are construed widely (see HMRC Capital Gains Manual CG13030). The exemption given in relation to vocation is extended by concession to an individual's trade or employment. See HMRC Extra-Statutory Concession D33 (referred to at 7.2 ASSETS). If the compensation relates to an asset (e.g. insurance recoveries), payment does constitute a disposal; see 10 CAPITAL SUMS DERIVED FROM ASSETS.

Enterprise investment scheme (EIS)

[23.26] Any gain arising on a disposal of shares more than, broadly, three years after the issue of them, where an amount of EIS income tax relief is attributable to them, is wholly or partly exempt. If a loss would otherwise arise on a disposal of shares where an amount of such relief is attributable to them, a reduction is made in the amount of allowable expenditure equal to the amount of relief. See 22 ENTERPRISE INVESTMENT SCHEME.

Compensation from foreign governments

[23.27] Gains on sums received by individuals from foreign governments by way of compensation for assets confiscated, destroyed or expropriated are exempt provided certain conditions are met. See 10.2 CAPITAL SUMS DERIVED FROM ASSETS.

Exempt amount for the year

[23.28] A specified amount of the taxable amount of gains for a year of assessment is exempt. See 2.5 ANNUAL RATES AND EXEMPTIONS.

Gains arising partly before 6.4.1965 or 31.3.1982

[23.29] Assets held on, and gains arising partly before, these dates are subject to special provisions. See 8 ASSETS HELD ON 31 MARCH 1982.

Individual Savings Accounts (ISAs)

[23.30] ISAs are available to individuals over 18 (though see below) who are residents in the UK. The accounts can be made up of cash, stocks and shares and, after 5 April 2016, innovative finance (i.e., broadly, peer-to-peer loans made through a regulated peer-to-peer lending platform). For 2017/18 to 2023/24, investors can subscribe up to £20,000 to an ISA in the tax year. See further details below. Cash ISAs could be opened by 16 and 17-year-olds before 6 April 2024, but with effect from that date, only those aged 18 years and older can open an adult ISA (see below for junior ISAs). There is no statutory lock-in, minimum subscription, minimum holding period or lifetime subscription limit. Withdrawals may be made at any time without loss of tax relief.

Where an ISA investor dies, their surviving spouse or civil partner is given an additional ISA allowance equivalent to the value of the deceased spouse or partner's ISAs (other than junior ISAs). There are provisions for an ISA to retain its tax-relieved status for a limited period following the death of the investor. See below under 'Closure and death'.

The terms and conditions of an account may allow an investor to replace cash withdrawn from an ISA earlier in the year without the replacement counting towards the annual subscription limit for that year.

From 1 December 2015, the Government introduced Help to Buy ISAs under which a bonus will be paid at the time savings are used to purchase a home. Lifetime ISAs have been introduced from 6 April 2017 for adults under the age of 40 under which a bonus will be paid at the time savings are used to purchase a home or on withdrawal of funds after age 60. Only one bonus from a Help to Buy or Lifetime ISA can be used to purchase a home.

Interest and dividends are free of income tax. With effect from 1 February 2016, where an amount is withdrawn from a Help to Buy ISA on the closure of that account, an equivalent amount may be invested in an ISA within 12 months without counting towards the annual limit if the house purchase falls through.

Gains arising from assets held within an ISA are not chargeable gains for CGT purposes (and losses are not allowable).

A 'junior ISA' is available for children who did not qualify for a child trust fund (see **23.24** above). Subscriptions of up to £9,000 (£4,368 before 6 April 2020; £4,260 before 6 April 2019; £4,128 before 6 April 2018; £4,080 before 6 April 2017) can be made in each tax year and can be saved in cash or stocks and shares. The funds are locked in until the child reaches adulthood. Child trust funds can be transferred to junior ISAs without using up any of the annual limit for the year of transfer.

[*TCGA 1992, s 151; ITTOIA 2005, ss 694–701; SI 2019 No 689, Regs 1, 13(4), 40; SI 2024 No 350*].

The Individual Savings Account Regulations 1998 (*SI 1998 No 1870* as amended) provide for the setting up of ISAs by HMRC-approved accounts managers, for the conditions under which they may invest and under which the accounts are to operate, for relief from tax in respect of account investments, and for general administration. The regulations are summarised below.

Eligibility

An application to subscribe to an ISA may be made by an individual resident in the UK (or a non-UK resident Crown employee with general earnings subject to UK tax within *ITEPA 2003, s 28* or an individual married to, or a civil partner of, such an employee). Joint accounts are not permitted. An investor who subsequently fails to meet the residence requirement may retain the account and the right to the accompanying tax exemptions but can make no further subscriptions to the account until they again come to meet that requirement. An application made on behalf of an individual suffering from mental disorder, by a parent, guardian, spouse, civil partner, son or daughter of his, is treated as if made by that individual.

Rules for accounts

An individual can subscribe to one or more of a cash account, a stocks and shares account and an innovative finance account in each tax year. A cash account consists of a single cash component, a stocks and shares account consists of a single stocks and shares component and an innovative finance account consists of a single innovative finance component. With effect from 6 April 2024, an individual can subscribe to more than one account of the same type in the same tax year. For details of investments qualifying for inclusion in each component, see Tolley's Income Tax. See above for the subscription limits.

Subscriptions

Subscriptions to an ISA must be made in cash (and must be allocated irrevocably to the agreed component or single component) except that:

(a) shares acquired by the investor under a savings-related (SAYE) share option scheme (see **21.23** EMPLOYEE SHARE SCHEMES); or

(b) plan shares (but not securities or other rights) of a tax-advantaged share incentive plan (see **21.16** EMPLOYEE SHARE SCHEMES) which have ceased to be subject to the plan but remain in his beneficial ownership, may be transferred to a stocks and shares component. See above for the reinvestment of non-cash assets to an ISA following the death of a spouse or civil partner. Transfers within (a) or (b) above count towards the annual subscription limits, by reference to the market value of the shares at the date of transfer. No chargeable gain or allowable loss arises on the transfer. A transfer of SAYE scheme shares must be made within 90 days after the exercise of the option. A transfer of share incentive plan shares must be made within 90 days after the shares ceased to be subject to the plan. In all cases, 'shares' includes a reference to shares held in the form of depositary interests.

Certain subscriptions do not count towards the annual investment limits where they are made within 180 days of a default or failure in relation to an exiting ISA.

Investments

ISA investments cannot be purchased from the investor or his spouse or civil partner.

The title to ISA investments (other than cash deposits, national savings products and certain insurance policies) is vested in the account manager (or his nominee) either alone or jointly with the investor, though all ISA investments are in the beneficial ownership of the investor.

Applications to subscribe to an ISA

The statements and declarations to be made when applying to subscribe to an ISA are specified. The maximum penalty for an incorrect statement or declaration is the amount (if any) of income tax and/or capital gains tax underpaid as a result. Assessments to withdraw tax relief or otherwise recover tax underpaid may be made on the account manager or investor. HMRC have power to require information from, and to inspect records of, account managers and investors.

Withdrawal of funds and transfer of accounts

The terms and conditions of an ISA cannot prevent the investor from withdrawing funds or from transferring his account (or a part of it) to another HMRC-approved account manager (subject to the conditions governing such transfers). It is possible to transfer both current year subscriptions and previous year subscriptions to a cash account into a stocks and shares account.

An investor may replace cash withdrawn from an ISA earlier in the year without the replacement counting towards the annual subscription limit for that year. Such a replacement may be by way of shares within (a) or (b) above. If the withdrawn cash was initially invested in the same year, the replacement subscription may be made into any account. Otherwise the replacement subscription must be made into the account from which the withdrawal was made. For this purpose, any withdrawal in a tax year is deemed to be made first out of a subscription made in that year and any replacement subscription is deemed to be a replacement first of any withdrawal made out of a previous year's subscription. Replacement subscriptions can only be made into accounts if the terms and conditions allow for them.

Where an amount is withdrawn from a Help to Buy ISA on the closure of that account, an equivalent amount may be invested in an ISA within 12 months without counting towards the annual limit if the house purchase falls through.

Help to Buy ISAs

Help to Buy ISAs are available from 1 December 2015. The scheme is intended to help first-time property buyers (for residential purposes, not buy-to-let) by adding a government bonus to savings at the point of purchase of a property costing up to £250,000 (£450,000 for London properties). The bonus is equal to 25% of the savings, including interest added, subject to a maximum of £3,000 and a minimum of £400. The bonus must be claimed by the conveyancers acting on behalf of the saver in connection with the property purchase. There is also a maximum amount of savings per month of £200, although up to £1,000 may be deposited on opening the account. An account may be opened before 1 December 2019 but can remain open indefinitely. Bonuses cannot be claimed after 1 December 2030 (or earlier date notified by the Treasury). An individual may only have one Help to Buy ISA in the lifetime of the scheme.

Help to Buy ISAs are subject to their own conditions but are otherwise subject to the normal ISA rules.

Lifetime ISAs

Lifetime ISAs are available from 6 April 2017. Accounts can be opened by individuals aged 18 or over but under 40 who are either resident in the UK or a Crown Servant. The maximum annual investment is £4,000 and investments can be made until the individual reaches 50. A government bonus of 25% of the amount invested (maximum £1,000) is added each tax year. Amounts invested in a Lifetime ISA count towards the investor's overall annual investment limit. Lifetime ISAs can hold cash, qualifying stocks and shares or a combination of both.

With effect from 6 April 2018, investors withdrawing amounts from a Lifetime ISA are liable to a 25% withdrawal charge. The charge is reduced to 20% for withdrawals in the period beginning 6 March 2020 and ending on 5 April 2021. The charge does not apply if the investor is aged 60 or over, if the funds are used towards the purchase of a first home (value up to £450,000) or if the investor is terminally ill with less than 12 months to live. With effect from 6 April 2024, relief from the charge will not apply where the purchase of a first home is funded by a loan from a person connected with the account holder. The account ends on death, with no withdrawal charge applying. Funds in a Lifetime ISA can only be used to purchase a first home if the account has been open for at least 12 months.

Holders of a Help to Buy ISA could transfer the savings into a Lifetime ISA in 2017/18 (without any amount saved before 6 April 2017 counting towards the annual limit) or could continue to save into both. Only the government bonus from one of the accounts can be used in buying a first home.

The UK ISA

At Spring Budget 2024, the government announced that it intends to introduce a new 'UK ISA' for investments in UK companies, with an annual investment limit of £5,000 (in addition to existing annual limits). The government is consulting on the design of the scheme. See www.gov.uk/government/consultations/uk-isa-consultation.

Maturing child trust funds

Where a child holder of a child trust fund (see **23.24** above) reaches the age of 18, the account provider must transfer the investments in the fund either to a 'matured CTF account' or an ISA to be held subject to the regulations applicable to such accounts and otherwise on the same terms and conditions which applied immediately before the transfer. If the transfer is to an ISA (also referred to in the legislation as a matured CTF account), the investments are held separately and no further contributions may be made to it (although amounts arising from the investments are credited) until the child makes an application for it to be treated as a normal ISA.

Alternatively, the child can give the account provider instructions as to what is to be done with the account investments either on their 18th birthday or subsequently in respect of a non-ISA matured CTF account. The transfer can be to the child directly or to an ISA (which is not subject to the restrictions above).

Where the investments from a fund are transferred to an ISA (either on instruction or automatically at maturity or on a subsequent instruction in relation to a non-ISA matured CTF account), the transfer does not count towards the overall subscription limit, but, if the transfer is to a Lifetime ISA, it does count towards the Lifetime ISA subscription limit.

Junior ISAs and children under 18

Before 6 April 2024, 16 and 17-year-olds who otherwise satisfied the general conditions above could subscribe to a cash account.

In addition, 'junior ISAs' can be opened on behalf of eligible children. The child must either have been born on or after 3 January 2011 or, if born before that date, must not have been eligible for a child trust fund (see **23.24** above) and must be resident in the UK (or be a non-UK resident Crown employee with general earnings subject to UK tax within *ITEPA 2003, s 28* or be married to, a civil partner of, or a dependant of, such an employee). An eligible child may hold only one cash account and one stocks and shares account (although provision is made for the transfer of accounts to a different account manager). An application for a junior ISA must normally be made by the person who has parental responsibility for the child but children over the age of 16 may apply on their own behalf. See above for the annual limit for subscriptions. No withdrawals can be made except where the child is terminally ill or dies. The child is treated as the beneficial owner of the funds in the junior ISA. When the child reaches the age of 18 the junior ISA ceases to be a junior ISA so that the normal ISA rules apply. Subscriptions and withdrawals can then be made accordingly.

Tax exemptions

Except as stated below, no income tax or capital gains tax is chargeable on the account manager or the investor in respect of interest, dividends, distributions, gains, alternative financial arrangement return or building society bonus on ISA investments. Capital losses are not allowable.

As regards ISAs, other than junior ISAs, held by children under 18 (see above), the exemption for interest on a cash account does not prevent the application of the settlements legislation of *ITTOIA 2005, s 629* (see Tolley's Income Tax under Settlements) whereby (subject to a *de minimis* limit) the income of an unmarried minor on capital provided by a parent is taxable as if it were the parent's income. Such income arising in an ISA is therefore taxable. The Government has indicated that this rule does not apply to junior ISAs.

Exempt income and gains do not have to be reported in the investor's personal tax return.

Further capital gains matters

A transfer of ISA investments by an account manager to an investor is deemed to be made at market value, with no capital gain or allowable loss arising. An investor is treated as holding shares or securities in an ISA in a capacity other than that in which he holds any other shares etc. of the same class in the same company, so that share identification rules (see **58.1** SHARES AND SECURITIES — IDENTIFICATION RULES) are applied separately to ISA investments (and separately as between different ISAs held by the same investor). The normal share reorganisation rules are disapplied in respect of ISA investments in the event of a reorganisation of share capital involving an allotment for payment, e.g. a rights issue. Shares transferred to an ISA in the limited circumstances described above are deemed for these purposes to have been ISA investments from,

- in the case of SAYE option scheme shares, their acquisition by the investor; or
- in the case of share incentive plan shares, the date when they ceased to be subject to the plan.

Where the investor held shares eligible for transfer to an ISA and other shares of the same class but not so eligible, disposals are generally identified primarily with the latter, thus preserving to the greatest possible extent the eligibility of the remaining shares.

Closure and death

Subject to the ISA terms and conditions, an investor may close an ISA at any time without affecting tax exemptions up to the date of closure.

Where an investor dies, ISA investments retain their tax-exempt status for a limited period following the death. This operates by exempting the income and gains from ISA investments received by the personal representatives of a deceased account holder, or by a legatee, during the administration of the deceased's estate. The exemption has effect for a maximum of three years after the account holder's death and applies only to investments retained in the ISA.

No new subscriptions can be made to the ISA account, and it cannot normally be transferred between ISA providers. Whilst the exemption has effect, the account is designated a '*continuing account of a deceased investor*'. When an investment is transferred from the personal representatives to a legatee whilst the account is so designated, the legatee is treated for CGT purposes as having acquired it at the date of transfer at its then market value. If the transfer occurs after the exemption ceases to have effect, the legatee is treated as having acquired the investment at the date of transfer but at its market value at the time the account ceased to be a continuing account of a deceased investor.

Bereaved investors are allowed to make an additional ISA subscription outside the normal subscription limits following the death of a spouse or civil partner. This is to enable the surviving spouse or partner to inherit the deceased's ISA tax advantages. The one-off subscription cannot exceed the total value held in the deceased's ISA(s) (disregarding junior ISAs) at the date of death or, if greater and the subscription has not then already been made, upon the account's ceasing to be a continuing account of a deceased investor (see above). The deceased and the surviving spouse or partner must have been 'living together' (as defined) at date of death. In the case of non-cash assets held in the deceased's ISAs the one-off subscription must be made in the period of 180 days beginning with the distribution of those assets by the deceased's estate to the surviving spouse or partner. The value of a subscription comprising non-cash assets is the value of the assets at the date of the subscription. In any other case the subscription must be made within three years after the date of death or, if later, within 180 days after the administration of the estate is completed. As far as the surviving spouse or partner is concerned, the normal rule that an investor can subscribe to only one cash account or one stocks and shares account in a tax year is ignored for these purposes, and the normal requirements as to UK residence status are disregarded with regard to the one-off subscription.

[*Savings (Government Contributions) Act 2017, ss 1, 3, Sch 1; SI 1998 No 1870; SI 2020 Nos 30, 506*].

Legatees

[23.31] No chargeable gain accrues to the personal representatives where a person acquires an asset from them as legatee, and the legatee is treated as if the personal representatives' acquisition of the asset had been his acquisition of it. See **18.14** DEATH.

Recovery of assets under Proceeds of Crime Act 2002, Pt 5

[23.32] *Proceeds of Crime Act 2002, Pt 5 Ch 2* provides for the recovery, in civil proceedings before the High Court (or, in Scotland, the Court of Session), of property which is, or represents, property obtained through 'unlawful conduct' (as defined in the Act). If the Court is satisfied that any property is recoverable under the provisions, it will make a '*recovery order*', vesting the property in an appointed trustee for civil recovery. Alternatively, the Court may make an order under *s 276* of the Act staying (or, in Scotland, sisting) proceedings on terms agreed by the parties. [*Proceeds of Crime Act 2002, ss 240(1), 266(1)(2), 276, 316(1)*].

A gain which is attributable to the vesting of property in a trustee for civil recovery or any other person either under a recovery order or in pursuance of an order under *s 276* (a '*Pt 5 transfer*'), and which accrues to the person who held the property immediately before the transfer (the '*transferor*'), is not a chargeable gain, unless a 'compensating payment' is made to the transferor. In the latter event, the amount of the compensating payment is treated as the consideration for the transfer of the property. Where property belonged, immediately before the *Pt 5* transfer, to joint tenants, and a compensating payment is made to one or more (but not all) of them, these provisions apply separately to each joint tenant.

A '*compensating payment*' for these purposes is any amount paid in respect of a *Pt 5* transfer by the trustee for civil recovery or another to a person who held the property in question immediately before the transfer. If a recovery order, or the terms on which an order under *s 276* is made, provides for the creation of any interest in favour of such a person, that person is treated as receiving (in addition to any actual compensating payment) a compensating payment equal to the value of the interest.

[*Proceeds of Crime Act 2002, s 448, Sch 10 paras 2(1)(3)–(5), 3(1)(2)*].

Proceeds of Crime Act 2002, s 298 provides for the forfeiture of 'cash' (which term includes coins and notes in any currency, postal orders, cheques of any kind (including travellers' cheques), bankers' drafts, bearer bonds and bearer shares) in summary proceedings before a magistrates' court (or, in Scotland, the sheriff). A gain attributable to such a forfeiture is not a chargeable gain if it accrues to the person who held the property immediately before the forfeiture and is attributable to property consisting of notes or coins in any currency other than sterling, of postal orders, cheques or bankers' drafts if expressed in any currency other than sterling or of bearer bonds or bearer shares. [*Proceeds of Crime Act 2002, s 289(6), Sch 10 para 3(3)*].

Seed enterprise investment scheme (SEIS)

[23.33] Any gain arising on a disposal of shares more than, broadly, three years after the issue of them, where an amount of SEIS income tax relief is attributable to them, is wholly or partly exempt. If a loss would otherwise arise on a disposal of shares where an amount of such relief is attributable to them, a reduction is made in the amount of allowable expenditure equal to the amount of relief. See **54** SEED ENTERPRISE INVESTMENT SCHEME.

Settled property

[23.34] No charge to capital gains tax arises:

(a) where a person disposes of an interest in settled property provided the interest either was created for his benefit or was not acquired for money or money's worth (see **56.15** SETTLEMENTS); or
(b) when a person becomes absolutely entitled to settled property on the termination of a life interest by the death of the person entitled to it (see **56.16** and **56.18** SETTLEMENTS); or

(c) on the termination, on the death of the person entitled to it, of a life interest in possession in settled property where the property does not cease at that time to be settled property (see **56.17** SETTLEMENTS).

Social investment relief

[23.35] Any gain arising on a disposal of an asset more than three years after its acquisition, where an amount of income tax social investment relief is attributable to it, is wholly or partly exempt. If a loss would otherwise arise on a disposal of an asset where an amount of such relief is attributable to it, a reduction is made in the amount of allowable expenditure equal to the amount of relief. Investments can no longer be made under the scheme after 5 April 2023. See **59** SOCIAL INVESTMENT RELIEF.

Substantial shareholdings of companies

[23.36] A gain on a disposal by a company of shares is exempt (and a loss is not allowable) where, throughout a continuous 12-month period beginning not more than six years before the disposal, the company held a 'substantial shareholding' (broadly, at least a **10%** interest) in the company whose shares are the subject of the disposal. The exemption extends to assets 'related to shares' (as defined). The investee company must be a trading company or the holding company of a trading group (or subgroup). A form of the exemption, with amended conditions, is available where the investee company is not a trading company but the investing company is owned by qualifying institutional investors. See **60** SUBSTANTIAL SHAREHOLDING EXEMPTION.

Venture capital trusts

[23.37] Any gain arising on a disposal of shares where an amount of income tax relief is attributable to them is wholly or partly exempt. A loss arising on a disposal of shares is not an allowable loss, except to the extent that a gain on the disposal would have been a chargeable gain. See **64.7** VENTURE CAPITAL TRUSTS.

Woodlands

[23.38] Where woodlands are managed by the occupier on a commercial basis and with a view to the realisation of profits:

(a) any consideration for the disposal of trees (whether standing, felled or cut thereon) and saleable underwood; and
(b) any capital sum received under an insurance policy in respect of the destruction of, or damage or injury to, trees or saleable underwood by fire or other hazard thereon,

is excluded from any capital gains tax computation on the disposal if the person making the disposal is the occupier.

In *any* capital gains tax computation on the sale of woodlands in the UK, there is excluded so much of the cost of the woodlands and/or consideration for the disposal as is attributable to trees, including saleable underwood, growing on the land. [*TCGA 1992, s 250*].

The cultivation of 'short rotation coppice' is regarded as farming for capital gains purposes and not as forestry, and any land on which such activity takes place is regarded as farm land or agricultural land, as the case may be, and not as woodlands. '*Short rotation coppice*' means a perennial crop of tree species at high density, the stems of which are harvested above ground level at intervals of less than ten years. [*FA 1995, s 154*].

Works of art etc.

[23.39] A gain is not a chargeable gain if it accrues on the disposal of property which has been (or could be) designated by HMRC under *IHTA 1984, s 31* where the disposal is:

(a) by way of sale by private treaty to a body mentioned in *IHTA 1984, Sch 3* (see **11.5** CHARITIES); or
(b) to such a body as in (a) above otherwise than by sale; or
(c) to HMRC in satisfaction of the payment of inheritance tax or capital transfer tax.

[*TCGA 1992, s 258(2)*].

See **23.79**(a)–(e) below for types of national heritage property which may be sold by private treaty within (a) above. See also **30.10** HOLD-OVER RELIEFS for relief for gifts of works of art etc.

The standard of objects which can be accepted under (c) above is very much higher. They have to satisfy a test of 'pre-eminence' either in the context of a national, local authority, or university collection, or through association with a particular building.

Exempt organisations and individuals

[23.40] The organisations and individuals detailed in **23.61** below are completely exempt from capital gains tax except where otherwise indicated.

Asbestos compensation settlements

[23.41] A gain on the disposal by the trustees of an 'asbestos compensation settlement' of any property comprised in the settlement is not a chargeable gain.

An '*asbestos compensation settlement*' is a settlement made before 24 March 2010 under certain insolvency arrangements where the sole or main purpose of the settlement is to make compensation payments to individuals suffering from an asbestos-related condition (or who suffered from such a condition before their death). The insolvency arrangements concerned are voluntary arrangements under *Insolvency Act 1986, Pt 1*, compromises or arrangements under *Companies Act 1985, s 425* or *Companies Act 2006, Pt 26*, or equivalent arrangements in Northern Ireland or under the law of a territory outside the UK.

[*TCGA 1992, s 271(1)(ea)(1ZA)(1ZB)*].

Bare trustees and nominees

[23.42] Where property is held by bare trustees or nominees for another person, capital gains tax is chargeable as if the property were held by that other person. Consequently, there is no liability where the property is transferred from the bare trustees etc. to that other person. [*TCGA 1992, s 60*]. See further **56.3** SETTLEMENTS.

British and Natural History Museums

[23.43] The British Museum and the Natural History Museum are entitled, on a claim, to exemption from tax on chargeable gains. [*TCGA 1992, s 271(6)(a)*].

Central banks

[23.44] Non-resident central banks as specified by Order in Council and the issue departments of the Reserve Bank of India and the State Bank of Pakistan are exempt from tax on chargeable gains. [*TCGA 1992, s 271(7A)–(8)*].

Charities

[23.45] Subject to restrictions, a gain is not a chargeable gain if it accrues to a charity and is applicable and applied for charitable purposes. See **11.2** CHARITIES.

Community amateur sports clubs

[23.46] On a claim, and subject to restrictions, a gain is not a chargeable gain if it accrues to a registered community amateur sports club and is wholly applied for qualifying purposes. See **11.10** CHARITIES.

The Crown

[23.47] The Crown is not liable to tax unless statute otherwise provides; see *Bank voor Handel v Administrator of Hungarian Property* HL 1954, 35 TC 311 and *Boarland v Madras Electric Supply Corporation* HL 1955, 35 TC 612. In addition, gains arising on the disposal of stock belonging to the Crown, or in the name of the Treasury or National Debt Commissioners under statutory schemes under which transfers are made in accounts at the Bank of England, are not chargeable gains. [*TCGA 1992, s 271(1)(a)*]. Property held under trusts contained in *Chevening Estate Act 1959* is exempt from capital gains tax. [*TCGA 1992, s 270*].

Diplomatic agents

[23.48] Diplomatic agents (i.e. heads of mission or members of the diplomatic staff) of foreign states are exempt from capital gains tax except on gains arising from private investments or immovable property in the UK. [*Diplomatic Privileges Act 1964*].

Similar exemption is given to official agents of Commonwealth countries or the Republic of Ireland. Consular officers and their personal staffs are exempt from gains arising out of disposals of assets which are situated outside the UK at the time of disposal. [*TCGA 1992, ss 11(2)–(4), 271(1)(f); ITA 2007, s 841*].

Friendly societies

[23.49] A friendly society registered under *Friendly Societies Act 1974* (a registered friendly society) is an unincorporated society of individuals. Under *Friendly Societies Act 1992*, societies are able to incorporate, take on new powers and form subsidiary companies. *TCGA 1992, ss 217A–217C* provide continuity of tax treatment between registered societies and incorporated societies and removes adverse tax consequences which would otherwise arise as a result of incorporation.

Friendly societies which are neither registered nor incorporated, the incomes of which do not exceed £160 per annum, are wholly exempt from corporation tax on chargeable gains, but a claim must be made. Exemption for other friendly societies is broadly restricted in respect of life or other long-term insurance business to the assurance of gross sums under contracts under which the total premiums payable in any period of twelve months do not exceed £270 or the granting of annuities not exceeding £156.

There are provisions to enable friendly societies to transfer existing tax exempt business to an insurance company or another friendly society without loss of the tax exemption.

[*FA 2012, ss 150–179, Schs 18, 19; TCGA 1992, ss 217A–217C; SI 2012 No 3008*].

The Historic Buildings and Monuments Commission for England

[23.50] The Historic Buildings and Monuments Commission for England is exempt from tax in respect of chargeable gains. [*TCGA 1992, s 271(7)*].

Housing associations

[23.51] Housing associations approved under *CTA 2010, ss 644–646* may make a claim (within two years of the end of the relevant accounting period) for exemption from corporation tax on chargeable gains arising from the sale of property which is, or has been, occupied by a tenant of the association. [*CTA 2010, s 643*].

Relief from corporation tax generally by specific grant made by the Secretary of State for the Environment may also be obtainable under *Housing Act 1988, s 54* for registered non-profit making housing associations which are approved as above. See Tolley's Corporation Tax under Housing Associations.

Disposals of land and other assets by a housing association (as defined) to the Regulator of Social Housing (or the Secretary of State or Scottish Homes) under certain statutory schemes, and subsequent disposals of those assets by the Regulator etc. to a single housing association, are treated as taking place on a no gain/no loss basis. The same applies to:

(a) transfers of land between the Regulator etc. and registered housing associations (as defined and see **23.58** below regarding self-build societies);
(b) transfers of land between such associations; and
(c) transfers under a direction from the Regulator etc. of property other than land between such associations.

Similar relief applies to NI housing associations.

[*TCGA 1992, ss 218–220*].

The disposal and corresponding acquisition of an estate or interest in land in the UK otherwise than under a bargain at arm's length to a registered housing association (as defined) is treated as being made for a no gain/no loss consideration (or for the actual consideration if the latter exceeds the disposer's allowable expenditure; see **16.12** COMPUTATION OF GAINS AND LOSSES) if a joint claim for such relief is made. On a subsequent disposal of the land by the association after a no gain/no loss acquisition its acquisition by the original donor is treated as the acquisition of the association. [*TCGA 1992, s 259*]. See **8.6** ASSETS HELD ON 31 MARCH **1982** and **32.4** INDEXATION for the consequential re-basing and indexation provisions which apply.

International organisations

[23.52] International organisations (e.g. the United Nations) may be specified by Order in Council as exempt from certain taxes [*International Organisations Act 1968*], as may certain financial bodies under the *Bretton Woods Agreement Act 1945* (e.g. the International Monetary Fund). Also exempt are the International Development Association and the International Finance Corporation [*International Development Act 2002, s 12* and *SI 1955 No 1954; SI 1960 No 1383*].

Securities issued by designated international organisations are treated as situated outside the UK. See **7.3** ASSETS.

Local authorities etc.

[23.53] Local authorities, local authority associations and health service bodies (as defined) are exempt from capital gains tax. [*TCGA 1992, s 271(3)*].

National Debt

[23.54] Gains accruing to trustees of a settlement the property of which is for the reduction of the National Debt and which qualifies under statute are not chargeable. [*TCGA 1992, s 271(1)(e)*].

The National Heritage Memorial Fund

[23.55] The National Heritage Memorial Fund is exempt from tax on chargeable gains. [*TCGA 1992, s 271(7)*].

Pension schemes

[23.56] Subject to the following, gains accruing to a person from investments forming part of the funds of certain pension schemes are not chargeable gains. The schemes covered by this exemption are registered pension schemes within *FA 2004, s 150(2)*, the House of Commons Members' Fund and certain overseas pension funds. Futures contracts and options contracts are included as investments (notwithstanding that one party to the contract will not be involved with a transfer of assets other than money). See **7.7** ASSETS.

The above exemption does not prevent a scheme sanction charge to income tax arising in the case of an investment-regulated pension scheme (as defined) on a gain on the disposal of certain taxable property (broadly, and subject to exceptions, residential and tangible moveable property). See Tolley's Income Tax.

[*TCGA 1992, s 99A(3), ss 271(1)(b)(c)(d)(g)(h)(j), (1A)(1B)(10)(11), 288(1)*].

The above exemption does not apply to gains accruing to a person as a member of a property investment limited liability partnership (see **44.17** PARTNERSHIPS). [*TCGA 1992, s 271(12)*].

Deregistration or withdrawal of approval of pension schemes

Where the registration of a registered pension scheme (within *FA 2004, s 150(2)*) is withdrawn and accordingly there is a charge to income tax under *FA 2004, s 242*, for capital gains purposes, the assets held for the purposes of the scheme in question are deemed to have been acquired immediately before the date of withdrawal of approval or registration (without any corresponding disposal) by the person who would be chargeable if there had been a disposal at that time giving rise to a gain. The acquisition cost of the assets is deemed to be equal to the amount on which income tax is charged as above. In all cases, that amount is the market value of the assets in question immediately before the date of withdrawal of approval or registration. Accordingly, only the gain accruing on the assets since approval or registration was withdrawn will be brought into account on a subsequent disposal. [*TCGA 1992, ss 239A, 239B, 288(1)*].

Pension Protection Fund

The Regulations provide that any gain accruing to the Board of the Pension Protection Fund from disposals of investments are not chargeable gains if, or to the extent that, they were held for the purposes of the Pension Protection Fund or Fraud Compensation Fund. Receipt of certain specified fraud compensation payments from the Board is not a disposal of an asset for tax purposes. [*FA 2005, s 102; SI 2005 No 1907; SI 2006 No 575*].

Scientific research associations

[23.57] Scientific research associations are exempt from tax on chargeable gains, provided that in each case:

(a) the association's object is the undertaking of 'research and development' (within the meaning of *CTA 2010, s 1138*) which may lead to or facilitate an extension of any class or classes of trade; and

(b) it is prohibited by its Memorandum or similar instrument from distributing its income or property to its members in any form other than that of reasonable payments for supplies, labour, power, services, interest and rent.

Treasury regulations (see *SI 2007 No 3426*) prescribe circumstances in which associations are deemed to comply, or not to comply, with the above conditions.

[*TCGA 1992, s 271(6)(b); CTA 2010, ss 469, 470; SI 2007 No 3426*].

Self-build society

[23.58] An approved self-build society (as defined) may claim relief from corporation tax on chargeable gains arising on the disposal of any land to a member, provided that none of its land is occupied by a non-member. Claims must be made within two years of the end of the accounting period. [*CTA 2010, ss 650–657*].

Disposals of land by unregistered self-build societies (as defined) to the Regulator of Social Housing, the Scottish Housing Regulator, the Secretary of State, Scottish Homes, the Homes and Communities Agency or the Greater London Authority are treated as made at a no gain/no loss price. [*TCGA 1992, s 219*]. See Tolley's Corporation Tax under Housing Associations and **23.51** above.

Trade unions

[23.59] Registered trade unions, provided that they are precluded from assuring more than £4,000 by way of gross sum or £825 by way of annuity (excluding annuities constituting or held in connection with a registered pension scheme) in respect of any one person. Exemption is granted in respect of chargeable gains which are applicable and are applied to 'provident benefits' i.e. sickness, injury and superannuation payments, payment for loss of tools, etc.

The above exemption also applies to employers' associations registered as trade unions and to the Police Federations for England and Wales, Scotland, and Northern Ireland and other police organisations with similar functions.

[*CTA 2010, ss 981–983*].

Unit and investment trusts, open-ended investment companies and venture capital trusts

[23.60] Authorised unit trusts, investment trusts, open-ended investment companies and venture capital trusts are exempt from corporation tax on their chargeable gains. See **63** UNIT TRUSTS ETC. and **64.6** VENTURE CAPITAL TRUSTS.

Visiting forces etc.

[23.61] A period during which a member of a visiting force, the staff of designated allied headquarters or the EU civilian staff to whom *ITA 2007, s 833* applies is in the UK solely because of such membership is not treated either as a period of residence in the UK or as creating a change in their residence or domicile. [*TCGA 1992, s 217ZA; ITA 2007, s 833*].

Reliefs and deferrals

[23.62] In addition to the exemption from capital gains tax detailed in 23.2–23.61 above, a number of reliefs are available to reduce or defer the amount of tax payable. The more common of these are outlined in 23.64–23.88 below as well as in certain provisions in 23.51 and 23.58 above.

Business asset disposal relief

[23.63] Business asset disposal relief can be claimed in respect of 'qualifying business disposals'. Qualifying gains are chargeable at a rate of only 10%. The relief applies for capital gains tax purposes only and is not available to companies. It is subject to a lifetime limit of net gains of, currently, £1 million. See 9 BUSINESS ASSET DISPOSAL RELIEF.

Capital distributions and sale of rights

[23.64] If small as compared with the value of the shares in respect of which it is made, a capital distribution may be treated not as a disposal but the proceeds deducted from the acquisition cost of the shares on a subsequent disposal. See 57.11 SHARES AND SECURITIES. This treatment also applies to any consideration received for the disposal of rights. See 57.4 SHARES AND SECURITIES.

Companies

[23.65] Reliefs and deferrals for companies are treated as follows:

(a) *Intra-group transfers of capital assets* are treated as if made at a no gain, no loss consideration (with certain exceptions). See 26.3 GROUPS OF COMPANIES.

(b) *Transfers of assets to non-UK resident company.* Where a UK resident company carrying on a trade outside the UK through a permanent establishment transfers that trade and its assets to a non-UK resident company partly or wholly for shares in that company, a proportion of the net chargeable gains relating to those shares may be claimed by the transferor company as being deferred. See 43.10 OVERSEAS MATTERS.

(c) *Transfers or divisions of UK businesses between companies resident in different EC member states* are treated as if made at a no gain, no loss consideration. See 43.12 OVERSEAS MATTERS.

Company reconstructions

[23.66] These do not normally constitute disposals, the original holding and the new holding being treated as the same asset acquired at the same date as the original shares. See 57.5 and 57.7 SHARES AND SECURITIES and 14.12 COMPANIES.

Constituency associations

[23.67] Where, as a result of the redistribution of parliamentary constituencies, an existing constituency association in a former parliamentary constituency disposes of any land:

(a) to a new association which is its successor, or
(b) to a body which is an organ of the political party (within *IHTA 1984, s 24*) and which, as soon as practicable thereafter, disposes of the land to a new association which is a successor to the existing association,

the disposal is treated as being made for such consideration as would secure that neither a gain nor loss accrues on disposal.

If the asset was originally held on 6 April 1965, time apportionment will be available (see **8.12** ASSETS HELD ON **28** MARCH **1982**) to the new association as if it had held the land from the original date of acquisition.

Where, as a result of the redistribution of parliamentary constituencies, an existing constituency association in a former parliamentary constituency disposes of any land used and occupied by it for the purposes of its functions and transfers the whole or part of the proceeds to a new association which is its successor, ROLLOVER RELIEF (53) may be claimed as if the land disposed of had been the property of the new association since its acquisition. Where only part of the proceeds is transferred, rollover relief may be claimed on a corresponding share. [*TCGA 1992, s 264*].

Corporate venturing scheme

[23.68] The corporate venturing scheme provided tax relief for shares issued before 1 April 2010. Under the scheme, certain trading companies were able to obtain corporation tax relief at 20% ('investment relief') on corporate venturing investments, i.e. acquisitions (by cash subscription) of minority shareholdings in 'small higher risk' trading companies. Despite the abolition of the scheme, the following capital gains issues may continue to be relevant to companies who made investments under it:

- an allowable capital loss on the disposal of a corporate venturing investment, computed net of investment relief, can be relieved against *income* of the accounting period in which the loss arises and accounting periods ending in the previous 12 months (or can be relieved against chargeable gains in the normal way); and
- investing companies were able to postpone chargeable gains ('deferral relief') on disposals of corporate venturing investments where they reinvested in other shares attracting investment relief. Such deferred gains are brought back into charge on disposal of the shares.

See the 2023/24 or earlier edition of this work for full coverage. **Simon's Taxes**, see **D8.3**.

Disposals — capital sums received as compensation etc.

[23.69] Where such a sum is received in respect of an asset which is damaged or, alternatively, lost or destroyed, a number of reliefs are available provided the capital sum is expended on restoration of, or a replacement for, the asset. See **10.3** and **10.4** CAPITAL SUMS DERIVED FROM ASSETS.

Enterprise investment scheme (EIS)

[23.70] Individuals and most trustees may defer all or part of a chargeable gain against a subscription for eligible shares under the EIS. The deferred gain becomes chargeable on a disposal of the EIS shares and in certain other circumstances. See 22.16 ENTERPRISE INVESTMENT SCHEME.

Gifts of business assets and assets on which inheritance tax is chargeable etc.

[23.71] A form of holdover relief applies to:

(a) gifts of business assets (see 30.2 HOLD-OVER RELIEFS); and
(b) gifts of assets on which inheritance tax is chargeable etc. (see 30.10 HOLD-OVER RELIEFS).

Gifts to charities etc.

[23.72] Disposals (otherwise than under a bargain at arm's length), by way of gift or at a consideration not exceeding the allowable expenditure, to charities or any of the bodies mentioned in *IHTA 1984, Sch 3* are deemed to have been made for a consideration giving neither a gain nor a loss. See 11.5 CHARITIES.

Hold-over — general relief for gifts

[23.73] After 5 April 1980 and before 14 March 1989, a general deferral relief for gifts applied to the disposal of an asset otherwise than at arm's length. See 30.12 HOLD-OVER RELIEFS.

Investors' relief

[23.74] Investors' relief can be claimed in respect of disposals of shares in unlisted trading companies made by individuals on or after 6 April 2019. Qualifying gains are chargeable at a rate of only 10%. The relief applies for capital gains tax purposes only and is not available to companies. It is subject to a lifetime limit of gains of, currently, £10 million. See 34 INVESTORS' RELIEF.

Land — compulsory acquisition

[23.75] Where *part* of a holding of land is transferred under a compulsory acquisition order, in certain circumstances the transferor may claim not to treat the transfer as a disposal and the consideration is then deducted from the allowable expenditure on a subsequent disposal. See 35.9 LAND for this and 35.10 for deferral of any gain arising on the compulsory purchase of land by means of a claim for rollover relief where the proceeds are re-invested in new land.

Land — part disposals

[23.76] Where the value of the consideration for a part disposal of a larger holding of land does not exceed £20,000, in certain circumstances the transferor may claim that the transfer is not treated as a disposal and the consideration is then deducted from the allowable expenditure on a subsequent disposal. See 35.6 LAND.

Localism Act 2011 transfers

[23.77] A transfer in accordance with a transfer scheme under *Localism Act 2011, s 190* of property, rights or liabilities of the Homes and Communities Agency where the transferee is a public body is regarded as made on a no gain, no loss basis. A transfer in accordance with a transfer scheme under *Localism Act 2011, s 191* is similarly regarded where the transferee is a public body. [*Localism Act 2011, Sch 24 para 6*].

Married persons and civil partners

[23.78] Transfers between married persons and between civil partners are regarded as made on a no gain, no loss basis where the spouses or partners are living together. See **40.4** MARRIED PERSONS AND CIVIL PARTNERS.

National heritage property

[23.79] The following types of property are within the term 'national heritage property' provided they are so designated by HMRC.

(a) Any picture, print, book, manuscript, work of art or scientific object, any collection or group of such items taken as a whole, and any other item not yielding income, which appears to HMRC to be pre-eminent for its national, scientific, historic or artistic interest (with regard being taken of any significant association of the item, collection or group with a particular place). '*National interest*' includes interest within any part of the UK.

(b) Land which in the opinion of HMRC is of outstanding scenic or historic or scientific interest.

(c) A building for the preservation of which special steps should in the opinion of HMRC be taken by reason of its outstanding historic or architectural interest.

(d) Any area of land which in the opinion of HMRC is essential for the protection of the character and amenities of such a building as is mentioned in (c) above.

(e) An object which in the opinion of HMRC is historically associated with such a building as is mentioned in (c) above.

[*IHTA 1984, s 31(1)(5)*].

Where any of the above assets, which have been (or could be) designated by HMRC under *IHTA 1984, s 31*, are disposed of by gift (including a gift into settlement) or deemed to be disposed of by trustees on a person becoming absolutely entitled to settled property (other than on the death of the life tenant), then the person making the disposal and the person acquiring the asset are treated for capital gains tax purposes as making the transaction for a consideration giving neither gain nor loss. [*TCGA 1992, s 258(3)(4)*].

Certain undertakings must be given by such persons as HMRC think appropriate in the circumstances of the case that, until the person beneficially entitled to the property dies or the property is disposed of, certain conditions regarding the property are kept, e.g. reasonable access to the public. [*TCGA 1992, s 258(9);*

IHTA 1984, ss 30(1), 31(2)(4)]. An undertaking may be varied by agreement between HMRC and the person bound by the undertaking or, in the absence of such agreement, by the Tribunal at HMRC's behest. [*TCGA 1992, s 258(8A); IHTA 1984, s 35A*].

If the asset is sold and inheritance tax is chargeable under *IHTA 1984, s 32* (or would be chargeable if an undertaking under that provision had been given), the person selling the asset is treated as having sold the asset for its market value. Similarly, if HMRC are satisfied that at any time during the period for which any undertaking was given that it has not been observed in a material respect, the owner is treated as having sold and immediately reacquired the asset for its market value. An undertaking for the purposes of these provisions is given for the period until the person beneficially entitled to the asset dies or disposes of the asset (whether by sale, gift or otherwise). [*TCGA 1992, s 258(5)(6)*].

If the asset subject to the undertaking is disposed of otherwise than on sale and without a further undertaking being given, the asset is treated as having been sold to an individual for its market value. [*TCGA 1992, s 258(6)*].

Where a person is treated as having sold for market value any asset within (c), (d) or (e) above, he is also treated as having sold and immediately reacquired at market value any asset 'associated' with it (unless HMRC direct otherwise). '*Associated*' assets are a building within (c) above and land or objects which, in relation to that building, fall within (d) or (e) above. [*TCGA 1992, s 258(7)*].

Where a person is treated as having sold an asset under these provisions and inheritance tax becomes chargeable on the same occasion, any capital gains tax payable is deductible in determining the value of the asset for inheritance tax purposes. [*TCGA 1992, s 258(8)*].

See also **30.10** HOLD-OVER RELIEFS for relief for gifts of works of art etc.

Exceptions

The above provisions do not apply where the disposal is by way of gift or sale by private treaty to a body within *IHTA 1984, Sch 3* or if the disposal is to HMRC in satisfaction of inheritance tax (or capital transfer tax). Such disposals are exempt. See **23.39** above.

Reinvestment relief

[23.80] Reinvestment relief enabled individuals and trustees to claim to roll-over chargeable gains accruing on any assets if the disposal proceeds were reinvested in a 'qualifying investment' within the 'qualifying period' and **before 6 April 1998**. The relief was given effect by reducing the sale proceeds of the disposed assets and the acquisition cost of the newly acquired investment by the lowest of the following amounts:

- the otherwise chargeable gain (net of any amount deferred by virtue of a previous claim for reinvestment relief);
- the acquisition cost of the new asset;
- if the new asset is not acquired at arm's length, the market value at the time of its acquisition;

- the amount specified by the individual in the claim.

These adjustments only affected the reinvestor claiming the relief and there was no consequential effect for either the complementary purchaser or vendor.

A '*qualifying investment*' was an acquisition of any 'eligible shares' in a 'qualifying company' (both as defined) unless, where the asset disposed of consisted of shares in or securities of any company, the qualifying company is that company or a member of that company's group. Where the eligible shares were acquired by their being issued to the taxpayer, the company was required to have an intention to employ the money raised by the issue wholly for the purposes of a 'qualifying trade' carried on by it.

For subsequent deferral reliefs applying for reinvestment in EIS and VCT shares, see respectively **22.16** ENTERPRISE INVESTMENT SCHEME and **64.8** VENTURE CAPITAL TRUSTS.

Withdrawal of relief

An effective withdrawal of reinvestment relief applied where certain events occurred within three years of the reinvestment. The withdrawal was made by deeming a chargeable gain equal to the whole or a proportion of the held-over gain to arise at the time of the event. In such circumstances so much of the held-over gain as is treated as the deemed gain is diregarded in computing a subsequent gain on disposal of the qualifying investment.

[*TCGA 1992, ss 164A–164N*].

Reorganisation of share capital

[23.81] Reorganisations do not normally constitute disposals, the original holding and the new holding being treated as the same asset acquired at the same date as the original shares. See **57.2** SHARES AND SECURITIES. See also **57.8** for conversion of securities into shares where the same principles apply.

Rollover relief — replacement of business assets

[23.82] A person disposing of certain qualifying assets used exclusively for the purposes of a trade who used the proceeds to purchase other qualifying assets so used may claim to defer the capital gains tax payable by deducting the otherwise chargeable gain on the old asset from the cost of the newly acquired one. See **53** ROLLOVER RELIEF.

Seed enterprise investment scheme (SEIS)

[23.83] A chargeable gain arising to an individual is exempt to the extent that it is matched with a subscription for shares in respect of which SEIS income tax relief is granted. For 2012/13 only, 100% of such a subscription may be matched with a gain, but for 2013/14 onwards only 50% of a subscription may be so matched. See **54.46** ENTERPRISE INVESTMENT SCHEME.

Settlements for the benefit of employees

[23.84] Where the circumstances surrounding a disposal are as in one of (a)–(c) below, the MARKET VALUE (**39.1**) rules do not apply to it; and if made gratuitously or for a consideration of an amount not exceeding the allowable expenditure attributable to the asset, the disposal, and the corresponding acquisition by the trustees, is treated as taking place on a no gain/no loss basis and the transferor's acquisition of the asset is imputed to the trustees.

The circumstances mentioned above are as follows.

(a) A close company (as in *CTA 2010, ss 439–454* but additionally including a non-UK resident company which would be close as defined by those provisions) disposes of an asset to trustees in circumstances such that the disposition is not a transfer of value for IHT purposes by virtue of *IHTA 1984, s 13* (employee trusts).

(b) An individual disposes of an asset to trustees in circumstances such that the disposal is an exempt transfer for IHT purposes by virtue of *IHTA 1984, s 28* (employee trusts).

(c) A company other than a close company (as in (a) above) disposes of property to trustees otherwise than under a bargain at arm's length in circumstances such that, broadly, had the disposition been made by a close company it would not be a transfer of value by virtue of *IHTA 1984, s 13*.

[*TCGA 1992, s 239(1)(2)(4)–(8)*].

For coverage of *IHTA 1984, s 13* and *s 28* (each of which refers to the provisions of *IHTA 1984, s 86*), see Tolley's Inheritance Tax under Trusts for Employees.

A gain accruing to the trustees of an 'employee trust' on the disposal of an asset of the trust to a 'beneficiary', or on a deemed disposal under *TCGA 1992, s 71* (person becoming absolutely entitled to settled property — see **56.16** SETTLEMENTS) is not a chargeable gain. This applies only if no actual consideration (as opposed to deemed consideration) is given for the asset, there is an income tax charge of the full market value of the asset and neither the beneficiary nor the person liable for the income tax (if different) is an 'excluded person'.

For this purpose, an '*employee trust*' is a trust within *IHTA 1984, s 86* but ignoring the restriction in *s 86(3)* (class defined by employment with a particular body to include all or most employees). An 'excluded person' is a participator (as defined) in a company of which shares or securities are comprised in the trust or a close company (as above) that has provided property comprised in the trust and any person who was a participator in such a company at any time during the ten years before the share, securities or property became comprised in the trust. Also excluded is any person 'connected' with any such participator. A '*beneficiary*' is a person within *IHTA 1984, s 86(1)(a)* or *(b)*. '*Connected*' has the same meaning as in **17 connected persons,** but as if 'relative' included uncle, aunt, nephew and niece.

[*TCGA 1992, s 239ZA*].

For the position of the shareholders in a close company transferor which makes a transfer within (a)–(c) above at less than market value, see **4.15** ANTI-AVOIDANCE.

See also **30** HOLD-OVER RELIEFS and **21.17** EMPLOYEE SHARE SCHEMES for alternative reliefs which may be available in respect of transfers to settlements for the benefit of employees.

Social investment relief

[23.85] Individuals may defer all or part of a chargeable gain against an investment in a social enterprise. Both the gain and the investment must be before 6 April 2023. The deferred gain becomes chargeable on a disposal of the investment and in certain other circumstances. See **59.14** SOCIAL INVESTMENT RELIEF.

Transfer of a business to a company — incorporation relief

[23.86] Where a person transfers a business and its assets to a company in return for shares in that company, any chargeable gain on disposal of the assets is deferred by reducing the amount otherwise chargeable in the proportion of the value of the shares received to the value of the overall consideration received by the transferor in exchange for the business. An election is available for the relief not to apply. See **31** INCORPORATION AND DISINCORPORATION RELIEFS.

Unremittable overseas gains

[23.87] On a claim, such gains may be treated as gains of the year in which conditions preventing remittance cease to apply. See **43.6** OVERSEAS MATTERS. See also **36.4** LATE PAYMENT INTEREST AND PENALTIES.

Venture capital trusts (VCTs)

[23.88] For 2003/04 and earlier years, individuals could defer all or part of a chargeable gain against subscriptions of up to £100,000 per tax year for shares in VCT companies by reference to which income tax investment relief is obtained. The deferred gain becomes chargeable on a disposal of the VCT shares and in certain other circumstances. The relief is abolished for VCT shares issued on or after 6 April 2004. See **64.8** VENTURE CAPITAL TRUSTS.

24

Furnished Holiday Accommodation

Introduction to furnished holiday accommodation

[24.1] Special provisions apply to the treatment for the purposes of tax on chargeable gains of the commercial letting of furnished holiday accommodation in the UK or the European Economic Area (EEA). The special provisions are to be abolished with effect from April 2025 (see below).

Definitions

'*Commercial letting*' is letting (whether or not under a lease) on a commercial basis and with a view to the realisation of profits (see *Brown v Richardson* (Sp C 129), [1997] SSCD 233 and Revenue Tax Bulletin October 1997 p 472), and accommodation is let '*furnished*' if the tenant is entitled to the use of furniture.

'*Holiday accommodation*' is accommodation which:

(a) must be available for commercial letting to the public generally as holiday accommodation for at least 210 days in a twelve month period (see below); and

(b) is so let for at least 105 such days.

It must, however, not normally be in the same occupation for more than 31 consecutive days at any time during a period (although not necessarily a continuous period) of seven months in that twelve month period which includes any months in which it is let as in (b) above.

In the case of an individual or partnership, these conditions must be satisfied in the tax year in which the profits or gains arise, unless:

(i) the accommodation was not let furnished in the preceding tax year but is so let in the following tax year, in which case they must be satisfied in the twelve months from the date such letting commenced in the tax year; or

(ii) the accommodation was let furnished in the preceding tax year but is not so let in the following tax year, in which case they must be satisfied in the twelve months ending with the date such letting ceased in the tax year.

For companies, the conditions must be satisfied in the 12 months ending on the last day of the accounting period in which the profits or gains arise, with similar variations as in (i) and (ii) above where the accommodation was not let furnished in the 12 months preceding or following the period in question.

In satisfying condition (b) above, averaging may be applied to letting periods of holiday accommodation already treated as such ('*qualifying accommodation*') and letting periods of any or all of other accommodation let by the same person which would be holiday accommodation if it satisfied the 105-day test. Any such other accommodation is then treated as holiday accommodation if the average of the days let in the 12-month period is at least 105. A claim for averaging must be made on or before the first anniversary of 31 January following the tax year for which it is to be applied. For companies, the time limit is two years after the end of the accounting period for which the averaging claim is to apply. Only one such claim may be made in respect of qualifying accommodation in any tax year or accounting period. Separate averaging claims must be made for accommodation in the UK and accommodation in the EEA.

If accommodation qualifies as holiday accommodation during a tax year, either by meeting conditions (a) and (b) above or as a result of an averaging election, the taxpayer may elect for the property to continue to qualify for the following tax year or the following two tax years if it would otherwise fail to do so only because it does not meet condition (b) for that year or years. The property is not, however, treated as qualifying for the purposes of averaging (or for the further application of this provision). An election can only be made if the taxpayer had a genuine intention to meet the condition in the affected tax years. A separate election is required for each tax year involved, but if no election is made for the first affected tax year, then an election cannot be made for the second. An election must be made on or before the first anniversary of 31 January following the tax year for which it is to be applied. A similar provision applies to companies by reference to accounting periods. An election must be made within two years after the end of the accounting period for which it is to apply.

Where there is a letting of accommodation only part of which is holiday accommodation, apportionments are made as are just and reasonable.

HMRC give the following examples of circumstances in which an election can be made: where the property was marketed to the same or a greater level than in successful years, or where the lettings are cancelled due to unforeseen circumstances, including extreme adverse weather. For 2020/21, HMRC accept that unforeseen circumstances include where the letting condition is not met due to coronavirus (COVID-19) measures such as enforced closure due to lockdown or travel ban. (HMRC Property Income Manual PIM4110).

[*ITTOIA 2005, ss 323–326A; CTA 2009, ss 265–268A; TCGA 1992, ss 241(1)(2)(7), 241A(1)–(3)(9)*].

Furnished holiday accommodation may include caravans (Revenue Press Release 17 May 1984).

See Tolley's Income Tax for income tax provisions for furnished holiday accommodation.

Abolition of the furnished holiday accommodation regime

The government announced at Spring Budget 2024 that the furnished holiday accommodation tax regime will be abolished from April 2025. To prevent the use of unconditional contracts to access the beneficial CGT treatment, the proposed legislation, which will be published in due course, will also include an anti-forestalling rule applying retrospectively from 6 March 2024. See www.gov.uk/government/publications/spring-budget-2024-overview-of-tax-legislation-and-rates-ootlar/spring-budget-2024-overview-of-tax-legislation-and-rates-ootlar#chapter2, para 2.7.

Capital gains tax treatment

[24.2] For the purposes of the following provisions, any UK property business which consists of, or so far as it consists of, the commercial letting of furnished holiday accommodation in the UK is treated as a trade, and all such lettings made by a particular person, partnership or body of persons are treated as one trade. Similarly, any overseas property business which consists of, or so far as it consists of, such letting in one or more EEA states is treated as a trade, and all such lettings made by a particular person, partnership or body of persons are treated as one trade. Note that a taxpayer who lets furnished holiday accommodation in both the UK and the EEA will be treated as carrying on two separate trades. This treatment is to be abolished with effect from April 2025 (see **24.1** above).

The provisions are as follows.

(a) ROLLOVER RELIEF (**53**).
(b) Relief for gifts of business assets (see **30.2–30.9** HOLD-OVER RELIEFS).
(c) Relief for loans to traders (see **38.11** LOSSES).
(d) The exemptions relating to SUBSTANTIAL SHAREHOLDINGS OF COMPANIES (**60**).
(e) BUSINESS ASSET DISPOSAL RELIEF (**9**).

Where, in any chargeable period, a person makes a commercial letting within these provisions, the let property is to be taken for the purposes of (a)–(e) above as being used throughout that period only for the purposes of the deemed trade of making such lettings except for any period when it is neither commercially let nor available to be so let (unless it is only works of construction or repair that make this the case).

For the purposes of (a) above, where the only or main residence exemption in *TCGA 1992, s 222* (see **47** PRIVATE RESIDENCES) is also available to any extent, the gain to which *TCGA 1992, s 222* applies is reduced by the amount of the rolled-over gain.

[*TCGA 1992, ss 241(3)–(6)(8), 241A(4)–(8)(10)(11)*].

Example

In May 2018, Isobel sells Heene Cottage for £120,000. The cottage had qualified as furnished holiday accommodation throughout Isobel's period of ownership and had originally cost £55,000. The whole proceeds are invested in the acquisition in June 2018 of Croft Cottage at a cost of £150,000 and Isobel claims rollover relief under *TCGA 1992, s 152*. The new property is used as furnished holiday accommodation until June 2022 when it becomes Isobel's only residence. Croft Cottage is sold in June 2024 for £290,000. The chargeable gain on disposal is computed as follows.

Disposal of Heene Cottage

	£	£
Allowable cost		55,000
Actual disposal consideration		120,000
Chargeable gain rolled over		£65,000
Deemed allowable cost of Croft Cottage (£150,000 – £65,000)		£85,000

Disposal of Croft Cottage

Disposal consideration		290,000
Allowable cost		85,000
Gain before main residence relief		£205,000
Main residence relief		
Gain before relief	205,000	
Less amount of rolled-over gain	65,000	65,000
Gain eligible for relief	140,000	
Less relief (2/6 × £140,000)	46,667	93,333
Chargeable gain 2024/25		£158,333

Key points concerning furnished holiday accommodation

[24.3] Points to consider are as follows:

- The furnished holiday accommodation tax regime will be abolished with effect from April 2025. To prevent the use of unconditional contracts to access the beneficial CGT treatment, an anti-forestalling rule will apply retrospectively from 6 March 2024.
- Where a furnished holiday accommodation business ceases, business asset disposal relief can normally be claimed where the assets are disposed of up to three years after cessation. For sole traders, provided the properties were used for the business at cessation, there should be no restriction on the relief. This may cover the properties being used for other purposes prior to sale, e.g. empty or let out but not qualifying as furnished holiday accommodations.
- Property is often acquired in joint names, e.g., husband and wife. Joint ownership does not necessarily indicate the existence of a partnership (PIM1030). However, where the owners provide significant additional services, a partnership may exist and the conditions for claiming business asset disposal relief are more restric-

tive. For a partnership, a gain on the disposal of a property used in the business may need to be time apportioned for any period when the property was not used for furnished holiday accommodation.

- Where the business contains several let properties and only some are disposed of, it is necessary to satisfy the 'part of a business' condition. Otherwise, no business asset disposal relief will be available. See **9.4** BUSINESS ASSET DISPOSAL RELIEF.

25

Gifts

Cross-references. See **33.2** INTERACTION WITH OTHER TAXES for inheritance tax interaction on lifetime gifts; and **45.5** PAYMENT OF TAX for payment by instalments on certain gifts etc.

Tax consequences of a gift

[25.1] The fact that no proceeds are received on a disposal of an asset does not mean that a chargeable gain will not arise. With certain exceptions, where a person acquires or disposes of an asset, otherwise than by way of a bargain made at arm's length *and in particular where he acquires or disposes of it by way of gift,* his acquisition or disposal of the asset is deemed to be for a consideration equal to the market value of the asset. [*TCGA 1992, s 17(1)(a)*]. Thus, the donor of an asset is normally treated as making a chargeable gain computed by reference to market value at the date of disposal.

The date of disposal where a person gifts property is the time when he has done everything within his power to transfer the property to the donee (see *Re Rose, Rose and Others v CIR* CA, [1952] 1 All ER 1217).

See **39** MARKET VALUE for the full market value rules and exceptions.

Exemptions

[25.2] Once the market value of a gift has been established, the ordinary capital gains tax provisions relating to exemptions apply to that gift. See **23** EXEMPTIONS AND RELIEFS. For example, the gift of a chattel with a market value of £6,000 or less is exempt. The following gifts are expressly exempt.

- Gifts for public benefit.
- Gifts of property to bodies mentioned in *IHTA 1984, Sch 3* for national purposes (see **23.39** EXEMPTIONS AND RELIEFS).
- Donatio mortis causa (see **18.5** DEATH).

Reliefs

[25.3] Reliefs are available for:

- gifts of business assets (see **30.2** HOLD-OVER RELIEFS);

- gifts to charities (see **11.5** CHARITIES);
- gifts of assets on which inheritance tax etc. is chargeable (see **30.10** HOLD-OVER RELIEFS);
- gifts to housing associations (see **23.51** EXEMPTIONS AND RELIEFS);
- gifts of national heritage property subject to certain undertakings (see **23.79** EXEMPTIONS AND RELIEFS); and
- gifts to settlements for the benefit of employees (see **23.84** EXEMPTIONS AND RELIEFS).

Recovery of tax from donee

[25.4] Where CGT arising on a gift (or any transaction not at arm's length) is not paid by the donor (or their personal representatives) within twelve months from the date it became payable, it may be recovered from the donee within two years after the date on which it became payable. The donee then has a right of recovery from the donor or his personal representatives. The recovery is done by assessment and the donee is assessed and charged (in the name of the donor) to CGT on an amount not exceeding the amount of the chargeable gain arising on the disposal, and not exceeding the grossed-up amount of the capital gains tax unpaid at the time such assessment is made, grossing up at the marginal rate of tax (i.e. by taking capital gains tax on a chargeable gain at the amount which would not have been chargeable but for that chargeable gain).

These provisions apply to a chargeable gain accruing to a transferor under *TCGA 1992, s 169C(7)* (clawback of relief under *TCGA 1992, s 165* or *s 260* if settlement becomes settlor-interested — see **30.8** HOLD-OVER RELIEFS) as they apply in relation to a gain accruing on a disposal by way of a gift. The transferor is taken to be the donor, and the trustees to whom the relevant disposal in question (see **30.8** HOLD-OVER RELIEFS) was made are taken to be the donee.

[*TCGA 1992, s 282*].

Key points concerning gifts

[25.5] Points to consider are as follows.

- Where a disposal is by way of a gift, the market value of the assets is substituted for the sale proceeds in the CGT calculation. The tax is then payable by the donor under the usual rules.
- As well as CGT, gifts may also be chargeable to inheritance tax. Practitioners should consider the implications of both taxes in relation to any gift. Where a gift is immediately chargeable to inheritance tax, capital gains tax hold-over relief may be available under *TCGA 1992, s 260*. See **30** HOLD-OVER RELIEFS for further details of hold-over relief.

26

Groups of Companies

Cross-references. See 8.1, 8.3 ASSETS HELD ON 6 APRIL 1965 and 8.3, 8.5 ASSETS HELD ON 31 MARCH 1982 for irrevocable election by principal company of a group; **14** COMPANIES.

Simon's Taxes. See D2.3, D2.4.

Introduction to groups of companies

[26.1] For certain chargeable gains purposes, the members of a group of companies are treated, in effect, as if they were one entity. This is achieved through the following reliefs:

(a) transfers of assets between group members are treated as if made for a disposal value giving rise to neither a gain nor a loss;
(b) an allowable loss of one group member can be set against a chargeable gain of another member, if both members elect for either the gain or the loss to be transferred from one to the other; and
(c) for the purposes of ROLLOVER RELIEF (53) on the replacement of business assets all the trades carried on by the members of the group are treated as a single trade (so that a gain of one member can be rolled over into the acquisition of an asset by another member).

For the detailed provisions and restrictions see **26.3** onwards below for (a) above, **26.13** below for (b) above and **53.10** ROLLOVER RELIEF for (c) above.

The relief for intra-group transfers at (a) above is withdrawn in certain circumstances. In particular, this applies where a company which acquired an asset by intra-group transfer subsequently leaves the group within six years of the transfer (the 'degrouping charge'). See **26.7** onwards below.

There are a number of anti-avoidance provisions which apply specifically to groups of companies as well as further such provisions which are more general but can apply to groups. The provisions are listed at **26.14** below and are mostly described in detail at **4** ANTI-AVOIDANCE. See, however, **26.15** onwards for the provisions dealing with gain and loss buying. These are designed to prevent groups of companies buying and selling companies in order to make use of capital losses suffered by another company or group.

The definition of a 'group' and other terms for the purposes of this chapter is given at **26.2** below.

Groups of companies — definitions

[26.2] For the purposes of this chapter, the following definitions apply.

Company

'*Company*' means a company within the meaning of the *Companies Act 2006, s 1(1)* (or the corresponding enactment in Northern Ireland) or a company (other than a limited liability partnership — see **44.17** PARTNERSHIPS) which is constituted under any other Act, Royal Charter, or letters patent or under the law of a country outside the UK. It also includes a registered society within *Co-operative and Community Benefit Societies Act 2014* or NI equivalent, a European Co-operative (see **14.17** COMPANIES), a trustee savings bank, a building society and an incorporated friendly society within the meaning of *Friendly Societies Act 1992*. There is no requirement for the company to be resident in the UK.

[*TCGA 1992, s 170(9); CTA 2010, s 1119*].

Group

A '*group*' comprises:

(a) a company ('*the principal company of the group*'); and
(b) that company's '75% subsidiaries' (as in *CTA 2010, s 1154(3)* i.e. where not less than 75% of the 'ordinary share capital' (see below under 'General') is beneficially owned directly or indirectly by the principal company), and those subsidiaries' 75% subsidiaries (and so on), except that any 75% subsidiary which is not 'an effective 51% subsidiary' of the principal company is excluded.

This definition is subject to the following rules.

(1) A company ('the subsidiary') which is a 75% subsidiary of another company cannot be a principal company of a group, unless,

   (i) because of the exclusion in (b) above, the two companies are not in the same group,
   (ii) the requirements of the definition of a group in (a) and (b) are otherwise satisfied, and
   (iii) no further company could, under this provision, be the principal company of a group of which the subsidiary would be a member.

(2) If a company would otherwise belong to more than one group (the principal company of each of which is called the 'head of a group' below), it belongs only to the group which can first be determined under the following tests.
   (i) The group to which it would belong if the exclusion of a company which is not an effective 51% subsidiary in (b) above were applied without the inclusion of any amount to which the head of a group is entitled of any profits available for distribution to equity holders of a head of another group or would be entitled to any assets of a head of another group available for distribution to its equity holders on a winding up.
   (ii) The group the head of which is entitled to a greater percentage than any other head of a group of its profits available for distribution to equity holders.
   (iii) The group the head of which would be entitled to a greater percentage than any other head of a group of its assets available for distribution to equity holders on a winding-up.
   (iv) The group the head of which owns (as in *CTA 2010, s 1154(2)*) directly or indirectly more of its ordinary share capital than any other head of a group.

(3) If a group was regarded as reconstituted purely because of the removal of the requirement for group companies to be UK-resident by *FA 2000*, such that the principal company of the 'old' group is not the principal company of the 'new' group, a subsidiary which is not 'an effective 51% subsidiary' of the new principal company remains part of the group for as long as it remains 'an effective 51% subsidiary' of the company which was the principal company of the old group.

A company ('the subsidiary') is '*an effective 51% subsidiary*' of another company ('the parent') at any time if and only if:

(A) the parent is entitled to more than 50% of any profits available for distribution to equity holders of the subsidiary; and
(B) the parent would be entitled to more than 50% of any assets available for distribution to the equity holders on a winding up.

CTA 2010, Pt 5 Ch 6 (group relief: equity holders and profits or assets available for distribution) applies with suitable modifications for the purposes of (2) and (A) and (B) above. One modification for these purposes disapplies the requirement that certain arrangements for changes in profit or asset shares are assumed to take place in applying the 50% tests above.

[*TCGA 1992, s 170(2)(b)(3)–(8)*].

For consideration of beneficial ownership of a company's shares where they are subject to cross-options by shareholders, see *J Sainsbury plc v O'Connor* CA 1991, 64 TC 208. Although legislation overturning the *Sainsbury* decision was introduced for group relief purposes, it does not apply for chargeable gains purposes.

A group remains the same group so long as the same company remains the principal company of the group, and if at any time the principal company of a group becomes a member of another group, the first group and the other group are regarded as the same, and the question whether or not a company has ceased to be a member of a group is determined accordingly. [*TCGA 1992, s 170(10)*].

Where the principal company of a group:

- becomes an SE (see **14.16** COMPANIES) by reason of being the acquiring company in the formation of an SE by merger by acquisition (in accordance with *Council Regulations (EC) No 2157/2001, Arts 2(1), 17(2)* and *29(1)*);
- becomes a subsidiary of a holding SE (formed in accordance with *Art 2(2)*); or
- is transformed into an SE (in accordance with *Art 2(4)*),

the group and any group of which the SE is a member on formation are regarded as the same, and the question whether or not a company has ceased to be a member of a group is determined accordingly. [*TCGA 1992, s 170(10A)*].

The passing of a resolution, or the making of an order, or any other act for the winding-up of a member of a group is not treated as an occasion on which any company ceases to be a member of the group. [*TCGA 1992, s 170(11)*].

Example

A Ltd, which is not itself a subsidiary of another company, owns 100% of the ordinary share capital of B Ltd and C Ltd. A Ltd also owns 75% of the ordinary share capital of D Ltd. In turn D Ltd owns 75% of the ordinary share capital of E Ltd and E Ltd owns 75% of the ordinary share capital of F Ltd. B Ltd and C Ltd have no subsidiaries. Each company has only one class of shares so that its percentage ownership of ordinary share capital of another company equates to its percentage entitlement to that company's profits available for distribution and to its assets on a winding up.

For chargeable gains purposes, A Ltd is the principal company of a group of companies consisting of itself, B Ltd, C Ltd, D Ltd and E Ltd.

F Ltd is excluded from the group. Although it satisfies the '75% subsidiary' test it is not an effective 51% subsidiary of the principal company, A Ltd. A Ltd would be entitled to only 42.19%(75% × 75% × 75%) of the profits and assets of F Ltd within (A) and (B) above.

General

'*Ordinary share capital*' means all issued share capital of a company except that carrying a fixed rate of dividend only. Any share capital of a registered industrial and provident society is treated as ordinary share capital. For HMRC's interpretation of 'ordinary share capital', see HMRC Company Taxation Manual CTM00511–CTM00516.

'*Group*' and '*subsidiary*' are construed with any necessary modifications where applied to a company incorporated under the law of a country outside the UK.

'*Profits*' means income and gains. '*Trade*' includes a vocation, office or employment (including the occupation of UK woodlands before 6 April 1993).

[*TCGA 1992, s 170(1)(2)(c)(d); CTA 2010, s 1119*].

For HMRC's own notes on the capital gains definition of a group of companies, see HMRC Capital Gains Manual CG45100–45140.

HMRC have confirmed that it is possible for a Delaware Limited Liability Company that issues shares to be a member of a capital gains group (Revenue Tax Bulletin February 2001 p 827). It is specifically provided that an open-ended investment company (see **63.7** UNIT TRUSTS, ETC.) cannot be the principal company of a group [*TCGA 1992, s 170(4A)*] or a member of a group (see HMRC Capital Gains Manual, CG45110).

Intra-group transfers

[26.3] Disposals of capital assets by one member of a group to another member (i.e. 'intra-group transfers') are treated as if made at a 'no gain/no loss' disposal value if:

(a) *either* the transferor company is UK-resident at the time of disposal *or* the asset is a 'chargeable asset' in relation to that company immediately before that time; *and*
(b) *either* the transferee company is UK-resident at the time of disposal *or* the asset is a 'chargeable asset' in relation to that company immediately after that time.

For these purposes, an asset is a '*chargeable asset*' in relation to a company at a particular time if, on a disposal by that company at that time, any gain would be a chargeable gain and would be within the charge to corporation tax (see **14.2**(a)–(c) COMPANIES).

A previous deemed disposal by the transferor company under *TCGA 1992, s 25(3)* (deemed disposal on asset ceasing to be chargeable asset — see **43.3** OVERSEAS MATTERS) is ignored in applying the no gain/no loss rule to the transferee company if no gain or loss was deemed to arise on the deemed disposal (as a result of *TCGA 1992, s 25ZA(2)*).

HMRC accept that the no gain/no loss rule can apply to the grant or surrender of a lease by one group company to another (HMRC Capital Gains Manual CG45325).

In *Gallaher Ltd v HMRC* FTT, [2019] UKFTT 207 (TC), the FTT found that the exclusion from *TCGA 1992, s 171* of an intra-group disposal to a transferee which is outside the UK tax net but located within an EU member state was a disproportionate restriction on the freedom of establishment. The tax charge arising on such a disposal was therefore disapplied. The Upper Tribunal ([2021] STC 247) referred the issue to the CJEU. The CJEU held ([2023] STC 408) that, although there was a restriction on the freedom of establishment, this was justified because it was proportionate to the objective of maintaining a balanced allocation of taxing powers between member states. See **45.10** PAYMENT OF TAX for CT payment plans for transactions with EEA resident group members which allow for payment by instalments where *s 171* is disapplied. The facility for such plans was introduced to prevent the disapplication of a tax charge in accordance with the FTT decision in *Gallaher*.

Exceptions

This rule does not, however, apply to the following.

(i) Assumed (as opposed to actual) disposals.

(ii) A disposal of a debt due from a group member effected by satisfying it (or part of it).

(iii) A disposal on redemption of redeemable shares.

(iv) A disposal of an interest in shares in consideration of a capital distribution within *TCGA 1992, s 122* whether or not involving a reduction of capital.

(v) The receipt of compensation for destruction etc. of assets (in that the disposal is treated as being to the insurer or other person who ultimately bears the burden of furnishing the compensation).

(vi) A disposal by or to an investment trust within *CTA 2010, s 1158* (and see also **26.11** below).

(vii) A disposal by or to a venture capital trust within *ITA 2007, Pt 6* (and see **26.12** below).

(viii) A disposal by or to a qualifying friendly society, i.e. an incorporated friendly society within *FA 2012, s 165* which is entitled to income tax and corporation tax exemptions on certain profits.

(ix) A disposal to a 'dual resident investing company' within *CTA 2010, s 109*.

(x) A disposal by or to a real estate investment trust (see **63.5** UNIT TRUSTS ETC.).

(xi) A disposal by one member of a group to another in fulfilment of its obligations under an option granted to that other member at a time when the two companies were not members of the same group.

(xii) An exchange of securities which is treated by *TCGA 1992, s 127* as it applies by virtue of *TCGA 1992, s 135* as not involving a disposal by the member of the group first mentioned above (see **57.2** and **57.5** SHARES AND SECURITIES).

For HMRC's views on this topic, see HMRC Capital Gains Manual CG45550.

[*TCGA 1992, s 171*].

As regards (iv) above, the assets acquired in the capital distribution are nevertheless transferred at a 'no gain/no loss' price (see *Innocent v Whaddon Estates Ltd Ch D 1981, 55 TC 476*).

Assets held on 6 April 1965

Where a company which is or has been a group member disposes of an asset which it acquired from another group member as a result of a no gain/no loss disposal, the provisions relating to assets held on 6 April 1965 (see **8.12** ASSETS HELD ON 31 MARCH **1982** apply as if all group members were one person. [*TCGA 1992, s 174(4)*].

Assets which are trading stock of one of the companies but not of the other

[26.4] Where a company (Company A) acquires an asset as trading stock of a trade from another member of the group (Company B), and the asset did not form part of the trading stock of a trade carried on by Company B, Company A is treated for the purposes of *TCGA 1992, s 161* (see **16.9** COMPUTATION OF GAINS AND LOSSES) as acquiring the asset otherwise than as trading stock and immediately appropriating it to trading stock. The effect is that, subject to an election being made for the alternative treatment in **16.9** COMPUTATION OF GAINS AND LOSSES, a chargeable gain or allowable loss accrues to Company A based on the difference between market value and the no gain/no loss (see **26.3** above) transfer value.

Where a company (Company C) disposes of an asset forming part of the trading stock of a trade to another member of the group (Company D), and the asset is acquired by Company D otherwise than as trading stock of a trade carried on by it, Company C is treated for the purposes of *TCGA 1992, s 161* as appropriating the asset immediately before the disposal for a purpose other than use as trading stock. The effect is that Company C is deemed to have acquired the asset at that time at the amount brought into the accounts of the trade for tax purposes (see **16.9** COMPUTATION OF GAINS AND LOSSES).

References above to a trade do not include a trade carried on by a non-UK resident company other than in the UK through a permanent establishment.

[*TCGA 1992, s 173*].

Acquisition 'as trading stock' implies a commercial justification for the acquisition, see *Coates v Arndale Properties Ltd* HL 1984, 59 TC 516, *Reed v Nova Securities Ltd* HL 1985, 59 TC 516, *N Ltd v Inspector of Taxes* (Sp C 90), [1996] SSCD 346 and *New Angel Court Ltd v Adam* CA, [2004] STC 779; [2004] EWCA Civ 242.

Indexation allowance

[26.5] See **8.6** ASSETS HELD ON **31** MARCH **1982** and **32.4** INDEXATION for re-basing and indexation provisions on 'no gain/no loss' disposals.

Intra-group transfers — clawback of relief

[26.6] In the following circumstances the relief given by treating an intra-group transfer as made at no gain and no loss is effectively clawed back:

(a) where the company to which the asset was transferred leaves the group within six years after the transfer (the 'degrouping charge');
(b) where the company to which the asset was transferred becomes an investment trust within six years after the transfer; and
(c) where the company to which the asset was transferred becomes a venture capital trust within six years after the transfer.

Broadly, the company concerned must still own the asset transferred. The clawback is made by treating the company as if, immediately after its acquisition of the asset, it had sold, and immediately reacquired, the asset at its then market value (although the resulting gain is treated as accruing at a time determined by the triggering event) or, where a share disposal causes the company to leave the group, by adjusting the gain or loss on that disposal. There are, however, a number of reliefs and exemptions which apply to the degrouping charge in (a) above. See **26.7–26.12** for the detailed provisions.

Degrouping charge

[26.7] A degrouping charge applies where a company ceases to be a member of a group at a time when it owns an asset previously transferred to it by another group member.

Note that these provisions do not apply if, before the chargeable company leaves the group (or leaves a second group — see below), it has become an investment trust or a venture capital trust and triggered the provisions at **26.11** or **26.12** below. [*TCGA 1992, s 179(2C)(2D)*].

The provisions apply where a company (the transferee company) has acquired an asset from another company (the transferor company) at a time when both companies are members of the same group and the transferee company ceases to be a member of the group within six years after the time of the acquisition. It is also a requirement that the asset be within the charge to UK corporation tax both before and after the transfer, the precise conditions being similar to those for intra-group transfers at **26.3** above.

If, when the transferee leaves the group it, or an 'associated' company also leaving the group, owns (not as trading stock) the asset, replacement property to which a gain on the disposal of the original asset has been carried forward under **53 ROLLOVER RELIEF** or an asset the value of which is wholly or partly derived from the original asset, the transferee is treated as if, immediately after its acquisition of the asset (subject to **26.9** below), it had sold, and immediately reacquired, the asset at its then market value. There will thus be a gain or loss by reference to the market value of the asset at that time and its 'no gain/no loss' acquisition consideration under **26.3** above. The gain or loss on the deemed sale is normally treated as accruing immediately after the beginning of the accounting period in which (or at the end of which, if that be the case) the company ceases to be a member of the group. This will apply in most cases but it is subject to the proviso that the time of accrual cannot be earlier than the time of transfer of the asset. Companies are '*associated*' for this purpose if one is a 75% subsidiary (as defined in **26.2** above) of the other or both are 75% subsidiaries of another company.

CTA 2010, ss 138–142 (limits on group relief — see Tolley's Corporation Tax) have effect as if the actual circumstances were as they are treated above as having been.

[*TCGA 1992, s 179(1)(1A)(3)(4)(10)(10A); FA 2019, Sch 1 para 65*].

Companies leaving the group at the same time

There is an exception to the degrouping charge where both the transferee and the transferor companies leave the group at the same time and either:

- the companies are both 75% subsidiaries and effective 51% subsidiaries (as defined in **26.2** above) of another company on the date of acquisition of the asset and continue to be so until immediately after they cease to be members of the group; or
- one of the companies is both a 75% subsidiary and an effective 51% subsidiary of the other on the date of acquisition and continues to be so until immediately after the companies cease to be members of the group.

Where either condition is satisfied, the degrouping charge does not apply.

However, the charge will nevertheless apply in certain circumstances where a company in a group transfers an asset intra-group and both transferor and transferee then leave that group to form a second group which, at the time the transferee leaves the first group, is 'connected' with the first. If the transferee company leaves the second group, the charge will apply (in relation to the departure from the second group) if the intra-group transfer, which is deemed for this purpose to have taken place in the second group, occurred within the preceding six years. Where the two groups cease to be connected (without the transferee having left the second group), the transferee company and any associated company are treated as having left the second group at that time and the provision applies accordingly. Where the above exception would otherwise apply in relation to the departure from the second group it does not do so if the transferee leaving the first group was part of arrangements a main purpose of which was the avoidance of a corporation tax liability. The two groups are '*connected*' at a particular time for this purpose if, broadly, at that time the second group is under the control of the first group or both groups are under the common control of a person or persons who control or have controlled the first group at any time since the chargeable company left the first group. The general definitions of *CTA 2010, ss 450, 451* (meaning of 'control') apply for this purpose (except for banking businesses). See Tolley's Corporation Tax under Close Companies.

[*TCGA 1992, s 179(2)–(2B)(9A)*].

Company leaving group due to share disposal

Where the conditions listed below are satisfied, a degrouping gain or loss under the above provisions is not treated as a separate gain or loss, but instead the gain or loss accruing on a 'group disposal' (see below) is adjusted to take account of the degrouping gain or loss. The conditions are as follows:

(A) the transferee company ceases to be a member of the group as a result of one or more disposals ('*group disposals*') by a group member of the transferee's shares or those of another group member;

(B) either:

(i) the company making the group disposal (or, if there is more than one such disposal, at least one of them) is UK resident at the time of disposal, the shares are within the charge to corporation tax (or would be but for the substantial shareholdings exemption — see **60** SUBSTANTIAL SHAREHOLDING EXEMPTION), or any part of the gains or loss on the disposal (or at least one of them) is treated as accruing to a person under *TCGA 1992, s 3* (previously *TCGA 1992, s 13(2)*; attribution of gains to members of non-resident companies — see **43.7** OVERSEAS MATTERS), or

(ii) had (i) above applied to the group disposal or to each of them, any gain arising would not have been a chargeable gain as a result of the substantial shareholdings exemption; and

(C) *CTA 2010, s 535* (UK real estate investment trusts: exemption of gains — see **63.5** UNIT TRUSTS AND OTHER INVESTMENT VEHICLES) would not apply to the degrouping gain or loss.

For these purposes, *TCGA 1992, s 127* (share reorganisations etc. treated as not involving disposal — see **57.2** onwards SHARES AND SECURITIES) is ignored in determining whether there has been a disposal.

Where the conditions are satisfied, a chargeable gain or allowable loss on a single group disposal is calculated by adding any degrouping gain which would have arisen but for these provisions to the consideration for the group disposal. Any degrouping loss which would have been allowable but for these provisions is treated as an allowable deduction (see **16.12** COMPUTATION OF GAINS AND LOSSES) in computing the gain or loss on the group disposal.

Where the group disposal is within *TCGA 1992, s 127* so that there is no disposal for chargeable gains purposes, the adjustments in respect of the degrouping gain or loss are made to any gain or loss on a disposal of the 'new holding' (see **57.2** SHARES AND SECURITIES) or a part of it. Where there is a degrouping gain, the amount of the gain reduces the allowable expenditure and any excess over the amount of that expenditure is treated as an additional gain on the new holding disposal. If the disposal is of only part of the new holding, only that part of the excess of the degrouping gain over the allowable expenditure that corresponds to the part of the new holding disposed of is treated as an additional gain in this way. Where there is a degrouping loss, it is added to the allowable expenditure.

If there is more than one group disposal, the degrouping profit or loss is apportioned to the group disposals as the companies making them jointly elect or, if no election is made, by dividing it equally between the group disposals. An election must be made to HMRC no later than two years after the end of the accounting period in which the first group disposal is made.

If a group disposal consists of shares of more than one class, the company can apportion any increase or deduction to be made under these provisions between the classes as it considers appropriate.

[*TCGA 1992, s 179(3A)–(3H)*].

If the vendor's gain on the share disposal qualifies for the SUBSTANTIAL SHAREHOLDING EXEMPTION (**60**), so does the degrouping charge added to it (HMRC Capital Gains Manual CG53235).

Company ceasing to be group member on principal company joining another group

Where the transferee company ceases to be a member of a group only because the principal company becomes a member of another, second, group (e.g. it is not an 'effective 51% subsidiary' of the principal company of the other group as in **26.2** above) the following provisions apply.

(I) The transferee company is not treated under the above provisions as selling the asset at that time.

(II) If:

(i) within six years of that time the company ceases at any time ('*the relevant time*') to satisfy the following conditions: namely that it is a '75% subsidiary' (as defined in **26.2** above) of one or more members of the other group mentioned in (a) above and an 'effective 51% subsidiary' (as defined in **26.2** above) of one or more of those members; and

(ii) at the relevant time the company or a company in the same group, owns (otherwise than as trading stock) the asset, or property to which a chargeable gain has been rolled over from the asset, or an asset the value of which is wholly or partly derived from the original asset,

the transferee company is treated as if, immediately after acquiring the asset (subject to **26.9** below), it had sold and reacquired it at its market value at the time of acquisition.

(III) (II) above does not apply if:

(i) the transferee company ceases at the relevant time to the conditions in (II)(i) above as a result of one or more disposals by a member of the second group of the transferee's shares or those of another group member;

(ii) either:

– the company making the share disposal (or, if there is more than one such disposal, at least one of them) is UK resident at the time of disposal, the shares are within the charge to corporation tax (or would be but for the substantial shareholdings exemption — see **60**), or any part of the gains or loss on the disposal (or at least one of them) is treated as accruing to a person under *TCGA 1992, s 13(2)* (attribution of gains to members of non-resident companies — see **43.7** OVERSEAS MATTERS); or

– had those conditions applied to the share disposal or to each of them, any gain arising would not have been a chargeable gain as a result of the substantial shareholdings exemption; and

(iii) in the absence of this provision *CTA 2010, s 535* (UK real estate investment trusts: exemption of gains — see **63.5** UNIT TRUSTS AND OTHER INVESTMENT VEHICLES) would not apply to the gain or loss in (II) above.

Instead the provisions above applying to a company leaving a group as a result of a share disposal (i.e. *TCGA 1992, s 179(3C)–(3H)*) apply (with appropriate modifications).

(IV) Any gain or loss on the deemed sale in (II) above is treated as arising immediately before the relevant time.

[*TCGA 1992, s 179(5)–(8)*].

Supplementary provisions

Ceasing to be a member of a group

Where a company ceases to be a member of a group in consequence of another member of the group ceasing to exist, the company is not treated as ceasing to be a group member for the purposes of the degrouping charge provisions. [*TCGA 1992, s 179(1)*]. HMRC consider that this let-out only applies to the case of a parent company ceasing to be a member of a group on the occasion of its only subsidiary ceasing to exist on dissolution (or all its subsidiaries ceasing to exist simultaneously on dissolution). HMRC have confirmed they do not apply the degrouping charge where the company receiving the asset ceases to be a group member as a result of its only subsidiary leaving the group (HMRC Capital Gains Manual CG45410 and see *Dunlop International AG v Pardoe* CA 1999, 72 TC 71).

Where, as part of a process of merger to which *TCGA 1992, s 140E* (European cross-border merger: assets left within UK tax charge — see **43.14** OVERSEAS MATTERS) applies, a company which is a member of a group ceases to exist and as a consequence assets, or shares in one or more companies which were also members of the group, are transferred to the transferee, the company which has ceased to exist and any company whose shares have been transferred to the transferee are, for the purposes of these provisions, not treated as having left the group. The transferee and the company which ceased to exist are treated as the same entity and, if the transferee is itself a member of a group following the merger, any company which was a member of the first group and became a member of the transferee's group as a result of the merger is treated as if the two groups were the same. [*TCGA 1992, s 179(1B)–(1D)*].

Where shares in a company are transferred as part of the process of the transfer of a business to which *TCGA 1992, s 140A* (see **43.12** OVERSEAS MATTERS) or *TCGA 1992, s 140C* (see **43.13** OVERSEAS MATTERS) applies, and as a result, the company ceases to be a member of a group, it is treated as not having left the group. If the company becomes a member of a second group, of which the transferee company is a member, as a result of the transfer, the company is treated as if the two groups were the same. [*TCGA 1992, s 179(1AA)*].

Value shifting

If under these provisions a deemed sale arises at any time, and if on an actual sale at market value at that time any loss or gain would, under the value shifting provisions (see **4.12** ANTI-AVOIDANCE), have been calculated as if the consideration were increased by an amount, the market value at the time of the deemed sale is treated as having been greater by that amount. [*TCGA 1992, s 179(9)*].

Assessments etc.

Any adjustment of tax or recomputation of liability on a disposal may be made by assessment or otherwise as a result of any deemed disposal and reacquisition mentioned above. [*TCGA 1992, s 179(13)*].

Example

C Ltd had the following transactions.

1.3.88	Purchased a freehold property £20,000.
1.12.18	Sold the freehold to D Ltd (a wholly-owned subsidiary) for £40,000 (market value £100,000).
31.7.24	Sold its interest in D Ltd (at which time D Ltd continued to own the freehold property).

Both C Ltd and D Ltd prepare accounts to 30 April.

The consideration for the sale of the shares is £1 million, and C Ltd purchased the shares in March 1986 for £120,000.

Relevant values of the RPI are: March 1986 96.73, March 1988 104.1, December 2017 278.1.

(i) C Ltd's disposal of the property to D Ltd is to be treated as one on which, after taking account of the indexation allowance, neither gain nor loss arises (see **26.3** above and **32.4 INDEXATION**).

Indexation factor 278.1 – 104.1/104.1 = 1.671

	£
Cost to C Ltd	20,000
Indexation allowance £20,000 × 1.671	33,420
Deemed cost to D Ltd	£53,420

(ii) On the sale of C Ltd's shares in D Ltd on 31.7.24 (i.e. within six years after the transaction in (i) above), *C Ltd* will have a deemed disposal as follows.

Deemed disposal by D Ltd on 1.12.18

	£
Market value at 1.12.18	100,000
Cost (as above)	53,420
Degrouping gain	£46,580
D Ltd's new base cost for future gains	£100,000

C Ltd's chargeable gain on disposal of D Ltd shares on 31.7.24

	£
Consideration	1,000,000
Add degrouping gain	46,580
	1,046,580
Less acquisition cost	120,000
Unindexed gain	926,580
Indexation allowance (278.1 – 96.73/96.73) × £120,000	225,000
Chargeable gain subject to CT	£701,580

Note to the example

For corporation tax purposes, indexation allowance is frozen at its December 2017 level. See **32.2** INDEXATION.

Deferral of degrouping charge

[26.8] Where a company is treated as making a gain under the degrouping charge provisions in **26.7** above or such a gain is taken into account in calculating a gain on a disposal of shares under those provisions a claim can be made to defer part of the gain.

Where the degrouping gain is taken into account in calculating a gain on a disposal of shares, the claim can be made by the company making the share disposal or, if there is more than one such disposal, the companies making those disposals acting jointly. In any other case the claim is to be made by the company to whom the degrouping gain is deemed to accrue. The effect is to reduce the amount of the gain by the amount specified in the claim. The reduction must be just and reasonable with regard, in particular, to any transaction as a direct or indirect result of which the asset to which the gain relates was acquired.

Where a gain is reduced in this way, the consideration for the deemed reacquisition of the asset (see **26.7** above) is taken to be its market value less the amount of the adjustment to the gain. In effect the part of the gain excluded is deferred until final disposal of the asset.

[*TCGA 1992, s 179ZA*].

Exemption for substantial shareholdings

[26.9] Where a company ceases to be a member of a group and is deemed under *TCGA 1992, s 179* to have sold and immediately reacquired at market value an asset transferred to it by another group member, then normally the time of the deemed sale is immediately after the transfer (see **26.7** above). However, where:

- a degrouping charge (as in **26.7** above) arises in relation to an asset, and
- a gain on a disposal of that asset (by the company then owning it) immediately before the time of degrouping would have been exempt under the provisions at **60** SUBSTANTIAL SHAREHOLDING EXEMPTION,

the deemed sale and reacquisition is instead treated as taking place immediately before the time of degrouping.

A comparable rule applies where the degrouping charge arises under *TCGA 1992, s 179(5)–(8)*. In this case, the rule applies by reference to the 'relevant time' (see **26.7** above) rather than the 'time of degrouping'.

[*TCGA 1992, Sch 7AC para 38*].

Exemption for mergers

[26.10] *TCGA 1992, s 179* in **26.7** above does not apply, subject to conditions, where, as part of a 'merger', a company (Company A) ceases to be a member of a group ('the A group'), and it is shown that the merger was carried out for bona fide reasons and that the avoidance of a liability to tax was not the main or one of the main purposes of the merger.

'*Merger*', in broad terms, means an arrangement whereby one or more companies ('the acquiring compan(y)(ies)') not in the A group acquire interests in the business previously carried on by Company A, and one or more members of the A group acquire interests in the business or businesses previously carried on either by the acquiring company or companies or by a company at least 90% of the ordinary share capital of which is owned by two or more of the acquiring companies. For this purpose a group member is treated as carrying on as one business the activities of that group. 25% of the value of the interests acquired must take the form of ordinary share capital, whilst the remainder of the interests acquired by the A group must consist of share capital or debentures or both. The value of the interests acquired must be substantially the same, and the consideration for the interests acquired by the acquiring companies must substantially consist of the interests acquired by the A group.

For these purposes, references to a company include a non-UK resident company.

[*TCGA 1992, s 181*].

See HMRC Capital Gains Manual CG45463 for examples on the operation of these provisions. See also **14.13** COMPANIES regarding demergers.

Company becoming an investment trust after acquiring asset intra-group

[26.11] Similar treatment as in **26.7** above (company leaving group) applies where a company (the '*acquiring company*') becomes an investment trust (within *CTA 2010, s 1158* — see **63.4** UNIT TRUSTS ETC.) not more than six years after the company acquired an asset from another company in its group, the disposal by which it acquired the asset (the corresponding disposal) having been treated by virtue of *TCGA 1992, s 171* (intra-group transfers — see **26.3** above) as a no gain/no loss disposal. The provisions apply where at the beginning of the said accounting period, the acquiring company owns, otherwise than as trading stock, either the asset itself or replacement property, i.e. property into which a chargeable gain on disposal of the asset has been rolled over as in **53** ROLLOVER RELIEF, whether directly (i.e. as a result of a single rollover relief claim) or indirectly (where two or more such claims have been made). For the purposes of these provisions, an asset acquired is deemed to be the same as an asset owned subsequently if the value of the latter asset is derived, wholly or partly, from the original asset (in particular where the original was a leasehold and the lessee has acquired the freehold reversion). The provisions do not apply if the acquiring company was an investment trust at the time of the corresponding disposal (in which case the no gain/no loss treatment would not have applied — see **26.3**(vi) above) nor if it has been an investment trust for any intervening accounting period.

The acquiring company is treated as if, immediately after the corresponding disposal, it had sold and immediately reacquired the asset at its market value at that time. The resulting chargeable gain or allowable loss is treated as accruing immediately before the end of the acquiring company's accounting period which immediately preceded that in which it became an investment trust. Notwithstanding normal time limits, any consequential corporation tax assessment may be made at any time within six years after the end of the accounting period in which the company became an investment trust. These provisions are disapplied if, prior to the company becoming an investment trust, the above treatment has already applied to the asset by virtue either of **26.7** above or **26.12** below (company becoming a venture capital trust).

[*TCGA 1992, s 101A*].

Company becoming a venture capital trust after acquiring asset intra-group

[26.12] The same treatment as in **26.11** above (company becoming an investment trust) applies where the acquiring company becomes a venture capital trust (VCT) (within *ITA 2006, Pt 6* — see **64** VENTURE CAPITAL TRUSTS) not more than six years after it acquired the asset intra-group by means of a no gain/no loss disposal under *TCGA 1992, s 171* (see **26.3** above). For this purpose, a company becomes a VCT at the time of the coming into effect of HMRC's approval (the time of approval). The provisions apply where, at the time of approval, the acquiring company owns, otherwise than as trading stock, either the asset itself (with the same rules as in **26.11** above as to derivation of assets) or replacement property (as in **26.11** above). The provisions do not apply if the acquiring company was a VCT at the time of the intra-group disposal and do not apply if it has been a VCT at any time in the intervening period. Nor do they apply if, prior to the company becoming a VCT, the said treatment has already applied to the asset by virtue either of **26.11** above or **26.7** above (company leaving group).

The chargeable gain or allowable loss resulting from the deemed disposal at market value immediately after the intra-group transfer is treated as accruing to the acquiring company immediately before the time of approval. Notwithstanding normal time limits, any consequential corporation tax assessment may, in a case in which HMRC's approval has effect as from the beginning of an accounting period, be made at any time within six years after the end of that accounting period.

[*TCGA 1992, s 101C*].

Election to transfer gain or loss within group

[26.13] Where two companies, X and Y, are members of a group, and a chargeable gain or allowable loss accrues to X, X and Y may make a joint election to transfer the gain or loss, or a specified part of it, from X to Y. The effect of the election is that, for the purposes of corporation tax on chargeable gains:

- the gain or loss, or specified part, is treated as accruing to Y (and not to X) at the time that, but for the election, it would have accrued to X; and

- if Y is not resident in the UK, the transferred gain or loss is taken to accrue in respect of a chargeable asset (i.e. an asset a gain on the disposal of which would be a chargeable gain forming part of Y's chargeable profits (see **14.2**(a)–(c) COMPANIES)).

An election will be disregarded if, taken together with any earlier elections, it would have the effect of transferring more than the total gain or loss. An election cannot be made in respect of a degrouping charge within **26.7** above (but see **26.9** above for the intra-group transfer of a degrouping charge).

The election must be made in writing to an HMRC officer on or before the second anniversary of the end of the accounting period of X in which the gain or loss accrued (or actual disposal was made). It can be made only if an actual transfer of the asset (or part) from X to Y would have been a no gain/no loss disposal within *TCGA 1992, s 171*. For this purpose, the condition at **26.3**(b) above is that, at the time of the deemed transfer, company Y is resident in the United Kingdom, or carrying on a trade in the United Kingdom through a permanent establishment or the asset is a chargeable asset in relation to company Y.

This provision is intended to facilitate the bringing together of chargeable gains and allowable losses within one group company. Any payment made by X to Y, or vice versa, in connection with the election is ignored in computing profits or losses of either company and is not treated as a distribution, *provided* it does not exceed the chargeable gain or allowable loss deemed to accrue to Y on the disposal.

An election cannot be made to transfer a gain made on the disposal of an interest in an oil field within *TCGA 1992, s 197* (or treated as so made under *TCGA 1992, s 197(4)*) from a company carrying on a 'ring fence trade' (as defined) to a company not carrying on such a trade.

[*TCGA 1992, ss 171A, 171B*].

Example

A Ltd and B Ltd are members of the same group of companies, preparing accounts each year to 31 March. On 30 September 2024, A Ltd sold an asset (asset 1) to an unconnected third party for £100,000. The asset had been acquired in June 2012 for £40,000. On 29 April 2024, B Ltd sold an asset (asset 2), which had cost £70,000 in January 2008, for £50,000 to an unconnected third party. B Ltd incurred costs on the disposal of £2,000. Neither company disposes of any other assets in the year ended 31 March 2025.

A Ltd and B Ltd jointly elect before 31 March 2027 under *TCGA 1992, s 171A* for the loss on asset 2 to be transferred to A Ltd.

The chargeable gains computation for the year ended 31 March 2025 for A Ltd is as follows:

Disposal of asset 1

	£
Consideration	100,000
Cost	40,000

Indexation allowance £40,000 × 0.150%		6,000
Chargeable gain		£54,000
Disposal of asset 2		
	£	£
Consideration		50,000
Cost to B Ltd	70,000	
Less Cost of disposal incurred by B Ltd	2,000	(72,000)
Allowable loss transferred to A Ltd		£(22,000)
Net chargeable gains £54,000 – £22,000 = £32,000		

Groups of companies — anti-avoidance

[26.14] There are a number of anti-avoidance provisions which apply specifically to groups of companies as well as further such provisions which are more general but can apply to groups. The provisions are covered in the paragraphs noted in the table below.

Depreciatory transactions within a group.	*TCGA 1992, s 176*	**4.19** ANTI-AVOIDANCE
Dividend stripping.	*TCGA 1992, s 177*	**4.20** ANTI-AVOIDANCE
Buying gains and losses: tax avoidance schemes.	*TCGA 1992, ss 184A–184F*	**26.16, 26.17**
Restriction on set-off of pre-entry losses where a company joins a group.	*TCGA 1992, Sch 7A*	**26.18–26.23**

Companies buying gains or losses

[26.15] Over the years, governments have introduced several sets of anti-avoidance provisions designed to prevent groups of companies buying and selling companies in order to make use of capital losses suffered by another company or group.

The first set of current provisions, described at **26.18–26.23** below, applies to prevent 'loss buying' where a group of companies with unrealised gains would acquire a company with losses. The provisions now operate by restricting the deduction of losses accruing to a company before the time it becomes a member of a group.

The second set of current provisions was introduced as part of a package of anti-avoidance provisions relating to capital losses of companies (see **14.6** COMPANIES). The provisions restrict the use of losses in both loss buying and gain buying situations where there is a change of ownership of a company as a result of arrangements with a tax avoidance purpose and are described at **26.16** and

26.17 below. The provisions apply in priority to the original loss buying provisions. The provisions are wide in scope and can apply in certain cases where there is no group of companies involved (see **26.16**(c) below). The stated intention of the provisions is to ensure that relief for a company's capital losses should only be available against its own capital gains or those of companies that were under the same economic ownership both when the capital loss was realised and when the loss is used to reduce other gains. (Treasury Explanatory Notes to the Finance Bill 2006.)

Restriction on buying gains and losses — tax avoidance schemes

[26.16] The loss buying and gain buying provisions described below apply where:

(A) there is a 'qualifying change of ownership' of a company (the '*relevant company*'), and
(B) the change occurs directly or indirectly in consequence of, or otherwise in connection with, any 'arrangements' the main purpose, or one of the main purposes, of which is to secure a 'tax advantage'.

For this purpose, there is a '*qualifying change of ownership*' of a company if any of the following occur.

(a) The company joins a group of companies. Whether a company is a member of a group is determined as in **26.2** above except that nothing in *TCGA 1992, s 170(10)* or *(10A)* is treated as preventing all the companies of one group from being regarded as joining another group when the principal company of the first group becomes a member of the other group at any time unless:
    (i) the same persons own the 'shares' of the principal company of the first group immediately before that time and the shares of the principal company of the other group immediately after that time;
    (ii) the principal company of the other group was not the principal company of any group immediately before that time; and
    (iii) immediately after that time the principal company of the other group had assets consisting entirely (or almost entirely) of shares of the principal company of the first group.

    References above to '*shares*' of a company are to the shares comprised in the company's issued share capital.
(b) The company ceases to be a member of a group.
(c) The company becomes subject to different control, i.e. one or more of the following occur:
    (I) a person who did not previously have control (within *CTA 2010, ss 450, 451*) of the company comes to have control (whether alone or together with one or more others);
    (II) a person who previously had control of the company alone comes to have control of the company together with one or more others; or
    (III) a person ceases to have control of the company (whether the person had control alone or together with one or more others).

> A company is not, however, treated as becoming subject to different control where it joins a group of companies in circumstances in which (a)(i)–(iii) above apply or where, although there is a change in the direct ownership of the company, it continues to be a 75% subsidiary of the same company.

'*Arrangements*' include any agreement, understanding, scheme, transaction or series of transactions, whether or not legally enforceable. '*Tax advantage*' means relief or increased relief from, or repayment or increased repayment of, corporation tax or the avoidance or reduction of a charge or assessment to corporation tax or the avoidance of a possible assessment to corporation tax.

[*TCGA 1992, ss 184A(1)(4), 184B(1)(4), 184C, 184D, 288(1)*].

For HMRC's views on the application of the terms 'arrangements', 'tax advantage' and 'main purpose', see **38.8** LOSSES and HMRC Capital Gains Manual CG47024–47029. For HMRC's views generally, see HMRC Capital Gains Manual CG47020–47338.

Loss buying

The loss buying provisions apply where conditions (A) and (B) above are met and the tax advantage under the arrangements involves the deduction from any chargeable gains of a loss (a '*qualifying loss*') accruing to the relevant company on a disposal of a 'pre-change asset' (see **26.17** below). In these circumstances, the qualifying loss is not deductible from a company's chargeable gains. It is immaterial whether the loss accrues before, after or at the time of the qualifying change of ownership, whether the loss accrues at a time when there are no gains from which it could be deducted, whether the tax advantage also involves something other than the deduction of a qualifying loss or whether the advantage would be secured for the company to which the loss accrues or any other company. [*TCGA 1992, s 184A(1)(2)(5)*].

Gain buying

The gain buying provisions apply where conditions (A) and (B) above are met and the tax advantage under the arrangements involves the deduction of a loss from a gain (a '*qualifying gain*') accruing to the relevant company or any other company on a disposal of a pre-change asset. In these circumstances, only a loss arising on a disposal before 21 March 2007 of a pre-change asset can be deducted from a qualifying gain. It is immaterial whether the gain accrues before, after or at the time of the qualifying change of ownership, whether the gain accrues at a time when there are no losses which could be deducted from it, whether the tax advantage also involves something other than the deduction of a loss from a qualifying gain or whether the advantage would be secured for the company to which the gain accrues or any other company. [*TCGA 1992, s 184B(1)(2)(5)*].

For HMRC examples of the operation of the provisions see HMRC Guidance 'Avoidance through the creation and use of capital losses by companies', 27 July 2006, available in the HMRC Capital Gains Manual CG-APP8.

Pre-change assets

[26.17] For the purposes of the provisions at **26.16** above, a '*pre-change asset*' is an asset held by the relevant company before the qualifying change of ownership occurs.

An asset ceases to be a pre-change asset on disposal by a company other than the relevant company if, after the qualifying change of ownership, it has been disposed of otherwise than by an intra-group no gain/no loss transfer within **26.3** above. If the company making the latter disposal retains an interest in or over the asset, that interest continues to be a pre-change asset.

If the relevant company or any other company holds an asset at or after the time of the qualifying change of ownership the value of which derives in whole or in part from a pre-change asset, the new asset is also treated as a pre-change asset provided that the company concerned did not acquire the asset as a result of a transfer other than an intra-group no gain/no loss transfer. For this purpose, the cases in which the value of an asset is derived from another asset include cases where assets have been merged or divided or have changed their nature and cases where rights or interests in or over assets have been created or extinguished.

Where a pre-change asset is the 'old asset' for the purposes of *TCGA 1992, s 116*, (reorganisation of share capital involving QUALIFYING CORPORATE BONDS (**48.4**)) the 'new asset' under that section is also a pre-change asset. Where a pre-change asset is the 'original shares' for the purposes of *TCGA 1992, ss 127–131* (reorganisation of share capital — see **57.2** SHARES AND SECURITIES), the 'new holding' under those provisions is also a pre-change asset.

Where one of the deferral provisions listed below applies to defer a gain on the disposal of a pre-change asset, so much of any gain or loss accruing on a subsequent occasion as accrues in consequence of the application of the deferral provision is treated as a gain or loss on the disposal of a pre-change asset. The provisions are:

- *TCGA 1992, s 139* (reconstruction involving transfer of business — see **14.12** COMPANIES);
- *TCGA 1992, s 140* (transfer of assets to non-resident company — see **43.10** OVERSEAS MATTERS);
- *TCGA 1992, s 140A* (transfer or division of UK business between companies in different EC member states — see **43.12** OVERSEAS MATTERS);
- *TCGA 1992, s 140E* (European cross-border merger leaving assets within UK tax charge — see **14.16** COMPANIES);
- *TCGA 1992, ss 152, 153* (**53** ROLLOVER RELIEF — REPLACEMENT OF BUSINESS ASSETS); and
- *TCGA 1992, s 187* (postponement of charge on deemed disposal on company ceasing to be UK resident — see **43.16** OVERSEAS MATTERS).

If a pre-change asset is transferred by the relevant company to another company directly or indirectly in consequence of, or in connection with the arrangements in **26.16**(A), and any of *TCGA 1992, ss 139, 140A* or *140E* apply to the transfer, the asset is a pre-change asset in the hands of the transferee company. The above provisions for determining when an asset ceases to be a pre-change asset then apply as if the transferee company were the relevant company.

Pooled assets

Special identification rules apply where a pre-change asset (whether held by the relevant company or, as a consequence of an intra-group no gain/no loss transfer, by another company) consists of a 'section 104 holding' or '1982 holding' (see **58.3** SHARES AND SECURITIES — IDENTIFICATION RULES) of shares, securities or other assets dealt in without identifying the particular asset disposed of or acquired. Such a holding (a '*pre-change pooled asset*') cannot be added to as a result of any disposal or acquisition taking place after the qualifying change of ownership. Any shares etc. that would otherwise be added to the pre-change pooled asset instead form or are added to a separate *s 104* holding (the '*other pooled asset*').

Shares etc. of the same class as those comprised in the other pooled asset which are disposed of at or after the time of the qualifying change of ownership are identified:

- first with shares etc. forming part of the other pooled asset;
- next with shares etc. forming part of the pre-change pooled asset; and
- finally, in accordance with the normal identification rules described at **58.3** SHARES AND SECURITIES — IDENTIFICATION RULES).

These identification rules apply even if some or all of the assets disposed of are separately identified by the disposal or by a transfer or delivery giving effect to it.

Shares etc. disposed of by a company in one capacity are not identified with shares etc. which are held, or which can only be disposed of, in some other capacity. Shares or securities of a company are not treated as being of the same class unless they are so treated by the practice of a recognised stock exchange (see **57.27** SHARES AND SECURITIES) or would be if dealt with on such an exchange.

[*TCGA 1992, ss 184A(3), 184B(3), 184E, 184F*].

Restriction on set-off of pre-entry losses where a company joins a group

[26.18] Where the loss buying provisions at **26.16** above do not apply, *TCGA 1992, Sch 7A* restricts the deduction of allowable losses ('pre-entry losses') which accrue to a company before the time it becomes a member of a group of companies (the '*relevant group*'). The restriction is described in detail at **26.19–26.23** below.

The restriction does not apply where the loss buying provisions at **26.16** above apply.

[*TCGA 1992, s 177A, Sch 7A para 1(1)*].

Before 19 July 2011, the provisions also applied to losses accruing to a company after the time at which it became a member of a group on assets held by it at that time. The restrictions on the use of such losses were removed by *FA 2011* as they are now considered unnecessary because of *TCGA 1992, s 184A* (see **26.16** above). The restrictions do, however, continue to apply to such losses realised before 19 July 2011 as if they had accrued immediately before the company became a member of the group. See earlier editions of this work for details.

Definitions

[26.19] A '*pre-entry loss*', in relation to a company, means any allowable loss that accrued to it at a time before it became a member of the relevant group. [*TCGA 1992, Sch 7A para 1(2)*].

If:

(a) the principal company of a group of companies ('*the first group*') has at any time become a member of another group ('*the second group*') so that the two groups are treated as the same under *TCGA 1992, s 170(10)* or *(10A)* (see **26.2** above), and
(b) the second group, together in pursuance of *TCGA 1992, s 170(10)* or *(10A)* with the first group, is the relevant group,

then, except where the circumstances are as listed below, the members of the first group are treated for the purposes of *Sch 7A* as having become members of the relevant group at that time, and not by virtue of *TCGA 1992, s 170(10)* or *(10A)* at the times when they became members of the first group. The circumstances are where:

(1) the persons who immediately before the time when the principal company of the first group became a member of the second group owned the shares comprised in the issued share capital of the principal company of the first group are the same as the persons who, immediately after that time, owned the shares comprised in the issued share capital of the principal company of the relevant group; and
(2) the company which is the principal company of the relevant group immediately after that time
    (i) was not the principal company of any group immediately before that time; and
    (ii) immediately after that time had assets consisting entirely, or almost entirely, of shares comprised in the issued share capital of the principal company of the first group.

[*TCGA 1992, Sch 7A para 1(6)(7)*].

For discussion of *Sch 7A para 1(6)(7)* see *Five Oaks Properties Ltd v HMRC (and related appeals)* (Sp C 563), [2006] SSCD 769, *HMRC v Prizedome Ltd; HMRC v Limitgood Ltd* CA, [2009] STC 980 and *ANO (No 1) Ltd v HMRC* FTT, [2019] SFTD 1147.

Where an allowable loss accrues to a company under *TCGA 1992, s 116(10)(b)* (gain or loss on shares exchanged on reorganisation, conversion or reconstruction for qualifying corporate bonds to crystallise when bonds sold; see **48.4** QUALIFYING CORPORATE BONDS), that loss is deemed to accrue at the time of the reorganisation etc. for the purposes of deciding whether a loss accrues before a company becomes a member of the relevant group. [*TCGA 1992, Sch 7A para 1(9)*]. Likewise, the annual deemed disposals of unit trust etc. holdings of a life assurance company's long-term insurance fund under *TCGA 1992, s 212* are deemed to occur for this purpose without regard to the 'spreading' provisions of *TCGA 1992, s 213*. [*TCGA 1992, Sch 7A para 1(10)*].

Restrictions on the deduction of pre-entry losses

[26.20] In the calculation of the amount to be included in respect of chargeable gains in any company's total profits for any accounting period:

(a) if in that period there is any chargeable gain from which the whole or any part of any pre-entry loss accruing in that period is deductible in accordance with the provisions in **26.21** below, the loss or, as the case may be, that part of it is deducted from that gain;

(b) if, after all the deductions in (a) above have been made, there is in that period any chargeable gain from which the whole or any part of any pre-entry loss carried forward from a previous accounting period is deductible in accordance with the provisions in **26.21**, the loss or, as the case may be, that part of it is deducted from that gain;

(c) the total of chargeable gains (if any) remaining after all the deductions in (a) or (b) above is subject to deductions in accordance with *TCGA 1992, s 2A(1)* (previously *TCGA 1992, s 8(1)*; chargeable gains less allowable losses of company to be included in chargeable profits; see **14.3** COMPANIES) in respect of any allowable losses that are not pre-entry losses; and

(d) any pre-entry loss which has not been the subject of a deduction under (a) or (b) above (as well as any other losses falling to be carried forward under *section 8(1)*) are carried forward to the following accounting period of that company.

[*TCGA 1992, Sch 7A para 6(1)*].

Further restrictions on the deduction of pre-entry losses may apply for accounting periods beginning on or after 1 April 2020 (subject to transitional rules for accounting periods straddling that date (see **14.11** COMPANIES under 'Deductions from chargeable gains')). Where the company's chargeable gains for the period exceed the amount of allowable losses arising in the period (including any pre-entry losses deductible under (a) above):

(1) deductions under (b) above cannot exceed the total of: (i) the amount of carried-forward pre-entry losses that would be so deductible on the assumption that such losses were subject to the restriction on deduction of carried-forward losses at **14.11**; and (ii) the amount of other carried-forward losses that would be deductible from gains in the period on the same assumption;

(2) deductions under (c) above cannot exceed the difference (if any) between the total in (1) above and the pre-entry losses actually deducted under (b) above.

[*TCGA 1992, Sch 7A para 6(1A)–(1C); FA 2020, Sch 4 paras 18, 42–46*].

Subject to (a)–(d) above, any question as to which or what part of any pre-entry loss has been deducted from any particular chargeable gain is decided in accordance with such elections as may be made by the company to which the loss accrued. An election must be made by notice to HMRC before the end of the period of two years beginning with the end of the company's accounting period in which the gain in question accrued. [*TCGA 1992, Sch 7A para 6(2)(3)*].

For the purposes of *Sch 7A* where any matter falls to be determined under the above provisions by reference to an election but no election is made, it is assumed, so far as consistent with any elections that have been made that losses are set against gains in the order in which the losses accrued, and that the gains against which they are set are also determined according to the order in which they accrued with losses being set against earlier gains before they are set against later ones. [*TCGA 1992, Sch 7A para 6(4)*].

Gains from which pre-entry losses are deductible

[26.21] A pre-entry loss that accrued to a company before it became a member of the relevant group is deductible from a chargeable gain accruing to that company if the gain is one accruing:

(a) on a disposal made by that company before the date on which it became a member of the relevant group ('*the entry date*');
(b) on the disposal of an asset which was held by that company immediately before the entry date; or
(c) on the disposal of any asset which:
  (i) was acquired on or after the entry date by the company to whom the loss accrued ('company A') or a company which, at the time of the acquisition, was a group company of company A (i.e. a member of the same group as company A), from a person who was not a member of the relevant group at the time of the acquisition; and
  (ii) since its acquisition from that person has not been used or held for any purposes other than those of a trade or business which was being carried on by company A immediately before the entry date and which continued to be carried on by company A, or a company which, when it carried on the trade or business, was a group company of company A, until the disposal.

Where the company subsequently becomes a member of another group, the above provision continues to apply to any loss which accrued before the company joined the relevant group by reference to the date it joined the relevant group (and does not apply separately to the loss by reason of it being a pre-entry loss in relation to the company becoming a member of the second group).

[*TCGA 1992, Sch 7A para 7(1)–(1C)*].

Where two or more companies become members of the relevant group at the same time and those companies were all members of the same group of companies immediately before they became members of the relevant group, then:

(I) an asset is treated for the purposes of (b) above as held, immediately before it became a member of the relevant group, by the company to which the pre-entry loss in question accrued if that company is one of those companies and the asset was in fact so held by another of those companies; and

(II) the acquisition of an asset is treated for the purposes of (c) above as an acquisition by the company to which the pre-entry loss in question accrued if that company is one of those companies and the asset was in fact acquired (whether before or after they became members of the relevant group) by another of those companies.

[*TCGA 1992, Sch 7A para 7(3)*].

An asset is not treated as a '*pre-entry asset*' (i.e. as held by a company immediately before the entry date) if the company which held the asset on the entry date is not the company making the disposal and since the entry date the asset has been disposed of in circumstances in which *TCGA 1992, s 171* (intra-group transfers at no gain/no loss — see **26.3** above) does not apply, except where the company making the disposal retains an interest in or over the asset (when the interest is treated as a pre-entry asset).

An asset ('*the second asset*') which derives wholly or partly its value from another asset ('*the first asset*') acquired or held by a company at any time, is treated as the same asset if the second asset is held subsequently by the same company, or by any company which is or has been a member of the same group of companies as that company (e.g. a freehold derived from a leasehold where the lessee acquires the reversion). Where this treatment applies, whether under this provision or not (*TCGA 1992, s 43* is similar; see **16.5** COMPUTATION OF GAINS AND LOSSES), the second asset is treated as a pre-entry asset in relation to a company if the first asset would have been.

[*TCGA 1992, Sch 7A para 7(4)–(4C)*].

Subject to *Sch 7A para 7(6)* below, where a gain accrues on the disposal of the whole or any part of:

(1) any asset treated as a single asset but comprising assets only some of which were held at the time mentioned in (b) above; or
(2) an asset which is treated as held at that time by virtue of a provision requiring an asset which was not held at that time to be treated as the same as an asset which was so held (see **26.19** above),

a pre-entry loss is deductible under (b) above from the amount of that gain to the extent only of such proportion of that gain as is attributable to assets held at that time or, as the case may be, represents the gain that would have accrued on the asset so held. [*TCGA 1992, Sch 7A para 7(5)*].

Where:

(A) a chargeable gain accrues under *TCGA 1992, s 116(10)* on the disposal of a qualifying corporate bond which has been exchanged for shares etc. (see **48.4** QUALIFYING CORPORATE BONDS and **26.19** above);
(B) that bond was not held as required by (b) above at the time mentioned in (b); and
(C) the whole or any part of the asset which is the 'old asset' for the purposes of *TCGA 1992, s 116* was so held,

the question whether that gain is one accruing on the disposal of an asset, the whole or any part of which was held by a particular company at that time, is determined for the purposes of *Sch 7A para 7* as if the bond were deemed to have been so held to the same extent as the old asset. [*TCGA 1992, Sch 7A para 7(6)*].

Change of a company's nature

[26.22] If:

(a) within any period of three years, a company becomes a member of a group of companies and there is (either earlier or later in that period, or at the same time) 'a major change in the nature or conduct of a trade or business' carried on by that company immediately before it became a member of that group; or

(b) at any time the scale of the activities in a trade or business carried on by a company has become small or negligible, and before any considerable revival of the trade or business, that company becomes a member of a group of companies,

the trade or business carried on before that change, or which has become small or negligible, is disregarded for the purposes of **26.21**(c) above in relation to any time before the company became a member of the group in question.

'*A major change in the conduct of a trade or business*' includes a reference to a major change in services or facilities provided or a major change in customers or, in the case of a company with investment business, a major change in the nature of investments held. Regard will also be had to appropriate changes in other factors such as the location of the company's business premises, the identity of the company's suppliers, management or staff, the company's methods of manufacture, or the company's pricing or purchasing policies to the extent that these factors indicate that a major change has occurred. Efficiency changes and technological advancements would not in themselves indicate that a major change in the nature or conduct of a trade or business has occurred.

HMRC will compare any two points in three years which include the date of change of ownership of the company. This applies even if the change is the result of a gradual process which began outside the period of three years mentioned in (a) above. HMRC take note of both qualitative and quantitative issues as discussed in the cases *Willis v Peeters Picture Frames Ltd* CA (NI) 1982, 56 TC 436 and *Purchase v Tesco Stores Ltd* Ch D 1984, 58 TC 46 respectively (HMRC Statement of Practice SP 10/91).

Where the operation of the above provisions depends on circumstances or events at a time after the company becomes a member of any group of companies (but not more than three years after), an assessment to give effect to the provisions may be made within six years from that time or the latest such time.

[*TCGA 1992, Sch 7A para 8*].

Miscellaneous

[26.23] Where, but for an election under *TCGA 1992, s 161(3)* (appropriation of asset to trading stock; see **16.9** COMPUTATION OF GAINS AND LOSSES), there would be deemed to have been a disposal on an appropriation prior to 8 March 2017 by a company of an asset, the amount by which the market value of the asset may be treated as increased under the election does not include the amount of any pre-entry loss that would have accrued on that disposal, and *Sch 7A* has effect as if the pre-entry loss of the last mentioned amount had accrued to the company at that time. [*TCGA 1992, Sch 7A para 10*].

The provisions of *Sch 7A* are prevented from applying where a loss arises, or a company joins a group, as a result of any enactment under which transfers of property etc. are made from a statutory body, a subsidiary of such a body or a company wholly owned by the Crown. [*TCGA 1992, Sch 7A para 11*].

For the purposes of *Sch 7A*, and without prejudice to the provisions in *Sch 7A para 11* above, where:

(a) a company which is a member of a group of companies becomes at any time a member of another group of companies as the result of a disposal of shares in or other securities of that company or any other company; and

(b) that disposal is one within the no gain/no loss provisions in **8.6** ASSETS HELD ON 31 MARCH **1982**,

Sch 7A has effect in relation to the losses that accrued to that company before that time and the assets held by that company at that time as if any time when it was a member of the first group were included in the period during which it is treated as having been a member of the second group. [*TCGA 1992, Sch 7A para 12*].

Key points on groups of companies

[26.24] Points to consider are as follows:

- Transfers of assets between companies within the same capital gains group can take place on a no gain/no loss basis. If a company leaves the group within six years after receiving an asset via a no gain/no loss transfer, degrouping charges may apply, clawing back the deferred gain.
- Rollover relief for gains on business asset disposals can be applied on a group-wide basis, rather than just at the individual company level.
- Any number of elections to transfer a gain can be made in respect of any given gain, so the gain can be split between several group companies (providing the total does not exceed the original gain). This means that part of the gain can be transferred to a company with some allowable losses, part to a company with current year trading losses, and so on.
- *TCGA 1992, s 181* is exceptionally useful in setting up joint ventures. It allows one or more groups to hive business assets down to a new subsidiary, which then leaves the group when the other member of the joint venture acquires more than 25% of its issued share capital (so it ceases to be a 75% subsidiary of the parent). Without *s 181*, the degrouping charge would make the formation of commercial joint ventures much more difficult. See **26.10.**

27

HMRC — Administration

Introduction — the Commissioners for HMRC

[27.1] The collection and management of capital gains tax and corporation tax is administered by the **Commissioners for His Majesty's Revenue and Customs.** [*TMA 1970, s 1*].

Under the Commissioners for HMRC are officers of Revenue and Customs ('HMRC officers') who are civil servants. They are responsible for processing returns, making assessments, dealing with claims, allowances and appeals, carrying out enquiries and collection and recovery of tax.

Criminal prosecutions of tax offences in England and Wales are conducted by an independent Revenue and Customs Prosecutions Office (now part of the Crown Prosecution Service), whose director is appointed by the Attorney General. [*CRCA 2005, ss 34–42, Sch 3*].

In this publication, 'HMRC' is generally used to mean both His Majesty's Revenue and Customs and their predecessors in relation to direct taxes, the Inland Revenue. Where the context requires, however, 'the Revenue' is used to refer to the Inland Revenue.

The remainder of this chapter looks at certain HMRC administrative powers and the rules for complaints about HMRC. Also included is the power for the National Crime Agency to take over HMRC's powers where a chargeable gain arises as a result of criminal conduct.

'Care and management' powers

[27.2] As noted at 27.1 above, the Commissioners for HMRC have responsibility for the 'collection and management' of taxes, including capital gains tax and corporation tax. Before 18 April 2005, the Board of Inland Revenue had responsibility for the 'care and management' of direct taxes. The extent and limits of these care and management powers were considered before the Courts on a number of occasions. These decisions may continue to be relevant to the powers of HMRC.

For the validity of amnesties by the Board, see *R v CIR (ex p. National Federation of Self-Employed and Small Businesses Ltd)* HL 1981, 55 TC 133. HMRC extra-statutory concessions have been the subject of frequent judicial criticism but their validity has never been directly challenged in the Courts. In *R v CIR (ex p. Fulford-Dobson)* QB 1987, 60 TC 168, it was held that there had been no unfair treatment by the Revenue when it failed to apply a published extra-statutory concession because it was clear from the facts of the case that it was one of tax avoidance and this was a clearly stated general circumstance in which concessions would not be applied (cf. *R v Inspector of Taxes, Hull, ex p. Brumfield and others* QB 1988, 61 TC 589 at **5.35** APPEALS). For a general discussion of the Board's care and management powers and an example of a ruling by the Court that the Board had acted reasonably, see *R v CIR (ex p. Preston)* HL 1985, 59 TC 1. See also *R v Attorney-General (ex p. ICI plc)* CA 1986, 60 TC 1, *R v CIR (ex p. MFK Underwriting Agencies Ltd and others)* QB 1989, 62 TC 607 and *R v CIR (ex p. Matrix-Securities Ltd)* HL 1994, 66 TC 587. See also **5.35** APPEALS regarding judicial review of Revenue powers.

The Inland Revenue policy of selective prosecution for criminal offences (see **46.31** PENALTIES) in connection with tax evasion did not render a decision in a particular case unlawful or *ultra vires*, provided that the case was considered on its merits fairly and dispassionately to see whether the criteria for prosecution were satisfied, and that the decision to prosecute was then taken in good faith for the purpose of collecting taxes and not for some ulterior, extraneous or improper purpose (*R v CIR (ex p. Mead and Cook)* QB 1992, 65 TC 1).

The making of a 'forward tax agreement' with a non-UK domiciled individual (see **52.6** REMITTANCE BASIS) was held to be 'not a proper exercise' of the Inland Revenue's 'duties of care and management' (*Fayed and Others v Advocate-General for Scotland (representing CIR)* SCS, [2002] STC 910).

HMRC have published a 'Code of Governance for resolving tax disuptes' which is intended to provide transparency and consistency to the Department's settlements of such disputes. See www.gov.uk/government/publications/resolving-tax-disputes.

Agreements to forgo corporation tax reliefs

There are provisions which prevent a company which has entered into an agreement with the Government under which it agrees to forgo a corporation tax relief, from obtaining that relief through the normal operation of tax legislation. The provisions were originally aimed in particular at banks using the Asset Protection Scheme announced on 19 January 2009. See *FA 2009, s 25*.

Payments to sanctioned persons

With effect from 1 March 2023, HMRC are prohibited from making any payment (such as a repayment of tax) to any person subject to financial sanctions under regulations made under *Sanctions and Anti-Money Laundering Act 2018*. The prohibition extends to indirect payments and payments to another person owned or controlled by the sanctioned person. [*F(No 2)A 2023, s 351*].

Exercise of officer functions by automated process

[27.3] HMRC can use automated processes or other means to perform functions which, under the applicable statute, must be performed by an HMRC officer. These include (but are not restricted to):

- notices to file returns under *TMA 1970, ss 8A* and *12AA* or *FA 1998, Sch 18 para 3* (see **52.5**, **52.21** RETURNS);
- assessment of tax under *TMA 1970, s 30A* (see **6.2** ASSESSMENTS);
- correction to a tax return under *TMA 1970, s 9ZB* (see **52.9**, RETURNS); and
- penalty determinations under *TMA 1970, s 100* (see **46.28** PENALTIES).

This rule was introduced following a number of tribunal decisions which held that notices issued automatically by computer were not valid. (The UT had, however, already overturned such a decision in *HMRC v Rogers* UT 2019, [2020] STC 220. In that case, the UT held that the requirement for a notice to deliver a return had to be given by an HMRC officer did not mean that a notice had to be given by an identified officer or that the return had to be submitted to that named officer. It was sufficient that the notice had been given under the authority of an officer.)

Although it was enacted by *FA 2020*, the rule is treated as always having been in force. It does not apply, however, to anything done by HMRC if a court or tribunal determined before 11 March 2020 that the act in question was invalid because it was not done by an HMRC officer (provided that the court or tribunal's decision had not been set aside or overturned on appeal before 11 March 2020).

[*FA 2020, s 103*].

The FTT held that the above provisions do not apply to a discovery assessment under *TMA 1970, s 29(1)* (see **6.10** ASSESSMENTS) in *Brown v HMRC* FTT [2024] UKFTT 245 (TC).

Non-statutory clearances

[27.4] HMRC's non-statutory clearance regime is covered at www.gov.uk/guidance/non-statutory-clearance-service-guidance and www.gov.uk/seeking-clearance-or-approval-for-a-transaction. HMRC will provide written confirmation of their view of the application of tax law to a specific transaction or event where a taxpayer has fully considered HMRC's guidance and been unable to find the necessary information or where a taxpayer remains uncertain about

HMRC's interpretation of recent tax legislation. In certain circumstances, HMRC will not give advice under the service; for example, if they do not think that there are genuine points of uncertainty or they consider that the transactions concerned are for the purposes of avoiding tax. HMRC will, in most cases, aim to respond to clearance applications within 28 days. Clearance applications can be made to HMRC Non-statutory Clearances Team, Wealthy, HMRC BX9 1BN. Large Business Service taxpayers should send clearance applications to their client relationship manager. Applications can be made by email to nonst atutoryclearanceteam.hmrc@hmrc.gov.uk.

Use of electronic communications

[27.5] HMRC have broad powers to make regulations, by statutory instrument (see *SI 2003 No 282*), to facilitate two-way electronic communication in the delivery of information, e.g. tax returns and the making of tax payments. Such regulations have effect notwithstanding any pre-existing legislation requiring delivery or payment in a manner which would otherwise preclude the use of electronic communications or intermediaries. [*FA 1999, ss 132, 133*].

See *the Income and Corporation Taxes (Electronic Communications) Regulations 2003* (*SI 2003 No 282*) and directions under those regulations by the Commissioners, which make provision for electronic communications in relation to delivery of tax returns and other information under various statutory provisions and payments or repayments in connection with the operation of those provisions.

In particular, agents are authorised to file clients' personal tax returns or company tax returns over the internet, subject to conditions as to authorisation of the agent by the client, authentication of the information by the client and use of Revenue approved software (see now Revenue Directions under *SI 2003 No 282, Reg 3*, 4 March 2003, 4 April 2008; HMRC Directions under *SI 2003 No 282, Regs 3* and *10*, 6 January 2010).

Regulations may also be made by the Commissioners for the provision of *incentives* to use electronic communications. [*FA 2000, s 143(1), Sch 38*]. Anything received by way of incentive is not regarded as income for tax purposes. [*ITTOIA 2005, s 778; CTA 2009, s 1287*].

Mandatory e-filing

HMRC have wide powers to make regulations requiring the use of electronic communication for the delivery of information required or authorised to be delivered under tax legislation. [*FA 2002, ss 135, 136*]. Companies are required to deliver tax returns electronically in a specified data format (known as iXBRL). See **52.3** RETURNS.

Power to give statutory effect to concessions

[27.6] The Treasury has the power, by order, to give statutory effect to any HMRC 'concession' made before 21 July 2008 which is in effect on that date.

For this purpose, a '*concession*' is a statement by HMRC, whether described as an extra-statutory concession, a statement of practice, an interpretation, a press release, or in any other way, that they will treat taxpayers as if they were entitled to a reduction in a tax liability or any other concession to which they are not, or may not be, entitled to by law.

[*FA 2008, s 160*].

Complaints etc.

HMRC error

[27.7] Where the taxpayer complains, HMRC will consider reimbursing any 'reasonable costs' incurred as a direct result of their mistake or delay. Such costs might include postage, telephone charges and professional fees. See www.gov.uk/complain-about-hmrc.

See also **36.5** LATE PAYMENT INTEREST AND PENALTIES and **45.32** PAYMENT OF TAX.

HMRC Charter

[27.8] HMRC are required to publish a Charter setting out standards of behaviour and values to which they aspire in dealing with taxpayers. The latest version of the Charter was published in November 2020. See www.gov.uk/government/publications/hmrc-charter/the-hmrc-charter.

The Charter must be regularly reviewed by HMRC and they must publish an annual report detailing the extent to which they have demonstrated the standards and values set out in the Charter. [*CRCA 2005, s 16A*].

Adjudicator

[27.9] A taxpayer who is not satisfied with the HMRC response to a complaint has the option of putting the case to an Adjudicator. The Adjudicator's office considers complaints about HMRC's handling of a taxpayer's affairs, e.g. excessive delays, errors, discourtesy or the exercise of HMRC discretion. Matters subject to existing rights of appeal are excluded.

Complaints will normally go to the Adjudicator only after they have been considered by the Director of the relevant HMRC office, and where the taxpayer is still not satisfied with the response received. The alternatives of pursuing the complaint to HMRC's Head Office, to an MP, or (through an MP) to the Parliamentary Ombudsman continue to be available. The Adjudicator will review all the facts, consider whether the complaint is justified, and, if so, make recommendations as to what should be done.

The Adjudicator publishes annual reports summarising the outcome of complaints made. Recent reports can be viewed on the Adjudicator's website (at www.gov.uk/government/organisations/the-adjudicator-s-office). To complain or request a review, contact should be made with the Adjudicator's Office using the online form (at www.gov.uk/guidance/contact-the-adjudicators-office) or by post at PO Box 11222, Nottingham, NG2 9AD. Tel: 0300–057 1111. Guidance on the actions a taxpayer should take and how the Adjudicator will respond to complaints is available on the Adjudicator's website.

HMRC functions carried out by the National Crime Agency

[27.10] Under *Proceeds of Crime Act 2002, Pt 6*, the National Crime Agency (NCA) is empowered to carry out the functions vested in HMRC in relation to (amongst other matters) capital gains tax and corporation tax. The NCA must have reasonable grounds to suspect either that:

(a) a gain accruing to a person in respect of a chargeable period is a chargeable gain and accrues as a result (whether wholly or partly, directly or indirectly) of the 'criminal conduct' of that person or another, or

(b) a company is chargeable to corporation tax on its profits arising in a chargeable period and the profits arise as a result (whether wholly or partly, directly or indirectly) of the criminal conduct of the company or another person,

and must serve a notice on HMRC specifying the person or company, the period or periods concerned, and the functions which he intends to carry out. The periods involved may include periods beginning before the *Act* was passed.

The NCA may cease carrying out the functions specified in the notice at any time (by notifying HMRC), but *must* so cease where the conditions allowing the notice to be made are no longer satisfied.

For the above purposes, '*criminal conduct*' is conduct which constitutes an offence anywhere in the UK or which would do so if it occurred there, but does not include conduct constituting an offence relating to a matter under the care and management of HMRC.

It should be noted that the vesting of a function in the NCA under these provisions does not divest HMRC of the function (so that, for example, they can continue to carry out routine work). Certain functions, as listed in *Proceeds of Crime Act 2002, s 323(3)* cannot be carried out by the NCA.

[*Proceeds of Crime Act 2002, ss 317, 323(1)(3), 326(1)(2)*].

28

HMRC — Confidentiality of Information

Introduction

[28.1] Officials of HMRC may not generally disclose information held by HMRC. All Commissioners and officers of HMRC must make a declaration acknowledging their duty of confidentiality as soon as reasonably practicable following their appointment. [*CRCA 2005, ss 3, 18*]. The exceptions to this rule are covered in this chapter at **28.2–31.5** below. See **28.5** below for the criminal offence of disclosing tax information held in the exercise of tax functions.

HMRC *are* permitted to use information held or acquired in connection with one function in connection with any other function. [*CRCA 2005, s 17(1)*].

HMRC were held to have breached their duty of confidentiality in *R (oao Ingenious Media Holding plc) v HMRC* SC, [2016] STC 2306.

Organisations to which HMRC may disclose information

[28.2] HMRC are authorised to disclose information to the following.

(a) **Charity Commissioners for England and Wales.** HMRC are authorised to disclose certain information to the Charity Commissioners regarding bodies which are or have been charities. Similar provisions apply in Scotland as regards disclosure to the Lord Advocate. [*Charities Act 1993, s 10; Law Reform (Miscellaneous Provisions) (Scotland) Act 1990, s 1; SI 2010 No 588*].

(b) **Department of Trade and Industry, Department of Employment or Statistics Board.** HMRC are authorised to disclose, for the purposes of statistical surveys, the names and addresses of employers and information concerning the number of persons employed by individual concerns. [*FA 1969, s 58*].

(c) **Tax authorities of other countries.** HMRC are authorised to disclose information concerning individual taxpayers where it is necessary to the administration or enforcement of double taxation agreements and may be required to disclose information to an advisory commission set up under the Arbitration Convention (*90/436/EEC*). [*TIOPA 2010, ss 126–129; TCGA 1992, s 277(4)*].

Council Directive 2011/16/EU on administrative cooperation in the field of taxation provides for the exchange of information between tax authorities of EU member states to enable them to correctly assess tax liabilities. This was transposed into UK domestic law by *SI 2012 No 3062*. Those regulations remained in force following Brexit but are revoked with effect from 31 December 2023 (see *Retained EU Law (Revocation and Reform) Act 2023, Sch 1*). The Directive was amended by Directive 2018/822/EU ('DAC 6') to provide for mandatory automatic exchange of information in relation to reportable cross-border arrangements. Following Brexit, the UK legislation giving effect to DAC 6 has been superseded by the Mandatory Disclosure Rules. See **19.7–19.8** DISCLOSURE OF TAX AVOIDANCE SCHEMES.

The UK may enter into agreements with other countries for mutual assistance in the enforcement of taxes. Such agreements may include provision for the exchange of information foreseeably relevant to the administration, enforcement or recovery of any UK tax or foreign tax. HMRC may disclose information under such agreements only if satisfied that the confidentiality rules applied by the foreign authorities concerned with respect to the information are no less strict than the equivalent UK rules. [*FA 2006, s 173; SI 2019 No 689, Reg 14*]. This power has been exercised to enter into the joint Council of Europe/Organisation for Economic Co-operation and Development Convention on Mutual Administrative Assistance in Tax Matters, signed on behalf of the UK on 24 May 2007. [*SI 2007 No 2126; SI 2011 No 1079*].

In addition to tax information agreements included as part of double tax treaties (see **20.2** DOUBLE TAX RELIEF), the UK has also signed tax information exchange agreements with various countries.

See also **45.34** PAYMENT OF TAX.

(d) **The Pensions Regulator.** HMRC are authorised to disclose information about pension schemes. [*Pensions Act 2004, s 88(1)(2)*].

(e) **Social Security Departments.** Information held by HMRC may be supplied to the social security authorities for use in relation to social security, employment or training, tax credits, child support, war pensions or prescribed evaluation or statistical studies.

Social security authorities are in turn permitted to supply information to HMRC.

[*Social Security Administration Act 1992, s 121E; FA 1997, s 110; Tax Credits Act 2002, Sch 5 para 4; Welfare Reform Act 2012, s 127; SI 2002 No 3036*].

(f) **Criminal investigations etc.** HMRC may disclose information to organisations such as the police, having a legitimate interest in, and capable of carrying out, criminal investigations and/or bringing proceedings for criminal offences and for the purposes of assisting criminal investigations or proceedings in the UK or elsewhere, including whether such investigations or proceedings should be initiated or brought to an end. Disclosures may also be made to the intelligence services for the purposes of facilitating the carrying out of their functions. [*Anti-terrorism, Crime and Security Act 2001, ss 19, 20*].

Also, HMRC can disclose information to the police to assist investigation into suspected murder or treason (*Royal Commission on Standards of Conduct in Public Life 1976, para 93*).

(g) **Non-UK resident entertainers and sportsmen.** In connection with the deduction of sums representing income tax from certain payments to such persons, HMRC may disclose relevant matters to any person who appears to HMRC to have an interest. [*ITA 2007, s 970(2)(3)*].

(h) **Local authorities and Health Departments etc.** As regards information held for the purposes of tax credit functions (see Tolley's Income Tax under Social Security) and functions relating to child benefit or guardian's allowance, HMRC may disclose information to a local authority (or authorised delegate) for use in the administration of housing benefit or council tax benefit. Information must also be provided in the opposite direction if the Board so require but only for use for purposes relating to tax credits etc. [*Tax Credits Act 2002, Sch 5 paras 7, 8*].

As regards information held for the above-mentioned purposes, HMRC may disclose information to Health Departments for use for purposes of prescribed functions relating to health, to relevant Government Departments for purposes of prescribed functions relating to employment or training (with provision also for certain information to pass in the opposite direction) and (as regards information held for child benefit and guardian's allowance functions only) to any civil servant or other person for purposes of prescribed functions relating to provision of specified services concerning participation by young persons in education and training. [*Tax Credits Act 2002, Sch 5 paras 5, 6, 9, 10*].

(i) **Financial Conduct Authority and Prudential Regulation Authority.** HMRC may authorise the disclosure of information to the Financial Conduct Authority or the Prudential Regulation Authority for the purpose of assisting or enabling that regulator to discharge its functions or to the Secretary of State for the purposes of investigations under *Financial Services and Markets Act 2000, s 168*. [*Financial Services and Markets Act 2000, s 350*]. Note that HMRC may only disclose information in this way if it was obtained or is held in the exercise of a function previously vested in the Inland Revenue. [*CRCA 2005, Sch 2 para 18*].

(j) **Proceeds of crime etc.** HMRC may disclose information to the Director of Public Prosecutions or the Director of the Serious Fraud Office for the purpose of the exercise of their functions under *Proceeds of Crime Act 2002, Pts 5 and 8*. [*Proceeds of Crime Act 2002, s 436*]. HMRC may also disclose information to the Lord Advocate and the Scottish Ministers in connection with the exercise of their functions in Scotland under *Proceeds of Crime Act 2002, Pt 3* and *Pt 5* respectively. [*Proceeds of Crime Act 2002, s 439*].

(k) **Financial Reporting Review Panel.** HMRC may disclose information to the Financial Reporting Review Panel for the purpose of facilitating the taking of steps by it to discover whether there are grounds for an application to the courts for a declaration that the annual accounts of a company do not comply with *Companies Acts* requirements or determining whether or not to make such an application. HMRC and the

Financial Reporting Review Panel have entered into a memorandum of understanding governing the disclosure of information under these provisions. See HMRC Internet Statement, 28 June 2005 and 2005 SWTI 1197.

(l) **National Crime Agency.** HMRC may disclose information to the National Crime Agency for the purpose of the exercise of the Agency's functions. [*Serious Organised Crime and Police Act 2005, s 34*].

(m) **Certification of British films, TV programmes and video games.** HMRC may disclose information to the Secretary of State for the purposes of his functions under *Films Act 1985, Sch 1* or *CTA 2009, ss 1179DK–1179DM, 1179FD–1179FF, 1216CB–1216CD, 1217CB–1217CD* (certification of films, TV films or video games as British for the purposes of the creative industries tax reliefs). Information so disclosed may be disclosed to the British Film Institute. [*CTA 2009, ss 1179DN, 1179FG, 1206; FA 2024, Sch 2 para 1*].

(n) **Criminal Assets Bureau in Ireland.** HMRC may disclose information to the Criminal Assets Bureau ('CAB') in Ireland for the purpose of enabling or assisting the CAB to exercise any of its functions in connection with the proceeds of crime. [*Serious Crime Act 2007, s 85*].

(o) **Prosecuting authorities.** HMRC are permitted to disclose information to the Director of Public Prosecutions for the purpose of enabling the Director to consider whether to institute criminal proceedings in respect of a matter considered in the course of an investigation by HMRC or to give advice in connection with a criminal investigation. In relation to Scotland, HMRC are similarly authorised to disclose information to the Lord Advocate or a procurator fiscal. In Northern Ireland disclosures to the Director of Public Prosecutions for Northern Ireland are likewise permitted. [*CRCA 2005, s 21*].

(p) **Council Directive on tax dispute resolution mechanisms in the EU.** Secrecy requirements under any enactment do not prevent HMRC or certain other persons from disclosing information required to be disclosed under any instrument, agreement or arrangement covered by regulations made to bring the Directive (2017/1852) into force. [*TIOPA 2010, s 128C; FA 2019, s 83*]. Following Brexit, those regulations have been repealed. See **20.9** DOUBLE TAX RELIEF.

(q) **Taxi, private hire vehicle and scrap metal licensing authorities.** HMRC are permitted to disclose to a licensing authority any confirmation or other information received by them in the course of a tax check undertaken by a person applying, on or after 4 April 2022, to renew a licence to drive a hackney carriage or private hire vehicle or to operate a private hire vehicle or scrap metal business. [*FA 2021, s 125, Sch 33 para 7; F(No 2)A 2023, s 342*]. A licensing authority cannot normally consider such a licence renewal application until it has received from HMRC confirmation that the applicant has completed a tax check, which requires the provision of certain information to HMRC to confirm the applicant's compliance with their tax obligations.

Publication of details of deliberate tax defaulters

[28.3] The Commissioners for HMRC can publish certain information about any person who, as a result of an investigation, has incurred one or more specified penalties, provided that the total potential lost revenue in respect of which the penalty or penalties were calculated is more than £25,000.

The Commissioners can publish the person's name, trading name, address or registered office, the nature of any business carried on, the amount of the penalties and the potential lost revenue, the period of time to which the offences relate and any other information which they consider appropriate in order to make the person's identity clear. The information can only be first published in the period of one year beginning with the last day on which any of the penalties becomes final. It cannot continue to be published for more than one year.

Before publishing the information the Commissioners must inform the taxpayer that they are doing so and provide a reasonable opportunity to make representations about whether it should be published. No information will be published if the penalty is reduced, by reason of disclosure, to the full extent possible.

The penalties concerned are those under *FA 2007, Sch 24 para 1* (see **46.11** PENALTIES) and *para 1A* (see **46.12** PENALTIES), *FA 2008, Sch 41 para 1* (see **46.3** PENALTIES) and certain VAT and duty penalties, where in each case the error, failure or other action was deliberate. See the relevant paragraph for the meaning of '*potential lost revenue*' in relation to each penalty.

The above applies also where a body corporate, a partnership or one or more of the trustees of a settlement has incurred a penalty under **46.11** PENALTIES in respect of a deliberate inaccuracy involving an offshore matter or an offshore transfer or a penalty under **46.3** PENALTIES in respect of a deliberate failure which involves an offshore matter or an offshore transfer. In this case, the Commissioners may publish information in respect of any individual who controls the body corporate or partnership ('control' being construed as in *CTA 2010, s 1124*) or any individual who is a trustee of the settlement, where in either case the individual has obtained a tax advantage (as in *FA 2013, s 208* — see **4.3** ANTI-AVOIDANCE) as a result of the inaccuracy or failure. This applies regardless of the amount of potential lost revenue, and the let-out applies only if the penalty is reduced, by reason of *unprompted* disclosure, to the full extent permitted.

[*FA 2009, s 94*].

Publication of details of persons failing to correct

[28.4] The Commissioners for HMRC may publish information about a person (P) if in consequence of an investigation they consider that:

- P has been found to have incurred (and been assessed to or had included in a contract settlement) one or more penalties under **46.17** PENALTIES (failure to correct offshore tax non-compliance) in relation to which the offshore potential lost revenue (offshore PLR) totals more than £25,000 in aggregate; or
- P has been found to have incurred five or more penalties under **46.17** PENALTIES.

Penalties relating to failure to correct offshore tax non-compliance existing at the end of 2016/17 of which P was aware at any time during the RTC period (see **46.17** PENALTIES) are taken into account for the above purposes only if P was aware at any time during the RTC period (see **46.17** PENALTIES) of the existence at the end of 2016/17 of the offshore tax non-compliance in question.

The Commissioners can publish P's name (including previous name or pseudonym), trading name, address, the nature of any business carried on, the amount of the penalties, the amount of the offshore PLR, the periods or times to which the uncorrected offshore tax non-compliance relates, and any other information which they consider appropriate in order to make P's identity clear. The information can only be first published in the period of one year beginning with the last day on which the penalty (or the latest day on which any of the penalties involved) becomes final. It cannot continue to be published for more than one year. No information can be published if the amount of the penalty is reduced for disclosure to no more than 100% of the offshore PLR or is reduced or stayed because of special circumstances (see **46.17** PENALTIES).

Before publishing any information, the Commissioners must inform P that they are considering doing so and afford P an opportunity to make representations about whether it should be published.

[*F(No 2)A 2017, Sch 18 paras 30, 31*].

Criminal offence of disclosure of tax information

[28.5] It is a criminal offence for a person to disclose tax information relating to an 'identifiable person' (as defined) held by him in the exercise of 'tax functions' or as a member of an advisory commission set up under the Arbitration Convention (*90/436/EEC*). '*Tax functions*' include functions relating to the First-tier and Upper Tribunals, HMRC and its officers. This applies equally as regards HMRC's tax credit functions and social security functions. It does not apply if the person has (or believes he has) lawful authority or the information has lawfully been made available to the public, or if the person involved has consented. The maximum penalty for an offence is imprisonment for up to two years, a fine, or both. The above applies equally as regards national insurance contributions, statutory sick pay, statutory maternity pay and tax credits. [*FA 1989, ss 182, 182A*].

29

HMRC Investigatory Powers

Cross-references. See **46** PENALTIES; **52** RETURNS.

Simon's Taxes. See A6.3.

Introduction to HMRC investigatory powers

[29.1] HMRC have wide powers to enforce compliance with tax legislation. There is a common set of information and inspection powers covering income tax, capital gains tax, corporation tax and other taxes, including inheritance tax and stamp duty land tax and VAT, enabling HMRC to conduct a single 'compliance check' into a taxpayer's tax position across any or, as relevant, all of those taxes. Evidence can be obtained both directly from the taxpayer and from third parties. The powers are described at **29.3–29.10** below and operate in tandem with those for enquiries into self-assessment returns, for which see **29.2** below and **52.11–52.14** RETURNS. *FA 2021* has extended HMRC's powers to include the issue of information notices for the purpose of collecting tax debts.

For compliance checks generally, see HMRC Compliance Handbook. HMRC have published a statement of the principles governing their litigation and settlements strategy. See now HMRC's Litigation and Settlement Strategy Manual which covers how HMRC enter into, handle and settle disputes about any of the taxes for which they are responsible. See also **29.11** below for HMRC's practice in cases of serious tax fraud.

In addition to the above powers, HMRC can obtain specialist and bulk information from specified 'data holders' and can obtain working papers from dishonest tax agents.

HMRC are able to exercise certain powers under the *Police and Criminal Evidence Act 1984* when conducting direct tax criminal investigations. See **29.12** below. Where those powers cannot be used, HMRC can in serious tax fraud cases seek judicial authority to require the delivery of documents (see **29.14** below).

There are special provisions relating to computer records (see **29.15** below).

For a discussion of HMRC's power to conduct an informal investigation outside of the above powers, see *R (oao JJ Management LLP) v HMRC* CA, [2020] STC 1422.

Communications data

Except in criminal investigation cases, HMRC are not generally prevented from obtaining information consisting of communications data from certain operators such as online banks because of the restrictions in *Investigatory Powers Act 2016, s 12(2)*. This rule was introduced in *F(No 2)A 2023* but is treated as always having had effect. There are transitional rules for cases where information to which HMRC were not entitled was sought before 11 July 2023 (the date of Royal Assent to *F(No 2)A 2023*) and where penalties were charged for non-compliance. [*F(No 2)A 2023, s 352*].

Self-assessment enquiries

[29.2] The self-assessment enquiry procedures are explained at **52.11–52.14** RETURNS; these operate in tandem with the provisions below. See in particular **29.5** below for restrictions on HMRC's power to issue an information notice where a tax return has been made.

Information and inspection powers under *FA 2008, Sch 36*

[29.3] *FA 2008, Sch 36* provides a common set of information and inspection powers for HMRC covering income tax, capital gains tax, corporation tax, and other taxes. The powers are covered at **29.4–29.10** below only to the extent that they apply for the purposes of capital gains tax and corporation tax on chargeable gains.

Definitions

For the purposes of the provisions at **29.4–29.10** below, the following definitions apply.

'*Checking*' includes carrying out an investigation or enquiry of any kind. '*Document*' includes a part of a document (unless the context requires otherwise).

An '*authorised HMRC officer*' is an HMRC officer who is, or who is a member of a class of officers, authorised by the Commissioners for HMRC for the particular purpose.

The carrying on of a business includes the letting of property and the activities of a charity, a government department, a local authority (within *ITA 2007, s 999*), a local authority association (within *ITA 2007, s 1000*) or any other public authority. HMRC can make regulations specifying activities as businesses.

'*Tax*' means any or all of income tax, capital gains tax, corporation tax, VAT, insurance premium tax, inheritance tax, stamp duty land tax, stamp duty reserve tax, petroleum revenue tax, aggregates levy, climate change levy, annual tax on enveloped dwellings, soft drink industry levy and landfill tax. It also includes taxes of EU member states in respect of which information can be disclosed or, where an information notice is issued for the purpose of collecting a tax debt, which are covered by the EU Directive on mutual assistance for the recovery of taxes (*Directive 2010/24/EU*, as it had effect immediately before 11pm on 31 December 2020 (Brexit IP completion day)) and taxes of territories to which a tax enforcement agreement apply (see **28.2**(c) HMRC — CONFIDENTIALITY OF INFORMATION).

A person's '*tax position*' is their position at any time and in relation to any period as regards any tax, including his position as to past, present and future liability to any tax, penalties and other amounts which have been paid or are, or may be, payable by or to them in connection with any tax, and any claims, elections, applications and notices that have or may be made or given in connection with their liability to pay any tax. References to a person's tax position also include the tax position of a company that has ceased to exist and an individual who has died.

'*Collecting a tax debt*' means taking any steps for, or in connection with, the recovery of an amount of tax or another amount (such as interest or a penalty) in connection with any tax. It does not matter that another person is also, or has been, liable to pay the amount (for example where the liability has been transferred as part of insolvency proceedings).

'*Parent undertaking*', '*subsidiary undertaking*' and '*undertaking*' have the same meanings as in *Companies Act 2006, ss 1161, 1162, Sch 7*.

For capital gains tax and corporation tax purposes, an '*involved third party*' is a person registered as a managing agent at Lloyd's in relation to a syndicate of underwriting members, and '*relevant information*' and '*relevant documents*' in relation to such a party, are information and documents relating to, and to the activities of, the syndicate.

[*FA 2008, Sch 36 paras 35(7), 58–60, 63, 63A, 63B, 64; FA 2021, s 127(6)–(8)*].

Responsibility of company officers

Everything to be done by a company under the provisions at **29.4–29.10** below must be done by it through the '*proper officer*' (i.e. the secretary of a corporate body, except where a liquidator or administrator has been appointed when the latter is the proper officer, or the treasurer of a non-corporate body) or, except where a liquidator has been appointed, any authorised officer. The service of a notice on a company may be effected by serving it on the proper officer. [*TMA 1970, s 108; FA 2008, Sch 36 para 56*].

Information and documents

[29.4] An HMRC officer may give a notice (an '*information notice*') in writing requiring a person to provide information or to produce a document if it is reasonably required:

(a) for the purpose of checking that person's tax position or the purpose of collecting a tax debt of that person; or
(b) for the purpose of checking the tax position, or collecting a tax debt, of another person whose identity is known to the officer; or
(c) for the purpose of checking the tax position, or collecting a tax debt, of a person whose identity is not known to the officer or of a class of persons whose individual identities are not known to the officer; or
(d) for the purpose of checking the tax position, or collecting a tax debt, of another person, or class of persons, whose identity or identities are not known by the officer but can be ascertained from information held by the officer.

A notice can only be given for the purpose of collecting a tax debt on or after 10 June 2021, but can be given in respect of a tax debt whenever arising.

A notice may require either specified information or documents or information or documents described in the notice (so that a notice is not restricted to information or documents which HMRC can specifically identify). An information notice requiring the taxpayer to carry out searches across its directors' emails for specified terms was held to be valid in *Parker Hannifin (GB) Ltd v HMRC* FTT, [2023] UKFTT 971 (TC), [2024] SFTD 576. The requirement in the notice to disclose all of the resulting emails was, however, held to be far too wide.

Where it is given with the approval of the Tribunal (see further below), the notice must say so.

The information or documents must be provided or produced within the time period and at the time, by the means and in the form (if any) reasonably specified in the notice. Documents must be produced for inspection either at a place agreed to by the recipient of the notice and an HMRC officer or at a place (other than one used solely as a dwelling) that an HMRC officer reasonably specifies. Subject to any conditions or exceptions set out in regulations made by HMRC, copies of documents can be produced unless the notice requires the production of the original document or an HMRC officer in writing subsequently requests the original document. Where an officer makes such a request, the document must be produced within the period and at the time and by the means reasonably requested by the officer.

An HMRC officer may take copies of, or make extracts from, a document (or copy) produced to him, and if it appears necessary to him, he may remove the document at a reasonable time and retain it for a reasonable period. The officer must, without charge, provide a receipt for a document which is removed where this is requested and must also provide, again without charge, a copy of the document, if the person producing it reasonably requires it for any purpose. Where a document which has been removed is lost or damaged, HMRC are liable to compensate the owner for expenses reasonably incurred in replacing or repairing it.

The production or removal of a document under these provisions does not break any lien (i.e. any right) claimed on it.

The taxpayer was held not to be able to rely on the right of a person not to self-incriminate in order to refuse to comply with a notice under these provisions in *Gold Nuts Ltd v HMRC* FTT, [2016] SFTD 371.

A taxpayer notice given to a UK national who was resident in Dubai was held to be valid in *R (oao Jimenez) v First-tier Tribunal* CA, [2019] STC 746.

Taxpayer notice

An information notice under (a) above can be given without the approval of the Tribunal (see **5.11** APPEALS), but where such approval is obtained the taxpayer has no right of appeal against the decision of the Tribunal to grant approval or against the notice or a requirement in it.

Where approval is sought from the Tribunal, the application for approval must be made by, or with the agreement of, an authorised HMRC officer. The taxpayer must normally have been told that the information or documents are required and have been given a reasonable opportunity to make representations to HMRC, but is not entitled to be present at the hearing. The Tribunal must be given a summary of any representations made. Where the Tribunal is satisfied that informing the taxpayer would prejudice the assessment or collection of tax, it can approve the giving of the notice without the taxpayer having been informed.

In *Perfectos Printing Inks Co Ltd v HMRC* FTT, [2020] SFTD 430, the FTT held that it had no power to direct that an application for tribunal approval should be decided at an *inter partes* oral hearing.

Third party notice

Except in the case of a financial institution notice (see further below), a notice within (b) above cannot be given without either the agreement of the taxpayer (i.e. the person whose tax position is to be checked) or the approval of the Tribunal and must normally name the taxpayer. Where approval is obtained from the Tribunal, there is no right of appeal against the decision of the Tribunal to grant approval or against the notice or a requirement in it.

Where approval is sought from the Tribunal, the application for approval must be made by, or with the agreement of, an authorised HMRC officer. The taxpayer must normally have been given a summary of the reasons why an officer requires the information or documents, but is not entitled to be present at the hearing. The person to whom the notice is to be given must normally have been told that the information or documents are required and have been given a reasonable opportunity to make representations to HMRC and the Tribunal must be given a summary of any such representations. These requirements can, however, be disapplied where the Tribunal is satisfied that informing the recipient of the notice or giving a summary of reasons to the taxpayer would prejudice the assessment or collection of tax.

The Tribunal can also disapply the requirement to name the taxpayer in the notice if it is satisfied that the officer has reasonable grounds for believing that naming them might seriously prejudice the assessment or collection of tax.

A copy of the notice must normally be given to the taxpayer. The Tribunal can, however, disapply this requirement if an application for approval is made by, or with the agreement of, an authorised HMRC officer and the Tribunal is satisfied that the officer has reasonable grounds for believing that giving a copy of the notice to the taxpayer might prejudice the assessment or collection of tax.

Where a third-party notice is given for the purpose of checking the tax position of a parent undertaking and any of its subsidiary undertakings, the above provisions apply as if the parent undertaking were the taxpayer. The requirement for the notice to name the taxpayer is satisfied by stating in the notice that its purposes is checking the tax position of the parent and subsidiary undertakings and naming the parent undertaking. Where a notice is given to a parent undertaking for the purpose of checking the tax position of one or more subsidiary undertakings, neither the agreement of the parent undertaking nor the approval of the Tribunal is required and a copy does not have to be given to the parent undertaking.

Where a third party notice is given for the purpose of checking the tax position of more than one of the partners in a business carried on in partnership, in their capacity as such, the above provisions apply as if the taxpayer were at least one of the partners. The requirement for the notice to name the taxpayer is satisfied by stating in the notice that its purpose is checking the tax position of more than one of the partners and giving a name in which the partnership is registered for any purpose. Where a third party notice is given to one of the partners for the purpose of checking the tax position of any of the other partners, neither the agreement of any of the partners nor the approval of the Tribunal is required and a copy does not have to be given to any other partners.

In *Kandore Ltd v HMRC* CA, [2021] STC 1524, the CA confirmed that there is no power for the FTT to direct that an application for tribunal approval should be decided at an *inter partes* oral hearing because approval was a 'judicial monitoring' of an investigation and not an adjudication in a dispute between the parties. At the Upper Tribunal stage of this case, the tribunal also held that it was open to the FTT to delay a determination of an application for a closure notice until after HMRC's application for approval of a third-party notice so that it would benefit from knowing whether HMRC had succeeded in the third party notice application before deciding whether to direct HMRC to close their enquiries.

Third party notices were held to have been validly issued to non-UK resident individuals in *Ex parte PQ* FTT 2019, [2020] SFTD 1.

Financial institution notices

A notice within (b) above can be given to a 'financial institution' without the agreement of the taxpayer or approval of the Tribunal if, in the reasonable opinion of the officer giving the notice, it would not be onerous for the institution to provide the information or produce the documents. Such a notice can only be given by, or with the agreement of, an authorised HMRC officer.

The notice must normally name the taxpayer to which it relates. The Tribunal can, however, disapply this requirement if it is satisfied that the officer has reasonable grounds for believing that naming the taxpayer might seriously prejudice the assessment or collection of tax.

A copy of the notice must normally be given to the taxpayer, together with a summary of why HMRC require the information or documents. These requirements can, however, be disapplied where the Tribunal is satisfied that giving a copy of the notice or giving a summary of reasons to the taxpayer would prejudice the assessment or collection of tax.

There is no right of appeal against the decision of the Tribunal to disapply any of these requirements.

A financial institution notice can only be given on or after 10 June 2021, but may relate to periods, liabilities or tax debts arising before that date.

A '*financial institution*' is a person treated as such under the OECD's Common Reporting Standard (CRS) or a person who issues credit cards. There is an exclusion for persons (such as family trusts and charities) which are within the CRS definition only because they are an investment entity within *section VIII(A)(6)(b)* of the CRS.

Non-disclosure of notice

With effect from 10 June 2021, where the Tribunal has disapplied the requirement for a copy of a third party notice or a financial institution notice to be given to the taxpayer, the notice can include a requirement that the recipient must not disclose the notice or anything relating to it to the taxpayer or (except for the purpose of complying with the notice) to any other person. The requirement not to disclose usually applies for 12 months beginning on the date the notice is given. HMRC may, however, by notice in writing, withdraw a requirement before the normal end date or extend it for a further period of 12 months (and may do so more than once). The notice must be given before the expiry of the 12-month period and must be given by, or with the agreement of, an authorised HMRC officer. A non-disclosure requirement can only be extended if the authorised HMRC officer has reasonable grounds for believing that not doing so might prejudice the assessment or collection of tax.

See **46.19** PENALTIES for the penalty for failure to comply with a requirement under these provisions.

Notice about persons whose identity is not known

The giving of a notice under (c) above requires the approval of the Tribunal. The Tribunal can approve the giving of the notice only if it is satisfied that:

- there are reasonable grounds for believing that the person or class of persons to whom the notice relates may have failed, or may fail, to comply with any law relating to tax (including the law of a territory outside the UK);
- any such failure is likely to have led, or to lead, to serious prejudice to the assessment or collection of tax; and
- the information or document is not readily available from another source.

There is no right of appeal against a decision of the Tribunal to grant approval.

The approval of the Tribunal is permitted but not required for a notice to be given to a parent undertaking for the purpose of checking the tax position of one or more subsidiary undertakings whose identities are not known to the HMRC officer giving the notice. Such approval is also permitted but not required for a notice to be given to a partner in a business carried on in partnership for the purpose of checking the tax position of partners whose identities are not known to the officer giving the notice.

Notice about person whose identity can be ascertained

A notice within (d) above must be given by an authorised HMRC officer and can only require the recipient to provide all or any of the name, last known address and date of birth of the taxpayer (or class of taxpayer) concerned. The officer must have reason to believe that the recipient of the notice will be able to ascertain the taxpayer's identity (or taxpayers' identities) from the information held by the officer and that the recipient obtained the information required in the course of carrying on a business. A notice cannot be given if the taxpayer's identity (or taxpayers' identities) can be readily ascertained by other means from the information held by the officer.

[*FA 2008, Sch 36 paras 1–9, 15, 16, 35, 37, 51A, 61ZA; FA 2021, ss 126(1)–(4)(9), 127(1)–(5)(8), Sch 34 para* 2].

For further restrictions on the above powers, see **29.5** below. For appeals against information notices, see **29.6** below.

Restrictions on information notice powers

[29.5] An information notice does not require a person to:

(i) produce a document if it is not in his possession or power;
(ii) provide or produce information that relates to the conduct of a pending tax appeal or any part of a document containing such information;
(iii) provide journalistic material (within *Police and Criminal Evidence Act 1984, s 13*) or information contained in such material;
(iv) subject to the exceptions below, provide or produce 'personal records' (within *Police and Criminal Evidence Act 1984, s 12*); or
(v) produce a document the whole of which originates more than six years before the giving of the notice, unless the notice is given by, or with the agreement of, an authorised officer.

With regard to (iv) above, an information notice may require a person to produce documents (or copies) that are personal records, omitting any personal information (i.e. information whose inclusion in the documents makes them personal records) and to provide any information in personal records that is not personal information.

[*FA 2008, Sch 36 paras 18–20*].

In *Brantjes v HMRC* FTT, [2020] UKFTT 177 (TC); 2020 SWTI 1233, the FTT held that a taxpayer could not be required by a notice to provide bank statements which she did not have and which the bank did not keep in hard copy form. A document which did not exist when the notices were issued was neither in the taxpayer's possession or power, even if it could be created at her instigation.

The making of a jeopardy amendment during an enquiry does not prevent HMRC from issuing an information notice in relation to matters dealt with by the amendment (*Foreign National v HMRC* FTT, [2023] UKFTT 475 (TC)).

Notice where tax return made

Where a person has made an individual, trustee, partnership or company tax return (see **52.5, 52.18** and **52.21** RETURNS) in respect of a tax year or accounting period, a taxpayer notice (see **29.4**(a) above) can be given for the purpose of checking their income tax, capital gains tax or corporation tax position for that year or period only if:

(a) an enquiry notice (see **52.11, 52.20** and **52.21** RETURNS) has been given in respect of either the return or a claim or election for the year or period to which the return relates and the enquiry has not been completed (or the enquiry has not been completed so far as relating to the matters to which the taxpayer notice relates);
(b) an HMRC officer has reason to suspect that, in relation to that person, an amount that ought to have been assessed to tax may not have been assessed, that an assessment for the period may be or have become insufficient or relief from tax for the period may be or have become excessive;
(c) the notice is given for the purpose of obtaining information or a document that is also required to check the taxpayer's position for any other tax other than income tax, capital gains tax or corporation tax; or
(d) the notice is given for the purpose of obtaining information or a document that is required to check the taxpayer's position as regards his obligation to make deductions or repayments under PAYE, the construction industry scheme or any other provision.

Similar provisions apply where a person has made a UK land disposal return (see **52.22** RETURNS) or an NRCGT return.

Where a third party notice (see **29.1** above) is given to a parent undertaking for the purpose of checking the tax position of one or more subsidiary undertakings, the above provisions apply as if the notice were a taxpayer notice (see **32.1**(a) above) or taxpayer notices given to the subsidiary undertaking or each of them.

Where a business is carried in partnership and a partnership return (see **52.21** RETURNS) or partnership claim or election (see **13.2** CLAIMS) has been made by one of the partners, the above provisions apply as if the return, claim or election had been made by each of the partners.

Where it appears to HMRC that there has been a change in ownership of a company (within *CTA 2010, Pt 14 Ch 7*) and, in connection with that change, a person (the '*seller*') may be or become liable to corporation tax under *CTA 2010, ss 710* or *713* (recovery of unpaid corporation tax from persons controlling company), the above restriction does not apply to a taxpayer notice given to the seller.

[*FA 2008, Sch 36 paras 21, 21ZA, 35(4), 36, 37(1)(2)*].

Deceased persons

An information notice for the purpose of checking the tax position of a deceased person cannot be given more than four years after death. [*FA 2008, Sch 36 para 22*].

Legal professional privilege

An information notice cannot require a person to provide information, or to produce any part of a document, in respect of which a claim to legal professional privilege (or, in Scotland, a claim to confidentiality of communications) could be maintained in legal proceedings.

Disputes as to whether information or a document is privileged are settled under the following procedures. If the information notice is given in the course of correspondence the procedure is as follows.

(A) The recipient of the notice, or a person acting on his behalf, must compile a list of the information or documents required under the notice which are in dispute by the date given in the notice for providing information or producing documents. The list must include a description of the nature and contents of each such item of information or document unless the description would itself give rise to a dispute over privilege.

(B) The list must then be served on HMRC within a reasonable time agreed between the parties but not later than 20 working days (i.e. days other than saturdays, sundays or public holidays) after the date given in the notice for providing information or documents. Proof of such service must be provided to HMRC.

(C) HMRC must then notify the person who provided the list of any documents on the list that they require to be produced and which they do not consider privileged.

(D) On receipt of HMRC's notification, the recipient of the information notice, or person acting on his behalf, must make an application to the First-tier Tribunal to consider and resolve the dispute. The application must include copies of the information or documents and must be made within a reasonable time agreed between the parties but not later than 20 working days of the date of HMRC's notification.

If the information notice is given in the course of an inspection of premises (see **29.8, 29.9** below), the recipient, or a person acting on his behalf, must indicate to the HMRC officer conducting the inspection each item of information or document required under the notice which is in dispute. The recipient of the notice or person acting on his behalf must then place the documents etc. (or copies) in a container which prevents the contents being visible. The container is then sealed, labelled and signed by that person and countersigned by the HMRC officer. That officer must then deliver the container to the First-tier Tribunal with the seal intact within 42 working days of having taken custody of it, together with an application to the Tribunal to consider and resolve the dispute.

A dispute may also be resolved at any time by HMRC and the recipient of the information notice reaching an agreement, in writing or otherwise.

These provisions do not affect the requirement to produce information or documents which are not in dispute.

[*FA 2008, Sch 36 para 23; SI 2009 No 1916*].

Legal professional privilege does not cover legal advice given by those who are not qualified lawyers (*R (oao Prudential plc) v Special Commissioner for Income Tax* CA, [2010] STC 2802), but see below for protections for auditors and tax advisers. The question of the extent to which an engagement letter was covered by legal professional privilege was considered in *Behague v HMRC* FTT, [2013] UKFTT 596 (TC), 2013 STI 3577.

The scope of legal professional privilege in relation to a conveyancing solicitor's client file was discussed in *HMRC v Taxpayer* FTT, [2023] UKFTT 71 (TC), [2023] SFTD 446.

Auditors

An information notice does not require an auditor (i.e. a person appointed as an auditor for the purpose of an enactment) to provide information held in connection with the performance of his functions under that enactment or to produce documents which are his property and which were created by him, or on his behalf, for or in connection with the performance of those functions.

This restriction does not apply to any information, or any document containing information, which explains any information or document which an auditor has, as tax accountant, assisted any client in preparing for, or delivering to, HMRC. Where the notice is given under **29.4**(c) above, the restriction also does not apply to information giving the identity or address of a person to whom the notice relates or of a person who has acted on behalf of such a person or to a document containing such information. Where the restriction is so disapplied, only that part (or parts) of a document which contains the relevant information has to be produced. The restriction is not disapplied if the information concerned, or a document containing the information, has already been provided or produced to an HMRC officer.

[*FA 2008, Sch 36 paras 24, 26, 27*].

Tax advisers

An information notice does not require a 'tax adviser' to provide information about, or to produce documents which are his property and which consist of, communications between him and a person in relation to whose tax affairs he has been appointed or between him and any other tax advisor of such a person, the purpose of which is the giving or obtaining of advice about any of those tax affairs. For this purpose, a '*tax adviser*' is a person appointed (directly or by another tax adviser) to give advice about the tax affairs of another person.

This restriction is disapplied in the same circumstances as the restriction applying to auditors is disapplied.

[*FA 2008, Sch 36 paras 25–27*].

Appeals against information notices

[29.6] A taxpayer can appeal against a taxpayer notice (see **29.4**(a) above) or any requirement in such a notice unless the notice was given with the approval of the Tribunal. No appeal can be made against a requirement to provide information or to produce a document which forms part of his 'statutory records'.

A person given a third-party notice (see **29.4**(b) above) can appeal against the notice or any requirement in it on the ground that compliance would be unduly onerous. An appeal can be made on any grounds by a parent undertaking against such a notice given to it for the purpose of checking the tax position of one or more subsidiary undertakings, by a partner against a notice given for the purpose of checking the tax position of other partners, or by an involved third party against a notice given for the purpose of checking the capital gains tax or corporation tax position of another person where the notice refers only to relevant information or relevant documents. No appeal can be made, however, where the notice was given with the approval of the Tribunal or against a requirement to provide information or produce a document forming part of the taxpayer's or involved third party's statutory records.

Where a third-party notice is given for the purpose of checking the tax position of a parent undertaking and any of its subsidiary undertakings, no appeal can be made against a requirement to provide information or produce a document forming part of the statutory records of the parent undertaking or any of its subsidiaries. No appeal can be made against a requirement, in a third-party notice given to a parent undertaking for the purpose of checking the tax position of one or more subsidiary undertakings, to produce a document forming part of the statutory records of the parent undertaking or any of its subsidiary undertakings.

Where a third-party notice is given for the purpose of checking the tax position of more than one of the partners in a business carried on in partnership, no appeal can be made against a requirement to provide information or produce forming part of the statutory records of any of the partners. No appeal can be made against a requirement, in a notice given to a partner for the purpose of checking the tax position of other partners, to produce a document forming part of the statutory records of the partner receiving the notice.

A person given a notice about persons whose identity is not known (see **29.4**(c) above) or a notice about persons whose identity can be ascertained (see **29.4**(d) above) can appeal against the notice or any requirement in it on the ground that compliance would be unduly onerous (or on any grounds where the notice is given to a parent undertaking for the purpose of checking the tax position of one or more unknown subsidiary undertakings, to a partner for the purpose of checking the tax position of unknown partners, or to an involved third party where the notice given for the purpose of checking the capital gains tax or corporation tax position of other persons and the notice refers only to relevant information or relevant documents). No appeal can be made against a requirement, in a notice given to a parent undertaking for the purpose of checking the tax position of one or more subsidiary undertakings, to produce a document forming part of the statutory records of the parent undertaking or any of its subsidiary undertakings. Likewise, no appeal can be made against a requirement, in a notice given to a partner in a business carried on in partnership for the purpose of checking the tax position of other partners, to produce a document forming part of the statutory records of the partner receiving the notice. No appeal can be made against a requirement in a notice given to an involved third party to provide any information or produce any document forming part of the involved third party's statutory records.

For this purpose, '*statutory records*' are information and documents which a taxpayer is required to keep and preserve for direct tax purposes (see **52.10**, **52.21** RETURNS), VAT purposes and the other taxes included in the definition of 'tax' at **29.3** above. To the extent that information or documents do not relate to the carrying on of a business and are not required to be kept or preserved for VAT purposes, they only form part of a taxpayer's statutory documents to the extent that the tax year or accounting period to which they relate has ended. Information and documents cease to be statutory records when the period for which they are required to be preserved ends. Private bank statements for an account used for both business and personal expenditure were held to be statutory records in *Beckwith v HMRC* FTT, [2012] UKFTT 181 (TC); 2012 STI 1842.

Procedure

Notice of appeal under the above provisions must be given in writing to the HMRC officer who gave the information notice within the period of 30 days beginning with the date on which the information notice was given. A decision on an appeal by the Tribunal is final (so that there is no further right of appeal to the Upper Tribunal or Court of Appeal — see *Jordan v HMRC* UT, [2015] STC 2314). Where the Tribunal confirms the notice or a requirement in it, the person to whom the notice was given must comply with the notice or requirement within the period specified by the Tribunal. If the Tribunal does not specify such a period, compliance must be within such period as an HMRC officer reasonably specifies in writing.

Subject to the above, the appeal provisions of *TMA 1970, Pt 5* (see **5** APPEALS) apply to an appeal against an information notice as they apply to an appeal against an income tax assessment.

[*FA 2008, Sch 36 paras 29–33, 34A, 35, 37, 62*].

Concealing, destroying or disposing of documents

[29.7] A person to whom an information notice is addressed must not conceal, destroy or otherwise dispose of, or arrange for the concealment, destruction or disposal of, a document that is the subject of the notice. This does not apply if he does so after the document has been produced to HMRC in accordance with the notice, unless an HMRC officer has notified him in writing that the document must continue to be available for inspection (and has not withdrawn the notification). It also does not apply if a copy of the document was produced in compliance with the notice and the destruction, etc. takes place after the end of the period of six months beginning with the day on which the copy was produced unless within that period, an HMRC officer makes a request for the original document.

Similarly, where a person has been informed that a document is, or is likely to be, the subject of an information notice addressed to him, he must not conceal, destroy or otherwise dispose of, or arrange for the concealment, destruction or disposal of, the document. This does not apply if he acts more than six months after he was so informed (or was last so informed).

[*FA 2008, Sch 36 paras 42, 43*].

Failure to comply with the above provisions may be a criminal offence or result in penalties. See **29.10** below.

Inspection of business premises

[29.8] An HMRC officer may enter a person's 'business premises' and inspect the premises and any 'business assets' and 'business documents' that are on the premises if the inspection is reasonably required for the purpose of checking that person's tax position. The officer may not enter or inspect any part of the premises used solely as a dwelling.

An HMRC officer may enter business premises of an involved third party (see **29.3** above) and inspect the premises and any business assets and relevant documents that are on the premises if the inspection is reasonably required for the purpose of checking the tax position of any person or class of persons. It is not necessary that the officer know the identity of the person or persons. Again, the officer may not enter or inspect any part of the premises used solely as a dwelling.

The officer may mark business assets and anything containing business assets to indicate that they have been inspected and may obtain and record information (electronically or otherwise) relating to the premises, assets and documents inspected. He may take copies of, or make extracts from, a document (or copy) which he inspects, and if it appears necessary to him, he may remove the document at a reasonable time and retain it for a reasonable period. He must, without charge, provide a receipt for a document which is removed where this is requested and must also provide, again without charge, a copy of the document, if the person producing it reasonably requires it for any purpose. Where a document which has been removed is lost or damaged, HMRC are liable to compensate the owner for expenses reasonably incurred in replacing or repairing it.

An inspection must normally be carried out at a time agreed to by the occupier of the premises. It can, however, be carried out at any reasonable time if:

(i) the occupier has been given at least seven days' notice (in writing or otherwise) of the time of the inspection; or

(ii) the inspection is carried out by, or with the agreement of, an authorised HMRC officer.

Where (ii) above applies, the officer carrying out the inspection must provide a notice in writing stating the possible consequences of obstructing the officer in the exercise of the power. If the occupier is present when the inspection begins, the notice must be given to him. If he is not present, the notice must be given to the person who appears to be the officer in charge of the premises, but if no such person is present, the notice must be left in a prominent place on the premises. The giving of such a notice does not require the approval of the Tribunal, but such approval can be applied for by, or with the agreement of, an authorised HMRC officer. A penalty for deliberate obstruction of an officer in the course of an inspection can only be charged where such approval has been obtained (see **29.10** below). A decision of the Tribunal to approve an inspection is final and there is no right of appeal.

An officer may not inspect a document if or to the extent that an information notice (see **29.4** above) given at the time of the inspection to the occupier of the premises could not require him to produce the document (see **29.5** above).

For the above purposes, '*business premises*' are premises (including any land, building or structure or means of transport), or a part of premises, that an HMRC officer has reason to believe are used in connection with the carrying on of a business by or on behalf of the taxpayer concerned. '*Business assets*' are assets, other than documents which are neither trading stock nor plant, that an HMRC officer has reason to believe are owned, leased or used in connection with the carrying on of any business. '*Business documents*' are documents, or copies of documents, relating to the carrying on of any business that form part of any person's statutory records.

[*FA 2008, Sch 36 paras 10–17, 28, 58*].

Inspection of other premises

[29.9] An HMRC officer can enter premises and inspect them and any other property there for the purpose of valuing them, measuring them or determining their character. The valuation, measurement of determination must be reasonably required for the purpose of checking any person's tax position (in this case restricted to capital gains tax, corporation tax on chargeable gains, inheritance tax, stamp duty land tax and stamp duty reserve tax). The officer can be accompanied by a valuation etc. expert.

The inspection must normally be carried out at a time agreed to by the occupier of the premises and he must be given notice in writing of the agreed time. If the occupier cannot be identified, agreement can be obtained from, and notice given to, a person who controls the premises. Where, however, the inspection has been approved by the Tribunal (see below), the only requirement is the occupier or person controlling the premises be given at least seven days' notice in writing of the time of the inspection. Where such notice is given it must state that the inspection has been approved by the tribunal and indicate the possible consequences of obstructing the inspection (see below).

The giving of a notice does not require the approval of the Tribunal, but such approval can be applied for by, or with the agreement of, an authorised HMRC officer. A penalty for deliberate obstruction of an officer in the course of an inspection can only be charged where such approval has been obtained (see **29.10** below). A decision of the Tribunal to approve an inspection is final and there is no right of appeal. Both the person whose tax position is in question and the occupier of the premises (unless he cannot be identified) must be given a reasonable opportunity to make representations to the HMRC officer and a summary of any representations must be given to the Tribunal.

An officer carrying out an inspection under these powers must produce evidence of his authority to do so if asked by the occupier or any other person who appears to be in charge of the premises or property. He may obtain and record information (electronically or otherwise) relating to the premises and property inspected.

[*FA 2008, Sch 36 paras 12A–14, 17*].

Offences and penalties under FA 2008, Sch 36

[29.10] For penalties for failure to comply with an information notice within **29.4** above, for deliberately obstructing an HMRC officer in the course of an inspection of premises under the powers at **29.8** and **29.9** above that has been approved by the Tribunal and for deliberate or careless inaccuracies in information or documents provided in compliance with an information notice, see **46.19** PENALTIES.

It is an offence for a person required to produce a document by an information notice within **29.4** above which has been approved by the Tribunal to conceal, destroy or otherwise dispose of the document or to arrange for its concealment, destruction or disposal. This does not apply if he does so after the document has been produced to HMRC in accordance with the notice, unless an HMRC officer has notified him in writing that the document must continue to be available for inspection (and has not withdrawn the notification). It also does not apply if a copy of the document was produced in compliance with the notice and the destruction, etc. takes place after the end of the period of six months beginning with the day on which the copy was produced unless within that period, an HMRC officer makes a request for the original document.

It is also an offence for a person to conceal, destroy or otherwise dispose of, or to arrange for the concealment, destruction or disposal of, a document after an HMRC officer has informed him in writing that the document is, or is likely to be, the subject of an information notice approval for which is to be obtained from the Tribunal. This does not apply if the person so acts more than six months after he was so informed (or was last so informed).

On summary conviction of either of the above offences the offender is liable to a fine not exceeding the statutory maximum. On conviction on indictment the punishment is imprisonment for a maximum of two years and/or a fine.

[*FA 2008, Sch 36 paras 53–55*].

HMRC practice in cases of serious tax fraud

[29.11] Under its published Criminal Investigation Policy (see www.gov.uk/government/publications/criminal-investigation/hmrc-criminal-investigation-policy), HMRC reserve complete discretion to conduct a criminal investigation in any case, with a view to prosecution by the Crown Prosecution Service ('CPS') in England and Wales or the appropriate prosecuting authority in Scotland and Northern Ireland. Examples of the kind of circumstances in which HMRC will generally consider commencing a criminal, rather than civil, investigation are, inter alia, cases involving organised or systematic fraud including conspiracy; cases where an individual holds a position of trust or responsibility; cases where materially false statements are made or materially false documents are provided in the course of a civil investigation; cases where deliberate concealment, deception, conspiracy or corruption is suspected; cases involving the use of false or forged documents; cases involving money laundering; cases where there is a link to suspected wider criminality; and repeated offences.

Where HMRC suspect fraud, it may instead commence an investigation under Code of Practice 9 (COP 9) with a view to recovery of tax and interest and the imposition of a civil penalty. Such cases can also lead to a criminal prosecution but it is HMRC's policy to offer the taxpayer the chance to avoid criminal prosecution by making a full disclosure under their contractual disclosure facility (CDF). Taxpayers have 60 days from date of receipt to either accept or formally reject the offer of a contract. If they accept, they must produce an Outline Disclosure within the same 60-day period; this should contain a brief description of the frauds committed, a formal admission of deliberately bringing about a loss of tax, details of any non-fraudulent irregularities and any proposals for a payment on account. If the Outline Disclosure is accepted, the taxpayer will be required to make progress towards the production of a Certificate of Full Disclosure.

Under the terms of the CDF contract, the taxpayer will not be criminally investigated, with a view to prosecution, for matters covered by the Outline Disclosure. The customer's co-operation will have the potential to maximise reductions in penalties. If the taxpayer rejects the offer of a contract or makes no response, HMRC have the option of starting a criminal investigation, though in most cases, they will pursue a civil investigation.

See *R v CIR (ex p Mead and Cook)* QB 1992, 65 TC 1 as regards HMRC discretion to seek monetary settlements or institute criminal proceedings. See *R v CIR (ex p Allen)* QB 1997, 69 TC 442 for an unsuccessful application for judicial review of a Revenue decision to take criminal proceedings.

The Crown Prosecution Service is not precluded from instituting criminal proceedings in circumstances where HMRC have accepted a monetary settlement (*R v W and another* CA, [1998] STC 550).

Statements made or documents produced by or on behalf of a taxpayer are admissible as evidence in proceedings against him, notwithstanding that reliance on HMRC's practice or on their policy for mitigating penalties (see **46.26** PENALTIES) may have induced him to make or produce them. [*TMA 1970, s 105*].

See generally HMRC Fraud Civil Investigation Manual.

Taxpayers wishing to own up to a fraud without waiting to be contacted by HMRC may complete form CDF1 (www.gov.uk/government/publications/voluntary-disclosure-contractual-disclosure-facility-cdf1) or use the digital disclosure service (see below); HMRC will then consider the taxpayer for a CDF contract.

Digital disclosure service

Taxpayers wishing to disclose unreturned or unpaid taxes (including capital gains tax and corporation tax) may do so online using HMRC's digital disclosure service. Disclosures may be made under any of HMRC's campaigns or otherwise. See www.gov.uk/government/publications/hm-revenue-and-customs-disclosure-service.

Simon's Taxes. See A7.423.

HMRC use of Police and Criminal Evidence Act 1984 powers

[29.12] HMRC are able to exercise certain powers under the *Police and Criminal Evidence Act 1984* when conducting direct tax criminal investigations. The powers involved include those concerning search warrants and arrest. Only HMRC officers authorised by the Commissioners for HMRC are able to exercise the powers. Similar powers are available to HMRC in Scotland and Northern Ireland.

As a result of the availability of the above police powers, the power to seek judicial authority to require the delivery of documents at **29.14** below is restricted to circumstances where the equivalent police power cannot be used because the material concerned is outside its scope.

[*Police and Criminal Evidence Act 1984, s 114; SI 2015 No 1783*].

In *Newcastle United Football Co Ltd v HMRC* KB, [2023] EWHC 3021 (Admin), [2024] STC 73, HMRC was permitted to retain digital copies of documents obtained using these powers in the course of a criminal investigation for the purposes of a civil investigation after the criminal case was discontinued.

HMRC use of Proceeds of Crime Act 2002 powers

[29.13] HMRC can exercise certain powers under the *Proceeds of Crime Act 2002* directly when conducting direct tax criminal investigations. The powers involved are those for search and seizure of cash, production orders, search and seizure warrants, customer information orders and account monitoring orders. Previously these powers could be exercised by the police on behalf of HMRC.

[*Proceeds of Crime Act 2002, Pts 5, 8*].

Order for delivery of documents in serious tax fraud cases

[29.14] Under *TMA 1970, s 20BA, Sch 1AA*, HMRC may apply to the appropriate judicial authority (a Circuit judge in England and Wales, a sheriff in Scotland or a County Court judge in NI) for an order requiring any person who appears to have in his possession or power documents specified or described in the order to deliver them to an HMRC officer within ten working days after the day of service of the notice, or such longer or shorter period as may be specified in the order. The judicial authority must be satisfied, on information on oath given by an authorised HMRC officer, that there is reasonable ground for suspecting that an offence involving serious tax fraud has been or is about to be committed, and that the documents may be required as evidence in proceedings in respect of the offence. In Scotland, a single sheriff may make orders in respect of persons anywhere in Scotland as long as one of the orders relates to a person residing or having a place of business at an address in the sheriff's own sherriffdom. Orders may not be made in relation to items subject to legal privilege (as defined) unless they are held with the intention of furthering a criminal purpose. Failure to comply with an order is treated as contempt of court, and there are severe penalties for falsification of documents.

These provisions are restricted to circumstances where the equivalent power under the *Police and Criminal Evidence Act 1984* (see **29.12** above) cannot be used because the material concerned cannot be obtained using those powers.

Schedule 1AA lays down detailed requirements in relation to applications under these provisions, and these may be supplemented by regulations (see now *SI 2000 No 2875*). In particular, a person is entitled to at least five days' notice of intention to apply for such an order, and to appear and be heard at the application, unless the judicial authority is satisfied that this would seriously prejudice investigation of the offence. Until the application has been dismissed or abandoned, or an order made or complied with, any person given such notice must not conceal, destroy, alter or dispose of any document to which the order sought relates, or disclose information etc. likely to prejudice the investigation, except with the leave of the judicial authority or the written permission of the Commissioners for HMRC. Professional legal advisers may, however, disclose such information etc. in giving legal advice to a client or in connection with legal proceedings, provided that it is not disclosed with a view to furthering a criminal purpose. Failure to comply with these requirements is treated as failure to comply with an order under these provisions. The procedural rules where documents are delivered in accordance with an order are as for Search and seizure under *TMA 1970, s 20CC(3)–(9)*. The regulations include procedural rules for resolving any dispute between HMRC and a person against whom an order is made as to whether a document (or part thereof) is an item subject to legal privilege.

[*TMA 1970, s 20BA, Sch 1AA; Police and Criminal Evidence Act 1984, s 14B*].

Computer records etc.

[29.15] The following applies to any tax provisions requiring a person to produce a document or cause a document to be produced or requiring a person to permit HMRC to inspect a document, to make copies of or extracts from, or remove, a document (i.e. including the provisions at **29.4**, **29.10**, **32.11**, and **29.14**).

For the purposes of such provisions, a reference to a document is a reference to anything in which information of any description is recorded, and a reference to a copy of a document is to anything onto which information recorded in the document has been copied, by whatever means and whether directly or indirectly. In *R (oao Glenn & Co (Essex Ltd) v HMRC* QB, [2010] EWHC 1469 (Admin), 2010 STI 2119, a computer was held to fall within this provision.

Where a document has been, or may be, required to be produced, inspected etc. under any such provisions, a person authorised by the Commissioners for HMRC can obtain access to any computer and associated apparatus or material used in connection with the document at any reasonable time in order to inspect it and check its operation. Reasonable assistance can be required from the person by whom or on whose behalf the computer has been so used or any person in charge of the computer etc. or otherwise concerned with its operation.

A penalty of £300 applies for obstruction of such access or refusal to provide assistance.

[*FA 2008, s 114*].

Key points on HMRC investigatory powers

[29.16] Points to consider are as follows.

- HMRC can inspect businesses and the taxpayer is required to cooperate or face a financial penalty. In cases where HMRC can demonstrate the taxpayer concealed, destroyed or disposed of information then the person can face imprisonment and/or a fine.
- The adviser needs to carefully review any information notice to ensure it is addressed to the correct person, the correct address, there is reason to suspect tax has been lost or overpaid, the time allowed to provide the information is sufficient and the information request is reasonable and relevant.
- The adviser should cooperate with HMRC as long it is clear the information request is correct and accurate. It is recommended advisors explain to clients that HMRC has a statutory power to request information.
- If at all possible, it is recommended that clients do not sign mandates for third parties. The adviser should use all available routes to gather the information needed first. Otherwise, the information request can be very damaging to the commercial and business relationship with the bank, for example.
- HMRC has to observe the Human Rights Act 1998 and the person's 'right to privacy'. This means minimising the damage and disruption that an enquiry can cause. HMRC cannot exchange information with other jurisdictions or departments outside of the legal gateways in place. HMRC does not need to inspect private dwellings and it is recommended that where possible the records are examined at a neutral venue such the adviser's offices.
- Requests for information created more than six years before the date of the notice need to be agreed with a senior officer within HMRC. These cases normally involve deliberate failure to report or return income or gains.

- Always seek legal professional advice straightaway if there is any suggestion or reference to criminal proceedings.
- Prevention is better than cure and advisers should attempt where possible to avoid HMRC using its formal powers due to the financial penalties and time constraints involved. HMRC perceives the need to use formal powers where there is a lack of cooperation on the client's part.
- Although some enquiries/requests for information are random, regard should be had to the significant volume of data released to HMRC via UK and overseas sources and warn clients to consider carefully whether they have accidentally omitted any information from their returns.

30

Hold-Over Reliefs

Cross-references. See **8.11** ASSETS HELD ON 31 MARCH **1982** for 50% relief etc. on held-over gains of companies relating to an asset acquired before 31 March 1982; **10.3**, **10.4** CAPITAL SUMS DERIVED FROM ASSETS for reliefs available where capital sums received as compensation are expended on restoration or replacement; **14.12** COMPANIES for the relief available on a scheme of reconstruction; **23** EXEMPTIONS AND RELIEFS generally; **25.3** GIFTS for summary of special reliefs relating to gifts; **26.3** GROUPS OF COMPANIES for relief on disposals within a group; **31** INCORPORATION AND DISINCORPORATION RELIEFS; **35.7**, **35.9**, **35.10** LAND for reliefs available on small part disposals and compulsory purchase of land; **43.3** OVERSEAS MATTERS for transfer of UK permanent establishment to UK resident company, **43.10** for transfers of assets to a non-UK resident company, **43.12** for transfer or division of business between companies in different EC member states and **43.13** for transfer or division of non-UK business between companies in different EC member states; **53** ROLLOVER RELIEF.

Simon's Taxes. See **C3.5**, **C3.1601–C3.1605**.

Introduction to hold-over reliefs

[30.1] There are currently two separate hold-over reliefs which apply to:

(a) disposals by individuals or trustees of business assets where the disposal is not at arm's length (for example, gifts); and
(b) disposals by individuals or trustees in respect of which inheritance tax is chargeable (or would be but for certain exemptions).

The effect of the reliefs is to reduce or eliminate the chargeable gain on the disposal and to make a corresponding reduction in the acquisition cost of the transferee. Relief must be claimed, usually by way of a joint claim by both transferor and transferee. Relief is denied in certain circumstances, including in most cases where the transferee is not UK-resident or is the trustee of a settlor-interested settlement. Relief already given is also clawed back in certain circumstances, including where the transferee subsequently emigrates. See **30.8** and **30.11** below.

The current restricted hold-over reliefs replaced wider reliefs in 1989. These superseded reliefs are described briefly at **30.9** and **30.12** below for their possible ongoing effect on acquisition costs.

Relief for gifts of business assets

[30.2] The hold-over relief described below applies where:

(a) an individual ('*the transferor*') makes a disposal not at arm's length (e.g. a gift) of an asset specified below, and
(b) a joint claim for relief is made by the transferor and the transferee, or, where the transferee is a trustee of a settlement, by the transferor alone.

[*TCGA 1992, s 165(1)*].

The relief is sometimes referred to as gift relief or business asset gift relief.

Note that the transferee need not be an individual and may, for example, be a company. See also **30.5** below regarding agricultural property and **30.6** below regarding settled property. The relief extends to direct and indirect disposals of UK land by or to a non-UK resident (see **30.4** below).

An asset is within (a) above if:

(i) it is, or is an interest in, an asset used for the purposes of a trade, profession or vocation carried on by the transferor, his 'personal company' or a member of a 'trading group' of which the 'holding company' is his personal company), or
(ii) it consists of shares or securities of a 'trading company', or of the holding company of a trading group, where *either* the shares etc. are not listed on a recognised stock exchange (within *ITA 2007, s 1005* — see **57.27** SHARES AND SECURITIES) *or* the trading company or holding company is the transferor's personal company.

[*TCGA 1992, s 165(2)*].

Hold-over relief does not apply on a disposal if:

- the disposal is a transfer of shares or securities and the transferee is a company;
- the gain arises by virtue of *TCGA 1992, s 116(10)(b)* (disposal of qualifying corporate bonds derived from shares giving rise to deferred gain, see **48.4** QUALIFYING CORPORATE BONDS); or
- hold-over relief is available (or would be if a claim were made) under *TCGA 1992, s 260* in **30.10** below for gifts on which inheritance tax is chargeable etc.

[*TCGA 1992, s 165(3)*].

See also the restriction and clawback provisions in 30.8 below.

Gifts of business assets — definitions

[30.3] For the purposes of 30.2 above, an individual's '*personal company*' is a company the voting rights in which are 'exercisable', as to not less than 5%, by that individual. ('*Exercisable*' means capable of being exercised, whether or not in fact exercised (*Hepworth v Smith* Ch D 1981, 54 TC 396).)

'*Trading group*', '*holding company*' and '*trading company*' have the following meanings. For the purposes of the definitions, the activities of group members are regarded as a single business, so that intra-group activities are disregarded.

A '*trading group*' is a 'group of companies' (see below), one or more of whose members carry on 'trading activities' and the activities of whose members, taken together, do not include to a 'substantial' extent activities other than trading activities. '*Trading activities*' means activities carried on by a member of the group, being activities that would fall within (A)–(D) below if these are interpreted by reference not only to that member but also to any other member of the group. A group member acquires a '*significant interest*' (see (D) below) if it acquires sufficient ordinary share capital in the other company to make that company a member of the same group as the acquiring company, or to give the acquiring company a qualifying shareholding in a 'joint venture company'. In determining whether a group of companies is a trading group, there is disregarded any 'qualifying shareholding' held by any member of the group in a 'joint venture company'. Each such member is regarded as carrying on a share of the joint venture company's activities (or, if the joint venture company is itself a holding company of a trading group, a share of that group's activities) proportionate to its percentage shareholding in that company. This does not apply if the joint venture company is itself a member of the group.

The views expressed in HMRC's Capital Gains Manual on the meaning of 'trading company' (see below) are also of relevance to 'trading groups', but intra-group activities are disregarded in applying the various tests.

A '*group of companies*' means a company and its '51% subsidiary(ies)' (within *CTA 2010, Pt 24 Ch 3*).

A '*holding company*' is a company with one or more 51% subsidiaries.

A '*trading company*' is a company carrying on 'trading activities' whose activities do not include to a 'substantial' extent activities other than trading activities. '*Trading activities*' means 'activities' carried on by the company:

(A) in the course of, or for the purposes of, a 'trade' being carried on by it; or
(B) for the purposes of a trade that it is preparing to carry on; or
(C) with a view to its acquiring or starting to carry on a trade; or
(D) with a view to its acquiring a 'significant interest' in the share capital of another company that is itself a trading company or the holding company of a trading group and that is not already a member of the same group as the acquiring company (where applicable).

Activities qualify under (C) or (D) above only if the acquisition is made, or the trade commenced, as soon as reasonably practicable in the circumstances. A company acquires a '*significant interest*' (see (D) above) if it acquires sufficient ordinary share capital in the other company to make that company its 51% subsidiary (within *CTA 2010, Pt 24 Ch 3*), or to give the acquiring company a qualifying shareholding in a joint venture company without making the two companies members of the same group. For further interpretation of (A)–(D) above, see HMRC Capital Gains Manual CG64060–64075.

In determining whether a company with a qualifying shareholding in a joint venture company is a trading company, any holding of shares by it in the joint venture company is disregarded. It is regarded as carrying on a share of the joint venture company's activities proportionate to its percentage shareholding in that company.

For the purposes of the above definitions (but not for the general purposes of the above relief — see below) '*trade*' means a trade, profession or vocation, as understood for income tax purposes, which is conducted on a commercial basis with a view to realisation of profits. Before April 2025, the expression also expressly includes the commercial letting of FURNISHED HOLIDAY ACCOMMODATION (**24**), but other letting of furnished property is excluded (*Patel v Maidment* Sp C 2003, [2004] SSCD 41, Sp C 384). The special treatment for furnished holiday accommodation is to be abolished with effect from April 2025 (and an anti-forestalling rule to prevent the use of unconditional contracts to access beneficial capital gains tax treatment will apply retrospectively from 6 March 2024). See **24.1** FURNISHED HOLIDAY ACCOMMODATION.

A '*joint venture company*' is a company:

(I) which is a trading company or the holding company of a trading group, *and*

(II) at least 75% in aggregate of the ordinary share capital (within *ITA 2007, s 989*) of which is held by no more than five persons (counting shares held by different members of a group of companies as held by a single company).

A company has a '*qualifying shareholding*' in a joint venture company if:

- it holds 10% or more of the ordinary share capital of the joint venture company, *or*
- (where the company is a member of a group of companies) the company and the other members of the group between them hold 10% or more of that ordinary share capital.

In interpreting whether a company's activities include non-trading activities to a substantial extent, HMRC consider that it is necessary to identify the trading and non-trading activities and then consider how best to measure the non-trading activities to see whether they are substantial in the context of the company's activities as a whole. There is no simple formula but some, or all, of the following are among the measures or indicators that might be taken into account by HMRC in reviewing a particular company's status:

- income from non-trading activities;
- the asset base of the company;
- expenses incurred, or time spent, by officers and employees of the company in undertaking its activities;
- the company's history.

These are factors, or indicators, that may be useful in establishing whether there is substantial overall non-trading activity. It may be that some indicators point in one direction and others the opposite way. HMRC instruct officers to weigh up the relevance of each in the context of the individual case and judge the matter in the round. Where neither the level of non-trading income nor the asset base of the company suggests that the non-trading element exceeds 20%, HMRC are unlikely to undertake a more detailed review.

(HMRC Capital Gains Manual CG64090).

In a business asset disposal relief case, *Allam v HMRC* UT 2021, [2022] STC 37, the Upper Tribunal agreed with the FTT that it was inappropriate to apply any numerical threshold in deciding whether there were 'substantial' non-trading activities. It was necessary instead to look at the nature of activities and to measure in some way the extent of those activities in the context of the company's activities as a whole. It also rejected the taxpayer's argument that 'activities' were restricted to actual human activities; what the directors and employees actually did. Since the holding of investment property and collecting rent involved little if any such activity, he argued that they should not be considered substantial non-trading activities. The UT held that 'activities' meant what the company did in commercial terms, so that the holding of investments was an activity. As a result, entrepreneurs' relief was not available.

'*Trade*', '*profession*' and '*vocation*' generally have the same meanings as in the *Income Tax Acts* but any UK property business which consists of, or so far as it consist of, the commercial letting of FURNISHED HOLIDAY ACCOMMODATION (24) in the UK is treated as a trade for relief purposes. Similarly, any overseas property business which consists of, or so far as it consists of, the commercial letting of such accommodation in one or more EEA states is treated as a trade. In determining whether for these purposes a company is a trading company, a '*trade*' includes the occupation of woodlands managed on a commercial basis by the occupier with a view to profit.

The special treatment for furnished holiday accommodation is to be abolished with effect from April 2025 (and an anti-forestalling rule to prevent the use of unconditional contracts to access beneficial capital gains tax treatment will apply retrospectively from 6 March 2024). See **24.1** FURNISHED HOLIDAY ACCOMMODATION.

[*TCGA 1992, ss 165(8)(9), 165A, 241(3)(3A), 241A(4)(5)*].

Nature of relief

[30.4] Where there is no actual consideration for the disposal (as opposed to a deemed MARKET VALUE (**39.1**) consideration under *TCGA 1992, s 17(1)*), or where an actual consideration does not exceed the allowable expenditure within *TCGA 1992, s 38* (see **16.12** COMPUTATION OF GAINS AND LOSSES) relating to the asset, the effect of a claim is that the gain otherwise chargeable on the transferor and the transferee's acquisition cost are each reduced by the 'held-over gain'.

The 'held-over gain' for this purpose is the gain otherwise chargeable (termed the '*unrelieved gain*') but subject to the reductions described below. Where actual consideration exceeds the allowable expenditure, the held-over gain is the unrelieved gain less that excess (see the *example* at **30.7** below) but again subject to the reductions below.

Where the disposal is a direct or indirect disposal of an interest in UK land to which the provisions at **35.23** or **35.24** LAND apply, (or, for disposals before 6 April 2019, a non-resident CGT disposal; see **35.31** LAND) to a UK-resident transferee, the 'held-over gain' is so much of the gain (for disposals before 6 April 2019, the NRCGT gain) that would otherwise be chargeable.

[*TCGA 1992, s 165(4)(6)(7)–(7D)*].

Where hold-over relief applies to a disposal the transferee may deduct for capital gains tax purposes on a subsequent disposal made by him any inheritance tax attributable to the value of the asset on the transfer to him which qualified for relief and which is either a chargeable transfer or a potentially exempt transfer which proves to be a chargeable transfer. The tax deductible may be varied on the subsequent death of the transferor within seven years or otherwise but it cannot in any circumstances give rise to an allowable loss on the subsequent disposal. [*TCGA 1992, s 165(10)(11)*]. See also **33.2** INTERACTION WITH OTHER TAXES.

Claims

Hold-over relief claims must be made on a standard claim form (which can be found attached to HMRC Helpsheet HS 295). As they are usually bilateral claims, they cannot be made in the self-assessment tax return itself and will fall within the provisions of *TMA 1970, Sch 1A* (claims not included in returns — see **13.3** CLAIMS). A unilateral claim by a settlor will usually form part of his tax return. (Revenue Tax Bulletin April 1997 pp 417, 418).

Due to measures put in place to stop the spread of coronavirus (COVID-19) in 2020, HMRC will allow the form to be completed using a digital signature rather than being physically signed by both transferor and transferee, until further notice (HMRC Capital Gains Manual CG66889).

In most circumstances, HMRC will admit a hold-over relief claim without requiring a computation of the gain, which would involve ascertaining the market value of the asset at the date of the transfer. Transferor and transferee must jointly request this in the standard claim form and must provide, in particular, a calculation incorporating informally estimated valuations and a statement that the claimants are satisfied that the value of the asset exceeds the allowable expenditure (plus any indexation allowance due). Once accepted by HMRC, a claim made on this basis cannot be withdrawn. In many cases, a formal valuation will never become necessary; in others, valuation may still be deferred until a subsequent disposal of the asset by the transferee. This practice applies equally to valuations on dates other than the date of transfer, where these are relevant to the computation of the gain. Where the asset was held by the transferor on 31 March 1982, then unless the transferee has paid *some* consideration, it will normally be necessary to agree a 31 March 1982 valuation only when the transferee disposes of the asset. (HMRC Statement of Practice SP 8/92).

Reductions in the held-over gain

If the qualifying asset disposed of was not used for the purposes of the trade, profession or vocation concerned throughout the period of its ownership by the transferor, the held-over gain is reduced by multiplying it by the fraction of which the denominator is the total period of ownership and the numerator the number of days in the period during which the asset was so used. (*Note.* In the determination of the period of ownership there is no exclusion of any period before 31 March 1982 as there is at **53.8** ROLLOVER RELIEF.) Where the qualifying asset disposed of is a building or structure part only of which has been used for the trade etc. concerned over all or a 'substantial' part of the period of its ownership, the held-over gain is reduced as is 'just and reasonable'. [*TCGA 1992, Sch 7 paras 4, 5(1), 6(1)*].

If the disposal of shares or securities of a company qualifies for relief and the company or group (as appropriate) then has 'chargeable assets' which are not 'business assets' and *either* at any time in the twelve months before the disposal the transferor could exercise 25% or more of the company's voting rights (as exercisable in general meeting) *or* the company is the personal company (see above) of an individual transferor at any time within that period of twelve months, the held-over gain is reduced by multiplying it by the fraction of which the denominator is the then market value of all of the company's or group's chargeable assets and the numerator is the then market value of the company's or group's chargeable business assets. In considering a group, a holding in the ordinary share capital of one group member by another is ignored, and if a 51% subsidiary is not wholly owned directly or indirectly by the holding company the values of its chargeable and business assets are reduced in proportion to the share capital owned; and for both purposes the expressions used are as in *ICTA 1988, s 838*. An asset is a '*business asset*' if it is or is an interest in an asset used for the purposes of a trade etc. carried on by the company or another group member, and an asset is a '*chargeable asset*' if a gain accruing on its disposal by the company or another group member would be a chargeable gain. [*TCGA 1992, Sch 7 paras 4, 7*].

Gifts of direct or indirect interests in UK land to non-residents

A disposal on or after 6 April 2019 of an asset within *TCGA 1992, s 1A(3)(b)* or *(c)* (direct or indirect interest in UK land — see **35.23** or **35.24** LAND) to a transferee who is not resident in the UK qualifies for relief (if the remaining conditions are met). Relief is available to both UK-resident and non-resident transferors. For disposals on or after 6 April 2015 and before 6 April 2019, this rule applied to disposals of a UK residential property interest (see **35.31** LAND). The full amount of the gain that would otherwise have been chargeable may be held over and no chargeable gain arises at the time of the disposal, although the amount of the gain that would have been chargeable but for the relief is not in this case deducted from the transferee's base cost. Instead, on a subsequent disposal by the transferee the whole or corresponding part of the held over gain is deemed to accrue at that time, in addition to any gain that actually accrues.

Relief for any inheritance tax payable on a disposal for which holdover relief has been claimed may be obtained by the transferee when he subsequently disposes of the asset. The actual chargeable gain accruing to the transferee on the disposal of the asset (and not the held over gain deemed to accrue at that time) is reduced by an amount equal to the lesser of the inheritance tax attributable to the value of the asset and the amount of the chargeable gain including the held-over gain.

[*TCGA 1992, s 167A*].

See HMRC Capital Gains Manual CG66886, 73986.

Agricultural property

[30.5] If an asset, or an interest in an asset:

(a) is 'agricultural property' within the inheritance tax provisions of *IHTA 1984, Pt V Ch II* and *either* qualifies for an inheritance tax reduction in value in relation to a chargeable transfer made simultaneously with the disposal *or* would so qualify if there were a chargeable transfer on the disposal *or* would so qualify but for *IHTA 1984, s 124A* (additional conditions for transfers within seven years before death of transferor) (assuming, where there is no chargeable transfer, that there were); but

(b) it fails to qualify for hold-over relief solely because the agricultural property is not used for the purposes of a trade etc. carried on as in **30.2**(i) above,

then, notwithstanding (b) above, hold-over relief is granted to the individual transferor. Hold-over relief is also granted to trustees (see under settled property below) where the agricultural property would not otherwise qualify for relief solely because it is not used for the purposes of a trade etc. carried on as in **30.6**(i) below. In these circumstances *TCGA 1992, Sch 7 para 4, para 5(1), para 6(1)* in **30.2** above do not apply. [*TCGA 1992, s 165(5), Sch 7 paras 1, 3, 5(2), 6(2)*]. Where development value over and above the agricultural value of the land is inherent in the property transferred, HMRC have in the past indicated that hold-over relief is available in respect of the whole of the gain, i.e. not just that part which reflects the land's agricultural value (Revenue Tax Bulletin November 1991 p 5).

Settled property

[30.6] If:

(a) trustees of a settlement make a non-arm's length disposal of an asset specified below, and

(b) a claim for relief under *TCGA 1992, s 165* is made by the trustees and the transferee or, if trustees are also the transferee, by the trustees making the disposal alone,

then, subject to *TCGA 1992, s 165(3)* (see **30.2** above) and the provisions in **30.8** below, hold-over relief given by *TCGA 1992, s 165(4)* (see **30.2** above) applies to the disposal.

An asset is within (a) above if:

(i) it is, or is an interest in, an asset used for the purposes of a trade, profession or vocation carried on by the trustees making the disposal or a beneficiary who had an interest in possession in the settled property immediately before the disposal; or

(ii) it consists of shares or securities of a trading company, or of the holding company of a trading group, where *either* the shares etc. are neither listed on a recognised stock exchange (see **57.27** SHARES AND SECURITIES) *or* not less than 25% of the voting rights as exercisable in general meeting are held by the trustees at the time of disposal.

Where hold-over relief is granted to trustees in this way, references to the trustees are substituted for references to the transferor in *TCGA 1992, s 165(4)(a)* above; and where hold-over relief is granted on a disposal deemed to occur by virtue of *TCGA 1992, s 71(1)* or *s 72(1)* (see **56.16–56.18** SETTLEMENTS and **30.8** below), no reduction in the held-over gain is made under *TCGA 1992, s 165(7)* in **30.2** above (reduction by excess of actual consideration over allowable expenditure). [*TCGA 1992, s 165(5), Sch 7 para* 2]. See also **30.5** above re agricultural property.

Example — partial consideration

[30.7]

Zoë owns a freehold property which she lets to the family trading company, Sphere Ltd, in which she and her father each own half the shares and voting rights. Zoë inherited the property in April 2001 at a probate value of £50,000, and since then, the whole of the property has been used for the purposes of the company's trade. In November 2024, Zoë transfers the property to her boyfriend. Its market value at that time is £115,000. The intention is that he should give sufficient consideration to leave Zoë with a chargeable gain exactly equal to the annual exempt amount (there being no other disposals in 2024/25).

Actual consideration should be £53,000 as shown by the following computation:

	£
Deemed consideration	115,000
Deduct: Cost	50,000
Unrelieved gain	65,000
Held-over gain (see below)	62,000
Chargeable gain covered by annual exempt amount	£3,000

Computation of held-over gain

	£	£
Unrelieved gain		65,000
Actual consideration	53,000	
Less allowable expenditure	50,000	3,000
Held-over gain		£62,000

Note to the example

(a) On a subsequent disposal of the property, the allowable expenditure would be £53,000 (deemed proceeds of £115,000 less held-over gain of 62,000).

Restrictions on, and clawback of, relief

[30.8] Hold-over relief under *TCGA 1992, s 165, Sch 7* is restricted or clawed back in the following circumstances.

Gifts to non-residents

Except where *TCGA 1992, s 167A* applies (see **30.4** above), relief cannot be claimed where the transferee is not resident in the UK. It also cannot be claimed where the transferee is an individual or company which, though resident in the UK, is regarded as resident elsewhere by virtue of DOUBLE TAX RELIEF (**20.2**) arrangements such that it would not under those arrangements be taxable in the UK on a gain arising on a disposal of the asset immediately after its acquisition. [*TCGA 1992, s 166*].

Gifts to foreign-controlled companies

Except where *TCGA 1992, s 167A* applies (see **30.4** above), relief under *TCGA 1992, s 165(4)* is also denied where the transferee is a company which is:

(1) controlled by a person who, or by persons each of whom, is not UK-resident and is connected (see **17** CONNECTED PERSONS) with the person making the disposal; or
(2) for disposals on or after 6 April 2021, controlled by the person or persons making the disposal where each of those persons is not UK-resident.

In determining a person's residence status for this purpose, a person who either alone or with others controls a company by virtue of holding assets relating to that or any other company and who is UK-resident is regarded as not UK-resident if he is regarded under a double tax agreement as resident overseas in circumstances in which he would not be liable to a UK tax charge on a gain arising on a disposal of the assets.

[*TCGA 1992, s 167; FA 2021, s 41*].

See *Foulser and another v MacDougall* CA, [2007] STC 973, in which a complex avoidance scheme failed because of the application of this provision. In the Ch D, the taxpayers' contention that the application of *section 167* to their case was incompatible with the EC Treaty was rejected and this decision was upheld by the CA.

The rule in (2) above in effect overrules the decision in *Reeves v HMRC* UT, [2018] STC 2056, in which the Upper Tribunal held that *s 167* did not apply where the taxpayer, who was non-UK resident, transferred a UK business to a new UK incorporated and resident company of which he was the sole shareholder. The Tribunal overturned the decision of the First-tier Tribunal that, because the taxpayer's wife was also not resident in the UK and as an associate of the taxpayer could be deemed to control the transferee company, so that (1) above applied. The Upper Tribunal concluded that it could not have been Parliament's intention that holdover relief should be withheld merely because there is someone connected to the transferor who is non-resident even if they have no interest in the transferee company. The attribution of interests between associates for the purpose of determining control of the transferee company should therefore be limited to connected persons holding assets relating to the company.

Gifts into dual resident trusts

Hold-over relief under *TCGA 1992, s 165* is not available where the transferees are trustees who are resident in the UK where, on a notional disposal of the asset by the trustees immediately after the disposal of it to them, the trustees would be regarded for double tax relief arrangements as resident overseas and as not liable to UK tax arising on the notional disposal. [*TCGA 1992, s 169*].

Emigration of transferee

Subject to the exceptions mentioned below, a gain held over under *TCGA 1992, s 165* (at a time when the transferee was a UK resident individual) will be clawed back if the individual transferee concerned ceases to be UK-resident. The clawback may be made within six years after the end of the tax year in which the disposal for which hold-over relief was claimed was made; otherwise (e.g. where trustees are the transferee) no time limit is specified. The charge, which is on a gain deemed to have accrued just prior to the cessation of UK residence, is reduced to the extent that the held-over gain has already been taken into account in a disposal by the transferee (e.g. on a part disposal). For the latter purpose, a disposal does not include a no gain/no loss disposal between married persons or civil partners (see **40.4** MARRIED PERSONS AND CIVIL PARTNERS) under *TCGA 1992, s 58*. If such a transfer occurs, a disposal by the acquiring spouse or civil partner is treated as made by the spouse or partner who originally acquired the asset to which the held-over gain related. If not paid within twelve months from the due date of payment, tax on the deemed gain assessed on the transferee can be assessed on the transferor within six years after the end of the tax year in which the disposal for which hold-over relief was claimed was made, although the transferor then has the right to recover any tax so paid from the transferee.

Where a deemed gain relating to a previously held-over gain has been assessed under the above, then on a subsequent disposal of the asset in question the allowable expenditure relating to it is not reduced by the held-over gain.

An exception to the above clawback applies where the disposal for which relief was claimed was made to an individual, and

(a) the reason for his becoming not resident in the UK is that he works in an employment or office, all of the duties of which are performed abroad, and
(b) he again becomes UK-resident within three years of ceasing to be so, and
(c) in the meantime, the asset which is the subject of the hold-over relief has not been subject to a disposal by him in connection with which the allowable expenditure attaching to the asset, if the individual had been UK-resident, would have been reduced by the held-over gain; for this purpose the same provisions as above for inter-spouse transfers apply.

Where (a) applies, and (b) and (c) *may* apply, no assessment under the main provisions outlined above will be made before the end of the three-year period.

A second exception is that, if the transferee so elects, a held-over gain does not accrue on the deemed disposal if the deemed disposal is of an interest in UK land (within **35.23** LAND). Where the deemed disposal is before 6 April 2019, this rule applies if the gain or loss on the deemed disposal would have been an NRCGT gain or loss on the assumption that the disposal was a non-resident CGT disposal (see **35.31** LAND). In either case, the gain or loss that would have accrued on the deemed disposal is treated as accruing at the time of any subsequent disposal of the interest, in addition to any gain or loss which actually accrues.

[*TCGA 1992, ss 168, 168A*].

Clawback of relief on life tenant's death

The exemption otherwise available for gains arising on deemed disposals under *TCGA 1992, s 71(1)* or *s 72(1)(a)* on the death of a life tenant etc. (see **56.16–56.18** SETTLEMENTS) does not apply to an asset (or part asset) where a claim for hold-over relief was made under *TCGA 1992, s 165* in relation to an original disposal of that asset to the trustees. Any chargeable gain accruing to the trustees will, however, be restricted to the held-over gain (or corresponding part) on the original disposal of the asset. Where the life tenant's interest was in part only of the settled property, and that property is subject to a deemed disposal under *TCGA 1992, s 71(1)*, the clawback is proportional to the life tenant's interest. [*TCGA 1992, s 74*]. If the termination of the life interest is a chargeable transfer for inheritance tax purposes, hold-over relief can be claimed under **30.10** below (HMRC Capital Gains Manual CG33550).

Limited liability partnerships (LLPs)

Where, when the transparency treatment afforded by *TCGA 1992, s 59A(1)* ceases to apply to an LLP (see **44.17** PARTNERSHIPS) (for example, by virtue of its going into liquidation), a member of the LLP holds an asset whose CGT acquisition cost is reduced by a gain held over under *TCGA 1992, s 165* on a disposal to a partnership, a chargeable gain equal to the amount of the reduction is treated as accruing to the member immediately before that time. [*TCGA 1992, s 169A*]. In the absence of such a rule, the held-over gain would have fallen out of charge as a result of the tax treatment of an LLP in liquidation.

Interaction with substantial shareholding exemption for companies

Where a company disposes of an asset whose CGT acquisition cost is reduced by a gain previously held over under *TCGA 1992, s 165*, and, by virtue of the provisions of *TCGA 1992, Sch 7AC*, any gain on the disposal would otherwise be exempt, the held-over gain, or an appropriate proportion of it, is treated as accruing to the company at that time (see **60.19** SUBSTANTIAL SHAREHOLDING EXEMPTION).

Gifts to settlor-interested settlements

Hold-over relief under *TCGA 1992, s 165* is not available in the case of a disposal (the '*relevant disposal*') to the trustees of a settlement if either:

(a) there is a 'settlor' who has an 'interest in the settlement' (or an 'arrangement' subsists under which such an interest will or may be acquired by a settlor) immediately after the making of the relevant disposal or at any time in the 'clawback period', or

(b) the following conditions are met:
   – disregarding any hold-over relief, a chargeable gain would accrue to the transferor on the relevant disposal,
   – in computing that gain, the allowable expenditure would be reduced in consequence, directly or indirectly, of a claim under *TCGA 1992, s 165* or *TCGA 1992, s 260* (see **30.10** below) in respect of an earlier disposal by an individual (whether or not to the transferor), and
   – that individual has an interest in the settlement (or an arrangement subsists under which such an interest will or may be acquired by him) immediately after the making of the relevant disposal or at any time in the 'clawback period'.

Where neither of the above conditions are met immediately after the relevant disposal and relief under *s 165* is claimed (and the claim is not revoked), if either of the conditions are subsequently met at a time during the clawback period, then a chargeable gain is treated as accruing to the transferor at the first such time (the '*material time*') of an amount equal to the held-over gain under *s 165*. This does not apply if the transferor is an individual who has died before the material time. Where the relief is clawed back in this way, the chargeable gains and allowable losses of the trustees or of any person whose title to any property derives to any extent from them (whether directly or indirectly) are determined on the basis that *s 165* never applied to the relevant disposal. Any necessary adjustments can be made to give effect to these provisions, whether by assessment, discharge or repayment of tax or otherwise, notwithstanding any time limits for the making of such adjustments.

Definitions

For these purposes, a person is a '*settlor*' in relation to a settlement if he is an individual and the settled property consists of or includes property originating from him. Property originates from a settlor where he provides it directly or indirectly for the purposes of the settlement (including property provided by another person under reciprocal 'arrangements') and where property represents such property (or a part thereof) or accumulated income from such property. '*Arrangements*' include any scheme, agreement or understanding, whether or not legally enforceable.

A settlor has an '*interest in a settlement*' if:

(i) any property which may at any time be comprised in the settlement or any 'derived property' is, or will or may become, payable to or applicable for the benefit of the settlor or his spouse or civil partner in any circumstances whatsoever, or

(ii) the settlor, or his spouse or civil partner, enjoys a benefit deriving directly or indirectly from any property which is comprised in the settlement or any derived property.

A settlor also has an interest in a settlement if:

(iii) any property which is or may at any time be comprised in the settlement or any derived property is, or will or may become, payable to or applicable for the benefit of a child of the settlor at any time when that child is a 'dependent child' of his, in any circumstances whatsoever, or

(iv) a dependent child of the settlor enjoys a benefit deriving directly or indirectly from any property which is comprised in the settlement or any derived property.

A '*dependent child*' of the settlor is, for this purpose, a child or stepchild under the age of 18 who is unmarried and does not have a civil partner.

References to the spouse or civil partner of the settlor in (i) and (ii) above do not include a spouse or civil partner from whom the settlor is separated under a court order, separation agreement or in circumstances such that the separation is likely to be permanent, or the widow, widower or surviving civil partner of the settlor. No account is taken of a term of the settlement relating to dependent children of the settlor at any time when he has no such children.

A settlor does not have an interest under (i) above if and so long as none of the property which may at any time be comprised in the settlement and no derived property can become applicable or payable as mentioned in (i) above except in the event of:

- in the case of a marriage settlement or civil partnership settlement, the death of both the parties to the marriage or partnership and all or any of the children of one or both of the parities to the marriage or partnership; or
- the death of a child of the settlor who had become beneficially entitled to the property or any derived property at an age not exceeding 25.

For these purposes, '*derived property*' in relation to any property means income from that property or any property directly or indirectly representing proceeds of, or proceeds of income from, that property or income therefrom.

Exclusions

The above provisions do not apply to a disposal to trustees of a heritage maintenance settlement if they have elected or, could have elected under *ITA 2007, s 508* that income arising under the settlement or part of the settlement involved is not to be treated as income of the settlor for the tax year in which the disposal is made.

The above provisions also do not apply if, immediately after the making of the relevant disposal:

(A) the settled property is held on trusts which secure that, during the lifetime of a 'disabled person';
   - if any of the property is applied for the benefit of a beneficiary it is applied for the benefit of the disabled person; and
   - either the disabled person is entitled to all the income (if any) arising from any of the property or that if any such income is applied for the benefit of a beneficiary, it is applied for the benefit of the disabled person.

(B) if one or more settlors has an interest in the settlement (disregarding any interest arising because of a spouse, civil partner or dependent child) or will or may acquire such an interest under subsisting arrangements, each such settlor is a disabled person and a beneficiary (or would be a beneficiary if he had the interest acquirable under the arrangements).

If the property is held on trusts of the kind described in *Trustee Act 1925, s 33* (protective trusts), the reference above to 'the lifetime of the disabled person' is to be interpreted as the period during which the property is held on trust for him.

'*Disabled person*' means either a person who by reason of mental disorder is incapable of administering his property or managing his affairs or a person in receipt of any one or more specified State benefits. A person is treated as being a disabled person for these purposes if he satisfies HMRC that he would be entitled to receive the State benefit in question were it not for his being resident outside the UK or in a care home, hospital or prison.

Condition (A) above is not treated as not met by reason only of:

(I) the trustees' having powers that enable them to apply in any tax year otherwise than for the benefit of the disabled person amounts (whether consisting of income or capital or both) not exceeding the 'annual limit'; or

(II) the trustees' having the powers conferred by *Trustee Act 1925, s 32* (powers of advancement) (or its NI equivalent); or

(III) the trustees' having those powers but free from, or subject to a less restrictive limitation than, the limitation imposed by *Trustee Act 1925, s 32(1)(a)* (or its NI equivalent); or

(IV) the trustees' having powers to the like effect as the powers mentioned in (II) or (III).

The '*annual limit*' in (I) above is £3,000 or, if lower, 3% of the maximum value of the settled property during the tax year in question.

[*TCGA 1992, ss 169B–169G*].

Miscellaneous

See also **25.4** GIFTS for the recovery by the trustees from the transferor of tax paid in respect of the deemed chargeable gain arising under the clawback provisions above and **45.5** PAYMENT OF TAX for payment of tax on such a gain by instalments.

Relief for gifts of business assets before 14 March 1989

[30.9] Hold-over relief was available where an individual ('*the transferor*') made a disposal before 14 March 1989 not at arm's length (e.g. a gift) to a person resident or ordinarily resident in the UK ('*the transferee*') of:

(a) an asset which was, or was an interest in, an asset which was used for the purposes of a trade, profession or vocation carried on by the transferor or by a company which was his 'family company' (as defined), or

(b) shares or securities of a 'trading company' (as defined) which was the transferor's family company.

The relief operated, as with other hold-over reliefs, by reducing the gain otherwise chargeable on the transferor and the transferee's acquisition cost by the held-over gain. Hold-over relief could also be claimed in certain circumstances where a trustee was deemed under *TCGA 1992, s 71(1)* (see **56.16** and **56.18** SETTLEMENTS) to have disposed of, and immediately reacquired, a business asset.

As a result of the availability of the general relief for gifts in **30.12** below, the rules relating specifically to gifts of business assets were of restricted application for gifts after 5 April 1980 and before 14 March 1989. None of the provisions in **30.8** above applied to the hold-over relief described above.

[*CGTA 1979, s 126, Sch 4*].

Gifts on which inheritance tax is chargeable etc.

[30.10] The hold-over relief described below is, subject to conditions, available if:

(a) an individual or trustees ('the transferor') make a disposal within (i)–(vii) below of an asset;
(b) the asset is acquired by an individual or trustees ('the transferee'); and
(c) a claim for relief is made by the transferor and transferee or, where trustees are the transferee, by the transferor alone.

[*TCGA 1992, s 260(1)*].

A disposal is within (a) above if it is made otherwise than under a bargain at arm's length (e.g. a gift) and it:

(i) is a chargeable transfer within *IHTA 1984* (or would be but for annual exemptions under *IHTA 1984, s 19*) and is not a potentially exempt transfer within the meaning of *IHTA 1984*; or
(ii) is an exempt transfer by virtue of *IHTA 1984, s 24, s 27* or *s 30* (political parties, maintenance funds for historic buildings and designated property); or
(iii) is a disposition to which *IHTA 1984, s 57A* applies and by which the property disposed of becomes held on trusts referred to in *IHTA 1984, s 57A(1)(b)* (maintenance funds for historic buildings); or
(iv) by virtue of *IHTA 1984, s 71(4)* (accumulation and maintenance trusts where property settled before 22 March 2006) does not constitute an occasion on which tax is chargeable under that provision; or
(v) by virtue of *IHTA 1984, s 71B(2)* (trusts for bereaved minors) does not constitute an occasion on which tax is chargeable under that provision; or
(vi) by virtue of *IHTA 1984, s 71E(2)* (age 18 to 25 trusts) does not constitute an occasion on which tax is chargeable under that provision; or
(vii) by virtue of *IHTA 1984, s 78(1)* (works of art etc., see also **23.39** and **23.79** EXEMPTIONS AND RELIEFS) does not constitute an occasion on which tax is chargeable under *IHTA 1984, Pt III Ch III*; or

(viii) is a disposal of an asset comprised in a settlement where, as a result of the asset or part of it becoming comprised in another settlement, there is no charge, or a reduced charge, to inheritance tax by virtue of *IHTA 1984, Sch 4 para 9, para 16* or *para 17* (maintenance funds for historic buildings).

[*TCGA 1992, s 260(2)*].

The '*held-over gain*' on a disposal is the chargeable gain otherwise accruing and relief is given by deducting this amount from the gain otherwise accruing to the transferor and from the consideration otherwise regarded as being given by the transferee. [*TCGA 1992, s 260(3)(4)*].

Hold-over relief is reduced or eliminated to nil on a disposal where there is actual consideration (as opposed to any deemed MARKET VALUE (**39**) consideration) which exceeds the allowable expenditure under *TCGA 1992, s 38* (see **16.12** COMPUTATION OF GAINS AND LOSSES). Any such excess is deducted from the held-over gain, but no deduction is made of any such excess where *TCGA 1992, s 260(3)* above applies to a deemed disposal under *TCGA 1992, s 71(1)* or *s 72(1)* (see **56.16–56.18** SETTLEMENTS). [*TCGA 1992, s 260(5)*].

Where the disposal is a direct or indirect disposal of an interest in UK land to which the provisions at **35.23** or **35.24** LAND apply (or, for disposals before 6 April 2019, a non-resident CGT disposal; see **35.31** LAND) to a UK-resident transferee, the 'held-over gain' is so much of the gain (for disposals before 6 April 2019, the NRCGT gain) that would otherwise be chargeable. [*TCGA 1992, s 260(6ZA)–(6ZD)*].

Hold-over relief does not apply to a disposal if it arises by virtue of *TCGA 1992, s 116(10)(b)* (disposal of qualifying corporate bonds derived from shares giving rise to deferred gain, see **48.4** QUALIFYING CORPORATE BONDS). [*TCGA 1992, s 260(6)*].

Where hold-over relief is claimed, or could have been claimed, on a transfer within (i) above, the transferee may deduct for capital gains tax purposes on a subsequent disposal made by him any inheritance tax attributable to the value of the asset on the transfer to him which qualified for hold-over relief. The tax deductible may be varied if the inheritance tax itself is varied but it cannot in any circumstances give rise to an allowable loss. [*TCGA 1992, s 260(7)(8)*]. See also **33.2** INTERACTION WITH OTHER TAXES.

Where a disposal is only partly within (i)–(vii) above, or is a disposal within (viii) above on which there is a reduced charge to inheritance tax, the foregoing provisions apply to an appropriate part of the disposal. [*TCGA 1992, s 260(10)*].

Partial claims are not permitted. Where, however, a single transaction involves the transfer of a number of separate assets (i.e. where a separate chargeable gain accrues on each asset), a claim is required for each asset and the parties are free to choose which assets are to be the subject of a claim. In such circumstances, some gains can be left in charge to be covered by annual exemptions or losses etc.

See **47.14** PRIVATE RESIDENCES for the exclusion from relief under *TCGA 1992, s 223* where relief is claimed under the above provisions.

Gifts of direct or indirect interests in UK land to non-residents

A disposal on or after 6 April 2019 of an asset within *TCGA 1992, s 1A(3)(b)* or *(c)* (direct or indirect interest in UK land — see **35.23** or **35.24** LAND) to a transferee who is not resident in the UK qualifies for relief. Relief is available to both UK-resident and non-resident transferors. For disposals on or after 6 April 2015 and before 6 April 2019, this rule applied to disposals of a UK residential property interest (see **35.31** LAND). The full amount of the gain that would otherwise have been chargeable may be held over and no chargeable gain arises at the time of the disposal, although the amount of the gain that would have been chargeable but for the relief is not in this case deducted from the transferee's base cost. Instead, on a subsequent disposal by the transferee the whole or corresponding part of the held over gain is deemed to accrue at that time, in addition to any gain that actually accrues.

Relief for any inheritance tax payable on a disposal for which holdover relief has been claimed may be obtained by the transferee when he subsequently disposes of the asset. The actual chargeable gain accruing to the transferee on the disposal of the asset (and not the held over gain deemed to accrue at that time) is reduced by an amount equal to the lesser of the inheritance tax attributable to the value of the asset and the amount of the chargeable gain including the held-over gain.

[*TCGA 1992, s 261ZA*].

Restrictions on, and clawback of, relief

[30.11] Hold-over relief under *TCGA 1992, s 260* is restricted or clawed back in the following circumstances.

Gifts to non-residents

Except where *TCGA 1992, s 261ZA* applies (see **30.10** above), relief is denied where the transferee is not UK-resident. Relief is also denied where the transferee is an individual who though UK-resident is regarded under a double tax agreement as resident overseas in circumstances where he would not be liable to a UK tax charge on a gain arising on a disposal of an asset immediately after its acquisition. [*TCGA 1992, s 261*].

Gifts into dual resident trusts

TCGA 1992, s 169 (see **30.8** above) operates, with appropriate modifications, for hold-over relief claimed under *TCGA 1992, s 260* in respect of gifts after 13 March 1989 as it does for hold-over relief under *TCGA 1992, s 165* in respect of gifts made after that date. [*TCGA 1992, s 169*].

Emigration of transferee

TCGA 1992, s 168 (see **30.8** above) operates, with appropriate modifications, for hold-over relief claimed under *TCGA 1992, s 260* as it does for hold-over relief under *TCGA 1992, s 165*. [*TCGA 1992, s 168*].

Clawback of relief on life tenant's death

TCGA 1992, s 74 (see **30.8** above) operates, with appropriate modifications, for hold-over relief claimed under *TCGA 1992, s 260* as it does for hold-over relief under *TCGA 1992, s 165*. [*TCGA 1992, s 74*].

Limited liability partnerships (LLPs)

Clawback under *TCGA 1992, s 169A* (see **30.8** above) applies in relation to hold-over relief under *TCGA 1992, s 260* as it does in relation to hold-over relief under *TCGA 1992, s 165*.

Gifts to settlor-interested settlements

TCGA 1992, ss 169B–169G (see **30.8** above) apply to hold-over relief under *TCGA 1992, s 260* as they apply to relief under *TCGA 1992, s 165*.

General relief for gifts from 1980 to 1989

[30.12] A general relief for gifts by individuals applied after 5 April 1980 and before 14 March 1989. It applied also for gifts by trustees after 5 April 1982.

The effect of the relief was that the gain otherwise chargeable (less any retirement relief), and the transferee's acquisition cost, were each reduced by the '*held-over gain*', i.e. the gain otherwise chargeable (less any retirement relief) less any excess of actual consideration over the aggregate of allowable expenditure within *TCGA 1992, s 38* and any retirement relief.

In computing any chargeable gain accruing on the subsequent disposal of the asset, the transferee may deduct any inheritance tax (or capital transfer tax) attributable to the value of the asset on the original transfer, being either a chargeable transfer or a potentially exempt transfer which proves to be a chargeable transfer. The tax deductible may be varied on the subsequent death of the original transferor or otherwise but cannot create an allowable loss on the subsequent disposal. See also **33.2** INTERACTION WITH OTHER TAXES.

Clawback of relief on life tenant's death

TCGA 1992, s 74 (see **30.8** above) operated (and continues to operate after 13 March 1989) *mutatis mutandis* for hold-over relief claimed under the above provisions where the original gift to the trustees was after 5 April 1981 and before 14 March 1989 as it does to hold-over relief under *TCGA 1992, s 165* in respect of gifts made after 13 March 1989. See **8.11** ASSETS HELD ON 31 MARCH **1982** for the treatment by HMRC of the clawback in relevant cases occurring after 5 April 1988.

[*TCGA 1992, ss 67, 74; CGTA 1979, s 56A; FA 1980, s 79*].

Key points on hold-over reliefs

[30.13] Points to consider are as follows.

- Hold-over relief under either *TCGA 1992, s 165* or *s 260* must be claimed on the form attached to the HMRC Helpsheet HS295. The time limit is four years after the end of the tax year in which the disposal took place.
- Gifts of business assets, such as the gift of a family company to the next generation, require careful planning. Where the family company is not a trading company then hold-over relief under *TCGA 1992, s 165* is unlikely to be available. The donor could consider a restructure of the company prior to the gift in order to meet the definition of a trading group and to qualify for hold-over relief.
- Where a donor is considering gifting agricultural property, he should determine whether holding on to such assets until they form part of the death estate is advantageous for tax purposes — agricultural property relief at 100% may be available on death, with a capital gains tax free uplift in base cost for the recipient.
- Transferors may wish to insure against a clawback of hold-over relief where they consider that this is a possibility. For example, gains held over may be clawed back where the transferee becomes non-resident in the UK within six years of the end of the year in which the disposal was made. Trustees who hold over gains on the distribution of capital to beneficiaries may wish to take reasonable precautions if they believe that a beneficiary may become non-resident within six years. Strictly the deemed gain is due for payment by the transferee (in this case, the beneficiary) but if the transferee cannot be located, the gain will be assessed on the transferor (the trustees). Depending on the circumstances, the trustees may wish to insure against such a claim.
- Hold-over relief under *TCGA 1992, s 260* is generally available where inheritance tax is immediately chargeable on a transfer. Before any gift is made, careful consideration of the effects of both taxes together is required. A client will be more interested in what a transaction will cost them in terms of tax, rather than which particular tax they are required to pay.
- Trustees of life interest settlements where there is an elderly or infirm life tenant should undertake sufficient planning where the trust holds assets upon which hold-over relief was claimed (either under *TCGA 1992, s 165* or *s 260*). This may include disposing of the assets over a number of tax years to utilise annual exempt amounts and avoid a clawback of the hold-over relief on the death of the life tenant. Keeping clear and accurate records is of utmost importance.
- Partially breaking the conditions for hold-over relief can enable a small gain to be realised that is covered by the annual exempt amount (hence low tax) whilst enabling a higher base cost to be carried forward. This can be particularly useful if the recipient of the asset is likely to make an onwards sale in the next few years. Hold over relief can be restricted where:
  - the consideration for the disposal exceeds the allowable cost;
  - the asset has not been used wholly for the purposes of the trade during the entire period of ownership;

   - the assets transferred are shares and the company's chargeable assets include non business assets.

  For example, a sole trader, Jack's only chargeable asset is goodwill worth £100,000 (nil base cost). If he sells the business to Chloe for £15,000 and claims hold-over relief, Jack will have a capital gain of £15,000 (less annual exempt amount) and Chloe will have a base cost of £15,000.

- Hold-over relief takes precedence over business asset disposal relief because it reduces the amount of the gain — if an entire gain is held-over, there is no relevant gain for business asset disposal relief purposes, but business asset disposal relief can be claimed on part of a gain that is not held over. If there is a risk that business asset disposal relief would not be available on a subsequent disposal, it may be better to claim that relief instead of hold-over relief and pay tax at 10% upfront.

31

Incorporation and Disincorporation Reliefs

Cross-references. See 30 HOLD-OVER RELIEFS; 53 ROLLOVER RELIEF.

Simon's Taxes. See B9.111–B9.116, B9.2.

Introduction to incorporation and disincorporation reliefs

[31.1] Incorporation relief is a form of rollover relief which applies where a person who is not a company transfers a business to a company as a going concern in exchange for shares issued by the company. The transfer must include the whole of the assets of the business (or the whole of those assets other than cash). The relief operates by reducing or eliminating the chargeable gain arising on the disposal and reducing the acquisition cost of the shares by a corresponding amount.

Where the conditions are satisfied, incorporation relief applies automatically without the need for a claim, but an election can be made to disapply it.

Disincorporation relief, now withdrawn, was also a form of rollover relief and could be claimed where certain small companies transferred their business to shareholders who were individuals before 1 April 2018. Goodwill and land and buildings used in the business were treated as transferred to the shareholders at a reduced value for chargeable gains purposes (and, in the case of goodwill, for the purposes of the intangible assets regime) so that no corporation tax was payable by the company on the transfer of the assets. Shareholders to whom the assets were transferred inherited the reduced transfer values for the purpose of capital gains tax and must use them for any subsequent disposals.

Transfer of business to a company — incorporation relief

[31.2] Where a person who is not a company transfers to a company a business as a going concern, together with the *whole* of the assets of the business (or together with the whole of those assets other than cash) ('the old assets') and the transfer is made wholly or partly in exchange for shares issued by the company to the transferor ('the new assets'), the chargeable gain on the disposal of the old assets is deferred. This is done by reducing the amount otherwise chargeable, by the fraction A/B, where 'A' is the 'cost of the new assets' and 'B' is the value of the overall consideration received by the transferor in exchange for the business. An election can be made to disapply this treatment (see **31.3** below).

'*The cost of the new assets*' means the total allowable expenditure under *TCGA 1992, s 38(1)(a)* if the new assets were disposed of as a whole in circumstances giving rise to a chargeable gain. (See **16.12** COMPUTATION OF GAINS AND LOSSES.)

The total expenditure otherwise allowable on the new assets is reduced by the amount of the chargeable gain deferred, and if the new assets comprise different classes of share, the reduction is apportioned by reference to the market value of each class of share at the time of their acquisition by the transferor. Deferment on part of the gain on the old assets therefore remains until the new assets are disposed of.

[*TCGA 1992, s 162*].

Whether a business is transferred 'as a going concern' is determined by reference to the circumstances at the time of transfer. If the business continues without interruption after that time, relief will be available notwithstanding the existence of a planned move of the entire assets of the business from one place to another (*Gordon v CIR (and cross-appeal)* CS 1991, 64 TC 173). For HMRC's interpretation of 'business' and 'going concern', see HMRC Capital Gains Manual CG65710, 65715. In *Ramsay v HMRC* UT, [2013] STC 1764, an activity consisting of letting flats in a large house in Belfast was held to amount to a business for the purpose of incorporation relief. The UT held that the activity undertaken in respect of the property outweighed 'what might normally be expected to be carried out by a mere passive investor'.

HMRC is prepared not to treat the assumption of business liabilities by the transferee company as consideration for the transfer; the relief is not precluded if some or all of the liabilities of the business are not taken over by the company. However, the assumption of *personal* liabilities, which includes tax liabilities pertaining to the unincorporated business, is treated as part of the consideration. (HMRC Extra-Statutory Concession D32; HMRC Capital Gains Manual CG65745). (See **4.21** ANTI-AVOIDANCE for the charge arising where concessions involving deferral of gains are abused.)

If some assets are retained by the original owner, relief under *TCGA 1992, s 162* above is not available and liability to CGT arises by reference to the market value of any chargeable assets transferred. Where *s 162* relief is not available, it is likely that a business asset hold-over relief claim under *TCGA 1992, s 165* (see **30.2** above) will prevail, provided that the transfer is by way of a non-arm's length bargain, including a transaction deemed to be such because it is between connected persons (see **4.13** ANTI-AVOIDANCE).

Incorporation relief is available to individuals who are members of a partnership (even if one of the partners is a company) where the whole of the partnership business is transferred to a company. Relief is computed separately for each individual partner and is not precluded by virtue of any other partner receiving all or part of his consideration otherwise than in shares. HMRC consider that relief is not available where a partnership incorporates into an existing corporate partner. As the corporate partner already owns a share of the business assets, the whole of the business is not transferred (HMRC Capital Gains Manual CG65700).

See HMRC Capital Gains Manual CG65700–65765.

Interaction with other reliefs

Subject to **31.3** below, incorporation relief under *TCGA 1992, s 162* is mandatory, although a claim for ROLLOVER RELIEF (**53**) takes precedence (HMRC Capital Gains Manual CG60201). Although *s 162* relief cannot be restricted to leave sufficient gains in charge to make use of the annual exempt amount or allowable losses, the same result can effectively be achieved by arranging for an appropriate part of the total consideration to be payable other than in the form of shares in the company, for example, in cash or by way of amount left to the credit of the transferor on loan account, so that a sufficient gain arises.

Example

W has carried on an antiquarian bookselling business for many years. He decides to form an unquoted company, P Ltd, to carry on the business. He transfers, in May 2024, the whole of the business undertaking, assets and liabilities to P Ltd, in consideration for the issue of shares, plus an amount left outstanding on interest-free loan. W becomes a director of P Ltd. The business assets and liabilities transferred are valued as follows:

		Value	Chargeable gain
	£	£	£
Freehold shop premises (acquired in 2000)		80,000	42,000
Goodwill		36,000	16,000
Fixtures and fittings		4,000	—
Trading stock		52,000	—
Debtors		18,000	—
		190,000	
Mortgage on shop	50,000		
Trade creditors	20,000	70,000	—
		£120,000	£58,000

The company issues 100,000 £1 ordinary shares, valued at par, to W in May 2024, and the amount left outstanding is £20,000. If W does not elect to disapply *TCGA 1992, s 162* treatment (see **31.3** below), the amount of the chargeable gain rolled over on transfer of the business is as follows:

$$\frac{100,000}{120,000} \times £58,000 \qquad £48,334$$

Of the chargeable gain, £9,666 (£58,000 – £48,334) remains taxable and is covered by the annual exempt amount.

The allowable cost of W's shares is £51,666 (£100,000 – £48,334).

Election to disapply incorporation relief

[31.3] On a transfer (of a business) that is within **30.13** above, the transferor may make an election to the effect that incorporation relief should not apply. The election must be made by notice in writing to HMRC. The deadline for making it is normally the second anniversary of 31 January following the tax year in which the transfer takes place. If, however, by the end of the tax year following that in which the transfer takes place, the transferor has disposed of *all* the 'new assets' (see below), the deadline is brought forward by one year. For this purpose, a transfer within *TCGA 1992, s 58* (see **40.4** MARRIED PERSONS AND CIVIL PARTNERS) is not counted as a disposal, but a subsequent disposal by the recipient spouse or civil partner (other than a transfer back to the original spouse or partner) counts as a disposal by the original spouse or partner.

As in **31.2** above, the '*new assets*' are the shares received by the transferor in exchange for the business, but in this case the expression also includes any shares or debentures treated by virtue of *TCGA 1992, s 127* (reorganisations of share capital — see **57.2** SHARES AND SECURITIES) as the same asset as the shares received in exchange for the business. The reference to *s 127* includes that *section* as applied by any other chargeable gains enactment (see, for example, **57.5**, **57.7**, **57.8** SHARES AND SECURITIES).

Where, immediately before the transfer of the business, it was owned by two or more persons (e.g. by a partnership, including a Scottish partnership), each person has a separate right to make the election in respect of his own entitlement to incorporation relief under *TCGA 1992, s 162* and by reference to his own share of the 'new assets'.

[*TCGA 1992, s 162A*].

Disincorporation relief

[31.4] Disincorporation relief could be claimed where certain small companies transferred their business to shareholders who are individuals **before 1 April 2018**. Where the relief was claimed, goodwill and land and buildings used in the business were treated as transferred to the shareholders at a reduced value for chargeable gains purposes (and, in the case of goodwill, for the purposes of the intangible assets regime) so that no corporation tax was payable by the company on the transfer of the assets. Shareholders to whom the assets were transferred inherit the reduced transfer values for the purpose of capital gains tax and must use them for any subsequent disposals.

See also HMRC Capital Gains Manual CG65800 onwards.

Effect of relief on subsequent disposal by shareholders

The disposal by the company and acquisition by the shareholders of any qualifying asset of the business included in the transfer is deemed to be for a consideration equal to the lower of:

(i) the total deductions allowable in computing the company's gain on the asset in question under the rules at **16.12** COMPUTATION OF GAINS AND LOSSES; and
(ii) the asset's market value.

Where the goodwill is dealt with in the company's hands under the intangible assets regime (see **15.13** COMPANIES—CORPORATE FINANCE AND INTANGIBLES), the acquisition by the shareholders is deemed to be for a consideration equal to the transfer value under that regime, as follows:

(A) If the goodwill has been written down under the regime, the transfer value is the lower of the tax written down value immediately before the transfer and the market value.
(B) If the goodwill is shown in the balance sheet but has not been written down, the transfer value is the lower of the cost of the goodwill (i.e. the cost recognised under the intangible assets regime) and its market value.
(C) If neither (A) nor (B) above apply, the transfer value is nil.

[*TCGA 1992, ss 162B, 162C; CTA 2009, s 849A; FA 2013, s 61*].

Key points on incorporation and disincorporation reliefs

[31.5] Points to consider are as follows.

- Incorporation relief is automatic if the conditions are met (but a taxpayer can elect to disapply it). However, it is quite easy to avoid wasting the annual exempt amount, for example by part of the consideration being paid in cash.
- Although it is often the case, the company to which the business is transferred does not have to be new. It can be an existing company.
- HMRC may challenge over optimistic valuations of goodwill. The post-transaction valuation procedure (form CG34) enables a value to be agreed with HMRC. Where practical it is advantageous to make the transfer early in the tax year and immediately file a CG34 as this enables a value to be agreed prior to the tax return being filed.

32

Indexation

Cross-references. See 8 ASSETS HELD ON 31 MARCH 1982; 16 COMPUTATION OF GAINS AND LOSSES; 35.12 LAND for concessionary treatment of indexation allowance on the merger of leases; 58 SHARES AND SECURITIES IDENTIFICATION RULES; 63.3, 63.4, 63.7 UNIT TRUSTS ETC. for HMRC practice in the case of unit trust units, investment trust shares and open-ended investment company shares acquired under monthly savings schemes.

Simon's Taxes. See C2.3.

Introduction to indexation

[32.1] Indexation allowance is intended to eliminate the effects of inflation from the calculation of chargeable gains. In effect, the allowance increases the amount of allowable expenditure in line with inflation, so that only any real-terms gain is taxed. The allowance applies **for corporation tax purposes only**, having been abolished for capital gains tax purposes (i.e. for disposals by individuals, trustees and personal representatives) in computing gains made on disposals on or after 6 April 2008. It is frozen at its December 2017 level.

Calculation of indexation allowance

[32.2] For corporation tax purposes only, an indexation allowance is deductible under certain circumstances from an 'unindexed' gain, i.e. the gain (if any) arrived at by deducting allowable expenditure from the amount of consideration realised (see 16 COMPUTATION OF GAINS AND LOSSES), or deemed to be realised, on a disposal. The amount of the indexation allowance is the aggregate of the 'indexed rise' in each item of 'relevant allowable expenditure' (see below). No indexation allowance is available in respect of expenditure incurred after 31 December 2017, and for expenditure incurred on or before that date and falling to be deducted on a disposal after that date, indexation allowance is computed up to and including December 2017 only.

Indexation allowance is given *only* against an unindexed gain. If the disposal gives rise to a loss, no indexation allowance is given and if the indexation allowance equals or exceeds the unindexed gain on a disposal so as to extinguish it, the disposal is regarded as one on which, after taking account of the indexation allowance, neither a gain nor a loss accrues.

'*Relevant allowable expenditure*' is allowable expenditure within *TCGA 1992, s 38(1)(a)* and *s 38(1)(b)*, i.e. basically acquisition cost or value, taken for these purposes as incurred when the asset is acquired or provided, and expenditure on enhancement and on establishing, preserving and defending title and rights to the asset (see **16.12**(a)–(c) COMPUTATION OF GAINS AND LOSSES). Such expenditure being taken for these purposes as incurred when it becomes due and payable. Disposal costs are excluded. In determining relevant allowable expenditure, account is taken of any provision of any enactment which, for the purpose of computing gains, increases, excludes or reduces any item of expenditure, or provides for it to be written down.

The '*indexed rise*' in each item of relevant allowable expenditure is computed by multiplying that item by a figure (rounded to the nearest third decimal place) calculated by the formula:

$$\frac{RD - RI}{RI}$$

where:

RD = retail prices index for the month in which the disposal occurs or, if earlier, December 2017; and
RI = retail prices index for March 1982 or the month in which the expenditure was incurred, whichever is the later.

If, in relation to any item of expenditure, RD in the formula is equal to, or less than, RI, there is no indexed rise for that item.

The freezing of indexation allowance at its December 2017 level for disposals after 31 December 2017 does not affect the computation of a gain which arose on an actual or deemed disposal on or before that date but by virtue of any capital gains enactment does not come into charge until after that date.

[*TCGA 1992, ss 53, 54, 288(1); ITA 2007, s 989*].

The above rules do not apply to 'section 104 holdings' (i.e. single asset pools) of shares or securities. Separate indexation provisions apply to such holding — see **58.4** SHARES AND SECURITIES — IDENTIFICATION RULES.

Special provisions apply to the calculation of indexation allowance in relation to disposals involving ASSETS HELD ON 31 MARCH **1982** (**8**).

The above rules are subject to the provisions in **32.3–32.8** below.

Indexation factors

The figure given by the above formula is commonly called the '*indexation factor*'. The consistent calculation of the indexation factor to more than three decimal places is generally accepted.

Indexation factors for disposals in December 2017 onwards are as follows:

	1982	1983	1984	1985	1986	1987	1988	1989	1990	1991
Jan	—	2.366	2.202	2.049	1.889	1.781	1.692	1.505	1.327	1.136
Feb	—	2.352	2.189	2.025	1.879	1.770	1.682	1.487	1.314	1.125
Mar	2.501	2.346	2.179	1.997	1.875	1.764	1.671	1.476	1.291	1.116
Apr	2.432	2.300	2.137	1.934	1.847	1.732	1.629	1.433	1.223	1.089
May	2.407	2.286	2.126	1.921	1.842	1.729	1.619	1.418	1.204	1.083
Jun	2.398	2.278	2.118	1.915	1.844	1.729	1.609	1.410	1.195	1.074
Jul	2.397	2.260	2.121	1.920	1.852	1.732	1.606	1.408	1.193	1.078
Aug	2.396	2.246	2.092	1.912	1.843	1.724	1.577	1.402	1.171	1.074
Sep	2.398	2.232	2.086	1.914	1.829	1.716	1.565	1.385	1.151	1.066
Oct	2.381	2.220	2.067	1.909	1.825	1.703	1.540	1.367	1.134	1.058
Nov	2.364	2.209	2.058	1.899	1.801	1.690	1.528	1.347	1.139	1.051
Dec	2.371	2.200	2.060	1.895	1.792	1.692	1.521	1.341	1.141	1.049

	1992	1993	1994	1995	1996	1997	1998	1999	2000	2001
Jan	1.051	1.017	0.968	0.905	0.852	0.801	0.744	0.702	0.669	0.625
Feb	1.040	1.004	0.957	0.893	0.843	0.794	0.735	0.699	0.660	0.617
Mar	1.034	0.996	0.952	0.885	0.836	0.790	0.729	0.695	0.651	0.615
Apr	1.004	0.978	0.929	0.866	0.822	0.779	0.710	0.683	0.635	0.607
May	0.996	0.971	0.922	0.859	0.819	0.772	0.701	0.679	0.629	0.596
Jun	0.996	0.972	0.922	0.856	0.818	0.766	0.702	0.679	0.625	0.595
July	1.004	0.977	0.931	0.865	0.825	0.766	0.706	0.684	0.631	0.605
Aug	1.002	0.968	0.922	0.855	0.816	0.755	0.699	0.680	0.631	0.598
Sep	0.995	0.960	0.918	0.847	0.808	0.746	0.692	0.673	0.620	0.593
Oct	0.988	0.961	0.915	0.856	0.808	0.744	0.691	0.670	0.621	0.596
Nov	0.991	0.964	0.914	0.856	0.807	0.742	0.692	0.668	0.616	0.602
Dec	0.998	0.960	0.905	0.845	0.801	0.738	0.692	0.662	0.615	0.604

	2002	2003	2004	2005	2006	2007	2008	2009	2010	2011
Jan	0.605	0.559	0.519	0.472	0.438	0.379	0.326	0.324	0.276	0.214
Feb	0.600	0.551	0.513	0.467	0.432	0.369	0.316	0.316	0.269	0.202
Mar	0.594	0.546	0.507	0.460	0.426	0.361	0.311	0.316	0.260	0.196
Apr	0.583	0.535	0.498	0.451	0.415	0.354	0.300	0.315	0.248	0.186
May	0.578	0.532	0.491	0.448	0.407	0.349	0.293	0.307	0.244	0.182
Jun	0.578	0.534	0.489	0.447	0.401	0.342	0.283	0.303	0.241	0.182
Jul	0.581	0.534	0.489	0.447	0.401	0.349	0.285	0.303	0.244	0.185
Aug	0.577	0.531	0.484	0.444	0.396	0.342	0.280	0.297	0.239	0.178
Sep	0.566	0.524	0.478	0.440	0.390	0.337	0.273	0.292	0.234	0.169
Oct	0.563	0.523	0.475	0.439	0.388	0.331	0.277	0.288	0.232	0.168
Nov	0.561	0.522	0.471	0.436	0.383	0.326	0.288	0.284	0.226	0.166
Dec	0.558	0.516	0.464	0.433	0.372	0.319	0.306	0.276	0.218	0.162

	2012	2013	2014	2015	2016	2017
Jan	0.168	0.131	0.101	0.089	0.075	0.047
Feb	0.159	0.123	0.094	0.083	0.070	0.036
Mar	0.155	0.118	0.091	0.082	0.065	0.033
Apr	0.147	0.115	0.088	0.078	0.064	0.028
May	0.147	0.112	0.087	0.076	0.061	0.024
Jun	0.150	0.114	0.085	0.074	0.057	0.021
Jul	0.149	0.114	0.086	0.075	0.056	0.019
Aug	0.144	0.108	0.082	0.070	0.052	0.012
Sep	0.139	0.104	0.080	0.071	0.050	0.011
Oct	0.132	0.104	0.079	0.072	0.050	0.010
Nov	0.132	0.103	0.082	0.070	0.047	0.008
Dec	0.127	0.101	0.080	0.067	0.041	—

Examples

(1) X Ltd acquired an asset in November 1985 for £28,000. It disposes of the asset on 11 August 2024 for £99,000. The indexation factor for November 1985 to December 2017 is 1.899.

	£
Sale consideration	99,000
Cost of asset	28,000
Unindexed gain	71,000
Indexation allowance	
1.899 × £28,000	53,172
Chargeable gain	£17,828

(2) Facts as in (1) above except that X Ltd receives consideration of £18,000.

	£
Sale consideration	18,000
Cost of asset	28,000
Allowable loss (no indexation allowance available)	£10,000

(3) Facts as in (1) above except that X Ltd received consideration of £40,000.

	£
Sale consideration	40,000
Cost of asset	28,000
Unindexed gain	£12,000

Indexation allowance is as in (1) above (£53,172), but as this exceeds the amount of the unindexed gain, the disposal gives rise neither to a gain nor to a loss.

Part disposals

[32.3] Where a disposal is a part disposal of an asset, apportionment of relevant allowable expenditure is to take place before computing the indexation allowance. The allowance is then only calculated for relevant allowable expenditure attributable to the part disposed of. [*TCGA 1992, s 56(1)*].

Example

X Ltd sells part of a plot of land on 18 January 2024 for £100,000. The then market value of the remaining part of the plot is £30,000. The cost, in September 1984, of the whole plot was £25,000. The indexation factor for September 1984 to December 2017 is 2.086.

	£
Allowable expenditure attributable to the part disposed of	
$\frac{100,000}{100,000 + 30,000} \times £25,000$	£19,231
Unindexed gain: £100,000 – £19,231	80,769
Indexation allowance	
2.086 × £19,231	40,116
Chargeable gain	£40,653

Notes to the example

(a) No indexation allowance is computed at this stage on the balance of expenditure to be carried forward of £5,769 (£25,000 – £19,231).

(b) Indexation allowance is frozen at its December 2017 level. See 32.2 above.

Disposals on a no gain/no loss basis

[32.4] On a 'no gain/no loss disposal' by a company, both the disposal consideration of the transferor and the corresponding acquisition consideration of the transferee are calculated for the purposes of *TCGA 1992* on the assumption that, on the disposal, an unindexed gain accrues to the transferor which is equal to the indexation allowance on that disposal, and so that after taking account of the indexation allowance the disposal is one on which neither a gain nor a loss accrues. This rule applied also to such disposals by individuals, trustees or personal representatives before 6 April 2008. Where the acquisition consideration for an asset was determined in this way, the amount of that consideration is not affected by the abolition of indexation allowance for capital gains tax purposes.

For the purposes of calculating indexation allowance under *TCGA 1992, ss 53, 54* (see **32.2** above), any enactment is disregarded to the extent to which it provides that, on a subsequent disposal of an asset by the transferee which was acquired by him on a no gain/no loss disposal as above, the transferor's acquisition of the asset is to be treated as the transferee's acquisition of it. [*TCGA 1992, ss 52A, 56(2)*]. For further applications of this provision, see **8.6** ASSETS HELD ON **31** MARCH **1982** and **58.4** SHARES AND SECURITIES — IDENTIFICATION RULES.

Where otherwise a loss would accrue on a disposal, and the sums allowable as a deduction in computing the loss would include an amount attributable to the application of the assumption contained in *TCGA 1992, s 56(2)* above on any no gain/no loss disposal, those sums are determined as if *TCGA 1992, s 56(2)* had not applied and the loss is reduced accordingly or, if those sums are then equal to or less than the consideration for the disposal, the disposal is to be one on which neither a gain nor a loss accrues. [*TCGA 1992, s 56(3)*].

For the purposes of *TCGA 1992, s 56(1)* (part disposals; see **32.3** above) and *TCGA 1992, s 56(2)(3)* above, a '*no gain/no loss disposal*' is one which, by virtue of any enactment other than *TCGA 1992, s 35(4)* (no gain/no loss disposal where the general re-basing rule of *TCGA 1992, s 35(1)(2)* would otherwise convert a gain into a loss and vice versa; see **8.2** ASSETS HELD ON **31** MARCH **1982**), *s 53(1)* (no gain/no loss disposal where indexation allowance equals or exceeds gain before indexation; see **32.2** above) or *s 56* itself, is treated as a disposal on which neither a gain nor a loss accrues. [*TCGA 1992, s 56(4)*]. For these purposes, the definition is not therefore confined to those no gain/no loss disposals mentioned in **8.6** ASSETS HELD ON **28** MARCH **1982**.

Receipts affecting allowable expenditure

[32.5] Where account is to be taken, in determining relevant allowable expenditure (see **32.2** above) of any provision which, for the purposes of computing gains, reduces such expenditure by reference to a '*relevant event*' (i.e. any event which is not treated as a capital gains tax disposal), the computation of the indexation allowance proceeds in three stages.

(i) The 'indexed rise' (see **32.2** above) is calculated for each item of expenditure ignoring the reduction.
(ii) The 'indexed rise' is calculated of a notional item of expenditure equal to the amount of the reduction, as if that notional amount had actually been incurred on the date of the 'relevant event'.
(iii) The figure calculated in (ii) above is deducted from that in (i) above.

[*TCGA 1992, s 57*]. Examples of such 'relevant events' are small part disposals of land as in **35.7** LAND and the sale of rights nil paid where the consideration received is small as in **57.2** SHARES AND SECURITIES.

Example

Z Ltd purchases a large area of land in April 1990 for £800,000. In June 1993, it sells a small part of that land at arm's length for £2,000. In August 2024, it sells all the remaining land for £4,500,000. The indexation factor for April 1990 to December 2017 is 1.223. For June 1993 to December 2017, it is 0.972.

	£	£
Sale consideration		4,500,000
Cost	800,000	

Small sale not treated as a disposal	2,000	798,000
Unindexed gain		£3,702,000
Indexation allowance on cost		£
1.223 × £800,000		978,400
Indexation allowance on notional expenditure equal to small sale consideration		
0.972 × £2,000		1,944
Reduced indexation allowance		£976,456
Chargeable gain = £(3,702,000 – 976,456)		£2,725,544

Reorganisation, reconstructions etc.

[32.6] In computing indexation allowance, any consideration given for 'the new holding' (treated under *TCGA 1992, s 127* as the same asset as 'the original shares' on a reorganisation etc.) is to be treated as an item of relevant allowable expenditure incurred when the consideration was, or was liable to be, given, i.e. not related back to the acquisition date of 'the original shares', as would normally be the case under *TCGA 1992, s 128(1)*.

'*Reorganisation*', the '*original shares*' and '*the new holding*' are as defined in *TCGA 1992, s 126(1)*. In addition the above provisions also apply where the treatment under *TCGA 1992, s 127* is adapted for a conversion of securities and for company reconstructions. See **57.2–57.8** SHARES AND SECURITIES. [*TCGA 1992, ss 131, 132(1), 135(3)*].

Example

In November 1989, Y Ltd purchases 5,000 shares in A plc for £3,500. In June 1991, it acquires, for £960, 1,000 further shares by way of a 1 for 5 rights issue. In August 2023, it sells all its holding for £150,000. The indexation factor for November 1989 to December 2017 is 1.347 and for June 1991 to December 2017 it is 1.347.

	£	£
Sale consideration		150,000
Original cost	3,500	
Cost of rights	960	
		4,460
Unindexed gain		£145,540
Indexation allowance on original cost		£
1.347 × £3,500		4,715
Indexation allowance on cost of taking up rights		
1.074 × £960		1,031

Total indexation allowance	£5,746
Chargeable gain = £(145,540 – 5,746)	£139,794

Notes to the example

(a) Strictly, the pooling provisions in 58.4 SHARES AND SECURITIES — IDENTIFICATION RULES apply, as the acquisition in November 1989 is a 'section 104 holding'. For practical purposes, where, as in this example, there is a single acquisition and disposal, the above computation gives essentially the same result.

(b) Indexation allowance is frozen at its December 2017 level. See 32.2 above.

Calls on shares

[32.7] Where the whole or part of the consideration for the issue of shares, securities or debentures is given after the period of 12 months beginning on the date of the issue of the shares etc., that consideration (or part) is treated as a separate item of expenditure for indexation purposes, incurred at the time it is given and not at the time at which the shares etc. were acquired or provided. [*TCGA 1992, s 113*]. Any calls paid within the 12-month period are thus treated as incurred at the time the shares etc. were acquired or provided.

Indexation allowance and options

[32.8] Where, on a disposal, relevant allowable expenditure includes both:

(a) the cost of acquiring an option binding the grantor to sell ('*the option consideration*'); and

(b) the cost of acquiring what was sold as a result of the exercise of the option ('*the sale consideration*'),

the option consideration and sale consideration are regarded as separate items of expenditure incurred when the option was acquired and when the sale took place respectively. An option binding the grantor both to sell and to buy is treated for these purposes as two separate options with one-half of the consideration attributable to each. These provisions do not apply where those at 58.4 SHARES AND SECURITIES — IDENTIFICATION RULES (under 'Consideration for options') apply. [*TCGA 1992, s 145*].

As in 7.7 ASSETS, the reference above to an 'option' includes a reference to an option binding the grantor to grant a lease for a premium, or enter into any other transaction which is not a sale. [*TCGA 1992, ss 144(6), 145(3)*].

In the case of the grantee of a 'cash-settled' option (see 7.7 ASSETS), the cost of the option is treated as incurred when the option was acquired for the purposes of calculating any indexation allowance. [*TCGA 1992, s 144A(3)(c)*].

33

Interaction with Other Taxes

Cross-references. See 2 ANNUAL RATES AND EXEMPTIONS for rates applicable to gains by reference to income tax bands; **30.10** HOLD-OVER RELIEFS for relief given to gifts on which inheritance tax is chargeable etc; **35.14–35.17** LAND for premiums on leases of land charged to income tax; 57 SHARES AND SECURITIES for interaction with income tax provisions.

General and income tax

[33.1] Any money or money's worth charged to income tax as income of, or taken into account as a receipt in computing income or profits or gains or losses of the person making the disposal is excluded from the consideration for the disposal of the asset for capital gains tax purposes. Also excluded are any amounts brought into account, by the person making the disposal, as a receipt under the cash basis for small businesses because the person ceases to use the asset in the trade (without disposing of it) or because there is an increase in the person's non-business use of the asset, these being deemed disposals for the purpose of the cash basis. This is the case provided such amounts have not already been excluded on a previous disposal of the asset. There are similar exclusions for such receipts brought into account under the cash basis for unincorporated property businesses. See Tolley's Income Tax for details of the cash basis.

However,

(a) this is not to be taken as excluding any money or money's worth:
- taken into account in making a balancing charge for the purposes of capital allowances (see *Hirsch v Crowthers Cloth Ltd* Ch D 1989, 62 TC 759); or
- brought into account as the disposal value of plant or machinery for capital allowances purposes; or
- brought into account as the disposal value of an asset representing qualifying expenditure under *CAA 2001, Pt 6* (research and development allowances);
- taken into account in computing a return on which income tax is charged under *ITTOIA 2005, Pt 4 Ch 2A* (disguised interest); and

(b) the capitalised value of a rentcharge (as in the case where a rentcharge is exchanged for another asset), ground annual or feu duty, or of a right of any other description to income or to payments in the nature of income over a period, or to a series of payments in the nature of income may be taken into account for capital gains tax purposes.

Income or profits charged or chargeable to tax include amounts from which a sum representing income tax is required to be deducted.

Where, under *ITA 2007, s 759(6)* or *CTA 2010, s 821(3)(5)*, the person charged to tax is a person other than the person by whom the gain was realised and the tax has been paid, then, for the purposes of the above provisions, the amount charged to tax is regarded as having been charged as the income of the person by whom the gain was realised.

Where, under *ITA 2007, s 517G(4)(6)* or *CTA 2010, s 356OG(4)(6)* (transactions in UK land — see **35.4** LAND), an amount is charged to tax as income of a person other than the person by whom the gain was realised and the tax has been paid, then, for the purposes of the above provisions, the amount charged to tax is regarded as having been charged as the income of the person by whom the gain was realised.

Similarly, where, under *ITA 2007, s 777(5)* (sales of occupation income — see Tolley's Income Tax), the person charged to tax is a person other than the person ('A') for whom the capital amount was obtained or by whom the property or right was sold or realised and the tax has been paid, then, for the purposes of the above provisions, the amount charged to tax is regarded as having been charged as the income of A.

See also **16.10** COMPUTATION OF GAINS AND LOSSES for the exclusion from disposal consideration of certain amounts under finance leases where anti-avoidance provisions apply.

[*TCGA 1992, ss 37, 39, 52(2)(3)(5), Sch 8 para 5(6)*].

In *Drummond v HMRC* CA, [2009] STC 2206, an individual (D) contracted to purchase five life assurance policies for a stated consideration of £1,962,233. On the following day he asked the vendor to surrender the policies. The surrender value was £1,751,376. In his tax return, D claimed that the effect of this was that he had made an allowable loss of £1,962,233 for CGT purposes. HMRC rejected the claim and D appealed, contending that the effect of *TCGA 1992, s 37* was that the 'surrender value' could be excluded from the computation of the gain or loss on the disposal. The Ch D reviewed the evidence in detail, rejected this contention, and rejected D's claim. Norris J observed that for income tax purposes the surrender had given rise to a 'chargeable event gain' of £1,351; and that the transactions had cost D £210,857. He held that this £210,857 represented professional fees which had not been 'wholly and exclusively expended in the acquisition of the policies'. Accordingly, for CGT purposes, the disposal had produced a loss of £1,351, being the amount chargeable to income tax and the only amount which fell to be excluded from the consideration charged to CGT by virtue of *TCGA 1992, s 37*. The CA unanimously upheld this decision. Rimer LJ held that 'the interpretation of legislation involves more than black letter literalism. In a case such as the present, in which there is a question as to which of limbs (i) and (ii) applies, it is necessary to give the statute a purposive construction'. The purpose of *TCGA 1992, ss 37–39* was 'to prevent the double taxation that might otherwise arise from the circumstance that the disposal of an asset will or may give rise to a charge to income tax and also be a disposal for CGT purposes. . . . It is not their purpose to enable the creation of an imaginary loss that the taxpayer can set against a real gain and so reduce a CGT liability'.

For income tax matters relating to know-how and patents (and which have a capital gains tax effect), see **7.4**, **7.5** ASSETS). See also **43.9** OVERSEAS MATTERS for offshore funds.

Expenditure

Expenditure which is deductible in computing profits or losses for income tax purposes (or would be so deductible if the asset were held as a fixed asset of a trade) is excluded from being allowable expenditure for capital gains tax purposes. For this purpose, where, under *ITA 2007, s 759(6)* or *CTA 2010, s 821(3)(5)*, the person charged to tax is a person other than the person by whom the gain was realised and the tax has been paid, then, for the purposes of the above provisions, the amount charged to tax is regarded as having been charged as the income of the person by whom the gain was realised. Where, under *ITA 2007, s 517G(4)(6)* or *CTA 2010, s 356OG(4)(6)* (transactions in UK land — see **35.4** LAND), an amount is charged to tax as income of a person other than the person by whom the gain was realised and the tax has been paid, then, for the purposes of the above provisions, the amount charged to tax is regarded as having been charged as the income of the person by whom the gain was realised. [*TCGA 1992, s 39(1)(2)(4)*]. See **16.14** COMPUTATION OF GAINS AND LOSSES.

Assessments etc.

Any assessment to income tax or decision on a claim under the *Income Tax Acts*, and any decision on an appeal in connection with it, is conclusive for capital gains tax purposes where liability to tax depends on the provisions of the *Income Tax Acts*. [*TCGA 1992, s 284*]. Where *alternative* income tax and capital gains tax assessments are made in respect of the same transactions, the fact that the capital gains tax assessment becomes final does not preclude the income tax assessment taking effect instead (*Bye v Coren* CA 1986, 60 TC 116). See also *Lord Advocate v McKenna* CS 1989, 61 TC 688 and *CIR v Wilkinson* CA 1992, 65 TC 28.

Income or capital?

Whether the gain arising on the disposal of an asset is of income or capital nature has been tested in the courts on numerous occasions and the outcome is likely to be one of fact and degree. In particular, see **35.3** LAND for isolated and speculative transactions in land. 'No part of our law of taxation presents such almost insoluble conundrums as the decision whether a receipt or outgoing is capital or income for tax purposes' (Lord Upjohn in *Strick v Regent Oil Co Ltd* HL 1965, 43 TC 1 which see for a comprehensive review of the law). A widely used test is the 'enduring benefit' one given by Viscount Cave in *Atherton v British Insulated & Helsby Cables Ltd* HL 1925, 10 TC 155.

Inheritance tax

[33.2] A lifetime disposal which contains an element of gift may incur liability to inheritance tax (IHT) as well as capital gains tax. For the purposes of IHT, no account is taken of any capital gains tax borne by the transferor in determining the reduction in value in his estate. [*IHTA 1984, s 164*].

> *Example 1*
>
> A makes a gift of land, to a non-UK resident discretionary trustee, B, which is valued at £20,000 and on which there is a capital gains tax liability of £3,000. The value for IHT purposes (subject to grossing-up for the IHT payable) is £20,000 (i.e. the same as if A had sold the land and given the £20,000 proceeds to B).

Relief for CGT against IHT

Capital gains tax paid will be taken into account for IHT purposes in the following instances.

(a) If the transferor fails to pay all or part of the capital gains tax within twelve months of the due date, an assessment may be made on the donee (see **25.4** GIFTS) and the amount of such tax borne by the donee is treated as reducing the value transferred. There is a similar effect when the transfer is from a settlement but, after 8 March 1982, this only applies if the capital gains tax is borne by a person who becomes absolutely entitled to the settled property concerned. [*IHTA 1984, s 165(1)(2)*].

(b) Where a person sells, or is treated as having sold, national heritage property on the breach or termination of an undertaking (see **23.79** EXEMPTIONS AND RELIEFS) any capital gains tax payable is deductible in determining the value of the asset for IHT purposes. [*TCGA 1992, s 258(8)*].

> *Example 2*
>
> In *Example 1* above, if A fails to pay the £3,000 capital gains tax and it is borne by B, the value transferred by A is £17,000 for the purposes of IHT (again subject to grossing-up for the IHT payable).

Relief for IHT against CGT

Where hold-over relief is granted under:

(i) *TCGA 1992, s 165* in relation to gifts made after 13 March 1989 (see **30.2** HOLD-OVER RELIEFS),

(ii) *TCGA 1992, s 260* in relation to gifts after 13 March 1989 (see **30.10** HOLD-OVER RELIEFS), or

(iii) *FA 1980, s 79* in relation to gifts after 5 April 1980 and before 14 March 1989 (see **30.12** HOLD-OVER RELIEFS),

the transferee may deduct on a subsequent disposal any IHT attributable to the value of the asset on the original transfer (being either a chargeable transfer or a potentially exempt transfer which proves to be a chargeable transfer). The tax deductible may be varied on the subsequent death of the transferor or otherwise but it cannot in any circumstances create an allowable loss on the subsequent disposal. [*TCGA 1992, ss 67(1)–(3), 165(10)(11), 260(7)(8)*].

There is no relief for IHT under (i) and (iii) above if hold-over relief is *not* claimed, so even where the gain otherwise arising is negligible or covered by reliefs, a hold-over relief claim may still be beneficial overall. A hold-over relief claim can be made even if an allowable loss arises on the original gift and so gives rise to an IHT deduction on a subsequent disposal by the donee whilst not affecting the loss relief position of the donor. Where only part of the asset gifted is subsequently disposed of, HMRC has indicated in the past that they accept that any IHT paid on the original gift can still be deducted in full on the part disposal (subject to the size of the gain arising) and there is no need to apportion IHT paid between the part disposed of and the part retained (Taxation 5 October 1989, pp 12, 14).

Valuation of assets

Valuations of assets made *at death* for the purpose of the application of an IHT charge on the value of a person's estate immediately before death are binding for capital gains tax purposes. [*TCGA 1992, s 274; IHTA 1984, s 168*]. See also Revenue Tax Bulletin April 1995 p 209. Therefore, quoted shares and securities are then valued using the IHT valuation (see **39.3** MARKET VALUE). In the case of land and quoted shares and securities, proceeds of certain post-death sales within a specified period may be substituted for values at date of death for IHT purposes. The value of related property (as defined for IHT purposes) may also be revised in the event of a post-death sale. If such substitutions/revisions are made for IHT purposes, they must be made for CGT purposes also (but see *Stonor and Another (Executors of Dickinson deceased) v CIR* (Sp C 288), [2001] SSCD 199 in which the executors failed in an attempt to use this rule to upgrade values of freehold properties for CGT purposes where there was no IHT liability). See Tolley's Inheritance Tax for details.

Value added tax

[33.3] If VAT is suffered on the purchase of an asset, but is available for set-off in full in the purchaser's VAT account (e.g. a capital asset purchased by a trader who is registered for VAT), then the cost of the asset for capital gains tax purposes is the cost exclusive of VAT. Where no VAT set-off is available, the cost is inclusive of VAT borne. On the disposal of an asset, VAT chargeable is disregarded in computing the disposal consideration for capital gains tax purposes (HMRC Statement of Practice SP D7).

A person whose output is partly exempt and partly taxable may set off only part of his VAT on inputs against his VAT on outputs. In such a case, although the computation of disposal proceeds is as above, it will be necessary to allocate the VAT ultimately suffered to the various expense payments made. HMRC will be prepared to consider any reasonable arrangements made to carry out this apportionment. A taxable person making both taxable and exempt supplies may therefore treat as part of the capital gains tax cost of an asset the input tax that was not available for credit in respect of the acquisition (HMRC Statement of Practice SP B1).

In some circumstances, such as under the capital goods scheme, the VAT is adjusted during the period of ownership of the asset. When this applies, only the adjusted amount of VAT should be included in the cost of the asset for capital gains tax purposes (HMRC Capital Gains Manual CG14325).

34

Investors' Relief

Cross-references. See 9 BUSINESS ASSET DISPOSAL RELIEF.

Introduction to investors' relief

[34.1] Investors' relief can be claimed by individuals or trustees in respect of qualifying disposals of qualifying ordinary shares in unlisted trading companies. The relief is not available to companies.

The main features of the relief are as follows:

- The relief can be claimed by individuals or trustees who dispose of ordinary shares, or an interest in ordinary shares, in unlisted trading companies or unlisted holding companies of trading groups for which they have subscribed on or after 17 March 2016.
- Gains on disposals of qualifying shares are chargeable to capital gains tax at a rate of 10% (after deduction of any allowable losses).
- Relief is subject to a lifetime limit of £10 million.
- Claims must be made on or before the first anniversary of 31 January following the tax year of disposal.
- The investor must hold the shares throughout the period beginning with the date the share was issued and ending with the date of disposal. That period must be at least three years.
- Relief is not available if the investor or a connected person has been an officer or employee of the company or a connected company at any time in the share-holding period;
- Where there have been previous disposals from a holding of shares, special identification rules apply to determine what proportion of the shares subsequently disposed of are qualifying shares.
- Shares are disqualified from relief if the investor receives any value worth, broadly, more than £1,000 from the company at any time in the period beginning one year before, and ending immediately before the third anniversary of, the date on which the shares were issued.

- There are provisions to determine the qualifying status of shares held following a reorganisation of share capital, exchange of shares or scheme of reconstruction. Broadly, shares held following such an event take on the history of the original shares proportionally.
- The investor can make an election to disapply the reorganisation provisions so that a claim to investors' relief can be made if the new shares would not qualify for relief.

See HMRC Capital Gains Manual CG635000 onwards.

Operation of investors' relief

[34.2] A 'qualifying person' can make a claim for investors' relief on the disposal of, or the disposal of an 'interest' in, a 'holding', or part of a holding, of shares in a company if, immediately before the disposal, some or all of the shares are 'qualifying shares' (see **34.7** below). See **34.3** below for the further condition applicable to disposals by trustees. Subject to the lifetime limit at **34.5** below, the relief applies as follows.

Where a claim is made and all of the shares in the holding are qualifying shares, the gain on the disposal (after deduction of any allowable losses) is taxable at the rate of 10%. If only some of the shares are qualifying shares, only a corresponding proportion of the gain (after deduction of any allowable losses) is taxable at the rate of 10%. The proportion is the number of qualifying shares treated as disposed of divided by the total number of shares disposed of. For this purpose, qualifying shares are treated as disposed of in priority to non-qualifying shares. See **34.4** below where there has been a previous disposal of shares from the holding.

A '*holding*' of shares means a holding which is treated as a single asset under *TCGA 1992, s 104(1)* (see **58.4** SHARES AND SECURITIES – IDENTIFICATION RULES). A '*qualifying person*' is an individual or the trustees of a settlement.

Disposal of an interest in shares

In relation to the disposal of an *interest* in a holding of shares, a 'holding' means a number of shares in a company of the same class which were acquired in the same capacity either by the qualifying person solely or by the same two or more persons including the qualifying person. An 'interest' in a holding means any interests of the qualifying person, in any of the shares in the holding, which are treated as a single asset under *TCGA 1992, s 104(1)*. An interest includes a part of an interest. References in this chapter to a holding of shares include the interest disposed of and references to the disposal of all or part of a holding include a disposal of an interest in the holding.

[*TCGA 1992, ss 169VC, 169VD, 169VJ, 169VY*].

Disposals by trustees

[34.3] Where the disposal is by the trustees of a settlement, investors' relief is not available unless there is at least one 'eligible beneficiary' in respect of the disposal. An individual is an '*eligible beneficiary*' if:

- he has an interest in possession (other than for a fixed term) in settled property that includes the holding of shares immediately before the disposal;
- he has had such an interest throughout the three years ending with the date of the disposal;
- he has not been a 'relevant employee' (see **34.7** below) in respect of the company at any time in the three-year period; and
- he has elected to be treated as an eligible beneficiary.

An election must be made to the trustees by the time of the claim for relief and can be withdrawn at any time until the claim is made.

[*TCGA 1992, s 169VH*].

If there is more than one person with an interest in possession in the settled property which includes the holding of shares immediately before the disposal, the trustees can only claim investors' relief in respect of the eligible beneficiary's share of the gain or, where there is more than one eligible beneficiary, on the aggregate of their shares. A person's share of a gain is the proportion of the gain equal to his interest in possession in the income from the holding of shares divided by all the interests in possession in that income. [*TCGA 1992, s 169VI*].

Previous disposal of shares in the holding

[34.4] Where, before a disposal in respect of which a claim to investors' relief is made, there have been one or more previous disposals of shares from the same holding, the following rules apply, where needed, to determine which shares are treated as having been previously disposed of (and therefore which shares are treated as in the holding immediately before the current disposal). The rules operate to preserve the maximum potential relief for future disposals.

Claim to investors' relief made in respect of previous disposal

Where a claim to investors' relief was made in respect of the previous disposal:

(a) all of the qualifying shares in the holding immediately before the previous disposal are treated as having been disposed of or, if less, so many of the qualifying shares as equals the total number of shares disposed of;

(b) if the number of qualifying shares in the holding immediately before the previous disposal was less than the total number of shares disposed of and excluded shares (broadly, shares which can never be qualifying shares: see **34.7** below) were in the holding at that time, then the excluded shares are also treated as having been disposed of, up to a maximum of the total number of shares in the disposal less those treated as having been disposed of in (a) above; and

(c) if the total number of shares treated as having been disposed of under (a) and (b) above is less than the total number of shares disposed of, so many of the potentially qualifying shares in the holding (i.e. shares which would be qualifying shares if they had been held by the qualifying person for sufficient time: see **34.7** below) as make up the difference are treated as having been disposed of (on a last in first out basis).

No claim made in respect of previous disposal

Where no claim to investors' relief was made in respect of the previous disposal, the identification order is altered so that:

(i) all of the excluded shares in the holding immediately before the previous disposal are treated as having been disposed of or, if less, so many of the excluded shares as equals the total number of shares disposed of;

(ii) if the number of excluded shares in the holding immediately before the previous disposal was less than the total number of shares disposed of and potentially qualifying shares were in the holding at that time, then the potentially qualifying shares are also treated as having been disposed of (on a last in first out basis), up to a maximum of the total number of shares in the disposal less those treated as having been disposed of in (i) above; and

(iii) if the total number of shares treated as having been disposed of under (i) and (ii) above is less than the total number of shares disposed of, so many of the qualifying shares in the holding as make up the difference are treated as having been disposed of.

[*TCGA 1992, ss 169VE–169VG*].

Lifetime limit on investors' relief

[34.5] Investors' relief is subject to a lifetime limit of £10 million, which applies as follows.

The amount to which relief would otherwise apply in respect of a disposal is added to any amounts to which relief applied in respect of earlier disposals. Where the total exceeds the limit, only so much (if any) of the amount to which relief would otherwise apply in respect of the current disposal as, together with the earlier amounts, does not exceed the limit qualifies for the 10% rate. Any part of the gain excluded by the application of this rule is chargeable at the normal rates of CGT.

The earlier disposals to be taken into account are:

(a) where the current disposal is made by an individual, earlier disposals made by him and earlier disposals by trustees in respect of which he is an eligible beneficiary; and

(b) where the current disposal is by trustees and an individual is an eligible beneficiary, earlier disposals by the trustees in respect of which that individual is an eligible beneficiary and earlier disposals made by that individual.

Where, in relation to an earlier disposal by trustees, there is more than one person with an interest in possession in the settled property, only the individual's share of the gain (see **34.3** above) is taken into account in (a) or (b) above.

[*TCGA 1992, ss 169VK, 169VL*].

Example 1

In May 2024, Sara sells her entire holding of shares in Watkins Ltd, an unlisted trading company, for £900,000. Sara subscribed for the shares in April 2017 for £200,000. She claims investors' relief in respect of the disposal. She has made no previous claim to the relief and makes no other disposals in 2024/25. Sara's capital gains tax liability for 2024/25 is calculated as follows.

	£
Sale consideration	900,000
Less cost of shares	200,000
Chargeable gain	700,000
Annual exemption	3,000
Gain chargeable to tax	£697,000
Capital gains tax payable (£697,000 × 10%)	£69,700

Example 2

In August 2024, Ms Moorer sells her entire shareholding in Alison Ltd, realising a gain of £10,050,000, which qualifies for investors' relief. Ms Moorer makes no other disposals in 2024/25 and has made no previous disposals qualifying for investors' relief. She is an additional rate income taxpayer for 2024/25. Ms Moorer's capital gains tax liability for 2024/25 is calculated as follows.

	£
Chargeable gain	10,050,000
Annual exemption	3,000
Gain chargeable to tax	£10,047,000
Capital gains tax payable	
£10,000,000 × 10%	1,000,000
£47,400 × 20%	9,480
	£1,009,480

Note to the example

(a) The annual exemption of £3,000 is allocated against the part of the gain chargeable to tax at 20% as this gives the greater tax saving.

Claims for relief

[34.6] Investors' relief must be claimed on or before the first anniversary of the 31 January following the tax year in which the disposal is made. In the case of a disposal by trustees, the claim must be made jointly by the trustees and the eligible beneficiary or beneficiaries. [*TCGA 1992, s 169VM*].

Shares qualifying for investors' relief

[34.7] A share which is in a holding of shares is a '*qualifying share*' immediately before a disposal of all or part of the holding if:

(a) it was subscribed for (solely or jointly) by the individual or trustees making the disposal (the '*investor*');
(b) it was issued to the investor for consideration wholly in cash;
(c) it was fully paid up at the time it was issued;
(d) it was subscribed for, and issued, for genuine commercial reasons and not as part of 'arrangements' with a main purpose of securing a 'tax advantage' to any person (as defined at 38.8 LOSSES);
(e) it was subscribed for, and issued, by way of a bargain at arm's length;
(f) the investor has held it continuously for the period beginning with its issue and ending with the disposal;
(g) it was issued on or after 17 March 2016;
(h) at the time it was issued, none of the shares or securities of the company were listed on a recognised stock exchange (see 57.27 SHARES AND SECURITIES);
(i) it was an 'ordinary share' when issued and immediately before the disposal;
(j) the company was a 'trading company' or the 'holding company of a trading group' when the share was issued and has been so throughout the share-holding period;
(k) neither the investor nor a connected person has been a 'relevant employee' (see below) in relation to the company at any time in the share-holding period; and
(l) the period beginning with the date the share was issued and ending with the date of disposal is at least three years.

A share is a '*potentially qualifying share*' if conditions (a) to (k) above are met but condition (l) above is not yet completed.

A share is an '*excluded share*' if it is neither a qualifying share nor a potentially qualifying share.

Where an individual (A) who has subscribed for shares transfers them to another individual (B) who is then living together with A as A's spouse or civil partner, B is treated as having subscribed for the shares and A's period of ownership is added to, and treated as part of, B's period of ownership.

In (i) above, '*ordinary shares*' means any shares forming part of the company's ordinary share capital within *ITA 2007, s 989*. In (j) above, '*trading company*' and '*holding company of a trading group*' have the same meaning as at 30.3 HOLD-OVER RELIEFS. A company is not, however, treated as ceasing to be a trading company or the holding company of a trading group only because of anything done as a result of the company or a subsidiary being in administration or receivership or of a resolution or order for winding-up. The entry into administration or receivership or the resolution or order and everything done as a result must be for genuine commercial reasons and not part of a scheme or arrangement a main purpose of which is tax avoidance.

In (k) above (and for the purposes of **34.3** above), a person who has at any time in the 'relevant period' been an officer or employee of the issuing company or a connected company is at that time a '*relevant employee*' in respect of the issuing company. An unremunerated director of the issuing company or a connected company is not, however, a relevant employee if neither he nor any person connected with him was connected with the issuing company or involved in carrying on any part of the trade, business or profession of the issuing company or a connected company at any time before the relevant period. A person who becomes an employee of the issuing company or a connected company within the relevant period, but not within its first 180 days, is not a relevant employee if there was, at the start of the relevant period, no 'reasonable prospect' of him becoming an employee within the relevant period and he is not a director at any time in that period. The '*relevant period*' for the purposes of (k) above is the share-holding period; for the purposes of **34.3** above it is the three-year period mentioned there. A company is a connected company if it is at any time in the relevant period connected with the issuing company There is a '*reasonable prospect*' of something if it is more likely than not.

An '*unremunerated director*' is a director who does not receive in the relevant period any 'disqualifying payment' from the issuing company or a 'related person' and who is not entitled to receive any such payment for that period or any part of it. A '*disqualifying payment*' is any payment other than:

- payment or reimbursement of travelling or other expenses wholly, exclusively and necessarily incurred in the performance of the director's duties;
- interest representing no more than a reasonable commercial return on money lent to the issuing company or a related person;
- a dividend or other distribution representing no more than a normal return on investment;
- a payment for the supply of goods not exceeding market value;
- payment of rent for any property occupied by the issuing company or a related person not exceeding a reasonable and commercial rent; or
- any necessary and reasonable remuneration for 'qualifying services' provided to the issuing company or a related person in the course of a trade or profession carried on wholly or partly in the UK which are taken into account in calculating the taxable profits of that trade or profession.

A 'related person' is a connected company of which the person concerned is a director or any person connected with such a company or the issuing company. 'Qualifying services' are services which are not secretarial or managerial services or services of a kind provided by the person to whom they are provided.

[*TCGA 1992, ss 169VH, 169VU-169VY*].

Disqualification of shares where value received

[34.8] Shares which would otherwise be qualifying shares or potentially qualifying shares for the purposes of investors' relief are disqualified from relief and treated as excluded shares if the investor receives any value, other than 'insignificant value', from the company at any time in the '*period of restriction*', i.e. the period beginning one year before, and ending immediately before the third anniversary of, the date on which the shares were issued.

The provisions apply equally to value received from a person connected with the company at any time in the period of restriction and to value received by an 'associate' (defined as in *CTA 2010, s 448*, but excluding a sibling) of the investor. References below to a payment or disposal to an investor include a payment or disposal to the person indirectly or to his order or for his benefit.

An investor '*receives value*' from the company if it:

(a) repays, redeems or repurchases any of its share capital or securities which are held by the investor, or makes any payment to him for giving up any right to any of the company's share capital or securities on its cancellation or extinguishment; or
(b) repays, under any 'arrangements' for, or in connection with, the acquisition of the shares, any debt owed to him other than one incurred by the company on or after the date of issue of the shares and otherwise than in consideration of extinguishing a debt incurred before that date; or
(c) makes any payment to the investor for giving up his right to any debt on its extinguishment; or
(d) releases or waives any liability of the investor to the company (which it is deemed to have done if discharge of the liability is twelve months or more overdue) or discharges or undertakes to discharge any liability of his to a third person; or
(e) makes a loan or advance to him (defined as including any debt, other than an 'ordinary trade debt', either to the company or to a third person but assigned to the company) which has not been repaid in full before the issue of the shares; or
(f) provides a benefit or facility for him; or
(g) disposes of an asset to him for no consideration or for consideration less than market value; or
(h) acquires an asset from him for consideration exceeding market value; or
(i) makes any other payment to him other than a 'qualifying payment'.

The investor also 'receives value' from the company if any person connected with the company purchases shares or securities of the company from him or pays him for giving up any right in relation to such shares or securities.

A debt or liability is not taken into account for these purposes if it would be discharged by the company making a qualifying payment. Similarly, any benefit or facility is excluded if, had a payment of equal value to the benefit or facility been made, that payment would have been a qualifying payment. A '*qualifying payment*' means:

(i) payment by any company of reasonable remuneration for services as an officer or employee;
(ii) payment or reimbursement by any company of travelling or other expenses wholly, exclusively and necessarily incurred by the investor in the performance of duties as an officer or employee;
(iii) payment by any company of interest representing a reasonable commercial return on money lent to it;
(iv) payment by any company of a dividend or other distribution not exceeding a normal return on any investment in its shares or securities;
(v) payment for the supply of goods of not more than market value;
(vi) payment for the acquisition of an asset not exceeding its market value;

(vii) payment of rent by any company for a property occupied by it of no more than a reasonable and commercial amount;

(viii) reasonable and necessary remuneration paid to any company for services rendered to it in the course of a trade or profession carried on wholly or partly in the UK and taken into account in calculating the taxable profits of the trade of profession; or

(ix) payment to discharge a debt for goods or services supplied in the ordinary course of a trade or business on normal credit terms of no more than six months.

The amount of value received by the investor is:

- where any of (a)–(c) above applies, the greater of the amount received by the investor and the market value of the share capital, securities or debt;
- where (d) above applies, the amount of the liability;
- where (e) above applies, the amount of the loan or advance not repaid before the shares are issued;
- where (f) above applies, the cost of providing the benefit or facility less any consideration given by the investor;
- where (g) or (h) above applies, the difference between market value and any consideration given;
- where (i) above applies, the amount of the payment;
- where a payment is made for purchase of, or for giving up rights in relation to, the company's shares or securities, the greater of the amount received by the investor and the market value of the shares or securities.

Insignificant value

An amount of '*insignificant value*' is an amount of value which does not exceed £1,000. If, at any time in the period beginning one year before the date of issue of the shares and ending with the date of issue, there are in existence arrangements (as broadly defined) providing for the investor (or an associate) to receive, or become entitled to receive, any value from the issuing company (or a connected person) at any time in the period of restriction, no amount of value received by the investor or associate is treated as an amount of insignificant value. References to an associate or person connected with the company include anyone who has such status at *any* time in the period of restriction.

There are provisions to aggregate a receipt of value, whether insignificant or not, with amounts of insignificant value received previously, and treating that aggregate, if it is not itself an amount of insignificant value, as an amount of value received at the time of the latest actual receipt.

Replacement value

The 'value received' provisions above (other than where (b) above applies) are disapplied if the person from whom the value was received (the '*original supplier*') receives, by way of a 'qualifying receipt', and whether before or after the original receipt of value, at least equivalent replacement value from the original recipient. A receipt is a '*qualifying receipt*' if it arises by reason of:

(A) any one, or any combination of, the following:

  (i) a payment by the original recipient to the original supplier other than a payment within (1) to (6) below or a payment covered by (C) below;

(ii) the acquisition of an asset by the original recipient from the original supplier for consideration exceeding market value;

(iii) the disposal of an asset by the original recipient to the original supplier for no consideration or for consideration less than market value; or

(B) (where the original receipt of value falls within (d) above) an event having the effect of reversing the original event; or

(C) (where the original receipt of value arose from the purchase from the individual by a person connected with the company of shares or securities of the company or from a payment for giving up any right in relation to them) the repurchase by the original recipient of the shares or securities in question, or reacquisition of the right in question, for consideration not less than the original value.

The amount of replacement value is:

- in a case within (A) above, the amount of any such payment plus the difference between the market value of any such asset and the consideration received;
- in a case within (B) above, the same as the amount of the original value; and
- in a case within (C) above, the consideration received by the original supplier.

A receipt of replacement value is disregarded if it occurs before the start of the period of restriction or, if it is received after the original value, it is not received as soon after the original value was received as is reasonably practicable in the circumstances.

A receipt of replacement value is also disregarded if it has previously been set against a receipt of value to prevent any shares being treated as excluded shares.

The following payments are excluded from (A)(i) above:

(1) a reasonable (in relation to their market value) payment for any goods, services or facilities provided (in the course of trade or otherwise) by the original supplier;

(2) a payment of interest at no more than a reasonable commercial rate on money lent to the original recipient;

(3) a payment not exceeding a reasonable and commercial rent for property occupied by the original recipient;

(4) a payment not exceeding market value for the acquisition of an asset;

(5) a payment in discharge of an ordinary trade debt;

(6) a payment for any shares or securities in any company in circumstances not within (A)(ii) above.

Each reference in (1)–(3) above to the original supplier or recipient includes a reference to any person who at any time in the period of restriction is an associate of his or, in the case of the supplier, is connected with him.

[*TCGA 1992, Sch 7ZB*].

Reorganisations

[34.9] The following rules apply to determine the qualifying status for the purposes of investors' relief of shares held following a reorganisation within *TCGA 1992, s 126* (see **57.2** SHARES AND SECURITIES), exchange of shares or scheme of reconstruction. For these purposes, a 'new holding' means a holding that is the new holding under the reorganisation provisions (see **57.2**) or, where that new holding consists of two or more actual holdings, any of those actual holdings. 'Original shares' means the shares held by the qualifying person immediately before the reorganisation that were original shares (as in **57.2**) in relation to the reorganisation. 'Consideration' has the same meaning as 'additional consideration' in **57.2**.

Reorganisation where no consideration given

Where a qualifying person disposes of shares which form all or part of a new holding following a reorganisation and that person did not give or become liable to give any consideration for any part of a new holding, the following assumption is made. If a number of the original shares were subscribed for by the qualifying person, were issued on a particular date and were held continuously for a period ending immediately before the reorganisation, an appropriate number of shares in the new holding are treated as having been subscribed for and as having been issued on, and held continuously from, the same date as those original shares. The number of shares so treated is found by multiplying the total number of shares in the new holding immediately after the reorganisation by the number of original shares so subscribed for, issued and held divided by the total number of original shares.

The provisions in **34.4** above apply, where needed, to determine which shares are included in a holding immediately before a reorganisation.

[*TCGA 1992, ss 169VN, 169VO*].

Reorganisation where consideration given

The following applies where a qualifying person disposes of shares which form all or part of a new holding following a reorganisation and that person gave or became liable to give consideration for shares issued to him on the reorganisation and which, immediately after the reorganisation, were in a new holding. In determining the qualifying status of shares in that new holding, the date of issue of the shares issued for consideration is taken to be their actual date of issue (and not the date of issue of any of the original shares). In determining the qualifying status of any shares forming any part of the new holding for which consideration was not given, the same assumption is made as above for reorganisations where no consideration was given but by reference only to that part of the new holding. That assumption is also made for any other new holding for which the qualifying person did not give or become liable to give consideration. [*TCGA 1992, s 169VP*].

Exchange of shares

Where *TCGA 1992, s 135* (see **57.5** SHARES AND SECURITIES) applies to an issue of shares in a company (company B) in exchange for shares in another company (company A), the reorganisation provisions above apply as if companies A and B were the same company and the exchange were a reorganisation of that company's share capital. [*TCGA 1992, s 169VQ*].

Scheme of reconstruction

Where *TCGA 1992, s 136* (see **57.7** SHARES AND SECURITIES) applies to an arrangement between a company (company A) and its shareholders (or a class of them) under which another company (company B) issues shares to those shareholders in exchange for shares in another company (company A) and the shareholders are treated as exchanging company A shares for the shares held by them as a result of the arrangement, the reorganisation provisions above apply as if companies A and B were the same company and the exchange were a reorganisation of that company's share capital. [*TCGA 1992, s 169VR*].

Conditions for being a qualifying share

On the disposal of a share which is in a new holding following an exchange of shares or deemed exchange under a scheme of reconstruction, the conditions at 34.7(j) and (k) above are met if, and only if:

- they are met by the original share for the period beginning with the issue of the original share and ending with the exchange; and
- they are met by a share representing the original share for the period beginning with the exchange and ending with the disposal.

Where there has been more than one exchange before the disposal, this rule applies to each stage of the sequence and must be met (with the necessary modifications) in respect of all of them.

[*TCGA 1992, s 169VS*].

Election to disapply reorganisation provisions

[34.10] Where a reorganisation within *TCGA 1992, s 126* or an exchange of shares treated as such a reorganisation by *TCGA 1992, s 135* or *s 136* takes place and *TCGA 1992, s 127* would otherwise apply to treat the 'original shares' and the 'new holding' as the same asset (see **57.2** SHARES AND SECURITIES), an election can be made to disapply that section so that a claim for investors' relief can be claimed in respect of the disposal of the original shares. (Note that the disapplication of *s 127* takes effect only where a claim to investors' relief is made; without such a claim the election has no effect.)

An election must be made on or before the first anniversary of the 31 January following the tax year in which the reorganisation etc. takes place. Where the disposal arising from the reorganisation etc. is by trustees, the election must be made jointly by the trustees and the eligible beneficiary or beneficiaries. An election may be beneficial if the original shares qualify for investors' relief but the shares in the new holding following the reorganisation do not.

[*TCGA 1992, s 169VT*].

35

Land

Cross-references. See **7.7** ASSETS for granting of options; **8.6** ASSETS HELD ON 6 APRIL **1965** for land reflecting development value and **8.7–8.12** for other land held at that date; **10.2** CAPITAL SUMS DERIVED FROM ASSETS for treatment of statutory compensation received by tenants of land and **10.4** for buildings destroyed and replaced out of compensation; **16.13**(k) COMPUTATION OF GAINS AND LOSSES for the deduction as enhancement expenditure of betterment levy; **23.38** for woodlands, **23.51** for housing associations, **23.58** for self-build societies and **23.79** for disposal by gift of national heritage property; **38.10** LOSSES for buildings becoming of negligible value; **39.6** MARKET VALUE; **41** MINERAL ROYALTIES; **45.5** PAYMENT OF TAX for payment by instalments on gifts of land; **47** PRIVATE RESIDENCES with land attached; **53** ROLLOVER RELIEF — REPLACEMENT OF BUSINESS ASSETS for a claim on disposal of land occupied for trade purposes.

Simon's Taxes. See **C2.11**, **C2.12**.

Introduction to land

[35.1] The general principles of tax on chargeable gains apply to disposals of land, but there are also a number of special provisions in the legislation relating to land.

In the first instance it is necessary to determine whether a gain on an isolated transaction in land may be taxable as income rather than as a chargeable gain, either under general principles or under specific legislation. Even if a gain is not itself chargeable to tax as income, in certain circumstances, part of the consideration may be so chargeable as income and excluded from the consideration. For the interaction with tax on income generally see **35.2–35.5** below and see **35.15** and **35.20** below for such interaction in relation to leases.

Special provisions apply where a disposal of land is a part disposal. HMRC will accept an alternative basis for apportioning allowable expenditure and, where the part disposed of is small, the taxpayer can claim for the transfer not to be treated as a disposal and for the consideration to be deducted from the allowable expenditure. See **35.6**, **35.7** below.

A similar relief is available where a small part disposal occurs as a result of a compulsory purchase. For compulsory purchases generally, rollover relief can be claimed where the proceeds are reinvested in new land. See **35.8–35.10** below. Rollover relief can also be claimed on the exchange of joint interests in land (see **35.11** below).

There are special provisions relating to leases of land, see **35.12–35.21** below. For contingent liabilities on the disposal of land, see **35.22** below.

This chapter also describes the charges on non-UK residents making disposals of interests in UK land and of assets deriving at least 75% of their value from UK land on or after 6 April 2019 (see **35.23** onwards below) which replace the previous CGT charge on disposals before 6 April 2019 of UK residential property interest by non-residents (see **35.31** below).

Meaning of 'land'

The definition of 'land' for the purposes of *TCGA 1992* is not exclusive and may lead to difficulties of interpretation, especially where property derives its existence from the existence of the physical land. '*Land*' includes for such purposes, except where the context otherwise requires, messuages, tenements and hereditaments, houses and buildings of any tenure. [*TCGA 1992, s 288(1)*]. This is the original 1851 definition and should be compared with the current *Interpretation Act 1978* definition which is that '*land*' includes buildings and other structures, land covered with water, and any estate, interest, easement, servitude or right in or over land. That said, many provisions in *TCGA 1992* refer to 'land' as including any interest in or right over land or to an interest in an asset which can include land or buildings etc. (e.g. *TCGA 1992, s 152* (ROLLOVER RELIEF (53), although *TCGA 1992, s 155* treats buildings and the underlying land as separate) and *TCGA 1992, s 247* (**35.10** below)). Deciding whether property is an interest or right over land can thus depend on general legal principles and the surrounding facts.

Interaction with tax on income

[35.2] In the first instance it is necessary to determine whether a gain on an isolated transaction in land may be taxable as income rather than as a chargeable gain. The following considerations are relevant.

(a) An isolated or speculative transaction may be liable to income tax rather than to capital gains tax as amounting to a venture in the nature of trade (see **35.3** below).

(b) Even where (a) above does not apply, capital gains from certain transactions in land may be treated as income (see **35.4** and **35.5** below).

Isolated or speculative transactions

[35.3] A line is drawn between realisations of property held as investment or as a residence (chargeable to tax as chargeable gains) and transactions amounting to a venture in the nature of a trade which are chargeable to tax as trading income. Per Lawrence LJ in *Leeming v Jones* HL 1930, 15 TC 333, 'in the case of an isolated transaction . . . there is really no middle course open. It is either an adventure in the nature of trade, or else it is simply a case of sale and resale of property.'

Whether the surplus on the purchase and resale of land, otherwise than in the course of an established commercial enterprise, is derived from a venture in the nature of trade depends upon the facts (see *Marson v Morton* Ch D 1986, 59 TC 381). In that case, the court applied the well-known 'badges of trade' but emphasised that they are not a comprehensive list and provide at most a common sense guidance as to whether a trade is being carried on. For more on the badges of trade and transactions in land, see Tolley's Corporation Tax, **Simon's Taxes, B5.216** and HMRC Business Income Manual BIM60001 onwards.

There have been many court and tribunal decisions over many years on the distinction between trading in land and investment. For detailed coverage of the case law, see **Simon's Taxes, B5.217–B5.218C.**

Transactions in UK land

[35.4] There are provisions which seek to ensure that the tax is charged on the full amount of profits from dealing in or developing land in the UK, regardless of whether the company is resident or non-resident in the UK.

The provisions override the general territorial rule for trading income whereby the charge on profits arising to a non-UK resident individual or company normally depends on the extent to which the trade is carried on in the UK.

The provisions apply specific income tax and corporation tax charges on profits from dealing in or developing UK land. The charge applies in specified circumstances to profits and gains of a capital nature arising when land is disposed of, and also to disposals of assets deriving their value from land in the UK. There is provision to ensure that the charge applies only to profits not otherwise chargeable to UK tax as income.

See Tolley's Income Tax and Tolley's Corporation Tax under Transactions in UK Land.

[*ITTOIA 2005, s 6B; ITA 2007, ss 517A–517U; CTA 2009, s 5B; CTA 2010, ss 356OA–356OT*].

Where a person is charged to income tax or corporation tax under the above provisions on the basis that a main purpose of developing the land was to realise a profit or gain from disposing of it once developed (i.e. where *ITA 2007, s 517B(7)* or *CTA 2010, s 356OB(7)* applies), that land is also to be treated for chargeable gains purposes (under *TCGA 1992, s 161*; see **16.9** COMPUTATION OF GAINS AND LOSSES) as having been transferred to stock. [*TCGA 1992, s 161(5)(6)*].

Land sold with right of reconveyance

[35.5] Where an interest in land is sold on terms requiring it to be subsequently reconveyed at a future date after the sale (or leased back one month or more after the sale) to the vendor, or a person connected with the vendor, and the price at which the interest is sold exceeds that at which it is to be reconveyed (or, in the case of a lease-back, the value of the reversionary interest plus any premium for the lease), the excess less 1/50th for each full year (minus one) between the sale and the date of the earliest possible reconveyance (or lease-back) is treated as a receipt of the vendor's property business. [*ITTOIA 2005, ss 284–286, 301, 302; CTA 2009, ss 224, 225*].

Any amount (as adjusted under *ITTOIA 2005, ss 301, 302* or *CTA 2009, ss 238, 239*) brought into account as a receipt of a property business under these provisions is excluded from the consideration brought into account in the computation for capital gains purposes *except* in the denominator of the part disposal fraction (A/(A+B); see **16.5** COMPUTATION OF GAINS AND LOSSES). This does not apply where what is disposed of is the remainder of a lease or a sub-lease out of a lease the duration of which does not exceed 50 years. See **35.16** below for the alternative provisions which apply. [*TCGA 1992, Sch 8 paras 5(3)(4), 6(3)*].

Part disposals

[35.6] The general provisions for part disposals in *TCGA 1992, s 42* apply to disposals of land. See **16.5** COMPUTATION OF GAINS AND LOSSES. These require the use of the market value of the part retained. HMRC will, however, accept an alternative basis of calculation in the case of land.

Under this basis, the part disposed of will be treated as a separate asset and any fair and reasonable method of apportioning part of the total cost to it will be accepted — e.g. a reasonable valuation of that part at the acquisition date.

The cost of the part disposed of will be deducted from the total cost of the estate (or the balance of total cost) to determine the cost of the remainder of the estate; thus the total of the separate amounts adopted for the parts will not exceed the total cost. The cost attributed to each part must also be realistic in itself and HMRC reserve the right to apply the general rule if not satisfied that apportionments are fair and reasonable. The taxpayer can always require that the general rule should be applied (except in cases already settled on the alternative basis). If he chooses the general rule it will normally be necessary to apply this rule to all subsequent disposals out of the estate; but where the general rule has been applied for a part disposal before the introduction of the alternative basis and it produced a result broadly the same as under the alternative basis, the alternative basis may be used for subsequent part disposals out of the estate.

Adoption of the alternative basis is without prejudice to the treatment of small disposals set out in 35.7 below (HMRC Statement of Practice SP D1).

Small part disposals

[35.7] Where there is a transfer of land forming part only of a holding of land (or an estate or interest in land) and the amount or value of the consideration does not exceed one-fifth of the market value of the holding as it existed immediately before the disposal, the transferor may claim under *TCGA 1992, s 242(2)* that the transfer is not treated as a disposal. The consideration which would have been brought into account in the capital gains tax computation is then treated as a reduction of allowable expenditure in relation to any subsequent disposal of the remaining holding.

The consideration for the transfer or, if the transfer is not for full consideration, the market value of the land transferred, must not exceed a limit of £20,000. Where the transferor has made other disposals of land in the tax year, the total amount or value of the consideration for all such disposals of land (other than those within 35.9 below) must not exceed the limit.

The provisions do not apply to:

(a) transfers treated as giving rise to neither a gain nor a loss between spouses or civil partners (see **40.4** MARRIED PERSONS AND CIVIL PARTNERS) or between companies in the same group (see **26.2** GROUPS OF COMPANIES); or
(b) an estate or interest in land which is a wasting asset (e.g. a short lease under 35.13 below).

A claim for small part disposals must be made for the purposes of capital gains tax on or before the first anniversary of 31 January following the tax year in which the transfer is made. For corporation tax purposes, the claim must be made within two years after the end of the accounting period in which the transfer is made.

Where the allowable expenditure is less than the consideration for the part disposal (or is nil), the claim referred to above cannot be made but, if the recipient elects under *TCGA 1992, s 244(2)* and there is allowable expenditure, the consideration for the part disposal is reduced by the amount of the allowable expenditure. None of that expenditure is then allowable as a deduction in computing the gain on the part disposal or any subsequent disposal.

[*TCGA 1992, ss 242, 244*].

Example

C owns land which cost £134,000 in May 1988. In February 1996, a small plot of land is exchanged with an adjoining landowner for another piece of land. The value placed on the transaction is £18,000. The value of the remaining estate excluding the new piece of land is estimated at £250,000. In March 2025, C sells the whole estate for £300,000. He makes no other disposals in 2024/25. The indexation factor for May 1988 to February 1996 is 0.421.

(i) No claim made under *TCGA 1992, s 242(2)*

		£	£
(a)	Disposal in February 1996		
	Disposal proceeds		18,000
	Allowable cost		
	$\frac{18{,}000}{18{,}000+250{,}000} \times £134{,}000$		9,000
	Unindexed gain		9,000
	Indexation allowance £9,000 × 0.421		3,789
	Chargeable gain 1995/96		£5,211
(b)	Disposal in March 2025		
	Disposal proceeds		300,000
	Allowable cost		
	Original land £(134,000 – 9,000)	125,000	
	Exchanged land	18,000	143,000
	Chargeable gain 2024/25		£157,000

(ii) Claim made under *TCGA 1992, s 242(2)*

		£	£
(a)	No disposal in February 1996		
	Allowable cost of original land		134,000
	Deduct disposal proceeds		18,000
	Adjusted allowable cost		£116,000
	Allowable cost of additional land		£18,000

		£	£
(b)	Disposal in March 2025		
	Disposal proceeds		300,000
	Allowable cost		
	Original land	116,000	
	Additional land	18,000	134,000
	Chargeable gain 2024/25		£166,000

Compulsory purchase

[35.8] The transfer of an interest in land to an 'authority exercising or having compulsory powers' (see **35.9** below) is a disposal for capital gains purposes.

If the land is acquired under a contract, the date of disposal is the time the contract is made (and not, if different, the time at which the asset is conveyed or transferred). If the contract is conditional, the date of disposal is the time when the condition is satisfied. See also **16.4** COMPUTATION OF GAINS AND LOSSES. Otherwise, the disposal and acquisition are made at the time at which compensation for the acquisition is agreed or otherwise determined (any variation on appeal against the original determination being disregarded).

[*TCGA 1992, ss 28, 246*].

Relief is available for small part disposals (see **35.9** below). Rollover relief may be claimed in certain circumstances (see **35.10** below).

In addition, where land or an interest in or right over land is acquired and the acquisition is (or could have been) made under compulsory powers, then the existence of the compulsory powers and any statutory provision treating the purchase price, compensation or other consideration as exclusively paid in respect of the land itself is disregarded in considering whether, under *TCGA 1992, s 52(4)* (just and reasonable apportionments), the purchase price etc. should be apportioned on a just and reasonable basis and treated in part as a capital sum within *TCGA 1992, s 22(1)(a)* (whether as compensation for loss of goodwill, for disturbance or otherwise) or should be apportioned in any other way. [*TCGA 1992, s 245(1)*]. The effect of this is that, where it is just and reasonable, part of the proceeds may be treated as a capital sum derived from an asset. See **10.2**(a) CAPITAL SUMS DERIVED FROM ASSETS.

The receipt of severance compensation or compensation for injurious affection where part of a holding of land is or could have been compulsorily purchased is treated as a part disposal of the remaining land. [*TCGA 1992, s 245(2)*]. Where the conditions are satisfied, a claim for rollover relief may be made (see **35.10** below) in which case the consideration rolled over will include such compensation and there will be no deemed disposal of the remaining land. [*TCGA 1992, s 247(6)*].

Example

(i) Rollover not claimed

D owns freehold land purchased for £77,000 in 1978. Part of the land is made the subject of a compulsory purchase order. The compensation of £70,000 is agreed on 10 August 2024. The market value of the remaining land is £175,000. The value of the total freehold land at 31 March 1982 was £98,000.

	£
Disposal consideration	70,000

Market value 31.3.82

$£98,000 \times \frac{70,000}{70,000 + 175,000}$	28,000
Chargeable gain	£42,000

(ii) Rollover claimed under *TCGA 1992, s 247*

If, in (i), D acquires new land costing, say, £80,000 in, say, December 2024, relief may be claimed as follows.

	£
Allowable cost of land compulsorily purchased	28,000
Actual consideration	70,000
Chargeable gain rolled over	£42,000
Allowable cost of new land (£80,000 – £42,000)	£38,000

Small part disposals

[35.9] Where a part of a holding of land (or an interest therein) is transferred to an 'authority exercising or having compulsory powers', the transferor may claim under *TCGA 1992, s 243(2)* that the transfer is not treated as a disposal, in which case the consideration which would have been brought into account is treated as a reduction of allowable expenditure in relation to any subsequent disposal of the remaining holding.

A claim must be made for the purposes of capital gains tax on or before the first anniversary of 31 January following the tax year in which the transfer is made. For corporation tax purposes the claim must be made within two years after the end of the accounting period in which the transfer is made.

[*TCGA 1992, s 243(2A)*].

A holding of land for these purposes comprises only the land in respect of which allowable expenditure would be apportioned under *TCGA 1992, s 42* if the transfer had been treated as a part disposal. The consideration for the transfer (or, if the transfer is not for full consideration, the market value of the land transferred) must be 'small' as compared with the market value of the holding immediately before the transfer. For this purpose, HMRC regard 'small' as meaning 5% or less but they also regard an amount of £3,000 or less as 'small', regardless of whether or not it would pass the 5% test (HMRC Capital Gains Manual CG57835, CG72200).

The transferor must not have taken any steps, by advertising or otherwise, to dispose of any part of the holding or to make his willingness to dispose of it known to anyone. The provisions do not apply to wasting interests in land (e.g. a short lease under **35.13** below) but subject to this any estate or interest in land is included as a holding.

Where the allowable expenditure is less than the consideration for the part disposal (or is nil) the claim referred to above cannot be made but, if the recipient elects under *TCGA 1992, s 244(2)* and there is allowable expenditure, the consideration for the part disposal is reduced by the amount of the allowable expenditure. For capital gains tax purposes, an election must be made on or before the first anniversary of the 31 January next following the tax year in which part disposal is made; and for corporation tax purposes it must be made within two years after the end of the accounting period in which the part disposal is made. None of that expenditure is then allowable as a deduction in computing the gain accruing on the part disposal or any subsequent disposal.

'*Authority exercising or having compulsory powers*' means, in relation to the land transferred, a person or body of persons acquiring it compulsorily or who has or have been, or could be, authorised to acquire it compulsorily for the purposes for which it is acquired, or for whom another person or body of persons has or have been, or could be, authorised so to acquire it.

[*TCGA 1992, ss 243, 244*].

Example

(i) No rollover relief claimed

T inherited land in June 1989 at a probate value of £290,000. Under a compulsory purchase order, a part of the land is acquired for highway improvements. Compensation of £32,000 and a further £10,000 for severance, neither sum including any amount in respect of loss of profits, is agreed on 14 May 2024. The value of the remaining land is £900,000. Prior to the compulsory purchase, the value of all the land had been £950,000.

	£
Total consideration for disposal (£32,000 + £10,000)	42,000
Deduct allowable cost $\frac{42,000}{42,000 + 900,000} \times £290,000$	12,930
Chargeable gain	£29,070

(ii) Rollover relief claimed under *TCGA 1992, s 243*

Total consideration for disposal is £42,000, less than 5% of the value of the estate before the disposal (£950,000). T may therefore claim that the consideration be deducted from the allowable cost of the estate.

Revised allowable cost (£290,000 – £42,000)	£248,000

Rollover relief

[35.10] ROLLOVER RELIEF (53) can be claimed by any landowner who disposes of land to an 'authority exercising or having compulsory powers' (see **35.9** above) where the landowner reinvests part or the whole of the proceeds in acquiring new land. Relief is not confined to land (or any interest in or right over land) which is used and occupied for the purposes of a trade.

Land which is a dwelling-house or part of one and on which the whole or part of the gain on a subsequent disposal within six years would be covered by the exemptions for PRIVATE RESIDENCES (47) is excluded. Where any land is not so excluded at acquisition, but becomes so within six years, relief is withdrawn.

The effect of a claim (under *TCGA 1992, s 247(2)*) is to defer capital gains tax by deducting the otherwise chargeable gain on the original land from the acquisition cost of the newly acquired land. Relief is restricted where part only of the proceeds is reinvested in qualifying land. See **53.8** ROLLOVER RELIEF.

The following further matters should be noted.

(a) The landowner must not have taken any steps, by advertising or otherwise, to dispose of the old land or to make his willingness to dispose of it known. In practice, any event which occurred more than three years before the date of disposal is ignored. (HMRC Capital Gains Manual CG61900, 72200).

(b) The new land must be acquired in the period beginning twelve months before and ending three years after the disposal or such longer period as HMRC may allow e.g. where it has not been practical to acquire new land within the time limit.

New town corporations and similar authorities may purchase land for development and then grant the previous owner a lease or tenancy of the land until they are ready to commence building. Where land is so acquired under a compulsory purchase order or under the threat of such an order and is immediately leased back to the previous owner HMRC are prepared, so long as there is a clear continuing intention that the sale proceeds will be used to acquire assets qualifying for rollover relief, to extend the time limit to a date three years after the land ceases to be used by him for his trade. An assurance to this effect will be given in appropriate cases subject to the reservation that it would be necessary to raise a protective assessment on the gain arising if exceptionally the lease or tenancy continued so long as to extend beyond the statutory time limit for making assessments (HMRC Statement of Practice SP D6).

(c) Where the new land is a depreciating asset, similar provisions apply as in **53.9** ROLLOVER RELIEF except that the gain is held over for ten years or until the new asset is disposed of, whichever is the sooner. For corporation tax purposes, and, for disposals before 6 April 2008, for capital gains tax purposes, a gain previously held over is never deemed to accrue in consequence of an event occurring after 5 April 1988 if the application of this provision would be directly attributable to the disposal of an asset before 1 April 1982.

(d) The normal treatment of severance compensation as a part disposal (see **35.8** above) is expressly excluded. Such compensation is treated as additional consideration for the old land.

(e) Claims under these provisions and under *TCGA 1992, s 243* (see **35.9** above) are mutually exclusive.

(f) Subject to all other conditions for the granting of relief being met, HMRC will accept a claim from a landlord whose leasehold tenant has exercised the following statutory rights:
- his right under the *Leasehold Reform Act 1967* or the *Leasehold Reform, Housing and Urban Development Act 1993* to acquire the freehold reversion of a property or an extension of the lease,
- his right to buy or to acquire the freehold or an extension of the lease under the *Housing Acts 1985* to *1996* (which covers the situation where a tenant's right to buy is preserved following a transfer of housing stock into the private sector) or the right to purchase tenanted property under the *Housing (Scotland) Act 1987*, or
- the right of a crofting community body to purchase croft land under *Land Reform (Scotland) Act 2003, Pt 3.*

HMRC will also accept a claim from a community group exercising its rights under *Land Reform (Scotland) Act 2003, Pt 3A* to buy abandoned, neglected or detrimental land.
(HMRC Capital Gains Manual CG61940).

(g) ROLLOVER RELIEF (**53**) is available where there is a compulsory purchase from one group member and acquisition of land by another.

[*TCGA 1992, ss 247, 248, Sch 4 paras A1, 4(5)*].

Provisional claims are permitted, in much the same way as for ROLLOVER RELIEF (**53.11**).

The claimant may make a declaration in his tax return for a tax year or company accounting period in which he has made a qualifying disposal of land that the whole or a specified part of the consideration will be invested, within the requisite time limits (see (b) above), in new land (or an interest in or right over land) and that the new land is not excluded by virtue of the availability of the private residence exemption (see above). As long as the declaration continues to have effect, the same consequences ensue as if both an acquisition and a valid rollover relief claim had been made. The declaration ceases to have effect on the day, and to the extent that, it is withdrawn or is superseded by a valid claim, if either occurs before the 'relevant day'. It otherwise ceases to have effect on the relevant day itself. On its ceasing to have effect, all necessary adjustments will be made to the claimant's tax position, even if otherwise out of time.

The '*relevant day*' means:

- in relation to capital gains tax, the third anniversary of 31 January following the tax year of disposal, e.g. 31 January 2029 for disposals in 2024/25; and
- in relation to corporation tax, the fourth anniversary of the last day of the accounting period of disposal.

[*TCGA 1992, s 247A*].

To the extent that a provisional claim is withdrawn or lapses, interest on unpaid tax is chargeable as if no such claim had been made.

Rollover relief for exchange of joint interests in land

[35.11] A form of rollover relief is available for certain exchanges of joint interests in land. Relief is available, where a claim is made, if:

(a) a 'holding of land' or two or more separate holdings of land are held jointly;
(b) one of the owners (the 'taxpayer') disposes of an interest in the holding or one or more of the holdings to one or more of the co-owners;
(c) the consideration for the disposal is or includes an interest in a holding of land held jointly by the taxpayer and the co-owners concerned;
(d) as a result of the exchange, the taxpayer and each of the co-owners become the sole owner of part of the holding or of one or more of the holdings; and
(e) the interest acquired by the taxpayer is not an interest in 'excluded land'.

For this purpose, '*holding of land*' includes an estate or interest in a holding of land and is to be construed in accordance with *TCGA 1992, s 243(3)* (see 35.9 above). Land is held jointly if it is held as joint tenants or tenants in common (in Scotland as joint owners or owners in common; in NI as joint tenants, tenants in common or coparceners). Land is '*excluded land*' to the extent that it is a dwelling-house (or part of, or an interest in or right over, a dwelling-house) and, under *TCGA 1992, ss 222–226* (see **47** PRIVATE RESIDENCES), the whole or part of any gain on a disposal of it within six years after the exchange would be exempt. If land is not excluded land at the time of the exchange but subsequently, and within the following six years, becomes excluded land, rollover relief is withdrawn. See below for relief on exchanges of interests in private residences.

Spouses or civil partners living together are treated as if they were one person for this purpose, so that an exchange of interests which results in such a couple alone becoming joint owners of land will meet the above conditions.

For disposals on or after 6 April 2023, the legislation explicitly allows for relief where the land is held by a partnership, treating the partners as the taxpayer and co-owners. This provision was introduced to ensure that relief is available to all types of partnerships, including LLPs and Scottish partnerships.

Where a claim for relief is made, the taxpayer is normally treated as if the disposal consideration were reduced to the amount which would secure that neither a gain nor a loss accrues and the acquisition cost of the acquired interest were reduced by the amount of the reduction in the disposal consideration. If this rule applies to exclude a gain which is not all chargeable gain (as a result of the rules for ASSETS HELD ON 6 APRIL **1965** (8)), the amount of the reduction in the acquisition is restricted to the amount of the otherwise chargeable gain.

If, however, the disposal consideration is greater than the market value of the interest disposed of the above relief is not available. Partial relief is, however, available if the excess of the consideration over the market value is less than the gain on the disposal (whether or not the gain is all chargeable gain). In that event, the gain is treated as reduced to the amount of the excess (and if the gain is not all chargeable gain, the chargeable part is reduced proportionately). The acquisition cost of the acquired interest is then reduced by the amount by which the chargeable gain is reduced.

[*TCGA 1992, ss 248A–248D; F(No 2)A 2023, s 43(1)(3)*].

Private residences

A similar rollover relief applies to the exchange of joint interests in private residences. The relief applies, on the making of a joint claim, where:

(i) interests in two or more dwelling-houses are held jointly (as above);
(ii) one of the owners (the 'taxpayer') disposes of an interest in one or more of the dwelling-houses to one or more of the co-owners;
(iii) the consideration for the disposal is or includes an interest in one of the other dwelling-houses;
(iv) as a result of the exchange, the dwelling-house in which the taxpayer acquires an interest becomes his only or main residence and each of the other dwelling-houses becomes the only or main residence of one (and only one) of the co-owners; and
(v) if each dwelling-house were disposed of immediately after the exchange, then under *TCGA 1992, ss 222, 223, 223B* (see **47** PRIVATE RESIDENCES) no part of each gain would be a chargeable gain.

Spouses or civil partners living together are treated as if they were one person for this purpose; an exchange of interests which results in such a couple alone becoming joint owners of a dwelling-house will meet the above conditions.

Where the taxpayer and the co-owners make a joint claim, the taxpayer is treated as if the disposal consideration were reduced to the amount which would secure that neither a gain nor a loss accrues. The taxpayer's acquisition is treated as made at the time of the acquisition of the joint interest and at the original base cost at that time.

For disposals on or after 6 April 2023, the legislation explicitly allows for relief where the land is held by a partnership, treating the partners as the taxpayer and co-owners. This provision was introduced to ensure that relief is available to all types of partnerships, including LLPs and Scottish partnerships.

[*TCGA 1992, s 248E; FA 2020, s 24(8); F(No 2)A 2023, s 43(2)(3)*].

Leases

[35.12] For capital gains tax purposes, a '*lease*' in relation to land includes an underlease, sub-lease or any tenancy or licence, and any agreement for a lease, underlease, sub-lease or tenancy or licence. In the case of land outside the UK, any interest corresponding to a lease as so defined is included. '*Lessor*', '*lessee*' and '*rent*' are construed accordingly. [*TCGA 1992, s 240, Sch 8 para 10(1)*].

Where a leaseholder of land acquires a superior interest in that land (whether a superior lease or the freehold reversion) so that the first lease is extinguished, the two interests are merged within the meaning of *TCGA 1992, s 43* (assets derived from other assets). On a subsequent disposal the allowable expenditure relating to the merged interest will include the cost of the first lease, after exclusion, in the case of a lease with less than 50 years to run, of the part which was wasted under *TCGA 1992, Sch 8* to the date of the acquisition of the superior interest (see **35.13** below) and the cost of the superior interest. Where the superior interest is itself a lease with less than 50 years to run, the total of these two amounts will also be wasted under *TCGA 1992, Sch 8* down to the date of disposal. Strictly, indexation allowance, where applicable, should be calculated on the total of these two amounts by reference to the date of acquisition of the superior interest, but, by concession, indexation on the expenditure on the earlier, inferior lease, is calculated by reference to the date of its acquisition. (HMRC Extra-Statutory Concession D42).

Where a lease is surrendered on terms which include the release of the tenant from a liability under the lease to make good any dilapidations or from any other onerous liability, the value attributable to the release is consideration for the surrender (HMRC Capital Gains Manual CG71260). No deduction was allowed, however, to the landlord in its capital gains tax computation on the grant of a subsequent lease for that value in *Wakelyn Trust v HMRC* FTT, [2022] UKFTT 23 (TC).

Leases as wasting assets

[35.13] A lease of land is not a wasting asset until the time when its duration does not exceed 50 years. [*TCGA 1992, Sch 8 para 1(1)*].

Duration of a lease

For this purpose, the duration of a lease is decided by reference to the facts known or ascertainable at the time when the lease was acquired or created. In determining the duration, the following provisions apply.

(a) Where the terms of the lease include provision for the determination of the lease by notice given by the landlord, the lease is not treated as granted for a term longer than one ending at the earliest date on which it could be determined by notice given by the landlord.
(b) Where any of the terms of the lease or any other circumstances render it unlikely that the lease will continue beyond a date earlier than the expiration of the terms of the lease, the lease is not treated as having been granted for a longer term than one ending on that date. This applies in particular where the lease provides for rent to go up after a given date, or for the tenant's obligation to become more onerous after a given date, but includes provision for the determination of the lease on that date, by notice given by the tenant, and those provisions render it unlikely that the lease will continue beyond that date.
(c) Where the terms of the lease include provision for the extension of the lease beyond a given date by notice given by the tenant, the duration of the lease applies as if the term of the lease extended for as long as it could be extended by the tenant, but subject to any right of the landlord to determine the lease by notice.

[*TCGA 1992, Sch 8 para 8*].

A lease granted under *Landlord and Tenant Act 1954* to follow on from another is not a continuation of the old lease and is to be treated as having been acquired on the date it was granted (*Bayley v Rogers* Ch D 1980, 53 TC 420).

A similar view was taken in *Lewis v Walters* Ch D 1992, 64 TC 489 regarding the right of a tenant to be granted a lease under *Leasehold Reform Act 1967* to follow on from another and where it was also held that (c) above did not apply since such a right was not included in the terms of the original lease.

Where a lease is 'extended' by surrender of an old lease and grant of a new one for a longer term, a disposal of the old lease will in strictness occur, the consideration for it normally being the value, if any, of the new lease. By concession, a disposal is not treated as arising in these circumstances provided that:

- the parties are not connected and the transaction is at arm's length (or the parties *are* connected but the terms of the transaction are equivalent to those to be expected in an arm's length transaction between unconnected parties);
- the transaction is not part of or connected with a larger scheme or series of transactions;
- no capital sum is received by the lessee;
- the extent of the property in which the lessee has an interest is unchanged; and
- the terms of the leases remain the same except as regards the duration and amount of rent payable. For this purpose, trivial differences will be ignored.

(HMRC Extra-Statutory Concession D39). (See **4.21** ANTI-AVOIDANCE for the charge arising where concessions involving deferral of gains are abused.)

Computation where lease is a wasting asset

If a lease of land is a wasting asset, its original cost and any enhancement expenditure are not written off on a straight line basis (as would otherwise be required under *TCGA 1992, s 46*) but on a reducing basis as set out in the table below.

Table for depreciation of leases

Years	Percentage	Years	Percentage	Years	Percentage
50 (or more)	100.000	33	90.280	16	64.116
49	99.657	32	89.354	15	61.617
48	99.289	31	88.371	14	58.971
47	98.902	30	87.330	13	56.167
46	98.490	29	86.226	12	53.191
45	98.059	28	85.053	11	50.038
44	97.595	27	83.816	10	46.695
43	97.107	26	82.496	9	43.154
42	96.593	25	81.100	8	39.399
41	96.041	24	79.622	7	35.414
40	95.457	23	78.055	6	31.195
39	94.842	22	76.399	5	26.722
38	94.189	21	74.635	4	21.983
37	93.497	20	72.770	3	16.959
36	92.761	19	70.791	2	11.629
35	91.981	18	68.697	1	5.983

Years	Percentage	Years	Percentage	Years	Percentage
34	91.156	17	66.470	0	0

The fraction of the *original cost* which is not allowed is given by the fraction

$$\frac{P(1) - P(3)}{P(1)}$$

where

P(1) = the percentage derived from the table for the duration of the lease at acquisition
P(3) = the percentage derived from the table for the duration of the lease at the time of disposal

The fraction of any *enhancement expenditure* which is not allowed is given by the fraction

$$\frac{P(2) - P(3)}{P(2)}$$

where

P(2) = the percentage derived from the table for the duration of the lease at the time when the item of expenditure is first reflected in the nature of the lease
P(3) = as above

If the duration of the lease is not an exact number of years, the percentage is that for the whole number of years plus one twelfth of the difference between that and the percentage of the next higher number of years for each odd month, counting an odd 14 days or more as one month.

[*TCGA 1992, Sch 8 para 1(3)(4)*].

The provisions above apply even if the period of ownership of the lease exceeds 50 years. Accordingly, in such a case, any cost or enhancement expenditure incurred before the lease becomes a wasting asset is not reduced until the lease does become a wasting asset. [*TCGA 1992, Sch 8 para 1(5)*]. In these circumstances P(1) and P(2) will each be 100 in the fractions given above.

Example

X purchases a 30-year lease of business premises in 2018 for £250,000. In 2021, when 27 years of the lease remain, he spends £25,000 on improvements which are at once reflected in the value of the lease and continue to be so until he disposes of it with 24 years remaining in 2024. His allowable expenditure is reduced as follows:

$$\text{Original cost } (£250{,}000) \times \frac{(87.330 - 79.622)}{87.330} \quad = \quad £22{,}066$$

$$\text{Additional cost (£25,000)} \times \frac{(83.816 - 79.622)}{83.816} = \underline{£1,251}$$

£23,317

The total allowable expenditure is then (£275,000 – £23,317) = £251,683

Exceptions

The above provisions do not apply in the following circumstances.

(i) If at the beginning of the period of ownership of a lease, it is subject to a *sub-lease not at a rackrent* and the value of the lease at the end of the sub-lease (estimated at the beginning of the period of ownership) exceeds the expenditure allowable in computing the gain accruing on the disposal of the lease (see **16.12**(a) COMPUTATION OF GAINS AND LOSSES), the lease is *not* a wasting asset until the end of the duration of the sub-lease. [*TCGA 1992, Sch 8 para 1(2)*].

(ii) Where the land, throughout the ownership of the person making the disposal, is used solely for the purposes of a trade, profession or vocation, and capital allowances have, or could have, been claimed in respect of its cost, or in respect of any enhancement expenditure. This also applies where the cost of land has otherwise qualified in full for any capital allowances. Where, however, the land disposed of has been used partly for non-business purposes, or has only partly qualified for capital allowances, the expenditure and consideration are apportioned and the restriction of allowable expenditure as above applies only to that portion of expenditure which has not qualified for capital allowances, or which relates to the period of non-business use. [*TCGA 1992, s 47, Sch 8 para 1(6)*].

Premiums for leases

[35.14] Where the payment of a 'premium' is required under a lease (or otherwise under the terms subject to which the lease is granted) there is a part disposal of the freehold or other interest out of which that lease is granted. [*TCGA 1992, Sch 8 para 2(1)*].

In the part disposal computation (which follows the normal rules in *TCGA 1992, s 42*, see **16.5** COMPUTATION OF GAINS AND LOSSES) the property which remains undisposed of includes a right to any rent or other payments (other than a premium) payable under the lease, and that right is valued at the time of the part disposal. [*TCGA 1992, Sch 8 para 2(2)*].

Meaning of 'premium'

'*Premium*' includes any like sum, whether payable to the intermediate or superior landlord and includes any sum (other than rent) paid on or in connection with the granting of a tenancy except when the other sufficient consideration for the payment can be shown to have been given. In Scotland, '*premium*' includes in particular a *grassum* payable to any landlord or intermediate landlord on the creation of a sub-lease. [*TCGA 1992, Sch 8 para 10(2)(3)*].

Capital sums treated as premiums

The legislation provides for other capital amounts payable under leases to be treated as if they were premiums. Where the landlord is a freeholder, or is a leaseholder and that lease has more than 50 years to run, and

(a) *under the terms of a lease*, a sum becomes payable by the tenant in lieu of the whole or part of the rent for any period ('commutation of rent'), or as consideration for the surrender of the lease, or
(b) a sum becomes payable by the tenant (otherwise than by way of rent) as consideration for the variation or waiver of any of the terms of the lease,

the lease is deemed to have required payment of a premium to the landlord (in addition to any actual premium) of the amount of that sum. This premium is treated as being due when the sum is payable by the tenant and as being in respect of, where (a) applies, the period in relation to which it is payable or, where (b) applies, the period from the time the variation or waiver takes effect to the time it ceases to have effect. The deemed receipt of the premium does not require a chargeable gain arising from the receipt of any other premium to be recomputed. Instead, it is regarded as a separate transaction effected at the time the premium is deemed to be due and as a part disposal (or further part disposal) of the freehold (or other asset out of which the lease is granted) or, in the case of a payment for surrender, as a disposal by the landlord of his interest in the lease.

Where a sum falls within (b) above and the transaction is not at arm's length and/or is entered into gratuitously, the amount actually payable is replaced in the tax computation by such sum as might have been required of the tenant in an arm's length transaction.

The rules are modified (but not where the payment is consideration for the surrender of a lease) if the landlord is himself a tenant under a lease with 50 years or less to run at the time the capital sum is paid. The premium is deemed to have been given by way of consideration for the grant of the part of the sub-lease covered by the period in respect of which the premium is treated as having been paid. It is *not* thereby treated as having been received at the time the sub-lease was granted; the date of disposal is determined under general principles — see **16.4** COMPUTATION OF GAINS AND LOSSES. See the worked example at HMRC Capital Gains Manual CG71371. As far as the sub-lessee is concerned, the payment is treated as allowable enhancement expenditure (see **16.12**(b) COMPUTATION OF GAINS AND LOSSES) incurred by him and attributable to the aforementioned part of the sub-lease.

[*TCGA 1992, Sch 8 para 3*].

See HMRC Capital Gains Manual CG71350–71371 for further commentary on the above and worked examples.

If a capital sum is paid by a tenant for commutation of rent and the terms of the lease do *not* provide for such a payment, the above rules do not apply. The transaction is treated as a part disposal within *TCGA 1992, s 22* (see **10.2** CAPITAL SUMS DERIVED FROM ASSETS). (HMRC Capital Gains Manual CG71350, 71372).

Reverse premiums

A reverse premium (as defined) is chargeable to income tax or corporation tax as a *revenue* receipt. See *CTA 2009, ss 96–100, 250; ITTOIA 2005, ss 99–106* and see Tolley's Income Tax for full coverage.

General

In *Clarke v United Real (Moorgate) Ltd* Ch D 1987, 61 TC 353, the taxpayer company contracted for a freehold site which it owned to be developed by a third party. Subsequently it entered into an 'agreement for a lease' with another third party ('A') under which A agreed to reimburse the company's development costs and the company was to grant him a long lease of the developed site at a rent below market value, which was to be ascertained by reference to his reimbursement payments to the company. The granting of the lease was agreed to be a part disposal. The reimbursement payments were held to be a premium within *TCGA 1992, Sch 8 paras 2(1), 10(2),* because they were made to the company in its capacity as landlord, and not to meet an obligation incurred by the company on behalf of A.

Premiums taxed as receipts of property business

[35.15] Where a premium is received for a lease not exceeding 50 years and part of it is liable to tax as a receipt of a UK property business under *CTA 2009, ss 217–221* or *ITTOIA 2005, ss 277–281A*, that part is excluded from the computation for capital gains purposes *except* in the denominator of the part disposal fraction of A/(A+B) given by *TCGA 1992, s 42*. '*Premium*' includes a deemed premium under (a) or (b) in **35.14** above. [*TCGA 1992, Sch 8 para 5(1)(5)*].

Where the terms of a lease impose an obligation on the tenant to carry out work on the premises concerned, an amount equal to the increase in value of the landlord's interest occasioned by the work is treated as a premium except insofar as the obligation relates to work which, had it been carried out by the landlord, would have been deductible as an expense of any property business carried on by the landlord. [*ITTOIA 2005, s 278; CTA 2009, s 218*]. For capital gains purposes the consequential effect is that the landlord is treated as incurring enhancement expenditure of that amount on the premises at the time of the grant of the lease. [*TCGA 1992, Sch 8 paras 7, 7A*].

Example

X grants a 14-year lease of premises for a premium of £5,000 in 2024/25 and retains the freehold interest. The amount chargeable to income tax for that year is:

£

Premium	5,000
Deduct $\frac{14-1}{50}$ × £5,000	1,300
Chargeable to income tax	£3,700

If the allowable expenditure on the original unencumbered freehold (acquired in 2009) is £30,000 and the value of the reversion £47,000, the gain is computed as follows:

	£
Consideration received (i.e. the premium)	5,000
Deduct amount chargeable to income tax	3,700
	£1,300
Allowable expenditure attributable to the part disposal	
$\frac{1,300}{(5,000+47,000)}$ × £30,000=	£750
Chargeable gain: £1,300 – £750 =	£550

Sub-leases granted out of short leases

[35.16] Where a sub-lease is granted out of a head-lease with less than 50 years to run, the normal part disposal rules do not apply. Instead, subject to below, a proportion of the cost and enhancement expenditure attributable to the lease is apportioned to the part disposed of as follows:

$$\frac{P(1)-P(3)}{P(2)}$$

where:

P(1) = the percentage derived from the table in **35.13** above for the duration of the lease at the date of granting the sub-lease

P(3) = the percentage for the duration of the lease at the date of termination of the sub-lease

P(2) = the percentage for the duration of the lease at the date of acquisition (for apportionment of cost) *or* the date when expenditure is first reflected in the nature of the lease (for apportionment of enhancement expenditure)

If the amount of the premium is less than what would be obtainable by way of premium for the sub-lease if the rent payable under the sub-lease were the same as the rent payable under the lease, the percentage attributable to the sub-lease as calculated above must be multiplied by the premium received over the premium so obtainable before being applied to cost or enhancement expenditure. [*TCGA 1992, Sch 8 para 4(1)(2)*].

Example

X purchases a 40-year lease of a flat in 2019 for £15,000. In 2024, he sub-lets the flat to Y for 20 years for a premium of £8,000. The premium obtainable on the basis of the rent paid under the head-lease is £10,000. X's original expenditure of £15,000 is apportioned as follows:

$$\frac{91.981 - 61.617}{95.457} = 0.3180908 \times \frac{8{,}000}{10{,}000} = 0.2544726$$

0.2544726 × £15,000 = £3,817

The expenditure attributable to the part disposal is therefore £3,817 as against £4,771 (£15,000 × 0.3180908) if the premium had been the maximum obtainable, £10,000.

Where the sub-lease is a sub-lease of part only of the land comprised in the lease, the cost and enhancement expenditure of the head-lease must be apportioned between the sub-lease and the remainder in proportion to their respective values. [*TCGA 1992, Sch 8 para 4(3)*].

Where a premium (including a deemed premium as in **35.15** above) is paid for the sub-lease, an amount of which is liable to tax as a receipt of a UK property business under *CTA 2009, ss 217–221* or *ITTOIA 2005, ss 277–281*, that amount is deducted from any *gain* accruing on the disposal for which the premium is consideration but not so as to convert the gain into a loss or to increase any loss. [*TCGA 1992, Sch 8 para 5(2)(5)*]. Similar provisions apply where, under *CTA 2009, ss 224, 225* or *ITTOIA 2005, ss 284–286* (see **35.5** above) what is disposed of is the remainder of a lease or a sub-lease out of a lease the duration of which does not exceed 50 years. [*TCGA 1992, Sch 8 para 5(4)*].

Allowances to payer for premiums paid

[35.17] Where a premium paid on the grant of a lease falls to be included in computing the property business profits of the recipient (see **35.15** above and **35.19** below), or would have done but for exemption, the tenant is treated as incurring an expense of a revenue nature at a rate equivalent to the amount so included spread over the period to which it relates. Where the lease is sub-let, this expense is an allowable deduction in computing the property business profits of the intermediate landlord. [*ITTOIA 2005, s 292; CTA 2009, s 232*]. If the sub-lease is granted for a premium, however, the deduction is restricted. See Tolley's Income Tax under Property Income for full details.

Where a person is treated in consequence of having granted a sub-lease as incurring revenue expenses under *ITTOIA 2005, s 292* or *CTA 2009, s 232*, the amount of any *loss* accruing for capital gains purposes to that person on the disposal by way of the grant of the sub-lease is reduced by the total amount of the expenses, but not so as to convert the loss into a gain. Any adjustment under *ITTOIA 2005, ss 301, 302* or *CTA 2009, ss 238, 239* (see **35.5** above) is taken into account. [*TCGA 1992, Sch 8 para 6(1)(3)*].

Example

On 21 January 2018, C is granted a lease of a shop for 21 years for a rent and a premium of £12,800. On 21 January 2025, he grants a sub-lease for a period of seven years for a premium of £1,000 and a rent equal to that payable under the terms of the head-lease. C is treated under *ITTOIA 2005, s 292* as incurring deductible expenses of £1,680. C's capital gains tax position is as follows.

	£	£
Premium received		1,000
Consideration given for lease	12,800	
Percentage applicable to lease of 21 years	74.635	
Percentage applicable to lease of 14 years	58.971	
Percentage applicable to lease of 7 years	35.414	
Amount allowable		
$\frac{58.971 - 35.414}{74.635} \times £12,800$		4,040
Loss		3,040
Deduct amount allowable in computing profits		1,680
Allowable loss		£1,360

Restriction of allowable expenditure of payer of premium

[35.18] Where a premium is paid for the acquisition of a short lease, and the person acquiring the lease uses the property for the purposes of his trade, profession or vocation, such that income tax or corporation tax relief under *CTA 2009, ss 62–67* or *ITTOIA 2005, ss 60–67* is available (see Tolley's Income Tax), then on a subsequent disposal of the lease, the allowable expenditure is reduced by the tax relief actually given. This reduction is made **before** the depreciation fraction at **35.13** above is applied, so that only the net expenditure is depreciated. (HMRC Capital Gains Manual CG71200).

Anti-avoidance provisions

[35.19] Where a lease not exceeding 50 years granted at *less than market value* is assigned for a consideration exceeding any premium for which it was granted (or the consideration on any previous assignment) the excess, up to the limit of the amount of any premium, or additional premium, which the grantor forwent when granting the lease, is treated as a receipt of the assignor's property business to the same extent that an additional premium would have been so treated (see **35.15** above). [*ITTOIA 2005, s 282; CTA 2009, s 222*].

Any assessment to income or corporation tax under these provisions is not taken into account in any capital gains computation. [*TCGA 1992, Sch 8 para 6(2)*]. There may, therefore, be a double charge to tax.

New lease of land after assignment or surrender — proportion of capital sum received to be taxed as income in certain circumstances

[35.20] The following applies where a lessee of land under a lease is entitled to one of a specified type of deduction for rent (i.e. a relevant deduction within *CTA 2010, s 860* or *ITA 2007, s 681BK*) and assigns or surrenders the lease. If the lease when so transferred or surrendered has no more than 50 years still to run and a new lease is granted to the lessee or a linked person for *15 years or less*, any increased rent payable, so far as it does not exceed a commercial rent, is allowable as a deduction from profits, but of the consideration received by the lessee for giving up the original lease (or undertaking to pay an increased rent) a proportion equivalent to one-fifteenth of that consideration multiplied by the number of years by which the term of the lease-back falls short of 16 years will be treated as an income receipt instead of a capital one.

Appropriate adjustment is made where the lease-back is of part only of the property previously leased.

For the above purposes, the term of the new lease is deemed to end on any date after which the rent payable is reduced, or, if the lessor or lessee has power to end the lease or the lessee has power to vary its terms, on the earliest date on which the lease can be so ended or varied.

[*ITA 2007, ss 861B–861BM; CTA 2010, ss 849–862*].

Value shifting — adjustment of leasehold rights

[35.21] Where an owner of land (or of any other description of property) enters into a transaction whereby he becomes the lessee of that property (e.g. a sale and lease-back) and there is a subsequent adjustment of rights and liabilities under the lease (whether or not involving the grant of a new lease) which is on the whole favourable to the lessor, such an adjustment is a disposal by the lessee of an interest in the property. [*TCGA 1992, s 29(4)*]. See **4.9** ANTI-AVOIDANCE for full coverage.

Contingent liabilities

[35.22] In the first instance, no allowance is made in a capital gains tax computation for:

(a) in the case of a disposal by way of assigning a lease of land or other property, any liability remaining with, or assumed by, the person making the disposal which is contingent on a default in respect of liabilities thereby or subsequently assumed by the assignee under the terms and conditions of the lease; and
(b) any contingent liability of the person making the disposal in respect of any covenant for quiet enjoyment or other obligation assumed as vendor of land, or of any estate or interest in land, or as a lessor.

If it is subsequently shown to the satisfaction of the inspector that any such contingent liability has become enforceable, and is being or has been enforced, such adjustment is made as is required in consequence.

[*TCGA 1992, s 49(1)(a)(b), (2)(3)*].

The receipt of a contingently repayable deposit in return for the grant of an option to purchase land was valued subject to the contingency because on the facts the contingency was not within (b) above (*Randall v Plumb* Ch D 1974, 50 TC 392).

Disposals of UK land by non-residents

[35.23] For 2019/20 onwards, a person who is not UK resident for a tax year is chargeable to capital gains tax on gains arising on the disposal in that year of any interests in UK land. Interests which have a connection to the person's UK branch or agency are, however, charged under the provisions at **43.3** OVERSEAS MATTERS. The charge applies also if the tax year is a split year for an individual under the statutory residence test (see **51.17** RESIDENCE AND DOMICILE) and the disposal is made in the overseas part of the year.

Similarly, for disposals on or after 6 April 2019, non-UK resident companies are chargeable to corporation tax on gains on interests in UK land (but interests with a connection to the company's UK permanent establishment are charged under the provisions at **43.3** OVERSEAS MATTERS).

An '*interest in UK land*' is an estate, interest, right or power in or over land in the UK, or the benefit of an obligation, restriction or condition affecting the value of such, but not including:

- any interest or right (other than a rentcharge or, in Scotland, a feu duty) held to secure payment of money or performance of any other obligation; or
- a licence to use or occupy land;
- in England, Wales or Northern Ireland, a tenancy at will or an advowson, franchise (i.e. a grant from the Crown, such as the right to hold a market or fair, or the right to take tolls) or manor; or
- any other interest or right specified in Treasury regulations.

'*Land*' includes buildings and structures and any land under the sea or otherwise covered by water.

The grant of an option (defined as at **7.7** ASSETS) binding the grantor to sell an interest in land is treated for these purposes as the disposal of an interest in land.

[*TCGA 1992, ss 1A(3)(b), 1C, 1G(1)(2), 2B(4)(a)(5)*].

These provisions replace and extend the provisions at **35.31** below for non-resident disposals of UK residential property, and are subject to the rebasing rules at **35.30** below. For the requirement to make a UK land disposal return and to pay an amount on account of CGT see **52.22** RETURNS and **45.3** PAYMENT OF TAX.

See also HMRC Capital Gains Manual CG73920–73990.

Registration and payment of tax by non-resident companies

A non-resident company or offshore collective investment vehicle which is not otherwise within the charge to UK corporation tax becomes chargeable when it makes a direct or indirect disposal of UK land on or after 6 April 2019.

Accordingly, HMRC consider that the company or vehicle must register with HMRC within three months of the date of the disposal (see **52.21** RETURNS). This does not apply if the company is registered with Companies House or, in the case of a collective investment vehicle, if it has made an election for transparent or exempt treatment (see **35.27** and **35.28** below). Dormant companies which have previously been registered with HMRC will need to register again.

HMRC consider that, where a company holds no other interests in UK land after the disposal, it will stop being chargeable to corporation tax. The company will therefore have a one-day accounting period (the day of the disposal). See **45.3** PAYMENT OF TAX for the application of the instalment payment rules for large companies to such accounting periods.

See www.gov.uk/guidance/register-a-non-resident-company-for-corporation-tax.

Rollover relief

Rollover relief under *TCGA 1992, s 152* (see **53** ROLLOVER RELIEF) is available if the old asset is an interest in UK land and any gain would otherwise be chargeable under the above provisions only if the new asset is also an interest in UK land (provided that any other necessary conditions for relief are satisfied).

For this purpose, references to the acquisition of new assets include references to acquisition of an interest in them or to entering into an unconditional contract for the acquisition of them. The reference to a disposal of an old asset includes the disposal of an interest in the old asset.

[*TCGA 1992, s 159A*].

Disposals of assets deriving 75% of value from UK land by non-residents

[35.24] For 2019/20 onwards, a person who is not UK resident for a tax year is chargeable to capital gains tax on gains arising on the disposal in that year of assets deriving at least 75% of their value from UK land if he has a 'substantial indirect interest' in that land. Assets which have a connection to the person's UK branch or agency are, however, charged under the provisions at **43.3** OVERSEAS MATTERS. The charge applies also if the tax year is a split year for an individual under the statutory residence test (see **51.17** RESIDENCE AND DOMICILE) and the disposal is made in the overseas part of the year.

Similarly, for disposals on or after 6 April 2019, non-UK resident companies are chargeable to corporation tax on gains on such assets (but assets with a connection to the company's UK permanent establishment are charged under the provisions at **43.3** OVERSEAS MATTERS).

These provisions are subject to the rebasing rules at **35.30** below. For the requirement to make a UK land disposal return and to pay an amount on account of CGT see **52.22** RETURNS and **45.3** PAYMENT OF TAX. See also **35.23** above for registration and payment of tax by non-resident companies.

[*TCGA 1992, ss 1A(3)(c), 1D, 1G(1)(2), 2B(4)(b)(6); FA 2019, Sch 1 paras 2, 120*].

For HMRC guidance, see HMRC Capital Gains Manual CG73930–73952. For a worked example of how these provisions apply, see CG73932.

An asset derives at least 75% of its value from UK land if it is a right or interest in a company and at least 75% of the market value of the company's 'qualifying assets' derives, directly or indirectly, from interests in UK land (defined as at **35.23** above) at the time of the disposal. For this purpose, market value can be traced through any number of companies, partnerships, trusts and other entities or arrangements (whether or not established under UK law), but not through a normal commercial loan (as defined by *CTA 2010, s 158(1)(b)* or *159(4)(b)*). In tracing market value in this way, the assets held by a company, partnership etc. must be attributed to the shareholders, partners, beneficiaries etc. in whatever way is appropriate.

Normal valuation principles apply in determining market value but HMRC accept that formal valuation may not always be necessary. They expect the basis of valuation to be appropriate to the value and complexity of the situation. Sources of information that would allow a taxpayer to conclude with strong confidence whether the company was UK property rich (i.e. it meets the 75% test above) or not might include informal valuations undertaken shortly before the disposal for other commercial purposes to report to independent parties (such as shareholders, banks and other similar creditors) or formal valuations undertaken for a recent balance sheet. (HMRC Capital Gains Manual CG73934).

'*Qualifying assets*' are all assets of the company other than any assets so far as they are matched to a 'related party liability'. Interests in UK land, however, remain qualifying assets even if so matched. An asset is matched to a 'related party liability' if the asset consists of a right under a transaction (including, but not restricted to, a right under a loan relationship or derivative contract) which entitles the company to require another person to meet a liability (including a contingent liability) under the transaction and that other person is relevant to the market value tracing exercise or is a 'related party' (defined, broadly, as under *CTA 2010, Pt 8ZB*) of the company on the day of the disposal. A person is relevant to the market value tracing exercise if he has assets which are taken into account in that exercise or has obligations (as trustee or otherwise) in relation to the holding of assets in any trust or other arrangement which are taken into account.

These provisions do not apply to a disposal of a right or interest in a company if it is reasonable to conclude that, so far as the market value of the company's qualifying assets derives from interest in UK land, all of those interests are used for trading purposes. Interests in UK land not used for trading purposes can, however, be ignored for this purpose provided that they have a total market value of no more than 10% of the total market value of interests used for trading purposes. An interest in UK land is used for trading purposes only if it is being used, or has been acquired for use, in or for the purposes of a 'qualifying trade'. A '*qualifying trade*' is one which has been carried on by the company or a connected person through the year ending with the disposal in question on a commercial basis with a view to the realisation of profits. It must be reasonable to conclude that the trade will continue to be so carried on for more than an insignificant period of time.

The provisions also do not apply to two or more disposals of rights or interests in companies if the disposals are 'linked' and:

- some but not all of the disposals would be disposals of assets deriving at least 75% of their value from UK land; but
- if one of the companies included all of the assets of the others, a disposal of an interest or right in it would not be a disposal of an asset deriving at least 75% of its value from UK land (on the assumption that all of the other companies are related parties of that company on the day of disposal).

For this purpose, disposals are '*linked*' if they are made under the same arrangements by the same person or connected persons and are made to the same person or to persons connected with each other. Additionally, the person making each disposal must be connected with the company in which the right or interest is disposed of. Whether or not two persons are connected is determined for this purpose immediately before the arrangements are entered into. '*Connected persons*' are defined as in **17** CONNECTED PERSONS, except that partners are treated as connected with each other and with each other's spouses, civil partners and relatives in all circumstances.

A person disposing of an asset deriving at least 75% of its value from UK land has a '*substantial indirect interest*' in that land if, at any time in the two years ending with the disposal, he has a '25% investment' in the company. A person's 25% investment is, however, ignored if it is only held for a period or periods forming an insignificant proportion of that part of his period of ownership of the interest or right in the company which is within the two-year period. As a general rule, HMRC consider 'insignificant' to be 10% or less of the time (HMRC Capital Gains Manual CG73936). See further below for disposals which have an appropriate connection with a collective investment vehicle.

A person (P) has a '*25% investment*' in a company (C) if:

- P possesses or is entitled to acquire 25% or more of the voting power in C;
- P would receive 25% or more of the proceeds of a disposal of the whole of the equity in C;
- P would receive 25% or more of the amount distributed if the income in respect of the equity of C was distributed among the equity holders; or
- P would receive 25% or more of the assets available for distribution to the equity holders on a winding-up of C.

The equity in C is made up of shares (including stock and any other members' interests) in C other than restricted preference shares (within *CTA 2010, s 160*), and loans to C other than normal commercial loans. If C does not have share capital, the definitions of 'normal commercial loan' and 'restricted preference share' are modified as necessary. Receiving any proceeds, amounts or assets includes both direct and indirect receipt and the direct or indirect application of the proceeds, amount or assets for a person's benefit (but not so as to give a person a 25% investment in a company due only to the existence of a normal commercial loan). It does not matter whether the receipt or application is at the time of the disposal, distribution etc. or subsequently.

If a person (A) directly receives any proceeds, amount or assets, or any proceeds etc. are directly applied for A's benefit, and another person (B) directly or indirectly owns a percentage of A's equity, B is treated as indirectly receiving that percentage of the proceeds etc. (or that percentage of the proceeds etc. are treated as indirectly applied for B's benefit). The percentage ownership for this purpose is determined by applying *CTA 2010, ss 1155–1157*, modified as necessary.

A person's entitlement to proceeds, amounts or assets includes, for these purposes, his share of the proceeds, amounts or assets of any partnership of which he is a member, determined on a just and reasonable basis. A person is also taken to have all of the rights and interests of any person connected with him (as defined).

For examples demonstrating situations in which a taxpayer has a 25% investment, see HMRC Capital Gains Manual CG73940.

Anti-avoidance

An anti-avoidance rule applies where a person enters into arrangements with a main purpose of obtaining a capital gains tax or corporation tax advantage as a result of any of the above provisions applying or not applying or as a result of 'treaty shopping' (i.e. where double tax arrangements apply despite the above provisions in circumstances where the advantage is contrary to the object and purpose of the double tax arrangements). Where the rule applies, just and reasonable adjustments are to be made to counteract the advantage, by way of assessment, modification of an assessment, amendment or disallowance of a claim or otherwise. The legislation specifically states that, in a treaty shopping case, the adjustments are to be made regardless of the effect of the double tax arrangements.
[*TCGA 1992, Sch 1A*].

Impact of double tax agreements

Where the UK has a double tax agreement with the territory in which the taxpayer is resident, the above provisions apply subject to the terms of that agreement. See **20** DOUBLE TAX RELIEF for agreements generally.

The OECD Model Agreement contains a 'securitised land provision', which gives the source state (the state where the immovable property is situated) the primary right to tax gains on indirect disposals. This is formulated as disposals of shares or similar interests in companies, partnerships and trusts, where more than 50% of the value is derived, directly or indirectly, from immovable property in the source state. Not all UK agreements contain a comparable provision, however, and those that do are frequently on different terms due to changes in the OECD Model and the preferences of both the UK and the treaty partner. See HMRC Capital Gains Manual CG73948.

Units in an authorised contractual scheme

A unit in an authorised contractual scheme which is a co-ownership scheme (CoACS) and is treated as an asset for chargeable gains purposes (see **63.12** UNIT TRUSTS ETC.) is treated for the purposes of the above provisions as if it were a share in a company. [*TCGA 1992, Sch 5AAA para 5*].

Disposals with a connection to a collective investment vehicle

Where a person disposes of an asset deriving at least 75% of its value from UK land and the disposal has an 'appropriate connection' to a 'collective investment vehicle', he is treated as having a substantial indirect interest in the UK land at the time of the disposal, even if not satisfying the 25% investment requirement above.

For this purpose, a 'collective investment vehicle' is defined as at **35.26** below. A disposal has an '*appropriate connection*' to a collective investment vehicle if:

(i) the asset disposed of consists of a right or interest in a collective investment vehicle;
(ii) the asset disposed of consists of a right or interest in a company at least half of whose market value derives from being a direct or indirect participant in one or more collective investment vehicles;
(iii) the vehicle is constituted by two or more persons carrying on a trade or business in partnership and the disposal is made by a person as a participant in the vehicle;
(iv) the vehicle is a company and the disposal is made by it; or
(v) a company (not the vehicle) makes the disposal and the vehicle and one or more other collective investment vehicles that are 'UK property rich' have a 50% investment in the company.

In (v) above, a collective investment vehicle is '*UK property rich*' if, on the assumption that it was a company, a disposal of a right or interest in it would be a disposal of an asset deriving at least 75% of its value from UK land but ignoring, with effect from 10 April 2020, the exceptions for interests in land used for trading purposes and for linked disposals. Whether collective investment vehicles have a 50% investment in a company is determined by treating them as a single person and applying the above 25% investment test by replacing references to 25% with references to 50% (and disregarding the requirement to attribute rights and interests of connected persons).

A disposal does not have an appropriate connection to a collective investment scheme if it would otherwise fall within (i), (ii), (iv) or (v) above and the vehicle or vehicles concerned each meet two conditions.

The first condition (the non-UK real estate condition) is that, at the time of the disposal, by reference to the vehicle's prospectus, no more than 40% of the expected market value of its investments is intended to derive from investments consisting of UK land or rights or interests in UK property rich companies.

The second condition depends on whether or not the vehicle is a company. If the vehicle is a company, the second condition (the non-close condition) is that the company must not be a close company (defined as at **35.26** below) or must be a close company only because it has a 'qualifying investor' (as defined to include various types of institutional investor) as a direct or indirect participator.

If the vehicle is not a company, the second condition (the genuine diversity of ownership condition) is that the vehicle must, broadly, fulfil the genuine diversity of ownership condition applicable to certain offshore funds under *SI 2009 No 3001, Reg 75* (as modified). With effect from 11 July 2023, if the vehicle is part of 'multi-vehicle arrangements', it can also meet the genuine diversity of ownership condition by reference to those arrangements taken as a whole. 'Multi-vehicle arrangements' are arrangements comprising two or more vehicles where an investor in any of them would reasonably regard their investment as an investment in the arrangements as a whole (rather than in any one of the vehicles exclusively).

Where (v) above would otherwise apply, and the vehicle in question is constituted by two or more persons carrying on a trade or business in partnership, the second condition is taken to be met if the company in (v) above meets the non-close condition.

[*TCGA 1992, Sch 5AAA paras 3, 6, 7; F(No 2)A 2023, Sch 4 para 1; SI 2020 No 315, Regs 4–6*].

Disposals of interests in UK land by non-residents — unascertainable consideration

[35.25] The following rules apply for capital gains tax purposes where, on or after 6 April 2019, a person makes a disposal resulting in a gain or loss within **35.23** or **35.24** above and receives all or part of the consideration in the form of a right for future consideration which is unascertainable. If the person subsequently receives all or part of that consideration (the 'ascertained consideration') in a tax year for which he is not UK resident, the consideration is not treated as accruing on the disposal of the right, and the amount by which it exceeds the original consideration relating to the right (if any) is instead treated as accruing on the original disposal. If the ascertainable consideration is less than the original consideration the latter is reduced. A gain or loss within **35.23** or **35.24** above will accrue accordingly at the time of receipt of the ascertained consideration.

For this purpose, a right is a right to unascertainable consideration only if it is a right to consideration the amount or value of which is unascertainable at the time the right is conferred on account of its being referable, in whole or part, to matters which are uncertain at that time because they have not yet occurred. Consideration is not regarded as unascertainable by reason only that the right to receive the whole or any part of it is postponed or contingent, but the amount or value, or the part of it in question, is taken into account in computing the gain on the disposal of the asset in question in accordance with *TCGA 1992, s 48* (see **16.14**(g) COMPUTATION OF GAINS AND LOSSES). Nor is it regarded as unascertainable by reason only that the right to receive it is postponed and may to any extent be satisfied by the receipt of property which some person has a right to select. A right is also not regarded as being a right to unascertainable consideration simply because either the amount or value of the consideration has not been fixed if the amount is to be fixed by reference to the value and the value is ascertainable or vice versa.

[*TCGA 1992, s 48A*].

Disposals of interests in UK land — collective investment vehicles

[35.26] The provisions at 35.23–35.25 above are subject to the following special rules relating to collective investment vehicles.

For HMRC guidance, see HMRC Capital Gains Manual CG73995P onwards.

Offshore collective investment vehicles treated as companies

An 'offshore collective investment vehicle' which is neither a company nor a partnership is treated for the purposes of the provisions at **35.23** and **35.24** above as if it were a company, and the rights of its 'participants' as if they were shares in that company. Accordingly, such vehicles are chargeable to corporation tax on direct and indirect disposals of UK land and non-resident participants may be subject to the charge in **35.24** above. This rule applies to authorised contractual schemes but does not displace the calculation rules on a disposal of units at **63.12** UNIT TRUSTS ETC. For a unit trust scheme, however, the rule applies instead of *TCGA 1992, s 99* (see **63.3**). This rule does not apply where an election for transparency has effect (see **35.27** below).

[*TCGA 1992, 103DB, Sch 5AAA para 4*].

Meaning of offshore collective investment vehicle

An '*offshore collective investment vehicle*' is a 'collective investment vehicle':

- constituted as a body corporate (other than a limited liability partnership) resident outside the UK;
- under which property is held on trust for the participants where the trustees are not UK-resident; or
- constituted by other arrangements that create rights in the nature of 'co-ownership' (defined so as not to be restricted to its meaning under UK law) which take effect as a result of the law of a territory outside the UK.

A '*collective investment vehicle*' is:

(i) a collective investment scheme (see **63.1** UNIT TRUSTS ETC.);
(ii) an alternative investment fund (within the *Alternative Investment Fund Managers Regulations 2013, Reg 3*);
(iii) a company which is a UK real estate investment trust (see **63.5**) or, for disposals on or after 10 April 2020, the principal company of a group UK real estate investment trust;
(iv) a company resident outside the UK which is not a member of a group and meets the property income conditions below;
(v) a company resident outside the UK which is the principal company of a group, which is not a 'close company' only because it has a 'qualifying investor' (as defined to include various types of institutional investor) as a direct or indirect participator, and meets the property income conditions below; or

(vi) a company resident outside the UK which is a member of a group but not the principal company, which is not a close company only because it has a qualifying investor or a company wholly (or almost wholly) owned by qualifying investors as a direct or indirect participator, and meets the property income conditions below

Before 10 April 2020, (iv)–(vi) above did not apply, but a company resident outside the UK which met the property income conditions was a collective investment vehicle.

For a company within (iv) above, the property income conditions are that:

- the company is not a close company (or is only a close company because it has a qualifying investor as a direct or indirect participator);
- at least half of its income derives directly or indirectly from long-term property investments (i.e. direct or indirect investments in land or estates, interests or rights in or over land which are made on a long-term basis);
- it distributes all (or substantially all) of its "profits" (excluding capital profits) from long-term property investments on an annual basis; and
- it is not liable to tax on its profits in any territory in which it is resident so far as the profits derive directly or indirectly from long-term property investments.

For a company within (v) or (vi) above, the property income conditions are that:

- at least half of the group's income derives directly or indirectly from long-term property investments;
- the group distributes all (or substantially all) of its profits from long-term property investments on an annual basis; and
- the company is not liable to tax on its profits in any territory in which it is resident so far as the profits derive directly or indirectly from long-term property investments.

Before 10 April 2020, the property income conditions were that:

- the company is not a close company (or is only a close company because it has a qualifying investor as a direct or indirect participator);
- at least half of its income is property income from long-term investments (i.e. income from direct or indirect investments in land or estates, interests or rights in or over land which are made on a long-term basis);
- it distributes all (or substantially all) of such property income on an annual basis; and
- it is not liable to tax on that income in any territory in which it is resident.

For this purpose, '*close company*' is defined, with certain modifications, in accordance with *CTA 2010, Pt 10 Ch 2*, but includes non-UK resident companies.

A '*participant*' in a collective investment vehicle is, in the case of a company, a shareholder in the company, or in other cases, a person who takes part in the arrangements or undertaking, whether by becoming the owner of any part of the property that is the subject of or held by the arrangements or undertaking or otherwise. A '*unit*' of a collective investment vehicle is either a share in the company or the rights or interests (however described) of the participant.

[*TCGA 1992, Sch 5AAA paras 1, 2, 46; F(No 2)A 2023, Sch 4 para 1; SI 2020 No 315, Regs 1–3, 15*].

Election for transparency

[35.27] The manager of an offshore collective investment vehicle (see **35.26** above) which is UK property rich and is transparent for income tax purposes (otherwise than as a result of being a partnership) may make an election to be treated for all purposes relating to chargeable gains as a partnership. Partnership treatment will then apply to all times on and after the vehicle's constitution (but not for disposals before 6 April 2019).

For this purpose, a vehicle is '*UK property rich*' if, on the assumption that it was a company, a disposal of a right or interest in it would be a disposal of an asset deriving at least 75% of its value from UK land as in **35.24** above but ignoring, with effect from 10 April 2020, the exceptions for interests in land used for trading purposes and for linked disposals. A vehicle is transparent for income tax purposes, if, were it to have any UK resident individual participants, they would be chargeable to income tax on part of the income of the vehicle under any of the provisions listed in *ITTOIA 2005, s 830(2)* (foreign income) or would have been so chargeable if the assets from which the income is derived were outside the UK.

An election can apply whether or not the vehicle would otherwise be chargeable to UK tax on chargeable gains. Where an election has effect, neither *TCGA 1992, s 103D* (tax transparent funds — see **63.12** UNIT TRUSTS ETC.) nor *TCGA 1992, s 99* (unit trust schemes — see **63.3**) apply to the vehicle. Neither do the provisions at **35.26** above. An election has no effect in relation to any units held by an insurance company for the purposes of its long-term business.

Where an election has effect and either the second or third sets of rebasing rules at **35.30** below would otherwise apply on a disposal, the first rebasing rule (for indirect disposals and direct disposals not chargeable before 6 April 2019) applies instead.

A notice requiring a partnership return may be given to the manager of the vehicle. Such a notice does not oblige the reporting of information other than to determine the capital gains liability of each partner, but a notice may require a return to be submitted whether or not any partnership property has been disposed of in the year in question.

An election requires the consent of the participants in the vehicle and must be made by notice to HMRC within the 12 months beginning with the earliest date on which an interest in UK land (defined as at **35.23** above) or a right or interest in a UK property rich company becomes part of the vehicle's property or, if later, before 1 October 2020. An election made on or after 10 April 2020 must include each participants' name, unique taxpayer reference, place of residence or business and, where relevant, date of birth. The election is irrevocable. If the vehicle was constituted before 6 April 2019, the election applies to disposals on or after 6 April 2019 and can be made at any time before 1 October 2020. For participants on 6 April 2019, the making of the election is not treated as a disposal of their units, and when any units are subsequently disposed of, any gains or losses of the participant are determined as if the election had applied throughout the vehicle's existence.

[*TCGA 1992, Sch 5AAA paras 3, 8–11, 49, 49A; SI 2020 No 315, Regs 1, 4, 8, 18, 19*].

Election for exemption from charge on interests in UK land

[35.28] An offshore collective investment vehicle (see **35.26** above) can make an election to be exempt from corporation tax on chargeable gains under the provisions at **35.23** and **35.24** above if:

- it is a company or is treated as a company under **35.26** above;
- it is 'UK property rich';
- in the case of an alternative investment fund (within the *Alternative Investment Fund Managers Regulations 2013, Reg 3*), it would also meet the definition of a collective investment vehicle for another reason; and
- either:
  - — it is a collective investment scheme and meets the 'genuine diversity of ownership condition';
  - — it is a collective investment scheme, it meets the 'UK tax condition' and is wholly, or almost wholly, owned by one or more other collective investment schemes each of which meets the genuine diversity of ownership condition;
  - — it is a company (but not a vehicle treated as a company under **35.26** above) and it meets the 'recognised stock exchange condition' and the 'non-close condition'; or
  - — it is a collective investment vehicle of any kind and meets both the 'UK tax condition' and the 'non-close condition'.

A company (wherever resident) which is not a collective investment vehicle can make an election with similar effect if:

- it is wholly (or almost wholly) and, for elections made on or after 10 April 2020, directly owned by a collective investment scheme which is either constituted by two or more persons carrying on a trade or business in partnership or is constituted by an authorised contractual scheme which is a co-ownership scheme (a 'CoACS' — see **63.12** UNIT TRUSTS ETC.);
- the company or, where the collective investment scheme is a CoACS, the CoACS is UK property rich; and
- either:
  - — the company meets both the 'UK tax condition' and the 'non-close condition'; or
  - — the collective investment scheme directly owning the company meets the 'genuine diversity of ownership condition' or is wholly (or almost wholly) and directly owned by one or more 'qualifying partnerships' each of which meets the genuine diversity of ownership condition.

A vehicle or company in respect of which an election has been made is referred to as a '*qualifying fund*' or a '*qualifying company*'.

A company or a collective investment vehicle is '*UK property rich*' if (on the assumption, in the latter case, that the vehicle was a company) a disposal of a right or interest in it would be a disposal of an asset deriving at least 75% of its value from UK land as in **35.24** above but ignoring, with effect from 10 April 2020, the exceptions for interests in land used for trading purposes and for linked disposals.

The '*genuine diversity of ownership condition*' is, broadly, that the scheme must fulfil the genuine diversity of ownership condition applicable to certain offshore funds under *SI 2009 No 3001, Reg 75* (as modified). With effect from 11 July 2023, if the vehicle is part of 'multi-vehicle arrangements', it can also meet the genuine diversity of ownership condition by reference to those arrangements taken as a whole. 'Multi-vehicle arrangements' are arrangements comprising two or more vehicles where an investor in any of them would reasonably regard their investment as an investment in the arrangements as a whole (rather than in any one of the vehicles exclusively).

The '*recognised stock exchange condition*' is that the company must have ordinary share capital which is regularly traded on a recognised stock exchange. The '*non-close condition*' is that the company must not be a close company (defined as at **35.26** above) or must be a close company only because it has a 'qualifying investor' (as defined to include various types of institutional investor) as a direct or indirect participator.

The '*UK tax condition*' is that the person making the election must reasonably consider that, if all of the company's shares were disposed of at market value, no more than 25% of the total proceeds would be left out of account for chargeable gains purposes as a result solely of double tax arrangements. If any of the proceeds would arise to a company wholly, or almost wholly, owned by investors within **35.29**(a)–(c) below, that company is treated for this purpose as if it were exempt from corporation tax on chargeable gains otherwise than as a result of double tax arrangements.

A company is wholly, or almost wholly, owned by a person if it is wholly owned by that person or if that person has a 99% investment in it. A company is wholly owned by a person if that person has a 100% investment in it. Whether a person has a 100% or 99% investment in a company is determined by applying the 25% investment test at **35.24** above by replacing references to 25% with references to 100% or 99% and making certain additional modifications (see *TCGA 1992, Sch 5AAA paras 40(3), 41(3)*).

A company is directly owned by a collective investment scheme or partnership if it is owned by the scheme or partnership otherwise than through a company, partnership, trust or other entity or arrangements. A '*qualifying partnership*' is a collective investment scheme constituted by two or more persons carrying on a trade or business in partnership.

[*TCGA 1992, Sch 5AAA paras 3, 7(8), 12, 13, 40, 41, 46; F(No 2)A 2023, Sch 4 para 1; SI 2020 No 315, Regs 1, 4, 9, 10*].

Effects of election

In addition to the exemptions noted above, the following rules apply where a qualifying fund or company has made an election under the above provisions.

If a person in which the qualifying fund or company has a 40% investment makes a direct disposal of any interests in UK land by reference to which the fund or company is UK property rich, a proportion of that person's gain is not a chargeable gain (and a proportion of a loss is not an allowable loss). This applies also where the person makes an indirect disposal within **35.24** above and the fund or company has a 40% investment in the company rights or an interest in which are disposed of. The proportion is that which so much of the consideration for the disposal as forms part (directly or indirectly) of the assets of the qualifying fund or company bears to the total consideration. Whether a qualifying fund or company has a 40% investment in a person is determined by applying the 25% investment test at **35.24** above by replacing references to 25% with references to 40% (and disregarding the requirement to attribute rights and interests of connected persons). If HMRC consider that the proportion of the gain which would otherwise be exempt would exceed the total gain, they may make just and reasonable adjustments to the exempt proportion to prevent that result. [*TCGA 1992, Sch 5AAA para 16; FA 2019, Sch 1 para 21*].

The exceptions for interests in land used for trading purposes and for linked disposals at **35.24** above do not apply to a disposal on or after 10 April 2020 of units in a vehicle in respect of which an election has been made. Likewise, in the case of an election by a qualifying company, those exemptions do not apply on a disposal of units in the relevant fund to the extent that the disposal constitutes the disposal of a right or interest in the company. [*TCGA 1992, Sch 5AAA para 33A, SI 2020 No 315, Reg 14*].

If a company (the 'investing company') which has ordinary share capital owned by one or more qualifying institutional investors within *TCGA 1992, Sch 7AC* (see **60.6** SUBSTANTIAL SHAREHOLDINGS OF COMPANIES) makes a gain or loss part of which is not chargeable or allowable under these provisions and some or all of the ownership (determined as at **60.6**) of those investors in the investing company is through the qualifying company, that ownership is ignored for the purposes of the exemption at **60.6**.

The following provisions apply where a participant (see **35.26** above) in the 'relevant fund' becomes entitled to receive an amount representing, in substance, value derived directly or indirectly from a disposal of UK land within **35.23** or **35.24** above if the amount is revenue in nature and is not subject to income tax or corporation tax on income (on the participant or anyone else). In the case of a qualifying fund, the participant is deemed for chargeable gains purposes to have sold all its units in the relevant fund at market value immediately before the time it became entitled to the amount, and to have reacquired the units at their market value immediately after that time. Likewise, in the case of a qualifying company, the participant is deemed to have sold, and immediately reacquired its rights and interests in the company or, where the relevant fund is a CoACS and the disposal is on or after 10 April 2020, the CoACS. For the calculation and treatment of gains arising from the deemed disposal see further below. This provision cannot result in a deemed gain arising to an investor within **35.29**(a)–(c) below other than an insurance company or to a company which is wholly (or almost wholly) owned by one or more such investors (none of which is an insurance company).

The '*relevant fund*' is the qualifying fund or, in the case of a qualifying company, the collective investment scheme which owns the company.

[*TCGA 1992, Sch 5AAA paras 21, 33(3), 34, 39; SI 2020 No 315, Regs 1, 11, 13*].

Disposal of company covered by election

Where a qualifying fund or company which has made an election, or a company covered by the election, disposes of all of its rights and interests in another company (company C) which is UK property rich and also covered by the election, company C is treated for chargeable gains purposes as selling and immediately reacquiring, at that time, the 'appropriate proportion' of every 'qualifying asset' the actual disposal of which would be a disposal of UK land within **35.23** or **35.24** above, at market value.

For this purpose, a company is covered by an election in respect of a disposal if the disposal would be wholly or partly exempt under *TCGA 1992, Sch 5AAA para 16* (see above). A '*qualifying asset*' is an asset held by company C, any other company covered by the election or by the qualifying fund or company throughout the period of one year ending on the day of the disposal. The '*appropriate proportion*' of a qualifying asset is equal to the proportion that would not be a chargeable gain under *para 16* on a sale of the asset for total consideration resulting in a gain of £100 immediately before the actual disposal of the rights and interests in company C.

[*TCGA 1992, Sch 5AAA para 31*].

Making an election

An election must be made by the manager of the relevant fund. It must be made by notice to HMRC and must specify the date from which it is to take effect. That date can be before the date the election is made, but can only more a date more than 12 months earlier with HMRC consent (whether general or particular).

An election must be accompanied by such information as may be specified by HMRC about disposals made by participants in the relevant fund in the two years ending the day before the election is made (or, if shorter, the period beginning with the constitution of the fund). If information has already been provided to HMRC, it is sufficient for the election to set out when it was provided. Information about disposals before 6 April 2019 is not required.

[*TCGA 1992, Sch 5AAA paras 14, 17, 39, 50*].

Information requirements following the making of an election

The qualifying fund or company must provide HMRC with information and documents in accordance with conditions specified by HMRC for each period of account ending at a time when the election is in force. Such information or documents must be provided within 12 months from the end of the period. For this purpose, a period of account is any period for which accounts of the relevant fund are drawn up, but a period of account cannot exceed 12 months (so that where accounts are drawn up for a longer period, the period is divided into two periods of account, the first of which is 12 months long (and so on)). [*TCGA 1992, Sch 5AAA para 15(1)–(3)(7)(8)*].

Election ceasing to have effect

An HMRC officer designated by the Commissioners for HMRC for the purpose may revoke an election if, in his opinion, there has been a breach of the above information requirements without reasonable excuse, HMRC can, however, waive a breach which is insignificant, having regard to the number and seriousness of any previous breaches.

A designated HMRC officer may also revoke an election if he considers it appropriate to do so in order to safeguard the public revenue.

Revocation of an election by HMRC must be made by notice by the designated officer to the manager of the relevant fund.

The manager of the relevant fund may also revoke an election by notice to HMRC.

A revocation notice must specify the date on which the election will cease to have effect; the election then no longer applies to disposals made on or after that day. Where the revocation is by the fund manager, the date specified may be before the date the notice is given if HMRC consent (whether by way of a general consent or consent in the particular case).

If HMRC revoke an election they must specify the grounds, and the manager of the relevant fund may appeal against the decision. An appeal must be made by notice to the designated HMRC officer within 30 days of the notice. The Tribunal cannot allow an appeal unless it considers that a designated HMRC officer could not reasonably have been satisfied that there were grounds for revocation.

If a qualifying fund or company ceases to meet the applicable exemption conditions, the election ceases to have effect automatically for disposals on or after the time at which the conditions cease to be met. This rule is subject to the following exceptions.

(i) If the fund or company ceases to meet the conditions otherwise than as a result of ceasing to be UK property rich and the manager of the relevant fund expects that all of the conditions will be met within 30 days of the failure, then if the conditions are in fact met within those 30 days, the failure is ignored. This exception can apply no more than four times in any 12-month period.

(ii) If the fund or company ceases to meet the conditions for any reason and the manager expects the failure to last for a temporary period of no more than nine months, then the conditions are treated as continuing to be met during that period, provided that they are in fact met within the nine-month period. This exception does not, however, disapply the provisions below for a deemed disposal to arise when an election ceases to have effect (so that a deemed disposal will arise at the beginning of the temporary period).

(iii) If the fund or company ceases to meet the conditions for any reason at a time when the manager is taking steps to dispose of all of the relevant fund's assets so that it can be wound up, then the conditions are treated as continuing to be met until the relevant fund is wound up. This exception does not, however, disapply the provisions below for a deemed disposal to arise when an election ceases to have effect (so that a deemed disposal will arise at the time the qualifying fund or company actually ceases to meet the conditions).

Where an election ceases to have effect (or where (ii) or (iii) above apply) in the case of a qualifying fund, each participant in the relevant fund is deemed for chargeable gains purposes to have sold its units in the relevant fund immediately before that time, and to have immediately reacquired them, at market value. Likewise, in the case of a qualifying company, each participant in the relevant fund is deemed to have sold its rights and interests in the company or, where the relevant fund is a CoACS and the disposal is on or after 10 April 2020, the CoACS, immediately before the election ceased to have effect, and to have immediately reacquired them, at market value. For the calculation and treatment of gains arising from the deemed disposals see further below.

[*TCGA 1992, Sch 5AAA paras 15(5)(6), 18–20, 22, 27, 28, 30, 38, 42; SI 2020 No 315, Regs 1, 12*].

Deemed disposals of UK land by company or fund

If an election which has been in effect continuously for at least five years ceases to have effect (otherwise than in 'disqualifying circumstances') or the manager of the relevant fund starts taking steps to dispose of all of the assets of the relevant fund so it can be wound up, the qualifying fund or company is treated for chargeable gains purposes as selling and immediately reacquiring, at that time, every asset the actual disposal of which would be a disposal of UK land within **35.23** or **35.24** above, at market value. In the case of any asset covered by the election for 12 months and held by a company at the time the election ceases to have effect or the steps are first taken, the company is deemed to have sold at that time, and immediately reacquired, the 'appropriate proportion' of the asset at its market value.

For this purpose, an election ceases to have effect in 'disqualifying circumstances' if it is revoked by a designated HMRC officer either because in his opinion there has been at least three serious breaches of the information requirements above or to safeguard the public revenue. An asset is covered by an election for 12 months if a disposal of it would be wholly or partly exempt under *TCGA 1992, Sch 5AAA para 16* (see above under 'Effect of election'). The '*appropriate proportion*' of an asset is equal to the proportion that would not be a chargeable gain under *para 16* on a sale of the asset for total consideration resulting in a gain of £100.

An election made by a fund or company is taken, for this purpose, to be the same election as a subsequent election made by another fund or company which owns the first fund or company.

[*TCGA 1992, Sch 5AAA para 32*].

Calculation and treatment of gains of participants on deemed disposals

The following provisions apply where a person is deemed to make a disposal of units in a qualifying fund or of rights or interests in a qualifying company either on becoming entitled to receive an amount not otherwise taxable where the value derives from a disposal of UK land or when an election ceases to have effect.

In calculating the deemed gain, a deduction is allowed for any allowable incidental costs which the person would reasonably have been expected to have incurred if the deemed sale had been an actual sale. [*TCGA 1992, Sch 5AAA para 24*].

A proportion of any deemed gain is deemed to arise only when, at the time of the deemed disposal or subsequently, the person actually disposes of a unit in the relevant fund or actually receives any part of the otherwise non-taxable amount. The proportion charged is equal to the consideration for the actual disposal or the amount of the receipt but not so as to exceed the amount of the deemed gain. Where part of a deemed gain becomes chargeable on more than one occasion, the total proportions brought into charge cannot be more than the total deemed gain. In the case of a deemed gain arising because of entitlement to an otherwise non-taxable amount, if not all of the gain has been charged when the relevant fund is wound up, the remaining part is treated as arising at that time. In the case of an election ceasing to have effect (but not where (ii) above applies), any part of the deemed gain not already charged is treated as arising three years after the deemed disposal or, if earlier, when the relevant fund is wound up. If the deemed gain arises as a result of (ii) above, any part of the gain not already charged is treated as arising when the relevant fund is wound up. If the deemed disposal arises because the election has ceased to have effect, these provisions apply only if the election ceased to have effect because the exemption conditions have ceased to be met. A deemed gain arising when an election is revoked is chargeable immediately. [*TCGA 1992, Sch 5AAA paras 23, 29*].

The manager of a relevant fund must notify any person in writing where:

- that person is deemed to have made a disposal on becoming entitled to an otherwise non-taxable amount;
- that person is deemed to have made a disposal as a result of the revocation of an election; or
- the remaining part of a deemed gain becomes chargeable as a result of the relevant fund being wound up or at the end of the three-year period after a deemed disposal.

Notice must be given within 30 days beginning with the event in question. If a manager fails to give notice he is liable to a penalty of up to £3,000. If the duty to notify applies to two or more managers, the total penalties cannot be more than £3,000. HMRC must assess a penalty under these provisions and notify the manager within 12 months of first becoming aware of the failure. An appeal can be made to HMRC against a decision to impose a penalty within 30 days after the penalty was notified. The appeal must be in writing and must specify the grounds of appeal.

The penalty must be paid within thirty days of the day on which the manager was notified of the penalty or, if an appeal is made, within 30 days of the day on which the appeal is finally determined or withdrawn.

[*TCGA 1992, Sch 5AAA paras 25, 26*].

UK real estate investment trusts

None of the above exemptions apply to gains made by a company which is, or is a member of, a UK real estate investment trust so far as the gain is exempt under *CTA 2010, s 535* or *s 535A* (see **63.5** UNIT TRUSTS ETC.) otherwise than as a result of a notice under *CTA 2010, s 586(1)* or *s 587(1)* (joint venture elections).

Where a gain is made by a company which is a member of a UK group real estate investment trust and the gain is exempt under *CTA 2010, s 535* or *s 535A* as a result of a notice under *CTA 2010, s 586(1)* or *s 587(1)* and both the company and the principal company of the group are covered by an election in respect of a qualifying fund, the exemption provided under the above provisions is reduced by the exemption under the real estate investment trust rules. For this purpose, a company is covered by an election in respect of a disposal if the disposal would be wholly or partly exempt under *TCGA 1992, Sch 5AAA para 16* (see above under 'Effects of election').

[*TCGA 1992, Sch 5AAA paras 35, 36*].

General

Where a person disposes of a right or interest in a company and parts of the gain or loss are not chargeable as a result of the operation of more than one exemption provision, then subject to any rules above which provide for a different basis, each exemption must be applied separately, without regard to the others, to the whole of the gain or loss. The total proportion which is exempt is then the total of the exempt proportions separately found (but not so as to exceed the total gain or loss). The exemption provisions to which this rule applies are any of the above exemptions, *TCGA 1992, Sch 7AC para 3* (see **60.6** SUBSTANTIAL SHAREHOLDING EXEMPTION) and any provision of *CTA 2010, Pt 12* (real estate investment trusts). [*TCGA 1992, Sch 5AAA para 37*].

The Treasury has power to make regulations to amend the above provisions and to allow managers of collective investment vehicles to report information and make payments of tax on behalf of participants. [*TCGA 1992, Sch 5AAA paras 43–45, 48*].

Exemption for disposals of interests in companies owned by certain investors

[35.29] A gain arising to a company which is wholly (or almost wholly) owned by one or more investors within (a)–(c) below) is not a chargeable gain if it arises on the disposal of a right or interest in a company whose assets consist wholly of units in:

(i) a collective investment vehicle in respect of which an election for transparency has been made (see **35.27** above);
(ii) a qualifying fund or company in respect of which an election for exemption has been made (see **35.28** above);
(iii) a company which is a UK real estate investment trust or the principal company of a group UK real estate investment trust; or

(iv) a property authorised investment fund which is 'UK property rich' (as defined at **35.28** above).

The investors in question are:

(a) a qualifying institutional investor within *TCGA 1992, Sch 7AC* (substantial shareholdings exemption — see **60.6** SUBSTANTIAL SHAREHOLDINGS OF COMPANIES);
(b) certain companies carrying on life assurance business or long-term business;
(c) a qualifying fund or company in respect of which an election under the provisions at **35.28** above is in force.

[*TCGA 1992, Sch 5AAA para 33; SI 2020 No 315, Reg 13*].

Rebasing for non-residents of interests in UK land held on 5 April 2019

[35.30] Subject to the following provisions, the normal CGT or corporation tax rules apply in calculating gains and losses charged under the provisions at **35.23** and **35.24** above. Broadly, only the part of the gain arising after 5 April 2019 is chargeable, unless the provisions at **35.31** below (non-resident CGT disposals of UK residential property) would have applied to a disposal of the asset on or before that date, in which case the part of the gain arising after 5 April 2015 is chargeable. Special rules are therefore needed to calculate the chargeable amount where the asset was held before 6 April 2019. The legislation divides assets into one of three separate categories, and for each category, provides a default method of calculation, rebasing the cost of the asset to its value at 5 April 2019 and/or 5 April 2015, and allowing elections to be made for an alternative method or methods of calculation.

Where the interest disposed of results from interests which have been acquired at different times, the date of acquisition of the first interest is taken, for these purposes, as the date on which all the interests were acquired. [*TCGA 1992, s 36A, Sch 4AA para 22(2)*].

The application of any of the rebasing rules which treat an asset as acquired on a different date to the date of its actual acquisition is ignored in determining whether or not the asset is a wasting asset (see **65** WASTING ASSETS). In calculating a gain or loss on a disposal where a rebasing rule has applied, *TCGA 1992, s 41* (restriction of losses by reference to capital allowances: see **16.14** COMPUTATION OF GAINS AND LOSSES) and *TCGA 1992, s 47* (wasting assets qualifying for capital allowances: see **65.2** WASTING ASSETS) apply in relation to any capital or renewals allowance made in respect of the expenditure actually incurred in acquiring or providing the asset as if that allowance were made in respect of the expenditure treated as incurred on the deemed acquisition date. [*TCGA 1992, Sch 4AA paras 19, 20*].

Indirect disposals and direct disposals not chargeable before 6 April 2019

The following rules apply to:

(i) all indirect disposals of UK land (i.e. disposals of assets within **35.24** above);

(ii) direct disposals of UK land (i.e. disposals of interests in UK land within **35.23** above) that were not fully residential before 6 April 2019; and

(iii) direct disposals of UK land by persons who were not chargeable before 6 April 2019.

In (ii) above, a disposal is not fully residential if there was no time in the period from date of acquisition (or 6 April 2015 if later) to 5 April 2019 inclusive at which the land in question consisted of, or included, a dwelling. An interest in UK land which subsists at any time before 6 April 2019 under a contract for an off-plan purchase of a dwelling (i.e. a contract for acquisition of land consisting of, or including, a building or part of a building that is to be constructed or adapted as a dwelling) is treated as fully residential before that date.

In (iii) above, a disposal is made by a person who was not chargeable before 6 April 2019 if, immediately before that date, the person was:

- a company other than a 'closely-held company' (as defined below; and for this purpose a divided company is treated as a closely-held company if the gain or loss is primarily or wholly attributable to a particular division of the company (as defined) and, if that division were a separate company, it would be closely-held);
- a unit trust scheme, or open-ended investment company (or non-UK equivalent), which is 'widely-marketed' (as defined) throughout the period from the date the scheme acquired the interest in land which is the subject of the disposal to the date of disposal, or if shorter, throughout the period of five years ending on the date of disposal;
- a unit trust scheme, or open-ended investment company (or non-UK equivalent), which has as an investor an offshore fund, open-ended investment company or authorised unit trust (the '*feeder fund*'), where the scheme and the feeder fund have the same manager, and the scheme is widely-marketed, after taking account of scheme documents for the feeder fund and the intended investors of the feeder fund, throughout the shortest of: the period from the date the scheme acquired the interest in land which is the subject of the disposal to the date of disposal; the period of five years ending on the date of disposal; and the period from the date the feeder fund first became an investor to the date of disposal; or
- a company carrying on life assurance business if immediately before 6 April 2019 the interest in land which is the subject of the disposal is held to provide benefits to policyholders in the course of that business.

Arrangements (as defined) with a main purpose of obtaining a tax advantage as a result of a person not being a closely-held company or being a widely-marketed scheme are ignored for these purposes.

Default rule — rebasing

In calculating the gain or loss on the disposal, the asset is treated as having been acquired at its market value on 5 April 2019.

Election for retrospective computation

Where the taxpayer so elects, rebasing does not apply and the gains or losses are computed (as for CGT or corporation tax) on the basis of the position over the whole period of ownership. Such an election may be beneficial where a loss arises, but in the case of an indirect disposal of UK land, such a loss is not an allowable loss.

If it is necessary to determine how much of a gain calculated on the retrospective basis is a residential property gain (to which the upper rates of CGT will apply), the provisions at **2.1** ANNUAL RATES AND EXEMPTIONS apply as if the 'applicable period' were the period beginning on the day on which the interest in land was acquired (or 31 March 1982 if later) and ending with the day before the disposal.

[*TCGA 1992, Sch 4AA paras 1(3), 2–5*].

Direct disposals of pre-April 2015 assets fully chargeable before 6 April 2019

The following rules apply to any direct disposal of UK land if the taxpayer held the interest in the land in question throughout the period from 6 April 2015 to the date of disposal and the land consisted of a dwelling on every day in the period from 6 April 2015 to 5 April 2019 inclusive. The rules do not apply if the disposal is of an interest subsisting under a contract for the acquisition of land that, at any time in that period, did not consist of a building to be constructed or adapted for use as a dwelling if the taxpayer was not chargeable before 6 April 2019 (see above).

Default rule — rebasing

In calculating the gain or loss on the disposal, the asset is treated as having been acquired at its market value on 5 April 2015.

Election for retrospective computation

Where the taxpayer so elects, rebasing does not apply and the gains or losses are computed (as for CGT or corporation tax) on the basis of the position over the whole period of ownership. Such an election may be beneficial where a loss arises.

If it is necessary to determine how much of a gain calculated on the retrospective basis is a residential property gain (to which the upper rates of CGT will apply), the provisions at **2.1** ANNUAL RATES AND EXEMPTIONS apply as if the 'applicable period' were the period beginning on the day on which the interest in land was acquired (or 31 March 1982 if later) and ending with the day before the disposal.

Election for straight-line time apportionment

Where the taxpayer so elects, rebasing does not apply and the gains or losses are computed (as for CGT or corporation tax) on the basis of the position over the whole period of ownership and then apportioned so that only the post-5 April 2015 part of it is treated as arising on the disposal. That part is found by multiplying the gain or loss by the number of days in the period beginning on 6 April 2015 and ending on the day of disposal, and dividing the result by the number of days in the period beginning on the day the taxpayer acquired the interest disposed of (or 31 March 1982 if later) and ending on the day of disposal.

If it is necessary to determine how much of a gain calculated on the straight-line time apportionment basis is a residential property gain, the 'applicable period' is deemed to be the period beginning on 6 April 2015 and ending with the day before the disposal.

[*TCGA 1992, Sch 4AA paras 6–11*].

Direct disposals of pre-April 2015 assets partly chargeable before 6 April 2019

The following rules apply to any direct disposal of UK land if none of the above provisions apply and the interest being disposed of was not a post-April 2015 asset (i.e. one acquired after 5 April 2015) which was 'fully residential before 6 April 2019'. For this purpose, an interest subsisting under a contract for the acquisition of land that, at any time in that period, did not consist of a building to be constructed or adapted for use as a dwelling is treated as not fully residential before 6 April 2019. An asset was *'fully residential before 6 April 2019'* if the land in question consisted of a dwelling throughout the period from acquisition to 5 April 2019.

Default rule — rebasing

In calculating the gain or loss on the disposal, the asset is treated as having been acquired at its market value on 5 April 2015 and then sold and immediately reacquired at its market value on 5 April 2019. The gain or loss arising on the deemed disposal on 5 April 2019 (under the non-resident disposal rules at **35.31** onwards below) is treated as a gain or loss arising on the actual disposal (in addition to the actual gain or loss). If the asset was in fact acquired after 5 April 2015, the assumption that it was acquired on that day does not apply.

Election for retrospective computation

Where the taxpayer so elects, rebasing does not apply and the gains or losses are computed (as for CGT or corporation tax) on the basis of the position over the whole period of ownership. Such an election may be beneficial where a loss arises.

If it is necessary to determine how much of a gain calculated on the retrospective basis is a residential property gain (to which the upper rates of CGT will apply), the provisions at **2.1** ANNUAL RATES AND EXEMPTIONS apply as if the 'applicable period' were the period beginning on the day on which the interest in land was acquired (or 31 March 1982 if later) and ending with the day before the disposal.

[*TCGA 1992, Sch 4AA paras 12–15*].

Making an election

An election for the retrospective or time-apportionment basis of computation can only be made in a self-assessment tax return for the tax year or accounting period in which the disposal is made or in the UK land disposal return for the disposal (or in an amendment to either type of return). An election made in a UK land disposal return can be revoked in the self-assessment return (or amendment), provided that the latter return is delivered by the filing date. Otherwise, an election is irrevocable. [*TCGA 1992, Sch 4AA para 21*].

Companies becoming, or ceasing to be, UK resident on or after 6 April 2019

If a company becomes UK-resident on or after 6 April 2019 and subsequently makes a direct or indirect disposal of UK land, the above provisions apply if they would otherwise have applied but for the fact that the disposal is made when the company is UK-resident. [*TCGA 1992, Sch 4AA para 16*].

The above provisions do not apply where a company ceases to be resident in the UK after 5 April 2019 and disposes of an asset held on that date which is a direct or indirect disposal of UK land (instead the gain or loss is chargeable or allowable in full). The asset disposed of is, however, excepted from the application of *TCGA 1992, s 185(2)(3)* (deemed disposal on company ceasing to be UK-resident — see **43.16** OVERSEAS MATTERS). [*TCGA 1992, Sch 4AA para 18*].

Trustees ceasing to be, UK resident on or after 6 April 2019

The above provisions do not apply where the trustees of a settlement cease to be resident in the UK after 5 April 2019 and dispose of an asset held on that date which is a direct or indirect disposal of UK land (instead the gain or loss is chargeable or allowable in full). The asset disposed of is, however, excepted from the application of *TCGA 1992, s 80(2)* (deemed disposal on trustees ceasing to be UK-resident — see **42.2** OFFSHORE SETTLEMENTS). [*TCGA 1992, Sch 4AA para 17*].

Non-resident CGT disposals of UK residential property before 6 April 2019

[35.31] For 2015/16 to 2018/19, capital gains tax is extended to disposals of UK residential property by non-residents. This means that CGT is charged on the basis of where such a property is located rather than where the seller is located. The provisions apply to disposals on or after 6 April 2015 and before 6 April 2019. The provisions are repealed for subsequent disposals and replaced with the expanded provisions for disposals of interest in UK land at **35.23–35.30** above. [*FA 2015, Sch 7 para 60*]. As a result of the provisions, changes were made to the main residence election rules (see **47.10** PRIVATE RESIDENCES) so that residences, wherever situated, may only qualify for main residence relief for a particular tax year, either as fact or by nomination, if a tax residency test and occupation test are met. It is therefore possible for properties subject to this non-resident CGT regime to qualify for main residence relief for tax years in which they meet these two tests.

The CGT charge can apply to non-resident individuals (including on disposals in the non-resident part of a split tax year), non-resident trustees, personal representatives of non-resident deceased persons, certain non-resident companies, and any such person who is a partner in a partnership.

For full commentary on the provisions, see the 2022/23 or earlier edition of this work. The main features are as follows:

- Capital gains tax is charged on gains ('*NRCGT gains*') accruing on a disposal before 6 April 2019 of a UK residential property interest by a non-UK resident person.
- Tax is charged on the total amount of the NRCGT gains arising in a tax year after deduction of any allowable losses on disposals of UK residential property interests (whether or not NRCGT losses) of the same tax year, and any unused such losses brought forward from previous years.
- Gains and losses are calculated as for CGT (or corporation tax) purposes but there are special rules for property interests held on 5 April 2015. Unless an election is made, only the gain arising after that date is charged. Alternatively an election can be made for time apportionment or, particularly where a loss arises, for the whole of the gain to be charged.
- There are special provisions for calculating the gain or loss where the disposal is, or includes, a disposal chargeable under the provisions for high-value disposals of dwellings.
- Relief for losses arising on non-resident CGT disposals can generally only be obtained against NRCGT gains but an NRCGT loss arising to an individual in the overseas part of a tax year which is a split year can be deducted against general chargeable gains arising in the UK part of the year and unused NRCGT losses can be carried forward and set against general chargeable gains of a later tax year.
- Companies are charged to capital gains tax (and not corporation tax) on the chargeable gains at 20%.
- Individuals are charged to capital gains tax at either 18% or 28% depending on the level of their taxable income. Trustees and personal representatives are charged at 28%. The annual exempt amount is available in the normal way.
- A person who makes a non-resident CGT disposal must, in most cases, make a special return reporting the disposal to HMRC within 30 days following the day of the completion of the disposal. HMRC have powers, similar to those for discovery assessments, to make a determination where no return is made or where the tax liability shown in the return is insufficient.
- Tax on NRCGT gains is generally due 30 days after completion of sale (i.e. on the date the return reporting the disposal is due), except where the person is registered for self-assessment, in which case payment may be made on the normal payment date for CGT, though the disposal must still be reported in a return within 30 days.
- Qualifying members of a group of companies may make an election to be treated as an NRCGT group. Disposals of UK residential property interests between members of the group are disregarded, and the charge to tax applies as if the members of the group were a single body.

[*TCGA 1992, ss 2(2A)(2B), 4(3B), 14B–14H, 48A, 188A–188K, Schs C1, 4ZZB*].

Key points on land

[35.32] Points to consider are as follows:

- A gain on the disposal of land could be taxed as income either as trading income or under the rules for profits from dealing in or developing UK land.
- The joint ownership of land does not in itself constitute a partnership, and where there is not otherwise a partnership, the share of a gain on disposal of a jointly owned investment property should simply be reported in the joint owners' self-assessment returns and, where relevant, their UK land disposal returns.
- Rollover relief is available for certain exchanges of joint interests in land. This can be a useful tool if joint owners want to go their separate ways.
- Lease termination payments can be structured so as to achieve a tax-free lease surrender receipt, a tax-deductible payment to exit an onerous lease, or a tax-free inducement to a new tenant.
- Where two individuals intend to enter into marriage or civil partnership, and one of them owns a property with a market value lower than the cost price, it may be possible to crystallise a loss by transferring an interest to the other individual prior to the marriage/civil partnership.
- In any transaction involving land, practitioners must always consider the possible impact of VAT and SDLT.
- Non-UK residents are chargeable to UK tax on gains on disposals of interests in UK land and on disposals of assets deriving at least 75% of their value from UK land.
- A special compliance regime applies to all direct disposals of UK land where a residential property gain arises. A UK land disposal return must be made together with a payment on account of CGT by the 60th day following the day of completion of the disposal. Non-UK residents must make returns and payments in respect of all UK land disposals. The regime does not apply to disposals by companies.
- HMRC have a toolkit 'capital gains tax for land and buildings' that considers the perceived risk areas such as access to historical data, date of disposal, valuations, qualifying expenditure and reliefs. Using the toolkit or an alternative checklist may help show that reasonable care has been taken. Showing reasonable care is important if the computation of the gain is subsequently challenged and found to be incorrect as it affects the penalty that can be charged.

36

Late Payment Interest and Penalties

Cross-references. See **6** ASSESSMENTS; **45** PAYMENT OF TAX; **46** PENALTIES.

Introduction to late payment interest and penalties

[36.1] A harmonised regime for interest applies to many of the taxes and duties administered by HMRC, including capital gains tax. In relation to interest on late payment of capital gains tax, the new regime is described at **36.2** below. For the purposes of income tax and capital gains tax self-assessment, it came into force on 31 October 2011. The harmonised regime was originally expected to be extended to corporation tax at a later date, but the extension has not yet occurred and in the meantime the rules at **36.3** below continue to apply.

Capital gains tax which is paid more than 30 days late is subject to the penalty provisions at **36.6** below. No late payment penalty currently applies to corporation tax.

The interest system mirrors that under which HMRC pay interest on overpaid tax (see **50** REPAYMENT INTEREST) but the rates of interest for overpaid tax are considerably lower.

Late payment interest

[36.2] A harmonised regime for interest applies to many of the taxes and duties administered by HMRC.

For the purposes of any 'self-assessment amount' payable by any person to HMRC, the regime came into force on 31 October 2011. A '*self-assessment amount*' means:

- any tax or other amount in relation to which, for any tax year, a personal, trustees' or partnership tax return falls to be made or a discovery assessment is made; and
- any penalties assessed in relation to that tax or amount.

Where interest was already accruing immediately prior to 31 October 2011 on a self-assessment amount, it accrues on and after that date under the new regime. Interest payable on or after 31 October 2011 on a self-assessment amount is known as '*late payment interest*'.

For the purposes of any amount payable on account of CGT on direct and indirect disposals of UK land under *FA 2019, Sch 2* (see **45.3** PAYMENT OF TAX), the regime came into force on 6 April 2019.

Late payment interest is payable without deduction of tax at source and is recoverable (as if it were tax) as a Crown debt. Interest is refundable to the extent that the tax concerned is subsequently discharged (and a tax repayment may be treated as a discharge for this purpose).

The rate of late payment interest is set by reference to the official bank rate set by the Bank of England Monetary Policy Committee; for details, see *SI 2011 No 2446, Reg 3*.

Rates of interest are:

7.75% p.a. from 22 August 2023
7.50% p.a. from 11 July 2023 to 21 August 2023
7.00% p.a. from 31 May 2023 to 10 July 2023
6.75% p.a. from 13 April 2023 to 30 May 2023
6.50% p.a. from 21 February 2023 to 12 April 2023
6.00% p.a. from 6 January 2023 to 20 February 2023
5.50% p.a. from 22 November 2022 to 5 January 2023
4.75% p.a. from 11 October 2022 to 21 November 2022
4.25% p.a. from 23 August 2022 to 10 October 2022
3.75% p.a. from 5 July 2022 to 22 August 2022
3.50% p.a. from 24 May 2022 to 4 July 2022
3.25% p.a. from 5 April 2022 to 23 May 2022
3.00% p.a. from 21 February 2022 to 4 April 2022
2.75% p.a. from 7 January 2022 to 20 February 2022
2.60% p.a. from 7 April 2020 to 6 January 2022

Period for which interest accrues

A payment of tax within these provisions carries interest at the late payment interest rate from the 'late payment interest start date' until the date on which payment is made. The '*late payment interest start date*' in respect of any amount is the date on which that amount becomes due and payable. (It matters not that it might be a non-business day.) However, see also below under Assessments and amendments to self-assessments.

A payment to HMRC may take the form of a set-off against an amount payable by HMRC, in which case the date on which the payment is made is the date from which the set-off takes effect. In general, for the date on which an amount is treated as paid to HMRC, see **45.12** PAYMENT OF TAX.

Assessments and amendments to self-assessments

A special rule applies to determine the late payment interest start date if:

(a) there is an amendment or correction to an assessment or self-assessment; or
(b) HMRC make an assessment in place of, or in addition to, an assessment made by a taxpayer; or
(c) HMRC make an assessment in place of an assessment that *ought to have been made* by a taxpayer.

In relation to any amount due and payable as a result of any of the above, the late payment interest start date is what it would have been if:

- the original assessment or self-assessment had been complete and accurate and had been made on the date (if any) by which it was required to be made; and
- accordingly, the amount had been due and payable as a result of that original assessment or self-assessment.

The above rule applies to any assessment or determination (however described) of any amount due and payable to HMRC. A case in which the taxpayer failed to give notice of chargeability to tax when required by law to do so (see **46.3** PENALTIES) falls within (c) above. Where the requirement arises after a notice to make a return was withdrawn (see **52.5** RETURNS), (c) above applies by reference to the assessment which the taxpayer would have been required to make had there been no withdrawal notice.

Tax postponed

If an amount of tax is postponed pending determination of an appeal against a capital gains tax assessment (see **45.18** PAYMENT OF TAX), this does not have the effect of deferring the late payment interest start date, which is the same as it would have been had there been no appeal.

Tax over-repaid

Where an assessment is raised to collect an amount of income tax previously over-repaid (see **45.33** PAYMENT OF TAX), the late payment interest start date in relation to that amount is 31 January following the tax year for which the assessment is made.

[*FA 2009, ss 101, 103, 104, Sch 53 paras 1, 2, 3–5, 15, 16; TMA 1970, s 69; SI 2011 No 2446*].

Miscellaneous

See **36.6** below for penalties for late payment of capital gains tax.

See also **36.5** below.

Companies

[36.3] Corporation tax carries interest (under *TMA 1970, s 87A*) from the due and payable date (see **45.4** PAYMENT OF TAX), even if it is a non-business day, until payment. Where corporation tax assessed on a company may be assessed on other persons in certain circumstances, the due and payable date is that which refers to the company's liability. Corporation tax is to be brought within the late payment interest regime at **36.2** above (with special additional rules) at a future date.

The interest rate is determined by criteria contained in Treasury regulations made by statutory instrument; see *SI 1989 No 1297, Regs 3ZA, 3ZB*.

The rates of interest (such interest being deductible for tax purposes — see below) as regards corporation tax becoming due **on or after the normal due date** (nine months and one day after the end of the accounting period) are:

7.75% p.a. from 22 August 2023
7.50% p.a. from 11 July 2023 to 21 August 2023
7.00% p.a. from 31 May 2023 to 10 July 2023
6.75% p.a. from 13 April 2023 to 30 May 2023
6.50% p.a. from 21 February 2023 to 12 April 2023
6.00% p.a. from 6 January 2023 to 20 February 2023
5.50% p.a. from 22 November 2022 to 5 January 2023
4.75% p.a. from 11 October 2022 to 21 November 2022
4.25% p.a. from 23 August 2022 to 10 October 2022
3.75% p.a. from 5 July 2022 to 22 August 2022
3.50% p.a. from 24 May 2022 to 4 July 2022
3.25% p.a. from 5 April 2022 to 23 May 2022
3.00% p.a. from 21 February 2022 to 4 April 2022
2.75% p.a. from 7 January 2022 to 20 February 2022
2.60% p.a. from 7 April 2020 to 6 January 2022

The rates for corporation tax payable by earlier **instalments**, under the quarterly accounting rules for large companies (see **45.4** PAYMENT OF TAX), are:

6.25% p.a. from 14 August 2023
6.00% p.a. from 3 July 2023 to 13 August 2023
5.50% p.a. from 22 May 2023 to 2 July 2023
5.25% p.a. from 3 April 2023 to 21 May 2023
5.00% p.a. from 13 February 2023 to 2 April 2023
4.50% p.a. from 26 December 2022 to 12 February 2023
4.00% p.a. from 14 November 2022 to 25 December 2022
3.25% p.a. from 3 October 2022 to 13 November 2022
2.75% p.a. from 15 August 2022 to 2 October 2022
2.25% p.a. from 27 June 2022 to 14 August 2022
2.00% p.a. from 16 May 2022 to 26 June 2022
1.75% p.a. from 28 March 2022 to 15 May 2022
1.50% p.a. from 14 February 2022 to 27 March 2022
1.25% p.a. from 27 December 2021 to 13 February 2022
1.10% p.a. from 30 March 2020 to 26 December 2021

The latter set of rates applies up to the earlier of the date of payment and the normal due date (whereafter the normal rates apply).

Interest on tax subsequently discharged is adjusted or repaid so as to secure that the total is as it would have been had the tax discharged never been charged. However, where surplus advance corporation tax of a later accounting period displaces mainstream corporation tax paid in respect of an earlier accounting period, or trading losses or non-trading deficits of a later accounting period are offset against profits of an earlier period, or there is a combination of such events, any such adjustment or repayment of interest is restricted. In considering an adjustment or repayment of interest, then, where relief for tax paid for an accounting period is given by way of repayment of tax, the amount repaid is, as far as possible, treated as if it were a discharge of the corporation tax charged for that period.

Interest is paid without deduction of income tax and is deductible in computing profits (as a non-trading debit under the loan relationship rules — see **15.2–15.6** COMPANIES — CORPORATE FINANCE AND INTANGIBLES and Tolley's Corporation Tax). It is recoverable (as if it were tax charged and due and payable under an assessment) as a Crown debt.

[*TMA 1970, ss 69, 87A, 90, 91(1A)(2A); FA 1989, s 178; SI 1998 No 3175, Reg 7*].

Exchange restrictions and delayed remittances

[36.4] Where gains arising overseas cannot be remitted to the UK due to government action in the country of origin etc., and HMRC agree to defer collection of the tax, interest under **36.3** above ceases to run from the date on which HMRC were first in possession of information necessary to enable them to agree to deferment. If that date is three months or less from the due and payable date, no interest is payable. But where a demand is later made for payment of the deferred tax, interest (from the date of demand) is only chargeable if the tax is not paid within three months of that demand. [*TMA 1970, s 92*]. HMRC may defer collection indefinitely. See **43.6** OVERSEAS MATTERS for an alternative relief under *TCGA 1992, s 279*.

Miscellaneous issues related to late payment interest

Death of taxpayer

[36.5] A special rule applies if a person chargeable to an amount of tax dies before the amount becomes due and payable and the executor or administrator is unable to pay the amount until he obtains probate or letters of administration (or, in Scotland, the executor is unable to pay the amount before he obtains confirmation). In relation to that amount, the late payment interest start date in **36.2** above is the *later* of:

- the date which would have been the late payment interest start date apart from this special rule; and
- the date falling 30 days after the date of grant of probate etc.

[*FA 2009, s 101, Sch 53 para 12*].

Disasters of national significance

No interest is chargeable on unpaid tax where HMRC agree that payment may be deferred by reason of circumstances arising from a disaster or emergency specified by order in a statutory instrument made for the purpose. This applies whether the agreement was made before or after the tax became due or the order was made.

The period for which interest does not arise is the period beginning with a date specified in the order or, if HMRC direct, a later date from which the agreement for deferred payment has effect and ending with the date on which that agreement ceases to apply or, if earlier, the date on which the order is revoked or amended so that it ceases to apply to the deferred amount. For this purpose, the agreement for deferred payment ceases to have effect at the end of the period of deferment specified in the agreement or, if HMRC agree to extend (or further extend) that period, with the end of the extended period. If the agreement is for payment by instalments, the period of deferment in relation to each instalment ends with the date by which it is to be paid, but if an instalment is not paid by the agreed date (and HMRC do not agree to extend the period of deferment), the whole agreement is treated as ceasing to apply on that date.

If no agreement for deferred payment is made, but HMRC are satisfied that one could have been made, these provisions apply as if one had been made on terms which HMRC are satisfied would have been agreed in the circumstances.

Where these provisions apply, no liability to a surcharge on the deferred amount arises during the deferment period.

The Treasury may make an order specifying a disaster or emergency for the purposes of these provisions only if they consider it to be of national significance.

[*FA 2008, s 135; FA 2020, s 105*].

This power has been used to allow for the deferral of the second self-assessment payment on account for 2019/20 from 31 July 2020 to 31 January 2021 as a consequence of the COVID-19 pandemic. See *SI 2020 No 934*.

Interest on judgment debts

The same rate of interest as under **36.2** above applies to interest payable to HMRC under *Judgments Act 1838, s 17* or under an order under *County Courts Act 1984, s 74* where the debt to which the interest relates arises from court proceedings relating to a tax matter. See *F(No 2)A 2015, s 52*. Similar rules apply in Scotland and Northern Ireland. See *FA 2016, ss 170, 171*.

Late payment penalty

[36.6] A unified penalty code for failure to make payments on time (the '*late payment penalty*') applies across a range of taxes including capital gains tax. The code does not yet apply for corporation tax purposes. The penalty code is described below, but only to the extent that it relates to capital gains tax and corporation tax.

For income tax self-assessment taxpayers, the penalty regime described at **36.7** below will replace the unified regime from a date to be appointed by the Treasury via regulations. For taxpayers with business or property turnover of more than £50,000 per year (who will be required to submit digital quarterly updates through making tax digital), the new regime will take effect from 6 April 2026. For taxpayers with turnover between £30,000 and £50,000, it will take effect from 6 April 2027. There will be further consultation before the regime is extended to other taxpayers. The new regime applies from 6 April 2024 to taxpayers who have elected to enter making tax digital voluntarily.

A penalty is payable under the code if a taxpayer fails to make a payment of tax on or before the date specified in the table below. For the purposes of the following provisions, the 'penalty date' is the day after the table date.

	Tax to which payment relates	Amount of tax payable	Date after which penalty is incurred
1	CGT	Amount contained in taxpayer's self-assessment.	30 days after the due date. The due date is normally 31 January following the tax year in question but is deferred in certain cases where tax return is issued late by HMRC — see **45.2** PAYMENT OF TAX.
2	CGT	Amount contained in simple assessment.	30 days after the date the amount becomes due and payable — see **45.2** PAYMENT OF TAX.
2A	CGT	Amount payable under *FA 2019, Sch 2 para 6* (UK land disposal returns) and not included in a self-assessment return.	30 days after 31 January following the tax year in question — see **45.3** PAYMENT OF TAX.
3	Corporation tax	Amount shown in company tax return.	The filing date for the tax return for the accounting period for which the tax is due (see **52.21** RETURNS).
4	Corporation tax	Amount payable under quarterly accounting rules (see **45.4** PAYMENT OF TAX).	The filing date for the tax return for the accounting period for which the tax is due (see **52.21** RETURNS).
5	CGT and corporation tax	Amount payable under a determination of tax where no return is made on time.	CGT: 30 days after the date by which the amount would have been required to be paid if it had been shown in the return (i.e. the same date as for 1 above). Corporation tax: The filing date for the tax return for the accounting period for which the tax is due (see **52.21** RETURNS).
6	CGT	Amount payable where a determination of tax under *TMA 1970, s 28C* (see **52.17** RETURNS) is superseded by a self-assessment.	30 days after the date on which the amount would have been payable had it fallen within 1 above — see **52.17** RETURNS.
7	CGT	Amount payable in respect of tax under appeal but not postponed (or of tax ceasing to be postponed) or amount payable on determination of appeal.	30 days after the due date (see **45.18, 45.19** PAYMENT OF TAX).
8	CGT	Amount payable as a result of a correction or amendment of a self-assessment.	30 days after the due date (see **45.2** PAYMENT OF TAX).

	Tax to which payment relates	Amount of tax payable	Date after which penalty is incurred
9	CGT	Amount payable under an assessment other than a self-assessment.	30 days after the due date (which itself is 30 days after the date of the assessment).
10	CGT and corporation tax	Amount (not within 7–9 above) shown in an amendment or correction of a return.	30 days after the later of the due date and the date on which the amendment or correction is made.
11	CGT and corporation tax	Amount (not within 7–9 above) shown in an assessment or determination made by HMRC in circumstances other than where the taxpayer was required to make a return but failed to do so on time and that return, had it been made, would have shown an amount of tax payable.	30 days after the later of the due date and the date on which the assessment or determination is made.
12	CGT	Amount payable under a CGT exit charge payment plan (see **45.8** PAYMENT OF TAX).	The later of 30 days after the normal due date and the date on which the amount is payable under the plan.
13	Corporation tax	Amount payable under a CT exit charge payment plan (see **45.9** PAYMENT OF TAX).	The later of the first day after the 12-month period beginning immediately after the migration accounting period and the date on which the amount is payable under the plan.
14	Corporation tax	Amount payable under a CT payment plan for transactions with EEA residents (see **45.10** PAYMENT OF TAX).	The later of the first day after the 12-month period beginning immediately after the accounting period to which the plan relates and the date on which the amount is payable under the plan.

If a failure is within more than one of the above categories, a penalty is payable in respect of each such category.

Amount of penalty

Where a failure to pay tax on or before the relevant specified date occurs, the taxpayer is liable to an initial penalty of 5% of the unpaid tax.

If any of the tax remains unpaid after the end of the five months beginning with the penalty date (three months where the tax is within 3 or 4 above), the taxpayer is liable to an additional penalty of 5% of the amount remaining unpaid at that time. A further additional penalty becomes due if any of the tax is unpaid after the end of the eleven months (nine months where the tax is within 3 or 4 above) beginning with the penalty date, again equal to 5% of the amount remaining unpaid.

HMRC will not charge the first 5% late payment penalty on income tax and/or capital gains tax due on 31 January 2021 if payment is made, or a time to pay plan set up, by 1 April 2021 (HMRC Press Notice 19 February 2021). Similarly, HMRC will not charge the first 5% late payment penalty on income tax and/or capital gains tax due on 31 January 2022 if payment is made, or a time to pay plan set up, by 1 April 2022 (HMRC Press Notice 6 January 2022).

Reduction in special circumstances

HMRC can reduce, stay or agree a compromise in relation to proceedings for a penalty if they think it right to do so because of special circumstances. Ability to pay and the fact that a potential loss of revenue from one taxpayer is balanced by a potential overpayment by another are not special circumstances for this purpose.

Suspension of penalty during time to pay agreement

A taxpayer is not liable to a penalty under the above provisions if, before the penalty arises, he makes a request to HMRC for the deferral of the tax concerned and HMRC agree (whether before or after the penalty date) to the deferral. See **45.5** PAYMENT OF TAX for 'time to pay' arrangements.

The taxpayer remains liable, however, for any penalty which arises after the end of the agreed deferral period. If the taxpayer breaks the agreement then he becomes liable to any penalty to which he would have been liable but for the agreement, provided that HMRC notify him to that effect. For this purpose, a taxpayer breaks an agreement if he fails to pay the tax when the deferral period ends or if he fails to comply with a condition forming part of the agreement.

Where a deferral agreement is varied, the above rules apply to the agreement as varied from the time of the variation.

Reasonable excuse

None of the above penalties are due in respect of a failure to make a payment if the taxpayer satisfies HMRC or, on appeal, the Tribunal, that there is a reasonable excuse for the failure. Insufficiency of funds is not a reasonable excuse for this purpose, unless attributable to events outside the taxpayer's control and neither is the taxpayer's reliance on another person to do anything, unless he took reasonable care to avoid the failure. If the taxpayer had a reasonable excuse, he is treated as continuing to have a reasonable excuse after the excuse has ceased if the failure is remedied without unreasonable delay.

See **46.2** PENALTIES for case law on reasonable excuse.

Double jeopardy

No penalty arises for a failure or action in respect of which the taxpayer has been convicted of an offence.

Procedure

For the making of assessments to penalties under these provisions see **46.28** PENALTIES. For the right of appeal against such an assessment see **46.30** PENALTIES

[*FA 2009, Sch 56 paras 1–4, 9, 10, 16, 17; FA 2020, Sch 7 para 3; FA 2021, Sch 27 para 40*].

FA 2021 late payment penalty

[36.7] For income tax self-assessment (ITSA) taxpayers, the penalty regime described below replaces that at **36.3** from a date to be appointed by the Treasury via regulations. [*FA 2021, s 117*]. For taxpayers with business or property turnover of more than £50,000 per year (who will be required to submit digital quarterly updates through making tax digital), the new regime will take effect from **6 April 2026**. For taxpayers with turnover between £30,000 and £50,000, it will take effect from **6 April 2027**. There will be further consultation before the regime is extended to other taxpayers. The regime applies from 6 April 2024 to taxpayers who have elected to enter making tax digital voluntarily. [*FA 2024, s 37; SI 2024 No 440*]. The government intends to extend the regime to corporation tax at a later date, but corporation tax is not included in the legislation in *FA 2021*.

In its application to capital gains tax, the late payment penalty has effect in relation to:

(1) amount of tax due under self-assessment;
(2) an amount of tax becoming due as a result of the amendment or correction of a self-assessment;
(3) an amount of tax payable by virtue of an assessment other than a self-assessment or a simple assessment;
(4) an amount of tax becoming due as a result of an HMRC determination being superseded by a self-assessment (see **52.17** RETURNS);
(5) an amount of tax payable by virtue of a simple assessment;
(6) an amount of tax becoming due following an application for postponement of tax pending determination of an appeal, including amounts postponed, amounts not postponed and additional tax becoming payable on determination of the appeal;
(7) an amount of tax (not within (4) above) shown in an assessment or determination made by HMRC 'in default of a return' (see below);
(8) an amount of tax (not within (2), (3) or (6) above) shown in an amendment or correction of a return; and
(9) an amount of tax (not within (2), (3) or (6) above) shown in an assessment or determination made by HMRC otherwise than 'in default of a return' (see below).

Penalties apply where a person fails to pay the amount in question on or before the date specified below.

Penalty within	*Specified date*

(1) above	The date specified in *TMA 1970, s 59B(3)* or *(4)* as the due date by which the amount must be paid. This date is normally 31 January following the tax year but is deferred in certain cases where the tax return is issued late by HMRC (see **45.2** PAYMENT OF TAX).
(2) above	The date specified in *TMA 1970, s 59B(5)* as the due date (see **45.2** PAYMENT OF TAX).
(3) above	The date specified in *TMA 1970, s 59B(6)* as the due date (see **45.2** PAYMENT OF TAX).
(4) above	The date specified in *TMA 1970, s 59B(5A)* as the due date. This is the date on which the amount would have been payable had it fallen within (1) above (see **52.17** RETURNS).
(5) above	The date specified in *TMA 1970, s 59BA(4)* or *(5)* as the due date (see **45.2** PAYMENT OF TAX).
(6) above	The date determined in accordance with *TMA 1970, s 55* as the due date. See **45.18** PAYMENT OF TAX as regards tax not postponed, and **45.19** PAYMENT OF TAX as regards tax becoming payable on determination of the appeal (whether it be tax previously postponed or additional tax).
(7) above	The date by which the amount would have been required to be paid if it had been shown in the return in question.
(8) above	The later of the date by which the amount must be paid and the date on which the amendment or correction is made.
(9) above	The later of the date by which the amount must be paid and the date on which the assessment or determination is made.

For the purposes of items (7) and (9) above, an assessment or determination by HMRC is made '*in default of a return*' if it is made where:

- a person is required to make or deliver a return falling within: (i) any *group* of returns in **46.8** PENALTIES; or (ii) any item in the table in *FA 2009, Sch 55 para 1* (late filing penalties);
- that person fails to make or deliver the return on or before the due date; and
- if the return had been made or delivered as required, it would have shown that an amount falling within the above table was due and payable.

When is a penalty chargeable?

No penalty is chargeable if the tax due is fully paid before the end of the period of 15 days ('*the 15-day period*') beginning with the day after the specified date in the table above.

No penalty is chargeable if 'the 15-day TTP condition' is met. '*The 15-day TTP condition*' is met if a 'time to pay agreement' (TTP agreement) is made (whether before or after the end of the 15-day period) as a result of proposals for paying the tax due made by the person before the end of the 15-day period. A '*time to pay agreement*' is defined for these purposes as an agreement between HMRC and a person to the effect that payment of an amount of tax due may be deferred for a period of time (the '*agreed deferral period*'); see **45.6** PAYMENT OF TAX for TTP arrangements generally. If a TTP agreement is varied at any time by a further agreement between the taxpayer and HMRC, references in these provisions to the agreement include the agreement as varied.

First penalty: tax outstanding after the 15-day period

A penalty ('*the first penalty*') is chargeable if the tax due is not paid in full before the end of the 15-day period and the 15-day TTP condition is not met.

If the tax due is paid in full after the end of the 15-day period but before the end of 'the 30-day period', the amount of the penalty is 2% of the tax unpaid at the end of the 15-day period.

If the tax due is not fully paid before the end of the period of 30 days ('*the 30-day period*') beginning with the day after the specified date, the amount of the penalty is:

- if 'the 30-day TTP condition' is met, 2% of the tax unpaid at the end of the 15-day period;
- otherwise, 2% of the tax unpaid at the end of the 15-day period plus 2% of the tax unpaid at the end of the 30-day period.

'*The 30-day TTP condition*' is met if a TTP agreement is made as a result of proposals for paying the tax due made by the person after the end of the 15-day period but before the end of the 30-day period. It does not matter whether the agreement itself is made before or after the end of the 30-day period. Where either the 15-day or the 30-day TTP condition was met but the taxpayer breaks the agreement in question, the first penalty is chargeable as if the TTP agreement in question had never been made. A person breaks a TTP agreement if:

- the person fails to pay the deferred amount within the agreed deferral period; or
- the deferral is subject to compliance with a condition, and the person fails to comply. This might, for example, be a condition that part of the deferred amount be paid within the agreed deferral period.

HMRC are to take a light-touch approach to the initial 2% penalty in the first year of operation of the new regime. Where a taxpayer is doing their best to comply, HMRC will not assess the first penalty at 2% after 15 days, allowing taxpayers 30 days to approach HMRC for a TTP agreement. (www.gov.uk/government/publications/penalties-for-late-payment-and-interest-harmonisation).

Second penalty: tax outstanding after the 30-day period

A penalty ('*the second penalty*') is chargeable if any amount of the tax due remains unpaid at the end of the 30-day period.

The amount of the penalty is calculated by applying a penalty rate of 4% per annum during 'the further penalty period' to so much of the tax due as is from time to time unpaid. '*The further penalty period*' begins with the day after the last day of the 30-day period and ends with the day on which the tax is paid in full.

If a TTP agreement has effect during any part of the further penalty period, the further penalty period does not include the period that begins with the day the taxpayer makes the proposals to HMRC for paying the tax, on the basis of which the TTP agreement is made, and ends with the day on which the tax is paid in full. If the taxpayer breaks the TTP agreement (see above), the second penalty is chargeable as if the TTP agreement had never been made.

Reasonable excuse

Liability to a late payment penalty does not arise in respect of a failure to make a payment if the person otherwise chargeable satisfies HMRC (or, on appeal, the Tribunal) that they had a reasonable excuse for the failure. Insufficiency of funds is not a reasonable excuse for this purpose and neither is the taxpayer's reliance on another person to do anything unless the taxpayer took reasonable care to avoid the failure. If the taxpayer had a reasonable excuse, he is treated as continuing to have a reasonable excuse after the excuse has ceased if the failure is remedied without unreasonable delay.

Reduction in special circumstances

HMRC may reduce or stay a penalty or agree a compromise in relation to proceedings for a penalty if they think it right to do so because of special circumstances. Ability to pay or the fact that a potential loss of revenue from a taxpayer is balanced by a potential overpayment by a taxpayer are not special circumstances for this purpose.

Double jeopardy

A person is not liable to a late payment penalty in respect of a failure or action in respect of which the person has been convicted of an offence.

[*FA 2021, Sch 26 paras 1–14, 22*].

Procedure

For the making of assessments to penalties under these provisions, see **46.28** PENALTIES. For the right of appeal against such an assessment, see **46.30** PENALTIES

A late payment penalty is recoverable (as if it were tax) as a Crown debt. [*TMA 1970, s 69; FA 2021, s 118, Sch 27 para 7*].

37

Life Insurance Policies and Deferred Annuities

Cross-reference. For the treatment of other kinds of insurance policy, see **23.10** EXEMPTIONS AND RELIEFS.

Disposal of rights

[37.1] A gain on the disposal of, or of an interest in, rights under a life insurance policy or contract for a deferred annuity is not a chargeable gain unless::

- in the case of a disposal of the rights, the rights or any interest in the rights; or
- in the case of a disposal of an interest in the rights, the rights, the interest or any interest from which all or part of the interest directly or indirectly derives,

have at any time been acquired by any person for 'actual consideration'.

For this purpose, '*actual consideration*' is consideration other than consideration deemed to be given under any provision relating to tax on chargeable gains. Amounts paid under the policy or contract by way of premiums or as lump sum consideration are not actual consideration. Actual consideration given for a disposal made by one spouse or civil partner to the other, an 'approved post-marriage disposal', an 'approved post-civil partnership disposal', or an intra-group transfer to which *TCGA 1992, s 171(1)* (see **26.3** GROUPS OF COMPANIES) applies, is treated as not being actual consideration. A disposal is an '*approved post-marriage disposal*' or an '*approved post-civil partnership disposal*' if it is one made in consequence of the dissolution or annulment of a marriage or civil partnership by one party to the marriage or partnership to the other, with the approval, agreement or authority of, or pursuant to an order of, a court (or other person or body) having jurisdiction under the law of any country or territory, where the rights or interest disposed of were held by the person making the disposal immediately before the marriage or partnership was dissolved or annulled. An '*interest*' in relation to any rights is an interest as co-owner of the rights, whether the rights are owned jointly or in common and whether or not the interests of the co-owners are equal.

Where an allowable loss would otherwise accrue on a disposal of, or of an interest in, the rights under a life insurance policy or contract for a deferred annuity but if *TCGA 1992, s 37* (exclusion from consideration of amounts charged to income tax — see **33.1** INTERACTION WITH OTHER TAXES) and *TCGA 1992, s 39* (exclusion from allowable expenditure of amounts deductible in computing profits or losses for income tax purposes — see **33.1** INTERACTION WITH OTHER TAXES) were disregarded there would be a loss of a smaller amount, that smaller amount is taken to be the loss on the disposal. Where, disregarding those provisions, either a gain or neither a gain nor a loss would accrue, the disposal is taken to be one on which neither a gain nor a loss accrue.

In the case of a life insurance policy, the receipt of the sum assured by the policy, the transfer of investments or other assets to the owner in accordance with the policy and the surrender of the policy are each treated as a disposal of the rights (or of all of the interests in the rights) under the policy. In the case of a contract for a deferred annuity, the receipt of the first instalment of the deferred annuity and the surrender of the rights under the contract are treated as a disposal of the rights (or of all the interests in the rights) under the contract. Where there is a disposal of (or of an interest in) the rights under a contract for a deferred annuity on receipt of the first instalment, the amount of the consideration for the disposal is deemed to be the aggregate of the amount or value of the first instalment and the then market value of the outstanding instalments (or, in the case of a disposal of an interest, such proportion of that aggregate as is just and reasonable), and no gain accruing on any subsequent disposal of the rights or any interest in them is a chargeable gain.

[*TCGA 1992, s 210*].

Where a policy-holder receives compensation for mis-selling of the policy, no chargeable gain arises in respect of that compensation provided that the exemption in *TCGA 1992, s 210(2)* above applies to the policy. In such circumstances, HMRC Extra-Statutory Concession D33 (see **7.2** ASSETS) applies (HMRC Capital Gains Manual CG69071).

Any transfer of investments or other assets to a policy-holder in accordance with a policy is deemed to be made at market value. [*TCGA 1992, s 204(3)(6)*].

Subject to the restriction noted above in relation to losses, in computing any chargeable gain or allowable loss under the above provisions, allowable expenditure will be:

(a) the base cost of the policy to the person to whom the gain accrues (this will be either market value or what that person paid for the policy), and
(b) any premiums paid by that person.

Corporation tax

[37.2] For corporation tax purposes, 'investment life insurance contracts' (broadly, life insurance policies which have a surrender value, contracts for a purchased life annuity and capital redemption policies) held by a company which is not a life insurance company are treated as creditor relationships of the company. See *CTA 2009, ss 560–569*.

For full details, see Tolley's Corporation Tax.

38

Losses

Cross-references. See also **4.33–4.37** ANTI-AVOIDANCE for restrictions on the use of losses under the serial avoiders regime; **10.2** for the loss arising to person in receipt of contribution allowances on demolition of a building or structure; **14.6** COMPANIES; **22.15** ENTERPRISE INVESTMENT SCHEME; **35.23** LAND; **49** REMITTANCE BASIS; **56.16, 56.21** SETTLEMENTS; **60.3–60.5** SUBSTANTIAL SHAREHOLDING EXEMPTION.

Simon's Taxes. See C1.5, C3.7.

Introduction to losses

[38.1] For capital gains tax purposes, allowable losses are calculated in the same way as chargeable gains. The basic rule is that losses incurred in a tax year are set off against gains of the same tax year, and to the extent that they cannot be so set off, are carried forward for set off against gains of subsequent years. Losses cannot, with two exceptions, be carried back to previous tax years. The exceptions are for certain losses on rights to deferred unascertainable consideration (see **38.18** below) and for losses carried back from the tax year of death (see **18.7** DEATH).

See **14.6** COMPANIES for losses incurred by companies. Relief for losses of a corporate body is restricted where any amount of an investment by the Government in the body is written off (see **38.19** below).

There are also a number of special rules giving rise to losses or providing for alternative reliefs as follows.

	Relief	Reference	Para
1	**Assets of negligible value.** Where an asset has become of negligible value, the owner may claim to crystallise a loss without disposing of the asset. Claim can be back-dated up to two years before tax year of claim.	*TCGA 1992, s 24(1A)–(3)*	**38.10**
2	**Loan to trader.** Loss relief is available where a loan used wholly for the purposes of a trade etc. becomes irrecoverable. Claim can be backdated up to two years before tax year of claim. **Payment made under guarantee.** Relief also applies to a payment made by a guarantor of such a loan. Claim cannot be backdated.	*TCGA 1992, s 253*	**38.11**
3	**Loan to trader evidenced by QCB.** Loss relief is available where a 'qualifying loan' backed by a qualifying corporate bond made before 17 March 1998 becomes irrecoverable. Claim can be backdated up to two years before tax year of claim.	*TCGA 1992, s 254*	**38.12**
4	**Losses on shares in unlisted trading companies — individuals.** Income tax relief can be claimed by an individual for a capital loss on shares in a qualifying trading company for which he subscribed or for shares to which EIS income tax relief is attributable. The loss can be relieved against income of the tax year in which the loss is incurred and/or the preceding tax year.	*ITA 2007, ss 131–151*	**38.14**
5	**Losses on shares in unlisted trading companies — investment companies.** An investment company may claim relief against income for a loss on shares in a qualifying trading company for which it subscribed. Relief is given first against income of the accounting period of loss, with any unrelieved balance set off against income of the preceding twelve months.	*CTA 2010, ss 68–90*	**38.17**

The final relief described in this chapter is relief for trading losses which can in certain circumstances be set off against the chargeable gains of a person other than a company. See **38.20** below.

Set-off of capital losses against chargeable gains

[38.2] The charge to capital gains tax is on all chargeable gains accruing to the taxpayer in the tax year, less any 'allowable losses' (see **38.4** below) accruing to them in that year and, so far as not allowed as a deduction from chargeable gains accruing in any previous tax year, any allowable losses accruing to them in any previous year (but not earlier than 1965/66). This rule applies subject to the annual exempt amount and, in particular, its interaction with losses brought forward (see **2.5** ANNUAL RATES AND EXEMPTIONS). [*TCGA 1992, s 1(3)*].

Losses are not deductible if, and so far as, other tax relief can be claimed in respect of them and may only be deducted once for capital gains tax purposes. They may not be deducted at all if already given relief for income tax (see **38.14** and **38.17** below regarding an election for capital losses arising on the disposal of certain shares in unquoted trading companies to be set off against general income). [*TCGA 1992, s 1F(4)(5)*].

Losses may be used in the most beneficial way, and so may be deducted from a gain irrespective of the rate of tax which would otherwise apply (see **2.1** ANNUAL RATES AND EXEMPTIONS).

For anti-avoidance provisions relating to allowable losses, see **38.8** below.

For provisions relating to losses of companies see **14.6** COMPANIES.

Set-off against attributed gains

A person's allowable losses, whether of the tax year under review or brought forward from previous years (or brought back from the year of death — see **18.7** DEATH), can be set off against attributed gains under *TCGA 1992, s 86* (charge on settlor of non-UK resident settlement in which he has an interest (see **42.5** OFFSHORE SETTLEMENTS)). Personal losses cannot be set off against gains treated under *TCGA 1992, ss 87, 87K, 87L* or *89(2)* as accruing to a beneficiary or the settlor of a non-UK resident settlement or the recipient of an onward gift from such a beneficiary (see **42.13–42.20** OFFSHORE SETTLEMENTS).

Where any personal losses are to be set against two or more attributed gains from different settlements and those gains are insufficient to extinguish them fully, a proportion of those losses is deducted from each of those gains on a pro rata basis. This rule will affect the amount recoverable by the settlor from the trustees in respect of tax on the attributed gains (see **42.11** OFFSHORE SETTLEMENTS).

[*TCGA 1992, s 1E(4)(5)*].

Remittance basis

See **49.2** REMITTANCE BASIS.

Miscellaneous

Short-term losses which accrued before 1971/72 but which were not relieved under *Sch D, Case VII* may be brought forward against gains chargeable to capital gains tax. [*TCGA 1992, Sch 11 para 12*]. This is the only instance where losses incurred before 6 April 1965 can be carried forward.

A person may be able to enjoy the benefit of an unutilised loss of trustees which has accrued to them in respect of property to which the person has become absolutely entitled. However, the loss can only be used against subsequent gains accruing to the beneficiary on disposal of the same asset. See **56.16** SETTLEMENTS. This facility to transfer losses does not apply as regards personal representatives and legatees (see **18.9** DEATH).

Losses of non-residents

[38.3] The following rules apply to losses arising to persons not resident in the UK or to losses arising in the overseas part of a split year for an individual under the statutory residence test (see **51.17** RESIDENCE AND DOMICILE).

A loss is not an allowable loss if it arises in a tax year at a time when, if a gain had arisen instead, it would not have been a chargeable gain.

Where a person who is not resident in the UK for a tax year has chargeable gains for that year, the only allowable losses that can be deducted from the gains are losses on the same types of assets on which such gains can arise, i.e.:

(i) UK-situated assets with a connection to the person's UK branch or agency (see **43.3** OVERSEAS MATTERS);
(ii) interests in UK land (see **35.23** LAND; and see below for NRCGT losses unrelieved at 6 April 2019); and
(iii) assets deriving at least 75% of their value from UK land where the person has a substantial indirect interest in that land (see **35.24** LAND).

Losses arising on disposals of assets within (i)–(iii) above in a tax year in which the taxpayer is UK-resident can be carried forward and set off against chargeable gains arising in a tax year of non-residence.

[*TCGA 1992, s 1E(1)–(3)*].

Where chargeable gains arise to an individual in the overseas part of a split tax year, and the assets disposed of are within (ii) or (iii) above, only losses on assets within (ii) or (iii) above (or which would be within those categories but for falling within (i) above) can be deducted from those gains. Losses on assets within (ii) or (iii) above which arise in the overseas part of a split year can, however, be set off against gains of any type arising in the UK part of the tax year. [*TCGA 1992, s 1G(1)(3)(4)*].

Non-resident CGT losses

See **35.31** LAND for relief for NRCGT losses. NRCGT losses unrelieved at 6 April 2019 can be carried forward as if they were losses within (i)–(iii) above. [*TCGA 1992, s 2(7B)*].

Computation of allowable loss

[38.4] Losses are computed as for gains (see **16** COMPUTATION OF GAINS AND LOSSES) except as in **38.20** below and where expressly provided otherwise (e.g. as in **32.2** INDEXATION).

Where an exemption is given so as to make a gain not a chargeable gain, that exemption applies similarly to losses so that they are not '*allowable losses*'.

[*TCGA 1992, s 16(1)(2); CTA 2010, s 1119*].

For anti-avoidance provisions relating to losses, see **38.8** below and for those applicable only for corporation tax purposes, see **14.6** COMPANIES.

Where a loss accrues on the disposal by a company of an asset held on 6 April 1965, there are provisions which may restrict the loss allowable. Similar observations may apply to disposals after 5 April 1988 of assets held on 31 March 1982. See **8** ASSETS HELD ON 31 MARCH **1982**. See also **16.14**(j) COMPUTATION OF GAINS AND LOSSES where an asset qualified for capital allowances.

For the treatment of losses arising to an individual not domiciled in the UK but resident here in respect of the disposal of an asset overseas, see **49** REMITTANCE BASIS.

Example

On 30 April 2024, Q sells for £40,000 a part of the land which he owns. The market value of the remaining estate is £160,000. Q bought the land for £250,000 in March 1993.

	£
Disposal consideration	40,000
Allowable cost $\dfrac{40{,}000}{40{,}000 + 160{,}000} \times £250{,}000$	50,000
Allowable loss	£10,000

Notification of capital losses

[38.5] A capital loss is not an allowable loss unless its amount is quantified and notified to HMRC. Such a notice is subject to the provisions of *TMA 1970, s 42*, and to the enquiry regime (see **52.11** RETURNS, **13.3** CLAIMS), as if it were a claim for relief (see **13.2** CLAIMS). For capital gains tax purposes, losses must, if possible, be notified on the self-assessment tax return or in an amendment to it, or failing that may be notified separately in writing within the normal time limits for claims (see **13.5** CLAIMS [*TCGA 1992, s 16(2A)*]).

No notification time limit applies to capital losses arising in 1995/96 and earlier years or in company accounting periods ending before 1 July 1999.

For the purposes of enquiring into the allowable loss for capital gains tax purposes, in *Cumming-Bruce v HMRC* UT, [2022] STC 1669, the UT found that capital losses reported on a tax return form part of the self-assessment and as such should be subject to an enquiry into the return rather than as an enquiry into a stand-alone claim.

Order of set-off

Losses arising to individuals, trustees and personal representatives in the year 1996/97 and subsequent years are to be treated as utilised before losses arising in earlier years. Similarly, losses accruing to companies for accounting periods ending on or after 1 July 1999 will have preference to losses arising in accounting periods ending before that date. [*FA 1995, s 113(2)*].

Carry-back prohibited

[38.6] Losses may not normally be carried back against the gains of an earlier year. There are two exceptions to this rule. See **18.7** DEATH for carry-back of losses from the year of death and **38.18** below for the election to treat a loss on a right to unascertainable consideration as accruing in an earlier year.

Disposals to connected persons — clogged losses

[38.7] A loss on a disposal to a CONNECTED PERSON (**17**) is deductible only from chargeable gains arising on other disposals to that same person while they are still connected. Such a loss is often referred to as a 'clogged loss'.

A disposal which settles capital and income wholly or primarily for educational, cultural or recreational purposes, the beneficiaries being 'an association of persons' most of whom are *not* connected persons, is not subject to this restriction on losses.

[*TCGA 1992, s 18(3)(4)*].

The restriction does not apply where a person becomes absolutely entitled as against the trustee to property in a settlement (see **56.16** SETTLEMENTS).

Where the disposal is of an option to enter into a transaction with the disposer, no loss accruing to a connected person who acquires the option is allowable unless it accrues on the disposal of the option at arm's length to a person unconnected with the acquirer. [*TCGA 1992, s 18(5)*].

Where a company has a clogged loss carried forward to an accounting period in which it makes a capital gain against which that loss could be offset and also makes a loss in the period which is not clogged, it can make a claim the effect of which is to treat a specified amount of the clogged loss as a loss of that period, and the same amount of the other loss as if it were a loss carried forward from a previous period. A claim must be made in the tax return for the period. The purpose of such a claim is to enable the clogged loss to be deducted in full where the corporate capital loss restriction (see **14.11** COMPANIES) would otherwise apply to restrict the deduction. Instead, that restriction applies to the current period loss as if it were a carried forward loss, leaving any part of it which cannot be deducted in the current period as an amount to carry forward which is not clogged. The claim is limited to the lowest of the total carried forward clogged losses, the gains of the accounting period against which they may be set and the losses of the accounting period. A claim may be made for an accounting period beginning on or after 1 April 2020 (subject to the transitional rule for periods straddling that date at **14.11**). [*TCGA 1992, s 18(9)–(12); FA 2020, Sch 4 paras 17, 42–46*].

See **4.13** ANTI-AVOIDANCE for special market value provisions for disposals between connected persons.

Debts

A loss on the disposal of a debt by a person (the 'subsequent creditor'), who acquired it from the 'original creditor' at a time when the original creditor or his personal representative or legatee was connected with the subsequent creditor, is not an allowable loss. Purchases through persons all of whom are connected with the subsequent creditor are also included as are acquisitions from the original creditor's personal representative or legatee. Where trustees of a settlement are the original creditor, any loss accruing to the subsequent creditor is not allowable if he is connected with any person (or his personal representative or legatee) who becomes absolutely entitled to the debt on its ceasing to be settled property. [*TCGA 1992, s 251(4)(5)*].

HMRC takes the view that these provisions do not apply to debts on a security (HMRC Capital Gains Manual CG53451). For debts generally, see **23.5** EXEMPTIONS AND RELIEFS.

Losses — anti-avoidance

[38.8] The following provisions apply to restrict losses in cases of avoidance.

Arrangements to secure tax advantage

An anti-avoidance provision applies so that a loss accruing on a disposal directly or indirectly in consequence of, or otherwise in connection with, any 'arrangements' the main purpose of which, or one of the main purposes of which, is to secure a 'tax advantage' is not an allowable loss. It does not matter whether the loss accrues at a time when there are no chargeable gains against which it could be set or whether the tax advantage would be secured for the person incurring the loss or another person.

'*Arrangements*' include any agreement, understanding, scheme, transaction or series of transactions, whether or not legally enforceable. '*Tax advantage*' means relief or increased relief from, or repayment or increased repayment of, capital gains tax, corporation tax or income tax or the avoidance or reduction of a charge or assessment to any of those taxes or the avoidance of a possible assessment to any of those taxes.

[*TCGA 1992, ss 16A, 184D*].

HMRC have published guidance on the operation of the provision. If, on the facts, any participant in arrangements is found to have a main purpose of achieving a tax advantage, that is considered to be sufficient to demonstrate that one of the main purposes of the arrangements is the securing of a tax advantage. Where there is more than one way of achieving a commercial objective and a course of action is chosen on commercial grounds, any incidental tax advantage is not relevant. However, where the tax advantage was material to the choice the anti-avoidance legislation may be in point, but HMRC have indicated that this is unlikely to be the case unless there is evidence of additional, complex or costly steps included solely for tax reasons. Using a marketed tax avoidance scheme will be taken as an indicator that securing a tax advantage was a main purpose of the arrangements.

The guidance also includes 18 examples demonstrating how HMRC think the provision operates in different circumstances.

(HMRC Capital Gains Manual CGAPP9).

Miscellaneous

Where a deemed disposal arises under *TCGA 1992, s 29(2)* on the transfer of value between different shares or rights in a company by the person controlling it, no loss is allowable on such a disposal. See **4.9** ANTI-AVOIDANCE. Value-shifting to give a tax free benefit may result in losses being allowable only to such extent as is just and reasonable. See **4.12** ANTI-AVOIDANCE.

Where there are depreciatory transactions within a group of companies or where there is 'dividend stripping' by one company holding 10% or more of a class of shares in another company, any related loss is only allowable to the extent that it is just and reasonable. See **4.19, 4.20** ANTI-AVOIDANCE.

A restriction of a loss of a company which is a member of a group may occur where the loss is wholly or partly referable to a time before it joined the group or the disposal of an asset which was held by another group member when that member company joined the group. See **26.18** GROUPS OF COMPANIES.

Trading losses effectively converted into allowable capital losses as in **38.20** below cannot be carried forward as a deduction against chargeable gains after the time the trade concerned ceases.

Special reliefs for losses

[38.9] There are a number of special rules giving rise to losses or providing for alternative reliefs and these are described at **38.10–38.18** below. See **38.1** above for a summary table.

Assets of negligible value

[38.10] Where the owner of an asset makes a 'negligible value' claim, he is treated as if he had sold, and immediately reacquired, the asset at the time of the claim or (subject to the following) at any earlier time specified in the claim for a consideration of an amount equal to the value specified in the claim.

An earlier time can be specified in the claim if the claimant owned the asset at that time, the asset had become of negligible value at that time and that time is not more than two years before the beginning of the tax year in which the claim is made or, for corporation tax, is on or after the first day of the earliest accounting period ending not more than two years before the time of the claim.

A negligible value claim can be made where either:

(a) the asset has become of negligible value while owned by the claimant; or
(b) the disposal by which the claimant acquired the asset was a no gain/no loss disposal at the time of which the asset was of negligible value and, between the time at which the asset became of negligible value and that disposal, any other disposal of the asset was a no gain/no loss disposal.

For the purposes of a negligible value claim, a building may be regarded as a separate asset from the land on which it stands, but where there is a deemed sale of a building, the land comprising the site of the building (including any land occupied for purposes ancillary to the use of the building) is likewise treated as if it was sold, and immediately reacquired, at its then market value.

[*TCGA 1992, s 24(1A)–(3)*].

'*Negligible value*' is not defined but is taken by HMRC to mean 'worth next to nothing' (HMRC Capital Gains Manual CG13125).

In *Director v Inspector of Taxes* (Sp C 161), [1998] SSCD 172, a negligible value claim was refused on the grounds that the shares in question had a nil acquisition cost by virtue of *TCGA 1992, s 17* (see **39.1** MARKET VALUE) and thus could not *become* of negligible value (but see (b) above).

In *Drown & Leadley (JJ Leadley's Executors) v HMRC* UT [2017] UKUT 111 (TCC), an individual (L) subscribed for shares in two companies which subsequently became insolvent. In May 2010 L was killed in a motoring accident. His executors submitted claims for relief under *ITA 2007, s 131* (see **38.14** below) on the basis that the shares had become of negligible value by the date of L's death. HMRC accepted that the shares had become of negligible value but rejected the claims on the basis that any claim had to be made by the shareholder and could not be made posthumously by a shareholder's executors. The UT agreed with HMRC, finding that there was no indication in the legislation that a negligible value claim could be taken as made at a time other than that at which it was submitted and *TCGA 1992, s 24* suggested that a claimant must still own the asset at the point such a claim is submitted in respect of it. A deceased person and his personal representatives could not be equated; *TCGA 1992, s 62* provided that the personal representatives were deemed to acquire the assets of a deceased person on his death for a consideration equal to their market value without a disposal (see **18.2** DEATH). The personal representatives could not submit a negligible value claim.

For certain qualifying corporate bonds becoming of negligible value where evidencing a 'qualifying loan', see **38.12** below.

The backdating facility above cannot be used by a company to obtain relief for a loss that would otherwise be non-allowable under the provisions for SUBSTANTIAL SHAREHOLDINGS OF COMPANIES (see **60.17**).

For HMRC practice and procedure, see HMRC Capital Gains Manual CG13120–13150. HMRC offer their post-transaction valuation checking service (see **52.7** RETURNS) to taxpayers making negligible value claims. Form CG34 must be submitted at the same time or after the claim is made. Acceptance by HMRC of the value submitted does not mean that they necessarily accept that all the conditions for the claim are met or that any allowable loss arises. (HMRC Internet Statement 31 January 2006).

Quoted securities

HMRC have accepted that certain quoted securities have become of negligible value within the meaning of *TCGA 1992, s 24(2)*. For securities so accepted in recent years, see the GOV.UK website (at www.gov.uk/guidance/negligible-value-agreements).

Example

In June 2024, John sells an asset, realising a chargeable gain of £27,800. In December 2024, John learns that his shareholding in Jones Ltd has become worthless. He acquired the shares in 1995 for their then market value of £15,000. John makes no other disposals in 2024/25.

If John makes a claim under *TCGA 1992, s 24* no later than 5 April 2027, then his taxable gains for 2024/25 are as follows.

	£
Chargeable gain	27,800
Less allowable loss	15,000
	12,800
Less annual exempt amount	3,000
Gains chargeable to tax 2024/25	£9,800

Loans to traders

[38.11] The following reliefs are available for losses on loans to traders.

Relief for lender on loan becoming irrecoverable

Loss relief is available to the extent that any outstanding amount of the principal of a 'qualifying loan' made by the claimant after 11 April 1978 has become irrecoverable otherwise than under the express terms of the loan or related arrangements, or by reason of any act or omission by the lender (or, as appropriate, the guarantor of a loan claiming the relief below). The relief is available provided that, at the time of the claim, the claimant and borrower were neither spouses or civil partners living together nor companies in the same 'group' when the loan was made or at any subsequent time, and that the claimant has not assigned his right of recovery.

The loss is treated as accruing either when the claim under *TCGA 1992, s 253(3)* is made or, within limits (see below), at an earlier specified time. The amount of the loss cannot include any amount falling to be relieved by way of a debit under the loan relationship provisions in **15.2–15.7** COMPANIES — CORPORATE FINANCE AND INTANGIBLES.

[*TCGA 1992, s 253(3)(12)(14)(a)(aa), (15)*].

For cases in which the Revenue failed in contending that the loans became irrecoverable by reason of acts of the lender, see *Cann v Woods* (Sp C 183), [1999] SSCD 77, and *Crosby and Others (Crosby's Trustees) v Broadhurst* (Sp C 416), [2004] SSCD 348.

The allowable loss accrues at the time of the claim or at whatever earlier time is specified in the claim, so long as the amount claimed was also irrecoverable at that earlier time. For capital gains tax purposes, the time specified cannot be earlier than two years before the beginning of the tax year in which the claim is made. For corporation tax purposes, the time specified must fall on or after the first day of the earliest accounting period ending within the two years ending with the date of claim. [*TCGA 1992, s 253(3)(3A)*].

Relief is not available and nor is a clawback of relief made (see below) if the amount in question is taken into account for computing income for the purposes of income tax or corporation tax. [*TCGA 1992, s 253(10)*].

A claim to relief was allowed in *Bunting v HMRC* [2024] UKFTT 275 (TC), where the loan had been converted into share capital of negligible value. The FTT considered that while the debt had been satisfied and discharged in consideration of shares with a nil market value, satisfaction did not represent recovery. Here, the taxpayer had been paid nil against the debt of £2.2 million which remained unpaid and thereby outstanding.

Qualifying loan

A '*qualifying loan*' is a loan where the money lent is used by the borrower wholly for the purposes of a trade, profession or vocation (not being a trade which consists of or includes the lending of money) carried on by him (and for this purpose money used by a borrower for setting up a trade which is subsequently carried on by him is treated as used for the purposes of that trade), and which is not a 'debt on a security'. For loans made before 24 January 2019, it is an additional requirement that the borrower must be UK-resident.

However, for guarantees see below, and for loans evidenced by securities which are qualifying corporate bonds, see **38.12** below.

The 'commercial letting' of 'furnished holiday accommodation' is treated as a trade. This treatment is, however, expected to be abolished with effect from April 2025. See **24** FURNISHED HOLIDAY ACCOMMODATION.

A '*debt on security*' is defined by reference to *TCGA 1992, s 132*, security therefore including any loan stock or similar security of any government or public or local authority in the UK or elsewhere, or of any company, and whether secured or unsecured. See further **23.5** EXEMPTIONS AND RELIEFS.

Where a company re-lends money to a 'trading company' in the same group, the original loan is treated as having been used by the first company as it is used by the second while the second remains a member of the group. For the purposes of these provisions, a group of companies is construed in accordance with **26.2** GROUPS OF COMPANIES. '*Trading company*' has the same meaning for this purpose as at **30.2** HOLD-OVER RELIEFS.

[*TCGA 1992, s 253(1)(2)(14)(b)(c); FA 2020, s 27*].

A loan was held not to be a qualifying loan in *Robson v Mitchell* CA, [2005] STC 893.

Relief for payment made under guarantee

The relief given above to a lender also applies (with the exception of the backdating facility) to a guarantor of a qualifying loan who makes a claim. The guarantor must have made a payment under the guarantee to the lender or a co-guarantor and he is treated as if an allowable loss of the amount of the payment had accrued to him when the payment was made. The guarantee must have been given after 11 April 1978. Relief is available even though the original loan is a 'debt on a security' (see above and **38.12** below).

Where loss relief is given, no allowable loss and no chargeable gain (otherwise than on a clawback of relief as below) will accrue on the disposal of rights consequent on the guarantor having made a payment (which may include a payment in respect of interest as well as principal) under the guarantee. Relief is reduced to the extent that any contribution is 'payable' to the claimant by any co-guarantor.

[*TCGA 1992, s 253(4)(11)(15)*].

Claims must be made not more than four years after the end of the tax year or accounting period in which the payment was made. [*TCGA 1992, s 253(4A)*].

'*Payable*' has its ordinary meaning, so that if under general legal principles the claimant could have made a recovery against one or more co-guarantors of part of a sum paid by him under a guarantee but chose not to do so, the relief given to him is reduced proportionately (*Leisureking Ltd v Cushing* Ch D 1992, 65 TC 400).

'*Guarantee*' covers the case where a person's property is charged as security for a qualifying loan. It does not include an indemnity, which creates a primary liability. In *Dennis v HMRC* FTT 2018, [2019] SFTD 593, a payment under a shareholders' agreement was held to be made under an indemnity and therefore not a guarantee.

For HMRC's views on the circumstances in which a payment is made 'under a guarantee', see HMRC Capital Gains Manual CG66010–66014.

Clawback of relief

Where loss relief has been obtained by the person who made the loan or a guarantor of it, and all or part of the outstanding amount of, or of interest in respect of (in the case of a guarantor), the principal of the loan is recovered, a chargeable gain is deemed to accrue to him at the time of recovery equal to so much of the allowable loss (for which relief was claimed) as corresponds to the amount recovered. Where a claimant has obtained loss relief in respect of a payment under a guarantee and recovers the whole or any part of that payment, he will be treated as if there had accrued to him at that time a chargeable gain equal to so much of the allowable loss as corresponds to the amount recovered.

A similar treatment will apply to a company ('the second company') which recovers the whole or any part of the outstanding amount of the principal of a loan which has become irrecoverable in circumstances where a company ('the first company'), which made the loan originally and is in the same group as the second company when the loan was made or at any subsequent time, has obtained loss relief in respect of that loan becoming irrecoverable. Where the first company has obtained loss relief in relation to a payment made under a guarantee in respect of a loan which has become irrecoverable, a similar treatment of the second company applies if it recovers the whole or any part of the outstanding amount of, or of interest in respect of, the principal of the loan, or the whole or any part of the guarantee payment made by the first company. An amount is treated as recovered if money or money's worth is received in satisfaction of the right of recovery. If this right is assigned otherwise than at arm's length, its full market value at that time is deemed to have been received.

[*TCGA 1992, s 253(5)–(9)(13)*].

Loans to traders evidenced by qualifying corporate bonds becoming irrecoverable

[38.12] A loss incurred on a qualifying corporate bond is not an allowable loss (see **48.2** QUALIFYING CORPORATE BONDS). However, special provisions apply for capital gains tax purposes only if, at the time of a claim under *TCGA 1992, s 254* by a person who has made a 'qualifying loan' **before 17 March 1998**, one of the three conditions given below is fulfilled. The claimant is treated as if an allowable loss equal to the 'allowable amount' had accrued to him either at the time of the claim or, within limits (see below), at an earlier specified time. The provisions are **repealed** in relation to loans made after 16 March 1998.

A 'qualifying loan' means a loan in the case of which:

(a) the borrower's debt is a debt on a security within *TCGA 1992, s 132* (see **38.11** above) issued after 14 March 1989 or issued before 15 March 1989 but held on 15 March 1989 by the person who made the loan;
(b) but for the borrower's debt being a debt on a security, the loan would be a qualifying loan within *TCGA 1992, s 253* (see **38.11** above); and
(c) the security is a **48** QUALIFYING CORPORATE BOND, other than a deeply discounted security (see **57.21** SHARES AND SECURITIES) and with certain other modifications (see *TCGA 1992, s 117(13)*), in particular so as to exclude building society permanent interest bearing shares.

The first condition is that:

(i) the value of the security has become negligible (but relief will still be available where the security ceases to have any value because it is redeemed early; HMRC Statement of Practice SP 8/90 and see (1) below for 'redemption date'),
(ii) the claimant has not assigned his right to recover any outstanding amount of the principal of the loan, and
(iii) the claimant and the borrower are not companies which have been in the same group (within *TCGA 1992, s 170*, see **26.2** GROUPS OF COMPANIES) at any time after the loan was made.

The second condition is that:

(1) the security's 'redemption date' (i.e. the latest date on which, under the terms under which the security was issued, the company or body which issued it can be required to redeem it) has passed,

(2) all the outstanding amount of the principal of the loan was irrecoverable (taking the facts existing on that date) or proved to be irrecoverable (taking the facts existing on a later date), and
(3) the requirements in (ii) and (iii) above are fulfilled.

The third condition is that:

(A) the security's redemption date (as at (1) above) has passed,
(B) sub-condition (2) of the second condition above was fulfilled on a similar basis as regards part (rather than the whole) of the outstanding principal of the loan, and
(C) the requirements in (ii) and (iii) above are fulfilled.

Where the first or second condition is fulfilled, '*the allowable amount*' is the lesser of the outstanding amount of the principal of the loan and the amount of the security's acquisition cost (i.e. the amount or value of the consideration in money or money's worth given, by or on behalf of the person who made the loan, wholly and exclusively for the acquisition of the security, together with the incidental costs to him of the acquisition). However, if any amount of the principal of the loan has been recovered the amount of the security's acquisition cost is for this purpose reduced (but not beyond nil) by the amount recovered. An amount is treated as recovered if money or money's worth is received in satisfaction of the right of recovery. If this right is assigned otherwise than at arm's length, its full market value at that time is deemed to have been received.

Where the third condition is fulfilled, then '*the allowable amount*' is an amount equal to the excess (if any) of the security's acquisition cost over the 'relevant amount' or nil (if there is no such excess). The '*relevant amount*' is the aggregate of the amount (if any) of the principal of the loan which has been recovered (as above) and the amount (if any) of the principal of the loan which has not been recovered but which is recoverable.

The allowable loss accrues at the time of the claim or at whatever earlier time is specified in the claim, so long as the relevant condition was also fulfilled at that earlier time. The time specified cannot be earlier than two years before the beginning of the tax year in which the claim is made.

Relief is not available and nor is a clawback of relief made (see below) if the amount in question is taken into account for computing income for the purposes of income tax or corporation tax. An amount is not treated as irrecoverable for the purposes of the relief if it becomes irrecoverable under the express terms of the loan or related arrangements, or by reason of any act or omission by the lender.

[*TCGA 1992, ss 254(1)–(8)(12), 255(1)(2)(4)(5)*].

Clawback of relief

Where the above relief has been given and the whole or any part of the 'relevant outstanding amount' is at any time recovered (as above) by the claimant, he is treated as if there had accrued to him at that time a chargeable gain equal to so much of the allowable loss as corresponds to the amount recovered. The '*relevant outstanding amount*' means, in a case where the first or second condition was fulfilled, the amount of the principal of the loan outstanding when the claim was allowed or, in a case where the third condition was fulfilled, the amount of the part (or the greater or greatest part) arrived at by the inspector under sub-condition (B) of the third condition above.

[*TCGA 1992, ss 254(9)–(11), 255(3)–(5)*].

Qualifying corporate bonds — reorganisations etc. and relief under 38.12 *above*

[38.13] *TCGA 1992, s 116(10)(11)* deals with the situation where, on a reorganisation etc. of shares (which are not qualifying corporate bonds), such shares ('the old asset') are replaced by securities ('the new asset') which are qualifying corporate bonds (and thus exempt from capital gains tax). The broad effect is to defer the chargeable gain or allowable loss that would have accrued on a disposal of the old asset at its market value immediately before the reorganisation until such time as a part or the whole of the new asset is disposed of, at which time the corresponding part or the whole of the deferred gain or loss is deemed to accrue. See **48.4** QUALIFYING CORPORATE BONDS for full details.

In such a case and where the new asset is a qualifying corporate bond in respect of which an allowable loss is treated as accruing under *TCGA 1992, s 254(2)* in **38.12** above, and the loss is treated as so accruing at a time falling after the reorganisation but before any actual disposal of the new asset subsequent to the reorganisation, then, for the purposes of *TCGA 1992, s 116(10)(11)*, a disposal of the new asset is deemed to have occurred at (and only at) the time the loss is deemed to have accrued. This applies whatever the time the reorganisation occurs. [*TCGA 1992, s 116(15)*]. The effect is that the deferred gain or loss relating to the old asset will be deemed to accrue at the same time as the loss arising on a claim under *TCGA 1992, s 254(2)* above in respect of the new asset is deemed to accrue, and any later disposal of the new asset is ignored for the purposes of ascertaining when and in what amount the deferred gain or loss is treated as arising.

A concessional practice, contained in HMRC Extra-Statutory Concession D38, applies as follows. Where a person acquired corporate bonds in respect of shares and securities and those bonds became, or would fall to be treated as, qualifying corporate bonds by virtue only of *FA 1989, s 139* (extension of definition to include a wider range of sterling bonds; see **48.3** and **48.4** QUALIFYING CORPORATE BONDS), an allowable loss, computed in accordance with the rules in *TCGA 1992, s 116* (see **38.12** above), will accrue if:

(a) the qualifying corporate bonds were issued in respect of shares or other securities before 14 March 1989 and were still retained at that date by the person to whom they were issued;
(b) the bonds were acquired in a transaction within *TCGA 1992, s 116(10)(11)* (see above) and on disposal after 13 March 1989 fall to be treated as qualifying corporate bonds as a result of *FA 1989, s 139*;
(c) relief under *TCGA 1992, s 254* would have been available had the loan been a qualifying loan within *TCGA 1992, s 254(1)*;
(d) the taxpayer claiming the concessional relief agrees that if all or part of the amount relieved is subsequently recovered, the relief will be clawed back in the same way as if *TCGA 1992, s 254* had applied, save that in all cases, the gain will be treated as accruing to the claimant; and

(e) when this concession applies, any gain or loss on the original shares or securities will be treated as accruing at the same time as the loss on the bonds in accordance with *TCGA 1992, s 116(15)* (see above and also **48.4** QUALIFYING CORPORATE BONDS for an additional relief which may apply in such circumstances where the bonds are gifted to a charity).

Under the concession the allowable loss will be treated as arising when a claim is made but it will be treated as arising in an earlier tax year or accounting period provided the claim is made not later than two years after the end of that year or accounting period, all the conditions for relief are satisfied at the date of claim, and the relief would have been available at the end of the tax year or accounting period for which relief is claimed.

Losses on shares in unlisted trading companies — individuals

[38.14] See generally HMRC Venture Capital Schemes Manual VCM10010 onwards, VCM70000 onwards.

An individual may claim relief from income tax, instead of from capital gains tax, for an allowable loss (as computed for capital gains tax purposes) on a disposal of 'qualifying shares'. The relief is often referred to as 'share loss relief'.

Relief is available only if:

- the disposal is at arm's length; or
- it is by way of a distribution on a winding-up; or
- the value of the shares has become negligible and a claim to that effect made under *TCGA 1992, s 24(2)* (see **38.10** above); or
- a deemed disposal occurs under *TCGA 1992, s 24(1)* (which deems the entire loss, destruction, dissipation or extinction of an asset to be a disposal — see **10.2** CAPITAL SUMS DERIVED FROM ASSETS).

Relief is not available where the shares are the subject of an exchange or arrangement within *TCGA 1992, ss 135* or *136* undertaken for tax avoidance purposes or other than for genuine commercial reasons so that a chargeable disposal under *TCGA 1992, s 137* arises. See **4.16** ANTI-AVOIDANCE.

The relief is one of the income tax reliefs capped by *ITA 2007, s 24A*. The relievable loss, aggregated where applicable with the other reliefs specified in *ITA 2007, s 24A* (including trade loss relief against general income), cannot exceed the greater of £50,000 and 25% of adjusted total income (as defined). The cap does not, however, apply to losses on the disposal of shares to which income tax relief under the enterprise investment scheme or seed enterprise investment scheme is attributable or to which social investment relief is attributable. See Tolley's Income Tax under Allowances and Tax Rates for details.

Qualifying shares

'*Qualifying shares*' are ordinary shares or stock:

- in a 'qualifying trading company' (see **38.15** below) for which the individual 'subscribed'; or
- to which EIS income tax relief is attributable (see **22** ENTERPRISE INVESTMENT SCHEME).

For this purpose, an individual '*subscribes*' for shares if they are issued to him by the company in consideration of money or money's worth, or were transferred to him *inter vivos* by his spouse or civil partner who had similarly subscribed for them. The spouses or civil partners concerned must be living together (see **40.3** MARRIED PERSONS AND CIVIL PARTNERS) at the time of the transfer, and the shares are treated as issued to the transferee at the time they were issued to the transferor. Where an individual has subscribed for shares, he is treated as having subscribed for any bonus shares subsequently issued to him in respect of those shares provided that the bonus shares are in the same company, of the same class and carry the same rights as the original shares. The bonus shares are treated as issued at the time the original shares were issued.

Where, for shares subscribed for before 10 March 1981, the consideration was deemed equal to the market value, the loss allowable on disposal cannot exceed what the loss would have been without applying that subsection. (For shares subscribed for after 9 March 1981, market value is not substituted where the consideration is less than market value.)

[*ITA 2007, ss 131, 135, 150, 151(1); FA 2020, s 38(2)*].

Shares issued to joint owners or nominees

HMRC accept that relief can be claimed by an individual even if the shares were subscribed for in joint names or through a nominee. (HMRC Brief 41/2010).

In *Murray-Hession v HMRC FTT*, [2016] UKFTT 612 (TC) the taxpayer was held to have subscribed for shares previously held by another person as nominee, agent or otherwise on his behalf.

Operation of and claims for relief

A loss may be claimed against income:

- of the tax year in which the loss is incurred; and/or
- of the tax year preceding that in which the loss is incurred.

If a claim is made in relation to both tax years, it must specify the year for which relief is to be given first. The loss is deducted in calculating net income for the specified tax year, and, if the claim relates to both tax years, any remaining part of the loss is then deducted in calculating net income for the other year.

Where, against income of the same year, claims are made both in respect of that year's loss and in respect of the following year's loss, the claim for the current year's loss takes precedence.

A claim for relief must be made in writing on or before the first anniversary of 31 January following the tax year *in which the loss is incurred*.

Relief under these provisions is given in priority to relief under *ITA 2007, s 64* (trading losses set against general income) and *ITA 2007, s 72* (further relief for trading losses to be set against general income in early years of a trade) for the same tax year.

To the extent that relief in respect of a loss is obtained under these provisions, the loss is not an allowable loss for capital gains tax purposes. Any part of the loss for which income tax relief is not given does, however, remain an allowable loss for capital gains tax purposes.

[*ITA 2007, ss 132, 133; TCGA 1992, s 125A(1)*].

Limits on relief

Where an individual claims relief under these provisions in respect of a loss on the disposal of qualifying shares which form part of a 'section 104 holding' (see 58 SHARES AND SECURITIES — IDENTIFICATION RULES) either at the time of disposal or at an earlier time, the relief is restricted to the sums that would have been allowable as deductions in computing the loss if the qualifying shares had not formed part of the holding.

Where the qualifying shares were acquired on the same day as other shares that are not capable of being qualifying shares (see below), such that, by virtue of *TCGA 1992, s 105(1)(a)* (see **58.2** SHARES AND SECURITIES — IDENTIFICATION RULES), all the shares are treated as acquired by a single transaction, the amount of relief is restricted to the sums that would have been allowable as deductions in computing the loss if the qualifying shares were treated as acquired by a single transaction and the other shares were not so treated.

Where the qualifying shares, taken as a single asset, and other shares or debentures in the same company which are not capable of being qualifying shares, also taken as a single asset, are treated for capital gains tax purposes as the same asset under *TCGA 1992, s 127* (see **57.2** SHARES AND SECURITIES), the amount of relief is restricted to the sums that would have been allowable as deductions in computing the loss if the qualifying shares and the other shares were not to be treated as the same asset.

For the above purposes, shares to which EIS income tax relief is not attributable are not capable of being qualifying shares at any time if they were acquired otherwise than by subscription, if condition (c) at **38.15** below was not met in relation to the issue of the shares. Additionally, for the purposes only of the 'same asset' restriction above, shares to which EIS income tax relief is not attributable are not capable of being qualifying shares at any time if they are shares of a different class from the qualifying shares concerned.

[*ITA 2007, s 147; FA 2020, s 38(2)(3)*].

Identification

The following provisions apply to identify whether a disposal of shares forming part of a mixed holding (i.e. a 'holding' of shares including shares that are not capable of being qualifying shares and other shares) is a disposal of qualifying shares and, if so, to which of any qualifying shares acquired at different times the disposal relates.

Except as noted below, the normal capital gains tax identification rules apply and where shares are thereby identified with the whole or any part of a section 104 holding, they are further identified with acquisitions on a last in/first out (LIFO) basis.

The above rules do not apply where the holding includes *any* of the following:

- shares in respect of which Business Expansion Scheme (BES) was given and was not withdrawn (see **23.22** EXEMPTIONS AND RELIEFS);

- shares to which Enterprise Investment Scheme (EIS) income tax relief is attributable (see **22** ENTERPRISE INVESTMENT SCHEME);
- shares to which EIS capital gains deferral relief is attributable (see **22.16** ENTERPRISE INVESTMENT SCHEME).

Instead, disposals are identified in accordance with the identification rules generally applicable to BES and EIS shares (first in/first out (FIFO), subject to certain special rules — see **22.15** ENTERPRISE INVESTMENT SCHEME, **23.22** EXEMPTIONS AND RELIEFS).

Where the above rules cannot identify the shares disposed of, the identification is to be made on a just and reasonable basis.

A '*holding*' of shares for the above purposes is any number of shares of the same class held by one individual in the same capacity, growing or diminishing as shares of that class are acquired or disposed of. Shares comprised in a 'new holding' following a reorganisation to which *TCGA 1992, s 127* applies are treated as having been acquired when the original shares were acquired. Any shares held or disposed of by a nominee or bare trustees for an individual are treated as held or disposed of by that individual.

[*ITA 2007, ss 148, 149*].

See the example at **38.16** below.

Anti-avoidance

Any claim to relief will bring in the provisions of *TCGA 1992, s 30* (value-shifting to give a tax-free benefit — see **4.11** ANTI-AVOIDANCE) so that the relief may be adjusted for any benefit conferred whether tax-free or not. [*TCGA 1992, s 125A(2)*].

Company reorganisations etc.

The following applies only to shares to which EIS income tax relief is not attributable. Where shares are disposed of and represent a new holding identifiable under *TCGA 1992, s 127* (see **57.2** SHARES AND SECURITIES) with 'old shares' after a reorganisation or reduction of share capital, relief is not available unless it could have been given if an allowable loss had arisen on the disposal of the old shares at arm's length at the reorganisation etc. had this legislation been in force. Where the reorganisation did not so qualify, but new consideration was given for the new shares, relief is limited to such of that new consideration as is an allowable deduction. '*New consideration*' is money or money's worth but excluding any surrender or alteration to the original shares or rights attached to them, and the application of assets of the company or distribution declared but not made out of the assets.

For new shares issued on or after 6 April 2007, the above does not apply where the share exchange provisions below apply.

[*ITA 2007, s 136*].

See HMRC Venture Capital Schemes Manual VCM75390.

Share exchanges

The following provisions apply in relation to shares to which EIS income tax relief is not attributable. Where, by means of an exchange of shares, all of the shares (the old shares) of a company (the old company) are acquired by a company (the new company) in which the only previously issued shares are subscriber shares, then, subject to the further conditions below being satisfied, the exchange is not regarded as involving a disposal of the old shares and an acquisition of the new company shares (the new shares). Where old shares held by an individual were subscribed for by him and EIS relief was not attributable to them, the new shares stand in the shoes of the old shares, e.g. as if they had been subscribed for and issued at the time the old shares were subscribed for and issued and as if any requirements under the above provisions met at any time before the exchange by the old company had been met at that time by the new company.

The further conditions are as follows.

(a) The shares must be issued after 5 April 1998.
(b) The consideration for the old shares must consist entirely of the issue of the new shares.
(c) The consideration for old shares of each description must consist entirely of new shares of the 'corresponding description'.
(d) New shares of each description must be issued to holders of old shares of the 'corresponding description' in respect of and in proportion to their holdings.
(e) The exchange of shares is not treated for capital gains tax purposes as involving a disposal of the old shares or an acquisition of the new shares by virtue of *TCGA 1992, s 127*.

For these purposes, old and new shares are of a '*corresponding description*' if, assuming they were shares in the same company, they would be of the same class and carry the same rights.

References above to 'shares' (other than those to 'shares to which EIS income tax relief is not attributable' or 'subscriber shares') include references to 'securities'.

An exchange within these provisions, or arrangements for such an exchange, does not breach the control and independence requirement at **38.15** below.

[*ITA 2007, ss 145, 146*].

Qualifying trading company

[38.15] As regards shares issued after **5 April 1998**, a '*qualifying trading company*' is a company which:

(a) either (i) on the date of disposal meets the trading, control and independence, qualifying subsidiaries and (for shares issued on or after 17 March 2004) the property managing subsidiaries requirements below, or (ii) has ceased to meet any of those requirements within three years before that date and has not since that cessation been an 'excluded company', an '*investment company*' (i.e. a company whose business consists wholly or mainly in, and the principal part of whose income derives from, making investments, but excluding the holding company of a 'trading group') or a '*trading company*' (i.e. a company, other than an excluded company, whose business consists wholly or mainly of the carrying on of a trade or trades, or which is the holding company of a trading group); *and*

(b) either (i) has met each of the requirements in (a)(i) above for a continuous period of at least six years prior to the disposal (or prior to the cessation in (a)(ii) above, as the case may be), or (ii) has met each of those requirements for a shorter continuous period ending with the disposal or cessation and has not previously been an excluded company, an investment company or a trading company; *and*

(c) met the gross assets requirement below both immediately before and immediately after the issue of the shares and (for shares issued after 6 March 2001) met the unquoted status requirement below at the 'relevant time'.

For shares issued before 7 March 2001, it was also a condition that the company be an 'unquoted' company (as defined for the purposes of the unquoted status requirement below) throughout that part of the period mentioned in (d) above that falls before 7 March 2001.

As regards shares issued **before 6 April 1998**, a '*qualifying trading company*' is a company none of whose shares have been listed on a recognised stock exchange at any time in the period ending with the date of disposal of the shares and beginning with the incorporation of the company, or, if later, one year before the date on which the shares were subscribed for, and which:

(1) either (i) is a trading company on the date of the disposal or (ii) has ceased to be a trading company within the previous three years and has not since that time been an investment company or an 'excluded company'; and

(2) either (i) has been a trading company for a continuous period of six years ending on the date of disposal of the shares or the time it ceased to be a trading company or (ii) if shorter, a continuous period ending on that date or that time and had not before the beginning of that period been an excluded company or an investment company.

An '*excluded company*' is a company which has a trade consisting mainly of dealing in land, in commodities or futures or in shares, securities or other financial instruments (as regards shares issued before 6 April 1998 — dealing in shares, securities, land, trades or commodity futures) or which is not carried on on a commercial basis with a reasonable expectation of profit, or a company which is the holding company of a group other than a trading group, or which is a building society (see **10** BUILDING SOCIETIES) or a registered society within *Co-operative and Community Benefit Societies Act 2014* or NI equivalent.

A '*trading group*' is a 'group' (i.e. a company and its 51% subsidiaries) the business of the members of which, taken together, consists wholly or mainly in the carrying on of a trade or trades (disregarding any trade carried on by a subsidiary which is an excluded company or, as regards shares issued before 6 April 1998, which is non-UK resident).

The six requirements referred to at (a) to (c) above are as follows.

The trading requirement

The company must either:

(i) exist wholly for the purpose of carrying on one or more 'qualifying trades' (see **22.11** ENTERPRISE INVESTMENT SCHEME) (disregarding purposes having no significant effect on the extent of its activities), or

(ii) be a '*parent company*' (i.e. a company that has one or more 'qualifying subsidiaries' (see **22.8** ENTERPRISE INVESTMENT SCHEME)) and the business of the '*group*' (i.e. the company and its qualifying subsidiaries) must not consist wholly or as to a substantial part in the carrying on of 'non-qualifying activities'.

Where the company intends that one or more other companies should become its qualifying subsidiaries with a view to their carrying on one or more qualifying trades, then, until any time after which the intention is abandoned, the company is treated as a parent company and those other companies are included in the group for the purposes of (ii) above.

For the purpose of (ii) above, the business of the group means what would be the business of the group if the activities of the group companies taken together were regarded as one business. Activities are for this purpose disregarded to the extent that they consist in:

- holding shares in or securities of any of the company's subsidiaries,
- making loans to another group company,
- holding and managing property used by a group company for the purposes of a qualifying trade or trades carried on by any group company, or
- holding and managing property used by a group company for the purposes of research and development from which it is intended either that a qualifying trade to be carried on by a 'group company' will be derived or, for shares issued after 5 April 2007, a qualifying trade carried on or to be carried on by a group company will benefit. '*Group company*' includes, for this purpose, any existing or future company which will be a group company at any future time.

Activities are similarly disregarded to the extent that they consist, in the case of a subsidiary whose main purpose is the carrying on of qualifying trade(s) and whose other purposes have no significant effect on the extent of its activities (other than in relation to incidental matters), in activities not in pursuance of its main purpose.

'*Non-qualifying activities*' are:

- excluded activities within **22.11** ENTERPRISE INVESTMENT SCHEME, and
- non-trading activities (other than research and development (as defined)).

References in the definition of 'qualifying trade' and 'excluded activities' at **22.11** ENTERPRISE INVESTMENT SCHEME to 'period B' are to be taken for the above purposes to refer to the continuous period mentioned in (b) above.

For the ascertainment of the purposes for which a company exists, see HMRC Venture Capital Schemes Manual VCM13050.

A company ceases to meet the trading requirement if before the time that is relevant for the purposes of (a) above a resolution is passed or an order is made for the winding-up of the company or if the company is dissolved without winding-up. This does not, however, apply if the winding-up is for genuine commercial reasons and not part of a scheme a main purpose of which is tax avoidance and the company continues, during the winding-up, to be a trading company. (Note that the continuation of trading condition now applies in relation to shares issued after 5 April 2001 but did originally apply up to and including 20 March 2000, after which a drafting error inadvertently altered the law.) For shares issued after 20 March 2000, a company does not cease to meet the trading requirement by reason of anything done as a consequence of its being in administration or receivership (both as defined by *ITA 2007, s 252*), provided everything so done and the entry into administration or receivership are for genuine commercial (and not tax avoidance) reasons. For shares issued after 16 March 2004, these provisions are extended to refer also to the winding-up, dissolution, administration or receivership of any of the company's subsidiaries.

The control and independence requirement

Subject to the share exchange provisions at **44.14** above, the issuing company must not:

(I) control another company other than a qualifying subsidiary (see **22.8** ENTERPRISE INVESTMENT SCHEME) or, for shares issued before 21 March 2000, have a 51% subsidiary other than a qualifying subsidiary, 'control' being construed as in *CTA 2010, ss 450, 451* and being considered with or without connected persons within *ITA 2007, s 993*,

(II) be a 51% subsidiary of another company or otherwise under the control of another company, 'control' being construed in accordance with *ITA 2007, s 995* (previously *ICTA 1988, s 840*) and again being considered with or without connected persons, or

(III) be capable of falling within (I) or (II) by virtue of any arrangements (as very broadly defined).

The qualifying subsidiaries requirement

The company must not have any subsidiaries other than qualifying subsidiaries (see **22.8** ENTERPRISE INVESTMENT SCHEME).

The property managing subsidiaries requirement

For shares issued on or after 17 March 2004, any 'property managing subsidiary' (see **22.7** ENTERPRISE INVESTMENT SCHEME) that the company has must be a 'qualifying 90% subsidiary' (see **22.9** ENTERPRISE INVESTMENT SCHEME).

The gross assets requirement

The value of the company's gross assets must not exceed £7 million immediately before the issue of the shares in respect of which relief is claimed and must not exceed £8 million immediately afterwards. In relation to shares issued before 6 April 2006, these limits were £15 million and £16 million respectively; the higher limits continue to apply in relation to shares issued after 5 April 2006 to a person who subscribed for them before 22 March 2006. If the issuing company is a parent company, the gross assets test applies by reference to the aggregate gross assets of the company and all its qualifying subsidiaries (disregarding certain assets held by any such company which correspond to liabilities of another).

The general approach of HMRC to the gross assets requirement is that the value of a company's gross assets is the sum of the value of all of the balance sheet assets. Where accounts are actually drawn up to a date immediately before or after the issue, the balance sheet values are taken provided that they reflect usual accounting standards and the company's normal accounting practice, consistently applied. Where accounts are not drawn up to such a date, such values will be taken from the most recent balance sheet, updated as precisely as practicable on the basis of all the relevant information available to the company. Values so arrived at may need to be reviewed in the light of information contained in the accounts for the period in which the issue was made, and, if they were not available at the time of the issue, those for the preceding period, when they become available. The company's assets immediately before the issue do not include any advance payment received in respect of the issue. Where shares are issued partly paid, the right to the balance is an asset, and, notwithstanding the above, will be taken into account in valuing the assets immediately after the issue regardless of whether it is shown in the balance sheet. (HMRC SP 2/00).

The unquoted status requirement

For shares issued on or after 7 March 2001, the company must be 'unquoted' at the time (the '*relevant time*') at which the shares are issued and no arrangements must then exist for it to cease to be unquoted. If, at the time of issue, arrangements exist for the company to become a wholly-owned subsidiary of a new holding company by means of a share exchange within the provisions below, no arrangements must exist for the new company to cease to be unquoted. A company is '*unquoted*' if none of its shares etc. are listed on a recognised stock exchange or on a foreign exchange designated for the purpose, or dealt in on the Unlisted Securities Market (now closed) or outside the UK by such means as may be designated for the purpose.

[*ITA 2007, ss 134, 137–144, 151(1)(7); FA 2020, s 38*].

Example

[38.16]

P subscribed for 3,000 £1 ordinary shares at par in W Ltd, a qualifying trading company, in June 1989. In September 1996, P acquired a further 2,200 shares at £3 per share from another shareholder. In December 2024, P sold 3,900 shares at 40p per share.

Establish 'section 104 holding' pool.

	Shares	Qualifying expenditure £
June 1989 subscription	3,000	3,000
September 1996 acquisition	2,200	6,600
	5,200	9,600
December 2024 disposal	(3,900)	(7,200)
Pool carried forward	1,300	£2,400

Step 1. Calculate the CGT loss in the normal way, as follows

	£
Disposal consideration 3,900 × £0.40	1,560
Allowable cost	7,200
Allowable loss	£5,640

Step 2. Applying a LIFO basis, identify the qualifying shares (1,700) and the non-qualifying shares (2,200) comprised in the disposal.

Step 3. Calculate the proportion of the loss attributable to the qualifying shares.

Loss referable to 1,700 qualifying shares $\frac{1,700}{3,900} \times £5,640$ £2,458

Step 4. Compare the loss in *Step 3* with the actual cost of the qualifying shares, *viz.*

Cost of 1,700 qualifying shares $\frac{1,700}{3,000} \times £3,000$ £1,700

The loss available against income is restricted to £1,700 (being lower than £2,458).

The loss not relieved against income remains an allowable loss for CGT purposes.

£5,640 – £1,700 = £3,940

Losses on shares in unlisted trading companies — investment companies

[38.17] Where an 'investment company' disposes of shares in a 'qualifying trading company' for which it has 'subscribed', and thereby incurs an allowable capital loss, it may claim relief for the loss against income instead of against chargeable gains.

The investment company must have been such on the date of the disposal and must either:

(a) have been an investment company for a continuous period of six years ending on that date; or
(b) have been an investment company for a shorter continuous period ending on that date, and must not have been, before the beginning of that period, a 'trading company' or an 'excluded company'.

It must also not have been 'associated' with, or have been a member of the same 'group' as, the qualifying trading company, at any time in the period beginning with the date of its (the investment company's) subscription for the shares, and ending with the date of disposal.

Relief is available only if:

- the disposal is at arm's length, or
- it is by way of a distribution on a winding-up, or
- the value of the shares has become negligible and a claim to that effect made under *TCGA 1992, s 24(2)* (see **38.10** above), or
- a deemed disposal occurs under *TCGA 1992, s 24(1)* (which deems the entire loss, destruction, dissipation or extinction of an asset to be a disposal — see **10.2** CAPITAL SUMS DERIVED FROM ASSETS).

Relief is not available where the shares are the subject of an exchange or arrangement within *TCGA 1992, ss 135* or *136* undertaken for tax avoidance purposes or other than for genuine commercial reasons so that a chargeable disposal under *TCGA 1992, s 137* arises. See **4.16** ANTI-AVOIDANCE.

For this purpose, '*qualifying trading company*', '*trading company*', '*excluded company*' and '*group*' are all defined as at **38.15** above. Companies are '*associated*' with each other if one controls the other, or both are under the control of the same person or persons. The general definitions of *CTA 2010, ss 450, 451* (meaning of 'control') apply for this purpose. See Tolley's Corporation Tax under Close Companies. A company 'subscribes' for shares in another company if they are issued to the company by the other company in consideration of money or money's worth. Any corresponding bonus shares subsequently issued to the company are treated as subscribed for on the date on which the original shares were subscribed for.

Operation of and claims for relief

A loss may be claimed against income of the accounting period in which it is incurred. Additionally, if the company was an investment company at that earlier time, it may claim to set off any balance of the loss remaining against income of the twelve months immediately preceding the accounting period in which the loss was incurred (income of the relevant accounting periods being time apportioned for this purpose where necessary).

Relief must be claimed within two years of the end of the accounting period in which the loss arises and is given before any deduction for expenses of management or other deductions, except that a claim for a loss on a Corporate Venturing Scheme investment to be relieved against income does take priority (see **19.5** CORPORATE VENTURING SCHEME).

To the extent that relief in respect of a loss is obtained under these provisions, the loss is not an allowable capital loss. Any part of the loss for which income relief is not given does, however, remain an allowable capital loss.

Limits on relief

Where a company claims relief under these provisions for a loss on the disposal of shares which form part of a 'section 104 holding' or a '1982 holding' (i.e. holdings of shares which are pooled for chargeable gains purposes) either at the time of the disposal or an earlier time, the relief is restricted to the sums that would have been allowable as deductions in computing the loss if the qualifying shares had not formed part of the holding.

Where the qualifying shares were acquired on the same day as other shares that are not capable of being qualifying shares (see below), so that under *TCGA 1992, s 105(1)(a)* all the shares are treated as acquired by a single transaction, the amount of relief is restricted to the sums that would have been allowable as deductions in computing the loss if the qualifying shares and the other shares were not so treated.

Where the qualifying shares, taken as a single asset, and other shares or debentures in the same company which are not capable of being qualifying shares, also taken as a single asset, are treated for chargeable gains purposes as the same asset under *TCGA 1992, s 127*, the relief is restricted to the sums that would have been allowable as deductions in computing the loss if the qualifying shares and the other shares or debentures were not to be treated as the same asset.

For these purposes, shares are not capable of being qualifying shares at any time if they were not acquired by subscription, if condition (c) at **38.15** above is not met. Additionally, for the purposes only of the 'same asset' restriction above, shares are not capable of being qualifying shares at any time if they are shares of a different class from the qualifying shares concerned.

Identification

Where it is necessary to determine whether a disposal of shares forming part of a mixed 'holding' (i.e. a holding which includes both shares for which the company has subscribed and other shares) qualifies for relief under these provisions, disposals are to be identified with acquisitions on a last in/first out (LIFO) basis. This does not apply where the holding includes shares to which investment relief under the Corporate Venturing Scheme is attributable and which have been held continuously by the company; the identification rules at **23.68** EXEMPTIONS AND RELIEFS (generally first in/first out) apply instead.

A '*holding*' of shares for these purposes is any number of shares of the same class held by one company in the same capacity, growing or diminishing as shares of that class are acquired or disposed of. Shares comprised in a 'new holding' following a reorganisation to which *TCGA 1992, s 127* applies are treated as having been acquired when the original shares were acquired. Any shares held or disposed of by a nominee or bare trustee for a company are treated as held or disposed of by the company.

Anti-avoidance

Any claim to relief will bring in the provisions of *TCGA 1992, s 30* (value-shifting to give a tax-free benefit — see **4.11** ANTI-AVOIDANCE) so that the relief may be adjusted for any benefit conferred whether tax-free or not.

Company reorganisations etc.

Where shares are disposed of and represent a new holding identifiable under *TCGA 1992, s 127* (see **57.2** SHARES AND SECURITIES) with 'old shares' after a reorganisation or reduction of share capital, relief under these provisions is not available unless it could have been given if an allowable loss had arisen on the disposal of the old shares at arm's length at the reorganisation etc. had this legislation been in force. Where the reorganisation did not so qualify, but new consideration was given for the new shares, relief is limited to such of that new consideration as is an allowable deduction. '*New consideration*' is money or money's worth but excluding any surrender or alteration to the original shares or rights attached thereto, and the application of assets of the company or distribution declared but not made out of the assets.

Share exchanges

Where, by means of an exchange of shares, all of the shares (the old shares) of a company (the old company) are acquired by a company (the new company) in which the only previously issued shares are subscriber shares, then, subject to the further conditions below being satisfied, the exchange is not regarded as involving a disposal of the old shares and an acquisition of the new company shares (the new shares). Where old shares held by a company were subscribed for by it, the new shares stand in the shoes of the old shares, e.g. as if they had been subscribed for and issued at the time the old shares were subscribed for and issued and as if any requirements under the above provisions met at any time before the exchange by the old company had been met at that time by the new company.

The further conditions are as follows.

(a) The shares must be issued after 5 April 1998.
(b) The consideration for the old shares must consist entirely of the issue of the new shares.
(c) The consideration for old shares of each description must consist entirely of new shares of the 'corresponding description'.
(d) New shares of each description must be issued to holders of old shares of the 'corresponding description' in respect of and in proportion to their holdings.
(e) For new shares issued on or after 6 April 2007, the exchange of shares is not treated for chargeable gains purposes as involving a disposal of the old shares or an acquisition of the new shares by virtue of *TCGA 1992, s 127*.
(f) For new shares issued before 6 April 2007, before the issue of the new shares, on the written application (for which see **4.16** ANTI-AVOIDANCE) of either the old or new company, HMRC must have notified to that company their satisfaction that the exchange:
    (i) is for genuine commercial reasons; and
    (ii) does not form part of a scheme or arrangements to which *TCGA 1992, s 137(1)* (see **4.16** ANTI-AVOIDANCE) applies.

    HMRC may, within 30 days of an application, request further particulars, which must then be supplied within 30 days of the request (or such longer period as they may allow in any particular case).

For these purposes, old and new shares are of a '*corresponding description*' if, assuming they were shares in the same company, they would be of the same class and carry the same rights.

An exchange within these provisions, or arrangements for such an exchange, do not breach the control and independence requirement at **38.15** above.

[*CTA 2010, ss 68–90, Sch 2 paras 27–51; TCGA 1992, s 125A; FA 2020, s 38*].

Deferred unascertainable consideration — election for treatment of loss as accruing in earlier year

[38.18] Where a person within the charge to capital gains tax makes a disposal of a right to future unascertainable consideration (see below) acquired as consideration for the disposal of another asset, and a loss accrues, they may, subject to conditions, make an election for the loss to be treated as arising in the year in which that other asset was disposed of. Accordingly, where the election is made, the loss on disposal of the right can be carried back to be set against the gain arising on the disposal of the original asset. The detailed provisions are described below.

Conditions for making election

The election is available where a person (the '*taxpayer*') disposes of a right and the following conditions are satisfied.

(1) An allowable loss (the '*relevant loss*') accrues on the disposal.
(2) The tax year in which the relevant loss actually accrues (the '*year of the loss*') is one in which the taxpayer is chargeable to capital gains tax in respect of chargeable gains accruing to him in that year, or would be so chargeable (apart from the deduction of any allowable losses and the annual exempt amount) were there any such gains.
(3) The right was, in whole or part, acquired by the taxpayer as the whole or part of the consideration for a disposal (the '*original disposal*') by him of another asset (the '*original asset*').
(4) The original disposal was made in a tax year earlier than that in which the disposal of the right is made. Where the right was acquired as consideration for two or more disposals, this condition must be satisfied with respect to all those disposals.
(5) On the taxpayer's acquisition of the right, there was no corresponding disposal of it.
(6) The right is a 'right to unascertainable consideration' (see below).
(7) A chargeable gain accrued to the taxpayer, or would have so accrued but for the deferral provisions of *TCGA 1992, Sch 5B para 2(2)(a)* (see **22.17** ENTERPRISE INVESTMENT SCHEME) or *Sch 5C para 2(2)(a)* (see **64.8** VENTURE CAPITAL TRUSTS), on one or more of the following events:
    (a) the original disposal,
    (b) an earlier disposal of the original asset by the taxpayer in the tax year of the original disposal, or
    (c) a later disposal of the original asset by the taxpayer in a tax year earlier than the actual year of the disposal of the right.

    Where the right was acquired as consideration for two or more original disposals, any reference in (a) to (c) above to the original disposal should be read as a reference to any of the original disposals, any reference to the original asset as a reference to the original asset in relation to that original disposal, and any reference to the tax year of the original disposal should be construed accordingly.

(8) There is a tax year (an '*eligible year*'), which is earlier than the year of the loss, in which a chargeable gain within (7) above accrued to the taxpayer and for which there remains a relevant amount on which capital gains tax is chargeable immediately before the election. Where the deferral provisions mentioned in (7) above applied to prevent a gain within (7) above from accruing, a tax year in which a chargeable gain is treated as accruing to the taxpayer in respect of that gain under *TCGA 1992, Sch 5B paras 4, 5* or *Sch 5C paras 4, 5* (chargeable events — see **22.17** ENTERPRISE INVESTMENT SCHEME and **64.8** VENTURE CAPITAL TRUSTS) will be an eligible year.
For these purposes, a tax year is one for which there remains a relevant amount on which capital gains tax is chargeable immediately before an election if, immediately before the making of the election, there remains for that year an amount in respect of which the taxpayer is chargeable to capital gains tax, after taking account of any previous elections under these provisions, after excluding any gains attributed under *TCGA 1992, ss 87, 87K, 87L* or *89(2)* and on the assumption that no losses fall to be deducted in consequence of any election under these provisions which could be, but has not been, made.

For the above purposes, any question as to whether a chargeable gain or loss is one that accrues (or would accrue but for any particular provision) on a particular disposal or a disposal of any particular description, or the time at which, or year in which, any particular disposal takes place, is determined without regard to *TCGA 1992, s 1M* (gains and losses accruing during period of temporary non-residence treated as accruing in period of return — see **43.5** OVERSEAS MATTERS). This provision does not, however, affect the determination of any question as to the period in which, by virtue of *TCGA 1992, s 1M*, the gain or loss is treated as accruing (apart from the effect of an election under these provisions), nor does it prevent a loss accruing during a period of temporary non-residence from being an allowable loss.

[*TCGA 1992, ss 279A, 279B(1)(7)(8)*].

Effect of election

Where an election is made under the above provisions, the relevant loss is treated for capital gains tax purposes as if it were a loss accruing in the earliest tax year which is an eligible year.

Where that year is 2008/09 or a subsequent year, the amount of the relevant loss that can be deducted from chargeable gains of that year is limited to the amount (the '*first year limit*') of the chargeable gains accruing to the taxpayer in the year, excluding any amounts attributed to him under *TCGA 1992, ss 87* or *89(2)* (see **42.13** OFFSHORE SETTLEMENTS), and after deducting any amounts in respect of allowable losses. Account must be taken of any previous elections made under these provisions, but no account must be taken of the relevant loss.

Where the earliest eligible year is 2007/08 or an earlier year, the first year limit is found by taking the following steps.

Step 1.

Take the total amount of chargeable gains accruing to the taxpayer in the year.

Step 2.

Exclude from that amount any amounts attributed to the taxpayer under *TCGA 1992, ss 77, 86, 87* or *89(2)* (see **2.5** ANNUAL RATES AND EXEMPTIONS).

Step 3.

Deduct from the remaining amount any amounts in respect of allowable losses except for any losses falling to be set against gains attributed to the taxpayer under *TCGA 1992, ss 77* or *86* (see **38.2** above). Account must be taken of any previous elections made under these provisions, but no account must be taken of the relevant loss.

Where the earliest eligible year is one of the years 2003/04 to 2007/08 inclusive, or where it is a year in respect of which an election under *FA 2002, Sch 11 para 8* has been made, two further steps must be taken to arrive at the first year limit, as follows.

Step 4.

Add to the remaining amount every amount attributed to the taxpayer as a chargeable gain under *TCGA 1992, ss 77* or *86.*

Step 5.

Deduct any losses falling to be set against such attributed gains.

To the extent that the relevant loss exceeds the first year limit (and so is not utilised in the first eligible year), it may be carried forward for set-off against gains of later years. In the case of tax years falling between the first eligible year and the year of the loss, any remaining part of the relevant loss can only be deducted if the year is an eligible year. For such years, the amount of the loss which may be deducted is limited to the amount (the '*later year limit*') in respect of which the taxpayer would be chargeable to capital gains tax for the year:

- on the assumption that no part of the relevant loss, or any other loss in respect of which an election under these provisions could be made but which, immediately after the making of the election in question, has not been made, falls to be deducted from the gains for the year;
- taking account of any previous elections under these provisions; and
- and any gains from which the taxpayer's personal losses are not deductible (see **38.2** above).

[*TCGA 1992, s 279C; FA 2008, Sch 2 paras 43, 56(2)*].

Where the right in respect of which an election is made is an earn-out right within the meaning of *TCGA 1992, s 138A* (see **57.6** SHARES AND SECURITIES) conferred before 10 April 2003, no election can be made under that section for the right to be treated as a security, whether at the same time as the election under these provisions or subsequently. [*FA 2003, s 162(2)(4)*].

Meaning of 'right to unascertainable consideration'

A right is a '*right to unascertainable consideration*' if, and only if, it is a right to consideration the amount or value of which is unascertainable when the right is conferred because it is referable, in whole or part, to matters which are uncertain at that time because they have not yet occurred.

The amount or value of any consideration is not regarded as unascertainable by reason only:

(i) that the right to receive all or part of the consideration is postponed or contingent, to the extent that the consideration is brought into account in accordance with *TCGA 1992, s 48* (see **16.14**(g) COMPUTATION OF GAINS AND LOSSES) in the computation of a gain accruing to the taxpayer on the disposal of an asset;

(ii) in a case where the right to receive all or part of the consideration is postponed and may be to any extent satisfied by the receipt of alternative types of property, that some person has the right to select the property or type of property that is to be received; or

(iii) that either the amount or the value of the consideration has not been fixed, if either the amount will be fixed by reference to the value, and the value is ascertainable, or the value will be fixed by reference to the amount, and the amount is ascertainable.

An earn-out right treated as a security by virtue of *TCGA 1992, s 138A* (see **57.6** SHARES AND SECURITIES) is not regarded as a right to unascertainable consideration for the purposes of these provisions.

[*TCGA 1992, s 279B(2)–(6)*].

Making of election

An election under the above provisions is irrevocable and must be made by notice in writing to HMRC on or before the first anniversary of 31 January following the year of the loss. The notice must specify the following:

- the amount of the relevant loss,
- the right disposed of,
- the tax year of the right's disposal, and, if different, the year of the loss,
- the tax year in which the right was acquired,
- the original asset or assets,
- the eligible year in which the relevant loss is to be treated as accruing,
- the first year limit, and
- the amount to be deducted from gains of that year.

If any part of the relevant loss is to be carried forward to later eligible years, the notice must also specify each such year and the later year limit and amount to be deducted for each such year.

A separate notice is required for each loss in respect of which an election is being made. Where two or more elections are made on the same day, the notices must specify the order in which they are to be treated as made. [*TCGA 1992, s 279D; FA 2019, Sch 1 para 85*].

Example

Tanya owns 2,000 £1 ordinary shares in Be Good Ltd, for which she subscribed at par in January 1994. On 31 March 2018, she and the other shareholders in Be Good Ltd sold their shares to another company for £20 per share plus a further unquantified cash amount calculated by means of a formula relating to the future profits of Be Good Ltd. The value in March 2018 of the deferred consideration was estimated at £5.10 per share. Tanya makes no other disposals of chargeable assets in 2017/18. On 30 April 2024, Tanya receives a further £3.60 per share under the sale agreement.

Without an election under *TCGA 1992, s 279A*, Tanya's capital gains position is as follows.

2017/18

	£	£
Disposal proceeds	40,000	
Value of rights	10,200	50,200
Cost of acquisition		2,000
Chargeable gain 2017/18		£48,200

2024/25

Disposal of rights to deferred consideration	
Proceeds 2,000 × £3.60	7,200
Deemed cost of acquiring rights	10,200
Allowable loss 2024/245	£3,000

If Tanya makes an election under *TCGA 1992, s 279A* by 31 January 2027, the 2024/25 loss is treated as arising in 2017/18 and can be set off against the gain of that year as follows.

2017/18

	£
Chargeable gain as above	48,200
Less Allowable loss	3,000
Taxable gains 2017/18 (subject to annual exempt amount)	£45,200

Restriction on losses — write-off of government investment

[38.19] Where any amount of an investment, by the Government, in a *company* other than an unincorporated association, is written off, an equal amount is to be set off against the body's tax 'losses', starting with losses available at the end of the accounting period ended before the write-off, and continuing for subsequent periods, until the investment is covered. The definition of '*losses*', for this purpose, includes, inter alia, unrelieved allowable capital losses. It should be noted, however, that the investment is only written off against capital losses as a last resort, i.e. after the extinction of other losses, unrelieved capital allowances, management expenses and charitable donations. The investment can also be written off against the losses of any member of the same 51% group. An investment is written off if the liability to repay any money lent is extinguished; if any shares subscribed for out of public funds are cancelled; or if 'commencing capital debts' (as defined) or 'public dividend capital' (as defined) is reduced otherwise than by being paid off or repaid. These provisions do not apply where the investment written off is replaced in some other form. [*CTA 2010, ss 92–96*]. See Tolley's Corporation Tax under Losses for further details.

Set-off of trading losses etc. against chargeable gains

[38.20] A person other than a company cannot normally set off his allowable losses for capital gains tax purposes against his income. A company, also, cannot normally set off its allowable losses for the purposes of corporation tax on chargeable gains against income but trading losses or management expenses of a company can, in certain cases, be set off against total profits, such profits including chargeable gains. See **14.3**, **14.6** COMPANIES. See, however, **38.14** and **38.17** above for the allowance of capital losses arising on the disposal of certain shares in unquoted trading companies against general income of *individuals* and *investment companies* respectively.

There are specific provisions enabling trading losses and certain other expenditure for income tax purposes to be set off against chargeable gains to the extent that they cannot be relieved against income (due to an insufficiency of income) for the tax year in question. These are described below.

Set-off of trading losses against gains of a person other than a company

Where trading losses arise so that relief is available under *ITA 2007, s 64* (set-off for income tax purposes of trading losses against general income — see Tolley's Income Tax under Losses) for a tax year and either a claim is made under that section or the person's total income for the year is either nil or does not include any income from which the loss can be deducted, a claim may also be made for the determination of the '*relevant amount*', which is so much of the trading loss as:

(a) is not deducted in calculating the claimant's net income for the year of claim, and
(b) has not already been relieved for any other year.

The claim is not deemed to be determined until the relevant amount for the year can no longer be varied, whether by the Tribunal on appeal or on the order of any court.

The relevant amount, as finally determined, is to be treated for the purposes of capital gains tax as an allowable loss accruing to the claimant in the tax year, except that it cannot exceed the 'maximum amount'. Any such excess remains an income tax loss.

The tax years for which relief may be claimed under *ITA 2007, s 64* against income, and consequently under *TCGA 1992, s 261B* against gains, are the year in which the trading loss is incurred or the preceding year.

The 'maximum amount' for this purpose is the amount on which the claimant would be chargeable to CGT for the year, disregarding the annual exempt amount and the effect of this relief provision.

In computing the maximum amount, no account is taken of any event occurring after the determination of the relevant amount and in consequence of which the amount chargeable to capital gains tax is reduced by virtue of any capital gains tax legislation (e.g. a claim for rollover relief in a later year having the effect of reducing the amount chargeable for the year for which this relief provision is claimed; in such a case the allowable capital losses flowing from a claim under this provision would be displaced by the effect of the rollover claim but would be available for carry forward to subsequent years).

No amount treated as an allowable loss under this provision may be deducted from chargeable gains accruing in a tax year which begins after the claimant has ceased to carry on the trade in which the loss was sustained. For the purpose of applying this rule, any such losses brought forward may be treated as set against gains in priority to genuine capital losses (HMRC Business Income Manual BIM85035).

A claim must be made on or before the first anniversary of the normal self-assessment filing date for the tax year in which the loss was made.

The above provisions apply also to employment losses relievable under *ITA 2007, s 128.*

[*ITA 2007, ss 71, 130; TCGA 1992, ss 261B, 261C*].

Anti-avoidance

No relief under the above provisions can be obtained where the loss arises directly or indirectly from arrangements which have as a main purpose the avoiding of a tax liability by means of sideways income tax relief or relief under the above provisions. See *ITA 2007, ss 74ZA* and *74B* and Tolley's Income Tax under Losses for the detailed provisions.

Where an individual carries on a trade in a non-active capacity and the above prohibition on relief does not apply the total amount of sideways income tax relief against non-trade income and capital gains relief under the above provisions for a tax year is restricted to £25,000. See *ITA 2007, s 74A* and Tolley's Income Tax under Losses for the detailed provisions.

Example

M has carried on a trade for some years, preparing accounts to 5 April each year. For the year ended 5 April 2025, he makes a trading loss of £17,000. His taxable profit for 2023/24 is £5,000 and his other income for both 2023/24 and 2024/25 amounts to £2,000. He makes a capital gain of £14,000 and a capital loss of £1,000 for 2024/25 and has capital losses brought forward of £6,800. M makes claims for loss relief, against income of 2023/24 and income and gains of 2024/25, under *ITA 2007, s 64* and *TCGA 1992, s 261B*.

Calculation of 'relevant amount'

	£
Trading loss — year ended 5.4.25	17,000
Relieved against other income for 2024/25	(2,000)
Relieved against income for 2023/24	(7,000)
Relevant amount	£8,000

Calculation of 'maximum amount'

		£
Gains for 2024/25		14,000
Deduct Losses for 2024/25		(1,000)
Unrelieved losses brought forward		(6,800)
Maximum amount		£6,200
Relief under *TCGA 1992, s 261B*		
	£	£
Gains for the year		14,000
Losses for the year	1,000	
Relief under *TCGA 1992, s 261B*	6,200	
		7,200
Gain		6,800
Annual exempt amount		3,000
		3,800
Losses brought forward (part)		3,800
Taxable gain		Nil
Loss memorandum		
		£
Capital losses brought forward		6,800
Claimed against gain of 2024/25		3,800
Capital loss carried forward		£3,000
Trading loss		17,000
Claimed against income of 2024/25		(2,000)
Claimed against income of 2023/24		(7,000)
Claimed under *TCGA 1992, s 261B*		(6,200)
Unutilised loss		£1,800

Set-off of post-cessation expenditure of a trade or property business against capital gains

Relief is available against both income and capital gains for individuals who incur qualifying business expenditure in connection with a trade, profession or property business which has ceased within seven years of its ceasing. Broadly, qualifying expenditure includes costs of remedying defective work or services rendered and damages in respect thereof, insurance premiums paid to insure against such costs and legal and other professional expenses incurred in connection therewith. Relief is also given for bad debts which prove to be bad or which are released in whole or in part, and for the costs of collecting debts which have been taken into account in the final accounts. The relief is reduced by accruals for costs in the final accounting period which remain unpaid. On a claim, the relief may be set against income and then against capital gains of the tax year in which the qualifying expenditure is incurred, otherwise it will have to be carried forward to be set only against any post-cessation receipts under *ITTOIA 2005, s 254*. Claims must be made within twelve months after the normal self-assessment filing date for the tax year in which the expenditure was incurred. A claim for relief cannot exceed the capital gains available, disregarding losses brought forward, the annual exemption and trading losses set against gains as above.

Relief under the above provisions is not available for a payment or event which is made or occurs directly or indirectly in consequence of, or otherwise in connection with, 'tax avoidance arrangements' to which the taxpayer is a party. For this purpose, '*tax avoidance arrangements*' are arrangements the main purpose, or one of the main purposes, of which is to obtain a reduction in tax liability under the above provisions, and '*arrangements*' include any agreement, understanding, scheme transaction or series of transactions, whether or not legally enforceable.

For full details of the provisions see Tolley's Income Tax under Post-Cessation Receipts and Expenditure.

[*ITA 2007, ss 98A, 101, 126; TCGA 1992, ss 261D, 261E*].

Set-off of post-employment deductions against capital gains

Relief against income or capital gains is available to former employees who bear the costs of indemnity insurance or certain work-related uninsured liabilities relating to their former employment where such costs are incurred by them up to six years after the year in which the employment ended. On a claim, the relief may be set against income and then against capital gains of the tax year in which the qualifying expenditure is incurred, otherwise it will be lost. Claims must be made four years after the end of the tax year to which the claim relates. A claim for relief cannot exceed the capital gains available, disregarding losses brought forward, the annual exemption, trading losses and post-cessation expenditure set against gains as above. For full details of the provisions, see Tolley's Income Tax under Employment Income. [*TCGA 1992, s 263ZA; ITEPA 2003, ss 555–564*].

Key points concerning losses

[38.21] Points to consider are as follows.

- A capital loss is not allowable unless it is quantified and notified to HMRC.
- A loss on a disposal carried out to secure a tax advantage is not allowable. In addition, the tax tribunals and courts now rarely rule in the taxpayer's favour in cases involving a loss arising from a scheme or arrangement where the taxpayer has suffered no economic loss.
- Relief for losses brought forward are more flexible than in year losses as they are offset to preserve the benefit of the annual exempt amount. Consideration should therefore be given to the timing of realising small gains potentially covered by the annual exempt amount and losses. Where beneficial and practical there may be an advantage to realising a small profit and loss in separate tax years.

- A loss on a disposal to a connected person can generally only be set against a gain on a disposal to that same person. This is often referred to as a 'clogged loss'.
- A settlor with an interest in a non-UK resident settlement (but not a beneficiary of such a settlement) can set personal losses against settlement gains attributed to them.
- Investment companies can claim relief for a loss on disposal of shares in a qualifying trading company for which they subscribed against income instead of gains. Similarly, individuals who subscribed for shares in an unquoted trading company can claim relief for a loss in respect of those shares against income. However, the conversion of a loan into shares in an attempt to obtain this relief may not succeed if the shares had already become of negligible value. At current personal tax rates, relief against income is normally more favourable.
- A penalty can be charged in respect of an overstated loss, even if not yet utilised, so particular care should be taken with negligible value claims and other losses involving asset valuations.

39

Market Value

Cross-references. See **4.13** and **4.14** ANTI-AVOIDANCE for anti-avoidance provisions which may override or amend the general rules given below; **5.4** APPEALS for appeals relating to market values; **16.12** COMPUTATION OF GAINS AND LOSSES for allowable expenditure relating to acquisition of assets at market value; **18.5** DEATH for valuation at death; **38.10** LOSSES for loss relief where the market value of an asset has become negligible; **44** PARTNERSHIPS for further valuation rules which apply to partnership assets.

Introduction to market value

[39.1] **Market value** is the price which assets might reasonably fetch in the open market, sold individually, with no allowance being made for any reduction in market value arising out of the whole of the assets being placed on the market at one and the same time. This provision applies subject to special rules applying under *TCGA 1992, s 25A* (deemed disposals of plant or machinery on commencement or termination of long funding lease — see **7.6** ASSETS) and *TCGA 1992, s 41A* (restriction on loss on disposal of fixture used for leasing under long funding lease — see **16.14**(j) COMPUTATION OF GAINS AND LOSSES). [*TCGA 1992, s 272(1)(2)(6)*].

Acquisition and disposal are treated as being made at market value (subject to any other provision and the exception below) if the transaction is:

(a) not at arm's length (which includes, in particular, any transaction between connected persons — see **4.13** ANTI-AVOIDANCE), or
(b) by way of gift, or
(c) on a transfer into settlement by a settlor, or
(d) a distribution from a company in respect of shares in that company, or
(e) wholly or partly for a consideration that cannot be valued (see *Fielder v Vedlynn Ltd* Ch D 1992, 65 TC 145), or
(f) in connection with their own or another's loss of office or employment, diminution of emoluments (see *Whitehouse v Ellam* Ch D, [1995] STC 503), or in consideration for or recognition of their or another's services (in any office, employment or otherwise), past or future.

Exception

The market value provisions in (a)–(f) above do not apply to the *acquisition* of an asset if there is no corresponding disposal of it *and* there is no consideration in money or money's worth (or the consideration is of an amount or value lower than the market value of the asset).

[*TCGA 1992, s 17*].

An attempt by a taxpayer to substitute market value for actual price paid in a transaction between unconnected persons failed in *Bullivant Holdings Ltd v CIR* Ch D 1998, 71 TC 22. For the application of the market value rule to shares acquired by reason of employment, see **21.3**, **21.5**, **21.22**, **21.23**, **21.24**.

Chargeable intangible assets

[39.2] Where there is a transfer of an intangible asset between 'related parties' (see below), at least one of which is a company, and the asset is a 'chargeable intangible asset' in the hands of the transferor or transferee (or both), the transfer is treated for *all* direct tax purposes (as regards both transferor and transferee) as being at 'market value'. For this purpose, the '*market value*' of an asset is the price it might reasonably be expected to fetch on a sale in the open market. An asset is a '*chargeable intangible asset*' if a gain on its realisation would give rise to a credit falling to be brought into account under the intangible assets regime summarised at **15.13** COMPANIES — CORPORATE FINANCE AND INTANGIBLES and covered in detail in Tolley's Corporation Tax under Intangible Assets.

There are a number of exceptions to the above rule, as follows.

(1) Where the consideration for the transfer falls to be adjusted under the transfer pricing rules in *TIOPA 2010, Pt 4* or, in certain circumstances, *would* fall to be so adjusted were it not for the fact that the consideration is an arm's length amount.

(2) Where the transfer is 'tax-neutral' under any provision of the intangible assets regime; this applies mainly in connection with intra-group transfers and certain transfers of a business.

(3) Where the asset is transferred to the company and a reduction is made under *TCGA 1992, s 165(4)(a)* (reduction of chargeable gain on gift of business asset — see **30.2** HOLD-OVER RELIEFS). In this case, for the purposes of the intangible assets regime, the transfer is treated as being at market value less the amount of the reduction.

(4) Where:
   - the asset is transferred from the company at less than its market value or to the company at more than market value;
   - the related party is not a company or, if it is a company, the asset is not a chargeable intangible asset in its hands; and
   - the transfer gives rise (or would but for the above rule) to an amount to be taken into account in computing any person's income, profits or losses for tax purposes under *CTA 2010, Pt 23 Ch 2* (company distributions) or *ITEPA 2003, Pt 3* (earnings and benefits treated as employment income).

In this case, the market value rule above is disapplied only for the purposes of the computation mentioned above.

(5) Where the transfer would be tax-neutral on a transfer within a group but for the transferor having at any time held the asset wholly or partly for the purposes of a non-UK permanent establishment and having made an election under *CTA 2009, s 18A* (exemption for foreign permanent establishments — see **43.8** OVERSEAS MATTERS) and the transferor has not so held the asset during any part of the period of ownership for which the election has applied. In this case, the transfer is treated as being for the tax written-down value of the asset plus the amount which would be the 'foreign permanent establishments amount' if the transfer were at market value.

(6) Where the provisions at **31.4** INCORPORATION AND DISINCORPORATION RELIEFS apply.

(7) Where the asset is a 'restricted asset' to which the special rules in *CTA 2009, ss 900E, 900F* apply (assets acquired on or after 1 July 2020).

The circumstances in which persons are treated as related parties (so that the market value rule above applies) include where the transfer pricing 'participation condition' (see *TIOPA 2010, s 147*) is met between them.

[*CTA 2009, ss 844–849A; FA 2020, s 31(3)*].

Parties are '*related parties*' in any of the following circumstances.

- Both are companies, and one has 'control' of, or holds a 'major interest' in, the other (as defined in *CTA 2009, ss 836, 837*).
- Both are companies, and both are under the 'control' of the same person (except, broadly, where that person is a state, a government or an international organisation).
- One is a close company (within the meaning given by *CTA 2010, ss 439–454*) and the other is, or is an 'associate' of, a 'participator' (both within *CTA 2009, s 841*) in that company.
- One is a close company and the other is, or is an associate of, a participator in a company that has control of, or holds a major interest in, that company.
- Both are companies within the same 'group' (as defined in *CTA 2009, ss 764–773*).

Parties are treated as related parties where they would be so treated under the above provisions but for any person (other than an individual) being the subject of 'insolvency arrangements'. For this purpose, '*insolvency arrangements*' include:

- arrangements under which a person acts as the liquidator, provisional liquidator, receiver, administrator or administrative receiver of a company or partnership;
- voluntary arrangements proposed or approved under *Insolvency Act 1986, Pt 1* (or NI equivalent); and
- equivalent arrangements under the law of any country or territory (whether made when the person is solvent or insolvent).

[*CTA 2009, ss 834, 835*].

Quoted shares and securities

[39.3] The market value of quoted shares and securities for capital gains tax purposes is determined as follows.

6 April 2015 onwards

The market value of shares, securities or strips which are included in the official UK list is:

- on any day the Stock Exchange is open, the lower of the two prices quoted in the Stock Exchange Daily Official List as the closing price for that day plus one-half of the difference between those prices; and
- on any day the Stock Exchange is closed, that value on the latest previous day on which it was open.

The above method of valuation does not apply for inheritance tax purposes but instead the method which was used for capital gains tax purposes before 6 April 2015 (see below) continues to apply. Where assets are valued to determine an inheritance tax charge *on death*, that value is also taken to be the market value on death for capital gains tax purposes under *TCGA 1992, s 274* (see **18.5** DEATH). Therefore, the value of quoted shares or securities for inheritance tax purposes (determined below) is also taken to apply for capital gains tax in such a scenario, even after 6 April 2015.

The above method of valuation does not apply for computing the value of shares or securities where special circumstances may affect the value.

The market value of securities or strips which are not included in the official UK list but are listed on a recognised foreign stock exchange is:

- on any day the exchange is open, the closing price shown in the exchange list for that day (or, if more than one price is shown, the lower of the two prices plus one-half of the difference between them; and
- on any day the exchange is closed, that value on the latest previous day on which it was open.

If securities are quoted in more than one foreign exchange list, then any foreign exchange list published for a foreign exchange which is regarded as the major exchange for such securities is to be used to determine the market value. If there is no such exchange, any foreign exchange list for an exchange in the territory in which the issuing company is resident is used in preference to any other such list. If a strip or a security exchanged for strips of that security is quoted in more than one foreign exchange list, any such list published for a foreign stock exchange in the territory of the issuing government is used in preference to any other such list and any such list published for a major exchange in that territory for such strips or securities is used in preference to any other such list.

[*TCGA 1992, s 272(3)(4); SI 2015 No 616*].

Before 6 April 2015

Before 6 April 2015, the market value of shares and securities quoted in The Stock Exchange Daily Official List is the lesser of:

(a) the lower of the two prices quoted in The Stock Exchange Daily Official List for the relevant date, plus a quarter of the difference between those prices (*'the quarter-up rule'*); and
(b) the average of the highest and lowest prices for normal bargains recorded on that date, if any.

If the London trading floor is closed on the relevant date, the prices are to be taken by reference to the latest previous date or to the earliest subsequent date, whichever produces the lower figure.

The above method of valuation continues to apply for inheritance tax purposes after 6 April 2015.

The above method of valuation does not apply for computing the value of shares as at 6 April 1965 (see **8.12** ASSETS HELD ON **28** MARCH **1982**), nor where special circumstances may affect the value.

[*TCGA 1992, s 272(3)(4)(6), Sch 11 para 6(1)(2)(4), para 7(1)*].

See *Hinchcliffe v Crabtree* HL 1971, 47 TC 419.

Units in unit trusts

Units in unit trusts, subject to similar valuation rules at 6 April 1965 (as above), are valued at the lower of the two prices published by the managers on the relevant date or if no price is published at that time, on the latest date before the relevant date. [*TCGA 1992, s 272(5)(6), Sch 11 para 6(1)(3)*].

Simon's Taxes. See **C2.122.**

Unquoted shares

[39.4] Market value of unquoted shares is determined on the assumption that all information is available which a prudent prospective purchaser might reasonably require before purchase by private treaty at arm's length from a willing vendor. [*TCGA 1992, s 273*].

Simon's Taxes. See **C2.123A.**

Alternative investment market (AIM) and other markets

[39.5] Shares traded on markets such as AIM and NEX Exchange are not treated as 'quoted' or 'listed'. For practical purposes, the closing mid-market price on the date of valuation may, in many cases, be viewed as the market value (HMRC Shares Valuation Manual SVM107080). This approach was rejected, however, in *Bell v HMRC* [2023] UKFTT 989 (TC) because the market in the particular shares involved was illiquid.

Land

[39.6] Where, at a certain date, freehold land was subject to a tenancy by a company controlled by the freeholder, the valuation had to be of the reversion in the land expectant on the determination of the tenancy and not of the unencumbered freehold (*Henderson v Karmel's Exors* Ch D 1984, 58 TC 201).

The valuation of trade-related property (in this case a care home) was considered in *HMRC v Denning* CA, [2022] STC 1223, CA.

40

Married Persons and Civil Partners

Cross-references. See 2 ANNUAL RATES AND EXEMPTIONS; 8.1 and 8.3 ASSETS HELD ON 6 APRIL 1965; 30 HOLD-OVER RELIEFS; 38.11 LOSSES for loss relief restrictions on qualifying loans between spouses; 47.2 and 47.7 PRIVATE RESIDENCES; 51 RESIDENCE AND DOMICILE for treatment of spouses.

Simon's Taxes. See C1.202.

Introduction to married persons and civil partners

[40.1] Married persons and civil partners are treated for capital gains tax purposes as separate individuals, so that each has their own annual exempt amount and losses of one cannot be set against gains of the other. Where the partners are living together, however, transfers of assets between them are treated as made on a 'no gain/no loss' basis. For disposals on or after 6 April 2023, no gain/no loss treatment continues for up to three tax years after that in which the couple stops living together and applies to transfers which are part of a divorce or separation settlement.

Independent taxation of married persons and civil partners

[40.2] Spouses and civil partners, whether or not 'living together' (see 40.3 below), are each treated as separate individuals so that:

(a) each spouse or partner is assessed and charged by reference only to their own gains and circumstances (e.g. the rate of tax applicable);
(b) losses of one spouse or partner are not deductible from the gains of the other; and
(c) each spouse or partner has a separate right to the whole of the annual exempt amount available to individuals generally.

Gains accruing to one spouse or civil partner as trustee or personal representative cannot affect the position of the other spouse or civil partner.

[*TCGA 1992, s 65(2)*].

Spouses or civil partners living together may claim exemption in respect of only one main residence. See 47.2 PRIVATE RESIDENCES.

See **58.2** SHARES AND SECURITIES – IDENTIFICATION RULES as regards joint shareholdings.

Transfers of assets between spouses or civil partners living together or in the process of separating are treated as made on a 'no gain/no loss basis' as in **40.4** below.

Jointly held assets

Where spouses or civil partners dispose of an asset which had been held jointly, any chargeable gain arising is apportioned between them in accordance with their respective beneficial interests in the asset at the time of the disposal.

HMRC consider beneficial interest to be a question of fact. If no factual evidence is available to determine each spouse's or civil partner's beneficial interest and they have joint legal title, HMRC will treat each as holder of a half interest (HMRC Capital Gains Manual CG22020).

If the spouses or civil partners have made a declaration under *ITA 2007, s 837* (on Form 17) in respect of their individual beneficial interests in, and in the income from, jointly held property and the declaration is still effective at the time of disposal of the property, HMRC will accept the same split in charging the gain on disposal. If no declaration has been made, HMRC will consider other factors, including who provided the cost price and received the disposal proceeds. See Tolley's Income Tax under Married Persons and Civil Partners for commentary on declarations under *ITA 2007, s 837*.

Transitional rule for delayed remittances

Where:

(i) a husband has made a claim under *TCGA 1992, s 279* (enforced delay in remitting gains from disposals of overseas assets, see **43.6** OVERSEAS MATTERS) in respect of gains accruing to their wife before 6 April 1990 (when gains of the wife were, with certain exceptions, assessed on the husband), and
(ii) under that provision, the gains are treated as accruing after 5 April 1990,

the gains are taxable on the wife (or her personal representatives) and not the husband.

[*TCGA 1992, s 279(7)*].

'Living together'

[40.3] Individuals who are married to, or are civil partners of, each other are treated as living together unless they are:

(a) separated under a court order or separation deed, or
(b) in fact separated in circumstances which render permanent separation likely.

[*ITA 2007, s 1011; TCGA 1992, s 288(3); F(No 2)A 2023, s 41(5)*].

Both (a) and (b) above require the marriage or civil partnership to have broken down (HMRC Capital Gains Manual CG22070).

Where either spouse or civil partner is non-UK resident, there is no authority for treating them as separated from a UK resident spouse or civil partner merely because of their residence status, even if an asset leaves the UK tax net as a result (HMRC Capital Gains Manual CG22300).

Transfers between spouses or civil partners

[40.4] For disposals on or after 6 April 2023, the rules applicable to transfers between spouses or civil partners extend to disposals made during the process of separating, when the couples are no longer living together. For convenience, the rules applying on or after that date are described below separately to the previous rules.

Transfers on or after 6 April 2023

A transfer of an asset between two individuals is treated as made on a 'no gain/no loss' basis where:

- the disposal is made while the two individuals are married to, or civil partners of, each other and are living together (see **40.3** above);
- the two individuals are married to, or civil partners of, each other but the disposal is made when they no longer live together but it is made:
  - on or before the last day of the third tax year after the tax year in which they ceased to live together; or
  - if earlier, the day on which the marriage or civil partnership is dissolved or annulled or the couple separate under a separation order; or
- the two have ceased to be married or civil partners (or are in the process of so ceasing) and the transfer is made as part of the divorce or separation settlement.

A divorce or separation settlement is defined at *TCGA 1992, s 225B(2)*, interpreting that definition to include agreements between former spouses or civil partners.

These rules apply to disposals on or after 6 April 2023, irrespective of when the couple stops living together, separate or divorce.

Transfers before 6 April 2023

Transfers of assets, in a tax year, between spouses or civil partners who are living together (see **40.3** above) in any part of that year are regarded as made on a 'no gain/no loss' basis. This treatment also applies to transfers between spouses or civil partners in the part of a year following the start of the marriage or civil partnership and in the whole of the year in which separation takes place, even though the spouses or civil partners may not be 'living together' at the time of transfer (but does not apply following a final order or decree absolute).

Transfers whilst spouses separated or treated as separated

In a case in which spouses, after several years of separation, were divorced and the court order (by consent) on the decree nisi (now known as a conditional order) provided for the transfer of certain property (which was not otherwise exempt), it was held that the property had been disposed of at the time of the decree nisi. As the divorce was not then final, the spouses were still connected persons and the consideration was to be taken as the market value. See **17.1** CONNECTED PERSONS and **39.1** MARKET VALUE and HMRC Capital Gains Manual CG22400–22505. The 'no gain/no loss' basis did not apply as the spouses were not living together (but see above for disposals on or after 6 April 2023). (*Aspden v Hildesley* Ch D 1981, 55 TC 609).

In *Wilmore v HMRC* [2023] UKFTT 858 (TC), the taxpayer (W) was held to have disposed of her beneficial interest in a property to her spouse in the year of separation, although the property was not sold until a subsequent year. W separated from her former spouse in September 2015 and they reached an informal agreement in December 2015 that he would become the sole owner of the relevant property. It was subsequently sold in September 2016. Although W's legal interest had not been transferred in the year of separation, the FTT concluded that due to the December 2015 agreement, a constructive trust arose under which W was a joint owner of the legal title, but had no beneficial interest in the property. She had therefore transferred her beneficial interest in the property in the year of separation and *TCGA 1992, s 58* applied to the transfer.

Exclusions from no gain/no loss treatment

The no gain/no loss treatment does not apply to transfers (whether on or after or before 6 April 2023): (i) by way of *donatio mortis causa* (see **18.6** DEATH); (ii) to or from trading stock of either spouse or civil partner; or (iii) of exempt employee shareholder shares where any gain would be wholly exempt (see **21.25** EMPLOYEE SHARE SCHEMES). Where a transfer of employee shareholder shares would only be partly exempt as a result of the lifetime limit for gains on such shares, the transfer is treated as made for a consideration equal to the amount (not exceeding market value) which results in a gain of an amount equal to the balance of the lifetime limit.

[*TCGA 1992, s 58; F(No 2)A 2023, s 41(2)(6)*].

Computation

The deemed consideration for a no gain/no loss transfer between spouses or civil partners is equal to the transferor's acquisition cost for CGT purposes, including any enhancement expenditure, plus, for transfers before 6 April 2008, indexation allowance if applicable (see **32.4** INDEXATION). The no gain/no loss rule cannot be disapplied, and any *actual* consideration given for the transfer is ignored. It should be noted that the transaction is still a disposal by the transferor spouse or partner and an acquisition by the transferee as at the date of transfer; the legislation does not operate by deeming no disposal to have taken place.

See **16.5** COMPUTATION OF GAINS AND LOSSES for part disposals between spouses or civil partners and **35.7** LAND for small part disposals of land.

Example

(A) No inter-spouse transfer

Paul and Heidi are a married couple. For 2024/25, Heidi's taxable income (after personal allowance) is £50,000 and Paul's is £15,000. On 4 July 2024, Heidi sells two paintings which she had acquired in June 1994 at a cost of £5,000 each. Net sale proceeds amount to £17,000 and £25,000. Neither spouse disposed of any other chargeable assets during 2024/25.

Chargeable gains — Heidi

	£
Net proceeds of painting 1	17,000
Cost	5,000
Chargeable gain	£12,000
Net proceeds of painting 2	25,000
Cost	5,000
Chargeable gain	£20,000
Total chargeable gains (£12,000 + £20,000)	32,000
Annual exempt amount	3,000
Taxable gains 2023/24	£29,000
Tax payable £29,000 × 20%	£5,800

(B) Inter-spouse transfer

The facts are as in (A) above except that in April 2024 Heidi gives painting 2 to Paul who then makes the sale on 4 July 2024.

Chargeable gains — Heidi

	£
Deemed consideration for painting 2 (April 4) note (a)	5,000
Cost	5,000
Chargeable gain	Nil
Net proceeds of painting 1	17,000
Cost	5,000
Chargeable gain	£12,000
Total chargeable gains	12,000
Annual exempt amount	3,000
Taxable gains 2023/24	£9,000
Capital gains tax £9,000 × 20%	£1,800

Chargeable gain — Paul

	£
Net proceeds (4.7.24)	25,000
Cost (April 2024)	5,000
Chargeable gain	20,000
Annual exempt amount	3,000
Taxable gain	£17,000
Capital gains tax £17,000 × 10%	£1,700
Tax saving compared with (A) above (£5,800 – (£1,800 + £1,700))	£2,300

Notes to the example

(a) The inter-spouse transfer is deemed to be for such consideration as to ensure that no gain or loss accrues.

(b) The fact that transfers of assets between spouses or civil partners are no gain/no loss transfers enables savings to be made by ensuring that disposals are made by a spouse with an unused annual exempt amount or who pays CGT at only 10%.

(c) An inter-spouse transfer followed by a sale could be attacked by HMRC as an anti-avoidance device. To minimise the risk, there should be a clear time interval between the two transactions and no arrangements made to effect the ultimate sale until after the transfer. The gift should be outright with no strings attached and with no 'arrangement' for eventual proceeds to be passed to the transferor. See also **38.8** LOSSES for anti-avoidance provisions applying where there are arrangements to secure a tax advantage involving a loss.

Unmarried couples

The no gain/no loss rule applies only to transfers between persons legally recognised as married or as civil partners under English or Scottish law. Polygamous marriages may be so recognised in limited circumstances (see HMRC Capital Gains Manual CG22070). The rule does not apply to a transfer to a so-called 'common-law' husband or wife. An unmarried couple or a couple who are not civil partners are not CONNECTED PERSONS (**17**) by reason of their relationship alone (though they may be for other reasons, for example if they are also business partners). However, a transfer of an asset between them is likely to be treated as taking place at MARKET VALUE (see **39.1**) unless made at arm's length in any case.

41

Mineral Royalties

Cross-reference. See 35 LAND.

[41.1] Before 6 April 2013 (1 April 2013 for corporation tax purposes), certain mineral royalties receivable in a tax year or accounting period were treated for tax purposes as one half income and the other half as a chargeable gain to which no allowable expenditure attached. This treatment may continue to be of relevance, as below, where a terminal loss arises.

Terminal loss

A 'terminal loss' which accrues on a 'relevant event' may (if the taxpayer so claims within four years of the event) be carried back and set against chargeable gains accruing in the tax years or accounting periods falling wholly or partly within a period of 15 years before the relevant event, taking later years first. This relief applies only where the mineral lease concerned is entered into before 6 April 2013 (1 April 2013 for corporation tax purposes).

A '*relevant event*' occurs on the expiry or termination of the mineral lease or the disposal (or deemed disposal under any provision) of the interest held in the land to which the lease relates ('*the relevant interest*'). The taxpayer must have been entitled to receive mineral royalties under the mineral lease and held the interest immediately before the relevant event.

A '*terminal loss*' is an allowable loss for chargeable gains purposes which arises:

(a) on the expiry or termination of the mineral lease, and on an additional claim within the same time limit as above, by which the taxpayer is treated as if he had disposed of and immediately re-acquired the relevant interest at its market value; or
(b) on the actual disposal (or any other deemed disposal under any provision) of the relevant interest.

Relief in any one tax year or accounting period is restricted to the chargeable gains previously assessed by reason of the treatment above in respect of the mineral lease in question, except that any unrelieved balance is treated as accruing at the date of the relevant event and as allowable against general gains. If no claim is made for the terminal loss to be treated as above, the whole of such loss is treated as accruing at the date of the relevant event and as an allowable loss against general gains. Repayments of tax are made as may be necessary.

[*TCGA 1992, ss 201–203; ITTOIA 2005, ss 157, 319, 340–343; CTA 2009, ss 274–276; FA 2012, s 227, Sch 39 paras 43–47*].

42

Offshore Settlements

Cross-references. See **43.3** OVERSEAS MATTERS for non-UK residents trading in the UK through branch or agency or permanent establishment; **51** RESIDENCE AND DOMICILE for the determination of a person's residence, ordinary residence and domicile status; and **56** SETTLEMENTS for settlements generally and provisions relating to UK resident settlements.

Simon's Taxes. See I5.12.

Introduction to offshore settlements

[42.1] The provisions set out in this chapter apply generally to settlements whose trustees are, or become, not resident and not ordinarily resident in the United Kingdom or where the trustees are regarded for the purposes of **20** DOUBLE TAX RELIEF arrangements as resident outside the UK. Such trustees are not, in general, chargeable to capital gains tax (see **43.1** and **43.3** OVERSEAS MATTERS) but trustees becoming non-resident are subject to an 'exit charge', and charges arise in certain circumstances on settlors and beneficiaries of such offshore settlements. See also **42.22** for information required to be provided to HMRC in relation to such settlements.

Residence of trustees

The trustees of a settlement are treated as if they were a single person (distinct from the persons who may from time to time be trustees). [*TCGA 1992, s 69(1)*].

The deemed single person is treated as resident in the UK at any time when either all the trustees are resident in the UK or:

(a) at least one trustee is resident in the UK and at least one is not so resident; and
(b) a settlor of the settlement was resident or domiciled in the UK (or deemed domiciled in the UK — see below) at a time when he made the settlement (or was treated as making the settlement — see below) or, where the settlement arose on his death, immediately before his death.

For the circumstances in which a settlor makes a settlement or is treated as making a settlement, see **56.5** SETTLEMENTS. In the case of a transfer of property between two settlements to which *TCGA 1992, s 68B* (identification of settlor on transfer of property between settlements — see **56.5** SETTLEMENTS) applies, (b) above is satisfied in relation to the transferee settlement if a settlor of the transferred property satisfied the condition in relation to the transferor settlement before the transfer.

An individual trustee who is resident in the UK for a tax year is treated as not UK-resident for these purposes if the year is a split year under the statutory residence test (see **51.17** RESIDENCE AND DOMICILE) and the individual begins or ceases to be a trustee during the year and is not a trustee during any part of the UK part of the year.

A trustee who is not resident in the UK (including an individual treated as not resident under the split year rule) is nevertheless treated for these purposes as if he were so resident at any time when he acts as trustee in the course of a business he carries on in the UK through a branch, agency or permanent establishment.

A deemed person not treated as resident in the UK under the above provisions is treated as not resident in the UK.

Condition (b) above is satisfied if the settlor is *deemed* domiciled in the UK (see **51.29** RESIDENCE AND DOMICILE) at the time of the settlement or, where the settlement arose on the settlor's death, immediately before his death.

[*TCGA 1992, s 69(2)–(2F)*].

In cases where a settlement would otherwise be treated as resident both in the UK and another territory, it is necessary to consider the 'tie-breaker' provision in the relevant double tax treaty (if there is one). This will often depend on the location of the place of effective management (PoEM) of the settlement. See, for example, *Smallwood v HMRC* [2010] STC 2045 and *Haworth v HMRC* [2024] UKUT 58 (TCC).

Most non-UK resident settlements are dealt with by HMRC Trusts BX9 1EL, telephone number 0300 123 1072.

Charge on trustees ceasing to be resident in the UK

[42.2] Where, at any time ('*the relevant time*'), trustees of a settlement become not resident in the UK (see **42.1** above), they are deemed for capital gains tax purposes to have disposed of 'the defined assets' immediately before the relevant time, and immediately to have reacquired them, at their market value at that time.

'*The defined assets*' are all assets constituting settled property of the settlement immediately before the relevant time. However, if immediately after the relevant time the trustees carry on a trade in the UK through a branch or agency or a permanent establishment, and any assets are situated in the UK and either used in or for the purposes of the trade or used or held for the purposes of the branch or agency or permanent establishment, those assets are not defined assets (see also **43.3** OVERSEAS MATTERS). In addition, assets are not defined assets if they are of a description specified in any DOUBLE TAX RELIEF (**20.2**) arrangements, and were the trustees to dispose of them immediately before the relevant time, the trustees would fall to be regarded for the purposes of those arrangements as not liable in the UK to tax on gains accruing to them on the disposal (but see below under Dual resident trustees).

TCGA 1992, s 152 (**53** ROLLOVER RELIEF) does not apply where the trustees have disposed of, or their interest in, 'the old assets' before the relevant time, and acquire 'the new assets', or their interest in them, after that time. However, this denial of relief does not apply to new assets if, at the time they are acquired, the trustees carry on a trade in the UK through a branch or agency or permanent establishment, and any new assets are situated in the UK and either used in or for the purposes of the trade or used or held for the purposes of the branch or agency or permanent establishment. '*The old assets*' and '*the new assets*' have the same meanings as in *TCGA 1992, s 152.*

[*TCGA 1992, s 80*].

In *Trustees of the P Panayi Accumulation and Maintenance Settlements v HMRC* CJEU, [2017] STC 2495, the court held that the requirement for immediate payment of tax under *TCGA 1992, s 80* without deferral is an unjustified restriction on freedom of establishment and therefore contravenes EU law. When the case was referred back to the First-tier Tribunal (see [2020] SFTD 209), it held that the legislation should be read to allow the option to defer payment in five equal annual instalments, without liability to interest. See below for exit charge payment plans which have now been introduced.

If the trustees so elect, a gain or loss on a deemed disposal of an interest in UK land (see **35.23** LAND) is deferred until a subsequent disposal of all or part of the interest. The gain or loss is then treated as arising on the subsequent disposal (in addition to any actual gain or loss on that disposal). On a disposal of only part of an interest, only a corresponding part of the deemed gain or loss is treated as arising.

[*TCGA 1992, s 80A*].

For HMRC's practice in this area, see HMRC Statement of Practice SP 5/92, paras 2 and 3.

The normal rules for assessment of trustees (see **6.6** ASSESSMENTS) are disapplied so that no assessment to CGT payable under *TCGA 1992, s 80* by the migrating trustees can be made on a person who ceased to be a trustee of the settlement before the relevant time and who shows that, when he did so cease, there was no proposal that the trustees might migrate. [*TCGA 1992, s 65(3)(4)*].

Exit charge payment plans

See **45.8** PAYMENT OF TAX for the availability of CGT exit charge payment plans under which trustees can defer the tax liability under the above provisions.

Death of trustee — special rules

Special rules apply where *TCGA 1992, s 80* above applies as a result of the death of a trustee of the settlement, and within the period of six months beginning with the death, the trustees of the settlement become resident in the UK. In such circumstances, *TCGA 1992, s 80* is to apply as if the defined assets were restricted to such assets (if any) as would, apart from this special rule, be defined assets and which either:

- are disposed of by the trustees in the period which begins with the death and ends when the trustees become resident in the UK, or
- are of a description specified in any double tax relief arrangements; constitute settled property of the settlement immediately after the trustees become resident in the UK; and, were the trustees to dispose of them at that time, the trustees would fall to be regarded for the purposes of the arrangements as not liable in the UK to tax on gains accruing to them on the disposal.

Further special rules apply where at any time the trustees of a settlement become resident in the UK as a result of the death of a trustee of the settlement, and *TCGA 1992, s 80* above applies as regards the trustees of the settlement in circumstances where the relevant time (within the meaning of that provision) falls within the period of six months beginning with the death. In such circumstances, *TCGA 1992, s 80* is to apply as if the defined assets were restricted to such assets (if any) as would, apart from this special rule, be defined assets and which the trustees acquired in the period beginning with the death and ending with the relevant time as a result of a disposal in respect of which relief is given under *TCGA 1992, s 165* (hold-over relief for gifts of business assets; see **30.2** HOLD-OVER RELIEFS) or in relation to which *TCGA 1992, s 260(3)* (hold-over relief for gifts on which inheritance tax is chargeable etc; see **30.10** HOLD-OVER RELIEFS) applies.

[*TCGA 1992, s 81*].

Past trustees: liability for tax

Where *TCGA 1992, s 80* above applies to the trustees of a settlement ('*the migrating trustees*'), and any resulting capital gains tax which is payable by them is not paid within six months from the time when it became payable, HMRC may act as below.

HMRC may, at any time before the end of the period of three years beginning with the time when the amount of tax is finally determined, serve on any person who, at any time within the 'relevant period', was a trustee of the settlement (but not so as to include a person ceasing to be a trustee before the end of the relevant period who can show that at the time he ceased to be a trustee there was no proposal that the trustees might migrate), a notice requiring the payment of outstanding tax and interest within 30 days from the service of the notice. The notified amount can be recovered from the person concerned as if it were tax due and payable; and he may recover from the migrating trustees any amount paid by him. No tax relief is given on any such payment in computing taxable profits etc.

The '*relevant period*' is the twelve months ending with the relevant time.

[*TCGA 1992, s 82*].

For HMRC's practice in this area, see HMRC Statement of Practice SP 5/92, paras 4–6.

Dual resident trustees

Charge on becoming dual resident

Where, at any time (the 'time concerned'), the trustees of a settlement, while continuing to be resident in the UK, become trustees who fall to be regarded for the purposes of any DOUBLE TAX RELIEF (**20.2**) arrangements as resident overseas and as not liable in the UK to tax on gains accruing on disposals of assets ('relevant assets') which constitute settled property of the settlement and fall within descriptions specified in the arrangements, they are deemed for capital gains tax purposes to have disposed of the relevant assets immediately before that time, and immediately to have reacquired them, at their market value at that time. [*TCGA 1992, s 83*].

Disapplication of rollover relief provision

TCGA 1992, s 152 (**53.2** ROLLOVER RELIEF) does not apply where:

- the new assets (as in **53.2** ROLLOVER RELIEF) are, or the interest in them is, acquired by the trustees of a settlement;
- at the time of acquisition the trustees are resident in the UK and fall to be regarded for the purposes of any double tax relief arrangements as resident overseas;
- the assets are of a description specified in the arrangements; and
- were the trustees to dispose of the assets immediately after the acquisition, the trustees would fall to be regarded for the purposes of the arrangements as not liable in the UK to tax on gains accruing to them on the disposal.

[*TCGA 1992, s 84*].

Trustees both resident and non-resident in tax year

[42.3] The following applies where a chargeable gain accrues to trustees of a settlement on a disposal of an asset in a tax year in which they are within the charge to capital gains tax but at a time when they are 'non-UK resident'.

Nothing in any **20** DOUBLE TAX RELIEF arrangements is to be read as preventing the trustees from being chargeable to capital gains tax (or as preventing a charge to tax arising, whether or not on the trustees) in respect of the gain.

For these purposes, trustees are within the charge to capital gains tax for a tax year if, during any part of the year they are resident in the UK and not 'treaty non-resident'. Trustees are '*non-UK resident*' at a particular time if they are then not resident in the UK or they are then resident in the UK but are treaty non-resident.

Trustees are '*treaty non-resident*' if they fall to be regarded as resident in a territory outside the UK for the purposes of **20** DOUBLE TAX RELIEF arrangements. For the meaning of 'resident', see **51** RESIDENCE AND DOMICILE.

[*TCGA 1992, ss 83A, 288(7B)*].

Disposal of settled interest

[42.4] The exemption in *TCGA 1992, s 76(1)* (see **56.15** SETTLEMENTS) by virtue of which no chargeable gain accrues in certain circumstances on the disposal of an interest created by or arising under a settlement does not apply to such disposals in either of the following circumstances.

(a) At the time of disposal, the trustees are not resident in the UK (see **42.1** above) and the disposal is not one which arises on a person becoming absolutely entitled to settled property as against the trustees and accordingly treated under *TCGA 1992, s 76(2)* (see **56.15** SETTLEMENTS) as made in consideration of his obtaining the settled property. [*TCGA 1992, s 85(1)*].
(b) Subject to the same exclusion as in (a) above, there has ever been a time when the trustees of the settlement were not resident in the UK or fell to be treated under a double tax agreement as resident in a territory outside the UK. Nor does the exemption apply if any property comprised in the settlement in question derives directly or indirectly from a settlement which is caught by this provision. [*TCGA 1992, s 76(1A)(1B)(3)*].

Calculation of gain on disposal of interest after trustees becoming non-resident

Subject to the exceptions below, for the purpose only of calculating any chargeable gain accruing to a person on the disposal of an interest created by or arising under a settlement, where:

(i) *TCGA 1992, s 80* at **42.2** above (charge on trustees becoming non-resident) applies as regards the trustees of the settlement;
(ii) the disposal is made after the 'relevant time' (see **42.2** above) and the circumstances are such that the exemption for disposal of an interest in a settlement is prevented from applying by (a) above; and
(iii) the interest was created for his benefit, or he otherwise acquired it, before the relevant time,

he is treated as if he had disposed of the interest immediately before the relevant time, and immediately reacquired it, at its market value at that time.

This treatment does not apply where:

- *TCGA 1992, s 83* at **42.2** above (charge on trustees ceasing to be liable to UK tax under double tax relief arrangements) applied as regards the trustees in circumstances where 'the time concerned' (see **42.2** above) fell before the time when the interest was created for the benefit of the person disposing of it or when he otherwise acquired it; or
- the settlement had 'relevant offshore gains' at the relevant time.

A settlement has '*relevant offshore gains*' at any time if, were the tax year to end at that time, chargeable gains would be treated under *TCGA 1992, s 89(2)* (see **42.17** below) or *TCGA 1992, Sch 4C para 8* as accruing in the following tax year to a beneficiary receiving a capital payment from the trustees in that year.

The above treatment is also disapplied where conditions (i)–(iii) above apply but, in addition, *TCGA 1992, s 83* at **42.2** above applied as regards the trustees in circumstances where 'the time concerned' (see **42.2** above) fell in the 'relevant period' (see below). In these circumstances, for the purposes only of calculating any chargeable gain accruing on the disposal of the interest, the person disposing of it is instead treated as if he had disposed of it immediately before the time concerned (where there is only one such time) or the earliest time concerned (where there is more than one because *TCGA 1992, s 83* applied more than once) and had immediately reacquired it at its market value at that time. This treatment does not apply where the settlement had relevant offshore gains (as defined above) at the time concerned or, as the case may be, the earliest time concerned.

For this purpose, the '*relevant period*' is the period which begins when the interest was created for the benefit of the person disposing of it or when he otherwise acquired it, and ends with the relevant time (within the meaning of *TCGA 1992, s 80* at **42.2** above).

[*TCGA 1992, s 85(2)–(11)*].

Charge on settlor with interest in settlement

[42.5] Where all the conditions listed below are fulfilled, chargeable gains of an amount equal to that referred to in (f) below are treated as accruing in a particular tax year to 'the settlor' (see **42.9** below) of a settlement such that they are treated as forming the highest part of the amount on which he is chargeable to capital gains tax for the year. Where the year is a split year under the statutory residence test (see **51.17** RESIDENCE AND DOMICILE), the gains are treated as accruing in the UK part of the year. See also **42.12** below.

The conditions are:

(a) the settlement is a 'qualifying settlement' (see **42.10** below) in a particular year of assessment;

(b) *either*:

  (i) there is not time in the year when the trustees are resident in the UK (see **42.1** above); or

  (ii) there is such a time but, whenever the trustees are resident in the UK during the year, they fall to be regarded for the purposes of any DOUBLE TAX RELIEF (20.2) arrangements as resident overseas.

(c) the person who is the settlor in relation to the settlement is domiciled in the UK (or deemed domiciled in the UK — see **51.29** RESIDENCE AND DOMICILE) at some time in the year and is resident in the UK for the year (and see **43.5** OVERSEAS MATTERS regarding 'temporary' non-residence);

(d) at any time during the year the settlor has an 'interest' (see **42.6** below) in the settlement;

(e) by virtue of disposals of any of the settled property 'originating' from the settlor (see **42.9** below), there is an amount on which the trustees would be chargeable to tax for the year under *TCGA 1992, s 1(3)*, previously *TCGA 1992, s 2(2)* (i.e. an amount of chargeable gains less current and brought forward allowable losses — see **38.2** LOSSES) if the assumption as to residence below were made; and

(f) the provisions in **42.8** below do not preclude a charge.

Where the residence condition specified in (b)(i) above applies, the assumption as to residence in (e) above is that the trustees are resident in the UK throughout the year; and where the residence condition specified in (b)(ii) above applies, the assumption as to residence in (e) above is that the double tax relief arrangements do not apply.

Where the disposal in (e) above is a non-resident disposal of a direct or indirect interest in land (see **35.23, 35.24** LAND), any amount on which the trustees are chargeable as such a gain is not attributed to the settlor.

Carried interest gains (see **44.19** PARTNERSHIPS) which would otherwise be included in the amount mentioned in (e) above are disregarded (.

In arriving at the amount to be charged on the settlor for a particular tax year, the effects of *TCGA 1992, s 1K* (annual exempt amount — see **56.8** and **56.9** SETTLEMENTS) are ignored. In addition, any deductions provided for by *TCGA 1992, s 1(3)* (current and brought forward allowable losses) are to be made in respect of disposals of any of the settled property originating from the settlor, and *TCGA 1992, s 16(3)* (losses of non-resident not to be allowable — see **43.3** OVERSEAS MATTERS) is to be assumed not to prevent losses accruing to trustees in one tax year from being allowed as a deduction from chargeable gains in a later year (so far as not previously set against gains).

Where trustees are participators in a company in respect of property which originates from the settlor, and under *TCGA 1992, s 3* (gains of non-resident close company assessable on shareholder — see **43.7** OVERSEAS MATTERS) gains or losses would be treated as accruing to the trustees in a particular tax year by virtue of so much of their interest as participators as arises from that property if the assumption as to residence in (e) above were made, the gains or losses are taken into account in arriving at the amount charged on the settlor as regards that year as if they had accrued by virtue of disposals of settled property originating from the settlor.

Where the trustees fall within the residence condition specified in (b)(i) above, further rules apply to arrive at the amount to be charged on the settlor as regards a particular tax year ('*the year concerned*'). If the conditions for the charge to apply are not fulfilled as regards the settlement in any tax year falling before the year concerned, no deductions are made for losses accruing before the year concerned. If those conditions are fulfilled as regards the settlement in any year or years of assessment falling before the year concerned, no deductions are made for losses accruing before that year (or the first of the years) so falling. However, these two prohibitions on deductions being made for losses are not to prevent deductions being made in respect of losses accruing in a tax year in which the conditions in (a) to (c) and (e) above are fulfilled as regards the settlement.

Where, as regards a particular tax year, there would otherwise be an amount to be charged on the settlor and the trustees fall within the residence condition specified in (b)(ii) above, the following assumptions and adjustments to the amount are made. It is to be assumed that references in the foregoing to settled property originating from the settlor were to such of it as constitutes 'protected assets' and that references in the foregoing to shares originating from the settlor were to such of them as constitute protected assets. The amount (if any) to be charged on the settlor is found on those assumptions, and if there is no amount found there is deemed to be no amount to be charged on the settlor, and if an amount is found on these assumptions it is compared with the amount which would otherwise be charged on the settlor, and the smaller of the two is taken to be the amount to be charged on the settlor.

Protected assets

Assets are '*protected assets*' if they are of a description specified in the double tax relief arrangements mentioned in connection with the residence condition specified in (b)(ii) above, and were the trustees to dispose of them at any 'relevant time', the trustees would fall to be regarded for the purposes of the arrangements as not liable in the UK to tax on gains accruing to them on the disposal. For this purpose, the alternative assumptions as to residence in (e) above are ignored, the '*relevant time*' is any time, in the tax year concerned, when the trustees fall to be regarded for the purposes of the arrangements as resident overseas, and if different assets are identified by reference to different relevant times, all of them are protected assets.

[*TCGA 1992, s 86(1)–(5), Sch 5 para 1*].

Test whether settlor has an interest

[42.6] A settlor has an interest in a settlement if:

(a) any property originating from the settlor ('*relevant property*') which is or may at any time be comprised in the settlement is, or will or may become, applicable for the benefit of or payable to a 'defined person' in any circumstances whatever;
(b) any income originating from the settlor ('*relevant income*') which arises or may arise under the settlement is, or will or may become, applicable for the benefit of or payable to a defined person in any circumstances whatever; or
(c) any defined person enjoys a benefit directly or indirectly from any relevant property which is comprised in the settlement or any relevant income arising under the settlement.

Each of the following is a '*defined person*':

- the settlor;
- the settlor's spouse;
- the settlor's civil partner;
- any child (which term includes stepchild) of the settlor or of the settlor's spouse or civil partner;
- the spouse or civil partner of any such child;
- any grandchild of the settlor or of the settlor's spouse or civil partner (see **42.7** below as regards the inclusion of grandchildren in the list of defined persons); ('*grandchild*' includes a child of a stepchild or a stepchild of a child or stepchild);
- the spouse or civil partner of any such grandchild (see **42.7** below as regards the inclusion of grandchildren and their spouses or civil partners in the list of defined persons);
- a company controlled by a person or persons mentioned in the foregoing (see **42.7** below as regards the inclusion of grandchildren and their spouses or civil partners in the fore-mentioned categories); ('*control*' is construed as in *CTA 2010, ss 450, 451* but for these purposes no rights or powers of (or attributed to) an associate or associates of a person are attributed to him under *CTA 2010, s 451(4)–(6)* if he is not a participator (within *CTA 2010, s 454*, but subject to restrictions on the definition of participator (see **42.9** below)) in the company);
- a company associated with any such company; ('*associated*' is construed as in *CTA 2010, s 449* but for these purposes where it falls to be decided whether a company is controlled by a person or persons, a similar relaxation to that for 'control' applies as above).

A settlor does not have an interest in a settlement at any time when none of the property or income concerned can become applicable or payable as mentioned above except in the event of:

- the bankruptcy of some person who is or may become beneficially entitled to that property or income;
- any assignment of or charge on the property or income being made or given by some such person;
- in the case of a marriage settlement or civil partnership settlement, the death of both parties to the marriage or civil partnership and of all or any of the children of one or both of the parties to the marriage or civil partnership; or
- the death under the age of 25 or some lower age of some person who would be beneficially entitled to the property or income on attaining that age.

He also does not have an interest in a settlement under (a) above at any time when some person is alive and under the age of 25 if during that person's life none of the property or income concerned can become applicable or payable as mentioned in (a) above except in the event of that person becoming bankrupt or assigning or charging his interest in the property or income concerned.

[*TCGA 1992, Sch 5 para 2*].

Inclusion of grandchildren in list of defined persons

[42.7] Grandchildren and their spouses or civil partners (and companies which they control or which are associated with such companies) are included in the list of defined persons in **42.6** above **in relation to disposals made on or after 17 March 1998**. Their inclusion applies as regards all disposals by settlements created on or after that date.

As regards settlements created before that date, post-16 March 1998 disposals (whether giving rise to gains or losses) to which the 'charge on settlor' provisions would not apply if the inclusion of grandchildren etc. to the list were disregarded are left out of account (i.e. are regarded as not falling within **42.5**(e) above) unless they are made in a tax year in which one of the following events occurs or in a subsequent tax year.

(a) Property or income is provided directly or indirectly for the purposes of the settlement (i.e. is added to the settlement) otherwise than under an arm's length transaction and otherwise than in pursuance of a liability incurred by any person before 17 March 1998. Property or income provided towards (and not beyond) an excess for a tax year of trust expenses (relating to administration and taxation) over trust income is ignored.
(b) The trustees cease to be UK resident or begin to fall to be regarded under a double tax agreement as resident in a territory outside the UK.
(c) The terms of the settlement are varied so as to enable for the first time any one or more of the persons mentioned below to benefit from the settlement.
(d) Any one or more of the persons mentioned below does enjoy a benefit for the first time but would not have been capable of doing so by reference to the terms of the settlement as they stood immediately before 17 March 1998.

The persons mentioned in (c) and (d) above are: any grandchild (as in **42.6** above) of the settlor or of the settlor's spouse or civil partner, the spouse or civil partner of any such grandchild, a company controlled by any such grandchildren and/or their spouses or civil partners (with or without other defined persons — see **42.6** above) and a company associated with any such company. (For these purposes, '*control*' and '*associated*' are to be construed as in **42.6** above.)

[*TCGA 1992, Sch 5 para 2A*].

Exceptions to charge

[42.8] There is no charge on the settlor if he dies in the year.

There is also no charge on the settlor where **both** (a) and (b) below apply.

(a) The settlor has no interest in the settlement at any time in the year except for one (or, where they are satisfied by reference to the same person, for two or all) of the following reasons:
  – property is, or will or may become, applicable for the benefit of or payable to a person, being the settlor's spouse or civil partner, any child (which term includes stepchild) or grandchild (defined as in

42.6 above, and see below for the addition of grandchildren to this list) of the settlor or of the settlor's spouse or civil partner, or the spouse or civil partner of any such child or grandchild;
- income is, or will or may become applicable for the benefit of or payable to such a person; or
- such a person enjoys a benefit from property or income.

(b) Either:
- the person referred to in (a) above dies in the year; or
- where the person referred to in (a) above is the settlor's spouse or civil partner or the spouse or civil partner of any child or grandchild of the settlor or of the settlor's spouse or civil partner, that person ceases to be married to, or to be a civil partner of, the settlor, the child or the grandchild concerned (as the case may be) during the year.

Again no charge arises on the settlor in the following circumstances:

(i) the settlor has no interest in the settlement at any time in the year except for the reason that there are two or more persons, each of whom is one of the following: the settlor's spouse or civil partner, any child (which term includes stepchild) or grandchild (defined as in **42.6** above, and see below for the addition of grandchildren to this list) of the settlor or of the settlor's spouse or civil partner, or the spouse or civil partner of any such child or grandchild and stands to gain for one or more of the following reasons:
- property is, or will or may become, applicable for his benefit or payable to him;
- the income is, or will or may become, applicable for his benefit or payable to him; or
- he enjoys a benefit from property or income, *and*

(ii) each of the persons referred to in (i) dies in the year.

References above to grandchildren apply only where the 'charge on settlor' provisions would otherwise apply by reference to grandchildren (see **42.6** and **42.7** above).

[*TCGA 1992, Sch 5 paras 3–5*].

Deemed domicile protection

A UK resident settlor who is *deemed* domiciled in the UK (see **51.29 RESIDENCE AND DOMICILE**) at some time in the year of the assessment, meets condition (c) in **42.5** above. However, protection provisions mean there is no charge on the settlor in a tax year ('*the particular year*') if all the following conditions are met:

(A) the particular year is 2017/18 or a later tax year;

(B) the settlor was not domiciled in the UK when the settlement was created, nor deemed domiciled in the UK at that time (for a settlement created on or after 6 April 2017);

(C) the settlor is not domiciled in the UK, nor deemed domiciled in the UK by virtue of being UK resident and born in the UK with a UK domicile of origin, at any time in the particular year; and

(D) the settlor, or the trustees of another settlement of which the settlor is the settlor or beneficiary, provides no property or income directly or indirectly for the purposes of the settlement, at a time during the period from 6 April 2017 (or, from the creation of the settlement, if later) to the end of the particular year when the settlor is domiciled or deemed domiciled in the UK.

Condition (C) above is narrowly-drawn in respect of deemed domicile such that a non-domiciled settlor who is deemed domiciled in the UK in the particular year by virtue of long-term residence *only* (see **51.29** RESIDENCE AND DOMICILE) is not excluded from this protection. However, the wider definition of deemed domicile is relevant to conditions (B) and (D) i.e. there is no exception from the charge for a settlor who was deemed domiciled in the UK by virtue of long-term residence when creating the settlement or when providing property or income to it.

Provision of property or income such that condition (D) is not met, '*taints*' the settlement (not a statutory term). If value is added to property in the settlement, this is also regarded for condition (D) as a direct provision of property for the purposes of the settlement, tainting the settlement. However, a settlement is not tainted by the provision of property or income where:

- property or income is provided under a transaction (other than a loan) on arm's length terms;
- property or income is provided (other than by way of a loan) without the intention to confer any gratuitous benefit;
- loans are made to the trustees on arm's length terms (here meaning interest is payable at least annually at the official rate or more), but see exception below;
- interest is paid to trustees under a loan made by them on arm's length terms (here meaning any interest payable is payable at no more than the official rate);
- a loan made by the trustees is repaid;
- property or income is paid pursuant to a liability incurred by any person before 6 April 2017; or
- the property or income constitutes a payment to cover the excess of taxation and administration expenses over settlement income.

In the case of a loan made to the trustees on arm's length terms by the settlor (or the trustees of a settlement of which the settlor is the settlor or a beneficiary), the loan *is* treated as provided (i.e. the settlement is tainted), if interest is not paid as required under the loan terms, or it is capitalised or if the loan is varied such that the terms become non-arm's length. The loan is treated as being provided at the time of the failure to pay interest, the interest capitalisation or the loan variation.

A settlor becoming deemed domiciled on a date (the '*deemed domicile date*') on or after 6 April 2017, may have made a loan to the trustees before this, or the trustees of a settlement of which the settlor is the settlor or a beneficiary may have made such a loan before the deemed domicile date. If the loan is not on arm's length terms and any outstanding amount of the loan on the deemed domicile date is payable or repayable on demand on or after that date, this outstanding amount is also treated as directly provided (i.e. taints the settlement) on the deemed domicile date. The exception to this is if the deemed domicile date is 6 April 2017 and either the loan is repaid (and all interest payable is paid) before 6 April 2018, or before 6 April 2018 the loan becomes a loan on arm's length terms and interest is paid as prescribed — effectively such that from 6 April 2017 it is on arm's length terms.

[*TCGA 1992, Sch 5 para 5A*].

Meaning of 'settlor'

[42.9] For the purposes of these provisions, a person is a '*settlor*' in relation to a settlement if the settled property consists of or includes property originating from him. [*TCGA 1992, Sch 5 para 7*].

Meaning of 'originating'

References to property originating from a person are taken as references to property provided by that person, property representing property provided by that person, and so much of any property provided by that person and other property as, on a just apportionment, can be taken to represent property provided by that person. References to income originating from a person are taken as references to income from property originating from that person and income provided by that person.

Where a person who is a settlor in relation to a settlement makes reciprocal arrangements with another person for the provision of property or income, then the property or income provided by the other person under the arrangements is treated as provided by the settlor, but property or income provided by the settlor under the arrangements is treated as provided by the other person (and not by the settlor).

Where property is provided by a '*qualifying company*' (i.e. a company which is a close company within *CTA 2010, ss 439–454* or which would be a close company if it were resident in the UK) controlled (construed as in *CTA 2010, ss 450, 451* but with the same relaxation as in **42.6** above) by one person alone at the time it is provided, that person is taken to provide it. Where property is provided by a qualifying company controlled by two or more persons (taking each one separately) at the time it is provided, those persons are taken to provide the property in equal shares. Where property is provided by a qualifying company controlled by two or more persons (taking them together) at the time it is provided, the persons who are participators (construed as in *CTA 2010, s 454*) in the company at the time it is provided are taken to provide it in just proportions (save that where a person would otherwise be treated under this last provision as providing less than 5% of any property, he is not taken as providing any property). A beneficiary in the settlement is not to be regarded as a participator in the company solely by virtue of his status as beneficiary.

References to property representing other property include references to property representing accumulated income from that other property. A person is treated as providing property or income if he provides it directly or indirectly.

[*TCGA 1992, Sch 5 para 8; SI 2017, No 495*].

See *Coombes v HMRC* Ch D 2007, [2008] STC 2984.

Qualifying settlements

[42.10] All settlements are '*qualifying settlements*' for the purposes of **42.5**(a) above except for certain settlements created before 19 March 1991.

A settlement created before 19 March 1991 which was not a qualifying settlement under the rules applicable for 1998/99 and earlier years, is not a qualifying settlement if it was a 'protected settlement' immediately after the beginning of 6 April 1999, it has not ceased to be a protected settlement and none of the four conditions set out below has been fulfilled. Such a settlement becomes a qualifying settlement with effect in and after any tax year in which either the settlement ceases to be a protected settlement or any of the four conditions becomes fulfilled.

A settlement is a '*protected settlement*' at any time if at that time the 'beneficiaries' are confined to persons falling within some or all of the following categories:

- children of a settlor or of a spouse or civil partner of a settlor who are under 18 either at that time or at the end of the immediately preceding tax year;
- unborn children of a settlor, of a spouse or civil partner of a settlor, or of a future spouse or civil partner of a settlor;
- future spouses or civil partners of any children or future children of a settlor, a spouse or civil partner of a settlor or any future spouse or civil partner of a settlor;
- a future spouse or civil partner of a settlor;
- persons who are not at that time defined persons (see **42.6** above) in relation to the settlement and by reference to any current settlor.

Despite the inclusion of grandchildren to the list of defined persons (see **42.7** above), HMRC do *not* regard the existence as beneficiaries of the settlor's (or his spouse's) grandchildren (of whatever age) as denying protected settlement status (Revenue Tax Bulletin December 1998 p 620).

The term 'children' includes stepchildren. For these purposes, a person is a '*beneficiary*' of a settlement if:

- there are any circumstances whatever in which:
  - (a) 'relevant property' which is, or may become, comprised in the settlement, or
  - (b) 'relevant income' which arises, or may arise, under the settlement,

  is, or will or may become, applicable for his benefit or payable to him; or
- he enjoys a benefit directly or indirectly from any 'relevant property' comprised in, or 'relevant income' arising under, the settlement.

'*Relevant property*' and '*relevant income*' mean, respectively, property and income originating (see **42.9** above) from a settlor.

The **four conditions** referred to above are as follows.

- The first condition is that after 18 March 1991 property or income is provided directly or indirectly for the purposes of the settlement otherwise than under a transaction entered into at arm's length and otherwise than in pursuance of a liability incurred by any person before 19 March 1991. However, if the settlement's expenses relating to administration and taxation for a year of assessment exceed its income for the year, property or income provided towards meeting those expenses is ignored for the purposes of this condition if the value of the property or income so provided does not exceed the difference between the amount of those expenses and the amount of the settlement's income for the year. By concession, a repayable on demand loan which was made to a relevant trust on non-commercial terms before 19 March 1991 was not caught by this condition provided that, before 31 July 1992, it was either repaid in full with any outstanding interest or made subject to fully commercial terms (HMRC Extra-Statutory Concession D41 — this concession contained further detailed notes on the treatment of amounts paid where the loan was put on a commercial basis. See also Revenue Tax Bulletin August 1993 p 83).
- The second condition is that the trustees cease after 18 March 1991 to be resident in the UK (or, before 6 April 2013 but after 18 March 1991 become neither resident nor ordinarily resident in the UK), or the trustees, while continuing to be resident (and, before 6 April 2013, ordinarily resident) in the UK, become after 18 March 1991 trustees who fall to be regarded for the purposes of any double tax relief arrangements as resident overseas.
- The third condition is that after 18 March 1991 the terms of the settlement are varied so that a defined person (see **42.6** above) becomes for the first time a person who will or might benefit from the settlement.
- The fourth condition is that after 18 March 1991 a defined person enjoys a benefit from the settlement for the first time and the person concerned is not one who (looking only at the terms of the settlement immediately before 19 March 1991) would be capable of enjoying a benefit from the settlement on or after that date.

For the purposes of the third and fourth conditions above, grandchildren (as in **42.6** above) and their spouses (and companies which they control or which are associated with such companies) are not defined persons in relation to events before 17 March 1998 (see also **42.7** above).

[*TCGA 1992, Sch 5 para 9*].

For HMRC's practice in this area, see HMRC Statement of Practice SP 5/92, paras 11–37.

Right of recovery

[42.11] Where a charge is made on a settlor, any tax he pays as a result may be recovered by him from any person who is a trustee of the settlement. For this purpose, the settlor may require certificated proof from HMRC of the amount of the gains concerned and the amount of tax paid. [*TCGA 1992, Sch 5 para 6*].

For HMRC's practice in this area, see HMRC Statement of Practice SP 5/92, paras 7–10.

Interaction with other provisions

[42.12] Where *TCGA 1992, s 87* (gains of overseas resident settlements chargeable on beneficiaries — see **42.13–42.20** below) applies to a settlement, any amounts chargeable on the settlor under the provisions in **42.5** above are deducted in arriving at the 'section 1(3) amount' (see **42.14** below). [*TCGA 1992, s 87(3)(4)*]. Where amounts chargeable on the settlor are so chargeable by virtue of *TCGA 1992, s 1M* (charge on temporary non-residents — see **43.5** OVERSEAS MATTERS), there are provisions (see below) to prevent a double tax charge where gains have been charged on beneficiaries.

Settlor temporarily non-resident

Where a charge on a settlor arises under the provisions in **42.5** above by virtue of the charge under *TCGA 1992, s 1M* (the charge on individuals temporarily non-resident in the UK — see **43.5** OVERSEAS MATTERS) in the year of his return to the UK, there is a limitation on the amount to be so charged.

These provisions interact with those of *TCGA 1992, s 87(4)(b)* (see **42.14** below) under which trust gains potentially chargeable on beneficiaries are reduced by amounts chargeable on settlors of the settlement.

The limitation applies if individuals are charged to tax in respect of the settlement under *TCGA 1992, ss 87, 87K, 87L* or *89(2)* (see **42.13** below) for one or more tax years each of which is earlier than the year of return (i.e. the tax year which includes the 'period of return' (see **43.5** OVERSEAS MATTERS)) and the amounts charged to tax are in respect of 'matched capital payments' received.

A '*matched capital payment*' is a capital payment all of which is matched with the section 1(3) amount for the year of return under the matching rules at **42.14** below.

Where the beneficiaries were charged to tax under *TCGA 1992, s 87* or *s 89(2)*, the amount of the gains otherwise chargeable on the settlor under the provisions in **42.5** above by virtue of *TCGA 1992, s 1M* is reduced by:

- the sum of the amounts charged on the beneficiaries for tax years earlier than the year of return to the extent that the matched capital payments are matched with the section 1(3) amount for the year of return; or
- where the settlement property has at any time included property not originating from the settlor, only so much (if any) of that sum as, on a just and reasonable apportionment, is property referable to the settlor.

Where, with respect to the year of return, an amount remains to be treated under *TCGA 1992, s 1M* as accruing to any of the settlors after having made the reductions under the above provisions, the aggregate of those amounts (for all the settlors) are applied in reducing so much of the section 1(3) amount for the year as has not already been matched with a capital payment for any prior year (but not so as to reduce the section 1(3) amount below zero).

[*TCGA 1992, s 86A*].

Charge in respect of capital payments received from settlement

[42.13] The following provisions apply to treat gains accruing to non-UK resident trustees of a settlement as the chargeable gains of beneficiaries who receive capital payments from them. In certain circumstances, the gains are treated as accruing to the settlor or to the recipient of an onward gift.

Where the charge applies to a non-UK domiciled individual who uses the REMITTANCE BASIS (**49**), settlement gains attributed to him are taxed on that basis irrespective of the location of the asset concerned.

The provisions apply to a settlement if there is no time in that year when the 'trustees' are resident in the UK.
[*TCGA 1992, s 87(1)(6)*].

As regards capital payments received by UK charities as beneficiaries, see **11.2** CHARITIES.

For allowable expenditure on a subsequent disposal of an asset transferred to a beneficiary, see **39.1** MARKET VALUE.

Definitions

'*Settlor*' is defined as at **56.5** SETTLEMENTS. '*Settlement*' is defined as in *ITTOIA 2005, s 620* and 'settled property' and references to property comprised in a settlement are construed accordingly. [*TCGA 1992, s 97(7)*].

In a case where a residuary legatee (who was domiciled and resident in the UK) settled the unadministered residue of the estate of a testator (who was domiciled and resident outside the UK) under a deed of family arrangement within *TCGA 1992, s 62(6)* (see **18.8** DEATH), it was held that the legatee was the settlor for the purposes of *TCGA 1992, s 87* (*Marshall v Kerr* HL 1994, 67 TC 56).

'*Trustee*' is specifically expressed to include, where a settlement would otherwise have no trustees, any person in whom the settled property or its management is vested. [*TCGA 1992, s 97(7A)*].

'*Beneficiary*' is not otherwise defined, but in any case where:

(1) a capital payment is received from the trustees of a settlement or is treated as so received by virtue of *TCGA 1992, s 96(1)* (see below under Payments by and to companies);
(2) it is received by a person, or treated as received by a person by virtue of *TCGA 1992, s 96(2)–(5)* (see below under Payments by and to companies);
(3) at the time it is received or treated as received, the person is not otherwise a beneficiary of the settlement; and
(4) certain exceptions do not apply;

then for the purposes of *TCGA 1992, ss 87–90* (for which see further below) and *TCGA 1992, Sch 4C* the person is treated as a beneficiary of the settlement as regards events occurring on or after that time. The first exception is where a payment within (1) above is made in circumstances where it is treated (otherwise than under the provision in the last sentence) as received by a beneficiary. The second exception is where the trustees of the settlement concerned or trustees of any other settlement are beneficiaries of the settlement concerned. [*TCGA 1992, s 97(8)–(10)*].

Capital payments

These are any 'payments' which are not chargeable to income tax on the 'recipient' or (under *ITTOIA 2005, ss 643A, 643J* or *643L* or *ITA 2007, ss 733A, 733C* or *733E*) on another person, or, in the case of a recipient not resident in the UK, are payments received otherwise than as income. A capital payment does not include a payment under a transaction entered into at arm's length. [*TCGA 1992, s 97(1)*].

A beneficiary is regarded as having received a capital payment from the trustees where:

- the beneficiary receives the payment from them, whether directly or indirectly;
- the trustees, directly or indirectly, apply the payment in settlement of any of the beneficiary's debts, or it is otherwise paid or applied for his benefit; or
- a third party receives it at the beneficiary's direction.

[*TCGA 1992, s 97(5)*].

In *Bowring v HMRC* UT 2015, [2016] STC 816, a trust had realised gains on the disposal of assets and transferred the funds to a new trust. The application of the anti-avoidance provisions in *TCGA 1992, Sch 4B* had been intentionally triggered by linking the transfer with trustee borrowings so that the provisions at **42.18** below were disapplied and the gains remained in the original trust. Capital payments were then made to the beneficiaries of the new trust. The Upper Tribunal rejected HMRC's contention that the new trust was a mere intermediary so that the above provisions applied. The capital payments had been made solely by the new trust.

'*Payment*' includes the transfer of an asset and the conferring of any other benefit. It also includes any occasion where settled property becomes property to which *TCGA 1992, s 60* applies (e.g. property held by nominees or on bare trusts for persons absolutely entitled). [*TCGA 1992, s 97(2)*]. A benefit treated (in whole or in part), under *ITTOIA 2005, ss 643A, 643J* or *643L* or *ITA 2007, ss 731–733E*, as an individual's income for a year of assessment *later* than the year of receipt, is not precluded from being treated as a capital payment in relation to any year *prior* to the year of assessment for which it is treated as income. It cannot, however, be treated as a capital payment in relation to the year for which it is treated as income, or in relation to any *subsequent* year. [*TCGA 1992, s 97(3)*].

The amount of capital payment made by way of loan, and of any other capital payment which is not an outright payment of money, is to be taken as the value of the benefit conferred by it. The value of the benefit conferred is determined by the following rules where a capital payment is made by a loan or by making tangible moveable property or land available.

In the case of a loan to a person P, the value of the benefit conferred on P, for each tax year in which the loan is outstanding, is the amount (if any) by which the interest that would have been payable on the loan at the official rate exceeds the interest actually paid by P.

The value of the benefit conferred by a capital payment consisting of making tangible movable property (other than money) available, without any transfer of the property in it, to P is, for each tax year in which the benefit is conferred:

$$((CC \times R \times D)/Y) - T$$

where:

CC	=	the capital cost of the movable property, when it is first made available to P in the tax year, where that capital cost is the consideration given for the property by the person conferring the benefit (or, if greater, its market value when acquired by that person) plus any enhancement expenditure incurred on it by that person;
D	=	the number of days in the tax year on which the property is made available to P (the '*relevant period*');
R	=	the official rate of interest (or the average official rate) for the relevant period;
Y	=	the number of days in the tax year; and
T	=	the total paid by P in the tax year, to the person conferring the benefit, in respect of the property's availability to P, plus any other amounts paid by P for the repair, insurance, maintenance or storage of the property.

The value of the benefit conferred by a capital payment consisting of making land available for the use of P (without the person conferring the benefit transferring the whole of their interest in the land to P) is, for each tax year in which the benefit is conferred, the excess of:

- the land's 'rental value' for the period of the tax year during which it is made available to P over
- the total paid by P in the tax year, to the person conferring the benefit, in respect of the land's availability to P, plus any other amounts paid by P for the repair, insurance or maintenance of the land.

The '*rental value*' of the land is broadly its letting value in the open market on the assumption that the tenant pays all taxes, rates and charges usually paid by a tenant, and the landlord bears the cost of repairs, maintenance and insurance.

[*TCGA 1992, ss 97(4), 97A, 97B, 97C*].

Calculation of chargeable gains in respect of chargeable payments

[42.14] Where 42.13 applies, chargeable gains are treated as accruing in the tax year concerned to a beneficiary of the settlement if he has received a capital payment from the trustees in that year or an earlier year and all or part of the payment is matched (as below) with the 'section 1(3) amount' for that year or any earlier year. The amount of the chargeable gains is equal to the capital payment or, if only part of the payment is matched, the matched part.

Where the year is a split year under the statutory residence test (see **51.17** RESIDENCE AND DOMICILE), the gains are treated as accruing in the UK part of the year.

For this purpose, the '*section 1(3) amount*' for a tax year for which the settlement is within *TCGA 1992, s 87* (i.e. where **42.13**(a) and, where relevant, (b) apply) is the amount which would have been chargeable on the trustees under *TCGA 1992, s 1(3)* (i.e. chargeable gains less current year and brought forward losses), had they been resident in the UK in that year *less*, if *TCGA 1992, s 86* (offshore settlement where settlor has interest — see **42.5** above) applies to the settlement for the year, any chargeable gains for the year under that section. The section 1(3) amount for a tax year for which *s 87* does not apply is nil.

In determining the section 1(3) amount, where the amount on which the trustees would be chargeable accrues on a non-resident disposal of a direct or indirect interest in land (for disposals on or after 6 April 2019 — see **35.23**, **35.24** LAND) or a non-resident CGT disposal (for disposals before 6 April 2019 — see **35.31** LAND) any amount on which the trustees are in fact chargeable as such a gain is not chargeable on the beneficiary.

Where the disposal in (f) above is a non-resident CGT disposal (see **35.31** LAND) any amount on which the trustees are chargeable as such a gain is not attributed to the settlor.

Carried interest gains (see **44.19** PARTNERSHIPS) which would otherwise be included in the *s 1(3)* amount are disregarded.

[*TCGA 1992, s 87; FA 2018, Sch 10 para 1(4)(11)(13)*].

Matching rules

Capital payments are matched with section 1(3) amounts on a last-in first-out basis by applying the following steps for each year to which to which *TCGA 1992, s 87* applies to the settlement.

Step 1.

Find the section 1(3) amount for the year concerned.

Step 2.

Find the total capital payments received by beneficiaries from the trustees in the year.

Step 3.

Match the section 1(3) amount for the year as follows:

(i) where the total capital payments received in the year do not exceed the section 1(3) amount for the year, match the amount with each capital payment so received; or

(ii) otherwise, apportion the section 1(3) amount between each of those capital payments.

Step 4.

Where (i) above applies, reduce the section 1(3) amount for the tax year by the total amount of capital payments for the year and reduce those payments to nil. Where (ii) above applies, reduce the section 1(3) amount for the year to nil and reduce the amount of each capital payment by the matched proportion.

Step 5.

Start again at Step 1. In doing so, if the section 1(3) amount for the year has not been reduced to nil, at Step 2 substitute the capital payments received in the latest tax year which is before the last tax year for which Steps 1 to 4 have been undertaken. If the section 1(3) amount for the year has been reduced to nil, at Step 1 substitute the section 1(3) amount for the latest tax year which is before the last year for which Steps 1 to 4 have been undertaken and for which the section 1(3) amount is not nil.

If either all the capital payments received in the year or any earlier year or the section 1(3) amounts for the year and any earlier years have been reduced to nil there is no need to return to Step 1.

Reductions made in Step 4 above are then taken into account in applying the above Steps for any subsequent tax year.

[*TCGA 1992, s 87A; SI 2022 No 230*].

Non-UK domiciled beneficiaries

Chargeable gains treated as accruing under *TCGA 1992, s 87, 87K* or *87L* (see **42.15** below) to a non-UK domiciled individual in a tax year to which *ITA 2007, ss 809B, 809D* or *809E* (see **49.2** REMITTANCE BASIS) apply to him are treated as gains on the disposal of assets situated outside the UK (so that the gains are taxed on the remittance basis). This applies regardless of the location of the assets disposed of.

In determining whether gains are remitted to the UK (see **49.2** REMITTANCE BASIS), property or benefits are treated as deriving from the gains if the capital payment (or onward gift — see **42.15** below) by reason of which the gains are treated as accruing consists of either the payment or transfer of the property or its becoming property to which *TCGA 1992, s 60* (property held by nominees and bare trustees — see **56.3** SETTLEMENTS) applies, or the conferring of the benefit.

[*TCGA 1992, s 87B*].

Election for re-basing of gains attributed to non-domiciled beneficiaries

Where *s 87* applied to a settlement for 2008/09, the trustees can make an irrevocable election (on Form RBE1) the broad effect of which is to re-base the settlement assets to the market value at 6 April 2008 so that the element of any gains relating to the period before that date will not be chargeable when attributed to a non-UK domiciled beneficiary.

An election must be made in the way and form specified by HMRC and must be made on or before 31 January following the end of the first tax year (beginning with 2008/09) in which either a capital payment is received (or treated as received) by a UK-resident beneficiary of the settlement (or, where the settlement has a *Sch 4C* pool), by a UK-resident beneficiary of a relevant settlement or the trustees transfer all or part of the settled property to another settlement and *TCGA 1992, s 90* (see **42.18** below) applies to the transfer.

The effect of the election is that where chargeable gains are treated under *ss 87, 89(2)* as accruing to an individual who is resident but not domiciled in the UK by virtue of the matching of a capital payment with a s 1(3) amount for 2008/09 or a subsequent year, the individual is only charged to capital gains tax on the 'relevant proportion' of the gains.

The '*relevant proportion*' for this purpose is equal to what would be the *s 1(3)* amount for the year if every 'relevant asset' had been sold immediately before 6 April 2008 and immediately reacquired at market value, divided by the actual section 1(3) amount for the year. An asset is a '*relevant asset*' if a chargeable gain or allowable loss accrues to the trustees in the year by reason of it, provided that it has been comprised in the settlement throughout the period from the beginning of 6 April 2008 to the time of the event giving rise to the gain or loss.

An asset is also a relevant asset if chargeable gains are treated as accruing to the trustees in the year under *TCGA 1992, s 13* (now *TCGA 1992, s 3* — attribution of gains of overseas resident companies — see **43.7** OVERSEAS MATTERS) by reason of it, but only if the company realising the actual gains owned the asset throughout the period from the beginning of 6 April 2008 to the time of the event giving rise to the gains (the '*relevant period*') and, if it had disposed of the asset at any earlier time in that period, part of the gains would have been attributed to the trustees under *s 13*. Where the proportion of chargeable gains treated as accruing to the trustees under *s 13* is greater than the smallest proportion of gains that would have been attributable to the trustees on a disposal of the asset in the relevant period, only a proportion of the asset is a relevant asset. The proportion is the smallest proportion of gains divided by the relevant proportion.

For the above purposes, where a company disposes of an asset to another company in the same group such that *TCGA 1992, s 171* (see **26.3** GROUPS OF COMPANIES) applies, the transferee company is treated as having owned the asset throughout the period when the transferor company owned it. Where an asset is a relevant asset as a result of this rule, then for the purpose of calculating the relevant proportion, the gains are treated as accruing to the company which owned the asset at the beginning of 6 April 2008 and the proportion of those gains attributable to the trustees under *s 13* are treated as the proportion of the gains actually accruing that are so attributable.

An asset is also a relevant asset if chargeable gains or allowable losses accrue to the trustees (or are treated as so accruing under *s 13*) by reason of it, the value of the asset derives wholly from another asset and *TCGA 1992, s 43* (assets derived from other assets — see **16.5** COMPUTATION OF GAINS AND LOSSES) applies to the calculation of the gains or losses. Either the new asset or the original asset must have been comprised in the settlement throughout the period from the beginning of 6 April 2008 to the time of the event giving rise to the gains or losses or, where the gains or losses are treated as accruing under *s 13*, the company realising the actual gains or losses must have owned the asset throughout the period from the beginning of 6 April 2008 to the time of the event giving rise to the gains or losses and, if it had disposed of the asset at any earlier time in that period, part of the gains would have been attributed to the trustees under *s 13*.

[*FA 2008, Sch 7 para 126*].

Disregard of capital payments to non-UK companies

Capital payments are disregarded for the above purposes if received (or treated as received) from the trustee by a company which is not resident in the UK and which would be a close company if it were so resident. This does not apply where the payment is treated under *TCGA 1992, s 96(3)–(5)* (see **42.19** below) as received by another person. [*TCGA 1992, s 87C*].

Disregard of capital payments to non-residents

Capital payments received in 2018/19 or a subsequent year are disregarded for the above purposes if received (or treated as received) from the trustee by a beneficiary who is non-UK resident throughout the tax year. This provision also applies for 2018/19 onwards to capital payments received before 2018/19 which have not been matched under the above provisions as they apply for 2017/18 and earlier years.

A capital payment received by a non-resident after 5 April 2018 is not disregarded under this provision if:

- the recipient is a 'close member' of the settlor's family at the time the payment is received (or treated as received) and the settlor is resident in the UK in the tax year of receipt (and see further below); or
- it is received in the tax year in which the settlement ceases to exist and capital payments are also received in that tax year by at least one beneficiary who is resident in the UK at some time in the year.

A '*close member*' of a settlor's family means the settlor's spouse or civil partner and any children of the settlor, spouse or civil partner aged under 18. Two people living together as if they were spouses or civil partners are deemed to be each other's spouses or civil partners. A person can only be a close member of the settlor's family while the settlor is alive.

If a capital payment is disregarded under these provisions and the recipient is only temporarily non-resident (see **43.5** OVERSEAS MATTERS) when the payment is received, the payment is treated as received in the beneficiary's 'period of return' (see **43.5**) and is taken into account for the purposes of the above provisions accordingly. If the year of departure was 2013/14 or later but the period of non-residence began before 8 July 2015, the deemed domicile rules at **51.29** RESIDENCE AND DOMICILE do not apply to the tax year which includes the period of return. If the disapplication of those rules enables the recipient to claim the remittance basis for that year, then, if that year is any of 2018/19 to 2020/21 inclusive, for that year only the remittance basis charge does not apply and he remains entitled to the annual exempt amount and income tax personal reliefs (see **49.2**, **49.5** REMITTANCE BASIS).

[*TCGA 1992, ss 87D–87F, 87H*].

Disregard of capital payments to migrating beneficiaries

A capital payment is disregarded for a particular tax year (2018/19 onwards) if it was received by a beneficiary in an earlier tax year to the extent that it has not been matched with the section 1(3) amount for any earlier year in which the 'relevant person' was UK-resident (or any year before 2018/19, regardless of the relevant person's residence status) if:

- the relevant person was UK-resident in the tax year the payment was received; but
- the relevant person is not UK-resident in the particular tax year.

For this purpose, the '*relevant person*' is the beneficiary unless *TCGA 1992, s 87G* applies (see below), in which case it is the settlor.

If a capital payment is disregarded under these provisions and the relevant person is only temporarily non-resident (see **43.5** OVERSEAS MATTERS), the payment is treated as received in the beneficiary's 'period of return' (see **43.5**) and is taken into account for the purposes of the above provisions accordingly. If the year of departure was 2013/14 or later but the period of non-residence began before 8 July 2015, the deemed domicile rules at **51.29** RESIDENCE AND DOMICILE do not apply to the tax year which includes the period of return. If the disapplication of those rules enables the recipient to claim the remittance basis for that year, then, if that year is any of 2018/19 to 2020/21 inclusive, for that year only the remittance basis charge does not apply and he remains entitled to the annual exempt amount and income tax personal reliefs (see **49.2**, **49.5** REMITTANCE BASIS).

[*TCGA 1992, ss 87N, 87P*].

Capital payment received by close member of settlor's family

Where a capital payment is received in 2018/19 or a later year by a beneficiary who is a close member (as above) of the settlor's family at the time of receipt and the settlor is resident in the UK in the tax year of receipt, the above provisions apply as if the payment were received by the settlor as a beneficiary (whether or not he is in fact a beneficiary) and not by the actual recipient. The settlor can recover any resulting tax from the actual recipient of the payment and can require HMRC to provide a certificate specifying the amount of the gains and the amount of tax for the purpose of recovering the tax. Any such certificate is conclusive evidence of the facts stated in it. [*TCGA 1992, s 87G; FA 2018, Sch 10 para 1(1)(13)*].

Losses

Where a loss accrues to the trustees in a tax year for which these provisions apply or *CGTA 1979, s 17* applied, the loss is allowable against gains accruing to the trustees in any later year (1981/82 onwards) insofar as it has not previously been set against gains for the purpose of a computation under these provisions, those of *CGTA 1979, s 17* or otherwise. [*TCGA 1992, s 97(6)*].

The beneficiary's own losses, whether of the current tax year of assessment or brought forward from previous years, cannot be set off against gains treated as accruing to him as above. See **38.2** LOSSES.

Example

C, born in 1982 and resident and domiciled in the UK, is the sole beneficiary of a discretionary settlement created by his father in 2006 and administered in the Cayman Islands. The trustees are all individuals resident in the Cayman Islands. The trustees make no gains or capital payments in 2020/21 or any earlier year, but make the following capital payments to C in 2021/22 onwards:

	£
2021/22	50,000
2022/23	60,000
2023/24	50,000
2024/25	70,000

In 2024/25, the trustees sell two settlement assets (shareholdings) realising a gain of £350,000 and a loss of £50,000. They make no other disposals in that year. C makes only one disposal in 2024/25, realising an allowable loss of £25,000, and pays income tax at the higher rate.

The settlement's 'section 1(3) amount' for 2024/25 is:

	£
Gain	350,000
Less Loss	50,000
Section 1(3) amount for 2024/25	£300,000

The section 1(3) amount is matched with the capital payments made to C on a last-in first-out basis as follows.

	£
Section 1(3) amount	300,000
2024/25 capital payment	70,000
202/24 capital payment	50,000
2022/23 capital payment	60,000
2021/22 capital payment	50,000
Unmatched amount carried forward	£70,000

C's liability to capital gains tax for 2024/25 is as follows.

	£
Matched section 1(3) amount (£70,000 + £50,000 + £60,000 + £50,000)	230,000
Less Annual exempt amount	,000
Amount chargeable to capital gains tax 2023/24	£227,000
Capital gains tax (£227,000 × 20%)	£45,400

Note

(a) C's personal loss of £25,000 for 2024/25 cannot be relieved against gains chargeable under *TCGA 1991, s 87* — see **38.2** LOSSES.

Recipients of onward gifts by beneficiaries

[42.15] There are provisions to tax capital payments by offshore settlements in circumstances where the beneficiary receiving the payment is not liable to CGT under the provisions at **42.14** above (because he is non-UK resident or a remittance basis user) and he makes an onward gift of the proceeds to a UK resident. Broadly, the UK resident is treated as if they had received the payment from the trust as a beneficiary. In detail, the provisions apply where a beneficiary receives a capital payment from the trustees of a settlement and:

(i) at the time of receipt by the beneficiary of the capital payment there are arrangements or an intention for the passing-on (directly or indirectly) of all or part of the payment and it is reasonable to expect that the person to whom the payment is to be passed on will be UK-resident when they receive at least part of what is passed on;

(ii) the beneficiary makes, directly or indirectly, a gift to (or confers a benefit on) a person (the '*subsequent recipient*') and the gift is made within the three years beginning with the day containing the 'start time' or, where it is reasonable to assume that the gift was made in anticipation of the capital payment, at any time before the capital payment is made;

(iii) the gift is of or includes the whole or part of the capital payment, anything which (wholly or in part, directly or indirectly) derives from or represents the whole or part of the capital payment or, if the capital payment is made with a view to enabling or facilitating (or otherwise in connection with) the making of the gift, any other property;

(iv) the subsequent recipient is UK-resident in the tax year in which the gift is received; and

(v) in the period beginning with the start of the tax year in which the capital payment is made and ending with the end of the tax year in which the gift is made, there is at least one tax year for which the 'otherwise-liable person' is not UK-resident or uses the remittance basis.

A gift which is made before the capital payment and which meets the condition in (ii) above is treated for the purposes of (iii) onwards above and of the provisions below as if it were made immediately after the capital payment and in the same tax year.

In (i) above, 'arrangements' include any agreement, understanding, scheme, transaction or series of transactions, whether or not legally enforceable. In (ii) above, the '*start time*' is the time the capital payment is received by the beneficiary (but see further below). In (v) above, the '*otherwise-liable person*' is the beneficiary receiving the capital payment or, where *TCGA 1992, s 87G* applies (see **42.14** above), the settlor.

If there is a series of two or more gifts, the last gift in the series is treated as if it were made by the original beneficiary of the capital payment (and not its actual maker) so that the intermediate gifts are effectively ignored, provided that:

- the first gift in the series is made, directly or indirectly, by the beneficiary within the time limits in (iii) above;
- the recipient of a gift in the series makes, directly or indirectly, the next gift in the series;
- the recipient of the last gift is UK-resident in the tax year in which the gift is received but all of the other recipients of gifts in the series are not UK-resident at any time in the tax year in which they received their gift; and
- each gift includes the whole or part of the capital payment, anything which (wholly or in part, directly or indirectly) derives from or represents the whole or part of the capital payment or, if the capital payment is made with a view to enabling or facilitating (or otherwise in connection with) the making of the gift, any other property.

Effect of provisions

Where the above conditions are met, the capital payment must first be divided into up to three slices as follows:

- the 'taxed part' (if any) of each 'matched amount' (if any);
- any untaxed part of each matched amount ('U'); and
- the rest of the payment ('R').

If all or part of the payment is, in a tax year (the '*matching year*') not later than the tax year of the gift, matched with the section 1(3) amount under the rules at **42.14** above for the matching year or an earlier year, the part so matched is a '*matched amount*'.

If, as a result of there being a matched amount, gains are treated by *TCGA 1992, s 87* as accruing to the otherwise-liable person, that person is UK-resident for the matching year and does not use the remittance basis for that year, the whole of the matched amount is its '*taxed part*' (and it has no untaxed part). If the otherwise-liable person uses the remittance basis for the matching year, so much of the matched amount as is equal to any part of the gains which are remitted to the UK in any tax year not later than the year of the gift and in which the person is UK-resident is the '*taxed part*'(and the remainder is the untaxed part).

If R is greater than nil, then the provisions at **42.14** above apply for the tax year of the gift and later years as if a capital payment was received by the subsequent recipient as a beneficiary of the settlement at the time of receipt of the gift. The amount of the deemed capital payment is equal to R or, if lower, G, where G is equal to so much of the gift as falls within (iii) above or, if lower, the amount of the actual capital payment. So much of the actual capital payment as is equal to the deemed capital payment is treated as not received by the otherwise-liable person.

If G is greater than R, and if U is greater than nil (i.e. where the otherwise-liable person uses the remittance basis for the matching year), chargeable gains are treated as accruing to the subsequent recipient in the tax year of the gift. The amount of the gains is U if (G–R) is greater than U or, if not, so much of U as is equal to (G–R). The chargeable gains treated as accruing to the otherwise-liable person under **42.14** above are treated as from the end of the tax year of the gift as reduced by the amount of the gains treated as accruing to the subsequent recipient. The reduction is made from so much of the gains as have not by then been remitted to the UK in a tax year in which the otherwise-liable person is UK-resident.

If this provision would apply in respect of two or more gifts received in the same tax year by reference to the same capital payment, it applies to the gifts as if they were a single gift equal in amount to the total value of all the gifts. Any resulting deemed capital payments and gains are then apportioned to each of the actual gifts according to their amounts or values. If the provision applies to gifts received in more than one tax year by reference to the same capital payment amounts R and U are reduced when applying the provision to the later gift. R is reduced by the amount of the deemed capital payment and U by the amount of the chargeable gain treated as accruing to the subsequent recipient in relation to the earlier gift.

Recipient close member of settlor's family

If the person treated as receiving a deemed capital payment in a tax year is a close member of the settlor's family (see **42.14** above) at the time of receipt and the settlor is UK-resident at any time in that year, the deemed capital payment is treated as received by the settlor as a beneficiary at the time of receipt (and not by the family member). A similar rule applies to chargeable gains otherwise treated as accruing to the subsequent recipient. The settlor can recover any resulting tax from the family member and can require HMRC to provide a certificate specifying the amount of the gains and the amount of tax for the purpose of recovering the tax. Any such certificate is conclusive evidence of the facts stated in it.

Recipient remittance basis user

Where a deemed capital payment is treated as arising to a person (other than the settlor) who uses the remittance basis for the tax year in which the payment is deemed to be made, these provisions are disapplied but, in the event of any further onward gift, the person is treated as having received a capital payment so that the provisions can be applied to that further gift. Where chargeable gains are deemed to accrue in a tax year to a person (other than the settlor) who uses the remittance basis for that year and not all of the gains are remitted to the UK in that year, the amount of the gains are reduced by the amount not so remitted. In the event of any further onward gift, the person is treated as having received a capital payment at the time the original gift was made equal to the amount of the reduction. The whole of that capital payment is then treated as the untaxed part of a matched amount (so that there is no taxed part). In either case, in applying these provisions to any further onward gift there is no requirement for condition (i) above to be met, the time limits in (ii) above apply by reference to the original gift instead of the original capital payment and condition (iii) above applies by reference to so much of the original gift as met that condition. The 'start time' in (ii) above remains the start time for the original capital payment.

[*TCGA 1992, ss 87I–87M*].

Dual resident settlements

[42.16] *TCGA 1992, s 87* (see **42.13–42.14** above) also applies to a settlement if the trustees are resident in the UK during any part of the year *and* at any time of such residence they fall to be regarded for the purposes of a double tax agreement as resident overseas.

The '*section 1(3) amount*' (see **42.14** above) for a tax year for which *TCGA 1992, s 87* applies by virtue of this provision is the 'assumed chargeable amount' *less*, if *TCGA 1992, s 86* (offshore settlement where settlor has interest — see **42.5** above) applies to the settlement for the year, any chargeable gains for the year under that section.

The '*assumed chargeable amount*' in respect of a tax year is the lesser of: the amount on which the trustees would be chargeable to tax for the year under *TCGA 1992, s 1(3)* on the assumption that the double tax relief arrangements did not apply; and the amount on which, by virtue of disposals of protected assets, the trustees would be chargeable to tax for the year under *TCGA 1992, s 1(3)* on the assumption that those arrangements did not apply. Assets are '*protected assets*' if they are of a description specified in the double tax relief arrangements, and were the trustees to dispose of them at any 'relevant time', the trustees would fall to be regarded for the purposes of the arrangements as not liable in the UK to tax on gains accruing to them on the disposal. For the purposes of this definition of protected assets: the second assumption in the first sentence of this paragraph is ignored; '*the relevant time*' is any time, in the tax year concerned, when the trustees fall to be regarded for the purposes of the arrangements as resident overseas; and if different assets are identified by reference to different relevant times, all of them are protected assets.

[*TCGA 1992, s 88*].

Migrant settlements

[42.17] A capital payment (see **42.13** above) made to a beneficiary in a period of one or more tax years 'for each of which *TCGA 1992, s 87* (see **42.13** above) does not apply to the settlement (a '*resident period*') is disregarded provided that the payment is not anticipatory of a disposal by the trustees in a succeeding period of one or more tax years for which *TCGA 1992, s 87* applies to the settlement (a '*non-resident period*'). [*TCGA 1992, s 89(1)*].

The following applies where a resident period follows a non-resident period and for the last year of the non-resident period all capital payments received by beneficiaries in that year or any earlier year have been reduced to nil under the matching rules at **42.14** above. Chargeable gains are treated as accruing to a beneficiary in any tax year in the resident period if he receives a capital payment from the trustees in that year and all or part of the payment is matched with the section 1(3) amount for the last non-resident year or any earlier year.

TCGA 1992, s 87C (disregard of capital payments to non-UK companies — see **42.14** above), *s 87B* (attributed chargeable gains treated as foreign chargeable gains — see **42.14** above), *ss 87D–87F* (disregard of capital payments to non-residents — see **42.14** above), *s 87G* (capital payments received by close member of settlor's family — see **42.14** above), *ss 87I–87M* (onward gifts of capital payments — see **42.15** above) and *ss 87N, 87P* (disregard of capital payments to migrating beneficiary — see **42.14** above) apply for the purposes of this provision as for the purposes of *TCGA 1992, s 87*.

[*TCGA 1992, s 89(1A)–(4)*].

Transfers between settlements

[42.18] There are provisions for the carry-over of unattributed gains under *TCGA 1992, s 87* or *s 89(2)* (apportioned where necessary), in cases where transfers of settled property are made from one settlement to another. If neither of the last mentioned provisions would otherwise apply to the transferee settlement for the year of transfer, *TCGA 1992, s 89(2)* is deemed to apply to it for that year and subsequent years. These provisions do not apply to a transfer to which *TCGA 1992, Sch 4B* (transfers of value by trustees linked with trustee borrowing) applies, or to any *s 1(3)* amount that is in a 'Schedule 4C pool'. [*TCGA 1992, ss 90, 90A; FA 2019, Sch 1 para 43*].

Where an election has been made by the transferor trustees under *FA 2008, Sch 7 para 126* (gains attributed to non-UK domiciled beneficiaries: re-basing — see **42.14** above) there are provisions to ensure that, following the transfer, any non-UK domiciled beneficiary is charged to capital gains tax only on the post-5 April 2008 element of gains of a non-UK resident company in which the transferor trustees were participators (so that *TCGA 1992, s 13* (now *TCGA 1992, s 3*) applies — see **43.7** OVERSEAS MATTERS). [*FA 2008, Sch 7 para 127*].

Payments by and to companies

[42.19] By virtue of *TCGA 1992, s 96(1)*, where a capital payment is received from a 'qualifying company' which is 'controlled' by the trustees of a settlement at the time it is received, it is treated for the purposes of *TCGA 1992, s 87* (see **42.13–42.14** above) and *ss 88–90* above as received from the trustees.

A '*qualifying company*' is a close company within *CTA 2010, ss 439–454* or a company which would be a close company if it were UK resident. A company is '*controlled*' by the trustees of a settlement if it is 'controlled' by the trustees alone or by the trustees together with a person who (or persons each of whom) is a settlor in relation to the settlement or is connected (see **17** CONNECTED PERSONS) with such a settlor. '*Control*' is to be construed in accordance with *CTA 2010, ss 450, 451* except that for this purpose no rights or powers of (or attributed to) an associate or associates of a person are attributed to him under *CTA 2010, s 451(4)–(6)* if he is not a participator (within *CTA 2010, s 454*) in the company. A beneficiary in the settlement is not to be regarded as a participator in the company solely by virtue of his status as beneficiary.

By virtue of *TCGA 1992, s 96(2)–(5)*, where a capital payment is received from trustees of a settlement (or treated as so received under the foregoing) and it is received by a '*non-resident qualifying company*' (i.e. a company which is not resident in the UK and would be a close company if it were so resident), the following provisions apply for the purposes of *TCGA 1992, ss 87–90*.

If the company is 'controlled' (construed as above) by one person alone at the time the payment is received, and that person is (or is deemed to be) then resident in the UK, it is treated as a capital payment received by that person.

If the company is controlled by two or more persons (taking each one separately) at the time the payment is received, then: if one of them is (or is deemed to be) then resident in the UK, it is treated as a capital payment received by that person; and if two or more persons are (or are deemed to be) then resident (or resident or ordinarily resident) in the UK ('*the residents*') it is treated as being as many equal capital payments as there are residents and each of them is treated as receiving one of the payments.

If the company is controlled by two or more persons (taking them together) at the time the payment is received, it is treated as being as many capital payments as there are participators in the company at the time it is received; and each such participator (whatever his residence) is treated as receiving one of the payments, quantified on the basis of just and reasonable apportionment. But where a participator would otherwise be treated as receiving less than 5% of the payment actually received by the company, he is not treated as receiving anything by virtue of the foregoing.

For HMRC's practice in this area, see SP 5/92, paras 38–40.

For the above purposes, an *individual* is deemed to be resident in the UK at any time in any tax year for which he is not so resident if the year falls within a temporary period of non-residence for the purposes of the charge to capital gains tax on temporary non-residents (see **43.5** OVERSEAS MATTERS). Where it appears after the end of a year of assessment that the rule does apply to an individual and consequential adjustments are required to the amounts of tax chargeable on any person under the above provisions, no time limits for making any assessment or claim prevent the making of those adjustments (whether by assessment, amended assessment, tax repayment or otherwise).

[*TCGA 1992, s 96*].

HMRC information powers

[42.20] HMRC may, by notice in writing, require any person, within such time as it directs (not less than 28 days), to furnish them with such particulars as they think necessary for the purposes of *TCGA 1992, ss 87–90* and *TCGA 1992, Sch 4C*. The very wide information powers of *ITA 2007, ss 748(3)–(5), 749, 750*, suitably adapted, are also expressly stated to apply. [*TCGA 1992, s 98*].

Further charge in respect of capital payments received from settlement

[42.21] Further provisions apply where the provisions in **42.13–42.20** above for taxing beneficiaries of overseas resident settlements apply. They provide for an increased tax charge on the beneficiary in certain cases.

The provisions apply where:

(I) chargeable gains are treated under *TCGA 1992, ss 87, 87K, 87L* or *89(2)* as accruing to an individual as a result of the matching of all or part of a 'capital payment' (see **42.13** above) with the '*section 1(3) amount*' (see **42.14** above) for a tax year (the '*relevant tax year*');

(II) the individual is charged to tax as a result of the matching; and
(III) the capital payment was made more than one year after the end of the relevant tax year.

Effect of provisions

Where the provisions apply, the tax payable by the individual in respect of the payment is increased by the amount found below, except that it cannot be increased beyond the amount of the payment.

The amount is equal to the interest that would be yielded if an amount equal to the tax which would be otherwise payable by him in respect of the payment carried interest for the 'chargeable period' at the rate of 10% per annum. The percentage may be amended by Treasury Order.

The '*chargeable period*' is the period which begins with the later of 1 December in the tax year immediately after the relevant tax year and 1 December falling six years before 1 December in the tax year following that in which the capital payment is made, and ends with 30 November in the tax year following that in which the capital payment is made.

In arriving, for the above purposes, at the amount of CGT payable by the individual in respect of the capital payment, that payment is deemed to form the lowest slice of the individual's total gains (HMRC Helpsheet HS 301). Therefore, it may, for example, be reduced by the annual exemption.

[*TCGA 1992, s 91*].

Information required to be returned in respect of settlements with a foreign element

[42.22] There are extensive requirements for information relating to 'settlements with a foreign element' to be returned to HMRC within certain time limits *without a notice to make a return having to be given by HMRC*. Penalties under *TMA 1970, s 98* apply for failure to comply although no failure will arise where information already has been returned or will be returned later under any other provision. In particular, the following requirements should be observed.

(a) Where property is transferred, otherwise than by way of an arm's length transaction or in pursuance of a liability, to a settlement created before 17 March 1998 which is non-UK resident at the time of transfer, a return of certain particulars must be made by the transferor within twelve months of the day ('the relevant day') of the transfer if he knows, or has reason to believe, the residence status of the settlement.
(b) Where a settlement is created which is either non-UK resident or both UK resident and, under double tax relief arrangements, resident elsewhere, a return of certain particulars must be made by the settlor within 12 months of the day ('*the relevant day*') he first fulfils the condition that he is UK domiciled (or deemed domiciled) and UK resident, not having met that condition at the time of the settlement's creation. Similarly, a return of certain particulars must be made by the settlor who meets the above condition at the time of the settlement's creation within *three months* of the day ('*the relevant day*') on which the settlement was created.

(c) Where a settlement becomes at any time ('*the relevant time*') non-UK resident or, whilst continuing to be UK resident becomes at any time ('*the relevant time*'), under double tax relief arrangements, resident elsewhere, a return of certain particulars must be made by a person who was a trustee immediately before the relevant time within *twelve months* of the day ('*the relevant day*') when the relevant time falls.

[*TCGA 1992, s 98A, Sch 5A*].

Key points concerning offshore settlements

[42.23] Points to consider are as follows.

- When determining the residence of the trustees, and where there are both resident and non-resident trustees, the residence or domicile of the settlor at the time the settlement was made is the deciding factor in determining the residence of the trust. Practitioners should be aware of the effect of the death of a trustee on the residence of the trust and take suitable steps to prevent any undesirable outcomes.
- In practice, many offshore settlements that were created (or expatriated) when the tax rules were more favourable have subsequently become regarded as settlor-interested. This is because the definition of a settlor-interested trust now includes those trusts in which the settlor, their children or grandchildren (or the spouses or civil partners of those people) can benefit from the trust. For many family trusts with a UK resident and domiciled settlor, the children and grandchildren are the most likely beneficiaries of these types of settlements. The gains of these settlements are therefore assessed on the settlor under *TCGA 1992, s 86*.
- For offshore settlements holding assets that are pregnant with gains, the capital gains tax charge on the settlor if the trust were to be wound up may be prohibitive, particularly if the trust assets are distributed to a beneficiary other than the settlor.
- A charge on the beneficiary(ies) under *TCGA 1992, s 87* arises where capital payments are made from offshore settlements where *s 86* does not apply. In practice, this may be for settlements where the settlor is deceased, or where the settlor was non-UK domiciled. In certain circumstances, the gains are treated as accruing to the settlor or to the recipient of an onward gift.
- Many offshore family settlements no longer offer a tax advantage and clients may consider repatriation of these trusts to the UK. Repatriation prevents stockpiled gains from accruing further, but does not eliminate the pool of stockpiled gains, which will continue to be matched against capital payments.
- The further charge in receipt of capital payments (known as the supplementary charge) is calculated as 10% 'interest' per year for each of the years between the gains arising and the capital distribution (up to a maximum of six years). Where the capital gains tax

rate is 20%, this means an effective maximum tax rate on capital distributions of 32% (20% tax plus the supplementary charge at 2% per year for six years). Where the lower rate of 10% capital gains tax applies, the maximum rate is reduced to 16%, making the cost of distributing capital to beneficiaries much more affordable. Trustees may wish to consider their distributions to take advantage of the lower rate where this is possible.

- Detailed records of the trust's gains history should be kept, as different capital gains tax rules may have applied in the past.
- Trust gains and capital payments should be disclosed to HMRC using Form 50(FS).

43

Overseas Matters

Cross-references. See **7.3** ASSETS for location of assets; **14.16** COMPANIES for European Companies (SEs); **16.13** COMPUTATION OF GAINS AND LOSSES for acquisitions from persons neither resident nor ordinarily resident in the UK after 9 March 1981 and before 6 April 1985; **20** DOUBLE TAX RELIEF for relief which may be claimable and for double tax agreements which may override or amend statutory provisions; **30** HOLD-OVER RELIEFS for clawback of relief where transferee becomes non-resident in the UK; **35** LAND for the charge on gains on disposals of direct and indirect interests in UK land by non-UK residents; **42** OFFSHORE SETTLEMENTS for provisions dealing with settlements whose trustees are, or become, non-resident in the UK; **44.2** PARTNERSHIPS for partnerships controlled and managed abroad; **51** RESIDENCE AND DOMICILE for the determination of a person's residence and domicile status; and **56.6** SETTLEMENTS for the residence status of settlements.

Simon's Taxes. See **C1.6, D4.811, D6.520–D6.536.**

Introduction to overseas matters

[43.1] A person who is not resident in the UK during any part of a tax year is chargeable to capital gains tax but only in respect of chargeable gains accruing in that year on the disposal of:

(i) UK-situated assets with a connection to the person's UK branch or agency (see **43.3** below);
(ii) interests in UK land (see **35.23** LAND) or (for disposals before that date but on or after 6 April 2015) interests in UK residential property (see **35.31** LAND); and
(iii) assets deriving at least 75% of their value from UK land where the person has a substantial indirect interest in that land (see **35.24** LAND).

Similar rules apply to charge corporation tax on chargeable gains made by non-resident companies. See **14.2** COMPANIES.

There are special rules which apply where an individual is not domiciled in the UK but resident here — **43.2** see below.

Gains on assets acquired by an individual whilst UK resident and disposed of during a period of temporary non-residence are charged in the tax year of their resuming UK residence — see **43.5** below.

Where a person's gains are taxed on the arising basis, they may be unable to remit overseas gains to the UK. See **43.6** below for the special relief available in such circumstances.

Persons may also be assessed by reference to chargeable gains accruing to non-UK resident persons with whom they have certain specified relationships. See **43.7** below for circumstances where a UK resident is a participator in a closely-held overseas resident company; and see **42** OFFSHORE SETTLEMENTS where an individual is a beneficiary of an overseas resident settlement and where a UK domiciled settlor has an interest in an overseas resident settlement.

A UK resident company can make an election for profits arising from its foreign permanent establishments, including chargeable gains, to be exempt from corporation tax (and for losses from those permanent establishments to be excluded). See **43.8** below.

Where a UK resident company has an interest in a 'controlled foreign company' and where a UK resident has 'offshore income gains' arising out of certain interests in 'offshore funds', there may be a capital gains tax effect. See **43.9** below.

A special relief is available where a UK resident company transfers the assets of an overseas trading branch or agency to an overseas resident company in exchange for shares in that company. See **43.10** below.

See **43.12** below for the special relief claimable where a UK business is transferred or divided between companies in different EC member states and **43.13** for the claim and double taxation relief available where a non-UK business is transferred or divided between companies in different EC member states. See **43.14** below for relief on European cross-border mergers and **43.15** below for the disapplication of these reliefs where a transparent entity is involved.

There are 'exit charges' and provisions for the recovery of unpaid tax where a company ceases to be UK resident etc. See **43.16** and **43.17** below. See also **42.2** OFFSHORE SETTLEMENTS for the 'exit charge' where trustees of a settlement cease to be UK-resident etc.

For exploration and exploitation rights to the UK territorial sea-bed, see **43.18** below.

For UK and European Economic Interest Groupings, see **43.19** below.

For the collection of tax where an overseas element is involved, see **43.20** below.

Individuals not domiciled in the UK disposing of overseas assets

[43.2] Individuals not domiciled in the UK, but resident here, are liable on gains arising in the UK. Gains from disposals of assets abroad are in certain circumstances subject to the remittance basis. See **49** REMITTANCE BASIS.

Trading in the UK through a permanent establishment or a branch or agency

[43.3] There are separate rules for companies and other persons.

Persons other than companies

Subject to any exceptions in the legislation, a person who is not resident in the UK for a tax year (see **1.2** INTRODUCTION) is chargeable to capital gains tax in respect of chargeable gains in respect of gains made at a time when he is carrying on a trade, profession or vocation in the UK through a 'branch or agency' where the disposal is of an asset situated in the UK which has a connection to the branch or agency. For this purpose, an asset has a connection to a UK branch or agency if:

(a) it is, or was, used in or for the purposes of the trade, profession or vocation at or before the time of disposal, or
(b) it is, or was, used or held for the purposes of the branch or agency at or before that time, or
(c) it is acquired for use by or for the purposes of the branch or agency.

The commercial letting of FURNISHED HOLIDAY ACCOMMODATION (**24.2**) in the UK, although treated as a trade for certain capital gains tax provisions, is not so treated for these purposes. Trade treatment generally is, in any event, expected to be abolished with effect from April 2025.

'*Branch or agency*' means, for capital gains tax provisions generally, any factorship, agency, receivership, branch or management. For consideration of this definition in relation to a partnership where two of the partners were resident outside the UK at the time of disposal of a partnership asset but the third partner was UK resident at that time, see *White v Carline* (Sp C 33), [1995] SSCD 186. See also *Puddu v Doleman* (Sp C 38), [1995] SSCD 236 (where a non-UK resident sole trader employed a supervisor to manage the UK trading activity) and *Willson v Hooker* Ch D 1995, 67 TC 585 (where a UK resident individual was held to be an agent of a non-UK resident company in relation to the company's purchase and subsequent sale of UK land, being transactions in which the individual was closely involved).

[*TCGA 1992, ss 1A(3)(a), 1B(1)(2)(5)*].

See **38.4** LOSSES for relief for losses arising on disposals where, had a gain arisen, it would have been chargeable under the above provisions.

Companies

Similar provisions to those above apply to non-resident companies, but with the substitution of the term 'permanent establishment' for 'branch or agency'. [*TCGA 1992, ss 2B(3), 2C(1)(2)*].

For this purpose, and for chargeable gains purposes generally, a company has a '*permanent establishment*' in a territory if:

(i) it has a 'fixed place of business' there through which the business of the company is wholly or partly carried on; or
(ii) an agent (other than one of independent status acting in the ordinary course of his business) acting on behalf of the company has and habitually exercises there authority to do business on behalf of the company,

unless the activities carried on there are only of a 'preparatory or auxiliary character' and are not part of a 'fragmented business operation'. A '*fixed place of business*' includes a place of management, a branch, an office, a factory, a workshop, an installation or structure for the exploration of natural resources, a mine, an oil or gas well, a quarry or other place of extraction of natural resources, or a building, construction or installation project. Activities of a '*preparatory or auxiliary character*' include the use of facilities for the purpose of storage, display or delivery of goods or merchandise belonging to the company; the maintenance of a stock of goods or merchandise belonging to the company for the purpose of storage, display, delivery or processing by another person; or purchasing goods or merchandise, or collecting information, for the company. Where 'alternative finance return' within *CTA 2009, ss 511–513* (alternative finance arrangements; see Tolley's Corporation Tax) is paid to a non-UK resident company, the company is not regarded as having a permanent establishment in the UK merely by virtue of anything done for the purposes of the arrangements by the other party or any other person acting for the company.

Activities are part of a '*fragmented business operation*' if they are carried on, either in the same place or in different places in the same territory, by the company or a person closely related to it, they constitute complementary functions that are part of a cohesive business operation and either:

- the overall activity resulting from the combination of the complementary functions is not of a preparatory or auxiliary character; or

- the company or a person closely related to it has a permanent establishment in the territory by reason of carrying on any of those functions. A person which is not a company is treated for this purpose as having a permanent establishment in the territory if it would be so treated if it were a company.

One person is '*closely related*' to another person if one is able to secure that the other acts in accordance with its wishes; if one can reasonably be expected to act, or typically acts, in accordance with the other's wishes; a third person is able to secure that both act in accordance with its wishes; both can be reasonably expected to act, or typically act, in accordance with a third person's wishes; or the 50% investment condition is met. The 50% investment condition is met if one person has a 50% investment (as defined at *TIOPA 2010, s 259ND*) in the other or a third person has a 50% investment in both. [*TCGA 1992, s 288(1); CTA 2010, ss 1141–1144*].

Deemed disposal on asset leaving UK

Where an asset ceases by virtue of becoming situated outside the UK to be a 'chargeable asset' (as below) in relation to a person, he is deemed to have disposed of the asset immediately before the time when the asset becomes situated outside the UK and immediately to have reacquired it, both such transactions being treated as made at market value. This does not apply where the asset becomes situated outside the UK contemporaneously with the person involved ceasing to carry on a trade, profession or vocation in the UK through a branch or agency or permanent establishment, or where the asset is an '*exploration or exploitation asset*' (i.e. an asset used in connection with 'exploration or exploitation activities' carried on in the UK or a 'designated area' as defined by *TCGA 1992, s 276* in **43.18** below; in this case comparable provisions apply). [*TCGA 1992, s 25(1)(2)(8)*].

Where an asset ceases to be a chargeable asset in relation to a person by virtue of his ceasing to carry on a trade, profession or vocation in the UK through a branch or agency or permanent establishment, he is deemed to have disposed of the asset immediately before the time when he ceased to carry on the trade, profession or vocation in the UK through the branch or agency or permanent establishment and immediately to have reacquired it, both such transactions being treated as made at market value. The deemed disposal and reacquisition does not apply to an asset which is a chargeable asset in relation to the person concerned at any time after he ceases to carry on the trade, profession or vocation in the UK through a branch or agency or permanent establishment and before the end of the chargeable period in which he does so. There is no deemed disposal and reacquisition on a transfer or division within *TCGA 1992, s 140A* of a UK business between companies in different EC member states (see **43.12** below).

There is no deemed disposal and reacquisition of an asset where, on a company ceasing to carry on the trade, the asset is disposed of in circumstances such that it is transferred at no gain/no loss by virtue of *TCGA 1992, s 139* or *171* (see, respectively, **14.12** COMPANIES and **26.3** GROUPS OF COMPANIES).

Unless an election is made (within two years of cessation in the case of a company), a gain or loss on a deemed disposal of an interest in UK land (see **35.23** LAND) on or after 6 April 2019 is deferred until a subsequent disposal of all or part of the interest. The gain or loss is then treated as arising on the subsequent disposal (in addition to any actual gain or loss on that disposal). On a disposal of only part of an interest, only a corresponding part of the deemed gain or loss is treated as arising. A transfer between group companies within *TCGA 1992, s 171* is not treated as a subsequent disposal for these purposes. Similar rules applied before 6 April 2019 to a deemed disposal where the gain or loss would have been an NRCGT gain or loss on the assumption that the disposal was a non-resident CGT disposal (see **35.31** LAND).

[*TCGA 1992, ss 25(3)–(6)(8), 25ZA, 140A(4)(b)*].

For the purposes of *TCGA 1992, s 25* above, an asset is at any time a '*chargeable asset*' in relation to a person if, were it to be disposed of at that time, any chargeable gains accruing to him on the disposal either would be chargeable under *TCGA 1992, s 1A(3)(a)* or chargeable to corporation tax under *TCGA 1992, s 2B(3)*. [*TCGA 1992, s 25(7)*].

Exit charge payment plans

See **45.8** and **45.9** PAYMENT OF TAX for the availability of CGT and CT exit charge payment plans under which certain taxpayers can defer the payment of tax in respect of a number of exit charge provisions, including the above provisions.

Rollover relief

Rollover relief under *TCGA 1992, s 152* (see **53** ROLLOVER RELIEF) is not available if the old assets are 'chargeable assets' (having the same meaning as in *TCGA 1992, s 25* above) in relation to the person concerned at the time of disposal unless the new assets are chargeable assets in relation to him immediately after the time they are acquired.

References to acquisition of the new assets include references to acquisition of an interest in them or to entering into an unconditional contract for the acquisition of them.

Rollover relief will, however, apply, where the acquisition of the new assets takes place after the disposal of the old assets and immediately after the time of acquisition the person concerned is resident in the UK, unless he is also then a 'dual resident' and the new assets are 'prescribed assets'. A '*dual resident*' is a person who is resident in the UK and falls to be regarded under any DOUBLE TAX RELIEF (**20.2**) arrangements as resident overseas. A '*prescribed asset*', in relation to a dual resident, is one which under any double tax relief arrangements would not give rise to a UK tax charge on him in respect of a gain accruing to him on a disposal of it.

[*TCGA 1992, s 159*].

Double tax agreements

No charge to tax under the branch or agency or permanent establishment rules applies to a person who, by virtue of any relevant double tax agreement, is exempt from income tax or corporation tax for the particular period in respect of profits or gains from the permanent establishment or branch or agency. [*TCGA 1992, ss 1B(3), 2C(3)*]. Note that the legislation for this provision was previously *TCGA 1992, ss 10(4), 10B(3)*.

UK representatives of non-residents

[43.4] Certain obligations and liabilities fall upon UK representatives of non-residents carrying on a trade in the UK through a branch or agency. Provided detailed conditions are satisfied, certain persons, e.g. casual agents, brokers, investment managers and persons acting in relation to alternative finance arrangements, are not treated as UK representatives for these purposes. Subject to this, a branch or agency in the UK through which a non-resident carries on (solely or in partnership) a trade, profession or vocation is his UK representative in relation to capital gains arising in connection with the branch or agency and chargeable under the provisions at **43.3** above. Where the non-resident ceases to carry on the trade etc. through the branch or agency, it continues to be his UK representative for tax purposes in relation to amounts arising during the period of the agency.

For corporation tax purposes a UK permanent establishment through which a non-resident company carries on a trade is its UK representative in relation to chargeable gains within the provisions at **43.3** above arising in connection with the permanent establishment. Where the company ceases to carry on the trade through the permanent establishment, it continues to be the UK representative for tax purposes in relation to amounts arising during the period of trading. Subject to detailed conditions, certain brokers, investment managers and Lloyd's agents in relation to certain transactions are not regarded as UK representatives of non-resident companies.

A UK representative is regarded as a legal entity distinct from the non-resident.

As regards the taxation of any amounts in relation to which a non-UK resident has a UK representative, legislation making provision for, or in connection with, the assessment, collection and recovery of income tax, corporation tax and capital gains tax, and interest on tax, has effect as if the obligations and liabilities of the non-resident were *also* obligations and liabilities of the UK representative. Obligations and liabilities attaching to the non-resident because of a notice or document are not, however, obligations or liabilities of the UK representative unless the notice or document was also served on the representative. A UK representative is not treated as committing any criminal offence committed by the non-resident unless the representative actually committed the offence or consented to or connived in its commission.

[*TCGA 1992, ss 271A–271J; ITA 2007, ss 835C–835Y; CTA 2010, ss 969–972, 1145–1153*].

For the full provisions, see Tolley's Income Tax under Non-Residents and Tolley's Corporation Tax under Residence.

Individuals temporarily non-resident in the UK

[43.5] The following provisions apply to tax chargeable gains made by an individual during a period of temporary non-UK residence when UK residence resumes.

An individual who is 'temporarily non-resident' is chargeable to capital gains tax as if the following gains or losses were chargeable gains or losses accruing in the 'period of return'. The gains or losses are:

(a) gains or losses accruing to the individual during the 'temporary period of non-residence';

(b) chargeable gains that would be treated as accruing to the individual, or losses that would be allowable to the individual, under *TCGA 1992, s 3* (previously *TCGA 1992, s 13*; gains of non-resident companies attributed to members — see **43.7** below) in that period if the 'residence assumption' were made; and

(c) chargeable gains that would be treated under *TCGA 1992, s 86* (attribution of gains to settlors with an interest in non-resident or dual-resident settlements — see **42.5** OFFSHORE SETTLEMENTS) as accruing to the individual in a tax year wholly within the temporary period of non-residence if he had been UK-resident for that year.

Gains which are otherwise chargeable are taxed in the normal way and therefore excluded from these provisions provided that a claim could not be made for exemption under any arrangements for DOUBLE TAX RELIEF (see **20**). Losses which are otherwise allowable are similarly excluded. See below for other exclusions.

The 'residence assumption' is that the individual had been resident in the UK for the tax year in which the gain or loss accrued to the company and that the year was not a split year under the statutory residence test (see **51.17** RESIDENCE AND DOMICILE).

Losses within (b) above are only treated as accruing in the period of return to the extent that, taking the losses for each tax year wholly or partly in the temporary period of non-residence separately, they would reduce or extinguish any gains within (b) above for that year.

Where (c) above applies, see **42.12** OFFSHORE SETTLEMENTS for details of the limitation on the amount to be brought into charge where beneficiaries of the settlement have been charged in respect of capital payments from the settlement.

If *ITA 2007, ss 809B, 809D* or *809E* (REMITTANCE BASIS — see **49.2**(a)–(c)) apply for the year of return (i.e. the tax year which includes the period of return), any gains within (a) above treated as arising in the period of return but remitted to the UK in the temporary period of non-residence are treated as so remitted in the period of return. Any part of any gains within (c) above treated as arising in the period of return which have not been remitted to the UK before the year of return are, however, treated as so remitted when actually so remitted. If the temporary period of non-residence began before 8 July 2015, the deemed domicile rules (see **51.29** RESIDENCE AND DOMICILE) do not apply in the year of return for these purposes, i.e. the remittance basis claim may be made in the year of return of an individual who is not domiciled in the UK under general law even if the individual would otherwise be treated as deemed domiciled in the UK under *ITA 2007, s 835BA*. In such a case, where a claim is made in any tax year of return from 2017/18 to 2020/21 inclusive, the individual does not pay the remittance basis charge and does not lose the personal allowance or annual exempt amount in that tax year.

Where these provisions apply, any assessment to capital gains tax may be made for the year of departure at any time before the second anniversary of 31 January following the year of return.

Nothing in any DOUBLE TAX RELIEF (**20**) arrangements is to be read as preventing the taxpayer from being chargeable to capital gains tax under the above provisions.

[*TCGA 1992, ss 1M, 3E*].

Temporary non-UK residence

An individual is regarded as 'temporarily non-resident in the UK' if:

(i) he has 'sole UK residence' for a 'residence period' ('period A');
(ii) immediately following period A, one or more residence periods occur for which the individual does not have sole UK residence;
(iii) at least four of the seven tax years immediately preceding the 'year of departure' were either:
   – a tax year for which the individual had sole UK residence; or
   – a split year (see **51.17** RESIDENCE AND DOMICILE) that included a residence period for which the individual had sole UK residence; and
(iv) the 'temporary period of non-UK residence', i.e. the period between the end of period A and the start of the next residence period for which the individual has sole UK residence, is five years or less.

A 'residence period' is normally a tax year. However, when a tax year is a split year, the UK part and overseas parts of the split year are separate residence periods.

An individual has 'sole UK residence' for a residence period consisting of an entire tax year if he is resident in the UK for that year and is not 'treaty non-resident' at any time in that year. An individual has 'sole UK residence' for a residence period consisting of the UK part of a split year if he is not treaty non-resident at any time in that part of the year.

An individual is 'treaty non-resident' at any time if at the time they fall to be regarded under a double tax treaty as resident in a country outside the UK.

In (iii) above, the 'year of departure' is the tax year that consists of or includes period A. The 'period of return' is the first residence period after period A for which the individual again has sole UK residence.

Transitional rule

Although the definition of 'temporarily non-resident in the UK' applies where the year of departure is 2013/14 or a subsequent year, it may be necessary to consider the taxpayer's residence status in earlier years for the purposes of the test in (iii) above. In relation to such a tax year, the test at (iii) above is that at least four of the seven tax years immediately preceding the year of departure were tax years meeting the following conditions:

- the individual was resident in the UK for the year; and
- there was no time in the year when the individual was treaty non-resident.

Whether an individual was resident in the UK for a tax year before 2013/14 is to be determined in accordance with the rules in force before the statutory residence test was introduced.

[*FA 2013, Sch 45 paras 109–115, 156*].

Exclusions from the charge

The gains or losses treated as accruing in the period of return do not include a gain or loss on the disposal of an asset if it was acquired by the taxpayer in the temporary period of non-residence, provided that:

(A) the asset was not acquired by means of a 'UK resident disposal' (see below) which is treated as having been a disposal on which neither a gain nor a loss accrued, by virtue of *TCGA 1992, s 58* (transfer between husband and wife — see **40.4** MARRIED PERSONS AND CIVIL PARTNERS), *TCGA 1992, s 73* (reversion of settled property to settlor on death of person entitled to interest in possession — see **56.18** SETTLEMENTS) or *TCGA 1992, s 258(4)* (gifts of national heritage property — see **23.79** EXEMPTIONS AND RELIEFS);

(B) that asset is not an interest created by or arising under a settlement; and

(C) the acquisition cost of the asset to the taxpayer does not fall, by reference to any 'UK resident disposal' (see below), to be treated as reduced under any of the following provisions:
   - *TCGA 1992, s 23(4)(b)* or *(5)(b)* (rollover where the replacement asset is acquired after receipt of compensation or insurance money — see **10.4** CAPITAL SUMS DERIVED FROM ASSETS);
   - *TCGA 1992, s 152(1)(b)* (rollover relief (see **53**) on business assets);
   - *TCGA 1992, s 153(1)(b)* (rollover relief (see **53**) on business assets where assets only partly replaced);
   - *TCGA 1992, s 162(3)(b)* (hold-over relief where shares are acquired on the disposal of a business to a company — see **31.2** INCORPORATION AND DISINCORPORATION RELIEFS);
   - *TCGA 1992, s 247(2)(b)* or *(3)(b)* (rollover relief where replacement land is acquired on the compulsory acquisition of other land — see **35.10** LAND).

For the purposes of (A) and (C) above, a 'UK resident disposal' is a disposal of an asset acquired by the person making the disposal at a time when that person was resident in the UK and was not treaty non-resident.

Note that this exclusion applies only to gains or losses arising on the disposal of assets and not to attributed gains within (B) or (C) above.

Where a chargeable gain has accrued on the disposal of an asset which is not within (A)–(C) above, but the gain falls to be postponed by virtue of one of the following CGT deferral provisions and treated as accruing on the disposal of the whole or part of another asset which is within (A)–(C) above, the above exclusion from the charge does not apply. The said provisions are:

- *TCGA 1992, s 116(10)* or *(11)* (deferral of gain arising on a company reconstruction where the new asset is a qualifying corporate bond (see **48.4**));
- *TCGA 1992, s 134* (deferral of gain arising where gilts are acquired as compensation for compulsory acquisition of shares and securities (see **57.8**));

- *TCGA 1992, s 154(2)* or *(4)* (deferral of gain on a business asset where a depreciating asset is acquired as replacement — see **53.9** ROLLOVER RELIEF).

[*TCGA 1992, s 1N*].

Relief for unremittable overseas gains

[43.6] Where chargeable gains accrue from assets situated abroad and the taxpayer is unable with reasonable endeavour to transfer those gains to the UK due to the laws of the territory where the assets were situated at the time of disposal, or to the executive action of its government, or to the impossibility of obtaining foreign currency in that territory, he may claim under *TCGA 1992, s 279(1)* that they be left out of account.

Claims must be made no later than four years after the end of the tax year or accounting period in which the gains arose.

Where a claim is made, the gains are then treated as gains of the year, if any, in which the conditions cease to apply. The claim is open to personal representatives.

[*TCGA 1992, s 279(1)–(3)(5)(6)(8)*].

These provisions cannot be relied upon as a defence against an assessment under *TCGA 1992, s 3* (see **43.7** below) if the taxpayer's inability to transfer the gain to the UK is owing to the company's failure to distribute the gain. Relief can only be given if the gain is represented by money, or money's worth, in the hands of the taxpayer (*Van Arkadie v Plunket*, Ch D 1982, 56 TC 310).

See **36.4** LATE PAYMENT INTEREST AND PENALTIES for an alternative relief given to interest on tax overdue, where collection of tax is deferred in similar circumstances.

Gains which are subject to payments made by the Export Credits Guarantee Department under statutory arrangements for export guarantees do not qualify for the relief above to the extent of such payments. [*TCGA 1992, s 279(4)*].

UK resident participator in overseas resident company

[43.7] The following provisions apply where chargeable gains accrue to a company which is not resident in the UK but which would be a close company (within *CTA 2010, ss 439–454*) if it were so resident if:

- the gain is connected to avoidance (see further below);
- the gain is not connected to a foreign trade or other economically significant foreign activities (see below); and
- some or all of the gain would not otherwise be chargeable to corporation tax on the company. (See **14.2** COMPANIES for circumstances in which a gain made by a non-resident company is chargeable to corporation tax.)

Subject to the following, so much of the gain not otherwise chargeable to corporation tax is apportioned among participators (within *CTA 2010, s 454*) or 'indirect participators' in the company who, at the time when the gain accrues to the company, are resident in the UK. The part of the gain apportioned to each participator or indirect participator is the part corresponding to his interest in the company and is treated as a chargeable gain accruing to him. See below for the application of the remittance basis for non-domiciled individual participators.

No amount is apportioned to a participator if:

- the participator is an individual, the tax year in which the gain accrues to the company is a split year under the statutory residence test (see **51.17** RESIDENCE AND DOMICILE) and the gain accrues in the overseas part of the year; or
- the total amount that would otherwise be apportioned to the participator and any connected persons is 25% or less of the amount of the gain which is to be apportioned.

The amount of the gain accruing to the non-resident company is computed as if the company were resident in the UK and within the charge to UK corporation tax on chargeable gains.

References to a person's interest as a participator in a company are references to the interest in the company which is represented by all the factors by reference to which he falls to be treated as such a participator. References to the extent of such an interest are references to the proportion of the interests as participators of all the participators in the company (including any who are not resident in the UK) which on a just and reasonable apportionment is represented by that interest.

Gains connected to avoidance

A gain is treated as connected to avoidance unless it is shown that neither the disposal of the asset by the company, nor the acquisition or holding of the asset by the company, formed part of a scheme or arrangements where a main purpose was the avoidance of a capital gains tax or corporation tax charge.

Gains connected to a foreign trade or other economically significant foreign activities

A gain is connected to a foreign trade if it arises on a disposal of an asset used only for the purposes of a trade carried on wholly outside the UK or for the purposes of the foreign part of a trade carried on partly within and partly outside the UK. Furnished holiday accommodation outside the UK is treated as used only for the purposes of a trade carried on wholly outside the UK if certain conditions are satisfied (see *TCGA 1992, s 3A(3)–(5))*. Trade treatment is expected to be abolished with effect from April 2025. See **24.1** FURNISHED HOLIDAY ACCOMMODATION.

A gain is connected to other economically significant foreign activities if the asset is used only for the purposes of activities consisting of the provisions of goods or services on a commercial basis carried on by the company wholly or mainly outside the UK. The activities must involve the use of staff and premises, and the addition of economic value to the customers, commensurate with the size and nature of the activities.

Indirect participators

A person is an '*indirect participator*' in a company (company A) if another company which is not resident in the UK but which would be a close company if it were so resident (company B) is a participator in company A and the person is a participator in company B (or in a third non-resident company which would be a close company if UK-resident which is itslef a participator in company B, and so on through any number of such companies). The person's interest in company A's gain is determined by apportioning the gain among company A's participators and then further apportioning the amount apportioned to company B among its participators (and so on through other companies).

Trustees and pension schemes

Gains of a company can be attributed to the trustees of a settlement who are participators, or indirect participators, in the company even if when the gain accrues to the company the trustees are not resident in the UK. See further in **42** OFFSHORE SETTLEMENTS.

For anti-avoidance provisions concerning the attribution of gains under these provisions to trustees of a UK-resident trust, see **56.22** SETTLEMENTS.

An interest held by trustees (other than bare trustees) is treated as the beneficial interest in determining if and how the gain of the non-resident company should be attributed to participators; the interests of the beneficiaries are disregarded.

A gain is not attributed under these provisions to a pension scheme or superannuation fund which is exempt from capital gains tax on disposals of assets forming part of the scheme etc. (see **23.56** EXEMPTIONS AND RELIEFS) if it would otherwise be attributed only if such exempt assets were taken into account in determining the extent of the scheme's interest as a participator.

Relief where company makes a distribution

Where any amount of tax (i.e. capital gains tax or corporation tax on chargeable gains) is paid by a participator as a result of the charge above and an amount in respect of the gain charged is distributed (either by way of dividend or distribution of capital or on the dissolution of the company) within a specified period, that amount of tax (so far as neither reimbursed by the company nor applied as a deduction under the further provisions below) is applied for reducing or extinguishing any liability of his to income tax, capital gains tax or corporation tax in respect of the distribution. For this purpose, a distribution to an individual is treated as the highest part of his income. The specified period is whichever of the following ends earlier:

- the period ending three years after the end of the period of account of the non-resident company in which the gain accrued; or
- the period of four years beginning with the date the gain accrued.

Deduction for tax paid

Any tax paid by the participator resulting from the above treatment (so far as neither reimbursed by the company nor applied as above for reducing any liability to tax) is treated as allowable expenditure in the computation of the gain arising on his disposal of any asset representing his interest as a participator in the company (e.g. shares in the company by reference to which he is a participator).

Losses

Any loss arising on the disposal of assets by a non-resident company which would be a close company if it were UK resident can be similarly treated as accruing to the participator concerned, but only insofar as it reduces or extinguishes gains apportioned to him under these provisions and treated as accruing in the same tax year. This rule applies to each participator separately. Losses can be set off against gains of the same company or different companies (HMRC Capital Gains Manual CG57295).

Payment of tax by company

If any tax payable by a participator as a result of a gain accruing to a non-resident company is paid by that company, or in a case where there are other intervening non-UK resident companies as above is paid by any such other company, the amount so paid is not a payment to that person for income tax, capital gains tax and corporation tax purposes.

Temporary non-residents

An individual who is 'temporarily' non-UK resident, such as to be within the charge to tax under the provisions at **43.5** above on his return to the UK, is chargeable for the tax year of return on gains that would have been attributed to him under the above provisions had he remained UK-resident. See **43.5** above.

Non-UK domiciled individual participators

Gains are attributed under the above provisions to individual participators who are not domiciled in the UK. Such a gain is a 'foreign chargeable gain' within *TCGA 1992, s 12* (and hence eligible to be taxed on the REMITTANCE BASIS (**49.2**)) only if the asset disposed of is situated outside the UK.

Where the remittance basis in fact applies to a gain attributed to an individual under the above provisions, in determining whether the gain is remitted to the UK, the consideration obtained by the company for the asset disposed of is treated as deriving from the attributed gain. Where the consideration was less than the market value of the asset, the asset itself is also treated as deriving from the attributed gain.

Where the remittance basis applies to an attributed gain, when that gain is remitted to the UK so that a chargeable gain accrues, that chargeable gain cannot be reduced or extinguished by a loss accruing to the company and attributed to the individual under the above provisions.

Non-resident groups

For the purposes of the above, the provisions at **26.3**, **26.4**, **26.7** GROUPS OF COMPANIES, *TCGA 1992, s 174(4)* at **8.1** ASSETS HELD ON **6** APRIL **1965** and *TCGA 1992, s 175(1)* at **53.10** ROLLOVER RELIEF apply, with appropriate modifications, in relation to non-UK resident companies which are members of a non-UK resident group of companies as they apply in relation to members of a CGT group as in **26.2** GROUPS OF COMPANIES. Those provisions are so applied not only where the UK-resident participator or shareholder on whom gains fall to be assessed is subject to corporation tax on chargeable gains but also where he is within the charge to capital gains tax (Revenue Tax Bulletin May 1993 p 74).

[*TCGA 1992, ss 3–3G*].

Double tax relief

The appropriate proportion of any overseas tax in respect of its gain which the company pays in its country of residence is deductible, by way of double tax relief, against UK capital gains tax payable by the participator. To the extent that the overseas tax cannot be relieved in this way, the deduction may be made in arriving at the amount of the gain chargeable on the participator. (HMRC Statement of Practice SP D23).

General

The relief for unremittable overseas gains (see **43.6** above) is not a defence to a liability under the above provisions.

Exemption for profits of foreign permanent establishments of UK resident company

[43.8] UK-resident companies are normally chargeable to corporation tax on gains arising worldwide, with double tax relief usually available for any foreign tax paid. See **14.2** COMPANIES and **20** DOUBLE TAX RELIEF. Such a company can, however, make an election for profits arising from its foreign permanent establishments, including chargeable gains, to be exempt from corporation tax (and for losses from those permanent establishments to be excluded). Profits and losses are not left out of account if they are profits or losses of a company's trade of dealing in or developing UK land (within *CTA 2009, s 5B*) or would be such profits or losses if the company were non-UK resident. Gains and losses which, if the company were non-resident, would be chargeable under the provisions at **35.23** or **35.24** LAND are also not left out of account. An election will apply to all accounting periods of the company beginning on or after the 'relevant day'. For this purpose, the 'relevant day' is the day on which, at the time of the election, the next or the first accounting period is expected to begin. If, in the event, an accounting period begins before and ends on or after the relevant day, then for corporation tax purposes that period is treated as two accounting periods, the first ending immediately before the relevant day and the second starting on that day. Profits and losses are to be apportioned to the two periods on a just and reasonable basis. An election can only be revoked by the company which made it before the relevant day, but it is revoked automatically where the company ceases to be UK resident. Otherwise the election is irrevocable.

An election can also be made by a non-UK resident company which expects to become UK resident. In such cases, the relevant day is the day on which the company becomes UK resident.

For each accounting period to which an election applies appropriate adjustments are made in calculating the company's total taxable profits to secure that profits and losses making up the 'foreign permanent establishments amount' are left out of account.

The '*foreign permanent establishments amount*' is the aggregate of the 'profits amount' for each territory outside the UK in which the company carries on, or has carried on, business through a permanent establishment, less the aggregate of the 'losses amount' for each such territory.

The calculation of the profits amount and losses amount differs depending on whether or not there is a double tax treaty between the territory and the UK which includes a provision (a '*non-discrimination provision*') that a permanent establishment of an enterprise of a contracting state is not to be taxed less favourably in the other state than an enterprise of that other state carrying on the same activities. Where there is such a treaty, the '*profits amount*' is the profits which would be taken to be attributable to the permanent establishment in ascertaining the amount of any credit relief for foreign tax (see **20.2**, **20.5** DOUBLE TAX RELIEF). The '*losses amount*' is calculated on the same basis. If an amount of credit relief does not depend on the profits taken to be attributable to the permanent establishment because, under the treaty, the foreign tax is not charged by reference to such profits, then only profits which would be taken to be attributable to the permanent establishment if the foreign tax were charged by reference to such profits are included in the profits amount (and only such losses are included in the losses amount).

Where there is no such treaty, the profits amount and losses amount are the amounts which would be taken to be so attributable to the permanent establishment if there were such a treaty and it was in the terms of the OECD model tax convention.

If a treaty does not include provisions for a credit to be allowed against tax computed by reference to the same profits as those by reference to which the tax was computed in the foreign territory concerned, it is assumed, for the above purposes, to do so.

Special rules apply to the calculation of the adjustments to the company's total taxable profits in relation to chargeable gains and gains taken into account in computing income, capital allowances, income from immovable property, profits and losses from investment business, payments subject to deduction of tax and certain employee share acquisitions. See below for the chargeable gains rules and see Tolley's Corporation Tax for the remaining rules.

[*CTA 2009, ss 18A, 18F, 18R, 18S*].

If, at any time in an accounting period to which an election applies, the company is a 'small company' then there is no profits amount or losses amount for that period for any permanent establishment in a territory which does not have a double tax treaty with a non-discrimination provision. A '*small company*' is a micro or small enterprise within the Annex to Commission Recommendation 2003/361/EC.

If the company is a close company (within *CTA 2010, s 439*) at any time during such an accounting period, so much of the company's profits which are derived from chargeable gains are not profits amounts or losses amounts. This exclusion does not apply to gains on the disposal of assets used only for the purposes of a trade carried on through the permanent establishment concerned or to gains on the disposal of foreign currency or a debt within *TCGA 1992, s 252(1)* (see **23.5** EXEMPTIONS AND RELIEFS) where the currency or debt is or represents money in use for the purposes of such a trade.

[*CTA 2009, ss 18P, 18S*].

Chargeable gains etc

The adjustments to be made under the above provisions include adjustments to remove the effect of any gains or losses relating to the disposal of assets taken into account in computing the foreign permanent establishments amount, so that, in appropriate cases, a gain may be increased to reflect a loss so taken into account or a loss increased to reflect a gain.

The profits to be taken into account in computing the 'profits amount' for a permanent establishment above include any gains in respect of immoveable property which has been used for the purposes of he business carried on through the permanent establishment, to an extent which is appropriate having regard to the extent which it has been so used. This also applies to the 'losses amount' and losses in respect of such property. Gains and losses which would be taken to be attributable to the permanent establishment for the purposes of ascertaining credit relief in respect of foreign tax payable before the election takes effect are excluded from the profits and losses amounts.

[*CTA 2009, s 18B*].

Where a company to which an election applies makes a no gain/no loss disposal (see **8.6** ASSETS HELD ON 31 MARCH **1982** but also including a disposal within *TCGA 1992, s 152* (ROLLOVER RELIEF (**53**)), the amount of the deemed consideration which results in that no gain/no loss, is to be arrived at after taking account of any adjustments under these provisions (so that the consideration includes the amount which would be the foreign permanent establishments amount attributable to the disposal for the accounting period in which it was made if the disposal were not a no gain/no loss disposal). [*TCGA 1992, s 276A*].

Pre-entry losses

Where losses have arisen in any of the company's foreign permanent establishments in the six-year period ending at the end of the accounting period in which the election is made and those losses have not been eliminated by profits from those establishments before the end of that period then the company will have an 'opening negative amount' and no adjustments can be made to the company's total taxable profits until that amount has been eliminated.

The '*opening negative amount*' is ascertained by calculating the foreign permanent establishments amount (excluding chargeable gains and allowable losses) for each accounting period ending less than six years before the end of the accounting period in which the election is made and for that accounting period. The earliest negative amount is carried forward to the next period where it is either increased by another negative amount or reduced or eliminated by a positive amount, but not so as to cause the result to be positive. This process continues through each accounting period and if there is a negative amount remaining after applying it to the last period, that amount is the opening negative amount.

In each subsequent accounting period (starting with the first to which the election applies) the total opening negative amount is then reduced by the aggregate of any profits amounts for the period. In the first accounting period in which that aggregate exceeds the remaining opening negative amount, adjustments can be made to the company's total taxable profits under the above provisions of an amount equal to the excess and the company can specify which profits are to be adjusted in its tax return for that period.

Alternatively, the company can elect for the opening negative amount to be streamed. If such an election is made then, in effect, the above provisions are applied separately to losses in a particular territory so that they do not delay the application of the exemption to other permanent establishments which would otherwise have no, or a shorter, transitional period. The election must be made at the same time as the exemption election and can only be revoked before the first accounting period to which the exemption election applies. It must specify the territories which are to be streamed. Where not all of the negative opening amount is streamed in this way, the residual amount must be eliminated against the residual profits amounts (i.e. for each accounting period, the total profits amount less the streamed profits amounts) in the same way.

Where a business carried on through a foreign permanent establishment is transferred to a connected company and the business has a 'transferred total opening negative amount', adjustments are made to ensure, broadly, that the above provisions apply to the same extent as they would have been had the business been carried on by the transferee throughout. Where the transferee makes an exemption election which takes effect after the transfer day and the accounting period of the transfer is to be taken into account in calculating its opening negative amount (as above), the transferred total opening negative amount is added to the foreign permanent establishments amount for that period, but only to the extent that it is attributable to the period by reference to which the opening negative amount is calculated. If the transferee's exemption election took effect before the transfer, the transferred total opening negative amount is treated as the transferee's opening negative amount (in addition to any such actual amount). A separate streaming election can be made in respect of the transferred amount, which does not have to be made at the same time as the exemption election. The transferred total opening negative amount is disregarded in applying the above provisions to the transferor after the day on which the transfer takes place.

If the transferor has not made an election for exemption before the transfer day, the '*transferred total opening negative amount*' is the amount that would have been that company's opening negative amount if it had carried on no business other than the transferred business, there had been no transfer and the company had made an election which took effect from the day after the transfer day. If the transferor made an election which took effect before the transfer day, the transferred opening negative amount is the remaining part of the transferor's opening negative amount insofar as it is attributable to the transferred business.

[*CTA 2009, ss 18J–18O*].

Anti-diversion

Anti-avoidance provisions apply to prevent a company using the exemption to divert profits to a low tax territory. The provisions apply by excluding the diverted profits from the profits amount for the affected territory, but this does not apply to chargeable gains and allowable losses. See *CTA 2009, ss 18G–18ID* and Tolley's Corporation Tax for full details.

Offshore funds

[43.9] Gains arising on disposals of certain investments in offshore funds are chargeable to income tax rather than capital gains tax. Broadly, this applies to investments that accumulate income rather than distribute it. Without special rules the accumulated income would be reflected in the value on disposal and would be converted into a chargeable gain. The tax treatment of participants in a fund depends on whether or not the fund is a 'reporting fund'.

For full coverage, see Tolley's Income Tax and Tolley's Corporation Tax. To the extent that it relates to tax on chargeable gains, the offshore funds regime is described below.

Meaning of offshore fund

For the purposes of the new tax regime, an '*offshore fund*' is one of the following:

(a) a 'mutual fund' constituted by a body corporate (other than a limited liability partnership) resident outside the UK;
(b) a mutual fund under which property is held on trust for the participants, where the trustees are not UK-resident; or
(c) a mutual fund constituted by other arrangements taking effect under the law of a territory outside the UK and creating co-ownership rights.

Broadly, '*mutual fund*' means arrangements whose purpose or effect is to enable the participants to participate in, or to receive profits or income from, the acquisition, holding, management or disposal of property without having day-to-day control of it. It is an additional condition that, under the terms of the fund, a reasonable investor would expect to be able to realise all or part of his investment on a basis calculated either by reference to the net asset value of the property or by reference to an index.

[*TIOPA 2010, ss 355–359*].

Participants in non-reporting funds

Any fund that is not a reporting fund (for which see below) is a '*non-reporting fund*'. [*SI 2009 No 3001, Reg 4*]. A charge to income tax or corporation tax on income normally arises if a person disposes of an interest (i.e. an investment) in a non-reporting fund and an offshore income gain (as defined) arises on the disposal. [*SI 2009 No 3001, Regs 17, 18*]. The above charge to income tax may also arise if the interest disposed of is an interest in a reporting fund which has been a non-reporting fund at some time since the interest was acquired.

A single disposal may give rise to both an offshore income gain chargeable to tax as income and a chargeable gain. To avoid a double charge, the following apply in such circumstances in place of *TCGA 1992, s 37(1)* (deduction of consideration chargeable to tax on income).

(i) The amount of the offshore income gain is deducted from the sum which would otherwise constitute the amount or value of the consideration in the calculation of the capital gain. The offshore gain is not, however, to be deducted in calculating the figure 'A' in the A/(A + B) fraction under the rules relating to part disposal (see **16.5** COMPUTATION OF GAINS AND LOSSES).

(ii) Where the disposal forms part of a transfer within *TCGA 1992, s 162* (see **31.2** INCORPORATION AND DISINCORPORATION RELIEFS) the offshore income gain is taken into account to reduce 'B' in the A/B fraction determined under those provisions.

(iii) Where, by virtue of *TCGA 1992, s 103G* or *103H* (collective investment schemes; see **63.2** UNIT TRUSTS ETC.) or *s 135* or *136* (reorganisation of shares or securities etc. (see **57.5** and **57.7** SHARES AND SECURITIES respectively)), the transaction does not constitute a disposal for capital gains purposes, but does constitute a disposal for the purposes of the offshore fund provisions, the amount of any offshore income gain to which the disposal gives rise is treated as consideration for the 'new holding' (within *TCGA 1992, s 128* — see **57.2** SHARES AND SECURITIES).

(iv) Where, by virtue of *TCGA 1992, s 127* (see **57.2** SHARES AND SECURITIES) an exchange of interests of different classes in an offshore fund does not constitute a disposal for capital gains purposes, but does constitute a disposal of an interest in an offshore fund, the amount of any offshore income gain to which the disposal gives rise is treated as consideration for the new holding.

[*SI 2009 No 3001, Regs 44–47*].

Interests in non-reporting funds are designated 'relevant securities' and amended identification rules apply. See **58.6** SHARES AND SECURITIES — IDENTIFICATION RULES.

Participants in reporting funds

A '*reporting fund*' is an offshore fund that has applied for and been approved by HMRC as a reporting fund. An existing offshore fund may apply to HMRC for reporting fund status, as may a fund that has yet to be established. [*SI 2009 No 3001, Regs 51, 55*]. A reporting fund must comply with various duties as to the preparation of accounts, the computation of its reportable income, the provision of information to HMRC and in particular, the provision of reports to participants. [*SI 2009 No 3001, Regs 57–93, 106, 107*]. Such reports must be made within six months of each 'reporting period' (as defined) and must include details of the amount distributed to participants per unit of interest in the fund in respect of the reporting period and of any excess of the reportable income per unit for the reporting period over the amount distributed. [*SI 2009 No 3001, Regs 90–93*]. Participants within the charge to income tax are then taxed on actual distributions from the fund plus their share of any such excess. For corporation tax purposes, the participant's share of the excess is exempt to the same extent as any actual distributions. [*SI 2009 No 3001, Regs 94–98*].

A disposal by a participant of his interest in a reporting fund is a disposal of an asset for chargeable gains purposes. An amount equal to the 'accumulated undistributed income' is treated for chargeable gains purposes as part of the acquisition cost of the asset within *TCGA 1992, s 38(1)(a)* (see **16.12** COMPUTATION OF GAINS AND LOSSES). For this purpose, the '*accumulated undistributed income*' is the aggregate of the amounts in respect of undistributed income on which the participant has been charged to tax under the above provisions. The deemed expenditure is normally treated as incurred on the fund distribution date for the reporting period concerned (i.e. the date on which the fund report is issued or, if the report is not issued within six months after the reporting period, the last day of the reporting period). Where, however, the participant receives an amount in respect of his interest in the fund after the disposal and that amount is chargeable to income tax, that amount is treated as received immediately before the disposal. Where the amount of any distributions to the participant has been treated as reduced under *SI 2009 No 3001, Reg 94A* (equalisation amounts not treated as distributions) the acquisition cost is treated as reduced by the amount of the reduction. This provision does not apply where the offshore fund is a transparent fund (see below). [*SI 2009 No 3001, Regs 94(4), 99*].

Fund becoming or ceasing to be a non-reporting fund

If an offshore fund ceases to be a reporting fund and becomes a non-reporting fund, a participant may make an election to be treated for chargeable gains purposes:

- as disposing of an interest in the reporting fund at the end of that fund's final period of account; and
- as acquiring an interest in the non-reporting fund at the beginning of that fund's first period of account.

The deemed disposal and acquisition are treated as made for a consideration equal to the net asset value of the participant's interest in the fund at the end of the period of account for which the final reported income is reported to him. The election must be made by being included in a tax return for the tax year or accounting period which includes the final day of the reporting fund's final period of account, but cannot be made if a report has not been made available to the participant for that period. The normal purpose of an election would be to crystallise the gain accrued to date as a chargeable gain; any subsequent gain on actual disposal would be an offshore income gain chargeable to income tax.

[*SI 2009 No 3001, Reg 100*].

A similar election can be made by a participant in a non-reporting fund which becomes a reporting fund in order to crystallise the gain accrued to date as an offshore income gain, leaving any subsequent gain on actual disposal to be taxed within the chargeable gains regime: see *SI 2009 No 3001, Reg 48*.

Transparent funds

Disposals of interests in an offshore fund which is a 'transparent fund' are dealt with under the same provisions as apply to authorised contractual schemes which are co-ownership schemes — see **63.12** UNIT TRUSTS AND OTHER INVESTMENT VEHICLES.

For this purpose, a fund is a '*transparent fund*' if:

(1) in the case of investors who are UK resident individuals, any sums forming part of the fund's income are of such a nature that they are chargeable to tax under a provision listed in *ITTOIA 2005, s 830(2)* (relevant foreign income); or

(2) (1) above would apply if not for the fact that the income is derived from assets within the UK.

[*TCGA 1992, s 103B; SI 2009 No 3001, Reg 11*].

Constant NAV funds

A '*constant NAV fund*' is an offshore fund whose net asset value (expressed in the currency in which units are issued) does not fluctuate by more than an insignificant amount throughout the fund's existence, as a result of the nature of the fund's assets, and the frequency with which it distributes its income. The reporting fund rules above are modified for such funds. If the value of such a fund's assets (expressed in the currency in which units are issued) does increase by more than an insignificant amount and the fund has not notified HMRC that it has ceased to be a constant NAV fund, a participant who subsequently disposes of his interest in the fund and who makes a chargeable gain on the disposal is treated as making an offshore income gain (chargeable to tax on income). [*SI 2009 No 3001, Regs 119–124*].

UK resident company transferring assets to overseas resident company

[43.10] The following deferral relief applies where a UK resident company carrying on a trade (which includes vocations, offices and employments) outside the UK through a permanent establishment transfers the whole or part of that trade together with its assets, or its assets other than cash, to a company not resident in the UK in exchange, wholly or partly, for shares (or shares and loan stock) in that company, so that thereafter it holds one quarter or more of the transferee company's ordinary share capital.

If the chargeable gains on the transfer exceed the allowable losses, a proportion of the resulting net chargeable gains relating to the shares (in the proportion that the market value of the shares at the time of the transfer bears to the market value of the whole consideration received) may be claimed by the transferor company as being deferred and not treated as arising until the happening of one of the following events.

(i) The transferor company disposes of all or any of the shares received. The 'appropriate proportion' of the deferred gain (insofar as not already charged under this specific provision or under (ii) below) is then treated as a chargeable gain arising at that time. In determining whether a gain is deemed to arise under this provision, the disapplication of *TCGA 1992, s 127* (reorganisations of share capital etc. — see **57.2** SHARES AND SECURITIES) under the provisions at **60.12** SUBSTANTIAL SHAREHOLDINGS OF COMPANIES is ignored (so that a reorganisation etc. within *s 127* is treated as not being a disposal of the shares). The gain is in addition to any gain or loss actually arising on the disposal of the shares. The '*appropriate proportion*' is the proportion which the market value of the shares disposed of bears to the market value of the shares held immediately before the disposal. However, for corporation tax purposes, no addition to the consideration is made under this provision if its application would be directly attributable to the disposal of an asset before 1 April 1982.

(ii) The transferee company disposes, within six years of the transfer, of the whole or part of the assets on which chargeable gains were deferred. The gain chargeable (insofar as it has not already been charged under this provision, or under (i) above) is the proportion which the deferred gain on the assets disposed of bears to the total deferred gain on assets held immediately before the disposal.

The following disposals are disregarded.

- For the purposes of (i) above, intra-group transfers within *TCGA 1992, s 171* (see **26.3** GROUPS OF COMPANIES). A charge will arise when a subsequent group company makes a disposal outside the group.
- For the purposes of (i) above, securities transferred by a transferor as part of the process of a merger to which *TCGA 1992, s 140E* applies (see **43.14** below). In relation to a subsequent disposal of the shares or disposal by the transferee company of assets within (ii) above, the transferee is treated as if it were the transferor company.
- For the purposes of (i) above, securities transferred by a transferor company as part of the process of the transfer of a business to which **43.12** or **43.13** below applies. In relation to a subsequent disposal of the securities or disposal by the transferee company of assets within (ii) above, the transferee is treated as if it were the transferor company.
- For the purposes of (ii) above, intra-group transfers which would be within *TCGA 1992, s 171* if for those purposes a group included (without qualification) non-UK resident companies. A charge will arise when a subsequent group company makes a disposal outside the group.

A claim under *TCGA 1992, s 140C* (transfer or division of non-UK business between different EC member states; see **43.13** below) precludes a claim under the above.

[*TCGA 1992, s 140, Sch 4 paras A1, 4(5)*].

Transfers, divisions and mergers within the European Union

Effect of Brexit

[43.11] The reliefs at **43.12** to **43.15** below give effect in UK law to the EU Mergers Directive *2009/133/EC*. After the end of the Brexit implementation period, i.e. after IP completion day (11pm on 31 December 2020), the Directive does not apply to the UK. *SI 2019 No 689, Reg 6*, however, provides for the retention of the reliefs as they apply to UK corporation tax. The effect of a transfer, division or merger in the home state of the companies involved (where that is not the UK) will depend on the tax laws of that state and any double tax treaties.

For the purposes of the reliefs a '*relevant state*' is an EU member state or, after IP completion day, the UK or an EU member state. [*TCGA 1992, s 140L(1)(ba); SI 2019 No 689, Regs 1, 6(12); European Union (Withdrawal Agreement) Act 2020, Sch 5 para 1(1)*].

Transfer or division of UK business between companies in different EC member states

[43.12] The following reliefs apply to transfers or divisions of UK businesses between companies resident in different relevant states (see **43.11** above).

Transfer of UK business

A special relief may be claimed where a company resident in one relevant state transfers the whole or part of a business carried on by it in the UK to a company resident in another relevant state wholly in exchange for shares or debentures in the latter company, provided that the further conditions below are satisfied.

A company is regarded as resident in a relevant state under the laws of which it is chargeable to tax because it is regarded as so resident (unless it is regarded under DOUBLE TAX RELIEF (**20.2**) arrangements entered into by the relevant state as resident in a territory not within any of the relevant states).

Division of UK business

The relief may also be claimed where a company resident in one relevant state transfers part of its business to one or more companies at least one of which is resident in another relevant state. The part of the transferor's business which is transferred must be carried on by the transferor in the UK and the transferor must continue to carry on a business after the transfer.

The transfer must be made in exchange for the issue of shares in or debentures of each transferee to the holders of shares in or debentures of the transferor, except where, and to the extent that, a transferee is prevented from meeting this requirement by reason only of *Companies Act 2006, s 658* (rule against limited company acquiring its own shares) or a corresponding provision in another member state.

The further conditions below must also be satisfied.

Further conditions

A claim for relief must be made by both the transferor and the transferee (or each of the transferees). The anti-avoidance provision below must not apply, and either:

(i) if the transferee company is, or each of the transferee companies are, non-UK resident immediately after the transfer, any chargeable gain accruing to it, or them, on a disposal of the assets included in the transfer would form part of its, or their, corporation tax profits under *TCGA 1992, s 2B(3)*; or
(ii) if it is, or they are, UK resident at that time, none of the assets included in the transfer is exempt from UK tax on disposal under double tax relief arrangements.

Effect of relief

Any assets included in the transfer are treated for the purposes of corporation tax on chargeable gains as transferred for a no gain/no loss consideration, and *TCGA 1992, s 25(3)* (deemed disposal by non-resident on ceasing to trade in the UK through a permanent establishment or a branch or agency, see **43.3** above) does not apply to the assets by reason of the transfer.

In the case of a division of a UK business, where the transfer is not made wholly in exchange for the issue of shares in or debentures of each transferee, neither *TCGA 1992, s 24* (deemed disposal where asset lost, destroyed or becoming of negligible value — see **16.4** COMPUTATION OF GAINS AND LOSSES and **38.10** LOSSES) nor *TCGA 1992, s 122* (capital distributions — see **57.11** SHARES AND SECURITIES) apply to the transfer.

Also in the case of a division of a UK business, where the transferor and transferee (or each of the transferees) are all resident in relevant states, but are not all resident in the same state, the transfer of assets is treated as if it were a scheme of reconstruction within *TCGA 1992, s 136* (see **57.7** SHARES AND SECURITIES) if it would not otherwise be so treated. Where *s 136* applies as a result of this provision, the anti-avoidance provision at *s 136(6)* does not apply (and neither does *s 137* (restrictions on company reconstructions — see **4.16** ANTI-AVOIDANCE)).

Anti-avoidance

The above provisions do not apply unless the transfer is effected for *bona fide* commercial reasons and not as part of a scheme or arrangement a main purpose of which is avoidance of income, corporation or capital gains taxes. Advance clearance may be obtained from HMRC on the application of the companies, to the same address and subject to the same conditions and appeal procedures as apply to clearances under *TCGA 1992, s 138* (see **4.16** ANTI-AVOIDANCE).

[*TCGA 1992, ss 140A, 140B, 140DA, 140L(2); SI 2019 No 689, Regs 1, 6(2)(4)(12); European Union (Withdrawal Agreement) Act 2020, Sch 5 para 1(1)*].

See also **53.9** ROLLOVER RELIEF.

Transfer or division of non-UK business between companies in different EC member states

[43.13] The following reliefs apply to the transfer or division of a non-UK business between companies in different relevant states (see **43.11** above).

Transfer of non-UK business

Special provisions apply, on a claim, where a company resident in the UK transfers to a company resident in another relevant state the whole or part of a business carried on by the UK company immediately before the transfer through a permanent establishment in a relevant state other than the UK. The transfer must be wholly or partly in exchange for shares or debentures in the non-UK transferee company and the further conditions below must be satisfied.

A company is not regarded as resident in the UK if it were regarded under any DOUBLE TAX RELIEF (20.2) arrangements to which the UK is a party as resident in a territory not within any of the relevant states. A company is regarded as resident in another relevant state under the laws of which it is chargeable to tax because it is regarded as so resident (unless it is regarded under a double tax relief arrangement entered into by the relevant state as resident in a territory not within any of the relevant states).

Division of non-UK business

The provisions may also apply where a company resident in the UK transfers part of its business to one or more companies at least one of which is resident in another relevant state other than the UK. The part of the transferor's business which is transferred must be carried on by the transferor immediately before the transfer in a relevant state other than the UK through a permanent establishment and the transferor must continue to carry on a business after the transfer.

The transfer must be made in exchange for the issue of shares in or debentures of each transferee to the holders of shares in or debentures of the transferor, except where, and to the extent that, a transferee is prevented from meeting this requirement by reason only of *Companies Act 2006, s 658* (rule against limited company acquiring its own shares) or a corresponding provision in another relevant state.

The further conditions below must also be satisfied.

Further conditions

The transfer must include all the UK company's assets used in the business or part (with the possible exception of cash) and the anti-avoidance provision below must be satisfied. The aggregate of the chargeable gains accruing to the UK company on the transfer must exceed the aggregate of the allowable losses so accruing.

The UK company must make a claim for the provisions to apply. No claim may, however, be made where a claim is made under *TCGA 1992, s 140* at **43.10** above in relation to the same transfer.

Effect of provisions

The transfer is treated as giving rise to a single chargeable gain of the excess of the aggregate of the chargeable gains accruing to the UK company on the transfer over the aggregate of the allowable losses so accruing.

In the case of a division of a non-UK business, where the transferor and transferee (or each of the transferees) are all resident in relevant states, but are not all resident in the same state, the transfer of assets is treated as if it were a scheme of reconstruction within *TCGA 1992, s 136* (see **57.7** SHARES AND SECURITIES) if it would not otherwise be so treated. Where *s 136* applies as a result of this provision, the anti-avoidance provision at *s 136(6)* does not apply (and neither does *s 137* (restrictions on company reconstructions — see **4.16** ANTI-AVOIDANCE)).

Anti-avoidance

The transfer must be effected for *bona fide* commercial reasons and not as part of a scheme or arrangement a main purpose of which is avoidance of income, corporation or capital gains taxes. Advance clearance may be obtained from HMRC on the application of the UK company, to the same address and subject to the same conditions and appeal procedures as apply to clearances under *TCGA 1992, s 138* (see **4.16** ANTI-AVOIDANCE).

[*TCGA 1992, ss 140C, 140D, 140DA, 140L; SI 2019 No 689, Regs 1, 6(3)(4)(12); European Union (Withdrawal Agreement) Act 2020, Sch 5 para 1(1)*].

Double tax relief

Where the above provisions apply, where gains accruing to the UK company would have been chargeable to tax under the law of the member state in which the trade was carried on immediately before the transfer but for the Mergers Directive, the amount of tax is treated for double tax relief purposes as tax paid in that other member state. In calculating the amount of the tax so treated it is assumed that, so far as permitted under the law of the member state, any losses arising on the transfer are set against the gains, and that the UK company claims any available reliefs.

These provisions apply also where *TCGA 1992, s 140F* (European cross-border merger: assets not left within UK tax charge — see **43.14** below) applies.

[*TIOPA 2010, s 122*].

European cross-border mergers

[43.14] The following provisions apply to:

(a) (before Brexit IP completion day (11pm on 31 December 2020)) the formation of an SE (see **14.16** COMPANIES) by the merger of two or more companies in accordance with *Council Regulation (EC) No 2157/2001, Arts 2(1), 17(2)*;
(b) (before Brexit IP completion day) the formation of an SCE (see **14.17** COMPANIES) by the merger of two or more 'co-operative societies', at least one of which is a registered society within *Co-operative and Community Benefit Societies Act 2014* or NI equivalent, in accordance with *Council Regulation (EC) No 1435/2003*;
(c) a merger effected by the transfer by one or more companies or co-operative societies of all their assets and liabilities to a single existing company or co-operative society; and
(d) a merger effected by the transfer by two or more companies of all their assets to a single new company (which is not an SE or SCE) in exchange for the issue by the transferee company of shares or debentures to each person holding shares in or debentures of a transferee company.

From Brexit IP completion day, no new SEs or SCEs can be formed in the UK.

For the purposes of (b) and (c) above, a '*co-operative society*' is a registered society within *Co-operative and Community Benefit Societies Act 2014* or NI equivalent (previously, a society registered under the *Industrial and Provident Societies Act 1965*) or a similar society established under the law of a relevant state (see **43.11** above) other than the UK.

Each of the merging companies or co-operative societies must be resident in a relevant state but they must not all be resident in the same state. A company resident in a relevant state for this purpose if it is within a charge to tax under the law of the State as being resident for that purpose and it is not regarded, for the purposes of any DOUBLE TAX RELIEF (**20**) arrangements to which the state is a party, as resident in a territory not within a relevant state.

Treatment of securities issued on merger

If it does not constitute or form part of a scheme of reconstruction within the meaning of *TCGA 1992, s 136* (see **57.7** SHARES AND SECURITIES), the merger is nevertheless treated as if it were a scheme of reconstruction for the purposes of that section, but the anti-avoidance provision at *section 136(6)* does not apply (and neither does *s 137* (restrictions on company reconstructions — see **4.16** ANTI-AVOIDANCE)). See, however, the anti-avoidance provision below.

Assets left within UK tax charge

If:

(i) *TCGA 1992, s 139* (reconstruction involving transfer of business — see **14.12** COMPANIES) does not apply to the merger;

(ii) where the merger is within (a), (b) or (c) above, the transfer of assets and liabilities is made in exchange for the issue of shares in or debentures of the transferee to the holders of shares in or debentures of a transferor, except where, and to the extent that, the transferee is prevented from meeting this requirement by reason only of *Companies Act 2006, s 658* (rule against limited company acquiring its own shares) or a corresponding provision in another relevant state; and

(iii) where the merger is within (d) above, in the course of the merger each transferor ceases to exist without being in liquidation (within the meaning of *Insolvency Act 1986, s 247*),

then any 'qualifying transferred assets' are treated for chargeable gains purposes as acquired by the transferee (i.e. the SE, SCE or merged company) for a consideration resulting in neither gain nor loss for the transferor company or co-operative society.

For this purpose, an asset transferred to the transferee as part of the merger process is a '*qualifying transferred asset*' if:

- either the transferor was resident in the UK at the time of the transfer or any gain accruing on disposal of the asset immediately before that time would have been a chargeable gain forming part of the transferor's chargeable profits by virtue of *TCGA 1992, s 2B(3)*); trade carried on via UK permanent establishment — see **43.3** above); and
- either the transferee is resident in the UK at the time of the transfer or any gain accruing to it on disposal of the asset immediately after the transfer would have been a chargeable gain forming part of its chargeable profits by virtue of *TCGA 1992, s 2B(3)*.

Where the condition at (ii) above applies, but the transfer is not made wholly in exchange for the issue of shares in or debentures of each transferee, neither *TCGA 1992, s 24* (deemed disposal where asset lost, destroyed or becoming of negligible value — see **16.4** COMPUTATION OF GAINS AND LOSSES and **38.10** LOSSES) nor *TCGA 1992, s 122* (capital distributions — see **57.11** SHARES AND SECURITIES) apply to the transfer.

Assets not left within UK tax charge

If:

- in the course of the merger a company or co-operative society resident in the UK (company A) transfers to a company or co-operative society resident in another member state all the assets and liabilities relating to a business carried on by company A in a member state other than the UK through a permanent establishment;
- the aggregate chargeable gains accruing to company A on the transfer exceed the aggregate allowable losses;
- where the merger is within (a), (b) or (c) above, the transfer of assets and liabilities is made in exchange for the issue of shares in or debentures of the transferee to the holders of shares in or debentures of a transferor, except where, and to the extent that, the transferee is prevented from meeting this requirement by reason only of *Companies Act 2006, s 658* or *Companies Act 1985, s 143* (rule against limited company acquiring its own shares) or a corresponding provision in another member state; and
- where the merger is within (c) or (d) above, in the course of the merger each transferor ceases to exist without being in liquidation (within *Insolvency Act 1986, s 247*),

the allowable losses are treated as set off against the chargeable gains and the transfer is treated as giving rise to a single chargeable gain equal to the excess. See **43.13** above for special double tax relief provisions applying where this provision applies.

Anti-avoidance

The above provisions do not apply if the merger is not effected for *bona fide* commercial reasons or if it forms part of a scheme or arrangements of which the main purpose, or one of the main purposes, is avoiding liability to UK tax. The advance clearance provisions of *TCGA 1992, s 138* (see **4.16** ANTI-AVOIDANCE) apply, with any necessary modifications, for this purpose as they apply for the purposes of *TCGA 1992, s 137*.

Subsidiary merging with parent

Where a merger is effected by the transfer by a company or all its assets and liabilities to a single company which holds the whole of its ordinary share capital and *TCGA 1992, s 139* does not apply, then, if, in the course of the merger, the transferor ceases to exist without being in liquidation, neither *TCGA 1992, s 24* nor *TCGA 1992, s 122* apply to the transfer.

[*TCGA 1992, ss 140E–140GA, 140L; SI 2019 No 689, Regs 1, 6(5)–(8)(12); European Union (Withdrawal Agreement) Act 2020, Sch 5 para 1(1)*].

Held-over gains

For the effect of a cross-border merger on various hold-over reliefs, see **43.10** above, **48.4** QUALIFYING CORPORATE BONDS and **53.9** ROLLOVER RELIEF.

Transparent entities — disapplication of reliefs

[43.15] The following provisions operate to disapply certain of the tax reliefs enacted to comply with the European Mergers Directive (*2009/133/EC*) where one of the parties to the transaction is a 'transparent entity'. In some cases, the disapplication of the reliefs is accompanied by a notional tax credit for the shareholder or interest holder in the transparent entity.

A '*transparent entity*' for this purpose is an entity resident in a relevant state (see **43.11** above) other than the UK which is listed as a company in Part A of Annex I to the Mergers Directive but which does not have an 'ordinary share capital' (within *CTA 2010, s 1119*) and, if it were UK-resident, would not be capable of being a company within the meaning of *Companies Act 2006*.

Except where the context requires otherwise, a '*company*' is, for the purposes of the provisions, an entity listed as a company in the Annex to the Mergers Directive. A company is regarded as resident in another relevant state under the laws of which it is chargeable to tax because it is regarded as so resident (unless it is regarded under a double tax relief arrangement entered into by the relevant state as resident in a territory not within any of the relevant states).

[*TCGA 1992, s 140L; SI 2019 No 689, Regs 1, 6(12); European Union (Withdrawal Agreement) Act 2020, Sch 5 para 1(1)*].

Share exchanges

Where a company (company B) issues shares or debentures to a person in exchange for shares in or debentures of another company (company A) and either of the companies is a transparent entity, the share exchange provisions at *TCGA 1992, s 135* (see **57.5** SHARES AND SECURITIES) are disapplied.

Where the exchange otherwise meets the conditions for *TCGA 1992, s 135* to apply, any tax which would, but for the Mergers Directive, have been chargeable on a gain accruing to a holder of shares in or debentures of company A on the exchange under the law of a relevant state other than the UK is treated, for the purposes of DOUBLE TAX RELIEF (**20**), as if it had been so chargeable. This notional tax is calculated on the basis that, so far as permitted under the law of the relevant state, losses arising on the exchange are set against gains arising from the exchange and that any relief available to company A under that law has been claimed.

[*TCGA 1992, s 140H; SI 2019 No 689, Regs 1, 6(9); European Union (Withdrawal Agreement) Act 2020, Sch 5 para 1(1)*].

Division of business or transfer of assets

Where:

- there is a transfer of a business, or part of a business, of a kind mentioned in *TCGA 1992, s 140A(1)* or *(1A)* (see **43.12** above) (or which would be of such a kind if the business or part transferred were carried on by the transferor in the UK and either **43.12**(i) or (ii) above were satisfied in relation to the transferee or each of the transferees), and

- either the transferor or transferee, or one of the transferees, is a transparent entity,

then, if the transferor is the transparent entity, neither *section 140A* nor *TCGA 1992, s 140DA* (transfer of assets treated as scheme of reconstruction — see **43.12** above) apply to the transfer. If a transferee is the transparent entity, *section 140DA* does not apply to the transfer to it.

Any tax which would, but for the Mergers Directive, have been chargeable on a 'transfer gain' under the law of a relevant state other than the UK is treated, for the purposes of DOUBLE TAX RELIEF (**20**), as if it had been so chargeable. This notional tax is calculated on the basis that, so far as permitted under the law of the relevant state, losses arising on the transfer are set against gains arising from the transfer and that any relief available under that law has been claimed. A '*transfer gain*' for this purpose is a gain accruing to a transparent entity (or which would be treated as accruing to such an entity were it not transparent) by reason of the transfer of assets by the transparent entity to the transferee.

[*TCGA 1992, s 140I; SI 2019 No 689, Regs 1, 6(10); European Union (Withdrawal Agreement) Act 2020, Sch 5 para 1(1)*].

Cross-border merger

Where there is a merger of a kind within **43.14**(a)–(d) above which meets the conditions at **43.14**(i)–(iii) and one or more of the merging companies is a transparent entity:

- if the assets and liabilities of a transparent entity are transferred to another company on the merger, *TCGA 1992, s 140E* (assets left within charge to UK tax — see **43.14** above) and *TCGA 1992, s 140G* (treatment of securities issued on merger — see **43.14** above) do not apply; and
- if the assets and liabilities of one or more companies are transferred to a transparent entity on the merger, *TCGA 1992, s 140G* does not apply.

Any tax which would, but for the Mergers Directive, have been chargeable on a 'merger gain' under the law of a relevant state other than the UK is treated, for the purposes of DOUBLE TAX RELIEF (**20**), as if it had been so chargeable. This notional tax is calculated on the basis that, so far as permitted under the law of the relevant state, losses arising on the merger are set against gains arising from the merger and that any relief available under that law has been claimed. A '*merger gain*' for this purpose is a gain accruing to a transparent entity (or which would be treated as accruing to such an entity were it not transparent) by reason of the transfer of assets by the transparent entity on the merger.

[*TCGA 1992, s 140J; SI 2019 No 689, Regs 1, 6(11); European Union (Withdrawal Agreement) Act 2020, Sch 5 para 1(1)*].

Taxation of transparent entity after merger or division

Where:

(i) a transparent entity (company A) is a transferee for the purposes of *TCGA 1992, s 140A(1A)* (division of UK business — see **43.12** above) or *TCGA 1992, s 140E* (cross-border merger: assets left within charge to UK tax — see **43.14** above);

(ii) a person ('X') with an interest in company A was or is also a shareholder or debenture holder of a company (company B);

(iii) X became entitled to an interest, or an increased interest, in company A in exchange for a disposal of shares in, or debenture of, company B on a merger to which *TCGA 1992, s 140E* applied or on a transfer to which *TCGA 1992, s 140(1A)* applied;

(iv) a chargeable gain accrued to X on the disposal of shares or debentures of company B;

(v) in calculating that gain account was taken of the value of an asset of company B; and

(vi) X makes a disposal of his interest in the asset,

then, in calculating the gain on the disposal in (vi) above, the amount allowed as the acquisition cost in relation to the interest, or proportion of the interest, which X acquired on the merger or transfer is the amount to be taken into account in computing the gain on the disposal of his shares in, or debentures of, company B.

References above to an interest in company A include an interest in the assets of, or shares in or debentures of, company A.

[*TCGA 1992, s 140K*].

Company ceasing to be UK resident etc.

[43.16] If, at any time ('*the relevant time*'), a company ceases to be resident in the UK and does not cease to exist:

(a) it is deemed to dispose of immediately before the relevant time, and immediately reacquire, all its 'assets' at market value at that time; and

(b) ROLLOVER RELIEF (53) under *TCGA 1992, s 152* is not subsequently available by reference to disposals of old assets made before that time and acquisitions of new assets after that time.

If at any later time the company carries on a trade in the UK through a permanent establishment (as defined in **43.3** above), the foregoing does not apply:

(i) for (a) above, to any assets which, immediately after the relevant time; or

(ii) for (b) above, to any new assets which, after the relevant time,

are situated in the UK and are used in or for a trade, or are used or held for the permanent establishment. '*Assets*' include various assets and rights relating to exploration or exploitation activities in the UK or a designated area of the sea, within *TCGA 1992, s 276* in **43.18** below. [*TCGA 1992, s 185*].

The excess of gains over losses arising on the foreign assets included in the deemed disposal is treated as a single chargeable gain not accruing to the company on the disposal. An equal amount ('*the postponed gain*') is instead treated as follows.

If within six years after the relevant time the company disposes of any assets (the '*relevant assets*') capital gains on which were taken into account in arriving at the postponed gain, a chargeable gain equal to the whole, or 'the appropriate proportion', of the postponed gain, so far as this has not already been treated as a chargeable gain under these provisions, is deemed to accrue to the principal company. '*The appropriate proportion*' is the proportion which the chargeable gain taken into account in arriving at the postponed gain in respect of the part of the relevant assets disposed of bears to the aggregate of the chargeable gains so taken into account in respect of the relevant assets held immediately before the time of the disposal.

If at any time:

(I) the company ceases to be a 75% subsidiary of the principal company on a disposal by the principal company of ordinary shares in it; or
(II) after the company otherwise ceases to be a 75% subsidiary, the principal company disposes of ordinary shares in it; or
(III) the principal company ceases to be resident in the UK,

a chargeable gain, equal to so much of the postponed gain as has not previously been charged under these provisions, is deemed to arise to the principal company. Payment of tax on the deemed gain can itself be further postponed by way of a CT exit charge payment plan (see **45.9** PAYMENT OF TAX).

If any part of the postponed gain becomes chargeable, and the subsidiary has unrelieved capital losses, the companies can elect within two years for part or all of the losses to be set against the amount chargeable.

For the purposes of the above provisions a company is a '*75% subsidiary*' of another company if and so long as not less than 75% of its ordinary share capital is owned *directly* by that other company.

The facility to postpone a charge under *TCGA 1992, s 185* under this provision is no longer available where a company ceases to be UK-resident on or after 1 January 2020. Payment of the charge can, however, still be postponed by way of a CT exit charge payment plan.

[*TCGA 1992, s 187*].

Unless a company so elects (within two years after ceasing to be UK-resident), neither a gain nor a loss accrue on the deemed disposal of an interest in UK land (as defined at **35.23** LAND). For deemed disposals before 6 April 2019, this rule applied if the gain or loss on the deemed disposal would have been an NRCGT gain or loss on the assumption that the disposal was a non-resident CGT disposal (see **35.31** LAND). In either case, the gain or loss that would have accrued on the deemed disposal is treated as accruing at the time of any subsequent disposal of the interest, in addition to any gain or loss which actually accrues. [*TCGA 1992, s 187B*].

CT exit charge payment plans

See **45.9** PAYMENT OF TAX for the availability of CT exit charge payment plans under which a company can defer the payment of tax in respect of a number of exit charge provisions, including the above provisions.

Compliance

[43.17] Before a company ceases to be resident in the UK, it must give HMRC:

(a) notice of its intention to cease to be resident, specifying the time when it intends to do so;
(b) a statement of the amount of tax which it considers payable for periods beginning before that time; and
(c) particulars of the arrangements which it proposes to make to secure the payment of that tax (which may include a proposal to enter into an exit charge payment plan (see **43.16** above).

Except to the extent that payment of that tax is to be secured by the company entering into an exit charge payment plan, the company must also make arrangements to secure the payment of the tax; and the arrangements must be approved by HMRC.

References to tax payable are not defined but include specified liabilities such as certain income tax payments, sub-contractors' deductions and amounts payable under *TMA 1970, s 77C* (territorial extension of charge of tax as in **43.18** below). Interest on unpaid tax is included in certain circumstances.

Any question as to the amount of tax payable is to be determined by the Tribunal. If any information provided by the company does not fully and accurately disclose all the material facts and considerations, any resulting approval is void.

A person who is, or is deemed to be, involved in a failure to comply with the foregoing provisions is liable to a penalty not exceeding the amount of unpaid tax for periods beginning before the failure occurred.

Any tax in respect of accounting periods beginning before the cessation of UK residence which is still unpaid six months after the time when it became payable can (see also **43.16** above), within three years of final determination of the tax due, be recovered from a person who is, or in the twelve months before the cessation of UK residence was, a member of the same group of companies (as in *TCGA 1992, s 170* (see **26.2** GROUPS OF COMPANIES) but substituting 51 per cent subsidiary for '75 per cent subsidiary') or a controlling director (as defined). Where the tax is subject to a CT exit charge payment plan, it can be recovered in this way within three years of the later of the first day after the twelve months following the migration accounting period and the date on which the tax is payable under the plan.

[*TMA 1970, ss 109B–109F*].

Guidance on the procedure to be followed under these provisions is given in HMRC Statement of Practice SP 2/90. In particular, notice under (a) above should be sent by email to clearances.companymigration@hmrc.gov.uk.

Exploration and exploitation rights to territorial sea-bed and continental shelf

[43.18] Any gains accruing on the disposal of 'exploration or exploitation rights' are treated for the purposes of *TCGA 1992* as gains accruing on the disposal of assets situated in the UK. For this and all other purposes of the taxation of chargeable gains, the territorial sea of the UK is deemed to be part of the UK. (Under the *Territorial Sea Act 1987, s 1*, the breadth of the territorial sea adjacent to the UK is 12 nautical miles, a nautical mile being approximately 1,852 metres.)

Gains accruing on the disposal of 'exploration or exploitation assets' which are situated in a 'designated area', or 'unquoted shares' (i.e. not listed on a recognised stock exchange — see **57.27** SHARES AND SECURITIES) deriving their value or the greater part of their value directly or indirectly from exploration or exploitation assets situated in the UK or a designated area or from such assets and exploration or exploitation rights taken together, are treated for the purposes of *TCGA 1992* as gains accruing on the disposal of assets situated in the UK. Gains accruing to a person not resident in the UK on the disposal of such rights or of such assets (the latter including for this purpose unquoted shares of the description above) are treated for the same purposes as gains accruing on the disposal of assets used for the purposes of a trade carried on by that person in the UK through a branch or agency or, in the case of a non-resident company, through a permanent establishment (for which see **43.3** above).

If exploration or exploitation rights or exploration or exploitation assets (the latter including for this purpose unquoted shares of the description above) are disposed of by a company resident in an overseas territory to either a company resident in the same territory or a UK-resident company, or by one UK-resident company to another, the provisions at **26.3**, **26.4**, **26.7**, **26.10** GROUPS OF COMPANIES apply, with appropriate modifications.

Definitions

'*Exploration or exploitation rights*' means rights to assets to be produced by 'exploration or exploitation activities' or to interests in or to the benefit of such assets. '*Exploration or exploitation activities*' means activities carried on in connection with the exploration or exploitation of so much of the seabed and subsoil and their natural resources as is situated in the UK or a designated area.

References in the above to the disposal of exploration or exploitation rights include references to the disposal of shares deriving their value or the greater part of their value directly or indirectly from such rights, other than shares listed on a recognised stock exchange. '*Shares*' includes stock and any security as defined in *CTA 2010, s 1117(1)*. '*Designated area*' means an area designated by Order in Council under the *Continental Shelf Act 1964, s 1(7)*.

For the above purposes, an asset disposed of is an '*exploration or exploitation asset*' if either:

(a) it is not a mobile asset and it is being or has at some time been used in connection with exploration or exploitation activities carried on in the UK or a designated area; or
(b) it is a mobile asset which has at some time been used in connection with exploration or exploitation activities so carried on and is dedicated to an oil field in which the person making the disposal, or a person connected with him, is or has been a participator;

and expressions used in (a) and (b) above have the same meanings there as if those paragraphs were included in *Oil Taxation Act 1975, Pt I*.

[*TCGA 1992, s 276*].

Compliance

There are comprehensive enforcement powers in relation to tax assessed by virtue of *TCGA 1992, s 276* above. In particular, unpaid tax so assessed on an overseas resident person may be recovered together with interest thereon from the holder of a licence granted under *Petroleum Act 1998* in respect of chargeable gains accruing on the disposal of exploration or exploitation rights connected with activities authorised, or carried on in connection with activities authorised, by the licence. An overseas resident liable to charge and who HMRC are satisfied will meet his obligations under the *Taxes Acts* may apply for a certificate to be issued to the licence holder exempting him (subject to detailed conditions) from a charge on the default of the applicant. [*TMA 1970, ss 77B–77K*].

Asset ceasing to be chargeable

Where an 'exploration or exploitation asset' (for this purpose, an asset used in connection with 'exploration or exploitation activities' carried on in the UK or a 'designated area', both expressions having the same meanings as in *TCGA 1992, s 276* above) ceases to be 'chargeable' in relation to a person by virtue of ceasing to be 'dedicated to an oil field' in which he, or a person connected with him, is or has been a 'participator' (these last two expressions having the same meanings as in *Oil Taxation Act 1975, Pt I*), he is deemed for all purposes of *TCGA 1992* to have disposed of the asset immediately before the time when it ceased to be so dedicated, and immediately to have reacquired it, at its market value at that time.

An asset is a '*chargeable*' asset at any time in relation to a person if, were it to be disposed of at that time, any chargeable gains accruing to him on the disposal would be brought into charge for capital gains tax or corporation tax by virtue of *TCGA 1992, s 1A(3)(a)* or *2B(3)* respectively.

Trade ceasing to be carried on through branch etc.

A similar deemed disposal and acquisition takes place where a person who is not resident in the UK for a tax year (as determined at **1.2** INTRODUCTION) ceases to carry on a trade through a branch or agency, or, in the case of a non-resident company through a permanent establishment, in respect of any exploration or exploitation asset, other than a mobile asset, used in or for the purposes of the trade at or before the time of the deemed disposal. No such deemed disposal and reacquisition takes place if, immediately after the cessation of the trade carried on through the UK branch or agency, the asset is used in or for the purposes of exploration or exploitation activities carried on by him in the UK or a designated area. However, on a person ceasing so to use the asset, there will be a deemed disposal and reacquisition.

[*TCGA 1992, s 199*].

As regards leasing of mobile drilling rigs and other assets by overseas resident companies, see HMRC Statement of Practice SP 6/84.

See also **51.30** RESIDENCE AND DOMICILE for the territorial extent of the UK.

European and UK Economic Interest Groupings

[43.19] There are special provisions governing the tax treatment of European Economic Interest Groupings (EEIGs), wherever registered, within *EEC Council Regulation No 2137/85* dated 25 July 1985. Following Brexit, from IP completion day (11pm on 31 December 2020), the ability to form an EEIG within the UK has been removed. Any EEIGs that were registered in the UK immediately before IP completion day were automatically converted into UK Economic Interest Groupings (UKEIGs). The UKEIG structure is expected to be a temporary structure, allowing entities more time to take more appropriate action, rather than a long term corporate choice. Without the European features, it is not believed that the structure will be an attractive long term corporate vehicle.

For the purposes of charging tax in respect of chargeable gains and subject to exceptions as below, an EEIG or UKEIG is regarded as acting as the agent of its members. Its activities are regarded for such purposes as those of its members acting jointly, each member being regarded as having a share of its property, rights and liabilities. Where the grouping carries on a trade or profession, the members are regarded for the purposes of tax on gains as carrying on that trade or profession in partnership. A person is regarded as acquiring or disposing of a share of the grouping's assets not only where there is an acquisition or disposal by it while he is a member but also where he becomes or ceases to be a member or there is a change in his share of its property. A member's share in a grouping's property, rights or liabilities is that determined under the contract establishing the grouping or, if there is no provision determining such shares, it will correspond to the profit share to which he is entitled under the provisions of the contract (or if the contract makes no such provision, members are regarded as having equal shares).

[*TMA 1970, ss 12A, 98B; TCGA 1992, s 285A; CTA 2010, s 990; SI 2019 No 689, Regs 1, 2, 6(15), 17(11); European Union (Withdrawal Agreement) Act 2020 Sch 5 para 1(1)*].

See also **52.23** RETURNS, and **46.6, 46.10** PENALTIES as regards non-compliance.

Collection of tax

[43.20] Although tax is legally assessable by notice served abroad, there can be difficulties in collection. See, however, **28.2**(c) **HMRC** — CONFIDENTIALITY OF INFORMATION for agreements for mutual assistance in the collection of taxes. See also **43.4** above for the assessment of UK resident agents of overseas resident traders and **43.17** above for arrangements required to secure payment of tax by a company ceasing to be UK resident or by a non-UK resident company. See also **42.2** OFFSHORE SETTLEMENTS for the arrangements where trustees become non-resident.

Key points concerning overseas matters

[43.21] Points to consider are as follows.

- A person is generally chargeable to capital gains tax on gains accruing in a tax year in which they are resident in the UK. Persons carrying on a trade in the UK through a branch or agency, and companies carrying on a trade in the UK through a permanent establishment, are also charged to tax on gains on disposal of trade-related assets situated in the UK. Non-UK residents are also taxable in respect of gains on direct or indirect disposals of UK land.
- Non-UK domiciled individuals can elect for the remittance basis to apply to gains on disposal of assets situated abroad.
- Gains on assets acquired by an individual whilst UK resident and disposed of whilst not UK resident for less than five years will be charged in the tax year when UK residence is resumed.
- Gains of a company which is not resident in the UK, and which would be a close company if UK resident, can be charged on UK resident participators.
- If a UK-resident settlement or company becomes non-resident, there is a deemed disposal and reacquisition of assets, which can give rise to an 'exit charge'.
- Where a gain is potentially taxable both in the UK and in another country, the terms of any double taxation agreement should always be consulted to determine which country has the taxing rights.

44

Partnerships

Cross-references. See **43.19** OVERSEAS MATTERS for UK and European Economic Interest Groupings deemed to carry on a trade in partnership; **53** ROLLOVER RELIEF and **55** SELF-ASSESSMENT.

Simon's Taxes. See **B7.406–B7.409**.

Introduction to partnerships

[44.1] A partnership is defined in *Partnership Act 1890, s 1* as 'the relation which subsists between persons carrying on a business in common with a view of profit'. This does not include purely capital transactions, e.g. the sale of a house by joint tenants.

An English partnership or firm is not a legal entity distinct from the partners themselves, but a collection of separate persons (which may be companies or individuals). In Scotland a firm is a legal person, but in general this does not affect the application of the *Taxes Acts*. A partnership cannot be a company for the purposes of *TCGA 1992*. [*TCGA 1992, s 288(1)*]. See **44.17** below as regards limited liability partnerships.

The taxation of partnership gains is based on a body of HMRC practice superimposed on the general capital gains rules. There are few specific references to partnerships in the capital gains legislation. For a useful codification of HMRC practice, reference should be made to HMRC Statements of Practice SP D12 (revised most recently in September 2015), SP 1/79 and SP 1/89 on which much of this chapter is based. The Statements of Practice are supplemented by the HMRC Capital Gains Manual at CG27000–28500.

Where a trade is carried on in partnership, tax is charged on each partner separately in respect of chargeable gains on the disposal of partnership assets. Each partner is treated as owning a fractional share of each asset. Consequently, a transfer of an asset to a partnership as a capital contribution by a partner is treated as a part disposal, and changes in sharing ratios result in the disposal or acquisition of a share in partnership assets by each partner as his share increases or decreases. A chargeable gain is likely to arise in such circumstances, however, only where assets have been revalued upwards in the partnership accounts or actual consideration is given for an increased share.

Special provisions apply to corporate partners and to limited liability partnerships.

For details of the requirement for partnership tax returns, see **52.18–52.20** RETURNS.

General rules

[44.2] Where two or more persons carry on a trade or business in partnership, tax is assessed and charged on them separately in respect of chargeable gains accruing to them on the disposal of any partnership assets. (The treatment of partnerships in Scotland as a legal person is ignored for this purpose.) Any partnership dealings are treated as dealings by the partners and not by the firm as such. [*TCGA 1992, s 59(1)(a)(b)*].

In general terms, it will be the residence and domicile circumstances of each partner (whether an individual or company) that will dictate the basis of charge. For example, an individual partner who is resident in the UK and domiciled there will be chargeable wherever partnership gains arise and whether remitted to the UK or not. An individual partner not resident in the UK would only be liable in respect of partnership assets connected with a UK branch or agency (see **43.3** OVERSEAS MATTERS) or on direct or indirect disposals of interests in UK land (see **35.23**, **35.24** LAND). However, it is specifically provided that, if, under a double tax agreement, any capital gains of a partnership which resides outside the UK or which carries on any trade, profession or business the control or management of which is situated outside the UK is relieved from tax in the UK, such relief is not to affect the liability of any UK resident partner's share of the capital gains. For this purpose, 'partner' includes any person entitled to a share of the partnership's capital gains. [*TCGA 1992, s 59(2)–(4)*].

Partners' fractional shares

[44.3] Each partner is regarded as owning a fractional share of each asset, which is calculated by reference to their asset-surplus-sharing ratio. Where no such ratio is specified, the share will follow the treatment in the accounts, subject to any external agreement. Failing that, regard will be had to the normal profit-sharing ratios. For appeals regarding apportionments of amounts etc., see 5 APPEALS and *White v Carline* (Sp C 33), [1995] SSCD 186.

The fraction is applied to the value of the total partnership interest in the asset disposed of, and no discount is allowed against market value for the size of an individual partner's share.

Expenditure on the acquisition of partnership assets will be allocated for capital gains tax purposes, in similar fashion to gains/losses, at the time of acquisition, subject to adjustment on any subsequent change in partnership sharing ratios.

(SP D12 introduction and sections 1, 2).

Examples

Each of the following partnerships disposes of its offices to outside parties at arm's length at a chargeable gain of £30,000. The gain is apportioned among the partners in the manner shown.

(a) *A & Co.* The partnership agreement states that each of the three partners shall be entitled to share equally in any surplus arising from assets disposed of by the partnership. Each partner is therefore treated as if he had made a gain of £10,000.

(b) *B & Co.* The three partners in B & Co have no formal agreement, but interest on capital contributed to the partnership is shown in the accounts at the same sum for each. The inference is that the capital has been equally contributed and can be equally withdrawn, so that the apportioned gain is £10,000 to each partner.

(c) *C & Co.* The three partners in C & Co, X, Y, and Z, have no formal agreement and the capital is shown in the accounts as a global sum. The profit-sharing ratio is 3:2:1, so that the apportioned gain is X–£15,000, Y–£10,000, and Z–£5,000.

A partner makes a disposal (or part disposal) of their fractional share of a partnership asset not only when the partnership disposes (or part disposes) of the asset as above but also when their share is extinguished (or reduced) for which see **44.6–44.11** below.

Transactions within the partnership

[44.4] Transactions within the partnership are not treated as made between CONNECTED PERSONS (17), provided they are pursuant to genuine commercial arrangements, unless the partners are otherwise connected. Market value will be substituted for actual consideration only if the consideration would have been different had the parties been at arm's length. Where market value is applied, the deemed disposal proceeds are treated in the same way as payments outside the accounts as in **44.11** below. (SP D12 sections 8.3, 8.4).

Contribution of assets to a partnership

[44.5] Where an asset is transferred to a partnership by means of a capital contribution by a partner, HMRC consider that the partner makes a part disposal of the asset equal to the fractional share that passes to the other partners. Where the market value rule does not apply, the consideration for the disposal is a proportion of the total consideration given by the partnership for the asset. The proportion is equal to the fractional share of the asset passing to the other partners. HMRC consider that a sum credited to the partner's capital account represents consideration for this purpose. Allowable costs are apportioned on a fractional basis as in **44.6** below.

(SP D12 section 5; HMRC Brief 3/2008).

Changes in sharing ratios

[44.6] Where changes occur in partnership sharing ratios (including partners joining or leaving the firm), each partner is treated as acquiring or disposing of part or the whole of a share in each of the partnership assets, insofar as their share increases or decreases.

Subject to (a) and (b) below, the disposal consideration of each chargeable asset is equal to the relevant fraction (i.e. the fractional share changing hands) of the current balance sheet value. In certain cases (where the partners' CGT base cost is equal to the balance sheet value), the disposal will be a *no gain/no loss disposal*. This is unlikely to be the case where, for example, the asset has been revalued in the partnership accounts, where a partner transferred the asset to the partnership for an amount that is not equivalent to the CGT base cost or where the partners' base costs were determined under *TCGA 1992, s 171* (see **26.3** GROUPS OF COMPANIES).

A partner whose share decreases will carry forward a smaller proportion of cost to set against any future disposal (including a disposal of one or more of the assets outside the partnership), and a partner whose share increases will carry forward a larger proportion of cost than before. An incoming partner will thereby take over a proportion of the cost of existing assets in accordance with his fractional entitlement. The *cost* of any part disposal under these provisions is calculated as a corresponding fraction of the total acquisition cost, and *not* by way of apportionment under *TCGA 1992, s 42* as in **16.5** COMPUTATION OF GAINS AND LOSSES.

(SP D12 section 4).

See the *example* at **44.8** below.

A different disposal consideration figure may have to be used in the following cases.

(a) Where a direct payment is made in connection with the change in sharing ratios (see **44.11** below).
(b) Where the change in sharing ratios results from a transaction made otherwise than at arm's length or made between CONNECTED PERSONS (**17**). The meaning of connected persons for these purposes is narrowed. See **44.4** above.

Re-basing to 1982 and indexation allowance (SP 1/89)

[44.7] HMRC have agreed that a disposal of a share of partnership assets which is treated under SP D12 section 4 above as on a no gain/no loss basis may be treated as if it were within the no gain/no loss provisions in **8.6** ASSETS HELD ON

31 MARCH **1982**. Such a disposal may also be treated as if it were a no gain/no loss disposal for the purposes of *TCGA 1992, s 36, Sch 4* (deferred charges — see **8.11** ASSETS HELD ON 31 MARCH **1982**).

Where such a disposal occurs, for capital gains tax (but not corporation tax) purposes, before 6 April 2008, the amount of the consideration is calculated on the assumption that an unindexed gain accrues to the transferor equal to the indexation allowance, so that after taking into account the indexation allowance due, neither a gain nor a loss accrues. Where under the above a partner is treated as having owned the asset on 31 March 1982 in relation to a disposal of all or part of his share of partnership assets, the indexation allowance on the disposal may be calculated as if he had acquired the share on 31 March 1982. A disposal of a share in a partnership asset (for capital gains tax (but not corporation tax) purposes, before 6 April 2008) which is treated under SP D12 section 4 above as on a no gain/no loss basis may be treated for the purposes of *TCGA 1992, s 55(5)(6)* as if it were a no gain/no loss disposal within those provisions (see **8.6** ASSETS HELD ON 31 MARCH **1982**). A special rule applies, however, where the share changed hands after 5 April 1985 (31 March 1985 in the case of an acquisition from a company) and before 6 April 1988: in these circumstances the indexation allowance is calculated by reference to the 31 March 1982 value *but* from the date of the last disposal of the share before 6 April 1988.

On a disposal after 5 April 2008 of an interest previously transferred on a no gain/no loss basis (whether under this provision or SP 1/89), the allowable expenditure to be taken into account then includes the value of the asset at 31 March 1982 and any indexation allowance for the period from 31 March 1982 to the earlier of the month in which the person making the disposal acquired the asset and April 1998.

(HMRC Statement of Practice SP 1/89; HMRC Brief 9/2009).

For indexation allowance in relation to no gain/no loss disposals generally, see **32.4** INDEXATION.

Note that, other than for companies, indexation allowance is abolished for disposals on or after 6 April 2008 and was previously frozen at its April 1998 level — see **32.2** INDEXATION. *TCGA 1992, s 36, Sch 4* applies only for corporation tax purposes for disposals on or after 6 April 2008, and for disposals on or after that date, re-basing to 31 March 1982 applies without exceptions for capital gains tax purposes (but not corporation tax purposes).

For further commentary, see HMRC Capital Gains Manual CG28100–28300.

Example

[44.8]

J and K have traded in partnership since 2002, sharing capital and income equally. The acquisition costs of the chargeable assets of the firm are as follows

	Cost
	£

Premises	60,000
Goodwill	10,000

The assets have not been revalued in the firm's balance sheet. On 1 June 2024, J and K admit L to the partnership and the sharing ratio is J 35%, K 45% and L 20%.

J and K are regarded as disposing of part of their interest in the firm's assets to L as follows

	£
J	
Premises	
Deemed consideration	
£60,000 × (50% – 35%)	9,000
Allowable cost	9,000
Chargeable gain	—
Goodwill	
Deemed consideration	
£10,000 × (50% – 35%)	1,500
Allowable cost	1,500
Chargeable gain	—
K	
Premises	
Deemed consideration	
£60,000 × (50% – 45%)	3,000
Allowable cost	3,000
Chargeable gain	—
Goodwill	
Deemed consideration	
£10,000 × (50% – 45%)	500
Allowable cost	500
Chargeable gain	—

The allowable costs of the three partners are now:

	Freehold land	Goodwill
	£	£
J	21,000	3,500
K	27,000	4,500
L (note (b))	12,000	2,000

Notes to the example

(a) The treatment illustrated above is taken from SP D12 section 4. Each partner's disposal consideration is equal to their share of current balance sheet value of the asset concerned, and each disposal treated as producing no gain and no loss.

(b) L's allowable costs comprise 20% of original cost.

Application of reliefs

[44.9] Where a partner is treated as making a disposal it may also qualify for HOLD-OVER RELIEFS (30), or ROLLOVER RELIEF (53). As regards a partner's acquisition, this may be used to cover a chargeable gain as in ROLLOVER RELIEF (53). A partner treated as disposing of a partnership asset (or share) can roll over any chargeable gain arising against an acquisition in another trade carried on, whether as sole trader or in another partnership trade, and *vice versa*. See 53.3 ROLLOVER RELIEF as regards assets owned personally by a partner and let to the partnership.

Accounting adjustments

[44.10] An upward revaluation of a partnership asset with the consequent credit to a partner's current or capital account does not give rise to a chargeable gain, but if after such a revaluation, a reduction occurs in a partner's sharing ratio (see **44.6** above), the disposal which he is thereby treated as making takes place at the increased value and may therefore give rise to a chargeable gain. Any acquisition is similarly treated.

Examples

(a) X, Y and Z are partners in D & Co and share both capital and income profits and losses in the ratio 3:2:1. X wishes to take a less active part in the business, and Z to devote more time to it. The asset-surplus-sharing ratio is amended to 2:2:2. X is treated as having disposed of a one-sixth interest in each chargeable asset belonging to the partnership for a consideration equal to one-sixth of their respective book values, and Z as having acquired that interest for the same consideration.

(b) The facts are as (a) above, save that before the ratio is altered, the partnership premises are written up in the books from £120,000 to £180,000. No charge arises on this occasion. On the change in sharing ratio, however, X is treated as having made a gain of £10,000 (one-sixth of the book gain) and this forms part of Z's acquisition cost on a future disposal.

A downward revaluation, even if following an upward revaluation, is similarly not treated as giving rise to an allowable loss, but a change in partnership shares following such a revaluation may do so.

(SP D12 section 6).

Consideration outside the accounts

[44.11] Where actual consideration is given in connection with an alteration in partnership sharing ratios (see **44.6** above), it is added to the consideration deemed to have been received under the rules in **44.6** and **44.10** above, and may therefore give rise to a chargeable gain or increased gain, the payer's acquisition cost being adjusted accordingly. Such an extraneous payment is often in respect of goodwill not included in the balance sheet. A payment is only deductible by the payer from a subsequent disposal (including a reduction in his share) of the asset, or on the payer's leaving the partnership. (SP D12 section 7).

Example

D, E and F are partners in a firm of accountants who share all profits in the ratio 7:7:6. G is admitted as a partner in May 2024 and pays the other partners £10,000 for goodwill. The new partnership shares are D $^3/_{10}$, E $^3/_{10}$, F $^1/_4$ and G $^3/_{20}$. The book value of goodwill is £18,000, its cost on acquisition of the practice from the predecessor in 1994.

The partners are treated as having disposed of shares in goodwill as follows:

	£	£
D		
$^7/_{20} - {}^3/_{10} = {}^1/_{20}$		
Disposal consideration		
Notional $^1/_{20}$ × £18,000	900	
Actual $^7/_{20}$ × £10,000	3,500	
		4,400
Allowable cost $^1/_{20}$ × £18,000		900
Chargeable gain		£3,500
E		
$^7/_{20} - {}^3/_{10} = {}^1/_{20}$		
Disposal consideration (as for D)		4,400
Allowable cost (as for D)		900
Chargeable gain		£3,500
F		
$^6/_{20} - {}^1/_4 = {}^1/_{20}$		
Disposal consideration		
Notional $^1/_{20}$ × £18,000	900	
Actual $^6/_{20}$ × £10,000	3,000	
		3,900
Allowable cost		900
Chargeable gain		£3,000
G's allowable cost of his share of goodwill is therefore		
Actual consideration paid		10,000
Notional consideration paid $^3/_{20}$ × £18,000		2,700
		£12,700

Annual payments to retired partner

[44.12] To the extent that annual payments (whether under covenant or not) to a retired partner exceed an amount regarded as a reasonable recognition of the partner's past work for the firm, the capitalised value of the annuity is treated as consideration for the disposal of their partnership share (and as allowable expenditure by the remaining partners). If the retired partner had been a partner for at least ten years, the maximum 'reasonable' annuity is two-thirds of their average share of the partnership profits (before capital allowances or charges on income) in the best three of the last seven years in which they were required to devote substantially the whole of their time to the partnership. The ten-year period includes any period during which the partner was a member of another firm which has been merged with the existing firm. For periods less than ten years, the relevant fractions are as follows (instead of two-thirds).

Complete years	Fraction
1–5	$^1/_{60}$ for each year
6	$^8/_{60}$
7	$^{16}/_{60}$
8	$^{24}/_{60}$
9	$^{32}/_{60}$

This treatment applies to certain cases in which a lump sum is paid as well as the annuity. (SP D12 section 9). Where the aggregate of the annuity and one-ninth of the lump sum does not exceed the appropriate fraction of the retired partner's average share of the profits (as above), the capitalised value is not treated as consideration in his hands. The lump sum continues to be treated as consideration. (HMRC Statement of Practice SP 1/79).

Fractional shares acquired in stages

[44.13] Where a partner's fractional share in one or more partnership assets is built up in stages, i.e. acquired at different times as a result of different transactions, such acquisitions are pooled for capital gains tax purposes. A subsequent part disposal is then regarded as a part disposal of a single asset and the pooled acquisition cost is apportioned accordingly (as in **44.6** above). However, pooling does not apply to any part of the fractional share that was acquired before 6 April 1965; part disposals are to be identified with each such acquisition separately, on a first in/first out basis, in priority to the post-5 April 1965 pool (unless this produces an unreasonable result when applied to purely temporary changes in partners' shares, for example, when a partner's departure and a replacement partner's admission are out of step by a few months). (SP D12 section 11).

Example

Q is a partner in a medical practice. The partnership's only chargeable asset is a freehold house used as a surgery. The cost of the house to the partnership was £3,600 in 1986 and it was revalued in the partnership accounts to £50,000 in 2002. Q was admitted to the partnership in June 1988 with a share of 1/6 of all profits. As a result of partnership changes, Q's profit share altered as follows:

1992 1/5
2000 1/4
2005 3/10

For capital gains tax, Q's allowable cost of his share of the freehold house is calculated as follows:

	£
1988 1/6 × £3,600	600
1992 (1/5 – 1/6) × £3,600	120
2000 (1/4 – 1/5) × £3,600	180
2005 (3/10 – 1/4) × £50,000	2,500
	£3,400

Note to the example

(a) On Q's acquisition of an increased share of the property in 2005 (subsequent to the revaluation in 1990), any partner with a reduced share will be treated as having made a disposal and thus a gain or loss (see **44.10** above).

Partnership assets distributed in kind

[44.14] The disposal of a partnership asset to one or more of the partners is treated as being made at market value which is apportioned among all the partners as in **44.6** above. Chargeable gains thus attributable to partners receiving no asset are taxed at the time of the disposal. Any gain notionally accruing to a receiving partner is treated as reducing his allowable expenditure on a subsequent disposal of the asset. The same principle applies where a loss arises. (SP D12 section 3).

Example

R, S and T are partners sharing all profits in the ratio 4:3:3. Farmland owned by the firm is transferred in November 2024 to T for future use by him as a market gardening enterprise separate from the partnership business. No payment is made by T to the other partners but a reduction is made in T's future share of income profits. The book value of the farmland is £50,000, its cost in 1993, but the present market value is £150,000.

		£
R		
Deemed disposal consideration	$^4/_{10}$ × £150,000	60,000
Allowable cost	$^4/_{10}$ × £50,000	20,000
Gain		£40,000
S		
Deemed disposal consideration	$^3/_{10}$ × £150,000	45,000
Allowable cost	$^3/_{10}$ × £50,000	15,000
Gain		£30,000
T		
Partnership share	$^3/_{10}$ × £50,000	15,000
Market value of R's share		60,000
Market value of S's share		45,000
Allowable cost of land for future disposal		£120,000

Miscellaneous

Mergers

[44.15] Mergers of existing partnerships are treated as in **44.6–44.11** above. If gains arise for reasons similar to **44.10** and **44.11** above, a continuing partner may claim ROLLOVER RELIEF (**53**) insofar as he disposes of his share of assets of the old firm and acquires a share in other assets of the new firm. (SP D12 section 10).

Corporate partners

[44.16] The above rules apply, with appropriate modifications, to company partners, but bearing in mind the differences listed at **14.2** COMPANIES between capital gains tax and corporation tax on chargeable gains. See also **15.3** COMPANIES — CORPORATE FINANCE AND INTANGIBLES.

Limited liability partnerships

[44.17] A limited liability partnership (LLP) is in law a body corporate (with legal personality separate from that of its members) incorporated under *Limited Liability Partnerships Act 2000*. [*LLPA 2000, s 1*]. But, for the purposes of income tax and corporation tax, a trade, profession or business carried on by an LLP with a view to profit is treated as if carried on instead by its members in partnership, and the property of the LLP is treated for those purposes as partnership property. [*ITTOIA 2005, s 863; CTA 2009, s 1273(1)*]. The essential feature of an LLP is that it combines the organisational flexibility and tax status of a partnership with limited liability for its members. LLPs are used mainly by professional partnerships.

Similarly, for the purposes of taxing chargeable gains, assets held by an LLP carrying on a trade or business with a view to profit are treated as held by its members as partners, and dealings by an LLP are treated as dealings by its members in partnership. As in **44.2** above, tax is assessed and charged on the members separately in respect of chargeable gains accruing to them on the disposal of LLP assets. [*TCGA 1992, s 59A(1)*].

All references to partnerships and partnership members in the legislation on taxation of chargeable gains are to be taken as including LLPs within *s 59A(1)* and members of such LLPs. [*TCGA 1992, s 59A(2)*]. Thus, the preceding paragraphs of this chapter generally apply as if an LLP were an ordinary partnership.

If an LLP *temporarily* ceases to carry on a trade or business with a view to profit, the treatment under *TCGA 1992, s 59A(1)* above continues. In the case of a permanent cessation, *s 59A(1)* treatment continues during an informal winding-up, provided the winding-up is not wholly or partly for tax avoidance reasons and is not unreasonably prolonged. *Section 59A(1)* treatment does, however, cease upon the appointment of a liquidator or (if earlier) the making of a winding-up order by the court (or upon the equivalent in each case under non-UK law). Neither the commencement of *s 59A(1)* treatment nor its ceasing to apply is to be taken as giving rise to the disposal of any assets by the LLP itself or by any of its members. During a liquidation period, an LLP is itself taxable (through its liquidator) on disposals of assets, under the normal corporate insolvency rules. Chargeable gains on assets disposed of in the liquidation period are taxed as if *s 59A(1)* tax treatment had never applied, and the only capital asset which a member then holds for tax purposes is his interest in the LLP. The proceeds of disposal of that interest is based on the amount of the liquidator's capital distributions (if any). In calculating the chargeable gain or allowable loss on that disposal, the member's interest is to be taken as acquired on the date he originally joined the LLP and by reference to the capital cost of his becoming a member. [*TCGA 1992, s 59A(3)–(6)*].

See **30.8**, **30.11** HOLD-OVER RELIEFS, **53.3** ROLLOVER RELIEF for other implications. See **52.18** RETURNS for the treatment of a return made by an LLP on the basis that it carries on a business with a view to profit as a valid partnership return even if in fact the LLP does not carry on a business with a view to profit.

HMRC Statement of Practice SP D12 (referred to throughout this chapter) applies equally to the members of an LLP for as long as it remains within *TCGA 1992, s 59A(1)*; the above treatment of an LLP in liquidation and of its members does not affect the tax treatment of pre-liquidation disposals, which will remain undisturbed.

Property investment LLPs

The normal exemptions for income and gains of pension funds, life insurance companies in respect of their pension business, and friendly societies in respect of their tax-exempt business do not apply where the income or gains accrue to the fund etc. in its capacity as a member of a 'property investment LLP'. See, for example, **23.56** EXEMPTIONS AND RELIEFS. A '*property investment LLP*' is an LLP whose business consists wholly or mainly in the making of investments in land

and the principal part of whose income is derived therefrom. Whether or not an LLP is within this definition must be judged for each period of account separately. [*TCGA 1992, s 288(1); CTA 2010, s 1135*].

Alternative investment fund management partnerships

[44.18] There are provisions under which members of an alternative investment fund management partnership can allocate certain profits to the partnership itself for income tax purposes rather than to individual or corporate partners. The profits concerned are certain amounts of 'variable remuneration' which partners cannot immediately access because of requirements of the Alternative Investment Fund Managers Directive (2011/61/EU), which will include remuneration which, if it vests in a partner, will vest in the form of instruments of the fund. See *ITTOIA 2005, ss 863H–863L*. The following applies where:

(1) under *ITTOIA 2005, s 863I* a partner in a partnership allocates to the partnership an amount of profit (the 'allocated profit') representing variable remuneration which, if it vests in the partner, will vest in the form of instruments;
(2) there is a disposal to the partner of instruments which are partnership assets of the partnership for the purposes of **44.2** above;
(3) by virtue of that disposal the variable remuneration vests in the partner; and
(4) where the disposal in (2) above is by a company which is a partner in the partnership, the company would, as such a partner, have been charged to tax on the allocated profit but for adjustments made under *CTA 2009, s 1264A(2)* or *ITTOIA 2005, s 850C(5)* (excess profit allocation to non-individual partners — see Tolley's Income Tax).

Both the persons making the disposal in (2) above and the partner are treated for capital gains purposes as if the instruments were acquired by the partner from those persons for a consideration equal to the allocated profit net of the income tax for which the partnership is liable under *ITTOIA 2005, s 863I* in respect of it.

[*TCGA 1992, ss 59B, 59C*].

Carried interest arising to investment managers

[44.19] Special provisions apply where an individual performs investment management services (as defined) directly or indirectly in respect of an '*investment scheme*' (either a 'collective investment scheme' or an investment trust) under 'arrangements' involving at least one partnership and 'carried interest' arises (see **44.21** below) to the individual under the arrangements.

A '*collective investment scheme*' includes arrangements which permit an external investor to participate in investments by the scheme without participating in the scheme itself and arrangements under which sums arise to an individual performing investment management services in respect of the scheme without those sums arising from the scheme itself. *Arrangements*' include any agreement, understanding, scheme, transaction or transactions, whether or not legally enforceable.

Where the carried interest arises in connection with the disposal of one or more assets of the partnership or partnerships, a chargeable gain equal to the amount of the carried interest less any permitted deductions (and no other such gain or loss) is deemed to accrue to the individual on the disposal at the time the carried interest arises. If the carried interest arises in any other circumstances, a chargeable gain equal to the amount of the carried interest less any permitted deductions is deemed to accrue to the individual at the time the carried interest arises. This treatment is subject to the making of an election to apply the accruals basis in charging gains, for which see **44.20** below.

These provisions do not apply to the extent that the carried interest is brought into account in calculating the individual's profits of a trade, profession or vocation for any tax year or if it constitutes a 'co-investment' repayment of return. There are statutory provisions which in effect require certain 'income-based' carried interest to be brought into account in calculating the profits of the trade etc. and so to exclude it from the CGT charge. See *ITA 2007, ss 809FZA–809FZZ* and Tolley's Income Tax.

'*Permitted deductions*' means so much of the following amounts as is just and reasonable:

(a) any consideration given to the scheme by or on behalf of the individual wholly and exclusively for entering into the arrangements (but excluding consideration in respect of co-investments);
(b) any amount which constituted earnings of the individual under *ITEPA 2003, Pt 3 Ch 1* in respect of the individual entering into the arrangements (but excluding any earnings in respect of co-investments and any exempt income within *ITEPA 2003, s 8*); and
(c) any amount which, due to events occurring no later that the time the carried interest arises, counts as the individual's income under *ITEPA 2003, s 426* (restricted shares — see **21.13**), *s 438* (conversion of convertible shares — see **21.14**), *s 446U* (shares acquired for less than market value — see **21.8**), or *s 447* (receipt of benefit — see **21.12**) or under *ITEPA 2003, s 476* (by virtue of *s 477(3)(a)* — acquisition of shares under employment-related share option — see **21.6**) or under *FA 2005, s 21* (transitional charge on shares in spin-out companies) in respect of the individual's participation in the arrangements (but excluding amounts in respect of co-investments).

No other amount may be deducted from the carried interest in computing the deemed gain.

For this purpose, a '*co-investment*' is an investment made directly or indirectly in the scheme by the individual where there is no return on the investment which is not an arm's length return (as defined by *ITA 2007, s 809EZB(2)*).

Where the carried interest arises as a result of the individual's acquisition of a right to it from another person for consideration in money given by or on behalf of the individual, the deemed chargeable gain is reduced by the amount of the consideration provided that the individual makes a claim to that effect.

Foreign chargeable gains

A gain accruing under the above provisions when carried interest arises is a chargeable gain arising on disposal of an asset situated outside the UK for the purpose of the REMITTANCE BASIS (**49.2**) only to the extent that the individual performs the investment management services outside the UK.

Anti-avoidance

In determining whether the above provisions apply to an individual, any arrangements a main purpose of which is to secure that the provisions do not apply to the individual (or the individual and one or more other individuals) are disregarded.

Relief for double taxation

An individual who is charged to CGT under these provisions may make a claim for adjustments to the charge where either:

- the individual has paid tax (i.e. income tax or another tax) charged in relation to the carried interest, the tax has not been repaid, and the amount on which the tax is charged is not a permitted deduction within (b) or (c) above; or
- tax (income tax or another tax) charged on another person in relation to the carried interest has been paid by that person and not repaid.

HMRC consider that this rule does not apply to non-UK tax charges (HMRC Investment Funds Manual IFM37410).

On a claim, HMRC must make such of the adjustments claimed (if any) as are just and reasonable. The value of the adjustments must not exceed the lesser of the two tax charges. Adjustments may be made for any period regardless of any time limits. Where both tax charges arise in the same tax year HMRC accept that a claim can be made in the appropriate tax return without the need to pay both tax liabilities. HMRC consider that, where a sum comprises a series of items, relief must be given on an item by item basis (i.e. it will only be possible to set the other tax due on a particular component of the sum arising against the CGT due on that component, rather than the CGT due on the sum as a whole) (HMRC Investment Funds Manual IFM37420).

Where the individual has capital losses brought forward which would be automatically set-off against his chargeable gains including those on carried interest and he makes a claim under these provisions, he may elect to reduce the losses to be set-off by an amount up to that on which the other tax is charged.

A claim cannot be made under this provision in respect of double taxation arising as a result of a deemed gain arising due to an election for the accruals basis (see **44.20** below). Instead, a claim can be made under the double taxation provisions at **44.20** below.

Relief for external investors on disposal of partnership asset

Where a chargeable gain arises to an 'external investor' in an investment scheme on the disposal of one or more partnership assets and the investor makes a claim, the gain is reduced by any part of the sum invested by the investor which, on a just and reasonable basis, is referable to the asset or assets disposed of, less any amount deducted in computing the gains for acquisition consideration. This relief reverses the effect of 'base cost shift' for the investor (as the above provisions are intended to reverse its effect for the fund manager). Base cost shift can arise as a result of the operation of HMRC Statement of Practice SP D12 and involves the effective transfer to the fund manager of base cost (i.e. the allowable deduction in respect of acquisition consideration) of underlying investments held by a fund partnership which is derived from contributions made by investors. When calculating their chargeable gains investors would therefore be entitled to deduct a smaller amount of base cost than the amount they themselves actually contributed to the fund. See the Appendix to HMRC's guidance referred to below.

An '*external investor*' is a participator in the scheme other than an individual who performs investment management services directly or indirectly in relation to the scheme or a person through whom sums are to, or may, arise directly or indirectly to such an individual from the scheme under the arrangements.

[*TCGA 1992, ss 103KA, 103KC–103KF, 103KFC(7), 103KH(1); ITA 2007, ss 809EZA(6)(7), 809EZE(1); F(No 2)A 2023, s 42*].

Carried interest—election for accruals basis

[44.20] For 2022/23 onwards, an individual who has received carried interest within the provisions at **44.19** above in respect of a particular investment scheme can make an election to apply an alternative 'accruals basis' to charge the carried interest from the scheme to capital gains tax. An individual can also make an election where it is reasonable to expect that they will receive such carried interest. This option has been introduced to prevent difficulties arising in obtaining double tax relief where carried interest gains are taxable in more than one country.

An election applies also to any 'associated' investment schemes, whether or not the conditions for making an election in respect of the associated scheme are met. Broadly, schemes are 'associated' for this purpose if both schemes have the same investment managers, the same investments and they act together.

The election is irrevocable and, once made, applies to all future tax years starting with the year identified in the election as the first year. For each tax year, the individual is treated as having a chargeable gain, calculated as below, arise to them immediately before the end of the year.

Calculating the deemed gain

The first step is to calculate the amount of carried interest that would arise to the individual in the tax year in question on the following assumptions:

(a) all of scheme's investments (held by it in the tax year or previously) which would be relevant to the individual's carried interest entitlement are disposed of in the year;
(b) where the investment has not yet actually been disposed of, the disposal consideration is equal to the acquisition cost;

(c) all income of the scheme for the year and previous years which would be relevant to the individual's carried interest entitlement is received in the year; and
(d) all of the scheme's profits from the disposals in (a) above and the income in (c) above are distributed to investors during the year.

Where distributions were made to external investors before the tax year in question and their timing affects the amount of carried interest that actually arises to the individual, the amount calculated as above must reflect the fact that those distributions were so made. But if the result is that an amount would otherwise be presumed to arise in an earlier tax year, that amount is instead presumed to arise in the tax year in question.

The resulting amount is then reduced by any gains deemed to arise in previous tax years for which the election had effect. A loss cannot arise under this calculation (see Treasury Explanatory Notes to the Finance (No 2) Bill 2023), but see further below for the loss that may be deemed to arise when the scheme comes to an end.

The deemed gain is a carried interest gain and is charged to capital gains tax at 18% and 28%. See **2.1** ANNUAL RATES AND EXEMPTIONS.

The deemed gain under this provision is treated as arising on disposal of an asset situated outside the UK only to the extent that the individual performs the investment management services outside the UK.

Relief for double taxation

The fact that an individual is charged to capital gains tax on the deemed gain as calculated above does not prevent another tax charge (whether to income tax, capital gains tax or any other tax) arising in respect of carried interest arising to the individual from the scheme.

Instead, where such a tax charge arises to the individual, they may make a claim for a just and reasonable adjustment to be made by HMRC reducing the tax chargeable. The reduction cannot be greater than the tax otherwise chargeable (or, if lower, the tax charged on deemed gains under the election).

Deemed loss on cessation of scheme

If, when all (or substantially all) of the scheme's investments have been disposed of, the amount of carried interest that has actually arisen to the individual since the start of the first tax year to which the election applies is less than the total of the deemed gains under the election, a loss is deemed to arise. It is a further condition that there must be no reasonable expectation that any further carried interest will arise.

The loss is treated as arising immediately before the end of the tax year in which these conditions are first met and is equal to the difference between the total deemed gains and the total carried interest.

Once the loss has arisen, no further deemed gains arise in subsequent tax years. If any further carried interest arises, no claim can be made under the relief for double taxation provisions above in respect of the tax chargeable.

Anti-avoidance

If an election is made with a main purpose of causing a loss to arise under the above provisions, the loss must be counteracted by the making of just and reasonable adjustments (by HMRC or the individual).

Making an election

An election must be made by notice in writing to HMRC no later than 31 January following the first tax year for which it is to apply and must indicate which year is the first tax year.

[*TCGA 1992, ss 103KFA–103KFE; ITA 2007, s 809FZZ; F(No 2)A 2023, s 42*].

Meaning of 'carried interest'

[44.21] '*Carried interest*' means a sum which arises to the individual under the arrangements by way of 'profit-related return'. A sum arises by way of '*profit-related return*' if under the arrangements:

- the sum can arise only if there are profits for a period on, or from the disposal of, the scheme investments or on particular scheme investments;
- the amount of the sum is variable, to a substantial extent, by reference to those profits; and
- returns to external investors are also determined by reference to those profits.

Where any part of the sum does not meet these conditions, that part is not to be regarded as arising by way of profit-related return. Where one or more sums arise to the individual under the arrangements by way of profit-related return in a tax year, but there was no significant risk that a sum of at least a certain amount would fail to arise, only the excess (if any) over that amount is carried interest. There are rules for determining how that amount is to be apportioned between the actual sums arising where more than one such sum arises in the tax year (see *ITA 2007, s 809EZC(7)(8)*). There are also rules for assessing the risk (see *ITA 2007, s 809EZC(4)–(6)*).

A sum is regarded as '*carried interest*', notwithstanding the above definition, if all, or substantially all, of the investments in the scheme made by the participants have been repaid to the participants, and each external investor has received a 'preferred return' on all, or substantially all, of his investments in the scheme. This also applies, with appropriate modification, where the scheme profits and preferred return are calculated on the basis of particular investments. '*Preferred return*' is an amount at least equivalent to compound interest on an investment at 6% per annum, with annual rests, for the whole of the period during which the investment was invested in the scheme.

Consideration received or receivable by an individual for the disposal, variation, loss or cancellation of a right to carried interest is treated as carried interest arising to that individual at the time of the disposal etc. This does not, however, apply to any extent that the consideration is a disguised fee within *ITA 2007, s 809EZA* (disguised investment management fees — see Tolley's Income Tax).

Carried interest '*arises*' to an individual if and only if it arises to him for the purposes of the disguised investment management fees provisions at *ITA 2007, ss 809EZA–809EZH*.

ITA 2007, s 809EZDB (which treats a sum as arising to the individual in certain cases where it arises to another person) does not apply in relation to a sum of carried interest arising to a company connected with the individual, or a person not connected with him, where the sum is 'deferred carried interest' in relation to him.

'*Deferred carried interest*' in relation to an individual is a sum of carried interest the provision of which to the individual or a connected person (other than, where relevant, the company to which the carried interest arises) is deferred (because, for example, further conditions need to be met) and it includes the individual's share, on a just and reasonable basis, of any carried interest the provision of which to the individual and one or more other persons, taken together, has been deferred. The sum is deemed to arise to the individual when it ceases to be deferred carried interest unless none of the enjoyment conditions below is met at that time and there is no reasonable likelihood that any of them will ever be met. The enjoyment conditions are:

(1) the sum, or part of it, is in fact calculated at some time to enure for the benefit of the individual or a connected person;
(2) the sum's ceasing to be deferred carried interest increases the value, either to the individual or a connected person, of any assets which they hold or which are held for their benefit;
(3) receives or is entitled to receive at any time any benefit provided or to be provided out of the sum or part of it;
(4) the individual or a connected person may become entitled to the beneficial enjoyment of the sum or part thereof if one or more powers are exercised or successively exercised (by anyone and with or without the consent of another person);
(5) the individual or a connected person can control directly or indirectly the application of the sum or part of it.

Where this provision applies because a sum arises to a company connected to the individual, in (1)–(5) above a connected person does not include that company.

In determining whether any of the above conditions is met regard must be had to the substantial result and effect of all relevant circumstances and all benefits which may at any time accrue to a person as a result of the sum ceasing to be deferred carried interest in relation to the individual must be taken into account (whatever their nature and whether or not there is a legal or equitable right to them).

Conditions (2), (3), and (4) above are not met if they would be met only because the individual holds shares or an interest in shares in a company. Conditions (1) and (5) are not met where the sum arises to a company connected with the individual and either the company includes the sum in it profits chargeable to corporation tax or the company is a controlled foreign company and the tax exemption in *TIOPA 2010, ss 371NA–371NE* applies for the accounting period in which the sum arises, or would be so apply if the company were a controlled foreign company. These provisions which prevent the conditions being met do not, however, apply where there are arrangements that have a main purpose of avoiding tax. This applies automatically where the sum is applied directly or indirectly as an investment in a collective investment scheme.

The disapplication of *ITA 2007, s 809EZDB* is ignored where the sum is applied directly or indirectly as an investment in a collective investment scheme and as a result, arrangements are deemed to be in place for the purposes of that section which have a main purpose of avoiding tax. The disapplication also does not apply where the deferral is not as a result of 'genuine commercial arrangements', or it is as a result of such arrangements but they have a main purpose of avoiding tax. '*Genuine commercial arrangements*' are arrangements involving the individual (alone or jointly with others performing investment management services) and external investors in the investment scheme.

[*TCGA 1992, ss 103KB, 103KG, 103KH(2); ITA 2007, ss 809EZC, 809EZD*].

Key points concerning partnerships

[44.22] Points to consider are as follows.

- A partnership is not treated as a separate entity for capital gains tax purposes. This also applies to a Limited Liability Partnership (LLP), except where it enters into a formal liquidation, when it is treated as a company.
- The legislation contains few specific rules in relation to partnership capital gains. HMRC's views on the application of the legislation to partnership matters are set out in Statements of Practice and the HMRC Capital Gains Tax Manual (CG27000–CG28500).
- Partners are treated as owning a share of each partnership asset, and are charged to tax separately on disposals. The market value of a partner's share is not discounted for the size of their partnership interest.
- For the purposes of transactions within a partnership, partners are not treated as connected simply because they are partners, so it is normally unnecessary to substitute market value for actual consideration.
- A partner who contributes an asset to a partnership makes a part-disposal of the share that passes to other partners. If a partnership asset is distributed to one or more partners, those who do not receive it are taxed on any gain at the time of distribution; for those who receive it, their base cost is reduced by the amount of any gain at the time of distribution.
- The revaluation of a partnership asset is not of itself an occasion of charge.
- Where there is a change in profit sharing ratios, a partner whose share increases or decreases is treated as acquiring or disposing of part or all of their share of each partnership asset.

- The incorporation of a partnership into an LLP does not of itself constitute a disposal by the partners of their interests in the old partnership's assets.
- A rolled-over or held-over gain in relation to any LLP assets crystallises if the LLP enters into formal liquidation.
- Transfers between partners who are spouses or civil partners are always treated as no gain/no loss disposals.
- Penalties for late filing of partnership tax returns are chargeable on each partner to whom the return relates. This can make the late filing of a partnership tax return very expensive. HMRC's free software for filing tax returns does not extend to partnerships. Paper returns should therefore be filed by 31 October or commercial software used to file online by 31 January following the end of the tax year.
- In normal circumstances, a partner's personal tax return includes the amount that the partnership statement says is their share of the partnership's profit or loss. Partnership returns are conclusive for tax purposes as to whether a person has a share in the profits or losses of the partnership for any period and what any person's share in those profits or losses is. This is subject to the right of any such person to refer any dispute about their share to the tribunal for determination. See **52.19** RETURNS.

45

Payment of Tax

Cross-references. See **5** APPEALS; **6** ASSESSMENTS; **36** LATE PAYMENT INTEREST AND PENALTIES; **42.2** OFFSHORE SETTLEMENTS as regards the liability of migrating trustees of a settlement; **43.6** OVERSEAS MATTERS for relief for unremittable overseas gains and **43.17** for companies ceasing to be UK-resident and non-resident companies; **55** SELF-ASSESSMENT.

Introduction to payment of tax

[45.1] Both capital gains tax and corporation tax operate under a system of self-assessment in which it is the taxpayer's responsibility to calculate their liability and pay the tax by the due date (although for capital gains tax, HMRC will normally calculate the liability if a return is made online or if the taxpayer does not wish to do so). The requirement to pay tax is not, therefore, dependent on the receipt of a demand from HMRC. Late payment will result in LATE PAYMENT INTEREST AND PENALTIES (36).

Capital gains tax is normally due on 31 January following the tax year. Corporation tax is due nine months and one day after the end of the accounting period, or, for large companies, by quarterly instalments. Tax may be paid by instalments where the disposal consideration is itself receivable in instalments or (capital gains tax only) where the disposal is by way of gift. Taxpayers can also negotiate with HMRC to enter into 'time to pay' arrangements. Certain 'exit charges' and transactions by companies with group members in EEA states may also be paid by instalments where the taxpayer enters into a payment plan.

A special compliance regime applies to all direct disposals of UK land where a residential property gain arises and to direct and indirect disposals of any UK land by non-UK residents. A UK land disposal return must be made together with a payment on account of CGT on or before the 60th day following the day of the completion of the disposal (the 30th day where the completion is before 27 October 2021). See **45.3** below and **52.22** RETURNS.

Tax may be paid by any one of a number of methods but HMRC operate rules to determine the effective date for each method and they charge a fee for payment by certain methods.

Where a taxpayer has appealed against an assessment or amendment to a self-assessment and considers that he is overcharged to tax he may apply to HMRC for the tax to be postponed pending the determination of the appeal. This does not affect the date from which interest on unpaid tax runs. When the appeal is determined any postponed tax must be paid in accordance with the decision, even if a further appeal is made to the Upper Tribunal or court.

See **45.20** below for HMRC's collection and enforcement powers. In certain circumstances tax which is unpaid may be collected from a person other than the person who made the disposal giving rise to the liability. HMRC also have powers to re-assess any tax which has been wrongly repaid.

In two limited situations, HMRC will not seek to collect tax which is legally due. The situations are where the arrears result from HMRC's failure to make proper use of information supplied by the taxpayer and where they accept a claim for special relief (see **13.7** CLAIMS).

HMRC have powers to collect certain foreign taxes under the EU Mutual Assistance Recovery Directive or under tax enforcement agreements with other countries.

Due date

Capital gains tax

[45.2] Subject to 45.3 below, capital gains tax becomes due and payable as part of a taxpayer's self-assessment or under a simple assessment (see below). The normal due date for payment (or repayment) is 31 January following the tax year (so that, for example, capital gains tax for 2023/24 becomes due on 31 January 2025). Where the taxpayer gave notice of chargeability under *TMA 1970, s 7* (see **46.3** PENALTIES) within six months after the end of the tax year, but was not given notice under *TMA 1970, s 8* or *s 8A* (personal and trustee's return; see **52.5** RETURNS) until after 31 October following the tax year, the due date is the last day of the three months beginning with the date of the said notice. Where a notice to file a return under *TMA 1970, s 8* or *s 8A* has been withdrawn (see **52.5** RETURNS) and a further such notice is subsequently given after 31 October following the tax year, the due date is the last day of the three months beginning with the date of the original withdrawn notice.

The amount of the payment so due is equal to the combined income tax (including certain Class 4 national insurance contributions treated as income tax) and capital gains tax liabilities contained in the self-assessment (see **52.8** RETURNS) less the aggregate of any payments on account (whether under *TMA 1970, s 59A*, *TMA 1970, s 59AA* (unless already repaid), *FA 2019, Sch 2* or otherwise) and any income tax deducted at source. This means that, in effect, the capital gains tax payable is reduced by any income tax overpayment for the year. If the second total exceeds the first, a repayment will be made. For this purpose, income tax deducted at source does not include, where the taxpayer is a charity, any income tax already repaid on a claim in respect of gift aid payments or other exempt income.

Where an HMRC officer enquires into the return (see **52.11** RETURNS) and a repayment is otherwise due, the repayment is not required to be made until the enquiry is fully completed (see **52.14** RETURNS) although the officer may make a provisional repayment at his discretion. [*TMA 1970, s 59B*]. Tax repayments arising from a partial closure notice (see **52.14** RETURNS) will not automatically be repaid, e.g. where tax is due in respect of other issues not covered by the partial closure notice (www.gov.uk/government/publications/tax-enquiries-closure-rules).

Simple assessments

In general, the due date for payment of the tax charged by a 'simple assessment' (see **6.9** ASSESSMENTS), net of any payments on account and income tax deducted at source, is 31 January following the tax year to which the assessment relates. However, where a person is given notice of the simple assessment after 31 October following the tax year to which it relates, the due date is deferred until the last day of the period of three months following the day on which the notice was given.

[*TMA 1970, s 59B(1)–(4A)(7)(8), s 59BA*].

Amendments and corrections

Where an amount of tax is payable (repayable) as a result of an amendment or correction to an individual's or trustees' self-assessment under any of (a)–(e) below, then, subject to the appeal and postponement provisions in, respectively, **5.2** APPEALS and **45.18** below, the due date for payment (repayment) is as stated below (if this is later than the date given under the general rules above). Note that these rules do *not* defer the date from which interest accrues, which is as in **36.2** LATE PAYMENT INTEREST AND PENALTIES (**50.2** REPAYMENT INTEREST).

(a) Taxpayer amendment to return as in **52.9** RETURNS: 30 days after the date of the taxpayer's notice of amendment.
(b) HMRC correction to return as in **52.9** RETURNS: 30 days after the date of the officer's notice of correction.
(c) Taxpayer amendment to return whilst enquiry in progress as in **52.15** RETURNS, where accepted by HMRC: tax payable 30 days after the date of a final or partial closure notice; tax repayable 30 days after the date of a final closure notice, regardless of whether or not a partial closure notice was previously given (see **52.14** RETURNS).
(d) HMRC amendment to return where amendment made by a final or partial closure notice on completion or part completion of an enquiry (see **52.14** RETURNS): 30 days after the date of the closure notice.
(e) HMRC amendment of self-assessment to prevent potential loss of tax to the Crown (see **52.15** RETURNS): 30 days after the date of the notice of amendment.

As regards amendments and corrections to partnership returns, (e) above is not relevant, and the equivalent date in each of (a)–(d) above as regards each partner is 30 days after the date of the officer's notice of consequential amendment to the partner's own tax return. The same applies in the case of a consequential amendment by virtue of an amendment of a partnership return on discovery (see **6.11** ASSESSMENTS) or following a determination by the tribunal of a dispute as to profit shares (see **52.19** RETURNS).

[*TMA 1970, s 59B(5), Sch 3ZA*].

Assessments other than self-assessments or simple assessments

Subject to the appeal and postponement provisions in **5.2** APPEALS and **45.18** below, the due date for payment of tax charged by assessment otherwise than by self-assessment or simple assessment, e.g. a discovery assessment under *TMA 1970, s 29* (see **6.10** ASSESSMENTS), is 30 days after the date of the assessment (but see also **36** LATE PAYMENT INTEREST AND PENALTIES). [*TMA 1970, s 59B(6)*].

Payments on account of CGT — UK land disposals

[45.3] Where a person is required to make a UK land disposal return (see **52.22** RETURNS) in respect of a disposal, he must make a payment on account of his liability to capital gains tax for the tax year of the disposal of an amount equal to the excess of the 'amount notionally chargeable' over any previous such payments on account for the tax year. The payment is due on the filing date for the return (the 60th day following the day of the completion of the disposal;

the 30th day where completion is before 27 October 2021). If the amount notionally chargeable is less than the previous payments on account, the difference is repayable to the taxpayer on the filing date.

The '*amount notionally chargeable*' at the filing date for a return is the amount of CGT which would be chargeable for the tax year ignoring any disposals with a completion date later than the completion date for the disposal in respect of which the return is made and any disposals on which gains arise but which are not UK land disposals in respect of which a return would be required. A loss on a disposal with a completion date after the completion date for the disposal in respect of which the return is made is not ignored if it arises before the latter completion date.

For these purposes, it must be assumed that a person has made any claim or election, or given any notice, if, at the time of completion, it is reasonable to expect that they will. Reasonable estimates (i.e. estimates on a fair and reasonable basis, having regard to person's knowledge and other circumstances) can be made about the values, apportionments and whether or not income tax will be chargeable for the year at a higher rate and, if not, how much of the basic rate band will be available in calculating the CGT liability.

For direct disposals of UK land by a UK resident (i.e where **52.22**(2) applies), *FA 2022* introduced an explicit rule that any proportion of the gain which is not a residential property gain (see **2.1** ANNUAL RATES AND EXEMPTIONS) is to be ignored in determining the amount notionally chargeable.

A UK land disposal return is treated as if it contained a self-assessment of an amount of capital gains tax, so that where an amount is payable on account (or repayable) as a result of an amendment or correction, *TMA 1970, Sch 3ZA* (see **45.2** above under 'Amendments and corrections') applies to determine the due date (but only where later than the normal due date).

[*TMA 1970, ss 12ZG, 59AZA, FA 2019, Sch 2 paras 6–8, 14, 21(2)(3), 24(3); FA 2022, s 23*].

Overpayments

Where payments on account for a tax year exceed the final CGT liability for the year (for example, because of a subsequent non-UK land allowable loss or because income for the year was lower than expected) and the taxpayer completes a self-assessment return for the year, HMRC's computer system could not, originally, automatically set the excess against other self-assessment liabilities or show it as a refund on the self-assessment account. HMRC adopted an interim solution for 2020/21 to allow for set-off or refunds to be made in these circumstances. Taxpayers should contact HMRC by telephone (0300 200 3300) to enable HMRC to make a manual adjustment.

For 2021/22 onwards, excess payments on account will automatically be offset against other self-assessment charges. If, following set-off, there remains an excess amount, taxpayers should contact HMRC by telephone (0300 200 3300) to enable repayment. If a repayment is not requested and no self-assessment return is filed, any overpayment will remain as a credit on the taxpayer's property disposal account.

Once the self-assessment return has been submitted, taxpayers should not attempt to amend their UK land disposal returns for the tax year.

See www.att.org.uk/technical/news/uk-property-reporting-service-its-interaction-self-assessment and HMRC Capital Gains Manual CGAPP18–180 and CGAPP18–320 para 3.2.1 onwards.

Corporation tax (on chargeable gains)

[45.4] Subject to the rules outlined below for payment by 'large' companies by quarterly instalments, corporation tax (including that in respect of chargeable gains) for an accounting period is due and payable on the day following the expiry of nine months from the end of the period.

If the company subsequently has grounds for believing that a change in circumstances has rendered payment for a period excessive, it may, by notice to an officer of the Board stating the grounds and the amount it considers should be repaid, claim repayment of the excess. Such notice may not be given before the date on which the tax became (or would have become) due and payable as above, or after an assessment for the period has become final. If the company wishes to claim repayment at a time when an assessment for the period is under appeal, the company must apply to the Tribunal for a determination of the amount to be repaid pending determination of the appeal. Such an application may be combined with an application for postponement of tax pending an appeal (see **45.18** below).

[*TMA 1970, ss 59D, 59DA*].

Quarterly instalments by large companies

'Large' companies pay corporation tax under a system of quarterly payment by instalments. [*TMA 1970, s 59E*].

'Large' companies are those with profits (including UK dividend income, other than intra-group dividends) exceeding £1,500,000 in an accounting period, divided by one plus the number of related 51% group companies (within *CTA 2010, s 279F*), if any, at the end of the preceding accounting period.

The timing of instalment payments depends on whether or not the company is a 'very large' company. 'Very large' companies are those with profits (including UK dividend income, other than intra-group dividends) exceeding £20,000,000 in an accounting period, divided by one plus the number of related 51% group companies.

However, a company is not treated as 'large' or 'very large' in respect of an accounting period if its total corporation tax liability for that period does not exceed £10,000, which might be the case if it would otherwise be large only by reference to the number of its related 51% group companies or the level of its dividend income. A company is also exempt from payment by instalments for an accounting period if it was not 'large' (nor 'very large') in the 12 months preceding the accounting period and its profits for the accounting period do not exceed £10 million, divided by one plus the number of related 51% group companies as at the end of the preceding accounting period.

Each of the above monetary limits is proportionately reduced for accounting periods of less than 12 months.

Where the company is very large, the first instalment is due two months and 13 days after the first day of the accounting period. The second, third and final instalments are then due at three-monthly intervals. If the accounting period is less than 12 months, the final instalment is generally due 14 days after the date falling one month before the end of the period. Earlier instalments are required only if they fall due before the final instalment date. If the accounting period does not end on the last day of the month and there is no day in the previous month with the same date, the final instalment is due 14 days after the last day of the previous month.

In all other cases, the first instalment is due six months and 14 days into the accounting period and the last is due three months and 14 days after the end of the accounting period. Interim instalments are due at quarterly intervals.

Except for accounting periods of less than 12 months, the amount of each instalment should be one quarter of the total liability. Interest on tax underpaid by any instalment will run from the due date of that instalment. In cases of deliberate or reckless non-payment or underpayment, a penalty of up to twice the amount of interest may be charged. Subject to similar penalty for fraud or negligence, a company may claim repayment of tax paid by instalments if its circumstances change such that the total liability is likely to be less than previously calculated. HMRC will accept claims for repayment that are dependent on events in subsequent accounting periods only in exceptional circumstances; for example, where the losses in the subsequent accounting period are so large they will comfortably exceed the profits in the previous accounting period. Full supporting evidence will be required from the company to confirm the exceptional circumstances. (HMRC Company Taxation Manual CTM92650).

HMRC are given extensive powers to require information and records to ascertain reasons for non-payment of an instalment, the validity of a repayment claim or whether the amount of an instalment is consistent with the quality and quantity of information available as to the company's likely corporation tax liability.

Companies chargeable to corporation tax only because of chargeable gains

If a company is chargeable to corporation tax for an accounting period only because of a chargeable gain and would otherwise be very large for that period, it is instead treated as only large.

Such companies are likely to have short accounting periods, in some cases of only one day. For a one day accounting period, this rule may apply to relatively small gains, owing to the requirement to reduce the relevant thresholds on a time basis. The effect for such a period is that the tax is due three months and 14 days after the one day accounting period instead of on the day itself. This rule affects, in particular, non-resident companies which dispose of direct or indirect interests in UK land.

[*SI 1998 No 3175; SI 2017 No 1072*].

HMRC have published guidance outlining the way in which they will use their information and penalty powers under the above regulations; the information powers are not intended for routine use, and the majority of cases of late or inadequate payment will attract only an interest charge, not a penalty. A penalty will be sought in only the most serious cases involving flagrant abuse of the regulations. (HMRC Enquiry Manual, EM8301; Revenue Press Release 8 June 1999).

Penalties are also chargeable for non-compliance with a notice to produce information, records etc. [*TMA 1970, s 98*].

Groups of companies

HMRC may enter into arrangements ('Group Payment Arrangements') with some or all of the members of a group of companies (defined to include all 51% subsidiaries) for one of them to discharge any liability of each of them for the accounting period to which the arrangements relate. [*TMA 1970, s 59F*]. See Revenue Tax Bulletins April 1999 pp 647–650 and April 2001 pp 831–836.

There are also provisions to allow two companies within a group (as defined for group relief purposes under *CTA 2010, Pt 5*) to jointly give notice to HMRC that a 'tax refund relating to an accounting period' which falls to be made to one of them should be surrendered in whole or part to the other. The surrendering company is then treated as having received on the 'relevant date' a payment equal to the refund (or part), and the recipient company as having paid on that date corporation tax equal to the amount of the refund (or part). [*CTA 2010, ss 963–966*]. These provisions are designed to enable group members to rearrange their tax liabilities without suffering a disadvantage because of the higher rates for interest on unpaid tax as compared with those for interest on overpaid tax. See Tolley's Corporation Tax under Groups of Companies for full coverage of the provisions.

Payment by instalments etc.

[45.5] Where the whole or part of the consideration for a disposal is receivable by instalments over a period exceeding 18 months, beginning not earlier than the date of disposal, the tax arising may at the option of the person making the disposal be paid by such instalments as HMRC allows, over a period not exceeding eight years (and ending not later than the time at which the last of the instalments of the consideration is payable). [*TCGA 1992, s 280*].

Example

Paul sells an asset on 31 March 2025 for £351,000. The consideration is to be paid by 12 annual instalments of £29,500 beginning on 31 March 2025. Paul originally purchased the asset for £13,000 in 1990 and his allowable costs of sale are £45,000. The gain is not chargeable at the higher rates and does not qualify for business asset disposal relief. Paul has no other chargeable gains in 2024/25.

Paul's liability to capital gains tax for 2024/25 is as follows:

	£
Consideration	351,000

	£
Less costs of sale	5,000
Acquisition cost	13,000
Chargeable gain 2024/25	333,000
Annual exempt amount	3,000
Gain chargeable to tax	£330,000
Capital gains tax payable (£330,000 × 20%)	£66,000

If Paul opts under *TCGA 1992, s 280* to pay the tax by instalments, the following payments will be due.

31 January 2026	£14,750
31 March 2026	£14,750
31 March 2027	£14,750
31 March 2028	£14,750
31 March 2029	£7,000

Notes to the example

(a) HMRC's practice is to ask for instalments of tax equal to half of each instalment of consideration until the total tax liability has been discharged. To the extent that instalments of consideration under the contract fall due on or before the normal due date for the payment of tax (31 January in the tax year following that in which the disposal occurred), the respective instalments of tax are payable on that normal due date. Where instalments of consideration fall due after that time, then the respective instalments of tax are payable on the dates when the taxpayer is contractually entitled to receive the consideration. (HMRC Capital Gains Manual CG14910).

(b) Interest on unpaid tax is charged on each instalment only if it is paid late and will run from the date when the instalment was due until the date of payment. (HMRC Self-Assessment Manual SAM80072).

(c) The instalment provisions do not apply to deferred consideration which is unquantified and contingent. See **10.2** CAPITAL SUMS DERIVED FROM ASSETS and **16.14** COMPUTATION OF GAINS AND LOSSES.

See HMRC Capital Gains Manual CG14910.

Gifts of land or shares etc.

Subject to the conditions below, capital gains tax chargeable on a gift may, on election in writing, be paid by ten equal yearly instalments. The first instalment is due on the ordinary due date and the unpaid tax will attract interest on unpaid tax in the usual way and which will be payable with each instalment. The outstanding balance together with accrued interest may be paid at any time. The deferral of payment is available where the whole or any part of specified assets is disposed of by way of gift or is deemed to be disposed of by trustees under *TCGA 1992, s 71(1)* or *s 72(1)* (see **56.16–56.18** SETTLEMENTS) and the disposal is *either* one to which neither *TCGA 1992, s 165(4)* nor *s 260(3)* (see

30.2 and 30.10 HOLD-OVER RELIEFS) applies (or would apply if a claim was made) *or* one to which either of those sections does apply but on which the held-over gain only partly reduces the gain otherwise arising or is nil.

The assets specified for this purpose are: land or any interest or estate in land; any shares or securities of a company which, immediately before the disposal, gave control to the person making or deemed to be making the disposal; and any shares or securities of a company not falling within the foregoing and not listed on a recognised stock exchange (see 57.27 SHARES AND SECURITIES) nor dealt in on the Unlisted Securities Market (now closed).

Tax and any accrued interest is payable immediately if the disposal was by way of a gift to a person connected (see 17 CONNECTED PERSONS) with the donor or was deemed to be made under *TCGA 1992, s 71(1)* or *s 72(1)* and the assets are disposed of for a valuable consideration under a subsequent disposal (whether or not made by the original donee). Interest on unpaid tax is chargeable on each instalment as if no election to pay by instalments had been made. Instalments and interest may be paid at any time with the interest calculation adjusted accordingly.

These provisions apply in relation to a chargeable gain accruing under *TCGA 1992, s 169C(7)* (clawback of relief under *TCGA 1992, s 165* or *s 260* if settlement becomes settlor-interested — see 30.8 HOLD-OVER RELIEFS) as they apply to a gain accruing on a disposal if:

- the 'relevant disposal' (see 30.8 HOLD-OVER RELIEFS) in question was a disposal of the whole or part of any asset of a type specified above, and
- at the time that the chargeable gain is deemed to accrue, no part of the subject-matter of the relevant disposal has been disposed of for valuable consideration under a subsequent disposal (whether or not by the trustees to whom the relevant disposal was made).

Tax and accrued interest are payable immediately if any part of the subject-matter of the relevant disposal is disposed of for valuable consideration under a subsequent disposal (whether or not by the trustees to whom the relevant disposal was made).

[*TCGA 1992, s 281*].

Example

On 1 June 2024, Chris gives a parcel of land to his son Scott. The market value of the land on that date was £392,000. Chris purchased the land in 1990 for £199,000, and makes no other disposals in 2024/25. For the purposes of this example only, the rate of interest on unpaid capital gains tax is taken to be 4% throughout.

Chris's liability to capital gains tax for 2024/25 is as follows:

	£
Consideration	392,000
Less acquisition cost	199,000
Chargeable gain 2024/25	193,000
Annual exempt amount	3,000

		£
Gain chargeable to tax		£190,000
Capital gains tax payable (£190,000 × 20%)		£38,000

If Chris elects under *TCGA 1992, s 281*, before 31 January 2026 to pay the tax by instalments, the following payments will be due.

	£	£
1st instalment due 31.1.26		3,800
2nd instalment due 31.1.27	3,800	
Interest 4% × £34,200	1,368	5,168
3rd instalment due 31.1.28	3,800	
Interest 4% × £30,400	1,216	5,016
4th instalment due 31.1.29	3,800	
Interest 4% × £26,600	1,064	4,864
5th instalment due 31.1.30	3,800	
Interest 4% × £22,800	912	4,712
6th instalment due 31.1.31	3,800	
Interest 4% × £19,000	760	4,560
7th instalment due 31.1.32	3,800	
Interest 4% × £15,200	608	4,408
8th instalment due 31.1.33	3,800	
Interest 4% × £11,400	456	4,256
9th instalment due 31.1.34	3,800	
Interest 4% × £7,600	304	4,104
10th instalment due 31.1.35	3,800	
Interest 4% × £3,800	152	3,952
Total tax and interest		£44,840

Notes to the example

(a) An election under *TCGA 1992, s 281* may be made at any time before the tax becomes payable (HMRC Capital Gains Manual CG66452).

(b) Interest on unpaid tax is charged as if no election had been made. The interest on the unpaid portion of the tax is added to each instalment and must be paid accordingly. (HMRC Self-Assessment Manual SAM80072).

For a summary of other reliefs available to disposals by way of gift etc., see **25.3** GIFTS.

'Time to pay' arrangements

[45.6] By concession, under a 'time to pay' arrangement, a taxpayer enters into a negotiated agreement with HMRC, which takes full account of his circumstances (e.g. illness, unemployment, unforeseen short-term business difficulties), and thereby commits to settle his tax liabilities by regular instalments. Clear reasons for allowing settlement over an extended period that runs beyond the due date must be established during negotiations and any such arrangement is normally subject to adequate provision being made to settle future liabilities on time. Interest on unpaid tax is chargeable in the normal way on the full amount unpaid at the due date and not just on overdue instalments. However, a late payment penalty may be avoided where a 'time to pay' arrangement is in force (see **36.6** LATE PAYMENT INTEREST AND PENALTIES). (HMRC Debt Management and Banking Manual DMBM800000 onwards). HMRC require all instalment payments under a 'time to pay' arrangement to be made by direct debit, unless the taxpayer is unable to set up a direct debit. (HMRC Notice 14 July 2015).

HMRC may require a business to produce an independent business review where they consider it appropriate (HMRC Debt Management and Banking Manual DMBM802230). HMRC originally announced that this would apply to tax debts of £1 million or more. (HMRC Press Notice 29 March 2010).

Self-assessment taxpayers with a payment due on 31 January 2021 or later of up to £30,000 can use a self-service time to pay facility in order to agree a plan with HMRC to spread their payment over 12 months. The taxpayer must have no other tax debts and have no other payment plans set up. See www.gov.uk/difficulties-paying-hmrc. Taxpayers with a payment due in excess of £30,000 must apply for a time to pay arrangement in the usual way.

Managed payment plans

[45.7] There is legislation providing for managed payment plans, under which a taxpayer agrees with HMRC to pay income tax, capital gains tax or corporation tax (other than corporation tax payable under a group payment arrangement — see **45.4** above) by instalments which are 'balanced' equally before and after the normal due date. Although the legislation was enacted in 2009, HMRC have not yet implemented the scheme.

[*TMA 1970, ss 59G, 59H*].

CGT exit charge payment plans

[45.8] Taxpayers liable to pay certain capital gains tax 'exit charges' can defer payment by entering into a CGT exit charge payment plan with HMRC. The facility is intended to ensure that the UK's exit charges comply with EU law but continue to be available following Brexit.

Where a person is treated as resident in a territory outside the EEA for the purposes of a double tax arrangement, he is also treated as resident in that territory for the purposes of these provisions.

See **45.9** below for exit charge payment plans available to companies which become non-UK resident.

Non-resident person

A person who is resident in an EEA state other than the UK can enter into a payment plan if he is liable to an exit charge under *TCGA 1992, s 25(1)* or *(3)* (deemed disposal of an asset used for UK branch or agency – see **43.3** OVERSEAS MATTERS) for a tax year. The plan can apply to any or all of the assets subject to the exit charge.

A person can only enter into a plan if either:

(a) at the time of the event giving rise to the charge he had a right to freedom of establishment under EU law or under the Agreement on the EEA; or
(b) at any subsequent time, he carries on a trade in an EEA state other than the UK through a branch or agency and the asset or assets to which the plan will apply are used in or for the purposes of that trade or are used or held for the purposes of the branch or agency.

The amount of the '*exit charge*' is equal to the difference between the actual CGT liability for the tax year and the amount that the CGT liability would be if gains arising under *TCGA 1992, s 25* were ignored. '*Trade*' includes a profession or vocation.

Trustees becoming non-resident

Trustees of a settlement can enter into a payment plan if they are liable to an exit charge under *TCGA 1992, s 80* (deemed disposal of assets where trustees cease to be UK-resident – see **42.2** OFFSHORE SETTLEMENTS) for a tax year. The plan can apply to any or all of the assets subject to the exit charge.

Trustees can only enter into a plan if:

(i) at the time they ceased to be UK-resident they had a right to freedom of establishment under EU law or under the Agreement on the EEA;
(ii) immediately before that time they used the asset or assets to which the plan will apply for an economically significant activity (as defined) carried on in the UK; and
(iii) immediately after that time, the trustees become resident in another EEA state and use the asset or assets for an economically significant activity carried on there.

The amount of the '*exit charge*' is equal to the difference between the actual CGT liability for the tax year and the amount that the CGT liability would be if gains arising under *TCGA 1992, s 80* were ignored.

Entering into a payment plan

The taxpayer must apply to HMRC to enter into the plan on or before the normal due date for payment of the exit charge. The application must include all of the required details of the plan. The plan must specify:

(A) where the exit charge is under *TCGA 1992, s 25*, the EEA state in which the taxpayer is resident and, if he has ceased to carry on a trade in the UK through a branch or agency, the date on which he did so;

(B) where the exit charge is under *TCGA 1992, s 80*, the date on which the trustees became non-UK resident and the EEA state in which they became resident; and

(C) the amount of the exit charge and the amount to be deferred under the plan.

If HMRC consider that there would otherwise be a serious risk to collection of the tax, the plan may include provision for HMRC to take security for the tax.

A payment plan is void if any information provided by the taxpayer does not fully and accurately disclose all facts and considerations material to HMRC's decision to enter into it or if an event giving rise to the exit charge is part of arrangements a main purpose of which is to defer the payment of the exit charge by the taxpayer.

A plan may relate to the whole of the exit charge or to only part. If the plan relates only to gains on some of the assets subject to the exit charge, the proportion of the exit charge attributable to each asset is equal to the proportion that the gain on that asset bears to the total gains.

Effect of payment plan

A payment plan takes effect where the taxpayer agrees to pay, and HMRC agree to accept payment of, the deferred exit charge (and any interest on it) in accordance with the plan. The plan must provide for payment of the deferred amount in six equal instalments, the first due on the normal due date (31 January following the tax year) and then at annual intervals.

The plan does not prevent the tax included in it from becoming due and payable in the normal way, but HMRC may not seek payment otherwise than in accordance with the plan. They may, however, make repayments of any amount of the tax paid, or amount paid on account of the tax, before the plan is entered into.

The tax deferred carries interest as if the plan had not been entered into. Each payment under the plan must include any interest on the tax. A late payment penalty (see **36.6** LATE PAYMENT INTEREST AND PENALTIES) will only be payable if the taxpayer fails to make payments in accordance with the plan. If the taxpayer becomes bankrupt or his estate is sequestered, or if he becomes resident in a state or territory outside the EEA, the entire outstanding balance of the deferred tax is payable on the date on which the next instalment would otherwise be due.

There is nothing to prevent a taxpayer paying any of the tax before the time it becomes payable under the plan.

[*TMA 1970, s 59BB, Sch 3ZAA*].

Corporation tax exit charge payment plans

[45.9] A company which ceases to be resident in the UK may enter into a CT exit charge payment plan with HMRC to defer payment of the exit charges which arise under a number of corporation tax provisions, including the chargeable gains provisions. The facility can also be used by certain non-resident companies which cease to carry on all or part of a trade in the UK through a permanent establishment. The facility is intended to ensure that the UK's exit charges comply with EU law. See *Redevco Properties UK 1 Ltd v HMRC* [2023] SFTD 1028, in which (before the introduction of payment plans) the charges were held to comply with EU law only with the addition of a conforming interpretation allowing for payment by annual instalments on similar lines to the payment plan rules.

For HMRC guidance, including information which the company will need to provide, see HMRC Company Taxation Manual CTM34131–34139.

See **45.8** above for exit charge payment plans available to certain individuals and trustees subject to exit charges. See also **14.18** COMPANIES for the treatment of assets subject to EU exit charges.

Company ceasing to be UK-resident

An 'eligible company' which ceases to be resident in the UK can enter into a CT exit charge payment plan if it becomes resident in another European Economic Area (EEA) state and is liable to pay 'qualifying corporation tax' in respect of the 'migration accounting period'. The following further conditions must be satisfied:

(i) on ceasing to be UK-resident the company must carry on a business in an EEA state; and
(ii) on becoming resident in the other EEA state, the company must not be treated as resident in a non-EEA territory for the purposes of any double tax arrangements.

The EEA state must either be a member of the EU or must be party to a mutual assistance agreement with the UK equivalent to the EU's Directive on mutual assistance (*Directive 2010/24/EU*) (a '*relevant EEA state*').

The company must apply to HMRC to enter into the plan before the end of the nine-month period following the migration accounting period and must include in the application all the required information (see below).

An '*eligible company*' is one that has a right to freedom of establishment under EU law or under the Agreement on the EEA. The '*migration accounting period*' is, if an accounting period comes to an end on the company ceasing to be UK-resident, that accounting period. In any other case, the migration accounting period is the accounting period during which the company ceases to be UK-resident.

A company is liable to pay '*qualifying corporation tax*' in respect of the migration accounting period if the corporation tax it is liable to pay for the period (CT1) is greater than the amount of corporation tax it would be liable to pay if any income, profits, gains, losses or debits arising only under the exit charge provisions listed below were ignored (CT2). The amount of the qualifying corporation tax is the difference between CT1 and CT2. The exit charge provisions are:

(a) *TCGA 1992, s 185* (deemed disposal of assets on company ceasing to be UK-resident; see **43.16** OVERSEAS MATTERS);

(b) *CTA 2009, s 162* as applied by *CTA 2009, s 41(2)(b)* (valuation of trading stock on ceasing to be within the charge to corporation tax);
(c) *CTA 2009, s 333* (deemed assignment of loan relationships on company ceasing to be UK-resident);
(d) *CTA 2009, s 609* (deemed assignment of derivative contract rights and liabilities on company ceasing to be UK-resident);
(e) *CTA 2009, s 859(2)(a)* (deemed realisation of intangible fixed asset on it ceasing to be chargeable intangible asset when company ceases to be UK-resident).

For the purposes of these provisions, '*exit charge assets*' and '*exit charge liabilities*' are assets or liabilities in respect of which income, profits or gains arise in the migration accounting period under the exit charge provisions above. '*TCGA or trading stock exit charge assets*' are exit charge assets in respect of which income, profits or gains arise under (a)–(c) above, other than any intangible fixed assets excluded from the intangible assets regime by that regime's commencement rules (see **15.13** COMPANIES — CORPORATE FINANCE AND INTANGIBLES). '*Financial exit charge assets or liabilities*' are exit charge assets or liabilities in respect of which income, profits or gains arise under (d) or (e) above. '*Intangible exit charge assets*' means exit charge assets in respect of which income, profits or gains arise under (f) or (g) above together with intangible assets excluded from being TCGA or trading stock exit charge assets as above.

[*TMA 1970, s 59FA, Sch 3ZB paras 1–3*].

Non-UK resident company with UK permanent establishment

An eligible company (defined as above) which is not resident in the UK but carries on a trade there through a permanent establishment in an accounting period (the '*migration accounting period*') can enter into a CT exit charge payment plan if one or more 'PE qualifying events' occurs and the company is liable to pay 'qualifying corporation tax' in respect of the migration accounting period.

The company must apply to HMRC to enter into the plan before the end of the nine-month period following the migration accounting period and must include in the application all the required information (see below).

A '*PE qualifying event*' occurs in relation to an asset or liability of the company (a PE qualifying asset or liability) if:

(I) an event occurs which triggers a deemed disposal and reacquisition of the asset or liability, or a valuation of the asset, under one of the exit charge provisions listed below;
(II) the event occurs during the migration accounting period or causes that period to end;
(III) at the time of the event, the company is not treated as resident in a non-EEA territory for the purposes of any double tax arrangements; and
(IV) immediately after the event, the asset or liability is held or owed by the company for the purposes of a permanent establishment in a relevant EEA state or, where the company is resident in a relevant EEA state, is held or owed by the company otherwise than for the purposes of a permanent establishment.

A company is liable to pay '*qualifying corporation tax*' in respect of the migration accounting period if the corporation tax it is liable to pay for the period (CT1) is greater than the amount of corporation tax it would be liable to pay if any income, profits, gains, losses or debits arising only under the exit charge provisions listed below were ignored (CT2). The amount of the qualifying corporation tax is the difference between CT1 and CT2. The exit charge provisions are:

(A) *TCGA 1992, s 25* (deemed disposal of assets leaving UK; see **43.3** OVERSEAS MATTERS);
(B) *CTA 2009, s 162* as applied by *CTA 2009, s 41(2)(b)* (valuation of trading stock on ceasing to be within the charge to corporation tax);
(C) *CTA 2009, s 334* (deemed assignment of loan relationship on company ceasing to hold relationship for UK permanent establishment);
(D) *CTA 2009, s 610* (deemed assignment of derivative contract rights and liabilities on company ceasing to hold contract for UK permanent establishment);
(E) *CTA 2009, s 859(2)(b)* (deemed realisation of intangible fixed asset on asset ceasing to be a chargeable intangible asset).

For the purposes of these provisions, '*exit charge assets*' and '*exit charge liabilities*' are PE qualifying assets or liabilities in respect of which income, profits or gains arise in the migration accounting period under the exit charge provisions above. '*TCGA or trading stock exit charge assets*' are exit charge assets in respect of which income, profits or gains arise under (A) or (B) above, other than any intangible fixed assets excluded from the intangible assets regime by that regime's commencement rules (see **15.13** COMPANIES — CORPORATE FINANCE AND INTANGIBLES). '*Financial exit charge assets or liabilities*' are exit charge assets or liabilities in respect of which income, profits or gains arise under (C) or (D) above. '*Intangible exit charge assets*' means exit charge assets in respect of which income, profits or gains arise under (E) above together with intangible assets excluded from being TCGA or trading stock exit charge assets as above.

[*TMA 1970, s 59FA, Sch 3ZB paras 4–6*].

Entering into a payment plan

A CT exit charge payment plan takes effect where the company agrees to pay, and HMRC agree to accept payment of, all or part of the qualifying corporation tax in accordance with the payment method below. The company must also agree to pay interest on the tax as described below. The plan must specify the following:

(1) where the company ceases to be UK-resident, the date on which it so ceases and the EEA state in which the company has become resident;
(2) where the company has a UK permanent establishment, the EEA state in which it is resident and, if the PE qualifying event is the company ceasing to trade in the UK through a permanent establishment, the date of cessation;
(3) the amount of qualifying corporation tax which the company considers is payable for the migration accounting period and the amount to be postponed;

(4) the amount of postponed tax attributable to each exit charge asset or liability;
(5) requirements for ongoing provision of information by the company to HMRC about the exit charge assets and liabilities.

The amount of tax attributable to each exit charge asset or liability for this purpose is the proportion of the tax postponed under the plan that the income, profits or gains arising in respect of that asset or liability under the exit charge concerned bears to the total income, profits or gains arising in respect of all the exit charges or liabilities under the exit charge provisions.

Where HMRC consider that entering into a plan would otherwise present a serious risk to collection of the tax, the plan may include provision for HMRC to take security for the tax. This would usually be in the form of a bank guarantee.

A payment plan is void if any information provided by the company does not fully and accurately disclose all facts and considerations material to HMRC's decision to enter into it.

[*TMA 1970, s 59FA, Sch 3ZB paras 7, 8, 10–12*].

Effect of payment plan

A CT exit charge payment plan does not prevent the tax included in it from becoming due and payable in the normal way, but HMRC may not seek payment otherwise than in accordance with the plan. HMRC may, however, make repayments of any amount of the tax paid, or amount paid on account of the tax, before the plan is entered into.

The tax deferred under the plan carries interest as if the plan had not been entered into. Each payment under the plan must include any interest on the tax.

A late payment penalty (when in force: see **36.6** LATE PAYMENT INTEREST AND PENALTIES) will only be payable if the company fails to make payments in accordance with the plan.

There is nothing to prevent a company paying any of the tax before the time it becomes payable under the plan.

[*TMA 1970, s 59FA, Sch 3ZB para 9*].

Payment method

The tax postponed under the plan is due in six equal annual instalments starting nine months and one day after the end of the migration accounting period.

Where the company becomes insolvent, enters administration or a liquidator is appointed, the balance of the tax is payable in full on the date on which the next instalment would otherwise be due. This applies also where the company becomes insolvent etc. under a corresponding law of a country or territory outside the UK, where the company ceases to be resident in an EEA state without becoming resident in another relevant EEA state and where the company fails to pay an amount due under the plan within 12 months of it becoming due.

A proportion of the postponed tax becomes due immediately if a 'trigger event' occurs in relation to an exit charge asset or liability before the final instalment becomes due (provided that there has been no previous trigger event in relation to that asset or liability). The amount due is:

$$(A - B) \times \frac{O}{T}$$

where:

A = the amount of postponed tax attributable to the asset or liability;
B = the amount of postponed tax that has previously become chargeable because of a 'partial trigger event' (see below);
O = the outstanding postponed tax at the time of the trigger event; and
T = the total postponed tax.

Where the asset is a TCGA or trading stock exit charge asset or an intangible exit charge, a '*trigger event*' occurs when the company disposes of it or ceases to hold it for the purposes of a business carried on by the company in a relevant EEA state without it then becoming held for the purposes of another such business. A trigger event in relation to a financial exit charge asset or liability occurs if the company ceases to be a party to the loan relationship or derivative contract or ceases to be a party to it for the purposes of a business carried on by the company in a relevant EEA state without it then becoming held for the purposes of another such business.

Part of the postponed tax also becomes due immediately if a 'partial trigger event' occurs in relation to an exit charge asset or liability before the final instalment becomes due (provided that there has been no previous trigger event in relation to that asset or liability). The amount that becomes due immediately must be calculated on a just and reasonable basis, taking account of the amount that would have been due if a trigger event had occurred. Where the asset is a TCGA or trading stock exit charge asset, a '*partial trigger event*' occurs if the company disposes of part (but not all) of it. In relation to a financial exit charge asset or liability, a partial trigger event occurs if there is a disposal of a right or liability under the loan relationship or derivative contract which amounts to a related transaction (within *CTA 2009, s 304* or *s 596*). Where the asset is an intangible exit charge asset, a partial trigger event occurs if there is a transaction resulting in a reduction in the accounting value of the asset but not resulting in the asset ceasing to be recognised on the company's balance sheet.

[*TMA 1970, Sch 3ZB paras 11–14*].

Corporation tax payment plans for transactions with EEA residents

[45.10] Companies liable to pay corporation tax on certain transactions with an EEA resident can defer payment by entering into a CT payment plan with HMRC. The facility is intended to ensure that the UK's rules for tax-neutral transfers within groups of companies comply with EU law following the FTT's decision in *Gallaher Ltd v HMRC* FTT, [2019] UKFTT 207 (TC) (see **26.3** GROUPS OF COMPANIES), although the CJEU has now held ([2023] STC 408) that the relevant UK legislation is compliant with EU law.

Given the UK's departure from the EU, the legislation providing for CT payment plans includes provisions for the rules to be repealed by statutory instrument. [*FA 2020, Sch 7 para 5*].

Qualifying transactions

A CT payment plan for an accounting period can be entered into in respect of corporation tax ('qualifying corporation tax') due as a result of any of the following 'qualifying transactions':

(i) a disposal of an asset to a non-UK resident company which is resident in an EEA state where the disposal would have been a no gain/no loss disposal within *TCGA 1992, s 139* (reconstructions involving transfer of business — see **14.12** COMPANIES) or *TCGA 1992, s 171* (intra-group transfers — see **26.3** GROUPS OF COMPANIES) if the transferee were UK-resident;

(ii) a transaction (or the first in a series of transactions) which results in the company being directly or indirectly replaced as a party to a loan relationship by a company resident outside the UK in an EEA state, where the transaction would have been within *CTA 2009, s 340(3)* (intra-group transfer at notional carrying value) if the transferee were UK-resident;

(iii) a transaction (or the first in a series of transactions) which results in the company being directly or indirectly replaced as a party to a derivative contract by a company resident outside the UK in an EEA state, where the transaction would have been within *CTA 2009, s 625(3)* (intra-group transfer at notional carrying value) if the transferee were UK-resident;

(iv) a transfer of an intangible asset to a non-UK resident company which is resident in an EEA state where the transfer would have been tax-neutral under *CTA 2009, s 775(1)* (transfers within a group) if the transferee were UK-resident.

The amount of 'qualifying corporation tax' for an accounting period is the excess of the corporation tax it is liable to pay for the period over the corporation tax it would be liable to pay if any gains, credits, losses or debits for qualifying transactions were ignored. A plan may include all or part of the qualifying corporation tax for the period.

Entering into a payment plan

The company must apply to HMRC to enter into the plan within nine months after the end of the accounting period. The application must include all of the required details of the plan. The plan must:

(a) specify the accounting period to which it relates;

(b) specify the amount of the qualifying corporation tax and the amount to be deferred under the plan;

(c) identify each qualifying transaction and, for each such transaction, the name of the transferee, the EEA state in which it is resident and the amount of tax to be deferred which is attributable to it.

In (c) above, the proportion of the deferred tax attributable to a transaction is equal to the proportion that the gain or credit on the transaction bears to the total gains or credits from all qualifying transactions in the period.

If HMRC consider that there would otherwise be a serious risk to collection of the tax, the plan may include provision for HMRC to take security for the tax.

A payment plan is void if any information provided by the company does not fully and accurately disclose all facts and considerations material to HMRC's decision to enter into it.

Effect of payment plan

A CT payment plan does not prevent the tax included in it from becoming due and payable in the normal way, but HMRC may not seek payment otherwise than in accordance with the plan. HMRC may, however, make repayments of any amount of the tax paid, or amount paid on account of the tax, before the plan is entered into.

The tax deferred under the plan carries interest as if the plan had not been entered into. Each payment under the plan must include any interest on the tax.

A late payment penalty (when in force: see **36.6** LATE PAYMENT INTEREST AND PENALTIES) will only be payable if the company fails to make payments in accordance with the plan.

There is nothing to prevent a company paying any of the tax (plus interest) before the time it becomes payable under the plan.

The tax postponed under the plan is due in six equal annual instalments starting nine months and one day after the end of the accounting period.

Where the company becomes insolvent, enters administration or a liquidator is appointed, the balance of the tax is payable in full on the date on which the next instalment would otherwise be due. This applies also where the company becomes insolvent etc. under a corresponding law of a country or territory outside the UK, where the company ceases to be within the charge to corporation tax and where the company fails to pay an amount due under the plan within 12 months of it becoming due.

A proportion of the postponed tax becomes due immediately if a 'trigger event' occurs in relation to a qualifying transaction included in the plan before the final instalment becomes due (provided that there has been no previous trigger event in relation to that transaction). The amount due is:

$$(A - B) \times \frac{O}{T}$$

where:

A = the amount of postponed tax attributable to the transaction;
B = the amount of postponed tax that has previously become chargeable because of a 'partial trigger event' (see below);
O = the outstanding postponed tax at the time of the trigger event; and
T = the total postponed tax.

A 'trigger event' occurs when the transferee disposes of the asset which is the subject of the transaction or ceases to be a party to the loan relationship or derivative contract. A trigger also occurs if the transferee ceases to be resident in an EEA state without becoming resident in another EEA state or if the company and the transferee cease to be members of the same group.

Part of the postponed tax also becomes due immediately if a 'partial trigger event' occurs in relation to a qualifying transaction before the final instalment becomes due (provided that there has been no previous trigger event in relation to that transaction). The amount that becomes due immediately must be calculated on a just and reasonable basis, taking account of the amount that would have been due if a trigger event had occurred. Where the qualifying transaction was within (i) above, a 'partial trigger event' occurs if the transferee disposes of part (but not all) of the asset. Where the transaction was within (ii) or (iii) above, a 'partial trigger event' occurs if there is a disposal by the transferee of a right or liability under the loan relationship or derivative contract which amounts to a related transaction (within *CTA 2009, s 304* or *s 596*). Where the qualifying transaction was within (iv) above, a 'partial trigger event' occurs if the transferee enters into a subsequent transaction resulting in a reduction in the accounting value of the asset but not resulting in the asset ceasing to be recognised on the company's balance sheet. If the asset has no balance sheet value, this rule applies as if, immediately before the subsequent transaction, it did have such a value.

[*TMA 1970, s 59FB, Sch 3ZC; FA 2020, Sch 7 paras 2, 4*].

Methods of payment

[45.11] Capital gains tax and corporation tax can be paid by any one of a number of methods, including cheques, postal orders, electronic transfer or credit card. Each method has its own effective date of payment for the purposes of calculating any interest or surcharges. See **45.12** below. Before 23 November 2023, capital gains tax could be paid by certificate of tax deposit. Capital gains tax under self-assessment can be paid via the HMRC app. HMRC may charge a fee for accepting certain types of payment — see **45.16** below.

Effective dates of payment

[45.12] HMRC take the date of payment in respect of each payment method to be as follows.

- Cheques, cash, postal orders handed in at HMRC offices or received by post (except as below): the day of receipt by HMRC.
- Cheques, cash, postal orders received by post following a day when the office has been closed for whatever reason (including a weekend): the day the office was first closed.
- Cheques, cash, postal orders for corporation tax where payment should have been made electronically: the day of receipt by HMRC plus two days.
- Electronic funds transfer — payment by BACS, CHAPS, government banking service or faster payment: the date HMRC receives cleared funds.
- Online payment service (debit or credit over the internet): the date of the transaction.
- Bank Giro: the date HMRC receives cleared funds.
- Direct debit using the National Direct Debit Service (NDDS) and Strategic Direct Debit Service (SDDS): one bank working day before the payment collection date as agreed in the payment plan.

[*TMA 1970, s 70A; SI 2003 No 282, Reg 3A*]. See also HMRC Debt Management and Banking Manual DMBM201020.

Certificates of tax deposit

[45.13] Such certificates, which enable money to be set aside for payment of future tax liability, may be used in payment of capital gains tax (but not corporation tax). New certificates cannot be purchased after 22 November 2017, but existing certificates will continue to be honoured until 23 November 2023. Interest is received on these certificates from the date of purchase until the date on which the tax in respect of which they are surrendered falls due. Certificates may also be encashed (with interest to the date of encashment) but a lower rate of interest is then paid. For further details, see Tolley's Income Tax.

Payment of tax in euros

[45.14] British businesses may, if they wish, pay tax in euros. The taxpayer will be credited with the sterling value actually received by HMRC after conversion at the prevailing rate. There is no facility for making tax repayments in euros. (Revenue Press Release 31 July 1998).

Mandatory electronic payment

[45.15] HMRC have wide powers to make regulations requiring payment by electronic means of any tax or duty for which they are responsible. [*FA 2003, ss 204, 205*].

Corporation tax

Companies are required to make the following payments by electronic means:

- corporation tax, including instalment payments;
- interest on overdue corporation tax; and
- any penalty (fixed or tax-related) under *FA 1998, Sch 18 paras 17, 18* for failure to deliver a company tax return (see **52.7** RETURNS).

See **45.12** above for cases in which such payments are nevertheless made by cheque.

[*SI 2003 No 282, Reg 3*].

Fee for payment by specified methods

[45.16] HMRC charge a fee for payment of tax by certain payment methods.

With effect from 1 November 2020, where a payment is made using a business credit card or business debit card, the fee is the sum of the merchant acquirer fee (i.e the fee for processing the payment charged to the payee by the merchant acquirer), the interchange fee (i.e. the fee charged to the merchant acquirer by the issuer of the card and recharged to the payee) and the scheme fee (i.e. the fee charged to the merchant acquirer by the person responsible for the card scheme applying to the card and recharged to the payee) for the payment. Previously, where a payment was made using a credit card, the fee was the percentage of the payment given by the following table. There was no fee in respect of payments by debit card. Tax cannot be paid by personal credit card.

	Rate %
	13.1.18–31.10.20
Visa Business	1.70
Visa Commerce	2.80
Visa Corporate	1.94
Visa Purchasing	1.92
Visa Commercial	1.94
Mastercard Business	1.80
Mastercard Corporate	1.98
Mastercard Purchasing	2.20
Mastercard Fleet	1.97
Mastercard Commercial	1.98

[*FA 2008, s 136; SI 2016 No 333; SI 2020 No 657*].

Effect of making an appeal

[45.17] Where a taxpayer appeals against an HMRC decision he can also apply for any tax due to be postponed pending the determination of the appeal. See **45.18** below. Note that postponement does not affect the date from which interest on the tax will run should it become payable on determination of the appeal.

Where a party to an appeal makes a further appeal against a decision of the Tribunal any tax due in accordance with that decision is nevertheless payable. See **45.19** below.

Postponement of tax pending appeal

[45.18] The following applies in the case of APPEALS (5) against:

(a) a conclusion stated or amendment made by a final or partial closure notice on completion or part completion of an enquiry into a personal, trustee or partnership tax return (see **52.14**, **52.20** RETURNS);
(b) an HMRC amendment made by a final or partial closure notice on completion or part completion of an enquiry into a company tax return (see *FA 1998, Sch 18 para 34*);
(c) an HMRC amendment to a self-assessment during enquiry to prevent potential loss of tax (see **52.15** RETURNS and, for companies, *FA 1998, Sch 18 para 30*); and
(d) an assessment other than a self-assessment.

In the absence of any application for postponement of tax as below, tax is due and payable as if there had been no appeal.

If the appellant has grounds for believing that he is overcharged to tax by the amendment or assessment or as a result of the conclusion stated (as the case may be), he (or his agent) may, by notice in writing, apply to HMRC for a determination by them of the amount of tax which should be postponed pending the determination of the appeal. The application must be made within 30 days of the 'specified date' and must state the amount believed to be overcharged and the grounds for that belief.

Where the taxpayer disagrees with HMRC's determination, he can refer the application to the Tribunal within 30 days from the date of the document notifying HMRC's decision.

The '*specified date*' is the date of issue of the notice of amendment or assessment or, in the case of an appeal within (a) above, the date of issue of the closure notice. The mount to be postponed is the amount in which it appears that there are reasonable grounds for believing that the taxpayer is overcharged.

If the taxpayer and HMRC come to an agreement as to the amount of tax to be postponed (if any), the agreement takes effect only if it is in writing or either the taxpayer or HMRC confirm it in writing.

On the determination of (or agreement on) the amount of tax to be postponed, the balance of tax not postponed (if any) becomes due and payable as if it had been charged by an amendment or assessment issued on the date of that determination or agreement (or on the date of notice of confirmation of the latter) and in respect of which there had been no appeal.

Application for postponement may be made outside the normal 30-day time limit if the appeal itself was made later or if there is a change in circumstances which gives grounds for belief that the appellant is overcharged by the amendment etc.

If, after the determination of an amount of tax to be postponed and as a result of a change in the circumstances of the case, either the appellant or HMRC have grounds for believing that the amount postponed is excessive or insufficient, and the parties cannot agree on a revised determination, either party can apply to the Tribunal for a revised determination of the amount to be postponed. If, on this further determination or agreement, an amount of tax ceases to be postponed, that amount is treated as charged by an assessment issued on the date of the further determination (or on the date of notice of confirmation of the agreement) and in respect of which no appeal is pending. If, on the other hand, an amount of tax has been overpaid, that amount becomes repayable.

A postponement application is subject to the normal appeal provisions, but the decision of the Tribunal is final and conclusive (so that there can be no further appeal to the Upper Tribunal or Court of Appeal).

Tax which is subject to an accelerated payment notice cannot be postponed. Tax which is postponed and subsequently becomes subject to such a notice becomes due and payable. See **4.32** ANTI-AVOIDANCE.

[*TMA 1970, s 55(1)–(3)(3A)(4)–(8)(8B)–(8E)(10)(10A)(10B)(11)*].

The giving of notice of appeal, whether or not accompanied by a postponement application, does *not* affect the date from which interest accrues.

Payment of tax on determination of appeal

[45.19] The following applies where tax is payable in accordance with the determination of an appeal within **45.18**(a)–(d) above and it is either tax postponed in accordance with **45.18** above or an addition to the tax charged by the amendment or assessment before appeal. Such tax becomes due and payable as if it were charged by an amendment or assessment issued on the date on which HMRC issued to the taxpayer a notice of the total amount payable in accordance with the determination and in respect of which there had been no appeal. Any tax found to be overpaid on determination of the appeal becomes repayable. [*TMA 1970, s 55(9)*].

Tax is payable or repayable in accordance with a decision of the Tribunal even if a party appeals to the Upper Tribunal. If the amount charged in the assessment concerned is subsequently altered by the Upper Tribunal, any amount undercharged is due and payable at the end of the thirty days beginning with the date on which HMRC issue the appellant with a notice of the amount payable in accordance with the Upper Tribunal's decision. Any amount overpaid will be refunded along with such interest as may be allowed by the decision. This provision applies equally to any further appeal from a decision of the Upper Tribunal to the Courts. See **4.32** ANTI-AVOIDANCE for applications to the court or Tribunal by HMRC to disapply the requirement to repay tax where an accelerated payment notice is in force. [*TMA 1970, s 56*]. HMRC have announced that they will apply this provision consistently to all cases except where to do so would drive the taxpayer into bankruptcy or liquidation. (HMRC Internet Statement, 11 March 2010).

Collection and enforcement

[45.20] The procedure in *TCEA 2007, Sch 12* (taking control of goods) is used by HMRC in England and Wales to recover unpaid sums. In Scotland, HMRC can apply to the sheriff for a summary warrant authorising the recovery of unpaid sums. In Northern Ireland, the Collector of Taxes may distrain. [*TMA 1970, s 61; FA 2008, ss 127–129*]. See also *Herbert Berry Associates Ltd v CIR* HL 1977, 52 TC 113.

Where an amount of CGT or corporation tax due is less than £2,000, the Collector may within one year after the due date take summary magistrates' court proceedings. HMRC may also recover tax by proceedings in the county court. [*TMA 1970, ss 65, 66; CRCA 2005, s 25(1A)(6); SI 1991 No 1877*]. But for limitations in Scotland and NI see *TMA 1970, ss 65(4), 66(3)(4), 67*, and see *Mann v Cleaver* KB 1930, 15 TC 367.

Unpaid tax (and arrears) may also be recovered (with full costs) as a Crown debt in the High Court. [*TMA 1970, s 68*].

The amount of an assessment which has become final cannot be re-opened in proceedings to collect the tax (*CIR v Pearlberg* CA 1953, 34 TC 57; *CIR v Soul* CA 1976, 51 TC 86), and it is not open to the taxpayer to raise the defence that the Revenue acted *ultra vires* in raising the assessment (*CIR v Aken* CA 1990, 63 TC 395).

For whether unpaid tax is a business liability for commercial etc. purposes, see *Conway v Wingate* CA, [1952] 1 All ER 782; *Stevens v Britten* CA, [1954] 3 All ER 385; *R v Vaccari* CA, [1958] 1 All ER 468; *In re Hollebone's Agreement* CA, [1959] 2 All ER 152.

HMRC can apply to the High Court for a freezing order where there is a risk of the dissipation of assets to avoid compliance with an assessment in the period before the tax is due and payable: *HMRC v Ali* Ch D 2011, [2012] STC 42.

Amounts payable on account of CGT under the provisions at **45.3** above are recoverable as if they were an amount of tax. [*TMA 1970, s 59AB*].

Set-off of amounts owed to taxpayer against amounts payable

HMRC may set a sum payable by them to a person under any enactment and certain sums repayable by them to that person (a '*credit*') against any sum payable to them by that person (a '*debit*') under any enactment or under a contract settlement (see **6.8** ASSESSMENTS). The sums repayable by HMRC that can be credits for this purpose are sums paid by the taxpayer in connection with any liability (including any purported or anticipated liability) to make a payment to HMRC under any enactment or under a contract settlement. For this purpose, sums paid or payable include sums that have been or are to be credited.

This provision applies without prejudice to any other power of HMRC to set off amounts (in relation to indirect taxes and national insurance contributions) but is subject to any obligation of HMRC to set the credit against any other sum.

The above provisions cannot be used, where an insolvency procedure has been applied to a person, to set a 'post-insolvency credit' against a 'pre-insolvency debit'. For this purpose, a '*post-insolvency credit*' is a credit which became due after the insolvency procedure was applied and which relates to, or to matters occurring at, times after it was applied, and a '*pre-insolvency debit*' is a debit which arose before the insolvency procedure was applied or which arose after it was applied but relates to, or to matters occurring at, times before it was applied. An insolvency procedure is applied when a bankruptcy order or winding up order is made, an administrator is appointed, a taxpayer is put into administrative receivership, a company passes a resolution for voluntary winding up, a voluntary arrangement comes into force or a deed of arrangement takes effect. An insolvency procedure is not treated as being applied to a person if it is applied at a time when another insolvency procedure applies to that person or if it is applied immediately upon another insolvency procedure ceasing to apply.

[*FA 2008, ss 130, 131, 139*].

Set-off of amounts assigned by original creditor

Where there has been a 'transfer' of a right to be paid a sum by HMRC, HMRC must set that sum against a sum payable to them by the original creditor if they would have had an obligation to do so under any enactment had the original creditor retained the right. If, but for the transfer, HMRC would have had the power under any enactment to set the sum against a sum payable to them by the original creditor, they may (but are not required to) do so. To the extent of any such set-off, the obligations of HMRC to the transferee creditor and the obligations of the original creditor are discharged. Where the right to be paid the transferred sum is dependent on a claim, these provisions apply only where such a claim is made.

In determining the amount of the sum to be paid, HMRC can make any reduction that they could have made but for the transfer, including a reduction arising from any defence to a claim for the sum.

A '*transfer*' for the above purposes includes a transfer by assignment, assignation or any other means. Where there has been more than one transfer of a right, the original creditor is the person from whom the right was first transferred.

[*FA 2008, s 133*].

Recovery of debts through the PAYE system

HMRC has the power to collect tax debts, including capital gains tax, through the PAYE system (where the taxpayer is an employee) by making adjustments to the taxpayer's tax code.

The power applies to unpaid self-assessment debts of taxpayers with a primary source of annual PAYE income of £30,000 or over. A graduated scale applies so that a maximum of £17,000 can be coded out for a person with earnings over £90,000. A £3,000 limit continues to apply to self-assessment balancing payments.

[*ITEPA 2003, s 684; SI 2003 No 2682, Reg 14A*].

See Tolley's Income Tax for full coverage of PAYE.

Power to obtain details of debtors

HMRC can by notice in writing require certain third parties to provide the details of a person who owes HMRC a sum by or virtue of an enactment or under a contract settlement. The third parties concerned are companies, local authorities, local authority associations and also other persons if HMRC have reasonable grounds to believe that they have obtained the details in the course of carrying on a business. Charities, and others providing services on behalf of a charity, are excluded if the details were obtained in the course of providing services free of charge to the recipient. HMRC must have reasonable grounds to believe that the third party has the details required.

Where such a notice is given, the third party must provide the details within such time, by such means and in such form as is reasonably indicated in the notice. There is a right of appeal against a notice or a requirement in a notice on the ground that compliance would be unduly onerous. A penalty of £300 (or a sum specified by Treasury regulations) applies for failure to comply with a notice.

[*FA 2009, s 97, Sch 49*].

Security for payments of corporation tax

[45.21] Where an HMRC officer considers it necessary for the protection of the revenue, he may require a company or its officers to give security for the payment of tax which it is or may become liable to pay. For this purpose, company officers are directors, company secretary, any similar officer or any person purporting to act in such a capacity. Security of a specified value may be required from one or more person and each is jointly and severally liable to give the security.

HMRC must give a notice to each person from whom security is required specifying the value of, the manner in which and the date on which, security is to be given and the period of time for which it is required. The date specified must not be earlier than the thirtieth day after the date the notice is given.

A person who has given security can apply to HMRC to reduce the value of security held by HMRC (i.e. to seek a repayment) if either his circumstances have changed because of hardship or having ceased to be a company officer or there has been a significant change in the company's circumstances so that either security is no longer needed to protect the revenue or a smaller value is so needed. A person who is jointly and severally liable for the security but has not made a payment cannot make such an application. If an application is made by a person who is jointly and severally liable on the grounds of a change in his circumstances, HMRC may notify the company or any other company officer to provide security in substitution for the original security.

A person given a notice requiring security can appeal against it or against any requirement in it. A person who has made an application to reduce the value of security given may appeal against HMRC's decision not to reduce the value or to make a smaller reduction than the application requested. Notice of appeal must be given within 30 days of the day on which the notice was given or HMRC notifies their decision and must state the grounds of appeal. On appeal against a notice requiring security, the Tribunal may confirm or vary the requirement or set aside the notice. On appeal against an HMRC decision on an application to reduce security, the Tribunal may confirm or vary the decision. On the final determination of an appeal, any security to be given is due by the thirtieth day after the determination.

Failure to comply with a requirement to give security by the due date is an offence punishable, on summary conviction, to a fine.

[*FA 1998, Sch 18 para 88A; SI 2019 No 384, Regs 1, 5–14*].

Security may in particular be required where a company has a poor compliance record or in cases of phoenixism (i.e. where a company accrues a tax debt, goes into liquidation or administration and the person responsible for running the business sets up again). See Treasury Explanatory Notes to the Finance (No 3) Bill 2018.

Enforcement by deduction from accounts

[45.22] HMRC have the power in England, Wales and Northern Ireland to enforce certain debts by direct recovery from the bank etc. account of the debtor. HMRC may issue a hold notice (see **45.24** below) to 'deposit-takers' effectively freezing the funds needed to pay the debt and giving the taxpayer and certain other interested parties an opportunity to object to HMRC against the issuing of the notice. If HMRC dismiss any objections there is a right of appeal to the county court. If there is no objection or appeal or if they are unsuccessful HMRC may issue a deduction notice (see **45.25** below) requiring the deposit-taker to deduct specified amounts from the taxpayer's accounts and pay them over to HMRC. Before issuing a hold notice HMRC may, but are not required to, issue an information notice (see **45.23** below) to ascertain which accounts are held by the taxpayer with a particular deposit-taker. All notices must be given in writing.

The power can be used to collect sums which are due and payable by a person to HMRC under or by virtue of an enactment or under a contract settlement where the following conditions are met:

(1) the sum is at least £1,000;
(2) the sum is an 'established debt' or is due under (or is the disputed tax specified in) an accelerated payment notice or partner payment notice (see **4.30** ANTI-AVOIDANCE onwards); and
(3) HMRC are satisfied that the taxpayer is aware that the sum is due and payable to them.

A sum is an '*established debt*' if there is no possibility that it, or any part of it, will cease to be due and payable to HMRC. This will be the case where there is no right of appeal, where the period for making an appeal has expired without an appeal having been made or where an appeal has been finally determined or withdrawn. Powers to grant permission to make a late appeal are disregarded for this purpose.

Before issuing an information notice or hold notice HMRC must consider whether, to the best of their knowledge, there are any matters as a result of which the taxpayer is, or may be, at a particular disadvantage in dealing with HMRC in relation to the unpaid sum. Any such matters must be taken into account in deciding whether or not to issue a notice. HMRC have published guidance on the factors which they consider to be relevant to deciding whether a person is at a particular disadvantage. The guidance sets out four indicators which HMRC will consider: a disability or long-term health condition; a temporary illness, physical or mental health condition; personal issues (such as redundancy, bereavement or trauma) and lower levels of literacy, numeracy and/or education. See www.gov.uk/government/publications/direct-recovery-of-debts-and-vulnerable-customers/direct-recovery-of-debts-vulnerable-customers.

A '*deposit-taker*' is, broadly, a person who may lawfully accept deposits in the UK in the course of a business. A deposit-taker is not liable for damages for anything done in good faith to comply with these provisions.

Joint accounts

References below to an account held by a person include a joint account held by that person and one or more others.

[*F(No 2)A 2015, s 51, Sch 8 paras 2, 5, 18, 22–24*].

Tax charged in a determination

Where HMRC are taking action under these provisions in respect of tax charged by a determination within **52.17** RETURNS (or a corporation tax determination, see **52.21** RETURNS) and the determination is superseded by a self-assessment, the action may be continued as if it were an action to recover so much of the tax charged by the self-assessment as is due and payable, has not been paid and does not exceed the amount charged in the determination. [*TMA 1970, s 28C(4A); FA 1998, Sch 18 para 40(5); F(No 2)A 2015, Sch 8 paras 25, 40*].

Regulations

The Treasury has wide powers to make regulations for supplementary provisions and to amend, revoke or repeal enactments in connection with these provisions. HMRC may make regulations to alter various amounts, thresholds and time limits, to exclude certain types of account or amount from the provisions and to prescribe the information which can be required by notices. [*F(No 2)A 2015, s 51, Sch 8 paras 19–21*].

Penalties

Penalties apply to deposit-takers for various failures to comply with the provisions and for disclosures likely to prejudice HMRC's ability to recover an unpaid sum using the provisions. See **46.23** PENALTIES.

Administrative costs

A deposit-taker may charge the account holder in respect of administrative costs incurred in complying with these provisions of up to £55. A charge may only be made if there is an agreement with the account holder or holders for such a charge. The deposit-taker must have made the final payment to HMRC in accordance with a deduction notice before the charge can be made. [*SI 2016 No 44*].

Information notice

[45.23] If it appears to HMRC that a person has failed to pay a sum meeting the above conditions and that the person holds one or more accounts with a deposit-taker, they may give the deposit-taker an information notice. Such a notice requires the deposit-taker to provide HMRC with the following information:

(1) the taxpayer's name and address, national insurance number, email addresses and phone numbers and, in respect of any joint accounts, the proportion of the balance to which the taxpayer is entitled; and

(2) for each account held by the taxpayer, any account number, roll number and sort code, the type of account (including whether it is a joint account), the account balance (in the currency in which it is held), whether, and what rate of, interest is payable, any minimum balance required to keep the account open, any contractual terms under which the taxpayer or any '*interested third parties*' (i.e. persons with a beneficial interest in an amount in the account) may suffer economic loss as a result of a hold notice or deduction notice, and, for each joint account holder, interested third party or person with power of attorney in respect of the account, the information specified in (1) above.

Information must be provided only if it is in the possession of, or immediately available to, the deposit-taker at the time the notice is given.

A notice must explain the time limit for complying with it and the penalties for non-compliance (see **46.23** PENALTIES). HMRC may issue a notice only for the purpose of determining whether to give the deposit-taker a hold notice (see below) in respect of the taxpayer concerned. The recipient of a notice must comply with it as soon as reasonably practicable and, in any event, within ten working days beginning with the day on which the notice was given.

[*F(No 2)A 2015, Sch 8 paras 3, 8(11); SI 2015 No 1986, Regs 2–4*].

Hold notice

[45.24] If it appears to HMRC that a person has failed to pay a sum meeting the conditions at **45.22** above and that the person holds one or more accounts with a deposit-taker, they may give the deposit-taker a hold notice. The notice must:

(a) specify the taxpayer's name and last known address;
(b) specify a 'specified amount';
(c) specify a 'safeguarded amount';
(d) set out any rules which are to decide the priority order to be used to determine the held amount for each account (see Step 3 below);
(e) explain the effects of the notice, the penalties for non-compliance and any provisions made by regulation excluding certain types of account and amounts from inclusion in a hold notice; and
(f) contain a statement about HMRC's compliance with the requirement to consider whether a taxpayer is at a particular disadvantage in dealing with HMRC (see above).

The notice may also specify any additional information which HMRC considers might assist the deposit-taker in identifying accounts. It may also exclude an account, type of account or specified amount from the notice.

In (b) above, the '*specified amount*' must not exceed what is left of the 'notified sum' after deducting the specified amounts in any other hold notices which relate to the same debts and which were either given on the same day to other deposit-takers or given on an earlier day to either the same or another deposit-taker. The specified amount of an earlier hold notice is not deducted if HMRC has received a notification from the deposit-taker that there are no affected accounts as a result of that notice (see further below). For this purpose, two hold notices relate to the same debts if at least one of the unpaid sums in respect of which they are issued is the same.

The '*safeguarded amount*' must, in general, be at least £5,000 but HMRC may specify a smaller amount (including nil) if they consider it appropriate to do so having regard to the value in sterling (determined in a manner prescribed by regulations) of any amounts in a non-sterling account which would be a 'relevant account' (see below) in relation to the notice if it were denominated in sterling. The safeguarded amount must be nil if HMRC has previously given a hold notice relating to the same debts and, within the 30 days ending with the date the current hold notice is given, HMRC have been notified that there is a held amount as a result of the earlier notice.

HMRC may not give more than one hold notice relating to the same debts to a single deposit-taker on the same day.

Effect of notice

A deposit-taker to whom a hold notice is given must, for each 'relevant account' determine whether or not there is a 'held amount' (greater than nil) for that account and if so must either:

(1) put in place arrangements to ensure that it does not do anything, or permit anything to be done, which would reduce the amount in the account below the held amount; or
(2) transfer an amount equal to the held amount into a specially-created 'suspense account' and put in place arrangements to ensure that it does not do anything, or permit anything to be done, which would reduce the amount in the suspense account below the held amount.

The deposit-taker must comply with these requirements as soon as reasonably practicable and, in any event, within five working days beginning with the day on which the notice is given and must maintain any arrangements made under (1) or (2) above until the notice ceases to be in force.

All accounts held by the taxpayer with the deposit-taker are '*relevant accounts*' unless they are not denominated in sterling or are suspense accounts or they have been excluded from the hold notice by HMRC or excluded from such notices generally by regulations. A relevant account is an '*affected account*' if as a result of the notice there is a held amount in relation to it.

A hold notice ceases to be in force when either HMRC cancel it or a deduction notice is given.

If the deposit-taker determines that there are one or more affected accounts it must give HMRC a notice setting out prescribed information about each account (and in the case of a joint account, about the other account holders) and the held amount for each account. The prescribed information is:

- the information within **45.23**(1) and (2) above;
- confirmation of which accounts are affected accounts;
- the date on which the deposit-taker complied with the requirements above;
- confirmation that the deposit-taker understands the penalties for making a disclosure likely to prejudice HMRC's ability to use these provisions to recover the unpaid tax (see **46.23** PENALTIES);
- the total of all held amounts;
- for each account, the amount not subject to action within (1) or (2) above; and
- a description of any economic loss suffered by an account holder or interested third party under any contractual term as a result of the hold notice.

Information must be provided only if it is the possession of, or immediately available to, the deposit-taker at the time the hold notice is given.

The notice must be given within five working days beginning with the day on which the deposit-taker complies with the hold notice. HMRC must then, as soon as reasonably practicable, give a copy of the hold notice to the taxpayer together with a notice which:

(A) specifies and states the amounts of the unpaid sums to which the hold notice relates;
(B) states the total of the unpaid amounts to which the notice relates; and
(C) states the 'notified sum' for the hold notice, i.e. the total in (B) above.

HMRC must also give a notice to any joint account holders other than the taxpayer and to any 'interested third parties' (see **45.23** above) in respect of whom information has been provided in the deposit-taker's notice. The notice must explain that a hold notice has been given in respect of the account concerned and explaining the effects of the notice and the objection and appeal provisions below.

Once it has complied with the hold notice, the deposit-taker may (but is not required to) notify the taxpayer, any joint account holders and any interested third parties stating that a hold notice has been received and the effect of the notice on the account concerned.

If the deposit-taker determines that there are no affected accounts as a result of the hold notice it must notify HMRC accordingly, including in the notice any information which it has taken into account to determine that there are no affected accounts. The notice must be given within five working days beginning with the day on which it makes the determination.

Held amounts

If there is only one relevant account, the '*held amount*' for that account is, if the 'available amount' exceeds the safeguarded amount, the excess up to the specified amount. If the available amount is not more than the safeguarded amount then the held amount is nil. If there is more than one relevant account, the held amount for each such account is found using the following steps:

Step 1. Determine the available amount for each relevant account.

Step 2. Add the available amounts together to determine the total of those amounts for all such accounts. If the total is no more than the safeguarded amount then the held amount for all of the accounts is nil.

Step 3. If the total in Step 2 is more than the safeguarded amount, the safeguarded amount is matched against the available amounts in the relevant accounts, taking the accounts in reverse priority order. The priority order is determined by the deposit-taker, but joint accounts must have a lower priority than other accounts and any rules included in the hold notice (see (d) above) must be followed. Note that it is the reverse of the priority order that is used in this Step.

Step 4. Match the specified amount against what remains of the available amounts by taking each account in priority order. The held amount for each account is then so much of the account balance as is so matched; if no part of an account balance is so matched, the held amount for that account is nil. Balances which are excluded from the effect of the hold notice by regulations are not matched.

The '*available amount*' is the amount standing to the credit of the account at the time the deposit-taker complies with the hold notice. In the case of a joint account, the available amount is restricted to the appropriate fraction of that amount, according to the number of account holders.

Cancellation or variation

HMRC may cancel or vary a hold notice by notifying the deposit-taker. Variation may take the form of cancelling the effect of the notice in relation to one or more accounts or in relation to part of the held amount for an account or accounts. HMRC must give a copy of the notice of cancellation or variation to the taxpayer and any other person HMRC consider is affected by it and who is a joint account holder or an interested third party.

On receipt of a notice the deposit-taker must cancel or adjust the arrangements made to comply with the hold notice as soon as reasonably practicable and, in any event, within five working days beginning with the day the notice of cancellation or variation was given.

Objections and appeals

The taxpayer, an interested third party or a joint account holder may notify HMRC of an objection to a hold notice on the grounds that:

- (i) the debts have been wholly or partly paid;
- (ii) at the time the hold notice was given there was no unpaid sum or the taxpayer did not hold an account with the deposit-taker;
- (iii) the notice is causing or will cause exceptional hardship to the person making the objection or another person; or
- (iv) there is an interested third party in relation to one or more of the affected accounts.

The objection notice must state the grounds of objection and must normally be made within 30 days beginning with the day on which a copy of the hold notice was given to the taxpayer. A joint account holder or independent third party who has received a notice from HMRC explaining that a hold notice has been issued may make an objection within 30 days beginning with the day on which that notice was given. HMRC may, however, agree to the making of a late objection and must do so if they are satisfied that there was reasonable excuse for not making the objection in time and that the person making the objection had sent a written request for agreement to the making of a late objection without unreasonable delay after the reasonable excuse ceased.

HMRC must consider any objections within 30 days of being given the objection notice. They must then decide whether to cancel or vary the hold notice (as above) or to dismiss the objection and must notify their decision to the taxpayer, any other person who objected and any other joint account holder or interested third party who HMRC consider to be affected. HMRC must also notify the deposit-taker if it has decided to cancel or vary the hold notice. A copy of HMRC's notice to the deposit-taker must be given to each of the persons to whom HMRC notified their decision.

The taxpayer, any joint account holder or any interested third party may appeal against HMRC's decision, but only on grounds within (i) to (iv) above. The appeal must state the grounds and must normally be made within 30 days beginning with the day on which the appellant was given notice of HMRC's decision. A joint account holder or independent third party who has not received a notice of HMRC's decision may appeal within 30 days beginning with the day on which the taxpayer was given notice of HMRC's decision. The appeal is to the county court which may cancel or vary the notice or dismiss the appeal.

Where an appeal is on the grounds of exceptional hardship (see (iii) above), the appellant may apply to the court to suspend the effect of the hold notice in full or in relation to a particular account or amount while the appeal is pending. Adequate security must be provided.

If the deposit-taker is served with a court order to cancel or vary the hold notice, it must make any necessary resulting arrangements as soon as reasonably practicable and, in any event, within five working days beginning with the day the order was given.

The normal provisions governing APPEALS (5) do not apply to objections or appeals under these provisions.

[*F(No 2)A 2015, Sch 8 paras 4, 6–12; SI 2015 No 1986, Regs 3, 5, 6*].

Deduction notice

[45.25] If it appears to HMRC that a person in respect of whom a hold notice given to a deposit-taker is in force has failed to pay a sum meeting the conditions at **45.22** above and that the person holds one or more accounts with the deposit-taker in respect of which there is a held amount relating to the unpaid sum, they may give the deposit-taker a deduction notice. The notice will specify one or more affected accounts (see **45.24** above) and require the deposit-taker to deduct and pay a 'qualifying amount' from each account to HMRC by the day specified in the notice. If a held amount for a particular account has been transferred to a suspense account (see **45.24** above), the deduction must be made from the suspense account. HMRC may amend or cancel the notice by notifying the deposit-taker.

A '*qualifying amount*' in an affected account is an amount not exceeding the held amount for that account. The total qualifying amounts specified in a deduction notice must not exceed the unpaid sum. The deposit-taker must not, while a deduction notice is in force, do anything or permit anything to be done that would reduce the amount in a specified account (or a suspense account) to fall below the amount required to make the deduction. A deduction notice must explain this provision and the penalties for non-compliance. A deduction notice comes into force when it is given to the deposit-taker and ceases to be in force when the deposit-taker is given a notice cancelling it or when the final required payment is made.

A deduction notice cannot be given in respect of an account unless the period for making an objection has passed and either no objections were made or any objections have been decided or withdrawn and, if objections were made and decided, unless the period for making an appeal has passed and any appeal or further appeal has been finally determined.

HMRC must give a copy of a deduction notice to the taxpayer and, for each account, must give a notice explaining that a notice has been given and its effect to any joint account holders other than the taxpayer and to any interested third parties about whom HMRC have sufficient information to do so. Similar copies and notices must be given where HMRC cancel or amend a deduction notice.

[*F(No 2)A 2015, Sch 8 para 13*].

Recovery of tax in respect of disposals by others

[45.26] There are instances in the legislation whereby HMRC can assess, and/or recover tax from, persons other than the person actually making the disposal which gives rise to the liability. This right usually follows from the non-payment of tax by the person originally assessed in respect of the chargeable disposal by him but may also arise because of specific legislation (e.g. UK-residents charged in respect of disposals made by certain overseas resident companies, see **43.7** OVERSEAS MATTERS). The person from whom tax is recovered is normally given a right of recovery from any person originally assessed.

The following table summarises the legislation relevant to tax on chargeable gains.

Description	Legislation	Location
Recovery of tax from officers. Tax may be recovered from the treasurer of a company which is not a body corporate.	*TMA 1970, s 108(2)(3)*	**45.27**
Collection of unpaid tax from other members of the group and controlling directors. Where corporation tax in respect of a chargeable gain remains unpaid for six months it may be collected from certain group members or, if the company is not UK-resident and the gain arises to a UK permanent establishment or from a direct or indirect disposal of UK land, from a controlling director.	*TCGA 1992, s 190*	**45.28**
Recovery from shareholders. Where a person connected with a UK-resident company receives, in respect of shares in that company, a capital distribution which is not a reduction of capital but which is derived from a disposal of assets from which a chargeable gain accrues to the company, and the company does not pay the corporation tax for the period of the gain within six months, the recipient of the distribution may be required to pay a proportion of the corporation tax.	*TCGA 1992, s 189*	**45.29**

Description	Legislation	Location
Joint and several liability of company directors etc. HMRC can issue a notice (a '*joint liability notice*') to individual directors or shadow directors of a company or to individual participators in a company making them jointly and severally liable for the company's tax liabilities or penalties. A notice can only be given in cases of insolvency or potential insolvency where stringent conditions are satisfied under one of three categories: tax avoidance or evasion; repeated insolvency and non-payment; and penalties for facilitation of tax avoidance or evasion. A notice can apply to any tax (not just tax on chargeable gains).	*FA 2020, Sch 13*	**45.30**
Company reconstructions. Tax charged under the anti-avoidance provision restricting the application of the relief for company reconstructions which is not paid within six months can be recovered from any person holding the shares issued to the original chargeable person following an inter-spouse or intra-group transfer.	*TCGA 1992, s 137(4)*	**4.16** ANTI-AVOIDANCE
Reconstructions involving transfer of business. Tax charged under the anti-avoidance provision restricting the application of the relief for such reconstructions which is not paid within six months can be recovered from the acquiring company or from any person holding the assets following an intra-group transfer.	*TCGA 1992, s 139 (6)(7)*	**14.12** COMPANIES
Gifts — recovery from donee. Where CGT on a gift is not paid within twelve months it may be recovered from the donee.	*TCGA 1992, s 282*	**25.4** GIFTS
Hold-over reliefs — emigration of transferee. Where tax arising on the clawback of hold-over relief when the transferee emigrates is not paid by the transferee within twelve months it may be recovered from the transferor.	*TCGA 1992, s 168(7)*	**30.8, 30.11** HOLD-OVER RELIEFS
Trustees becoming non-resident. Tax charged on trustees as a result of their becoming non-resident which is not paid within six months may be recovered from certain former trustees.	*TCGA 1992, s 82*	**42.2** OFFSHORE SETTLEMENTS
Company ceasing to be UK-resident. Tax in respect of accounting periods beginning before the cessation of UK residence which is not paid within six months can be recovered from a member of the same group or a controlling director.	*TMA 1970, s 109E*	**43.17** OVERSEAS MATTERS

Description	Legislation	Location
Exploration or exploitation rights. unpaid tax assessed on an overseas resident person may be recovered from the holder of a licence granted under *Petroleum Act 1998* in respect of chargeable gains accruing on the disposal of such rights under the licence.	*TMA 1970, ss 77B–77E*	**43.18** OVERSEAS MATTERS
Recovery from beneficiary. Tax charged on trustees which is not paid within six months may be recovered from any beneficiary to whom the asset concerned or the proceeds from the disposal have been transferred.	*TCGA 1992, s 69(4)*	**56.10** SETTLEMENTS
Change in company ownership. Unpaid corporation tax due from a company can be recovered from persons controlling the company, in certain circumstances where there has been a change of ownership.	*CTA 2010, ss 706–718*	Tolley's Corporation Tax
Non-UK resident companies. Unpaid corporation tax due from a non-UK resident company can be recovered from other companies within the same group, from any member of a consortium owning the company, or from any member of the same group as a member of that consortium.	*CTA 2010, ss 973–980*	Tolley's Corporation Tax

Recovery of tax from officers

[45.27] Tax which has fallen due may be recovered from the treasurer or acting treasurer (the 'proper officer') of a company which is not a body corporate or not incorporated under a UK enactment or by charter. That officer then has a right of reimbursement out of moneys coming into his hands on behalf of that company, and to be indemnified by the company for any balance. [*TMA 1970, s 108(2)(3)*].

Collection of unpaid tax from other members of the group and controlling directors

[45.28] Where a chargeable gain accrues to a company (hereafter referred to as the taxpayer company) and either:

– that company is UK-resident at the time the gain accrues, or
– the gain is within the charge to corporation tax by virtue of *TCGA 1992, s 2B(3)(4)* (non-UK resident company — see **14.2**(a)–(c) COMPANIES),

the following rules apply where all or part of the corporation tax assessed on the company for the relevant accounting period (i.e. the accounting period in which the gain accrues) remains unpaid six months after it became payable.

HMRC may serve on any of the following persons a notice requiring that person to pay, within 30 days, the unpaid tax or, if less, an amount equal to corporation tax on the chargeable gain at the appropriate rate.

(a) If the taxpayer company was a member of a 'group' at the time the gain accrued:
- a company which was at that time the 'principal company of the group'; and
- any other company which, in any part of the period of 12 months ending with that time, was a member of the group *and* owned the asset, or any part of the asset, disposed of (or, where that asset is an interest in, or a right over, another asset, owned either asset or any part of either asset).

(b) If the taxpayer company was not UK-resident when the gain accrued, any person who is, or has been during the 12 months ending with the time the gain accrued, a controlling director of the taxpayer company or of a company which has, or has had within that 12-month period, control over the taxpayer company.

For the purpose of (a) above, '*group*' and '*principal company of the group*' are construed as in **26.2** GROUPS OF COMPANIES but as if references there to 75% subsidiaries were references to 51% subsidiaries. For the purposes of (b) above and in determining whether a director is a controlling director, 'control' is construed in accordance with *CTA 2010, ss 450, 451*, and 'director' has the wide meaning given by *ITEPA 2003, s 67(1)(2)* and *CTA 2010, s 452(1)*.

The notice must state the amount of tax assessed, the original due date and the amount required from the person on whom it is served. It has effect, for the purposes of collection, interest and appeals, as if it were a notice of assessment on that person. The notice must be served within three years beginning with the date on which the liability of the taxpayer company for the relevant accounting period is finally determined. That date varies according to whether the unpaid tax is charged in a self-assessment (and, if so, whether there is an enquiry into the tax return in question), in a discovery assessment (and, if so, whether there is an appeal) or in consequence of a 'determination' (see Tolley's Corporation Tax under Returns). In the simplest case of a self-assessment and no enquiry, the liability is determined on the last date on which notice of enquiry could have been given.

A person paying an amount under these provisions may recover it from the taxpayer company, but such an amount is not deductible for any tax purpose.

[*TCGA 1992, s 190*].

Recovery from shareholders

[45.29] Where a person connected with a UK-resident company (see **17** CONNECTED PERSONS) receives, or becomes entitled to receive, in respect of shares in that company, a capital distribution within *TCGA 1992, s 122* (see **57.11** SHARES AND SECURITIES) which is not a reduction of capital but which constitutes, or is derived from, a disposal of assets from which a chargeable gain accrues to the company, and the company does not pay, within six months after the later of the due date and the date the assessment was made, the corporation tax due for the accounting period in which the gain accrued, the recipient of the distribution may be required to pay so much of that corporation tax as relates to chargeable gains but not exceeding the lesser of:

(i) part of that tax, at the rate in force when the gain accrued, proportionate to his share of the total distribution made by the company, and
(ii) the value of the distribution he received or became entitled to receive.

The recipient then has a right of recovery against the company, which extends to any interest on unpaid tax which he has paid on the outstanding tax. The assessment on the recipient must be made within two years after the later of the date the tax became due and payable by the company and the date the assessment was made on the company. These provisions do not affect any liability of the recipient in respect of any chargeable gain accruing to him as a result of the capital distribution. [*TCGA 1992, s 189*].

Joint and several liability of company directors etc.

[45.30] HMRC can issue a notice (a '*joint liability notice*') to individual directors or shadow directors of a company or to individual participators in a company making them jointly and severally liable for the company's tax liabilities or penalties. Such a notice can apply to any amount payable to HMRC by the company under any enactment and includes liabilities under a contract settlement. A notice can only be given in cases of insolvency or potential insolvency where stringent conditions are satisfied under one of three categories: tax avoidance or evasion; repeated insolvency and non-payment; and penalties for facilitation of tax avoidance or evasion.

The provisions apply to tax liabilities for periods ending on or after 22 July 2020 and to tax liabilities not related to a period arising from an event or default occurring on or after that date.
[*FA 2020, s 100, Sch 13 paras 1, 19*].

For HMRC's guidance on the provisions, see www.gov.uk/guidance/joint-and-several-liability-notices-for-tax-avoidance-and-tax-evasion-cases.

A company is subject to an insolvency procedure if, broadly, it is undergoing, or has undergone, a winding up, it is in administration or receivership, it has moved from administration to dissolution, it is subject to a compromise or arrangement under *Companies Act 2006, Pt 26* or NI or overseas equivalent, or it has been struck off the register under *Companies Act 2006, s 1000* or *1003*. See *FA 2020, Sch 13 para 8*.

Where a company has ceased to exist, the effect of a joint liability notice is to make the individual solely liable for the amount specified in the notice or, where a notice is given to more than one individual in respect of the same liability, jointly and severally liable with the other individuals. The tax liability of such a company is taken, for the purposes of these provisions, to be whatever it was immediately before the company ceased to exist. [*FA 2020, Sch 13 para 17*].

The provisions apply also to liabilities of limited liability partnerships. References below to directors and shadow directors include members and shadow members of such partnerships. A shadow member is, broadly, a person in accordance with whose instructions the members of the partnership are accustomed to act. [*FA 2020, Sch 13 paras 18, 19*].

Tax avoidance and evasion

An authorised HMRC officer may issue a joint liability notice to an individual if it appears that:

(1) a company has entered into 'tax avoidance arrangements' or has engaged in 'tax-evasive conduct';

(2) the company is subject to an insolvency procedure or there is a serious possibility that it will be;

(3) either:

  (i) at a time when the individual was a director, shadow director or participator, the individual was responsible (alone or with others) for the company entering into the arrangements or engaging in the conduct or the individual received a benefit which, to his knowledge, arose (at least partly) from the arrangements or conduct; or

  (ii) at a time when the individual was a director or shadow director or was otherwise concerned or taking part in the management of the company (directly or indirectly), the individual took part in, assisted with or facilitated the arrangements or conduct;

(4) there is, or is likely to be, a tax liability referable to the arrangements or conduct;

(5) there is a serious possibility that some or all of that tax liability will not be paid.

In (3)(i) above, an individual is taken to know anything that he could reasonably be expected to know. Benefits received by a connected person are treated as received by the individual.

The notice makes the individual jointly and severally liable with the company, and any other individuals to whom a notice is given, for the tax liability in (4) above. The amount for which an individual is so liable is reduced by any penalty paid by that individual in relation to that liability.

A notice under these provisions must specify the company to which it relates and set out the reasons why it appears to the officer that the above conditions are met. It must state the effect of the notice and explain the individual's right of review and appeal. It must also specify the amount of the tax liability, but if this is not yet known, the amount can be specified in a further notice.

'*Tax avoidance arrangements*' are:

- arrangements in respect of which a final notice has been given under the general anti-abuse rule (see **4.3** ANTI-AVOIDANCE) stating that a tax advantage is to be counteracted under the rule;
- arrangements in respect of which a follower notice (see **4.26**) has been given and not withdrawn;
- 'DOTAS arrangements' within **4.31**;
- arrangements to which HMRC have allocated a reference number or in respect of which a promoter must provide information under the disclosure of tax avoidance schemes rules for VAT and other indirect taxes;
- arrangements in relation to which a Tribunal has made an order that they are notifiable under the disclosure of tax avoidance schemes rules for direct taxes or VAT etc.; or
- arrangements that are substantially the same as arrangements (involving the same or different parties) in respect of which such an order has been made and which have the same promoter.

'*Tax-evasive conduct*' means giving HMRC any deliberately inaccurate return, claim, document or information or deliberately failing to comply with an obligation to notify etc. within the Table in *FA 2008, Sch 41 para 1*.

[*FA 2020, Sch 13 paras 2, 6, 7, 9*].

Repeated insolvency and non-payment

An authorised HMRC officer may issue a joint liability notice to an individual if it appears that:

(a) the individual had a 'connection' with at least two companies (the old companies) at any time during the five years ending with the day the notice is given and each of those companies became subject to an insolvency procedure during those five years at a time when:
- it had a tax liability; or
- it had failed to submit a return or other document or to make a declaration or application that it was required to and which was relevant to the question whether the company had a tax liability or how much its tax liability was; or
- it had submitted such a return or other document or made such a declaration or application but an act or omission on its part had prevented HMRC from dealing with it;

(b) another company (the new company) is or has been carrying on a trade or activity that is the same as, or similar to, that carried on previously by each of the old companies (or at least two of them if there are more than two);

(c) the individual has had a connection with the new company at any time in the five-year period in (a) above; and

(d) at the time the notice is given, at least one of the old companies has a tax liability and the total tax liabilities of all of the old companies within (b) above is more than £10,000 and is more than 50% of the total of those companies' liabilities to unsecured creditors.

For these purposes, an individual has a connection with an old company if that individual is a director, shadow director or participator. An individual has a connection with the new company if that individual is a director, shadow director or participator or is otherwise concerned, or takes part, in the management of the company (directly or indirectly).

The notice makes the individual jointly and severally liable with the new company and any other individuals to whom a notice is given for any tax liability which the new company has on the day the notice is issued or which arises during the following five years (or while the notice continues in effect if that is less than five years). The individual is also made jointly and severally liable with any old company within (b) above and any other individuals to whom a notice is given for any liability which that company has on the day the notice is given. The amount for which an individual is so liable in respect of any liability is reduced by any penalty paid by that individual in relation to that liability.

A notice must be issued within the two years beginning with the day on which HMRC first become aware of sufficient facts for them reasonably to conclude that the above conditions are met. It must set out the reasons why it appears to the officer that the above conditions are met and specify any amounts for which the individual is liable. It must also state the effect of the notice and explain the individual's right of review and appeal.

The Treasury may amend the amount and percentage in (d) above by statutory instrument.

[*FA 2020, Sch 13 paras 3, 4, 9*].

HMRC have indicated that the power to issue a joint liability notice under this provision will not be used in respect of those such as 'turnaround specialists' whose connection with companies is part of a genuine attempt to save the company from failing. When a person falls within the above conditions solely by virtue of being a participator in the company, HMRC will not issue a notice to that person where it is satisfied the person acted in good faith and had no material influence over the company's affairs. (Treasury Explanatory Notes to the 2020 Finance Bill).

Penalty for facilitating avoidance or evasion

An authorised HMRC officer may issue a joint liability notice to an individual if it appears that:

(I) HMRC have imposed a penalty under one of the following provisions on a company or proceedings have commenced before the First-tier Tribunal for the imposition of such a penalty. Penalties imposed, or in respect of which proceedings commenced, before 22 July 2020 are excluded. The provisions are:
- *TMA 1970, s 98C* (failure to disclose tax avoidance scheme; see **49.27** PENALTIES);
- *FA 2014, Sch 35 paras 2, 3* (high-risk promoters of avoidance schemes);
- *FA 2016, Sch 20 para 1* (enabling offshore tax evasion);
- *F(No 2)A 2017, Sch 16 Pt 1* (enablers of defeated tax avoidance);
- *F(No 2)A 2017, Sch 17 Pt 2* (disclosure of tax avoidance schemes (VAT etc.));
- *FA 2022, Sch 13* (facilitating avoidance schemes involving non-resident promoters);

(II) the company is subject to an insolvency procedure or there is a serious possibility that it will be;

(III) the individual was a director or shadow director of, or participator in, the company at the time of any act or omission in respect of which the penalty was imposed or proceedings commenced; and

(IV) there is a serious possibility that some or all of the penalty will not be paid.

The notice makes the individual jointly and severally liable for the penalty with the company and any other individuals to whom a notice is given.

A notice under these provisions must specify the company to which it relates and set out the reasons why it appears to the officer that the above conditions are met. It must state the effect of the notice and explain the individual's right of review and appeal. It must also specify the amount of the penalty but if this is not yet known because proceedings before the Tribunal have not concluded, the amount can be specified in a further notice.

[*FA 2020, s 100(4), Sch 13 para 5; FA 2022, s 91(2)*].

Withdrawal or modification of notice

HMRC must withdraw a joint liability notice if any of the conditions were not in fact met when the notice was given or if it is not necessary for the protection of the revenue for the notice to continue in effect. They must also withdraw a notice in a repeated insolvency and non-payment case if any of the old companies was being wound up by way of a members' voluntary winding-up and it pays its debts in full, together with interest at the official rate, before the end of the winding-up and condition (a) above would not have been met if that company (or each of them) had not been subject to an insolvency procedure.

HMRC may withdraw a notice if they think it appropriate to do so. They may also issue a further notice varying the amount to which the individual is liable if it seems to them that the amount specified in the notice is too much or not enough.

Withdrawal of a joint liability notice is by HMRC giving a further notice. A withdrawn notice is of no effect but does not give the individual any right to repayment of any amount paid under it, except where the notice is withdrawn because the conditions were not met when the notice was given.

Reviews and appeals

An individual who is given a joint liability notice (or a further notice specifying the amount to which he is liable) can request a review of HMRC's decision to give the notice. A request must be in writing and made within the 'permitted period', i.e. normally the period ending on the 30th day after the day the notice was given. HMRC can allow an extended period by notice given before the end of what would otherwise be the permitted period. It must specify a date at least 30 days after the date of the extension notice. The permitted period can be extended more than once. HMRC must accept a late request for a review if they are satisfied that the individual had a reasonable excuse for the late request and that there was no unreasonable delay after the excuse ceased to apply.

HMRC can conduct their review in a way that appears appropriate in the circumstances but they must have regard to steps taken before the review by HMRC in reaching their decision to issue the notice or by another person in seeking to resolve disagreement about the decision. They must take account of any representations by the individual but the individual cannot challenge the existence or amount of the tax liability to which the notice relates.

HMRC must set aside the notice if it appears on review that any of the conditions were not met when the notice was given or that it is not necessary for the protection of the revenue for it to continue in effect. They must set aside the notice or vary the amount of the liability specified in it if it appears to them that the amount specified is incorrect. Otherwise, HMRC must uphold the notice. If a notice is set aside on the basis that it is not necessary for the protection of the revenue for it to continue in effect, the individual does not have a right to recover any amounts already paid.

They must normally notify the individual of their conclusions and reasoning in writing within 45 days of the date the review request was received or, in the case of a late request, within 45 days of their decision to undertake the review. HMRC may agree a later date with the individual. If HMRC fail to meet the deadline, the notice is nevertheless upheld, and HMRC must notify the individual accordingly.

HMRC are not required to conduct or continue a review if the individual appeals against the notice.

An individual may appeal to the First-tier Tribunal against a joint liability notice (or a further notice specifying the amount to which he is liable) within the permitted period, i.e. normally, the 30 days beginning with the day on which the notice is given. HMRC can allow an extended period by notice given before the end of what would otherwise be the permitted period. It must specify a date at least 30 days after the date of the extension notice. The permitted period can be extended more than once.

If a review has been conducted by HMRC an appeal can be made within 30 days beginning with the date of the notice of HMRC's conclusions. Where a late request for a review has been made, no appeal can be made unless HMRC have notified the individual as to whether or not a review will be conducted. If HMRC do conduct a review, an appeal must be made within the 30 days beginning with the date of the notice of HMRC's conclusions. If HMRC do not conduct a review, an appeal can only be made with the Tribunal's permission. If HMRC have failed to notify their conclusions following a review within the time limit, an appeal can be made within the 30 days beginning with the date of HMRC's notice that the joint liability notice is upheld.

Late appeals may be made with the Tribunal's permission.

The Tribunal must set aside the notice if it appears that any of the conditions were not met when the notice was given or that it is not necessary for the protection of the revenue for it to continue in effect. It must set aside the notice or vary the amount of the liability specified in it if it appears that the amount specified is incorrect. Otherwise, the Tribunal must uphold the notice. If a notice is set aside on the basis that it is not necessary for the protection of the revenue for it to continue in effect, the individual does not have a right to recover any amounts already paid.

An individual cannot challenge the existence or amount of any tax liability of a company on appeal against a joint liability notice. An individual subject to such a notice is, however, entitled to be a party to any ongoing appeal by the company in respect of the liability to which the notice relates if the company is subject to an insolvency procedure. If the company is unwilling or unable to continue the appeal, the individual may do so. If the company has not appealed (but is subject to an insolvency procedure), an appeal may be made in the name of the individual. Such an appeal must be made within the 30 days beginning with day on which the joint liability notice was given and may be made even if the time limit for the company to appeal has expired.

In a penalty for facilitating avoidance or evasion case where penalty proceedings were commenced before the joint liability notice was issued but the penalty had not then been imposed, the individual to whom the notice was issued is entitled to be a party to those proceedings.

[*FA 2020, Sch 13 paras 11–16*].

Cases in which HMRC do not pursue payment

[45.31] HMRC will not seek to collect tax which is due and payable where the concession at **45.32** below applies or where a claim for the special relief at **13.7** CLAIMS is accepted.

Remission of tax in cases of HMRC delay

[45.32] Arrears of income tax or capital gains tax may be given up if they result from HMRC's failure to make proper and timely use of information supplied by:

- a taxpayer about his or her own income, gains or personal circumstances;
- an employer where the information affects a taxpayer's coding; or
- the Department for Work and Pensions about a taxpayer's State retirement, disability or widow's pension.

Tax will normally be given up only where the taxpayer could reasonably have believed that his or her tax affairs were in order; and

- was notified of the arrears more than twelve months after the end of the tax year in which HMRC received the information in question; or
- was notified of an over-repayment after the end of the tax year following the year in which the repayment was made.

In exceptional circumstances arrears of tax notified twelve months or less after the end of the relevant tax year may be given up if HMRC either failed more than once to make proper use of the facts they had been given about one source of income or allowed the arrears of tax to build up over two whole tax years in succession by failing to make proper and timely use of information they had been given.

(HMRC Extra-Statutory Concession A19).

A decision by HMRC not to apply this concession can only be challenged by way of judicial review (*Prince v HMRC* FTT, [2012] SFTD 786).

Under *TMA 1970*, unless a longer or shorter period is prescribed, no statutory claim for relief is allowed unless it is made on or before the fifth anniversary of 31 January following the tax year to which it relates. However, repayments of tax will be made in respect of claims made outside the statutory time limit where an overpayment of tax has arisen because of an error by HMRC or another Government Department, and where there is no dispute or doubt as to the facts (HMRC Extra-Statutory Concession B41).

Over-repayments of tax

[45.33] If not otherwise assessable under *TMA 1970, s 29* (discovery assessments — see **6.10** ASSESSMENTS), capital gains tax repaid in error, or over-repaid, by HMRC may be assessed and recovered as if it were unpaid tax. For this purpose, a repayment includes an amount allowed by way of set-off. HMRC's right to assess under these provisions is subject to the same exceptions (modified as appropriate) as apply to discovery assessments. Excess repayment supplement may be similarly assessed or may be included in an assessment of over-repaid tax. The normal deadline for raising assessments is extended in the above cases to the later of:

- the end of the tax year following that in which the repayment was made, and
- in the event of an HMRC enquiry into a return, the day on which the enquiry is fully completed (see **52.14** RETURNS).

Comparable provisions apply for the purposes of corporation tax (and interest on overpaid corporation tax). The normal deadline for raising assessments is extended to the later of:

- the end of the accounting period following that in which the repayment was made, and
- in the event of an HMRC enquiry into a relevant company tax return, the end of the period of three months following the day on which the enquiry is completed (in accordance with *FA 1998, Sch 18 para 32*).

[*TMA 1970, s 30; FA 1998, s 117, Sch 18 paras 52, 53*].

The exercise by HMRC of their discretion to raise an assessment under *TMA 1970, s 30* can be challenged only by way of judicial review (see **5.35** APPEALS) and not by appeal (*Guthrie v Twickenham Film Studios Ltd* Ch D, [2002] STC 1374).

Recovery of foreign taxes etc.

[45.34] **EU member states.** Provision is made for the recovery in the UK of direct taxes (and interest and penalties) in respect of which a request for enforcement has been made in accordance with the Mutual Assistance Recovery Directive (MARD) (*Directive 2010/24/EU*) by an authority in another EU member state. Disclosure of information by a UK tax authority (e.g. HMRC) for these purposes (or for the purposes of a request by the UK for enforcement elsewhere) is not generally precluded by any obligation of secrecy.

Broadly, the UK tax authority has the same powers it would have for a corresponding claim in the UK, in particular in relation to interest and penalties. Treasury regulations may make provision for procedural and supplementary matters. Regulations may also be made by the UK tax authority for the application, non-application or adaptation of the law applicable to corresponding UK claims.

No proceedings may be taken against a person under these provisions if he shows that proceedings relevant to the liability in question are pending (i.e. still subject to appeal), or are about to be instituted, before a competent body in the relevant member state. This does not apply to any steps which could be taken in similar circumstances in the case of a corresponding UK claim or if the foreign proceedings are not prosecuted or instituted with reasonable expedition. If a final decision on the foreign claim (i.e. one no longer appealable) (or a part of it) has been given in the taxpayer's favour by a competent body in the relevant member state, no proceedings may be taken under these provisions in relation to the claim (or part).

Following Brexit, the UK legislation is amended (with effect from IP completion day on 31 December 2020) to reflect the fact that MARD is extended to the UK as a third country by the EU Withdrawal Agreement and to ensure that the legislation continues to give effect to MARD. MARD will apply to the UK for the five years following IP completion day for amounts that became due or transactions that occurred before that day and, if the debt falls under the Northern Ireland Protocol, for as long as that Protocol remains in force.

[*FA 2011, s 87, Sch 25; SI 2011 No 2931; SI 2020 No 996*].

Tax enforcement agreements

Provision is made for the Treasury to make regulations for the recovery in the UK of foreign taxes covered by a tax enforcement agreement with another country (see also **28.2**(c) HMRC — CONFIDENTIALITY OF INFORMATION). See now *SI 2007 No 3507*. [*FA 2006, s 175*].

Key points concerning payment of tax

[45.35] Points to consider are as follows.

- For individuals and trustees, tax due on capital gains tax is usually payable by 31 January following the year of assessment (ending 5 April) in which the gains arise. Tax for 2023/24 is therefore payable by 31 January 2025.
- A special compliance regime applies to all direct disposals of UK land by individuals or trustees where a residential property gain arises and to direct and indirect disposals of any UK land by non-UK residents. A UK land disposal return must be made together with a payment on account of CGT on or before the 60th day following the day of the completion of the disposal. See **45.3** above and **52.22** RETURNS.
- If HMRC was notified of chargeability by the taxpayer within six months of the end of the year of assessment but did not issue a tax return or a notice to complete one by the following 31 October then the tax becomes due three months after such a return or notice is issued.
- Penalties for failure to notify can normally be avoided if the tax is **paid** by a specific date; for income tax and capital gains tax by the normal due date (31 January) and for corporation tax by the notification date (one year after the end of the accounting period).
- Penalties apply for late payment of capital gains tax. The penalty code does not apply for corporation tax purposes except to corporation tax due under an exit charge payment plan.

- Capital gains tax arising from an amendment to a self-assessment tax return (made after 1 January following the year of assessment) or from a discovery assessment is due and payable 30 days after the date of the amendment or assessment although interest will run from the normal due date.
- Capital gains tax is not taken into account in the calculation of self-assessment payments on account for a subsequent year.
- HMRC may be flexible regarding payments if a taxpayer is having difficulty and allow arrangements to pay by instalments. Penalties for late payment of tax can be suspended where the taxpayer agrees a time to pay arrangement, subject to meeting the terms of the arrangement.
- Tax can be paid by business credit card or debit card but HMRC will charge a fee.
- For companies (who pay corporation tax on chargeable gains), the tax is paid as part of normal corporation tax and is generally due nine months and one day following the end of the accounting period. Large and very large companies must pay the tax in quarterly instalments. Payments of corporation tax must be made using an electronic means.

46

Penalties

Cross-references. See **36** LATE PAYMENT INTEREST AND PENALTIES; **43.17** OVERSEAS MATTERS for companies ceasing to be UK resident; **45** PAYMENT OF TAX; **52** RETURNS.

Simon's Taxes. See **A6.340–A6.345**, **A6.431**.

Introduction to penalties

[46.1] Financial penalties can be charged or sought by HMRC for a substantial number of offences by taxpayers or their agents. The current penalties relevant to capital gains tax and corporation tax on chargeable gains and which are described in detail in this chapter or elsewhere in this work are summarised in the table below.

Offence	Penalty	Para
1. Failure to notify chargeability to tax. Failure to comply with the obligation to notify chargeability to CGT within six months of tax year or to CT within one year of accounting period. *FA 2008, Sch 41.*	Deliberate and concealed failure: 100% of potential lost revenue. Deliberate but unconcealed failure: 70% of potential lost revenue. Any other case: 30% of potential lost revenue. A statutory reduction in the amount of the penalty is made for disclosure of a failure. HMRC can also reduce a penalty in special circumstances. Where the failure is linked to an offshore matter relating to certain categorised territories the amount of the penalty is increased.	**46.3**
2. Failure to deliver corporation tax return on time. *TMA 1970, s 7; FA 1998, Sch 18 paras 17, 18.*	(i) £100 if up to 3 months late (£500 if previous two returns also delivered late);	**46.4**
	(ii) £200 if over 3 months late (£1,000 if previous two returns also late);	
Failure continuing at later of final day for delivery of return and 18 months after return period	Further penalty of 10% of tax unpaid 18 months after return period (20% of tax unpaid at that date if return not made within 2 years of return period)	
3. Failure to make return on time (income tax and capital gains tax). *FA 2009, Sch 55*	(i) initial penalty of £100.	**46.5**
	(ii) if failure continues three months after penalty date and HMRC give notice, a further penalty of £10 per day for each day failure continues in 90-day period beginning with date specified in notice.	
	(iii) if failure continues six months after penalty date, a further penalty of the greater of 5% of the tax liability and £300.	

Offence	Penalty	Para
To be replaced by late filing penalty under *FA 2021, s 24* on the introduction of making tax digital (MTD).	(iv) if failure continues twelve months after penalty date and the withholding of information is deliberate or concealed a further penalty of the greater of 100% of the tax liability and £300; if the withholding is deliberate and not concealed, the greater of 70% of the liability and £300; or otherwise, greater of 5% of the liability and £300.	
	A statutory reduction in the amount of the penalty is made for disclosure of a failure. HMRC can also reduce a penalty in special circumstances. Where the failure is linked to an offshore matter relating to certain categorised territories the amount of the penalty is increased.	
4. Late filing (MTD). *FA 2021, Sch 24* Applies from 6 April 2024 for voluntary MTD adopters	£200 when maximum number of penalty points have been awarded.	**46.8**
5. Late filing—deliberate withholding of information (MTD). *FA 2021, Sch 25* Applies from 6 April 2024 for voluntary MTD adopters	If return filed late and the withholding of information is deliberate and concealed a further penalty of the greater of 100% of the tax liability and £300; if the withholding is deliberate and not concealed, the greater of 70% of the liability and £300.	**46.9**
	A statutory reduction in the amount of the penalty is made for disclosure of a failure. HMRC can also reduce a penalty in special circumstances. Where the failure is linked to an offshore matter relating to certain categorised territories the amount of the penalty is increased.	

Offence	Penalty	Para
6. Failure to make payment of CGT on time. *FA 2009, Sch 56*	A 5% penalty applies if full amount not paid within 30 days of due date. If amount remains unpaid six months after due date a penalty of 5% applies; a further 5% penalty applies if amount is still unpaid after a further six months.	**36.6** LATE PAYMENT INTEREST AND PENALTIES
7. Late payment (MTD). *FA 2021, Sch 26* Applies from 6 April 2024 for voluntary MTD adopters	16 days late — 2%	**36.7** LATE PAYMENT INTEREST AND PENALTIES
	31 or more days late First penalty — 2% of tax unpaid after 15 days plus 2% of tax unpaid after 30 days. Second penalty — 4% per annum of tax from time to time unpaid until tax is paid in full.	
8. Error in taxpayer's document. Careless or deliberate error in document amounting to or leading to understatement of liability, overstatement or loss or false or inflated claim to repayment of tax. *FA 2007, Sch 24 para 1.*	Deliberate and concealed error: 100% of potential lost revenue. Deliberate but unconcealed error: 70% of potential lost revenue. Any other case: 30% of potential lost revenue. A statutory reduction in the amount of the penalty is made for disclosure of an error. HMRC can also reduce a penalty in special circumstances. Where the error is linked to an offshore matter relating to certain categorised territories the amount of the penalty is increased.	**46.11**

Offence	Penalty	Para
9. Error in taxpayer's document attributable to another person. Deliberately supplying false information to, or deliberately withholding information from, a person giving a document to HMRC resulting in document containing an inaccuracy amounting to or leading to understatement of liability, overstatement of loss or false or inflated claim to repayment of tax. *FA 2007, Sch 24 para 1A.*	100% of potential lost revenue subject to statutory reduction for disclosure or in special circumstances.	**46.12**
10. Failure to notify HMRC of error in assessment. Failure to take reasonable steps to notify HMRC of an under-assessment within the 30 days beginning with the date of the assessment. *FA 2007, Sch 24 para 2.*	30% of potential lost revenue subject to statutory reduction for disclosure or in special circumstances.	**46.13**
11. Arrangements counteracted under the GAAR. A person is liable to a penalty if HMRC counteract a tax advantage by making adjustments under the general anti-abuse rule ('GAAR'). *FA 2013, ss 212A, 212B.*	60% of the counteracted advantage.	**46.14**
12. Offshore asset move where taxpayer becomes liable to another penalty under 1, 3 or 5 above. *FA 2015, Sch 21.*	50% of original penalty.	**46.15**
13. Asset-based penalty for offshore inaccuracies and failures. *FA 2016, Sch 22.*	Lower of (i) 10% of value of the asset, and (ii) the offshore potential lost revenue x 10, subject to statutory reduction for disclosure.	**46.16**
14. Failure to correct offshore tax non-compliance. *F(No 2)A 2017, Sch 18.*	200% of potential lost revenue subject to statutory reduction for disclosure or in special circumstances to minimum of 100% of potential lost revenue.	**46.17**

Offence	Penalty	Para
15. Failure to maintain records. Failure to keep and preserve appropriate records supporting personal and trustees' returns or partnership returns. *TMA 1970, s 12B; FA 1998, Sch 18 para 23.*	Up to £3,000	**46.18**
16. Failure to comply with HMRC investigatory powers. Failure to comply with an information notice within *FA 2008, Sch 36 Pt 1* or deliberately obstructing an HMRC officer in the course of an inspection of business premises under *FA 2008, Sch 36 Pt 2* which has been approved by the First-tier Tribunal (FTT). *FA 2008, Sch 36.*	(i) Initial penalty of £300. (ii) If failure/obstruction continues, a further penalty up to £60 per day. (iii) If failure/obstruction continues after penalty under (i) imposed, a tax-related amount determined by the Upper Tribunal.	**46.19**
17. Disclosure of a third party notice or a financial institution notice. Failure to comply with requirement in a third party notice or a financial institution notice not to disclose notice to taxpayer or other person. *FA 2008, Sch 36.*	£1,000	**46.19**
18. HMRC investigatory powers: inaccurate information and documents *FA 2008, Sch 36.*	Up to £3,000	**46.19**
19. Special returns etc. Failure to comply with a notice to deliver any return or other document, to furnish any particulars, to produce any document or record, to make anything available for inspection or give any certificate under specified provisions. *TMA 1970, s 98.*	Up to £300 (£3,000 in specified cases)	**46.22**

Offence	Penalty	Para
20. Failure to disclose tax avoidance scheme. Failure to comply with any of a number of requirements under the disclosure of tax avoidance schemes rules. *TMA 1970, s 98C.*	(i) Initial penalty of £5,000. (ii) Daily penalty of £600 (£5,000 in specified cases). (iii) Penalty of £100 for failure of party to notifiable arrangements to notify HMRC of scheme reference number. Increased to £500 for second failure in three-year period and £1,000 for third failure.	**49.27**
21. Powers of enforcement by deduction from accounts. [*F(No 2)A 2015, Sch 8*]. Various compliance failures or making disclosure likely to prejudice HMRC's ability to use the powers to recover the sum in question.	(i) Initial penalty of £300. (ii) If failure continues, a further penalty up to £60 per day.	**46.23**
22. Penalties under the serial avoiders regime. [*FA 2016, Sch 18*]. Where a person suffers a defeat of an avoidance scheme used whilst in a warning period.	Penalty of 20% of the value of the counteracted advantage. If, before the relevant defeat is incurred, the person was liable to be given prior warning notices, the penalty is increased. It is increased to 40% where there has been a single prior warning notice, and to 60% where there has been more than one such notice.	**46.24**
23. Uncertain tax treatment. Failure to make notification of uncertain tax treatment by large business. *FA 2022, Sch 17 para 20*	Where treatment is uncertain when return filed: £5,000 for first failure; £25,000 for second failure; £50,000 for further failures. For each failure, only failures in the previous three years are counted. Where treatment becomes uncertain after return filed, £5,000.	**46.25**

The following table summarises penalties which may be relevant to capital gains tax and corporation tax on chargeable gains but which are not described in detail in this work.

Offence	Penalty
24. HMRC data-gathering powers: failure to comply *FA 2011, Sch 23.*	(i) Initial penalty of £300. (ii) If failure continues, a further penalty up to £60 per day. (iii) If failure continues for more than 30 days after penalty under (ii) imposed, a further daily penalty determined by the Upper Tribunal up to £1,000 per day.
25. HMRC data-gathering powers: inaccurate data *FA 2011, Sch 23.*	Up to £3,000
26. Dishonest conduct by tax agents *FA 2012, Sch 38 para 26.*	Up to £50,000 (minimum £5,000)
27. Tax agents: failure to comply with file access notice *FA 2012, Sch 38 paras 22, 23.*	(i) Initial penalty of £300.
	(ii) If failure continues, a further penalty up to £60 per day.
28. Enabling offshore tax evasion. *FA 2016, s 162, Sch 20*	Higher of 100% of the potential lost revenue and £3,000. If the original tax non-compliance resulted in a penalty under *FA 2015, Sch 21* (see 9 above), higher of 50% of the potential lost revenue in respect of the original tax non-compliance and £3,000.
29. Enablers of defeated tax avoidance. *F(No 2)A 2017, s 65, Sch 16.*	The total amount or value of the consideration received or receivable by the enabler for anything done by him which enabled the arrangements.
30. Failure to disclose tax avoidance scheme. Failure to comply with any of a number of requirements under the disclosure of tax avoidance schemes rules. *TMA 1970, s 98C.*	(i) Initial penalty of £5,000. (ii) Daily penalty of £600 (£5,000 in specified cases). Tribunal may increase total up to £1 million. (iii) Penalty of £100 for failure of party to notifiable arrangements to notify HMRC of scheme reference number. Increased to £500 for second failure in three-year period and £1,000 for third failure.

Offence	Penalty
31. Follower notice. [*FA 2014, ss 208, 208A*].	Up to 30% of the value of the denied tax advantage or 12% in partnership cases for failure to comply with notice. An additional penalty of up to 20% (8% in partnership cases) where there is an unreasonable appeal.
32. Failure to make accelerated payment. [*FA 2014, s 226*].	A 5% penalty applies if full amount is not paid by due date. If amount remains unpaid five months after due date a penalty of 5% applies; a further 5% penalty applies if amount is still unpaid after a further six months.
33. Facilitating avoidance schemes involving non-resident promoters. *FA 2022, Sch 13*	The total value of the consideration received by all members of the promotion structure in connection with the proposal or arrangements in question of other proposals or arrangements which are substantially the same.
34. Failure to comply with requirement to publish tax strategy. [*FA 2016, Sch 19*].	(i) Initial penalty of £7,500. (ii) If failure continues for six months, a further penalty of £7,500. (iii) If failure continues, a further penalty of £7,500 at the end of each subsequent month.

For the procedure for charging penalties see **46.28** onwards below. See **46.31** below for potential liability under the criminal law.

Reasonable excuse

[46.2] It is generally provided for the purposes of *TMA 1970* that a person is deemed not to have failed to do anything required to be done where there was a reasonable excuse for the failure and, if the excuse ceased, provided that the failure was remedied without unreasonable delay after the excuse had ceased. Similarly, a person is deemed not to have failed to do anything required to be done within a limited time if he did it within such further time as HMRC may have allowed. [*TMA 1970, s 118(2)*].

There are separate 'reasonable excuse' let-outs as regards penalties for failure to notify chargeability (see **46.3** below), penalties for late returns (see **46.4, 46.5, 46.8** below) and penalties for late payment of tax (see **36.6, 36.7** LATE PAYMENT INTEREST AND PENALTIES).

Appeals against penalties on the grounds that the taxpayer has a reasonable excuse are heard frequently by the FTT. In determining whether a taxpayer has a reasonable excuse for a failure, the Tribunal will generally follow the principles laid down by the Upper Tribunal in *Perrin v HMRC* UT, [2018] UKUT 156 (TCC). This involves a four-step approach as follows:

(1) Establish what facts the taxpayer asserts give rise to a reasonable excuse (including the belief, acts or omissions of the taxpayer or any other person, the taxpayer's own experience or relevant attributes, the situation of the taxpayer at any relevant time and any other relevant external facts).

(2) Decide which of those facts are proven.

(3) Decide whether, viewed objectively, those proven facts amount to an objectively reasonable excuse for the default and the time when that objectively reasonable excuse ceased. In doing so, the Tribunal should take into account the experience and other relevant attributes of the taxpayer and the situation in which the taxpayer found themselves at the relevant times. Was what the taxpayer did (or omitted to do or believed) objectively reasonable for them in those circumstances?

(4) Having decided when any reasonable excuse ceased, decide whether the taxpayer remedied the failure without unreasonable delay after that time. The Tribunal should again decide the matter objectively, but taking into account the experience and other relevant attributes of the taxpayer and the situation in which the taxpayer found themselves at the relevant times.

The following cases are just a sample of the many decisions of the FTT on reasonable excuse. For a more detailed discussion, see **Simon's Taxes, A4.568** onwards.

The taxpayer was found to have a reasonable excuse in the following cases:

- *Hauser v HMRC* FTT 2015, [2016] SFTD 423. The taxpayer submitted her return online but HMRC did not receive it owing to a glitch in the computer system.
- *McDonald v HMRC* FTT, [2017] SFTD 993. The taxpayer submitted her return late due to a period in which she cared for her sick parents and subsequently managed their financial affairs after their deaths, which occurred within six months of each other.
- *Pokorowski v HMRC* FTT, [2019] UKFTT 86 (TC). The taxpayer was essentially homeless or living in temporary hostels.
- *Ferguson v HMRC* FTT, [2020] UKFTT 66 (TC). Difficulties accessing HMRC's online systems from China.
- *Pearson v HMRC* FTT, [2017] UKFTT 780 (TC). The taxpayer was held to have a reasonable excuse for late payment of CGT resulting from the sale of shares because his lack of funds was attributable to circumstances outside his control; a catastrophic fall in the price of the remaining shares which he needed to sell to pay the CGT.
- *McGreevy v HMRC* FTT, [2017] UKFTT 690 (TC). The taxpayer was found to have a reasonable excuse for late filing of an NRCGT return as the Tribunal observed that the return was in the first year of operation and it had been reasonable for the (non-resident) taxpayer to think that

she only needed to mention the gain on her self-assessment tax return. The Tribunal rejected HMRC's contention that the taxpayer should have stayed up to date with legislation affecting her activities in the UK, finding that this obligation identified by HMRC had no source; it was not the law.

The taxpayer was held not to have a reasonable excuse in the following cases:

- *Smith v HMRC* FTT, [2020] SFTD 362. A taxpayer who had signed up for electronic communications and deleted an email from HMRC as spam without reading it. This email had advised him that a notice to file a return had been posted to his online personal tax account. As a result, he was found not to have a reasonable excuse for late filing.
- *Chartridge Developments Ltd v HMRC* FTT, [2017] UKFTT 766 (TC). The company had delegated the task of submitting a return to an employee who had failed to do so. The company was held not to have a reasonable excuse as there was no evidence that it had taken any steps to ensure that the return would be submitted on time or to check that it had in fact been submitted other than delegating the task to the employee.
- *Hesketh v HMRC* FTT, [2017] UKFTT 871 (TC). The judge disagreed with the decisions in *McGreevy* above, holding that ignorance of the law was not a reasonable excuse in the circumstances of the case.
- *Bieliauskas v HMRC* FTT, [2020] UKFTT 346 (TC). The taxpayer's reliance on his accountant to file his tax return did not provide a reasonable excuse; it remained his responsibility to file the return and he should have sought confirmation around the time of the filing deadline that it had been submitted.
- *Exclusive Promotions Ltd v HMRC* UT, [2023] UKUT 269 (TCC), [2023] STC 1919. Belief that a judicial review against an accelerated payment notice would succeed was not a reasonable excuse.

Coronavirus

A taxpayer's inability to meet an obligation such as a payment date or filing deadline due to coronavirus (COVID-19) will be accepted as a reasonable excuse. However, this is on the condition that the taxpayer remedies the failure as soon as they are able to do so. Additionally, taxpayers will need to explain how they were affected by coronavirus when making their appeal. See www.gov.uk/tax-appeals/reasonable-excuses.

Notification of chargeability

[46.3] Taxpayers who do not automatically receive tax returns for completion have an obligation to notify HMRC of their chargeability to capital gains tax or corporation tax within specified time limits. Penalties apply for failure to do so as described below.

Capital gains tax (and income tax)

A person chargeable to income tax or capital gains tax for a particular tax year who has not received a notice under *TMA 1970, s 8* (see **52.5** RETURNS) to deliver a return for that year of their income and chargeable gains has until 5 October following that tax year to notify HMRC that they are so chargeable. Where a person chargeable to income tax or capital gains tax has received such a notice, but the notice has subsequently been withdrawn (see **52.5** RETURNS), they must notify HMRC that they are chargeable within 30 days after the date on which the notice was withdrawn (or before 6 October if later).

Where an asset is disposed of and acquired under a contract, the gain or loss arises at the time the contract is made (see **16.4** COMPUTATION OF GAINS AND LOSSES) or, if the contract is conditional, when the conditions are satisfied, and therefore in the tax year in which that time falls. Where the contract is entered into on or after 6 April 2023, but the asset is not conveyed or transferred until after 5 October following the tax year in which the contract is made, the time limit for notifying chargeability in respect of the gain or loss arising is extended. In such a case, notification must be made no later than 5 October following the tax year of conveyance or transfer.

A person is excepted from the requirement to notify HMRC if their total income is fully taxed at source or chargeable at a nil rate (see Tolley's Income Tax for the detailed provisions) *and* they have no chargeable gains for the year; in practice, this is taken to mean no chargeable gains in excess of the annual exempt amount — see HMRC Self Assessment Legal Framework Manual SALF210.

The above applies equally to 'relevant trustees' of settlements by reference to a notice under *TMA 1970, s 8A* (see **52.5** RETURNS) to deliver a tax return. Trustees must make a notification via HMRC's online Trusts Registration Service.

Where a 'simple assessment' is made for a tax year (see **6.9** ASSESSMENTS), the requirement to notify chargeability does not then apply for that year unless the person is chargeable to any income tax or capital gains tax that is not included in the simple assessment.

[*TMA 1970, s 7; TCGA 1992, s 28A; FA 2022, s 98; F(No 2)A 2023, s 40*].

The trustees of pension schemes which have income or capital gains are also within these provisions (see Revenue Press Release 29 August 1997, Pension Schemes Office Update 30, 5 September 1997 and see generally Revenue Tax Bulletin, February 1999, pp 628, 629).

A person is not required to notify chargeability by reference only to a chargeable gain on a disposal in respect of which they have made a UK land disposal return (see **52.22** RETURNS) within the time limit for notification above. However, notification is required if the amount notionally chargeable (see **45.3** PAYMENT OF TAX) at the filing date for the return is less than the CGT liability for the tax year. [*FA 2019, Sch 2 para 18*].

Corporation tax

A company chargeable to corporation tax for a particular accounting period which has not received a notice to deliver a company tax return has twelve months after the end of the accounting period in which to notify HMRC that it is so chargeable. [*FA 1998, s 117, Sch 18, para 2*].

Where an asset is disposed of and acquired under a contract, the gain or loss arises at the time the contract is made (see **16.4** COMPUTATION OF GAINS AND LOSSES) or, if the contract is conditional, when the conditions are satisfied, and therefore in the accounting period in which that time falls. Where the contract is entered into on or after 1 April 2023, but the asset is not conveyed or transferred until more than 12 months after the end of the accounting period in which the contract is made, the time limit for notifying chargeability in respect of the gain or loss arising is extended. In such a case, notification must be made no later than 12 months after the end of the accounting period in which the conveyance or transfer takes place. [*TCGA 1992, s 28A; FA 2020, s 40*].

See also **52.21** RETURNS for the requirement to give notice of coming within the charge to corporation tax within three months of the *beginning* of an accounting period.

Penalties for non-compliance with obligations to notify chargeability

Penalties for non-compliance with the above provisions are charged under a unified penalty code for failures relating to a range of taxes. The code is described below, but only to the extent that it relates to the above provisions.

A person is not liable to a penalty for a failure in respect of which he has been convicted of an offence.

Amount of penalty

The amount of the penalty depends on whether or not the failure is deliberate and is subject to reduction as detailed below. It also depends on which of four categories the failure falls in. The categories are as follows.

- **Category 0.** Not yet in operation — see below under Future developments.
- **Category 1.** Failures involving a 'domestic matter' or inaccuracies involving an 'offshore matter' where the territory concerned is a category 1 territory or the tax involved is neither income tax nor capital gains tax.
- **Category 2.** Failures involving an offshore matter or an 'offshore transfer' where the territory involved is a category 2 territory and the tax is income tax or capital gains tax.
- **Category 3.** Failures involving an offshore matter or an offshore transfer where the territory involved is a category 3 territory and the tax is income tax or capital gains tax.

If a failure is within more than one category it is treated as if it were separate failures, one in each of the categories concerned according to the matters it involves, and the 'potential lost revenue' (see below) is calculated separately for each deemed failure.

A failure involves an '*offshore matter*' if it results in potential lost revenue charged on, or by reference to, income arising from a source in, or assets (including sterling) held or situated in, a territory outside the UK, activities carried on wholly or mainly in such a territory or anything having effect as if it were such income, assets or activities.

A failure involves an *offshore transfer* if:

- it does not involve an offshore matter;
- it is deliberate (whether or not concealed) and results in a potential loss of revenue; and

- the proceeds of the disposal on (or by reference to which) the tax is charged (or any part of those proceeds):
  - are received in a territory outside the UK; or
  - are transferred to a territory outside the UK before the date by reference to which the potential lost revenue is to be calculated. The reference to the transfer of proceeds is to be read as including a reference to the transfer of any assets derived from or representing those proceeds.

Where more than one category of territory is involved in an offshore transfer, the level of penalty is to be determined by reference to the highest category of territory involved.

A failure involves a '*domestic matter*' if it does not involve an offshore matter or an offshore transfer. The classification of territories to categories 1, 2 or 3 is as follows.

- **Category 1:** Anguilla; Aruba; Australia; Belgium; Bulgaria; Canada; Cayman Islands; Cyprus; Czech Republic; Denmark (not including Faroe Islands and Greenland); Estonia; Finland; France; Germany; Greece; Guernsey; Hungary; Ireland; Isle of Man; Italy; Japan; Latvia; Liechtenstein (from 24 July 2013); Lithuania; Malta; Montserrat; Netherlands (not including Bonaire, Sint Eustatius and Saba); New Zealand (not including Tokelau); Norway; Poland; Portugal; Romania; Slovakia; Slovenia; South Korea; Spain; Sweden; Switzerland (from 24 July 2013); United States of America (not including overseas territories and possessions).
- **Category 2:** All territories (except the UK) not within categories 1 or 3.
- **Category 3:** Albania; Algeria; Andorra; Bonaire, Sint Eustatius and Saba; Brazil; Cameroon; Cape Verde; Colombia; Republic of the Congo; Cook Islands; Costa Rica; Curaçao; Cuba; Democratic People's Republic of Korea; Dominican Republic; Ecuador; El Salvador; Gabon; Guatemala; Honduras; Iran; Iraq; Jamaica; Kyrgyzstan; Lebanon; Macau; Marshall Islands; Federated States of Micronesia; Monaco; Nauru; Nicaragua; Niue; Palau; Panama; Paraguay; Peru; Seychelles; Sint Maarten; Suriname; Syria; Tokelau; Tonga; Trinidad and Tobago; United Arab Emirates; Uruguay. The following territories were originally in category 3 but moved to category 2 with effect from 24 July 2013: Antigua and Barbuda; Armenia; Bahrain; Barbados; Belize; Dominica; Grenada; Mauritius; Saint Kitts and Nevis; Saint Lucia; Saint Vincent and the Grenadines; San Marino.

The amount of the penalty (subject to the reductions below) is the percentage of the potential lost revenue found using the table below.

	Percentage of potential lost revenue		
Type of failure	*Category 1*	*Category 2*	*Category 3*
deliberate and concealed	100	150	200
deliberate but not concealed	70	105	140

any other	30	45	60

A deliberate and concealed failure occurs where the failure was deliberate and the taxpayer made arrangements to conceal the situation giving rise to the obligation. A deliberate but not concealed failure occurs where the failure was deliberate but the taxpayer did not make arrangements to conceal the situation giving rise to the obligation.

For income tax and capital gains tax purposes, the '*potential lost revenue*' is in most cases equal to the amount of tax payable for the year that, by reason of the failure, remains unpaid on 31 January following that year. Where an obligation to notify chargeability arises following the withdrawal of a notice to make a return (see **52.5** RETURNS), the '*potential lost revenue*' is the amount of tax that is, by reason of the failure to comply with the obligation:

(a) where the period for notification is extended to 30 days after the date of the withdrawal notification and that period ends after the 'relevant date', unpaid at the end of that period; or
(b) in any other case, unpaid on the relevant date.

The '*relevant date*' for this purpose is 31 January following the tax year or, where, after that date, HMRC refund a payment on account for the year, the day after the refund is issued.

For corporation tax purposes, the '*potential lost revenue*' is equal to the amount of tax payable for the accounting period that, by reason of the failure, remains unpaid twelve months after the end of the period. Tax payable is computed disregarding any deferred relief arising from the repayment of loans made to close company participators.

The fact that potential lost revenue may be balanced by a potential overpayment by another person is ignored, except to the extent that that person's tax liability is required or permitted to be adjusted by reference to the taxpayer's.

No penalty is due in relation to a failure that is not deliberate if the taxpayer satisfies HMRC or, on appeal, the Tribunal, that there is a reasonable excuse for the failure. Insufficiency of funds is not a reasonable excuse for this purpose and neither is the taxpayer's reliance on another person to do anything, unless he took reasonable care to avoid the failure. If the taxpayer had a reasonable excuse, he is treated as continuing to have a reasonable excuse after the excuse has ceased if the failure is remedied without unreasonable delay. See **46.2** above for the approach of the Tribunal to reasonable excuse.

Reduction for disclosure — necessary disclosures

A reduction in a penalty will be given where the taxpayer discloses a failure to notify. The penalty will be reduced to a percentage which reflects the quality of the disclosure and the amount of the reduction will depend on whether the disclosure is 'prompted' or 'unprompted' and is subject to a minimum percentage (see tables below). A disclosure is '*unprompted*' if made when the taxpayer has no reason to believe HMRC have discovered or are about to discover the failure. In all other cases, disclosures are '*prompted*'.

In the case of a failure that involves a domestic matter, or in the case of a *non-deliberate* failure involving an offshore matter, a person is treated as making a disclosure for these purposes only if he tells HMRC about the failure, gives them reasonable help in quantifying the tax unpaid and allows them access to records for the purpose of checking how much tax is unpaid.

In the case of a *deliberate* failure (whether concealed or not) involving an *offshore matter* or any failure involving an *offshore transfer*, a person (P) will be treated as making a disclosure only if P tells HMRC about the failure, gives them reasonable help in quantifying the tax unpaid, and allows them access to records for the purpose of checking how much tax is unpaid. P must also tell HMRC if there is:

- any person who encouraged, assisted or otherwise facilitated the failure; and
- any asset situated or held outside the UK that is held on P's behalf by another person,

and must provide further specified details if either is the case.

Reduction for disclosure — domestic matters

The minimum percentage (i.e. the percentage below which a penalty may not be reduced) for each level of penalty in relation to domestic matters is as follows. Where relevant, the 'Case A' minimum applies where HMRC become aware of the failure less than twelve months after the time when the tax first becomes unpaid by reason of the failure; otherwise the 'Case B' minimum applies.

Standard percentage	Minimum percentage for prompted disclosure	Minimum percentage for unprompted disclosure
30	case A: 10 case B: 20	case A: 0 case B: 10
70	35	20
100	50	30

Reduction for disclosure — offshore matters

For a failure involving an offshore matter or offshore transfer, the penalty cannot be reduced below a minimum percentage shown in the table below. Where relevant, the 'Case A' minimum applies where HMRC become aware of the failure less than 12 months after the time when the tax first becomes unpaid by reason of the failure; otherwise the 'Case B' minimum applies.

Standard percentage	Minimum percentage for prompted disclosure	Minimum percentage for unprompted disclosure
30	case A: 10 case B: 20	case A: 0 case B: 10
45	case A: 15 case B: 30	case A: 0 case B: 15

Standard percentage	Minimum percentage for prompted disclosure	Minimum percentage for unprompted disclosure
60	case A: 20 case B: 40	case A: 0 case B: 20
70	45	30
100	60	40
105	62.5	40
140	80	50
150	85	55
200	110	70

Reduction in special circumstances

HMRC can also reduce, stay or agree a compromise in relation to proceedings for a penalty if they think it right to do so because of special circumstances. Ability to pay and the fact that a potential loss of revenue from one taxpayer is balanced by a potential overpayment by another are not special circumstances for this purpose.

Reduction for other penalty or surcharge

The amount of a penalty in respect of a failure is reduced by the amount of any other penalty or late payment surcharge, the amount of which is determined by reference to the same tax liability. No reduction is made for a tax-related penalty within **46.19** below or for a penalty within **46.16, 49.28** or **49.29** below.

No reduction is made for a penalty within **36.6** or **36.7** LATE PAYMENT INTEREST AND PENALTIES.

Agents

A person is liable to a penalty under the above provisions where the failure is by a person acting on his behalf. He is not, however, liable to a penalty in respect of anything done or omitted by his agent, if he satisfies HMRC or, on appeal, the tribunal, that he took reasonable care to avoid the failure.

Company officers

Where a company is liable to a penalty under the above provisions for a deliberate failure and the failure was attributable to a company 'officer', the officer is liable to pay such part (including all) of the penalty as HMRC specify by written notice. In relation to a body corporate other than a limited liability partnership, a director, shadow director, manager or secretary of the company is an '*officer*'; in relation to a limited liability partnership, a member is an '*officer*'; and in any other case, a director, manager, secretary or any other person managing or purporting to manage any of the company's affairs is an '*officer*'. The procedural provisions (see **46.28** onwards below) apply to a part of a penalty payable by a company officer as if it were itself a penalty.

Future developments

With effect on and after a day to be appointed by the Treasury, a new category (category 0) is to be introduced alongside categories 1 to 3 above. A category 0 territory will be a territory designated as such by Treasury order. The intention is that only territories that adopt automatic exchange of information under the Common Reporting Standard (see Tolley's Income Tax for details of international co-operation including the Common Reporting Standard) will be given category 0 status.

Category 0 will have the same penalty levels as the current category 1 (and all penalties for domestic matters and corporation tax will be moved to category 0). The current penalty levels for category 1 will be increased from 100%, 70% and 30% to 125%, 87.5% and 37.5% respectively. The penalty levels for categories 2 and 3 will remain the same. The new category 1 penalty levels can be reduced for unprompted disclosure to a minimum of 50%, 35% and 0% respectively and for prompted disclosure to a minimum of 72.5%, 53.75% and 12.5% respectively. If, however, HMRC do not become aware of the failure until 12 months or more after the time tax first becomes unpaid by reason of the failure, the 37.5% penalty cannot be reduced below 12.5% for unprompted disclosure and 25% for prompted disclosure.

[*FA 2008, s 123, Sch 41 paras 1, 5–7, 11–15, 20–24; FA 2021, Sch 26 para 15; SI 2017 No 345*].

See **46.15** below as regards a possible further penalty where assets are moved between overseas territories in order to prevent or delay the discovery of a potential loss of revenue giving rise to the above penalty.

Failure to deliver tax return on or before filing date (late filing penalty)

Company returns

[46.4] A company which fails to deliver a company tax return for an accounting period on or before the 'filing date' when required to do so by notice under *FA 1998, Sch 18 para 3* is liable to a flat-rate penalty of:

- £100, if the return is delivered within three months after the filing date; or
- £200, if the return is delivered more than three months after the filing date.

The '*filing date*' is the last day of whichever of the periods at **52.21**(a)–(c) RETURNS is the last to end (see *FA 1998, Sch 18 para 14*). In the straightforward case, it will be the last day of the twelve months following the accounting period in question.

For a third successive failure, the above amounts are increased to £500 and £1,000 respectively. Such a failure occurs where a company is within the charge to corporation tax throughout three successive accounting periods, is required to deliver a return for each such period, is liable to a flat-rate penalty in respect of each of the first two such periods, and is again liable in respect of the third such period.

The flat-rate penalty does not apply if the period for which the return is required (the 'return period') is one for which accounts are required under *Companies Act 2006* or *Companies Act 1985* (or NI equivalent) and the return is delivered to HMRC no later than the last day for delivery of the accounts to the Registrar of Companies.

If a failure to deliver a return continues beyond the 18 months following the end of the accounting period in question (or beyond the filing date if, exceptionally, it falls later than that), then, in addition to a flat-rate penalty, the company is liable to a tax-related penalty. This is equal to 10% of the 'unpaid tax', increasing to 20% if the return is still not delivered within two years after the end of the return period. The '*unpaid tax*' is so much of the tax payable for the accounting period in question as remains unpaid beyond the 18-month period referred to above (or beyond the filing date if later). Tax payable is computed for this purpose in accordance with *FA 1998, Sch 18 para 8* (but disregarding any deferred relief arising from the repayment of loans made to close company participators).

[*FA 1998, s 117, Sch 18 paras 17–19*].

Replacement of penalty

The above provisions were to be replaced by the new penalties at **46.5** below at a future date. Following the forthcoming replacement of those penalties with the *FA 2021* penalties at **46.8** below, it appears to be unlikely that those penalties will ever apply to corporation tax. In particular, the government has indicated that the *FA 2021* penalties are to be extended to corporation tax in due course.

Cross-tax penalty for failure to make returns

[46.5] A unified penalty code for failure to make a return applies across a range of taxes including capital gains tax. The code was originally intended to be extended to corporation tax, but this has not yet happened. The penalties are described below, but only to the extent that they relate to capital gains tax and may in future relate to corporation tax. Given that the Government now intends to extend the *FA 2021* penalty rules (see **46.7** below) to corporation tax, it seems unlikely that the penalties described here will ever apply to corporation tax.

Where a return is required under any of the provisions listed below, a penalty under the code is payable if the taxpayer fails to make or deliver the return to HMRC on or before the 'filing date'. For this purpose a requirement to make a return includes the requirement to deliver any accounts, statement or document which must be delivered with the return. The provisions are:

(a) *TMA 1970, s 8* (personal tax return — see **52.5** RETURNS);
(b) *TMA 1970, s 8A* (trustee's tax return — see **52.5** RETURNS);
(c) *FA 2019, Sch 2* (UK land disposal return (other than a voluntary return — see **52.22** RETURNS));
(d) *TMA 1970, s 12AA* (partnership tax return — see **52.18** RETURNS); and
(e) *FA 1998, Sch 18 para 3* (corporation tax return — see **52.21** RETURNS).

For returns within (a) and (b) above, the '*filing date*' is:

- if the return is a non-electronic return, 31 October following the tax year to which it relates or, if later, within three months beginning with the date of the notice;
- if the return is an electronic return, 31 January following the tax year to which it relates or, if later, within three months beginning with the date of the notice.

For returns within (e) above, the '*filing date*' is the last day of whichever of the periods at **52.21**(a)–(c) RETURNS is the last to end (see *FA 1998, Sch 18, para 14*). In the straightforward case, it will be the last day of the 12 months following the accounting period in question. See **52.18** RETURNS for the filing date for partnership returns. See **52.22** for the filing date for returns within (c) above.

If a failure to make a return falls within the terms of more than one of the following penalties, the taxpayer is liable to each of those penalties (subject to the overall limit for tax-geared penalties below). A taxpayer is not liable to a penalty for a failure or action in respect of which he has been convicted of an offence.

Where HMRC issue a notice withdrawing a notice to make a return within (a), (b) or (e) above (see **52.5, 52.18** RETURNS), the notice may also cancel a penalty under these provisions for failing to make a return.

Coronavirus (COVID-19)

Due to the coronavirus, HMRC suspended late filing penalties in respect of returns within (c) above in respect of disposals that were completed between 6 April 2020 and 30 June 2020, provided that the return was filed by 31 July 2020.

HMRC did not charge late filing penalties for 2019/20 self-assessment returns (including partnership and trustee returns) if the return is filed **online** by 28 February 2021 (HMRC Press Notice 25 January 2021). Similarly, HMRC did not charge late filing penalties for 2020/21 self-assessment returns (including partnership and trustee returns) if the return is filed online by 28 February 2022 (HMRC Press Notice 6 January 2022).

Initial penalty

An initial penalty of £100 is payable for failure to make a return on or before the filing date.

Daily penalty

HMRC can impose a daily penalty where the taxpayer's failure to make the return continues after the end of three months beginning with the day after the filing date (the '*penalty date*').

The amount of the penalty is £10 for each day that the failure continues during the period of 90 days starting with a date specified by HMRC. HMRC must notify the taxpayer of the starting date, which date cannot be earlier than the end of the three-months beginning with the penalty date. The date can, however, be earlier than the date of the notice.

Tax-geared penalties

First tax-geared penalty

If the failure continues after the end of six months starting with the penalty date the taxpayer is liable to a penalty equal to the greater of £300 and 5% of any tax liability which would have been shown in the return.

For this purpose (and that of the second tax-geared penalty below), the tax liability which would have been shown in a return is the amount which, had a correct and complete return been delivered on the filing date, would have been shown to be due and payable in respect of the tax for the period concerned. If a penalty is assessed before the return is made, HMRC must determine the tax liability to the best of their information and belief. Then, when the return is subsequently made, the penalty must be re-assessed by reference to the amount of tax shown in the return to be due and payable (but subject to any amendments or corrections to the return). Any deferred relief arising from the repayment of loans made to close company participators is disregarded.

In *HMRC v D. Hansard* UT 2019, [2020] STC 336, the Tribunal held that the above rules provide for an iterative process where a return has not been submitted. HMRC can assess, as a first step, a penalty of £300 in the knowledge that it cannot be excessive and top up the penalty to 5% of the tax liability when the amount of the tax is known.

Second tax-geared penalty

A further tax-geared penalty is payable if the failure continues the end of twelve months starting with the penalty date. The amount of the penalty depends on whether or not, by failing to make the return, the taxpayer deliberately withholds information which would enable or assist HMRC to assess the tax liability.

If there is deliberate withholding of information, the amount of the penalty further depends on whether the withholding is concealed and on which of four categories the information falls within. The categories are as follows.

- **Category 0.** This category is not yet in operation — see below under Future developments.
- **Category 1.** Information involving a 'domestic matter' or involving an 'offshore matter' or an 'offshore transfer' where the territory concerned is a category 1 territory or the tax involved is neither income tax nor capital gains tax.
- **Category 2.** Information involving an offshore matter or an offshore transfer where the territory involved is a category 2 territory and the tax is income tax or capital gains tax.
- **Category 3.** Information involving an offshore matter or an offshore transfer where the territory involved is a category 3 territory and the tax is income tax or capital gains tax.

If the information withheld is within more than one category, the failure is treated as if it were separate failures, one in each of the categories concerned and the tax liability which would be shown in the return is apportioned on a just and reasonable basis.

Information involves an '*offshore matter*' if the liability which would have been shown in the return includes a liability to tax charged on, or by reference to, income arising from a source in, or assets (including sterling) held or situated in, a territory outside the UK, activities carried on wholly or mainly in such a territory or anything having effect as if it were such income, assets or activities.

Information involves an '*offshore transfer*' if:

- it does not involve an offshore matter;
- it is information which would enable or assist HMRC to assess the taxpayer's liability to income tax;
- by failing to make the return, the taxpayer deliberately withholds the information (whether or not the withholding of the information is also concealed); and
- the proceeds of the disposal on (or by reference to which) the tax is charged (or any part of the proceeds):
  - are received in a territory outside the UK; or
  - are transferred to a territory outside the UK before the date on which the taxpayer becomes liable to the second tax-geared penalty. The reference to the transfer of proceeds is to be read as including a reference to the transfer of any assets derived from or representing those proceeds.

Where more than one category of territory is involved in an offshore transfer, the level of penalty is to be determined by reference to the highest category of territory involved.

Information involves a '*domestic matter*' if it does not involve an offshore matter or an offshore transfer. The classification of territories to categories 1, 2 or 3 is as at **46.3** above.

The amount of the penalty is the greater of £300 and the percentage of the tax liability which would be shown in the return found using the table below.

	Percentage of tax liability		
	Category 1	*Category 2*	*Category 3*
deliberate and concealed withholding of information	100	150	200
deliberate but not concealed withholding of information	70	105	140
any other	5	5	5

For this purpose, the withholding of information by a taxpayer is concealed if the taxpayer makes arrangements to conceal that it has been withheld.

See **46.15** below as regards a possible further penalty where the second tax-geared penalty is chargeable and assets are moved between overseas territories in order to prevent or delay the discovery by HMRC of the loss of tax revenue.

Maximum tax-geared penalty

Where both the first and second tax-geared penalties are due in relation to the same tax liability, the total of those penalties cannot exceed the 100%, 150% or 200% limit as appropriate.

Partnerships

In the case of a partnership return, where the partner required to make the return or his successor (see **52.18** RETURNS) fails to make the return on or before the filing date, a penalty is payable by each person who was a partner at any time in the period for which the return is required.

Reasonable excuse

None of the above penalties are due in respect of a failure to make a return if the taxpayer satisfies HMRC or, on appeal, the Tribunal, that there is a reasonable excuse for the failure. Insufficiency of funds is not a reasonable excuse for this purpose and neither is the taxpayer's reliance on another person to do anything, unless he took reasonable care to avoid the failure. If the taxpayer had a reasonable excuse, he is treated as continuing to have a reasonable excuse after the excuse has ceased if the failure is remedied without unreasonable delay. See further **46.2** above.

Reduction for disclosure

A reduction in the second tax-geared penalty above will be given where the taxpayer discloses information which has been withheld by a failure to make a return. The penalty will be reduced to a percentage which reflects the quality of the disclosure (including its timing, nature and extent) and the amount of the reduction will depend on whether the disclosure is 'prompted' or 'unprompted' and is subject to a minimum percentage. In all cases the amount of the penalty cannot be reduced below £300.

For penalties involving a *domestic* matter, the minimum percentage (i.e. the percentage below which a penalty may not be reduced) is as follows.

Standard percentage	Minimum percentage for prompted disclosure	Minimum percentage for unprompted disclosure
70	35	20
100	50	30

In the case of information involving an *offshore matter* or *offshore transfer*, the minimum percentage shown in the table below in each case applies.

Standard percentage	Minimum percentage for prompted disclosure	Minimum percentage for unprompted disclosure
70	45	30
100	60	40

Standard percentage	Minimum percentage for prompted disclosure	Minimum percentage for unprompted disclosure
105	62.5	40
140	80	50
150	85	55
200	110	70

In the case of a failure that involves a domestic matter, or a *non-deliberate* failure that involves an offshore matter, a person (P) is treated as making a disclosure for these purposes only if P tells HMRC about the information, gives them reasonable help in quantifying the tax unpaid by reason of the information having been withheld and allows them access to records for the purpose of checking how much tax is unpaid. In addition, in the case of a *deliberate* failure (whether concealed or not) involving an *offshore matter*, or in the case of any failure involving an *offshore transfer*, P must also tell HMRC if there is:

- any person who encouraged, assisted or otherwise facilitated the withholding of the information; and
- any asset situated or held outside the UK that is held on P's behalf by another person,

and must provide further specified details if either is the case.

A disclosure is '*unprompted*' if made when the taxpayer has no reason to believe HMRC have discovered or are about to discover the information. In all other cases, disclosures are '*prompted*'.

Reduction in special circumstances

HMRC can also reduce, stay or agree a compromise in relation to proceedings for a penalty if they think it right to do so because of special circumstances. Ability to pay and the fact that a potential loss or revenue from one taxpayer is balanced by a potential overpayment by another are not special circumstances for this purpose.

Reduction for other penalty

The amount of a tax-geared penalty is reduced by the amount of any other penalty the amount of which is determined by reference to the same tax liability. No such reduction is made for another penalty under the above provisions (but see above for the maximum tax-geared penalty under these provisions), for a tax-related penalty for late payment of tax within **36.6** LATE PAYMENT INTEREST AND PENALTIES or for a penalty within **46.16**, **49.28** or **49.29** below.

Future developments

For income tax self-assessment taxpayers, the penalty regime at **46.7** below will replace the unified code from a date to be appointed by the Treasury via regulations. For such taxpayers with business or property turnover of more than £50,000 per year (who will be required to submit digital quarterly updates through Making Tax Digital), the new regime will take effect from **6 April 2026**. For those with turnover of more than £30,000, it will take effect from **6 April 2027**. The new regime applies from 6 April 2024 to taxpayers who elect to enter MTD voluntarily.

With effect on and after a day to be appointed by the Treasury, a new category (category 0) was to be introduced for the second tax-geared penalty alongside categories 1 to 3 above. Given the passage of time since it was legislated for in 2015, and the absence of a category 0 in the new penalty regime at **46.9** below, there must be some doubt now as to whether this will go ahead for income tax and capital gains tax taxpayers. A category 0 territory was to be a territory designated as such by Treasury order. The intention was that only territories that adopted automatic exchange of information under the Common Reporting Standard (see Tolley's Income Tax for details of the Common Reporting Standard) would be given category 0 status. Category 0 was to have the same penalty levels as the current category 1 (and all penalties for domestic matters were to be moved to category 0). The higher current penalty levels for category 1 were to be increased from 100% and 70% to 125% and 87.5% respectively, with the 5% level staying unchanged. Where both the first and second tax-geared penalties were due in relation to the same tax liability, the total of those penalties would not be able to exceed the new 125% limit. The penalty levels for categories 2 and 3 were to remain the same. The new higher category 1 penalty levels would have been reduced for unprompted disclosure to a minimum of 50% and 35% respectively and for prompted disclosure to a minimum of 72.5% and 53.75% respectively; the overriding minimum was to continue to be £300.

[*FA 2009, Sch 55 paras 1–6AB, 14–17B, 23–27; FA 2019, Sch 2 para 29; FA 2021, s 118, Sch 27 para 39; SI 2011 No 976; SI 2017 No 345*].

European Economic Interest Grouping returns

[46.6] For income tax and capital gains tax purposes, a failure by a UK or European Economic Interest Grouping (see **43.19** OVERSEAS MATTERS) or a member thereof to deliver a return under *TMA 1970, s 12A* (see **52.23** RETURNS) is subject to a fixed penalty of £300 multiplied by the number of members of the grouping at the time of failure. For continuing failure, there is a further daily penalty of up to £60 multiplied by the number of members of the grouping at the end of the day on which the grouping or member is notified of a direction to impose such a penalty by the Tribunal on an application by an HMRC officer, such daily penalty to start from the day after the taxpayer is so notified (but not for any day for which such a daily penalty has already been imposed). Neither the fixed nor the daily penalty can be imposed after the failure is remedied, and the aggregate of any fixed and daily penalties cannot exceed £100 if there is no income or chargeable gain to be included in the return. [*TMA 1970, s 98B(1)–(4)*].

FA 2021 late filing penalties

[46.7] For income tax self-assessment (ITSA) taxpayers, the FA 2021 penalty regime described at **46.8** and **46.9** below replaces that at **46.5** above from a date to be appointed by the Treasury via regulations. [*FA 2021, s 116*]. See www.g

ov.uk/government/publications/penalties-for-late-submission. For income tax self-assessment taxpayers with business or property turnover of more than £50,000 per year (who will be required to submit digital quarterly updates through MTD), the new regime will take effect from **6 April 2026**. For those with turnover of more than £30,000, it will take effect from **6 April 2027**. The regime applies from 6 April 2024 to taxpayers who have elected to enter MTD voluntarily. No penalties will apply during the voluntary testing phase in respect of quarterly returns. [*FA 2024, s 37; SI 2024 No 440*].

Although not included in the FA 2021 legislation, the Government intends to extend the FA 2021 penalty rules to corporation tax at a later date.

The FA 2021 regime replaces existing late filing penalties with a points-based system (see **46.8** below). It also replicates (see **46.9** below) the penalty for deliberately withholding information described in **46.5** above under Second tax-geared penalty, but with the significant difference that the penalty will be potentially applicable as soon as a return is late, rather than after a return has been outstanding for 12 months.

Late filing penalty: points-based system

[46.8] The new regime replaces existing late filing penalties with a points-based system. See **46.7** for the dates from which the penalty will take effect. The points-based system provides for a person to be liable to penalty points in respect of each group of returns, with returns being grouped according to the frequency with which they are required to be made. A penalty of £200 becomes chargeable when a maximum penalty points total is reached for a group of returns. A similar points-based regime will apply to VAT (not covered here) but taxpayers will have separate points totals for direct taxes and VAT. See www.gov.uk/government/publications/penalties-for-late-submission.

Groups of returns

For self-assessment taxpayers, returns are grouped (according to the frequency with which returns are required to be made) as set out below. References in this commentary to a 'return' include any return, information, statement, account or other document specified in any of the groups.

Income tax or capital gains tax (persons other than trustees or partnerships)

Group 1A (annual returns). This group applies where there is no requirement to provide information under regulations under *TMA 1970, Sch A1 para 7*. *TMA 1970, Sch A1 para 7* is to do with periodic reporting under MTD.

The group consists of the following items:

- personal tax return under *TMA 1970, s 8* (see **52.5** RETURNS);
- such accounts, statements or documents as are required to accompany the return.

Group 1B (quarterly returns). This group applies where there is a requirement to provide information under regulations under *TMA 1970, Sch A1 para 7*. The group consists of the following items:

(1) personal tax return under *TMA 1970, s 8* as prospectively amended by *F(No 2)A 2017, Sch 14 para 3* (making tax digital);
(2) such accounts, statements or documents as are required to accompany the return;
(3) statement to be provided digitally under Making Tax Digital (MTD) regulations to be made under *TMA 1970, Sch A1 para 8* (end of period statement containing specified information about the person's business or property business in relation to the tax year or basis period);
(4) information required to be provided digitally under MTD regulations to be made under *TMA 1970, Sch A1 para 7* (specified information about the person's business or property business).

Income tax or capital gains tax (trustees)

Group 2A (annual returns). This group applies where there is no requirement to provide information under regulations under *TMA 1970, Sch A1 para 7*. The group consists of the following items:

- trust tax return under *TMA 1970, s 8A* (see **52.5** RETURNS);
- such accounts, statements or documents as are required to accompany the return.

Group 2B (quarterly returns). This group applies where there is a requirement to provide information under regulations under *TMA 1970, Sch A1 para 7*. The group consists of the following items:

(1) trust tax return under *TMA 1970, s 8A* as prospectively amended by *F(No 2)A 2017, Sch 14 para 4* (making tax digital);
(2) such accounts, statements or documents as are required to accompany the return;
(3) statement to be provided digitally under Making Tax Digital (MTD) regulations to be made under *TMA 1970, Sch A1 para 8* (end of period statement containing specified information about the trustees' business or property business in relation to the tax year or basis period);
(4) information required to be provided digitally under MTD regulations to be made under *TMA 1970, Sch A1 para 7* (specified information about the trustees' business or property business).

Income tax or corporation tax (partnerships)

Group 3A (annual returns). This group applies where there is a requirement to provide information under regulations under *TMA 1970, Sch A1 para 7*. The group consists of the following items:

- partnership tax return under *TMA 1970, s 12AA* (see **52.18** RETURNS);
- such accounts, statements or documents as are required to accompany the return.

Group 3B (quarterly returns). This group applies where there is a requirement to provide information under regulations under *TMA 1970, Sch A1 para 7*. The group consists of the following items:

(1) partnership return to be provided digitally under Making Tax Digital (MTD) regulations to be made under *TMA 1970, Sch A1 para 10* (return containing specified information about the partnership's business);

(2) information required to be provided digitally under MTD regulations to be made under *TMA 1970, Sch A1 para 7* (specified information about the partnership's business or property business).

Digital reporting sub-groups

Each numbered item in group 1B, 2B or 3B is referred to in the points-based penalty provisions as a '*digital reporting sub-group*' of returns.

Person carrying on more than one business

Special rules apply where a person carries on more than one business and in relation to two or more of those businesses (the '*relevant businesses*'), is required to make returns belonging to the same group of returns. These should be read in conjunction with what is said below under Penalty points.

If the group of returns is group 1A, 2A or 3A, the person makes a single return belonging to that group for all the relevant businesses; there is thus a single group of returns for those businesses. If the group of returns is group 1B, 2B or 3B, there is treated as being a single group of returns for all the relevant businesses notwithstanding that the person makes separate returns belonging to that group for each business.

Where, accordingly, there is a single group of returns for two or more relevant businesses:

- the person has a single liability for penalty points and penalties for those businesses; and
- any change to the number of relevant businesses does not affect the continuity of the group of returns or the penalty points that the person has for that group.

[*FA 2021, Sch 24 paras 1–4*].

Penalty points

Whenever a person fails to make a return on or before the due date, the person is liable to one penalty point for the group of returns to which the return belongs, but with the following exceptions.

(a) A person is not liable to a penalty point for a group of returns if that person already has the maximum number of penalty points for that group of returns. The maximum is two points for group 1A, 2A or 3A and 4 points for group 1B, 2B or 3B.

(b) A person is not liable to more than one penalty point per month for group 1A, 2A or 3A, even if in that month there is more than one failure to make a return in that group.

(c) A person is not liable to more than one penalty point per month in respect of a failure to make a return in a digital reporting sub-group of returns, even if in that month there is more than one failure in that sub-group. For this purpose, digital reporting sub-groups (1) and (2) of group 1B or 2B are treated as a single digital reporting sub-group.

For other exceptions, see below under Reasonable excuse, Withdrawal of notice to make a return and Double jeopardy.

In certain circumstances involving a person carrying on more than one business, the references in (c) above to a month are to be taken as references to a 'calendar quarter'. (A '*calendar quarter*' is the period of three months beginning with 1 January, 1 April, 1 July or 1 October.) This occurs where:

- in relation to two or more of the businesses carried on by them, the person is required to make returns belonging to digital reporting sub-group 1B(4), 2B(4) or 3B(2); and
- the due dates for the returns belonging to the digital reporting sub-group in question do not all fall within the same month of a calendar quarter.

If there is more than one failure in a month or calendar quarter (as the case may be) to make a return in a group of returns, or in a digital reporting sub-group, the one penalty point for the month or calendar quarter to which the person is liable is for all of those failures.

Award of penalty points

Where a person is liable to a penalty point for a group of returns, HMRC can award the person a penalty point for that group. They must notify the taxpayer, and must state in the notice the failure(s) and the group of returns for which the point is awarded.

An award of a penalty point cannot be made after the later of:

(i) the end of the period of 48 weeks or 11 weeks (whichever is applicable — see below) beginning with:
  - if the penalty point is to be awarded in respect of a single failure, the day on which the failure occurred;
  - if the penalty point is to be awarded in respect of more than one failure in the same month or, where applicable (see above), the same calendar quarter, the day on which the latest failure occurred; and

(ii) the last day of the period of 12 months beginning with:
  - the end of the 'appeal period' for the assessment of the tax liability which would have been shown in the 'relevant return'; or
  - if there is no such assessment, the date on which that liability is ascertained (or is ascertained to be nil).

In (i) above, 48 weeks applies if the return is in group 1A, 2A or 3A, and 11 weeks applies if the return is in group 1B, 2B or 3B.

The '*appeal period*' is the period during which an appeal could be brought (ignoring any possibility of a late appeal) or during which an appeal that has been brought has not been determined or withdrawn. The '*relevant return*' is:

- if the penalty point is to be awarded in respect of a single failure to make a return on or before the due date, that return;
- if the penalty point is to be awarded in respect of more than one failure to make a return in the same month or, where applicable, the same calendar quarter, the return which had the latest due date in the month or quarter. If this means there is more than one relevant return, and these would produce different dates for (ii) above, the latest of those dates should be taken.

If the penalty point is to be awarded in respect of failure to make, on or before the due date, a return in digital reporting sub-group 1B(3) or (4), 2B(3) or (4) or 3B(2), the award cannot be made after the later of the date given by (i) above and, where it applies, Date X. Date X applies where, on the date given by (i) above, it was not reasonable to expect HMRC to be aware that the person was required to make the return(s). Date X is then the last day of the period of 12 months beginning with the first day on which it was reasonable to expect HMRC to be aware that the person was required to make the return (or one of the returns).

Expiry of individual penalty points

A penalty point awarded for a group of returns expires at the end of the 24 months starting on the first day of the month following that in which the failure(s) for which the point was awarded occurred, unless the person has reached the maximum number of points for that group of returns. Where the penalty point was awarded in respect of more than one failure in a calendar quarter rather than a month (see above), the expiry date is instead the end of the 24 months starting on the first day of the calendar quarter following that in which the failures occurred.

There is one exception. In a case as above where the award could not be made after the later of the date given by (i) above and Date X, and the penalty point was awarded after the first of those dates but on or before Date X, the expiry date for that point is instead the end of the 24 months beginning after the day on which the point was awarded.

Expiry of all penalty points for a group of returns

It will be seen above that individual penalty points cannot expire once the taxpayer has reached the maximum number of points for the group of returns in question. However, *all* of a person's penalty points for a group of returns expires at the beginning of the first day on which both of conditions A and B are met in relation to that group.

- Condition A is that all returns have been made on time over a period of at least 24 months or 12 months (whichever is applicable) beginning with the first day of the month following that in which the most recent failure occurred. Twenty four4 months applies if the return is in group 1A, 2A or 3A, and 12 months applies if the return is in group 1B, 2B or 3B.
- Condition B is met on any day if the person has made (whether on time or not) all returns whose due date fell within the last 24 months.

HMRC must notify the taxpayer that all of their points for a group of returns have expired.

Effect of moving between groups of returns

The points-based regime recognises that the submission frequency of a taxpayer's returns may change from time to time; for example, a taxpayer may move from group 1A ('*the old group*') to group 1B ('*the new group*'). The following rules apply only where the returns in the old group relate to a business or businesses carried on by a person and the returns in the new group also relate to that business or all of those businesses.

If the person (P) has no penalty points for the old group, P has no penalty points for the new group. If P does have penalty points for the old group, the number of penalty points P has for the new group is determined by adjusting the number of points P has for the old group. If the move is from group 1A, 2A or 3A to group 1B, 2B or 3B, two points are added to the total. If the move is in the opposite direction, two points are deducted. If the adjustment would otherwise give a minus figure, it is treated instead as giving an adjusted total of zero.

If the adjusted points total for the new group is greater than zero but less than the actual points total for the old group:

- P is treated as having, for the new group, the points which were awarded in respect of the *x* most recent failures for which points were awarded in the old group (where x = the adjusted points total for the new group); and
- the points awarded in respect of the other failures for which points were awarded in the old group are treated as having expired, so that P is left with no penalty points for the old group.

If the adjusted points total for the new group is greater than the actual points total for the old group:

- all the penalty points for the old group become penalty points for the new group; and
- the surplus points are treated as having been awarded in respect of failures occurring on the same day as the most recent failure for which a point was awarded in the old group.

In applying the provisions above concerning expiry of all penalty points for a group of returns, the starting point for Condition A (all returns made on time over a period) is the first day of the month following the first month for all or part of which a return in the new group is required to be made. The reference in Condition B to all returns includes returns in the old as well as the new group.

Liability to penalties

If a person fails to make a return on or before the due date and either of the following two conditions is met, the person is liable to a penalty of £200. The first condition is that:

- the person is awarded a penalty point in respect of the failure; and
- on being awarded that penalty point, or on being awarded after that failure a penalty point in respect of an earlier failure (or earlier failures), the person has the maximum number of penalty points for the group of returns to which the return belongs. The maximum is two points for group 1A, 2A or 3A and 4 points for group 1B, 2B or 3B.

The second condition is that the failure occurs on a day on which the person has the maximum number of penalty points for the group of returns to which the return belongs, i.e. every failure after the maximum is reached incurs a penalty (until such time as all the penalty points for the group of returns have expired).

A person is not liable to more than one penalty per month in respect of a failure to make a return in a digital reporting sub-group, even if there is more than one such failure in the month in relation to that sub-group. For this purpose, digital reporting sub-groups (1) and (2) of group 1B or 2B are treated as a single digital reporting sub-group. In certain circumstances involving a person carrying on more than one business, the references here to a month are to be taken as references to a 'calendar quarter'. This rule is similar to the 'calendar quarter' rule above under Penalty points.

If there is more than one failure in a month or calendar quarter (as the case may be) to make a return in a digital reporting sub-group, the one penalty for the month or calendar quarter to which the person is liable is for all of those failures.

[*FA 2021, Sch 24 paras 5–13, 15, 18*].

Reasonable excuse

Liability to a penalty point or a penalty under these provisions does not arise in respect of a failure to make a return if the person satisfies HMRC (or on appeal, the Tribunal) that there is a reasonable excuse for the failure. Insufficiency of funds is not a reasonable excuse for this purpose and neither is the taxpayer's reliance on another person to do anything, unless the taxpayer took reasonable care to avoid the failure. If the taxpayer had a reasonable excuse, they are treated as continuing to have a reasonable excuse after the excuse has ceased if the failure is remedied without unreasonable delay. For HMRC's approach to reasonable excuse for late filing of a return, see **46.17** below, HMRC Compliance Handbook CH160000 and www.gov.uk/tax-appeals/reasonable-excuses.

Withdrawal of notice to make a return

Where a person is liable to a penalty or a penalty point in relation to a failure to make a return in group 1A or in (1) or (2) of group 1B and HMRC withdraw the notice to make the return (see **52.5** RETURNS), whether of their own volition or at the taxpayer's request, the notification of withdrawal may include provision cancelling liability to the penalty or penalty point from the date of withdrawal. The same applies to trustees (by reference to returns in group 2A or in (1) or (2) of group 2B) and to partnerships (by reference to returns in group 3A).

Partnerships and settlements

For the purposes of these provisions, the partners in a partnership are together treated as if they were a single person (the '*deemed single person*') (distinct from the persons who are partners). A failure by one or more partners to make a return on time is treated as a failure by the deemed single person. Other things done by or in relation to a partner are also treated as done by or in relation to the deemed single person. That deemed single person is treated as continuing in existence even if there is a change in the members of the partnership. Where the deemed single person is assessed to a penalty, every 'relevant partner' is jointly and severally liable for the penalty. A '*relevant partner*' is a person who is a member of the partnership on the day on which the penalty is assessed. A person is a relevant partner even if that person was not a partner when liability was incurred to one or more of the penalty points by virtue of which liability to the penalty arose (the '*relevant penalty points*'). The relevant partners are jointly and severally liable even if none of them were partners when liability was incurred to the relevant penalty points.

The above applies to the trustees of a settlement as it does to the partners in a partnership.

Double jeopardy

A person is not liable to a penalty or a penalty point in respect of a failure in respect of which that person has been convicted of an offence.

Assessment and appeals

See **46.28** below for assessment of penalties, and see **46.30** below as regards appeals. An appeal can be brought against the award of a penalty point as well as against the imposition of a penalty.

[*FA 2021, Sch 24 paras 19–21, 25, 26*].

Penalty for deliberate withholding of information

[46.9] The new *FA 2021* penalty regime introduced at **46.7** above also replicates the pre-existing penalty for deliberately withholding information described at **46.5** above under Second tax-geared penalty, but with the significant difference that the penalty will be potentially applicable as soon as a return is late, rather than after a return has been outstanding for 12 months. See **46.7** for the dates from which the penalty will take effect.

The deliberate withholding of information penalty

The penalty will be payable by a person who, by failing to make a return listed in the third column of the table below on or before the due date for that return, deliberately withholds information which would enable or assist HMRC to assess that person's liability to tax.

	Tax to which return relates	*Return*
(1)	Income tax or capital gains tax	Personal or trust tax return under *TMA 1970, s 8* or *TMA 1970, s 8A* (see **52.5** RETURNS)
		Such accounts, statements or documents as are required to accompany the return
(2)	Income tax or corporation tax	Partnership tax return under *TMA 1970, s 12AA* (see **52.18** RETURNS)
		Such accounts, statements or documents as are required to accompany the return
(3)	Income tax or corporation tax	Partnership return to be provided digitally under Making Tax Digital regulations to be made under *TMA 1970, Sch A1 para 10* (return containing specified information about the partnership's business)

In this commentary, 'return' means any return, accounts, statement or document specified in the third column of the above table.

A person who fails to make a return on or before the due date is liable to the penalty if (and only if) at any time, by failing to make the return, the person is deliberately withholding information which would enable or assist HMRC to assess the person's liability to tax. The amount of the penalty depends on whether or not the withholding is concealed and into which of three categories the information falls. The categories are as in **46.5** above under Second tax-geared penalty, except that there is no provision for a potential category 0. Categories 1–3 read slightly differently to those in **46.5** and are as follows:

- **Category 1.** Information involving a domestic matter or involving an offshore matter where the territory concerned is a category 1 territory.
- **Category 2.** Information involving an offshore matter or offshore transfer where the territory involved is a category 2 territory and it is information which would enable or assist HMRC to assess the person's liability to the tax in question.
- **Category 3.** Information involving an offshore matter or offshore transfer where the territory involved is a category 3 territory and it is information which would enable or assist HMRC to assess the person's liability to the tax in question.

Whether a territory is a category 1, 2 or 3 territory is determined as in **46.5**, and 'domestic matter', 'offshore matter' and 'offshore transfer' have the same meanings.

The amount of the penalty is the *greater* of £300 and a percentage of the tax liability which would have been shown in the return. The tax liability which would have been shown in the return is the amount of income tax which, had a complete and accurate return been delivered on the due date, would have been shown to be due and payable for the period covered by the return. If the information withheld is in more than one category, the failure is treated as if it were separate failures, one in each of the categories concerned, and the tax liability which would have been shown in the return is apportioned on a just and reasonable basis. The percentage is found from the table below.

	Percentage of tax liability		
	Category 1	*Category 2*	*Category 3*
Deliberate and concealed withholding of information	100%	150%	200%
Deliberate but not concealed withholding of information	70%	105%	140%

For this purpose, the withholding of information by a taxpayer is concealed if the taxpayer makes arrangements to conceal that it has been withheld.

Reduction for disclosure

A reduction in the deliberate withholding of information penalty will be given where the taxpayer discloses information that they were withholding by virtue of their failure to make a return. The penalty will be reduced to a percentage which reflects the quality of the disclosure; the amount of the reduction will depend on whether the disclosure is prompted or unprompted, but cannot be reduced below a minimum percentage as shown in the tables below, and cannot in any case be reduced below £300.

Standard percentage	Minimum percentage for prompted disclosure	Minimum percentage for unprompted disclosure
70%	45%	30%
100%	60%	40%
105%	62.5%	40%
140%	80%	50%
150%	85%	55%
200%	110%	70%

Whether a disclosure is prompted or unprompted is determined as in **52.5** above, as is the question of when a person makes a disclosure. Where the information disclosed involves an offshore matter or an offshore transfer, the Treasury must make regulations setting out what additional information is required.

Reasonable excuse

The legislation does not provide a reasonable excuse defence for this penalty.

Determination of penalty where no return made

If a penalty is assessed before the return is made, then, for this purpose only, HMRC may determine that tax liability to the best of their information and belief. Alternatively, they may proceed on the assumption that the minimum £300 penalty applies. When the return is subsequently made, the penalty must be re-assessed by reference to the amount of tax shown in the return to be due and payable (subject to any amendments or corrections to the return).

Reduction in special circumstances

HMRC can also reduce, stay or agree a compromise in relation to proceedings for a penalty if they think it right to do so because of special circumstances. Ability to pay and the fact that a potential loss of revenue from a taxpayer is balanced by a potential overpayment by a taxpayer are not special circumstances for this purpose.

Reduction for other penalties

Where a person is liable to a deliberate withholding of information penalty based on a percentage of the tax liability (as opposed to the minimum £300), amount of the penalty is reduced by the amount of any other penalty incurred by that person, the amount of which is determined by reference to the same tax liability. This does not, however, include a late payment penalty within **36.6** or **36.7** LATE PAYMENT INTEREST AND PENALTIES or a penalty within **49.28** below (follower notices) or **49.29** below (accelerated payment notices).

Partnerships

Where the partner responsible for dealing with the return or a successor (see **52.18** RETURNS) fails to make a return within item (2) in the above table, or the nominated partner (see *TMA 1970, Sch A1 para 5(5)*) fails to make a return within item (3), the question of whether the condition for a deliberately withholding information penalty is met is judged by reference to the liability to tax of each '*relevant partner*', i.e. each person who was a partner at any time in the period for which the return was required. Where the condition is met as regards any relevant partner, every relevant partner is liable to a penalty. The penalty in each case is fixed at £300, regardless of the amount of the tax liability and with no reductions for disclosure. An appeal (see **46.30** below) can be brought only by the responsible partner, successor or nominated partner, as the case may be. Where such an appeal is brought in connection with a penalty payable in respect of a failure, the appeal is to be treated as if it were in connection with every penalty payable in respect of that failure.

Withdrawal of notice to make a return

Where a person or member of a partnership is liable to a deliberately withholding information penalty and HMRC withdraw the notice to make the return (see **52.5** RETURNS), whether of their own volition or at the taxpayer's request, the notification of withdrawal may include provision cancelling liability to the penalty from the date of withdrawal.

Double jeopardy

A person is not liable to a penalty for a failure or action in respect of which that person has been convicted of an offence.

Assessment and appeals

See **46.28** below for assessment of the penalty, and see **46.30** below as regards appeals.

[*FA 2021, Sch 25 paras 1–11, 15, 16, 20*].

European Economic Interest Groupings — negligence or fraud in connection with return or accounts

[46.10] If a UK or European Economic Interest Grouping (see **43.19** OVERSEAS MATTERS) or a member thereof fraudulently or negligently delivers an incorrect return, accounts or statement under *TMA 1970, s 12A* (see **52.23** RETURNS) or makes an incorrect declaration in such a return, the grouping or member is liable to a maximum penalty of £3,000 multiplied by the number of members of the grouping at the time of delivery. [*TMA 1970, s 98B(5); SI 2019 No 689, Regs 1, 2(4)*].

Careless or deliberate errors in documents

[46.11] The following provisions apply to a wide range of documents relating to both direct and indirect taxes which may be given by a taxpayer to HMRC, including the following which are relevant for the purposes of capital gains tax and corporation tax on chargeable gains:

- a tax return under *TMA 1970, s 8* or *s 8A* (personal or trustees' return — see **52.5** RETURNS);
- a company tax return under *FA 1998, Sch 18 para 3* (see **52.21** RETURNS);
- a return, statement or declaration in connection with a claim for an allowance, deduction or relief;
- accounts in connection with ascertaining liability to tax;
- a partnership return;
- a statement or declaration in connection with a partnership return;
- accounts in connection with a partnership return;
- a UK land disposal return under *FA 2019, Sch 2*; and
- any other document (other than one in respect of which a penalty is payable under *TMA 1970, s 98* — see **46.22** below) likely to be relied on by HMRC to determine, without further inquiry, a question about the taxpayer's liability to tax, his payments by way of or in connection with tax, other payments (such as penalties) by the taxpayer or repayments or any other kind of payment or credit to him.

A penalty is payable by a person who gives HMRC such a document if it contains a careless or deliberate inaccuracy which amounts to, or leads to, an understatement of his (or another person's) tax liability or a false or inflated statement of a 'loss' or claim to 'repayment of tax'. If there is more than one inaccuracy in the document a penalty is payable for each inaccuracy. See **46.12** for the penalty payable where an inaccuracy in a document is attributable to the supply of false information or the withholding of information by another person.

For this purpose, giving HMRC a document includes making a statement or declaration in a document and giving HMRC information in any form and by any method (including post, fax, email or telephone). A '*loss*' includes a charge, expense, deficit or any other amount which may be available for, or relied on to claim, a deduction or relief. '*Repayment of tax*' includes allowing a credit against tax and payment of a corporation tax credit (as defined).

A person is not liable to a penalty for an inaccuracy in respect of which he has been convicted of an offence.

See **46.15** below as regards a possible further penalty where assets are moved between overseas territories in order to prevent or delay the discovery of a potential loss of revenue giving rise to the above penalty.

Amount of penalty

The amount of the penalty depends on whether the inaccuracy is careless or deliberate and is subject to reduction as detailed below. For this purpose, an inaccuracy in a document which was neither careless nor deliberate is treated as careless if the taxpayer or a person acting on his behalf discovered the inaccuracy after giving HMRC the document but did not take reasonable steps to inform them. Reasonable steps to inform HMRC would, in their view, include consulting with an accountant or agent to discuss the position so that they can inform HMRC, or contacting HMRC directly to discuss the inaccuracy (HMRC Guidance Note, 1 April 2008).

The amount of the penalty also depends on which of four categories the inaccuracy falls in. The categories are as follows.

- **Category 0.** Not yet in operation — see below under Future developments.
- **Category 1.** Inaccuracies involving a 'domestic matter' or inaccuracies involving an 'offshore matter' where the territory concerned is a category 1 territory or the tax involved is neither income tax nor capital gains tax.
- **Category 2.** Inaccuracies involving an offshore matter or (for documents relating to 2016/17 onwards) an 'offshore transfer' where the territory involved is a category 2 territory and the tax is income tax or capital gains tax.
- **Category 3.** Inaccuracies involving an offshore matter or an offshore transfer where the territory involved is a category 3 territory and the tax is income tax or capital gains tax.

If an inaccuracy is within more than one category it is treated as if it were separate inaccuracies, one in each of the categories concerned according to the matters it involves, and the 'potential lost revenue' (see below) is calculated separately for each deemed inaccuracy.

An inaccuracy involves an '*offshore matter*' if it results in potential lost revenue charged on, or by reference to, income arising from a source in, or assets (including sterling) held or situated in, a territory outside the UK, activities carried on wholly or mainly in such a territory or anything having effect as if it were such income, assets or activities.

An inaccuracy involves an *offshore transfer* if:

- it does not involve an offshore matter;
- it is deliberate (whether or not concealed) and results in a potential loss of revenue; and
- the proceeds of the disposal on (or by reference to) which the tax is charged (or any part of those proceeds):
  - is received in a territory outside the UK; or
  - is transferred to a territory outside the UK before the date when the document containing the inaccuracy is given to HMRC. The reference to the transfer of proceeds is to be read as including a reference to the transfer of any assets derived from or representing those proceeds.

Where more than one category of territory is involved in an offshore transfer, the level of penalty is to be determined by reference to the highest category of territory involved.

An inaccuracy involves a '*domestic matter*' if it does not involve an offshore matter or an offshore transfer. The classification of territories to categories 1, 2 or 3 is as at **46.3** above.

The amount of the penalty (subject to the reductions below) is the percentage of the potential lost revenue found using the table below.

Type of action	Percentage of potential lost revenue		
	Category 1	*Category 2*	*Category 3*
careless	30	45	60
deliberate but not concealed	70	105	140
deliberate and concealed	100	150	200

Type of action

For this purpose, careless action occurs where the taxpayer or a person acting on his behalf failed to take reasonable care. HMRC consider that what constitutes 'reasonable care' has to be viewed in the light of each person's abilities and circumstances. They do not expect the same level of knowledge or expertise from an unrepresented self-employed individual as from a large multinational company. They expect a higher degree of care to be taken over large and complex matters than simple straightforward ones. In HMRC's view, it is reasonable to expect a person encountering a transaction or other event with which they are not familiar to take care to check the correct tax treatment or to seek suitable advice. (HMRC Brief 19/2008).

In *Mariner v HMRC* FTT 2013, [2014] SFTD 504, a taxpayer who had relied on the professional advice of an accountant was held not to have been careless. Taxpayers who had relied on professional advice were, by contrast, found to have been careless in *Magic Carpets (Commercial) Ltd v HMRC* FTT 2023, [2024] SFTD 113. The company implemented an EBT scheme which did not work. The directors made no attempt to understand the steps in the scheme beyond a vague understanding that it involved an EBT and they did not understand the documents that the company was entering into or whether the documents were properly executed. A prudent and reasonable taxpayer would have sought further information about the scheme either from their agents or another advisor.

In that case, however, the FTT allowed the company's appeal against the penalty because HMRC failed to demonstrate a causal link between the lack of reasonable care and the inaccuracies. This approach was rejected in *Delphi Derivatives Ltd v HMRC* FTT, [2023] UKFTT 722 (TC). There, the FTT held that the concept of a 'causal link' in the sense of a proximate cause for the inaccuracy was the wrong model to construe the harmonised penalty legislation. Instead, in relation to carelessness, the legislation required that the inaccuracy can be accounted for by 'a mode of behaviour', a broader consideration than a focus on a specific action or particular omission.

There is a presumption of carelessness where a document contains a non-deliberate inaccuracy as a result of its being submitted on the basis that particular 'avoidance arrangements' had an effect which in fact they did not have. The presumption is disapplied if the taxpayer satisfies HMRC or an Appeal Tribunal that he took reasonable care to avoid inaccuracy, but neither HMRC nor the Tribunal can take any account of any evidence of any reliance by the taxpayer on 'disqualified advice'.

Arrangements (as widely defined) are '*avoidance arrangements*' for this purpose if it would be reasonable to conclude that the obtaining of a tax advantage (also widely defined) was a main purpose of them. There is a let-out for arrangements which accord with established practice accepted by HMRC. Where arrangements are caught by specified anti-avoidance or anti-abuse legislation, they are automatically avoidance arrangements for this purpose, and the let-out does not apply.

'*Disqualified advice*' is defined in broadly similar terms as in **46.17** below. There is a limited exemption for certain advice received in connection with 'avoidance-related rules' (as in **4.37** ANTI-AVOIDANCE). The question of whether the taxpayer has taken reasonable steps to find out whether or not advice is disqualified, and believes it not to be so, is judged as at the time when the document containing the inaccuracy is given to HMRC. Where a document is given to HMRC by the personal representative of a deceased person, the disqualified advice rules are applied by reference both to the deceased and the personal representative.

See **14.21** COMPANIES for circumstances in which an error is treated as careless if made when a special measures notice is in force.

Deliberate but not concealed action occurs where the inaccuracy was deliberate but the taxpayer did not make arrangements to conceal it. Deliberate and concealed action occurs where the inaccuracy was deliberate and the taxpayer made arrangements to conceal it (for example, by submitting false evidence in support of an inaccurate figure).

Reduction for disclosure

A reduction in a penalty will be given where the taxpayer discloses an inaccuracy in a document. The penalty will be reduced to a percentage which reflects the quality of the disclosure and the amount of the reduction will depend on whether the disclosure is 'prompted' or 'unprompted' and is subject to a minimum percentage.

In the case of a failure involving a domestic matter, the minimum percentage (i.e. the percentage below which a penalty may not be reduced) for each level of penalty is as follows.

Standard percentage	Minimum percentage for prompted disclosure	Minimum percentage for unprompted disclosure
30	15	0
70	35	20
100	50	30

For an inaccuracy involving an *offshore matter* or *offshore transfer* the penalty cannot be reduced below a minimum percentage as shown below.

Standard percentage	Minimum percentage for prompted disclosure	Minimum percentage for unprompted disclosure
30	15	0
45	22.5	0
60	30	0
70	45	30
100	60	40
105	62.5	40
140	80	50
150	85	55
200	110	70

A person (P) is treated as making a disclosure for these purposes only if P tells HMRC about the inaccuracy, gives them reasonable help in quantifying the inaccuracy and allows them access to records for the purpose of ensuring that the inaccuracy is fully corrected. In the case of a *deliberate* inaccuracy (whether concealed or not) that involves an *offshore matter*, or any inaccuracy involving an *offshore transfer*, P must also tell HMRC if there is:

- any person who encouraged, assisted or otherwise facilitated the inaccuracy etc.; and
- any asset situated or held outside the UK that is held on P's behalf by another person,

and must provide further specified details if either is the case.

A disclosure is '*unprompted*' if made when the taxpayer has no reason to believe HMRC have discovered or are about to discover the inaccuracy. In all other cases, disclosures are '*prompted*'.

Example 1

Alec, a trustee of a settlement, included a capital gain in the trust's tax return. The gain is the subject of a compliance check. During the check, Alec discloses that he has used the wrong acquisition value as there was a held-over gain on the transfer of the asset to the settlement. This is related to the subject under review and so is a prompted disclosure.

Example 2

Tessa is the subject of a compliance check into her employment expenses. There is no intention to expand the scope of the check. She discloses that she has not declared a capital gain. This is an unprompted disclosure.

Note to the examples

The above examples are based on the examples given by HMRC in their Compliance Handbook at CH82422. They therefore reflect HMRC's view of what constitutes a prompted or unprompted disclosure.

Reduction in special circumstances

HMRC can also reduce, stay or agree a compromise in relation to proceedings for a penalty if they think it right to do so because of special circumstances. Ability to pay and the fact that a potential loss of revenue from one taxpayer is balanced by a potential overpayment by another are not special circumstances for this purpose. It is expected that this power will be used only in rare cases (see Treasury Explanatory Notes to the 2007 Finance Bill). See *Roche v HMRC* FTT, [2012] UKFTT 333 (TC); 2012 STI 2364 in which the Tribunal granted a reduction due to special circumstances where the taxpayer was suffering stress at the time of completing her return. In *White v HMRC* FTT, [2012] UKFTT 364 (TC); 2012 STI 2502, special circumstances were held to apply in a case in which the taxpayer failed to include a redundancy payment in her return. She had received confusing information from her employer and had made genuine efforts to resolve the confusion. The Tribunal reduced the penalty by 60%. The Tribunal reduced a penalty to nil in *Usher and another v HMRC* FTT, [2016] UKFTT 50 (TC); 2016 STI 1410.

Reduction for other penalty or surcharge

The amount of a penalty in respect of a document relating to a particular tax year or accounting period is reduced by the amount of any other penalty or late payment surcharge, the amount of which is determined by reference to the same tax liability. Where a penalty is imposed under these provisions and those at **46.12** below in respect of the same inaccuracy, the aggregate of the penalties cannot exceed 100% of the potential lost revenue for a Category 1 inaccuracy, 150% of the potential lost revenue for a Category 2 inaccuracy and 200% of the potential lost revenue for a Category 3 inaccuracy. No reduction is made for a tax-related penalty within **46.19** below or for a penalty within **46.16, 49.28** or **49.29** below.

No reduction is made for a penalty within **36.6** or **36.7** LATE PAYMENT INTEREST AND PENALTIES.

Potential lost revenue

The '*potential lost revenue*' is the additional tax due or payable as a result of correcting the inaccuracy in the document. This includes any amount payable to HMRC having been previously repaid in error and any amount which would have been repayable by HMRC had the inaccuracy not been corrected. Relief under *CTA 2010, s 458* (close company loans) and group relief are ignored (but this does not prevent a penalty being charged for an inaccurate claim for relief). 'Tax' includes, for this purpose, amounts payable on account of CGT under *TMA 1970, s 59AA* or *FA 2019, Sch 2* (see **45.3** PAYMENT OF TAX).

Where the amount of potential lost revenue depends on the order in which inaccuracies are corrected, careless inaccuracies are taken to be corrected before deliberate inaccuracies, and deliberate but not concealed inaccuracies are taken to be corrected before deliberate and concealed inaccuracies. Where there are inaccuracies in one or more documents relating to a particular tax year or accounting period and those inaccuracies include both understatements and overstatements, the overstatements are taken into account in calculating the potential lost revenue and are set off against understatements in the order which reduces the level of penalties the least (i.e. against understatements not liable to a penalty first, then against careless understatements, and so on). The fact that potential lost revenue may be balanced by a potential overpayment by another person is also ignored.

Special rules apply where an inaccuracy leads to there being a wrongly recorded loss which has not been wholly used to reduce a tax liability. The potential lost revenue in respect of that part of the loss which has not been so used is restricted to 10% of the unused part. Where, however, there is no reasonable prospect of a loss being used to support a claim to reduce a tax liability (of any person) because of the taxpayer's circumstances or the nature of the loss, the potential lost revenue is nil.

Where an inaccuracy results in an amount of tax being declared later than it would have been (otherwise than because of a wrongly recorded loss), the potential lost revenue is 5% of the delayed tax for each year of delay (applied pro rata for periods of less than a year).

Suspension of penalty

HMRC can suspend all or part of a penalty for a careless inaccuracy. A notice in writing must be given to the taxpayer setting out what part of the penalty is to be suspended, the period of suspension (maximum two years) and the conditions of suspension with which the taxpayer must comply. The conditions can specify an action to be taken and a period within which it must be taken. A penalty can be suspended only if compliance with a condition of suspension will help the taxpayer to avoid further penalties under these provisions.

A suspended penalty will become payable:

- at the end of the suspension period, if the taxpayer does not satisfy HMRC that the conditions have been complied with; and
- if, during the suspension period, the taxpayer incurs another penalty under these provisions.

Otherwise, the penalty is cancelled at the end of the suspension period.

Agents

A person is liable to a penalty under the above provisions where a document containing a *careless* inaccuracy is given to HMRC on his behalf. He is not, however, liable to a penalty in respect of anything done or omitted by his agent, if he satisfies HMRC that he took reasonable care to avoid inaccuracy.

Company officers

Where a company is liable to a penalty under the above provisions for a deliberate inaccuracy and the inaccuracy was attributable to a company 'officer', the officer is liable to pay such part (including all) of the penalty as HMRC specify by written notice. In relation to a body corporate (other than a limited liability partnership), a director, shadow director, manager or secretary of the company is an '*officer*'; in relation to a limited liability partnership, a member is an '*officer*'; and in any other case, a director, manager, secretary or any other person managing or purporting to manage any of the company's affairs is an '*officer*'. The procedural provisions (see **46.28** onwards below) apply as if the part payable by the officer were itself a penalty.

Partnerships

Where a partner is liable to a penalty arising from an inaccuracy in, or in connection with, a partnership return, and the inaccuracy affects the amount of tax payable by another partner, that other partner is also liable to a penalty. The potential lost revenue is calculated separately for each partner by reference to the proportions of any tax liability that would be borne by each of them. The suspension provisions above are, however, applied jointly to the partners' penalties.

Powers to amend provisions

The Treasury may by order make any incidental, supplemental, consequential, transitional, transitory or saving provision in connection with these provisions and those at **46.12** and **46.13** below.

Future developments

With effect on and after a day to be appointed by the Treasury, a new category (category 0) is to be introduced alongside categories 1 to 3 above. A category 0 territory will be a territory designated as such by Treasury order. The intention is that only territories that adopt automatic exchange of information under the Common Reporting Standard will be given category 0 status.

Category 0 will have the same penalty levels as the current category 1 (and all penalties for domestic matters will be moved to category 0). The current penalty levels for category 1 will be increased from 30%, 70% and 100% to 37.5%, 87.5% and 125% respectively. The penalty levels for categories 2 and 3 will remain the same. The new category 1 penalty levels can be reduced for unprompted disclosure to a minimum of 0%, 35% and 50% respectively and for prompted disclosure to a minimum of 18.75%, 53.75% and 72.5% respectively.

Where penalties are imposed as described in this section and **46.12** below in respect of the same inaccuracy, the aggregate penalty cannot exceed 100% of the potential lost revenue for an inaccuracy in new category 0 or 125% of the potential lost revenue for an inaccuracy in amended category 1.

[*FA 2007, s 97, Sch 24 paras 1, 3–12, 14, 18–28; FA 2009, Sch 56 para 9A; FA 2019, Sch 2 paras 27, 32(1); FA 2021, Sch 26 para 15; SI 2011 No 976; SI 2017 Nos 259, 345*].

Error in taxpayer's document attributable to another person

[46.12] Where a document (of a type listed at **46.11** above) given to HMRC contains an inaccuracy which amounts to, or leads to, an understatement of a tax liability or a false or inflated statement of a 'loss' or claim to 'repayment of tax', and the inaccuracy is attributable to a person deliberately supplying false information to the person giving the document to HMRC (whether directly or indirectly) or deliberately withholding information from that person, with the intention of the document containing the inaccuracy, a penalty is payable by the person supplying or withholding the information. See **46.11** above for the meaning of 'loss' and 'repayment of tax'.

The penalty is 100% of the potential lost revenue (defined as at **46.11** above, with the necessary modifications), subject to the same reductions that apply under the provisions at **46.11** above for special circumstances or disclosure. Where a penalty is imposed under these provisions and those at **46.11** above in respect of the same inaccuracy, see **46.11** above for the maximum aggregate of the penalties.

A person is not liable to a penalty for an inaccuracy in respect of which he has been convicted of an offence.

[*FA 2007, Sch 24 paras 1A, 4, 4B, 5, 7–12, 21*].

Failure to notify HMRC of error in assessment

[46.13] A penalty is payable by a person if an assessment or determination issued to him by HMRC understates his liability to tax and he or a person acting on his behalf has failed to take reasonable steps to notify HMRC of the under-assessment, within the 30 days beginning with the date of the assessment.

The penalty is 30% of the potential lost revenue (defined as at **46.11** above, with the necessary modifications), subject to the same reductions that apply under the provisions at **46.11** above for special circumstances or disclosure. HMRC must consider whether the taxpayer or a person acting on his behalf knew, or should have known, about the under-assessment and what steps would have been reasonable to take to notify HMRC.

A person is not liable to a penalty under this provision in respect of anything done or omitted by his agent, if he satisfies HMRC that he took reasonable care to avoid unreasonable failure to notify HMRC.

The amount of a penalty under this provision in respect of a document relating to a particular tax year or accounting period is reduced by the amount of any other penalty the amount of which is determined by reference to tax liability for the period (but see **46.11** above for exclusions from this rule)

A person is not liable to a penalty for a failure in respect of which he has been convicted of an offence.

[*FA 2007, s 97, Sch 24 paras 2, 4–12, 18, 21, 28*].

Arrangements counteracted by the general anti-abuse rule

[46.14] A person (P) is liable to a penalty if:

- P has been given a final counteraction notice stating that a tax advantage arising from tax arrangements is to be counteracted under the general anti-abuse rule ('GAAR'; see **4.3** ANTI-AVOIDANCE) and the advantage has been counteracted by the making of adjustments under the GAAR;

- a tax document has been given to HMRC on the basis that the tax advantage arises to P from the arrangements; and
- the document was given to HMRC by P or by another person and P knew, or ought to have known, that the document was given on the basis that the tax advantage arises to P from the arrangements.

With effect from 10 June 2021, in relation to tax arrangements entered into at any time, a partner (P) in a partnership is liable to a penalty if the partnership's responsible partner (see **4.7** ANTI-AVOIDANCE) has been given a final counteraction notice stating that a tax advantage is to be counteracted and the advantage, so far as arising to P, has been counteracted by the making of adjustments under the GAAR.

The penalty is 60% of the 'value of the counteracted advantage'. For this purpose, a '*tax document*' means a return, claim or other document submitted in compliance (or purported compliance) with any provision of an Act.

See **4.4–4.7** ANTI-AVOIDANCE for certain circumstances in which a penalty cannot be charged.

The '*value of the counteracted advantage*' is the additional amount due or payable by P in respect of tax as a result of the counteraction. This includes any amount previously repaid by HMRC which is now payable, together with any amount which would be repayable by HMRC if the counteraction were not made and any consequential adjustments. If the counteraction affects P's liability to more than one tax, each of the taxes is considered together in determining the value of the counteracted advantage. Group relief and relief in connection with loans to participators (under *CTA 2010, s 458*) are ignored in the calculation of the additional amount. Where the tax advantage counteracted under the GAAR created or increased a 'loss', and the loss was used to reduce the amount of tax payable, the additional amount due or payable can be ascertained, and the penalty calculated, in the normal way. However, where the loss has not been wholly used in this way, the value of the counteracted advantage is deemed to be 10% of any part of the loss not so used. In the case of an aggregate loss recorded for a group of companies, group relief may be taken into account. The value of the counteracted advantage in respect of a loss is nil where there is no prospect of the loss being used to support a claim to reduce a tax liability (of any person). To the extent that the tax advantage is a deferral of tax, the value of the counteracted advantage is the lower of:

(a) 25% of the deferred tax for each year of deferral (or a proportionate amount for part years); and
(b) 100% of the deferred tax.

For these purposes, a '*loss*' includes a charge, expense, deficit or other amount which may be available for, or relied on to claim, a deduction or relief. A repayment of tax includes a reference to allowing a credit against tax or to a payment of certain corporation tax credits. Giving a document to HMRC includes communicating information in any form and by any method (post, fax, email, telephone or otherwise).

Interaction with other penalties

The following applies where more than one penalty arises in respect of the same amount, one of those penalties is a GAAR penalty, and one or more of the others is incurred under *FA 2007, Sch 24* (errors; see **46.11–46.13** above), *FA 2008, Sch 41* (failure to notify; see **46.3** above), *FA 2009, Sch 55* (failure to make return; see **46.5** above), *FA 2016, Sch 18* (serial avoiders; see **46.24** below) or *FA 2021, Sch 25* (deliberate withholding of information (prospective); see **46.9** above). The general rule is that the aggregate penalty must not exceed 100% of the amount in question or, if at least one of the penalties is a £300 penalty under *FA 2009, Sch 55*, £300 (if greater). Where the maximum penalty under one of the other provisions is more than 100% because of the rules for offshore matters and offshore transfers, the aggregate penalty must not exceed that higher maximum percentage. See **49.28** below for the maximum aggregate penalties where a GAAR penalty and a penalty under *FA 2014, s 212* (follower notices) is incurred in respect of the same tax.

[*FA 2013, ss 212A, 212B, Sch 43C paras 1–4, 8; FA 2021, Sch 27 para 42, Sch 32 paras 7, 8, 13*].

Penalty for offshore asset moves

[46.15] A penalty (the '*offshore asset moves penalty*') applies where assets are moved between overseas territories and a main purpose of that movement is to prevent or delay the discovery by HMRC of a potential loss of revenue that itself gives rise to one of the penalties listed below. The offshore asset moves penalty is intended to address a risk that assets will be moved from territories committed to exchanging information under the Organisation for Economic Co-operation and Development's Common Reporting Standard to other territories for the purpose of continuing to conceal past failures or actions for which other penalties are chargeable.

The offshore asset moves penalty applies where the person concerned (P) becomes liable to another penalty (the '*original penalty*') and this is either:

- the penalty for failure to notify chargeability in **46.3** above; or
- the second tax-geared late filing penalty in **46.5** above; or
- the deliberately withholding information penalty in **46.9** above; or
- the penalty for careless or deliberate errors in documents in **46.11** above; or
- the penalty for failure to correct offshore tax non-compliance in **46.17** below.

However, the offshore asset moves penalty applies only where the original penalty is for a deliberate failure or action (regardless of whether or not it was concealed) and where the tax involved is income tax, capital gains tax or inheritance tax (or, for a penalty under **46.3** or **46.9**, income tax or capital gains tax). In the case of a penalty for failure to correct, the failure is deliberate if P was aware at any time during the RTC period (see **46.17** below) that at the end of 2016/17 he had offshore tax non-compliance to correct.

The amount of the offshore asset moves penalty is 50% of the amount of the original penalty payable by P. Even though the original penalty may be determined by reference to a liability to tax, the offshore asset moves penalty is not.

For the offshore asset moves penalty to apply, there has to be a 'relevant offshore asset move' which occurs after the 'relevant time'. There is a '*relevant offshore asset move*' if, at a time when P is the beneficial owner of an 'asset' and without his ceasing entirely to be the beneficial owner of it:

- the asset ceases to be situated or held in a 'specified territory' and becomes situated or held in a non-specified territory; or
- the person who holds the asset ceases to be resident in a specified territory and becomes resident in a non-specified territory; or
- there is a change in the arrangements for the ownership of the asset.

Where P disposes of an asset and reinvests all or part of the proceeds in another, the original and new asset are to be treated as the same asset for the purposes of determining whether there is a relevant offshore asset move. '*Asset*' has the same meaning as for capital gains tax purposes (see **7.2** ASSETS) but also includes sterling. The question of whether or not a territory is a specified territory is to be determined as at the time one of these events occurs. A '*specified territory*' is a territory designated as such by the Treasury by means of statutory instrument (see *SI 2015 No 866*). The intention is that a territory will be so designated once it has committed to exchanging information under the Common Reporting Standard (Treasury Explanatory Notes to the first 2015 Finance Bill).

The '*relevant time*' for capital gains tax purposes is determined according to the nature of the original penalty as follows.

- Where the original penalty is a penalty for failure to notify chargeability, the relevant time is the beginning of the tax year to which the obligation to notify relates.
- Where the original penalty is a second tax-geared late filing penalty, the relevant time is the beginning of the tax year to which the return or document relates.
- Where the original penalty is a deliberately withholding information penalty, the relevant time is the beginning of the tax year to which the return or document relates.
- Where the original penalty is a penalty for careless or deliberate errors in documents, the relevant time is the beginning of the tax year to which the document containing the inaccuracy relates.
- Where the original penalty is a penalty for failure to correct offshore tax non-compliance, the relevant time is the date of Royal Assent of *F(No 2)A 2017*.

Interest on penalties

Late payment interest on a penalty under the above provisions is charged in accordance with *FA 2009, s 101* where the late payment interest start date is on or after 6 September 2019. Repayment interest under *FA 2009, s 102* on an overpaid penalty is similarly available where the repayment date is on or after that date.

[*FA 2015, Sch 21 paras 1–6, 9; F(No 2)A 2017, Sch 18 para 27; FA 2021, Sch 27 para 44; SI 2015/866; SI 2017/989; SI 2019/1238*].

Asset-based penalty for offshore inaccuracies and failures

[46.16] An asset-based penalty is payable by a person where:

(a) one or more 'offshore tax penalties' have been imposed on a person in relation to 2016/17 or a subsequent tax year; and

(b) the potential lost revenue threshold is met in relation to that year.

Where the above conditions are met in relation to more than one tax year falling within the same 'investigation period', only one asset-based penalty is payable in that investigation period in relation to any given asset. This penalty is charged by reference to the tax year within the investigation period that has the highest 'offshore PLR' (see below under Potential lost revenue threshold). In relation to a person (P), the first '*investigation period*' begins on the day on which the asset-based penalty regime comes into force and ends on 5 April in the last tax year before P is notified of an asset-based penalty in respect of an asset. Subsequent investigation periods begin on the day following the end of the previous investigation period and end on 5 April in the last tax year before P is notified of a subsequent asset-based penalty in respect of the asset. Different investigation periods may apply in relation to different assets. The investigation period rules do not apply where the offshore tax penalty is a penalty under *F(No 2)A 2017, Sch 18* (failure to correct offshore tax non-compliance). Where such a penalty is imposed, and (b) above is met, only one asset-based penalty is payable in relation to any given asset.

Meaning of 'offshore tax penalty'

For the purposes of (a) above and these provisions generally, an '*offshore tax penalty*' is any of the following:

- a penalty under *FA 2007, Sch 24 para 1* (errors in documents) imposed for deliberate action (whether or not concealed) where the inaccuracy for which the penalty is imposed involves an offshore matter or an offshore transfer (see **46.11** above);
- a penalty under *FA 2008, Sch 41 para 1* (failure to notify chargeability) imposed for deliberate failure (whether or not concealed) where the failure involves an offshore matter or an offshore transfer (see **46.3** above);
- a penalty under *FA 2009, Sch 55 para 6* (the second tax-geared late filing penalty) imposed for deliberate withholding of information (whether or not concealed) where the withholding of information involves an offshore matter or an offshore transfer (see **46.5** above);
- a penalty under *FA 2021, Sch 25* (the deliberately withholding information penalty) where the withholding of information involves an offshore matter or an offshore transfer (see **46.9** above); or
- a penalty under *F(No 2)A 2017, Sch 18* (failure to correct offshore tax non-compliance) where the person was aware at any time during the RTC period that at the end of 2016/17 he had offshore tax non-compliance to correct (see **46.17** below),

but only if the tax at stake is (or includes) a tax within the asset-based penalty regime, i.e. 'asset-based income tax', capital gains tax and, where applicable, inheritance tax. Where the tax at stake includes any taxes other than those, the offshore tax penalty is the part of the penalty which relates to those taxes. 'Asset-based income tax' is income tax that is charged under any of a significant number of charging provisions listed at *FA 2016, Sch 22 para 13(2)*; see also below under Identification and valuation of assets. Where the inaccuracy etc. for which a penalty is imposed also involves a domestic matter, the offshore tax penalty is only that part of the penalty that involves the offshore matter or offshore transfer; this is not relevant to a penalty for failure to correct.

For the purposes of (a) above, as regards income tax or capital gains tax, the tax year to which an offshore tax penalty relates is the tax year to which the document containing the inaccuracy, the obligation to notify chargeability, the failure to deliver a return or other document or the offshore tax non-compliance relates.

Potential lost revenue threshold

For the purposes of (b) above, the potential lost revenue threshold is reached where the 'offshore PLR' in relation to a tax year exceeds £25,000. The '*offshore PLR*', in relation to a tax year, is the total of:

- the potential lost revenue (as in **46.3** and **46.11** above and **46.17** below); and
- the liability to tax (as in **46.5** or **46.9** above),

by reference to which all of the offshore tax penalties imposed in relation to the tax year are assessed. Where a penalty assessed relates to an offshore tax penalty and one or more other penalties (a '*combined penalty*'), only the potential lost revenue or liability to tax relating to the offshore tax penalty is taken into account in calculating the offshore PLR. Where necessary for the purposes of calculating the offshore PLR in such a case, income and gains relating to domestic matters are taken to have been taxed before income and gains relating to offshore matters and offshore transfers, and income and gains relating to taxes within the asset-based penalty regime are taken to have been taxed before income and gains relating to taxes outside the regime. Where it cannot otherwise be determined, the potential lost revenue or liability to tax relating to the offshore tax penalty is taken to be such share of the total potential lost revenue or liability to tax by reference to which the combined penalty was calculated as is just and reasonable. Where an offshore tax penalty or combined penalty relates to two or more taxes, including asset-based income tax and capital gains tax, then where necessary for the purposes of calculating the offshore PLR, income and gains relating to asset-based income tax are taken to have been taxed before income and gains relating to capital gains tax.

Amount of penalty

The penalty is the lower of (i) 10% of the value of the asset (see below) and (ii) the offshore PLR (see above) x 10.

HMRC must reduce the penalty where the taxpayer makes a disclosure of the inaccuracy or failure relating to the offshore tax penalty, provides HMRC with a reasonable valuation of the asset and provides HMRC with information or access to records that HMRC require for the purposes of valuing the asset. The reduction must reflect the quality of the disclosure, valuation and information provided (and for these purposes 'quality' includes timing, nature and extent). The maximum amount by which a penalty can be reduced is 50% of the standard amount in a case involving only unprompted disclosures and 20% of the standard amount in a case involving prompted disclosures. A case involves only unprompted disclosures if all the offshore tax penalties to which the asset-based penalty relates were reduced on the basis of unprompted disclosures. A case involves prompted disclosures if any of the offshore tax penalties to which the asset-based penalty relates was reduced on the basis of a prompted disclosure.

HMRC may also reduce, stay, or agree a compromise in relation to proceedings for, an asset-based penalty because of special circumstances if they think it right to do so. Ability to pay and the fact that a potential loss of revenue from one taxpayer is balanced by a potential overpayment by another are not special circumstances for this purpose.

Identification and valuation of assets

Where the 'principal tax at stake' is capital gains tax, the asset is the asset which is the subject of the disposal by reference to which the capital gains tax to which the offshore tax penalty relates is charged. The value of the asset is taken to be the consideration for the disposal for capital gains tax purposes. Where the disposal is a part disposal of an asset, the asset-based penalty is calculated by reference to the full market value of the asset. The '*principal tax at stake*' is the tax to which the offshore tax penalty relates. If the offshore tax penalty relates to more than one tax, it is the tax which gives rise to the highest offshore PLR value, i.e. the potential lost revenue or liability to tax by reference to which the part of the penalty relating to each tax was assessed. An asset-based penalty may relate to more than one asset.

Where an asset-based penalty is chargeable in relation to an asset that is jointly held by the taxpayer (P) and another person (A), the value of the asset is the value of P's share of it. If P and A are living together in a marriage or civil partnership, the asset is taken to be jointly owned by them in equal shares, unless it appears to HMRC that this is not the case.

Interest on penalties

Late payment interest on a penalty under the above provisions is charged in accordance with *FA 2009, s 101* where the late payment interest start date is on or after 6 September 2019. Repayment interest under *FA 2009, s 102* on an overpaid penalty is similarly available where the repayment date is on or after that date.

[*FA 2016, s 165, Sch 22 paras 1–11, 14, 19; F(No 2)A 2017, Sch 18 para 28; FA 2021, Sch 27 para 48; SI 2017 Nos 277, 334; SI 2019 No 1238*]

Failure to correct offshore tax non-compliance

[46.17] A penalty is payable by a person who has 'offshore tax non-compliance' to correct at the end of 2016/17 and fails to correct it within the period 6 April 2017 to 30 September 2018 inclusive (known as the '*RTC* *period*'). [*F(No 2)A 2017, Sch 18 para 1*]. The penalty applies to income tax, capital gains tax and inheritance tax non-compliance; the coverage below focuses on its application to capital gains tax. The penalty does not apply to capital gains tax payable by companies in respect of NRCGT gains.

Meaning of offshore tax non-compliance

For this purpose, '*offshore tax non-compliance*' means 'tax non-compliance' which involves an 'offshore matter' or an 'offshore transfer', whether or not it also 'involves an onshore matter'. Any of the following is '*tax non-compliance*' for this purpose:

(a) failure to notify chargeability to capital gains tax by the required date (see **46.3** above);
(b) failure to deliver a tax return or other document (as listed in *F(No 2)A 2017, Sch 18 para 8(3)*) by the required date (see **46.5** above); and
(c) delivery of a return or other document (as listed in *F(No 2)A 2017, Sch 18 para 8(3)(4)*) containing an inaccuracy (whether or not careless or deliberate) amounting to, or leading to, an understatement of a tax liability or a false or inflated statement of a loss or claim to repayment of tax.

Tax non-compliance '*involves an onshore matter*' if and to the extent that it does not involve an offshore matter or an offshore transfer. The question of whether tax non-compliance involves an '*offshore matter*' is determined in the same way as for other penalties to which this is relevant. See **46.3**, **46.5** and **46.11** above. The determination is made by reference, in a case within (a) above, to the potential loss of revenue; in a case within (b) above, to the tax liability (if any) that would have been shown in the return etc.; and, in a case within (c) above, to the information that should have been given in the document.

Tax non-compliance involves an '*offshore transfer*' if it does not involve an offshore matter and:

- in a case within (a) or (b) above, the proceeds of the disposal on (or by reference to which) tax is charged (or any part of those proceeds) were received in a territory outside the UK or were transferred before 6 April 2017 to a territory outside the UK; and
- in a case within (c) above, the information that should have been given in the document relates to proceeds of disposal which were received in a territory outside the UK or were transferred before 6 April 2017 to a territory outside the UK.

In any of these cases, the reference to the transfer of proceeds is to be read as including a reference to the transfer of any assets derived from or representing those proceeds. '*Assets*' has the same meaning as for capital gains tax purposes (see *TCGA 1992, s 21(1)*) but also includes sterling.

It is an overriding condition that tax non-compliance can involve an offshore matter or offshore transfer only, in a case within (b) above, where a complete and accurate return etc. would have included information enabling or assisting HMRC to assess the person's tax liability; and, in a case within (c) above, if the inaccuracy relates to information that would have enabled or assisted HMRC to assess the person's liability.

[*F(No 2)A 2017, Sch 18 paras 7–12*].

When the rules apply

A person has offshore tax non-compliance to correct at the end of 2016/17 if:

- Conditions A and B below are met in respect of any offshore tax non-compliance committed before 6 April 2017 (the '*original offshore tax non-compliance*'); and
- Condition C below is met.

Condition A is that the original offshore tax non-compliance has not been fully corrected before the end of 2016/17. Condition B is that the original offshore tax non-compliance involved a potential loss of revenue when it was committed and that, in the case of partial correction before the end of 2016/17, the uncorrected part of that time involved a potential loss of revenue.

Condition C is that on 6 April 2017 HMRC would in law have been able to assess the taxpayer to the tax liability arising from the non-compliance if they had been aware at that time of the information missing as a result of the failure to correct. What is said below under Extension of period for assessment of offshore tax is disregarded for the purpose of applying Condition C.

[*F(No 2)A 2017, Sch 18 paras 3–6*].

Correcting offshore tax non-compliance

Offshore tax non-compliance can be corrected by giving HMRC the 'relevant information' by:

- in a case within (a) above, delivering a tax return;
- in a case within (b) above, delivering the requisite return or document;
- in a case within (c) above, amending the document or delivering a new document;
- using the digital disclosure service (see below) or any other service provided by HMRC as a means of correcting tax non-compliance;
- communicating it to an HMRC officer in the course of an enquiry; or
- using any other method agreed with an HMRC officer.

The '*relevant information*' is the information relating to offshore tax that, were it not for the non-compliance, would have enabled or assisted HMRC to calculate the offshore tax due.

[*F(No 2)A 2017, Sch 18 para 13*].

Amount of penalty

The penalty is **200%** of the 'offshore PLR' attributable to the offshore tax non-compliance remaining uncorrected when the RTC period ends. The '*offshore PLR*' is the potential loss of revenue (PLR) attributable to the offshore tax non-compliance in question, and is determined as follows:

- in a case within (a) above, it is calculated in similar matter as in **46.3** above and is thus usually the amount of tax payable that, by reason of the non-compliance, remains unpaid on 31 January following the tax year in question.

- In a case within (b) above, it is the tax liability that would have been shown as due or payable in a complete and accurate return delivered on the due date.
- In a case within (c) above, it is calculated in similar manner as in **46.11** above and is thus usually the additional tax due or payable as a result of correcting the inaccuracy in the document. *F(No 2)A 2017, Sch 18 para 15(3)* modifies the rules in **46.11** for this purpose; the principal modification is that where the amount of PLR depends on the order in which inaccuracies are corrected, the PLR attributable to any offshore tax non-compliance constituted by any one of those inaccuracies is taken to be such amount as is just and reasonable.

Any 'combined tax non-compliance' is treated for these purposes as if it were two separate acts of tax non-compliance. '*Combined tax non-compliance*' is tax non-compliance that involves an offshore matter or an offshore transfer but also involves an onshore matter. The PLR attributable to the offshore tax non-compliance is to be taken to be such share of the total PLR as is just and reasonable.

Reductions

HMRC must reduce the penalty if the person liable discloses any of the following matters that is relevant to the non-compliance or its correction or to the assessment or enforcement of the offshore tax attributable to it: chargeability to tax (where the tax non-compliance is a failure to notify chargeability); a missing tax return; an inaccuracy in a document; a supply of false information or a withholding of information; or a failure to disclose an under-assessment. The reduction must reflect the quality of the disclosure (and for these purposes 'quality' includes timing, nature and extent) but the penalty cannot be reduced below 100% of the offshore PLR. A person discloses a matter for these purposes only by: telling HMRC about it; giving HMRC reasonable help in relation to it (for example by quantifying an inaccuracy in a document); informing HMRC of any person who acted as an enabler of the offshore tax non-compliance or the failure to correct it; and allowing HMRC access to records for any reasonable purpose connected with resolving the matter and to ensure that HMRC can identify all persons who may have acted as enablers. A person acts as an enabler of offshore tax non-compliance by another if he encourages, assists or otherwise facilitates the conduct constituting the non-compliance.

HMRC may also reduce, stay, or agree a compromise in relation to proceedings for, the penalty because of special circumstances if they think it right to do so. Ability to pay and the fact that a potential loss of revenue from one taxpayer is balanced by a potential overpayment by another are not special circumstances for this purpose.

Reasonable excuse

Liability to the above penalty does not arise in relation to a particular failure to correct any offshore tax non-compliance within the RTC period if the taxpayer (T) satisfies HMRC or, on appeal, the Appeal Tribunal, that there is a reasonable excuse for the failure. Insufficiency of funds is not a reasonable excuse for this purpose, unless attributable to events outside T's control, and nor is reliance on another person to do anything (unless T took reasonable care to avoid the failure) or reliance on 'disqualified' advice. A person with a reasonable excuse is treated as having continued to have it if the failure in question was remedied without unreasonable delay after the excuse ceased.

Advice is '*disqualified*' if it (i) was given to T by an interested person; or (ii) was given to T as a result of arrangements between an 'interested person' and the person who gave the advice; or (iii) was given by a person without the appropriate expertise; or (iv) did not take account of all T's individual circumstances (so far as relevant); or (v) was addressed to, or given to, a person other than T. However, the advice is not disqualified if, at the end of the RTC period, T has taken reasonable steps to find out whether or not the advice falls within any of (i)–(iv) and reasonably believes that it does not. An '*interested person*' is one who participated in 'relevant avoidance arrangements' or any transaction forming part of them, or one who, for consideration, facilitated T's entering into such avoidance arrangements. Avoidance arrangements are arrangements (as widely defined) in respect of which it would be reasonable to conclude that a main purpose is the obtaining of a tax advantage (also as widely defined). However, arrangements are not avoidance arrangements if they accord with established practice, and HMRC had, at the time the arrangements were entered into, indicated their acceptance of that practice. Where any offshore tax non-compliance arose originally because information was submitted to HMRC on the basis that particular avoidance arrangements had an effect which they did not have, those avoidance arrangements are '*relevant avoidance arrangements*' in relation to that non-compliance.

Double jeopardy

A person is not liable to the above penalty in respect of any conduct (or any failure to act) for which he has been convicted of an offence or for which he is liable to, and has been assessed to, a penalty under other provisions (provided the assessment has neither been successfully appealed against nor withdrawn). The reference here to a penalty under other provisions includes the second tax-geared late filing penalty but does not include any of the other late filing penalties in **46.5** above. Where a person is thus liable to both the above penalty and the *first* tax-geared late filing penalty in **46.5**, and the amount of the latter has been determined by reference to a liability to tax, the aggregate penalty must not exceed 200% of that liability to tax.

[*F(No 2)A 2017, Sch 18 paras 14–17, 23, 24; FA 2021, Sch 27 para 51*].

Extension of period for assessment of offshore tax

Where:

- at the end of 2016/17 a person has offshore tax non-compliance to correct; and
- the last day on which it would otherwise be lawful for HMRC to assess the person to any 'offshore tax' falls within the period 6 April 2017 to 4 April 2021 inclusive,

the period in which it is lawful for HMRC to assess the person to the offshore tax is extended so as to end with 5 April 2021. This would appear to enable offshore tax for any of the years 2013/14 to 2015/16 (as well as 2016/17) to be assessed at any time on or before 5 April 2021. '*Offshore tax*' is tax corresponding to the offshore PLR in respect of the offshore tax non-compliance in question.

[*F(No 2)A 2017, Sch 18 para 26*].

Interest on penalties

Late payment interest on a penalty under the above provisions is charged in accordance with *FA 2009, s 101* where the late payment interest start date is on or after 6 September 2019. Repayment interest under *FA 2009, s 102* on an overpaid penalty is similarly available where the repayment date is on or after that date [*SI 2019/1238*].

Power to publish details

The Commissioners for HMRC may in some circumstances publish information about an individual who incurs penalties under the above provisions — see **28.4** HMRC — CONFIDENTIALITY OF INFORMATION.

Failure to keep and preserve records

[46.18] The maximum penalty for non-compliance with *TMA 1970, s 12B* (records to be kept and preserved for the purposes of self-assessment tax returns — see **52.10** RETURNS) in relation to any tax year is £3,000. [*TMA 1970, s 12B(5)–(5B)*]. The same applies for companies under corporation tax self-assessment. [*FA 1998, s 117, Sch 18 para 23*].

A separate maximum £3,000 penalty applies in relation to records relating to a claim made otherwise than in a self-assessment tax return (see **13.3** CLAIMS). [*TMA 1970, Sch 1A para 2A(4)(5)*]. This also applies in relation to certain claims by companies under corporation tax self-assessment. [*FA 1998, s 117, Sch 18 paras 57(4), 58(3), 59*].

Penalties in respect of investigatory powers under FA 2008, Sch 36

[46.19] The penalties below apply to offences under the investigatory powers of *FA 2008, Sch 36*.

Failure to comply — fixed and daily penalties

Where a person (P) fails to comply with an information notice within *FA 2008, Sch 36 Pt 1* (see **29.4 HMRC** INVESTIGATORY POWERS), P is liable to a fixed penalty of £300 and, for each subsequent day of continuing failure, a further penalty not exceeding £60. If the failure continues for more than 30 days beginning with the date on which notice of an assessment to a daily penalty is given, an HMRC officer may make an application to the Tribunal for an increased daily penalty. Such an application can only be made if P has been told that it may be made. If the Tribunal decides that an increased daily penalty should apply, it must also determine the day from which it will apply. Subject to a maximum of £1,000 per day the Tribunal, in determining the amount of the increased penalty, must have regard to the likely cost to P of complying with the notice and any benefits to P or anyone else of non-compliance. Before 10 June 2021, the procedure for imposing an increased daily penalty was slightly different. The Tribunal imposed the increased penalty directly by way of an HMRC notice (rather than HMRC assessing the increased penalty determined by the Tribunal) and the day on which the increase took effect was determined by HMRC in that notice.

For this purpose, failing to comply with a notice includes concealing, destroying or otherwise disposing of, or arranging for the concealment, destruction or disposal of, a document in breach of *FA 2008, Sch 36 paras 42, 43* (see **29.7 HMRC INVESTIGATORY POWERS**).

Where a person deliberately obstructs an HMRC officer in the course of an inspection of business premises under *FA 2008, Sch 36 Pt 2* (see **29.8 HMRC INVESTIGATORY POWERS**) which has been approved by the First-tier Tribunal he is liable to a fixed penalty of £300 and, for each subsequent day of continuing obstruction, a further penalty not exceeding £60.

No penalty is due where a person fails to do anything required to be done within a limited time period if he does it within such further time as an HMRC officer allows. A person is not liable to a penalty if he satisfies HMRC or (on appeal) the First-tier Tribunal that there is a reasonable excuse for the failure or obstruction. An insufficiency of funds is not a reasonable excuse for this purpose unless it is attributable to events outside the person's control. Where a person relies on another person to do anything, that is not a reasonable excuse unless the first person took reasonable care to avoid the failure or obstruction. Where a person has a reasonable excuse which ceases, he is treated as continuing to have a reasonable excuse if the failure is remedied or the obstruction stops without unreasonable delay.

The Treasury can make regulations amending the amounts of the above penalties.

[*FA 2008, s 108, Sch 36 paras 39–41, 44, 45, 49A, 49B; FA 2021, Sch 34 paras 5, 6*].

In *Qubic Tax Ltd v HMRC* FTT, [2020] SFTD 769, a company appealed against an information notice given during enquiries into its corporation tax returns. The FTT rejected the appeal but allowed the company's appeal against initial and daily penalties for failure to comply with an information notice. The penalties had been issued after the company had appealed against the information notice but before it had received HMRC's review conclusion letter and before the hearing into its appeal against the notice. The FTT held that it must be reasonable not to comply with a notice while it is being challenged in the Tribunal or in the courts. Otherwise, any such appeals would be 'rendered nugatory'. The company therefore had a reasonable excuse for not complying and the appeal was upheld.

The FTT also upheld an appeal against a penalty for failure to comply with an information notice in *Ahmed v HMRC* FTT, [2020] UKFTT 337 (TC), 2020 SWTI 1900. The information required under the notice merely repeated that required by two earlier notices in respect of which the time limit for issuing a penalty had expired. It was not possible for HMRC to refresh the time limit by issuing a new notice.

Failure to comply — tax-related penalty

A tax-related penalty may be imposed by the Upper Tribunal where a person's failure or obstruction continues after a fixed penalty has been imposed under the above provisions. An HMRC officer must have reason to believe that the amount of tax that that person has paid, or is likely to pay is significantly less than it would otherwise have been as a result of the failure or obstruction, and the officer must make an application to the Upper Tribunal before the end of the twelve months beginning with the 'relevant date'. In deciding the amount of the penalty (if any), the Upper Tribunal must have regard to the amount of tax which has not been, or is likely not to be, paid by the person.

The '*relevant date*' is the date on which the person became liable to the penalty. Where, however, the penalty is for a failure relating to an information notice against which a person can appeal, the relevant date is the later of the end of the period in which notice of such appeal could have been given and, where an appeal is made, the date on which the appeal is determined or withdrawn.

A tax-related penalty is in addition to the fixed penalty and any daily penalties under the above provisions. No account is taken of a tax-related penalty for the purposes of **46.20** below and no reduction in a penalty charged under *FA 2007, Sch 24* (see **46.11–46.13** above) or *FA 2008, Sch 41* (see **46.3** above) is to be made in respect of a penalty under these provisions.

[*FA 2008, Sch 36 para 50*].

Penalties under these provisions were imposed in *HMRC v Tager* CA, [2018] STC 1755 and *HMRC v AML Tax (UK) Ltd* UT, [2022] UKUT 81 (TCC), 2022 SWTI 531.

Failure to comply with requirement not to disclose third party notice or financial institution notice

A penalty of £1,000 applies for failure to comply with a requirement in a third party notice or financial institution notice not to disclose the notice or anything related to it to the taxpayer or any other person. The Treasury can make regulations amending the amount of the penalty. [*FA 2008, Sch 36 paras 41, 51B(1)(4); FA 2021, Sch 34 para 2*].

Inaccurate information or documents

A penalty not exceeding £3,000 applies if, in complying with an information notice, a person provides inaccurate information or produces a document that contains an inaccuracy. The penalty is due if the inaccuracy is careless (i.e. due to a failure to take reasonable care) or deliberate; or the person complying with the notice later discovers the inaccuracy and fails to take reasonable steps to inform HMRC; or knows of the inaccuracy at the time the information or document is provided but does not inform HMRC at that time. If the information or document contains more than one inaccuracy, a penalty is payable for each of them.

The Treasury can make regulations amending the amounts of the above penalties.

[*FA 2008, Sch 36 paras 40A, 41*].

A person is not liable to a penalty under any of the above provisions in respect of anything for which he has been convicted of an offence. [*FA 2008, Sch 36 para 52*].

Two or more tax-related penalties in respect of same tax

[46.20] Where two or more tax-related penalties are determined by reference to the same income tax, capital gains tax or corporation tax liability, the aggregate penalty is reduced to the greater or greatest of those separate penalties. Note that the penalties at **46.11**, **46.13**, **46.14**, **46.16** and **46.19** above and **46.24** below are not taken into account for the purposes of this provision (as they have their own equivalent provision). Penalties under **36.6** or **36.7** LATE PAYMENT INTEREST AND PENALTIES are also not taken into account for the purposes of this provision. [*TMA 1970, s 97A; FA 1998, s 117, Sch 18 para 90, Sch 19 para 3; FA 2007, Sch 24 para 12(3); FA 2008, Sch 36 para 50(6); FA 2009, Sch 56 para 9A; FA 2013, Sch 43C para 8(4), Sch 50 paras 13, 16(3); FA 2014, s 212(3); FA 2016, s 158(3), Sch 18 para 40(3), Sch 22 para 21; FA 2021, Sch 26 para 15; Sch 28 para 5(3), Sch 32 para 13(8)*]. See **46.26** below for mitigation of penalties.

Interest on penalties

[46.21] Penalties charged under *TMA 1970* or *FA 1998, Sch 18* carry interest, calculated from the due date (broadly, 30 days after issue of a notice of determination by an HMRC officer — see **46.28** below, or immediately upon determination by the Tribunal or judgement of the High Court — see **49.40**, **49.41** below) to the date of payment. [*TMA 1970, s 103A; FA 1998, s 117, Sch 19 para 40; SI 1998 No 311*]. For income tax and capital gains tax, rates of interest on penalties are synonymous with those on late paid tax — see **36.2** LATE PAYMENT INTEREST AND PENALTIES. For interest on other penalties, see the relevant paragraph of this chapter.

Special returns etc.

[46.22] Failure to render any information or particulars or any return, certificate, statement or other document which is required, whether by notice or otherwise, under the provisions listed in *TMA 1970, s 98* is the subject of a maximum penalty of £300, plus £60 for each day the failure continues after that penalty is imposed (but not for any day for which such a daily penalty has already been imposed). The maximum penalty for an incorrect return etc. given fraudulently or negligently is £3,000. Penalties for failure to render information etc. required by notice cannot be imposed after the failure is rectified, and daily penalties can similarly not be imposed where the information etc. was required other than by notice. [*TMA 1970, s 98*].

Penalties in respect of powers of enforcement by deduction from accounts

[46.23] Under the powers of HMRC to enforce collection of unpaid tax by deduction from the taxpayer's account (see **45.22** PAYMENT OF TAX), a deposit-taker is liable to a penalty of £300 if it:

(a) fails to comply with an information notice;
(b) fails to comply with a hold notice or deduction notice;
(c) fails to comply with an obligation to notify HMRC of the effects of a hold notice;
(d) fails to comply with an obligation to cancel or modify the effect of a hold notice;
(e) fails to comply with an obligation to cancel or adjust arrangements to give effect to HMRC's decision about an objection to a hold notice; or
(f) after receiving an information or hold notice, makes a disclosure of information (other than the required notice) to the taxpayer or any other person which is likely to prejudice HMRC's ability to use their powers to deduct the unpaid tax.

If a failure within (a) to (e) above continues after the day on which notice of a penalty is given, the deposit-taker is liable to a further penalty or penalties of up to £60 per day on which the failure continues.

A failure to comply does not give rise to a penalty if the deposit-taker complies within such further time as HMRC allow. No penalty applies if the deposit-taker satisfies HMRC or the Tribunal that there is a reasonable excuse for the failure or disclosure. Relying on another person to do something is not, for this purpose, a reasonable excuse unless the deposit-taker took reasonable care to avoid the failure or disclosure. Where a reasonable excuse ceases, the deposit-taker is treated as continuing to have the excuse if the failure is remedied without unreasonable delay.

[*F(No 2)A 2015, Sch 8 para 14*].

Penalties under the serial avoiders regime

[46.24] A person is liable to a penalty if he incurs a relevant defeat (see **4.35** ANTI-AVOIDANCE) in relation to any arrangements which he has used whilst in a warning period (see **4.34** ANTI-AVOIDANCE). The time at which a person has 'used' arrangements is determined by *FA 2016, Sch 18 para 55* (see **4.37** ANTI-AVOIDANCE). The standard penalty is 20% of the 'value of the counteracted advantage'. If, before the relevant defeat is incurred, the person has been given (or become liable to be given) 'prior warning notices', the penalty is increased.

It is increased to 40% where there has been a single prior warning notice, and to 60% where there has been more than one such notice. A '*prior warning notice*' is a warning notice in relation to the defeat of arrangements which the person has used in the warning period.

If a person incurs simultaneously two or more relevant defeats in relation to different arrangements, then for the purpose of determining the penalty those defeats are placed in order of value, the defeat of greatest value being deemed to be the first incurred; the value of a defeat is the value of the counteracted advantage. If a person has been given a single warning notice in relation to two or more relevant defeats, he is treated for penalty purposes as having been given a separate warning notice in relation to each defeat.

The Commissioners for HMRC have discretion to mitigate a penalty under these provisions, or stay or compound any proceedings for such a penalty. They may also, after judgment, further mitigate or entirely remit the penalty.

Value of the counteracted advantage

The '*value of the counteracted advantage*' is the additional amount of tax due or payable as a result of the counteraction or corrective action. To the extent that the counteracted advantage has resulted in a loss being wrongly recorded or increased but the counteracted loss has not been wholly used to reduce tax payable, the value of the counteracted advantage is increased by 10% of the part of the counteracted loss not so used. However, the value of a counteracted loss is nil if, due to the nature of the loss or the person's circumstances, there is no reasonable prospect of the loss ever being used to reduce the tax liability of any person. To the extent that the counteracted advantage is a deferral of tax, the value of the advantage is 25% of the amount of deferred tax for each year of the deferral, but not so as to exceed 100% of the total amount of deferred tax.

Interaction with other penalties

The amount of a penalty is to be reduced by any other penalty incurred by the person if the amount of that other penalty is determined by reference to the same tax liability. Other penalties do not for this purpose include the GAAR penalty at **46.14** above and the penalties at **49.28** and **49.29** above (follower notices and accelerated payments notices).

Reasonable excuse

A person is not liable to a penalty in respect of a relevant defeat if he satisfies HMRC or, on appeal, the Tribunal that he had a reasonable excuse for the failures or inaccuracies in question. In determining the rate of penalty an earlier warning notice is disregarded if it relates to a relevant defeat in respect of which the person had a reasonable excuse. Otherwise, the same comments apply regarding 'reasonable excuse' as in **4.37** ANTI-AVOIDANCE.

[*FA 2016, Sch 18 paras 30–35, 40, 42–44*].

Failure to make notification of uncertain tax treatment

[46.25] A company or partnership which fails to make a notification of an uncertain tax treatment (see **52.24** RETURNS) in respect of an amount which is uncertain at the time it makes its affected tax return is liable to a penalty of

£5,000 for a first failure, £25,000 for a second failure or £50,000 for any further failure. In determining whether a failure is the first, second or a further failure, only the period of three years prior to the period for which the affected return is made are considered.

Note that, although the uncertain tax treatment rules apply to corporation tax, income tax, PAYE and VAT, each tax is treated separately in determining the number of failures.

Failure to make a notification of an uncertain tax treatment which becomes uncertain after the time the return is made attracts a penalty of £5,000.

Failures to which a penalty can apply are: not notifying within the time limit; not submitting a required notification at all; and submitting an incomplete or incorrect notification (HMRC Uncertain Tax Treatment Manual UTT17100).

No penalty arises if the taxpayer satisfies HMRC or, on appeal, the Tribunal, that they have a reasonable excuse for the failure. Insufficiency of funds is not a reasonable excuse, and reliance on another person can be a reasonable excuse only if the taxpayer took reasonable care to avoid the failure. A reasonable excuse which has come to an end is treated as continuing if the failure is remedied without unreasonable delay.

The Treasury can amend the specified penalty amounts by statutory instrument. [*FA 2022, Sch 17 paras 20–22, 26*].

Mitigation of penalties

[46.26] The Commissioners for HMRC may mitigate penalties before or after judgment. [*TMA 1970, s 102; FA 2013, Sch 43C para 10; FA 2016, s 157(3), Sch 18 para 44*]. This rule does not apply to penalties under *FA 2007, Sch 24* (see **46.11–46.12** above), *FA 2008, Sch 36* (see **46.19** above) and *Sch 41* (see **46.3** above), *FA 2009, Sch 55* (failure to make returns — see **46.5** above) and *Sch 56* (late payment penalty — see **36.6** LATE PAYMENT INTEREST AND PENALTIES), *FA 2016, Sch 18 Pt 5* (see **46.24** above) and *FA 2016, Sch 22* (asset-based penalty for offshore inaccuracies and failures — see **46.16** above), *F(No 2)A 2017, Sch 18* (see **46.17** above), *FA 2021, Sch 24* (see **46.8** above), *Sch 25* (see **46.9** above) and *Sch 25* (see **36.7** LATE PAYMENT INTEREST AND PENALTIES) which include specific rules for the reduction of penalties in certain cases. [*TMA 1970, s 103ZA; FA 2021, Sch 27 para 8*]. A binding agreement by a taxpayer to pay an amount in composition cannot be repudiated afterwards by him or his personal representatives (*A-G v Johnstone* KB 1926, 10 TC 758; *A-G v Midland Bank Executor and Trustee Co Ltd* KB 1934, 19 TC 136; *CIR v Richards* KB 1950, 33 TC 1).

See also **46.2** above as regards *TMA 1970, s 118(2)* (reasonable excuse for failure etc.).

For the validity of tax amnesties, see *R v CIR (ex p. National Federation of Self-Employed and Small Businesses Ltd)* HL 1981, 55 TC 133.

Other HMRC action where a penalty is chargeable

[46.27] Where it is established that a penalty is chargeable HMRC may also take the following actions.

Certificates of full disclosure

HMRC may request that the taxpayer complete a certificate of full disclosure stating that complete disclosure has been made of, inter alia, all banking, savings and loan accounts, deposit receipts, building society accounts and accounts with other financial institutions; all investments including savings certificates and premium bonds and loans (whether interest-bearing or not); all other assets, including cash and life assurance policies, which the taxpayer now possesses, or has possessed, or in which he has or has had any interest or power to operate or control during the stated period; all gifts in any form, by the taxpayer to his spouse, domestic partner, children or other persons during the stated period; all sources of income and all income derived therefrom; and all facts bearing on liability to income tax, capital gains tax and other duties for the stated period. Great care must be exercised before signing such a certificate, since subsequent discovery of an omission could lead to heavy penalties including, in serious cases, criminal prosecution.

Managing serious defaulters programme

HMRC closely monitor the tax affairs of individuals and businesses who meet certain criteria to be serious defaulters for a period of up to five years. The circumstances meeting the criteria include where the individual or business has been charged a penalty because of deliberate behaviour. Monitoring may include:

- making announced or unannounced inspection visits to carry out pre-return checks of books and records;
- requiring that additional information or documents are submitted with tax returns;
- conducting in-depth compliance checks into all or any part of the taxpayer's affairs.

See www.gov.uk/guidance/managing-serious-defaulters-msd-programme.

Procedure for charging penalties

[46.28] Where a penalty is due, HMRC may, in certain cases, seek to negotiate a contract settlement with the taxpayer. In the absence of such a settlement, the following formal procedures apply to impose penalties.

Assessment

Except where indicated below, penalties are charged by HMRC assessment.

An assessment is treated in the same way as a tax assessment and can be enforced by HMRC accordingly. Where the penalty relates to a tax year or accounting period, the notice of assessment must state the year or period in respect of which it is assessed.

Subject to the time limit for making an assessment, HMRC can make a supplementary assessment if an existing assessment operates by reference to an underestimate (of the 'potential lost revenue' etc.).

Where an assessment of a penalty for failure to make a return on time, failure to pay CGT on time or failure to correct offshore tax non-compliance is excessive, HMRC may issue an amendment. Such an amendment does not affect when the penalty must be paid and can be made even if the time limit for making the assessment has passed.

Where the person liable to a penalty relating to the GAAR (*FA 2013, ss 212A, 212B* — see **46.14** above) is a partner and the final counteraction notice was given to the partnership's responsible partner (see **4.7** ANTI-AVOIDANCE), a notice of assessment must also be sent to the responsible partner.

An assessment of a penalty relating to the GAAR or under the serial avoiders regime (*FA 2016, Sch 18* — see **46.24** above) may be revised if it overestimates the value of the counteracted advantage. Where, following the making of a GAAR penalty assessment, consequential adjustments are made (see **4.3** ANTI-AVOIDANCE under 'Effect of the GAAR'), HMRC must make any just and reasonable alterations to the penalty assessment to take account of those adjustments and may do so regardless of any time limits which would otherwise prevent them.

A penalty must be paid within the 30-day period beginning with the date on which HMRC issue notification of the penalty assessment or for penalties. The time limit is extended for penalties relating to the enforcement of tax debts by deduction (*F(No 2)A 2015, Sch 8* — see **46.23** above), HMRC's investigatory powers (*FA 2008, Sch 36* — see **46.19** above) or for failure to notify uncertain tax treatment (*FA 2022, Sch 17* — see **46.25** above) if an appeal against the penalty is made. In such cases, the penalty must be paid within the 30-day period beginning with the date on which the appeal is determined or withdrawn.

[*FA 2007, Sch 24 para 28; FA 2008, Sch 36 paras 46, 49, 49A, 51B; Sch 41 para 16; FA 2009, Sch 55 para 18, Sch 56 para 11; FA 2013, Sch 43C paras 5–7, Sch 50 paras 1, 7, 10, 14; FA 2015, Sch 21 para 7; F(No 2)A 2015, Sch 8 paras 15(1), 17; FA 2016, Sch 18 para 39, Sch 22 para 15; F(No 2)A 2017, Sch 18 para 18; FA 2021, Sch 24 para 16, Sch 25 paras 12, 13, Sch 26 paras 16, 17, Sch 28 para 4, Sch 32 para 13(7), Sch 34 paras 2, 5; FA 2022, Sch 17 paras 23(1), 25*].

Determination

The following penalties are imposed by an authorised HMRC officer making a determination imposing a penalty of an amount which they consider correct or appropriate:

(a) failure to deliver corporation tax return on time (*FA 1998, Sch 18 paras 17, 18* — see **46.4** above);
(b) penalties in respect of special returns (other than the initial penalty for failure to comply) (*TMA 1970, s 98* — see **46.22** above);
(c) failure to keep records (*TMA 1970, s 12B; FA 1998, Sch 18 para 23* — see **46.18** above).

See **27.3** HMRC—ADMINISTRATION for the exercise of functions of an HMRC officer by automated process.

The notice of determination must state the date of issue and the time within which an appeal can be made. It cannot be altered unless:

(i) there is an appeal;
(ii) an authorised officer discovers that the penalty is or has become insufficient (in which case he may make a further determination); or
(iii) the penalty arises under *FA 1998, Sch 18 para 18(2)* and an authorised officer subsequently discovers that the amount of tax is or has become excessive (in which case it is to be revised accordingly).

A penalty under these provisions is due 30 days after the date of issue of the notice of determination and is treated as tax charged under an assessment and due and payable.

[*TMA 1970, ss 100, 100A*].

In *Partito Media Services Ltd v HMRC* FTT, [2012] UKFTT 256 (TC), it was held that a penalty notice had not been validly served because it had been sent to the company's old registered office (notwithstanding that the company had failed to inform HMRC of the change of registered office). Judge Redston rejected HMRC's contention that the effect of *TMA 1970, s 115(2)(a)* was that the notice had been validly served by being sent to P's last known registered office, and held that the phrase 'usual or last known place of residence' was only applicable to sole traders and partners, and did not include companies.

Proceedings before the FTT

An initial penalty for failure to file a special return (*TMA 1970, s 98(1)(i)* — see **46.22** above) is imposed using the following procedure.

An authorised HMRC officer may commence proceedings before the FTT. The proceedings are by way of information in writing to the FTT, and upon summons issued by them to the defendant (or defender), and are heard and decided in a summary way. An appeal lies to the Upper Tribunal on a question of law or, by the defendant (defender), against the amount. The court can confirm, set aside or vary the determination as deemed appropriate. The penalty is treated as tax charged in an assessment and is due and payable.

[*TMA 1970, s 100C*].

Increased daily penalties for failure to comply with HMRC investigatory powers (*FA 2008, Sch 36* — see **46.19** above) are also imposed by the FTT. With effect from 10 June 2021, the penalty is nevertheless charged by HMRC assessment (see above) and HMRC must notify the person assessed.

Penalty imposed by Upper Tribunal

A tax-related penalty for failure or obstruction under HMRC's investigatory powers must be imposed by the Upper Tribunal — see **47.11** above.

General matters

Statements made or documents produced by or on behalf of a company are admissible evidence in proceedings against it, notwithstanding that reliance on HMRC's practice in cases of full disclosure may have induced it to make or produce them. [*TMA 1970, s 105*].

The imposition of penalties calculated as a percentage of unpaid tax was held to be in the nature of 'criminal' (rather than 'civil') proceedings for the purposes of the European Convention on Human Rights in *King v United Kingdom (Application 13881/02)* [2004] STC 911, ECHR.

In *P & H Cleaning Co Ltd v HMRC* [2013] UKFTT 669 (TC), the FTT (following *HMRC v Hok Ltd* [2012] UKUT 363) confirmed that it is not within its jurisdiction to set aside penalties for the late payment of PAYE on the ground of unfairness and disproportionality. The doctrine of proportionality can affect direct tax penalties only through the door of the *Human Rights Act 1998*.

Time limits for charging penalties

[46.29] HMRC must make any penalty assessment within specified time limits.

For the purposes of the time limits, where relevant, the 'appeal period' is the period during which an appeal could be brought (ignoring any possibility of a late appeal) or during which an appeal that has been brought has not been determined or withdrawn.

The time limits are:

- Incorrect returns etc — *FA 2007, Sch 24.*
  - (i) If the penalty is payable under *FA 2007, Sch 24 paras 1, 1A* (see **46.11**, **46.12** above), the assessment must be made within 12 months from the end of the appeal period for the assessment correcting the inaccuracy. If there was no assessment, the 12-month period runs from the date on which the inaccuracy was corrected.
  - (ii) If the penalty is payable under *FA 2007, Sch 24 para 2* (see **46.13** above), the time is 12 months from the end of the appeal period for the amended assessment which corrected the understatement (or if there is no assessment, the date on which the understatement is corrected).

  [*FA 2007, Sch 24 para 13*].
- Failure to notify chargeability — *FA 2008, Sch 41.*

  An assessment of a penalty within **46.3** above must be made before the end of the 12 months beginning with the end of the appeal period for the assessment of tax unpaid by reason of the failure or, where there is no such assessment, the date on which the amount of tax unpaid by reason of the failure is ascertained.

  [*FA 2008, Sch 41 para 16*].
- Failure to deliver a return (not applicable to corporation tax) — *FA 2009, Sch 55.*

  Time limit for assessing a penalty within **46.5** above is the latest of:
  - (i) the last day of the period of two years beginning with the filing date; and
  - (ii) the last day of the 12 months beginning with the end of the appeal period for the assessment to recover the tax unpaid or, where no such assessment has been made, the date on which that liability is ascertained (or found to be nil).

[*FA 2009, Sch 55 para 19*].

- Late filing penalty (MTD) — *FA 2021, Sch 24*.

The assessment of a penalty under **46.8** above cannot be made after the later of:

(i) the end of the period of two years beginning with:
- if the penalty is to be assessed in respect of a single failure, the day on which the failure occurred;
- if the penalty is to be assessed in respect of more than one failure in the same month or, where applicable (see **46.8** above), the same calendar quarter, the day on which the latest failure occurred; and

(ii) the last day of the period of 12 months beginning with the end of the appeal period for the assessment of the tax liability which would have been shown in the 'relevant return' or, if there is no such assessment, the date on which that liability is ascertained (or is ascertained to be nil). The 'relevant return' is:
- if the penalty is to be assessed in respect of a single failure to make a return on or before the due date, that return;
- if the penalty is to be assessed in respect of more than one failure to make a return in the same month or, where applicable, the same calendar quarter, the return which had the latest due date in the month or quarter. If this means there is more than one relevant return and these would produce different dates for (ii) above, the latest of those dates should be taken.

If the penalty is to be assessed in respect of failure to make, on or before the due date, a return in digital reporting sub-group 1B(3) or (4), 2B(3) or (4) or 3B(2) (see **46.8** above), the assessment of the penalty cannot be made after the later of the date given by (i) above and, where it applies, Date X. Date X applies where on the date given by (i) above it was not reasonable to expect HMRC to be aware that the person was required to make the return(s). Date X is then the last day of the period of 12 months beginning with the first day on which it was reasonable to expect HMRC to be aware that the person was required to make the return (or one of the returns).

An exception to the above timing rules has effect where:
- a person is liable to a penalty in respect of a failure to make a return upon reaching the maximum number of penalty points for the group of returns to which the return belongs;
- the penalty point by virtue of which the person reaches the maximum is awarded in respect of an earlier failure (or earlier failures) to make a return; and
- when the penalty point is awarded in respect of the earlier failure(s), an assessment of the penalty could no longer be made under the above timing rules.

In such a case, the above timing rules are disapplied, and the assessment of the penalty can instead be made during the 12 months beginning with the first day on which it was reasonable to expect HMRC to be aware of the earlier failure (or one of the earlier failures).

[*FA 2021, Sch 24 para 17*].

- Penalty for deliberate withholding of information (MTD) — *FA 2021, Sch 25*.

  An assessment of penalty for deliberate withholding of information (see **46.9** above) cannot be made after the later of:
  - the end of the two years beginning with the due date for delivery of the return; and
  - the last day of the 12 months beginning with the end of the appeal period for the assessment of the liability to tax which would have been shown in the return (or, in the absence of any such assessment, the date on which that liability is ascertained (or is ascertained to be nil)).

  The above time limit does not apply to a re-assessment of a penalty (see **46.9** above under 'Determination of penalty where no return made'). A re-assessment must instead be made before the end of the two years beginning with the day on which the return is made.

  [*FA 2021, Sch 25 para 14*].
- Late payment of tax (not applicable to corporation tax) — *FA 2009, Sch 56*:

  An assessment must be made on or before the later of:

  (1) the last date on which payment could have been made without incurring a penalty (i.e. the last day of the two years beginning with the date specified in the table at **36.6** LATE PAYMENT INTEREST AND PENALTIES); and

  (2) the last day of the 12 months beginning with the end of the appeal period for the assessment of the tax in respect of which the penalty is assessed or, if no such assessment, the date on which that tax is ascertained.

  These time limits do not, however, apply to a re-assessment of a tax-geared penalty following the payment of the tax.

  [*FA 2009, Sch 56 para 12*].
- Late payment penalty (MTD) — *FA 2021, Sch 26*.

  The assessment of a late payment penalty (see **36.7** LATE PAYMENT INTEREST AND PENALTIES) must be made on or before the later of:
  - the last day of the two years beginning with the last date on which payment of the tax could have been made without incurring a late payment penalty; and
  - the last day of the 12 months beginning with the end of the appeal period for the assessment of the amount of tax in question (or if there is no such assessment, the 12 months beginning with the date on which that amount of tax is ascertained).

  [*FA 2021, Sch 26 para 18*].
- Penalty in respect of arrangements counteracted under the general anti-avoidance rule — *FA 2013, s 212A*.

  An assessment to a penalty (see **46.14** above) must be made within the 12 months beginning with the latest of the dates on which the counteraction under the GAAR (see **4.3** ANTI-AVOIDANCE) becomes final. Where a person becomes liable to a penalty before 22 July 2020, the assessment must be made within the 12 months beginning with the end of the appeal period for the assessment giving effect to the counteraction or, if there is no such assessment, the 12 months beginning with the latest of the dates on which the counteraction becomes final. For this purpose, counteraction becomes final when the adjustments made, and any amounts resulting from them, can no longer be varied, on appeal or otherwise. [*FA 2013, Sch 43C para 5; FA 2020, Sch 14 paras 9, 14, 15*].

- offshore asset moves penalty — *FA 2015, Sch 21*.

  The time within which an assessment must be made is the same as that allowed for the assessment of the 'original penalty' (see **46.15** above) to which the offshore asset moves penalty is linked. [*FA 2015, Sch 21 para 7(4)*].
- Asset-based penalty for offshore inaccuracies and failures — *FA 2016, Sch 22*.

  An assessment to an asset-based penalty for offshore inaccuracies and failures (see **46.16** above) must be made within the period allowed for making an assessment of the offshore tax penalty to which the asset-based penalty relates (or, where the asset-based penalty relates to more than one offshore tax penalty, within the latest of those periods). [*FA 2016, Sch 22 para 15*].
- Penalty for failure to correct offshore tax non-compliance — *F(No 2)A 2017, Sch 18*.

  Where the non-compliance is the delivery of a tax document containing an inaccuracy (see **46.17** above), the assessment must be made before the end of the 12 months beginning with the end of the appeal period for the decision correcting the inaccuracy or, if there is no assessment to tax, the date on which the inaccuracy is corrected. In other cases, the assessment must be made before the end of the 12 months beginning with the end of the appeal period for the assessment of tax unpaid by reason of the non-compliance, or where there is no such assessment, the date on which the amount of tax unpaid by reason of the non-compliance is ascertained. [*F(No 2)A 2017, Sch 18 para 19*].
- HMRC investigatory powers — *FA 2008, Sch 36*.

  An assessment to a fixed or daily penalty within **46.19** above must be made within 12 months of the date on which the liability arose. Where, however, the penalty is for a failure relating to an information notice against which a person can appeal, the assessment must be made within 12 months of the end of the appeal period. An assessment to a penalty for an inaccuracy must be made within 12 months of HMRC first becoming aware of the inaccuracy and within six years of the person becoming liable to the penalty. An assessment for a failure to comply with a requirement not to disclose a third-party notice or financial institution notice must be made within twelve months of HMRC first becoming aware of the breach of the requirement.

  [*FA 2008, Sch 36 paras 46, 51B(3); FA 2021, Sch 34 para 2*].
- Fixed and daily penalties under the enforcement of tax debts by deduction from accounts provisions — *F(No 2)A 2015, Sch 8*.

  An assessment to a penalty within **46.23**(a) above must be made within 12 months beginning with the date on which the liability to the penalty arose. An assessment to a penalty within **46.23**(b)–(f) above must be made within 12 months beginning with the latest of the date on which the liability to the penalty arose, the end of the period in which an appeal against the hold notice could have been made and, if such an appeal is made, the date on which the appeal is finally determined or withdrawn. [*F(No 2)A 2015, Sch 8 para 15(2)(3)*].

- Penalty under the serial avoiders regime — *FA 2016, Sch 18*.
  An assessment to a penalty under *FA 2016, Sch 18* (see **46.24** above) must be made within the 12 months beginning with the date of the relevant defeat in question. [*FA 2016, Sch 18 para 38*].
- Penalty for failure to make notification of uncertain tax treatment — *FA 2022, Sch 17*.
  An assessment to a penalty (see **46.25** above) must be made within the six months after the failure first comes to the attention of an HMRC officer and cannot be made more than six years after the end of the financial year to which the failure relates. [*FA 2022, Sch 17 para 23(2)*].

Penalty charged otherwise than by assessment

Where a penalty is not imposed by assessment, the time within which it can be determined, or proceedings commenced, is as follows.

(a) If the penalty is ascertainable by reference to tax payable, the time is the later of six years after the penalty was incurred and three years after the determination of the amount of the tax.
(b) In any other case, the time is six years from the time when the penalty was, or began to be, incurred.

[*TMA 1970, s 103*].

Provisional agreement of the amount due subject to HMRC's being satisfied with statements of assets, etc. is not final determination for these purposes (*Carco Accessories Ltd v IRC* CS 1985, 59 TC 45).

The application of the rule in (b) above to a penalty for failure to disclose a tax avoidance scheme (see **47.10** above) was considered by the Upper Tribunal in *Root2 Tax Ltd v HMRC* UT, [2022] UKUT 353 (TCC), [2023] STC 171. HMRC applied to the FTT for a penalty in 2019 which the taxpayer argued was out of time because the penalty was incurred on the first occasion on which it became aware of any transaction taking place which formed part of the scheme in question. As this was in 2011, it was more than six years before HMRC made the application. HMRC argued that a penalty was in principle incurred on each occasion on which the company became aware of a transaction forming part of any implementation of the scheme. As the last such occasion was in 2017, the application was not time-barred. The Upper Tribunal agreed with the company and dismissed HMRC's appeal.

Appeals against penalties

[46.30] Appeals may be made against penalties charged by HMRC.

Penalties charged by assessment

An appeal may be brought against a penalty assessment. The appeal may be against:

- the imposition of a penalty; and/or
- (except in the case of a fixed penalty) the amount of the penalty.

An appeal is treated in the same way as an appeal against an assessment to the tax in question (see **5** APPEALS), but not so as to require the taxpayer to pay the penalty before an appeal against its assessment is determined.

Notice of appeal must normally be given within 30 days after the date of issue of the penalty assessment (see **5.3** APPEALS).

If the appeal is against the imposition of a penalty and it goes to the Tribunal, the Tribunal may affirm or cancel HMRC's decision to impose. If the appeal is against the amount of the penalty and it goes to the Tribunal, the Tribunal may affirm the amount charged or substitute its own amount (but only an amount that HMRC had the power to charge).

The Tribunal has power to make a reduction for disclosure or special circumstances, where relevant, to the same extent as HMRC, which may mean applying the same percentage reduction as HMRC but to a different starting point. It may make a reduction to a different extent to HMRC, but only if it thinks that HMRC's decision was flawed when considered in the light of the principles applicable in proceedings for judicial review.

Specific issues arising in relation to particular penalties are discussed below.

Penalty under *FA 2007, Sch 24* (inaccuracies)

An appeal can also be made against a decision not to suspend a penalty or against conditions of suspension. The powers of the Tribunal are restricted in such cases, to where it thinks that HMRC's decision was flawed when considered in the light of principles applicable in proceedings for judicial review.

Penalty under *FA 2009, Sch 55* (failure to make return)

In partnership cases, an appeal can be brought only by the partner required to make the return or his successor. Such an appeal is treated as an appeal against every penalty payable by any partner in respect of the failure concerned. This provision was applied in *Dyson v HMRC* FTT, [2015] SFTD 529, despite the Tribunal holding that it contravened the European Convention on Human Rights.

Penalty under *FA 2013, ss 212A, 212B* (counteraction under GAAR)

Where the person liable to the penalty is a partner and the final counteraction notice was given to the partnership's responsible partner (see **4.7** ANTI-AVOIDANCE), an appeal can only be made by the responsible partner. An appeal against the imposition of a penalty can only be made on the grounds that the arrangements concerned were not abusive or that there was no tax advantage to be counteracted (see **4.3** ANTI-AVOIDANCE). An appeal against the amount of a penalty can only be made on the grounds that the penalty is based on an overestimate of the counteracted advantage (see **46.14** above).

Penalty points under *FA 2021, Sch 24* (late filing — MTD)

An appeal may be brought against the award of a penalty point under *FA 2021, Sch 24* (late filing — see **46.8** above). Notice of appeal must be given within 30 days after the date of award of the penalty point.

Where an appeal is made against the imposition of a penalty based on penalty points, the Tribunal may affirm or cancel HMRC's decision that the person was liable to any of the penalty points by virtue of which they were liable to the penalty. This applies in relation to a penalty point even if the time limit for appealing against it expired before the appeal against the penalty was brought. It does not apply in relation to a penalty point if HMRC's decision that the person was liable to the point was affirmed on an earlier appeal.

In a case where the Tribunal has cancelled both a penalty and one or more penalty points, HMRC have 12 months, after the date of the Tribunal's decision, to award penalty points that would have accrued before the Tribunal's decision but did not because the taxpayer already had the maximum number of points. The normal timing rules in **46.8** above on awards of penalty points are disapplied in such a case.

[*FA 2007, Sch 24 paras 15–17; FA 2008, s 123, Sch 36 paras 47, 48, 51C(1)(2), Sch 41 paras 17–19; FA 2009, Sch 55 paras 20–22, 25(4)(5), Sch 56 paras 13–15; FA 2013, Sch 43C para 9; FA 2015, Sch 21 paras 8, 9; F(No 2)A 2015, Sch 8 para 16; FA 2016, Sch 18 para 41, Sch 22 paras 16–18; F(No 2)A 2017, Sch 18 paras 20–22; FA 2021, Sch 24 paras 22–24, Sch 25 paras 17–19, Sch 26 paras 19–21, Sch 32 para 13(9), Sch 34 paras 2–4; FA 2022, Sch 17 para 24*].

Penalties charged by HMRC determination

Subject to the following points, the general APPEALS (5) provisions apply to an appeal against a determination of a penalty as in **46.28** above.

TMA 1970, s 50(6)–(8) (see **5.20** APPEALS) do not apply. Instead (subject to below), on appeal the First-tier Tribunal can:

- in the case of a penalty which is required to be of a particular amount, set the determination aside, confirm it, or alter it to the correct amount; and
- in any other case, set the determination aside, confirm it if it seems appropriate, or reduce it (including to nil) or increase it as seems appropriate (but not beyond the permitted maximum).

Neither *TMA 1970, s 50(6)–(8)* nor the above apply on an appeal against a determination of an automatic late filing penalty for personal or partnership tax returns (see **46.4**, **45.5** above), where the 'reasonable excuse' let-out may have effect (see **46.4** above for the options open to the Tribunal in those cases).

In addition to the right to appeal to the Upper Tribunal on a point of law, the taxpayer can so appeal (with permission) against the amount of a penalty determined by the First-tier Tribunal.

[*TMA 1970, ss 100B, 103ZA; FA 2021, Sch 27 para 8*].

Liability under criminal law

[46.31] 'False statements to the prejudice of the Crown and public revenue' are criminal offences (*R v Hudson* CCA 1956, 36 TC 561). False statements in income tax returns, or for obtaining any allowance, reduction or repayment may involve liability to imprisonment for up to two years, under *Perjury Act 1911, s 5,* for 'knowingly and wilfully' making materially false statements or returns for tax purposes. Also, in Scotland, summary proceedings may be taken under *TMA 1970, s 107*.

Criminal prosecutions for tax fraud in England and Wales are conducted by the Crown Prosecution service. For HMRC practice in considering whether to accept a money settlement or institute criminal proceedings for fraud, see **29.11 HMRC** INVESTIGATORY POWERS.

Falsification etc. of documents which are required to be produced, as in **29.14 HMRC** INVESTIGATORY POWERS, is a criminal offence punishable, on summary conviction, by a fine of the statutory maximum or, on indictment, by a fine or imprisonment for up to two years or both. [*TMA 1970, s 20BB; FA 2012, Sch 38 para 46*]. Similar punishments apply for the concealment, destruction or disposal of documents required to be produced as in **29.4, 32.11 HMRC** INVESTIGATORY POWERS. See **29.10** and **32.11**.

The fraudulent evasion of *income tax* (not capital gains tax or corporation tax) on behalf of oneself or another person is itself a criminal offence. [*TMA 1970, s 106A*].

Offshore evasion

A criminal offence applies for failure to properly declare offshore income or chargeable gains as set out below. It applies only if a threshold limit is exceeded for any particular tax year. The threshold is £25,000. There is no requirement for the prosecution to prove intent to evade tax.

The offence covers the following:

(a) failure to give timely notification of chargeability to tax (as in **46.3** above), where the tax in question is chargeable (wholly or partly) on offshore income, assets or activities and the threshold limit is exceeded (by which is meant that the total income tax and CGT chargeable for the tax year on offshore income, assets or activities exceeds the threshold);

(b) failure to file a personal tax return before the end of the period during which the notice under *TMA 1970, s 8* to file the return can be withdrawn (see **52.5** RETURNS), where an accurate return would have disclosed liability to income tax or CGT (or both) chargeable for the tax year on offshore income, assets or activities and the threshold limit is exceeded (as in (a) above); and

(c) an inaccuracy in a personal tax return required by notice under *TMA 1970, s 8*, where (i) the return contains the inaccuracy at the end of the 'amendment period'; (ii) its correction would result in an increase in the income tax or CGT (or both) chargeable for the tax year on offshore income, assets or activities; and (iii) the amount of that increase exceeds the threshold limit. The '*amendment period*' is the period during which the taxpayer can amend the return (see **52.9** RETURNS).

References to tax being chargeable on offshore income, assets or activities include tax being chargeable by reference to offshore income, assets or activities. The offence does not apply in relation to offshore income, assets or activities reportable to HMRC in accordance with the Common Reporting Standard or article 8 of Council Directive 2011/16/EU on administrative cooperation in the field of taxation. Whether the threshold limit has been exceeded is determined by reference to *SI 2017 No 988, Regs 4–9*. With regard to (a) and (c) above, these regulations operate by reference to the potential lost revenue provisions at, respectively, **46.3** and **46.11** above.

A person guilty of an offence is liable, on summary conviction, to, in England and Wales, an unlimited fine and/or imprisonment for up to six months for offences committed before the coming into force of *Criminal Justice Act 2003, s 281(5)* and 51 weeks thereafter and, in Scotland and NI, a fine of up to level 5 on the standard scale and/or imprisonment for up to six months.

It is a defence for a person to prove that he had a reasonable excuse for failing to give the notice required in (a) or deliver the return in (b) or to prove that he took reasonable care to ensure that the return in (c) was accurate. Where a deadline is extended under *TMA 1970, s 118(2)*, the extension applies for the purposes of the deadlines relevant to (a)–(c) above. A person is not guilty of an offence if the capacity in which he is required to give the notice or file the return is as a relevant trustee of a settlement or as executor or administrator of a deceased person.

Offshore income, assets or activities means income arising from a source in, assets situated or held in, or activities carried on wholly or mainly in, a territory outside the UK. 'Assets' has the meaning given in *TCGA 1992, s 21(1)* (see **7.2** ASSETS), but also includes sterling.

[*TMA 1970, ss 106B–106H; SI 2017 No 988*].

Key points concerning penalties

[46.32] Points to consider are as follows.

- There are a number of reasons that HMRC can charge penalties and these apply across several taxes and not just capital gains tax. In general penalties are imposed for doing something wrong either in error or deliberately such as:
  - (a) Failure to notify chargeability.
  - (b) Late submission or errors in a tax return or other documents.
  - (c) Failure to keep records.
  - (d) Disclosing information.
  - (e) Failure to tell HMRC that an assessment or determination is insufficient.
  - (f) Late payment of tax.
- Some penalties are fixed but others fall within a range (as a percentage of the tax involved). The seriousness and magnitude of the offence as well as the level of cooperation from the taxpayer will determine the level of the penalties imposed by HMRC. Where it can be shown that an inaccuracy in a return was made despite

taking reasonable care no penalty may be charged. HMRC have issued various toolkits which focus on the errors HMRC officers find commonly occur. Using the toolkits does not supplant the taxpayer's obligation to ensure that their returns are complete and accord with the taxes act but their use, or use of an alternative checklist, may, depending on the precise facts, help support an argument that reasonable care was taken. The main toolkits currently in issue relevant to capital gains tax are:

- Capital gains tax for land and buildings;
- Capital gains tax for shares;
- Capital v revenue expenditure;
- Chargeable gains for companies;
- Capital gains tax for trusts and estates.

- The penalty regimes also allow for a penalty to be set aside where the taxpayer had a reasonable excuse. Interesting quotes from Tribunals are:
  - 'An excuse is likely to be reasonable where the taxpayer acts in the same way as someone who seriously intends to honour their tax liabilities and obligations would act.' *B&J Shopfitting Services* TC00390.
  - 'HMRC argues that a "reasonable excuse" must be some exceptional circumstance which prevented timeous filing. That, as a matter of law, is wrong. Parliament has provided the penalty will not be due if the appellant can show it has "reasonable excuse". If Parliament had intended to say that the penalty would not be due only in exceptional circumstances, it would have said so in those terms. The phrase "reasonable excuse" uses ordinary English words in everyday usage which must be given their plain and ordinary meaning.' *NA Dudley Electrical Contractors Ltd* TC01124.
- Where more than one tax geared penalty applies to the same tax the amount charged is usually limited to the larger of the separate penalties.
- There are often commercial reasons why accurate figures cannot be shown on a tax return, for example, admission of new partners to an existing partnership. Late filing penalties can normally be avoided by filing a return containing provisional or estimated figures and amending the return as soon as the actual figures become available. The estimate must be reasonable and clearly marked.

47

Private Residences

Cross-references. See **35** LAND generally and **21.19** for restriction on rollover relief arising from disposal of shares to a tax-advantaged share incentive plan, where replacement asset is or becomes exempt as a private residence.

Simon's Taxes. See **C3.17**.

Introduction

[47.1] An exemption from capital gains tax applies on the disposal by an individual of a dwelling-house which has been his only or main residence. The exemption also extends to garden or grounds held for the individual's own occupation and enjoyment with that residence. The exemption is either total or fractional, depending on whether and to what extent the residence has been the only or main residence of the individual throughout his period of ownership (and for this purpose certain periods of absence from the property are ignored). The relief is restricted when the residence is in a country where neither the person making the disposal nor their spouse or civil partner is tax resident.

The exemption is variously known as the main residence exemption, principal private residence (PPR) relief, private residence relief or main residence relief.

An individual can only have one main residence at a time, and this applies also to an individual and spouse or civil partner so long as they are living together. Where an individual or couple has more than one residence an election may be made for one of the residences to be treated as the main residence. The election may subsequently be varied.

The exemption is extended to situations where a residence is occupied under the terms of a settlement or by will or intestacy and to occupation by a dependant relative which began before 6 April 1988.

A further exemption is available where partial relief under the above provisions is available and, at a time when part of the dwelling-house was the taxpayer's main residence, part of it was let as residential accommodation. See **50.15–50.17** below.

A special compliance regime applies to all direct disposals of UK land where a residential property gain arises (i.e. where the main residence exemption does not apply or does not apply in full). A UK land disposal return must be made together with a payment on account of CGT on or before the 60th day following the day of the completion of the disposal (the 30th day where the completion date is before 27 October 2021). See **45.3** PAYMENT OF TAX and **52.22** RETURNS. Previously, the regime applied only to non-UK residents (see **52.22**).

Main residence exemption generally

[47.2] Where a gain accrues to an individual so far as attributable to the disposal of, or of an interest in:

(a) a dwelling-house or part of a dwelling-house (see **47.3** below) which is, or has at any time in their period of ownership been, their only or main residence (see **47.4** below), or
(b) land which they have for their own occupation and enjoyment with that residence as its garden or grounds up to the 'permitted area' (see **47.5** below),

then either the whole or a fraction of the gain is exempt as below. [*TCGA 1992, s 222(1)*].

Any loss accruing is similarly treated as being wholly or partly a non-allowable loss. [*TCGA 1992, s 16(2)*].

Note that the exemption is *not* restricted to dwelling-houses situated in the UK.

Quality of occupation required

It is a requirement of the relief that the individual must occupy the dwelling-house (or part) as their 'residence'. Whether occupation amounts to 'residence' has been the subject of several tax cases. Miller J in *Moore v Thompson* [1986] STC 170, 61 TC 15 commented that 'even occasional and short residence in a place can make that a residence; but the question [is] one of fact and degree'.

In the following cases, the taxpayer's occupation was held **not** to constitute residence.

- Occupation of a farmhouse for 32 days. The nature, quality, length and circumstances of the taxpayer's 32-day occupation of a farmhouse were such that he had moved into it on a temporary basis and his occupation did not qualify as residence (*Goodwin v Curtis* CA 1998, 70 TC 478).
- A taxpayer's occupation of a house for short periods of time whilst deciding whether to live in it permanently or to sell it (*Harte v HMRC* FTT, [2012] UKFTT 258 (TC)).

- Occupation of a house for several months after the taxpayer separated from his wife and before purchasing a house with his new partner, 'did not have any degree of permanence or expectation of continuity'. The taxpayer had never envisaged the house as a long-term home (*Moore v HMRC* FTT, [2013] UKFTT 433 (TC)).
- Camping on a site on which the taxpayer's previous dwelling-house had been situated during the building of a replacement house which he planned to sell (*Gibson v HMRC* FTT, [2013] UKFTT 636 (TC)).
- Occupation of a flat for 25 days (*Ive v HMRC* FTT, [2014] UKFTT 436 (TC)).

In the following cases, the taxpayer's occupation did constitute residence.

- Occupation of a London flat for seven weeks. It was clear that the taxpayer hoped to live in the flat on a continuous basis at the time he moved in but was aware that circumstances might arise which would require him to live elsewhere (*Dutton-Forshaw v HMRC* FTT, [2015] UKFTT 478 (TC)).
- Occupation of a property for two short periods of a few months each, the taxpayer moving out once because he could not secure a suitable mortgage and for the second time after deciding to sell due to health problems. The FTT found that each time he had moved into the property, he had intended it would be his home (*Bailey v HMRC* FTT, [2017] UKFTT 658 (TC)).
- Occupation of three houses, bought and sold sequentially after significant improvements were made. The evidence of the taxpayer and the witnesses he called showed that the properties were furnished and enjoyed socially as would be expected for an ordinary family home (*Ives v HMRC* FTT, [2023] UKFTT 968 (TC)).

In *Patwary v HMRC* FTT, [2024] UKFTT 053 (TC), the taxpayer failed to demonstrate that he had occupied the property at all. The FTT noted that the burden of proof was on the taxpayer and that there was 'remarkably little evidence' to demonstrate a period of residence. There was a distinction between evidence demonstrating residence at a property and evidence that might be addressed to a property owner. This case contrasts with *Ives* (see above) where the taxpayer's witness evidence was an important factor in persuading the FTT to rule for the taxpayer.

Spouses and civil partners

There can only be one main residence in the case of an individual and their spouse or civil partner living with them, so long as they are 'living together' (see **40.3** MARRIED PERSONS AND CIVIL PARTNERS). [*TCGA 1992, s 222(6)*]. As regards separation or divorce, see **47.7** and **47.11** below.

Total exemption

Total exemption (under *TCGA 1992, s 223(1)*) applies to a gain within *TCGA 1992, s 222(1)* above if the dwelling-house or part of a dwelling-house has been the individual's only or main residence throughout the period of ownership, or throughout the period of ownership except for all or any part of the last nine months of that period (18 months for disposals before 6 April 2020). A 36-month final period applies to certain disposals by disabled persons and long-term residents in a care home (see further below).

Fractional exemption

Fractional exemption (under *TCGA 1992, s 223(2)*) applies where total exemption does not apply to a gain. The fraction of the gain that is exempt is given by:

(i) the length of the part or parts of the period of ownership during which the dwelling-house (or part) was the individual's only or main residence, but inclusive of the last nine months of the period of ownership in any event (18 months for disposals before 6 April 2020; and see further below for disposals by disabled persons and long-term residents in care homes), divided by;

(ii) the length of the period of ownership.

Disposals by disabled persons or persons in care homes

The final period of ownership that qualifies for exemption even where the dwelling-house was not then the only or main residence is extended to 36 months where, at the time of the disposal:

(1) the individual is a 'disabled person' or a 'long-term resident' in a 'care home' and does not have any other right in a private residence (see below); or

(2) the individual's spouse or civil partner is a disabled person or a long-term resident in a care home and neither the individual nor the spouse or civil partner has any other right in a private residence.

'Disabled person' is defined for this purpose at *FA 2005, Sch 1A*. An individual is a 'long-term resident' in a care home at the time of a disposal if at that time they are resident there and have been resident, or can reasonably be expected to be resident there, for at least three months. A 'care home' is an establishment providing accommodation together with nursing or personal care.

An individual has any other right in a private residence at the time of a disposal if:

- at that time either they own or hold an interest in a dwelling-house, or part of one, other than that on which the gain in question arises or the trustees of a settlement own or hold such an interest and the individual is entitled to occupy that dwelling-house or part under the settlement's terms; and
- a gain on the disposal of that dwelling-house or interest (or of part of it) at that time would have qualified for exemption, or would have qualified if an election under **47.10** below had been made.

Period of ownership

In considering the 'period of ownership' for the purposes of applying total or fractional exemption, any period before 31 March 1982 is ignored.

Any period before 6 April 2015 is also excluded if the whole or part of the gain is a residential property gain (see **2.1** ANNUAL RATES AND EXEMPTIONS) which arises as a result of the charge on non-resident disposals of interest in UK land in **35.23**

LAND (or, for disposals before 6 April 2019, an NRCGT gain (i.e. a gain on a non-resident disposal of an interest in UK residential property — see **35.31** LAND)) unless an election for the retrospective basis of calculation is made (see **35.30, 35.31** LAND).

See **47.7** below for certain periods of ownership that additionally qualify for the purposes of total and fractional exemption.

[*TCGA 1992, s 223(1)(2)(5)–(7A), s 225E; FA 2019, Sch 1 paras 74, 120; FA 2020, s 24(3)(7)(11)*].

The UT held in *HMRC v Lee* UT, [2023] UKUT 242 (TCC), [2023] STC 1846 that the 'period of ownership' refers to the length of ownership of the dwelling actually disposed of. In that case, the taxpayers had bought a freehold interest in land, demolished the existing house and built a new house in which they then lived for 15 months. As a result they had occupied the property as their residence for only 15 months of the 43 months for which they owned the freehold interest. The UT held that the taxpayers qualified for total exemption. As a matter or straightforward textual interpretation, the period of ownership could only refer to the ownership of the dwelling-house in question. There was no concept of ownership of anything else. Furthermore, there was nothing to suggest that the legislation should be read in a different way. The Tribunal rejected HMRC's arguments based on the proposition that a dwelling-house is not capable of ownership separately from the ground on which its stands. The taxpayers' interpretation did not involve the notion of separate interests in land and the dwelling-house. An 'interest in a dwelling-house' within *TCGA 1992, s 222(1)* would include the ground on which it stands, but the crucial distinction between such an interest and an interest in land more generally was that an interest in a dwelling-house required that a dwelling-house should exist.

The tribunal in *Lee* explicitly declined to follow the Special Commissioners' decision in *Henke v HMRC* Sp C, [2006] SSCD 561 (Sp C 550) which had previously confirmed HMRC's approach that the period of ownership was the length of ownership of the plot of land.

Following the decision in *Lee*, HMRC accept that where a person acquires land on which they build a house, the period of ownership begins at the time the building comes to be a dwelling-house (HMRC Helpsheet HS283 (2023)).

Off-plan purchases

In *Higgins v HMRC*, CA [2019] STC 2312, the taxpayer entered into a contract in 2006 for the purchase of a flat off-plan. He did not have any right to occupy it until January 2010 when he completed the purchase, and the flat did not exist for most of the period before then. It was accepted that he occupied the flat as his principal residence from January 2010 until its sale in 2012 and so some relief was available under *TCGA 1992, s 222* but the issue was the period of ownership. The CA held that, for the purposes of main residence relief, the taxpayer's period of ownership began only on the date when the purchase was completed, rather than the date of the contract. The mere fact of contracting to buy a property did not give a person ownership 'such as could allow him to possess, occupy or even use the property, let alone to make it his "only or main residence"'. The Court also concluded that *TCGA 1992, s 28* (see **16.4**

COMPUTATION OF GAINS AND LOSSES), which determines for CGT purposes the date of acquisition of an asset acquired under a contract as the date the contract is made, did not dictate the conclusion that the period of ownership must run from that date.

See also **47.7**(b) below for further case law on when the period of ownership begins.

Change in interest

Where the individual has had different interests at different times, the period of ownership is taken to begin from the first acquisition taken into account in arriving at the amount of the allowable expenditure deductible in the computation of the gain. In the case of an individual living with their spouse or civil partner:

(A) if one disposes of, or of their interest in, a dwelling-house (or part) to the other, and in particular if it passes on death to the other as legatee, the other's period of ownership is treated as beginning with the beginning of the period of ownership of the one making the disposal, and
(B) if (A) above applies, but the dwelling-house (or part) was not the only or main residence of both throughout the period of ownership of the one making the disposal, account is taken of any part of that period during which it was their only or main residence as if it were also that of the other.

Where the disposal or death is before 6 April 2020, the rule in (A) above applies only where the dwelling-house (or part) was the only or main residence of the transferring spouse or civil partner at the time of the transfer.

[*TCGA 1992, s 222(7); FA 2020, s 23(2)(10)*].

Apportionments

Apportionments of consideration must be made wherever required, and, in particular, where a person disposes of a dwelling-house only part of which is their only or main residence. [*TCGA 1992, s 222(10)*].

What is a dwelling-house?

[47.3] An immobilised caravan with main services installed has been held to be a dwelling-house (*Makins v Elson* Ch D 1976, 51 TC 437) but one still on wheels and with no services installed was not so held (*Moore v Thompson* Ch D 1986, 61 TC 15).

A houseboat will often be an exempt asset in its own right (see **23.4** EXEMPTIONS AND RELIEFS regarding tangible movable wasting assets). If this is not the case, it may qualify as a dwelling-house if it is permanently located on a site and connected to all mains services. Such a houseboat *will* be regarded as a dwelling-house if it has been used as an immobile residence for a period of six months or more and has had its engines removed. Other cases will be considered on their merits. (HMRC Capital Gains Manual CG64325).

Green v CIR CS 1982, 56 TC 10 involved the disposal of a mansion (occupied by the taxpayer) and its two wings. The Commissioners' finding that the wings were not part of his dwelling-house was upheld.

In *Gibson v HMRC* FTT, [2013] UKFTT 636 (TC) the taxpayer knocked down an existing house and built a new house because it was cheaper than extending the house. The tribunal held that the two dwelling-houses could not be treated as the same dwelling-house for the purposes of the exemption.

Which is the main residence?

[47.4] Where a taxpayer has more than one residence, the question as to which is the main residence is a question of fact, subject to the making of an election as in **47.10** below.

See *Frost v Feltham* Ch D 1980, 55 TC 10 (which concerned mortgage interest relief for income tax purposes). See also HMRC Capital Gains Manual CG64545 for factors which HMRC will consider in deciding if a residence is a main residence in the absence of an election.

In *Regan v HMRC (No 2)* TC 2247 [2012] UKFTT 570 (TC) the First-tier Tribunal held that when considering the facts of what constitutes a main residence it should be determined based on the quality of the occupation not the quantity of the occupation.

What is the permitted area?

[47.5] In addition to the residence itself, main residence relief applies to land which the individual has for their own occupation and enjoyment with that residence as its garden or grounds up to the 'permitted area'.

The '*permitted area*' in **47.2**(b) above means an area (inclusive of the house itself) of 0.5 hectares (i.e. 5,980 sq. yards or 5,000 sq. metres) or larger area if required for the reasonable enjoyment of the whole or part of the dwelling-house as a residence having regards to its size and character.

Where the land occupied with a residence is larger than the permitted area, then (up to the permitted area), the part of the land that qualifies for relief is that part which would be most suitable for occupation and enjoyment with the residence if the remainder were separately occupied.

[*TCGA 1992, s 222(2)–(4)*].

HMRC consider that no relief is due on any sale of a garden or grounds taking place after a prior sale of the dwelling-house, relying on *Varty v Lynes* Ch D 1976, 51 TC 419. Land must be held together with the residence on the date of disposal (HMRC Capital Gains Manual CG64377–64385). It is also a requirement that the land must be garden or grounds at the time of the disposal (*Nunn v HMRC* FTT, [2024] UKFTT 298 (TC)).

Land which is disposed of separately before the dwelling-house is not therefore precluded from relief on that basis, provided that the land is occupied as part of the garden or grounds at the time of disposal. HMRC may, however, argue that a separate disposal of part of the garden or grounds of a residence may be prima facie evidence that the part disposed of was not required for the reasonable enjoyment of the dwelling-house as a residence. This only becomes of relevance where the area of the garden or grounds exceeds 0.5 hectares. However, it accepts that there are two common circumstances where this inference may be incorrect. The first is where the owner of the land makes a disposal to a member of his family where he may be prepared to tolerate some curtailment of the reasonable enjoyment of the residence. The second is where financial necessity may force the owner to sell land which would be regarded as part of the most suitable area of garden or grounds to be included in the permitted area (HMRC Capital Gains Manual CG64832).

In deciding whether an area of garden or grounds larger than 0.5 hectares is 'required for the reasonable enjoyment' of the dwelling-house as a residence, the following words of Du Parcq J in the compulsory purchase case of *Re Newhill Compulsory Purchase Order 1937, Payne's Application* KB 1937, [1938] 2 All ER 163 provide useful guidance:

> ' "Required", I think, in this Section does not mean merely that the occupiers of the house would like to have it, or that they would miss it if they lost it, or that anyone proposing to buy the house would think less of the house without it than he would if it was preserved to it. "Required" means, I suppose that without it there will be such a substantial deprivation of amenities or convenience that a real injury would be done to the property owner.'

The 'required' test is an objective one. In *Longson v Baker* Ch D 2000, 73 TC 415, in which a permitted area of 7.56 hectares was unsuccessfully claimed and in which the taxpayer stressed the equestrian aspect of the property, it was not objectively *required*, in other words necessary, to keep horses at a house to enjoy it *as a residence*. An individual taxpayer may subjectively wish to do so but that was not the same thing.

In *Ritchie v Revenue and Customs Commissioners* [2017] UKFTT 449 (TC), [2017] All ER (D) 112 (Jun), the Ritchies disposed of house and grounds on a site greater than 0.5 hectares. Having found that a large shed on the site was part of the dwelling-house (see more about whether subsidiary buildings form part of a residence at **47.6** below), the First-tier Tribunal concluded that the approach path to the shed was part of the permitted area but not land lying on the other side. In deciding how to apportion the gain between the permitted and unpermitted areas, the Tribunal found that all of the land was of equal value to a developer.

There is no requirement that the land occupied and used with the residence as garden or grounds at the time of disposal has to adjoin the land on which the dwelling-house stands. See *Wakeling v Pearce* (Sp C 32), [1995] SSCD 96 where the distance between the garden (which was disposed of) and the land including the dwelling-house (which was retained) was less than 10 metres. However, HMRC consider that it will be rare for exemption to be given to land (even if used as a garden) separated from the residence by other land which is not in the same ownership as the residence (see HMRC Capital Gains Manual CG64367).

Subsidiary buildings

[47.6] The courts have considered whether a building which is separate from the main dwelling-house building can fall within the exemption a number of times.

The leading case is *Lewis v Rook* CA 1992, 64 TC 567. A finding by Commissioners that a gardener's cottage some 170 metres from the main dwelling-house formed part of the taxpayer's residence was initially upheld in the High Court, but was rejected in the Court of Appeal. The true test was declared to be whether the cottage was 'within the curtilage of, and appurtenant to [the main house], so as to be part of the entity which, together with [the main house], constituted the dwelling-house occupied by the taxpayer as her residence'.

The curtilage concept was derived from a non-tax case, *Methuen-Campbell v Walters* CA, [1979] QB 525 (and see also *Dyer v Dorset County Council* CA, [1989] QB 346), in which Buckley LJ stated that 'for one corporeal hereditament to fall within the curtilage of another, the former must be so intimately associated with the latter as to lead to the conclusion that the former in truth forms part and parcel of the latter'. The cottage in *Lewis v Rook* was not 'intimately associated' with the main house as it was some way off and separated from it by a large garden. The total area of land involved was around 10.5 acres and Balcombe LJ remarked that as

> 'the "permitted area" of garden and grounds which is exempt from capital gains tax is limited to one acre [now 0.5 hectares] or such larger area as [is] required for the reasonable enjoyment of the dwelling-house as a residence, it does seem to me to be remarkable that a separate lodge or cottage which by any reasonable measurement must be outside the permitted area can nevertheless be part of the entity of the dwelling-house'.

HMRC consider that whether or not a particular building is within the curtilage of the main house is a matter of fact and degree. The building must be geographically close to the main house and be an integral part of it. However, as the necessary proximity required will vary in each case HMRC do not attempt to set a generally acceptable limit. Buildings within the curtilage of the main house will of necessity be 'appurtenant' to it. See HMRC Capital Gains Manual CG64245, 64255 for further discussion.

In *Honour v Norris* Ch D 1992, 64 TC 599, the taxpayer owned four separate, self-contained flats in a London square. Two of these were adjacent and were converted to form a single property, the other two being some way off and not adjacent to each other. Although the taxpayer and his wife had occasionally used the non-adjacent flats themselves, their main function was to provide sleeping accommodation for guests and a nanny. The Appeal Commissioners upheld the taxpayer's contention that one of the distant flats, which had been sold, was part of his main residence. However, the Revenue's appeal was upheld in the High Court, Vinelott J remarking that the proposition that the flat which had been sold formed part of the taxpayer's main residence was 'an affront to common sense'.

Periods of ownership qualifying for exemption

[47.7] The following rules apply in determining whether a gain qualifies for total exemption or, if not, what proportion (if any) qualifies for fractional exemption.

(a) **Periods of absence.** A '*period of absence*' means a period during which the dwelling-house (or part) was not occupied by the individual as a residence. In applying total or fractional exemption (ignoring periods of ownership before 31 March 1982):

   (i) a period of absence not exceeding three years (or periods of absence which together did not exceed three years), and in addition,
   (ii) any period of absence throughout which the individual worked in an employment or office all the duties of which were performed outside the UK or lived with a spouse or civil partner who worked in such an office or employment, and in addition,
   (iii) any period of absence not exceeding four years (or periods of absence which together did not exceed four years) throughout which the individual was prevented from residing in the dwelling-house (or part) in consequence of the situation of his place of work or in consequence of any condition imposed by his employer requiring him to reside elsewhere, being a condition reasonably imposed to secure the effective performance by the employee of his duties, and in addition,
   (iv) any period of absence not exceeding four years (or periods of absence which together did not exceed four years) throughout which the individual lived with a spouse or civil partner to whom (iii) above applied for that period or periods,

   is treated as if in that period of absence the dwelling-house (or part) was occupied by the individual as a residence. This rule applies only where, before the period, there was a time when the dwelling-house (or part) was the individual's only or main residence and after the period, either:

   (A) where any of (i)–(iv) above apply, there was a time when the dwelling-house (or part) was again the individual's only or main residence;
   (B) where any of (ii)–(iv) above apply, the individual was prevented from resuming residence in the dwelling-house because of the situation of their place of work or a condition imposed by the terms of their employment requiring them to reside elsewhere (the condition being reasonably imposed to secure the effective performance of the duties); or
   (C) where any of (ii)–(iv) above apply, the individual lived with a spouse or civil partner to whom (B) above applied.

   Where the period of ownership is deemed to begin on 6 April 2015 (because the gain is a residential property gain subject to the charge in **35.23** LAND or, for disposals before 6 April 2019, an NRCGT gain — see **47.2** above under 'Period of ownership'), then in establishing whether any of the above permitted periods of absence apply, the rule that the dwelling-house or part must have been occupied as the only or main residence at some time before the period of absence is determined ignoring times before 6 April 2015. However, pre-6 April 2015 periods can be used to satisfy the requirement if the individual so elects. An election must be made in the UK land disposal return (or NRCGT return) for the disposal (see **52.22** RETURNS) and specify the day before

6 April 2015 relied on in relation to the period of absence. The prior period of absence (i.e. that before 6 April 2015) is deducted from the amount of absence available for relief after 5 April 2015.
[*TCGA 1992, ss 223(3)–(3B)(7)(7B), 223A; Sch 2 paras 26(3), 32(1)*].
See **47.2** above for the quality of occupation required to constitute 'residence'.
Where the periods of absence exceed the three or four years mentioned in (i) and (iii) above, it is only the excess which does not qualify for the exemption treatment. See the example at HMRC Capital Gains Manual CG65066.
These provisions treat the dwelling-house as a residence during a period of absence. They do not treat it as their only or main residence. If there is another residence in which the individual has a legal or equitable interest during the period of absence, a main residence election as in **47.10** below nominating the residence from which the taxpayer is absent may be needed in order to qualify that residence for relief for the period of absence. See HMRC Capital Gains Manual CG65047.

Example

T purchased a house on 1 August 1981, from which date, it was used as her only residence until 10 February 1982 when she moved to France to live in rent-free accommodation provided by her employer whilst she carried out all the duties of the employment there. She returned from France on 4 August 1990 when she again occupied the house as her only residence. On 30 November 2018, she left the house empty and moved to live with her elderly father in a residence owned by him, intending to sell her own house. In the event, the house was not sold until 1 November 2024 when an otherwise chargeable gain of £150,000 was realised.

	£
Gain on sale	150,000
Deduct ((8y4m + 28y4m + 9m)/42y7m) × £150,000 (see note 2)	131,800
Chargeable gain	£18,200

Notes to the example

(1) The period of ownership for the exemption calculation does not include any period before 31 March 1982.

(2) All of the period spent in France (ignoring the period before 31 March 1982), eight years and four months, counts as a period of residence under (ii) above. It is assumed that the supply of accommodation to T in France was such that it was not eligible for relief under *TCGA 1992, s 223* (e.g. a licence). The period of occupation as main residence from 4 August 1990 to 30 November 2018, 28 years and four months, is eligible for relief. None of the period from 30 November 2018 to 1 November 2024 can count as a period of residence under (i) above as there was not a time afterwards that the house was T's only or main residence. However, the last nine months of ownership are exempt provided the house has, at some time during the period of ownership (not restricted to periods after 31 March 1982), been the only or main residence. The total period of ownership from 1 April 1982 to 1 November 2024 was 42 years and seven months.

(b) **Delay in taking up residence.** Where a dwelling-house (or part) does not become an individual's only or main residence immediately on acquisition but does so within the first 24 months of the period of ownership, then in certain circumstances it is nevertheless treated as the only or main residence from the beginning of that period. The circumstances are where, before the individual moves in, either:

(i) the construction, renovation, redecoration or alteration of the dwelling-house or part is completed; or

(ii) the individual disposes of any other dwelling-house (or part) which was then their only or main residence.

The dwelling-house (or part) must not be any other person's residence at any time during the period of ownership up to the moving-in date. In determining when a disposal within (ii) above takes place, for this purpose, the normal rule for determining when a disposal under a contract occurs (see **16.4** COMPUTATION OF GAINS AND LOSSES) is disregarded. [*TCGA 1992, s 223ZA; FA 2020, s 24(4)(11)*].

See also *HMRC v Lee and another* (**47.2** above) in which the taxpayers demolished the existing house on a plot of land and built a new one and *Higgins v HMRC* (**47.2** above) in which the taxpayer entered into a contract for the purchase of a flat off-plan but had no right to occupy it until the purchase was completed four years later.

(c) **Separation of married persons or civil partners.** Special rules apply where an individual ceases to live with their spouse or civil partner and subsequently, as part of a divorce or separation settlement (defined at *TCGA 1992, s 225B(2)*), disposes of the home which had been their only or main residence, or an interest in it, to the other partner.

For disposals on or after 6 April 2023, the disposal is treated as made at no gain/no loss under the rules at **40.4** MARRIED PERSONS AND CIVIL PARTNERS. For disposals before that date, no gain/no loss treatment is unlikely to apply, but the transferring partner may instead make a claim for the home to be regarded for the purposes of the main residence exemption as continuing to be their only or main residence from the date occupation ceased until the date of transfer. Throughout this period, the home must have continued to be the other partner's only or main residence, and the transferring partner must not elect for another house to be treated as their main residence for any part of the period.

Disposal to third party on or after 6 April 2023. Where the disposal is to a third party rather than to the other partner and takes place on or after 6 April 2023, the transferring partner may make a claim for the home to be regarded for the purposes of the main residence exemption as continuing to be their only or main residence from the date occupation ceased until the date of transfer. Throughout this period, the home must have continued to be the other partner's only or main residence, and the transferring partner must not elect for another house to be treated as their main residence for any part of the period.

[*TCGA 1992, s 225B; Divorce, Dissolution and Separation Act 2020, Schedule para 53; F(No 2)A 2023, s 41(3)(6)*].

See also **47.11** below for deferred sale agreements.

(d) **'Job-related' accommodation.** If at any time during an individual's period of ownership (including any period before 31 March 1982) they reside in 'job-related' living accommodation and the individual intends in due course to return and occupy the dwelling-house (or part) as their only or main residence, they are deemed at that time to occupy the dwelling-house (or part) as a residence for the purposes of *TCGA 1992, ss 222–226* (i.e. all the provisions contained in this chapter). Living accommodation is 'job-related' for these purposes if it is provided for a taxpayer by reason of their employment or is provided for their spouse or civil partner by reason of their employment in any of the following cases:

  (i) Where it is necessary for the proper performance of the duties of the employment that the employee should reside in that accommodation.

  (ii) Where the provision of such accommodation is customary and it is provided for the better performance of the duties of employment.

  (iii) Where there is a special threat to the employee's security, special security arrangements are in force, and the employee resides in the accommodation as part of those arrangements.

With certain exceptions, (i) and (ii) above do not apply to accommodation provided to its directors by a company (or associated company). In respect of residence after 5 April 1983, living accommodation is also job-related if either the person claiming the relief or their spouse or civil partner is carrying on a trade, profession or vocation on premises or other land provided by another person, under tenancy or otherwise, and is bound under an arm's length contract to live in those premises or on other premises provided. Relief is not given if the accommodation is provided, in whole or in part, by a company in which the borrower, or their spouse or civil partner, has a material interest (as defined) or by any person or persons with whom they carry on a business in partnership. Living accommodation is also job-related if an 'armed forces accommodation allowance' for or towards the cost of the accommodation is paid to, or in respect of, the person claiming the relief or their spouse or civil partner. 'Armed forces accommodation allowance' is an allowance which is exempt for income tax purposes under *ITEPA 2003, s 297D*. [*TCGA 1992, s 222(8)(8A)–(8D)(9); FA 2020, s 24(2)(c)(d)*].

The above treatment still applies if the dwelling-house is disposed of without having been occupied by the individual (but subject to the test of intention to occupy being satisfied previously) or if the property has been let (see **50.17** below).

These provisions treat the dwelling-house as a residence during a period of residence in job-related accommodation. They do not treat it as their only or main residence. If there is another residence in which the individual has a legal or equitable interest during the period in question, a main residence election as in **47.10** below nominating the residence from which the taxpayer is absent may be needed in order to qualify that residence for relief for the period.

(e) **Relocation of employees.** The exemption is extended to cases where an individual sells their home, or an interest in it, as a consequence of a change in their place of work or that of a 'co-owner' (i.e. another individual holding an interest in the home jointly or in common), if the change is required by the individual's or co-owner's employer. The disposal must be made under a relocation agreement with the employer (or a person operating under an agreement with the employer) which must include a term entitling the individual to a share of any profit made on the subsequent disposal of the house or interest by the purchaser. If, within three years of the initial disposal, the individual receives such a profit share and that share would otherwise fall within *TCGA 1992, s 22* (CAPITAL SUMS DERIVED FROM ASSETS (**10**)), it is instead treated as a gain attributed to the individual's disposal of the home or interest, but accruing at the time the sum is received. The result is that the profit share will generally be exempt to the same extent as the home itself. [*TCGA 1992, s 225C*]. Where the provision does not apply, the receipt of the profit share cannot itself attract any private residence relief as it is not a disposal of an interest in a residence (HMRC Capital Gains Manual CG14970, 64611).

Non-qualifying tax years

[47.8] A dwelling-house or part of a dwelling-house is not treated as being occupied as a residence by an individual at any time in their period of ownership which falls into a 'non-qualifying' tax year or non-qualifying 'partial tax year'. A '*non-qualifying*' tax year is a tax year in the individual's period of ownership where neither the individual nor their spouse or civil partner is tax resident in the territory in which the dwelling house is situated, and the individual does not meet the day count test for that year. The restriction therefore applies broadly where either:

- a non-UK resident has a dwelling house in the UK and does not spend at least 90 days in that house in the tax year in question; or
- a UK resident has a dwelling house overseas and is not present in that house for at least 90 days in the tax year.

Where only part of the tax year falls into the period of ownership that part is a '*partial tax year*' and the day count test is applied to the partial tax year (see below).

A tax year before 2015/16 can only be a non-qualifying tax year if the disposal is of an interest in UK land on which a residential property gain or loss (see **2.1** ANNUAL RATES AND EXEMPTIONS) arises as a result of the charge on non-residents in **35.23** LAND.

The effect of this provision is that the property can neither be exempt as the individual's factual only or main residence, nor as their main residence by election (see **47.10** below), for a non-qualifying tax year. The rule applies to any property, wherever situated, and any gain attributable to the non-qualifying tax year(s) is chargeable to capital gains tax when the property is sold, at which date the owner may be resident or non-resident.

For the purposes of the restriction, an individual is resident in a non-UK territory for a tax year if either they are liable to tax in the overseas territory, under its law relating to residency or domicile, for periods making up more than half of the year or they would be resident there under the UK statutory residence test (see **51.2** RESIDENCE AND DOMICILE) if the rules of the test were applied to that territory.

The exemption for periods of absence (see **47.7**(a) above) can still apply for a non-qualifying tax year. The exemption for job-related accommodation (see **47.7**(d) above) may also apply. However, the treatment of visiting forces as non-UK resident is disregarded for these purposes (see **23.61** EXEMPTIONS AND RELIEFS).

Day count test

The day count test applies to any property that is occupied as a residence, wherever situated. The test is met if either the individual or their spouse or civil partner spends at least 90 days (prorated for a partial tax year, rounded up to the nearest whole day) in one or more houses which are situated in the same overseas territory, and which either the individual or their spouse or civil partner has an interest in. A day is spent at the house if the person is there at midnight or was there at some time on that day and the following day and had stayed overnight. The 90 days do not need to be consecutive, and days spent in different houses can be aggregated, but a day which both the individual and the spouse or civil partner spend at a house is not counted twice.

[*TCGA 1992, ss 222B, 222C*].

Part-business use, changes of use etc.

[47.9] If a gain accrues on the disposal of a dwelling-house or part of a dwelling-house and part of it is used *exclusively* for the purposes of a trade or business, or of a profession or vocation, the gain is apportioned. The main residence exemption rules are then applied in relation to the part of the gain apportioned to the part which is not exclusively used for those purposes. The apportionment also applies for the purpose of calculating any exemption for letting (see **50.15** onwards). [*TCGA 1992, s 224(1); FA 2020, s 24(6)*].

It will be noted that the apportionment applies only where part of the house is used *exclusively* for business purposes. A room used partly for business and partly for residential purposes does not give rise to any restriction. However, in determining exclusivity, occasional and very minor residential use of a business room, for example, its use for the keeping of private possessions, is disregarded by HMRC (HMRC Capital Gains Manual CG64663). An apportionment based on the number of rooms used respectively for business and residential purposes will often suffice in cases of relatively small business use. It may not produce a result acceptable to HMRC if the residential part of a mixed property is likely to have a disproportionately lower value than the business part, as is probable in the case of, for example, accommodation above a public house (see the worked example at HMRC Capital Gains Manual CG64663). An apportionment fraction already in use for income tax purposes is not necessarily appropriate for CGT purposes (HMRC Capital Gains Manual CG64663 and, as regards farmhouses, CG64680).

The legislation does not specifically address the question of part of a residence used for the purposes of an employment, though it is arguable that the reference in *TCGA 1992, s 224(1)* to a 'business' includes the business carried on by the individual's employer. In practice, HMRC do not require a restriction to be made for the use (exclusive or otherwise) for employment purposes of a small part of a residence, for example a room used as a study, and this remains the case even if an expenses allowance has been given against employment income. If, however, a 'substantial part' of the property is used exclusively in connection with the employment, they will insist on a restriction of the CGT exemption on the more general grounds that relief is available only for a dwelling-house (or part) which has been the individual's only or main *residence* (see **47.2** above). (HMRC Capital Gains Manual CG64690).

If at any time in the period of ownership there is a change in what is occupied as the individual's residence, whether on account of a reconstruction or conversion of a building or for any other reason, or there have been changes as regards the use of part of the dwelling-house for the purpose of a trade etc. or for any other purpose, main residence relief may be adjusted in such manner as is just and reasonable. [*TCGA 1992, s 224(2); FA 2020, s 24(6)*].

HMRC's approach in such cases is to deal with each case on its merits, and to require an adjustment which as far as possible reflects the extent to which, and the length of time over which, each part of the dwelling-house has been used as part of residence. Where part of a residence has been used for part of the period of ownership for other (e.g. business) purposes, but has *at some time* during the period of ownership been used as part of the main residence, the last nine months of ownership is an exempt period by virtue of the rule at **47.2**(i) above, and this applies regardless of actual use during those last nine months (HMRC Capital Gains Manual CG64760, 64985).

ROLLOVER RELIEF (**53**) may be available in respect of any chargeable gain arising on the business portion of a dwelling-house if a new dwelling-house is acquired, part of which will also be used *exclusively* for the purposes of a trade etc. The rolled over gain will be set against the acquisition cost of the business part of the new property.

Letting the dwelling-house may restrict the exemption given by **47.2** and **47.7** above (subject to the relief at **47.15** below) but there is no restriction where a lodger lives as part of a family, sharing their living accommodation and taking meals with them (HMRC Statement of Practice SP 14/80). A restriction may be applied if there are two or more lodgers — see HMRC Capital Gains Manual CG64702. Participation in the 'rent a room' income tax relief scheme of *ITTOIA 2005, ss 784–802* will not normally lead to any capital gains tax liability (HL Written Answers, 27 January 1993, Vol 514 col 94).

Adult placement carers

The occupation of part of a dwelling-house by a person under an 'adult placement scheme' is disregarded in determining the period during which the dwelling-house is the main residence of the individual making the disposal. For the purposes of the part-business use provisions above, the occupation of the part of the residence under the scheme is not regarded as the use of that part exclusively for the purposes of a trade etc. The effect of theses provisions is that no restriction on the amount of relief will be required in such cases.

An '*adult placement scheme*' is a scheme to which a registration requirement under *Care Standards Act 2000, s 11* applies and under which an individual agrees to provide care and support, including accommodation, to an adult. In Scotland this relief applies by reference to arrangements constituting an adult placement service (as defined). In Northern Ireland it applies by reference to arrangements made with an adult placement agency (as defined) for the provision of accommodation to an adult.

[*TCGA 1992, s 225D*].

Election for main residence

[47.10] An individual may have more than one residence. Because, broadly, only one residence can qualify for the main residence exemption at a particular time, it is necessary to determine which is the individual's main residence. The individual may conclude that question for any period by written notice to an HMRC officer. Such a notice is usually referred to as a main residence election.

In the absence of a nomination covering any particular period of time, the question of which is the main residence is decided on the facts. The main residence will not necessarily be the one at which the taxpayer spends most of their time, although it commonly will be; for other criteria taken into account by HMRC, see HMRC Capital Gains Manual CG64545.

Subject to the exception below, the notice must be given within two years from the date on which the individual has a particular combination of residences and its effect may be backdated by up to two years (but not before that date).. Each time there is a change in the individual's combination of residences a new two-year period begins and there is a new opportunity to make a nomination.

Where a dwelling house is acquired, the date on which there is a new combination of residences will not necessarily be the date of acquisition, it will be the date on which the dwelling house was first occupied as a residence. Similarly, where an individual ceases to occupy a dwelling house as a residence, the date on which there is a new combination of residences will be the date on which the dwelling house is no longer used as a residence, it will not necessarily be the date on which that dwelling house is disposed of (HMRC Capital Gains Manual CG64495).

It is worth emphasising that the choice is not between two or more properties but between two or more *residences*. A property never occupied by the taxpayer as a residence cannot enter the equation (see *Harte and another v HMRC* FTT, [2012] UKFTT 258 (TC); 2012 STI 2219).

Once the individual has made a nomination, they may vary that notice by a further written notice to an HMRC officer with effect for any period beginning not earlier than two years before the giving of the further notice.

[*TCGA 1992, s 222(5)*].

A notice or further notice can, however, be given more than two years after the beginning of the period for which it is to apply if the individual has not held an interest of more than a negligible market value in more than one of the residences during the period. [*TCGA 1992, s 222(5A); FA 2020, s 24(2)(9)*]. This may apply where, for example, one of the residences is a weekly rented flat or accommodation provided by an employer.

There is a separate, more restricted election available where a non-UK resident taxpayer disposes of a residence in the UK (see **35.23** LAND) (referred to here as a 'section 222A election').

In the case of spouses or of civil partners, there can only be one residence or main residence for both, so long as 'living together' (see **40.3** MARRIED PERSONS AND CIVIL PARTNERS) and, where a notice specifying the main residence affects both spouses or civil partners, it must be given by both. [*TCGA 1992, s 222(6)*]. If when a couple marry or register a civil partnership they each have a residence and they continue to use both, the two-year period for jointly nominating the main residence begins on the date of marriage or registration (HMRC Capital Gains Manual CG64525).

The nomination of a residence as the main residence has effect until the earlier of, if any, the date from which the original notice is varied and the date on which the taxpayer's combination of residences changes (such that a new nomination becomes possible) (HMRC Capital Gains Manual CG64497).

The above interpretation was confirmed in *Griffin v Craig-Harvey* Ch D 1993, 66 TC 396. In the judgment in that case, the following hypothetical situations were put forward.

(1) The taxpayer owns two houses, each of which he occupies as a residence. More than two years have elapsed since he began to have two residences. He then begins to use a third house as a residence. A new two-year period begins to run at that time so that he can make an election as between all three residences during that two-year period.
(2) If on the same facts the taxpayer ceased, after acquiring a third residence, to use one of them as a residence a new period will begin at the time of cessation so that, again, he will have a period of two years during which he can elect between the remaining residences.
(3) The taxpayer owns two houses which he occupies as residences. The taxpayer conveys one of the houses to the trustees of the settlement under which he has a beneficial interest and the trustees have power which they exercise to permit him to continue to reside in the residence. A new two-year period begins at the time when he creates the settlement and again an election can be made (jointly by the taxpayer and the trustees; see **47.12** below) within the subsequent two years.
(4) The taxpayer has two residences, one owned by him and the other by the trustees of a settlement under which the trustees have power to permit the taxpayer to occupy it as a residence. No election is made during the two years following the inception of this state of affairs. If the trustees have and exercise a power to transfer the residence which they own to the taxpayer he can elect that that residence is to be his main residence at any time during the subsequent two years.

Where a *s 222(5)* nomination has been made, it does not cease to be effective at any time simply because at that time another residence is treated as not being occupied as a residence for the tax year because it is a non-qualifying tax year (see **47.8** above). [*TCGA 1992, s 222(6A)*].

Example 1

S purchased the long lease of a London flat on 1 June 2016. He occupied the flat as his sole residence until 31 July 2018 when he acquired a property in Shropshire. Both properties were thereafter occupied as residences by S until the lease of the London flat was sold on 28 February 2025, realising an otherwise chargeable gain of £75,000. S is UK-resident throughout.

The possibilities open to S are:

(i) Election for London flat to be treated as main residence throughout

Exempt gain	£75,000

(ii) Election for Shropshire property to be treated as main residence from 31 July 2018 onwards

Exempt gain $£75,000 \times \dfrac{2y2m + 9m}{8y9m}$	£25,000

(iii) Election for London flat to be treated as main residence up to 31 May 2024, with election for the Shropshire property to be so treated thereafter

Exempt gain $£75,000 \times \dfrac{8y + 9m}{8y9m}$	£75,000

Notes to the example

(a) S owned the London flat for eight years and nine months, giving the denominators in (ii) and (iii) above. In (ii) above, the London flat is treated as the main residence for the period 1 June 2016 to 31 July 2018, two years and two months. The final nine months are also exempt. In (iii) above, the London flat is treated as the main residence for the eight years from 1 June 2016 to 31 May 2024 and the final nine months are also exempt.

(b) The elections in (iii) are the most favourable, provided they could have been made by 31 July 2020 in respect of the London flat, and by 31 May 2026 in respect of the Shropshire property. The advantage of (iii) over (i) is that the period of ownership from 1 May 2024 to 28 February 2025 of the Shropshire property will be treated as a period of residence as regards any future disposal of that property.

Example 2

HMRC themselves give the example of an individual with two residences, X and Y, on which this example is based. The individual has long since nominated X as his main residence, but on 15 January 2025, he disposes of Y at a substantial gain. On, say, 1 March 2025, he gives notice of variation, nominating Y as his main residence from 1 March 2023. On 8 March 2025, he gives further notice of variation, renominating X as his main residence from 8 March 2023.

The outcome is that Y has been the individual's main residence at some time during the period of ownership, albeit for only one week at the beginning of March 2023. This is enough to give the individual the benefit of the 'final nine months' exemption at **47.2** above, so he has secured nine months' relief on Y at a cost of just one week's relief on X.

(HMRC Capital Gains Manual CG64510).

Section 222A elections

Where the disposal is of an interest in UK land by a non-UK resident and a residential property gain or loss (see **2.1** ANNUAL RATES AND EXEMPTIONS) arises as a result of the charge on non-residents in **35.23** LAND, a *s 222A* election can be made in the online UK land disposal return which must be submitted within 60 days of completion of the disposal (see **52.22** RETURNS). The election allows for the nomination of a residence as the main residence retrospectively. While such an election can generally vary a previously made *s 222(5)* election, it cannot vary a previous election for a residence which has already been disposed of (in whole or in part). In addition, a *s 222A* election cannot subsequently be varied, either under *TCGA 1992, s 222A* or *s 222(5)*.

This provision gives an opportunity for an election where a non-resident individual who has a main residence abroad retains a UK residential property which is sold while they are non-resident rather than re-occupied (for example, because their employer assigns them to a new location, rather than returning them to the UK). Note however that the election can only be made for years which are not non-qualifying tax years.

If a *s 222A* election affects the individual's spouse or civil partner who was living with them, and both the individual and the spouse or civil partner must submit a UK land disposal return or NRCGT return, an election by the individual is only effective in relation to a period when they were living together as spouses or civil partners if the spouse or civil partner also so elects. If they are not both required to submit a return, the election made by the individual is only effective for that period if it is accompanied by a written notice of agreement by the spouse or civil partner.

[*TCGA 1992, s 222A*].

Deferred sale agreements on separation or divorce

[47.11] Where a married couple or civil partners break up, one option for dealing with the couple's main residence is to enter into a deferred sale agreement under which one partner (A) transfers their interest in the home to the other partner (B), who continues to live there. Often, the agreement will require B to sell on the happening of a specified event, such as the youngest child reaching 18 or B's remarriage. A remains entitled to a share of the profits when B eventually sells the property and the receipt of that share will result in a chargeable gain (see **10.2** CAPITAL SUMS DERIVED FROM ASSETS).

Where the disposal by B occurs on or after 6 April 2023, a relief applies so that the gain arising to A on their share of the profits is effectively treated in the same way as the gain arising on the initial transfer of A's interest in the property to B. If that initial gain qualifies for the main residence exemption, the later gain will do so to the same extent. If the initial gain was no gain/no loss (see **40.4** MARRIED PERSONS AND CIVIL PARTNERS), the later gain will also be no gain/no loss. The relief applies where the following conditions are met:

(a) A ceases to live with B in a dwelling-house (or part of a dwelling-house) which was, immediately before A moved out, A's only or main residence;
(b) A disposes of the dwelling-house or part, or disposes or an interest in it, to B in accordance with a separation or divorce settlement (within *TCGA 1992, s 225B*) which includes a term entitling A to a share of the profit made by B when B disposes of the property;
(c) in accordance with the settlement, A receives a share of the profits made by B on the disposal of the dwelling-house or part, or of an interest in it; and
(d) the receipt of the profit share by A would otherwise be treated as a disposal within *TCGA 1992, s 22* (see **10.2** CAPITAL SUMS DERIVED FROM ASSETS).

The relief operates by treating A's receipt of the profit shares as a gain attributable to A's initial disposal (in (b) above) but arising when A receives the profit share.

[*TCGA 1992, s 225BA; F(No 2)A 2023, s 41(4)(6)*].

Occupation under terms of settlement or by will or intestacy

[47.12] The main residence exemption provisions in **47.2–47.10** above also apply in relation to a gain accruing to the trustees of a settlement on a disposal of settled property where, during the period of ownership of the trustees, the dwelling-house (or part) has been the only or main residence of a person entitled to occupy it under the terms of the settlement.

In the application of those provisions, references to the individual are taken as references to the trustees except in relation to the occupation of the dwelling-house, residence in a territory and meeting the day count test at **47.8** above. References to an individual being, or being the spouse or civil partner of, a disabled person or long-term resident in a care home are taken as references to the person entitled under the settlement so being. Any *s 222(5)* election for main residence treatment under **47.10** above must be made jointly by the trustees and the person entitled to occupy. Any *s 222A* election under **47.10** above given by the trustees must be accompanied by a written notification from the beneficiary agreeing to its terms.

The trustees must make a claim for exemption to apply in this way.

[*TCGA 1992, ss 225, 225E(7)*].

The exemption was held to apply in *Wagstaff v HMRC* FTT, [2014] UKFTT 43 (TC).

A person is 'entitled' to occupy if they do so by permission of the trustees of a discretionary trust of which they are a beneficiary (*Sansom v Peay* Ch D 1976, 52 TC 1). See **56.4** SETTLEMENTS as to HMRC's views on whether an 'interest in possession' is created in such circumstances.

The main residence exemption provisions in **47.2–47.10** above similarly apply in relation to a gain accruing to personal representatives provided that:

(a) *immediately before and after* the deceased's death the dwelling-house (or part) was the only or main residence of one or more individuals, one or more of whom have a 'relevant entitlement'; and
(b) the aggregate relevant entitlements of those individuals account for at least 75% of the 'net proceeds of disposal' of the property.

For this purpose, a '*relevant entitlement*' is an entitlement as legatee of the deceased to, or to an interest in possession in, the whole or any part of the net proceeds of disposal. The '*net proceeds of disposal*' are the disposal proceeds realised by the personal representatives less any incidental costs allowable as a deduction under *TCGA 1992, s 38(1)(c)* (see **16.12** COMPUTATION OF GAINS AND LOSSES) but on the assumption that none of the proceeds is needed to meet the liabilities of the estate, including any inheritance tax liability.

In the application of the provisions, references to the individual are taken as references to the personal representatives except in relation to the occupation of the dwelling-house (or part), residence in a territory and meeting the day count test at **47.8** above. Any *s 222(5)* election for main residence treatment under **47.10** above must be made jointly by the personal representatives and the individuals entitled to occupy. Any *s 222A* election under **47.10** above given by the personal representatives must be accompanied by a written notification from the individuals entitled to occupy agreeing to its terms.

The personal representatives must make a claim for exemption to apply in this way.

[*TCGA 1992, s 225A*].

Occupation by dependent relative

[47.13] Main residence exemption as in **47.2–47.10** above can be claimed by an individual in respect of a gain so far as it is attributable to the disposal of, or of an interest in, a dwelling-house (or part) which, on 5 April 1988 or at any earlier time in their period of ownership, was the *sole* residence of a 'dependent relative' of the individual, provided 'rent-free and without any other consideration'.

Such relief is given in respect of the dwelling-house and its garden and grounds as would be given under *TCGA 1992, ss 222–224* if the dwelling-house had been the individual's only or main residence in the period of residence by the dependent relative. Any such relief is in addition to any relief already available under those provisions. Not more than one dwelling-house (or part) may qualify for relief as the residence of a dependent relative at any one time. In the case of an individual and their spouse or civil partner living together, no more than one dwelling-house may qualify as the residence of a dependent relative of the claimant or of the claimant's spouse or civil partner at any one time.

[*TCGA 1992, s 226(1)(2)(4)*].

Where the conditions are met, periods before 6 April 1988 can qualify as periods of residence and, provided that the dependent relative occupied the dwelling-house on 5 April 1988, so can periods after that date. If, however, the dwelling-house (or part) ceases, whether before 6 April 1988 or later, to be the sole residence (provided as mentioned above) of the dependent relative, any subsequent period of residence beginning after 5 April 1988 by that or any other dependent relative does not qualify for relief. [*TCGA 1992, s 226(3)*].

The condition that the dwelling-house must have been provided 'rent-free and without any other consideration' will be regarded as satisfied where the dependent relative paid all or part of the occupier's rates or council tax and the cost of repairs to the dwelling-house attributable to normal wear and tear. In addition, the exemption will not be lost where the dependent relative made other payments in respect of the property either to the individual claiming the exemption or to a third party, provided that no net income was receivable by the individual, taking one year with another. For this purpose, the income receivable and allowable deductions will be computed in accordance with normal property business income tax rules, except that account will be taken of mortgage payments (including both income and capital elements) and of other payments made by the dependent relative as consideration for the provision of the property, whether such payments were made directly to the mortgagee or other recipient or indirectly via the individual (HMRC Extra-Statutory Concession D20).

Dependent relative

'*Dependent relative*' means, in relation to an individual:

(a) any 'relative' of the individual or of their spouse who is incapacitated by old age or infirmity from maintaining themselves, or
(b) the mother of the individual or of their spouse who, whether or not incapacitated, is widowed, separated, or a single woman in consequence of dissolution or annulment of marriage.

[*TCGA 1992, s 226(5)(6)*].

If the mother has never been married, she cannot fall within any of the categories in (b) above, but HMRC allow relief if, had she been married, one of the categories would have applied to her (HMRC Capital Gains Manual CG65579). '*Relative*' is undefined, but HMRC accept that the following are relatives: a blood relation; a person who, while under the age of 16 years was an adopted child of the claimant; the husband or wife (or widow or widower) of a blood relation; a stepbrother (or sister) and a stepson (or daughter) — whether a blood relation or not; a foster parent and a foster brother (or sister) where the foster parent had custody of and maintained the foster child at his or her own expense when the child was under the age of 16; and a blood relation of the claimant's deceased wife (or husband). (HMRC Capital Gains Manual CG65574).

Old age, according to HMRC, is reached at an age of 65 years in any case, and can be reached at an age greater than 54 years if the individual becomes, only because of age, not capable of working again 'in his own industry' (i.e. a man aged 57 years is not considered to have reached old age if he chooses not to work again or is unemployed because of a general lack of jobs). An individual is regarded as infirm if they are prevented by physical or mental illness from supporting themselves by working. (HMRC Capital Gains Manual CG65575–65577).

Exclusions from the main residence exemption

[47.14] The following exclusions from the main residence and letting exemptions described in this chapter apply.

Dwelling-house acquired for profit

The main residence exemption (see **47.2** above) and the letting exemption (see **50.15–50.17** below) do not apply to a gain if the acquisition of, or of the interest in, the dwelling-house (or part) was made wholly or partly for the purpose of realising a gain from the disposal of it. They also do not apply to a gain *so far as attributable to* any expenditure which was incurred after the beginning of the period of ownership and was incurred wholly or partly for the purpose of realising a gain from the disposal. [*TCGA 1992, s 224(3); FA 2020, s 24(6)*].

HMRC's practice is not to take into account expenditure incurred in obtaining planning permission or in removing restrictive covenants when considering whether to apply the second of these rules.

The two most common applications of the second rule are:

- acquisition by a leaseholder of a superior interest in the property, and
- conversion of an undivided house into self-contained flats.

(HMRC Capital Gains Manual CG65243).

In *Jones v Wilcock* (Sp C 92), [1996] SSCD 389, a married couple incurred a loss on the sale of their house. They contended that the loss was an allowable loss because a gain would have been a chargeable gain as the house had been purchased 'wholly or partly for the purpose of realising a gain'. However, from the facts of the case, it was decided that the house was purchased to be used as the couple's home.

Relief obtained under *TCGA 1992, s 260* on earlier disposal

Anti-avoidance provisions apply to prevent perceived historical exploitation of the interaction between the exemption for private residences and hold-over relief under *TCGA 1992, s 260* (see **30.10** HOLD-OVER RELIEFS). Subject to the transitional rules below, the provisions apply where:

- exemption under *s 223* would otherwise be available in relation to a gain (or part of a gain) accruing after 9 December 2003 to an individual or the trustees of a settlement on a disposal (the '*later disposal*'), and
- in computing the chargeable gain which would (apart from *s 223*) accrue on that disposal, the allowable expenditure falls to be reduced to any extent in consequence, directly or indirectly, of a claim or claims under *s 260* in respect of one or more earlier disposals (whether or not made to the person making the later disposal).

Where the claim to relief under *s 260* in respect of the earlier disposal (or, if there is more than one earlier disposal, any of them) is made on or before the making of the later disposal (or, in the case of trustees, on or before the making of a claim for relief under *s 223*), the main residence exemption does not apply in relation to the gain (or part of the gain) on the later disposal. Where the claim (or any of the claims) is made after the later disposal (or claim for the main residence exemption), the exemption is treated as never having applied to the gain (or part of the gain) on the later disposal and any adjustments required, whether by assessment, discharge or repayment of tax or otherwise, can be made notwithstanding any time limit for the making of adjustments.

Where a claim under *s 260* is revoked, it is treated for the purposes of these provisions as having never been made.

The above provisions do not apply to a later disposal made by the trustees of a settlement if they have elected for *ITA 2007, s 508* (certain income from heritage maintenance property not to be income of settlor — see Tolley's Income Tax) to apply in relation to each tax year in which there is an earlier disposal in respect of which a claim under *s 260* is made.

Transitional provisions

The above provisions are modified where the earlier disposal, or, if more than one, each of them, is made before 10 December 2003. Total exemption is excluded as above, but fractional exemption can be obtained. In calculating the fractional exemption, the dwelling-house (or part) in question is taken not to have been the individual's only or main residence at any time after 9 December 2003, and the period of ownership after that date is taken not to form part of the last nine months of the period of ownership.

[*TCGA 1992, ss 226A, 226B*].

Exemption for letting of part of main residence

[47.15] Where a gain to which fractional main residence exemption (see **47.2** above) applies accrues to an individual, further relief is available where, at any time in the period of ownership, part of the dwelling-house is the individual's only or main residence and another part is let out by them as residential accommodation.

The part of the gain which would otherwise be chargeable by reason of the letting is exempt to the extent of the lower of:

(a) £40,000; and

(b) the amount of the gain otherwise exempt under *TCGA 1992, s 223* (see **47.2** and **47.7** above).

Where an individual's period of ownership is treated as beginning with the start of the period of ownership of that individual's spouse or civil partner (see **47.2** above under 'Change in interest'), the exemption is available for periods during the spouse or partner's period of ownership when part of the dwelling-house was the spouse or partner's only or main residence and another part was let out as residential accommodation.

[*TCGA 1992, s 223B; FA 2020, s 24(5)(11)*].

These provisions do not apply to restrict an allowable loss.

The availability of the above exemption extends to gains accruing to trustees and qualifying for the main residence exemption under *TCGA 1992, s 225* (see **47.12** above).

See **50.17** below for consideration of whether let accommodation is part of the owner's dwelling-house (in which case, the above exemption will be available), or is itself a separate dwelling-house (in which case it will not).

For the capital gains tax consequences of a lodger living as part of a family and of eligibility for 'rent a room' income tax relief, see **47.9** above.

For reliefs applicable to the commercial letting of furnished holiday accommodation before April 2025, see **24** FURNISHED HOLIDAY ACCOMMODATION.

Example 1

Gino sells a house in October 2024, realising a gain before relief of £250,000. He has lived in the house as his main residence throughout his period of ownership, but throughout that period, 50% of the floor area of the house has been let as residential accommodation. His chargeable gain for 2024/25 on the house is:

	£	£
Gain before reliefs		250,000
Less: Main residence relief (50%)		(125,000)
		125,000
Less: letting relief—lowest of:		
Main residence relief	125,000	
Gain attributable to letting	125,000	
£40,000	40,000	(40,000)
Chargeable gain		£85,000

Key points

[47.16] Points to consider are as follows.

- Even if the property does not qualify as the only or main residence since 31 March 1982, such occupation before that date will provide for the last nine months of ownership to be exempt.
- Where ownership is transferred between spouses or civil partners, the previous period of occupation and exemption profile is also transferred whether or not the property was the only or main residence at the time of the transfer. This rule may be disadvantageous if the property was not exempt before the transfer (for example where it had been let out).
- Periods of absence — to gain the benefit of exempt periods of absence the property must be the only or main residence after the period of absence (unless employment elsewhere prevents occupation). The legislation does not prevent the subsequent period being the subject of an election (if it qualifies) to make it the only or main residence thus securing the extra exempt periods.
- The treatment of the family home when married couples or civil partners separate has changed for disposals on or after 6 April 2023. Where the family home is disposed of on or after that date by one spouse or partner to the other as part of the divorce or separation settlement, the disposal is treated as at no gain/no loss (see **40.4** MARRIED PERSONS AND CIVIL PARTNERS). If the marital home is sold to a third party, it continues to be the only or main residence of the departing spouse or civil partner until it is disposed of, even though that spouse or partner no longer occupies the property. A claim must be made for the latter relief to apply. A further relief applies where, as part of the divorce or separation settlement, one spouse or partner transfers their interest in the family home to the other but retains an entitlement to a share of the ultimate sale proceeds. The gain which is deemed to arise in respect of that share is treated in the same way as the gain arising on the initial transfer. It may therefore qualify for the main residence exemption or be treated as a no gain/no loss disposal.
- Where there is more than one residence an election in favour of one or other property can be beneficial. A two year window to make an election opens when there is a change in the combination of residences. Once made, an election can be varied outside this window but it should be noted that when the combination of residences again changes any existing election ceases to have effect.
- Private residence relief is not intended to relieve speculative gains or gains arising from development (**47.14**). Property owners normally expect a gain and are often willing to undertake a variety of activities to enhance a potential gain. Activities comparable to property development can create planning opportunities and pitfalls and considerable care is required. However, simply, obtaining planning permission for future alternations is often acceptable. (See CG65243).
- It is increasingly common for individuals to work from home. In such cases, a taxpayer may be keen to maximise the proportion of expenses allowable for income tax. If the fixed-rate deduction is not used, the normal method of apportionment for income tax is

based upon floor space and time used, e.g. an outbuilding designated as an office makes up 30% of floor space and is so used 100% of the time. Where an area is used **exclusively** for business purposes, private residence relief is restricted. It is important when considering income tax claims to remember the impact exclusive use will have on the capital gains tax exemption. If practical and possible, retaining a reasonable element of private use may in the long term be preferable.

- If a property was occupied by a 'dependent relative' before 6 April 1988 or by a beneficiary of a settlement then some period of exemption may apply.

48

Qualifying Corporate Bonds

Simon's Taxes. See **C3.1814A, D6.111–D6.115.**

Introduction to qualifying corporate bonds

[48.1] Gains on qualifying corporate bonds (QCBs) are exempt from tax on chargeable gains. This chapter describes the exemption and also the special provisions which apply to reorganisations of share capital where either the original shares or the new shares are qualifying corporate bonds.

The definition of a qualifying corporate bond is also given. Different rules apply for corporation tax and capital gains tax purposes. For corporation tax purposes, any asset representing a loan relationship of a company is a qualifying corporate bond. For capital gains tax, broadly, a qualifying corporate bond is a security on which the debt is a normal commercial loan and which is expressed in sterling with no provision for its conversion into, or redemption in, another currency. See **48.3** below for the detailed provisions.

See **38.12** LOSSES for allowable loss relief in respect of certain qualifying corporate bonds evidencing loans made before 17 March 1998 which become irrecoverable etc.

Exemption rules for QCBs

[48.2] A gain on the disposal of a qualifying corporate bond (as defined in **48.3** below) is not a chargeable gain, and a loss is not an allowable loss. [*TCGA 1992, s 115(1)(a)*].

The same applies to disposals of options or contracts to acquire or dispose of qualifying corporate bonds (see **7.7, 7.8** ASSETS).

See **48.4** below re share capital reorganisations involving qualifying corporate bonds.

QCBs — definitions

[48.3] Different definitions apply for the purposes of corporation tax and capital gains tax.

Corporation tax

For corporation tax purposes 'qualifying corporate bond' means *any* asset representing a loan relationship of a company (see **15.5** COMPANIES — CORPORATE FINANCE AND INTANGIBLES).

[*TCGA 1992, s 117(A1)*].

Capital gains tax

Definition of corporate bond

Before defining a 'qualifying corporate bond', it is first necessary to define a 'corporate bond'. Subject to the specific inclusion of certain securities within this definition (see below) and the exclusion of some (again, see below), a '*corporate bond*' is a 'security' which fulfils both the following conditions.

(a) The debt on the security represents, and has at all times represented, a 'normal commercial loan'.
'*Normal commercial loan*' is as would be defined by *CTA 2010, s 162* if, for *subsection (2)(a)–(c)* of that section, there were substituted the words 'corporate bonds (within the meaning of *TCGA 1992, s 117*)'. The broad effect of the modification is that securities can be treated as corporate bonds if they carry conversion rights into other corporate bonds but not if the conversion rights relate to securities other than corporate bonds. Securities carrying an indirect right of conversion into ordinary shares were held not to be corporate bonds in *Weston v Garnett* CA, [2005] STC 1134.

(b) The security is expressed in sterling and no provision is made for its conversion into, or redemption in, a currency other than sterling.
A security is *not* treated as expressed in sterling if the amount of sterling falls to be determined by reference to the value at any time of any other currency or asset. A provision for redemption in a currency other than sterling is disregarded provided the rate of exchange to be used is that prevailing at redemption.
Securities carrying an option for redemption in a foreign currency do not become corporate bonds when the option lapses (*Harding v HMRC* CA, [2008] STC 3499). In *Blumenthal v HMRC* FTT, [2012] SFTD 1264, however, the variation of the terms of securities to remove an option for redemption in a foreign currency was held to have the effect of converting the securities into corporate bonds. In *Trigg v HMRC* CA 2017, [2018] STC 281, bonds which were denominated in sterling but which had been issued with a provision for their conversion into euros if the UK were to adopt the euro were held to be qualifying corporate bonds notwithstanding the provision.

'*Security*' includes any loan stock or similar security of any government or public or local authority in the UK or elsewhere, or of any company, and whether secured or unsecured.

[*TCGA 1992, ss 117(1)(2), 132(3)(b)*].

Inclusion of other securities within the definition of corporate bond

A deeply discounted security (within **57.21** SHARES AND SECURITIES) is a corporate bond (and is also a qualifying corporate bond — see below). [*TCGA 1992, s 117(2AA)*].

Save in relation to the application of this definition for the purposes of *TCGA 1992, s 254* (loss relief for irrecoverable loans made before 17 March 1998 to traders and evidenced by qualifying corporate bonds — see **38.12** LOSSES), 'corporate bond' also includes a share in a building society (within *Building Societies Act 1986*) which meets the condition in (b) above and which is a 'qualifying share' (i.e. a share which is either a 'permanent interest bearing share', as defined, or is of a description specified in Treasury regulations for this purpose). [*TCGA 1992, s 117(4)–(6), (11)(b), (12), (13)*].

'Corporate bond' also includes any debenture issued after 15 March 1993 which is not a 'security' as defined above but would fall to be treated as such under *TCGA 1992, s 251(6)* (see **23.5** EXEMPTIONS AND RELIEFS). This does not apply to debentures acquired by a person following a prior disposal of a qualifying corporate bond derived from shares giving rise to a deferred gain (where the general exemption in *TCGA 1992, s 115* has had effect in accordance with *TCGA 1992, s 116(10)(c)* — see **48.4** below). (This provision and *TCGA 1992, s 251(6)* prevent, in certain circumstances, the issue of a debenture which neither represents a debt on a security nor is a qualifying corporate bond.) [*TCGA 1992, s 117(6A)*].

An alternative finance arrangement which is an investment bond arrangement within *TCGA 1992, s 151N* (see **3.3** ALTERNATIVE FINANCE ARRANGEMENTS) is a 'corporate bond' if:

- the 'capital' is expressed in sterling;
- the arrangements do not include provision for the 'redemption payment' to be in a currency other than sterling;
- entitlement to the redemption payment is not capable of conversion into an entitlement to the issue of securities other than other such arrangements; and
- the 'additional payments' are not determined wholly or partly by reference to the value of the bond assets.

For this purpose, '*capital*', '*redemption payment*' and '*additional payments*' are all defined as at **3.3** ALTERNATIVE FINANCE ARRANGEMENTS.

[*TCGA 1992, ss 117(6D), 151T*].

Securities excluded from being corporate bonds

An excluded indexed security (as defined by *ITTOIA 2005, s 433* and meaning broadly a security the amount payable on redemption of which is linked to the value of chargeable assets) issued after 5 April 1996 is not a corporate bond. An excluded indexed security issued before that date is a corporate bond only if it satisfies the general conditions above and if the question of whether or not it is a corporate bond arises only for the purposes of *TCGA 1992, s 116(10)* (reorganisation of share capital involving the issue of a qualifying corporate bond — see **48.4** below). [*TCGA 1992, s 117(6B)(6C)*].

Definition of qualifying corporate bond

A corporate bond:

(A) is a '*qualifying corporate bond*' if it is issued after 13 March 1984; and
(B) becomes a '*qualifying corporate bond*' if, having been issued before 14 March 1984, it is acquired by any person after 13 March 1984 unless
  (i) the acquisition is as the result of *any* disposal treated as a no gain/no loss transaction or a disposal where the consideration is reduced by an amount of held-over gain under *TCGA 1992, s 165* or *s 260* (see **30.2–30.12** HOLD-OVER RELIEFS); and
  (ii) the bond was not a qualifying corporate bond before the disposal.

[*TCGA 1992, s 117(7)(8)*].

See the example below.

Where a right to a security is comprised in a provisional letter of allotment or similar instrument, the security is not deemed to be issued until acceptance has been made. [*TCGA 1992, s 117(11)(a)*].

A security which is a corporate bond due to its being a deeply discounted security (see above) is a qualifying corporate bond whatever its date of issue. [*TCGA 1992, s 117(8A)*].

Example

B has the following transactions in 5% unsecured loan stock issued in 1983 by F Ltd.

		£
11.11.83	Purchase £2,000	1,800
10.7.89	Gift from wife £1,000 (original cost £800)	—
30.9.97	Purchase £2,000	2,100
5.6.24	Sale £4,000	(3,300)

Apart from the gift on 10.7.89, all acquisitions were arm's length purchases. B's wife acquired her £1,000 holding on 11.11.83. Indexation allowance of £266 arose on the transfer from wife to husband.

For the purposes of the accrued income scheme, the sale is without accrued interest and the rebate amount is £20. The stock is a corporate bond as defined by *TCGA 1992, s 117(1)* and therefore a 'relevant security'.

Under the rules for matching relevant securities in *TCGA 1992, s 106A* (see **58.2** SHARES AND SECURITIES — IDENTIFICATION RULES), the stock disposed of is identified with acquisitions as follows.

(i) Identify £2,000 with purchase on 30.9.97 (LIFO)

		£
Disposal consideration	$£3,300 \times \frac{2,000}{4,000}$	1,650
Add rebate amount	$£20 \times \frac{2,000}{4,000}$	10
		1,660
Allowable cost		2,100
Loss		£440

The loss is *not* allowable as the £2,000 stock purchased on 30.9.97 is a qualifying corporate bond (note (a)). [*TCGA 1992, s 115*].

(ii) Identify £1,000 with acquisition on 10.7.89

		£
Disposal consideration	$£3,300 \times \frac{1,000}{4,000}$	825
Add rebate amount	$£20 \times \frac{1,000}{4,000}$	5
		830
Allowable cost (including indexation to 10.7.89)		1,066
Allowable loss		£236

The loss is allowable as the stock acquired on 10.7.89 is not a qualifying corporate bond (note (b)).

(iii) Identify £1,000 with part of purchase on 11.11.83

		£
Disposal consideration	$£3,300 \times \frac{1,000}{4,000}$	825
Add rebate amount	$£20 \times \frac{1,000}{4,000}$	5
		830
Allowable cost	$£1,800 \times \frac{1,000}{4,000}$	900
Allowable loss		£70

The loss is allowable as the stock acquired on 11.11.83 is not a qualifying corporate bond (note (c)).

Notes to the example

(a) The acquisition on 30.9.97 is a qualifying corporate bond as it was acquired after 13 March 1984 otherwise than as a result of an excluded disposal.

(b) The acquisition on 10.7.89 was the result of an excluded disposal, being a no gain/no loss transfer between spouses where the first spouse had acquired the stock before 14 March 1984. It is therefore not a qualifying corporate bond.

(c) Securities acquired before 14 March 1984 cannot be qualifying corporate bonds in the hands of the person who so acquired them.

Reorganisation of share capital involving QCBs

[48.4] Special provisions apply to a transaction ('*relevant transaction*') where otherwise *TCGA 1992, ss 127–130* (share reorganisation rules for 'original shares' and 'new holding'; see **57.2** SHARES AND SECURITIES) would apply under any provision contained in *TCGA 1992, Pt IV Ch II* (reorganisation of share capital, conversion of securities etc.), and either the original shares would consist of or include a qualifying corporate bond and the new holding would not, or the original shares would not and the new holding would consist of or include such a bond.

The provisions apply equally to a conversion of securities effected other than by means of a transaction, for example in consequence of the terms of the security. Where the qualifying corporate bond would constitute the original shares it is referred to as '*the old asset*', the shares and securities constituting the new holding being referred to as '*the new asset*'. Where the qualifying corporate bond would constitute the new holding it is referred to as '*the new asset*', the shares and securities constituting the original shares being referred to as '*the old asset*'.

TCGA 1992, ss 127–130 do not apply to the relevant transaction so far as it relates to the old asset and the new asset. Where shares are exchanged, converted etc. for a new holding consisting partly of qualifying corporate bonds and partly of shares etc., then *TCGA 1992, ss 127–130* are only disapplied to the extent that the consideration takes the form of qualifying corporate bonds, any apportionment of the base cost of the original shares being on a just and reasonable basis under *TCGA 1992, s 52(4)* by reference to the respective market values at the time of exchange of the shares etc. and qualifying corporate bonds received in exchange etc. (HMRC Capital Gains Manual CG53718).

Where the qualifying corporate bond would constitute the old asset, the shares or securities which constitute the new asset are to be treated as being acquired on the date of the relevant transaction and for a consideration of the market value of the old asset immediately before the relevant transaction. Similar provisions apply where the qualifying corporate bond constitutes the new asset. Where a sum of money by way of consideration for the old asset is received, in addition to the new asset, that sum is to be deducted from the deemed market value consideration and where a sum of money is paid by way of consideration, in addition to the old asset, that sum is to be added to the deemed market value consideration. See also (ii) below.

Old asset consisting of qualifying corporate bond

Where the old asset consists of a qualifying corporate bond, then so far as it relates to the old and the new asset, the relevant transaction is to be treated as a disposal of the old asset and an acquisition of the new asset. [*TCGA 1992, s 116(9)*].

Other cases

In all other cases (e.g. where the new asset consists of a qualifying corporate bond) then so far as it relates to the old asset and to the new asset the relevant transaction is *not* to be treated as a disposal of the old asset but:

(a) the chargeable gain or allowable loss is calculated that would have accrued had the old asset been disposed of at the time of the relevant transaction at its market value immediately before that time, and

(b) subject to the exclusions below, the whole or a corresponding part of the calculated chargeable gain or allowable loss at (a) above is to be deemed to accrue on a subsequent disposal of the whole or part of the new asset. The exemption provided by **48.2** above applies only to the gain or loss that actually accrues on that disposal and not to the gain or loss that is deemed to accrue. [*TCGA 1992, s 116(10)*].

Exclusions

The following exclusions are made to the above provisions.

(i) The provisions in (b) above do not apply to disposals falling within: *TCGA 1992, s 58(1)* (see **40.4** MARRIED PERSONS AND CIVIL PARTNERS); *s 62(4)* (see **18.14** DEATH); *s 139* (see **14.12** COMPANIES); *s 140A* (see **43.12** OVERSEAS MATTERS); *s 140E* (see **43.14** OVERSEAS MATTERS); *s 171(1)* (see **26.3** GROUPS OF COMPANIES). Where there is such a disposal (and without there having been a previous disposal other than such a disposal or a devolution on death) the person who has acquired the new asset is treated for the purposes of (b) above as if the new asset had been acquired by him at the same time and for the same consideration as it was acquired by the person making the disposal.

(ii) Where a chargeable gain arises under (a) above and part of the consideration for the old asset is received as money, a proportion of the chargeable gain is deemed to accrue at that time. The proportion is the ratio which the sum of money bears to the market value of the old asset immediately before the relevant transaction. On a later disposal of a part or the whole of the new asset, the proportion already deemed to have accrued is to be deducted from the gain accruing under (b) above. However, if the sum of money is 'small' in comparison with the market value of the old asset immediately before the relevant transaction, HMRC may direct that no chargeable gain accrues at that time. The money consideration is then deducted from allowable expenditure on any subsequent disposal (see **10.3** CAPITAL SUMS DERIVED FROM ASSETS).

For the purpose of the above, HMRC regard 'small' as meaning 5% or less and also regard an amount of £3,000 or less as 'small', regardless of whether or not it would pass the 5% test (HMRC Capital Gains Manual CG53717, 57835).

(iii) The treatment at (a) and (b) above) is disapplied in certain circumstances (with the result that the transaction is treated as a disposal of the old asset and an acquisition of the new asset) where the old asset consists of shares or securities that have qualified for tax relief under the corporate venturing scheme or the community investment tax credit scheme. See **19.7** CORPORATE VENTURING SCHEME and Tolley's Income Tax under Community Investment Tax Relief. See also **60.12** SUBSTANTIAL SHAREHOLDINGS OF COMPANIES.

[*TCGA 1992, s 116(1)–(14)*].

In *Hancock v HMRC* SC, [2019] STC 1084, a married couple held the entire share capital of a company (B). In 2000 they sold the shares to another company (L), receiving loan notes as consideration. The terms of issue of the loan notes included a provision enabling the noteholders to require repayment in US dollars, which prevented the loan notes from constituting qualifying corporate bonds within *TCGA 1992, s 117*. The sale agreement also included provision for further consideration depending on the subsequent performance of B's business. In 2001 the couple received further loan notes under this provision. These further notes initially also included a provision enabling the noteholders to require repayment in US dollars, but that provision was removed by deeds of variation in 2002, with the result that these further notes did constitute qualifying corporate bonds. In May 2003 the couple exchanged both their QCB and non-QCB holdings of loan notes for further loan notes, which constituted qualifying corporate bonds, and which were redeemed in June 2003. HMRC issued assessments charging CGT under *TCGA 1992, s 116*. The couple appealed. They contended that there had been only one conversion so that the original gain (realised on the disposal of the shares) had been rolled into exempt qualifying corporate bonds. The Upper Tribunal found however that the overall structure of the provisions suggested that each conversion was a different transaction and that each original single asset or single security should be treated as the subject of a conversion. The Tribunal therefore concluded that the conversion of the first set of loan notes into the further loan notes was a conversion to which *s 116(1)* applied so that on their redemption, the frozen gain was realised, triggering a taxable gain calculated at the earlier point of the removal of the dollar redemption provision. The Supreme Court upheld the decision that the transaction should be treated as two separate conversions so that the gain did not disappear. It acknowledged the strength of the appellants' argument that *s 116* contemplates the possibility of a single transaction 'which involves a pre-conversion holding of both QCBs and non-QCBs'. But the Court also observed that if the appellants' interpretation was correct, taxpayers would be able to use the roll-over provisions to avoid CGT, rather than defer it, with 'extreme ease'. The Court added that the word 'include' in *s 116(1)(b)* made it clear that 'the intention of Parliament was that each security converted into a QCB should be viewed as a separate conversion.'

Miscellaneous

See also **60.18** SUBSTANTIAL SHAREHOLDINGS OF COMPANIES.

Where the new asset is a qualifying corporate bond which is subsequently gifted to a charity (within **11.5** CHARITIES), HMRC take the view that no deferred gain or loss will arise to the donor (or the charity) under (b) above (HMRC Capital Gains Manual CG66624).

A special rule has effect where, before 15 February 1999, there occurred a transaction (the original transaction) to which *TCGA 1992, ss 127–130* applied and the new holding consisted of or included something (the new asset) which becomes a 'deeply discounted security' (and thus a qualifying corporate bond — see **48.3** above) by virtue of the widening of the definition of that term to take further account of potential redemptions before maturity (see **57.21** SHARES AND SECURITIES). In relation to any disposal or part disposal of the new asset after 14 February 1999, there is deemed to have been a transaction subsequent to the original transaction whereby the holder of the new asset disposed of it and immediately re-acquired it. The re-acquired asset is deemed to consist of a qualifying corporate bond and the subsequent transaction is deemed to be one to which *TCGA 1992, s 116* applies, with the same consequences as in (a) and (b) above. The subsequent transaction is deemed to have occurred immediately after the original transaction, except that where the original transaction occurred before 5 April 1996 the subsequent transaction is deemed to have occurred on that date. [*FA 1999, s 66*].

See **38.12** LOSSES for the interaction of the provisions above with the now repealed provisions relating to loss relief by reference to certain qualifying corporate bonds evidencing loans which become irrecoverable etc.

Example

D holds 5,000 £1 ordinary shares in H Ltd. He acquired the shares in April 2001 by subscription at par. On 1 August 2010, he accepted an offer for the shares from J plc. The terms of the offer were one 25p ordinary share of J plc and £10 J plc 10% unsecured loan stock (a qualifying corporate bond) for each H Ltd ordinary share. Both the shares and the loan stock are listed on the Stock Exchange. In December 2024, D sells £20,000 loan stock at its quoted price of £105 per cent.

The value of J plc ordinary shares at 1 August 2010 was £3.52 per share and the loan stock was £99.20 per cent.

The cost of the H Ltd shares must be apportioned between the J plc ordinary shares and loan stock.

	£
Value of J plc shares	
5,000 × £3.52	17,600
Value of J plc loan stock	
£50,000 × 99.2%	49,600
	£67,200
Allowable cost of J plc shares	

$$\frac{17,600}{67,200} \times £5,000 \qquad £1,310$$

Allowable cost of J plc loan stock

$$\frac{49,600}{67,200} \times £5,000 \qquad £3,690$$

Chargeable gain on H Ltd shares attributable to J plc loan stock to date of exchange

	£
Deemed disposal consideration	49,600
Allowable cost	3,690
Deferred chargeable gain	£45,910

Deferred chargeable gain accruing on disposal of loan stock in December 2024

Loan stock sold (nominal)	£20,000
Total holding of loan stock before disposal (nominal)	£50,000

Deferred chargeable gain accruing in 2024/25

$$\frac{20,000}{50,000} \times £45,910 \qquad £18,364$$

Notes to the example

(a) The gain on the sale of J plc loan stock is exempt (as the stock is a qualifying corporate bond) except for that part which relates to the gain on the previous holding of H Ltd shares. [*TCGA 1992, ss 115, 116(10)*]. There will also be income tax consequences under the accrued income scheme.

(b) The qualifying corporate bond is treated as acquired at the date of the reorganisation, so even if the original shares had been held at 31 March 1982, re-basing would *not* apply on the subsequent disposal of the loan stock.

(c) The exchange of J plc ordinary shares for H Ltd shares is dealt with under *TCGA 1992, ss 127–130* (see **57.2** SHARES AND SECURITIES), and no gain or loss will arise until the J plc shares are disposed of.

49

Remittance Basis

Cross-references. See **7.3** ASSETS for the location of assets; **20.5** DOUBLE TAX RELIEF for relief available where remittance basis applies; **43.6** OVERSEAS MATTERS for relief available where overseas gains are unremittable to the UK; **51** RESIDENCE AND DOMICILE.

Simon's Taxes. See **C1.603, E6.324A–E6.333B.**

Introduction to the remittance basis

[49.1] UK residents are, subject to any DOUBLE TAX RELIEF (**20**), normally liable to capital gains tax on the whole of their worldwide chargeable gains arising in a tax year (the arising basis). The remittance basis is available to UK resident individuals who are not domiciled in the UK. In most cases (but see **49.2** below), the individual must also not be deemed domiciled in the UK (see **51.29** RESIDENCE AND DOMICILE) for the remittance basis to apply. The remittance basis provides for foreign source chargeable gains to be charged to tax by reference to the extent to which they are remitted to, or received in, the UK. The government intends to abolish the remittance basis from 6 April 2025 (see below).

A claim for the remittance basis is required in most cases. The claim applies for income tax purposes also. An individual who claims the remittance basis loses entitlement to the annual exempt amount and, if he is a 'long-term UK resident', he is also liable to an additional tax charge (see **49.5** below). See **49.2–49.5** below.

HMRC's views on the practical operation of the remittance basis are contained in HMRC Capital Gains Manual CG25300–25431.

Abolition of remittance basis

As noted above, the government has announced its intention to abolish the remittance basis from 6 April 2025. It is expected that it will be replaced by a new regime linked to the number of years of UK residency.

Under the new regime, individuals will not be taxed in the UK on their foreign income and gains for the first four tax years of UK residency. They will be free to bring the foreign income and gains arising in those tax years to the UK without suffering a UK tax liability, in a departure from the existing remittance basis rules. They will also not pay tax on non-resident trust distributions. They will not however be entitled to a UK personal allowance or annual exempt amount. From the fifth year, the individual will be fully taxable on their worldwide income and gains.

Years of UK tax residency under the statutory residence test prior to 6 April 2025 will be counted when deciding whether the individual qualifies for the new regime. However, split tax years and years of treaty residence will be ignored for these purposes.

The following transitional rules are expected to apply.

- Individuals paying tax on the remittance basis who are not eligible for the new foreign income and gains regime will be taxed in the UK on 50% of their foreign income arising in 2025/26. For 2026/27 onwards, UK tax will be due on all worldwide income and gains in the normal way.
- Individuals who have claimed the remittance basis and are not UK domiciled or deemed domiciled by 5 April 2025 who become taxable on their worldwide income and gains can choose to rebase any chargeable assets held on 5 April 2019 to that date. It is unclear whether the individual can choose to rebase assets on an asset-by-asset basis or whether it will be an election that covers all assets held at 5 April 2019.
- Individuals who have been taxed on the remittance basis will be able to elect to pay UK tax at a reduced rate of 12% on remittances of pre-6 April 2025 foreign income and gains under a temporary repatriation facility that will be available for 2025/26 and 2026/27 only. The facility will not apply to pre-6 April 2025 foreign income and gains generated within trusts and trust structures.

To the extent that previously unremitted income and gains are not brought to the UK under the temporary repatriation facility and are instead remitted later, these will continue to be taxed on the remittance basis.

See www.gov.uk/government/publications/changes-to-the-taxation-of-non-uk-domiciled-individuals/technical-note-changes-to-the-taxation-of-non-uk-domiciled-individuals.

The remittance basis for 2008/09 and subsequent years

[49.2] Chargeable gains ('*foreign chargeable gains*') arising to an individual in a tax year on the disposal of assets situated outside the UK are taxed on the remittance basis if the individual is resident in the UK for that year but not domiciled in the UK in that year and:

(a) they make a claim for the remittance basis to apply under *ITA 2007, s 809B*; or

(b) their 'unremitted foreign income and gains' for the year are less than £2,000; or

(c) they have no UK income or gains for the year other than taxed investment income (as defined) not exceeding £100, no relevant foreign income or gains are remitted to the UK in that year (see below) and either they are under 18 throughout the year or they have been UK residents in not more than six of the immediately preceding nine tax years.

For 2017/18 and subsequent tax years, the individual must also not be deemed domiciled in the UK in that tax year (see **51.29** RESIDENCE AND DOMICILE) in order to make a claim under (a) above, or for the automatic remittance basis treatment under (c) above to apply. The remittance basis *does* still apply automatically in the case of (b) above for an individual who is deemed domiciled in the UK, but who is not domiciled in the UK under general law.

Where the above applies, the remittance basis applies for the year concerned for both capital gains tax and income tax purposes. Where (a) above applies, the remittance basis is subject to the charge on nominated income or chargeable gains at **49.5** below. Where (b) or (c) above apply, the individual can notify HMRC in their tax return for that year that the remittance basis is not to apply.

If the tax year is a split year under the statutory residence test (see **51.17** RESIDENCE AND DOMICILE), foreign chargeable gains arising in the overseas part of the year are not taxed on the remittance basis regardless of the part of the year in which they are remitted; such gains are either exempt or chargeable under the provisions for temporary non-residents (see **43.5** OVERSEAS MATTERS) or for disposals of UK land.

In (b) above, an individual's '*unremitted foreign income and gains*' for a tax year are his 'foreign income and gains' for the year less so much of those income and gains as are remitted to the UK in that year. In (c) above, the foreign income and gains which must not be remitted to the UK in the year are any foreign income and gains for that year, for every other year for which (a), (b) or (c) above apply and every year before 2008/09 in which the taxpayer was UK resident but was not UK domiciled. An individual's '*foreign income and gains*' for a tax year are:

(i) chargeable overseas earnings (within *ITEPA 2003, s 23*);
(ii) non-UK general earnings within *ITEPA 2003, s 26(1)*;
(iii) foreign securities income within *ITEPA 2003, s 41F* (previously *ITEPA 2003, s 41A*);
(iv) amounts chargeable as disguised remuneration under *ITEPA 2003, ss 554Z9(2)* or *553Z10(2)*;
(v) relevant foreign income within *ITTOIA 2005, s 830* (but for 2007/08 and earlier years, relevant foreign income is included only if the remittance basis applied to that income); and
(vi) where he is not domiciled in the UK, chargeable gains on the disposal of foreign assets.

[*TCGA 1992, s 12(1)(1A)(4); ITA 2007, ss 809B–809E, 809Z7*].

Chargeable gains treated as accruing to an individual under *TCGA 1992, s 87* in 2008/09 or a subsequent year are foreign chargeable gains regardless of the location of the assets disposed of. See **42.14** OFFSHORE SETTLEMENTS.

Effect of remittance basis

Chargeable gains are treated as accruing to the individual at the time in any tax year at which any of the foreign chargeable gains are remitted to the UK. If the tax year is a split year under the statutory residence test (see **51.17** RESIDENCE AND DOMICILE) this means that the gains are treated as accruing in the part of the year (i.e. the UK part of the year or the overseas part of the year) in which the gains are remitted. The amount of the gains treated as accruing is equal to the full amount of those gains remitted. [*TCGA 1992, Sch 1 paras 1, 5*]. Where the remittance basis applied for 2007/08 or an earlier year and gains arising in any such year are not remitted to the UK before 6 April 2008, this provision applies to those gains for 2008/09 onwards as if the taxpayer had made a claim under (a) above for the year in which the gain arose. [*FA 2008, Sch 7 para 84*].

For the circumstances in which chargeable gains are treated as remitted to the UK, see **49.3** below.

Annual exempt amount

No annual exempt amount (see **2.5** ANNUAL RATES AND EXEMPTIONS) is available for a tax year in respect of which a claim for the remittance basis under (a) above has been made. [*TCGA 1992, s 1K(6)*].

Losses

An individual who is not domiciled in the UK who claims the remittance basis (see (a) above) for the first time can make an irrevocable election for the year concerned so that the following provisions apply in that and subsequent years. From 2017/18, the deemed domicile rules apply here (see **51.29** RESIDENCE AND DOMICILE). If no such election is made in respect of that year, losses accruing in that year and any subsequent year (other than one in which he is domiciled in the UK) on the disposal of assets situated outside the UK ('*foreign losses*') are not allowable losses.

If an individual has made such an election, but then later, in a tax year (from 2017/18 onwards) becomes domiciled in the UK (for example, by becoming deemed domiciled through long-term residence), the election no longer applies to that or subsequent tax years. However, from 2017/18, the election can also be made by an individual who is not domiciled in the UK, in the first tax year in which they claim the remittance basis following a period of UK domicile. Therefore, an individual whose previous election lapsed on becoming UK domiciled, is not prevented from making the election again once the conditions are met.

The election must be made within the normal time limit for CLAIMS (**13.5**). [*TCGA 1992, s 16ZA*].

Gains remitted in tax year after year in which they accrue

Where an election has effect, allowable losses and the annual exempt amount (where available) cannot be set off against chargeable gains treated as accruing as a result of the remittance to the UK of foreign chargeable gains in a year subsequent to that in which they arose. (The gains may, however, already have been reduced by losses matched with them — see below.) [*TCGA 1992, s 1K(3), Sch 1 para 2*].

Calculation of taxable amount for year to which remittance basis applies

Where an election has effect, the amount on which an individual who is not domiciled in the UK is charged to capital gains tax in respect of a year to which the remittance basis applies under (a)–(c) above is calculated as follows.

Step 1.

Allowable losses (including brought forward losses) are matched with chargeable gains (excluding gains attributed under *TCGA 1992, ss 87, 87K, 87L* or *89(2)* (see **42.13** OFFSHORE SETTLEMENTS)) in the following order:

(I) foreign chargeable gains arising in the year and remitted to the UK in the year or, where the year is a split year under the statutory residence test (see **51.17** RESIDENCE AND DOMICILE), the UK part of the year;
(II) foreign chargeable gains arising in the year but either not remitted to the UK or, where the year is a split year, remitted to the UK in the overseas part of the year; and
(III) all other chargeable gains arising in the year (other than gains treated as accruing on the remittance to the UK of foreign chargeable gains arising in a previous year).

If the losses reduce but do not exhaust gains within (II) above, the losses are matched with those gains in reverse chronological order (starting with the last gain to arise in the year). Where necessary, losses are deducted from gains arising on the same day on a pro rata basis.

Step 2.

Only the amounts matched in Step 1 with gains within (I) and (III) above are deducted as allowable losses in calculating the amount on which the individual is chargeable to capital gains tax for the year.

Any losses matched with gains under Step 1 above cannot be carried forward, but where a loss is matched with a foreign chargeable gain within (II) above, the amount of that gain is reduced by the matched amount (so that relief for the loss is effectively obtained if the gain is subsequently remitted to the UK).

[*TCGA 1992, Sch 1 paras 3, 4*].

Example

Danish is a resident but not domiciled in the UK. He claims the remittance basis for the first time in 2023/24 and also claims that basis for 202/25. He makes the following gains and losses.

2023/24	£
Foreign chargeable gain — remitted to the UK in 2024/25	£20,000
2024/25	
Foreign chargeable gain — remitted to the UK in 2024/25	£10,000
Foreign chargeable gain — not remitted to the UK	£12,000
Foreign loss	£27,000
UK chargeable gain	£25,000

If Danish makes an election under *TCGA 1992, s 16ZA* for 2023/24, his chargeable gains computation for 2024/25 is as follows.

Matching of allowable loss with gains

£

(i)	2024/25 foreign gain remitted in 2024/25	10,000
(ii)	2024/25 foreign gain not remitted to UK	12,000
(iii)	2024/25 UK chargeable gain (part)	5,000
		£27,000

Chargeable gains 2024/25	
2023/24 foreign gain remitted in 2024/25	20,000
2024/25 foreign gain remitted in 2024/25	10,000
UK chargeable gain	25,000
	55,000
Less allowable loss (£10,000 + £5,000)	15,000
Taxable gains	£40,000

Notes to the example

(a) Danish is not entitled to the annual exempt amount for 2024/25 (or 2023/24).

(b) The part of the loss (£12,000) which is allocated against the foreign gain not remitted to the UK may be given effect by reducing that gain to nil if it is remitted to the UK in a subsequent year.

Chargeable gains remitted to the UK

[49.3] Subject to the exceptions below, an individual's chargeable gains are remitted to the UK in any of circumstances (a)–(c) below.

(a) Property (which may include money) is brought to, or received or used in, the UK by, or for the benefit of, a 'relevant person' or a service is provided in the UK to, or for the benefit of, a relevant person, and
  - (i) the property, service or consideration for the service (as the case may be) is (wholly or in part) the gains; or
  - (ii) the property, service or consideration derives from the gains and, in the case of property or consideration, is property of a relevant person or consideration given by a relevant person; or
  - (iii) gains are used outside the UK (directly or indirectly) in respect of a 'relevant debt'; or
  - (iv) anything deriving from the gains is used as mentioned in (iii) above.

  The references in (ii) and (iv) above to something 'deriving from the gains' are references to its so deriving wholly or in part and directly or indirectly.

  Property is brought to the UK where there is a direct transfer of funds from an offshore bank account to a UK bank account (*Alimahomed v HMRC* FTT, [2024] UKFTT 432 (TC). In that case also, the use of an offshore credit card to make purchases in the UK created a relevant debt within (iii) above, so that payment of the card with an offshore bank account amounted to the use of income or gains outside the UK in respect of a relevant debt.

(b) 'Qualifying property' of a 'gift recipient':
   (i) is brought to, or received or used in, the UK, and is enjoyed by a relevant person; or
   (ii) is consideration for a service that is enjoyed in the UK by a relevant person; or
   (iii) is used outside the UK (directly or indirectly) in respect of a relevant debt.

(c) Property of a person other than a relevant person (apart from qualifying property of a gift recipient as in (b) above):
   (i) is brought to, or received or used in, the UK, and is enjoyed by a relevant person; or
   (ii) is consideration for a service that is enjoyed in the UK by a relevant person; or
   (iii) is used outside the UK (directly or indirectly) in respect of a relevant debt,

   in circumstances where there is a 'connected operation'.

In (a)(iii), (b)(iii) and (c)(iii) above, 'in respect of a relevant debt' would appear to mean 'to satisfy, or partly satisfy, a relevant debt'. In addition, if property (including income or gains) is used to pay interest on a debt, it is regarded as used in respect of the debt. HMRC consider that foreign income and gains used as collateral for a loan are used in respect of the relevant debt, so there is a taxable remittance when the loan is brought to the UK. Where foreign income and gains are also used to pay interest on the debt or to repay the borrowed capital the income or gains are also used in respect of a relevant debt and are treated as a remittance. In such circumstances there are potentially two possible sources of a taxable remittance. See HMRC Residence, Domicile and Remittance Basis Manual RDRM33170.

A 'service' in (a)–(c) above refers to services in the ordinary sense of the word which are normally provided on a commercial basis in exchange for payment (*HMRC v Sehgal* UT, [2024] UKUT 74 (TCC)).

In a case where (b)(i) or (ii) or (c)(i) or (ii) above applies to the importation or use of property, the gains are taken to be remitted at the time the property or service is first enjoyed by a relevant person by virtue of that importation or use.

Enjoyment of property or a service by a relevant person is to be disregarded for the above purposes if it is minimal (i.e. the property or service is enjoyed virtually to the entire exclusion of all relevant persons); if the relevant person gives full consideration in money or money's worth for the enjoyment; or if the property or service is enjoyed by relevant persons in the same way (and on the same terms) that it may be enjoyed by the public (or a section of the public).

[*ITA 2007, ss 809L(1)–(6)(9)–(10), 809N(9), 809O(6)*].

In determining whether a remittance has been made in the case of a foreign chargeable gain on a disposal at undervalue (and if so, how much), the amount of the gain is taken to be the gain that would have arisen if the disposal had been at market value. [*ITA 2007, s 809T*].

If a foreign chargeable gain would otherwise be treated as remitted to the UK before it accrues, by virtue of anything done in relation to anything regarded as deriving from the gain, the remittance is instead treated as made at the time the gain accrues. [*ITA 2007, s 809U*].

The following are '*relevant persons*' for the above purposes: the individual; the spouse or civil partner of the individual; a child or grandchild (under 18) of any of the aforementioned; a close company in which any other person within this definition is a participator (as defined) or a company which is a 51% subsidiary (within *CTA 2010, Pt 24 Ch 3*) of such a company; a company which would be close if it were UK resident and in which any other person within this definition is a participator or a company which is a 51% subsidiary of such a company; the trustees of a settlement of which any other person within this definition is a beneficiary; and a body connected with such a settlement. For this purpose, a cohabiting couple are treated as husband and wife or, as the case may be, civil partners; a body is 'connected with' a settlement if the body falls within **17.2**(c) or (d) CONNECTED PERSONS as regards the settlement; in relation to a settlement that would otherwise have no trustees, a 'trustee' means any person in whom the settled property or its management is for the time being vested.

The question of whether a person whose property is dealt with as in (c) above is a relevant person is to be determined at the time the property is so dealt with.

In relation to an individual's income or chargeable gains for any year before 2008/09, only the individual himself is a relevant person.

[*ITA 2007, ss 809M, 809O(2)*].

A '*relevant debt*' is a debt that relates (wholly or in part, and directly or indirectly) to property within (a) above; a service within (a) above; property dealt with as in (b)(i) or (c)(i) above; or a service falling within (b)(ii) or (c)(ii) above. [*ITA 2007, s 809L(7)(8)*].

A '*gift recipient*' is a person (other than a relevant person) to whom the individual makes a gift of money or property that is (or derives from) chargeable gains of the individual. The question of whether a person is a relevant person is determined by reference to the time of the gift; but if a person subsequently becomes a relevant person, he then ceases to be a gift recipient. A disposition of property at less than full consideration is a gift to the extent of the deficit. Property is considered to have been gifted even in a case where the disponor retains an interest in it or a right to benefit from it.

'*Qualifying property*' in (b) above, in relation to a gift recipient, means the property gifted or anything that derives from it (as widely defined). It also means any other property if it is dealt with as in (b)(i), (ii) or (iii) above by virtue of an operation effected with reference to, or to enable or facilitate, the gift of the property to the gift recipient.

In relation to an individual's income or chargeable gains for any year before 2008/09, the initial reference in the definition of 'gift recipient' above to a relevant person is to the individual, and the subsequent references are to be disregarded.

[*ITA 2007, s 809N(1)–(8)(10)*].

A '*connected operation*' in relation to property dealt with as mentioned in any of (c)(i)–(iii) above is an operation which is effected with reference to, or to enable or facilitate, a 'qualifying disposition'. A '*qualifying disposition*' is a disposition made by a relevant person to or for the benefit of the person whose property is dealt with as in (c) above, which is a disposition of money or other property that is, or derives from, chargeable gains of the individual. There is no qualifying disposition if the disposition represents, or is part of, the giving of full consideration for the fact that the property is so dealt with. In relation to an individual's income or chargeable gains for any year before 2008/09, only the individual is a relevant person for this purpose. [*ITA 2007, s 809O(1), (3)–(5), (7)*].

Determining the amount remitted to the UK

ITA 2007, s 809P provides rules to determine the amount remitted by reference to (a)–(c) above. In the most straightforward case, where the property, service or consideration for a service is the chargeable gains, or derives from them, the amount remitted is equal to the amount of the gains or (as the case may be) the amount of gains from which the property, service or consideration derives. If the gains, or anything deriving from them, are used outside the UK in respect of a relevant debt, the amount remitted is equal to the amount of gains used, or the amount from which what is used derives. In cases within (b) above, the amount remitted is, broadly, equal to the gains of which the property in question consists or consisted, or from which it derives or derived. In cases within (c) above, the amount remitted is equal to the gains which are the qualifying disposition or from which the qualifying disposition is derived.

In all cases involving a relevant debt, if the debt relates only partly to the property or service in question, the amount remitted is limited (if it would otherwise be greater) to the amount the debt would be if it related wholly to the property or service.

In all cases, where the amount remitted, together with amounts previously remitted, would otherwise exceed the amount of the gains, the amount remitted is limited to an amount equal to the amount of gains.

If the property remitted is part of a set only part of which is in the UK, the amount remitted is a just and reasonable portion of the amount that would have been remitted if the complete set had been brought to, or received or used in, the UK when the part was.

[*ITA 2007, s 809P*].

Transfers from mixed funds

Where money or other property is brought to, or received or used in, the UK by, or for the benefit of, a relevant person or a service is provided in the UK to, or for the benefit of, a relevant person (i.e. the first leg of (a) above), the property or the consideration for the service may be, or may derive from, a transfer from a 'mixed fund' (or part of it may), or a transfer from a mixed fund (or something deriving from such a transfer) may be used in respect of a relevant debt (as in (a)(iii) above). In such cases, there are rules to determine if the second leg of (a) above (i.e. any of (a)(i)–(iv)) applies and, if so, to determine the amount remitted.

A '*mixed fund*' means money or other property which immediately before the transfer consists of (or derives from) income or capital of more than one of the following nine categories, or for more than one tax year:

(A) employment income (other than income within (B) or (C) below or income subject to a foreign tax);
(B) amounts within **49.2**(i) or (ii) above, other than those subject to a foreign tax;
(C) amounts within **49.2**(iii) above, other than income subject to a foreign tax;
(D) relevant foreign income within *ITTOIA 2005, s 830*, other than income subject to a foreign tax;
(E) foreign chargeable gains, other than gains subject to a foreign tax;
(F) employment income subject to a foreign tax;
(G) 'relevant foreign income' subject to a foreign tax;
(H) foreign chargeable gains subject to a foreign tax; and
(I) any income or capital not within any of (A)–(H) above.

For this purpose, references to anything derived from income or capital within (I) above do not include income or gains within (A)–(H) above, or anything derived from such income or gains.

For each of categories (A)–(I), find the amount of income and capital for the 'relevant tax year' in the mixed fund immediately before the transfer in question. The '*relevant tax year*' is the tax year in which the transfer takes place. For the purpose of determining the composition of the mixed fund, property which derives (wholly or in part, and directly or indirectly) from an individual's income or capital for a tax year is treated as consisting of or containing that income or capital. Similarly, if a debt relating (wholly or partly, and directly or indirectly) to property is satisfied (wholly or partly) at any time by an individual's income or capital for a particular tax year, or by anything deriving from it, the property is to be treated from that time as consisting of or containing that income or capital if, and to the extent that, it is just and reasonable to do so. If an 'offshore transfer' is made from a mixed fund, it is to be regarded as containing the same proportion of each kind of income or capital as was contained in the fund before the transfer (except where the provisions for cleansing mixed funds apply, as described below). A transfer is an '*offshore transfer*' if these rules (i.e. the rules in *ITA 2007, s 809Q*) do not apply to it; a transfer is *treated as* an offshore transfer if, and to the extent that, these rules do not apply to it at the end of the tax year in which it is made and will not do so on the best estimate that can reasonably be made at that time. If the rules in *ITA 2007, s 809Q* apply to part of a transfer, they are to be applied before applying the offshore transfer rules to the rest of the transfer.

If the amount in category (A) does not exceed the amount of the transfer in question, regard the transfer as containing the income and gains in that category for the relevant tax year. Reduce the amount of the transfer by the amount in (A) and compare what remains with the amount in category (B). Continue by reference to each category, in the order in which they are listed, until the amount of the transfer is reduced to nil.

If, after going through all the categories, the amount of the transfer is still not fully matched, repeat the process by reference to income and capital of the preceding tax year, and so on until the amount of the transfer is fully matched.

If the amount in category (A) does exceed the amount of the transfer, regard the transfer as containing the appropriate proportion of each kind of income and gains in that category for the relevant tax year; similarly if the amount in subsequent category exceeds what remains of the amount of the transfer.

[*ITA 2007, ss 809Q, 809R*].

See also Tolley's Income Tax for special rules for income from mixed employments.

The mixed fund rules do not apply for the purposes of determining whether income or chargeable gains for any tax year before 2008/09 are remitted to the UK in 2008/09 or any subsequent year (or of determining the amount of any such income or chargeable gains so remitted). However, specific rules *do* apply in relation to the cleansing of mixed funds containing pre-6 April 2008 income or gains as described below. [*FA 2008, Sch 7 para 89; F(No 2)A 2017, Sch 8 para 46*].

If, by reason of an arrangement (as widely defined) a main purpose of which is to secure an 'income tax advantage' or a 'CGT advantage', a mixed fund would otherwise be regarded as containing income or capital within any of (F) to (J) above, the mixed fund should be treated as containing so much of such income or capital as is just and reasonable. For this purpose, an '*income tax advantage*' means a relief or increased relief from income tax, a repayment, or increased repayment of income tax, the avoidance or reduction of a charge or assessment to income tax or the avoidance of a possible assessment to income tax. '*CGT advantage*' is similarly defined. [*ITA 2007, s 809S*].

Cleansing of mixed funds

The deemed domicile rules introduced by *F(No 2)A 2017* (see **51.29** RESIDENCE AND DOMICILE) include a one-off opportunity for qualifying individuals to 'cleanse' mixed funds i.e. to separate such funds into their constituent parts. A '*qualifying individual*' is one who has used the remittance basis in any tax year from 2008/09 to 2016/17 inclusive, either by claim (*ITA 2007, s 809B*) or automatically (under *ITA 2007, s 809D* or *ITA 2007, s 809E*), and who was *not* born in the UK with a UK domicile of origin. If the prescribed conditions (below) are met, an offshore transfer made in either 2017/18 or 2018/19 is *not* regarded as containing a proportion of each kind of income or capital in the mixed fund before transfer. Instead the individual specifies the kind of income or capital, or the amounts and kinds of different income and capital, to be regarded as contained in the transfer, in a nomination. The amount specified for a kind of income or capital in such a nomination cannot exceed the amount of that kind which is in the mixed fund immediately before the transfer.

For this treatment to apply to an offshore transfer, the transfer must be a transfer of money made in 2017/18 or 2018/19, from a mixed fund (account A) to another account B and the qualifying individual must make the nomination for the treatment to apply. There cannot have been a previous nomination, in respect of a transfer from account A to account B.

The rules are extended to a transfer from a mixed fund (overseas account A) which contains income or chargeable gains for the tax year 2007/08 or earlier (*'pre-6 April 2008 income or chargeable gains'*), to another overseas account B. However, this requires specific provisions to determine the composition of such a mixed fund as the above mixed fund rules (*ITA 2007, ss 809Q–809R*) do not apply to pre-6 April 2008 amounts.

- **Transfer of money before 6 April 2008 from the mixed fund to another overseas account.** Calculate the total income and gains in the mixed fund immediately before transfer, and then the proportion of this which is income, and the proportion which is gains. If the transfer amount is less than the total income and gains, the transfer is treated as consisting of income and chargeable gains in these proportions. If the transfer amount exceeds the total income and gains, the transfer is treated as consisting of all the income and gains in the mixed fund prior to transfer, plus other capital in the mixed fund making up the balance.
- **Transfer of money before 6 April 2008 from another overseas account to the mixed fund, where there is insufficient evidence to determine the composition of the transfer.** Calculate the total income and gains in the other overseas account immediately before transfer, and then the proportion of this which is income, and the proportion which is gains. The transfer consists of income and gains in these proportions. Where there is insufficient evidence to determine whether an amount in the other overseas account is income or gains, treat it as income.

[*F(No 2)A 2017, Sch 8 paras 44–46*].

Foreign chargeable gains where disposal not for full consideration

For the purposes of the above provisions, where foreign chargeable gains accrue on the disposal of an asset for consideration of less than the market value, the asset is treated as deriving from those chargeable gains. [*ITA 2007, s 809T*].

Property treated as not remitted to the UK

To the extent described below, money and other property brought into the UK are treated for tax purposes as not remitted to the UK.

- **Payment of the remittance basis charge.** Direct payments to HMRC from untaxed foreign income or gains in settlement of the charge in **49.5** below are not treated for tax purposes as remittances to the UK. This exemption applies only if the amount is paid in respect of the tax due for a tax year for which the remittance basis has been claimed and for which the charge applies. The exemption covers any number of direct payments up to the total amount of the charge. If any of the money is repaid by HMRC, for example because the taxpayer withdraws his claim, the exemption is to that extent deemed never to have applied. [*ITA 2007, s 809V; FA 2012, Sch 12 paras 4, 5*].

  To qualify for this exemption, the money must be sent direct from an overseas bank account to HMRC by way of a cheque drawn on the overseas bank account or a form of electronic transfer, and not via a UK bank account (Treasury Explanatory Notes to the 2008 Finance Bill).

Where an individual is liable to the charge for a tax year (year A), any income tax self-assessment payments on account (see **55.2** SELF-ASSESSMENT) that are made for the following tax year (year B) will be at least partly based on that charge. If the individual does not claim the remittance basis for year B, and is thus not liable to the charge for that year, a repayment may be due from HMRC of all or part of the payments on account. If the payments on account were made out of untaxed foreign income or gains, that repayment constitutes a taxable remittance.

An exemption applies in relation to payments on account. The 'relevant amount of income or gains' is treated as not remitted to the UK if money equal to that amount is taken offshore by 15 March in the tax year following year B or such later date as HMRC may allow on a claim by the individual. A claim may be made only if the individual has submitted a personal tax return for year B and reasonably expects to receive a tax repayment for that year; it must be made no later than 5 April in the tax year following year B.

The '*relevant amount of income or gains*' is the lower of:

- the amount brought to the UK by virtue of the making of the payments on account; and
- the amount of the remittance basis charge for year A (see **49.5** below).

See **49.4** below as to what is meant by taking money offshore. Money that is thus taken offshore is treated as having the same composition of kinds of income and capital as the money used to make the payments on account.

[*ITA 2007, ss 809UA, 809Z9*].

- **Property used to make qualifying investments (business investment relief).** Where a 'relevant event' occurs, and income or chargeable gains of an individual would otherwise be regarded as remitted to the UK by virtue of that event, the income or gains are treated as not remitted to the UK if the individual makes a claim under *ITA 2007, s 809VA*. See **49.4** below.
- **Consideration for certain services.** An exemption applies if:
  - gains would otherwise be treated as remitted to the UK because of (a) above;
  - the first leg of (a) is met because a service is provided in the UK;
  - the second leg of (a) is met because (a)(i) or (ii) applies to the consideration for that service; and
  - both Conditions A and B below are met.

  Where this exemption applies, income or gains are treated as not remitted to the UK.

  Condition A is that the service provided relates wholly or mainly to property situated outside the UK.

  Condition B is that the whole of the consideration for the service is given by way of payments to bank accounts held outside the UK by or on behalf of the person providing the service.

The exemption does not apply if the service relates to the provision in the UK either of a benefit treated as deriving from the income under *ITA 2007, s 735* or a benefit treated under *TCGA 1992, s 87B* as deriving from the chargeable gains (see **42.14** OFFSHORE SETTLEMENTS).
[*ITA 2007, s 809W*].
Condition A would cover, for example, fees paid to a UK bank for managing an individual's overseas investments. It would also cover legal or brokerage fees in respect of offshore assets, such as legal fees on the sale of a foreign house. The term 'wholly or mainly' in Condition A is not statutorily defined, but will be taken to mean more than half. (Treasury Explanatory Notes to the 2008 Finance Bill).

- **Exempt property.** 'Exempt property' which is brought to, or received or used in, the UK, such that the first leg of (a) above applies, is treated as not remitted to the UK. The following are '*exempt property*' for this purpose.
  - Property which meets the 'public access rule'. This rule allows certain property to be imported into the UK, without giving rise to a tax charge on the remittance basis, if all the conditions set out below are met.
    The property must be available for public access (as defined) at an approved museum, gallery or similar establishment or in storage at, or in transit to or from, the establishment (or other commercial premises in the UK used by the establishment for storage) pending or following public access.
    During the 'relevant period', the property must meet the above condition for no more than two years (or such longer period as HMRC may in a particular case allow). The '*relevant period*' is the period beginning with the importation of the property and ending when it next ceases to be in the UK, except that if the property is lost or stolen the relevant period is suspended.
    The property must attract a 'relevant VAT relief' (for which see *ITA 2007, s 809Z1*). This condition is abolished on and after 6 April 2013 or, in the case of property already in the UK on that date, from the time it ceases to be in the UK or is lost or stolen.
  - Clothing, footwear, jewellery and watches which meet certain additional conditions.
  - Property where the 'notional remitted amount' (as defined) is less than £1,000, or if the property meets certain conditions as to temporary importation or importation for repair.

For these purposes, 'property' does not include money (or specified items equivalent to money). Subject to the exceptions below, if property ceases to be exempt property at any time after it is brought to, or received or used in, the UK, it is treated as remitted to the UK at that time. Property ceases to be exempt property if it (or part of it) is sold (or otherwise converted into money or specified items equivalent to money) whilst in the UK. Property which is exempt by virtue of one or more of the 'public access rule', the 'personal use rule', the 'temporary importation rule' and the 'repair rule' also ceases to be exempt property if it ceases to meet the rule(s) relied upon whilst in the UK, provided it does not meet any of the remaining rules. Property which ceases to be exempt property as a result of ceasing to meet one of those rules is not, however, treated as remitted to the UK at that time if, no later than the time it ceases to be exempt property, it has been donated in circumstances within *FA 2012, Sch 14 para 1* (gifts to the nation — see **11.7** CHARITIES). In such a case the property continues to be treated as not remitted to the UK.

Property used to make qualifying investments. With effect where property ceases to be exempt property and a claim for this relief is made, it is *not* treated as remitted to the UK at that time if the property is used by a relevant person (as above) to make a qualifying investment (as in **49.4** below) within the 45 days beginning with the day on which it ceased to be exempt property. The claim must be made (by the individual whose income or gains would otherwise be treated as remitted) no later than the first anniversary of 31 January following the tax year in which the property ceases to be exempt property. The relief also applies where the formerly exempt property is disposed of or otherwise converted into money and the disposal proceeds or the money are used to make the investment.

Where this relief has effect, the potentially chargeable event rules at **49.4** below if there is subsequently such an event in relation to the qualifying investment. If the investment is made using more than just the formerly exempt property, only the part made using that property is treated as the qualifying investment for the purposes of applying those rules.

In applying the mixed fund rules, the formerly exempt property (or thing into which it was converted) used to make the investment is treated as containing (or deriving from) an amount of each kind of income and gain mentioned in (A)–(H) above equal to the amount of that kind of income or gain contained in the property when it was brought to, or received or used in, the UK.

Sales of exempt property. If property ceases to be exempt property because the whole of it is sold whilst in the UK, it is *not* treated as remitted to the UK at that time if all the conditions listed at (1)–(6) below are met. This relief does not apply if the sale is made as part of, or as a result of, a tax avoidance scheme or arrangements.

(1) The sale is to a person other than a relevant person (as above).
(2) The sale is by way of a bargain made at arm's length.
(3) Once the sale is completed, no relevant person:
  – has any interest in the property;
  – is able or entitled to benefit from the property by virtue of any interest, right or arrangement; or
  – has any right to acquire any such interest, ability or entitlement.
(4) The whole of the disposal proceeds are 'released' (whether all at once or in instalments) on or before the first anniversary of 5 January following the tax year in which the property ceases to be exempt property.
(5) The whole of the disposal proceeds are taken offshore or used by a relevant person to make a qualifying investment (as in **49.4** below) within the 45 days beginning with the day on which the proceeds are 'released'. If the disposal proceeds are paid in instalments, the condition is that each instalment is taken off-

shore or used in that way within the 45 days beginning with the day on which the instalment is released. In both cases, there is an overriding deadline of the first anniversary of 5 January following the tax year in which the property ceases to be exempt property, if this falls within the 45 days normally permitted.

(6) If (5) above is satisfied wholly or partly by the making of a qualifying investment, a claim for relief must be made (by the individual whose income or gains would otherwise be treated as remitted) on or before the first anniversary of 31 January following the tax year in which the property is sold.

For the purposes of (5) and (6) above, proceeds or instalments are '*released*' on the day on which they first become available for use by or for the benefit of any relevant person. An officer of HMRC may (on the request of the individual whose income or gains would otherwise be treated as remitted) agree to extend any deadline within (5) above if circumstances are exceptional.

In applying the mixed fund rules, where this relief has effect, the disposal proceeds are treated as containing (or deriving from) an amount of each kind of income and gain mentioned in (A)–(H) above equal to the amount of that kind of income or gain contained in the exempt property when it was brought to, or received or used in, the UK. Also where this relief has effect and (5) above was satisfied by the making of a qualifying investment, the potentially chargeable event rules at **49.4** below apply if there is subsequently such an event in relation to the investment. If the investment is made using more than just the disposal proceeds, only the part made using those proceeds is treated as the qualifying investment for the purposes of applying those rules.

Where a chargeable gain (but not a loss) accrues to an individual on a sale of exempt property, and this relief applies to prevent the property being treated as remitted to the UK, the gain is treated for the purpose of applying the remittance basis as a foreign chargeable gain (see **49.2** and (E) above) and, for the purposes of **49.2**(c) above as not being part of the individual's UK income and gains. Where this rule applies, *ITA 2007, s 809U* (see above) is disregarded, and anything done in relation to any part of the disposal proceeds before the part is taken offshore or used to make a qualifying investment does not count as a remittance to the UK of any of the gain. This rule applies also to an individual to whom part of such a gain is apportioned under *TCGA 1992, s 3* (see **43.7** OVERSEAS MATTERS). The rule can, however, be disapplied by notice in writing to HMRC. Such a notice must be given on or before the first anniversary of the 31 January following the tax year in which the gain is made or, where the taxpayer is temporarily non-UK resident in that year (see **43.5** OVERSEAS MATTERS), the year of return. A notice is irrevocable after the expiry of the time limit for making it.

Property lost, stolen or destroyed. In relation to property lost, stolen or destroyed whilst in the UK, the property cannot cease to be exempt property in the circumstances outlined above after it is lost, stolen and destroyed and (in the case of loss or theft followed by recovery) before it is 'recovered'. For this purpose, property is '*recovered*' on the day it becomes available to be used or enjoyed in the UK by or for the benefit of a relevant person (as above).

Property ceases to be exempt property where a payment of compensation (whether under an insurance policy or otherwise) is 'released' in respect of exempt property that has been lost, stolen or destroyed. A compensation payment is '*released*' on the day on which it first becomes available for use in the UK by or for the benefit of any relevant person.

However, property is not treated as remitted to the UK by virtue of a release of compensation as above if the whole of the compensation payment is taken offshore or used by a relevant person to make a qualifying investment (as in **49.4** below) within the 45 days beginning with the day on which the payment is released. To the extent that this relief arises from the making of a qualifying investment, a claim for the relief must be made no later than the first anniversary of 31 January following the tax year in which the payment is released.

For the purposes of the mixed fund rules, the compensation payment is treated as containing (or deriving from) an amount of each kind of income and gain mentioned in (A)–(H) above equal to the amount of that kind of income or gain contained in the exempt property when it was brought to, or received or used in, the UK.

Where this relief has effect by virtue of the making of a qualifying investment, the rules at **49.4** below apply if there is subsequently a potentially chargeable event in relation to the investment. If the investment is made using more than just the compensation payment, only the part made using that payment is treated as the qualifying investment for the purposes of applying those rules.

[*ITA 2007, ss 809X–809Z5, 809Z10*].

- **Offshore mortgages.** In certain circumstances, relevant foreign income of an individual used outside the UK before 6 April 2028 to pay the interest on a debt is treated as not remitted to the UK. A similar exemption applies to interest on a subsequent replacement loan. [*FA 2008, Sch 7 para 90*].

Property used to make qualifying investments (business investment relief)

[49.4] Where a 'relevant event' occurs, and income or chargeable gains of an individual would otherwise be regarded as remitted to the UK by virtue of that event, the income or gains are treated as not remitted to the UK if the individual makes a claim under *ITA 2007, s 809VA* for the relief. A '*relevant event*' occurs if money or other property:

(a) is used by a relevant person (as in **49.3** above) to make a 'qualifying investment' (see below); or

(b) is brought to or received in the UK in order to be used by a relevant person for the purpose of making such an investment (but see below for 45-day time limit).

The relief (known as **business investment relief**) is equally available where income or gains would otherwise be treated under the exempt property rules at **49.3** above as remitted to the UK by virtue of the relevant event, e.g. because exempt property is sold to raise the capital for the investment.

A claim for relief must be made no later than the first anniversary of 31 January following the tax year in which the income or gains would otherwise be regarded as remitted to the UK. No relief is available if the relevant event occurs, or the investment is made, as part of, or as a result of, a tax avoidance scheme or arrangement.

HMRC can be asked for their view on whether a proposed investment will qualify for relief. Applications for advance clearance should be sent by email to nonstatutoryclearanceteam.hmrc@hmrc.gov.uk or to Business Investment Relief, HMRC, BX9 1BN.

45-day rule

Relief by virtue of (b) above is available to the extent only that the investment is made within the period of 45 days beginning with the day on which the money etc. is brought to or received in the UK. If this requirement is only partly satisfied, the portion of the income or gains which attracts the relief is determined on a just and reasonable basis. Where money etc. is brought to the UK with the intention of making a qualifying investment but some or all of that money etc. is not invested within the 45-day limit, the income or gains thereby not qualifying for the relief are nevertheless treated as not remitted to the UK if and to the extent that the unused money etc. is taken offshore within the same 45-day period. Where only part of the unused amount is taken offshore within the time limit, the portion of the income or gains which attracts the relief is again determined on a just and reasonable basis.

[*ITA 2007, ss 809VA, 809VB, 809Z10*].

Qualifying investments

For the above purposes, a person makes an investment if shares in, or securities of, a company are issued to him or acquired by him or if he makes a loan (whether secured or unsecured) to a company. In order to be a '*qualifying investment*', the investment must satisfy both conditions A and B below at the time it is made.

Where a loan agreement authorises a company to draw down amounts of a loan over time, entry into that loan agreement is not treated as the making of a loan for these purposes. Instead, a separate loan is treated as being made each time an amount is drawn down; each drawdown will thus be a separate investment.

Condition A

The company in which the investment is made (the '*target company*') must be an 'eligible trading company', an 'eligible stakeholder company', an 'eligible holding company' or an 'eligible hybrid company'.

A company is an '*eligible trading company*' if:

- it is a 'private limited company';

- it carries on one or more 'commercial trades' or is preparing to do so within the next five years; and
- carrying on commercial trades is all or substantially all of what it does (or of what it is expected to do when it begins trading).

A company is a '*private limited company*' if none of its shares are listed on a recognised stock exchange; limited liability partnerships are not private limited companies.

A company is an '*eligible stakeholder company*' if:

- it is a 'private limited company' (as above);
- it exists wholly for the purpose of making investments (as defined above) in eligible trading companies (ignoring any minor or incidental purposes); and
- it holds one or more such investments or is preparing to do so within the next five years.

A company is an '*eligible holding company*' if:

- it is a member of an 'eligible trading group' or of an 'eligible group' that is reasonably expected to become an eligible trading group within the next five years; and
- an eligible trading company in the group is a 51% subsidiary of it. Where the eligible holding company owns the share capital of the eligible trading company indirectly, each intermediary company must also be a member of the group.

A company is an '*eligible hybrid company*' if:

- it is a 'private limited company' (as above), and neither an eligible trading company nor an eligible stakeholder company;
- it carries on one or more 'commercial trades' or is preparing to do so within the next five years;
- it holds one or more investments in eligible trading companies or is preparing to do so within the next five years; and
- the carrying on of commercial trades and the making of investments in eligible trading companies are all (or substantially all) of what it does (or of what it is reasonably expected to do once it begins operating).

For the above purposes, a group means a parent company and its 51% subsidiaries. A group is an '*eligible group*' if the parent company and each of its 51% subsidiaries are private limited companies. An eligible group is an '*eligible trading group*' if carrying on 'commercial trades' is all or substantially all of what the group does (taking the activities of its members as a whole).

A trade is a '*commercial trade*' if it is conducted on a commercial basis and with a view to the realisation of profits. For this purpose, a trade includes anything that is treated for corporation tax purposes as if it were a trade and also includes a business carried on for 'generating income from land' (as defined by *CTA 2009, s 207*). It includes the carrying on of research and development activities from which it is intended that a commercial trade will be derived or will benefit. A corporate partner in a partnership is not regarded for these purposes as carrying on a trade carried on by the partnership.

Condition B

Condition B is that no relevant person (as in **49.3** above) has (directly or indirectly) obtained, or become entitled to obtain, any related benefit, and that no relevant person expects to obtain any such benefit. A benefit is related if it is directly or indirectly attributable to the making of the investment or if it is reasonable to assume that the benefit would not be available in the absence of the investment. A benefit includes the provision of anything which would not be provided to the relevant person in the ordinary course of business or would be provided on less favourable terms. It does not include the provision of anything to the relevant person in the normal course of business and on arm's length terms.

[*ITA 2007, ss 809VC–809VF, 809Z10*].

Potentially chargeable events

Where relief has been given as above, the occurrence of a 'potentially chargeable event' (PCE) may result in the 'affected income or gains' being treated as having been remitted to the UK. This can be avoided if appropriate steps are taken in mitigation but each step must be taken within a specified period of grace allowed for that step. In the absence of one or more mitigation steps, the remittance is deemed to take place immediately after the end of the appropriate grace period. The '*affected income or gains*' means such portion of the income or gains relieved as above as reflects the portion of the qualifying investment affected by the PCE. This will usually be the whole of the qualifying investment, but where the event is a part disposal it is the portion disposed of. Where there is a second or subsequent PCE in relation to a single investment, the relieved income or gains that may then be treated as remitted do not include any amounts treated as remitted or used in mitigation as a result of a previous PCE.

Where an investment is made which consists partly of funds which qualify for relief under the qualifying investment provisions and partly of other funds, the investment is treated as two separate investments for these purposes.

Meaning of 'potentially chargeable event'

Any of the following is a '*potentially chargeable event*':

- the target company (see above) is for the first time neither an eligible trading company nor an eligible stakeholder company nor an eligible holding company nor an eligible hybrid company;
- the relevant person who made the investment disposes of all or part of it;
- the extraction of value rule is breached (see below); or
- the five-year start-up rule is breached (see below).

If consideration for a disposal is paid in instalments, the disposal is treated for these purposes as if it were separate disposals, one for each instalment and each giving rise to a separate PCE.

If a PCE occurs because of an 'insolvency step' taken for genuine commercial reasons, it will not be treated as a PCE. However, this does not prevent the receipt of value as a result of the insolvency step from being a PCE. Broadly, an '*insolvency step*' is taken if a company enters into administration or receivership, or is wound up or dissolved (or the overseas equivalent in each case).

Extraction of value rule

The extraction of value rule is breached if the relevant person who made the investment or any other relevant person receives, or receives the benefit of, value in money or money's worth from any person in circumstances that are directly or indirectly attributable to the investment. For a case in which the extraction of value rule was breached, see *D'angelin v HMRC* FTT, [2024] UKFTT 462 (TC).

The extraction of value rule is not breached if the value is received as a result of a disposal that is itself a PCE. Also, the rule is not breached merely because a relevant person receives value which is treated as income for tax purposes (or would be if the relevant person were liable to income tax or corporation tax), provided the value is paid or provided on arm's length terms and in the ordinary course of business; an example of such value would be director's remuneration.

Five-year start-up rule

The five-year start-up rule is breached if:

- immediately after the end of the five years beginning with the day on which the investment was made, the target company is not operational; or
- at any time after the end of that period, the target company ceases to be operational.

In order to be operational, the target company must either be trading (i.e. carrying on a commercial trade), be a stakeholder in at least one eligible trading company which is trading, be a member of an eligible trading group and have at least one 51% subsidiary which is trading or be an eligible hybrid company which is trading or is a stakeholder in at least one eligible trading company which is trading.

Mitigation steps and periods of grace

If the PCE is a disposal, the appropriate mitigation step is to take the proceeds offshore or use them to make another qualifying investment (whether in the same or a different company). If the proceeds are themselves a qualifying investment (for example on a share for share exchange), the appropriate step is regarded as having been taken. Otherwise, the period of grace allowed to take the step is the 45 days beginning with the day on which the disposal proceeds first become available for use by, or for the benefit of, the investor or any other relevant person. See below for the meaning of disposal proceeds and for what is meant by taking proceeds offshore.

If the PCE is anything other than a disposal, the appropriate mitigation step is twofold, as follows. Firstly, the investor must dispose of the entire investment (or so much of it as he still holds when the PCE occurs). Secondly, he must take the proceeds of that disposal offshore or use them to make another qualifying investment. The period of grace allowed for the first leg of this mitigation step is the 90 days beginning (if the PCE is a breach of the extraction of value rule) with the day on which value is received or (in any other case) with the day on which a relevant person first became aware, or ought reasonably to have become aware, of the PCE. The period of grace allowed for the second leg is the 45 days beginning with the day on which the disposal proceeds first become available for use by, or for the benefit of, the investor or any other relevant person. If the first leg is not carried out within the 90 days allowed, it is immediately after the end of those 90 days that the affected income or gains is deemed to have been remitted to the UK.

The above does not apply if the PCE is a breach of the five-year start-up rule by virtue of the target company ceasing to be operational after the end of the five-year period. Instead, the total period of grace allowed for carrying out both legs of the mitigation step is the two years beginning with the day on which the investor or any other relevant person first became aware, or ought reasonably to have become aware, of the PCE.

Where a breach of the extraction of value rule takes place in connection with the winding-up or dissolution of the target company, there is no need to dispose of the holding, and references to the disposal proceeds in these provisions are to the value received.

Applicable proceeds

In any case where proceeds need to be taken offshore or reinvested, the amount of proceeds to which this applies is the total disposal proceeds or, if less, so much of those proceeds as equals the sum originally invested (as defined). For this purpose, the sum originally invested is deemed to be reduced by so much of it as has, on previous occasions involving the same investment:

- been taken into account in determining the amount of income and gains treated as remitted after a PCE; or
- been taken offshore or reinvested as an appropriate mitigation step; or
- been used to purchase a certificate of tax deposit (see below under Retention of funds to meet CGT liabilities).

For example, in Year 1 an individual invests £3 million of foreign income in an eligible trading company. In Year 5, he sells half the holding for £2 million. The appropriate mitigation step is to take £2 million offshore or reinvest it. In Year 6, he sells the remaining holding for £3.5 million. The appropriate mitigation step is to take £1 million (£3 million less £2 million) offshore or reinvest it. In all, he has invested £3 million and realised £5.5 million; the amount he has been required to take offshore or reinvest is limited to £3 million.

Extension of grace periods

An officer of HMRC may agree in a particular case to extend the grace period allowed for an appropriate mitigation step:

- where the target company has ceased to be a private limited company by virtue of having some or all of its shares listed on a recognised stock exchange or has become a subsidiary of another company (the 'new company') which is a body corporate some or all of whose shares are (or are to be) so listed, and the investor is unable to comply with an appropriate mitigation step without breaching the terms of a 'lock-up agreement';
- where the investor is prevented from taking an appropriate mitigation step by a prohibition imposed by or under any enactment;
- where taking an appropriate mitigation step would breach the terms of a court order; or

- in exceptional circumstances (to be defined in HMRC published guidance).

A '*lock-up agreement*' is a contract entered into by the investor with one or more of the target company, the new company or professional advisors retained by the target or new company in relation to the listing of the shares, where the contract is directly related to the listing of the shares and imposes restrictions on the time or manner in which the investor may dispose of some or all of his holding in the target company or of any shares in the new company received by him in return for his holding in the target company.

The extension may be for a length of time that is indefinite but is capable of becoming definite by means identified in advance, such as the satisfaction of conditions.

Amounts reinvested

Where disposal proceeds are used to make another qualifying investment as part of appropriate mitigation steps, these provisions apply with the necessary modifications to the new investment as they applied to the original investment; for example, references to the sum originally invested are henceforth to the sum reinvested. Where the new investment is made in a greater sum than is required to satisfy the rules, it is treated as two separate investments, one of an amount equal to the minimum amount required to meet the rules and the other of an amount equal to the balance; the latter then falls outside these provisions.

A reinvestment of proceeds requires a further claim under *ITA 2007, s 809VA* (see above). This must be made no later than the first anniversary of 31 January following the tax year in which the reinvestment is made. If the claim is not made, the appropriate mitigation steps will not be regarded as having been taken.

Retention of funds to meet CGT liabilities

The legislation recognises that the disposal proceeds of a qualifying investment may have to be retained in the UK to meet a CGT liability on that disposal. It deals with this by enabling the amount otherwise required to be taken offshore or reinvested to be reduced by a set amount, provided the amount is used to purchase a certificate of tax deposit (CTD) (see **45.13** PAYMENT OF TAX) within the 45-day grace period allowed as above. It must be confirmed in writing to HMRC that the CTD purchased is intended to relate to *ITA 2007, s 809VK* and that the amount of the deposit is no greater than the 'shortfall'. The '*shortfall*' is the amount (if any) by which the actual disposal proceeds fall short of Amount Y, where Amount Y is the sum of the amount otherwise required to be taken offshore or reinvested and the amount resulting when the highest potential CGT rate is applied to the chargeable gain on the disposal. (The shortfall is calculated by reference to proceeds actually received even if the disposal was not made on arm's length terms.) The set amount can be anything up to the amount of the shortfall.

If the CTD is used to pay the individual's CGT liability for the tax year in which the disposal took place, this does not count as remitting to the UK the portion of the affected income or gains that is represented by the payment. If, however, any of the 'CTD conditions' is breached, the portion of the affected income or gains to the UK that is affected by the breach are treated as having been remitted to the UK immediately after the day on which the breach occurs. The '*CTD conditions*' are as follows.

- The CTD must not be used to pay any other tax liability.
- If any of the amount deposited is withdrawn by the depositor, the amount withdrawn must be taken offshore or invested in a qualifying company within the 45 days beginning on the date of withdrawal.
- Any part of the amount deposited that has been neither used to pay a tax liability nor withdrawn by the due date for payment of the said CGT liability must be withdrawn by the depositor and taken offshore or invested in a qualifying company within the 45 days beginning with that date.

Where an amount withdrawn is invested in a qualifying company, these provisions apply with the necessary modifications to the new investment as they applied to the original investment. Again, a further claim is required under *ITA 2007, s 809VA*.

Order of disposals

There are rules to determine the order in which disposals are treated as being made where there are multiple acquisitions and disposals in the same target company or group and also where both qualifying and non-qualifying investments have been made.

The first rule applies where income or gains of an individual are treated as not remitted to the UK as a result of more than one qualifying investment in either the same target company or the same eligible trading group or in both an eligible trading company and its eligible stakeholder company or its eligible hybrid company. The investments are treated as a single investment for the purpose of applying the PCE rules. A disposal of all or part of that deemed single investment affects it in the order in which the qualifying investments were made, i.e. first in, first out. It does not matter whether the investments in question are held by the same relevant person (as in **49.3** above) or different ones.

The second rule applies where income or gains of an individual are treated as not remitted to the UK as a result of one or more qualifying investments and a relevant person holds at least one non-qualifying investment in the same target company, the same eligible trading group or a 'related eligible company'. The investments are treated as a single investment for the purpose of applying the PCE rules. A disposal of all or part of that deemed single investment is taken to be a disposal from a qualifying investment until all the qualifying investments have been disposed of. It does not matter whether the investments in question are held by the same relevant person or different ones. Two companies are '*related eligible companies*' if one is an eligible trading company and the other is its eligible stakeholder company or its eligible hybrid company.

Meaning of disposal proceeds

For these purposes, in relation to a sale or any other disposal, the disposal proceeds are the amount of consideration for the disposal less any fees or other incidental costs deducted from the consideration before it is accounted for to the person making the disposal or to any relevant person (as in **49.3** above). If the consideration is provided in the form of property rather than money, the amount of the consideration is the market value of the property at the time of the disposal. If the disposal is not at arm's length, it is deemed to be made for a consideration equal to the market value of the thing being disposed of. A disposal made to another relevant person or to a person connected with a relevant person is always treated as made other than at arm's length.

Fees and other incidental costs are not deductible if payable by one relevant person to another except to the extent that they relate to a service actually provided by the recipient in connection with effecting the disposal and do not exceed what would normally be charged for that service on arm's length terms.

Taking proceeds etc. offshore or investing them

For the purposes of these provisions, things (e.g. disposal proceeds) are to be regarded as '*taken offshore*' if (and only if) they are taken outside the UK such that, on leaving the UK, they cease to be available to be used or enjoyed in the UK by, or for the benefit of, a relevant person (as in **49.3** above) or used or enjoyed in any other way that would count as remitting income or gains to the UK. If money needs to be taken offshore or invested in order to satisfy a statutory requirement, and it is paid temporarily into an account pending satisfaction of that requirement, the requirement is satisfied only if the money actually taken offshore or invested is taken from the same account. If the thing required to be taken offshore or invested is something in money's worth, the requirement can be satisfied either by taking the thing offshore or investing it or by taking offshore or investing money or other property of equivalent value. A requirement to take something offshore or invest it can be met by taking part of it offshore and investing the other part. If a disposal is deemed to be made at market value (see above under Meaning of disposal proceeds), the requirement can be satisfied by taking offshore or investing money or other property of a value equal to the amount of the deemed consideration less any deductible fees or other incidental costs.

Where, as above, a statutory requirement can be met by taking offshore or investing property of equivalent value, that property is treated as deriving from the thing required to be taken offshore or invested and as having the same composition of kinds of income and capital as that thing (see **49.3** above). Such property must not be exempt property (as in **49.3** above) or consideration for a disposal of exempt property, and it must not be consideration for the disposal of all or part of a qualifying investment.

[*ITA 2007, ss 809VG–809VP, 809Z8, 809Z9, 809Z10; SI 2012 No 1898*].

Investments made from mixed funds

The following applies if, but for the above relief, income or gains would have been remitted to the UK by virtue of a relevant event and *ITA 2007, s 809Q* (transfers from mixed funds — see **49.3** above) would have applied in determining the amount that would have been so remitted. The relevant event counts as an offshore transfer for the purposes of *ITA 2007, s 809R(4)*. The investment holding is treated as containing a proportion of each of the kinds of income and capital in **49.3**(A)–(H) equal to the proportion of that kind of income or capital contained in the money or other property used to make the investment.

The following applies where, under the rules for potentially chargeable events above, money or other property is treated as not remitted to the UK because an amount is taken offshore, reinvested or used to purchase a certificate of tax deposit. The amount in question is treated, immediately after the step is taken, as containing the same proportion of each kind of income and capital contained in the investment holding.

The following applies where income and gains are treated as remitted to the UK because the appropriate mitigation steps were not taken within the grace period. The mixed fund rules at **49.3** above do not apply to determine the amounts remitted. The affected income and gains (see above) are so much of the 'fixed amount' of each kind of income or gain that would have been remitted to the UK by virtue of the relevant event as reflects the portion of the investment affected by the potentially chargeable event. The '*fixed amount*' is the amount of that kind of income or gain that the investment holding is treated as containing (as above).

The anti-avoidance rule at *ITA 2007, s 809S* (see **49.3** above) applies equally in relation to the above.

[*ITA 2007, s 809VO*].

Charge for claiming the remittance basis

[49.5] An individual who claims the remittance basis for 2008/09 or any subsequent tax year (see **49.2**(a) above) incurs an additional tax charge for that year if the following circumstances apply to him:

- he is 18 years of age or over in that tax year; and
- he meets the 'seven-year residence test' or the 'twelve-year residence test'.

If the individual meets the 12-year test, the charge is £60,000 and if he meets the seven-year test, it is £30,000.

The '*seven-year residence test*' is met for a tax year if the individual does not meet the 12-year residence test but has been UK resident in at least seven of the nine tax years immediately preceding that year. These preceding years may include years prior to 2008/09.

The '*twelve-year residence test*' is met for a tax year if the individual has been UK resident in at least 12 of the 14 tax years immediately preceding that year. These preceding years may include years prior to 2012/13 and indeed prior to 2008/09.

The charge is made on income and gains not remitted to the UK and is thus in addition to the tax charge on remitted income and gains. The individual can nominate the income and/or gains on which this charge is to be levied, and the remittance basis does not then apply to the nominated amount. For example, a taxpayer liable to the £30,000 charge could nominate a £107,143 chargeable gain on the disposal of a foreign residential property on which tax is then chargeable at 28%, giving a liability of £30,000. The point of nominating is that the nominated income and/or gains are not then charged to tax again if they are remitted in a later year. The nomination is made in the individual's claim within **49.2**(a) above, and the nominated amount must be part (or all) of his 'foreign income and gains' for the year (see **49.2** above). If the nominated amount is insufficient to increase the taxpayer's total income tax and CGT liability by the required amount (after taking into account all reliefs and deductions due, but ignoring any income tax charged under *ITA 2007, s 424* (Gift Aid)), he is treated for this purpose only as if he had nominated sufficient additional *income* to bring the tax increase up to that amount; this remains the case even if in reality he has insufficient income to nominate. Income *treated as* nominated does not count as nominated income for the purpose of the subsequent remittances rule below).

As the charge is a charge to tax (whether it be income tax or CGT), the normal self-assessment payment dates apply. It is also available to cover Gift Aid payments. The Treasury are of the view that it should be recognised as tax for the purposes of double tax agreements. If, however, insufficient income and gains are nominated, the income *treated as* nominated, and the tax on that income, does not qualify for double tax relief as it is not tax on specific income. (Treasury Explanatory Notes to the 2008 Finance Bill). The US Internal Revenue Service has ruled that the charge is a tax on income and that credit is allowed under US tax law (www.irs.gov/pub/irs-drop/rr-11-19.pdf).

[*ITA 2007, ss 809C, 809H*].

Direct payments to HMRC from untaxed foreign gains (or income) in settlement of the charge are not treated for tax purposes as remittances to the UK (see **49.3** above).

Nominated income and gains subsequently remitted

For the purpose of applying the exemption from charge of nominated income and gains if later remitted, nominated income and gains are treated as not remitted (even if, in fact, they have been) until all other previously unremitted foreign income and gains have been remitted. In considering the extent to which other previously unremitted foreign income and gains have been remitted, one takes into account income and gains arising in the tax year under review and all other years for 2008/09 onwards for which the remittance basis has applied to the individual (on a claim or otherwise).

'Nominated income and gains' means income and gains actually nominated and does not include income merely treated as nominated as above.

The above treatment is disapplied (and the steps below do not need to be taken) if the cumulative total of nominated income and gains from each year that have been remitted in years up to and including the current year does not exceed £10.

Where nominated income and gains are, in fact, remitted in a tax year but are to be treated as above as having not been remitted, the following steps determine the income and gains that are to be treated as having been remitted instead.

Step 1.

Add the amount of nominated income and gains for the tax year and any earlier tax year which are remitted in the tax year to the amount of other foreign income and gains remitted in the tax year that has arisen in any year for 2008/09 onwards for which the remittance basis has applied to the individual.

Step 2.

Next, find the amount (if any) of the individual's foreign income and gains for the year (other than nominated income and gains) that fall within each of the following categories:

- amounts within **49.2**(i) or (ii) above other than those subject to a foreign tax;
- income within **49.2**(iii) above other than income subject to a foreign tax;
- income within **49.2**(iv) above other than income subject to a foreign tax;
- foreign chargeable gains, other than gains subject to a foreign tax;
- amounts within **49.2**(i) or (ii) above subject to a foreign tax;
- income within **49.2**(iii) above subject to a foreign tax;
- income within **49.2**(iv) above subject to a foreign tax; and
- foreign chargeable gains subject to a foreign tax.

If the tax year is one to which the remittance basis does not apply, ignore this Step and Step 3 below.

Step 3.

Compare the total in Step 1 to each of the amounts in Step 2 in the order in which those amounts are listed.

If the first such amount does not exceed the total in Step 1, regard the total in Step 1 as containing the income and gains in that category. Reduce the total in Step 1 by the amount of that income and gains and compare what remains with the next of the amounts in Step 2 and so on.

If the first such amount does exceed the total in Step 1, regard the total in Step 1 as containing the appropriate proportion of each kind of income and gains in that category; similarly if the amount in any subsequent category exceeds what remains of the amount in Step 1.

Step 4.

If the total in Step 1 is still not fully matched, repeat Steps 2 and 3 by reference to income and gains of the 'appropriate tax year' that had not yet been remitted (or treated under these provisions as remitted) by the beginning of the tax year in question. The '*appropriate tax year*' is the latest of the preceding years (ignoring years before 2008/09) for which the remittance basis applied.

If the tax year in question is one to which the remittance basis does not apply, carry out this Step instead of Steps 2 and 3.

Step 5.

If the total in Step 1 is still not fully matched, repeat Steps 2 and 3 by reference to the next latest of the preceding years for which the remittance basis applied, and so on.

[*ITA 2007, ss 809I, 809J*].

Key points concerning the remittance basis

[49.6] Points to consider are as follows.

- The remittance basis can be claimed by non-domiciled UK residents who are not deemed UK-domiciled and applies to foreign capital gains and income. It cannot be claimed for gains (or income) in isolation.
- The remittance basis can be claimed on a year by year basis.
- Claiming the remittance basis causes the loss of the capital gains tax annual exempt amount (and income tax personal allowances).
- Long-term residents (aged over 18) may need to pay the remittance basis charge. The level of charge depends upon the number of years the individual is resident; £30,000 for at least seven years and £60,000 for at least 12 years. The charge can be paid out of foreign gains without this being a remittance of those gains.
- The definition of a remittance is very wide and includes virtually anything where a 'relevant person' brings, receives or uses the gain in the UK. However when considering the remittance of gains that arose before 6 April 2008 the definition of a relevant person is restricted to the individual. There is a relief for remittances used for the purpose of making qualifying commercial investments.
- If an individual disposed of an asset, realising a foreign capital gain, before 6 April 2008 in a year for which the remittance basis applied, and remits that gain to the UK in 2024/25, that gain is taxable in 2024/25. However, if the proceeds of the disposal are gifted (offshore) to another person (including a spouse or civil partner), those proceeds can be brought to the UK tax free. It is important that the individual who realised the gain does not benefit from the funds remitted to the UK. The difficulty here is isolating the pre-2008 capital gains to enable the remittance, especially where the mixed fund rules apply.
- Foreign capital losses cannot be remitted to the UK and are not allowable. However, a once and for all election can be made, so that foreign losses are allowable but the order in which all losses (including UK losses) must be utilised will generally mean that such an election will not be worthwhile.

50

Repayment Interest

Cross-reference. See **45** PAYMENT OF TAX.

Introduction to repayment interest

[50.1] A harmonised regime for interest applies to many of the taxes and duties administered by HMRC. In relation to interest on capital gains tax repaid by HMRC, the harmonised regime is described at **50.2** below. The regime was originally expected to apply to corporation tax, but this has not yet happened and in the rules at 50.3 below continue to apply.

The repayment interest system mirrors that under which HMRC charge interest on late paid tax (see **36** LATE PAYMENT INTEREST AND PENALTIES) but the rates of interest for overpaid tax are considerably lower.

Repayment interest

[50.2] A harmonised regime for interest applies to many of the taxes and duties administered by HMRC, including income tax and capital gains tax under self-assessments, including tax charged by discovery assessment and penalties. The regime also applies to amounts paid on account of CGT under *FA 2019, Sch 2* (see **45.3** PAYMENT OF TAX).

An amount carries interest only if it is payable by HMRC to any person under or by virtue of an enactment or if it is a repayment by HMRC of any sum that was paid in connection with any liability (including any purported or anticipated liability) to make a payment to HMRC under or by virtue of an enactment.

Interest added to a repayment is known as '*repayment interest*'.

Rates of repayment interest are significantly lower than those by reference to which late payment interest is charged (see **36.2** LATE PAYMENT INTEREST AND PENALTIES). The rates are set by reference to the official bank rate set by the Bank of England Monetary Policy Committee; for details, see *SI 2011 No 2446, Reg 4*. There is a minimum rate of repayment interest of 0.5%, so that some interest will be due even when the official rate would otherwise be too low.

Rates of interest are:

- **4.25% p.a. from 22 August 2023;**
- 4.00% p.a. from 11 July 2023 to 21 August 2023;
- 3.50% p.a. from 31 May 2023 to 10 July 2023;
- 3.25% p.a. from 13 April 2023 to 30 May 2023;
- 3.00% p.a. from 21 February 2023 to 12 April 2023;
- 2.50% p.a. from 6 January 2023 to 20 February 2023;
- 2.00% p.a. from 22 November 2022 to 5 January 2023;
- 1.25% p.a. from 11 October 2022 to 21 November 2022;
- 0.75% p.a. from 23 August 2022 to 10 October 2022;
- 0.50% p.a. from 31 October 2011 to 22 August 2022.

Period for which interest accrues

A repayment within these provisions carries interest at the repayment interest rate from the 'repayment interest start date' until the date on which the repayment is made. The '*repayment interest start date*' is arrived at as set out below. It matters not that the repayment interest start date might be a non-business day.

- Where the repayment is of an amount which has been paid to HMRC, the repayment interest start date is the *later* of date A and date B, where:
  date A = the date on which the amount was paid to HMRC; and
  date B = the date on which payment of the amount to HMRC became due and payable to HMRC (where the amount was paid in connection with a liability to make a payment to HMRC).
- Where the repayment is of an amount which has not been paid to HMRC but is payable by them by virtue of a return having been filed or a claim having been made, the repayment interest start date is the *later* of date C and date D, where:
  date C = the date (if any) on which the return was required to be filed or the claim was required to be made; and
  date D = the date on which the return was in fact filed or the claim was in fact made.
- Where the repayment is the result of a loss relief claim affecting two or more years (see **13.2** CLAIMS), the repayment interest start date is 31 January following the *later* year in relation to the claim, i.e. on a claim to carry back a loss, the tax year in which the loss arises.

A repayment may take the form of a set-off against an amount owed to HMRC, in which case the date on which the repayment is made is the date from which the set-off takes effect.

As regards the date on which an amount is treated as paid to HMRC, see **45.12** PAYMENT OF TAX.

Supplementary

Repayment interest is not payable on an amount payable in consequence of an order or judgment of a court having power to allow interest on the amount.

[*FA 2009, ss 102, 103, 104, Sch 54 paras 1–5, 7; FA 2019, Sch 2 para 31; SI 2011 Nos 701, 2401, 2446*].

Companies

[50.3] Where a repayment of corporation tax falls to be made to a company, the repayment carries interest (under *ICTA 1988, s 826*) from the 'material date' until the order for repayment is issued. Corporation tax is to be brought within the repayment interest regime at **50.2** above (with special additional rules) in future.

The '*material date*' is the later of the date the corporation tax was paid and the date on which it became (or would have become) due and payable, i.e. the day following the expiry of nine months from the end of the accounting period (see **45.4** PAYMENT OF TAX).

In the case of large companies which are required to make instalment payments under the quarterly accounting rules (see **45.4** PAYMENT OF TAX) a special rate applies to any excess instalment payments until nine months after the end of the accounting period concerned, and the normal rate applies after that time. The special rate also applies to payments made by a company outside the quarterly accounting regime before the day following the expiry of nine months after the end of the accounting period concerned. Such interest is payable from the date of payment until that day although not for periods before the first instalment date (or the date which would be the first instalment date were the company within the quarterly accounting regime).

The interest rates are determined by criteria contained in Treasury regulations made by statutory instrument, see *SI 1989 No 1297, Regs 3BA, 3BB*.

The rates of interest for amounts overpaid **on or after the normal due date** for payment of corporation tax (see above) are:

- **4.25% p.a. from 22 August 2023;**
- 4.00% p.a. from 11 July 2023 to 21 August 2023;
- 3.50% p.a. from 31 May 2023 to 10 July 2023;
- 3.25% p.a. from 13 April 2023 to 30 May 2023;
- 3.00% p.a. from 21 February 2023 to 12 April 2023;
- 2.50% p.a. from 6 January 2023 to 20 February 2023;
- 2.00% p.a. from 22 November 2022 to 5 January 2023;
- 1.25% p.a. from 11 October 2022 to 21 November 2022;
- 0.75% p.a. from 23 August 2022 to 10 October 2022;
- 0.50% p.a. from 29 September 2009 to 22 August 2022.

The rates for amounts overpaid **before the due date, for example under the quarterly accounting rules for large companies,** are:

- **5.00% p.a. from 14 August 2023;**
- 4.75% p.a. from 3 July 2023 to 13 August 2023;
- 4.25% p.a. from 22 May 2023 to 2 July 2023;
- 4.00% p.a. from 3 April 2023 to 21 May 2023;
- 3.75% p.a. from 13 February 2023 to 2 April 2023;
- 3.25% p.a. from 26 December 2022 to 12 February 2023;
- 2.75% p.a. from 14 November 2022 to 25 December 2022;
- 2.00% p.a. from 3 October 2022 to 13 November 2022;
- 1.50% p.a. from 15 August 2022 to 2 October 2022;
- 1.00% p.a. from 27 June 2022 to 14 August 2022;

- 0.75% p.a. from 16 May 2022 to 26 June 2022;
- 0.50% p.a. from 21 September 2009 to 15 May 2022.

The latter set of rates applies up to the earlier of the date of repayment and the normal due date (after which the normal rates apply).

There are restrictions on the amount of the interest where surplus advance corporation tax of a later accounting period displaces mainstream corporation tax paid in respect of an earlier accounting period, or trading losses or non-trading deficits of a later accounting period are offset against profits of an earlier period or there is a combination of such events.

Interest is paid without deduction of income tax and is chargeable to corporation tax as a non-trading credit under the loan relationship rules (see **15.2–15.7** COMPANIES — CORPORATE FINANCE AND INTANGIBLES and Tolley's Corporation Tax). Corporation tax repayments are as far as possible treated as repayments of tax paid on a later date rather than an earlier date.

Interest on overpaid tax paid to a company which becomes recoverable because of a change in the company's assessed corporation tax liability and not because of HMRC error can be recovered without an assessment.

[*ICTA 1988, ss 826, 826A; FA 1989, ss 178, 179(1)(c)(ii), 180(6); FA 2009, s 105(6); FA 2019, s 88(1)(2); SI 1989 No 1297; SI 1998 No 3175, Reg 8*].

Miscellaneous

[50.4] See **45.33** PAYMENT OF TAX as regards assessment of repayment supplement or interest overpaid.

Unauthorised demands for tax

There is a general right to interest under *Supreme Court Act 1981, s 35A* in a case where the taxpayer submits to an unauthorised demand for tax, provided that the payment is not made voluntarily to close a transaction (*Woolwich Equitable Building Society v CIR* HL 1992, 65 TC 265).

Interest on judgment debts

A special rate of interest applies to interest payable by HMRC under *Judgments Act 1838, s 17* or under an order under *County Courts Act 1984, s 74* where the debt to which the interest relates arises from court proceedings relating to a tax matter. The annual rate is the Bank of England official rate plus 2%. See *F(No 2)A 2015, s 52*. Similar rules apply in Scotland and Northern Ireland. See *FA 2016, ss 170, 171*.

51

Residence and Domicile

Cross-references. See **18.9** DEATH for residence etc. status of personal representatives; **20** DOUBLE TAX RELIEF for double tax agreements which may override or amend statutory provisions or HMRC practice for the purposes of such agreements; **42** OFFSHORE SETTLEMENTS; **43** OVERSEAS MATTERS; **44.2** PARTNERSHIPS for overseas resident partners and partnerships; and **56.6** SETTLEMENTS for residence etc. status of trustees.

Simon's Taxes. See **C1.201**, **C1.6**, **E6.1**, **E6.3**.

Introduction to residence and domicile

[51.1] An individual is chargeable to capital gains tax on gains made in a tax year during any part of which they are resident in the UK. Individuals who are not domiciled in the UK can claim to use the remittance basis. Non-UK resident individuals and companies are chargeable only in respect of direct and indirect disposals of UK land. This chapter looks at the meaning of 'residence' and 'domicile'. It also considers the residence status of companies.

For 2013/14 and subsequent years, an individual's residence status is determined under the statutory residence test at **51.2** below onwards.

The term 'domicile' is governed by the general legal meaning such that each case rests on its own facts. However, from 2017/18 a 'deemed domicile' rule applies for income tax and capital gains tax purposes, with statutory definition. See **51.29** below.

The extent of the UK for tax purposes is given in **51.30** below.

Statutory residence test

[51.2] Statutory rules apply to determine whether an individual is resident or not resident in the UK for **2013/14** or any subsequent tax year. [*FA 2013, Sch 45 para 153(1)*]. These rules are known collectively as the '*statutory residence test*'. [*FA 2013, s 218, Sch 45*]. References in the rules to an individual are to one acting in any capacity, including as trustee or personal representative. [*FA 2013, Sch 45 para 145*]. The rules do not apply to determine whether an individual is resident or not resident in England, Wales, Scotland or Northern Ireland specifically (rather than in the UK as a whole). [*FA 2013, Sch 45 para 1(3)*]. Any reference in any capital gains tax enactment to an individual being resident (or not resident) in the UK is to be taken as a reference to his being resident (or not resident) in the UK in accordance with the statutory residence test. [*FA 2013, Sch 45 paras 2(1)(2), 145*].

Subject to the split year treatment at **51.17** below where there are certain changes of circumstances, an individual who, in accordance with the statutory residence test, is resident (or not resident) in the UK *for* a tax year is regarded as being UK resident (or not UK resident) at *all* times in that tax year. [*FA 2013, Sch 45 para 2(3)(4)*].

For HMRC guidance, with examples, on the statutory residence test, see HMRC Residence, Domicile and Remittance Basis Manual RDRM11000.

HMRC stress the importance of individuals keeping records and documents to support statements made when considering the statutory residence test, and give some examples of the types of records required (see HMRC Residence, Domicile and Remittance Basis Manual RDRM12900).

Coronavirus (COVID-19) special measure

The statutory residence test is amended by *FA 2020, s 109* with the effect that days between 1 March 2020 and 1 June 2020 inclusive spent by individuals in the UK for specified reasons connected with the detection, treatment or prevention of coronavirus (see **51.6** below) will not count towards the relevant tests. See also **51.3**(2), (3), **51.4**(3), **51.6**, **51.8**, **51.12**, **51.13**, **51.14**, **51.15** and **51.16** below.

This special measure applies for the purposes of determining:

- whether an individual was or was not resident in the UK for 2019/20; and
- if an individual was not resident in the UK for 2019/20 (including the case where the individual's non-resident status was as a result of the special measure), whether the individual is or is not resident in the UK for 2020/21.

[*FA 2020, s 109(1)*].

The basic rule

Under the statutory residence test an individual (P) is resident in the UK for a tax year if for that year:

- the 'automatic residence test' is met; or

- the 'sufficient ties test' (see **51.10** below) is met.

If neither of those tests is met, P is not resident in the UK for that year.

[*FA 2013, Sch 45 paras 3, 4*].

Automatic residence test

The '*automatic residence test*' is met for a year if P meets at least one of the 'automatic UK tests' (see **51.3** below) and none of the 'automatic overseas tests' (see **51.3** below). [*FA 2013, Sch 45 para 5*].

The automatic UK tests

[51.3] There are four '*automatic UK tests*'. As stated in **51.2** above, an individual (P) need meet only one of them to pass the automatic residence test.

(1) The first automatic UK test is that P spends at least 183 days in the UK in the tax year in question (year X). See **51.6** below as regards days spent in the UK.

(2) The second automatic UK test is that:
   - P has a home (see **51.7** below) in the UK for at least part of year X;
   - P is present at that home (while it is a home of his) for at least some of the time on at least 30 days (whether consecutive or intermittent) in year X;
   - while it is a home of P's, there is at least 1 period of 91 consecutive days throughout which condition A or condition B (or a combination of those conditions) is met; and
   - at least 30 days of that 91-day period fall within year X.

   Condition A is that P has no home overseas. Condition B is that P does have 1 or more homes overseas but each of them is a home at which he is present for at least some of the time on fewer than 30 days (whether consecutive or intermittent) in year X.

   If, in fact, P has more than 1 home in the UK, the test must be applied to each of those homes individually, but the test has to be met only in relation to at least 1 of them.

   The coronavirus (COVID-19) special measure at **51.2** above applies to this test, and does so for the purposes stated there. In this respect, the special measure is that a day does not count as a day when P is present at a home of P's in the UK if it is a day that would fall within the coronavirus relaxation at **51.6** below if P were present in the UK at the end of it.

(3) The third automatic UK test is that:
   - P works 'sufficient hours in the UK' (see **51.8** below), as assessed over a period of 365 days;
   - there are no 'significant breaks' from UK work within that period;
   - at least part of that period falls within year X;
   - of the total number of days in that period when P does more than 3 hours' work, more than 75% of them are days when he does more than 3 hours' work in the UK; and
   - at least 1 day in year X is a day on which P does more than 3 hours' work in the UK.

For these purposes, there is a '*significant break*' from UK work if at least 31 days go by and not one of them is a day on which P does more than three hours' work in the UK (or would have done so but for being on annual leave, sick leave, parenting leave or emergency volunteering leave under *Coronavirus Act 2020, Sch 7*). The reference here to emergency volunteering leave is part of the coronavirus (COVID-19) special measure at **51.2** above, and it applies for the purposes stated there.

See **51.8** below as regards work generally.

The third automatic UK test does not apply to P if:

- at any time in year X he has a 'relevant job' on board a vehicle, aircraft or ship (see **51.9** below); and
- at least six of the trips that he makes in year X as part of that job are cross-border trips that begin or end in the UK (or both begin and end in the UK).

(4) The fourth automatic UK test is that:

(a) P dies in year X;

(b) for each of the previous three tax years, P was resident in the UK by virtue of meeting the automatic residence test;

(c) the tax year preceding year X would not be a split year (see **51.18** below) as regards P, even if he is non-UK resident for year X;

(d) when P died, his home (see **51.7** below) (or at least one of his homes if more than one) was in the UK; and

(e) if P had a home overseas during all or part of year X, P did not spend a sufficient amount of time there in year X.

In (e) above, P spent a sufficient amount of time in year X at the overseas home if there were at least 30 days in the year when P was present there on that day for at least some of the time (no matter how short a time) or P was present there for at least some of the time (no matter how short a time) on each day of year X up to and including the day of P's death. There is no requirement for the 30 days to be consecutive, but P is only treated as present at a home if it is a home of P's at the time of his presence. If P had more than one overseas home each must be considered separately.

[*FA 2013, Sch 45 paras 6–10, 29(1), 145, 146, 154(5); FA 2020, s 109(3)(7)*].

The automatic overseas tests

[51.4] There are five '*automatic overseas tests*'. As stated in **51.2** above, the automatic residence test is failed if an individual (P) meets at least one of the automatic overseas tests.

(1) The first automatic overseas test is that:

- P was resident in the UK for one or more of the three tax years preceding the tax year in question (year X);
- the number of days in year X that P spends in the UK is less than 16; and
- P does not die in year X.

(2) The second automatic overseas test is that:

- P was resident in the UK for none of the three tax years preceding year X; and

- the number of days in year X that P spends in the UK is less than 46.

(3) The third automatic overseas test is that:

- P works 'sufficient hours overseas' (see **51.8** below), as assessed over the course of year X;
- there are no 'significant breaks' from overseas work during year X;
- the number of days in year X on which P does more than 3 hours' work in the UK is less than 31; and
- the number of days spent by P in the UK in year X is less than 91 (disregarding any days *treated* as spent in the UK under the 'deeming rule' in **51.6** below).

For these purposes, there is a '*significant break*' from overseas work if at least 31 days go by and not one of them is a day on which P does more than three hours' work overseas (or would have done so but for being on annual leave, sick leave, parenting leave or emergency volunteering leave under *Coronavirus Act 2020, Sch 7*). The reference here to emergency volunteering leave is part of the coronavirus (COVID-19) special measure at **51.2** above, and it applies for the purposes stated there.

See **51.8** below as regards work generally.

The third automatic overseas test does not apply to P if:

- at any time in year X he has a 'relevant job' on board a vehicle, aircraft or ship (see **51.9** below); and
- at least six of the trips that he makes in year X as part of that job are cross-border trips that begin or end in the UK (or both begin and end in the UK).

(4) The fourth automatic overseas test is that:

(a) P dies in year X;
(b) P was resident in the UK for neither of the two tax years preceding year X; and
(c) the number of days that P spends in the UK in year X is less than 46.

P also meets the condition in (b) above if he was not resident in the UK for the tax year preceding year X but the year before that was a split year as regards P because the circumstances fell within Case 1, Case 2 or Case 3 at **51.19–51.21** below.

(5) The fifth automatic overseas test is that:

(a) P dies in year X;
(b) P was resident in the UK for neither of the two tax years preceding year X because he met the third automatic overseas test for each of those years; and
(c) P would meet the third automatic overseas test for year X if that test were assessed by reference to the period from the start of year X up to (but not including) the date of death.

P also meets the condition in (b) above if he was not resident in the UK for the tax year preceding year X because he met the third automatic overseas test for that year but the year before that was a split year as regards P because the circumstances fell within Case 1 at **51.19** below.

[*FA 2013, Sch 45 paras 11–16, 29(2), 145, 146; FA 2020, s 109(7)*].

See 51.6 below as regards days spent in the UK.

Automatic tests — supplementary

[51.5] The following paragraphs (51.6–51.9) supplement, and provide definitions for the purposes of, the automatic UK and overseas tests at 51.3 and 51.4 above and these provisions generally.

Days spent in the UK

[51.6] Generally, if an individual (P) is present in the UK at the end of a day, that day counts as a day spent by P in the UK for the purposes of the statutory residence test. If, however, P arrives in the UK on one day and departs on the next, he is not treated as spending a day in the UK (despite his presence at the end of the day of arrival) if between arrival and departure he does not engage in activities that are to a substantial extent unrelated to his passage through the UK, i.e. he is merely a passenger in transit. Note that this precludes not only his engaging in activities relating to business or employment but also in many activities of a non-business nature such as spending time with family.

A day at the end of which P is present in the UK due only to exceptional circumstances beyond their control that prevent their leaving the UK does not count as a day spent by P in the UK. Exceptional circumstances include, for example, a sudden or life-threatening illness or injury and national or local emergencies such as war, civil unrest or natural disasters; in all cases it must be P's intention to leave the UK as soon as those circumstances permit. The maximum number of days in a tax year on which P can rely on this exclusion is limited to 60. Accordingly, once the number of days for which the exclusion applies reaches 60 (counting forward from the start of the tax year), any subsequent days, whether involving the same or different exceptional circumstances, will count as days spent by P in the UK.

Moral obligations and obligations of conscience, such as to a sick relative, do not amount to exceptional circumstances (*HMRC v A Taxpayer* UT, [2023] UKUT 182 (TCC), [2023] STC 1498). The taxpayer in that case had remained in the UK to care for a relative suffering from alcoholism and depression who had threatened suicide.

For more on how HMRC interpret the term 'exceptional circumstances', see HMRC Residence, Domicile and Remittance Basis Manual RDRM13240. See HMRC Residence, Domicile and Remittance Basis Manual RDRM11005 for circumstances resulting from the impact of COVID-19 (coronavirus) that are accepted by HMRC as being exceptional.

Coronavirus (COVID-19) relaxation

A day at the end of which P is present in the UK due where the following circumstances are present does not count as a day spent by P in the UK:

- the day in question falls within the period 1 March 2020 to 1 June 2020 inclusive;
- on that day P is present in the UK for an 'applicable reason' related to coronavirus; and

- in the tax year under consideration (whether it be 2019/20 or 2020/21), P is resident in a territory outside the UK, i.e. P is considered for tax purposes to be a resident of that territory in accordance with that territory's laws.

The following are 'applicable reasons':

- that P is in the UK as a medical or healthcare professional for purposes connected with the detection, treatment or prevention of coronavirus;
- that P is in the UK for purposes connected with the development or production of medicinal products (including vaccines), devices, equipment or facilities related to the detection, treatment or prevention of coronavirus.

The Treasury have power to make regulations to defer the 1 June 2020 date above (provided the revised date is no later than 5 April 2021) and/or to add one or more 'applicable reasons'.

This is an integral part of the coronavirus special measure at **51.2** above, and it applies for the purposes stated there.

The 'deeming rule'

If P is not present in the UK at the end of a day, that day does not count as a day spent by P in the UK, but this is subject to a rule known as the 'deeming rule'. The '*deeming rule*' applies if:

- P has at least three 'UK ties' (see **51.11** below) for a tax year (year X) (determined without reference to the deeming rule itself);
- P was resident in the UK for at least one of the three tax years preceding year X; and
- the number of days ('*visiting days*') in year X when P is present in the UK at some point in the day, but *not* at the end of it, is more than 30.

The deeming rule is that, once the number of visiting days in year X reaches 30 (counting forward from the start of the tax year), each subsequent visiting day in year X is treated as a day spent by P in the UK.

The coronavirus special measure at **51.2** above applies to the deeming rule, and does so for the purposes stated there. In this respect, the special measure is that a day does not count as a visiting day if it is a day that would fall within the COVID-19 relaxation above if P were present in the UK at the end of it.

[*FA 2013, Sch 45 paras 22–24; FA 2020, s 109(4)(5)*].

An individual's home

[51.7] For the purposes of the statutory residence test, an individual's home could be a building or part of a building or, for example, a vehicle, vessel or structure of any kind. Whether, for a given building etc., there is sufficient degree of permanence or stability about an individual's arrangements there for it to count as his home (or one of his homes) depends on all the circumstances of the case. A place that an individual uses periodically as nothing more than a holiday home or temporary retreat (or similar) does not count as a home of his.

A place can count as an individual's home whether or not he holds any estate or interest in it; but the mere fact that he still holds an estate or interest does not continue to make a place an individual's home once he has moved out. [*FA 2013, Sch 45 para 25*].

For further information about how HMRC interpret the term 'home' in the context of applying the statutory residence test, see HMRC Residence, Domicile and Remittance Basis Manual RDRM13020–13060.

Work

[51.8] For the purposes of the statutory residence test, an individual (P) is considered to be 'working' (or 'doing work') at any time when he is doing something either in performing the duties of an employment or in the course of a trade carried on by him (whether alone or in partnership). A voluntary post for which P has no contract of service does not count as an employment for these purposes. Throughout these provisions 'trade' includes a profession or vocation, anything treated as a trade for income tax purposes and the commercial occupation of woodlands. Whilst in most cases it will be obvious, *FA 2015, Sch 43 para 26(2), (3)* contain extra rules for determining whether something is being done in performing the duties of an employment or in the course of a trade etc.

Time spent *travelling* counts as time spent working:

- if the cost of the journey would, if incurred by P, be deductible in calculating his taxable earnings or, as the case may be, taxable profits (on the assumption that P is within the charge to income tax); or
- to the extent that P does something else during the journey that would itself count as work.

Time spent undertaking *training* counts as time spent working if:

- in the case of employment, the training is provided or paid for by the employer and is undertaken to help P in performing his duties; and
- in the case of a trade etc., the cost of the training is deductible in calculating taxable profits (on the assumption that P is within the charge to income tax).

[*FA 2013, Sch 45 paras 26, 145*].

Location of work

Work is regarded as done where it is actually done, regardless of where the employment is held or the trade is carried on. However, work done by way of, or in the course of, travelling to or from the UK by air, sea or tunnel is assumed to be done overseas even during the part of the journey in or over the UK. For this purpose, the travelling begins when P boards the aircraft, ship or train that will take him to another country from the UK or vice versa and ends when he disembarks.

In the case of people with relevant jobs on board vehicles, aircraft or ships (see **51.9** below), the above is subject to **51.14** below.

[*FA 2013, Sch 45 para 27*].

Working sufficient hours

For the purposes of the third automatic UK test at **51.3**(3) above, P works '*sufficient hours in the UK*' if his weekly 'net UK hours' are at least 35.

P's total '*net UK hours*' are determined by identifying, for any given period of 365 days and including all employments held and trades carried on by him, the total number of hours that P works in the UK during that period. However, any hours that he works in the UK on 'disregarded days' are not to be included in this total. A '*disregarded day*' is a day on which P does more than three hours' work overseas (even if he also does work in the UK on the same day).

Similarly, for the purposes of the third automatic overseas test at **51.4**(3) above, P works '*sufficient hours overseas*' if his weekly 'net overseas hours' are at least 35. P's total '*net overseas hours*' are determined by identifying, for year X and including all employments held and trades carried on by him, the total number of hours that P works overseas during that period. Any hours that he works overseas on 'disregarded days' are not to be included in the total. A '*disregarded day*' is a day on which P does more than three hours' work in the UK (even if he also does work overseas on the same day).

The reference period

P's weekly net UK hours is his total net UK hours divided by the number of weeks in the 'reference period'. The '*reference period*' is calculated by subtracting from 365 the total number of disregarded days as above and, if appropriate, reducing the total as described below. The number of weeks in the reference period is calculated by dividing the reference period by 7; the result is rounded down to the nearest whole number, unless it is less than 1 in which case it is rounded up to 1.

P's weekly net overseas hours are computed in similar fashion, except that if year X is a leap year the starting point in calculating the reference period is 366. Where **51.4**(5)(c) is in point, the starting point is the number of days in the period from the start of year X up to (but not including) the date of P's death.

In all cases the reference period can be reduced to take account of:

(a) reasonable amounts of annual leave or parenting leave taken (having regard to, for example, the nature of the work and the country in which it is performed);
(b) reasonable sick leave taken;
(c) absences from work at times during the period specified in an emergency volunteering certificate issued to P under *Coronavirus Act 2020, Sch 7* (emergency volunteering leave); and
(d) any 'non-working days' 'embedded' within a block of leave for which a reduction is made under (a) or (b).

No such reduction can be made in respect of a disregarded day. If the total days for which a reduction is available under (a) or (b) is not a whole number, the number is rounded down (but the rounding is ignored for the purposes of (d)). A '*non-working day*' is any day on which P is not normally expected to work (according to his contract of employment or usual pattern of work) and does not in fact work. Non-working days are '*embedded*' within a block of leave only if there are at least three consecutive days of leave taken both before and after the non-working day (or series of non-working days) in question.

If there is a change of employment during the reference period, with a gap in between the two jobs, the reference period is reduced by the number of days in the gap. The reduction for any 1 gap is limited to 15 days; if there is more than 1 such gap, the maximum reduction for all the gaps is limited to 30 days.

Item (c) above is part of the coronavirus (COVID-19) special measure at **51.2** above, and it applies for the purposes stated there.

[*FA 2013, Sch 45 paras 9(2), 14(3), 16(3), 28, 145, 146; FA 2020, s 109(3)*].

Relevant job on board vehicle, aircraft or ship

[51.9] For the purposes of the statutory residence test, an individual (P) has a relevant job on board a vehicle, aircraft or ship if conditions A and B are both met. Condition A is that:

(a) P holds an employment, the duties of which consist of duties to be performed, or
(b) carries on a trade, the activities of which consist of work to be done or services to be provided,

on board a vehicle, aircraft or ship while it is travelling. The condition at (b) is met only if, in order to do the work or provide the services, P has to be present (in person) on board the vehicle etc. while it is travelling.

Condition B is that substantially all of the trips made in performing those duties or carrying on those activities are trips that involve crossing an international boundary ('*cross-border trips*').

In determining whether conditions A and B are met, duties or activities of a purely incidental nature are ignored.

[*FA 2013, Sch 45 para 30*].

See also **51.14** below.

The sufficient ties test

[51.10] As stated in **51.2** above, the sufficient ties test is an alternative to the automatic residence test. The '*sufficient ties test*' is met by an individual (P) for the year in question (year X) if P meets none of the automatic UK tests (**51.3** above) and none of the automatic overseas tests (**51.4** above), but P has sufficient 'UK ties' (see **51.11** below) for the year. Whether P has sufficient UK ties for year X depends upon whether he was resident in the UK for any of the previous three tax years and the number of days he spends in the UK in year X. See the tables below, and note the modifications where death occurs in year X. See **51.6** above as regards days spent in the UK.

Sufficient UK ties tables

Where P was UK resident for at least 1 of the 3 tax years preceding year X

Days spent by P in the UK in year X	*Number of UK ties that are sufficient*
More than 15 but not more than 45	At least 4
More than 45 but not more than 90	At least 3
More than 90 but not more than 120	At least 2
More than 120	At least 1

Where P was UK resident for none of the 3 tax years preceding year X

Days spent by P in the UK in year X	*Number of UK ties that are sufficient*
More than 45 but not more than 90	4
More than 90 but not more than 120	At least 3
More than 120	At least 2

Modification of tables on death in year X

If P dies in year X, the first modification is that in the first table the top row of the first column reads 'not more than 45' instead of 'more than 15 but not more than 45'.

The second and final modification is that if the death occurs before 1 March in year X, both tables have effect as if each number of days quoted in the first column were reduced by the 'appropriate number'. The '*appropriate number*' is found by multiplying the number of days quoted, in each case, by $^A/_{12}$, where A = the number of 'whole months' in year X after the month in which P dies. A '*whole month*' means an entire calendar month, e.g. the month of January. If the appropriate number is not a whole number it is rounded down if the first figure after the decimal point is less than 5; otherwise it is rounded up. If P dies on, say, 17 December in year X, the number of whole months is 3. So, for example, in the top row of the first column of the second table, the figure of 45 is reduced by 11 (45 x $^3/_{12}$) and the figure of 90 is reduced by 23. The top row then reads 'more than 34 but not more than 67', reflecting the fact that P is alive for approximately only three-quarters of the tax year.

[*FA 2013, Sch 45 paras 17–20, 145*].

UK ties

[51.11] If the individual (P) was resident in the UK for at least one of the three tax years preceding the tax year in question (year X), each of the following counts as a '*UK tie*' for the purposes of **51.10** above and these provisions in general:

(a) a 'family tie' (**51.12** below);
(b) an 'accommodation tie' (**51.13** below);

(c) a 'work tie' (**51.14** below);
(d) a '90-day tie' (**51.15** below); and
(e) a 'country tie' (**51.16** below).

If P was resident in the UK for none of the three tax years preceding year X, each of the types of tie listed at (a)–(d) above, but not (e) above, counts as a UK tie.

In order to have the requisite number of UK ties for year X, each of P's ties has to be of a different type.

[*FA 2013, Sch 45 para 31*].

Family ties

[51.12] For the purposes of **51.11**(a) above, P has a '*family tie*' for year X if:

(a) in year X, a 'relevant relationship' exists at any time between P and another person; and
(b) that other person is resident in the UK for year X (see further below).

A '*relevant relationship*' exists at any time between P and another person if at that time:

- they are spouses or civil partners and are not separated (whether by court order, deed of separation or in circumstances where the separation is likely to be permanent);
- they are living together as if they were spouses or civil partners; or
- the other person is a child of P and is under 18.

P does not have a family tie by virtue of the last of these conditions if P sees the child in the UK on fewer than 61 days in total in year X (or, where relevant, in the part of year X before the child's 18th birthday); a day counts as a day on which P sees the child if he sees the child in person for all or part of the day. But a day does not count as a day on which P sees the child if the day on which P sees the child would be a day falling within the coronavirus (COVID-19) relaxation at **51.6** above if P were present in the UK at the end of it; this is part of the coronavirus special measure at **51.2** above, and it applies for the purposes stated there.

Whether 'other person' is UK resident

The following rules apply in determining whether a person is resident in the UK for year X for the purposes of (b) above (and only for those purposes).

A family tie based on the fact that a family member has, by the same token, a relevant relationship with P is to be disregarded in deciding whether that family member is someone who is resident in the UK for year X.

A family member who:

- is a child of P under 18,
- is in full-time education in the UK at any time in year X, and
- is resident in the UK for year X but would not be so resident if time spent in full-time education in the UK were disregarded,

is treated as being not resident in the UK for year X if the number of days that he spends in the UK in the part of year X outside term-time is less than 21. Half-term breaks, and any other breaks when teaching is not provided during a term, are considered to form part of term-time for these purposes.

[*FA 2013, Sch 45 paras 32, 33; FA 2020, s 109(8); SI 2019 No 1458, Sch 3 para 36(2)*].

For further information about how HMRC interpret the term 'family tie', see HMRC Residence, Domicile and Remittance Basis Manual RDRM13310–13330.

Accommodation ties

[51.13] For the purposes of **51.11**(b) above, P has an '*accommodation tie*' for year X if:

(a) P has a place to live in the UK;
(b) that place is available to P during year X for a continuous period of at least 91 days (but see below); and
(c) P spends at least one night at that place in that year (but see below).

For the purposes of (a) above, P is considered to have a place to live in the UK if:

- P's home or at least one of his homes (if more than one) is in the UK; or
- P has a holiday home or temporary retreat (or similar) in the UK; or
- accommodation is otherwise available to P where he can live when in the UK. Accommodation may be regarded as available to P even if he holds no estate or interest in it and even if he has no legal right to occupy it.

See **51.7** above for what is meant by an individual's home.

For the purposes of (b) above, if there is a gap of fewer than 16 days between periods in year X when a particular place is available to P, that place is treated as continuing to be available to P during the gap.

For the purposes of (c) above, if the accommodation is the home of a 'close relative' of P, the condition is met only if P spends a total of at least 16 nights there in year X (as opposed to 1 night). For this purpose, a '*close relative*' means a parent or grandparent, a brother or sister, a child aged 18 or over or a grandchild aged 18 or over; it is irrelevant whether the relationship subsists by blood or half-blood or by virtue of marriage or civil partnership.

The coronavirus (COVID-19) special measure at **51.2** above applies to the conditions at (a)–(c) above, and does so for the purposes stated there. In this respect, the special measure is that:

- if the place in (a) above is available to P on a day that would fall within the coronavirus relaxation at **51.6** above if P were present in the UK at the end of it, that day is to be disregarded for the purposes of (b) above; and
- a night spent by P at the place immediately before or after a day that would fall within the coronavirus relaxation is to be disregarded for the purposes of (c) above.

[*FA 2013, Sch 45 para 34; FA 2020, s 109(9)*].

For further information about what HMRC consider to be an accommodation tie see HMRC Residence, Domicile and Remittance Basis Manual RDRM13070–13090.

Work ties

[51.14] For the purposes of **51.11**(c) above, P has a '*work tie*' for year X if he works in the UK for at least 40 days (whether continuously or intermittently) in year X. For these purposes, P works in the UK for a day if he does more than 3 hours' work in the UK on that day. See **51.8** above for what is meant by working.

The coronavirus (COVID-19) special measure at **51.2** above applies to the above rule, and does so for the purposes stated there. In this respect, the special measure is that a day that would fall within the coronavirus relaxation at **51.6** above, if P were present in the UK at the end of it, does not count as a day on which P works in the UK.

Relevant job on board vehicle, aircraft or ship

If P has a relevant job on board a vehicle, aircraft or ship (see **51.9** above), he is assumed for the above purposes to do more than three hours' work in the UK on any day on which he starts a cross-border trip (as part of that job) that begins in the UK. He is assumed to do fewer than three hours' work in the UK on any day on which he completes a cross-border trip (as part of that job) that ends in the UK. Any day on which P both starts and completes a cross-border trip is treated as one on which he does more than three hours' work in the UK. In the case of a cross-border trip to or from the UK that is undertaken in stages, the day on which the trip begins or, as the case may be, ends is the day on which the stage of the trip that involves crossing the UK border begins or ends. Any day on which a stage of the trip is undertaken by P solely within the UK is to be counted, if it lasts for more than three hours, as a day on which P does more than three hours' work in the UK.

[*FA 2013, Sch 45 paras 35, 36; FA 2020, s 109(10)*].

90-day ties

[51.15] For the purposes of **51.11**(d) above, P has a '*90-day tie*' for year X if P has spent more than 90 days in the UK in either or both of the 2 tax years preceding year X.

The coronavirus (COVID-19) special measure at **51.2** above applies to the above rule, and does so for the purposes stated there. In this respect, the special measure is that a day that would fall within the COVID-19 relaxation at **51.6** above, if P were present in the UK at the end of it, does not count as a day P has spent in the UK in the tax year in question.

[*FA 2013, Sch 45 para 37; FA 2020, s 109(11)*].

Country ties

[51.16] For the purposes of **51.11**(e) above, P has a '*country tie*' for year X if the country in which P meets the 'midnight test' for the greatest number of days in year X is the UK. P meets the '*midnight test*' in a country for a day if he is present in that country at the end of that day. In the event that the greatest number of days is equal for two or more countries, P has a country tie for year X if one of those countries is the UK.

The coronavirus (COVID-19) special measure at **51.2** above applies to the midnight test, and does so for the purposes stated there. In this respect, the special measure is that P is to be treated as not being present in the UK at the end of a day that would fall within the coronavirus relaxation at **51.6** above.

[*FA 2013, Sch 45 para 38; FA 2020, s 109(12)*].

Split year treatment

[51.17] The effect of a tax year being a split year is to relax the general rule in **51.2** above that treats individuals who are UK resident (or not resident) *for* a tax year as being UK resident (or not resident) at all times in that tax year. A split year is divided into a UK part and an overseas part as set out in each of **51.19–51.26** below.

The effect of split year treatment on the various capital gains tax charging rules is covered throughout this work where relevant: see in particular **1.2** INTRODUCTION, **42.5** OFFSHORE SETTLEMENTS, **52.5** RETURNS.

Split year treatment does not apply to personal representatives, and applies to only a limited extent to trustees (see **42.1** OFFSHORE SETTLEMENTS). The existence of special charging rules for cases involving split years is not intended to affect any question as to whether an individual would fall to be regarded under a double tax treaty as UK resident.

[*FA 2013, Sch 45 paras 39–42, 153(2)*].

What is a split year?

[51.18] For the purposes of **51.17** above and the statutory residence test generally, a tax year (year X) is a '*split year*' as regards an individual (P) if he is resident in the UK for year X and the circumstances of the case fall within any of Cases 1–8 at **51.19–51.26** below. Cases 1–3 involve departure from the UK, and Cases 4–8 involve arrival in the UK. [*FA 2013, Sch 45 para 43*].

If the taxpayer falls within two or all of Cases 1–3, Case 1 takes priority over Cases 2 and 3, and Case 2 takes priority over Case 3. [*FA 2013, Sch 45 para 54*].

If the taxpayer falls within two or more of Cases 4–8 the following priority rules apply.

- If both Case 5 and Case 6 apply, Case 6 takes priority unless the 'split year date' for Case 5 is earlier than the split year date for Case 6, in which case, Case 5 takes priority.
- If Case 7 and Case 5 (but not Case 6) apply Case 7 takes priority unless the split year date for Case 5 is earlier than the split year date for Case 7, in which case, Case 5 takes priority.
- If two or all of Cases 4, 5 and 8 apply but neither Case 6 nor Case 7 apply, the Case with the earliest split year date has priority. If two or all of the Cases share the earliest split year date, those Cases take priority.

The '*split year date*' means the first day of the UK part of the year under the Case concerned.

[*FA 2013, Sch 45 para 55*].

Case 1

[51.19] The circumstances of a case fall within Case 1 if they are of the description below. The overseas part of the split year is the part beginning with the first day of the period mentioned in (2) below. If there is more than one such period, the overseas part of the split year is the part beginning with the first day of the longest of those periods. The UK part of the split year is the part that is not the overseas part.

(1) P was resident in the UK for the tax year preceding year X (whether or not that previous year was itself a split year).

(2) There is a period that:
- begins with a day in year X on which P does more than three hours' work overseas;
- ends with the last day of year X; and
- satisfies the 'overseas work criteria'.

There may be more than one such period.

(3) P is not resident in the UK for the tax year following year X, and this is because he meets the third automatic overseas test (see **51.4**(3) above) for that following year.

For the purposes of (2) above, a period satisfies the '*overseas work criteria*' if:

- P works 'sufficient hours overseas', as assessed over that period;
- there are no 'significant breaks' from overseas work during that period (see **51.4**(3) above);
- the number of days in that period on which P does more than three hours' work in the UK does not exceed the 'first permitted limit'; and
- the number of days in that period spent by P in the UK does not exceed the 'second permitted limit'. (Any days *treated* as spent in the UK under the 'deeming rule' in **51.6** above do not count for this purpose.)

The question of whether P works '*sufficient hours overseas*' is determined as in **51.8** above except that the starting point in calculating the reference period is the number of days in the period mentioned in (2) above. The maximum number of days by which the reference period may be reduced for multiple gaps between employments is equal to the 'first permitted limit' (instead of 30 as in 51.8).

The '*first permitted limit*' is 30 minus the 'appropriate number'; the '*second permitted limit*' is 90 minus the 'appropriate number'. The '*appropriate number*' is the product of:

$$A \times \frac{B}{12}$$

A = either 30 or 90, depending on whether one is calculating the first or second permitted limit; and

B = the number of whole months in the part of year X before the day on which begins the period mentioned in (2) above. A '*whole month*' means an entire calendar month, e.g. the month of January; the period from 6 April to 30 April inclusive also counts as a whole month.

If the appropriate number is not a whole number it is rounded down if the first figure after the decimal point is less than 5; otherwise it is rounded up.

[*FA 2013, Sch 45 paras 29(2), 44, 52–56, 145; FA 2020, s 109(7); SI 2019 No 1458, Sch 3 para 36(3)*].

Case 2

[51.20] The circumstances of a case fall within Case 2 if they are of the description below. The UK part of the split year is the part of the tax year ending immediately before the 'deemed departure day' in (4) below; the remainder of the tax year is the overseas part of the split year.

(1) P was resident in the UK for the tax year preceding year X (whether or not that previous year was itself a split year).
(2) P has a 'partner' whose circumstances fall within Case 1 at **51.19** above for year X or the previous tax year. '*Partner*' means a spouse or civil partner or a person with whom P is living as if they were a married couple or civil partners.
(3) On a day in year X, P moves overseas in order to continue living with the partner while the partner is working overseas.
(4) In the part of year X beginning with the 'deemed departure day':
   - P either has no home (see **51.7** above) in the UK or has homes in both the UK and overseas but spends the greater part of the time living in the overseas home; and
   - the number of days that P spends in the UK does not exceed the 'permitted limit'. (See **51.6** above as regards days spent in the UK.)
(5) P is not resident in the UK for the tax year following year X.

If (2) above applies by reference to year X itself, the '*deemed departure day*' is the later of the day mentioned in (3) above and the first day of what is, for P's partner, the overseas part of the year (see **51.19** above). If (2) above applies by reference to the previous tax year, the '*deemed departure day*' is the day mentioned in (3) above.

The '*permitted limit*' is 90 minus the 'appropriate number. The '*appropriate number*' is the product of:

$$A \times \frac{B}{12}$$

A = 90

B = the number of whole months in the part of year X before the deemed departure day. A '*whole month*' means an entire calendar month, e.g. the month of January; the period from 6 April to 30 April inclusive also counts as a whole month.

If the appropriate number is not a whole number it is rounded down if the first figure after the decimal point is less than 5; otherwise it is rounded up.

[*FA 2013, Sch 43 paras 45, 52–56, 145*].

Case 3

[51.21] The circumstances of a case fall within Case 3 if they are of the description below. The UK part of the split year is the part of the tax year ending immediately before the day mentioned in (2)(a) below; the remainder of the tax year is the overseas part of the split year.

(1) P was resident in the UK for the tax year preceding year X (whether or not that previous year was itself a split year).
(2) At the start of year X P had one or more homes (see **51.7** above) in the UK but:
  (a) there comes a day in year X when P ceases to have any home in the UK; and
  (b) from then on, P has no home in the UK for the rest of that tax year.
(3) In the part of year X beginning with the day mentioned in (2)(a) above, P spends fewer than 16 days in the UK. (See **51.6** above as regards days spent in the UK.)
(4) P is not resident in the UK for the tax year following year X.
(5) At the end of the period of six months beginning with the day mentioned in (2)(a) above, P has a 'sufficient link' with a country overseas.

For the purposes of (5) above, P has a '*sufficient link*' with a country overseas if (and only if):

- he is considered for tax purposes to be a resident of that country in accordance with its domestic laws; or
- he has been in that country at the end of each day of the six-month period mentioned in (5) above; or
- his only home is in that country or, if he has more than one home, they are all in that country.

[*FA 2013, Sch 45 paras 46, 52–56*].

Case 4

[51.22] The circumstances of a case fall within Case 4 if they are of the description below. The UK part of the split year is the part of the tax year beginning on the day mentioned in (2) below; the earlier part of the tax year is the overseas part of the split year.

(1) P was not resident in the UK for the tax year preceding year X.

(2) At the start of year X, P did not meet the 'only home test', but there comes a day in year X when he starts to meet that test and he then continues to meet it for the remainder of the tax year; or
The '*only home test*' is met if P has only one home (see **51.7** above) and it is in the UK or if P has more than one home and all of them are in the UK.

(3) For the part of year X before the day mentioned in (2) above, P does not have sufficient UK ties.

The sufficient ties test at **51.10** above applies for the purposes of (3) above, but with the following modifications:

- references to 'year X' are to be read as references to the part of year X in question (except that when applying the family ties test in **51.12** above, the residence of the 'other person' is still determined by reference to year X); and
- both tables have effect as if each number of days quoted in the first column were reduced by the 'appropriate number'.

For this purpose, the '*appropriate number*' is found by multiplying the number of days quoted, in each case, by $^{A}/_{12}$, where A = the number of 'whole months' in year X beginning with the day mentioned in (2) above. A '*whole month*' means an entire calendar month, e.g. the month of January. If the appropriate number is not a whole number it is rounded down if the first figure after the decimal point is less than 5; otherwise it is rounded up.

[*FA 2013, Sch 45 paras 47, 52–56, 145*].

Case 5

[51.23] The circumstances of a case fall within Case 5 if they are of the description below. The overseas part of the split year is the part before the period mentioned in (2) below begins. If there is more than one such period, the overseas part of the split year is the part before the first of those periods begins. The UK part of the split year is the part that is not the overseas part.

(1) P was not resident in the UK for the tax year preceding year X.

(2) There is at least one period of 365 days beginning in year X in respect of which all the following conditions are met:

  (a) the period begins with a day on which P does more than three hours' work in the UK;
  (b) in the part of year X before the period begins, P does not have sufficient UK ties;
  (c) P works 'sufficient hours in the UK' (see **51.8** above), as assessed over the period;
  (d) there are no 'significant breaks' from UK work (see **51.3**(3) above) during that period; and
  (e) of the total number of days in the period when P does more than three hours' work, at least 75% of them are days when he does more than three hours' work in the UK.

The sufficient ties test at **51.10** above applies for the purposes of (2)(b) above, but with the same modifications as in **51.22** above; the appropriate number is computed in the same way as in **51.22** but by reference to the number of whole months in year X beginning with the day on which the 365-day period in (2) begins.

[*FA 2013, Sch 45 paras 48, 52–56, 145*].

Case 6

[51.24] The circumstances of a case fall within Case 6 if they are of the description below. The overseas part of the split year is the part ending with the last day of that period. If there is more than one such period, the overseas part of the split year is the part ending with the last day of the longest of those periods. The UK part of the split year is the part that is not the overseas part.

(1) P was not resident in the UK for the tax year preceding year X, and this is because he met the third automatic overseas test (see **51.4**(3) above) for that preceding year.

(2) There is a period that:
- begins with the first day of year X and ends in that year;
- ends with a day on which P does more than three hours' work overseas; and
- satisfies the 'overseas work criteria'.

There may be more than one such period.

(3) P is resident in the UK for the tax year following year X (whether or not that following year is itself a split year).

In (2) above, '*overseas work criteria*' has the same meaning as in Case 1 at **51.19** above, except that, in computing the 'appropriate number', B = the number of whole months in the part of year X after the period in (2) ends.

[*FA 2013, Sch 45 paras 49, 52–56, 145*].

Case 7

[51.25] The circumstances of a case fall within Case 7 if they are of the description below. The UK part of the split year is the part of the tax year beginning with the 'deemed arrival day' in (4) below; the earlier part of the tax year is the overseas part of the split year.

(1) P was not resident in the UK for the tax year preceding year X.

(2) P has a 'partner' whose circumstances fall within Case 6 at **51.24** above for year X or the previous tax year. '*Partner*' means a spouse or civil partner or a person with whom P is cohabiting as if they were a married couple or civil partners.

(3) On a day in year X, P moves to the UK in order to continue living with the partner on the partner's return or relocation to the UK.

(4) In the part of year X before the 'deemed arrival day':
- P either has no home (see **51.7** above) in the UK or has homes in both the UK and overseas but spends the greater part of the time living in the overseas home; and
- the number of days that P spends in the UK does not exceed the 'permitted limit'. (See **51.6** above as regards days spent in the UK.)

(5) P is resident in the UK for the tax year following year X (whether or not that following year is itself a split year).

If (2) above applies by reference to year X itself, the '*deemed arrival day*' is the later of the day mentioned in (3) above and the first day of what is, for P's partner, the UK part of the year (see **51.24** above). If (2) above applies by reference to the previous tax year, the '*deemed arrival day*' is the day mentioned in (3) above.

In (4) above, '*permitted limit*' is the same as in Case 2 at **51.20** above, except that, in computing the 'appropriate number', B = the number of whole months in the part of year X beginning with the deemed arrival day.

[*FA 2013, Sch 45 paras 50, 52–56, 145*].

Case 8

[51.26] The circumstances of a case fall within Case 8 if they are of the description below. The UK part of the split year is the part of the tax year beginning on the day mentioned in (2)(a) below; the earlier part of the tax year is the overseas part of the split year.

(1) P was not resident in the UK for the tax year preceding year X.
(2) At the start of year X, P had no home (see **51.7** above) in the UK, but:
  (a) there comes a day when, for the first time in that year, P does have a home in the UK; and
  (b) from then on, he continues to have a home in the UK for the remainder of year X and for the whole of the following tax year.
(3) For the part of year X before the day mentioned in (2)(a) above, P does not have sufficient UK ties.
(4) P is resident in the UK for the tax year following year X, and that following year is not a split year as regards P.

The sufficient ties test at **51.10** above applies for the purposes of (3) above, but with the same modifications as in **51.22** above; the appropriate number is computed in the same way as in **51.22** but by reference to the number of whole months in year X beginning with the day mentioned in (2)(a) above.

[*FA 2013, Sch 45 paras 51–56, 145*].

Members of Parliament

[51.27] A person who for any part of a tax year is a member of the House of Commons or, with certain exceptions, the House of Lords is treated for income tax and capital gains tax purposes as resident and domiciled in the UK for the whole of that tax year. [*Constitutional Reform and Governance Act 2010, ss 41, 42*].

Companies

[51.28] A company incorporated in the UK is regarded for corporation tax purposes as resident there, irrespective of any rule of law giving a different place of residence. [*TCGA 1992, s 286A; CTA 2009, s 14*].

A company which would otherwise be regarded as resident in the UK for corporation tax purposes, and is regarded for the purposes of any double tax relief arrangements as resident in a territory outside the UK and not resident in the UK (on the assumption that a claim for relief under those arrangements has been made and under the claim it falls to be decided whether the company is to be so regarded for the purposes of those arrangements), is treated for corporation tax purposes as resident outside the UK and not resident in the UK. This treatment applies whether the company would otherwise be regarded as resident in the UK for corporation tax purposes under the 'incorporation test' above, the test for SEs below or by virtue of some other rule of law (see below). [*TCGA 1992, s 286A; CTA 2009, s 18*].

For companies incorporated outside the UK there is no statutory definition of residence. The courts have determined that such a company resides where its real business is carried on, i.e. '*where its central management and control actually abide*'. This was the criterion applied to all companies prior to the introduction of the above provisions.

A company doing business abroad but controlled from the UK is therefore resident in the UK (subject to any overriding provisions contained in relevant double taxation agreements). In the following cases, the company was held to be managed and controlled from, and hence resident in, the UK:

- *Calcutta Jute Mills Co Ltd v Nicholson* Ex D 1876, 1 TC 83 (UK company operating abroad but directors and shareholders meeting in UK);
- *De Beers Consolidated Mines Ltd v Howe* HL 1906, 5 TC 198 (South African company operating there but important affairs controlled from UK where majority of directors resided);
- *New Zealand Shipping Co Ltd v Thew* HL 1922, 8 TC 208 (New Zealand company with New Zealand directors, but overall control lay with separate London board);
- *American Thread Co v Joyce* HL 1913, 6 TC 163 (UK company operating in USA with US directors in charge of current business, but overall control in London);
- *John Hood & Co Ltd v Magee* KB (I) 1918, 7 TC 327 (company registered in both UK and USA, with the only director resident in USA, but general meetings and material trading activities in UK);
- *Laerstate BV v HMRC* FTT, [2009] SFTD 551 (Netherlands company with policy, strategic and management matters decided in UK sby sole shareholder).

But in *A-G v Alexander* Ex D, [1874] 10 Ex 20, a foreign state bank with a UK branch was held resident abroad, notwithstanding that shareholders' meetings were held in London. See also *Wood v Holden* CA, [2006] STC 443 where a subsidiary company registered in the Netherlands with Netherland's directors was held to be non-resident. Even though the subsidiary was formed for a limited purpose as part of a plan devised purely for tax purposes of UK taxpayers, the board of directors in the Netherlands was independent.

A contrasting decision was reached in *Development Securities plc v HMRC* CA, [2020] EWCA Civ 1705, in which Jersey-registered companies were held to be residents in the UK. The companies were set up solely to implement a tax avoidance scheme. The court upheld the FTT's decision that the Jersey directors had merely formally approved what the UK parent had already decided so that central management and control was in the UK.

HMRC's approach to applying the basic test of the place of central management and control is first to ascertain whether the directors in fact themselves exercise central management and control; if so, to determine where that central management and control is exercised (not necessarily where they meet); if not, to establish where and by whom it is exercised. The concept of the place of central management and control is directed at the highest level of control of the company's business, rather than the place where the main business operations are to be found. This must always be a question of fact in any particular case, but the place of directors' meetings will usually be of significance if they are the medium through which central management and control is exercised. If, however, central management and control is in reality exercised by, for example, a single individual, the company's residence will be where that individual exercises his powers. With regard to the particular problem of residence of a subsidiary, HMRC would not normally seek to impute to the subsidiary the residence of its parent unless the parent in effect usurps the functions of the Board of the subsidiary. Matters taken into account would include the extent to which the directors of the subsidiary take decisions on their own authority as to investment, production, marketing and procurement without reference to the parent (and see below).

In all cases, HMRC will seek to determine whether a major objective of the existence of any particular factors bearing on residence is the obtaining of tax benefits from residence or non-residence, and to establish the reality of the central management and control (HMRC Statement of Practice SP 1/90).

A company may be resident in more than one country. See *Swedish Central Railway Co Ltd v Thompson* HL 1925, 9 TC 342, and for an authoritative discussion of dual residence, *Union Corporation Ltd v CIR* HL 1953, 34 TC 207.

A company may have a domicile (see *Gasque v CIR* KB 1940, 23 TC 210), but it would seem from the *Union Corporation* case above that, for a company, ordinary residence and residence are synonymous. In the light of *CTA 2009, s 19* and *TCGA 1992, s 2C* it would seem, anyway, that ordinary residence is not relevant to the chargeable gains of companies.

European Companies (SEs) and European Co-operatives (SCEs)

An SE (a European Company — see **14.16** COMPANIES) which transfers its registered office to the UK in accordance with *Council Regulation (EC) 2157/2001, Art 8* is regarded upon registration in the UK as resident in the UK for tax purposes. If a different place of residence is given by any rule of law, that place is not taken into account for tax purposes. Where this rule applies, the SE is not treated as ceasing to be UK-resident by reason only of the subsequent transfer from the UK of its registered office. The same rules apply also to an SCE (a European Co-operative — see **14.17** COMPANIES) which transfers its registered office to the UK in accordance with *Council Regulation (EC) 1435/2003, Art 7*. [*TCGA 1992, s 286A; CTA 2009, ss 16, 17*]. These provisions are subject to the double tax agreement provisions above.

Redomiciliation

At the Autumn Budget 2021, the government published a consultation seeking views on its intention to allow companies to relocate to the UK, by enabling the 'redomiciliation' of companies. Such a change would bring the UK in line with several other common law jurisdictions, including Canada, New Zealand, Australia, Singapore, and a number of US states. A specific redomiciliation regime would enable a foreign-incorporated company to change its place of incorporation to the UK, while retaining the same legal identity. Currently, a foreign company wishing to become domiciled in the UK must create a new UK entity to which it transfers assets, or establish a new UK holding company which then acquires shares in the foreign company. Such reorganisations can involve substantial cost and complexity for the foreign company and its shareholders: for example, the insertion of a UK holding company above a foreign holding company via a share for share exchange might crystallise foreign tax charges for shareholders in the foreign holding company. It should be noted that the consultation does not deal with another type of redomiciliation, where a foreign entity remains incorporated outside the UK, but establishes its tax residence in the UK. The government also sought views on outward redomiciliation, whereby UK-incorporated companies could move their domicile from the UK to a foreign jurisdiction. See www.gov.uk/government/consultations/corporate-re-domiciliation.

Domicile and deemed domicile

[51.29] An individual may have only one domicile under general law at any given time, denoting the country or state considered his natural home. Domicile does not necessarily correspond with either residence or nationality and is essentially a question of fact (*Earl of Iveagh v Revenue Commissioners* SC (RI), [1930] IR 431).

Under rules introduced by *F(No 2)A 2017*, certain long-term residents and returning expatriates are *deemed* domiciled in the UK by statute (see further below) for specific purposes in relation to income tax and capital gains tax, even if they do not have a UK domicile under general law as described here.

Under general law, a *domicile of origin* is acquired at birth (normally that of the taxpayer's father, see below), but may be replaced by a *domicile of choice* (to be proved by subsequent conduct). A domicile of choice may be replaced by another domicile of choice (if the necessary proof is forthcoming), but if a domicile of choice is lost without another being acquired, the domicile of origin immediately revives (*Fielden v CIR* Ch D 1965, 42 TC 501).

It is normally more difficult to show the displacement of a domicile of origin than that of a domicile of choice. See *CIR v Bullock* CA 1976, 51 TC 522 where a taxpayer with a domicile of origin in Canada lived in England and intended to remain here during his wife's lifetime. He was held not to have acquired an English domicile of choice (the judgements in this case give a useful review of the law relating to domicile). In *Buswell v CIR* CA 1974, 49 TC 334, the taxpayer had a domicile of origin in South Africa. He came to England to school in 1928, and was called up into the British Army during the Second World War, serving in India. On his return, he signed a written declaration that he intended to remain permanently in the UK. In 1955, he took out a South African passport. In 1961, he married an English lady and their children were brought up in the UK, though registered as South African nationals. In 1968, he and his wife visited South Africa for the first time for 40 years and, with the intention of eventually settling there permanently, bought property there in which they spent three months in each year. He was held never to have abandoned his domicile of origin.

In *Re Clore (decd.) (No 2), Official Solicitor v Clore and Others* Ch D, [1984] STC 609, it was held that an English domicile of origin was never lost as, on the evidence, the taxpayer never formed a settled intention to reside permanently elsewhere. Contrast *Qureshi v Qureshi* Fam D, [1972] Fam D 173, and *In re Lawton* Ch D 1958, 37 ATC 216. Actual settlement abroad is necessary as well as intention; see *Plummer v CIR* Ch D 1987, 60 TC 452.

In *Steiner v CIR* CA 1973, 49 TC 13, a Jewish man who had acquired a German domicile of choice, but who fled to England in 1939 and obtained British naturalisation was held to have acquired an English domicile of choice. In *F and Another (Personal Representatives of F deceased) v CIR* 1999 (Sp C 219), [2000] SSCD 1, an Iranian who had obtained British naturalisation following the 1979 Islamic Revolution was held on the facts to have had a settled intention to return to Iran permanently and thus not to have abandoned his domicile of origin.

In *Henderson v HMRC* FTT, [2017] UKFTT 556 (TC), 2017 SWTI 2044, the determination of the domicile of the appellants depended on whether their grandfather had acquired a domicile of choice in Brazil at the time of the birth of their father (thereby giving their father a Brazilian domicile of origin subsequently passed on to the appellants).

In *Strachan v HMRC* FTT, [2023] UKFTT 617 (TC), [2023] SFTD 1133, the Tribunal held that, where a person has two homes, a domicile of choice can only be established in a jurisdiction if the person had their 'chief' or 'principal' home in that jurisdiction. Whether or not that was the position required consideration of all of the relevant facts. In that case, a taxpayer with an English domicile of origin, who lived in London but retained a property in the USA to which he intended to retire, failed to establish that he had acquired a domicile of choice in the USA.

See also *Moore's Executors v CIR* (Sp C 335), [2002] SSCD 463, *Surveyor v CIR* (Sp C 339), [2002] SSCD 501; *Johnson's Executors v HMRC* (Sp C 481), [2005] SSCD 614; and *Gaines-Cooper v HMRC* Ch D 2007, [2008] STC 1665.

In determining domicile for capital gains tax, relevant action taken by a person in connection with electoral rights is disregarded unless otherwise requested by the person whose liability is in question. Relevant action refers to prospective or actual registration as an overseas elector or use of such vote. [*FA 1996, s 200*].

Married women

Up to 31 December 1973, a woman automatically acquired the domicile of her husband on marriage. From 1 January 1974 onwards, the domicile of a married woman is ascertained in the same way as any other individual capable of having an independent domicile, except that a woman already married on that date will retain her husband's domicile until it is changed by acquisition or revival of another domicile. [*Domicile and Matrimonial Proceedings Act 1973, ss 1, 17(5)*]. See *CIR v Duchess of Portland* Ch D 1981, 54 TC 648. But a woman who is a national of the USA and who married a man with UK domicile before 1974 is treated in determining her domicile, as if the marriage had taken place in 1974. See Article 4(6) of the US/UK Double Tax Agreement and any similar provisions in double tax agreements with other countries. A widow retains her late husband's domicile unless she later acquires a domicile of choice (or reverts to a domicile of origin) (*In re Wallach* PDA 1949, [1950] 1 All ER 199).

Minors

The domicile of a minor follows that of a person on whom he is legally dependent (usually his father). Under *Domicile and Matrimonial Proceedings Act 1973, s 3* (which does not extend to Scotland), a person first becomes capable of having an independent domicile when he attains 16 (in Scotland, 14 for boys and 12 for girls) or marries under that age. Under *section 4* of that Act, where a child's father and mother are living apart, his domicile is that of his mother if he has his home with her and has no home with his father.

Deemed domicile

Rules of deemed domicile apply for specific income tax and capital gains tax purposes (such as the REMITTANCE BASIS in **49.2**). An individual who is not domiciled in the UK under general law at a time in 2017/18 or a subsequent tax year is treated as domiciled in the UK for certain capital gains tax provisions for that year if either:

(A) the individual was born in the UK with a UK domicile of origin and is UK resident in that tax year; or
(B) the individual has been resident in the UK for at least 15 out of the last 20 tax years, immediately preceding that tax year (although this does not apply if the individual is not resident in the UK at any time from 6 April 2017 onwards).

Capital gains tax re-basing: deemed domicile

An individual who is deemed domiciled under (B) above may re-base a foreign asset held on 5 April 2017 to its market value on that date, if he is a 'qualifying individual' and the asset is disposed of on or after 6 April 2017. The asset must not have been situated in the UK at any time from 16 March 2016 (or the date of acquisition by the individual, if later) to 5 April 2017 inclusive (the '*relevant period*'), but with some exceptions (see below). A '*qualifying individual*' is one who:

(a) has paid the remittance basis charge under *ITA 2007, s 809H* in a tax year prior to 2017/18 (see **49.5** REMITTANCE BASIS);
(b) is *not* an individual who was born in the UK and whose domicile of origin was in the UK;
(c) was *not* domiciled in the UK under general law at any time in a tax year from 2017/18 until the tax year of the disposal inclusive ('*relevant tax years*'); and

(d) was deemed domiciled under (B) above in each relevant tax year.

The re-basing is automatic on a disposal where the conditions are met. However, the conditions are tested for each disposal such that re-basing does not apply universally to all foreign assets held by an individual on 5 April 2017. An irrevocable election may be made in respect of a particular disposal for the re-basing *not* to apply. The claim must be made within four years of the end of the tax year of disposal.

Where *TCGA 1992, s 127* applies to a reorganisation such that an original holding of shares and a new holding are treated as a single asset (see **57.2** SHARES AND SECURITIES), neither holding must have been situated in the UK in the relevant period.

Re-basing applies where the conditions are met notwithstanding the nil gain nil loss treatment for disposals between spouses under *TCGA 1992, s 58(1)* (see **40.4** MARRIED PERSONS AND CIVIL PARTNERS).

A foreign asset brought into the UK before the end of the relevant period is still treated as being outside the UK (and so can benefit from re-basing) if it falls into one of the following exceptions.

(i) It meets the conditions of *ITA 2007, s 809Z(3)* being available for public access (as defined) at an approved museum, gallery or similar establishment or being in storage at, or in transit to or from, the establishment (or other commercial premises in the UK used by the establishment for storage) pending or following public access.
(ii) It meets the conditions of *ITA 2007, s 809Z3(3)* being under repair or restoration, or being in storage at, or in transit to or from, UK premises used for the repair or restoration (or other commercial premises in the UK used by the restorer for storage), pending or following repair or restoration.
(iii) It is brought into the UK with the sole or principal purpose of selling it.
(iv) It is clothing, footwear, jewellery or a watch for the personal use of the individual or their husband, wife or civil partner (or a child or grandchild of such a person if the child or grandchild is under 18 years old). For these purposes, couples living together as husband and wife or civil partners are treated as such.
(v) It is not treated as remitted as the notional remitted amount is less than £1,000 (under *ITA 2007, s 809X(5)(c)*).
(vi) It meets certain conditions as to temporary importation (under *ITA 2007, s 809Z4*).

[*ITA 2007, s 835BA*].

United Kingdom

[51.30] The United Kingdom for tax purposes comprises England, Scotland, Wales and Northern Ireland. The Channel Islands (Jersey, Guernsey, Alderney, Sark, Herm and Jethou) and the Isle of Man are excluded. Great Britain comprises England, Scotland and Wales only.

See 43.18 OVERSEAS MATTERS for the territorial extension of the UK in certain circumstances.

Key points concerning residence and domicile

[51.31] Points to consider are as follows.

- Non-resident individuals are usually outside the scope of UK capital gains tax, except in the case of UK land held directly or indirectly (see 35.23 LAND).
- A statutory residence test applies to determine an individual's residence status. There have been a number of tax cases dealing with residence.
- Residence status depends on number of days and other facts. Detailed record keeping and supporting evidence is vital.
- It is possible to be resident in more than one country at the same time and reference then needs to be made to any double taxation agreements between the jurisdictions involved.
- Non-residents who are returning to the UK after an absence during which they were temporarily non-resident (see 43.5 OVERSEAS MATTERS) will be taxable on any gains arising during their absence on assets which they held before they left the UK.
- Individuals becoming resident in the UK for the first time or following a period of absence of more than five years should consider uplifting the base cost of shares and securities by means of a 'bed & breakfast' transaction. This is because the '30 day' rule does not apply to non-residents.
- A UK resident non-domiciled individual is entitled to claim the remittance basis of taxation. Such a claim means that non-UK gains are only taxable in the UK to the extent that they are remitted to the UK. One of the costs of claiming the remittance basis is, in most cases, the loss of the capital gains tax annual exempt amount.
- It is difficult for an individual to change their domicile but care needs to be taken when considering future intentions not to inadvertently acquire a domicile of choice in the UK. A long-term resident or an individual returning to the UK who was originally born in the UK with a UK domicile of origin, may become deemed domiciled in the UK. Domicile is expected to lose its significance in relation to income tax and capital gains tax from April 2025 due to the planned abolition of the remittance basis.

52

Returns

Cross-references. See **46** PENALTIES as regards late or incorrect returns; **46.3** PENALTIES as regards duty to notify chargeability to tax.

Introduction to returns

[52.1] Both capital gains tax and corporation tax are administered through a system of self-assessment under which the key document is the tax return (but see **52.2** below for future changes to the system under 'making tax digital'). Individuals, partnerships, trustees, personal representatives and companies all have obligations to file returns of their income and gains where HMRC, by notice, require them to do so. Such returns must also include a self-assessment of the taxpayer's liability for the period concerned (although for taxpayers other than companies, this requirement need not be complied with if the return is made within specified time limits). In practice, where a return is filed electronically the tax due is automatically computed during the filing process. Failure to make a return will result in penalties and enable HMRC to make a determination of tax liability which can only be displaced by filing the return.

A special compliance regime applies to all direct disposals of UK land where a residential property gain arises. A UK land disposal return must be made together with a payment on account of CGT on or before the 60th day following the day of the completion of the disposal (the 30th day where the date of completion is before 27 October 2021). See **52.22** below and **45.3** PAYMENT OF TAX. Previously, the regime applied only to non-UK residents (see **52.22** below). The regime also applies to direct disposals of non-residential UK land and indirect disposals of UK land by non-UK residents.

The obligations under self-assessment of individuals and others within the charge to capital gains tax are covered at **52.5–52.17** below, together with HMRC's powers to enquire into filed returns. For convenience, income tax obligations are also covered to some extent, but see Tolley's Income Tax for full coverage of those. Partnership obligations are covered at **52.18–52.20** below. For companies see **52.21** below.

As well as the powers to require self-assessment returns, HMRC can also require certain other types of return. To the extent that these are relevant to tax on chargeable gains, see **52.23** onwards below.

See also **6.9** ASSESSMENTS for simple assessment by HMRC of an individual's or trustee's income tax or capital gains tax liability without the taxpayer first being required to complete a self-assessment tax return on the basis of information already held by HMRC.

Making tax digital for income tax

[52.2] Individuals carrying on a trade, profession or vocation or a property business will be subject to 'making tax digital' (MTD) for 2026/27 if the business has qualifying income exceeding £50,000. Individuals with qualifying income in excess of £30,000 will be subject to MTD for 2027/28 onwards. The dates from which MTD will apply to partnerships are yet to be announced. Under MTD, taxpayers are required to keep digital records of business income and expenses and send them digitally to HMRC as cumulative quarterly updates. At the end of the tax year, the taxpayer must submit a final declaration confirming any personal income and claims for any other reliefs. The deadline for the end-of-period statement is 31 January after the end of the tax year, the same as the deadline for a self-assessment tax return. HMRC are running an MTD pilot under which self-employed individuals and landlords, other than those renting out furnished holiday lettings, can volunteer to use software to keep business records digitally and send income tax updates to HMRC for 2022/23 onwards. See www.gov.uk/guidance/sign-up-your-business-for-making-tax-digital-for-income-tax. See generally www.gov.uk/guidance/using-making-tax-digital-for-income-tax. Note that late filing penalties and late payment penalties apply to voluntary MTD users under the FA 2021 rules with effect from 6 April 2024. See **36.7** LATE PAYMENT INTEREST AND PENALTIES and **46.7** PENALTIES.

MTD is not initially applicable to capital gains tax so that the existing requirements to notify chargeability and make returns will continue.

The Government also intends for MTD to be extended to corporation tax. See www.gov.uk/government/consultations/making-tax-digital-for-corporation-tax.

Electronic filing of returns

[52.3] Individuals and companies can file tax returns electronically via the online gateway on gov.uk.

Agents are authorised to file individual and company clients' tax returns over the internet subject to certain conditions (see **27.5** HMRC — ADMINISTRATION).

See also **27.5** HMRC — ADMINISTRATION for HMRC's powers to make regulations requiring electronic filing of information (including returns).

Corporation tax returns

Companies are *required* to file their tax returns online using a specified data format (known as iXBRL). This does not apply to companies which are subject to a winding-up order, or in administration or administrative receivership. A further exception applies where the use of electronic communications is contrary to the beliefs of a religious group of which all the company's directors are practising members (or, in the case of an unincorporated association, of which all the individuals in the association are practising members). [*SI 2003 No 282, Reg 3*].

Real-time capital gains service

[52.4] UK resident individuals can use HMRC's real-time capital gains service to report capital gains, other than UK residential property gains arising on or after 6 April 2020, via the online Government Gateway. The service is aimed particularly at unrepresented taxpayers who do not submit tax returns annually, although it is not restricted to such taxpayers. The service can be used to report gains at any time up to 31 December following the tax year. There is, however, no need to wait until after the end of the tax year. See www.gov.uk/report-and-pay-your-capital-gains-tax/if-you-have-other-capital-gains-to-report.

The service is accessed using the taxpayer's Government Gateway details and requires a PDF or JPG file to be uploaded showing both the amount of the gains and the CGT due. HMRC will then send a letter or email with a payment reference number and details of how to pay. The payment date remains 31 January following the tax year of the gains, although payment can be made early. It is possible to amend a report via the service once the reference number has been received.

Using the service does not displace the requirements of self-assessment. In particular, the requirement to notify chargeability by 5 October following the tax year in which the gains arise. If HMRC subsequently issue a notice to file a self-assessment tax return, the gains must be included in the return in the normal way. This may happen, for example, where HMRC wish to open a formal enquiry into the gains.

Returns by individuals etc.

Annual tax returns

[52.5] For the purposes of establishing the amounts in which a person is chargeable to income tax and capital gains tax for a tax year, an HMRC officer may by notice require that person to deliver a return (i.e. a self-assessment tax return) within the following time limits.

Returns must be delivered on or before 31 January following the tax year, except that returns which are not 'electronic returns' must be delivered on or before 31 October following the tax year. Where the notice to make a return is given on or after 1 August but before 1 November following the tax year the return must be delivered within three months beginning with the date of the notice or, in the case of an electronic return, on or before 31 January. Where notice is given after 31 October following the tax year, the return must be delivered within three months beginning with the date of the notice.

The return must contain such information and be accompanied by such accounts, statements and documents as may reasonably be required. The return must include a declaration that, to the best of the knowledge of the person making it, it is complete and correct. The information, accounts and statements required by the notice may differ in relation to different periods, or different sources of income, or different descriptions of person.

For 2025/26 onwards, HMRC have the power to make regulations requiring taxpayers to include additional information which is relevant to the general collection and management of tax (as opposed to establishing the amounts in which the taxpayer is chargeable to income tax and capital gains tax). Failure to comply with a requirement to include such information will result in a penalty of £60. HMRC have indicated that this power is to be used initially to obtain three types of information, none of which are relevant to capital gains tax. See Treasury Explanatory Notes to the 2023/24 Finance Bill.

[*TMA 1970, s 8; FA 2024, s 36(1)*].

See **27.3** HMRC—ADMINISTRATION for the exercise of functions of an HMRC officer by automated process.

'Establishing the amounts in which a person is chargeable' means 'calculating and assessing the amounts'. In *HMRC v Goldsmith* UT, [2019] STC 2512, a return was therefore validly made because, although the amounts of tax were known before it was issued, a return was needed to create a debt due from the taxpayer.

An '*electronic return*' is a return delivered using HMRC's Self-Assessment Online service (see **52.3** above). (Revenue Directions under *SI 2003 No 282, Reg 3* and prescribing of electronic returns, 4 April 2008).

Where an individual makes a return for a tax year without having been given a notice to do so (i.e. the return is made voluntarily), then for all tax purposes the return is treated as made pursuant to such a notice issued on the date the return was made (and therefore as a return made under the above provisions), provided that HMRC decide to treat it in that way. This rule in effect overturns the decision in *Patel v HMRC* FTT, [2018] SFTD 1000, where it was held that a voluntary return was not a return under the above provisions and therefore HMRC could not open an enquiry into it. [*TMA 1970, s 12D*].

Similar provisions apply in relation to returns by trustees. [*TMA 1970, ss 8A, 12*].

See **46.5, 46.7** PENALTIES as regards automatic and possible daily penalties for non-compliance (i.e. late returns).

Withdrawal of notice to make return

HMRC may withdraw a notice to an individual or trustee to make a return. The notice can be withdrawn within two years of the end of the tax year to which the notice relates or, in exceptional circumstances, within such extended period as HMRC may determine.

A notice may not be withdrawn if the taxpayer has already filed their return for the year or if HMRC have made a determination under the provisions at

52.17 below.

If HMRC withdraw a notice they do so by giving a withdrawal notice specifying the date on which the notice is withdrawn. Withdrawing a notice in this way does not prevent HMRC subsequently issuing a further notice for the same year.

A withdrawal notice may also cancel a penalty for failing to make a return (see **46.5, 46.8, 46.9** PENALTIES).

[*TMA 1970, s 8B; FA 2009, Sch 55 para 17A; FA 2021, Sch 27 para 2*].

Reporting limits

Where an individual's chargeable gains for a year do not exceed the annual exempt amount (see **2.5** ANNUAL RATES AND EXEMPTIONS) *and* the aggregate amount or value of the consideration for all disposals of chargeable assets other than those treated under *TCGA 1992, s 58* as giving rise to neither a gain nor a loss (see **40.4** MARRIED PERSONS AND CIVIL PARTNERS) does not exceed £50,000, a statement in the self-assessment tax return to that effect complies with the above obligations so far as they relate to chargeable gains (though not so as to prejudice HMRC's right to more detailed information). For returns for 2022/23 and earlier years, the limit for aggregate consideration was equal to *four times* the annual exempt amount. For this purpose, the amount of an individual's chargeable gains is, where allowable losses are to be deducted, the amount before the deduction of such losses. These reduced reporting requirements do not apply where a claim for the REMITTANCE BASIS (**49.2**(a)) applies for the year or where gains accruing in a previous year are remitted to the UK, and are chargeable, in the current year and an election under *TCGA 1992, s 16ZA* has effect for both years.

Where the year is a split year under the statutory residence test (see **51.17** RESIDENCE AND DOMICILE), the above rules apply by reference to the UK part of the year only.

These provisions apply to personal representatives as they apply to individuals but only for the year of assessment in which the individual concerned dies and the next two tax years. [*TCGA 1992, s 3A(4)*]. Similar provisions apply to the trustees of settlements. The total gains limit applies by reference to reduced annual exempt amounts (see **56.8** SETTLEMENTS) where applicable, but the aggregate consideration limit is four times the annual exempt amount *for an individual.*

[*TMA 1970, s 8C; FA 2023, s 8(7)(9)*].

The above-mentioned statement should *not*, however, be made if a net capital loss has been incurred: a claim has to be made for such a loss to be allowable (see **38.5** LOSSES) and this requires full disclosure.

Informal procedure for personal representatives of deceased estates

In respect of income tax and capital gains tax liabilities arising during the administration period of a deceased estate, HMRC operate an informal procedure under which self-assessment tax returns are not required. HMRC will normally operate the procedure where the estate is not complex and the tax arising during the whole of the administration period is less than £10,000. Where this procedure is used, only a simple computation of the estate's liability needs to be submitted to HMRC, who in turn provide the personal representative with a payslip to enable payment of the tax due. Self-assessment returns are required in all cases not meeting the conditions. Further conditions are that value of the estate is not more than £2.5 million at the date of death and the proceeds of any assets (whether chargeable or not) sold in any one tax year do not exceed £500,000. See HMRC Trusts Settlements and Estates Manual TSEM7410.

See **52.9** below for amendments of returns and self-assessments. See **52.10** below for record-keeping requirements and **52.11** below for enquiries into returns. See **52.17** below for determination of tax liability where no return delivered.

Form and delivery of returns

[52.6] The power of the Commissioners for HMRC to prescribe the form of returns is given by *TMA 1970, s 113(1)*. The basic self-assessment tax return does not include a space to enter details of chargeable gains and allowable losses. These must be entered on supplementary pages, which form part of the return. If the taxpayer is making a paper return, the supplementary pages can be downloaded from www.gov.uk/government/publications/self-assessment-capital-gains-summary-sa108, along with any required Helpsheets. If the statement mentioned in **52.5** above under 'Reporting limits' can be made, it is made in the basic return, and the supplementary pages are not then required. Similarly, if the only gain arises from the disposal of the taxpayer's main residence and it is wholly exempt under the provisions in **47** PRIVATE RESIDENCES, a statement in the basic return to this effect is sufficient. Following submission of the return, HMRC have the power, under the enquiry provisions at **52.11** below, to require full details of gains and losses.

The capital gains supplementary pages do not include space to enter details of individual gains and losses, so that computations for each disposal must be submitted along with the pages. It is necessary in any case to indicate on the return that a valuation (for which see also **52.7** below) or an estimate had been used in calculating a gain or loss. The return also includes space for additional information to be entered.

Provisional figures

A return containing a provisional figure will be accepted provided that the figure is reasonable, taking account of all available information, and is clearly identified as such. An explanation should be given as to why the final figure is not available, all reasonable steps having been taken to obtain it, and when it is expected to be available (at which time it should be notified without unreasonable delay). The absence of such explanation and expected date will influence HMRC in selecting returns for enquiry (see **52.11** below). Pressures of work and complexity of tax affairs are not regarded as acceptable explanations. If the provisional figure is accepted but the final figure is not provided by the expected date, HMRC will take appropriate action to obtain it, which may mean opening an enquiry. Note that a provisional figure is different in concept to an estimate that is not intended to be superseded by a more accurate figure.

Where the replacement of a provisional figure by a final figure leads to a *decrease* in the self-assessment, and the time limit for making amendments (see **52.9** below) has passed, the amendment may be made by way of a claim for repayment of tax (see **13.7** CLAIMS) where the conditions for such relief are otherwise met. Where such replacement leads to an *increase* in the self-assessment, a discovery assessment (see **6.10** ASSESSMENTS) may be made to collect the additional tax due.

Post-transaction valuation checks

[52.7] Individuals, trustees and companies may submit asset valuations used in their capital gains tax calculations to HMRC for checking before they make their returns (**post-transaction valuation checks**). The service is free of charge, but valuations will be considered only *after* the relevant transaction has occurred. Full information about the transactions to which they relate together with any relevant tax computations must be submitted to HMRC with the valuations using Form CG34. The service extends to valuations of assets that are the subject of a negligible value claim (see **38.10** LOSSES).

Most forms CG34 for individuals and partnerships should be sent to PAYE and Self Assessment, HMRC, BX9 1AS. Taxpayers dealt with by High Net Worth Units or Public Departments 1 should send the form to the relevant tax office. Companies should send the form to the nominated customer compliance manager if they have one, or otherwise to Corporation Tax Services, HM Revenue and Customs BX9 1AX.

If HMRC agree the valuations they will not be challenged when the return is submitted unless information affecting the valuation was not provided. If HMRC disagree with the valuations they will suggest alternatives. HMRC should be allowed a minimum of three months to agree a valuation or suggest an alternative. The due date for filing the return or UK land disposal return cannot be deferred.

(Revenue Press Release 4 February 1997; HMRC Working Together Publication 38, November 2009).

Under the principles at **16.12**(d) COMPUTATION OF GAINS AND LOSSES, costs reasonably incurred in making a valuation or apportionment submitted for a post-transaction valuation check are deductible in arriving at the gain, but any costs incurred in making the submission or in subsequent negotiations cannot be so deducted (HMRC Capital Gains Manual CG15260, 16615).

See also **27.4** HMRC — ADMINISTRATION for procedures for non-statutory clearances.

Self-assessments

[52.8] Every return under *TMA 1970, s 8* or *s 8A* (see **52.5** above) must include, subject to the exception below, an assessment (a self-assessment) of the liability, based on the information in the return and taking into account all reliefs, allowances, tax credits, tax at source and tax repayments, of the person making the return to income tax and capital gains tax for the year of assessment. HMRC's Tax calculation summary notes, available online with the tax calculation summary pages at www.gov.uk/government/publications/self-assessment-tax-calculation-summary-sa110, are designed to assist in the calculation of the tax liability.

Taxpayers need not comply with this requirement if they make and deliver their return on or before 31 October following the tax year or, where the notice to deliver a return is given after 31 August following the tax year, within two months beginning with the date of the notice. In such cases, HMRC will compute the tax due. For returns submitted outside these time limits, HMRC will calculate the tax and make the assessment if the taxpayer fails to do so, but will not guarantee to do so before the due date for payment of tax.

Assessments made as above by an HMRC officer are treated as self-assessments by the person making the return and as included in the return.

[*TMA 1970, ss 8, 8A, 9(1)–(3A)*].

The 31 October deadline is of no significance where returns are filed over the internet (see **52.6** above) as the tax due is automatically computed during the filing process.

Time limits

Subject to any provision allowing a longer period, a self-assessment contained in a return under *TMA 1970, s 8* or *s 8A* cannot be made more than four years after the end of the tax year. This provision does not, however, prevent a person who has received a notice to make a return within the four-year period from making a return including a self-assessment within three months beginning with date of the notice where the three months expires after the end of the four-year period. Similarly, the provision does not prevent a person from making a self-assessment to supersede a determination under *TMA 1970, s 28C* (see **52.17** below) within the time limits at **52.17** below.

[*TMA 1970, s 34A*].

Amendments of returns other than where enquiries made

[52.9] A person may by notice to an HMRC officer amend his return at any time within twelve months after the filing date (for this purpose treated as 31 January following the tax year or, where the notice to deliver the return is given after 31 October following the tax year, the end of the three-month period beginning with the date of the notice).

At any time within nine months after the delivery of a person's return, an HMRC officer may by notice to that person amend his return to correct obvious errors and omissions (whether of principle, arithmetical or otherwise). An HMRC officer may also correct anything else in the return that he has reason to believe is incorrect in the light of information available to him. Where the correction is required in consequence of an amendment by the taxpayer as above, the nine-month period begins immediately after the date of the taxpayer's amendment. The taxpayer has a legal right to reject an officer's correction, by notice within 30 days beginning with the date of the notice of correction.

[*TMA 1970, ss 9(4)(6), 9ZA, 9ZB*].

For amendments to returns subject to an HMRC enquiry, see **52.14**, **52.15** below.

Record-keeping

[52.10] For capital gains tax and income tax, any person who may be required to make and deliver a personal or trustee tax return (see **52.5** above) for a tax year or a partnership tax return (see **52.18** below) for any period is required by law to keep all records necessary for the preparation of a complete and correct return *and* to preserve them until the end of the 'relevant day'. The 'relevant day' is initially:

(a) in the case of a person carrying on a trade (including for these purposes any letting of property), profession or business, whether alone or in partnership, the fifth anniversary of 31 January following the tax year or, for partnership returns, the sixth anniversary of the end of the period covered by the return;
(b) otherwise, the first anniversary of 31 January following the tax year; or
(c) (with effect from a date to be fixed by order) in either case, such earlier day as may be specified in writing by HMRC.

Where, as is normal, notice to deliver the return is given before the day given by whichever is the applicable of (a) and (b) above, the '*relevant day*' is the *later* of that day and whichever of the following applies:

(i) where HMRC enquiries are made into the return, the day on which the enquiries are fully completed (see **52.14** below);
(ii) where no such enquiries are made, the day on which HMRC no longer have power to enquire (see **52.11** below).

Where notice to deliver a return is given *after* the day given by whichever is the applicable of (a) and (b) above, (i) and (ii) above still apply to determine the relevant day but only in relation to such records as the taxpayer has in his possession at the time the notice is given.

HMRC have the power to make regulations specifying records which are required to be kept and preserved under these provisions and specifying that those records include specified supporting documents. Subject to this, in the case of a person within (a) above, the records to be preserved include records concerning business receipts and expenditure and, in the case of a trade involving dealing in goods, all sales and purchases of goods. All supporting documents (including accounts, books, deeds, contracts, vouchers and receipts) relating to such items must also be preserved.

Generally, copies of documents may be preserved instead of the originals and are admissible in evidence in proceedings before the Tribunal. (For computer records in particular, see HMRC Compliance Handbook CH13400.) Exceptions to this are vouchers, certificates etc. which show tax credits or deductions at source of UK or foreign tax and evidence of tax deducted from payments to sub-contractors under the construction industry tax deduction scheme, which must be preserved in their original form. The right to preserve copies of documents is subject to any conditions or further exceptions specified in writing by HMRC.

The maximum penalty for non-compliance in relation to any tax year or accounting period is £3,000. This does not apply to records only required for claims, elections or notices not included in the return, as there are separate record-keeping requirements (and a separate penalty) for those (see **13.3** CLAIMS) nor does it apply in respect of original dividend vouchers and interest certificates where HMRC are satisfied that other documentary evidence supplied to them proves any facts they reasonably require to be proved and which such vouchers etc. would have proved.

[*TMA 1970, s 12B*].

Enquiries into returns

[52.11] An HMRC officer may enquire into a personal or trustees' return, and anything (including any claim or election) contained (or required to be contained) in it. An enquiry can also extend to consideration by HMRC of whether to give the taxpayer a transfer pricing notice under *TIOPA 2010, s 168(1)*.

Notice of enquiry

The officer must give notice that he intends to carry out an enquiry (notice of enquiry) within whichever of the following periods is appropriate:

(a) in the case of a return delivered on or before the filing date (i.e. the date on or before which the return must be delivered — see **52.5** above), the twelve months after the day on which the return was delivered;

(b) in the case of a return delivered after the filing date, the period ending with the 'quarter day' next following the first anniversary of the delivery date;

(c) in the case of a return amended by the taxpayer under **52.9** above, the period ending with the 'quarter day' next following the first anniversary of the date of amendment.

For these purposes, the '*quarter days*' are 31 January, 30 April etc. A return cannot be enquired into more than once, except in consequence of an amendment (or further amendment). If notice under (c) above is given at a time when the deadline in (a) or (b) above, as the case may be, has expired or after an enquiry into the return has been fully completed, the enquiry is limited to matters affected by the amendment. The same applies if a partial closure notice has been issued (see **52.14** below) in relation to the matters to which the amendment relates.

[*TMA 1970, s 9A*].

The 'giving' of notice under *TMA 1970, s 9A* is effected not when the notice is issued or posted but at the time it would be received in the ordinary course of post (generally taken to be four working days for second class mail) or, if proved, the time of actual receipt (*Holly v Inspector of Taxes* 1999 (Sp C 225), [2000] SSCD 50, and see also *Wing Hung Lai v Bale* (Sp C 203), [1999] SSCD 238). HMRC accept this to be the case.

In *R (oao Spring Salmon and Seafood Ltd) v CIR* CS, [2004] STC 444 it was held that, under the corporation tax self-assessment enquiry powers of *FA 1998, Sch 18 para 24*, a notice of enquiry need not be in writing. Furthermore, it need not be sent to a company's registered office but is valid if sent to a company's place of business.

In *Tinkler v HMRC* SC, [2021] STC 1546, HMRC sent a letter opening an enquiry into the taxpayer's return to an old address rather than the address which he had included in the return. A copy of the letter was sent to his agents, BDO. The enquiry continued through correspondence and phone calls between HMRC and BDO, culminating in the issue of a closure notice in 2012. The taxpayer appealed against the notice and subsequently amended his notice of appeal to contend that HMRC had failed to give a valid notice of enquiry because the enquiry notice was not sent to his last known place of residence. The Supreme Court held that the taxpayer was prevented, under estoppel by convention, from denying that a valid enquiry had been opened. (Broadly, estoppel by convention can apply where the parties have acted on the basis of a mistaken common assumption, communicated between them, as to the law or facts.)

An appeal against a closure notice was upheld on the grounds that no valid notice of enquiry had been given in *Credit Suisse Securities (Europe) Ltd v HMRC* FTT, [2020] UKFTT 86 (TC); 2020 SWTI 403.

Conduct of enquiry

[52.12] HMRC have published an Enquiry Manual as part of their series of internal guidance manuals and, as an extended introduction to the material on operational aspects of the enquiry regime covered in the manual, a special edition of their Tax Bulletin (Special Edition 2, August 1997). The following points are selected from the Bulletin.

- Early submission of a tax return will not increase the likelihood of selection for enquiry.
- HMRC do not have to give reasons for opening an enquiry — and they *will not* do so (but see further below).

- Enquiries may be full enquiries or 'aspect enquiries'. An aspect enquiry will fall short of an in-depth examination of the return (though it may develop into one), but will instead concentrate on one or more aspects of it.
- Greater emphasis is placed on examination of underlying records. HMRC will make an informal request for information before, if necessary, using their powers under *FA 2008, Sch 36* (see **52.13** below).
- Where penalties are being sought, HMRC will aim to conclude the enquiry by means of a contract settlement (see **6.8** ASSESSMENTS) rather than issue a final closure notice under *TMA 1970, s 28A* (see **52.14** below).

Where an enquiry remains open beyond the period during which notice of intention to enquire had to be given (see above) and solely because of an unagreed valuation for capital gains tax purposes, HMRC will not take advantage of the open enquiry to raise further enquiries into matters unrelated to the valuation or the CGT computation except in circumstances where a 'discovery' (see **6.10** ASSESSMENTS) could in any case have been made if the enquiry had been completed (HMRC Statement of Practice SP 1/99).

Information powers

[52.13] See **29.3–29.10** HMRC INVESTIGATORY POWERS for HMRC's powers to require the production of information and documents. See in particular **29.5** for the restriction on those powers where a return has been made.

Completion or part completion of enquiry

[52.14] An enquiry is completed when an officer of HMRC gives the taxpayer notice (a final closure notice) that he has completed his enquiries. An HMRC officer can also issue a partial closure notice, which completes the enquiry insofar as it concerns the matters specified in the notice. The enquiry is not fully completed until a final closure notice has been issued to inform the taxpayer that the officer has completed his remaining enquiries. A partial or final closure notice takes effect when it is issued and must state the officer's conclusions and make the necessary amendments to the return to give effect to those conclusions or state that no amendment is required. An amendment made by a closure notice is in the nature of an assessment by HMRC (*R (oao Archer) v HMRC* CA 2017, [2018] STC 38).

During the course of an enquiry, the taxpayer may apply to the tribunal for a direction requiring HMRC to issue a partial or final closure notice within a specified period, such application to be heard and determined in a similar manner to an appeal. The tribunal must give the direction unless satisfied that there are reasonable grounds for not issuing the partial or final closure notice within a specified period. [*TMA 1970, s 28A*].

Guidance is given to HMRC officers as to when they might agree to an application to issue a closure notice without the need for a Tribunal hearing (HMRC Enquiry Manual EM1976, 1980). HMRC will make use of partial closure notices where the taxpayer's affairs are complex or where there is tax avoidance or large amounts of tax at risk; HMRC officers may issue a partial closure notice at their own discretion by agreement with the taxpayer (www.gov.uk/government/publications/tax-enquiries-closure-rules).

In *Embiricos v HMRC* CA, [2022] STC 232, the Court of Appeal held that HMRC could not issue a partial closure notice denying the taxpayer's claim to the remittance basis without specifying the amount of tax due. A similar decision was reached in *Executors of Levy (decd) v HMRC* FTT, [2019] SFTD 1045. That case also concerned an application for a direction to be made for a partial closure notice in relation to a taxpayer's domicile status, and it was held that there was no power to issue a partial closure notice in respect of a matter at a time when the tax effect of the determination is unknown.

In *Eastern Power Networks plc v HMRC* CA, [2021] EWCA Civ 283, the Court of Appeal criticised the approach of four companies in using an application for a closure notice to avoid providing information to HMRC. HMRC opened enquiries into the consortium relief claims made by the companies. The companies provided much, but not all, of the information requested by HMRC and applied to the FTT for a direction for closure notices. HMRC considered that an anti-avoidance rule might apply and so opposed the application, arguing that they required the outstanding information to determine the purpose of the 'arrangements'. The companies contended that HMRC did not need the information because, as a matter of law, there were no arrangements and therefore no need to consider their purpose. The FTT considered that it had jurisdiction to decide the point of law, on the authority of *Vodafone 2 v HMRC* [2006] EWCA Civ 1132, as to do so would determine the application for the closure notices. It held that there were arrangements but that the anti-avoidance rule did not apply and therefore directed HMRC to issue closure notices. The Court of Appeal was highly critical of the approach taken by the taxpayers and the FTT. It would often be the case, as here, that a statutory provision set a number of cumulative conditions. Those conditions could require varying amounts of information to determine and 'taxpayers should not be encouraged to pick and choose which information they provide and then ask the tribunal to decide the applicability of one element in the hope that a "quick win" will bring the rest of the enquiry to a halt'. The approach adopted by the FTT required the tribunals to apply the statute without any clear findings of fact or agreed statement of facts. The jurisdiction to decide an incidental point of law in a closure notice application was useful, as in *Vodafone*, but only if used sparingly; applications for closure notices were not generally a suitable vehicle for deciding points of law.

See **5.2** APPEALS for right of appeal against any conclusion stated or amendment made by a partial or final closure notice.

Amendments of returns where enquiries made

[52.15] If a return is amended by the taxpayer under **52.9** above or in accordance with the requirements of a follower notice (see **4.28** ANTI-AVOIDANCE) while an enquiry is in progress in relation to any matter affected by the amendment, the amendment does not restrict the scope of the enquiry but may itself be taken into account in the enquiry. The amendment does not take effect to alter the tax payable until a partial closure notice is issued in relation to the matters to which the amendment relates or, if no such notice is issued, a final closure notice is issued. See **52.14** above for partial and final closure notices. The amendment may then be taken into account separately or, if the officer so states in the closure notice, in arriving at the amendments contained in that notice. It does not take effect if the officer concludes in the closure notice that the amendment is incorrect.

[*TMA 1970, s 9B*].

If in his opinion there is otherwise likely to be a loss of tax in relation to any matter, an officer may amend a self-assessment contained in the return while an enquiry is still in progress in relation to that matter. If the enquiry is itself limited to an amendment to the return (see **52.11** above), the officer's power in this respect is limited accordingly. [*TMA 1970, s 9C*].

Referral of questions during enquiry

[52.16] There are provisions as below to enable specific contentious points to be litigated while the enquiry is still open, instead of waiting until it is completed. This applies while an enquiry is still open into any matter (allowing for the fact that such an enquiry may be partly completed by the issue of a partial closure notice as in **52.14** above).

At any time whilst the enquiry is in progress, any one or more questions arising out of it may be referred, jointly by the taxpayer and an HMRC officer, to the Appeal Tribunal for its determination. More than one notice of referral may be given in relation to the enquiry. Either party may withdraw a notice of referral. Until the questions referred have been finally determined (or the referral withdrawn), no final closure notice may be given or applied for in relation to the enquiry, and no partial closure notice relating to the question referred may be given or applied for.

The determination of the question(s) by the Tribunal is binding on both parties in the same way, and to the same extent, as a decision on a preliminary issue in an appeal. HMRC must take account of it in concluding their enquiry. Following completion of the enquiry, the question concerned may not be reopened on appeal except to the extent (if any) that it could have been reopened had it been determined on appeal following the enquiry rather than on referral during the enquiry.

[*TMA 1970, ss 28ZA–28ZE*].

Determination of tax where no return delivered

[52.17] Where a notice has been given under *TMA 1970, s 8* or *s 8A* (notice requiring an individual or trustee to deliver a return — see **52.5** above) and the return is not delivered by the 'filing date', an HMRC officer may make a determination of the amounts of taxable income, capital gains and income tax payable which, to the best of his information and belief, he estimates for the tax year. The officer must serve notice of the determination on the person concerned. Tax is payable as if the determination were a self-assessment, with no right of appeal (see *Bartram v HMRC* UT, [2012] STC 2144). No determination may be made after the expiry of three years beginning with the filing date.

A determination is automatically superseded by any self-assessment made (whether by the taxpayer or HMRC), based on information contained in a return. Such self-assessment must be made within the three years beginning with the filing date or, if later, within twelve months beginning with the date of the determination. Any tax payable or repayable as a result of the supersession is deemed to have fallen due for payment or repayment on the normal due date, usually 31 January following the tax year (see **45.2** PAYMENT OF TAX). Any recovery proceedings commenced before the making of such a self-assessment may be continued in respect of so much of the tax charged by the self-assessment as is due and payable and has not been paid.

The '*filing date*' for these purposes is 31 January following the tax year or, where the notice to deliver the return is given after 31 October following the tax year, the end of the three-month period beginning with the date of the notice.

See also **45.22** PAYMENT OF TAX for the continuation of action under the provisions for enforcement of tax debts by deduction from accounts where a determination is superseded by a self-assessment.

[*TMA 1970, ss 28C, 59B(5A)*].

Partnership returns

[52.18] Any partner (including a company) may be required by notice to complete and deliver a return of the partnership profits (a partnership return) together with accounts, statements etc. The return must include the names, addresses and (subject to an exception for certain overseas partners in investment partnerships) tax references of all persons (including companies) who were partners during the period specified in the notice and such other information as may reasonably be required by the notice, which may include information relating to disposals of partnership property. The general requirements are similar to those for personal returns under *TMA 1970, s 8* and include the requirement to include prescribed information relevant to the collection and management of tax (see **52.5** above). The notice will specify the period (the relevant period – normally a period of account of the partnership) to be covered by the return and the date by which the return should be delivered (the filing date – see below). The provisions relating to voluntary returns at **52.5** above apply also to partnership returns.

Where the partner responsible for dealing with the return ceases to be available, a successor may be nominated for this purpose by a majority of the persons (or their personal representatives) who were partners at any time in the period covered by the return. A nomination (or revocation of a nomination) does not have effect until notified to HMRC. Failing a nomination, a successor will be determined according to rules on the return form or will be nominated by HMRC.

In relation to returns for 2018/19 onwards, where a partner in a partnership is a partner only as trustee for a beneficiary absolutely entitled to their share of partnerships profits and the beneficiary is chargeable to tax on those profits, the beneficiary is also treated as a partner for these purposes. Where a partner is itself a partnership, any partner in the latter partnership (whether he is a partner directly or as a result of any previous application of this rule) is treated as a partner in the reporting partnership.

A return made on the basis that the activities of an LLP are treated as carried on in partnership by its members (because it carries on a business with a view to profit — see **44.17** PARTNERSHIPS) is treated as a valid partnership return even if in fact the LLP does not carry on a business with a view to profit. Accordingly, HMRC may open an enquiry into the return under the provisions at **52.20** below or issue a follower notice or partnership payment notice as if it were a partnership return. This rule was introduced to reverse the effect of a number of FTT decisions (although the UT overturned the FTT decision in one of the cases, *Inverclyde Property Renovation LLP v HMRC* UT, [2020] STC 1348).

Although it was enacted by *FA 2020*, the rule is treated as always having been in force. It does not apply, however, to a return if a court or tribunal determined before 11 March 2020 that the return in question was not a valid partnership return (provided that the court or tribunal's decision had not been set aside or overturned on appeal before 11 March 2020).

Filing date — partnership including at least one individual

Two different filing dates may be specified in the notice, depending on whether or not the return will be an 'electronic return' (see **52.5** above). For an electronic return, the filing date will be no earlier than 31 January following the tax year concerned (normally that in which the period of account ends); for non-electronic returns it will be no earlier than 31 October following the tax year. Where, however, the notice to make the return is given on or after 1 August but before 1 November following the tax year, the filing date must be at least three months after the date of the notice or, in the case of an electronic return, no earlier than 31 January. Where notice is given after 31 October following the tax year, the filing date must be at least three months after the date of the notice.

In *Fitzpatrick and Co Solicitors v HMRC* FTT, [2012] SFTD 816, a partnership return submitted as a PDF attached to the online personal returns of the partners was held to constitute an electronic return.

Filing date — partnership including at least one company

Two different filing dates may be specified in the notice, depending on whether or not the return will be an electronic return. For an electronic return, the filing date will be no earlier than the first anniversary of the end of the relevant period; for non-electronic returns, it will be no earlier than nine months after the end of the relevant period. Where notice is given more than nine months after the end of the relevant period, the filing date must be at least three months after the date of the notice.

[*TMA 1970, ss 12AA, 12BZA; FA 2020, s 104; FA 2024, s 36(3)*].

See **46.5, 46.7** PENALTIES regarding penalties for non-compliance. For the capital gains tax position as regards partnership transactions, see **44** PARTNERSHIPS.

Withdrawal of notice to make return

A partner who has received a notice to make a partnership return may request HMRC to withdraw the notice. Such a request can be made within the two years of the end of the tax year or relevant period to which the notice relates or, in exceptional circumstances, within such extended period as HMRC may agree. A partner cannot make such a request if he has already filed the return for the year.

If HMRC agree to withdraw the notice they do so by giving a withdrawal notice specifying the date on which the notice is withdrawn. Withdrawing a notice in this way does not prevent HMRC subsequently issuing a further notice for the same year or period.

A withdrawal notice may also cancel a penalty for failing to make a return (see **46.5** PENALTIES).

[*TMA 1970, s 12AAA; FA 2009, Sch 55 para 17B; FA 2021, Sch 27 para 3*].

Partnership statements

[52.19] Each partnership return must include a statement (a partnership statement) showing, in respect of the period covered by the return and (if that period is not a single period of account) each period of account ending within that period:

- the amount of the partnership income or loss from each source;
- the amounts of tax deducted at source from or tax credits on partnership income;
- the amount of consideration for each disposal of partnership property,

and each partner's share of each of those amounts. Additional information must be included where the reporting partnership is a partner in another partnership or where the reporting partnership includes a partner which is itself a partnership. [*TMA 1970, s 12AB(1)–(1D)(5); ITA 2007, s 989*].

Where a company carries on a trade etc. in partnership the company tax return (see **52.21** below) for any period must include amounts in respect of the company's share of any income, loss, consideration, tax credit or charge stated in any relevant statement falling to be made by the partnership for a period which includes, or includes any part of, the period in respect of which the return is required. [*FA 1998, s 117, Sch 18 para 12*]. In the case of an individual carrying on a trade etc. in partnership, a return under *TMA 1970, s 8* (see **52.5** above) must include each amount, which according to any 'relevant partnership statement' is his share of any income, loss, tax, credit or charge for the period covered by the statement. A '*relevant partnership statement*' is a statement falling to be made, as respects the partnership, under the above provisions for a period which includes, or includes any part of, the year of assessment or its basis period. [*TMA 1970, s 8(1B)(1C)*].

Partners' shares

Partnership returns are conclusive for tax purposes as to whether a person has a share in the profits or losses of the partnership for any period and what any person's share in those profits or losses is. This is subject to the right of any such person to refer any dispute about his share to the tribunal for determination. The right to make such a referral does not extend to a dispute to the extent that it is in substance about the amount of the partnership's profits or losses before sharing. A referral must be made within the 12 months beginning with the day after the day the return was delivered or, where the dispute relates to an amendment to the return, the day on which the amendment was made. The tribunal has no power to extend these time limits (*Anderson v PricewaterhouseCoopers* FTT, [2022] UKFTT 457 (TC), [2023] SFTD 575). A person who makes a referral must notify HMRC and the reporting partner, and the reporting partner must then notify every other partner and any other person who appears to be a party to the dispute.

Where the tribunal determines a referral, HMRC must, if necessary, amend the partnership return in accordance with the tribunal's determination and make any consequential amendments to the partners' own returns.

At any time before the referral is determined by the tribunal, the dispute may be settled by the partners. All of the partners must agree in writing either that the return is correct or that it requires correcting in a particular way and the reporting partner must notify HMRC accordingly. Where such an agreement is reached, the referral is treated as if it had been determined by the tribunal. A partner may, however, withdraw from the agreement within 30 days by written notice to the other partners and HMRC may, within 30 days of receiving notice, notify the reporting partner of their objections to the agreement. In either case, the agreement is disregarded.

Usually, only one referral can be made in respect of a return, but a further referral can be made in respect of a dispute arising as a result of an amendment to the return.

[*TMA 1970, s 12ABZB*].

Amendments to partnership returns

Provisions similar to those in **52.9** above apply as regards amendments and corrections to partnership returns. Where a partnership return is so amended or corrected (and the correction is not rejected by the taxpayer), the partners' returns will be amended by HMRC accordingly, by notice to each partner concerned. [*TMA 1970, ss 12ABA, 12ABB*].

Enquiries into returns

[52.20] Provisions similar to those at **52.11** above apply as regards enquiries into a partnership return. The notice of enquiry may be given to a successor (as defined) of the person who made the return (see **52.18** above). The giving of such notice is deemed to include the giving of notice under *TMA 1970, s 9A* (see **52.11** above) (or, where applicable, the equivalent corporation tax provision of *FA 1998, Sch 18 para 24*) to each partner affected. [*TMA 1970, ss 12AC, 118(1)(3)*].

HMRC's power to call for documents at **52.13** above also applies here.

Similar provisions to those at **52.14–52.16** above apply in the case of an enquiry into a partnership return. However, there is no equivalent provision to *TMA 1970, s 9C* in **52.15** above (amendment by HMRC while enquiry in progress).

Where a partnership return is amended under the relevant provisions in **52.14**, **52.15** above, HMRC will, by notice, make any necessary consequential amendments to the partners' returns (including those of company partners). Similar provisions apply where a referral of a dispute under *TMA 1970, s 12ABZB* (see **52.19** above) is made during an enquiry. [*TMA 1970, ss 12AD, 28ZA–28ZE, 28B*].

Company tax returns

[52.21] The following provisions apply to companies.

Notification of coming within charge to corporation tax

A company must give notice to HMRC of the beginning of its first accounting period and of the beginning of any subsequent accounting period that does not immediately follow the end of a previous accounting period (i.e. the first accounting period following a period of dormancy). The notice must be given in writing to an HMRC officer not later than three months after the beginning of the accounting period. It must state when the accounting period began and include the following information:

- the company's name, registered number, registered office and principal place of business;
- the nature of the business carried on;
- the date to which accounts are to be drawn up;
- the full name and home address of each of the directors;
- if the company has taken over a business, the name and address of that former business and the name and address of the person from whom it was acquired;
- the name of any parent company and its registered office; and
- if the company then has any PAYE obligations, the date on which those obligations first arose.

The requirement does not apply to unincorporated associations or partner-'ships. [*FA 2004, s 55; SI 2004 No 2502*].

Note that *FA 2004, s 55* is removed from the list of provisions in respect of which a penalty can be charged under *TMA 1970, s 98* by *FA 2008, Sch 41 para 25* obligations arising on or after 1 April 2010. No replacement penalty provision has been enacted.

Notification of chargeability

A company chargeable to corporation tax for any accounting period which has neither made a return of its profits for that period nor received a notice requiring such a return (see below) must give notice of its chargeability to HMRC within 12 months after the end of that accounting period. [*TMA 1970, s 10(1); FA 1998, s 117, Sch 18 para 2*].

See **46.3** PENALTIES regarding failure to meet the requirement.

Self-assessment returns

If so required by notice, a company must make a return of such information, relevant to its corporation tax liabilities, as is required under the notice. Supporting accounts, statements and reports may also be required, although the accounts required of companies resident in the UK throughout the period to which the return relates (*'the return period'*), and required to prepare accounts under *Companies Act 2006* or *Companies Act 1985* (or NI equivalent) for any period consisting of or including the return period, are only those it is so required to prepare.

The return must include a declaration to the effect that, to the best of the knowledge of the person making it, it is correct and complete. *TMA 1970, s 108(1)* requires that person to be *'the proper officer of the company'* (i.e. the secretary of a corporate body, except where a liquidator or an administrator has been appointed when the latter is the proper officer, or the treasurer of a non-corporate body) or, except where a liquidator has been appointed, any authorised person.

Where a company makes a return for an accounting period without having been given a notice to do so (i.e. the return is made voluntarily), then for all tax purposes the return is treated as made pursuant to such a notice issued on the date the return was made (and therefore as a return made under the above provisions), provided that HMRC decide to treat it in that way. This rule in effect overturns the decision in *Patel v HMRC* FTT, [2018] SFTD 1000, where it was held that a voluntary return was not a return under the above provisions and therefore HMRC could not open an enquiry into it. The rule applies with retrospective effect to any voluntary return, whenever made, but it does not apply to a return if, before 29 October 2018, the company made an appeal or a claim for judicial review and one of the grounds for the appeal or claim was that the voluntary return was not a return under the above provisions because no notice to make a return was given.

Similar self-assessment provisions as in **52.8**, **52.9** above apply, except that a company does not have the option of requiring HMRC to compute the tax liability.

[*FA 1998, s 117, Sch 18, paras 3, 7, 8, 11, 13, 15, 16, 20A*].

The return must be made by the later of:

(a) twelve months after the end of the period to which it relates,
(b) twelve months after the end of the period for which the company makes up accounts (*'period of account'*) in which falls the last day of the accounting period to which it relates (except that periods of account in excess of 18 months are treated as ending after 18 months for this purpose), and
(c) three months after service of the notice requiring the return.

If the period specified by the notice for the making of a return (*'the specified period'*) is not an accounting period of the company, but the company is within the charge to corporation tax for some part of the specified period, the notice is to be taken as referring to all company accounting period(s) ending in or at the end of the specified period. If there is no such accounting period, but there is a part of the specified period which does not fall within an accounting period, the notice is to be treated as requiring a return for that part of the period. Otherwise, the notice is of no effect, and the company is not required to make any return pursuant to it. For the determination of a company's accounting period, see Tolley's Corporation Tax under Accounting Periods. See also **52.19** above where a company carries on a trade in partnership.

[*FA 1998, s 117, Sch 18 paras 5, 14*].

All companies are required to file their tax returns online using a specified data format (known as iXBRL). Companies with less complex tax affairs are able to use HMRC's own filing software to do so. (HMRC News Release 20 August 2009; HMRC Directions under *SI 2003 No 282, Regs 3* and *10*, 6 January 2010).

In the absence of a return, HMRC have power to determine the corporation tax liability. [*FA 1998, s 117, Sch 18 paras 36–40*].

An enquiry regime analogous to that in **52.11–52.16** above applies to companies. Note that in addition to the matters mentioned at **52.11** above in respect of which an enquiry can be made, for corporation tax purposes an enquiry can also extend to consideration of whether to give the taxpayer a notice under *TIOPA 2010, s 232* or *s 249* or *TCGA 1992, s 184G* or *s 184H* (avoidance utilising losses — see **14.7** COMPANIES). [*FA 1998, Sch 18 paras 24–35; F(No 2)A 2017, Sch 15 paras 24–28, 44*].

Similar record-keeping requirements as in **52.10** above apply to companies under corporation tax self-assessment. A company must preserve its records for six years from the end of its return period (subject, from a date to be fixed by order, to HMRC specifying, in writing, an earlier date). [*FA 1998, s 117, Sch 18 paras 21–23*].

Corporation tax self-assessment is covered in full in Tolley's Corporation Tax.

HMRC offer post-transaction (pre-return) valuation checks to companies (in relation to their chargeable gains) as they do to individuals (see **52.7** above).

Where an enquiry remains open beyond the period during which notice of intention to enquire had to be given and solely because of an unagreed valuation for chargeable gains purposes, HMRC will not take advantage of the open enquiry to raise further enquiries into matters unrelated to the valuation or the chargeable gains computation except in circumstances where a 'discovery' (see **6.10** ASSESSMENTS) could in any case have been made if the enquiry had been completed (HMRC Statement of Practice SP 1/02).

See **46.4** PENALTIES regarding non-compliance. See also **14.16** COMPANIES regarding the application of these provisions where a company ceases to be UK-resident in the course of the formation of an SE and where an SE becomes non-UK resident.

UK land disposal returns

[52.22] Where a person makes a direct or indirect disposal of UK land meeting the conditions below, that person must make a return to HMRC in respect of the disposal on or before the 60th day following the day of the 'completion' of the disposal (the 30th day where the completion date is before 27 October 2021) and, where appropriate, make a payment on account of CGT — see **45.3**

PAYMENT OF TAX. Only one return is required where two or more disposals are made in the same tax year and have the same completion date. A return must contain the information specified by HMRC and include a declaration by the person making it that it is to the best of that person's knowledge correct and complete.

In completing a return, reasonable estimates (i.e. estimates on a fair and reasonable basis, having regard to person's knowledge and other circumstances) can be made about the values, apportionments and whether or not income tax will be chargeable for the year at a higher rate and, if not, how much of the basic rate band will be available in calculating the CGT liability.

The requirement to make a return applies for capital gains tax purposes to:

(1) any direct or indirect disposal of UK land to which the provisions at **35.23** or **35.24** LAND (disposals by non-residents or in the overseas part of a split tax year) apply, whether or not a gain is made; and
(2) any other direct disposal of UK land where a residential property gain (see **2.1** ANNUAL RATES AND EXEMPTIONS) arises.

The return should generally be made using HMRC's online Capital Gains Tax on UK Property service: see www.tax.service.gov.uk/capital-gains-tax-uk-property/start/report-pay-capital-gains-tax-uk-property. For the procedure for agents to file returns on clients' behalf (including the digitally excluded), see HMRC Capital Gains Manual CGAPP18-130. Anyone unable to use the online service can download an interactive paper return for 2022/23 onwards at www.gov.uk/guidance/report-your-capital-gains-tax-on-uk-property-by-post. For earlier years, paper returns must be requested from HMRC. For the circumstances in which HMRC will accept paper returns, see CGAPP18-110.

Where an allowable loss arises on a disposal which would have been within (2) above if a gain had arisen, the taxpayer may choose to make a return under these provisions in order to secure a repayment of tax under the payment on account rules at **45.3** PAYMENT OF TAX. Such a return cannot be made if (a) or (b) below apply.

If, in determining whether or not a return is required, a question arises as to whether a particular capital gains provision applies and the answer to that question requires taking account of events after the completion of the disposal, it must be assumed that the provision does apply if, at the time of completion, it is reasonable to expect that it will.

For this purpose, the '*completion*' of a disposal occurs at the time of the disposal or, where the disposal is under a contract completed by conveyance, transfer or other instrument, at the time the instrument takes effect. The completion date may, therefore, not be the same as the date of the disposal for CGT purposes (and could in some cases be in a later tax year). This is because the date of disposal under an unconditional contract is the date the contract is made rather than the date of conveyance etc. (see **16.4** COMPUTATION OF GAINS AND LOSSES).

Where the disposal is of property which is the subject of a collective investment scheme in respect of which an election for transparency (see **35.27** LAND) is in effect, and the disposal takes place before the election is made, then if a person is required to make a return in respect of the disposal, the disposal is treated as if completion was on the day on which the election is made.

In the case of a deemed disposal by a participant of units in a qualifying fund or of rights or interests in a qualifying company (either on becoming entitled to receive an amount not otherwise taxable where the value derives from a disposal of UK land or when an election for exemption ceases to have effect — see **35.27** LAND), the completion of the disposal occurs on the day on which the manager of the relevant fund notifies the participant of the deemed disposal. Where, however, the deemed gain is deferred, each occasion on which any part of the gain is subsequently treated as arising is treated as a separate disposal for which a return is required. The time at which each such disposal is treated as completing is the later of the time at which the part of the gain is treated as arising and the time at which notification is given by the fund manager.

The requirement to make a return does not apply to an '*excluded disposal*', i.e. where the disposal is a no gain/no loss disposal (see **8.6** ASSETS HELD ON **28** MARCH **1982**), the grant of a lease at arm's length to an unconnected person for no premium or a disposal by a charity or of pension scheme investments.

No UK land disposal return is required in respect of a disposal within (2) above if the taxpayer is not required to make a payment on account of CGT under the provisions at **45.3** PAYMENT OF TAX. A return is also not required where:

(a) the taxpayer has filed an ordinary tax return which includes a self-assessment taking account of the disposal before the date by which the UK land disposal return would otherwise have to be made; or
(b) HMRC have issued a notice requiring the taxpayer to make an ordinary tax return for the tax year of the disposal and the filing date for that return is no later than the time limit for making the UK land disposal return.

In (a) above, a self-assessment is not treated as taking account of the disposal if the self-assessed CGT is less than the amount that would be payable on account under the provisions at **45.3** PAYMENT OF TAX. The exclusions in (a) and (b) are only likely to apply where the completion date is in a later tax year than that in which the disposal is treated as occurring. The requirement to file a UK land disposal return is only displaced by the making of a self-assessment return where (a) above applies. If an ordinary return is not made before the filing date for the UK land disposal return, the filing of the ordinary return does not negate the requirement for a UK land disposal return.

A return is also not required where a disposal has an 'appropriate connection' to a collective investment scheme (see **35.24** LAND) and the taxpayer is not required to make a payment on account of CGT.

For the purposes of the above provisions, it must be assumed that a person has made any claim or election, or given any notice, if, at the time of completion, it is reasonable to expect that they will.

If, after a disposal has completed and a return has been filed, an expectation or estimate used in the return changes, the taxpayer may (but is not required to) make a further return (and, where applicable, obtain a repayment of tax). The further return is made on the basis that a notional additional disposal has been made, which is treated as completing at the time of the change and, except for that change, as a replication of the actual disposal. In calculating the tax due on the additional disposal, the actual disposal is then ignored. This provision applies where:

- it becomes reasonable to assume that a particular capital gains provision will apply by reference to the taxpayer's residence;
- it becomes reasonable to conclude that a relief is available on the disposal;
- it becomes known whether or not income tax will be chargeable for the year at a higher rate and, if not, how much of the basic rate band will be available in calculating the CGT liability, or it becomes reasonable to make a different estimate of those issues than was made in the original return; or
- the value of anything, or of an amount to be apportioned, becomes known where an estimate was used in the return.

See **46.5** PENALTIES for the penalty for failure to make a return and **46.11** PENALTIES for the penalty for errors in a return.

Options

Where the grant of an option binding the grantor to sell an interest in asset is, on exercise, treated for CGT purposes as the same transaction as the sale (see **7.7** ASSETS), the grantor must nevertheless make a return and any payment on account (see **45.3** PAYMENT OF TAX) in respect of the grant of the option (if the grant is a disposal to which the above provisions apply).

[*FA 2019, Sch 2 paras 1–5, 10–17; FA 2022, s 23(2)(4)*].

Amendments to a return

Subject to the following, the provisions at **52.9** above for amendments and corrections to self-assessment returns apply to UK land disposal returns. Amendments are allowed, however, only so far as the original UK land disposal return could have included the amendment by reference to things already done. No amendments can be made on or after the date on which the taxpayer filed an ordinary tax return which includes a self-assessment taking account of the disposal or the date on which he is required to do so. If the taxpayer is not required to file an ordinary tax return for the year concerned, no amendment to the UK land disposal return can be made more than 12 months after 31 January following the tax year. [*FA 2019, Sch 2 para 19*].

Enquiries into UK land disposal returns

Subject to certain modifications, the enquiry provisions at **52.11–52.15** above apply to a UK land disposal return as the apply to an ordinary self-assessment return. The modifications are as follows.

- If the taxpayer is required to make an ordinary return for the tax year, the time limit for giving a notice of enquiry into a UK land disposal return is the same as that for the ordinary return.
- Otherwise, the time limit is what would have been the time limit for giving a notice of enquiry into an ordinary return for the tax year on the assumption that such a return was made on the later of 31 January following the tax year or the date on which the UK land disposal return was made.

- HMRC are not required to make any repayment of tax under the payment on account provisions at **45.3 PAYMENT OF TAX** before the enquiry is completed, but they may do so on a provisional basis to the extent they think fit.
- An enquiry into an ordinary tax return for a tax year is taken also to be an enquiry into any UK land disposal returns for disposals in that year.
- A final closure notice which completes an enquiry into an ordinary tax return for a tax year is taken also to be a final closure notice in respect of any enquiries into UK land disposal returns for disposals in that year if no such notice has previously been given in respect of such returns.

[*FA 2019, Sch 2 paras 20, 21(1)*].

HMRC determinations

Subject to certain modifications, the provisions for making determinations at **52.17** above apply to a UK land disposal return as the apply to an ordinary self-assessment return. The provisions apply where a person is required to make UK land disposal return and does not do so by the filing date. A determination must be made within three years of 31 January following the tax year concerned. If a determination is superseded by a return, any amount of CGT which is payable or repayable as a result is treated as so payable or repayable on the filing date for the return. [*FA 2019, Sch 2 para 22*].

UK or European economic interest groupings

[52.23] A UK or European Economic Interest Grouping (see **43.19 OVERSEAS MATTERS**) registered in the UK or having an establishment there must make and deliver a return (through its manager or the individual representative of its manager) containing such information and accompanied by such accounts and statements as may be required by a notice given by the inspector. In the case of any other grouping, a return is required from any member of it resident in the UK, or, if none is, from any member. [*TMA 1970, s 12A; SI 2019 No 689, Regs 1, 2*]. See **46.6 PENALTIES** as regards non-compliance.

Notification of uncertain tax treatment

[52.24] *FA 2022* introduced a requirement for large businesses to notify HMRC when they take a tax position in a return that is 'uncertain', broadly where a provision is made in their accounts to reflect the probability that a different treatment will be applied or where the treatment diverges from HMRC's view as published or expressed directly to the taxpayer. The requirement applies to corporation tax returns, partnership returns, PAYE returns and VAT returns but are discussed here only so far as they apply to corporation tax and partnership returns. Only businesses with UK turnover of at least £200 million or a UK balance sheet total of more than £2 billion are subject to the rules, the limits being applicable to a group of companies as a whole. Notification is only required where the tax advantage from taking the uncertain position (together with certain related tax advantages) is more than £5 million.

The requirement applies to returns for which the filing date is on or after 1 April 2022. [*FA 2022, Sch 17 para 33*].

For HMRC guidance on the provisions, see the Uncertain Tax Treatments by Large Businesses Manual which is referred to below.

Companies subject to the requirement to notify

The notification requirement applies only to a company which makes a company tax return for a financial year in which it is a 'qualifying company'.

A company is a '*qualifying company*' in a financial year if, in the previous year, its UK turnover exceeded £200 million or its UK balance sheet total exceeded £2 billion. If the company was a member of a group at the end of the previous year, the UK turnover and UK balance sheet total for the purpose of this test are that of all of companies which were members of the group at that time which were within the charge to corporation tax on income at any time in that year. Where a group company does not draw up accounts to the same date as the company under consideration (C), its UK turnover and UK balance sheet total for the last year ending before C's financial year end are taken.

For this purpose, a '*company*' is any body corporate other than a limited liability partnership, a public authority, an open-ended investment company or a registered co-operative and community benefit society. A '*group*' is defined by reference to 51% subsidiaries but certain qualifying asset holding companies (QAHCs) are excluded if they are not part of the same worldwide group for the purposes of the corporate interest restriction (see **63.8** UNIT TRUSTS ETC).

'*Turnover*' has the same meaning as in *Companies Act 2006, s 474* and '*UK turnover*' means, in the case of a UK resident company, all of its turnover. The UK turnover of a non-UK resident company is that part of its turnover which is attributable to activities within the charge to corporation tax on income, apportioned on a just and reasonable basis. '*Balance sheet total*' means the aggregate amounts shown as assets in the balance sheet at the end of the financial year and '*UK balance sheet total*' means, in the case of a UK resident company, its balance sheet total. The UK balance sheet total of a non-UK resident company is that part of its balance sheet total which is attributable to activities within the charge to corporation tax on income, again apportioned on a just and reasonable basis.

[*FA 2022, Sch 17 paras 2, 3, 7*].

Partnerships subject to the requirement to notify

The notification requirement applies only to a a partnership which makes a partnership return for a financial year in which it is a 'qualifying partnership.

A partnership is a '*qualifying partnership*' in a financial year if, in the previous year, its UK turnover (as above) exceeded £200 million or its UK balance sheet total (as above) exceeded £2 billion.

A 'partnership' for this purpose is a partnership (wherever formed) or a LLP incorporated in the UK that carries on a trade, business or profession with a view to profit. Collective investment schemes and alternative investment funds are excluded.

[*FA 2022, Sch 17 para 4*].

Requirement to notify

Where a qualifying company makes a company tax return or a qualifying partnership makes a partnership return, it must notify HMRC if the return includes an 'uncertain amount' (including a nil amount) which is brought into account for corporation tax or income tax purposes. The company or partnership must also notify HMRC if the amount becomes uncertain after the return has been submitted (see below). The requirement to notify extends to amounts included as a result of an amendment to the return. If there is more than one amount in a return which is uncertain at the time it is made, a single notification must be given covering all of them.

Notification must be made on or before the filing date for the return or for companies, if later, the last day for the delivery of the accounts to the registrar of companies under *Companies Act 2006*. If the uncertain amount is one which only becomes uncertain after the return has been submitted, notification must be made by the filing date for the return for the year in which the provision is recognised in the accounts or for companies, if later, the last day for delivery of those accounts to the registrar of companies. An uncertain amount included in a return by amendment must be notified within the 30 days beginning with the day on which HMRC are notified of the amendment.

The form of the notification and the information to be included are those specified in an HMRC notice with the force of law. The online notification form is at www.gov.uk/guidance/check-if-you-need-to-notify-hmrc-about-an-uncertain-tax-treatment#how-to-notify-us.

These provisions apply only if the 'threshold test' below is met and is subject to the following exemptions. Notification is not required where:

- it is reasonable for the taxpayer to conclude that HMRC already have all, or substantially all, of the information about the uncertain amount which would have been included in a notification; or
- (for companies) the uncertain amount relates to a transaction between group members the net effect of which is that the tax advantages which would be obtained by the group as a whole do not exceed £5 million. HMRC give the example of an asset transferred intra-group and then sold outside the group in the same accounting period. If there is subsequently uncertainty that the intra-group disposal provisions apply, although the transferring company would gain a tax advantage by applying the provisions, overall the group obtains no advantage (as the transferee company's acquisition cost would be increased by the same amount as the transferor's gain). (HMRC Uncertain Tax Treatment Manual UTT16300).

[*FA 2022, Sch 17 paras 8, 9, 18, 19*].

Meaning of 'uncertain amount'

An amount brought into account by a company or partnership is an 'uncertain amount' if it meets either (or both) of the following conditions.

(1) A provision has been recognised in the company's accounts reflecting the probability that a different treatment will be applied to the 'transaction' to which the amount relates. Often the provision will be made in the

accounts for a year later than that in which the amount to which it relates is recognised in the accounts, in which case, the amount in question becomes uncertain in the later year (unless (2) below also applies). If it becomes uncertain after the return for the earlier year is made, the extended time limit for notification applies as above.

(2) The tax treatment applied relies on an interpretation or application of the law which does not accord with HMRC's known interpretation or application. This applies whether HMRC's views are known from guidance, statements etc. of general application and in the public domain or through dealings with HMRC by the company.

In (1) above, '*transactions*' includes any arrangements, agreements or understanding, whether or not legally enforceable.

[*FA 2002, Sch 15 paras 10, 30*].

HMRC consider that they can be treated as having no known public position where their position is unclear, for example where publications have not been updated to reflect changes. Where HMRC's publications are contradictory, the known position should be taken as the most recently published statement. HMRC expect a level of familiarity with its published material and that a business would want to ascertain whether HMRC are likely to take a different view. In considering whether a business has a reasonable excuse for not making a notification, they will consider whether their guidance on the issue is easy to find (for example by inclusion in a guidance manual), whether an online search using relevant search terms finds HMRC's published view and whether the issue is novel, contentious, high-value or high-risk so that a careful examination of HMRC's view would be warranted (HMRC Uncertain Tax Treatment Manual UTT13200).

Threshold test

The '*threshold test*' is met if it is reasonable to conclude that the company or partnership will obtain a 'tax advantage' it would not obtain if the uncertain amount were replaced by the 'expected amount' and the total value of all such tax advantages that would be obtained from the uncertain amount and any other uncertain amounts arising from substantially the same tax treatment for the same accounting period is more than £5 million. If the accounting period is less than 12 months, the £5 million threshold is increased or decreased accordingly.

A '*tax advantage*' for this purpose includes a relief or increased relief, repayment or increased repayment of tax, avoidance or reduction of a charge to tax, avoidance of a possible assessment, deferral of payment, advance of a repayment and avoidance of an obligation to deduct or account for tax. The value of the tax advantage is the additional tax which would be due if the uncertain amount were replaced by the expected amount. The effects of any group relief or group relief for carried forward losses and of any tax repaid following the release or repayment of a loan to a close company participator are ignored. Where the tax advantage results in a loss which cannot be set off, the value of the tax advantage is 10% of the loss. But if there is no reasonable prospect of the loss ever being used the value is nil.

The '*expected amount*' is, where the uncertain amount is within (1) above, the amount of the provision. Where the uncertain amount is within (2) above, the expected amount is the amount that would be wholly in accordance with HMRC's view. If more than one tax treatment is wholly in accordance with HMRC's view, the expected amount is that given by adopting the treatment which gives the smallest tax advantage from using the uncertain amount. If both (1) and (2) above apply and result in different expected amounts, the amount which gives the greatest tax advantage is taken.

[*FA 2022, Sch 17 paras 11, 12, 14–17*].

Penalties

For the penalty for failure to make a required notification, see **46.25** PENALTIES.

Key points about returns

[52.25] Points to consider are as follows.

- The deadline for submitting self-assessment tax returns for individuals, partnerships and trustees is generally 31 January following the year of assessment for electronic returns or 31 October following the year of assessment for paper returns. These returns include details of income and allowances as well as capital gains.
- A company generally has twelve months after the end of its accounting period to submit a self-assessment return which would include any chargeable gains and allowable losses.
- Capital gains only need reporting on a personal return if the chargeable gains (before losses) are less than the annual exempt amount and the proceeds for all disposals do not exceed £50,000. For this purpose the following are not taken into account:
  (a) The disposal of exempt assets such as a principal private residence.
  (b) Transactions between spouses or civil partners.
- If the remittance basis of taxation is claimed the annual exempt amount is not generally available and so the above reporting limits do not apply. All disposals of chargeable assets must be disclosed.
- If there are net losses for the year a disclosure will be required whatever the level of proceeds.
- Returns can be amended within twelve months of the normal filing date and HMRC can raise an enquiry within twelve months of the date of delivery of a return if filed before the normal filing date. The enquiry window may be longer when the return is late.
- A special compliance regime applies to all direct disposals of UK land where a residential property gain arises. A UK land disposal return must be made together with a payment on account of CGT on or before the 60th day following the day of the completion of the disposal (the 30th day where completion is before 27 October 2021). See **52.22** above and **45.3** PAYMENT OF TAX. Previously, the

regime applied only to non-UK residents (see **52.22** above). The regime also applies to direct disposals of non-residential UK land and indirect disposal of UK land by non-UK residents for disposals.

53

Rollover Relief — Replacement of Business Assets

Cross-references. See **8.11** ASSETS HELD ON **28** MARCH **1982** for 50% relief on rolled-over gains of companies relating to an asset acquired before 31 March 1982; **24.2** FURNISHED HOLIDAY ACCOMMODATION for application of rollover relief to such accommodation before April 2025; **30** HOLD-OVER RELIEFS generally; **35.10** and **35.11** LAND for rollover relief on compulsory purchase of land and exchanges of joint interests in land respectively; **35.23** and **35.31** LAND for rollover relief for certain disposals of land by non-residents; **42.2** OFFSHORE SETTLEMENTS for disapplication of rollover relief where trustees cease to be UK-resident or liable to UK tax; **43.3**, **43.16** and **43.18** OVERSEAS MATTERS for restriction on rollover relief in certain cases.

Simon's Taxes. See C3.3.

Introduction to rollover relief

[53.1] Rollover relief enables traders and certain others (see **53.5** below) to defer chargeable gains on the disposal of qualifying assets used for business purposes where they invest the proceeds in other qualifying assets for use in the business. The replacement assets must normally be acquired within one year before or three years after the disposal of the old assets (see **53.2** below). The relief must be claimed (see **53.11** below).

There are nine classes of qualifying asset, including land, fixed plant and machinery and certain Lloyd's assets. Goodwill and certain agricultural and fishing quotas and payment entitlements are also qualifying assets for capital gains tax purposes, but following the introduction of the corporation tax intangible fixed assets regime (see **15.13** COMPANIES — CORPORATE FINANCE AND INTANGIBLES), these assets are not normally qualifying assets for corporation tax purposes. See **53.4** below.

The way in which relief is given depends on the nature of the new assets. If the new assets are not depreciating assets (see **53.9** below), the disposal consideration for the old assets is reduced to an amount which results in neither a gain nor a loss and the acquisition cost of the new assets is decreased by the amount of that reduction (see **53.6** below). If the new assets are depreciating assets, the gains on the old assets are not rolled over into the acquisition cost of the new assets but simply deferred until the earlier of the disposal of the new assets, their ceasing to be used for business purposes, or ten years after their acquisition (see **53.9** below). Partial relief is available in certain cases where the proceeds from the old assets are not fully reinvested or where the old assets were only partly used for business purposes or not used for business purposes for the whole of the period of ownership (see **53.8** below).

Groups of companies are able to claim rollover relief where the disposal is made by one group company and the acquisition by another. See **53.10** below.

Conditions for rollover relief

[53.2] Rollover relief can be claimed where:

(a) a person carrying on a trade disposes of, or of their interest in, assets (the 'old assets') used, and used only, for the purposes of the trade throughout the period of ownership (excluding any period before 31 March 1982);

(b) they apply the consideration obtained for the disposal, within a specified period (see below), in acquiring other assets, or an interest in other assets (the 'new assets') which on the acquisition are taken into use, and used only, for the purposes of the trade; and

(c) the old assets and the new assets are within the classes of assets listed at **53.4** below.

[*TCGA 1992, s 152(1)(3)(9)*].

Partial relief is available in certain cases where the proceeds from the old assets are not fully reinvested or where the old assets were only partly used for business purposes or not used for business purposes for the whole of the period of ownership. See **53.8** below.

'*Trade*' has the same meaning as for income tax purposes, but not so as to apply the provisions of the *Income Tax Acts* as to the circumstances in which, on a change in the persons carrying on a trade, a trade is to be regarded as discontinued, or as set up and commenced. [*TCGA 1992, s 158*]. '*Trade*' includes any venture in the nature of trade. [*ITA 2007, s 989*]. For discussion of the meaning of 'trade' for rollover relief purposes, see *CIR v Richmond and Jones (Re Loquitur Ltd)* Ch D 2003, 75 TC 77.

Commercial letting of 'furnished holiday accommodation' is treated as a trade for the purposes of the relief. This treatment is, however, expected to be abolished with effect from April 2025 (and an anti-forestalling rule to prevent the use of unconditional contracts to access beneficial capital gains tax treatment will apply retrospectively from 6 March 2024). See **24.1** FURNISHED HOLIDAY ACCOMMODATION. HMRC have indicated that both parties to a genuine share farming agreement may be considered to be carrying on a farming trade for taxation purposes (HMRC Business Income Manual BIM55075).

For the application of rollover relief to certain qualifying undertakings other than trades, see **53.5** below.

The old assets must actually be used for the trade in question. Any original intention for such use is ignored. Relief was refused, for example, where land was purchased on which it was proposed to build a factory for use in the taxpayer's trade but was sold without the factory being built (*Temperley v Visibell Ltd* Ch D 1973, 49 TC 129).

It is not normally necessary for the purposes of (b) above to establish a direct link between the actual disposal proceeds and their application: the taxpayer is simply required to reinvest an amount equal to the proceeds received (HMRC Capital Gains Manual CG60270). The Inland Revenue indicated in 1991 that there was no reason why in principle relief should not be available where the acquisition consideration is satisfied by the issue of shares by a company (Institute of Taxation TIR/11/91, 1991 STI 1097). They have also confirmed that relief is available where assets are exchanged (CCAB Statement TR 508 9 June 1983).

Use of new assets

Subject to the concession below, the new assets must be taken into trading use immediately on acquisition. Again any original intention to attempt at immediate use is ignored. See *Campbell Connelly & Co. Ltd v Barnett* CA 1993, 66 TC 380. On the authority of statements of Knox J in the Ch D in that case, HMRC consider that the time at which the asset must be taken into use is normally the time that any contracts are completed by conveyance or delivery and possession has been obtained. (HMRC Capital Gains Manual CG60270).

Where a new asset is not, on acquisition, immediately taken into trading use it will nevertheless qualify for relief by concession provided:

(i) the owner proposes to incur capital expenditure for the purpose of enhancing its value;
(ii) any work arising from such capital expenditure begins as soon as possible after acquisition, and is completed within a reasonable time;
(iii) on completion of the work the asset is taken into use for the purpose of the trade and for no other purpose; and
(iv) the asset is not let or used for any non-trading purpose in the period between acquisition and the time it is taken into use for the purposes of the trade.

Where a person acquires land with a building on it, or with the intention to construct a building on it, the land is treated as qualifying for the above concession provided that the building itself qualifies for relief whether under the above concession or otherwise and provided that the land is not let or used for any non-trading purpose between its acquisition and the time that both it and the building are taken into use for the purposes of the trade.

(HMRC Extra-Statutory Concession D24).

In *Steibelt v Paling* Ch D 1999, 71 TC 376, Sir Richard Scott V-C commented that on the facts of the case the taxpayer had failed to comply with condition (ii) above.

Tonnage tax regime

Rollover relief is not available to the extent that the new asset is used wholly and exclusively for the purposes of a shipping company's activities within the tonnage tax regime (see **23.17** EXEMPTIONS AND RELIEFS). If a new asset begins to be used for such purposes after rollover relief has been given, the rolled over gain becomes a chargeable gain, which is, however, deferred until the new asset is disposed of. [*FA 2000, Sch 22 para 67*].

Disposal and acquisition of same asset

Relief is not strictly available where there is a disposal and reacquisition of the same asset. By concession, however, where an asset is repurchased for purely commercial reasons after having been sold, HMRC will not object to a rollover relief claim on those grounds (HMRC Extra-Statutory Concession D16). This concessional treatment also applies to partnership changes which result in reacquisition of fractional shares in partnership assets. (HMRC Capital Gains Manual CG60280).

In *Watton v Tippett* CA 1997, 69 TC 491, a trader made a part disposal of some business premises and attempted unsuccessfully to roll over the gain against the previous acquisition of the part of those premises still retained. It was held that the premises had been acquired as, and until the part disposal continued to be, a single asset, and that the acquisition cost could not be divided between the part of the premises sold and the part retained and treated as having been given for two separate assets.

Proceeds used to enhance or acquire further interest in existing asset

Where the proceeds from the disposal of an old asset are used to enhance the value of other assets already held, the expenditure is treated for rollover relief purposes (and for the purposes of *TCGA 1992, Sch 4* (deferred charges on gains before 31 March 1982; see **8.11** ASSETS HELD ON 31 MARCH **1982**)) as incurred in acquiring other assets provided the other assets are used only for the purposes of the trade or, on completion of the enhancement work, the assets are immediately taken into use and used only for the purposes of the trade. (HMRC Extra-Statutory Concession D22). Similar treatment is given where a further interest is acquired in another asset which is already in use for the purposes of the trade (HMRC Extra-Statutory Concession D25).

Time limit for replacement of assets

The acquisition of the new assets must take place within one year before, or three years after, the disposal of the old assets or at such later or earlier time as HMRC allow by notice. It is sufficient if an unconditional contract for acquisition is entered into within the specified periods, but if, in such circumstances, relief is given on a provisional basis, any necessary adjustments can be made, without time limit, if the contract is not completed. [*TCGA 1992, s 152(3)(4)*].

HMRC's practice is to extend the above time limits where the trader can show that they had a firm intention to acquire new assets within the time limit but were prevented from doing so by some fact or circumstance outside their control and that they acted as soon as they reasonably could after ceasing to be so prevented (HMRC Capital Gains Manual CG60300). The non-exercise of HMRC's statutory discretion to extend the time limit may be challenged by judicial review but cannot be reviewed by the Tribunal (*Steibelt v Paling* Ch D 1999, 71 TC 376). Such a challenge was unsuccessful in *R (oao Barnett) v CIR* QB 2003, [2004] STC 763.

Non-resident taxpayer

HMRC accept that a rollover relief can be validly made where the taxpayer has become non-resident in the UK before the acquisition of the new assets if the new assets are chargeable assets in relation to the taxpayer immediately after they are acquired. (HMRC Capital Gains Manual CG60260). Note, however, the restrictions in **42.2** OFFSHORE SETTLEMENTS and **43.3**, **43.16** and **43.18** OVERSEAS MATTERS in certain cases.

See also **35.23** and **35.31** LAND for disposals of certain interests in UK land by non-residents qualifying for rollover relief.

Anti-avoidance

Relief is denied if the acquisition of the new assets was made wholly or partly for the purpose of realising a gain from their subsequent disposal. [*TCGA 1992, s 152(5)*]. See also **4.21** ANTI-AVOIDANCE for the charge arising where concessions involving deferral of gains are abused, including those relating to rollover relief.

Application of rollover relief to particular traders

[53.3] Rollover relief applies as follows to certain types of trader.

Taxpayer with more than one trade

Rollover relief is available to a person who, either successively or at the same time, carries on two or more trades as if both or all of them were a single trade. [*TCGA 1992, s 152(8)*].

Where a trader ceases carrying on one trade and, within three years, commences carrying on another, HMRC will treat the trades as carried on 'successively'. If the disposal or acquisition takes place in the intervening period, relief will be restricted in respect of the period during which the assets disposed of were not used for trade purposes (see **53.8** below), and will be conditional on the replacement assets not being used or leased for any purpose prior to commencement of the new trade, and on their being taken into use for the purposes of the new trade on its commencement (HMRC Statement of Practice SP 8/81). In *Steibelt v Paling* Ch D 1999, 71 TC 376, a nine-year gap between trades meant that they could not be said to be carried on successively.

Trade carried on by individual's personal company

Where:

(i) the person disposing of the old assets and acquiring the new assets is an individual, and
(ii) the trade or trades in question are carried on not by that individual but by a company, which, both at the time of disposal and at the time of the acquisition referred to in (i) above, is his 'personal company',

then, for rollover relief purposes, references to the person carrying on the trade include a reference to that individual.

For this purpose, an individual's '*personal company*' is a company the voting rights in which are 'exercisable', as to not less than 5%, by that individual. ('*Exercisable*' means capable of being exercised, whether in fact exercised (*Hepworth v Smith* Ch D 1981, 54 TC 396).) See also *Boparan v HMRC* (Sp C 587), [2007] SSCD 297.

[*TCGA 1992, s 157*].

Assets must be disposed of and acquired by the individual for use by the same personal company. (HMRC Capital Gains Manual CG60260).

Partnerships

Relief is available to the owner of assets let to a trading or professional partnership of which he is a member, provided they are used for the purposes of the partnership's trade or profession (HMRC Statement of Practice D11). See also **44.9** PARTNERSHIPS as regards disposals by partners and **44.15** as regards mergers of partnerships and **53.10** below for partnerships involving a member of a group of companies.

Where land or other assets used for the purposes of a trade carried on in partnership are partitioned by the partners, the asset acquired is treated as a newly acquired asset provided the partnership is dissolved immediately thereafter (HMRC Extra-Statutory Concession D23).

Limited liability partnerships (LLPs)

Where a member of an LLP (see **44.17** PARTNERSHIPS) has rolled over a gain into an LLP asset and, at a later time but before any disposal of the asset, the transparency treatment afforded by *TCGA 1992, s 59A(1)* ceases to apply to the LLP (for example, by virtue of its going into liquidation), a chargeable gain equal to the amount rolled over is treated as accruing to the member immediately before that later time. Similarly, a postponed gain under **53.9** below (where the LLP asset is a depreciating asset) is brought back into charge immediately before that time. [*TCGA 1992, s 156A*]. In the absence of such a rule, the rolled over or postponed gain would have fallen out of charge as a result of the tax treatment of an LLP in liquidation.

Companies

For the application of the relief to groups of companies, see **53.10** below.

Rollover relief is not available where one company makes a disposal and an associated company makes an acquisition (*Joseph Carter & Sons Ltd v Baird; Wear Ironmongers & Sons Ltd v Baird* Ch D 1998, 72 TC 303).

Where a company ceases to be a member of a group such that a gain (a 'degrouping charge') arises under *TCGA 1992, s 179* (see **26.7** GROUPS OF COMPANIES) on a deemed sale and reacquisition of an asset, and the asset is a qualifying asset for rollover relief purposes, the company may claim rollover relief if it acquires a new qualifying asset. The rollover relief rules described in this chapter apply in modified form.

Intangible fixed assets

Due to the intangible assets regime (see **15.13** COMPANIES — CORPORATE FINANCE AND INTANGIBLES), the rollover relief provisions are amended for corporation tax purposes only.

- **Disposals.** A gain on the disposal of an asset that is both an intangible fixed asset and within one of the classes of qualifying assets at **53.4** below does not qualify for rollover relief. Disposals of intangible fixed assets (whether or not within one of the classes of qualifying assets) excluded from the intangible assets regime by virtue of its commencement rules do, however, qualify for relief under the intangible fixed assets rollover relief provisions (see now *CTA 2009, ss 898, 899*), which are modified for this purpose. Where relief is claimed in such a case, then in calculating the chargeable gain on the disposal of the asset, the consideration is treated as reduced by the amount available for relief. Note that intangible asset rollover relief is an entirely separate relief from the capital gains relief; for details of the relief see Tolley's Corporation Tax under Intangible Assets.
- **Acquisitions.** Assets within Classes 4 to 7 and 9 at **53.4** below are not qualifying assets for corporation tax purposes if they are 'chargeable intangible assets'. An asset is a '*chargeable intangible asset*' if a gain on its realisation would give rise to a credit falling to be brought into account under the intangible assets regime.

[*TCGA 1992, ss 156ZA, 156ZB; CTA 2009, s 870A*].

Assets qualifying for rollover relief

[53.4] Subject to the overriding requirement of use for the purposes of a trade (see 53.2 above), qualifying assets are divided into the classes listed below (the Treasury having power to specify additional classes or amend the existing classes). Further comment on certain classes is made after the list under relevant headings. Both the old and the new assets must fall within these classes though not necessarily within the same class.

For capital gains tax purposes, the classes are as follows.

(1) Assets within (a) and (b) below.
  - (a) Land, buildings (including parts thereof) and any permanent or semi-permanent structures in the nature of buildings, all such assets being occupied (as well as used) only for the purposes of the trade.
  - (b) Fixed plant or machinery (see *Williams v Evans* 2 Ch D, 1982, 59 TC 509) which does not form part of a building or of a permanent or semi-permanent structure in the nature of a building.

(2) Ships, aircraft and hovercraft.
(3) Satellites, space stations and spacecraft (including launch vehicles).
(4) Goodwill.
(5) Assets within (a) and (b) below.
  (a) 'Milk quotas' (now abolished); i.e. rights to sell dairy produce without liability to pay milk levy, or to deliver dairy produce without liability to pay a milk levy contribution.
  (b) 'Potato quotas' (now abolished); i.e. rights to produce potatoes without liability to pay more than the ordinary contribution to the Potato Marketing Board's fund.
(6) 'Ewe and suckler cow premium quotas' (now abolished), i.e. rights in respect of any ewes or suckler cows to receive payments by way of any subsidy entitlement to which is determined by reference to limits contained in a European Community instrument.
(7) Fish quota, i.e. an allocation of quota to catch fish stocks, which derives from the Total Allowable Catches set in pursuance of specified European Community instruments (see also below).
(8) Assets within (a) and (b) below.
  (a) Syndicate rights of an individual (i.e. non-corporate) underwriting member of Lloyd's.
  (b) Syndicate rights of an individual (i.e. non-corporate) underwriting member of Lloyd's held through a Members' Agent Pooling Arrangement (MAPA) and treated by *FA 1999, s 82* as a single asset.
(9) Assets within (a) and (b) below.
  (a) Payment entitlements under the single payment scheme (now abolished), i.e. the scheme of income support for farmers under Title III of EC Council Regulation 73/2009 (previously EC Council Regulation 1782/2003).
  (b) Payment entitlements under the basic payment scheme, i.e. the scheme of income support for farmers under European Parliament and Council Regulation 1307/2013.

For corporation tax purposes, Classes 4 to 7 and 9 do not apply as regards the acquisition of new assets that are 'chargeable intangible assets' for the purposes of the intangible fixed assets regime (see **53.3** above).

[*TCGA 1992, ss 155, 156ZB*].

Land and buildings

Land and buildings are treated as separate assets for rollover relief purposes (HMRC Capital Gains Manual CG60281).

Where the trade is one of dealing in or developing land or of providing services for the occupier of land in which the trader has an interest, the trader's disposal of the land does not qualify for relief. However, this does not apply where a profit on the sale of any land held for the purposes of a trade of dealing in or developing land would not form part of the trading profits. [*TCGA 1992, s 156(1)–(3)*]. See also **24** FURNISHED HOLIDAY ACCOMMODATION.

A lessor of tied premises, within *CTA 2009, s 42* or *ITTOIA 2005, s 19*, is treated as occupying (as well as using) those premises for the purposes of the trade (to the extent that the conditions of *CTA 2009, s 42(1)* or *ITTOIA 2005, s 19(1)* are met in relation to the premises). [*TCGA 1992, s 156(4)*].

Where a building is rebuilt after having been destroyed by fire, gains on other assets may be rolled over into the cost of rebuilding (subject to any claim made under *TCGA 1992, s 23* in respect of insurance proceeds, see **10.3** and **10.4** CAPITAL SUMS DERIVED FROM ASSETS).

In *Anderton v Lamb* Ch D 1980, 55 TC 1, it was held that houses occupied by farm employees were not occupied for the purposes of the business, and, therefore, were not qualifying assets. The taxpayer appealed to the CA where the appeal was stayed on agreed terms: see 1982 STI 179.

Options over land

Provided relief would be due on the disposal of the underlying land which is the subject of the grant of an option, HMRC accepts that any gain arising on the grant of the option can be the subject of a rollover relief claim (HMRC Capital Gains Manual CG60281). For options generally, see **7.7** ASSETS.

Goodwill

See HMRC Capital Gains Manual CG68000–68330 for consideration of what constitutes goodwill. In *Balloon Promotions Ltd v Wilson* (Sp C 524) [2006] SSCD 167 the Special Commissioner questioned the applicability of HMRC's then approach to goodwill. HMRC have subsequently rewritten their internal guidance accordingly.

See also *Kirby v Thorn EMI plc* CA 1987, 60 TC 519, and *Mertrux Ltd v HMRC* CA, [2013] STC 2199.

In *The Leeds Cricket Football & Athletic Co Ltd v HMRC* [2019] UKFTT 568 (TC), the question was whether there was a sale of a business with attached goodwill or was a disposal of land with attached income streams. The company owned the freehold to a cricket ground, which it leased to Yorkshire County Cricket Club ('YCCC'). It retained the right to carry on hospitality, catering and advertising at the property. For instance, it sold corporate hospitality packages and advertising on the boards at the ground. The company then sold the ground to YCCC and, after the sale, provided assistance to YCCC to ensure a smooth handover, which included the transfer of client details and the benefit of agreements of third parties.

The First-tier Tribunal rejected HMRC's submission that the company had only received income streams ancillary to the land. It noted that the income streams continued even when cricket was not played at the ground and it found that the company was not a passive recipient of income but was actively carrying on a business. For instance, it employed 19 full-time catering staff. The Tribunal also found that the business had goodwill attached to it; it had an established client base and reputation developed over the years 'through a professional sales, marketing and delivery operation which would distinguish it from a similar, but newly established operation'.

Fish quota

These are amounts of various types of fish that were allocated by the EU to the UK and sub-allocated to UK fishermen according to rules prescribed by the Fisheries Departments. They are one of a number of items that may be involved in a disposal of a fishing vessel (and may be disposed of separately in certain circumstances). The vessel itself is a qualifying asset for rollover relief. A fishing vessel licence and a 'track record' (being the amount of particular stocks of fish caught in previous years) are separate chargeable assets; each is treated as constituting goodwill and thus eligible for rollover relief in its own right. Fish quota is also a separate chargeable asset but is not regarded as goodwill. (Revenue Press Release 2 March 1999).

Other undertakings eligible for rollover relief

[53.5] Rollover relief applies with necessary modifications to the following activities as it applies to a trade.

(a) The discharge of the functions of a public authority.
(b) The occupation of woodlands where the woodlands are managed by the occupier on a commercial basis and with a view to the realisation of profits.
(c) A profession, vocation, office or employment.
(d) Such of the activities of a body of persons whose activities are carried on otherwise than for profit and are wholly or mainly directed to the protection or promotion of the interests of its members in the carrying on of their trade or profession as are so directed.
(e) The activities of an unincorporated association or other body chargeable to corporation tax, being a body not established for profit whose activities are wholly or mainly carried on otherwise than for profit, but in the case of assets within (1)(a) in **53.4** above only if they are both occupied and used by the body, and in the case of other assets only if they are used by the body.
(f) The activities of a company owned by an association or body within (e) above (the '*parent body*'), but in the case of assets within 1.(a) in **53.4** above only if they are both occupied and used by the parent body, and in the case of other assets only if they are used by the parent body. For this purpose, a parent body owns a company if it holds at least 90% of the ordinary share capital, is beneficially entitled at least 90% of the profits available for distribution to equity holders and would be so entitled on a winding up to at least 90% of the assets available for distribution to equity holders.

'Profession', 'vocation', 'office' and 'employment' have the same meanings as in the Income Tax Acts.

[*TCGA 1992, s 158*].

If land or a building is owned by an employee or office-holder but is made available to the employer for general use in his trade, the employee etc. may nonetheless satisfy the occupation test of *TCGA 1992, s 155* (see **53.4** above at (1)) provided the employer does not make any payment (or give other consideration) for his use of the property nor otherwise occupy it under a lease or tenancy. The qualifying use of assets by an employee etc. for the purposes of *TCGA 1992, s 152* (see **53.1** above) will include any use or operation of those assets by him, in the course of performing the duties of his employment or office, as directed by the employer (HMRC Statement of Practice 5/86). The practice may be compared with the relief available under *TCGA 1992, s 157* (see **53.3** above) where the trade is carried on by the individual's personal company, although in relation to SP 5/86 consideration passing or the existence of a lease or tenancy would deny relief.

Effect of rollover relief

[53.6] Where the conditions at **53.2**(a)–(c) above are met and the taxpayer makes a claim (see **53.11** below), he is treated for capital gains purposes:

(a) as if the consideration for the disposal of, or of the interest in, the old assets were (if otherwise of a greater amount or value) of such an amount as would secure that on the disposal neither a gain nor a loss accrues to him, and

(b) as if the amount or value of the consideration for the acquisition of, or of the interest in, the new assets were reduced by the excess of the amount or value of the actual consideration for the disposal of, or of the interest in, the old assets over the amount of the consideration which he is treated as receiving under (a) above.

This treatment does not affect the treatment for capital gains purposes of the other party to the transaction involving the old assets, or of the other party to the transaction involving the new assets.

Where (a) above applies to exclude a gain which, in consequence of *TCGA 1992, Sch 2* (ASSETS HELD ON 6 APRIL **1965** (8)), is not all chargeable gain, the amount of the reduction to be made under (b) above is the amount of the chargeable gain, and not the whole amount of the gain.

[*TCGA 1992, s 152(1)(2)(9)*].

For partial relief where the proceeds from the old assets are not fully reinvested or where the old assets were only partly used for business purposes or not used for business purposes for the whole of the period of ownership, see **53.8** below. For relief where the new assets are depreciating assets, see **53.9** below.

Example

L Ltd carries on a vehicle repair business. In December 2003 it sells a workshop for £90,000 net of costs. The workshop had cost £45,000 inclusive in April 1995. A new workshop is purchased for £144,000 (including incidental costs of acquisition) in January 2005 and is sold for £168,000 in January 2025.

Indexation factors:	April 1995 to December 2003	0.232
	January 2005 to December 2017	0.472

	£
Allowable cost of original workshop	45,000
Indexation allowance £45,000 × 0.232	10,440
	55,440
Actual disposal consideration	90,000
Chargeable gain rolled over	£34,560
Cost of new workshop	144,000
Deduct amount rolled over	34,560
Deemed allowable cost	£109,440
Disposal consideration, replacement workshop	168,000
Allowable cost	109,440
Unindexed gain	58,560
Indexation allowance £109,440 × 0.472	51,656
Chargeable gain	£6,904

Note to the example

For corporation tax purposes, indexation allowance is frozen at its December 2017 level. No indexation allowance is available in respect of expenditure incurred after 31 December 2017, and for expenditure incurred on or before that date and falling to be deducted on a disposal after that date, indexation allowance is computed up to and including December 2017 only. See **32.2** INDEXATION.

Interaction of rollover relief with other provisions

[53.7] Any provision which fixes the amount of consideration deemed to be given for the acquisition or disposal of assets is applied before operating the relief. [*TCGA 1992, s 152(10)*]. However, the relief is not affected by the fact that the new asset may have attracted a grant such as to reduce the expenditure allowable on a subsequent disposal — see **16.14**(c) COMPUTATATION OF GAINS AND LOSSES (*Wardhaugh v Penrith Rugby Union Football Club* Ch D 2002, 74 TC 499). The Revenue indicated that in its view gifts of assets are within *TCGA 1992, s 152(10)*. (Institute of Taxation TIR/11/91, 1991 STI 1097).

HMRC accept that rollover relief can be claimed where the disposal of the old assets is a deemed disposal, for example, under either *TCGA 1992, s 22* (see **10.2** CAPITAL SUMS DERIVED FROM ASSETS) or *TCGA 1992, s 161(1)* (asset appropriated from capital to trading stock — see **16.9** COMPUTATION OF GAINS AND LOSSES). They also accept that relief can be claimed where the acquisition of the new assets is a deemed acquisition. (HMRC Capital Gains Manual CG60270).

Although relief under *TCGA 1992, s 162* (transfer of a business to a company — see **31.2** INCORPORATION AND DISINCORPORATION RELIEFS) is mandatory (unless disapplied by election — see **31.3**), a valid claim for rollover relief takes precedence (HMRC Capital Gains Manual CG60201).

Partial rollover relief

[53.8] Partial rollover relief is available in the following circumstances.

Disposal consideration not reinvested in full

Partial rollover relief is available where not all of the amount or value of the consideration received for the disposal of the old assets is applied in acquiring the new assets. Provided that the part of the disposal consideration not applied in acquiring the new assets is less than the amount of the gain (whether all chargeable gain or not) otherwise accruing on the disposal of the old assets, the claimant is treated for capital gains purposes:

(a) as if the gain accruing on the disposal of the old assets were reduced to the amount of the said part, and
(b) as if the amount or value of the consideration for the acquisition of the new assets were reduced by the amount by which the gain is reduced in (a) above.

If not all the gain is a chargeable gain, (a) above applies but with a proportionate reduction in the amount of the chargeable gain, and in (b) above the reduction in consideration is the amount by which the chargeable gain is proportionately reduced. Neither (a) nor (b) above affects the capital gains treatment of the other parties to the transactions involving the old and new assets. [*TCGA 1992, s 153*].

Only part of building or structure used for trade purposes. If, over the period of ownership (excluding any period before 31 March 1982) or any substantial part of the period of ownership, part of a building or structure is, and part is not, used for the purposes of a trade, rollover relief applies as if the part so used, with any land occupied for purposes ancillary to the occupation and use of that part of the building or structure, were a separate asset, and subject to any necessary apportionments of consideration for an acquisition or disposal of the building or structure and other land. [*TCGA 1992, s 152(6)(9)*].

Where the taxpayer acquires an undivided share in the new asset which is only partly used for trade purposes, relief is limited to the proportion so used of the individual's undivided share of the asset (*Tod v Mudd* Ch D 1986, 60 TC 237).

Old assets not used for trade purposes throughout period of ownership

If the old assets were not used for the purposes of the trade throughout the period of ownership (excluding any period before 31 March 1982) rollover relief applies as if a part of the asset representing its use for the purposes of the trade having regard to the time and extent to which it was, and was not, used for those purposes, were a separate asset which had been wholly used for the purposes of the trade, and this treatment applies in relation to that part subject to any necessary apportionment of consideration for an acquisition or disposal of the asset. [*TCGA 1992, s 152(7)(9)*].

Apportionment

Without prejudice to *TCGA 1992, s 52(4)* (just and reasonable apportionments of consideration and expenditure; see **16.5** COMPUTATION OF GAINS AND LOSSES), where consideration is given for the acquisition or disposal of assets some or part of which are assets in relation to which a rollover relief claim applies, and some or part of which are not, the consideration is apportioned in such manner as is just and reasonable. [*TCGA 1992, s 152(11)*].

Examples

(a) In 1997, X purchased a factory for £40,000. It was used and occupied entirely for carrying on his trade until sold for £100,000 in October 2024. In the same month, X bought another factory for £120,000 which was immediately used and occupied for carrying on a new trade carried on by him. He claimed rollover relief, computed as follows.

	£
Proceeds of sale of factory 1	100,000
Allowable expenditure on factory 1	40,000
Chargeable gain eligible to be rolled over	£60,000
Cost of factory 2	120,000
Rolled-over gain	60,000
Base cost for factory 2 on subsequent disposal	£60,000

(b) Facts as in (a) above, except factory 2 is bought for £90,000. The part of the £100,000 disposal consideration of factory 1 which is not applied in acquiring factory 2 is £10,000. This is less than the gain otherwise arising on the disposal of factory 1 (£60,000). The gain deemed to arise on the disposal of factory 1 is therefore £10,000. The gain so arising has therefore been reduced by £50,000, with the result that this amount is deducted from the £90,000 consideration given for factory 2, and so producing a base cost of £40,000 on a subsequent disposal.

(c) In September 2024, Y purchased a new factory for £100,000, having sold his old one in the same month for £52,000. The original factory had been bought in September 2013 for £20,000 but had only been used for his trade since September 2016. He claimed rollover relief. It is accepted that one-quarter of the new factory is not used for trade purposes.

	£
Proceeds of sale of old factory	52,000
Cost of old factory	20,000
Chargeable gain	£32,000

$$\frac{\text{Period of trading use of old asset}}{\text{Period of ownership}} = \frac{8\text{years}}{10\text{years}}$$

Gain on old asset eligible for relief	
£32,000 × $^{8}/_{10}$	£25,600
Cost of qualifying part of new factory	
($^{3}/_{4}$ × £100,000)	75,000
Rolled-over gain	25,600
Base cost of qualifying part of new factory	£49,400

£

The unrelieved gain of £6,400 (£32,000 – £25,600) is brought into charge on the disposal of the old factory. The base cost of the non-qualifying part of the new factory, treated as separate, is £25,000.

Rollover relief and depreciating assets

[53.9] Where rollover relief is claimed and the new asset is a 'depreciating asset', the gain on the disposal of the old asset is not deducted from the acquisition consideration of the new asset, but held over until ten years after the time of acquisition of the new asset, or until the new asset is disposed of, or until the new asset ceases to be used for the trade, whichever is the sooner. When the relevant event occurs, the held-over gain becomes chargeable as a capital gain. For corporation tax purposes and, for disposals before 6 April 2008, for capital gains tax purposes, however, the held-over gain is not brought into charge under this provision in consequence of an event after 5 April 1988 if its application would be directly attributable to the disposal of an asset before 1 April 1982. [*TCGA 1992, s 154(1)(2)(7), Sch 4 paras A1, 4(5)*].

If, however, not later than the time when the held-over gain would be brought into charge, a further asset is acquired which is not a depreciating asset, the trader may claim rollover relief as if it had been acquired within the time limits of *TCGA 1992, s 152(3)* for the application of the proceeds of the disposal of the old asset, the depreciating asset being effectively disregarded. The trader may claim relief if only part of the proceeds can be treated in this way, the balance remaining held over until crystallisation by virtue of one of the events specified. [*TCGA 1992, s 154(4)–(6)*].

See 53.3 above for a special rule where the new asset is held by a limited liability partnership at the time of its going into liquidation.

Meaning of 'depreciating asset'

For the above purposes, an asset is a '*depreciating asset*' if, at the time of acquisition, it is a WASTING ASSET (65) or will become so within ten years beginning at that time.

A building constructed on leasehold land where the lease has less than 60 years to run at the time of construction is considered by HMRC to be a depreciating asset. This is despite the treatment of land and buildings as separate assets for rollover relief purposes (and contrary to the general rule for land as in 35.2 LAND).

If, as contemplated by *TCGA 1992, s 155*, an item of fixed plant or machinery has effectively become a part of a building or structure, it will be so treated for rollover relief purposes, with the result that such assets acquired for installation in a building etc. then held freehold or on a lease with more than 60 years to run will not be treated as depreciating assets. Subject to this, because an item of plant and machinery is always to be treated as being a wasting asset (see 65.2 WASTING ASSETS), it will also be treated as a depreciating asset. Deciding whether an item of fixed plant or machinery has become part of a building etc. will normally be done by reference to the size and nature of the item in question, how it is attached to the building and whether damage to the fabric of the building would be caused if the item was removed (Revenue Tax Bulletin May 1993 p 73).

Cross-border mergers

A transfer of the new asset or of shares in a company which holds the new asset as part of the process of a cross-border merger to which *TCGA 1992, s 140E* (European cross-border mergers: assets left within UK charge to tax — see **43.14** OVERSEAS MATTERS) applies does not bring the held-over gain into charge under the above provisions. In such circumstances, if the transferee holds the new asset it is treated as if it had claimed the rollover relief. If the transferee holds shares in the company which holds the new asset, *TCGA 1992, s 175* (see **53.10** below) applies as if the transferee's group were the same group as any group of which the company claiming the rollover relief was a member before the merger. [*TCGA 1992, s 154(2A)(2C)*].

Where, as part of the process of a cross-border merger to which *TCGA 1992, s 140E* applies, the transferee becomes a member of a group of which a company which has claimed rollover relief in respect of a wasting asset is a member, *TCGA 1992, s 175* (see **53.10** below) applies for the purposes of determining when the held-over gain is brought into charge as if the group of which the transferee is a member were the same group as the group of which the claimant was a member before the merger. [*TCGA 1992, s 154(2B)(2C)*].

The above cross-border merger provisions apply also to the transfer of an asset in circumstances where *TCGA 1992, s 140A* (transfer or division of UK business between companies in different EC member states — see **43.12** OVERSEAS MATTERS) applies (with references to a merger being treated as references to the transfer). [*TCGA 1992, s 154(2D)*].

Example

In March 2020, a father and son partnership carrying on a car-dealing trade sold a freehold showroom for £400,000, realising a chargeable gain of £190,000. On 30 June 2020, the firm purchased, for £450,000, the remaining term of a lease due to expire on 30 June 2050 and used the premises as a new showroom. The whole of the gain on the old asset was held over under *TCGA 1992, s 154* on the acquisition of the new asset. In consequence of the father's decision to retire from the business and the resulting need to downsize the operation, the firm assigns the lease for £490,000 on 1 July 2024.

The chargeable gains to be apportioned between the two partners for 2024/25 are as follows:

	£	£
Proceeds of assignment		490,000
Cost (see note (a))	450,000	
Deduct Wasted $\frac{87.330 - 82.496}{87.330} \times £450{,}000$	24,909	425,091

	£	£
Chargeable gain 2024/25		£64,909
Held-over gain becoming chargeable under *TCGA 1992, s 154(2)(a)*		£190,000

Note to the example

(a) The gain is deferred as opposed to being rolled over and does not reduce the cost of the new asset.

Rollover relief and groups of companies

[53.10] For rollover relief purposes, all the trades carried on by members of a group of companies (within **26.2** GROUPS OF COMPANIES) are treated as a single trade. Any trade carried on by a non-UK resident company otherwise than in the UK through a permanent establishment is, however, excluded. Acquisitions as a group member by a 'dual resident investing company' within *ICTA 1988, s 404* are excluded from this treatment. [*TCGA 1992, s 175(1)(1A)(2)*].

Where there is a disposal by a member of a group of companies and an acquisition by another member of the same group and both companies make a claim, then for rollover relief purposes, the companies are treated as if they were the same person. The following conditions must be met:

- either the company making the disposal is UK-resident at the time of disposal or the assets in question are 'chargeable assets' in relation to that company immediately before that time; and
- either the acquiring company is UK-resident at the time of acquisition or the assets are 'chargeable assets' in relation to that company immediately after that time.

For these purposes, an asset is a 'chargeable asset' in relation to a company at a particular time if, on a disposal by that company at that time, any gain would be a chargeable gain and would be within the charge to corporation tax by virtue of *TCGA 1992, s 2B(3)*; non-UK resident company trading in the UK through a permanent establishment — see **43.3** OVERSEAS MATTERS.

Rollover relief is also available where a non-trading member of a group makes a disposal or acquisition of assets used only for trading purposes by other members of the same group.

However, rollover relief will not apply where there is an acquisition of new assets by a member of a group from another member of that group resulting from a disposal within the no gain/no loss provisions (see **8.6** ASSETS HELD ON **31** MARCH **1982**) or one where, under *TCGA 1992, ss 195B, 195C* or *195E* (oil licence swaps) the disposal gives rise to neither a gain nor a loss.

[*TCGA 1992, s 175(2A)–(2C)*].

Where the new asset is a depreciating asset, *TCGA 1992, s 154(2)* (see **53.9** above) applies where the company making the claim is a member of a group of companies as if all members of the group for the time being carrying on trades within these provisions (see above) were the same person (and, in accordance with *TCGA 1992, s 175(1)* above, as if all those trades were the same trade) and so that the gain accrues to the member of the group holding the asset concerned on the occurrence of the event mentioned in *TCGA 1992, s 154(2)* (i.e. the earlier of the disposal of the depreciating asset, cessation of its trading use or the expiry of ten years from its acquisition). [*TCGA 1992, s 175(3)*].

The disposing company must be a member of a group at the time of disposal, and the acquiring company must be a member of the same group at the time of acquisition, but HMRC does not insist that either company be a member of that group at the time of the transaction carried out by the other (HMRC Statement of Practice SP D19). Where this applies in a case where one member of a group makes the disposal and a second makes the acquisition, it may be that the disposal takes place after the first company has ceased to trade or the acquisition takes place before the second company commences trading. Relief will then be restricted for the period during which the assets disposed of were not used for business purposes, and will be conditional on the replacement assets not being used or leased for any purpose prior to the second company's commencing trading, and being taken into use for the purposes of the trade on its commencement (HMRC Statement of Practice SP 8/81, and see also **53.8** above).

If a qualifying unincorporated association uses property owned by a company in which at least 90% of the shares are held by or on behalf of the association or its members, rollover relief can be claimed subject to the usual conditions. (HMRC Extra-Statutory Concession D15). (See **4.21** ANTI-AVOIDANCE for the charge arising where concessions involving deferral of gains are abused.)

See **35.10**(g) LAND above with regard to rollover relief in cases of compulsory purchase of land.

Claims for rollover relief

[53.11] A claim for rollover relief relates to both a disposal and an acquisition of assets and so cannot be made until both have occurred (but see below re provisional claims under self-assessment).

Form of claim

A claim for relief must be made in writing and must specify:

- the old assets which have been disposed of;
- the amount received for each of those assets;
- the date of disposal of each of those assets;
- the new assets which have been acquired;
- the date of acquisition of each of those assets or the dates on which unconditional contracts for the acquisition of each of those assets were entered into;
- the cost of each of those assets; and
- the amount of the proceeds from each of the old assets which has been used to acquire each new asset.

(HMRC Helpsheet HS 290).

Where the disposal is made by one group company and the acquisition made by another (see **53.10** above), a rollover relief claim must be made by both companies. [*TCGA 1992, s 175(2A)*].

Time limits for claims

As no time limit is specified, the general time limits in *TMA 1970, s 43* and *FA 1998, Sch 18 para 55* apply (see **13.5** CLAIMS). For rollover relief purposes, the period of time allowed for the making of a claim (four years) begins with the later of:

- the end of the tax year or company accounting period in which the disposal takes place, and
- the end of the tax year or company accounting period in which the new assets are acquired.

A claim to relief is not prevented by the finality of any assessment.

(HMRC Capital Gains Manual CG60310).

Provisional claims

It would be anomalous to require a taxpayer, who intends to roll over gains, to pay the tax on those gains under self-assessment and thus reduce the funds available to invest in the new assets. Provisional rollover relief claims are therefore possible as outlined below.

The claimant may make a declaration in his tax return for a tax year or company accounting period in which he has made a disposal of qualifying assets (see **53.4** above) that the whole or a specified part of the consideration will be invested, within the time limits (see **53.2** above), in qualifying assets which on acquisition will be taken into use exclusively for the purposes of the trade. The form in HMRC Helpsheet HS 290 may be used by an individual for this purpose. As long as the declaration continues to have effect, the same consequences ensue as if both an acquisition and a valid rollover relief claim had been made. The declaration ceases to have effect on the day, and to the extent that it is withdrawn or is superseded by a valid claim, if either occurs before the 'relevant day'. It otherwise ceases to have effect on the relevant day itself. On its ceasing to have effect, all necessary adjustments will be made to the claimant's tax position, even if they would otherwise be out of time.

The '*relevant day*' means:

- in relation to capital gains tax, the third anniversary of 31 January following the tax year of disposal, e.g. 31 January 2025 for disposals in 2020/21; and
- in relation to corporation tax, the fourth anniversary of the last day of the accounting period of disposal.

[*TCGA 1992, s 153A*].

The disapplication of the normal time limits for making an assessment under this provision did not allow HMRC to make a discovery assessment (see **6.10** ASSESSMENTS) in circumstances where the discovery was 'stale' before the assessment was made in *Oriel Developments Ltd v HMRC* FTT, [2019] SFTD 1288.

To the extent that a provisional claim is withdrawn or lapses, interest on unpaid tax is chargeable as if no such claim had been made. There is nothing to prevent a valid claim from subsequently being made if new assets are acquired within the normal time limit or further time allowed by HMRC (see 53.2 above).

Key points on rollover relief

[53.12] Points to consider are as follows.

- Rollover relief must be claimed.
- The replacement assets must normally be acquired within the period of one year before or three years after the disposal of the old assets, but HMRC can extend the limit if the taxpayer can show that an intention to do so was prevented by circumstances beyond their control, and that they acted as soon as they could thereafter. Where a taxpayer intends to reinvest (i.e. in years two or three), they can make a provisional claim to avoid the payment of the tax on the gain.
- It is the consideration (deemed or actual) that must be reinvested and not as in the case of EIS deferral relief the gain.
- Partial relief may be available where sale proceeds are not fully reinvested in replacement assets, or where the old assets were either only partly used for business purposes or were not so used for the whole of the period of ownership. It may be possible to use this to ensure the annual exemption is not wasted.
- Relief will generally be available where a UK-resident company in a group disposes of an asset and another UK-resident group company acquires a replacement asset.
- Spouses and civil partners are separate persons for rollover relief. *Tod v Mudd (1986)* demonstrates the apportionment for joint ownership of a new asset (plus its only partial business use).
- Relief can be claimed on a deemed disposal of old assets or a deemed acquisition of replacement assets.
- Rollover relief takes precedence over business asset disposal relief — if an entire gain is rolled over, there is no relevant gain for business asset disposal relief purposes, but relief can be claimed on part of a gain that is not rolled over. If it appeared that business asset disposal relief would not be available on disposal of the replacement asset, it may be worth considering a claim to that relief instead of rollover relief and paying tax at 10% upfront.
- Rolled-over gains normally arise on the disposal of the replacement asset. However, provided the conditions are met, this gain can also be rolled over. Rolled-over gains normally escape capital gains tax on the death of the taxpayer. (Separate rules apply where the new assets are depreciating assets).

54

Seed Enterprise Investment Scheme

Introduction to the Seed Enterprise Investment Scheme

[54.1] The Seed Enterprise Investment Scheme (SEIS) is a tax-advantaged venture capital scheme similar to the ENTERPRISE INVESTMENT SCHEME (22) but focused on smaller, early stage companies. [*ITA 2007, s 257A*]. The main features of the SEIS are as follows.

- Income tax relief is available for investment in small companies (i.e. those with 25 or fewer employees and assets of up to £350,000 (£200,000 for shares issued before 6 April 2023)) that are carrying on, or preparing to carry on, a new qualifying business.
- The relief is available on share subscriptions of up to £200,000 per individual (£100,000 before 6 April 2023). Relief can be carried back to the preceding year.
- The maximum relief is 50% of the amount subscribed.
- The shares must be retained for at least three years.
- The scheme incorporates many of the requirements of the Enterprise Investment Scheme (EIS), for example the requirement that the investor have no more than a 30% stake in the investee company.
- Any one company may raise investment of up to £250,000 under the SEIS in any three-year period (£150,000 before 6 April 2023).
- Chargeable gains on disposals of SEIS shares are exempt from CGT provided the shares are held for the requisite three-year period.
- Chargeable gains realised from disposals of any assets are exempt from CGT if invested via the SEIS in the same year.

This chapter concentrates on the capital gains tax reliefs but the conditions for income tax relief are included in detail at **54.2** onwards. For completeness, a brief summary of the income tax relief is also included at **54.33** — for full details see Tolley's Income Tax under Seed Enterprise Investment Scheme. See also HMRC Venture Capital Schemes Manual VCM30000 onwards for both income tax and CGT reliefs.

Advance assurance

A company may apply to HMRC for assurance, in advance of a share issue, that it will meet the qualifying conditions of the SEIS. Application can be made using the online form at www.gov.uk/guidance/venture-capital-schemes-apply-for-advance-assurance. HMRC will not provide advance assurances for investments that, taking into account all the facts that HMRC have available, will fail, or appear likely to fail, the risk-to-capital condition at **54.4** below (HMRC Venture Capital Schemes Manual VCM8550).

Conditions for income tax relief

[54.2] An individual investor is eligible for SEIS income tax relief in respect of an amount subscribed by him on his own behalf for an issue of shares in a company if:

- the risk-to-capital condition is met (see **54.4** below);
- the shares are issued to the investor;
- the six general requirements at **54.5** below are met in respect of the shares;
- the investor is a 'qualifying investor' (see **54.12** below) in relation to the shares; and
- the company issuing the shares is a 'qualifying company' (see **54.18** below) in relation to the shares.

[*ITA 2007, s 257AA*].

Bare trustees and nominees

[54.3] SEIS relief is available where shares which satisfy the requirement at 54.6(a) below are held on a bare trust for two or more beneficiaries as if each beneficiary had subscribed as an individual for all of those shares, and as if the amount subscribed by each was the total subscribed divided by the number of beneficiaries.

Shares subscribed for, issued to, held by or disposed of for an individual by a nominee are treated for the purposes of SEIS relief as subscribed for, issued to, held by or disposed of by the individual.

[*ITA 2007, s 257HE*].

The risk-to-capital condition

[54.4] The risk-to-capital condition mentioned at **54.2** above is an overarching condition which is met if, having regard to all existing circumstances at the time of issue of the SEIS shares, it would be reasonable to conclude that:

- the issuing company has objectives to grow and develop its trade in the long term; and
- there is a significant risk of loss of capital of an amount greater than the net investment return, i.e. the net return to investors (whether by way of income or capital growth) taking into account the value of SEIS relief. The risk and the return is to be determined with reference to the investors in general, and a loss of capital means a loss of at least part of the amounts subscribed for the shares by the investors.

[*ITA 2007, s 257AAA*].

The intention is to prevent tax-relieved investment in companies whose activities are geared towards preservation of investors' capital rather than the company's long-term growth and development. *ITA 2007, s 257AAA(3)* provides an illustrative, non-exhaustive list of the types of circumstance that may be taken into account in reaching any conclusion. For HMRC guidance on the condition, with examples, see HMRC Venture Capital Schemes Manual VCM8500–8560.

The risk-to-capital condition (under the EIS or SEIS scheme) was held to be satisfied in *Inferno Films Ltd v HMRC* FTT, [2022] UKFTT 141 (TC) and *Cry Me A River Ltd v HMRC* FTT, [2022] UKFTT 182 (TC), in which funds were raised to make, develop and sell films. The condition was also satisfied in *Hoopla Animation Ltd (formerly known as Daisy Boo and Monkey Too Ltd) v HMRC* FTT, [2023] UKFTT 24 (TC) but the companies' appeals against HMRC's decision not to issue compliance certificates were dismissed because there were 'disqualifying arrangements' (see **22.5** below). The condition was also held to be satisfied by the FTT in *Coconut Animated Island Ltd v HMRC* UT, [2024] STC 880, but the issue was not considered by the UT (which dismissed the company's appeal because there were disqualifying arrangements).

The condition was held not to be met in *Valyrian Bloodstock Ltd v HMRC* FTT, [2022] UKFTT 306 (TC). The company was established to carry on a business of buying racehorses at six to twelve months old and selling them at three years or older (known as 'pinhooking'). The only contemporaneous evidence (the company's website) indicated that there was no intention to grow and develop the business, but instead, the company was a one-off investment for a three-year term which would be wound up after the last horse was sold. The condition was also held not to be met in *Legend of Golden Temple Ltd v HMRC* FTT, [2023] UKFTT 988 (TC).

General requirements of Seed Enterprise Investment Scheme

[54.5] The six general requirements mentioned in **54.2** above are described at **54.6–54.11** below.

The shares requirement

[54.6] The shares must:

(a) be ordinary shares which do not, at any time during 'period B' below, carry (subject to below) any present or future preferential right to dividends or to assets on a winding-up or any present or future right to be redeemed; and

(b) unless they are bonus shares, be subscribed for wholly in cash and be fully paid up at the time of issue.

Shares are, however, permitted to carry a preferential right to dividends provided the amount and timing of the dividends do not depend on a decision of the company, the shareholder or any other person and provided the dividends are not cumulative.

Period B

'*Period B*' is the three-year period beginning with the issue of the shares.

[*ITA 2007, ss 257AC, 257CA*].

The 'purpose of the issue' requirement

[54.7] The shares (other than any bonus shares) must be issued to raise money for the purposes of a 'qualifying business activity' (see **54.31** below) carried on, or to be carried on, by the issuing company or a 'qualifying 90% subsidiary' (see **54.30** below) of that company. [*ITA 2007, ss 257CB, 257HJ(1)*].

The 'spending of the money raised' requirement

[54.8] Before the end of period B (as in **54.6** above) all of the money raised by the issue of the shares (other than any of them which are bonus shares) must be spent for the purposes of the qualifying business activity (see **54.31** below) for which the money was raised. However, this requirement does not fail to be met merely because an amount of money which is not significant is spent for another purpose or remains unspent at the end of period B. The spending of money on the acquisition of shares or stock in a company does not of itself amount to spending it for the purposes of a qualifying business activity.

[*ITA 2007, ss 257CC, 257HJ(1)*].

The 'no pre-arranged exits' requirement

[54.9] The 'issuing arrangements' must not:

(a) provide for the eventual disposal by the investor of the shares in question or other shares or securities of the issuing company; or

(b) provide for the eventual cessation of a trade of the company or of a person connected with it; or

(c) provide for the eventual disposal of all, or a substantial amount (in terms of value) of, the assets of the company or of a person connected with it; or

(d) provide (by means of any insurance, indemnity, guarantee or otherwise) complete or partial protection for investors against what would otherwise be the risks attached to making the investment (disregarding any arrangements which merely protect the issuing company and/or its subsidiaries against normal business risks).

Arrangements with a view to the company becoming a wholly-owned subsidiary of a new holding company within the terms of *ITA 2007, s 257HB(1)* (see **54.43** below) are excluded from (a) above. Arrangements with a view to shares in the company being exchanged for, or converted into, shares of a different class in that company, are also excluded from (a) above. Arrangements applicable only on an unanticipated winding-up of a company for genuine commercial reasons are excluded from (b) and (c) above.

'*Issuing arrangements*' means the arrangements under which the shares are issued to the individual or any arrangements made, before the shares were issued, in relation to or in connection with the issue. If, before the shares were issued, information on pre-arranged exits, i.e. information indicating the possibility of making during period B (as in **54.6** above) arrangements of the kind described in any of (a)–(d) above, was made available to prospective subscribers, the term also includes any arrangements made during period B. The term 'arrangements' is broadly defined.

[*ITA 2007, ss 257CD, 257HJ(1)*].

The 'no tax avoidance' requirement

[54.10] The shares must be issued for genuine commercial reasons and not as part of a scheme or arrangement a main purpose of which is the avoidance of tax. [*ITA 2007, s 257CE*].

The 'no disqualifying arrangements' requirement

[54.11] The shares must not be issued, nor any money raised by the issue spent, in consequence or anticipation of, or otherwise in connection with, 'disqualifying arrangements'. Arrangements (as broadly defined) are '*disqualifying arrangements*' if they are entered into with the purpose of ensuring that any of the 'relevant tax reliefs' (see below) are available in respect of the issuing company's business (or, where applicable, that of its qualifying 90% subsidiary) and either or both of conditions A and B below are met. It is immaterial whether the issuing company is a party to the arrangements.

Condition A is that, as a result of the money raised by the issue of the shares being spent as required by **54.8** above, an amount representing the whole or most of the amount raised is, in the course of he arrangements, paid to (or for the benefit of) one or more parties to the arrangements or a person or persons connected with such a party (within **17** CONNECTED PERSONS). Condition B is that, in the absence of the arrangements, it would have been reasonable to expect that the whole or greater part of the component activities (as defined) of the qualifying business activity for which the issue of the shares raised money would have been carried on as part of another business by one or more parties to the arrangements or a person or persons connected with such a party.

The 'relevant tax reliefs' are those listed at **22.5** ENTERPRISE INVESTMENT SCHEME.

[*ITA 2007, ss 257CF, 257HJ(1)*].

Disqualifying arrangements were found to exist in *Coconut Animated Island Ltd v HMRC* UT, [2024] STC 880 and *Hoopla Animation Ltd (formerly known as Daisy Boo and Monkey Too Ltd) v HMRC* FTT, [2023] UKFTT 24 (TC) (an EIS case). Both companies were formed by a group to exploit the rights to a cartoon concept for children. In both cases, it was found that a substantial proportion of the money raised by the share issues was paid to or for the benefit of one of the parties to the arrangements; in this case, another group member which had carried out development and production work.

Qualifying investor

[54.12] An individual is a '*qualifying investor*' in relation to shares if the requirements at **54.13–54.17** are met.

The 'no employee investors' requirement

[54.13] Neither the investor nor an associate (see below) of the investor may at any time during period B (as in **54.6** above) be an employee of the issuing company or of any 'qualifying subsidiary' (see **54.30** below) of that company. However, for this purpose a person is not to be treated as an employee of the issuing company etc. at any time when he is a director of the company.

Meaning of 'associate'

The SEIS provisions adopt the EIS definition of 'associate' in *ITA 2007, s 253*. An '*associate*' of any person is any 'relative' (i.e. spouse, civil partner, ancestor or linear descendant) of that person, the trustee(s) of any settlement in relation to which that person or any relative (living or dead) is or was a settlor and, where that person has an interest in any shares of obligations of a company which are subject to any trust or are part of a deceased estate, the trustee(s) of the settlement or the personal representatives of the deceased. For this purpose, 'settlor' is defined as in *ITA 2007, ss 467–473*.

[*ITA 2007, ss 257BA, 257HJ(1)*].

The 'no substantial interest in the issuing company' requirement

[54.14] The investor must not have a 'substantial interest' in the issuing company at any time during 'period A' below.

An individual has a '*substantial interest*' in a company if:

(a) he directly or indirectly possesses, or is entitled to acquire, more than 30% of the ordinary or issued share capital of, or more than 30% of the voting power in, the company or any 'subsidiary'; or
(b) he directly or indirectly possesses, or is entitled to acquire, such rights as would entitle him to more than 30% of the assets of the company or a subsidiary that are available for distribution to equity holders in, for example, a winding-up; or
(c) he has control (within *ITA 2007, s 995*) of the company or any subsidiary.

For these purposes a company (Y) is a '*subsidiary*' of another (Z) if Y is a 51% subsidiary of Z at any time in period A. For the purposes of (b), *CTA 2010, Pt 5 Ch 6* has effect, with appropriate modifications, to determine the persons who are equity holders of a company and the percentage of assets to which an individual would be entitled.

An individual is treated as entitled to acquire anything which he is entitled to acquire at a future date or will at a future date be entitled to acquire. Rights or powers of associates (see **54.13** above) are attributed to the individual.

An individual does *not* have a substantial interest in a company merely because one or more shares in the company are held by him, or by his associate, at a time when the company has not issued any shares other than subscriber shares and has not begun to carry on, or make preparations for carrying on, a trade or business.

Period A

'*Period A*' is the period beginning with the incorporation of the issuing company and ending immediately before the third anniversary of the issue of the shares.

[*ITA 2007, ss 257BB, 257BF, 257HJ(1)*].

The 'no related investment arrangements' requirement

[54.15] The investor must not subscribe for the shares as part of an arrangement (as broadly defined) which provides for another person to subscribe for shares in another company in which the investor, or any other individual who is party to the arrangement, has a 'substantial interest' (see **54.14** above). [*ITA 2007, ss 257BC, 257HJ(1)*].

The 'no linked loans' requirement

[54.16] No loan may be made by any person to the investor or to an associate (see **54.13** above) at any time in period A (as in **54.14** above) if it would not have been made, or would not have been made on the same terms, if the investor had not subscribed, or had not been proposing to subscribe, for the shares. The giving of credit to, or the assignment of a debt due from, the investor or associate is counted as a loan for these purposes. [*ITA 2007, s 257BD*].

It seems likely that, in their interpretation of the above, HMRC will apply SP 6/98 which already covers the similar requirement under the EIS — see **22.6** ENTERPRISE INVESTMENT SCHEME.

The 'no tax avoidance' requirement

[54.17] The shares must be subscribed for by the investor for genuine commercial reasons and not as part of a scheme or arrangement a main purpose of which is the avoidance of tax. [*ITA 2007, s 257BE*].

Qualifying company

[54.18] The issuing company is a '*qualifying company*' in relation to the shares if the requirements at **54.19–54.30** below are met.

The trading requirement

[54.19] The company must meet the 'trading requirement' throughout period B (as in **54.6** above). The '*trading requirement*' is that:

(a) the company exists wholly for the purpose of carrying on one or more new qualifying trades (see **54.32** below) (disregarding purposes having no significant effect on the extent of its activities); or
(b) the company is a '*parent company*' (i.e. a company with one or more 'qualifying subsidiaries' — see **54.30** below) and the business of the '*group*' (i.e. the company and its qualifying subsidiaries) does not consist wholly or as to a substantial part (i.e. broadly 20% — see HMRC Venture Capital Schemes Manual VCM3010) in the carrying on of 'non-qualifying activities'.

If period B begins after the incorporation of the company, the requirement must have been complied with since incorporation, apart from any interval between incorporation and commencement of business.

Where the company intends that one or more other companies should become its qualifying subsidiaries with a view to their carrying on one or more new qualifying trades, then, until any time after which the intention is abandoned, the company is treated as a parent company and those other companies are included in the group for the purposes of (b) above.

For the purpose of (b) above, the business of the group means what would be the business of the group if the activities of the group companies taken together were regarded as one business. Activities are for this purpose disregarded to the extent that they consist in:

(i) holding shares in or securities of any of the company's qualifying subsidiaries;
(ii) making loans to another group company;
(iii) holding and managing property used by a group company for the purposes of one or more qualifying trades (see **54.32** below) carried on by a group company; or
(iv) holding and managing property used by a group company for the purposes of research and development from which it is intended either that a qualifying trade to be carried on by a group company will be derived or that a qualifying trade carried on or to be carried on by a group company will benefit.

References in (iv) above to a group company include references to any existing or future company which will be a group company at any future time.

Activities are similarly disregarded to the extent that they consist, in the case of a subsidiary whose main purpose is the carrying on of qualifying trade(s) and whose other purposes have no significant effect on the extent of its activities (other than in relation to incidental matters), in activities not in pursuance of its main purpose.

Non-qualifying activities

'*Non-qualifying activities*' are:

- excluded activities within **22.11** ENTERPRISE INVESTMENT SCHEME; and
- non-trading activities (not including research and development — see **54.31** below).

Winding-up etc.

A company is not regarded as ceasing to meet the trading requirement merely because of anything done in consequence of the company or any of its subsidiaries being in administration or receivership (both as defined by *ITA 2007, s 252*) or because the company or any of its subsidiaries is wound up or otherwise dissolved. The entry into administration or receivership, winding-up or dissolution, and anything done as a consequence of the company concerned being in administration or receivership, must be for genuine commercial reasons and not part of a tax avoidance scheme or arrangements.

[*ITA 2007, ss 257DA, 257DB, 257HJ(1)(2)*].

The 'issuing company to carry on the qualifying business activity' requirement

[54.20] At no time in period B (as in **54.6** above) must any of the following be carried on by a person other than the issuing company or a 'qualifying 90% subsidiary' (see **54.30** below) of that company:

- the '*relevant new qualifying trade*', i.e. the 'new qualifying trade' (see **54.32** below) which is the subject of the qualifying business activity referred to in **54.7** above;
- '*relevant preparation work*', i.e. preparations to carry on a new qualifying trade where such preparations are the subject of that qualifying business activity (see **54.31**(a) below);
- research and development which is the subject of that qualifying business activity (see **54.31**(b) below); and
- any other preparations for the carrying on of the new qualifying trade.

Where relevant preparation work is carried on by the issuing company or a qualifying 90% subsidiary, the carrying on of the relevant new qualifying trade by a company other than the issuing company or a qualifying 90% subsidiary is disregarded for these purposes if it occurs before the issuing company (or subsidiary) carries on that trade.

The requirement is not regarded as failing to be met if, by reason only of a company being wound up or dissolved or being in administration or receivership (both as defined by *ITA 2007, s 252*), the relevant new qualifying trade ceases to be carried on in period B by the issuing company or a qualifying 90% subsidiary and is subsequently carried on in that period by a person who is not connected (within **17** CONNECTED PERSONS) with the issuing company at any time in period A (as in **54.14** above). This let-out applies only if the winding-up, dissolution or entry into administration or receivership (and everything done as a consequence of the company concerned being in administration or receivership) is for genuine commercial reasons and not part of a tax avoidance scheme or arrangements.

[*ITA 2007, ss 257DC, 257HJ(2)*].

The UK permanent establishment requirement

[54.21] Although the issuing company need not be UK resident, it must have a permanent establishment in the UK. The company must meet this requirement throughout period B (as in **54.6** above).

In determining whether or not a company has a permanent establishment in the UK, the same rules apply as for the identical requirement under the EIS — see **22.7** ENTERPRISE INVESTMENT SCHEME.

[*ITA 2007, ss 257DD, 257HJ(1)*].

The financial health requirement

[54.22] This requirement must be met at the beginning of period B (as in **54.6** above). The requirement is that the issuing company is not 'in difficulty'. A company is '*in difficulty*' if it is reasonable to assume that it would be regarded as a firm in difficulty for the purposes of the *EU Guidelines on State Aid for Rescuing and Restructuring Firms in Difficulty (2004/C 244/02)*. Following Brexit, the definition applies by reference to the Guidelines as they had effect immediately before 11pm on 31 December 2020 (IP completion day). [*ITA 2007, s 257DE; SI 2020 No 1499*].

The 'unquoted status' requirement

[54.23] The issuing company must be 'unquoted' at the beginning of period B (as in **54.6** above), and no arrangements must then exist for it to cease to be unquoted. If, at the time of issue, arrangements exist for the company to become a wholly-owned subsidiary of a new holding company by means of a share exchange within **54.43** below, no arrangements must exist for the new company to cease to be unquoted. A company is '*unquoted*' if none of its shares etc. are listed on a recognised stock exchange or on a foreign exchange designated for the purpose, or dealt in outside the UK by such means as may be designated for the purpose.

[*ITA 2007, s 257DF*].

The control and independence requirement

[54.24] The issuing company must not at any time in period A (ignoring any on-the-shelf period) (as in **54.14** above) either:

(a) control another company (other than a 'qualifying subsidiary' — see **54.30** below), 'control' being construed in accordance with *CTA 2010, ss 450, 451* and being considered with or without CONNECTED PERSONS (**17**); or

(b) (subject to **54.43** below) be under the control of another company, 'control' being construed in accordance with *ITA 2007, s 995* and again being considered with or without connected persons; or

(c) be capable of falling within (a) or (b) by virtue of any arrangements which are in existence for a company to control another (as broadly defined).

An on-the-shelf period is defined as a period during which the issuing company has not yet issued any shares other than subscriber shares and has not made preparations to begin carrying on a trade or business.

[*ITA 2007, ss 257DG, 257HJ(3)*].

The 'no partnerships' requirement

[54.25] Neither the issuing company nor any 'qualifying 90% subsidiary' (see **54.30** below) of that company may, at any time during period A (as in **54.14** above), be a member of a partnership. This includes a limited liability partnership and a foreign entity of similar nature to a partnership. [*ITA 2007, s 257DH*].

The gross assets requirement

[54.26] The value of the issuing company's assets must not exceed £350,000 immediately before the issue of SEIS shares (£200,000 for shares issued before 6 April 2023). If the issuing company is a parent company, the gross assets test applies by reference to the aggregate gross assets of the company and all its qualifying subsidiaries (disregarding certain assets held by any such company which correspond to liabilities of another). [*ITA 2007, ss 257DI, 257HJ(1); F(No 2)A 2023, s 15(3)(7)*].

For HMRC's approach to the gross assets requirement see HMRC Venture Capital Schemes Manual VCM34100.

The 'number of employees' requirement

[54.27] The issuing company must have fewer than the equivalent of 25 full-time employees when the SEIS shares are issued. If the company is a parent company, this rule applies by reference to the aggregate number of full-time employees of itself and its qualifying subsidiaries. To ascertain the equivalent number of full-time employees of a company, take the actual number of full-time employees and add to it a just and reasonable fraction for each employee who is not full-time. For this purpose, an 'employee' includes a director but does not include anyone on maternity or paternity leave or a student on vocational training. [*ITA 2007, ss 257DJ, 257HJ(1)*].

HMRC consider that a full-time employee is one whose standard working week (excluding lunch breaks and overtime) is at least 35 hours (HMRC Venture Capital Schemes Manual VCM34110).

The 'no previous other risk capital scheme investments' requirement

[54.28] This requirement is that:

- no EIS investment or VCT investment is or has been made in the issuing company on or before the day on which the SEIS shares are issued; and
- no EIS investment or VCT investment has been made on or before that day in a company which at the time the SEIS shares are issued is a 'qualifying subsidiary' (see **54.30** below) of the issuing company.

An EIS investment is made if the company issues shares (for which money has been subscribed) and provides a compliance statement under *ITA 2007, s 205* in respect of the shares. The investment is made when the shares are issued. A VCT investment is made if an investment (of any kind) in the company is made by a VCT (see **64** VENTURE CAPITAL TRUSTS). [*ITA 2007, s 257DK*].

The 'amount raised through the SEIS' requirement

[54.29] The total amount of SEIS investments made in the issuing company, together with any other de minimis State aid received by the company, in the period of three years and one day ending on the date of the current issue must not exceed an upper limit of £250,000 (£150,000 for shares issued before 6 April 2023).

A SEIS investment is made if the company issues shares (for which money has been subscribed) and provides a compliance statement under **54.35** below in respect of them; the investment is made on the day the shares are issued. De minimis aid is defined by reference to Article 2 of Commission Regulation (EC) No 1998/2006; the amount of the aid is the amount of the grant or, if the aid is not in the form of a grant, the gross grant equivalent amount (within the meaning of that Regulation).

Where the current share issue would take the total amount of SEIS investments (plus de minimis aid) to more than the upper limit, the requirement is treated as met in relation to an appropriate proportion of the shares in the issue (and in any other issue made on the same day). For example, if 300,000 shares are issued for £1 each on 6 April 2023 and there has been no previous issue in the last three years (and no de minimis aid), 250,000 of the shares can be SEIS shares. Those shares and the remainder of the shares comprised in the issue are then treated as two separate issues for SEIS purposes.

The definition of de minimis aid above has not been amended despite the revocation of the de minimis Regulation in the UK following Brexit.

[*ITA 2007, s 257DL; F(No 2)A 2023, s 15(4)(7)*].

The subsidiaries requirements

[54.30] At all times in period B (as in **54.6** above), any subsidiary of the issuing company must be a 'qualifying subsidiary' (see below). [*ITA 2007, s 257DM*].

The company must not at any time in period B have a 'property managing subsidiary' which is not a 'qualifying 90% subsidiary' (see below) of the company. A '*property managing subsidiary*' is a subsidiary whose business consists wholly or mainly in the holding or managing of land or any 'property deriving its value from land'. For this purpose, '*property deriving its value from land*' includes any shareholding in a company, and any partnership interest or interest in settled property, which derives its value directly or indirectly from land and any option, consent or embargo affecting the disposition of land. [*ITA 2007, s 257DN*].

Qualifying subsidiary and qualifying 90% subsidiary

Both '*qualifying subsidiary*' and '*qualifying 90% subsidiary*' have the same meanings as they do for EIS purposes. See respectively **22.8** and **22.9** ENTERPRISE INVESTMENT SCHEME. [*ITA 2007, s 257HJ(1)*].

Qualifying business activity

[54.31] Either of the following is a '*qualifying business activity*' in relation to the issuing company:

(a)
- (i) the carrying on of a 'new qualifying trade' (see **54.32** below) which, on the date of issue of the shares, the company or a 'qualifying 90% subsidiary' (see **54.30** above) is carrying on; or
- (ii) the activity of preparing to carry on such a trade which, on the date of issue of the shares, is intended to be carried on by the company or any such subsidiary and which is eventually carried on by the company or any such subsidiary; or

(iii) the eventual carrying on of the trade mentioned in (ii) above; and

(b) the carrying on of 'research and development' which, on the date of issue of the shares, the company or a 'qualifying 90% subsidiary' is carrying on or which the company or any such subsidiary begins to carry on immediately afterwards, and from which it is intended on that date that a new qualifying trade which the company or any such subsidiary will carry on will be derived or will benefit.

For the purposes of (b) above, when research and development is begun to be carried on by a qualifying 90% subsidiary of the issuing company, any carrying on of the research and development by it before it became such a subsidiary is ignored. '*Research and development*' has the meaning given by *ITA 2007, s 1006*. References in (a) and (b) above to a qualifying 90% subsidiary include, in cases where the new qualifying trade is not carried on at the time of issue of the shares, references to any existing or future company which will be such a subsidiary at any future time.

[*ITA 2007, ss 257HG, 257HJ(1)*].

New qualifying trade

[54.32] '*Qualifying trade*' is defined as for EIS purposes — see **22.11** ENTERPRISE INVESTMENT SCHEME. A qualifying trade carried on by the issuing company or a 'qualifying 90% subsidiary' (see **54.30** above) of that company is a '*new qualifying trade*' if (and only if):

- the trade does not begin to be carried on (whether by the company concerned or any other person) before the period of three years ending immediately before the day on which the shares are issued (two years for shares issued before 6 April 2023); and
- at no time before the company concerned begins to carry on the trade was any other trade being carried on by the issuing company or by any company that was a 51% subsidiary of the issuing company at the time in question.

[*ITA 2007, s 257HF; F(No 2)A 2023, s 15(5)(7)*].

Form of SEIS income tax relief

[54.33] Subject to the carry-back facility described below, relief is given for the tax year in which the shares are issued. It is given by means of a reduction in what would otherwise be the individual's income tax liability (a '*tax reduction*') equal to tax at the SEIS rate for the year on the amount (or aggregate amounts) subscribed for shares in respect of which he is eligible for and claims SEIS relief. The SEIS rate is 50%. Investors can restrict their claim for SEIS relief to only some of the shares issued to them at any one time.

There is an upper limit of £200,000 on the amount of investment on which an individual may obtain relief in a tax year. For shares issued before 6 April 2023, the upper limit was £100,000.

For the order in which tax reductions are given against an individual's tax liability see Tolley's Income Tax under Allowances and Tax Rates. A tax reduction must be restricted to the extent (if any) that it would otherwise exceed the individual's remaining income tax liability after making all prior reductions.

Carry-back

Where shares in respect of which an individual is eligible for SEIS relief are issued at any time in any tax year, the individual may claim relief as if any number of shares up to the full number issued to him had been issued in the tax year preceding that in which they were actually issued. This carry-back is subject to the overriding rule that the total amount of investment on which relief can be obtained for any one year cannot exceed the annual maximum for that year.

[*ITA 2007, s 257AB; F(No 2)A 2023, s 15(2)(7)*].

Attribution of relief to shares

[54.34] Subject to any reduction or withdrawal of relief (see **54.36** *et seq.* below), where an individual's income tax liability is reduced for a tax year as in **54.33** above by reason of an issue or issues of shares made (or treated as made) in that year, the tax reduction is attributed to that issue or those issues (being apportioned in the latter case according to the amounts claimed for each issue). Issues of shares of the same class by a company to an individual on the same day are treated as a single issue for this purpose. A proportionate amount of the reduction attributed to an issue is attributed to each share in the issue in respect of which the claim was made and is adjusted correspondingly for any subsequent bonus issue of shares of the same class and carrying the same rights.

An issue to an individual part of which is treated as having been made in the preceding tax year (as in **54.33** above) is treated as two separate issues, one made on a day in the previous year.

Where relief attributable to an issue of shares falls to be withdrawn or reduced, the relief attributable to each of the shares in question is reduced to nil (if relief is withdrawn) or proportionately reduced (where relief is reduced).

[*ITA 2007, ss 257E, 257HI*].

Claims for relief

[54.35] A claim for SEIS income tax relief is valid only if it is made no later than the fifth anniversary of 31 January following the tax year in which the shares are issued.

The claimant must have received, with the authority of HMRC, a compliance certificate from the issuing company before making the claim. The certificate must state that the requirements for relief, except in so far as they fall to be satisfied by the investor, are for the time being satisfied in relation to the shares in question.

Before issuing such a certificate, the company must supply to HMRC a compliance statement that the requirements for relief are satisfied for the time being and have been satisfied at all times since the shares were issued.

If a certificate or statement is made fraudulently or negligently, or a certificate was issued when it should not have been, the issuing company is liable to a fine of up to £3,000.

No application for postponement of tax pending appeal can be made on the ground that relief is due under these provisions unless a claim has been duly submitted.

[*ITA 2007, ss 257EA–257EG*].

Reduction or withdrawal of relief

[54.36] The following provisions apply to reduce or withdraw SEIS income tax relief in certain circumstances. References to a reduction of relief include its reduction to nil, and references to the withdrawal of relief in respect of any shares are to the withdrawal of the relief attributable to those shares (see **54.34** above). Where no relief has yet been given, a reduction applies to reduce the amount which would otherwise be available for relief, and a withdrawal means the shares cease to be eligible for relief. [*ITA 2007, s 257HJ(4)*].

An assessment to income tax withdrawing or reducing SEIS relief is made for the tax year for which the relief was given.

Disposal of shares

[54.37] Where, before the end of period B (as in **54.6** above), the investor disposes of shares to which relief is attributable (see **54.34** above) or grants an option the exercise of which would bind him to sell the shares, then:

(a) if the disposal is at arm's length, relief attributable to those shares (see **54.34** above) is withdrawn or, if that relief is greater than an amount equal to tax at the SEIS rate (see **54.33** above) on the disposal consideration, is reduced by that amount; or
(b) if the disposal is not at arm's length, the relief is withdrawn.

Where the relief attributable to the shares is less than tax at the SEIS rate on the amount subscribed for the issue, the amount referred to in (a) above is correspondingly reduced. An issue to an individual part of which is treated as having been made in the preceding tax year (as in **54.33** above) is treated as two separate issues, one made on a day in the previous year. Where the relief attributable to the shares has been reduced (otherwise than as a result of an issue of bonus shares — see **54.34** above) before the relief was obtained, then in calculating the amount referred to in (a) above the relief attributable to the shares before that reduction is used.

A share exchange within *TCGA 1992, s 136* is treated as a disposal of shares for these purposes, as is a disposal of an interest or right in or over shares. If, at any time in period A (as in **54.14** above), a person grants the investor an option the exercise of which would bind the grantor to purchase any shares to which relief is attributable, the relief is withdrawn.

These provisions do not apply to a disposal of shares occurring as a result of the investor's death. See **54.42** below for transfers of shares between spouses or civil partners.

Identification rules

For the above purposes, disposals are identified with shares of the same class issued on an earlier day before shares issued on a later day, i.e. first in/first out (FIFO). Where shares within two or more of the categories listed below were acquired on the same day, any of those shares disposed of (applying the FIFO basis) are treated as disposed of in the order in which they are listed, as follows:

- shares to which no SEIS income tax relief is attributable;
- shares to which SEIS income tax relief, but not SEIS reinvestment relief (see **54.46** below), is attributable;
- shares to which both SEIS income tax relief and SEIS reinvestment relief are attributable.

Shares transferred between spouses or civil partners living together are treated as if they were acquired by the transferee spouse or partner on the day they were issued (see also **54.42** below). Shares comprised in a 'new holding' following a reorganisation to which *TCGA 1992, s 127* applies (see **57.2** SHARES AND SECURITIES) are treated as having been acquired when the original shares were acquired.

[*ITA 2007, ss 257FA–257FD, 257HA, 257HH*].

Value received by investor

[54.38] If, at any time in period A (as in **54.14** above), the investor receives value (other than insignificant value) from the issuing company, any relief attributable to those shares (see **54.34** above), and not previously reduced in respect of the value received, is withdrawn or, if that relief exceeds an amount equal to tax at the SEIS rate on the value received, is reduced by that amount.

If an individual to whom shares in a company have been issued enters into a convertible loan agreement with the company under the Future Fund on or after 20 May 2020, and subsequently receives value from the company under the terms of that agreement, the value received is ignored in relation to any SEIS relief attributable to shares issued before the individual entered into the agreement. This is to ensure that investors in a company who also support the company using a Future Fund convertible loan note will not lose relief on any previous SEIS investments when that loan is redeemed or converted into shares. The Future Fund was set up as part of Government support to companies impacted by the 2020 coronavirus (COVID-19) pandemic (see www.gov.uk/guidance/future-fund).

[*ITA 2007, ss 257FE–257FI, 257FM; FA 2020, s 110*].

For full details of the provisions, see Tolley's Income Tax.

Acquisition of trade or trading assets

[54.39] Relief attributable (see **54.34** above) to any shares in a company held by an individual is withdrawn if:

(a) at any time in period A (as in **54.14** above), the company or any 'qualifying subsidiary' (see **54.30** below)

- begins to carry on as its trade, business or profession (or as part of its trade etc.) a trade etc. previously carried on at any time in that period by someone other than the company or any qualifying subsidiary; or
- acquires the whole or the greater part of the assets used for the purposes of a trade etc. previously so carried on; and

(b) the individual is a person or one of a group of persons:
   (i) who owned at any time in period A more than a half share in the trade etc. previously carried on, and also own or owned at any such time such a share in the trade etc. carried on by the company; or
   (ii) control (within *CTA 2010, ss 450, 451*), or at any time in period A has controlled, the company, and also, at any such time, controlled another company which previously carried on the trade etc.

In determining, for the purposes of (b)(i) above, the ownership of a trade and, if appropriate, the shares owned by multiple owners, *CTA 2010, s 941(6)* and *s 942* apply. Interests, rights or powers of 'associates' (see **54.13** above) of a person are treated as those of that person.

[*ITA 2007, ss 257FP, 257HJ(3)*].

Acquisition of share capital

[54.40] Relief attributable (see **54.34** above) to any shares in a company held by an individual is withdrawn if:

- the company, at any time in period A (as in **54.14** above), comes to acquire all the issued share capital of another company, and
- the individual is a person, or one of a group of persons, who control (within *CTA 2010, ss 450, 451*) or has, at any time in period A, controlled the company and who also, at any such time, controlled the other company.

[*ITA 2007, ss 257FQ, 257HJ(3)*].

Relief subsequently found not to have been due

[54.41] Relief is withdrawn if it is subsequently found not to have been due. If relief is to be withdrawn on the ground that the issuing company is not a qualifying company (see **54.18** above) or that the purpose of the issue or spending of the money raised requirements at **54.8** are not met:

- the issuing company must have given notice to that effect under *ITA 2007, s 257GF*; or
- an HMRC officer must have given notice to the issuing company of his opinion that the whole or part of the relief was not due because of the ground in question.

The issuing company may appeal against an HMRC notice as though it were refusal of a claim by the company.

[*ITA 2007, ss 257FR, 257GA*].

Married persons and civil partners

[54.42] The provisions for withdrawal of relief on the disposal of shares in respect of which relief has been given (see 54.37 above) do not apply to transfers between spouses or civil partners living together. On any subsequent disposal or other event, the spouse or partner to whom the shares were so transferred is treated as if:

- he or she were the person who subscribed for the shares;
- the amount he or she subscribed for the shares were the same amount as subscribed by the transferor spouse or partner;
- his or her liability to income tax had been reduced in respect of the shares by the same amount, and for the same tax year, as applied on the subscription by the transferor spouse or partner; and
- that amount of SEIS income tax relief had continued to be attributable to the shares despite the transfer.

Where the amount of SEIS relief attributable to the shares had been reduced before the relief was obtained by the transferor spouse or partner, the transferee is treated as if his or her relief had been correspondingly reduced before it was obtained.

Any assessment for reducing or withdrawing relief is made on the transferee spouse or partner. The identification rules for disposals at 54.37 above apply to determine the extent (if any) to which shares to which relief is attributable are comprised in the transfer.

[*ITA 2007, ss 257FA(4), 257H, 257HA(1)*].

Issuing company acquired by new company

[54.43] Where a company (Company A) has issued shares under the SEIS (and has issued a compliance certificate — see 54.35 above) and subsequently, by means of an exchange of shares, all of its shares (the old shares) are acquired by a company (Company B) in which the only previously issued shares are subscriber shares, then, subject to the further conditions below being satisfied:

- the exchange is not regarded as involving a disposal of the old shares (and a consequent withdrawal of relief) and an acquisition of the Company B shares (the new shares); and
- SEIS relief attributable to the old shares is regarded as attributable instead to the new shares for which they are exchanged. For SEIS purposes generally, the new shares stand in the shoes of the old shares, e.g. as if they had been subscribed for and issued at the time the old shares were subscribed for and issued and as if anything done by or in relation to Company A had been done by or in relation to Company B.

The further conditions are as follows.

(a) The consideration for the old shares must consist entirely of the issue of the new shares.

(b) The consideration for old shares of each description must consist entirely of new shares of the 'corresponding description'.
(c) New shares of each description must be issued to holders of old shares of the 'corresponding description' in respect of and in proportion to their holdings.
(d) Before the issue of the new shares, on the written application (for which see **4.16** ANTI-AVOIDANCE) of either Company A or Company B, HMRC must have notified to that company their satisfaction that the exchange:
  - is for genuine commercial reasons; and
  - does not form part of a scheme or arrangements designed to avoid liability to corporation tax or capital gains tax.

  HMRC may, within 30 days of an application, request further particulars, which must then be supplied within 30 days of the request (or such longer period as they may allow in any particular case).

For the purposes of (b) and (c) above, old and new shares are of a '*corresponding description*' if, assuming they were shares in the same company, they would be of the same class and carry the same rights.

References above to 'shares' (other than those to 'shares issued under the SEIS' or 'subscriber shares') include references to securities.

An exchange within these provisions does not breach the control and independence requirement at **54.24** above.

[*ITA 2007, ss 257HB–257HD; TCGA 1992, s 138(2)*].

Capital gains tax

[54.44] See also **54.46** below for SEIS reinvestment relief.

Gains

Gains arising on the disposal by the investor, after the end of period A (as in **54.14** above), of shares on which SEIS income tax relief has been given are not chargeable gains. (There is no such exemption for shares disposed of before the end of period A, and any SEIS income tax relief given will be withdrawn — see **54.37** above.)

Where SEIS income tax relief was not given on the full amount subscribed for the shares (other than by reason of the income tax liability being insufficient to support the relief), the capital gains tax exemption is restricted to a proportion of the gain. Where this arises, it will usually be because the investor's SEIS subscriptions exceeded the annual maximum on which relief is available (see **54.33** above). The exempt gain is the proportion of the gain found by applying the multiple R/T where:

R = the actual income tax relief given (expressed in terms of the reduction in the tax liability); and
T = tax at the SEIS rate on the amount subscribed for the issue.

[*TCGA 1992, s 150E(2)(4)(5)*].

Losses

If a disposal of shares on which SEIS income tax relief has been given results in a capital loss, the loss is allowable *regardless* of whether the disposal occurs within or without period A (see above). However, in calculating the loss, or in ascertaining whether a loss has indeed arisen, the cost of the shares for CGT purposes is reduced by the amount of SEIS income tax relief attributable to the shares disposed of (expressed in terms of the reduction in the tax liability) to the extent that this has not been, or does not fall to be, withdrawn.

[*TCGA 1992, s 150E(1)(3)*].

Identification rules

The normal identification rules (see **58.2** SHARES AND SECURITIES — IDENTIFICATION RULES) are each disapplied as regards SEIS shares. Instead, the rules described at **54.37** above apply to match disposals with acquisitions of shares of the same class in the same company, and they apply where at least some of those shares have attracted SEIS income tax relief. [*TCGA 1992, s 150E(6)(7)*].

Rights issues

If, immediately following a rights issue, EIS relief is attributable either to the original holding or the rights shares, the share reorganisation rules of *TCGA 1992, ss 127–130* (see **57.2** SHARES AND SECURITIES) are disapplied, with the result that the rights shares are treated as a separate acquisition. [*TCGA 1992, s 150E(8)*].

Company reconstructions

If as part of a reconstruction, shares or debentures in another company are issued to an SEIS shareholder in exchange for SEIS shares to which income tax relief remains attributable, then the shares in the new company are not generally deemed to stand in the place of shares in the old company under *TCGA 1992, s 135* or *s 136* (see **57.5**, **57.7** SHARES AND SECURITIES) and there is thus a disposal of the shares in the old company. However, *section 135* or *136* does apply in the normal way if:

- the new holding consists of new ordinary shares issued after the end of period A (applied by reference to the original shares and the company which issued them) and carrying no present or future preferential rights to dividends or assets or right to redemption; and
- the company issuing the new shares has previously issued shares under the SEIS and has issued the appropriate compliance certificate (see **54.35** above) enabling investors to obtain relief on that earlier issue.

In addition, *TCGA 1992, s 135* is not disapplied in a case to which *ITA 2007, s 257HB* (see **54.43** above) applies. That provision is instead applied for CGT purposes also.

[*TCGA 1992, s 150E(9)–(11)(13)*].

Example 1

On 8 November 2020, P subscribes £130,000 for 65,000 shares in the SEIS company, S Ltd, and obtains the then maximum SEIS income tax relief of £50,000 (£100,000 × 50%) for 2020/21. On 3 April 2025, he sells the entire holding for £240,000.

The chargeable gain arising is calculated as follows.

	£
Disposal proceeds	240,000
Cost	130,000
Gain	110,000
Less TCGA 1992, s 150E(2)(4)(5) exemption	
$£110{,}000 \times \frac{50{,}000\ (R)}{65{,}000 (T)} =$	84,615
Chargeable gain 2024/25	£25,384

Note:

R = relief given (£100,000 × 50%) = £50,000

T = £130,000 × 50% = £65,000

Example 2

Assuming the facts otherwise remain the same as in *Example 1* above but that the shares are sold for £50,000 on 3 April 2025.

The allowable loss arising is calculated as follows.

	£	£
Disposal proceeds		50,000
Less Cost	130,000	
Less Income tax relief given (and not withdrawn)	50,000	80,000
Allowable loss 2024/25		£30,000

Example 3

The facts are otherwise as in *Example 2* above except that the shares are sold in an arm's length bargain on 3 April 2022, i.e. within three years after their issue.

Income tax relief given for 2020/21 is withdrawn as follows.

Relief attributable (£100,000 @ 50%)	£50,000 (1)
Consideration	
$£50{,}000 \times \frac{50{,}000\ (£100{,}000\ @\ 50\%)}{65{,}000\ (£130{,}000\ @\ 50\%)}$ @ 50%	£19,230 (2)

The amount at (1) is greater than that at (2), so income tax relief of £19,230 is withdrawn. [*ITA 2007, ss 257FA, 257FB*].

The relief not withdrawn is therefore £(50,000 – 19,230) =	£30,770

The allowable loss arising is calculated as follows.

	£	£
Disposal proceeds		50,000
Less Cost	130,000	
Less Income tax relief not withdrawn	30,770	99,230
Allowable loss 2021/22		£49,230

Reduction of relief where value received etc.

[54.45] Where a gain on disposal of SEIS shares would otherwise be exempt due to their having been held until after the end of period A (as in **54.14** above), a special rule applies if SEIS income tax relief has been, or falls to be, reduced (though not fully withdrawn) as a result of the investor receiving value from the company (see **54.38** above).

The CGT exemption applies only to so much of the gain as remains after deducting so much of it as is represented by the fraction A/B where:

A = the reduction(s) made, as mentioned above, to the income tax relief given; and
B = the income tax relief given before applying such reductions.

Where the CGT exemption has already been restricted because EIS income tax relief was not given on the full amount subscribed for the shares (see **54.44** above), the fraction is applied to the part of the gain otherwise exempt and the deduction made from that part.

[*TCGA 1992, s 150F*].

SEIS reinvestment relief

[54.46] A CGT exemption is available where:

- an individual realises a chargeable gain on a disposal at any time in a tax year; and
- he is eligible for, and claims, SEIS income tax relief for the year in which the disposal is made in respect of an amount subscribed for an 'issue of shares' in a company made to him (or treated as made to him) in that year.

If the issue of shares or any corresponding bonus shares (i.e. shares issued other than for payment which are in the same company and class and carry the same rights as the SEIS shares) precedes the disposal, it is an additional condition that the individual continue to hold those shares at the time of the disposal. For this purpose, an '*issue of shares*' means an issue of shares in a company which are of the same class and are issued to the individual in one capacity and on the same day.

On a claim by the individual, 50% of so much of the 'unused' acquisition cost of the SEIS shares as is specified in the claim and does not exceed so much of the chargeable gain as is 'unmatched' is set against the gain. To the extent that an amount is set against the gain, the gain ceases to be a chargeable gain. For this purpose, the acquisition cost is '*unused*' to the extent that it has not already been set against a gain either under these provisions or under EIS deferral relief (see **22.16** ENTERPRISE INVESTMENT SCHEME); and a gain is '*unmatched*' to the extent that the acquisition costs of other SEIS shares or EIS shares have not already been set against it.

The total amount that can be set against gains cannot exceed 50% of an upper limit of £200,000 (£100,000 for shares issued before 6 April 2023), i.e. the maximum amount on which SEIS income tax relief is available. Where the individual's SEIS income tax relief is restricted to the upper limit (see **54.33** above), the amount of the limit is apportioned between share issues. If the amount of SEIS income tax relief attributable (see **54.34** above) to any of the shares has been reduced by any of the provisions at **54.36–54.41** above (otherwise than because of corresponding bonus shares being issued) before the income tax relief was obtained, the amount which can be set against gains under these provisions is correspondingly reduced. If both of these restrictions apply, the upper limit restriction is applied first.

The chargeable gain eligible for relief is the gain after taking into account any mandatory reductions, and any other reliefs or elections claimed or made in computing the chargeable gain, but before the deduction of losses or the annual exemption (HMRC Venture Capital Schemes Manual VCM45010).

Claims

A claim for SEIS reinvestment relief must be made no later than five years after the 31 January following the tax year in which the shares are issued. Where SEIS shares issued in one tax year and treated as issued in the previous tax year as a result of a SEIS income tax relief carry-back claim (see **54.33** above), they will thereby qualify to be used in a reinvestment relief claim (HMRC Venture Capital Schemes Manual VCM45010) for the earlier year. This does not, however, affect the time limit for making a claim.

Attribution of relief to shares

A proportionate part of the expenditure set off against a chargeable gain is attributed to each of the SEIS shares concerned and the attribution is adjusted correspondingly for any subsequent issue of corresponding bonus shares.

Removal or reduction of relief

If SEIS income tax relief attributable (see **54.34** above) to shares is withdrawn (see **54.35** onwards above), any SEIS reinvestment relief attributable to those shares is also withdrawn. If SEIS income tax relief attributable to shares is reduced, any SEIS reinvestment relief attributable to those shares is reduced in the same proportion. In either case, a chargeable gain is then deemed to accrue to the individual in the tax year in which the shares were issued of an amount equal to the amount of reinvestment relief to be withdrawn or the amount by which reinvestment relief falls to be reduced.

Transfer to spouse or civil partner

Where shares to which SEIS income tax relief is attributable are transferred by the individual to whom they were issued ('A') to that individual's spouse or civil partner ('B') during their lives, then, if that relief was not withdrawn or reduced on that transfer (see **54.42** above), any chargeable gain arising to remove or reduce SEIS reinvestment relief attributable to the shares is treated as arising to B.

[*TCGA 1992, s 150G, Sch 5BB; F(No 2)A 2023, s 15(6)(7)*].

Example

On 1 June 2024, X sells an asset for £365,000. The asset had cost X £240,000 in 2005. X makes no other disposals in 2023/24. On 1 February 2024, X acquires by subscription 100,000 shares in ABC Ltd at a total price of £200,000. X claims SEIS income tax relief in respect of the acquisition.

If X makes a claim under *TCGA 1992, Sch 5BB*, then his CGT position for 2024/25 is as follows.

	£
Consideration	365,000
Less Acquisition cost	240,000
Gain	125,000
Less Reinvestment relief	100,000
Chargeable gain	25,000
Less annual exempt amount	3,000
Taxable gain 2024/25	£22,000

55

Self-Assessment

Simon's Taxes. See **E1.2**.

Introduction to self-assessment

[55.1] Both CGT and corporation tax on chargeable gains are administered under a system of self-assessment. CGT is largely incorporated within the income tax self-assessment system, although there is an additional compliance regime for disposals of UK land. A separate (but similar) system applies for corporation tax purposes (but there is no special regime for UK land).

The term 'self-assessment' refers to the system whereby the tax return for the year or accounting period includes the taxpayer's own assessment of the tax liability. Payment of tax is then due automatically, based on the self-assessment.

A summary of the CGT/income tax system is given at **55.2** below, and that for corporation tax at **55.3** below.

For the phased introduction of 'Making Tax Digital', see **52.1** RETURNS.

Capital gains tax (and income tax)

[55.2] The main features of the self-assessment regime for individuals, personal representatives and trustees are summarised below. The detailed provisions are covered as indicated.

- A special compliance regime applies to direct disposals of UK land where a residential property gain arises (regardless of the residence status of the taxpayer) and to all direct or indirect disposals of UK land by non-UK residents. A UK land disposal return must be made together with a payment on account of CGT on or before the 60th day following the day of the completion of the disposal (the 30th day where completion is before 27 October 2021). See **45.3** PAYMENT OF TAX and **52.22** RETURNS.
- A person chargeable to CGT (and/or income tax) for a particular tax year who has not received a notice to deliver a return for that year has until 5 October following that year to notify HMRC that they are so chargeable (see **46.3** PENALTIES).

- HMRC may withdraw a notice to an individual or trustee to make a return. The notice must normally be withdrawn within two years of the end of the tax year to which the notice relates. If HMRC withdraw a notice, they will issue a withdrawal notice and no return needs to be submitted. See **52.5** RETURNS.
- HMRC can instead make a 'simple assessment' of an individual's or trustee's income tax or CGT liability without the taxpayer first being required to complete a self-assessment tax return. The simple assessment will be made on the basis of information already held by HMRC, whether it was received from the taxpayer or a third party. HMRC operate a real-time capital gains service under which UK resident individuals can report capital gains via the online Government Gateway. See **52.4** RETURNS.
- Returns of income and gains must normally be filed with HMRC by 31 January following the tax year, except that the deadline is brought forward to 31 October following the tax year if the return is not delivered electronically via HMRC's Self-Assessment Online service (see **52.5** RETURNS). The return must, subject to the exception below, include a self-assessment of the tax liability, based on the information in the return, although in practice the tax due is computed automatically during the filing of an electronic return. Electronic returns must be filed by 30 December following the tax year if the taxpayer wishes unpaid tax (where this is less than £3,000) to be collected via their tax code.
- Taxpayers who are not filing their return electronically and who prefer not to compute their own liabilities do not have to do so if they file their return by 31 October following the tax year (or, if later, within two months of the date of the notice to file the return) (see **52.8** RETURNS). In such cases, HMRC will compute the tax due and make an assessment. Such an assessment is treated as a self-assessment included in the return.
- A separate return must be filed by a partnership (in addition to the returns of each partner). This must include a statement of the allocation of partnership income between the partners. See **52.18–52.20** RETURNS.
- Penalties are imposed for failure to notify and for late submission of returns, subject to appeal on the grounds of reasonable excuse (see **46.3**, **46.4**, **46.5** and **46.7** PENALTIES).
- Before making a return, a taxpayer can ask HMRC to check any valuations used for CGT purposes in completing the return (see **52.7** RETURNS).
- Taxpayers may amend their return at any time within 12 months after the filing date (treated, for this purpose, as 31 January following the tax year in most cases). HMRC may amend a return to correct obvious errors, omissions or anything else which they have reason to believe is incorrect in the light of information available to them at any time within nine months after its delivery, but the taxpayer can reject such a correction within 30 days. See **52.9** RETURNS.
- HMRC are given broadly one year from the day the return is delivered to give notice of their intention to enquire into the return (see **52.11** RETURNS). A formal procedure is laid down for such enquiries (see

52.11–52.16 RETURNS). HMRC can also make use of their powers under *FA 2008, Sch 36* to carry out 'compliance checks' (see **29.3** HMRC INVESTIGATORY POWERS).

- If HMRC do not give such notice, the return becomes final and conclusive, subject to any claim for recovery of overpaid tax by the taxpayer (see **13.7** CLAIMS) or 'discovery' assessment (see **6.10** ASSESSMENTS).
- In the event of non-submission of a return, HMRC can make a determination of the tax liability; there is no right of appeal but the determination is superseded on submission of the return (see **52.17** RETURNS).
- A self-assessment contained in a return cannot normally be made more than four years after the end of the tax year. See **52.8** RETURNS.
- Income tax (on all sources of taxable income) for a tax year is payable by means of two interim payments of equal amounts, based normally on the liability for the previous tax year and due on 31 January in the tax year and the following 31 July. A final balancing payment is due on the following 31 January which is also the due date for CGT liability (see **45.2** PAYMENT OF TAX). Interim payments are not required where substantially all of a taxpayer's income is subject to deduction of tax at source or where the amounts otherwise due are below de minimis limits. See Tolley's Income Tax for more on interim payments.
- Interest on overdue payments runs from the due date to the date of payment (see **36.2** LATE PAYMENT INTEREST AND PENALTIES). Interest on tax overpaid normally runs from the date of payment to the date of repayment (see **50.2** REPAYMENT INTEREST); the rate of interest is lower than that on overdue tax.
- Late payment penalties apply where tax due is unpaid more than 30 days after the due date. See **36.6** LATE PAYMENT INTEREST AND PENALTIES.
- There is a statutory requirement for taxpayers to keep records for the purpose of making returns and to preserve such records for specified periods (see **52.10** RETURNS).
- For the procedures for making claims, elections and notices, see **13.2** CLAIMS.
- For appeals see **5.2** APPEALS.

See also HMRC Self Assessment Legal Framework Manual.

Corporation tax

[55.3] The main features of the corporation tax self-assessment regime are summarised below. The detailed provisions are covered as indicated and in Tolley's Corporation Tax.

- A company must notify HMRC of the start of its first accounting period (and of the beginning of any subsequent accounting period that does not immediately follow a previous accounting period) within three months after the start of the period (see **52.21** RETURNS).
- A company chargeable to corporation tax for an accounting period which has neither made a return for that period nor received a notice to deliver a return must notify HMRC of its chargeability within twelve months after the end of that period (see **52.21** RETURNS).

- Returns of profits and gains must normally be filed with HMRC within twelve months after the end of the period to which they relate (see **52.21** RETURNS). The return must include a self-assessment of the tax liability, based on the information in the return. Returns must be filed online using a specified data format (iXBRL).
- Penalties are imposed for failure to notify chargeability and for late submission of returns, subject to appeal on the grounds of reasonable excuse (see **46.3** and **46.4** PENALTIES).
- Before making its return, a company can ask HMRC to check any valuations used for chargeable gains purposes in completing the return (see **52.21** RETURNS).
- Companies may amend their return at any time within twelve months after the filing date. HMRC may amend a return to correct obvious errors, omissions or anything else which they have reason to believe is incorrect in the light of information available to them at any time within nine months after its delivery. The company can reject such a correction by amending its return or, where the time limit for amendment has passed, by notice within three months.
- HMRC are given broadly one year from the day the return is delivered to give notice of their intention to enquire into the return (see **52.21** RETURNS).
- If HMRC do not give such notice, the return becomes final and conclusive, subject to any claim for recovery of overpaid tax by the company (see **13.7** CLAIMS) or 'discovery' assessment (see **6.10** ASSESSMENTS).
- In the event of non-submission of a return, HMRC can make a determination of the tax liability; there is no right of appeal but the determination is superseded on submission of the return (see **52.17** RETURNS).
- For companies other than 'large' companies, corporation tax (including that in respect of chargeable gains) for an accounting period is due and payable on the day following the expiry of nine months from the end of the period. Large companies pay corporation tax under a system of quarterly instalments. See **45.4** PAYMENT OF TAX.
- Interest on overdue payments runs from the due date to the date of payment (see **36.3** LATE PAYMENT INTEREST AND PENALTIES). A different rate of interest applies to unpaid instalments under the quarterly instalment rules from the due date to the earlier of the date of payment and the normal due date (i.e. the day following the expiry of nine months from the end of the accounting period). Interest on tax overpaid normally runs from the date of payment to the date of repayment (see **50.3** REPAYMENT INTEREST); again, a different rate of interest applies up to the normal due date (whether or not the quarterly instalment rules apply).
- There is a statutory requirement for companies to keep records for the purpose of making returns and to preserve such records for six years from the end of the return period (see **52.21** RETURNS).
- For the procedures for making claims, elections and notices, see **13.4** CLAIMS.
- For appeals see **5.2** APPEALS.

See also **Simon's Taxes, D1.13.**

56

Settlements

Cross-references. See **2** ANNUAL RATES AND EXEMPTIONS; **6.6** ASSESSMENTS for assessments on trustees; **11** CHARITIES; **12.2** CHILDREN for bare trustees for children; **18** DEATH for provisions relating to death and to personal representatives; **23.84** EXEMPTIONS AND RELIEFS for settlements for the benefit of employees; **25** GIFTS and **30** HOLD-OVER RELIEFS for disposals not at arm's length and the availability of hold-over reliefs generally; **42** OFFSHORE SETTLEMENTS for overseas resident settlements etc.; **47.12** PRIVATE RESIDENCES for reliefs applicable to trustees; **52.12** RETURNS for returns by trustees; **57.10** SHARES AND SECURITIES for stock dividends received by trustees; **65.7** WASTING ASSETS for the situation where a disposal of a life interest in settled property gives rise to a chargeable event.

Simon's Taxes. See I5.9–I5.13.

Introduction to settlements

[56.1] Trustees of a settlement are liable to Capital gains tax (CGT) on disposals of settled property, as if they were a single person. This chapter describes the liability of trustees as well as that of settlors and beneficiaries of settlements. Special rules apply to certain trusts with vulnerable beneficiaries (see **56.13** below).

Also covered in this chapter are the disposals which may arise during the life-cycle of a settlement, from its creation to the termination of a life interest. There are a number of anti-avoidance provisions relevant to settlements and these are covered at **56.19** onwards below.

For the capital gains tax rules which apply where the trustees of a settlement are not resident in the UK see **42** OFFSHORE SETTLEMENTS.

Settlements: definitions

[56.2] The following definitions apply for the purposes of this chapter.

Meaning of 'settled property'

[56.3] '*Settled property*' means any property held in trust other than property held by 'nominees' or 'bare trustees' (see below). References in *TCGA 1992*, however expressed, to property comprised in a settlement are references to settled property. Property held by a trustee or assignee in bankruptcy or under a deed of arrangement (see below) is not settled property. Property under a unit trust scheme (as defined) is also excluded from being settled property. [*TCGA 1992, ss 66(4), 68, 99*]. See also **63.3** UNIT TRUSTS ETC.

Nominees and bare trustees

Where property is held by a person:

(i) as nominee for another or others; or
(ii) as trustee for a person (or persons) 'absolutely entitled' as against them,

capital gains tax is chargeable as if the property were held by that other person or persons and such property were not settled property.

A person is '*absolutely entitled*', for these purposes, if they have the exclusive right (subject only to satisfying any outstanding charge, lien or other right of the trustee to resort to the property for the payment of duty, tax, costs or other outgoings) to direct how that property shall be dealt with, or would have that right but for being an infant or under some other legal disability (e.g. a mentally handicapped person).

[*TCGA 1992, s 60*].

The disability must arise from the general law and not from the wording of the trust deed (see *Tomlinson v Glyns Exor and Trustee Co* CA 1969, 45 TC 600 where the trustees were held assessable to capital gains tax because the beneficiary's interest was contingent on his attaining majority and could not be deemed to be vested in him). In *Booth v Ellard* CA 1980, 53 TC 393, several taxpayers, by agreement, transferred their shares in a company to trustees. The trusts were determinable by a majority of the beneficiaries (who were also the settlors), each beneficiary had a right of pre-emption over the others' shares, and the income was to be distributed in proportion to the number of shares to which each beneficiary was entitled (which corresponded with the number to which he had settled). It was held that each beneficiary retained his interest in the same number of shares as he had settled (albeit not the identical shares). Despite the restraints, it was within the beneficiaries' collective power to terminate the trusts, and each beneficiary was therefore absolutely entitled as against the trustees.

Kidson v Macdonald Ch D 1973, 49 TC 503 laid down that tenants in common of land held on trust for sale were jointly absolutely entitled. It is not necessary that particular assets to which the beneficiaries are entitled should be identifiable (*Stephenson v Barclays Bank Trust Co Ltd* Ch D 1974, 50 TC 374), but see *Cochrane's Exors v CIR* CS 1974, 49 TC 299 (entitlement to residue) and *Crowe v Appleby* CA 1975, 51 TC 457.

Trustees of bare trusts treated as such for tax purposes are not required to complete self-assessment tax returns or make tax payments, the 'beneficiaries' being liable to give details of the income and gains in their own tax returns. The trustees may, *if they wish*, make a self-assessment return of income, and account for basic or lower rate income tax thereon. Capital gains and capital losses *cannot* be included in any such return, these being the sole responsibility of the beneficiaries. (HMRC Trusts, Settlements and Estates Manual TSEM1563).

Insolvents' assets

Assets held by a trustee or assignee in bankruptcy or under a 'deed of arrangement' are treated as if still owned by the bankrupt or debtor (the trustee's acquisitions from, or disposals to, the bankrupt being disregarded) and as if the trustee's acts in relation to those assets were acts of the bankrupt. But tax on chargeable gains arising from such acts is assessable on, and payable by, the trustee, etc. '*Deed of arrangement*' means a deed to which the *Deeds of Arrangement Act 1914* (or any corresponding Act in Scotland or NI) applies. [*TCGA 1992, s 66(1)(5)*].

If, when a person is discharged from bankruptcy, that person reacquires the beneficial ownership of property previously held by a trustee or assignee in bankruptcy, this too is ignored for CGT purposes. The effect is that the person is treated as owning the property throughout the period from original acquisition (*Newfield v HMRC* FTT, [2024] UKFTT 116 (TC)).

When the bankrupt etc. dies, the assets held by the trustee are deemed for the purposes of *TCGA 1992, s 62(1)* (see **18.2** DEATH) to have then been acquired by the trustee as if he were a personal representative. The provisions above do not then apply after death. But if the bankrupt is dead before the trustee is appointed, the provisions above also do not apply, the assets being regarded as held by the deceased's personal representative. [*TCGA 1992, s 66(2)–(4)*].

In re McMeekin QB (NI) 1973, 48 TC 725 it was held that capital gains tax is an administration cost of bankruptcy.

Interests in settled property

[56.4] Interests in settled property take a variety of forms as outlined below. Their treatment for capital gains tax purposes is given in **56.15** to **56.18** below. See **56.3** above as regards bare trusts.

Interests created by or arising under a settlement

These include, in particular, an annuity or life interest (see below), and the reversion to an annuity or life interest, but are otherwise not specifically defined. [*TCGA 1992, s 76*].

Interest in possession in all or part of settled property

Interpretation of the term 'interest in possession' arose in *Pearson and Others v CIR* HL, [1980] STC 318 where the point at issue was the meaning of the term as used in certain capital transfer tax legislation dealing with settled property. The majority opinions of the HL indicated the following.

(a) There must be a *present right to the present enjoyment* of something for there to be an interest in possession in settled property. So a person with an interest in possession will have an immediate right to trust income as it arises.
(b) If the trustees have *any power to withhold income* as it arises there is no interest in possession. There is a distinction between a power to terminate a present right to present enjoyment and a power which prevents a present right of present enjoyment arising. It follows that:
    (i) a power to accumulate income is sufficient to prevent a beneficiary from having an interest in possession. The position is the same if there is a trust to accumulate. Whether or not income is in fact accumulated is irrelevant;
    (ii) an overriding power of appointment which could be used to defeat the interest of a beneficiary does not prevent that interest from being in possession if it does not affect the right of the beneficiary to the income which has already arisen;
    (iii) the possibility of future defeasance of an interest does not prevent it from being in possession until the occurrence of the relevant event; and
    (iv) a power of revocation does not prevent an interest from being in possession until it is exercised.
(c) There is a distinction between trustees' *administrative powers,* such as those to pay duties, taxes etc., and their *dispositive powers* to dispose of the net income of the trust. The existence of the former does not prevent an interest from being in possession. Any interest in possession will be in the net income of the trust after deduction of administrative expenses.
(d) The fact that an interest in settled property is not in remainder or reversion or contingent does not automatically make it an interest in possession.

If, in exercise of their powers under the settlement, the trustees grant a beneficiary an exclusive or joint right to occupy a dwelling-house which forms part of the settled property with the intention of providing the beneficiary with a permanent home, HMRC regard this as creating an interest in possession, even if the right is revocable or for a limited period. A right granted for non-exclusive occupation or for full consideration is not so regarded (HMRC Statement of Practice SP 10/79). See **47.12** PRIVATE RESIDENCES for the exemption available on the disposal of a dwelling-house which has been occupied in the above circumstances.

Meaning of 'settlor'

[56.5] The following extended definition of 'settlor' applies for all capital gains purposes, unless the context otherwise requires. There are, however, also definitions for the purposes of particular provisions.

Subject to the above, a '*settlor*' of a settlement is the person, or any of the persons, who has made, or is treated as having made, the settlement. A person is a settlor of property which is settled property by reason of his having made the settlement or of an event which causes him to be treated as having made the settlement or which derives from such property (see below).

For these purposes, a person is treated as having made a settlement if he has, directly or indirectly, made or entered into the settlement. In particular, a person is so treated if he has provided, or undertaken to provide, property directly or indirectly for the purposes of the settlement. Where the settlement arises by will, intestacy or otherwise on a person's death, that person is treated as having made the settlement if the settled property, or property derived from it, is or includes property of which he was 'competent to dispose immediately before his death'. A person making or entering into a settlement in accordance with reciprocal 'arrangements' with another person is not treated as having made the settlement by reason only of those arrangements. Instead, the other person is treated as having made the settlement.

A settlor is treated as ceasing to be a settlor of a settlement if:

- no property of which he is a settlor remains in the settlement;
- he has not undertaken to provide property directly or indirectly for the purposes of the settlement in the future; and
- he has not made reciprocal arrangements with another person to enter into the settlement in the future.

For the purposes of these provisions, 'arrangements' include a scheme, agreement or understanding, whether or not legally enforceable. Property is derived from other property if it derives, directly or indirectly, wholly or partly, from that property or any part of it or from income from that property or any part of it. Property of which a person was '*competent to dispose immediately before his death*' is any property which (otherwise than in right of a power of appointment or of the testamentary power conferred by statute to dispose of entailed interests) he could, if of full age and capacity, have disposed of by his will, assuming that all the property was situated in England and, if he was not domiciled in the United Kingdom, that he was domiciled in England, and include references to his severable share in any property to which, immediately before his death, he was beneficially entitled as joint tenant.

[*TCGA 1992, ss 62(10), 68A*].

Transfers between settlements

Where there is a 'transfer of property' from the trustees of one settlement to the trustees of a second settlement otherwise than for full consideration or at arm's length, the settlor or settlors of the property so transferred are treated from the time of the transfer as settlors of the second settlement. If there is more than one settlor of the property transferred, each is treated in relation to the second settlement as the settlor of a proportionate part of the 'transferred property'.

There is a '*transfer of property*' for these purposes if there is a disposal of property by the trustees of one settlement and the acquisition by the trustees of the second settlement either of property disposed of by the trustees of the first settlement or property created by the disposal. References above and below to '*transferred property*' are to property acquired by the trustees of the second settlement on the disposal. Where a transfer of property is between trustees who are CONNECTED PERSONS (17) the transfer is not treated as being otherwise than at arm's length by reason of the connection.

If and to the extent that property disposed of by the trustees of the first settlement was provided for the purposes of that settlement or is derived from property so provided, the transferred property is treated from the time of the disposal as having been provided for the purposes of the second settlement by the person or persons who provided the property disposed of or the property from which it was derived (and hence those persons are treated as having made the second settlement). If there is more than one such person each of them is treated as having provided a proportionate part of the transferred property. This does not apply to a transfer of property:

- occurring by reason of the assignment or assignation by a beneficiary of the first settlement of an interest in that settlement to the trustees of the second settlement;
- occurring by reason only of the exercise of a general power of appointment; or
- resulting from a variation of a will or intestacy within the provisions below such that property of which the deceased person is a settlor is comprised in a settlement immediately before the variation and immediately afterwards the property, or property derived from it, becomes comprised in another settlement.

[*TCGA 1992, s 68B*].

Variation of will or intestacy

The following provisions apply where, within two years of a person's death, there is a variation in a disposition of property of which the deceased was competent to dispose to which *TCGA 1992, s 62(6)* (deeds of family arrangement etc. — see **18.8** DEATH) applies.

Where property becomes settled property as a result only of the variation, the following persons are treated as having made the settlement and as having provided property for the purposes of the settlement:

- a person who immediately before the variation was entitled absolutely as legatee to the property or property from which it derives, or who would have been so entitled but for being an infant or other person under a disability; and
- a person who would, but for the variation, have become absolutely entitled as legatee to the property or property from which it derives or who would have become so entitled but for being an infant or other person under a disability.

In determining for this purpose whether a person was, or would be entitled absolutely as legatee, property taken under a testamentary disposition or on an intestacy or partial intestacy includes any property appropriated by the personal representative in or towards satisfaction of a pecuniary legacy or any other interest or share in the property devolving.

Where property which would, but for the variation, have become comprised in an existing settlement (whether or not the deceased was the settlor) or a settlement arising on the death of the deceased person (by will, intestacy or otherwise) instead becomes comprised in another settlement as a result of the variation, the deceased person is treated as having made that other settlement. Unless that settlement arose on the deceased's death, he is treated as having made it immediately before his death.

Where property of which the deceased person is a settlor is comprised in a settlement immediately before the variation and immediately afterwards the property, or property derived from it, becomes comprised in another settlement, the deceased person is treated as having made that other settlement. Unless that settlement arose on the deceased's death, he is treated as having made it immediately before his death.

[*TCGA 1992, s 68C*].

Liability of trustees, settlors and beneficiaries

[56.6] Trustees of a settlement are liable to capital gains tax, under provisions relating to the tax generally, on disposals or deemed disposals of settled property. The exempt amount for a tax year available to trustees is given in **56.8** and **56.9** below.

The trustees of a settlement are treated as if they were a single person (distinct from the persons who may from time to time be trustees). [*TCGA 1992, s 69(1)*]. For the residence etc. status of the deemed person, see **42.1** OFFSHORE SETTLEMENTS. See **56.12** below for the election available for the sub-fund of a settlement to be treated as a separate settlement.

Where an invalid appointment of trustees is made, the trustees of the settlement remain, for this purpose, the validly-appointed trustees, even if the latter believe that they have retired (see *Jasmine Trustees Ltd v Wells and Hind* Ch D, [2007] STC 660). Acts of the purported trustees are attributed to the actual trustees.

Special rules apply to overseas resident settlements etc. See **41** OFFSHORE SETTLEMENTS.

Where part of the property comprised in a settlement is vested in one trustee or set of trustees and part in another (and in particular settled land within the meaning of the *Settled Land Act 1925* is vested in the tenant for life and investments representing capital money are vested in the trustees of the settlement), all the trustees are treated as together constituting and, insofar as they act separately, as acting on behalf of a single body of trustees. [*TCGA 1992, s 69(3)*].

Rates of tax

[56.7] The rates of tax are shown in the table below. [*TCGA 1992, ss 1H(7)(8), 4(3)*].

	2024/25 onwards	2023/24 and earlier
Residential property gains	24%	28%
Gains to which business asset disposal relief applies	10%	10%
Gains to which investors' relief applies	10%	10%
All other chargeable gains	20%	20%

Any allowable losses and annual exempt amounts can be set against the gains in the most beneficial way. [*TCGA 1992, ss 1F(1), 1K(5)*].

Annual exemptions

[56.8] An annual exempt amount (sometimes known as an annual exemption) is allowed to trustees in the same way as it is to individuals, and the same rules apply as to the interaction between this amount and allowable losses. See **2.5** ANNUAL RATES AND EXEMPTIONS.

The level and availability of the exemption are subject to conditions. These are given below or, in the case of settlements for the disabled etc., in **56.9** below.

Settlements made before 7 June 1978

An outright exemption of *one-half* of the full annual exempt amount for individuals is available to trustees of such settlements. The exemption limit is thus £1,500 for 2024/25. Limits for earlier years are as follows.

2023/24	£3,000
2022/23	£6,150
2021/22	£6,150
2020/21	£6,150
2019/20	£6,000

Settlements made after 6 June 1978

The same exemption is available as for settlements made before 7 June 1978 above with the addition of special provisions for 'groups' of settlements. Where a settlement is one of two or more 'qualifying UK settlements' comprised in a group and is not a settlement for the benefit of a disabled person (see **56.9** below), the annual exempt amount is the amount given by dividing one-half of the full annual exempt amount for individuals (see above) by the number of settlements in the group. However, there is a minimum exemption per settlement of one-tenth of the full annual exempt amount for individuals. These provisions apply without regard to any sub-fund settlement elections (see **56.12** above), so that a principal settlement and its sub-fund settlements count as only one settlement for the purpose of dividing up the exempt amount. See also below regarding sub-fund settlements.

A '*qualifying UK settlement*' is any settlement made after 6 June 1978 (or 9 March 1981 in the case of a settlement for the benefit of a disabled person) where:

(i) the trustees are resident in the UK during any part of the tax year in question (see **42.1** OFFSHORE SETTLEMENTS); and
(ii) the property in the settlement is not held for a 'charitable purpose' or a 'pensions purpose'.

For this purpose, property is held for a '*charitable purpose*' if it is held solely for charitable purposes and cannot become applicable for other purposes. Property is held for a '*pensions purpose*' if it is held for the purposes of certain pension schemes and funds which are exempt from a charge on capital gains.

A '*group*' of settlements constitutes all those qualifying UK settlements with the same 'settlor'. Where, in consequence of this, a settlement is comprised in two or more groups because that settlement was made by two or more settlors, then, in determining the level of annual exempt amount available as above, it is deemed to be in the group comprised of the greatest number of settlements.

'*Settlor*' is as in **56.5** above.

[*TCGA 1992, Sch 1C paras 5–7; FA 2021, s 40; FA 2023, s 8; SI 2020 No 333*].

Sub-fund settlements

Where a settlement has been divided for tax purposes into a principal settlement and one or more sub-fund settlements (see **56.12** above), the exempt amount available to the trustees of each deemed settlement is, initially, the amount that would be available to the trustees of the principal settlement under the provisions above or those at **56.9** below if no sub-fund settlement elections had been made. The amount available to each set of trustees is reduced, however, where the deemed settlements include two or more qualifying UK settlements. In such circumstances, the exempt amount available to each set of trustees is equal to the amount otherwise available divided by the number of qualifying UK settlements. For this purpose only, qualifying UK settlements are not restricted to those made after 6 June 1978 (or in the case of a settlement for the benefit of a disabled person, 9 March 1981). [*TCGA 1992, Sch 1C paras 7(4), 8*].

Settlements for the disabled etc.

[56.9] Subject to the 'grouping' provisions below, the same annual exempt amount as for individuals (£3,000 for 2024/25) (applied, in general, as for individuals: see **2.5** ANNUAL RATES AND EXEMPTIONS for this and for exemptions for earlier years) is available to trustees of such settlements if the following conditions are satisfied.

The conditions are that, during the whole or part of the tax year concerned, the settled property is held on trusts which secure that, during the lifetime of a disabled person:

(i) if any of the property is applied for the benefit of a beneficiary it is applied for the benefit of the disabled person; and
(ii) either the disabled person is entitled to all the income (if any) arising from any of the property or that if any such income is applied for the benefit of a beneficiary, it is applied for the benefit of the disabled person.

'*Disabled person*' means either a person who by reason of mental disorder is incapable of administering his property or managing his affairs or a person in receipt of any one or more specified State benefits. A person is treated as being a disabled person for these purposes if he satisfies HMRC that he would be entitled to receive the State benefit in question were it not for his being resident outside the UK or in a care home, hospital or prison.

A trust is not disqualified from the relief by reason only of:

(I) the trustees' having powers that enable them to apply in any tax year otherwise than for the benefit of the disabled person amounts (whether consisting of income or capital or both) not exceeding the 'annual limit'; or
(II) the trustees' having the powers conferred by *Trustee Act 1925, s 32* (powers of advancement) (or its NI equivalent); or
(III) the trustees' having those powers but free from, or subject to a less restrictive limitation than, the limitation imposed by *Trustee Act 1925, s 32(1)(a)* (or its NI equivalent); or
(IV) the trustees' having powers to the like effect as the powers mentioned in (II) or (III).

The '*annual limit*' in (I) above is £3,000 or, if lower, 3% of the maximum value of the settled property during the tax year in question. The Treasury may amend the amount of the annual limit and its application by statutory instrument.

Groups

Where a settlement for the benefit of a disabled person is one of two or more 'qualifying UK settlements' comprised in a 'group', the annual exempt amount is the full annual exempt amount for individuals divided by the number of settlements in the 'group'. However, there is a minimum exemption of one-tenth of the full annual exempt amount. These provisions apply without regard to any sub-fund settlement elections (see **56.12** below), so that a principal settlement and its sub-fund settlements count as only one settlement for the purpose of dividing up the exempt amount. See also **56.8** above.

'*Settlor*', '*qualifying UK settlement*' and '*group*' are as defined in **56.8** above.

[*TCGA 1992, Sch 1C paras 2–4, 6; FA 2021, s 40*].

Collection of unpaid tax from beneficiaries etc.

[56.10] If tax assessed on trustees in respect of a chargeable gain accruing to them is not paid within six months from the date when it becomes payable *and* before or after that date the asset in respect of which the gain accrued, or any part of the proceeds of sale of that asset, is transferred to a person who becomes absolutely entitled to it, or the proceeds etc., that person may be assessed and charged in the name of the trustees within two years from the time when the tax became payable. The tax chargeable is not to exceed the tax chargeable on an amount equal to the chargeable gain and, where only a part of the asset or of the proceeds was transferred, is not to exceed a proportionate part of that amount. [*TCGA 1992, s 69(4)*].

Relevant trustees

[56.11] For the purposes of the assessment and collection of tax on trust income and gains where there is more than one trustee, anything done by a 'relevant trustee' is regarded as done by all the relevant trustees, including the making of returns and self-assessment. Liability for penalties, interest or surcharges may be recovered (but only once) from any one or more of the relevant trustees other than one who was not a relevant trustee at the relevant time (as defined by *TMA 1970, s 107A(3))*. In relation to chargeable gains, the 'relevant trustees' of a settlement are the persons who are trustees in the tax year in which the gains accrue and any persons who subsequently become trustees. [*TMA 1970, ss 7(2)(9), 8A(1)(5), 107A, 118(1); FA 2021, Sch 27 para 9*].

Chargeable gains which accrue to a settlement can be assessed on any relevant trustee (see **6.6** ASSESSMENTS).

Sub-fund settlements

[56.12] Trustees of a settlement (the '*principal settlement*') may make an irrevocable election under which a specified part (a '*sub-fund*') of the settled property is treated for capital gains tax purposes as a separate settlement, known as a '*sub-fund settlement*'. [*TCGA 1992, s 69A, Sch 4ZA paras 1, 13*].

The election applies also for income tax purposes (see *ITA 2007, s 477* and Tolley's Income Tax).

For an election to be made, the principal settlement must not be itself a sub-fund settlement, and the following conditions must be satisfied when the election is made and throughout the period (if any) beginning with the time the election is treated as taking effect (see below) and ending immediately before it is made.

(i) The sub-fund must not be the whole of the property comprised in the principal settlement.

(ii) On the assumption that the election had then taken effect, the sub-fund settlement would not include an 'interest' in any asset in which an interest was retained by the principal settlement. The provisions of *TCGA 1992, s 104* and *s 109* treating certain holdings of shares etc. as a single asset (see **58.2** shares and securities — identification rules) are ignored for this purpose. An '*interest*' in an asset means an interest as co-owner, whether the asset is owned jointly or in common and whether or not the interests of the co-owners are equal.

(iii) On the assumption that the election had then taken effect, nobody would be a beneficiary of both the sub-fund settlement and the principal settlement. A person is a beneficiary of a settlement for this purpose if any property which is or may at any time be comprised in the settlement, or any 'derived property', is or will or may be payable to him or applicable for his benefit in any circumstances whatsoever, or if he enjoys a benefit deriving directly or indirectly from any property comprised in the settlement or any derived property. '*Derived property*' means income from other property, property directly or indirectly representing proceeds of, or of income from, other property or income from property which is itself derived property.

A person is not treated as a beneficiary, however, if property comprised in the settlement or any derived property will or may become payable to him or applicable for his benefit by reason only of:

- his marrying or becoming a civil partner of a beneficiary;
- the death of a beneficiary;
- the exercise by the trustees of the principal settlement of a power of advancement within *Trustee Act 1925, s 32* (or Northern Ireland equivalent), a similar power conferred by the law of a jurisdiction other than England and Wales or Northern Ireland, or a power of advancement which is subject to the same restrictions as those specified in *Trustee Act 1925, s 32(1)(a)(c)* and which is conferred by either the instrument creating the settlement or another instrument made in accordance with the terms of the settlement; or
- the failure or determination of protective trusts within *Trustee Act 1925, s 33*.

[*TCGA 1992, Sch 4ZA paras 3–9*].

Making an election

An election, which is irrevocable, must be made by notice in writing to HMRC in such form as HMRC may require. The notice must specify the date on which the election is to be treated as having taken effect, which must not be later than the date on which it is made. The election must be made within one year after 31 January following the tax year in which the date on which it is to be treated as taking effect falls. An election must include:

- a declaration of consent by each trustee of the principal settlement;
- a statement by those trustees that the conditions for making an election are satisfied;
- such information as HMRC may require in relation to the principal settlement including, in particular, information relating to the trustees, the trusts, property comprised in the settlement, the settlors and the beneficiaries;
- a declaration by the trustees of the principal settlement that the information given in the election is correct to the best of their knowledge and belief; and
- such other declarations as HMRC may require.

A penalty under *TMA 1970, s 98* applies for fraudulently or negligently providing incorrect information in an election.

[*TCGA 1992, s 288(1), Sch 4ZA paras 10–16*].

Consequences of an election

A sub-fund settlement election takes effect at the beginning of the day specified in the election. If there is a deemed disposal by the trustees of the principal settlement at the beginning of that day under the provisions below, the election is deemed to take effect on that day immediately after that disposal.

The sub-fund settlement is treated as having been created at the time the election takes effect. Each trustee of the trusts on which the property in the sub-fund settlement is held is treated as a trustee of the sub-fund settlement and, unless he is also a trustee of trusts on which property in the principal settlement is held, as ceasing to be a trustee of the principal settlement from the time the election takes effect. A trustee of the principal settlement is not treated as a trustee of the sub-fund settlement unless he is also a trustee of trusts on which property in that settlement is held.

The trustees of the sub-fund settlement are treated as becoming absolutely entitled to the property comprised in that settlement as against the trustees of the principal settlement at the time the election takes effect.

The taking effect of the election may trigger deemed disposals by the trustees of the principal settlement under:

(a) *TCGA 1992, s 71(1)* (person becoming absolutely entitled to settled property — see **56.16** below); and
(b) *TCGA 1992, s 80(2)* (see **42.2** OFFSHORE SETTLEMENTS) where the principal settlement becomes non-UK resident as a result of the trustees of the sub-fund settlement ceasing to be trustees of the principal settlement.

Such a deemed disposal is treated as being made at the beginning of the day on which the election takes effect. No deemed disposal of an asset is treated as being made by virtue of (b) above if there is a deemed disposal of the same asset by virtue of (a) above. Any assets acquired by the trustees of the sub-fund settlement in respect of which there is a deemed disposal are treated as acquired by them at the time the election takes effect.

If the trustees of the sub-fund settlement are treated as becoming absolutely entitled as above to money expressed in sterling they are treated as acquiring it at the time the election takes effect and the trustees of the principal settlement are treated as disposing of it at the beginning of the day on which the election takes effect.

In the case of non-resident settlements, if there is a deemed disposal of an asset within (a) above when the election takes effect, then for the purposes of the provisions charging beneficiaries to capital gains tax in respect of capital payments (see **42.13** OFFSHORE SETTLEMENTS) and the further charge on such beneficiaries (see **42.21** OFFSHORE SETTLEMENTS), the trustees of the principal settlement are treated as having transferred the asset to the sub-fund settlement trustees (so that the relevant provisions for transfers between settlements may apply). This applies also if there would have been such a deemed disposal at that time of money expressed in sterling if (a) above applied to such property.

[*TCGA 1992, Sch 4ZA paras 2, 17–22*].

HMRC accept that where the transaction creating the sub-fund settlement is a chargeable transfer for inheritance tax purposes and it takes place on the day the election takes effect, the deemed disposal will qualify for relief under *TCGA 1992, s 260* (see **30.10** HOLD-OVER RELIEFS). (HMRC Capital Gains Manual, CG33330).

Trusts with vulnerable beneficiary

[56.13] The trustees of a settlement may claim special tax treatment for a tax year if:

- in that year they hold property on 'qualifying trusts' for the benefit of a 'vulnerable person', and
- a 'vulnerable person election' has effect for all or part of that year in relation to those trusts and that person.

[*FA 2005, ss 23, 24, 45*].

The claim has effect for both income tax and capital gains tax purposes; for the income tax consequences see Tolley's Income Tax.

Definitions

A '*vulnerable person*' is a 'disabled person' or a 'relevant minor'.

The meaning of '*disabled person*' is given by *FA 2005, Sch 1A*. It means either a person who by reason of mental disorder is incapable of administering his property or managing his affairs or a person in receipt of any one or more specified State benefits. A person is treated as being a disabled person for these purposes if he satisfies HMRC that he would be entitled to receive the State benefit in question were it not for his being resident outside the UK or in a care home, hospital or prison.

A person under the age of 18 is a '*relevant minor*' if at least one of his parents has died.

Where property is held on trusts for the benefit of a disabled person, those trusts are '*qualifying trusts*' if they secure that, during the lifetime of the disabled person or until the termination of the trusts (if earlier) the following conditions are satisfied. The conditions are:

- that if any of the property is applied for the benefit of a beneficiary it is applied for the benefit of the disabled person; and
- either that the disabled person is entitled to all the income (if any) arising from any of the property or that if any such income is applied for the benefit of a beneficiary, it is applied for the benefit of the disabled person.

But, the trusts are not to be treated as failing to secure that the above conditions are met by reason only of:

(a) the trustees' having powers that enable them to apply in any tax year otherwise than for the benefit of the disabled person amounts (whether consisting of income or capital or both) not exceeding the 'annual limit'; or

(b) the trustees' having the powers conferred by *Trustee Act 1925, s 32* (powers of advancement) (or its NI equivalent); or
(c) the trustees' having those powers but free from, or subject to a less restrictive limitation than, the limitation imposed by *Trustee Act 1925, s 32(1)(a)* (or its NI equivalent); or
(d) the trustees' having powers to the like effect as the powers mentioned in (b) or (c).

The '*annual limit*' in (a) above is £3,000 or, if lower, 3% of the maximum value of the settled property during the tax year in question.

If the property is held on trusts of the kind described in *Trustee Act 1925, s 33* (protective trusts), the reference above to 'the lifetime of the disabled person' is to be interpreted as the period during which the property is held on trust for him.

Where property is held on trusts for the benefit of a relevant minor, those trusts are '*qualifying trusts*' if they are:

(i) statutory trusts for the relevant minor under *Administration of Estates Act 1925, ss 46, 47(1)* (succession on intestacy and statutory trusts in favour of relatives of intestate);
(ii) trusts established under the will of a deceased parent of the relevant minor; or
(iii) trusts established under the Criminal Injuries Compensation Scheme (i.e. schemes established under *Criminal Injuries Compensation Act 1995*, arrangements made by the Secretary of State for compensation for criminal injuries in operation before the commencement of those schemes or the scheme established under the *Criminal Injuries (Northern Ireland) Order 2002 SI 2002 No 796*).

Trusts within (ii) or (iii) above must secure that:

- when the relevant minor reaches 18 he will become absolutely entitled to the property, any income arising from it, and any income that has arisen from property held on the trusts for his benefit which has been accumulated before that time;
- until the relevant minor reaches 18 (so long as he is living), any property applied for the benefit of a beneficiary is applied for his benefit; and
- until the relevant minor reaches 18 (so long as he is living), either the minor is entitled to all the income (if any) arising from any of the property or if any such income is applied for the benefit of a beneficiary, it is applied for the benefit of the minor.

But trusts are not to be regarded as failing to secure the meeting of these conditions by reason only of the trustees' having powers as in (a)–(d) above.

For the purposes of these provisions, property held on trusts includes a part of an asset if that part (and any income arising from it) can be identified for the purpose of determining whether the trusts are qualifying trusts.

[*FA 2005, ss 23(7), 34–36, 38, 39, Sch 1A*].

The above definitions apply in Scotland with certain modifications (see *FA 2005, s 42*).

Vulnerable person election

A '*vulnerable person election*' can be made jointly by the trustees and a beneficiary if the trusts are qualifying trusts and the beneficiary is a vulnerable person. The election is irrevocable and must be made by notice in writing to HMRC in such form as they may require. It must specify the date from which it will take effect and be made within twelve months of 31 January following the tax year in which that date falls or within such further time as HMRC may by notice allow. The notice of election must include a statement that the trusts are qualifying trusts, a declaration that all the information included is correct to the best of the knowledge and belief of the trustees and beneficiary, a declaration by the beneficiary that he authorises the trustees to make a claim under these provisions for any tax year as they consider appropriate, and any other information and declarations as HMRC may require.

An election is effective until the beneficiary ceases to be a vulnerable person or the trusts cease to be qualifying trusts or are terminated. Where the trustees become aware that one of these events has occurred, they must, subject to a penalty under *TMA 1970, s 98* for failure, notify HMRC that the election has ceased to have effect within 90 days beginning on the day on which they first became aware of the event.

Where property held on trusts in respect of which an election is in force is treated for tax purposes as comprised in a sub-fund settlement (see **56.12** above) and the election was not made by the trustees of that settlement, the election applies to those trusts as if it had been made by those trustees and the vulnerable person. This treatment does not relieve the trustees of the principal settlement (see **56.12** above) from their notification obligations under the above provisions in relation to matters arising before the sub-fund settlement election took effect.

HMRC have powers to require the trustees or the vulnerable person by notice in writing to provide any particulars that they may require to determine whether the requirements for an election were met at the time it was made or whether an event has occurred such that the election ceases to be effective. The notice must specify the time (at least 60 days) within which the information must be provided. If HMRC determine that the requirements were not so met or that such an event has occurred they may give notice in writing to the trustees and the vulnerable person that the election never had effect or, as appropriate, that it ceased to have effect from a specified date. This is subject to a right of appeal, which must be made within 30 days after the notice was given. The provisions above which treat an election as made by trustees of a sub-fund settlement do not prevent HMRC from issuing a notice to the trustees of the principal settlement in relation to matters arising before the sub-fund settlement election took effect.

[*FA 2005, ss 37, 40, 41(1), 43*].

Capital gains tax

The special capital gains tax treatment described below applies for a tax year if:

(1) chargeable gains (the '*qualifying trusts gains*') accrue in that year to the trustees of a settlement from the disposal of settled property (see **56.3** above) which is held on qualifying trusts for the benefit of a vulnerable person;
(2) the trustees would (apart from these provisions) be chargeable to capital gains tax in respect of those gains;
(3) the trustees are resident in the UK during any part of the year (see **56.6** above); and
(4) a claim for special tax treatment for the year is made by the trustees. (Note that a claim applies for income tax purposes also.)

The treatment does not apply for a tax year in which the vulnerable person dies.

The qualifying trusts gains in (1) above include attributed gains of non-resident companies within **43.7** OVERSEAS MATTERS.

[*FA 2005, s 30*].

UK resident vulnerable person

If the vulnerable person is UK resident for the tax year, then the trustees' liability to capital gains tax for the year is reduced by an amount equal to:

TQTG – (TLVA –TLVB)

where:

TQTG = the amount of capital gains tax to which the trustees would, apart from these provisions, be liable for the tax year in respect of qualifying trust gains;
TLVB = the total amount of capital gains tax to which the vulnerable person is liable for the tax year; and
TLVA = what TLVB would be if the qualifying trust gains accrued to the vulnerable person instead of the trustees, and no allowable losses were deducted from them.

[*FA 2005, ss 31, 41(2)(a)*].

Example

Harry was born in 2009. In June 2015, both of his parents were killed in a road accident. Neither parent has made a will, so that a statutory trust is established for Harry under the intestacy rules of *Administration of Estates Act 1925, ss 46, 47(1)*. The trustees and Harry's guardian make a vulnerable person election (by 31 January 2019) to take effect on 6 April 2016. On 16 May 2024, the trustees sell an asset, realising a chargeable gain of £20,000. The trustees (who are resident in the UK throughout) make no other disposals in 2024/25. Harry is resident in the UK throughout the tax year and has no personal chargeable gains. If the gain had been taxable on Harry, CGT would have been payable at 10%.

If the trustees make a claim for special tax treatment under *FA 2005, s 24* for 2024/25, their capital gains tax liability is calculated as follows.

	£
Gain	20,000

	£
Annual exempt amount	1,500
Taxable gain 2024/25	£18,500
CGT £18,500 × 20%	3,700.00
Less reduction under *FA 2005, s 31*	2,000.00
CGT payable by trustees	£1,700.00

The reduction under *FA 2005, s 31* is equal to:

TQTG – (TLVA – TLVB)

In this case, TQTG = £3,700.00 (as above), TLVB is nil, and TLVA is calculated as follows.

	£
Gain	20,000
Annual exempt amount	3,000
Taxable gain	£17,000
CGT £17,000 × 10% (TLVA)	£1,700.00
The reduction is therefore £3,700 – (£1,700 – Nil) =	£2,000.00

Non-resident vulnerable person

If the vulnerable person is not UK resident for the tax year, the trustees' liability to capital gains tax for the year is reduced by an amount equal to:

TQTG – (TLVC –TLVD)

where:

TQTG = the amount of capital gains tax to which the trustees would, apart from these provisions, be liable for the tax year in respect of qualifying trust gains;
TLVD = the total amount of capital gains tax to which the vulnerable person would be liable for the tax year if his 'taxable amount' for capital gains tax purposes for the tax year were equal to his 'deemed CGT taxable amount'; and
TLVC = what TLVD would be if his taxable amount for capital gains tax were equal to the aggregate of his deemed CGT taxable amount and the amount of the qualifying trust gains.

For this purpose, the vulnerable person's '*actual income*' for a tax year is the income which would be assessable to income tax for the year on the assumption that he was resident and domiciled in the UK throughout the year. The '*trustees' specially taxed income*' for a tax year is the income of the trustees for the year from property held on qualifying trusts for the benefit of the vulnerable person in connection with which special income tax treatment applies by virtue of a claim under these provisions.

The vulnerable person's '*taxable amount*' for a tax year is the amount on which he would be chargeable to CGT for the year if no annual exempt amount were deducted. The *deemed CGT taxable amount*' for a tax year is the total of his taxable amount for the year calculated by reference only to 'actual gains' and 'actual losses' and his taxable amount calculated only by reference to 'assumed gains' and 'assumed losses'. Any claims or elections made in relation to any assumed gains are disregarded. In calculating the taxable amount by reference to assumed gains and assumed losses, no deduction is made for losses brought forward or, on the death of the vulnerable person, for losses carried back.

The '*actual gains*' are any chargeable gains accruing to the vulnerable person in respect of which he is chargeable to capital gains tax for the tax year. '*Actual losses*' are allowable losses, including losses brought forward. '*Assumed gains*' are any chargeable gains, other than actual gains, in respect of which the vulnerable person would be chargeable to capital gains tax on the assumption that:

(A) he is resident and domiciled in the UK throughout the tax year; and
(B) he has given a notice to HMRC quantifying the amount of any losses accruing in the tax year (see **38.5** LOSSES).

Note that assumption (A) above does not apply for the purposes of *TCGA 1992, s 1M* (previously *TCGA 1992, s 10A*; temporary non-residents — see **43.5** OVERSEAS MATTERS).

'*Assumed losses*' are any allowable losses, other than actual losses, which would accrue to the vulnerable person for the tax year on the same assumptions as apply for calculating assumed gains.

[*FA 2005, ss 32, 33, 41(2), Sch 1*].

For HMRC guidance on trusts with vulnerable beneficiaries, see HMRC Capital Gains Manual CG35500–35543.

Disposals during the life-cycle of a settlement

Creation of a settlement

[56.14] The provisions described at **56.14–56.18** apply to the various occasions during the life-cycle of a settlement when chargeable gains may arise.

A transfer into settlement, whether revocable or irrevocable, is a disposal of the entire property settled even if the transferor is a beneficiary or trustee of the settlement. [*TCGA 1992, s 70*]. The acquisition and disposal are treated as being made at MARKET VALUE (**39**) subject to the exclusion at **39.1** MARKET VALUE. HOLD-OVER RELIEFS (**30**) may be available in respect of chargeable gains that would otherwise arise to the settlor. The settlor of a settlement and the trustees of that settlement are CONNECTED PERSONS (**17**) and further rules may operate as to valuation and losses (in particular see **4.13** and **4.14** ANTI-AVOIDANCE, **39.1** MARKET VALUE and **38.7** LOSSES).

Example

In December 2024, C transfers to trustees of a settlement for the benefit of his disabled daughter 10,000 shares in W plc, a quoted company. The value of the gift is £85,000. C bought the shares in 2001 for £35,000.

	£
Deemed disposal consideration	85,000
Acquisition cost	35,000
Chargeable gain	£50,000
Trustees' allowable cost	£85,000

Note to the example

(a) If the transfer is a chargeable lifetime transfer for inheritance tax purposes, or would be one but for the annual inheritance tax exemption and C does not have an interest in the settlement within *TCGA 1992, s 169F* (see **30.8** HOLD-OVER RELIEFS), C could elect under *TCGA 1992, s 260* to hold the gain over against the trustees' base cost of the shares. The trustees do not join in any such election.

Exercise of power of appointment or advancement

For the consequences of the exercise of such a power see *Hoare Trustees v Gardner*; *Hart v Briscoe* Ch D 1977, 52 TC 53; *Chinn v Collins* HL 1980, 54 TC 311; *Roome v Edwards* HL 1981, 54 TC 359; *Eilbeck v Rawling* HL 1981, 54 TC 101; *Bond v Pickford* CA 1983, 57 TC 301; *Swires v Renton* Ch D 1991, 64 TC 315.

Following the decision in *Bond v Pickford* above, the Revenue issued Statement of Practice SP 7/84 to set out their views on the capital gains tax implications of the exercise of a power of appointment or advancement when continuing trusts are declared.

The Revenue stated in SP 7/84 that the judgments in *Roome v Edwards* emphasised that, in deciding whether or not a new settlement has been created by the exercise of a power of appointment or advancement, each case must be considered on its own facts, and by applying established legal doctrine to the facts in a practical and commonsense manner. The Court of Appeal judgments in *Bond v Pickford* explained that the consideration of the facts must include examination of the powers which the trustees purported to exercise, and the determination of the intention of the parties, viewed objectively.

HMRC consider that a deemed disposal under *TCGA 1992, s 71(1)* (see **56.16** below) cannot arise unless the power exercised by the trustees, or the instrument conferring the power, expressly or by necessary implication, confers on the trustees authority to remove assets from the original settlement by subjecting them to trusts of a different settlement. Such powers (which may be powers of advancement or appointment) were referred to by the Court of Appeal in *Bond v Pickford* as 'powers in the wider form'. HMRC consider that a deemed disposal will not arise when such powers are exercised and trusts are declared in circumstances such that:

(a) the appointment is revocable; or
(b) the trusts declared of the advanced or appointed funds are not exhaustive so that there exists a possibility at the time when the advancement or appointment is made that the funds covered by it will, on the occasion of some event, cease to be held upon such trusts and once again come to be held upon the original trusts of the settlement.

HMRC also consider it unlikely a deemed disposal will occur when trusts are declared following the exercise of such a power if the duties of trusteeship as regards the appointed assets fall to the trustees of the original settlement. This follows from the provision in *TCGA 1992, s 69(1)* that the trustees of a settlement form a single and continuing body (see **56.6** above).

In conclusion, HMRC accept that a power of appointment or advancement can be exercised over only a part of settled property and that the foregoing would apply to that part.

Disposal of an interest in settled property

[56.15] Subject to the exclusions below for settlements which are, or have ever been, non-resident settlements, no chargeable gain accrues on the disposal of an interest created by or arising under a settlement (see **56.4** above) if the disposal was made:

(a) by the person for whose benefit the interest was created by the terms of the settlement; or
(b) by any other person except one who acquired, or derives his title from one who acquired, the interest for a consideration in money or money's worth, other than consideration consisting of another interest under the settlement.

Subject to the above, where a person who has acquired an interest in settled property becomes, as the holder of that interest, absolutely entitled (see **56.3** above) as against the trustee to any settled property, he is treated as disposing of the interest in consideration of obtaining the property so received (but without prejudice to any gain accruing to the trustee on the deemed disposal by the trustee under *TCGA 1992, s 71(1)* (see **56.16** below)).

[*TCGA 1992, s 76(1)(2)*].

Where the disposal of a life interest in settled property does give rise to a chargeable event, the interest may be treated as a wasting asset in certain circumstances. See **65.7** WASTING ASSETS.

See **56.20** below for anti-avoidance provisions deeming there to be, in specified circumstances, a disposal of underlying assets at the same time as an actual disposal of an interest in settled property for consideration.

Exclusion for non-resident settlements

The exemption above does not apply to disposals of interests in settlements which are, or have ever been, non-resident. See **42.4** OFFSHORE SETTLEMENTS.

Person becoming absolutely entitled to settled property

[56.16] Subject to the exception below, where a person becomes absolutely entitled to any settled property as against the trustee, all the assets forming part of the settled property to which he becomes so entitled are deemed to have been disposed of by the trustee and immediately reacquired by him in the capacity of bare trustee or nominee within *TCGA 1992, s 60(1)* (see **56.3** above) for a consideration equal to the market value of the assets. [*TCGA 1992, s 71(1)*].

See *Figg v Clarke* Ch D 1996, 68 TC 645 for interpretation of date of absolute entitlement. See also *McLaughlin v HMRC* FTT, [2012] SFTD 1003 for discussion of circumstances in which a person becomes absolutely entitled.

Where an interest in possession in part of settled property terminates (whether voluntarily or involuntarily) and the part can properly be identified with one or more specific assets, or where within a reasonable time, normally three months, of the termination, the trustees appropriate specific assets to give effect to the termination, HMRC will treat the deemed disposal and reacquisition as applying to those assets, and not to any part of the other assets comprised in the settlement. In particular, agreement will be made of lists of assets properly identifiable with the termination, and any such agreement will be regarded as binding on HMRC and the trustees (HMRC Statement of Practice SP D10).

Any resulting net chargeable gain is assessed on the trustee in the usual way (subject to a claim for HOLD-OVER RELIEFS (**30**)).

Losses

Where a person (the beneficiary) becomes absolutely entitled to any settled property as against the trustee and a loss accrues to the trustee on the resulting deemed disposal under *TCGA 1992, s 71(1)* (see above) of an asset comprised in that property, then, subject to the restrictions below, the loss is treated as a loss accruing to the beneficiary instead of to the trustee.

Such treatment is mandatory, but applies only to the extent that the loss cannot be deducted from gains accruing to the trustee either on the deemed disposal of other assets on that occasion or on disposals made earlier in the same year of assessment, and for this purpose only such a loss is treated as deductible in priority to any other allowable losses accruing to the trustee in that year.

Where a loss is so treated as accruing to the beneficiary, it is allowable *only* against chargeable gains accruing to him on disposal by him of the same asset, i.e. the asset on the deemed disposal of which the loss occurred, or, where the asset is land, any asset which is 'derived' from it (as defined). The loss can be carried forward to subsequent years of assessment until such time as it has been fully allowed against such gains. Where there is such a gain, the loss in question is treated as deductible in priority to any other allowable losses accruing to the beneficiary in the year of assessment concerned and, where it is brought forward, is deductible as if it were a loss accruing in that year (see **38.2** LOSSES for set-off of losses generally). For a worked example, see Tolley's Tax Computations.

These provisions are equally applicable where it is another set of trustees who become absolutely entitled as against the trustees with the losses (HMRC Capital Gains Manual CG37209).

[*TCGA 1992, s 71(2)–(2D)*].

The position should be contrasted with that of allowable losses made by personal representatives as in **18.9** DEATH.

Where trust losses are transferable to a beneficiary as above, HMRC do not restrict those losses under *TCGA 1992, s 18(3)* (see **38.7** LOSSES) where the trustees and the person becoming absolutely entitled are CONNECTED PERSONS (**17**) (Revenue Tax Bulletin February 1993 p 57).

No loss is transferable to beneficiaries unless it has been notified by the trustees under the normal self-assessment rules at **38.5** LOSSES (HMRC Capital Gains Manual CG37210).

Miscellaneous

References in the above to the case where a person becomes absolutely entitled to settled property as against the trustee include references to the case where a person would become so entitled but for being an infant or other person under disability. [*TCGA 1992, s 71(3)*].

Where a person disposes of an asset held by another person as trustee to which he became absolutely entitled as against the trustee, any incidental expenditure incurred by that person or the trustee in relation to the transfer of the asset to him is allowable as a deduction in the computation of the gain arising on the disposal. [*TCGA 1992, s 64(1)*].

Exception where an interest is terminated by the death of the person entitled thereto

Where, as above, a person becomes absolutely entitled as against the trustee to assets forming part of settled property and that occasion is the termination of an interest in possession by the death of the person entitled to that interest then, where that interest meets certain conditions (and, subject to exceptions), *no* chargeable gain arises on the deemed disposal. See **56.18**(a) below for full details.

Termination of interest in possession on death of person entitled — assets remaining settled property

[56.17] Where an interest in possession in all or part (see SP D10 in **56.16** above) of settled property is terminated on the death of the person entitled to it (e.g. a life tenant), the whole or a corresponding part of each of the assets forming part of the settled property and not at that time ceasing to be settled property is deemed to be disposed of and immediately reacquired by the trustee at that time for a consideration equal to the whole or a corresponding part of the market value of the asset. However, any gain arising on such a deemed disposal is not a chargeable gain. Where the deceased became entitled to the interest in possession on or after 22 March 2006, this applies only if:

(i) the deceased died under the age of 18 and, immediately before his death, *IHTA 1984, s 71D* (age 18 to 25 trusts) applies to the property in which the interest subsists; or

(ii) immediately before his death:
  (a) the interest in possession is an immediate post-death interest within *IHTA 1984, s 49A*;
  (b) the interest is a transitional serial interest within *IHTA 1984, s 49B*;
  (c) the interest is a disabled person's interest within *IHTA 1984, s 89B*; or
  (d) *IHTA 1984, s 71A* (trusts for bereaved minors) applies to the property in which the interest subsists.

[*TCGA 1992, s 72(1)–(1C)*].

(See the exception below as regards previously held-over gains.)

The above provisions also apply where the person entitled to an interest in possession in all or part of the settled property dies but the interest does not then terminate. Again, where the deceased became entitled to the interest in possession on or after 22 March 2006, this applies only if, immediately before his death, one of (ii)(a) to (c) above applies. [*TCGA 1992, s 72(2)(2A)*].

Annuities

The above provisions apply on the death of the person entitled to any annuity payable out of, or charged on, settled property or the income of settled property as it applies on the death of a person whose interest in possession in the whole or any part of settled property terminates on his death. Where, in the case of any entitlement to an annuity created by a settlement some of the settled property is appropriated by the trustees as a fund out of which the annuity is payable, and there is no right of recourse to, or to the income of, settled property not so appropriated, then without prejudice to *TCGA 1992, s 72(5)* below, the settled property so appropriated is, while the annuity is payable, and on the occasion of the death of the person entitled to the annuity, treated for the purposes of *TCGA 1992, s 72* as being settled property under a separate settlement. [*TCGA 1992, s 72(3)(4)*]. In the case where the annuity is not paid out of specified funds, HMRC treats the corresponding part (see above) of the assets forming the settled property as being given by the proportion which the amount of the annuity bears to the whole of the settlement income arising in the year prior to the date of death.

Part interests and income interests

For the purposes of the above provisions, an interest which is a right to part of the income of settled property is treated as such an interest in a corresponding part of the settled property. [*TCGA 1992, s 72(1)*].

If there is an interest in income in a part of settled property such that there is no right of recourse to, or to the income from, the remainder of the settled property, then the part of the settled property in which such interest subsists is similarly treated as being settled property under a separate settlement for so long as such an interest subsists. [*TCGA 1992, s 72(5)*].

Disabled person's interests

Disabled person's interests within *IHTA 1984, s 89B(1)(a)(b)* (which are treated as interests in possession for inheritance tax purposes) are treated as interests in possession for the purposes of the above provisions. [*TCGA 1992, s 72(6)*].

Exception where hold-over relief under *TCGA 1992, s 165* or *s 260* or *FA 1980, s 79* claimed previously

In certain circumstances where a claim has been made for hold-over relief in respect of the disposal of an asset to the trustee and, subsequently, the trustee is deemed to dispose of and immediately reacquire the asset so that under *TCGA 1992, s 72* above there would otherwise be no chargeable gain arising, it is specifically provided by *TCGA 1992, s 67* or *s 74* that a chargeable gain, restricted to the amount of the held-over gain, is to accrue to the trustee. See **30.8**, **30.11** and **30.12** HOLD-OVER RELIEFS.

Termination of interest on death of person entitled — person becoming absolutely entitled

[56.18] The following applies on the termination of an interest in possession where property leaves the trust.

(a) Where, under *TCGA 1992, s 71(1)* in **56.16** above, the assets forming part of any settled property are deemed to be disposed of and reacquired at market value by the trustee on the occasion when a person becomes, or would but for a disability become, absolutely entitled thereto as against the trustee, then, if that occasion is the death of a person entitled to an interest in possession in the settled property (e.g. the death of a life tenant):
   (i) no chargeable gain accrues on the deemed disposal; and
   (ii) if on the death the property reverts to the disponer (e.g. the original settlor), the disposal and reacquisition by the trustee is treated as taking place on a no gain/no loss basis, and if the acquisition by the trustee was at a time prior to 31 March 1982, the reversion is related back to that date.

   In relation to a sub-fund settlement (see **56.12** above), (ii) above is treated as applying if the property does not revert to the trustees of the principal settlement (see **56.12** above) only because it becomes comprised in another sub-fund of the principal settlement in respect of which a sub-fund settlement election is in force.

(b) Where the interest is an interest in part (see SP D10 in **56.16** above) only of the settled property to which the person becomes absolutely entitled, (a)(i) above does not apply but although a chargeable gain will accordingly arise as under *TCGA 1992, s 71(1)* in **56.16** above it is reduced by a proportion corresponding to that represented by the part in which the interest subsisted. Any remaining chargeable gain may be the subject of a claim for one of the HOLD-OVER RELIEFS (**30**).

Where the deceased became entitled to the interest in possession on or after 22 March 2006, these provisions apply only if either **56.17**(i) or (ii) above applies.

[*TCGA 1992, s 73(1)(2)(2A)*].

(See the exception below as regards previously held-over gains.)

Annuities

The above provisions apply on the death of the person entitled to any annuity payable out of, or charged on, settled property or the income of settled property as it applies on the death of a person whose interest in possession in the whole or any part of settled property terminates on his death. Where, in the case of any entitlement to an annuity created by a settlement some of the settled property is appropriated by the trustees as a fund out of which the annuity is payable, and there is no right of recourse to, or to the income of, settled property not so appropriated, then without prejudice to *TCGA 1992, s 72(5)* below, the settled property so appropriated is, while the annuity is payable, and on the occasion of the death of the person entitled to the annuity, treated for the purposes of *TCGA 1992, s 72* as being settled property under a separate settlement. [*TCGA 1992, ss 72(3)(4), 73(3)*]. In the case where the annuity is not paid out of specified funds, HMRC treats the 'proportion corresponding to that represented by the part in which the interest subsisted' (see (b) above) of the assets forming the settled property as being given by the proportion which the amount of the annuity bears to the whole of the settlement income arising in the year prior to the date of death.

Part interests and income interests

For the purposes of (a) and (b) above, an interest which is a right to part of the income of settled property is treated as such an interest in a corresponding part of the settled property. [*TCGA 1992, ss 72(1), 73(3)*].

If there is an interest in income in a part of settled property such that there is no right of recourse to, or to the income from, the remainder of the settled property, then the part of the settled property in which such interest subsists is similarly treated as being settled property under a separate settlement for so long as such an interest subsists. [*TCGA 1992, ss 72(5), 73(3)*].

Disabled person's interests

Disabled person's interests within *IHTA 1984, s 89B(1)(a)(b)* (which are treated as interests in possession for inheritance tax purposes) are treated as interests in possession for the purposes of the above provisions. [*TCGA 1992, ss 72(6), 73(3)*].

Exception where hold-over relief under *TCGA 1992, s 165* or *s 260* or *FA 1980, s 79* claimed previously

In certain circumstances where a claim has been made for hold-over relief in respect of the disposal of an asset to the trustee and, subsequently, the trustee is deemed to dispose of and immediately reacquire the asset so that under *TCGA 1992, s 73* above there would otherwise be no chargeable gain arising, it is specifically provided by *TCGA 1992, s 67* or *s 74* that a chargeable gain, restricted to the amount of the held-over gain, is to accrue to the trustee. See **30.8, 30.11** and **30.12** HOLD-OVER RELIEFS.

Anti-avoidance

[56.19] A number of anti-avoidance provisions apply specifically to settlements and these are described at 56.20–56.22 below.

Deemed disposal of underlying assets on certain disposals of interests in settled property

[56.20] Cross-reference. See 56.15 above for the general exemption from CGT on a disposal of an interest in settled property.

Deemed disposal

Where:

- a disposal of an 'interest in settled property' is made, or is effectively completed (see below under Time lapse before effective completion),
- the disposal is 'for consideration', and
- specified conditions are present as detailed below (as to UK residence of trustees and settlor and as to settlor interest in the settlement),

the trustees of the settlement are deemed for all CGT purposes to have disposed of and immediately reacquired the underlying assets (see below) at market value. The deemed disposal takes place at the same time as the actual disposal of the interest in settled property. It is regarded as made under a bargain at arm's length (which effectively precludes a claim for the gain to be deferred as in 30.2 or 30.10 HOLD-OVER RELIEFS).

[*TCGA 1992, s 76A, Sch 4A paras 1, 4(1)(3), para 9*].

See below for modifications to the above where there is a time lapse before effective completion of the actual disposal.

Where the trustees have made an election under *ITA 2007, s 508* in respect of income arising from heritage maintenance property, no charge arises under these provisions in relation to the settlement for that year. [*TCGA 1992, Sch 4A para 14*].

For these purposes, an '*interest in settled property*' is any interest created by or arising under the settlement. This includes the right to enjoy any benefit arising from the exercise of a discretion or power by the trustees of a settlement or by any person in relation to a settlement. A disposal is '*for consideration*' if actual consideration is given or received by any person for, or in connection with, any transaction by which the disposal is effected. Consideration deemed to have been given under any CGT provision is disregarded for these purposes. Consideration in the form of another interest under the same settlement is also disregarded, as long as that interest has not previously been disposed of by any person for consideration. [*TCGA 1992, Sch 4A paras 2, 3*].

HMRC consider that consideration for these purposes does not include incidental costs, in particular reasonable fees charged by professional advisers for legal and tax advice as to the effects of the transaction or for drafting and executing the relevant paperwork. Where there are no payments other than in respect of such costs, the transaction does not fall within these provisions. (Revenue Tax Bulletin August 2003 p 1048).

Underlying assets

Where the interest disposed of is in the whole of the settled property, the deemed disposal is of each of the assets comprised in that property. Where the interest disposed of is in a specific fund or other defined part of the settled property, the deemed disposal is of each of the assets comprised in that fund or part. In either case, the deemed disposal is of the whole of each of the assets concerned, unless the interest disposed of is an interest in a specified fraction or amount of the income or capital, in which case the deemed disposal is of a corresponding part of each of the assets concerned. Where part only of an asset is comprised in a specific fund or other defined part of the settled property, that part of the asset is treated as a separate asset for the purposes of these provisions. [*TCGA 1992, Sch 4A para 8*].

See also below under Time lapse before effective completion.

Conditions

All the following conditions must be present for the disposal of underlying assets to be deemed to take place (and see also the modifications below under Time lapse before effective completion).

UK residence of trustees

The trustees must have been resident in the UK during any part of the tax year of disposal and not regarded under a double tax agreement as resident elsewhere.

UK residence of settlor

In the tax year of disposal or in any of the previous five tax years, a person who is a 'settlor' (see below) in relation to the settlement must have resident in the UK (see **1.2** INTRODUCTION).

Settlor interest in the settlement

At some time during the 'relevant period', either:

- a person who is a 'settlor' in relation to the settlement must have had an interest in the settlement (see below); or
- the settlement must have comprised property derived, directly or indirectly, from another settlement in which a settlor had an interest at any time in the relevant period.

'*Settlor*' is defined for this purpose as in **42.9** OFFSHORE SETTLEMENTS, but excluding the provisions there relating to property provided by a qualifying company. The circumstances in which a settlor has an interest in a settlement are defined as for the purposes of the gifts to settlor-interested settlements provisions at **30.8** HOLD-OVER RELIEFS.

The '*relevant period*' is the period beginning two years before the beginning of the tax year of disposal and ending with the date of the disposal of the interest in settled property.

The above condition is treated as not present in a tax year in which the settlor dies or where:

- he has an interest in a settlement only because property is, or will or may become, payable to or applicable for the benefit of his spouse or civil partner *or* his spouse or civil partner enjoys a benefit from property, or for both such reasons, and his spouse or civil partner dies, or he and his spouse or civil partner cease to be married to or to be civil partners of each other, during the year; or
- he has an interest in a settlement only because property is, or will or may become, payable to or applicable for the benefit of a dependent child of his *or* a dependent child of his enjoys a benefit from property, or for both such reasons, and he ceases during the year to have (and does not in that year subsequently come to have) any such dependent children.

A '*dependent child*' of the settlor is, for this purpose, a child or stepchild under the age of 18 who is unmarried and does not have a civil partner.

[*TCGA 1992, Sch 4A para 4(2), paras 5–7, 12*].

Prevention of double charge

Where there would be a deemed disposal as above and the actual disposal of the interest in settled property is not itself exempt by virtue of *TCGA 1992, s 76* (see **56.15** above), the following provisions apply to ensure that there is no double charge or double allowance of a loss.

- If both the deemed disposal and the actual disposal give rise to a chargeable gain (or in the case of the deemed disposal a net chargeable gain by reference to all the assets involved), the lower gain is disregarded.
- If both disposals give rise to an allowable loss (or net allowable loss), the lower loss is disregarded.
- If one disposal gives rise to a (net) chargeable gain and the other a (net) allowable loss, the loss is disregarded.
- If the actual disposal gives rise to neither a chargeable gain nor an allowable loss, any net chargeable gain on the deemed disposal is taken as accruing instead.

[*TCGA 1992, Sch 4A para 10*].

Trustees' right of recovery

Where tax becomes chargeable in respect of a deemed disposal as above and either it is chargeable on the trustees or it is chargeable on the settlor and recovered by him from the trustees, the trustees have the right to recover the tax from the person who made the actual disposal (i.e. of an interest in the settlement) giving rise to the deemed disposal. For this purpose, they may require an inspector to certify the gain and the tax paid.

[*TCGA 1992, Sch 4A para 11*].

Time lapse before effective completion

The above provisions are subject to the modifications below where there is a period between the beginning of the disposal of the interest in settled property and the effective completion of that disposal. For these purposes, the disposal begins when a contract is entered into or, where relevant, an option is granted. It is effectively completed when the person acquiring the interest becomes for all practical purposes unconditionally entitled to the whole of the intended subject matter of the disposal.

Where the beginning of the disposal and the effective completion take place in different tax years:

- the deemed disposal is treated as taking place in the tax year of effective completion;
- the conditions as to UK residence of trustees and settlor are treated as present if they are present by reference to either of those tax years or any intervening year;
- the '*relevant period*' for the purpose of the condition as to settlor interest in the settlement is the period beginning two years before the beginning of the first of those tax years and ending with the effective completion.

If the identity or value of the underlying assets changes during the period between the beginning of the disposal and its effective completion, an asset is subject to the deemed disposal rules if it was comprised in the settled property (or specific fund or other defined part) at any time during that period, unless it was disposed of (and not reacquired) by the trustees during that period under a bargain at arm's length. The market value of an asset for the purposes of the deemed disposal is its highest market value at any time in that period.

[*TCGA 1992, Sch 4A para 13*].

HMRC have given examples of circumstances in which they would consider that the person acquiring the asset is for all practical purposes unconditionally entitled to the intended subject matter of the disposal (as above). These are where the buyer has the power to compel the trustees to transfer the property to him on giving due notice, and where the buyer has a right to enjoy the property now, but is not entitled to it until a particular contingency is fulfilled, and there is no real likelihood of its not being fulfilled. (Revenue Tax Bulletin August 2003 p 1049).

Restriction on set-off of settlement losses

[56.21] **Cross-reference.** See **56.16** above for restrictions on transfer of settlement losses to beneficiary becoming absolutely entitled to settled property.

Where the circumstances set out below apply in relation to a chargeable gain accruing to the trustees of a settlement, no allowable losses accruing to the trustees (whether in the same tax year or brought forward from an earlier year) may be set against any part of that gain.

The circumstances are as follows.

- In computing the gain in question, the allowable expenditure would be greater if it were not for a claim having been made for gifts hold-over relief under *TCGA 1992, s 165* or *s 260* (see **30.2**, **30.10** HOLD-OVER RELIEFS) in respect of an earlier disposal (not necessarily of the same asset) to the trustees; and

- the person who made that earlier disposal, or a person connected with him (within *TCGA 1992, s 286* — see **17** CONNECTED PERSONS), has at any time acquired an 'interest in the settled property' (defined as in **56.20** above), or entered into an arrangement to acquire such an interest, as a result of which any person has at any time received (or become entitled to receive) any consideration.

[*TCGA 1992, s 79A*].

Attribution to trustees of gains of non-resident companies

[56.22] The following apply where the trustees of a settlement are participators (within *CTA 2010, s 454*) in a close company (within *CTA 2010, ss 439–454* — broadly a company under the control of five or fewer participators or of directors who are participators, see Tolley's Corporation Tax under Close Companies) or in a non-UK resident company which would otherwise be a close company.

Where, by reason of such participation by the trustees, any part of a chargeable gain accruing to a non-UK resident company falls to be attributed to them under *TCGA 1992, s 3* (see **43.7** OVERSEAS MATTERS), nothing in any double tax agreement (see **20.2** DOUBLE TAX RELIEF) is to be taken as averting the tax charge otherwise arising.

Where:

(a) a chargeable gain accrues to a non-UK resident company which would otherwise be a close company;

(b) all or part of the gain is attributed under *TCGA 1992, s 3* to a close company which, by reason of a double tax agreement, is not chargeable to corporation tax on the gain; and

(c) had that close company been a non-UK resident company, all or part of the chargeable gain would have been attributed to the trustees by reason of such participation as is mentioned above;

then, for the purposes of the provisions in **43.7** OVERSEAS MATTERS which enable a gain to be attributed through a chain of companies to an indirect participator, the company in (b) above is treated as a non-UK resident company, with the result that the gain can be attributed to the trustees. This treatment also applies to any other company which, if it were non-UK resident, would have been part of the chain, such that all or part of the gain in question would have been attributed as in (c) above.

[*TCGA 1992, s 79B*].

Key points related to settlements

[56.23] Points to consider are as follows.

- In general, capital gains tax is calculated in the same way for trustees as it is for individuals. The highest rate of capital gains tax for trustees is 28%. With the current 45% rate of income tax for discretionary trusts, many trustees may be keen to move towards assets that are assessed to capital gains, rather than to income tax.
- The trustees' annual exempt amount (which is, in general, one half of the individual annual exempt amount) is further divided by the number of settlements created by the same settlor after 6 June 1978. Be aware that different restrictions apply to the capital gains tax annual exempt amount and the income tax standard rate band. For example, a father creates a settlement for the benefit of each of his four children when they are born, in 1977, 1979, 1981 and 1983. For income tax purposes there are four qualifying settlements, therefore each trust's standard rate band will be divided by four. For capital gains tax purposes, the earliest settlement is pre-6 June 1978 and it will therefore be eligible for the full trustees' annual exempt amount. The remaining three settlements form a qualifying group and will each receive one-third of the trustees' annual exempt amount.
- Additionally, if in the above example the child born in 1983 was disabled, then the capital gains tax annual exempt amount available to that trust would be one third of the full annual exempt amount (the amount due to individuals), rather than half of this amount, being the amount due to trustees (in general). This would have no effect on the amounts due to the other two trusts in the qualifying group.
- The creation of a settlement (or subsequent transfer of assets into an existing settlement) is a chargeable event for capital gains tax purposes. The settlor of the assets is treated as having disposed of them at full market value, and the gain is calculated thereon. In many cases involving settlements, an immediate charge to inheritance tax arises on the same occasion, and in order to prevent a double taxation charge, gifts hold-over relief may be available — see 30 HOLD-OVER RELIEFS.
- In qualifying interest in possession trusts (interest in possession settlements created before 22 March 2006, or those created after that date which are classed as an immediate post-death interest, a transitional serial interest, a disabled person's interest or a trust for bereaved minors) the underlying assets of the trust are treated as those of the life tenant and the life tenant is absolutely entitled to the income generated by those assets. The life tenant does not usually have a right to the capital of the trust and therefore the gains are assessable on the trustees for capital gains tax purposes.

57

Shares and Securities

Cross-references. See 4 ANTI-AVOIDANCE; 5.6 APPEALS for appeals regarding values of unquoted shares; 7.3 ASSETS for location of shares; 7.7 ASSETS for options to acquire shares; 8 ASSETS HELD ON 31 MARCH 1982; 14 COMPANIES; 15.2–15.6 COMPANIES — CORPORATE FINANCE AND INTANGIBLES; 23.5 EXEMPTIONS AND RELIEFS for meaning of 'debt on a security'; 23.22 EXEMPTIONS AND RELIEFS for business expansion scheme shares; 28 GOVERNMENT SECURITIES; 30 HOLD OVER RELIEFS for relief in respect of gifts of shares in certain cases and transfers to companies in exchange for shares; 39 LOSSES for reliefs available for losses arising from certain share disposals and for negligible value claims; 34 INVESTORS' RELIEF; 39 MARKET VALUE; 43 OVERSEAS MATTERS for shares in certain overseas resident companies and funds; 48 QUALIFYING CORPORATE BONDS; 53 ROLLOVER RELIEF — REPLACEMENT OF BUSINESS ASSETS for relief where shares etc. are held in certain companies; 63 UNIT TRUSTS ETC.; 64 VENTURE CAPITAL TRUSTS.

Simon's Taxes. See C2.7–C2.8, D6.1, D6.2, D6.6, D9.10, E1.435, E1.436.

Introduction to shares and securities

[57.1] There are many complex tax rules dealing with capital gains on shares and securities. The main provisions are listed below and described in more detail in this chapter or as indicated. For further relevant provisions, see 57.19–57.27 below and the list of cross-references at the head of the chapter.

Identification rules

Because one batch of shares or securities of the same class in a company are (unless numbered) effectively indistinguishable from another batch, special rules are needed to match disposals with multiple acquisitions. There are different rules for capital gains tax purposes and for corporation tax purposes. See 58 SHARES AND SECURITIES — IDENTIFICATION RULES.

Reorganisation of share capital

Such reorganisations, including bonus and rights issues, are not normally treated as disposals. Instead, the 'new holding' is treated as the same asset, acquired at the same date, as the 'original shares'. See 57.2–57.4 below.

Exchanges, schemes of reconstruction, etc.

The share reorganisation provisions apply also to the exchange of securities for those in another company (for example, in the course of a takeover, grouping exercise or buy-out). See 57.5 below. Similarly, the provisions also apply to certain arrangements made as part of a scheme of reconstruction involving the issue of securities (such as a merger or division) and on the conversion of securities. See 57.7 and 57.8 below.

Stock dividends (aka scrip dividends)

See 57.10–57.13 below.

Capital distributions

A capital distribution, on liquidation or otherwise, is normally treated as a disposal of an interest in the shares. See 57.11 below.

Substantial shareholding exemption (SSE)

A corporation tax exemption is available for a disposal by a company of shares. The company making the disposal must have held a 'substantial shareholding' in the company whose shares are the subject of the disposal throughout a continuous 12-month period beginning not more than six years before the disposal. See 60 SUBSTANTIAL SHAREHOLDING EXEMPTION.

Employee share schemes

For the CGT consequences where employees receive shares in their employing companies, see 21 EMPLOYEE SHARE SCHEMES.

Venture capital schemes

There are currently three schemes under which various tax reliefs are available for investment in shares of qualifying companies. Individuals can invest in such companies directly via the ENTERPRISE INVESTMENT SCHEME (see **22**) or the SEED ENTERPRISE INVESTMENT SCHEME (see **54**) or indirectly through VENTURE CAPITAL TRUSTS (see **64**). Before 1 April 2010, companies could make direct investments using the corporate venturing scheme.

Sale of controlling interest in company to employee-ownership trust

A relief from CGT applies to a disposal of certain shares in a trading company to the trustees of a settlement which operates for the benefit of all the employees of the company. The relief is available only if the settlement acquires a controlling interest in the company in the tax year of the disposal. See **57.14** below.

Reorganisation of share capital

[57.2] A 'reorganisation' does not normally constitute a disposal. Instead, the 'new holding' is treated as the same asset, acquired at the same date, as the 'original shares'.

For this purpose:

- '*original shares*' means shares held before, and concerned in, the reorganisation, and
- '*new holding*' means, in relation to any original shares, the shares in and debentures of the company which, following the reorganisation, represent the original shares, and any remaining original shares.

[*TCGA 1992, ss 126(1), 127*].

In certain cases involving BUSINESS ASSET DISPOSAL RELIEF (**9.17**), an election may be made for the reorganisation to be treated as an actual disposal and reacquisition.

Separate rules apply to a reorganisation of share capital involving qualifying corporate bonds. See **48.4** QUALIFYING CORPORATE BONDS.

See **57.9** below where a quoted option to subscribe for shares in a company is dealt in (on the stock exchange where it is quoted) within three months after (or such longer period after as may be allowed in written notice by HMRC) a reorganisation within these provisions.

Scope of provisions

A 'reorganisation' is defined as a '*reorganisation or reduction of a company's share capital*'. '*Reorganisation of a company's share capital*' includes the making of bonus and rights issues of shares or debentures in proportion to the original holdings (see **57.3** and **57.4** below), the reduction of share capital and the alteration of rights attaching to the original shares. '*Reduction of share capital*' does not include the paying off of redeemable share capital, and where shares in a company are redeemed by the company otherwise than by the issue of shares or debentures (with or without other consideration) and otherwise than in a liquidation, the shareholder is treated as disposing of the shares at the time of the redemption. [*TCGA 1992, s 126*].

In strictness, the alteration of rights attaching to shares is a reorganisation only where there is already more than one class of shares in issue. HMRC, however, accept that a reorganisation can occur where there is only one class of shares in issue. (HMRC Capital Gains Manual CG51780).

In *Dunstan v Young Austen and Young Ltd* CA 1988, 61 TC 448, the CA held that an increase in share capital can be a reorganisation even if it is not a conventional bonus or rights issue, 'provided that the new shares are acquired by existing shareholders because they are existing shareholders and in proportion to their existing beneficial holdings'. See also *Unilever (UK) Holdings Ltd v Smith* CA, 2002 STI 1806 and *Fletcher v HMRC* (Sp C 711), [2008] SSCD 1219.

HMRC will treat any subscription for shares under an 'open offer', which is equal to or less than the shareholder's minimum entitlement under the offer, as a share reorganisation. Any shares subscribed for in excess of the minimum entitlement will be treated as a separate acquisition. (An 'open offer' is where a company invites its shareholders to subscribe for shares subject to a minimum entitlement based on their existing holdings, and possibly enabling them to subscribe also for shares which other shareholders do not want.) (HMRC Capital Gains Manual CG51756).

No part of any acquisition of shares by existing shareholders under a 'vendor placing' can be treated as a share reorganisation. For this purpose, a '*vendor placing*' takes place where a company wishes to pay for the purchase of an asset by issuing its own shares and, with the vendors not wanting the shares, the company makes arrangements to sell the shares on the vendors' behalf to its existing shareholders. (HMRC Capital Gains Manual CG51763).

For HMRC's views on the treatment of rights to acquire shares in other companies, see HMRC Capital Gains Manual CG52065.

The share reorganisation provisions also apply to exchanges of securities for those in another company within **57.5** below, to schemes of reconstruction within **57.7** below and on the conversion of securities (see **57.8** below).

Consideration given by shareholder

Any additional consideration given by the shareholder at the time of reorganisation (e.g. as a subscription for a rights issue — see **57.4** below) is added to the cost of the original holding for the purpose of computing the unindexed gain on a subsequent disposal.

The surrender, cancellation or alteration of the original holding or the rights attached thereto, and any consideration met out of the assets of the company (e.g. on a bonus issue) or represented by a dividend or other distribution declared but not paid are not regarded as 'additional consideration'. Similarly, in the case of a reorganisation occurring after 9 March 1981, any consideration given, otherwise than by way of a bargain made at arm's length, for part or all of the new holding will be disregarded, to the extent that its amount or value exceeds the amount by which the market value of the new holding, immediately after the reorganisation, exceeds the market value of the original shares immediately before the reorganisation. (See also *CIR v Burmah Oil Co. Ltd* HL 1981, 54 TC 200.)

[*TCGA 1992, s 128(1)(2)*].

See **32.6** INDEXATION for the calculation of indexation allowance in respect of the additional consideration.

Consideration received by shareholder

Where, on a reorganisation, a person receives (or is deemed to receive), or becomes entitled to receive, any consideration, other than the new holding, for the disposal of an interest in the original shares, and in particular:

(i) where under *TCGA 1992, s 122* he is to be treated as if he had in consideration of a capital distribution disposed of an interest in the original shares (see **57.11** below and note the procedure where the amount of the capital distribution is small or exceeds the allowable expenditure attaching to the original shares), or

(ii) where he receives (or is deemed to receive) consideration from other shareholders in respect of a surrender of rights derived from the original shares,

he is treated as if the new holding resulted from his having for that consideration disposed of an interest (but without prejudice to the original shares and the new holding being treated in accordance with *TCGA 1992, s 127* above as the same asset). [*TCGA 1992, s 128(3)*].

Collective investment schemes

See **63.3** UNIT TRUSTS ETC. for the treatment (generally, and therefore for the purposes of the share reorganisation provisions) of an authorised unit trust as a company and the rights of unit holders as shares in that company. See **63.2** UNIT TRUSTS ETC. for the disapplication of the above provisions as regards collective investment schemes entitling participants to exchange rights in one part of a scheme property for rights in another.

Valuation of different classes of share on subsequent disposal

Where the new holding consists of more than one class of share, security, debenture, etc. none of which is quoted on a recognised stock exchange within three months of the reorganisation, the allowable acquisition cost is arrived at on the basis of the market value of the various classes at the date of a chargeable disposal of the new holding or part thereof. This also applies where consideration, other than the new holding, is received as in *TCGA 1992, s 128(3)* above. [*TCGA 1992, ss 128(4), 129*].

However, in the case of shares and securities any one class or more of which is or are listed on a recognised stock exchange (see **57.27** below) (or, in the case of unit trust rights, of which the prices were published daily by the managers) within three months after the reorganisation takes effect (or such longer time as HMRC may allow), the base value is determined *once and for all* by reference to the respective market value, on the first day on which the market values or prices of the shares are quoted or published (whether published before or after the actual reorganisation). The provisions apply also to the reorganisation of rights under unit trusts. See **63** UNIT TRUSTS AND OTHER INVESTMENT VEHICLES. A reorganisation which involves the allotment of holdings is deemed to take effect on the day following the day on which the right to renounce any allotment expires. [*TCGA 1992, ss 130, 288(1)*].

For the application of the indexation provisions to holdings of shares arising out of these rules, see **32.6** INDEXATION and **58.4, 58.5** SHARES AND SECURITIES — IDENTIFICATION RULES.

Assets held on 6 April 1965

See **8.12** ASSETS HELD ON 31 MARCH **1982** for certain situations that may still arise in relation to reorganisations.

Example

A Ltd, an unquoted company, was incorporated in 1996 with an authorised share capital of £50 million denominated into 500 million ordinary shares of 10p each, of which 300 million were issued at par on incorporation. In 2012, the directors decided to reorganise the company's share capital by issuing the balance of the authorised share capital in the form of a bonus issue of 200 million ordinary shares of 10p so that two such shares are issued for every three of such shares already held. The 500 million ordinary shares of 10p each in issue are then consolidated into 50 million new ordinary shares of £1 each. A rights issue is then made on the basis of one 7% cumulative preference share of £1 issued at par for every five new ordinary shares of £1 already held.

X was issued 90,000 Ordinary Shares of 10p on incorporation and has held them continually since then. Assuming he takes up the rights issue, his new holding after the reorganisation is as follows.

	No. of shares	Par value	Cost
			£
Original holding: 10p Ords	90,000	10p	9,000
Bonus issue: 10p Ords	60,000	10p	Nil
	150,000		£9,000
Consolidation: 10p Ords to £1			
New Ords	15,000	£1	9,000
Rights issue: £1 Prefs	3,000	£1	3,000
Cost of complete new holding			£12,000

X disposes of 1,500 £1 Prefs in 2024 when each such share is worth £3 and each £1 New Ord is worth £1.80. The apportionment is as follows.

		£
Total value of £1 Prefs: (£3 × 3,000)	=	9,000
Total value of £1 New Ords: (£1.80 × 15,000)	=	27,000
		£36,000
Proportional value of £1 Prefs × original cost		
9/36 × £12,000	=	£3,000
Allowable cost of 1,500 £1 Prefs (£3,000 × 2)	=	£1,500

Note

If X later disposes of the remainder (1,500) of the £1 Prefs when their value is £4 each and that of the £1 Ords is £2 each, the calculation will be made as follows:

		£
Total value of £1 Prefs: (£4 × 1,500)	=	6,000
Total value of £1 Ords: (£2 × 15,000)	=	30,000
		£36,000
Original cost (as reduced by previous disposal)	=	£10,500
Proportional value of £1 Prefs × original cost		
6/36 × £10,500	=	£1,750
Allowable cost of 1,500 £1 Prefs	=	£1,750

Bonus issues (aka scrip issues)

[57.3] A bonus issue is a reorganisation within **57.2** above, but see **57.10** below for stock dividends.

Where a company has acquired its own shares and holds them as treasury shares (see **57.19** below) a bonus issue in respect of shares of the same class can be a reorganisation whether or not bonus shares are issued in respect of the treasury shares (HMRC Capital Gains Manual CG51750).

In practice, where a bonus issue follows a repayment of share capital (e.g. under *CTA 2010, s 1022*), and is treated as income of the recipient, the net amount of the distribution is treated as the acquisition cost of the new shares (HMRC Capital Gains Manual CG51825).

Example

X plc, a quoted company, makes a bonus issue in September 2024 of one preference share for every eight ordinary shares held. On first trading after issue, the preference shares were valued at £10 and the ordinary shares at £6.

Mr A had purchased 1,000 ordinary shares in December 2015 for £7,000. After the issue of preference shares, the allowable expenditure on a subsequent disposal of the ordinary and preference shares is computed as follows.

		£
Initial value of preference shares (125 × £10)		1,250
Initial value of ordinary shares (1,000 × £6)		6,000
Total		£7,250
Allowable cost of 1,000 ordinary shares	$\frac{6,000}{7,250} \times 7,000$ =	£5,790
Allowable cost of 125 preference shares	$\frac{1,250}{7,250} \times 7,000$ =	£1,210

Rights issues

[57.4] A rights issue of shares or debentures in respect of shares already held in a company is a reorganisation within **57.2** above. A company cannot grant rights in respect of treasury shares, but this will not in itself prevent the rights issue being a reorganisation (HMRC Capital Gains Manual CG51750).

Disposal of rights

Where a person receives or becomes entitled to receive in respect of any shares in a company a provisional allotment of shares in or debentures of the company and he disposes of his rights, *TCGA 1992, s 122* applies as if the amount of consideration for the disposal were a capital distribution received by him from the company in respect of the first-mentioned shares, and as if he had, instead of disposing of the rights, disposed of an interest in those shares. This rule also applies to rights obtained in respect of any debentures of a company. [*TCGA 1992, s 123*].

See **57.11** below for *TCGA 1992, s 122* and note the procedure where the amount of the capital distribution is small or exceeds the allowable expenditure attaching to the original shares etc.

Example

W plc is a quoted company which, in June 1992, made a rights issue of one £1 ordinary share for every eight £1 ordinary shares held, at £1.35 payable on allotment. V, who held 16,000 £1 ordinary shares purchased in May 1984 for £15,000, took up his entitlement in full and was allotted 2,000 shares. In December 2024, he sells 6,000 of his shares for £30,000.

'Section 104 holding'	Shares	Qualifying expenditure
		£
May 1984 acquisition	16,000	15,000
June 1992 rights issue	2,000	2,700
	18,000	17,700
December 2024 disposal	(6,000)	(5,900)
Pool carried forward	12,000	£11,800

Calculation of chargeable gain		£
Disposal consideration		30,000
Allowable cost	$\frac{6,000}{18,000} \times £17,700$	5,900
Chargeable gain 2024/25		£24,100

Exchange of securities for those in another company ('share for share exchange')

[57.5] The share reorganisation provisions at 57.2 above apply also where a company (company B) issues shares or debentures in exchange for the shares or debentures of another company (company A), provided that one of the following conditions is satisfied. This is often referred to as a 'share for share exchange' or a 'paper for paper exchange'. The conditions are that:

- company B holds, or in consequence of the exchange will hold, more than 25% of company A's 'ordinary share capital';
- company B holds, or in consequence of the exchange will hold, more than 50% of the voting power in company A; or
- company B issues the shares etc. as the result of a general offer made to the members of company A (or any class of them) and the offer is initially made on a condition which, if satisfied, would give company B control of company A. (This covers abortive takeover bids which become unconditional, but which do not succeed.)

In applying the share reorganisation provisions, company A and company B are treated as if they were the same company. Following the exchange, therefore, the shares etc. in company B (which form the 'new holding' for the purposes of the reorganisation provisions) are treated, in the hands of the original holders of the exchanged company A shares etc., as the same asset, acquired at the same date, as the exchanged shares etc. (which form the 'original shares').

For this purpose, the '*ordinary share capital*' of a company is all its issued share capital (by whatever name called), other than shares carrying only a right to fixed rate dividends and no other right to participate in profits and also includes units in a unit trust and, in relation to a company with no share capital, interests in the company possessed by its members. In relation to such a company, references above to shares or debentures include any such interests.

These provisions are subject to the anti-avoidance rule below.

[*TCGA 1992, s 135; CTA 2010, s 1119*].

The above provisions can be used in several different commercial situations, including straightforward takeovers, reverse takeovers, forming groups out of associated companies and buy-outs. See HMRC Capital Gains Manual CG52570. Where the conditions are satisfied, the provisions apply automatically, without claim.

See **63.2** UNIT TRUSTS ETC. for the application of the provisions as regards collective investment schemes entitling participants to exchange rights in one part of a scheme for rights in another.

For the tax consequences of a share exchange before 14 March 1988 within a group of companies, see *Westcott v Woolcombers Ltd* CA 1987, 60 TC 575 and *NAP Holdings UK Ltd v Whittles* HL 1994, 67 TC 166 at **26.3** GROUPS OF COMPANIES.

See **57.9** below where a quoted option to subscribe for shares in a company is dealt in (on the stock exchange where it is quoted) within three months after (or such longer period after as may be allowed in written notice by HMRC) an exchange within these provisions.

Treasury shares

Where company A has acquired its own shares and is holding them as treasury shares (see **57.19** below) at the time of the exchange, no issue of shares by Company B can be made in respect of the treasury shares. The treasury shares do not count as issued share capital in determining whether the conditions for the above treatment are met. A disposal of its treasury shares by Company B is treated as the company issuing those shares. (HMRC Capital Gains Manual CG52521).

Incidental costs of acquisition and disposal and warranty payments in respect of contingent liabilities

Any such costs or payments attributable to the new holding of shares or debentures are by concession treated as consideration given for that holding. In the case of warranty payments, relief under this concession and *TCGA 1992, s 49(1)(c)* (see **16.14** COMPUTATION OF GAINS AND LOSSES) will in total be restricted to what would have been allowed under *TCGA 1992, s 49(1)(c)* had *TCGA 1992, s 135* not applied (HMRC Extra-Statutory Concession D52).

Anti-avoidance

The above provisions do not apply unless the exchange is made for genuine commercial reasons and does not form part of a scheme or arrangements of which the main purpose, or one of the main purposes, is the avoidance of capital gains tax or corporation tax. In such cases, a chargeable disposal is treated as taking place except where a person to whom the new shares or debentures are issued owns (or he and persons connected with him together own) less than 5% of, or any class of, the shares or debentures of company A. There are provisions for advance clearance of an exchange by HMRC. [*TCGA 1992, ss 137, 138*].

For full coverage, see **4.16** ANTI-AVOIDANCE.

Where the provisions are disapplied, then under general principles the disposal proceeds will be the value in money's worth of the shares or debentures issued by the acquiring company or, if the transaction is not a bargain made at arm's length, the market value of the shares or debentures sold (if different).

See also **4.17** ANTI-AVOIDANCE for provisions which treat shares or debentures held by an individual following a share exchange as located in the UK in certain circumstances.

Miscellaneous

TCGA 1992, s 135 is disapplied in certain circumstances (with the result that an exchange of securities is treated as a disposal of the original holding and an acquisition of a new holding) in relation to shares and securities that have qualified for tax relief under one of the various venture capital tax schemes or the community investment tax credit scheme. See **23.68** EXEMPTIONS AND RELIEF, **22.15**, **22.19** ENTERPRISE INVESTMENT SCHEME, **23.22** EXEMPTIONS AND RELIEFS (as regards the Business Expansion Scheme), **64.7** VENTURE CAPITAL TRUSTS and Tolley's Income Tax under Community Investment Tax Relief. See also **60.12** SUBSTANTIAL SHAREHOLDINGS OF COMPANIES.

Example

Wendy buys 10,000 shares in Never Ltd for £20,000 in November 2004. Never Ltd is taken over by Ryan plc on 1 May 2024 and Wendy receives 4,000 shares in Ryan plc in exchange for her Never Ltd shares.

Wendy is not treated as making a disposal of the Never Ltd shares on 1 May 2024. Instead, her Ryan plc shares are treated as acquired in November 2004 at the same cost (£20,000) as her shares in Never Ltd.

Earn-out rights

[57.6] An agreement for the sale of shares in a company may include the right to receive deferred consideration which is itself unascertainable at the time of the agreement, usually because it depends on the future profit performance of the company. Such a right was held to be a separate asset in *Marren v Ingles* HL 1980, 54 TC 76 (see **10.2** CAPITAL SUMS DERIVED FROM ASSETS). In certain circumstances, where the right (known as the 'earn-out right') is a right to receive securities, the right itself is treated as a security so that the share exchange provisions at **57.5** above can apply. The subsequent issue of the actual securities in pursuance of the right is then treated as a conversion of securities within **57.8** below. Such treatment is mandatory, subject to the option to disapply it by election.

Detailed provisions

Where a person ('the seller') transfers securities (i.e. shares or debentures) of a company and, as all or part of the consideration for the transfer, has conferred upon him a right to receive securities ('the new securities') of another company ('the acquiring company'), the value or quantity of which is 'unascertainable' (see below) at that time, such right is known as an '*earn-out right*'. It is a further condition that the terms of the right are such that it cannot be discharged otherwise than by the issue of the new securities. Any right to receive cash and/or an ascertainable amount of securities as part of the total consideration does not fall within these provisions and must be distinguished from the earn-out right.

Provided that *TCGA 1992, s 135* (exchange of securities — see **57.5** above) would have applied if the earn-out right were an ascertainable amount of securities of the acquiring company, the right is treated for capital gains purposes as if it were itself a security of the acquiring company (so that *s 135* may apply). This treatment does not apply if the seller so elects.

An election is irrevocable and must be made by written notice to an HMRC officer by the first anniversary of 31 January following the tax year in which the earn-out right is conferred, or, where made by a company, within two years after the end of the accounting period in which the right is conferred. In *Adams v HMRC* FTT, [2009] SFTD 184, the making of a return on the basis that an election applied was held to amount to a valid election.

Where security treatment applies, it is then assumed, as regards the seller and any subsequent owner of the earn-out right, that:

(a) the earn-out right is a security within the definition in *TCGA 1992, s 132* (see **57.8** below);
(b) the notional security represented by the earn-out right is not a QUALIFYING CORPORATE BOND (**48**);
(c) all references in *TCGA 1992* to a debenture include references to such a notional security; and
(d) the eventual issue of actual securities in pursuance of the earn-out right constitutes a conversion of the right, insofar as it is discharged by the issue, into those securities (see **57.8** below re conversion of securities).

Where an earn-out right is treated as a notional security of a company as above and it is extinguished and replaced with a new right to be issued with securities of the same company, the value or quantity of which is 'unascertainable' (see below) at that time, the new right is treated for CGT purposes as if it were a security of the company, with the same consequences as above. The person on whom the new right is conferred may make an election to disapply this treatment. The time limits for election operate by reference to the tax year or accounting period in which the new right is conferred.

Meaning of 'unascertainable'

(1) The value or quantity of securities to be issued in pursuance of an earn-out right is unascertainable at a particular time if, and only if, it is made referable to matters relating to any business or assets of one or

more 'relevant companies' and those matters are then uncertain on account of future business or future assets being included in the business or assets to which they relate. A *'relevant company'* is either the acquiring company or the acquired company or any company in the same group of companies as either of those. A group of companies is construed in accordance with **26.2** GROUPS OF COMPANIES.

(2) The value or quantity of securities to be issued in pursuance of an earn-out right is *not* to be taken as unascertainable merely by reason of any part of the consideration for the transaction being contingent or of any risk of its being irrecoverable. In such cases, *TCGA 1992, s 48* (consideration due after time of disposal — see **16.14** COMPUTATION OF GAINS AND LOSSES) applies in computing the gain.

(3) The existence of an option to choose between shares in and debentures of the acquiring company does not in itself render unascertainable the value or quantity of such securities. However, neither does such option prevent the above provisions from applying.

(4) If the value of securities to be issued in pursuance of an earn-out right is ascertainable and the quantity is to be fixed by reference thereto, or *vice versa*, this does not in itself render the value or quantity unascertainable.

[*TCGA 1992, s 138A*].

Note that an earn-out right treated as a security by virtue of *TCGA 1992, s 138A* is not regarded as a right to unascertainable consideration for the purposes of *TCGA 1992, ss 279A–279D* (loss on right to unascertainable consideration treated as accruing in earlier year — see **38.18** LOSSES). [*TCGA 1992, s 279B(6)*].

In *Briggs v HMRC* FTT, [2019] SFTD 952, the buyer of a company was liable to pay a 'pass-through payment' to the sellers if the buyer received a settlement payment in respect of litigation in progress at the time of the sale of the company. The right to receive the payment (in the form of securities in the company) was held to be an earn-out right within these provisions. In the event, a deed of variation was entered into so that the sellers received cash in respect of the pass-through payment. The cash payment was held to be a capital sum derived from the earn-out right and so a disposal within *TCGA 1992, s 22*.

For HMRC's views on earn-outs, see HMRC Capital Gains Manual CG58000–58095.

Example

K owns 10,000 ordinary shares in M Ltd, which he acquired for £12,000 in December 2005. In July 2023, the whole of the issued share capital of M Ltd was acquired by P plc. Under the terms of the takeover, K receives £2 per share plus the right to further consideration up to a maximum of £1.50 per share depending on future profit performance. The initial consideration is receivable in cash, but the deferred consideration is to be satisfied by the issue of shares in P plc. In December 2024, K duly receives 2,000 ordinary shares valued at £6 per share in full settlement of his entitlement. The right to future consideration is valued at £1.40 per share in July 2023.

If K elects to disapply *TCGA 1992, s 138A* the position would be

2023/24

	£	£
Disposal proceeds 10,000 × £2	20,000	
Value of rights 10,000 × £1.40	14,000	34,000
Cost		12,000
Chargeable gain		£22,000

2024/25

	£
Disposal of rights to deferred consideration:	
Proceeds — 2,000 P plc shares @ £6	12,000
Deemed cost of acquiring rights	14,000
Allowable loss	£2,000
Cost for CGT purposes of 2,000 P plc shares	£12,000

Without an election, the position would be

2023/24

	£
Proceeds (cash) (as above)	20,000
Cost $£12{,}000 \times \dfrac{20{,}000}{20{,}000 + 14{,}000}$	7,059
Chargeable gain	£12,941
Cost of earn-out right for CGT purposes (£12,000 – £7,059)	£4,941

2024/25

The shares in P plc stand in the place of the earn-out right and will be regarded as having been acquired in December 2005 for £4,941. No further gain or loss arises until a disposal of the shares takes place.

Scheme of reconstruction involving issue of securities

[57.7] The share reorganisation provisions at 57.2 above apply also where certain arrangements between a company (company A) and its share- or debenture-holders (or any class of them) are entered into for the purposes of, or in connection with, a 'scheme of reconstruction'. Under the arrangement, another company (company B) must issue shares or debentures to those holders in respect of, or in proportion to (or as nearly as may be in proportion to), their original holdings, which latter are then retained, cancelled or otherwise extinguished.

In such a case, the holders are treated as exchanging their holdings in company A for the shares or debentures held by them as a consequence of the arrangement and the share reorganisation provisions apply as if company A and company B were the same company and the exchange were a reorganisation of its share capital. Any shares in or debentures of company A that are of a class involved in the scheme and that are retained are treated as if they had been cancelled and replaced by a new issue.

Where company A carries out an actual reorganisation of its share capital as a prelude to a scheme of reconstruction the above provisions apply to the position after the preliminary reorganisation has been carried out.

References above to shares or debentures being retained include their being retained in altered form, whether as a result of reduction, consolidation, division or otherwise. In relation to a company with no share capital, references to shares or debentures include any interests in the company possessed by its members.

[*TCGA 1992, s 136*].

See **57.9** below where a quoted option to subscribe for shares in a company is dealt in (on the stock exchange where it is quoted) within three months after (or such longer period after as may be allowed in written notice by HMRC) a scheme of reconstruction within these provisions.

Meaning of 'scheme of reconstruction'

A '*scheme of reconstruction*' is a scheme of merger, division or other restructuring that meets the following conditions.

(1) The scheme must involve the issue of 'ordinary share capital' of a company or companies (the '*successor company(ies)*') to holders of 'ordinary share capital' of another company (the '*original company*') (or, where relevant, to the holders of one or more particular classes of 'ordinary share capital' involved in the scheme). Where there is more than one original company involved in the scheme, the issue must be to holders of 'ordinary share capital' of (or of one or more particular classes of 'ordinary share capital' of) any of those companies. The scheme must *not* involve the issue of ordinary share capital of the successor company(ies) to anyone else. For this purpose a transfer of treasury shares (i.e. of the company's own shares acquired and held by it — see **57.19** below) is treated as an issue of shares (HMRC Capital Gains Manual CG52707A).

(2) Holders of a class of ordinary share capital (of the original company(ies)) involved in the scheme must each have the same proportionate entitlement to acquire ordinary share capital of the successor company(ies) (see example at HMRC Capital Gains Manual CG52707B). This does not apply to treasury shares because such shares are treated as if they had been cancelled (HMRC Capital Gains Manual CG52707B).

(3) Unless condition (4) below is satisfied, the effect of the restructuring must be that the business or substantially the whole of the business carried on by the original company is carried on either by a successor

company which is not the original company or by two or more successor companies (which may include the original company). Where there is more than one original company, the effect must be that all or part of the business(es) carried on by one or more of the original companies is carried on by a different company *and* the whole or substantially the whole of the businesses carried on by the original companies is carried on:

- by the successor company (which may be one of the original companies) where there is only one such company, or
- by the successor companies (which may be the same as the original companies or include any of them) where there are two or more such companies.

For the above purposes, the whole or substantially the whole of a business (or businesses) is carried on by two or more successor companies if, inter alia, the activities of those companies taken together embrace the whole or substantially the whole of that business (or those businesses). A business carried on by a company that is under the control (within *CTA 2010, s 1124*) of another company is treated as carried on by each of them. This enables a holding company with no business of its own to meet condition (3) by reference to the business of its subsidiary.

For the purposes of this condition, there are disregarded any assets retained by an original company in order to make a capital distribution within *TCGA 1992, s 122* (see **57.11** below), for example to any significant minority of shareholders who indicated their unwillingness to maintain their investment in the business following the reconstruction.

(4) If condition (3) above is not satisfied, the scheme must be carried out in pursuance of a compromise or arrangement under *Companies Act 2006, Pt 26* (previously *Companies Act 1985, s 425*) (or NI or foreign equivalent) without involving any transfer of the business of the original company(ies).

For these purposes, '*ordinary share capital*' is as defined in **57.5** above, including the extension to units in a unit trust and, in relation to a company with no share capital, interests in the company possessed by its members.

Where any of the original companies 'reorganise' (within **57.2** above) their share capital as a prelude to a scheme of reconstruction, conditions (1) and (2) above apply to the position after the preliminary reorganisation has been carried out. For the purposes of those two conditions, there is disregarded any issue of shares in or debentures of any of the successor companies which is made after the latest date on which any of the successor companies issues shares or debentures:

- in consideration of the transfer of any business (or part of a business) under the scheme, or
- (where applicable) in pursuance of the compromise or arrangement mentioned in condition (4) above.

[*TCGA 1992, s 136(4), Sch 5AA*].

For practical illustrations of schemes of reconstruction, including demergers, see HMRC Capital Gains Manual CG52720–52728.

Anti-avoidance

The same anti-avoidance rules apply as in **57.5** above [*TCGA 1992, s 136(6)*].

For full coverage see **4.16** and **4.17** ANTI-AVOIDANCE.

Incidental costs of acquisition and disposal and warranty payments in respect of contingent liabilities

Any such costs or payments attributable to the new holding of shares or debentures are by concession treated as consideration given for that holding. In the case of warranty payments, relief under this concession and *TCGA 1992, s 49(1)(c)* (see **16.14** COMPUTATION OF GAINS AND LOSSES) will in total be restricted to what would have been allowed under *TCGA 1992, s 49(1)(c)* had *TCGA 1992, s 136* not applied (HMRC Extra-Statutory Concession D52).

Miscellaneous

TCGA 1992, s 136 is disapplied in certain circumstances (with the result that a scheme of reconstruction is treated as a disposal of the original holding and an acquisition of a new holding) in relation to shares and securities that have qualified for tax relief under one of the various venture capital tax schemes or the community investment tax credit scheme. See **19.8** CORPORATE VENTURING SCHEME, **22.15**, **22.19** ENTERPRISE INVESTMENT SCHEME, **23.22** EXEMPTIONS AND RELIEFS (as regards the Business Expansion Scheme), **64.7** VENTURE CAPITAL TRUSTS and Tolley's Income Tax under Community Investment Tax Relief. See also **60.12** SUBSTANTIAL SHAREHOLDINGS OF COMPANIES.

Cross-border divisions and mergers

Certain transfers of assets on the division of a business between companies in different EC member states and certain transfers of assets and liabilities on cross-border mergers are treated as schemes of reconstruction. See **43.12–43.14** OVERSEAS MATTERS.

Example

N Ltd carries on a manufacturing and wholesaling business. In 1995, it was decided that the wholesaling business should be carried on by a separate company. Revenue clearance under *TCGA 1992, s 138* was obtained, and a company, R Ltd, was formed which, in consideration for the transfer to it by N Ltd of the latter's wholesaling undertaking, issued shares to the shareholders of N Ltd. Each holder of ordinary shares in N Ltd received one ordinary share in R Ltd for each N Ltd share he held. W, who purchased his 2,500 N shares for £10,000 in December 1993, received 2,500 R shares. None of the shares involved are quoted. In August 2024, W sells 1,500 of his N shares for £6 each, a total of £9,000, agreed to be their market value. The value of W's remaining N shares is also £6 per share, and the value of his R shares is £4.50 per share.

	£
Disposal consideration	9,000
Allowable cost $\pounds 10{,}000 \times \dfrac{9{,}000}{9{,}000 + (1{,}000 \times \pounds 6) + (2{,}500 \times \pounds 4.50)}$	3,429

Chargeable gain 2024/25	£5,571

Conversion of securities

[57.8] The share reorganisation provisions at **57.2** above apply also to the '*conversion of securities*', which phrase includes:

(a) a conversion of securities of a company into shares in that company;
(b) a conversion of a security which is not a qualifying corporate bond (QCB) (see **48** QUALIFYING CORPORATE BONDS) into a security of the same company which is a QCB;
(c) a conversion of a QCB into a security of the same company which is not a QCB;
(d) a conversion in lieu of redemption at the option of the holder of the securities; and
(e) any exchange of securities in pursuance of compulsory purchase powers.

Any of the above is a conversion of securities regardless of whether effected by a transaction or occurring as a result of the operation of the terms of any security or debenture.

'*Security*' includes any loan stock or similar security issued by national or local government or public authority in the UK or elsewhere, or by a company, and whether secured or unsecured. Certain company debentures are deemed under *TCGA 1992, s 251* to be securities for the purposes of that section (see **23.5** EXEMPTIONS AND RELIEFS). There are provisions to ensure that (b) and (c) above operate in relation to such debentures.

[*TCGA 1992, s 132*].

An amendment to the terms of loan notes which was intended to transform the notes into a QCB by removing the right to redeem them in dollars was held to be a conversion of the notes within the above provisions in *Klincke v HMRC* UT, [2010] STC 2032.

A premium in money (in addition to a new holding) on a conversion of securities is treated in virtually identical terms as under *TCGA 1992, s 122* for a capital distribution in **57.11** below. (It would appear that the case of *O&Rourke v Binks* CA 1992, 65 TC 165 mentioned therein applies equally to premiums on conversion within this provision as it does to capital distributions within *TCGA 1992, s 122*.) Similar rules as in *s 122* apply if the premium is 'small' (which is as defined in **57.11** below). [*TCGA 1992, s 133*].

See **57.9** below where a quoted option to subscribe for shares in a company is dealt in (on the stock exchange where it is quoted) within three months after (or such longer period after as may be allowed in written notice by HMRC) a conversion within these provisions.

Alternative rules apply to the conversion of securities of a company involving qualifying corporate bonds. See **48.4** QUALIFYING CORPORATE BONDS.

See also **63.2** UNIT TRUSTS ETC. for the disapplication of *TCGA 1992, s 132* as regards collective investment schemes entitling participants to exchange rights in one part of a scheme for rights in another.

Example

N bought £10,000 of 8% convertible loan stock in S plc, a quoted company, in June 2006. The cost was £9,800. In August 2010, N exercised his right to convert the loan stock into 'B' ordinary shares of the company, on the basis of 50 shares for £100 loan stock, and acquired 5,000 shares. In June 2024, N sells 3,000 of the shares for £10.00 each.

		£
Disposal consideration		30,000
	Cost $\frac{3,000}{5,000} \times £9,800$	5,880
Chargeable gain 2024/25		£24,120

Notes to the example

(a) The shares acquired on the conversion in 1999 stand in the shoes of the original loan stock. [*TCGA 1992, s 132*].

(b) The loan stock cannot be a corporate bond (and thus cannot be a qualifying corporate bond) as it is convertible into securities other than corporate bonds, i.e. into ordinary shares. [*CTA 2010, s 162; TCGA 1992, s 117(1)*].

Compensation stock

Instead of *TCGA 1992, s 132* above applying, where gilt-edged securities are issued on the compulsory acquisition of shares or securities the gain that would have accrued had the shares or securities been disposed of at their value at that time is not treated as arising until the gilt-edged securities are disposed of. However, for corporation tax purposes, where the gilt-edged securities received are disposed of after 5 April 1988 no gain arises under this provision if its application would be directly attributable to the disposal of an asset before 1 April 1982.

Disposals are, so far as possible, identified with gilts issued under the above provisions rather than with other gilts of the same kind and subject to this, with gilts issued at an earlier time rather than with those issued at a later time.

The deferment of the gain otherwise arising on the issue of the gilt-edged securities is extended to the recipient where their later disposal is within *TCGA 1992, s 58(1)* (spouses or civil partners), *s 62(4)* (legatee acquiring asset from personal representatives) and *s 171(1)* (groups of companies).

[*TCGA 1992, s 134, Sch 4 paras A1, 4(5)*].

Euroconversion of securities

A 'small' cash payment received on a 'euroconversion' of a security, not involving a disposal of the security and therefore not within *TCGA 1992, s 132* (see above), is treated in virtually identical terms as a 'small' capital distribution under *TCGA 1992, s 122* (see **57.11** below). '*Euroconversion*' for these purposes refers to the redenomination into euros of a security expressed in the currency of an EU member state participating in the European single currency. [*TCGA 1992, s 133A*].

Quoted option granted following reorganisation

[57.9] If a quoted option (within *TCGA 1992, s 144(8)* — see **7.7** ASSETS) to subscribe for shares in a company is dealt in (on the stock exchange where it is quoted) within three months after (or such longer period after as may be allowed in written notice by HMRC) a reorganisation, reduction, conversion, exchange or scheme of reconstruction (within the provisions in **57.2–57.8** above) relating to the company granting the option, then:

(a) the option is regarded for those provisions as the shares which could be acquired following the reorganisation etc. by exercising the option; and
(b) the ordinary market value rules for quoted securities apply (see **39.3** MARKET VALUE).

[*TCGA 1992, s 147*].

Stock dividends (aka scrip dividends)

[57.10] Stock or 'scrip' dividends are issues of shares in lieu of a dividend and are treated for tax purposes as described below.

Issues of shares in lieu of dividend to individuals by non-UK resident companies are treated as bonus issues, and no allowance for capital gains tax purposes is made for the cash dividend forgone. Issues made by a UK resident company are subject to income tax (see Tolley's Income Tax under Savings and Investment Income).

An issue of shares by a UK resident company does not constitute a reorganisation but is treated in the hands of the recipient shareholder as a free-standing acquisition made at the time of the issue for a consideration equal to the 'cash equivalent of the share capital'. [*TCGA 1992, s 142*]. This rule applies also to stock dividends issued by a UK real estate investment trust ('REIT') or the parent company of a UK group REIT where the issue is attributed to the property rental business within the REIT regime (see **63.5** UNIT TRUSTS AND OTHER INVESTMENT VEHICLES). [*TCGA 1992, s 142A*].

The above provisions apply not only where the shares are issued as a consequence of an option to receive additional shares instead of a cash dividend but also where they are issued as a bonus issue in a case where the existing shares carry the right under the original terms of issue (or original terms as extended or varied) to receive bonus share capital of the same or a different class. [*ITTOIA 2005, s 410(1)*].

The '*cash equivalent of the share capital*' in the case of an issue of shares in lieu of dividend is the amount of the cash dividend alternative, except where the difference between that amount and the market value of the shares issued is 15% or more of the market value, in which case, the cash equivalent is the market value. In the case of a bonus issue of share capital, the cash equivalent is the market value of the shares issued. [*ITTOIA 2005, s 412*].

If two or more persons are entitled to the shares issued, those shares (and the appropriate amount in cash) are apportioned among them by reference to their interests in the shares at the date of issue. [*ITTOIA 2005, s 413(5)(6)*].

Settlements and personal representatives

The position above applies equally to personal representatives, to trustees of discretionary and accumulation trusts where the dividend would have been chargeable at the trust rate if received in cash, and to trustees of interest in possession trusts. [*TCGA 1992, s 142; ITTOIA 2005, s 410(2)–(4)*]. The trustees' acquisition cost of the original shareholding remains unaltered and the beneficiaries are regarded as acquiring the stock dividend shares as at the dividend date for the appropriate amount in cash. However, see SP 4/94 below re enhanced stock dividends.

The beneficiaries of a bare trust are treated in the same way as individuals, the trust being ignored for this purpose (HMRC Capital Gains Manual CG33800).

In the case of a discretionary or accumulation trust where the dividend would have been chargeable at the trust rate if received in cash, the appropriate amount in cash forms part of the trustees' allowable expenditure. Any subsequent distribution of the stock dividend shares to the beneficiaries is a part disposal at market value by the trustees, with the normal identification rules applying (see **58** SHARES AND SECURITIES — IDENTIFICATION RULES).

In the case of an *enhanced stock dividend*, i.e. one which is worth significantly more than the cash dividend forgone, there was some doubt as to whether the position for interest in possession trusts outlined above could apply, the point being that the stock dividend may under trust law be capital rather than income. It is up to the trustees to decide in the light of the trust deed whether the enhanced stock dividend should properly be regarded as income or as capital. The Revenue issued Statement of Practice SP 4/94 setting out their views. They are prepared to accept whichever of the three approaches listed below the trustees conclude that they should adopt, provided that their conclusion is supportable on the facts of the case.

- If the trustees treat the dividend as income, the beneficiary is chargeable to income tax under *ITTOIA 2005, s 410* and is treated as acquiring the shares for the 'appropriate amount in cash'. The issue is not treated as a reorganisation.
- If the trustees treat the dividend as capital, the issue is a reorganisation within *TCGA 1992, s 126* (see **57.2** above) and the trustees are not regarded as having made any payment for the shares.
- If the trustees treat the dividend as capital but pay compensation to a beneficiary in the form of shares for forgoing the cash dividend alternative, the transfer constitutes a part disposal of the new holding.

See HMRC Capital Gains Manual CG33800 for a full discussion of the above.

Close companies

The appropriate amount in cash relating to shares issued in lieu of a dividend made by a UK resident company to a close company in accounting periods ending before 1 April 1989 was treated as part of its apportionable income for income tax purposes, and any income tax in respect of such income apportioned (but not paid) to a participator can be added to his allowable expenditure, for capital gains tax purposes, on a disposal of shares in the close company. The close company's allowable expenditure in respect of the shares was increased by the cash equivalent of the share capital. [*TCGA 1992, s 124; ICTA 1988, Sch 19 para 12*]. See further in **57.23** below. There is no addition to allowable expenditure of the shares held for later accounting periods or, for any accounting period, where the shares are held by a non-close company.

Example

D holds ordinary 20p shares in PLC, a quoted company. The company operates a scrip dividend policy whereby shareholders are given the option to take dividends in cash or in new fully-paid ordinary 20p shares, the option being exercisable separately in relation to each dividend. D purchased 2,000 shares for £1,500 in March 1980 and a further 3,000 shares for £8,100 in May 1992 and up until the end of 1997, he had always taken cash dividends. In January 1998, he opted for a scrip dividend and received 25 shares instead of a cash dividend of £100. On 20 April 1998, he purchased a further 1,000 shares for £3,950. In July 1998, he opted for a scrip dividend of 44 shares instead of a cash dividend of £180. He opted for cash dividends thereafter. In May 2024, he sells 2,069 shares for £8,550 (ex div), leaving himself with a holding of 4,000.

In the case of both scrip dividends taken by D, the market value of the new shares is equivalent to the cash dividend forgone. The 'cash equivalent of the share capital' is thus the amount of that dividend. The market value at 31 March 1982 of 20p shares in PLC is 80p.

The 'section 104 holding' is as follows.

Section 104 holding

	Shares	Qualifying expenditure
		£
March 1980 acquisition	2,000	1,600
May 1992 acquisition	3,000	8,100
January 1998 scrip dividend	25	100
April 1998 acquisition	1,000	3,950
July 1998 scrip dividend	44	180
	6,069	13,930
May 2024 disposal	(2,069)	(4,749)
Pool carried forward	4,000	£9,181

	£
Proceeds	8,550
Cost £13,930 × 2,069/6,069	4,749
Chargeable gain 2024/25	£3,801

Capital distributions

[57.11] A capital distribution (other than of a new holding within 57.2 above) is treated as accruing to the shareholder from the disposal of an interest in the shares.

For this purpose, a '*capital distribution*' is any distribution, on liquidation or otherwise, in money or money's worth by a company to a shareholder, which is not treated as income for tax purposes.

The circumstances in which a distribution is treated as income for tax purposes include where a distribution to which the charge to corporation tax on income under *CTA 2009, Pt 9A* would apply were the distribution not exempt for the purposes of that Part.

[*TCGA 1992, s 122(1)(5)(6)*].

If the amount or value of the capital distribution is 'small' as compared with the value of the shares in respect of which it is made, the capital distribution shall not be treated as a disposal, in which case no immediate capital gains tax liability arises, but the proceeds are deducted from the acquisition cost of the shares on a subsequent disposal. [*TCGA 1992, s 122(2)*].

For this purpose, HMRC regard 'small' as meaning 5% or less and additionally regard an amount of £3,000 or less as 'small', regardless of whether or not it would pass the 5% test (see HMRC Capital Gains Manual CG57835).

Where the amount or value of the capital distribution exceeds any allowable expenditure on the shares, the taxpayer may elect to have *all* such expenditure set against the distribution with the balance of the distribution being treated as on a part disposal and the expenditure deducted not allowable on that or any subsequent disposal. [*TCGA 1992, s 122(4)*]. In *O'Rourke v Binks* CA 1992, 65 TC 165, it was held that the right to make the election under *TCGA 1992, s 122(4)* was constrained by the requirement of *TCGA 1992, s 122(2)* that the amount or value of the capital distribution be small as compared with the value of the shares in respect of which it was made.

Example 1

T holds 10,000 ordinary shares in a foreign company M SA. The shares were bought in April 2013 for £80,000. In February 2025, M SA has a capital reconstruction involving the cancellation of one-fifth of the existing ordinary shares in consideration of the repayment of £10 to each shareholder per share cancelled. T's holding is reduced to 8,000 shares, valued at £96,000.

	£
Disposal consideration (2,000 × £10)	20,000
Allowable cost $\dfrac{20,000}{20,000 + 96,000} \times £80,000$	13,793

Chargeable gain 2024/25	£6,207
The allowable cost of the remaining shares is £80,000 – £13,793	£66,207

Example 2 (Sale of rights)

X is a shareholder in K Ltd, owning 2,500 £1 ordinary shares which were purchased for £7,000 in October 1997. K Ltd makes a rights issue, but X sells his rights, without taking them up, for £700 in August 2024. The ex-rights value of X's 2,500 shares at the date of sale is £14,500.

'Section 104 holding' of K Ltd £1 ordinary shares

	Shares	Qualifying expenditure
		£
October 1997 acquisition	2,500	7,000

HMRC cannot require the capital distribution to be treated as a disposal, as the £700 received for the rights does not exceed 5% of (£700 + £14,500) and in any case does not exceed £3,000. If the transaction is not treated as a disposal, the £700 is deducted from the acquisition cost of the shares leaving a balance of £6,300. If the transaction is treated as a disposal (possibly because X wishes to utilise part of his annual exempt amount), the computation is as follows.

	£
Disposal proceeds	700
Allowable cost $\frac{700}{700 + 14{,}500} \times £7{,}000$	322
Chargeable gain 2024/25	£378

The allowable cost of the shares is then reduced to £6,678 (£7,000 – £322).

Distributions in a liquidation — unquoted shares

[57.12] Instead of requiring a strict valuation of unquoted shares for the purposes of the part disposal arising on a distribution, HMRC are prepared to accept a reasonable estimate of the residual value of the shares if the liquidation is expected to be completed within two years of the first distribution. If the distribution takes longer, the valuations may be reopened. Where the taxpayer is a company and time apportionment (see **8.12** ASSETS HELD ON **28 MARCH 1982**) applies, HMRC are prepared to calculate the gain on each distribution by applying the time apportionment fraction as at the date of the first distribution (HMRC Statement of Practice SP D3).

Distributions of assets in specie in a liquidation

[57.13] Where a company-owned asset, for example shares in a subsidiary, is distributed by the liquidator in specie to shareholders, *TCGA 1992, s 17* (see **39.1** MARKET VALUE) must be applied in determining the acquisition cost of an asset so received by a shareholder. For this purpose, each distribution to each shareholder is considered in isolation from the others. For example, if an asset is distributed equally to each of five shareholders, the acquisition cost for capital gains tax purposes of the part received by each (and also its disposal value from the point of view of the company) is the value of a 20% share, and not one-fifth of the value of a 100% share which may have produced a different (and almost certainly higher) figure. In a case in which the company is controlled by persons connected with each other, so that each such person is connected with the company (see **17.5** CONNECTED PERSONS), it is understood that the above nevertheless applies and that HMRC would not normally invoke the linked transactions provisions of *TCGA 1992, s 19* (see **4.14** ANTI-AVOIDANCE) so as to value each distribution as a percentage of the whole.

Disposal of shares to employee-ownership trust

[57.14] A relief from capital gains tax applies to a disposal of certain shares in a trading company to the trustees of a settlement which operates for the benefit of all the employees of the company. The relief is available only if the settlement acquires a controlling interest in the company in the tax year of the disposal. The person making the disposal must make a claim for the relief.

The requirements for relief are as follows:

(a) a person other than a company disposes of any 'ordinary share capital' of a company to the trustees of a settlement;
(b) the person making the disposal makes a claim for relief;
(c) the company meets the trading requirement at **57.15** below at the time of the disposal and continues to meet that requirement for the remainder of the tax year;
(d) the settlement meets the all-employee benefit requirement at **57.16** below at the time of the disposal and continues to meet that requirement for the remainder of the tax year;
(e) the settlement does not meet the controlling interest requirement at **57.17** below immediately before the tax year in which the disposal is made, but does meet it at the end of that year and, if it meets the requirement before the end of that year (whether before or after the time of the disposal) it continues to meet it throughout the remainder of that year;
(f) the limited participation requirement at **57.18** below is met; and
(g) relief under these provisions does not apply to any 'related' disposal by the person making the disposal in question or a person connected with him in an earlier tax year.

For the purposes of (d) above, unless the settlement met the all-employee benefit requirement at the time of disposal on the basis that it was created before 10 December 2013 and satisfied the conditions at **57.16**(A), (B) below, that basis cannot be used to determine whether the settlement continues to meet the requirement. If the settlement initially met the requirement on that basis but subsequently meets the requirement on the basis of meeting the conditions at **57.16**(a)–(d) below, it cannot revert to meeting the requirement on the original basis.

'*Ordinary share capital*' means all issued share capital of a company except that carrying a fixed rate of dividend only. For the purposes of (g) above, a disposal in an earlier tax year is '*related*' to the disposal in question if both are of ordinary share capital of the same company or the earlier disposal is of ordinary share capital of a company which is, or was at the time of the earlier disposal, a member of the same group (see **57.15** below) as the company in question. In determining whether a person is connected with another, the provisions in **17** CONNECTED PERSONS apply as if 'relative' included any aunt, uncle, niece or nephew.

Relief is also available where the trustees of a settlement (the 'acquiring settlement') become absolutely entitled to settled property consisting of ordinary share capital of a company as against the trustee of that settled property (the 'transferring trustee') so that a deemed disposal arises under *TCGA 1992, s 71(1)* (see **56.16** SETTLEMENTS) and the conditions at (c)–(f) above are met. The transferring trustee must make a claim.

Effect of the relief

Where the above requirements are met, the disposal and the trustees' acquisition (or the deemed disposal and acquisition) are treated as made for a consideration resulting in no gain and no loss.

Disqualifying events

If there is one or more 'disqualifying event' in the tax year following that in which the disposal is made, no claim for relief may be made on or after the day of the first such event, and, if a claim has been made before that day, the claim is treated as revoked and all affected chargeable gains and allowable losses of any person are recalculated as if the claim had never been made. A 'disqualifying event' occurs if and when:

(i) the company ceases to meet the trading requirement (see **57.15** below); or
(ii) the settlement ceases to meet the controlling interest requirement (see **57.17** below); or
(iii) the settlement ceases to meet the all-employee benefit requirement (see **57.16** below); or
(iv) the participation fraction exceeds 2/5 (see **57.18** below); or
(v) the trustees act in a way which the trusts, as required by the all-employee benefit requirement, do not permit.

For the purposes of (iii) above, unless the settlement met the all-employee benefit requirement at the time of acquisition on the basis that it was created before 10 December 2013 and satisfied the conditions at **57.16**(A), (B) below, that basis cannot be used to determine whether the settlement continues to meet the requirement. If the settlement initially met the requirement on that basis but subsequently meets the requirement on the basis of meeting the conditions at **57.13**(a)–(d) below, it cannot revert to meeting the requirement on the original basis.

Where the participator fraction exceeds two fifths for a period lasting no more than six months, any time in that period is ignored for the purposes of (iv) above if the fraction exceeded the limit because of events outside the reasonable control of the trustees.

Where relief is obtained under these provisions, the relief is effectively clawed back on the acquiring trustees on the first occasion after the tax year following the tax year of the disposal on which there is a disqualifying event. The trustees are treated as having disposed of and immediately reacquired any ordinary share capital of the company acquired in circumstances in which relief was obtained (and not previously disposed of and reacquired) at market value immediately before the event.

Claims

A claim for relief must include information to identify the settlement acquiring the share capital, the name of the company and its registered office address, the date of disposal and the number of shares disposed of or deemed to be disposed of.

Share identification

Shares held by trustees which are acquired or deemed to be acquired in circumstances in which the above relief applied (and which have not been subsequently disposed of and reacquired) are treated as of a different class to any other shares held by the trustees for the purposes of the share identification provisions (see 58 SHARES AND SECURITIES — IDENTIFICATION RULES). Where the trustees hold shares which would be of the same class but for this rule and they dispose of some, but not all, of them, they may determine what proportion of the shares disposed of are shares to which the above relief applied (up to the number of such shares held). This rule does not, however, apply to a disposal deemed to arise on the happening of a disqualifying event.

[*TCGA 1992, ss 104(4A), 236H, 236NA–236Q, 236S(1)(3)*].

Trading requirement

[57.15] A company meets the trading requirement if it is either a '*trading company*' which is not a member of a group or the 'principal company' of a 'trading group'.

For this purpose a '*trading company*' is a company carrying on trading activities (i.e. activities carried on in the course of, or for the purposes of, a trade) and not carrying on any other activities to a substantial extent. A '*trade*' means one conducted on a commercial basis and with a view to the realisation of profits.

A '*trading group*' is a group one or more of whose members carry on trading group activities (i.e. activities carried on by a group member in the course of, or for the purposes of, a trade being carried on by any group member) and the activities of whose members, taken together, do not include to a substantial extent any activities which are not trading group activities.

In determining whether a company is a trading company or the principal company of a trading group, the activities of the group's members are treated as one business (so that intra-group activities are ignored) and a business carried on in partnership is treated as not being a trading activity or trading group activity.

'*Group*', membership of a group and '*principal company*' of a group are defined for these purposes in *TCGA 192, s 170* (see **26.2** GROUPS OF COMPANIES). Where applied to a company incorporated outside the UK, references to a group must be construed with any necessary modifications.

[*TCGA 1992, ss 236I, 236S(1)(2)*].

All-employee benefit requirement

[57.16] A settlement meets the all-employee benefit requirement if the trusts of the settlement do not permit at any time:

(a) any settled property or income arising from it to be applied otherwise than for the benefit of all the 'eligible employees' on the same terms;
(b) the trustees to apply at any time any settled property or income arising from it by creating a trust or transferring property to the trustees of another settlement other than by an 'authorised transfer';
(c) the trustees to make loans to beneficiaries; and
(d) the trustees or any other person to amend the trusts so that they would not comply with any of (a)–(c) above.

In (a) above, employees and office-holders of the company or any group member are '*eligible employees*' unless:

(i) they are a participator in the company or a group member;
(ii) they are a participator in a close company which has made a disposition under which property became comprised in the settlement if that disposition would have been a transfer of value for inheritance tax purposes but for *IHTA 1984, ss 13, 13A* (dispositions by close company for benefit of employees or to employee-ownership trusts);
(iii) they have been a participator in a company within (i) or (ii) above at any time on or after the first day of the 10 years ending on later of the 10 December 2013 and the day on which any property first entered the settlement; or
(iv) they are connected (see **57.14** above) with any person within (i) to (iii) above.

A participator who is not beneficially entitled to (or to rights entitling him to acquire) 5% or more of (or of any class of the shares in) the company's capital and who on a winding-up would not be entitled to 5% of more of the assets is not, however, excluded from being an eligible employee by (i)-(iv) above. Where the company has ceased to meet the trading requirement or the trustees have ceased to hold any shares in the company, an individual who was an eligible employee at any time in the two years before that event continues to be an eligible employee. '*Close company*' and '*participator*' are defined for these purposes as in *IHTA 1984, s 102*. If the company is not a close company, 'participator' means a person who would be a participator by applying that definition if the company were close.

The condition in (a) above is not infringed by reason only that the trusts:

(1) permit the settled property or income from it to be applied as if the spouse, civil partner or dependant of a deceased eligible employee were themselves an eligible employee for up to a year after the death;

(2) prevent the settled property or income from it being applied for the benefit of employees who have not been eligible employees for a continuous period of up to twelve months;
(3) permit the trustees to comply with a written request by a person not to receive the benefit of any settled property or income from it; or
(4) prevent the settled property or income from it being applied for the benefit of all office-holders.

The condition in (a) above is also not infringed by reason only that the trusts also permit the settled property or income from it to be applied for charitable purposes. Subject to these exceptions, the condition in (a) above is infringed if the trusts permit the settled property or any income from it to be applied by reference to factors other than remuneration, length of service or hours worked. The condition is not infringed by reason only that the trusts permit the settled property or any income from it to be applied for the benefit of all the eligible employees by reference to those factors unless the terms of the trusts are such that some (but not all) eligible employees receive no benefits (other than where (2)–(4) above apply). Where settled property or income is applied by reference to more than one of those factors, each such factor must give rise to a separate entitlement to benefits and the total entitlement must be the sum of those separate entitlements.

In (b) above, an '*authorised transfer*' is a transfer of property which includes any ordinary share capital of a company which meets the trading requirement in **57.15** above to the trustees of a settlement which meets the controlling interest requirement in **57.17** below in relation to the company immediately after the transfer and meets the all-employee benefit requirement (ignoring the provisions below which deem that requirement to be met in certain cases).

Where a settlement would not otherwise meet the all-employee benefit requirement at any time it is treated as doing so at that time if it was created before 10 December 2013 and:

(A) on that date *IHTA 1984, s 86* (trusts for the benefit of employees) applied to the settled property, the trustees held a 'significant interest' in the company and the settlement did not otherwise meet the all-employee benefit requirement; and
(B) the trustees do not, during the twelve months ending with the time in question: apply any of the settled property or income from it otherwise than for the benefit of all eligible employees on the same terms; apply any of that property or income by creating a trust or by transferring property to the trustees of a settlement other than by an authorised transfer; or make loans to beneficiaries.

For the purposes of (A) above, the trustees held a 'significant interest' in the company on 10 December 2013 if on that date:

(I) they held 10% or more of the ordinary share capital of the company and had voting powers in the company which would yield 10% or more of the total available votes;
(II) they were entitled to 10% or more of the profits available for distribution to the company's equity holders;
(III) they would have been entitled, on a winding-up of the company, to 10% or more of the assets available for distribution to equity holders; and

(IV) there were no provisions in any agreement or instrument affecting the company's constitution or management or its shares or securities under which the conditions in (I)-(III) above could cease to be satisfied without the trustees' consent.

The provisions of *CTA 2010, ss 157–182* (group relief: equity holders and profits available for distribution) apply for the purposes of (I)–(IV) above. For the purposes of (II) above, trustees are treated as entitled to dividends on shares even if they are required or permitted by the trusts to waive their entitlement. In determining whether (IV) above applies, any provision of a mortgage or charge granted by the trustees to a third party to secure any debt and any agreement in respect of a loan made to the trustees by a third party are ignored if they confer an entitlement on the third party in the event of a default by the trustees. '*Third party*' for this purpose means a person other than the company, a group member, a person who is, or has at any time in the preceding twelve months been, a participator in the company or a group member, or a person connected with such a person.

The requirement in (B) above that the trustees must not apply property or income otherwise than for the benefit of all eligible employees on the same terms is treated as infringed or not infringed in the same circumstances as apply to the condition in (a) above. Anything done by the trustees before 10 December 2013 is ignored for the purposes of (B) above.

[*TCGA 1992, ss 236J–236L, 236R*].

Controlling interest requirement

[57.17] A settlement meets the controlling interest requirement if:

(a) the trustees hold more than 50% of the ordinary share capital of the company and have voting powers in the company which would yield a majority of the total available votes;
(b) they are entitled to more than 50% of the profits available for distribution to the company's equity holders;
(c) they would be entitled, on a winding-up of the company, to more than 50% of the assets available for distribution to equity holders; and
(d) there are no provisions in any agreement or instrument affecting the company's constitution or management or its shares or securities under which the conditions in (a)-(c) could cease to be satisfied without the trustees' consent.

The provisions of *CTA 2010, ss 157–182* (group relief: equity holders and profits available for distribution) apply for the purposes of (a)–(d) above. For the purposes of (b) above, trustees are treated as entitled to dividends on shares even if they are required or permitted by the trusts to waive their entitlement. In determining whether (d) above applies, any provision of a mortgage or charge granted by the trustees to a third party to secure any debt and any agreement in respect of a loan made to the trustees by a third party are ignored if they confer an entitlement on the third party in the event of a default by the trustees. '*Third party*' for this purpose means a person other than the company, a group member, a person who is, or has at any time in the preceding twelve months been, a participator in the company or a group member, or a person connected with such a person.

[*TCGA 1992, ss 236M, 236R*].

Limited participation requirement

[57.18] The limited participation requirement is met if:

(1) there was no time in the twelve months ending immediately after the disposal when the person making the disposal was a 'participator' in the company and the 'participator fraction' exceeded two fifths; and

(2) the participator fraction does not exceed 2/5 at any time in the period beginning with that disposal and ending at the end of the tax year in which it occurs.

Where, however, the participator fraction exceeds two fifths for a period lasting no more than six months, any time in that period is ignored for the purposes of (1) and (2) above if the fraction exceeded the limit because of events outside the reasonable control of the trustees.

The '*participation fraction*' is NP/NE where:

NP is the sum of the number of persons who are both participators and employees or office-holders of the company and the number of other persons who are both connected with such persons and are also employees or office-holders of the company or a member of the group.

NE is the number of employees of the company or any member of the group.

Participators who are not beneficially entitled to, or to rights entitling them to acquire, 5% or more of, or of any class of, the company's share capital and who would be entitled to less than 5% of the company's assets on a winding-up are excluded in calculating the participation fraction.

'*Participator*' for the purposes of the above provisions is defined as in *CTA 2010, s 454*. If the company is not a close company, 'participator' means a person who would be a participator by applying that definition if the company were close.

[*TCGA 1992, s 236N*].

Company purchase of own shares (aka share buy-back)

[57.19] *Companies Act 2006, Pt 18* provides the authority for a company to buy back its own shares from its shareholders, subject to various conditions. This facility can be useful in providing an exit route for investors where an external buyer for shares is not available. A company can buy back its own shares out of distributable profits or proceeds from a new share issue. Normally, the repurchased shares are cancelled but a company may purchase and hold its own shares (known as treasury shares).

Treasury shares

The following provisions ensure that for tax purposes own shares held without cancellation are treated as if cancelled, and as newly issued shares if they are subsequently sold.

Where a company acquires any of its shares, whether by purchase, bonus issue or otherwise, it is not treated for tax purposes as acquiring an asset. The company is not treated as a result of acquiring or holding the shares, or of being entered on its register of members in respect of any of them, as a member of itself. The company's issued share capital is treated as reduced by the nominal value of the shares acquired. Any shares not cancelled on acquisition are treated as cancelled, and any subsequent cancellation is disregarded (and is therefore not a disposal of an asset and does not give rise to an allowable loss). If the shares were issued to the company as bonus shares (i.e. share capital issued as paid up otherwise than by the receipt of new consideration within *CTA 2010, s 1115*) they are treated as if they had not been issued.

Where a company holds any treasury shares and it issues bonus shares in respect of those shares or any class of those shares, the above provisions do not prevent the existing shares being the company's 'holding' of shares for the purposes of the application of *TCGA 1992, s 126* (reorganisation of share capital — see **57.2** above) other than its application in modified form by virtue of any chargeable gains provision (see, for example, *TCGA 1992, s 192(2)* at **14.13** COMPANIES).

Where a company disposes of any of its treasury shares, the shares are not treated as having been disposed of by the company at the time of the disposal but are treated as having been issued as new shares by the company at that time. The person acquiring the shares is treated as having subscribed for them for an amount equal to any consideration payable for the disposal of the shares by the company. If that consideration does not exceed the nominal value of the shares, the share capital of the shares is treated for the purposes of *CTA 2010, Pt 23* (company distributions etc.) as being the amount of the consideration. If the consideration exceeds the nominal value, the shares are treated as issued at a premium equal to that excess.

The above provisions do not apply to a company purchasing its own shares if the price payable by the company is taken into account in computing its trading profits.

[*FA 2003, s 195*].

Treatment of vendor on company purchasing own shares

Any consideration given by a company for the redemption, repayment or purchase of its own shares (whether or not those shares are then held as treasury shares), *except* insofar as it represents repayment of share capital, is normally treated as a distribution, and hence as income in the hands of the recipient (see Tolley's Corporation Tax under Distributions).

The purchase by the company is nevertheless still a disposal by the shareholder concerned for capital gains purposes, but, for a non-corporate shareholder, the element of the consideration representing a distribution is excluded in the computation under *TCGA 1992, s 37* (see **33.1** INTERACTION WITH OTHER TAXES), as it is taken into account for the purposes of computing income.

For a corporate shareholder, it is likely that the distribution will be treated as exempt from corporation tax. Consequently, the whole of the purchase price must be brought into account in the calculation of any chargeable gain on the disposal. Only if a company receives a non-exempt distribution will the element of the consideration representing a distribution be excluded in the computation.

Payments in respect of shares in unquoted trading companies (or holding companies) are *not* treated as distributions where certain conditions are met, and thus give rise to liability to capital gains tax (or corporation tax on chargeable gains) on the recipient in the normal way. See Tolley's Corporation Tax under Purchase by a Company of its Own Shares for detailed conditions. [*CTA 2010, ss 1033–1048*].

HMRC have published guidance on some of the main tax issues that may arise where employees of unquoted companies sell shares to their employer. See www.gov.uk/government/publications/purchase-of-own-shares-by-non-quoted-companies-tax-implications-for-employees-selling-shares.

Example

Paul has 50 £1 shares in Tracy Ltd bought back by the company at £6 per share in August 2024. Paul had originally purchased the shares for £150 in July 2011 from a person who had subscribed from them at par. The buy back does not qualify for capital treatment.

Paul is treated as receiving a distribution from Tracy Ltd as follows.

	£
Disposal proceeds	300
Less nominal value	50
Dividend	£250

Paul has also made a capital disposal and the allowable loss is calculated as follows.

	£
Disposal proceeds	300
Less amount charged to income tax	250
	50
Less acquisition cost	150
Allowable loss	£100

Accrued income scheme

[57.20] The accrued income scheme provisions (see now *ITA 2007, ss 615–681*) apply, broadly, to transfers of any government, public authority or company loan stock. (See further **58.6** SHARES AND SECURITIES — IDENTIFICATION RULES.)

The accrued income scheme does not apply for the purposes of corporation tax. [*ICTA 1988, s 710(1A)*].

It also does not apply on a transfer to which *ITTOIA 2005, ss 427–460* apply (charge to or relief from tax on the profit or loss realised from the discount on a deeply discounted security — see **57.21** below).

If a transfer is with accrued interest, a payment (calculated under *ITA 2007, s 632* and broadly representing the accrued interest) is treated as made by the transferee to the transferor in the interest period in which the settlement day falls. If the transfer is without accrued interest, a payment (calculated under *ITA 2007, s 633* and broadly representing the interest accruing from the settlement day to the next interest payment day) is treated as made by the transferee to the transferor in the relevant interest period. Special rules apply to transfers with unrealised interest and of variable rate securities. For each kind of security transferred by or to a person in an interest period, the deemed payments are then used to calculate (under *ITA 2007, ss 628–631*) his accrued income profits or losses. Profits are chargeable to income tax and losses are carried forward as payments made in the next interest period.

Capital gains

Where there is a transfer within the accrued income provisions either with or without accrued interest, neither *TCGA 1992, s 37* nor *s 39* applies (see **33.1** INTERACTION WITH OTHER TAXES). Instead, where a transfer is with accrued interest, an amount equal to deemed payment under *ITA 2007, s 632* is excluded from the transferor's disposal consideration, and the same amount is excluded from the transferee's allowable expenditure when he makes a subsequent disposal. Where the transfer is without accrued interest, an amount equal to the deemed payment under *ITA 2007, s 633* is added to the transferor's disposal consideration, and the same amount is added to the transferee's allowable expenditure when he makes a subsequent disposal. Similar rules apply to transfers with unrealised interest and of variable rate securities and where there is a disposal (e.g. a deemed disposal) without there being a contemporaneous transfer within the scope of the accrued income provisions.

Where on a 'conversion' (being one within *TCGA 1992, s 132*; see **57.8** above) or an 'exchange' (being one which is not treated as a disposal: see generally **57.2** above) of securities, a payment is treated under the accrued income provisions as made to the transferor (or an accrued income profit is treated as accruing to him in respect of variable rate securities), an equal amount less any consideration received on the conversion or exchange (other than the new holding of securities) is treated for the purposes of *TCGA 1992* as consideration given on the conversion or exchange. Where the consideration received on the conversion or exchange (other than the new holding of securities) equals or exceeds an amount equal to the accrued amount, that consideration is treated for the purposes of *TCGA 1992* as reduced by that amount. If on a conversion or exchange of securities, a payment is treated under the accrued income provisions as made by the transferor, an equal amount is treated for the purposes of *TCGA 1992* as consideration received on the conversion or exchange.

[*TCGA 1992, s 119*].

See Tolley's Income Tax for full details of the accrued income scheme.

The above procedures will not be required for the purposes of computing a chargeable gain where the security is otherwise exempt. See 28 GOVERNMENT SECURITIES and 48 QUALIFYING CORPORATE BONDS.

Deeply discounted securities

[57.21] When a person transfers a 'deeply discounted security', or becomes entitled, as holder, to any payment on its redemption, he is chargeable to **income tax** on the excess of the amount payable on the transfer or redemption over the amount paid for its acquisition. In the event of a loss on a transfer or redemption of listed securities held on 26 March 2003 or strips of government securities, a claim may be made for relief against income of the tax year of transfer or redemption. There are anti-avoidance provisions denying loss relief in respect of strips of government securities where there is a scheme for the manipulation of the acquisition, sale or redemption price. The provisions are extended to prevent an allowable loss arising for capital gains tax purposes as a result of the making of a payment under such a scheme otherwise than in respect of the acquisition or disposal of a strip (see now *TCGA 1992, s 151C*). Similar provisions prevent an allowable loss arising for capital gains tax as a result of the making of a payment under a scheme for the manipulation of the acquisition, sale or redemption price of a 'corporate strip' (see below) acquired after 1 December 2004 (see now *TCGA 1992, s 151D*).

See Tolley's Income Tax for the detailed provisions. The provisions do **not** apply for corporation tax purposes.

Meaning of 'deeply discounted security'

A '*deeply discounted security*' is, except as excluded below, any security such that the amount payable on redemption (excluding interest) is or might be an amount involving a '*deep gain*', i.e. the issue price is less than the amount payable on redemption by 15% of that amount or, if less, by $^1/_2$% per annum of that amount (counting months and part months as $^1/_{12}$th of a year) to the redemption date. This comparison is made as at the time of issue of the security and assuming redemption in accordance with the terms of issue. 'Redemption' for these purposes referred originally to redemption on maturity or, if the holder of the security could opt for earlier redemption, the earliest occasion on which the holder might require redemption. In addition to redemption on maturity, possible earlier occasions on which a security might be redeemed must also be considered. The security will be a deeply discounted security if it would be such by reference to at least one such occasion. One need not take into account any occasion on which there may be a redemption other than at the option of the holder *unless* issuer and holder are connected or the obtaining of a tax advantage (as defined) is a main benefit that might be expected to accrue from the redemption provision. Additionally, where the holder has an option entitling him to redeem only on the occurrence of an 'event adversely affecting the holder' (as defined) or of a person's default *and* such entitlement is unlikely, judged at time of issue, to arise, the potential redemption is disregarded.

Gilt strips and strips of overseas government securities acquired after 26 March 2003 are always deeply discounted securities regardless of their issue terms. Strips of interest-bearing corporate securities ('*corporate strips*') acquired after 1 December 2004 are likewise always deeply discounted securities regardless of their issue terms.

Special rules apply to determine the issue price of (and the amount paid for the acquisition of) securities issued to a person in accordance with the terms of a 'qualifying earn-out right' (as defined). See Tolley's Income Tax for details.

The following are not deeply discounted securities:

(i) shares in a company;
(ii) gilt-edged securities (but see above concerning gilt strips and strips of overseas government securities);
(iii) excluded indexed securities (as defined);
(iv) life assurance policies;
(v) capital redemption policies; and
(vi) (with exceptions) securities issued under the same prospectus as other securities issued previously but not themselves deeply discounted securities.

Securities within (iii) and (vi) above may, however, be treated as deeply discounted securities in certain circumstances involving their being held by a person connected with the issuer. *ITA 2007, s 993* applies to determine whether persons are connected for the purposes of these provisions but without taking any account of the security under review or any security issued under the same prospectus.

[*ITTOIA 2005, ss 427–460; TCGA 1992, ss 151C, 151D*].

Avoidance of double charge

For the avoidance of a double charge, i.e. to both income tax and capital gains tax (and double relief for losses), any deeply discounted security, whatever its date of issue, is brought within the definition of a QUALIFYING CORPORATE BOND (**48**). [*TCGA 1992, s 117(2AA)(8A)*]. However, a deeply discounted security does not qualify for the relief at **38.12** LOSSES for irrecoverable pre-17 March 1998 loans on securities.

Depositary receipts

[57.22] Depositary receipts are used as substitute instruments indicating ownership of shares and securities and designed primarily to enable investors to hold and deal in shares of companies located outside the investor's country. They are issued by a bank or other financial institution (the depositary), with whom the share certificate is deposited. Where a depositary receipt is issued in the UK, HMRC's view is that its holder retains beneficial ownership of the underlying shares. This has the following results.

- A transfer of shares by a shareholder to a depositary in exchange for an issue of depositary receipts is not a disposal of the shares for CGT purposes.

- A disposal of the depositary receipts is a disposal of both the depositary receipts and the underlying shares. In practice, the value of depositary receipts will track the value of the underlying shares and to that extent HMRC regard the consideration for the disposal of the depositary receipts as consideration for the disposal of the shares.
- In a share exchange (see 57.5 above) or company reconstruction (see 57.7 above) in which shareholders have an option to receive depositary receipts instead of being issued with shares, HMRC accept that the shares are treated for the purpose of *TCGA 1992, s 135* as being issued to the shareholders.
- If the holder of depositary receipts converts them back into the underlying shares, there is no change of ownership of those shares and so no disposal of the shares. There will have been a disposal of the depositary receipts and the usual computational rules will apply. If no consideration is received for the disposal of the depositary receipts there will be no chargeable gain.
- Where a person holds the same class of shares directly and through depositary receipts, then they may be regarded as constituting a single holding for share identification purposes.

Following the decision in the stamp duty reserve tax case of *HSBC Holdings and Bank of New York Mellon v HMRC* FTT, [2012] UKFTT 163 (TC), HMRC consider that, where a depositary receipt is issued outside the UK, the beneficial ownership of the underlying shares should be determined by reference to the law of the territory in which the depositary receipt was issued. If the beneficial ownership cannot be determined conclusively, HMRC will consider the holder of a depsoitary receipt as holding the beneficial interest in the underlying shares, with the same consequences as above. If the relevant law means that the holder of a depositary receipt is not the beneficial owner of the underlying shares, the consequences are as follows.

- A transfer of shares by a shareholder to a depositary in exchange for an issue of depositary receipts is a disposal of the shares for CGT purposes.
- A disposal of the depositary receipts is not a disposal of the underlying shares.
- In a share exchange (see 57.5 above) or company reconstruction (see 57.7 above) in which shareholders have an option to receive depositary receipts instead of being issued with shares, HMRC consider that *TCGA 1992, s 135* will not apply to shareholders taking depsoitary receipts as they will not have been issued with shares.
- Where a holder of depositary receipts converts them into the underlying shares there will be a disposal of the depositary receipts and an acquisition of the shares.

(HMRC Capital Gains Manual CG50240). See **7.3** ASSETS as regards location of shares held in depositary receipt form.

Close companies

[57.23] Income tax which has been charged on a participator as a result of an apportionment under *ICTA 1988, ss 423–430, Sch 19* (broadly only in relation to accounting periods ending before 1 April 1989) and paid by him in respect of income of a close company which has not subsequently been distributed (including stock dividends; see **57.10** above), may be deducted, pro rata, in computing a gain on the disposal of any of his shares in that company. Shares are identified on a first in, first out basis. [*TCGA 1992, s 124*].

Tax paid which is referable to gains of a non-resident company charged on a UK participator or shareholder under *TCGA 1992, s 3* (previously *TCGA 1992, s 13*; see **43.7** OVERSEAS MATTERS) is similarly deductible. See also **16.13** COMPUTATION OF GAINS AND LOSSES for an alternative concessional treatment.

Life assurance policies

[57.24] Investments or other assets transferred to a policy holder by an insurance company, in accordance with a life assurance policy, are deemed to be transferred at market value. [*TCGA 1992, s 204(3)(6)*].

Stock lending arrangements

[57.25] The following provisions apply in relation to 'stock lending arrangements'.

Definition

A '*stock lending arrangement*' is an arrangement between two persons ('the borrower' and 'the lender') under which:

(a) the lender transfers 'securities' to the borrower otherwise than by way of sale; and
(b) a requirement is imposed on the borrower to transfer those securities back to the lender otherwise than by way of sale.

Subject to the following provisions, the disposals and acquisitions made in pursuance of any stock lending arrangement *are disregarded* for the purposes of capital gains tax. [*TCGA 1992, s 263B(1)(2)*].

Disposals by the borrower

If the borrower under any stock lending arrangement disposes of any securities transferred to him under the arrangement such that that disposal is made otherwise than in the discharge of the requirement for the transfer of securities back to the lender, and that requirement, so far as it relates to the securities disposed of, has been or will be discharged by the transfer of securities other than those transferred to the borrower, any question relating to the acquisition of the securities disposed of shall be determined as if the securities disposed of were the securities with which that requirement (so far as relating to the securities disposed of) has been or will be discharged. [*TCGA 1992, s 263B(3)*].

Transfer back to the lender not taking place

The ensuing consequences will occur in the case of any stock lending arrangement, where it becomes apparent, at any time after the making of the transfer by the lender, that the requirement for the borrower to make a transfer back to the lender will not be complied with.

(i) The lender is deemed to have made a disposal at that time of the securities transferred to the borrower;
(ii) The borrower is deemed to have acquired them at that time; and
(iii) *TCGA 1992, s 263B(3)* (above) shall have effect in relation to any disposal before that time by the borrower of securities transferred to him by the lender as if the securities deemed to have been acquired by the borrower were to be used for discharging a requirement to transfer securities back to the lender.

The disposal in (i) above and acquisition in (ii) above are at market value.

This provision does not apply where the insolvency provisions below apply.

[*TCGA 1992, s 263B(4)*].

References, in relation to a person to whom securities are transferred, to the transfer of those securities back to another person are to be construed as if the cases where those securities are taken to be transferred back to that other person included any case where securities of the same description as those securities are transferred to that other person either:

(a) in accordance with a requirement to transfer securities of the same description; or
(b) in exercise of a power to substitute securities of the same description for the securities that are required to be transferred back.

[*TCGA 1992, s 263B(5)*].

Securities are not taken to be of the same description as other securities unless they are in the same quantities, give the same rights against the same persons and are of the same type and nominal value as the other securities. '*Securities*' means shares of any company resident in the United Kingdom (*UK shares*), securities of the Government of the United Kingdom, any public or local authority in the United Kingdom or of any company or other body resident in the United Kingdom (*UK securities*) or shares, stock or other securities issued by a government or public or local authority of a territory outside the United Kingdom or by any other body of persons not resident in the United Kingdom *(overseas securities)*. [*TCGA 1992, s 263B(6)(7); CTA 2010, ss 806, 814*].

Provisions to ensure continuity of treatment for stock lending arrangements involving securities redenominated in euros following the introduction of the European single currency in certain EU member states other than the UK are contained in *SI 1998 No 3177, Regs 20–23*.

Stock lending involving redemption

A transfer back to a person of securities transferred by him shall be taken to include references to the payment to him, in pursuance of an obligation arising on any person's becoming entitled to receive an amount in respect of the redemption of those securities, of an amount equal to the amount of the entitlement. Where, in pursuance of any such obligation, the lender under any stock lending arrangement is paid any amount in respect of the redemption of any securities to which the arrangement relates:

(A) that lender shall be deemed to have disposed, for that amount, of the securities in respect of whose redemption it is paid ('*the relevant lent securities*');

(B) the borrower shall not, in respect of the redemption, be taken to have made any disposal of the relevant lent securities; and

(C) *TCGA 1992, s 263B(3)* (see above) shall have effect in relation to disposals of any of the relevant lent securities made by the borrower before the redemption as if:

  (i) the amount paid to the lender were an amount paid for the acquisition of securities, and

  (ii) the securities acquired were to be used by the borrower for discharging a requirement under the arrangement to transfer the relevant lent securities back to the lender.

[*TCGA 1992, s 263C*].

Provisions to ensure continuity of treatment for stock lending arrangements involving securities redenominated in euros following the introduction of the European single currency in certain EU member states other than the UK are contained in *SI 1998 No 3177, Regs 20–23*.

Insolvency of borrower

Subject to the commencement provisions below, the following applies where the borrower under a stock lending arrangement becomes 'insolvent' after the lender has transferred the securities and as a result, the buyer's requirement to make a transfer back to the lender will not be fully complied with.

If 'collateral' is used directly or indirectly to enable the lender to acquire replacement securities of the same description as those which will not be transferred back within 30 days beginning with the date of the insolvency, then, for chargeable gains purposes:

(i) the transfer of the original securities by the lender is not treated as a disposal (but see further below);

(ii) the borrower is treated as having acquired the securities which will not be transferred back at market value on the date of the insolvency; and

(iii) the lender's acquisition of the replacement securities is treated as if it were a transfer back of securities under the arrangement (and so is not treated as an acquisition).

If the number of replacement securities is less than the number of securities the buyer is treated as acquiring as in (ii) above, the lender is treated as disposing of the difference on the date of the insolvency. The consideration for the disposal is nil if all of the collateral is used to enable the lender to acquire the replacement securities. If not all of the collateral is used, the consideration is the difference between the market value on the date of the insolvency of the number of securities which could have been acquired using the collateral, and the market value on that date of the number of securities which were acquired. If the lender subsequently receives an amount in respect of the buyer's liability in respect of the securities treated as disposed of by the lender, that amount is treated as a chargeable gain of the lender at the time the amount is received.

For this purpose, the borrower becomes '*insolvent*' if a company or individual voluntary arrangement takes effect, if an administration application is made or a receiver or manager, or administrative receiver is appointed, on the commencement of a winding up, on the presentation of a bankruptcy petition, if a compromise or arrangement under *Companies Act 2006, Pt 26* takes effect, or a bank insolvency or administration order takes effect, or on the occurrence of a corresponding event under Scottish, NI or non-UK law. '*Collateral*' is an amount of money or property provided under the stock lending arrangement (or arrangements of which it forms part) which is payable to or made available for the benefit of the lender to secure the discharge of the requirement to transfer securities back to him.

[*TCGA 1992, s 263CA*].

Agreements for sale and repurchase of securities ('repos')

[57.26] There are special income tax and corporation tax provisions dealing with agreements for sale and repurchase of securities (commonly known as 'repos'). Such an agreement involves one party agreeing to sell securities (typically these would be corporate bonds, gilts or other Government securities or shares) to another, with a related agreement (either a forward contract or an option) to buy back the securities at an agreed date and price. Broadly, any difference between the sale and repurchase price is treated for the purposes of tax on income as interest, and the sale and repurchase are ignored for the purposes of tax on chargeable gains. Separate rules apply for corporation tax purposes, based on accounting principles. See Tolley's Income Tax and Tolley's Corporation Tax under Anti-Avoidance for the detailed income provisions. The chargeable gains provisions are detailed below.

Corporation tax on chargeable gains

Debtor repos

Where a company (the '*borrower*') has a 'debtor repo' and, having sold the securities under the repo arrangement to another party (the '*lender*'), is the only person with the right or obligation under the arrangement to repurchase those or similar securities, the sale and repurchase are ignored for the purposes of corporation tax on chargeable gains.

Where, however, at any time after the initial sale, it becomes apparent that the borrower will not make the repurchase or the accounting condition below ceases to be met, the borrower is treated for chargeable gains purposes as disposing of the securities at that time at market value. If the borrower does in fact subsequently make the repurchase this is not then ignored under the above provision.

The accounting condition mentioned above ceases to be met if, under generally accepted accounting practice, the borrower's accounts for any period after the one in which the 'advance' (i.e. the money or other asset received from the lender) is made do not record a financial liability in respect of the advance (except as a result of the subsequent purchase of the securities or similar securities).

For this purpose, a '*debtor repo*' is defined in *CTA 2009, s 548* as, broadly, a repo from the point of view of the company selling and repurchasing the securities. References above to the borrower include a partnership of which the borrower is a member.

[*FA 2007, s 47, Sch 13 para 6*].

Creditor repos

Similarly, where a company (the '*lender*') has a 'creditor repo' and, having bought the securities under the repo arrangement from another party (the '*borrower*'), is the only person with the right or obligation under the arrangement to sell those or similar securities, the purchase and sale under the arrangement are ignored for the purposes of corporation tax on chargeable gains.

Where, however, at any time after the initial sale, it becomes apparent that the lender will not make the sale under the agreement or the accounting condition below ceases to be met, the lender is treated for chargeable gains purposes as acquiring the securities at that time at market value. If the seller does in fact subsequently make the sale this is not then ignored under the above provision.

The accounting condition ceases to be met if, under generally accepted accounting practice, the lender's accounts for any period after the one in which the 'advance' (i.e. the money or other asset received by the lender) is made do not record a financial asset in respect of the advance (except as a result of the subsequent sale of the securities or similar securities).

For this purpose, a '*creditor repo*' is defined in *CTA 2009, s 543* as, broadly, a repo from the point of view of the company buying and then selling the securities. References above to the lender include a partnership of which the lender is a member.

[*FA 2007, s 47, Sch 13 para 11*].

Redemption arrangements

The above provisions apply with modifications in cases involving 'redemption arrangements'. For this purpose, a case involves '*redemption arrangements*' where arrangements, corresponding to those in repo cases, are made in relation to securities that are to be redeemed in the period after the sale, and a person, instead of having the right or obligation to buy back those or other securities, has a right or obligation in respect of the benefits that will result from the redemption. The definitions of 'debtor repo' and 'creditor repo' are modified to include such arrangements, and for chargeable gains purposes, the company selling the securities under the arrangement is treated as disposing of the securities when the redemption takes place, and the company buying the securities is treated as acquiring them at that time, for an amount equivalent to the redemption proceeds. [*FA 2007, Sch 13 para 15(6); SI 2007 No 2485, Regs 3, 4*].

Treasury power to amend provisions

The Treasury may, by regulations, modify the above provisions in relation to certain non-standard repos and cases involving redemption arrangements. This may include modification of *TCGA 1992* in relation to cases where, as a result of the regulations, an acquisition or disposal is excluded from those ignored for chargeable gains purposes under the above provisions. Regulations have been made in respect of redemption arrangements (see above) and non-standard repos involving the substitution of securities. [*FA 2007, Sch 13 para 15; SI 2007 No 2485*].

Capital gains tax

Where *ITA 2007, s 607(1)* applies to treat the price differential on sale and repurchase as an interest payment, the acquisition and disposal by the interim holder, and (except where the repurchaser is or may be different from the original owner) the disposal and acquisition (as repurchaser) by the original owner, are disregarded for chargeable gains purposes. For these purposes a repurchase arrangement is also deemed to exist where the repurchaser is connected to the original owner (see **17** CONNECTED PERSONS). Arrangements for repurchase include:

(a) requirement to buy back the securities by the agreement or related agreement;
(b) requirement to buy back the securities by exercise of an option under the agreement or related agreement; or
(c) exercise of an option to buy back the securities which was acquired under the agreement or related agreement.

References to buying back securities include the purchase of similar securities by the original owner or the repurchase of the original or similar securities by someone connected to the original owner. Similar securities are defined as securities which:

(a) give the same rights against the same person to capital, distributions, interest and dividends; and
(b) the same remedies to enforce those rights.

This definition extends to situations where there may be differences in the total nominal value of the securities, the form in which they are held or the manner in which they can be transferred.

This does not, however, apply:

(a) if the agreement(s) in question are non-arm's length agreements, or if all the benefits or risks arising from fluctuations in the market value of the securities accrue to, or fall on, the interim holder; or
(b) in relation to any disposal or acquisition of QUALIFYING CORPORATE BONDS (**48**) where the securities disposed of by the original owner, or those acquired by him or another person as repurchaser, are not such bonds.

Where, however, at any time after the initial sale, it becomes apparent that the interim holder will not dispose of the securities to the repurchaser, he is treated for capital gains tax purposes as acquiring the securities at that time at market value. Similarly, where at any time it becomes apparent that the original owner will not acquire the securities as repurchaser, he is treated for capital gains tax purposes as disposing of the securities at that time at market value.

In a case involving 'redemption arrangements' (defined, broadly as above, at *ITA 2007, s 613(2)*), the original owner is treated as disposing of the securities when the redemption takes place, and the interim holder is treated as acquiring them at that time, for an amount equivalent to the redemption proceeds.

[*TCGA 1992, s 263A–263AA; SI 2007 No 2486, Regs 3, 4*].

Where *ITA 2007, s 607* applies but *TCGA 1992, s 263A* does not, the repurchase price is, as the case may be, either reduced by the excess of that price over the sale price or increased by the excess of the sale price over that price for chargeable gains purposes. [*TCGA 1992, s 261G*].

Where the repurchase price falls to be computed by reference to the provisions of *ITA 2007, s 604* (deemed increase in repurchase price: price differences under repos) and *TCGA 1992, s 263A* does not apply, the deemed increase in that price also has effect for chargeable gains purposes. For capital gains tax purposes, where *ITA 2007, s 604* applies, either there must be no difference for the purposes of *ITA 2007, s 607* between the sale and repurchase price as a result of the increase, or that section must not apply as a result of an exemption in *ITA 2007, s 608*. [*TCGA 1992, s 261F*].

Gain accruing to person paying manufactured dividend

The following provisions apply where a person resident in the UK, other than a company,

(a) disposes of 'UK shares' (as defined in *ITA 2007, s 566(2)*)
   (i) transferred to him as the interim holder under a repurchase agreement which is a 'repo' within *ITA 2007, Pt 11*,
   (ii) transferred to him as the borrower under a stock lending arrangement (as above), or
   (iii) under a 'short sale transaction' (i.e. a contract or other arrangements for the transfer of the equities which is neither a repurchase agreement nor a stock lending arrangement) to which he is a party; and

(b) pays a 'manufactured dividend' under that agreement, arrangement or transaction, which is representative of a dividend on those equities.

If a chargeable gain accrues to that person on the disposal, an allowable loss is treated as accruing to him on the same date, deductible only from that gain. The amount of the loss is the lowest of: the chargeable gain, the manufactured dividend and the dividend of which the manufactured dividend is representative. For manufactured dividends paid (or treated as paid) before 31 January 2008, the amount of the loss is the lesser of the chargeable gain and the 'adjusted amount'. For this purpose the '*adjusted amount*' is equal to the lesser of the manufactured dividend and the dividend of which the manufactured dividend is representative less so much of the manufactured dividend as is allowable as a deduction for income tax purposes under *ITA 2007, ss 574, 575*.

A 'manufactured dividend' is as defined in *ITA 2007, Pt 11 Ch 2*, and references above to a manufactured dividend being paid include deemed payment under *ITA 2007, s 602(1)* but do not include deemed payment under *ITA 2007, s 596(2)*. See Tolley's Income Tax under Anti-Avoidance.

[*TCGA 1992, s 263D*].

Recognised stock exchanges

[57.27] The expression '*recognised stock exchange*' means:

(i) the London Stock Exchange and any other market of a 'recognised investment exchange' which is designated as a recognised stock exchange by Order; and
(ii) any overseas stock exchange designated by Order.

A '*recognised investment exchange*' is, for this purpose, an exchange in relation to which a recognition order is in force under *Financial Services and Markets Act 2000, s 285*.

A list of designated overseas stock exchanges is available at www.gov.uk/government/publications/designated-recognised-stock-exchanges-section-1005-income-tax-act-2007. Certain exchanges have been designated as recognised stock exchanges for the purposes only of investment bond arrangements within 3.3 ALTERNATIVE FINANCE ARRANGEMENTS. See www.gov.uk/government/publications/recognised-stock-exchanges-section-48a-finance-act-2005/list-of-recognised-stock-exchanges-designated-solely-for-the-purposes-of-the-alternative-finance-investment-bonds-rules.

Securities, shares or stock are listed on a recognised stock exchange if:

- they are admitted to trading on that exchange; and
- they are either included in the 'official UK list' (i.e. the official list within *Financial Services and Markets Act 2000, Pt 6*) or are officially listed, in a country outside the UK which has a recognised stock exchange, under provisions corresponding to those generally applicable in European Economic Area countries.

[*ITA 2007, s 1005; CTA 2010, s 1137; TCGA 1992, s 288(1)(5A)(5B)*].

Shares traded on markets such as AIM and NEX Exchange are not treated as 'quoted' or 'listed' (HMRC Shares Valuation Manual SVM107080).

Key points on shares and securities

[57.28] Points to consider are as follows.

- The tax treatment of a reorganisation (as defined in *TCGA 1992, s 126*) is mandatory. You cannot normally elect out of the regime and HMRC cannot refuse to apply it. There is no motive test associated with this relief. See 57.2. An election can, however, be made to disapply reorganisation treatment to enable a claim to BUSINESS ASSET DISPOSAL RELIEF (9.17) or INVESTORS' RELIEF (34.10).
- A rights issue is still a reorganisation even if some shareholders do not take up their entitlements. It is the initial allotment or allocation of shares that must be pro rata to the original shareholding, so the actual take-up of the offer doesn't matter. See 57.2.

- It is important to keep records of the amounts paid and received for shares and of any reorganisations events, throughout your period of ownership. Otherwise, it can become difficult to compute any gains or losses on eventual disposal. See **57.2** onwards.
- The tax treatment of an exchange of securities or of a scheme of reconstruction as if they were a reorganisation is only mandatory so long as the appropriate motive tests are satisfied (genuine commercial reasons and not for the avoidance of capital gains tax of corporation tax). But if those conditions are satisfied, you cannot elect out of the regime (except as indicated above) and HMRC cannot refuse to apply it. See **57.5** and **57.7**.
- While HMRC are mandatorily required to consider clearance applications (see **4.16**), it is your responsibility to ensure that the transactions you are intending to carry out will constitutes an exchange of securities reorganisation or a scheme of reconstruction, as defined as *TCGA 1992, Sch 5AA*. See **57.5** and **57.7**.
- The generic term 'earn-out right' can apply to any situation where an amount of consideration falls to be ascertained by reference to future events, it is not restricted to future profits of the business sold. Another common example is where the further consideration being predicated on low levels of customer turnover. See **57.6**.
- Earn outs give at least two different CGT disposals (the share sale and the part/final disposal of the earn out right). Historically, sellers preferred to minimise the gain on the first disposal by giving a low value to the earn out right. However, where sellers have business asset disposal relief capacity (current limit £1 million) and with low interest rates the opposite can be true. This is because only the first disposal normally qualifies for business asset disposal relief; the subsequent disposals are usually taxable at 20%. Giving a high value to the earn out right gives a cash flow disadvantage in paying tax earlier but a 10% tax saving. Also if the initial value of the earn out is overly optimistic the seller can claim to carry back the loss.
- In the *Strand Options and Futures* case, the Courts upheld the finding that the buy back of the shares was a disposal and chargeable under *TCGA 1992, s 1*, without any need for the intervention of *s 122*. See **57.19**.
- HMRC have a toolkit 'capital gains tax for shares' that considers the perceived risk areas such as access to historical data, date of disposal, valuations, qualifying expenditure and reliefs. Using the toolkit or an alternative checklist may help show that reasonable care has been taken. Showing reasonable care is important if the computation of the gain is subsequently challenged and found to be incorrect as it affects the penalty that can be charged.

58

Shares and Securities — Identification Rules

Cross-references. See **32** INDEXATION; **57** SHARES AND SECURITIES.

Simon's Taxes. See **C2.7–C2.8, D1.920.**

Introduction to shares and securities — identification rules

[58.1] Because one batch of shares or securities of the same class in a company are (unless numbered) effectively indistinguishable from another batch, special rules ('identification rules') are needed to match disposals with multiple acquisitions. There are different rules for capital gains tax purposes and for corporation tax purposes.

Capital gains tax

Disposals of shares (and securities) on or after 6 April 2008 are to be identified with acquisitions by the same person of shares (and securities) of the same class in the same company in the following order:

(1) acquisitions on the same day as the disposal;
(2) acquisitions within 30 days after the day of disposal (thus countering 'bed and breakfasting');
(3) shares comprised in the 'section 104 holding' in **58.4** below; and
(4) if the shares disposed of are still not exhausted, shares acquired subsequent to the disposal (and beyond the above-mentioned 30-day period).

The detailed provisions are covered at **58.2** below.

Corporation tax

The rules applying for the purposes of corporation tax on chargeable gains are covered at **58.3** below. In summary disposals are to be identified with acquisitions in the following order:

(1) acquisitions on the same day as the disposal;
(2) acquisitions in the previous nine days;
(3) shares acquired after 5 April 1982 and comprised in the 'section 104 holding' in **58.4** below;
(4) shares acquired before 6 April 1982 and comprised in the '1982 holding' in **58.5** below;
(5) shares acquired on or before 6 April 1965 on a LIFO basis;
(6) if the shares disposed of are still not exhausted, shares acquired subsequent to the disposal, taking the earliest acquisition first.

Capital gains tax — identification rules on or after 6 April 2008

[58.2] See 58.1 above for **a summary** of the capital gains tax identification rules for disposals on or after 6 April 2008 as detailed below. **The provisions described below do not apply for the purposes of corporation tax on chargeable gains.**

The identification rules detailed below apply to disposals on or after 6 April 2008 for the purposes of capital gains tax. They apply for the purpose of identifying a disposal of shares with an acquisition of shares etc. of the same class made by the person making the disposal and held by him in the same capacity as that in which he makes the disposal. For identification purposes, disposals are considered in the date order in which they take place. These rules override any identification purporting to be made by the disposal itself or by a transfer or delivery giving effect to it.

Shares etc. held by a person who acquired them as an employee of the company concerned or of anyone else and on terms which for the time being restrict his right to dispose of them (known as 'clogged shares') are treated as being of a different class from both:

- shares etc. held by him in the same company and acquired otherwise than as an employee; and
- shares etc. held by him in the same company which are not, or are no longer, subject to the same restrictions.

Upon the removal of restrictions, where the clogged shares form a separate section 104 holding (see below) that holding is merged with any such holding for shares of the same class in the same company which are not clogged. (HMRC Capital Gains Manual CG51580).

Shares held by trustees which are acquired or deemed to be acquired in circumstances in which the relief at **57.14** SHARES AND SECURITIES (disposals to employee-ownership trusts) applied (and which have not been subsequently disposed of and reacquired) are treated as of a different class to any other shares held by the trustees.

The rules below do not apply to shares (or securities) to which Enterprise Investment Scheme relief, venture capital trust scheme relief or community investment tax relief is attributable or to shares in respect of which relief has been given (and not withdrawn) under the Business Expansion Scheme (BES).

Disposals of such shares retain their own identification rules — see **22.15**, **22.17**, **22.20** ENTERPRISE INVESTMENT SCHEME, **64.7**, **64.8** VENTURE CAPITAL TRUSTS, **23.22** EXEMPTIONS AND RELIEFS (as regards the BES) and Tolley's Income Tax under Community Investment Tax Relief. The rules also do not apply to assets to which income tax social investment relief is attributable — again such assets retain their own identification rules — see **59.13** SOCIAL INVESTMENT RELIEF.

Different rules apply to '*relevant securities*' (i.e. securities within the accrued income ('bondwashing') provisions, QUALIFYING CORPORATE BONDS (**48**) and securities which are, or have been, material interests in non-qualifying offshore funds or which are interests in a non-reporting offshore fund) and 'relevant EMI shares'. See below.

Application of rules to other assets

These identification rules apply not only to shares but also to securities of a company and also to any other assets of such nature as to be dealt in without identifying the particular assets disposed of or acquired, e.g. units in a unit trust, such assets being known as *fungible* assets. Shares and securities are treated as being of the same class only if they are, or would be, so treated by the practice of a recognised stock exchange (as defined by *ITA 2007, s 1005* – see **57.27** SHARES AND SECURITIES).

Identification rules

The rules apply **in the order set out below**, so that each rule is taken into account only to the extent that the shares disposed of are not exhausted by the preceding rule(s).

(1) **Same day rule.** Where two or more acquisitions of shares etc. of a particular class are made on the same day by the same person in the same capacity, they are treated as a single acquisition. The same applies to disposals. A disposal is then identified first and foremost and as far as possible with an acquisition made on the same day. In certain limited circumstances, an election is available for alternative treatment of same-day acquisitions by individuals (see below). Where some of the shares acquired are relevant EMI shares, they are treated as a single acquisition separate from the remainder of the shares (which are also treated as a single acquisition). The relevant EMI shares are then treated as disposed of after the remainder of the shares.

(2) **30-day rule.** If within the period of 30 days after a disposal, the person making it acquires shares of the same class, the disposal is identified with those acquisitions, taken in the order in which they occur within that period. Where the person acquires relevant EMI shares in the 30-day period, the disposal is matched with shares which are not relevant EMI shares first. This rule does not require shares to be identified with shares which the person making the disposal acquires at a time when they are not residents in the UK or when they are '*treaty non-resident*' (i.e. at a time when they fall to be regarded as resident in a territory outside the UK for the purposes of DOUBLE TAX RELIEF (**20**) arrangements). See also below under 'Bed and breakfasting'.

It is confirmed by HMRC Capital Gains Manual CG51560 that a disposal of rights attached to shares (see **57.4** SHARES AND SECURITIES) does not fall to be matched under the 30-day rule with a subsequent acquisition of shares of the same class but with no rights attached. Nor does a disposal of shares fall to be matched with shares of the same class subsequently acquired by a scrip or rights issue (as the reorganisation rules deem such shares to have been acquired at the same time as the original shares to which they attach — see below).

(3) **Section 104 holding.** The disposal is then identified with the 'section 104 holding' (if any), i.e. the single asset pool for shares, whenever acquired (see above and **58.4** below). Acquisitions matched under the same day or 30-day rules above do not form part of the section 104 holding.

(4) **Shares acquired subsequent to the disposal.** To the extent, if any, that the rules at (1)–(3) above have not exhausted the shares disposed of, the disposal is finally identified with shares acquired after the disposal (and after the expiry of the 30-day period in (2) above), taken in the order in which such acquisitions occur.

Same-day rule — election for alternative treatment

An election is available (under *TCGA 1992, s 105A*) to modify the application of the same-day rule at (1) above, as it relates to acquisitions, where:

(a) an individual acquires shares of the same class on the same day in the same capacity; and

(b) some, but not all, of those shares are acquired on the exercise of an option under an enterprise management incentive scheme (see **21.21** EMPLOYEE SHARE SCHEMES), or under a tax-advantaged employee share option scheme (see **21.23–21.25** EMPLOYEE SHARE SCHEMES) in circumstances such that no income tax charge arises.

Where the election is made:

(i) the shares in (b) above (the '*tax-advantaged-scheme shares*') and the balance of the shares in (a) above (the '*remainder shares*') are treated as *separate* acquisitions; and

(ii) any disposal falling to be matched (under the identification rules above) with the shares acquired on the day in question is matched with the remainder shares in priority to the tax-advantaged-scheme shares.

The election must be made by written notice to an HMRC officer on or before the first anniversary of 31 January following the tax year in which the individual first makes a disposal within (ii) above. It then has effect in relation to that disposal and all subsequent disposals within (ii) above. In determining, for these purposes, which is the first disposal, any capital distribution treated as a disposal by *TCGA 1992, s 122(1)* (see **57.11** SHARES AND SECURITIES) is disregarded, as is a receipt of consideration, on a capital reorganisation etc., treated as a disposal by virtue of any application of *TCGA 1992, s 128(3)* (see **57.2** SHARES AND SECURITIES).

Where the election is made, any 'clogged shares' (see above) acquired on the same day and in the same capacity as the shares in (a) above are automatically brought within the election from the time they cease to be treated as being of a different class from the shares in (a) above. Shares or securities received on a capital reorganisation etc. and treated by virtue of any application of *TCGA 1992, s 127* (see **57.2**, **57.5**, **57.7**, **57.8** SHARES AND SECURITIES) as the same asset as the shares in (a) above are split proportionately between the tax-advantaged-scheme shares and the remainder shares and continue to be covered by the election.

The election cannot be made in respect of ordinary shares in VENTURE CAPITAL TRUSTS (**64**).

[*TCGA 1992, ss 104(4A), 105A(1)–(3)(5)(6), 105B*].

'Bed and breakfasting'

The 30-day rule at (2) above is designed to counter the previously common practice known as 'bed and breakfasting' whereby shares are sold and bought back the next day or very shortly afterwards, the purpose being to realise a gain by reference to historical cost. (The 30-day rule applies equally to disposals of 'relevant securities' (see **58.6** below).)

'Bed and breakfasting' remains feasible for couples where the disposal is by one partner and the acquisition is by the other. This is subject to the transaction not falling within the anti-avoidance provision at **38.8** LOSSES for losses arising from arrangements to secure a tax advantage.

Scrips, rights issues etc.

For the purpose of applying the above identification rules, shares and securities acquired as a result of a reorganisation, e.g. a scrip or bonus issue or a rights issue, and treated under *TCGA 1992, s 127* (see **57.2** SHARES AND SECURITIES) as equating to shares already held are regarded as having been acquired at the time the original shares were acquired.

Relevant securities

The above identification order does not apply in relation to disposals of relevant securities (see above). Instead, disposals are identified in the following order.

(i) **30-day rule.** If within the period of 30 days after a disposal, the person making it acquires relevant securities of the same class, the disposal is identified with those acquisitions, taken in the order in which they occur within that period. This rule does not require securities to be identified with securities which the person making the disposal acquires at a time when they are not residents in the UK or when they are '*treaty non-resident*' (i.e. at a time when they fall to be regarded as resident in a territory outside the UK for the purposes of DOUBLE TAX RELIEF (**20**) arrangements).

(ii) **LIFO basis.** The disposal is then identified with acquisitions made at any time on a last in/first out (LIFO) basis.

See HMRC Capital Gains Manual CG51565.

Relevant EMI shares

Subject to the rules in (1) and (2) above, disposals of company shares are identified with relevant EMI shares before other shares, and with relevant EMI shares on a first in/first out basis. Relevant EMI shares cannot form part of a new or existing section 104 holding.

'*Relevant EMI shares*' are defined at **9.4** BUSINESS ASSET DISPOSAL RELIEF, broadly as shares acquired on or after 6 April 2012 by exercising a qualifying option within the enterprise management incentives scheme (see **21.21** EMPLOYEE SHARE SCHEMES). In certain cases, an election had to be made under *FA 2013, Sch 23 para 6(3)* for shares acquired in 2012/13 to be treated as relevant EMI shares.

[*TCGA 1992, ss 104, 105, 106A, 288(7B)*].

Deemed disposals and reacquisitions

Where under any capital gains tax legislation shares are deemed to be disposed of and immediately reacquired by the same person (see, for example, **38.10** LOSSES as regards negligible value claims), it is HMRC's view that neither the same day rule at (1) above nor the 30-day rule at (2) above require the deemed disposal to be matched with the deemed reacquisition (Revenue Tax Bulletin April 2001 pp 839, 840).

Example

Z, who is resident in the UK throughout, has made the following acquisitions/disposals of ordinary 25p shares in MIB plc. MIB's ordinary 25p shares were worth 210p per share on 31 March 1982. In 2024/25, Z made no disposals of chargeable assets other than as shown below.

Date	No. of shares bought/(sold)	Cost/(proceeds)
		£
1 May 1980	1,000	2,000
1 October 1983	2,000	4,500
1 December 1996	500	1,800
1 May 2024	(1,000)	(3,900)
25 May 2024	2,000	7,600
2 January 2025	(3,000)	(18,000)
Remaining holding	1,500	

The disposal on 1 May 2024 is matched with 1,000 of the shares acquired on 25 May 2024 (under the 30-day rule at (2) above). The resulting chargeable gain is as follows.

	£
Proceeds 1.5.24	3,900
Cost (£ 7,600 × 1,000/2,000)	3,800
Chargeable gain	£100

The disposal of 3,000 shares on 2 January 2025 is matched with 3,000 of the 4,500 forming the 'section 104 holding' (see (3) above) as follows.

	No. of shares	Qualifying expenditure
		£
Shares acquired 1 May 1980 (note (a))	1,000	2,100
Additional shares 1 October 1983	2,000	4,500
Additional shares 1 December 1996	500	1,800
Additional shares 25 May 2024	1,000	3,800
	4,500	12,200
Disposal 2 January 2025	(3,000)	(8,133)
Pool carried forward	1,500	£4,067

The chargeable gain is as follows.

	£
Proceeds 2.1.25	18,000
Cost (£12,200 × 3,000/4,500)	8,133
Chargeable gain	£9,867
Total chargeable gains 2024/25 £100 + £9.867	£9,967

Note to the example

(a) Re-basing to market value at 31 March 1982 applies automatically for capital gains tax purposes for disposals on or after 6 April 2008. Accordingly, the qualifying expenditure included in the section 104 holding in respect of the shares acquired on 1 May 1980 is the market value of those shares on 31 March 1982. See **58.4** below.

Identification rules for shares and securities for corporation tax purposes

[58.3] For disposals for corporation tax purposes on or after 1 April 1985 (referred to as the '*1985 date*') the identification rules for securities are as set out below.

Special rules apply to the following.

(a) Shares to which Enterprise Investment Scheme relief or venture capital trust scheme relief is attributable, shares in respect of which relief has been given (and not withdrawn) under the Business Expansion Scheme (BES) and shares or securities held by companies to which investment relief under the corporate venturing scheme or community investment tax relief is attributable. Disposals of such shares retain their own identification rules – see **22.15, 22.17, 22.20** ENTERPRISE INVESTMENT

SCHEME, **64.7**, **64.8** VENTURE CAPITAL TRUSTS, **23.22** EXEMPTIONS AND RELIEFS (as regards the BES), **23.68** EXEMPTIONS AND RELIEFS and Tolley's Income Tax under Community Investment Tax Relief.

(b) '*Relevant securities*', i.e. securities within the accrued income ('bondwashing') provisions, QUALIFYING CORPORATE BONDS (**48**) and securities which are, or have been, material interests in non-qualifying offshore funds. See **58.6** below for further details.

For shares and securities not falling within (a) and (b) above and any other assets dealt in without identifying the particular assets disposed of or acquired, then, subject to the rules for:

(i) disposals on or before the day of acquisition (see below); and
(ii) acquisitions and disposals within a ten day period (see below),

securities disposed of are identified, in order of priority, with:

(A) securities acquired on or after the '1982 date' (see **58.4** below) and forming part of a 'section 104 holding' (see **58.4** below);
(B) securities forming part of a '*1982 holding*' (see **58.5** below); and then
(C) other securities on a 'last in, first out' basis. (Broadly, those held on 6 April 1965, which are not subject to an election for 6 April 1965 value.)

Securities held by a person in one capacity cannot be identified with similar securities which he holds or can dispose of only in some other capacity (e.g. as a trustee).

[*TCGA 1992, ss 104(1)–(3), 107(1)(1A)(2)(7)–(9), 150(5), 150A(5)*].

Disposals and acquisitions on the same day

Securities disposed of on a particular day are matched with securities acquired on the same day by the same person in the same capacity and the pooling rules do not apply for this purpose. Where more securities are disposed of than are acquired, and the excess can neither be identified with previous acquisitions or a 'section 104 holding' (see **58.4** below), that excess is matched with a subsequent acquisition or acquisitions, taking the earliest first. [*TCGA 1992, s 105*].

Acquisitions and disposals within a ten-day period

Subject to the rules for disposals on or before the day of acquisition (see above) if, within a ten-day period, a number of securities are acquired which would otherwise increase or constitute a 'section 104 holding' (see **58.4** below) and subsequently a number of securities are disposed of, which would otherwise decrease or extinguish the same 'section 104 holding', then the securities disposed of are identified with those acquired and are not regarded as forming part of, or constituting, a 'section 104 holding'. If the number of securities acquired exceeds the number disposed of, the excess is regarded as forming part of, or constituting, a 'section 104 holding' and where securities were acquired at different times within the ten-day period, securities disposed of are first identified with those acquired at an earlier time (first in/first out). If the number of securities disposed of exceeds the number acquired, the excess is not identified under this rule. Any securities which are identified under this rule do not qualify for indexation allowance. [*TCGA 1992, s 107(3)–(6)*].

Example

B Ltd has the following transactions in 25p ordinary shares of H plc, a quoted company. At no time did B Ltd's holding amount to 2% of H plc's issued shares.

		Cost/(proceeds)
		£
6.6.78	Purchased 500 at £0.85	425
3.11.81	Purchased 1,300 at £0.80	1,040
15.5.82	Purchased 1,000 at £1.02	1,020
8.9.82	Purchased 400 at £1.08	432
1.2.86	Purchased 1,200 at £1.14	1,368
29.7.87	Sold 2,000 at £1.30	(2,600)
8.6.90	Purchased 1,500 at £1.26	1,890
21.12.93	Received 1,000 from group company (cost £1,250, indexation to date £250)	1,500
10.4.24	Sold 3,900 at £4.00	(15,600)

The shares stood at £1.00 at 31.3.82.

Indexation factors	**March 1982 to December 2017**	2.501
	May 1982 to April 1985	0.161
	September 1982 to April 1985	0.158
	April 1985 to February 1986	0.019
	February 1986 to July 1987	0.054
	July 1987 to June 1990	0.245
	June 1990 to December 1993	0.120
	December 1993 to December 2017	1.017

Disposal on 10 April 2024

The 'section 104 holding' pool immediately prior to the disposal should be as follows

	Shares	Qualifying expenditure	Indexed pool
		£	£
15.5.82 acquisition	1,000	1,020	1,020
Indexation to April 1985			
£1,020 × 0.161			164
8.9.82 acquisition	400	432	432
Indexation to April 1985			
£432 × 0.158			68
Pool at 6.4.85	1,400	1,452	1,684
Indexed rise: April 1985 – Feb. 1986			
£1,684 × 0.019			32
1.2.86 acquisition	1,200	1,368	1,368

	Shares	Qualifying expenditure £	Indexed pool £
	2,600	2,820	3,084
Indexed rise: February 1986 – July 1987			
£3,084 × 0.054			167
	2,600	2,820	3,251
29.7.87 disposal	(2,000)	(2,169)	(2,501)
	600	651	750
Indexed rise: July 1987 – June 1990			
£750 × 0.245			184
8.6.90 acquisition	1,500	1,890	1,890
	2,100	2,541	2,824
Indexed rise: June 1990 – December 1993			
£2,824 × 0.120			339
21.12.93 acquisition	1,000	1,250	1,500
	3,100	3,791	4,663
Indexed rise: December 1993 – December 2017			
£4,663 × 1.017			4,742
	3,100	3,791	9,405

The '1982 holding' is as follows

	Shares	Allowable expenditure £
6.6.78 acquisition	500	425
3.11.81 acquisition	1,300	1,040
	1,800	1,465

(i) Identify 3,100 shares sold with 'section 104 holding'

	£
Disposal consideration 3,100 × £4.00	12,400
Allowable cost	3,791
Unindexed gain	8,609
Indexation allowance £9,405 – £3,791	5,614
Chargeable gain	£2,995

(ii) Identify 800 shares sold with '1982 holding'

	£	£
Disposal consideration 800 × £4.00	3,200	3,200
Cost $\frac{800}{1,800} \times £1,465$	651	
Market value 31.3.82 $\frac{800}{1,800} \times £1,800$		800
Unindexed gain	2,549	2,400
Indexation allowance £800 × 2.501	2,001	2,001
Gain after indexation	£548	£399
Chargeable gain		£399
Total chargeable gain 10 April 2024 (£2,995 + £399)		£3,394

Note to the example

For corporation tax purposes, indexation allowance is frozen at its December 2017 level. No indexation allowance is available in respect of expenditure incurred after 31 December 2017, and for expenditure incurred on or before that date and falling to be deducted on a disposal after that date, indexation allowance is computed up to and including December 2017 only. See **32.2** INDEXATION.

'*Section 104* holdings' of securities

[58.4] Different provisions apply for the purposes of capital gains tax and corporation tax.

Capital gains tax

In relation to disposals on or after 6 April 2008, securities are pooled to form a 'section 104 holding' regardless of when they were acquired (subject to the rules at **58.2**(1)(2) above).

Corporation tax

Pooling applies to securities acquired on or after 1 April 1982.

Effect of pooling

Any securities of the same class to which pooling applied and held by the same person in the same capacity immediately before the '1985 date' (see **58.3** above) are pooled as a single asset which grows or diminishes as acquisitions and disposals are made on or after that date. Securities of the same class acquired for the first time on or after the '1985 date' are pooled as a single asset in the same way. This treatment has no effect on any market value that has to be ascertained.

Shares and securities of a company are not to be treated as being of the same class unless they are so treated by the practice of the Stock Exchange or would be so treated if dealt with on the Stock Exchange.

The single asset is referred to as the 'section 104 holding') and the part disposal rules apply on any disposal other than one of the whole holding.

A separate 'section 104 holding' applies in relation to any securities held by a person to whom they were issued as an employee of the company or of any other person on terms which restrict his rights to dispose of them, so long as those terms are in force (known as 'clogged shares'). While such a separate 'section 104 holding' exists the owner of it is treated as holding it in a different capacity to that in which he holds any other securities of the same class. Upon the removal of restrictions, two such separate 'section 104 holdings' merge. (HMRC Capital Gains Manual CG51580).

Indexation allowance

For corporation tax purposes, on any disposal from a 'section 104 holding' (other than the whole of it) the 'qualifying expenditure' and the 'indexed pool of expenditure' are apportioned between the part disposed of and the remainder in the same proportions as, under the normal capital gains tax rules for part disposals, the relevant allowable expenditure is apportioned (see **16.5** COMPUTATION OF GAINS AND LOSSES). The indexation allowance on the disposal is the amount by which the part of the indexed pool of expenditure apportioned to the part disposed of exceeds the equivalent part of the qualifying expenditure. On a disposal of the whole of the 'section 104 holding', the indexation allowance is the amount by which the indexed pool of expenditure at the time of disposal exceeds the qualifying expenditure at that time. For disposals after December 2017, indexation allowance is frozen at its December 2017 level.

The '*qualifying expenditure*' is, at any time, the amount which would be the aggregate of the 'relevant allowable expenditure' in relation to a disposal of the whole of the holding at that time. See **32.2** INDEXATION for '*relevant allowable expenditure*'.

The '*indexed pool of expenditure*' in the case of a 'section 104 holding' in existence immediately before the '1985 date' comes into existence immediately before that date. It consists of the aggregate of the qualifying expenditure at that time and the indexation allowance which would have been available if all the securities in the holding were disposed of at that time on the assumption that the twelve-month qualifying period and restrictions on loss-making disposals (which applied before the '1985 date') had never applied. In the case of any other 'section 104 holding', the indexed pool of expenditure is created at the same time as the holding (or, if earlier, when any of the qualifying expenditure is incurred) and is equal, at that time, to the qualifying expenditure.

Where a disposal on or after 30 November 1993 to a person acquiring or adding to a 'section 104 holding' is treated under any enactment as one on which neither a gain nor a loss accrues to the person making the disposal, *TCGA 1992, s 56(2)* (general treatment on no gain/no loss disposal; see **32.4** INDEXATION) does not apply to the disposal (so that the amount of the consideration on the disposal is not calculated on the assumption that an unindexed gain of an amount equal to the indexation allowance accrues to the person making the disposal). However, an amount equal to the indexation allowance on the disposal is added to the indexed pool of expenditure for the holding acquired or, as the case may be, held by the person to whom the disposal is made, and in such a case where there is an addition to the indexed pool of a 'section 104 holding' already held, the addition is made after any increase required by (a) below.

Whenever there is an event, called an '*operative event*', which has the effect of increasing or reducing the qualifying expenditure, a change is made to the indexed pool of expenditure.

(a) The indexed pool of expenditure is increased by the 'indexed rise' since the last operative event or, if none, since the pool came into being. This is done before the calculation of the indexation allowance on a disposal.
(b) If the operative event increases the qualifying expenditure, the indexed pool of expenditure is increased by the same amount.
(c) If there is a disposal resulting in a deduction in the qualifying expenditure, the indexed pool of expenditure is reduced in the same proportion. This is done after the calculation of the indexation allowance on the disposal.
(d) If the qualifying expenditure is reduced but there is no disposal, the indexed pool of expenditure is reduced by the same amount.

The '*indexed rise*' is the sum obtained by multiplying the value of the indexed pool of expenditure immediately before the operative event by a figure (expressed as a decimal but with no express requirement as to the number of decimal places to be calculated) calculated by the formula:

$$\frac{RE - RL}{RL}$$

where:

RE = the retail prices index for the month in which the operative event occurs or, if earlier, December 2017; and
RL = the retail prices index for the month of the immediately preceding operative event or, if none, that in which the indexed pool of expenditure came into being.

The indexed rise is nil if the month in RL (i.e. the month of the preceding operative event) is after December 2017 or if RE is equal to or less than RL.

See **32.2** INDEXATION for values of the retail price index for March 1982 and subsequent months.

Note

Reorganisations of shares do not normally constitute disposals or acquisitions but they may constitute an operative event as above; e.g. an issue of shares of the same class for payment under a rights issue would be an operative event as the qualifying expenditure is increased, but a bonus issue of shares of the same class would not be. Where the reorganisation involves shares of a different class this automatically gives rise to an operative event as the qualifying expenditure attributable to the 'section 104 holding' consisting of the original class of shares is decreased. An additional 'section 104 holding' is created as only shares of the same class can be pooled in the original 'section 104 holding'. The rules in **57.2** SHARES AND SECURITIES determine the proportions of qualifying expenditure to be attributed to holdings of shares following a reorganisation and these also apply to the indexed pool of expenditure.

Consideration for options

Where an increase in qualifying expenditure under (b) above is wholly or partly attributable to the cost of acquiring an option binding the grantor to sell, then the indexed pool of expenditure is additionally increased by a sum obtained by multiplying the consideration for the option by a figure (expressed as a decimal but without any clarification as to the number of decimal places to be calculated) calculated by the formula:

$$\frac{RO - RA}{RA}$$

where:

RO = the retail prices index for the month in which the option is exercised or, if earlier, December 2017; and
RA = the retail prices index for the month in which the option was acquired, or March 1982 if later.

The indexed rise is nil if the month in RA (i.e. the month in which the option was acquired) is after December 2017 or if RO is equal or less than RA.

The freezing of indexation allowance at its December 2017 level for disposals after 31 December 2017 does not affect the computation of a gain which arose on an actual or deemed disposal on or before that date but by virtue of any capital gains enactment does not come into charge until after that date.

[*TCGA 1992, ss 104(1)(3)–(6), 110, 114*].

Capital gains tax: no gain/no loss transfer before 6 April 2008

For disposals on or after 6 April 2008, where there were any additions to a 'section 104 holding' between 30 November 1993 and 5 April 2008 resulting from a no gain/no loss disposal, the amount of the original cost will not include any element of indexation (as the indexation element would, as described above, have been allocated to the indexed pool of expenditure) (Treasury Explanatory Notes to the 2008 Finance Bill). In such cases, the indexation allowance is lost, which differs from the position for other types of asset where *TCGA 1992, s 56(2)* (see **32.4** INDEXATION) applied to the no gain/no loss disposal. See, however, *Taxation* Magazine, 25 September 2008, pp. 340–342 for an argument that this only applies to no gain/no loss disposals before 6 April 1998, as later such disposals would not have resulted in an addition to a 'section 104 holding'.

Securities held on 31 March 1982

In relation to disposals on or after 6 April 2008, for capital gains tax purposes, a 'section 104 holding' can include or consist of securities held on 31 March 1982. Where this is the case, the re-basing provisions of *TCGA 1992, s 35(2)* (see **8.2** ASSETS HELD ON 31 MARCH **1982**) apply to any of the securities constituting or forming part of the section 104 holding which were held on 31 March 1982 by the person making the disposal. [*TCGA 1992, s 104(3A)*].

'1982 holding'

[58.5] For corporation tax purposes, the '1982 holding' comprises all shares of the same class in the same company acquired between 7 April 1965 and 31 March 1982 in so far as those shares have not been identified with disposals under current or previous identifiction rules. The pooled holding includes quoted securities held on 6 April 1965 where an election had been made that their actual cost be ignored and computations made by reference to their market value at 6 April 1965 only. See **8.3** and **8.4** ASSETS HELD ON 6 APRIL **1965**.

The 1982 holding is a single asset but one which cannot grow by the acquisition of additional securities of the same class. The relevant allowable expenditure attributable to it for capital gains tax purposes is the aggregate of that for the assets of which it is comprised.

[*TCGA 1992, s 109*].

Relevant securities

[58.6] Separate rules apply for capital gains tax and for corporation tax purposes.

Capital gains tax

For disposals on or after 6 April 2008, see **58.2** above.

Corporation tax

The identification rules in **58.3** above do not apply to disposals of 'relevant securities'. Instead, the following rules apply.

'*Relevant securities*' are as follows.

(a) Qualifying corporate bonds.
(b) Securities within the accrued income ('bondwashing') scheme (other than those within (a) above). These comprise any loan stock or similar security of any government, public or local authority in the UK or elsewhere or any company or other body other than:
    (i) shares in a company (except qualifying shares in a building society);
    (ii) national savings and war savings certificates;
    (iii) certificates of deposit;
    (iv) any security which is redeemable, for which the amount payable on redemption exceeds the issue price and in respect of which no return other than the amount of that excess is payable; and
    (v) any deeply discounted security within **57.21** SHARES AND SECURITIES transferred or redeemed after 26 March 2003.
(c) Securities which are, or at any time have been, interests in a non-reporting offshore fund.

Relevant securities are not subject to pooling. The identification rules direct how disposals of such securities are to be identified with acquisitions of securities of the same class held by the same person in the same capacity. Where relevant securities were held on 6 April 1965, special rules apply. See **8.4** and **8.9** ASSETS HELD ON 6 APRIL **1965** for quoted and unquoted securities respectively.

The general rules are subject to special rules for 'contangos' (see below) and, in order of priority, are as follows.

(a) For identification purposes, disposals are to be taken in chronological order. The identification of relevant securities comprised in an earlier disposal therefore determine (by elimination) which securities can be comprised in a later disposal.

(b) Securities disposed of for transfer or delivery on a particular date (e.g. a stock exchange settlement date) or in a particular period (e.g. a stock exchange account) are not to be identified with securities acquired for transfer or delivery on a later date or in a later period. They must be identified with acquisitions of securities for transfer or delivery on or before that date, or, in or before that period. However, subject to this, they have to be first identified with acquisitions for *transfer or delivery* on or after the contract disposal date. (The 'transfer or delivery', i.e. settlement, date is generally different from the contract date. See also *MacPherson v Hall* Ch D 1972, 48 TC 210.)

(c) Disposals are to be identified, on a 'first in, first out' basis, with acquisitions within the twelve months preceding the disposal. Otherwise, disposals are to be identified with acquisitions on a 'last in, first out' basis.

(d) Disposals are to be identified with acquisitions at different times on the same day in as nearly as may be equal proportions.

Contangos

Where, under arrangements designed to postpone the transfer or delivery of securities disposed of, a person by a *single bargain* acquires relevant securities for transfer or delivery on a particular date or in a particular period (the 'earlier date' or 'earlier period'), and disposes of them for transfer or delivery on a later date or in a later period, then the disposal and acquisition covered by the single bargain are matched. Any previous disposal which, apart from the above matching provisions, would have been identified with the acquisition under the contango arrangement must (subject to the general rule that disposals must be taken in chronological sequence) be identified with any 'available securities' acquired for transfer or delivery on the earlier date or in the earlier period. '*Available securities*' are securities which have not been matched under the above 'single bargain' rule, or under the general identification rules, with disposals for transfer or delivery on the earlier date or in the earlier period. Insofar as the previous disposal cannot be identified with 'available securities', the disposal is to be treated as being for transfer or delivery on the later date, or in the later period. Where any of the securities within (c) or (d) above are disposed of on or after the '1985 date' and within a period of ten days beginning on the day on which the expenditure was incurred, no indexation allowance is due.

[*TCGA 1992, ss 54(2), 108*].

59

Social Investment Relief

Introduction to social investment relief

[59.1] Income tax and capital gains tax reliefs are available to an individual making an eligible investment before 6 April 2023 in a 'social enterprise' (as defined). The measure of the income tax relief ('social investment relief') is 30% of the amount invested, and this is deducted from the individual's income tax liability for the tax year in which the investment is made. The investment may be a subscription for shares or a 'qualifying debt investment' (see **62.3** below). There is a £1 million limit on the annual amount of investment per investor that can qualify for relief, but relief can be carried back to the previous tax year.

Chargeable gains attributable to an increase in the value of an eligible investment are not liable to capital gains tax if the investment is held for a minimum period. Tax on chargeable gains on other assets can be deferred in certain circumstances where the individual invests in a social enterprise. See **59.13, 59.14** below.

The reliefs ceased to be available for investments made after **5 April 2023**. [*ITA 2007, s 257K(1)(5); FA 2021, s 20*].

The relief is administered by HMRC's Venture Capital Reliefs Team.

This chapter concentrates on the capital gains tax reliefs. For completeness, a brief summary of the income tax relief is also included at **59.2** – but for full details of the relief and the conditions for it, see Tolley's Income Tax under Social Investment Tax Relief.

Income tax relief

[59.2] Where an individual who is eligible for income tax social investment relief makes a claim for relief, he is entitled to a reduction in his income tax liability for the year in which the investment is made. The claim may be for all or part of the amount invested. The reduction is equal to 30% (the 'SI rate') of the amount on which relief is claimed for the year, subject to a maximum relief for any year of 30% of £1 million.

For the order in which tax reductions are given against an individual's tax liability see Tolley's Income Tax under Allowances and Tax Rates. A tax reduction must be restricted to the extent (if any) that it would otherwise exceed the individual's remaining income tax liability after making all prior reductions.

Income tax relief ceased to be available for investments made after **5 April 2023**.

Carry-back of relief

A claim for income tax social investment relief may be made as if all or part of the amount eligible for relief had been invested in the tax year preceding that in which the investment was, in fact, made. This carry-back is subject to the overriding rule that the total amount of investment on which relief can be obtained for any one year cannot exceed the maximum referred to above.

[*ITA 2007, s 257JA*].

Attribution of relief to investments

[59.3] Subject to any withdrawal or reduction of relief (see **59.5** below), where an individual's income tax liability is reduced for a tax year as in **59.2** above by reason of one or more 'distinct investments' made (or treated as made) in that year, the tax reduction is attributed to that investment or those investments (being apportioned in the latter case according to the amounts claimed by the investor in respect of each of those investments). A 'distinct investment' is an investment, made on a single day, in:

(a) a single share or a single 'qualifying debt investment' (see **62.5** above); or
(b) two or more shares, or two or more qualifying debt investments, where the shares or qualifying debt investments are in the same social enterprise and of the same class.

A proportionate amount of the tax reduction attributed to a distinct investment within (b) above is attributed to each of the shares, or qualifying debt investments, concerned. An investment of which part is treated as having been made in the preceding tax year (as in **59.2** above) is treated for these purposes as two separate investments, one made on a day in the preceding year. If bonus shares (in the same company, of the same class, and carrying the same rights) are issued to an investor in respect of any shares to which relief is attributed, the bonus shares are treated as if they had been issued to the investor on the same day as the original shares, and the tax reduction attributed to the original shares is then apportioned between the increased number of shares now held.

[*ITA 2007, s 257N*].

Claims to relief

[59.4] A claim for relief must be made no later than the fifth anniversary of 31 January following the tax year in which the investment is made (or, in the case of a carry-back claim as in 59.2 above, in which it is treated as made).

The claimant must have received a compliance certificate from the social enterprise before making the claim, stating that the requirements for relief, except in so far as they fall to be satisfied by the investor, are for the time being fulfilled in relation to the investment. A certificate may not be issued without the authority of an HMRC officer.

No application for postponement of tax pending appeal can be made on the ground that relief is due under these provisions unless a claim has been duly submitted.

[*ITA 2007, ss 257P–257PC*].

Withdrawal or reduction of relief

[59.5] The following provisions apply to withdraw or reduce income tax social investment relief in certain circumstances. References to a reduction of relief include its reduction to nil, and references to the withdrawal of relief in respect of an investment are to the withdrawal of the relief attributable to that investment (see 59.3 above). Where no relief has yet been given, a reduction applies to reduce the amount which would otherwise be available for relief, and a withdrawal means the investment ceases to be eligible for relief.

For the procedure for withdrawing or reducing relief see Tolley's Income Tax.

Disposal of investment

[59.6] The rules below apply where the investor disposes of the whole or part of an investment to which income tax social enterprise relief is attributable (see 59.3 above) before the end of 'Period B'. Reference to a 'disposal', in relation to any shares or other investments, includes a disposal of an interest or right in or over them.

If the disposal is at arm's length, the relief attributable to the investment is normally withdrawn. However, if that relief exceeds an amount equal to tax at the SI rate (see 59.2 above), for the tax year for which the relief was obtained, on the disposal consideration, the relief is instead reduced by that amount. If the disposal is not at arm's length, the relief is always withdrawn.

Where the relief attributable to the investment is less than tax at the SI rate on the amount on which relief is claimed, the amount referred to in (a) above is correspondingly reduced. Where the relief attributable has been reduced (otherwise than as a result of an issue of bonus shares — see 59.3 above) before the relief was obtained, then in calculating the amount referred to in (a) above, the gross relief attributable to the investment before that reduction is used.

If the investor grants an option, the exercise of which would bind him to sell the whole or part of the investment, the grant of the option is treated for the above purposes as a disposal. Relief is also withdrawn where, during 'Period A', an option is granted to the investor, the exercise of which would bind the grantor to purchase the whole or part of the investment, where applicable. There are rules for identifying the part of an investment to which an option relates.

These provisions do not apply to a disposal occurring as a result of the investor's death. See **59.12** below for transfers of shares between spouses or civil partners.

'Period A' is the period beginning with the incorporation or establishment of the social enterprise or, if later, the day one year before the investment is made and ending with the third anniversary of the date of the investment. 'Period B' is the period beginning with the date of the investment and ending with the third anniversary of that date.

[*ITA 2007, ss 257KC, 257R–257RC, 257TE*].

Identification rules

For the above purposes, disposals are identified with investments of the same class made on an earlier day before those made on a later day (i.e. first in/first out (FIFO)). Investments made on the same day are treated as disposed of in the following order:

(i) firstly, investments to which neither social investment income tax relief nor social investment capital gains deferral relief (see **59.14** below) is attributable;
(ii) next, those to which capital gains deferral relief, but not income tax relief, is attributable;
(iii) next, those to which income tax relief, but not capital gains deferral relief, is attributable; and
(iv) finally, any to which both income tax relief and capital gains deferral relief are attributable.

Any investment within (iii) or (iv) above which is treated as issued on an earlier day by virtue of the carry-back provisions at **59.2** above is to be treated as disposed of before any other investment within the same category. Investments transferred between spouses or civil partners living together are treated as if they were acquired by the transferee spouse or partner on the day they were made (see also **59.12** below). Shares comprised in a 'new holding' following a reorganisation to which *TCGA 1992, s 127* applies (see **57.2** SHARES AND SECURITIES) are treated as having been acquired when the original shares were acquired.

[*ITA 2007, s 257TA*].

Value received by investor

[59.7] If the investor receives value (other than an insignificant receipt) from the social enterprise at any time in Period A (see **59.6** above), any income tax social investment relief given in respect of the investment is normally withdrawn. However, if that relief exceeds an amount equal to tax at the SI rate (see **59.2** above), for the tax year for which the relief was given, on the value received, the relief is instead reduced by that amount.

[*ITA 2007, ss 257Q–257QI*].

For full details of the provisions see Tolley's Income Tax.

Repayments etc. of share capital to other persons

[59.8] If social investment relief is attributable (see **59.3** above) to the whole or any part of an investment and, at any time in Period A (see **59.6** above), the social enterprise or any 'subsidiary':

(a) repays, redeems or repurchases any of its share capital which belongs to any member other than:
  (i) the investor; or
  (ii) a person whose relief is thereby withdrawn or reduced by virtue of **59.6** or **59.7**(a) above; or
(b) makes any payment to any such member for giving up his right to any of the share capital of the social enterprise or subsidiary on its cancellation or extinguishment,

the relief is normally withdrawn. If, however, the relief exceeds an amount equal to tax at the SI rate (see **59.2** above), for the tax year for which the relief was obtained, on the sum received by the member, the relief is instead reduced by that amount. There is an exception for insignificant payments.

[*ITA 2007, ss 257QJ–257QP*].

For full details of the provisions see Tolley's Income Tax.

Acquisition of trade or trading assets

[59.9] Income tax social enterprise relief attributable to an investment is withdrawn if, at any time in Period A (see **59.6** above), the social enterprise or any qualifying subsidiary begins to carry on as its trade, business or profession (or part), a trade etc. (or part) previously carried on at any time in that period otherwise than by the social enterprise or a qualifying subsidiary, or acquires the whole or the greater part of the assets used for a trade etc. previously so carried on, and the investor is a person who, or one of a group of persons who together, either:

(a) owned at any time in Period A more than a half share in the trade etc. previously carried on, and also own or owned at any such time such a share in the trade etc. carried on by the social enterprise; or
(b) 'control' (as defined), or at any time in Period A, have controlled the social enterprise, and also, at any such time, controlled another company which previously carried on the trade etc.

In determining, for the purposes of (a) above, the ownership of a trade and, if appropriate, the shares owned by multiple owners, *CTA 2010, s 941(6)* and *s 942* apply. For those purposes, interests etc. of 'associates' (see **62.9** above) are taken into account.

There are special rules relating to shares held by certain directors of, or of a partner of, the social enterprise or any subsidiary.

[*ITA 2007, s 257QQ*].

Acquisition of share capital

[59.10] Income tax social enterprise relief attributable to an investment (see 59.3 above) is withdrawn if:

- the social enterprise, at any time in Period A (see **59.6** above), comes to acquire all the issued share capital of another company; and
- the investor is a person, or one of a group of persons, who control (as defined) or has, at any time in Period A, controlled the social enterprise and who also, at any such time, controlled the other company.

There are special rules relating to investments held by certain directors of, or of a partner of, the social enterprise or any subsidiary.

[*ITA 2007, s 257QR*].

Relief subsequently found not to have been due

[59.11] Income tax social investment relief is withdrawn if it is subsequently found not to have been due.

[*ITA 2007, s 257QS*].

Married persons and civil partners

[59.12] The provisions for withdrawal of relief on the disposal of investments to which income tax social investment relief is attributable (see **59.5** above) do not apply to transfers between spouses or civil partners living together. On any subsequent disposal or other event, the spouse or partner to whom the investment was transferred is treated as if:

- he or she were the person who made the investment;
- his or her liability to income tax had been reduced in respect of the investment by the same amount, and for the same tax year, as applied on the making of the investment by the transferor spouse or partner; and
- that amount of social investment relief had continued to be attributable to the investment despite the transfer.

Where the amount of relief attributable to the investment had been reduced before the relief was obtained by the transferor spouse or partner, the transferee is treated as if his or her relief had been correspondingly reduced before it was obtained.

Any assessment for withdrawing or reducing relief is made on the transferee spouse or partner. The identification rules for disposals at **59.6** above apply to determine the extent (if any) to which investments to which relief is attributable are comprised in the transfer.

[*ITA 2007, ss 257R(1)(d), 257T, 257TA(1)*].

Capital gains tax

[59.13] See also **59.14** below for deferral relief.

In determining the gain or loss on a disposal of an asset to which any income tax social enterprise income tax relief is attributable (see **59.3** above):

(a) if a loss would otherwise arise, the consideration the individual is treated as having given for the asset is treated as reduced by the amount of the relief;
(b) if the disposal is after the end of the three years beginning with the day the individual acquired the asset, and a gain would otherwise arise, the gain is not a chargeable gain (although this does not prevent a loss arising in these circumstances from being an allowable loss).

Where social enterprise income tax relief was not given on the full amount invested (other than by reason of the income tax liability being insufficient to support the relief), the capital gains tax exemption in (b) above is restricted to a proportion of the gain. This will usually be because the individual's social enterprise investments exceeded the annual maximum on which relief is available (see **59.2** above). The exempt gain is the proportion of the gain found by applying the multiple A/B where:

A = the income tax relief given; and
B = tax at the SI rate (see **59.2** above), for the tax year for which the relief was obtained, on the amount invested in the asset.

Where, because of (b) above, a gain (or part of a gain) on a disposal would not be a chargeable gain, but the income tax relief on the asset disposed of is reduced on account of value received from the company by the claimant or by other persons (see **59.7**, **59.8** above) before the disposal, then a corresponding proportion of the gain is chargeable. This rule applies after applying any restriction on the exemption where the maximum income tax relief was not originally obtained.

[*TCGA 1992, ss 255B–255D*].

Identification rules

The normal identification rules (see **58.2** SHARES AND SECURITIES — IDENTIFICATION RULES) are each disapplied as regards assets to which income tax social investment relief is attributable. Instead, the rules described at **59.6** above apply to match disposals with acquisitions of shares of the same class in the same company, and they apply where at least some of those shares have attracted SEIS income tax relief. [*TCGA 1992, s 255B(4)(6)*].

Reorganisations of share capital

Where income tax social investment relief has been given on some shares in a particular company but not others and there is a reorganisation within the meaning of *TCGA 1992, s 126*, then *TCGA 1992, s 127* (see **57.2** SHARES AND SECURITIES) applies separately as regards the shares attracting and not attracting relief so that, in each case, the new shares will stand in the place of the old shares. A distinction is also made, as regards shares attracting income tax relief, between those (if any) to which deferral relief (see **59.14** below) is attributable and those to which it is not, and the separate treatment described above also applies to each of those two categories.

Rights issues

If, immediately following a rights issue, EIS relief is attributable either to the original holding or the rights shares, the share reorganisation rules of *TCGA 1992, ss 127–130* (see **57.2** SHARES AND SECURITIES) are disapplied, with the result that the rights shares are treated as a separate acquisition.

[*TCGA 1992, s 255E(1)–(4)*].

Company reconstructions

If as part of a reconstruction, shares or debentures in another company are issued to a shareholder in exchange for shares to which income tax social investment relief remains attributable, then the shares in the new company are not generally deemed to stand in the place of shares in the old company under *TCGA 1992, s 135* or *s 136* (see **57.5**, **57.7** SHARES AND SECURITIES) and there is thus a disposal of the shares in the old company. However, *section 135* or *136* does apply in the normal way if:

- the new holding consists of new ordinary shares issued after the end of the three years beginning with the day the individual acquired the original shares and which meet conditions A and B at **62.5** above; and
- the company issuing the new shares has previously issued shares eligible for income tax social investment relief and has issued the appropriate compliance certificate (see **62.32** above) enabling investors to obtain relief on that issue.

[*TCGA 1992, s 255E(5)–(7)*].

Capital gains deferral relief

[59.14] If an amount equal to the amount of a chargeable gain is invested in a social enterprise within a specified time then the individual making the gain and the investment may claim for the gain be treated as accruing when the investment is disposed of and not at an earlier time.

This deferral relief applies where:

(a) a chargeable gain accrues to an individual on the disposal of any asset or on the occurrence of a chargeable event within (3) or (4) below or an aggregate chargeable gain is deemed to arise as in **9.12** BUSINESS ASSET DISPOSAL RELIEF (but only to the extent that the deemed gain would not be chargeable to capital gains tax at the 10% rate);

(b) the individual makes an investment on his own behalf in a social enterprise on which he is eligible for social investment income tax relief;

(c) the gain accrues on or after 6 April 2014 and **before 6 April 2023**;

(d) the individual is UK resident both when the gain accrues and when he makes the investment; and

(e) the investment is made **before 6 April 2023** and either during the three years beginning with the day the gain accrues or during the 12 months immediately preceding that day.

Deferral relief also applies if:

(i) a gain accrues as a result of a chargeable event within (1)–(3) below;
(ii) the chargeable event is the disposal to a social enterprise of shares in or debentures of the enterprise or the cancellation, extinguishment, redemption or repayment by a social enterprise of its shares or debentures;
(iii) as part of the chargeable event or in connection with it, and in place of the shares or debentures, the investor acquires one or more assets from the social enterprise, being shares in or debentures of the enterprise and the investor suffers no detriment in return for the acquisition of those shares or debentures (other than ceasing to hold the original shares or debentures);
(iv) but for **62.6** above (consideration for acquisition to be wholly in cash and fully-paid) the investor would be eligible for social investment income tax relief in respect of consideration given for the assets thus acquired; and
(v) conditions (c) to (e) above are met by reference to the above-mentioned acquisition.

For the purposes of (i)–(v) above, 'debenture' includes any instrument creating or acknowledging indebtedness.

Where (a)–(e) above apply, the investor may make a claim for the chargeable gain to be reduced by the amount invested or by a smaller amount specified in the claim. Where (i)–(v) above apply, the investor may make a claim for the gain to be reduced to the extent specified in the claim. The reduction may not be more than the original gain or, if the gain has already been reduced under these provisions or as a result of a claim for deferral relief under the ENTERPRISE INVESTMENT SCHEME (**22.16**) or the SEED ENTERPRISE INVESTMENT SCHEME (**54.46**), the reduced gain.

The total of all such reductions claimed for any tax year cannot exceed £1 million.

Claims

Subject to what is said at **13.2** CLAIMS regarding claims being included in a self-assessment tax return if possible, there is no statutory form in which a claim *must* be made. The provisions for income tax relief claims (see **59.4** above) are applied, with modifications, to deferral relief claims. Thus, a deferral relief claim cannot be made later than the fifth anniversary of 31 January following the tax year in which the shares were issued. A claim cannot be made until, with the authority of HMRC, the company has furnished the individual with a compliance certificate to the effect that, from its point of view, the conditions for deferral relief are satisfied.

Attribution of relief to assets

Relief is attributable to the asset or assets acquired as in (b) or (iii) above. Relief ceases to be attributable to any particular asset (or any part of an asset) when a chargeable event (see below) occurs in relation to it or the person holding it dies.

Deferred gain becoming chargeable

The deferred gain will become chargeable when any of the chargeable events listed below occurs (without any chargeable event having previously occurred) in relation to the '*social holding*' (i.e. the assets acquired as in (b) or (iii) above). If a chargeable event occurs in relation to part only of the social holding (without any chargeable event having previously occurred in relation to that part) only a proportion of the deferred gain becomes chargeable. The proportion is found by attributing a proportionate part of the deferred gain (as reduced by any previous application of this rule) to each part of the social holding held immediately before the chargeable event by the investor or by a person who has acquired it from the investor on a transfer between spouses or civil partners within *TCGA 1992, s 58*.

A chargeable event occurs in relation to an asset forming the whole or any part of the social holding if (after the acquisition of the holding):

(1) the investor disposes of the asset otherwise than by a transfer between spouses or civil partners within *TCGA 1992, s 58*;
(2) the asset is disposed of, otherwise than by a disposal to the investor, by a person who acquired it by a transfer between spouses or civil partners within *TCGA 1992, s 58*;
(3) the asset is cancelled, extinguished, redeemed or repaid; or
(4) any of the eligibility conditions for income tax social enterprise relief (see **62.4–62.28** above) fails to be met.

For this purpose, references above to an asset include a part of an asset.

Where the chargeable event is within (1) or (2) above, the deferred gain is treated as accruing to the person making the disposal. Where (3) or (4) above apply, the gain is treated as accruing to the person who held the asset, or part, when the chargeable event occurs.

Nothing which occurs at or after the time of the investor's death or the death of a person who acquired the whole or part of a social holding by a transfer between spouses or civil partners within *TCGA 1992, s 58* is a chargeable event.

Identification rules

In determining whether any assets of a particular class disposed of are assets to which deferral relief is attributable, the normal identification rules (see **58.2** SHARES AND SECURITIES — IDENTIFICATION RULES) are disapplied and, instead, the same rules as in **59.6** above apply (broadly, first in/first out but with special rules where shares acquired on the same day fall into different specified categories).

Where at the time of the chargeable event, any asset that formed the whole or part of the social holding is regarded under capital gains tax legislation as represented by assets which consist of or include assets other than that asset, the deferred gain attributable to that asset is to be apportioned between those other assets on a just and reasonable basis. As between different assets regarded as representing the same asset, the identification of those assets follows the same identification rules as above. For this purpose, the deferred gain attributable to an asset is found by attributing a proportionate part of the gain to each asset forming the whole or part of the social holding held, immediately before the chargeable event, by the investor or a person who acquired any part of the social holding from the investor by a transfer between spouses or civil partners within *TCGA 1992, s 58*.

[*TCGA 1992, s 255A, Sch 8B; FA 2021, s 40*].

60

Substantial Shareholding Exemption

Simon's Taxes. See D1.10.

Introduction to substantial shareholding exemption

[60.1] Under the substantial shareholding exemption ('SSE'), a gain on a disposal by a company of shares is exempt (and a loss is not allowable) where, throughout a continuous 12-month period beginning not more than six years before the disposal, the company (the '*investing company*') held a 'substantial shareholding' (broadly and usually, at least a **10%** interest) in the company (the '*investee company*') whose shares are the subject of the disposal. The exemption extends to assets related to shares (as in **60.4** below).

The investee company must be a trading company or the holding company of a trading group (or subgroup). Shares held by members of a worldwide group are aggregated in determining whether a company holds a substantial shareholding.

There is also a specific exemption (see **60.6** below) where the investee company is not a trading company but the *investing company* is owned by qualifying institutional investors (as defined). In such a case, a full or partial exemption may apply depending on the level of ownership by such investors, and the substantial shareholding condition may be met if the investing company's shareholding is below a 10% interest but costs more than £20 million (see **60.8**).

For HMRC's coverage of the SSE, see HMRC Capital Gains Manual CG53000–53240. For clearance applications, see **27.4** HMRC – ADMINISTRATION.

The exemptions are of no application to a disposal the gain (or loss) on which would, by virtue of some other enactment, not be a chargeable gain (or an allowable loss). Neither do they apply to a disposal which, by virtue of any chargeable gains enactment, is a no gain/no loss disposal. [*TCGA 1992, Sch 7AC para 6(1)*].

Minor definitions

[60.2] For the purposes of these provisions, a '*company*' is as defined at **26.2** GROUPS OF COMPANIES. A '*group of companies*' is also as defined at **26.2** but as if each reference there to '75%' were a reference to '51%'. Thus, subject to the detailed rules there, a '*group*' comprises a company and its effective '51% subsidiaries' (within *CTA 2010, Pt 24 Ch 3*), and may include non-UK resident companies. A '*holding company*' of a group is the principal company of the group (within the meaning given in **26.2**). A '*subgroup*' is a number of companies that *would* form a group were it not for the fact that one of them (the '*holding company*' of the subgroup) is itself a 51% subsidiary. [*TCGA 1992, Sch 7AC para 26*].

The exemptions

Exemption for shares

[60.3] A gain accruing to a company (the '*investing company*') on a disposal of shares (or an interest in shares — see **60.22** below) in another company (the '*investee company*') is not a chargeable gain i.e. the substantial shareholding exemption (SSE) applies if:

(a) the investing company held a 'substantial shareholding' (see **60.8** below) in the investee company throughout any continuous period of 12 months beginning not more than **six** years prior to the disposal (see **60.9** below); and

(b) the requirements at **60.10** below are met in relation to the investee company.

See also the anti-avoidance rule at **60.7** below.

[*TCGA 1992, Sch 7AC paras 1, 7, 28*].

A loss on a disposal is not an allowable loss if a gain on that disposal would not have been a chargeable gain (see **23.2** EXEMPTIONS AND RELIEFS).

The nature of the condition at (a) above is such that part disposals out of a once-substantial shareholding can continue to attract the exemption for up to five years after the shareholding has ceased to be substantial.

Note that the exemption is available even where the shares disposed of are not the shares that meet the substantial shareholding requirement at (a) above. If (a) above is met in relation to ordinary shares (and (b) and (c) above are also met as necessary), a disposal of a holding of, say, fixed-rate preference shares in the investee company will qualify for the exemption, irrespective of the size and duration of that holding (HMRC Capital Gains Manual CG53155).

The exemption is automatic and does not require the making of a claim.

A disposal of shares qualified in full for the exemption in *Williamson Tea Holdings Ltd v HMRC* FTT, [2010] SFTD 1101 even though part of the consideration was given in return for the taxpayer company entering into a non-competition agreement.

Example

Martin Ltd is a trading company with 20,000 issued shares. In 2017, 3,000 of the shares are acquired by Steve Ltd. Steve Ltd then sells 1,200 of the shares on 31 July 2020, 800 of the shares on 30 June 2025 and the remaining 1,000 shares on 31 August 2025. The SSE applies as follows.

Disposal on 31 July 2020

Steve Ltd has held at least 10% of the ordinary share capital throughout the period from acquisition in 2017 to disposal on 31 July 2020. The exemption applies.

Disposal on 30 June 2025

Steve Ltd holds only 9% of the shares in Martin Ltd on 30 June 2025. There is, however, a 12-month period beginning within the six years immediately before the disposal throughout which it held at least 10% of the shares. That is the period 1 August 2019 to 31 July 2020. The exemption applies.

Disposal on 31 August 2025

Steve Ltd holds only 5% of the shares in Martin Ltd on 31 August 2025. In the six years prior to that date (i.e. 1 September 2019 to 31 August 2025), Steve Ltd held at least 10% of the shares only in the period 1 September 2019 to 31 July 2020. As this period is less than 12 months, the exemption does not apply.

Exemption for assets related to shares

[60.4] A gain accruing to a company (Company A) on a disposal of an asset 'related to shares' in another company (Company B) is not a chargeable gain (i.e. the substantial shareholding exemption (SSE) applies) (and a loss is not an allowable loss) if:

- at the time of the disposal, Company A holds shares (or an interest in shares — see **60.22** below) in Company B; and
- any gain on a disposal at that time of those shares (or that interest) would be exempt under **60.3** above (disregarding *TCGA 1992, Sch 7AC para 6(1)* at **60.1** above).

This exemption also applies where:

- the shares etc. are held not by Company A itself but by another member of a group of companies (see **60.2** above) of which Company A is a member; and
- any gain on a disposal at that time of those shares etc., on the assumption that they were held by Company A, would be exempt under **60.3** above (disregarding *TCGA 1992, Sch 7AC para 6(1)* at **60.1** above).

Where assets of a company are vested in a liquidator, the above applies as if they were vested in the company and as if the acts of the liquidator were the acts of the company (disposals by the company to the liquidator, and vice versa, being disregarded).

See also the anti-avoidance rule at **60.7** below.

[*TCGA 1992, Sch 7AC paras 2, 6(2)*].

The exemption is automatic and does not require the making of a claim.

For this purpose, an asset is '*related to shares*' in a company if it is:

(a) an option to acquire or dispose of shares (or an interest in shares — see **60.22** below) in that company; or

(b) (broadly) a security that is convertible or exchangeable into shares (or an interest in shares) in that company, or into an option within (a) above, or into another security within this definition; or

(c) an option to acquire or dispose of a security within (b) above (or an interest in any such security); or

(d) an interest in, or option over, any option or security within (a)–(c) above; or

(e) an interest in, or option over, any interest or option within (d) above (or an interest in, or option over, any interest or option within this sub-paragraph).

As regards (b) above, a convertible or exchangeable security is not an asset related to shares if when the conversion etc. rights were granted, there was no more than a negligible likelihood they would be exercised to any significant extent. Therefore, it is not possible to bring a security within the scope of the exemption by attaching spurious or extremely remote rights to convertibility in the event of an unlikely occurrence (HMRC Capital Gains Manual CG53010).

Note that certain securities, options etc. are outside the scope of corporation tax on chargeable gains, and thus outside the exemption, due to their falling within the special rules for loan relationships, derivative contracts etc. (see HMRC Capital Gains Manual CG53010).

An '*interest*' in a security or option has a similar meaning to an 'interest in shares' at **60.22** below.

[*TCGA 1992, Sch 7AC para 30*].

Exemption where main conditions previously met

[60.5] A further possibility of exemption under the SSE is provided where either of the exemptions at **60.3** or **60.4** above does not apply because some of the conditions were not satisfied at the time of the disposal even though they *had been* satisfied at a time in the two years immediately preceding the disposal.

A gain accruing to a company (Company A) on a disposal of shares (or an interest in shares – see **60.22** below), or an asset related to shares (see **60.4** above), in another company (Company B) is not a chargeable gain (and a loss is not an allowable loss) if the conditions at **60.3** or **60.4** above, whichever is relevant, are not fully met (so that a chargeable gain or allowable loss would otherwise arise on the disposal) *but all* of the following conditions *are* met.

(a) At the time of disposal, Company A had held a 'substantial shareholding' (see **60.8** below) in Company B throughout any continuous period of 12 months beginning not more than six years prior to the disposal (see also **60.9** below).

(b) At the time of disposal, either Company A is UK-resident or any chargeable gain accruing to it on the disposal would form part of its corporation tax profits by virtue of *TCGA 1992, s 2B(3)(4)* (non-resident companies – see **14.2**(a)–(c) COMPANIES).

(c) There was a time within the two years ending with the disposal (the '*relevant period*') when a gain on a hypothetical disposal by:
   - Company A, or
   - a company that at any time in the relevant period was a member of the same group (see **60.2** above) as Company A,

   being a disposal of shares (or an interest in shares) in Company B that the disposing company then held, would have been exempt under **60.3** above (disregarding *TCGA 1992, Sch 7AC para 6(1)* at **60.1** above, and see also below).

(d) If, at the time of disposal, the requirements at **60.10** below as to the investee company are not met in relation to Company B, there was a time within the relevant period (as defined at (c) above) when Company B was controlled by:
   - Company A; or
   - Company A together with any persons connected with it (within *TCGA 1992, s 286* — see **17** CONNECTED PERSONS); or
   - a company that at any time in the relevant period was a member of the same group (see **60.2** above) as Company A; or
   - any such company together with persons connected with it.

   'Control' is to be construed in accordance with *CTA 2010, ss 450, 451*.

For the purpose only of determining the 'relevant period' for the purposes of (c) or (d) above, the time of disposal is taken as the time the contract is made, notwithstanding that the contract may be conditional. In determining whether the gain on the hypothetical disposal in (c) above would have attracted the exemption at **60.3** above, the requirements at **60.10**(b) below as to the status of the investee company immediately after the time of disposal are taken to be satisfied.

See also the anti-avoidance rule at **60.7** below.

[*TCGA 1992, s 288(1), Sch 7AC para 3(1)–(4)(7)(8), para 6(2)*].

Thus, for example, where the investee company ceases to trade on being put into liquidation so that it can no longer meet the requirements at **60.10** below, disposals by the investing company (including capital distributions) can continue to attract the exemption for a further two years.

It should be noted, however, that the above exemption also contains an anti-avoidance element in that if, for example, the investee company's trade is transferred elsewhere (within a group, for instance) and the conditions above are all met, a loss on a disposal by the investing company within the two years following the transfer will not be an allowable loss.

A further anti-avoidance rule applies to prevent the exemption from applying where value has been transferred into the investee company within the said two-year period. Where the above exemption would otherwise apply but:

(i) immediately before the disposal by Company A, Company B holds an asset; and
(ii) the allowable expenditure attributable to that asset has been reduced by a claim for gifts hold-over relief under *TCGA 1992, s 165* (see **30.2** HOLD-OVER RELIEFS) on an earlier disposal of the asset within the relevant period (as defined above),

a gain on the disposal by Company A does not attract the exemption *but* a loss on the disposal is not an allowable loss. (Where assets of Company B are vested in a liquidator, (i) above applies as if they were vested in the company.)

[*TCGA 1992, Sch 7AC para 3(5)(6)*].

The exemption is automatic and does not require the making of a claim.

Exemption: qualifying institutional investors

[60.6] A full or partial exemption (see below) applies under the SSE in respect of a gain accruing to an investing company on the disposal of shares in an investee company, if the *investing company* is fully or partially owned by 'qualifying institutional investors' and if:

(a) the investing company held a substantial shareholding (as modified — see **60.8** below) in the investee company throughout a period of 12 months beginning not more than six years prior to the disposal (the substantial shareholder requirement);
(b) the investee company does *not* meet the requirements at **60.10**; and
(c) the investing company is not a 'disqualified listed company'.

Certain bodies would usually be exempt from tax in their own right if they had owned the shares in a non-trading investee company directly. This exemption gives relief where such shares are held indirectly by a 'qualifying institutional investor' through an investing company. Specifically, a 'qualifying institutional investor' is defined as any of the following persons:

(a) the trustee or manager of a registered pension scheme (not an investment-regulated scheme as defined in *FA 2004, Sch 29A*) or an overseas pension scheme as per *FA 2004, Part 4*;
(b) a company carrying on life assurance business under *FA 2012, s 56*, where immediately before the disposal, the company's shareholding in the investing company is part of the company's long-term business fixed capital as defined by *FA 2012, s 137*;
(c) a person not liable for corporation tax or income tax because of sovereign immunity (sovereign wealth funds etc);

(d) a charity or investment trust;
(e) an authorised investment fund under *SI 2006 No 964* meeting the genuine diversity of ownership condition;
(f) the trustees of an exempt unauthorised unit trust meeting the genuine diversity of ownership condition (*SI 2006 No 964*).

A '*disqualified listed company*' is a company with any ordinary share capital listed on a recognised stock exchange, which is not a qualifying institutional investor itself, and which is not a qualifying UK REIT. A qualifying UK REIT for these purposes is a UK REIT as per *CTA 2010, Part 12* which is not treated as a close company because it is controlled by or on behalf of the Crown (*CTA 2010, s 443*), or is a close company only because it has an institutional investor as a participator. The list of institutional investors (in *CTA 2010, s 528*) is similar to, but not the same as, that above for qualifying institutional investors.

In determining the proportion of the investing company's ordinary shares owned by qualifying institutional investors, both direct and indirect holdings are taken into account in accordance with the rules set out in *CTA 2010, ss 1155–1157*, but with modifications. It is not possible to trace ownership through a disqualified listed company but it is possible to trace ownership through an exempt unauthorised unit trust (as per *SI 2013 No 2819*), which is treated as a body corporate for these purposes. For these purposes, under a repurchase agreement or stock lending arrangements (see **60.9** below), the original owner of the shares is regarded as owning them. Shares held by a partnership are treated as being owned by each partner in accordance with that partner's proportionate interest in the shares.

Amount of the exemption

The exemption applies in full i.e. no chargeable gain or allowable loss accrues to an investing company on the disposal of shares in an investee company, if qualifying institutional investors own 80% or more of the ordinary share capital of the *investing* company immediately before the disposal.

If qualifying institutional investors own at least 25% but less than 80% of the ordinary share capital of the investing company immediately before the disposal, the amount of the chargeable gain or loss is reduced by the percentage owned by such investors. For example, if two qualifying institutional investors together hold 75% of the investing company, the latter's gain on disposing of a holding in the investee company is reduced by 75%, i.e. the investing company pays tax on only 25% of the gain.

[*TCGA 1992, Sch 7AC paras 3A, 3B, 30A, 31*].

Anti-avoidance

[60.7] None of the exemptions in **60.3–60.6** above are available where:

(a) an 'untaxed' gain accrues to an investing company (Company A) on a disposal of shares (or an interest in shares — see **60.22** below), or an asset related to shares (see **60.4** above), in another company (Company B); and

(b) before the accrual of that gain, either:
- Company A acquired control of Company B, or the same person(s) acquired control of both companies; or
- there was a 'significant change of trading activities affecting Company B' at a time when it was controlled by Company A or when both companies were controlled by the same person(s);

and these circumstances occur in pursuance of arrangements (as very widely defined) from which the sole or main benefit that could be expected is that the gain would be exempt under any of **60.3–60.6** above.

For the above purposes:

(i) a gain is '*untaxed*' if it (or all but an insubstantial part of it) represents profits that have not been brought into account (in the UK or elsewhere and including profits apportioned to a UK resident company under the controlled foreign company rules) for the purposes of tax on profits for a period ending on or before the date of the disposal; 'profits' means income or gains (including unrealised income or gains);

(ii) 'control' is defined as in *CTA 2010, ss 450, 451*; and

(iii) there is a '*significant change of trading activities affecting Company B*' if:
- there is a 'major change in the nature or conduct of a trade' carried on by Company B or a 51% subsidiary of Company B; or
- there is a major change in the scale of the activities of a trade carried on by Company B or a 51% subsidiary; or
- Company B or a 51% subsidiary begins to carry on a trade.

By virtue of *CTA 2010, s 673*, a '*major change in the nature or conduct of a trade*' includes a major change in the type of property dealt in or services or facilities provided, or in customers, outlets or markets. Some of the circumstances which may amount to a major change are set out in HMRC Statement of Practice SP 10/91.

[*TCGA 1992, s 288(1), Sch 7AC para 5*].

HMRC expect cases where this anti-avoidance rule is in point to be unusual and infrequent. It is a question of fact as to whether a gain wholly (or wholly but for an insubstantial part of it — interpreted by them as 20% or less) represents untaxed profits; this involves looking at how the consideration obtained for the disposal by Company A is derived from assets held directly or indirectly by Company B. Profits are not 'untaxed' if they are simply covered by a specific relief or if they represent dividends which are themselves paid out of taxed profits. If a gain represents both taxed and untaxed profits, it should be taken as first representing taxed profits, with only the balance representing untaxed profits. See HMRC Statement of Practice SP 5/02.

'Substantial shareholding' requirement

Meaning of substantial shareholding

[60.8] A company holds a '*substantial shareholding*' in another company if it holds shares (or interests in shares — see **60.22** below) in that company by virtue of which:

- it holds at least 10% of the company's ordinary share capital;
- it is beneficially entitled to at least 10% of the profits available for distribution to equity holders of the company; and
- it would be beneficially entitled on a winding-up to at least 10% of the assets of the company available for distribution to equity holders.

CTA 2010, Pt 5 Ch 6 applies, with suitable modifications, to define an 'equity holder' and to determine the profits or assets available for distribution.

[*TCGA 1992, Sch 7AC para 8*].

Additionally, where qualifying institutional investors own at least 25% of the ordinary share capital of the investing company (see **60.6** above), the investing company also holds a 'substantial shareholding' if it holds ordinary shares (or interests in ordinary shares) in the investee company that cost it at least £20 million (in one or over several acquisitions), whether representing a 10% interest or not. The shares (or any other shares in the investee company) must give the investing company beneficial entitlement to a percentage of profits and assets on a winding up at least equal to that percentage of ordinary shares held by the investing company, although this condition is treated as met if a shortfall is insignificant. This alternative way to satisfy the substantial shareholding condition is not restricted to the exemption at **60.6** above but can apply in respect of the other exemptions of *TCGA 1992, Sch 7AC*, but only where the investing company is owned at least 25% by qualifying institutional investors.

[*TCGA 1992, Sch 7AC para 8A*].

For the purposes of deciding whether the 'substantial shareholding' test is satisfied, holdings of shares (and interests in shares) by members of the same group of companies (which may be a worldwide group — see **60.2** above) are aggregated. [*TCGA 1992, Sch 7AC para 9(1)*].

Where assets of the investing company, or of a member of the same group as the investing company, are vested in a liquidator, they are treated for the purposes of the substantial shareholding requirement (and those of **60.13, 60.14** below) as if they were vested in the company and as if the acts of the liquidator were the acts of the company (disposals by the company to the liquidator, and vice versa, being disregarded). [*TCGA 1992, Sch 7AC para 16*].

Special rules apply in relation to assets held for the purposes of long-term insurance business where the investing company is an insurance company, or in certain cases a 51% subsidiary of an insurance company, or a member of the same group as an insurance company. [*TCGA 1992, Sch 7AC paras 9(2), 17*].

Holding period

[60.9] As stated at **60.3**(a) above, the investing company must have held a substantial shareholding in the investee company throughout a continuous period of 12 months beginning not more than six years prior to the disposal. Shares are treated as having been held for such a period if, for example, they were acquired at any time on 15 June 2023 and sold at any time on 14 June 2024; they do not have to be held on the anniversary of the acquisition (HMRC Capital Gains Manual CG53008). The following special rules apply.

No gain/no loss transfers

Where the investing company acquired any shares from another company by means of a no gain/no loss transfer, i.e. under any chargeable gains enactment that states that a disposal is to be treated as made for such consideration that no gain or loss accrues, the period during which it is treated as holding those shares is extended to include the period during which the previous owner held them. The period is further extended back through any series of no gain/no loss transfers by which the shares arrived in the hands of the present owner. The present owner is treated as having had the same entitlements, to shares and to any rights enjoyed by virtue of holding shares, as the company or companies by which they were held at any earlier time in the extended period. These include any entitlements etc. arising from the aggregation rule for groups of companies in **60.8** above. These rules also cover interests in shares (see **60.22** below), and the extension also covers any period during which the asset held by any of the previous companies concerned in the no gain/no loss series consisted of shares (or an interest in shares) from which the current shares (or interest) are 'derived'.

For the above purposes, any transfer falling within **26.3**(xii) GROUPS OF COMPANIES (intra-group share exchanges), and which would otherwise have been a no gain/no loss transfer within *TCGA 1992, s 171*, is treated as if it had been a no gain/no loss transfer. A transfer between non-UK resident group companies even where the shares are not chargeable assets of the transferor company immediately before transfer or of the transferee company immediately after transfer, but which would otherwise have been a no gain/no loss transfer within *TCGA 1992, s 171*, is treated as a no gain/no loss transfer.

Shares (or interests in shares) are '*derived*' from other shares (or interests) only where:

- a company becomes co-owner of shares previously owned by it alone, or vice versa;
- a company's interest in shares as co-owner changes (but co-ownership continues);
- a shareholding is treated by virtue of *TCGA 1992, s 127* (including its application by virtue of another enactment — see, for example, **57.2**, **57.5**, **57.7**) as the same asset as another shareholding; or
- there is a sequence of two or more of the above occurrences.

[*TCGA 1992, Sch 7AC para 10*].

> *Example*
>
> X Ltd has a wholly-owned subsidiary, Y Ltd. On 1 April 2023, X Ltd buys 20% of the ordinary share capital of Z Ltd. On 1 March 2024, X Ltd transfers its Z Ltd shares to Y Ltd. On 30 September 2024, Y Ltd sells the shares.
>
> The transfer of the Z Ltd shares on 1 March 2024 is a no gain/no loss transfer under *TCGA 1992, s 171* (see **26.3** GROUPS OF COMPANIES). In determining whether, therefore, the substantial shareholding exemption applies to Y Ltd's sale of the Z Ltd shares on 30 September 2024, Y Ltd is treated as holding the shares throughout the period 1 April 2023 to 30 September 2024.

Deemed disposals and reacquisitions

Where, under any corporation tax enactment, shares have been deemed to be disposed of and immediately reacquired by a company, the company is regarded as not having held the shares during any part of the holding period falling before the deemed disposal and reacquisition. This rule extends to interests in shares (see **60.22** below) and to shares (or interests) from which the current shares (or interest) are 'derived' (as above).

A deemed disposal and reacquisition of qualifying shares on the entry of a company into the QAHC regime (see **63.8** UNIT TRUSTS ETC.), on an asset crossing the QAHC ring fence or on a company leaving the QAHC regime is not treated as a deemed disposal and reacquisition for these purposes.

[*TCGA 1992, Sch 7AC para 11; FA 2022, Sch 2 paras 14, 22(8), 31(4)*].

Sale and repurchase agreements (repos)

Where the company that holds shares transfers them under a repo (as defined), such that, by virtue of *FA 2007, Sch 13 para 6* or *TCGA 1992, s 263A* (see **57.26** SHARES AND SECURITIES), the disposal falls to be disregarded, it is similarly disregarded for the purposes of the provisions in this chapter. Thus, during the period covered by the repo, the ownership of the shares, and the entitlement to any rights attached to them, rests with the original owner and not the interim holder. If, at any time during that period, the original owner, or a member of the same group (see **60.2** above) as the original owner, becomes the *actual* holder of any of the shares transferred (or any shares directly or indirectly representing them), this rule ceases to have effect at that time in relation to the shares concerned. [*TCGA 1992, Sch 7AC para 12*].

Stock lending arrangements

Rules identical to those above for repos apply where shares are transferred under a stock lending arrangement (as defined), such that, by virtue of *TCGA 1992, s 263B(2)* (see **57.25** SHARES AND SECURITIES), the disposal falls to be disregarded. [*TCGA 1992, Sch 7AC para 13*].

Transfer of trading assets within a group

The period in which the investing company is treated as holding a substantial shareholding in the investee company is extended if the following conditions are met:

(1) immediately before the disposal the investing company holds a substantial shareholding in the investee company;
(2) an asset which, at the time of the disposal, is being used for the purposes of a trade carried on by the investee company was transferred to it by the investing company or another company;
(3) at the time of the transfer company the investee company, the investing company and, where relevant, the company transferring the asset were all members of the same group (as in **60.2** above); and
(4) the asset was previously used by a member of the group, other than the investee company, for the purposes of a trade carried on by it at a time when it was such a member.

Where these conditions are satisfied, the investing company is treated as having held the substantial shareholding at any time during the 12 months ending with the time of disposal when the asset was used as in (b) above if it did not otherwise hold a substantial shareholding at that time.

[*TCGA 1992, Sch 7AC para 15A*].

The extended holding period provided by these provisions was held not to apply in a case where a stand-alone company created a new subsidiary and then hived down its trade and assets before selling the share in the subsidiary (*M Group Holdings Ltd v HMRC* UT, [2023] UKUT 213 (TCC), [2023] STC 1556). As the company, M Ltd, only owned the subsidiary, MCS Ltd, for a period of just under 11 months, it relied on the extension. The UT held that it was not possible to have a 'group' consisting of just one company. The ordinary and natural meaning of 'group' required there to be more than one company in the group and this was consistent with the context and purpose of the relevant legislation. The tribunal held that the ownership period could only be extended for periods during which the assets were in use by a member of the group. The purpose of the legislation was to provide a benefit to groups of companies; the wording was entirely focussed on groups and what was happening to assets used by group members when they were members.

Requirements relating to investee company

[60.10] The requirements to be met in relation to the investee company for the purposes of the exemption at **60.3** above are that:

(a) it must have been a 'qualifying company' throughout the period:
  - beginning with the start of the latest 12-month period for which the substantial shareholding requirement (see **60.3**(a) above) was met; and
  - ending with the time of the disposal; and

(b) it must, in certain limited circumstances, be a 'qualifying company' immediately after the time of the disposal.

A '*qualifying company*' is a 'trading company' or the holding company (as in **60.2** above) of a 'trading group' or 'trading subgroup' (see **60.11** below).

Where the conditions at **60.9**(2)–(4) above (transfer of trading asset within a group) are satisfied in relation to a disposal, then, for the purposes of (a) above, the investee company is treated as having been a trading company at any time during the 12 months ending with the disposal when the asset concerned was used as in **60.9**(2) above.

The requirement at (b) above needs to be met only if the disposal is to a person connected with the investing company, or if the substantial shareholding holding period at **60.9** above is met because of the transfer of trading assets within the group as described in **60.9** above. For these purposes *CTA 2010, s 1122* applies for the meaning of 'connected persons'.

Where the disposal is made under a contract and, by virtue of *TCGA 1992, s 28* (see **16.4** COMPUTATION OF GAINS AND LOSSES), the time of disposal for tax purposes precedes the conveyance or transfer of the asset disposed of, the requirements at both (a) and (b), where necessary, above must be met by reference to the time of the conveyance or transfer as well as the time of the disposal.

[*TCGA 1992, Sch 7AC para 19*].

[60.11] For the purposes of this chapter, a '*trading subgroup*' is a subgroup (as in **60.2** above), one or more of whose members carry on 'trading activities' and the activities of whose members, taken together, do not include to a 'substantial' extent activities other than 'trading activities'. '*Trading activities*' are defined in relation to a subgroup as they are in relation to a group, with the appropriate modifications; the activities of subgroup members are regarded as a single business, so that intra-subgroup activities are disregarded, but this does not extend to activities between a member of the subgroup and a company that is a member of the main group but not the subgroup (Revenue Tax Bulletin December 2002 p 983).

[*TCGA 1992, Sch 7AC para 22*].

It is worth noting that it is possible to have a trading subgroup within an otherwise non-trading group. See **60.15** below as regards the treatment of holdings in joint venture companies.

Share reorganisations etc.

[60.12] Without the special rules below, the SSE would be of no relevance to any of the following events (in relation to shares held by the investing company in the investee company):

(a) A reorganisation of share capital, company take-over/reconstruction or conversion of securities which, by virtue of *TCGA 1992, s 127*, does not constitute a disposal (see **57.2, 57.5, 57.7, 57.8** SHARES AND SECURITIES), the 'new holding' standing in the shoes of the original shares.

(b) An event which would have been within (a) above but for the fact that the 'new asset' consists of a qualifying corporate bond and which, by virtue of *TCGA 1992, s 116(10)*, is not treated as a disposal (see **48.4** QUALIFYING CORPORATE BONDS).

(c) A tax-exempt distribution on a demerger which, by virtue of *TCGA 1992, s 192* (see **14.13** COMPANIES), does not constitute a capital distribution within **57.11** SHARES AND SECURITIES).

To the extent that a gain would thereby be exempt (or a loss non-allowable) under **60.3–60.6** above, the enactment mentioned in (a), (b) or (c) above, whichever is relevant, is disapplied, so that an event in (a) or (b) is treated as a disposal, a distribution in (c) is treated as a capital distribution and the new shares or securities are normally treated as acquired at market value. This disapplication does not, however, have effect if the result would be a withdrawal or reduction (under *FA 2000, Sch 15 para 46*) of investment relief under the CORPORATE VENTURING SCHEME. Where it does have effect, the provisions at **19.9** CORPORATE VENTURING SCHEME, where relevant, are modified accordingly.

[*TCGA 1992, Sch 7AC para 4*].

HMRC have provided illustrations of how these and related provisions operate in two different types of intra-group transaction and also in relation to a share exchange outside a group in CG53170a.

Effect of earlier company reconstruction etc.

[60.13] The following applies where:

(a) shares held by the investing company in the investee company were acquired as a result of either:
   (i) an exchange of securities within *TCGA 1992, s 135* (see **57.5** SHARES AND SECURITIES); or
   (ii) a scheme of reconstruction within *TCGA 1992, s 136* (see **57.7** SHARES AND SECURITIES); and
(b) *TCGA 1992, s 127* (see **57.2** SHARES AND SECURITIES) applied, such that the event was not treated as a disposal and the 'new holding' stood in the shoes of the original shares; and
(c) *TCGA 1992, s 127* did not fall to be disapplied by **60.12** above (because, for example, the conditions for the exemptions at **60.3–60.6** above were not satisfied or the event took place before 1 April 2002).

The question of whether, at any time *before* the event in (a)(i) or (ii) above, the substantial shareholding requirement at **60.8** above was met, or the requirements relating to the investee company at **60.10** above were met, is determined by reference to the shares held by the investing company at that time. This rule can apply more than once, i.e. where there has been more than one event within (a)(i) or (ii) above, and it can apply in combination with the rule at **60.14** below where there have been one or more transfers within that paragraph as well as one or more events within (a)(i) or (ii) above.

[*TCGA 1992, Sch 7AC paras 14, 25*].

Example

On 1 October 2023, Prosser Ltd acquires 40% of the ordinary share capital of Cooper Ltd. On 30 April 2024, Cooper Ltd is acquired by Oyster Ltd, Prosser Ltd receiving Oyster Ltd shares in exchange for its Cooper Ltd shares. As a result, Prosser Ltd holds 12% of the ordinary share capital of Oyster Ltd.

The substantial shareholding exemption is not available at the time of the share exchange because Prosser Ltd did not hold the Cooper Ltd shares for at least 12 months. Instead *TCGA 1992, s 127* applies so that there is no disposal and no acquisition and the Oyster Ltd shares are treated as the same asset as the Cooper Ltd shares.

If on 30 September 2024, Prosser Ltd sells its shares in Oyster Ltd, the period over which the substantial shareholding requirement and the investee company requirements must be satisfied for exemption to apply is 1 October 2023 to 30 September 2024. The tests must be determined by reference to the Cooper Ltd shares in the period 1 October 2023 to 30 April 2024 and by reference to the Oyster Ltd shares from 30 April 2024 to 30 September 2024.

Effect of earlier demerger

[60.14] The following applies where:

- shares held by the investing company in the investee company were acquired as a result of a transfer by a parent company of shares in its subsidiary; and

- the demerger provisions of *TCGA 1992, s 192* applied (see **14.13** COMPANIES), such that the transfer was not treated as a capital distribution and the transferred shares in the subsidiary fell to be treated as received as a result of a reorganisation of share capital and thus (by virtue of *TCGA 1992, s 127*) as standing in the shoes of the shares previously held in the parent company.

Whether, at any time *before* the transfer, the substantial shareholding requirement at **60.8** above is met, or the requirements relating to the investee company at **60.10** above are met, is determined by reference to the shares held by the investing company at that time. This rule can apply more than once, i.e. where there has been more than one such transfer, and it can apply in combination with the rule at **60.13** above where there have been one or more events within that rule as well as one or more transfers within this paragraph.

[*TCGA 1992, Sch 7AC paras 15, 25*].

Treatment of holdings in joint venture companies (JVCs)

[60.15] For the following purposes, a company is a '*joint venture company*' (JVC) if (and only if):

(i) it is a 'trading company' or the holding company (as in **60.2** above) of a 'trading group' or 'trading subgroup' (see **60.11** below); *and*
(ii) there are five or fewer persons who between them hold **75% or more** of its ordinary share capital (within *CTA 2010, s 1119*) (counting members of a group, as in **60.2** above, as if they were a single company).

The following provisions apply only where a company has a 'qualifying shareholding' in a JVC. A company has a '*qualifying shareholding*' in a JVC if (and only if):

(a) it is a sole company (i.e. not a member of a group) and it holds shares, or an interest in shares (see **60.22** below), in the JVC by virtue of which it holds **10% or more** of the JVC's ordinary share capital, or
(b) it is a member of a group, the group members between them hold 10% or more of the ordinary share capital of the JVC *and* the company itself holds part of that ordinary share capital.

Where the above conditions are satisfied, definitions of 'trading company', 'trading group' and 'trading subgroup' have effect with the modifications in (1)–(3) below. Where the JVC is itself a 'holding company' (as in **60.2** above), the references in (1), (2) and (3) below to its activities are to the activities (other than intra-group activities) of the JVC and its '51% subsidiaries' (within *CTA 2010, Pt 24 Ch 3*). Each reference below to a holding of shares in a JVC includes securities of the JVC or an interest in shares in, or securities of, the JVC.

(1) In determining whether a company with a qualifying shareholding in a JVC is a 'trading company', its holding of shares in the JVC is disregarded. It is treated as carrying on a share of the JVC's activities proportionate to its percentage shareholding in the JVC. This does not apply if the company and the JVC are members of the same group of companies.

(2) In determining whether a group, of which a company with a qualifying shareholding in a JVC is a member or is the holding company, is a 'trading group', there is disregarded any holding of shares in the JVC by any member of the group which has a qualifying shareholding in the JVC. Each such member is treated as carrying on a share of the JVC's activities proportionate to its percentage shareholding in the JVC. This does not apply if the JVC is itself a member of the group.

(3) In determining whether a company with a qualifying shareholding in a JVC is the holding company of a 'trading subgroup' (see **60.11** above), there is disregarded any holding of shares in the JVC by the company and by any of its 51% subsidiaries which itself has a qualifying shareholding in the JVC. The company and each such subsidiary is treated as carrying on a share of the JVC's activities proportionate to its percentage shareholding in the JVC. This does not apply if the JVC is a member of the same group as the company.

[*TCGA 1992, Sch 7AC paras 23, 24, 26(4)*].

HMRC consider that where a group has an interest in a joint enterprise not falling within the above definition of a 'joint venture company' it is not necessarily the case that the interest must be treated as a non-trading activity. Whether it represents part of the group's overall trading activities will be a question of fact and will depend on the circumstances of the case. (HMRC Capital Gains Manual CG53114).

Consequential rules

Degrouping charge

[60.16] See **26.9** GROUPS OF COMPANIES for interaction between the exemptions in this chapter and the charge where a company ceases to be a member of a 75% group of companies and has had an asset transferred to it by another group member within the preceding six years.

Negligible value claims

[60.17] Where:

- a company makes a negligible value claim under *TCGA 1992, s 24(2)* (see **38.10** LOSSES) in respect of an asset; and
- by virtue of the provisions in this chapter, a loss on a disposal of that asset at the time of the claim would not be an allowable loss,

the consequent deemed disposal and reacquisition is regarded as taking place at the time of the claim and cannot be backdated to an earlier time. Thus, in these circumstances, a negligible value claim cannot result in an allowable loss. [*TCGA 1992, Sch 7AC para 33*].

Reorganisation involving qualifying corporate bond

[60.18] Where, on a reorganisation of share capital, the 'new asset' consists of a qualifying corporate bond (see **48.4** QUALIFYING CORPORATE BONDS), the exemptions in this chapter do not apply to or affect the chargeable gain or allowable loss deemed to accrue under *TCGA 1992, s 116(10)(b)* on a subsequent disposal of the whole or part of the new asset. This does not apply if the 'reorganisation' occurred in a period of account beginning before 1 January 2005 and was, in fact, a deemed disposal and reacquisition within *FA 1996, s 92(7)* (asset ceasing to be a 'convertible security' but continuing to be a creditor relationship of the company). [*TCGA 1992, Sch 7AC para 34*].

Note that the above is of no application where the reorganisation has itself been treated as an exempt disposal by virtue of **60.12** above.

Held-over gains on gifts of business assets

[60.19] Where:

- (a) a company disposes of an asset;
- (b) the allowable expenditure attributable to that asset would have been greater were it not for a claim for gifts hold-over relief under *TCGA 1992, s 165* (see **30.2** HOLD-OVER RELIEFS) having been made in respect of an earlier disposal; and
- (c) by virtue of the provisions in this chapter, any gain on the disposal in (a) above would not be a chargeable gain,

the amount of the held-over gain is treated as a gain accruing to the company at the time of the disposal in (a) above and as being a gain which is outside the exemptions in this chapter. If the disposal in (a) above is a part disposal, only an appropriate proportion of the held-over gain becomes chargeable on that occasion. [*TCGA 1992, Sch 7AC para 37*].

FOREX matching regulations

[60.20] No gain or loss is treated as arising under the provisions for matching of foreign exchange differences on foreign currency assets with loan relationships or derivative contracts on a disposal on which any gain would be exempt under the provisions in this chapter — see **15.3** COMPANIES — CORPORATE FINANCE AND INTANGIBLES.

Miscellaneous

[60.21] The question of whether an asset is a chargeable asset for the purposes of corporation tax on chargeable gains generally is to be determined without regard to the availability, or potential availability, of the exemptions covered in this chapter, and references throughout this book to 'chargeable assets' should be read accordingly. [*TCGA 1992, Sch 7AC para 32*].

[60.22] For SSE purposes, an 'interest in shares' is an interest as a co-owner of shares (whether they be owned jointly or in common and whether the interests of the co-owners are equal or disparate). [*TCGA 1992, Sch 7AC para 29*].

Key points concerning the substantial shareholding exemption

[60.23] Points to consider are as follows.

- If the conditions are satisfied for the exemption to apply, a gain is exempt even on shares that have only been held for a short time. For example, a trading company holds 10% of the shares in another trading company for the requisite period, then acquires the other 90% of the shares. A few days later, 50% of the shares are sold at a gain. The whole gain is exempt, even though the majority of the shares had only been held for a few days. See **60.3**.
- The anti-avoidance rule at *TCGA 1992, Sch 7AC para 5* is of limited scope and is rarely applicable in practice. See **60.7**.
- The words 'by virtue of' in the 10% substantial shareholding requirement can be crucial. If a company owns 100% of the shares of a subsidiary as well as, say, a convertible loan note of that subsidiary, it could be that all the assets of the subsidiary would pass to the parent under the terms of the loan note, not the share capital. In that case, the parent is not beneficially entitled to the assets of the subsidiary by virtue of its substantial shareholding and the test is failed. See **60.8**.
- The mere holding of cash, for example, the consideration of a disposal of a subsidiary, is not generally considered by HMRC to be an activity. Therefore, it is unlikely that holding cash will constitute a non-trading activity.
- It is recommended that you review the case law on trading activities in cases of doubt. See **60.10–60.11**.

61

Time Limits — Fixed Dates

Cross-references. See also **13.5** CLAIMS; **62** TIME LIMITS — MISCELLANEOUS.

Introduction to time limits: fixed dates

[61.1] This chapter lists fixed date time limits (for capital gains tax) falling in the **12 months to 30 September 2025**. It also notes time limits for corporation tax on chargeable gains where these are dependent upon the company's accounting date (see also Tolley's Corporation Tax).

Exercise of HMRC discretion

For HMRC's approach to late claims and elections, see HMRC Capital Gains Manual CG13800 and Self Assessment Claims Manual SACM10025, 10040.

Time limits of one year or less

[61.2] Time limits of one year or less are as follows:

(a) **5 October 2024** for action in respect of **2023/24**.
Chargeability to tax. A person chargeable to CGT for a tax year must, unless they have received a tax return for completion, notify HMRC, within six months after the end of that year, that they are so chargeable. (In limited circumstances for 2023/24 onwards, the time limit applies by reference to the tax year in which conveyance or transfer takes place, rather than the tax year in which the disposal takes place for CGT purposes, usually on exchange of contracts.) See **46.3** PENALTIES.

(b) **31 October 2024** for action in respect of **2023/24**.
Self-assessment. Tax returns other than electronic returns must be delivered on or before 31 October following the tax year to which it relates. See **52.5** RETURNS.

(c) **Nine months from end of company accounting period.**
Payment of tax. Payment of corporation tax in respect of chargeable gains is normally required by the day following the expiry of nine months from the end of the accounting period if interest on unpaid tax is to be avoided. ('Large' companies must pay by instalments.) See **45.4** PAYMENT OF TAX.

(d) **31 January 2025** for action in respect of **2023/24.**
(i) *Returns.* A person other than a company who has received a self-assessment tax return for completion and is filing electronically must generally do so on or before 31 January following the tax year to which it relates. See **52.5** RETURNS.
(ii) *Payment of tax.* CGT is normally due on or before 31 January following the tax year. See **45.2** PAYMENT OF TAX.

(e) **5 April 2025** for action in respect of **2023/24.**
(i) *Claims following late assessments.* A claim (including a supplementary claim) which could not have been allowed but for the making of an assessment to CGT after the tax year to which it relates or the making of an HMRC amendment to a self-assessment issued as part of an enquiry closure notice (see **52.14** RETURNS), may be made at any time before the end of the tax year following that in which the assessment or amendment was made. See **13.5** CLAIMS.
(ii) *Claims following discovery assessments.* Where a discovery assessment is made otherwise than to make good a loss of tax brought about carelessly or deliberately, a relevant claim, election etc. can be made, revoked or varied within a year after the end of the tax year (or company accounting period) in which the assessment was made. See **13.5** CLAIMS.
(iii) *Tax over-repaid.* This (and any associated excess repayment interest) may be recovered by the end of the tax year (or company accounting period) following that in which the repayment was made, where the normal time limit for assessment has expired. This deadline is extended in the event of an HMRC enquiry into a self-assessment tax return. See **45.33** PAYMENT OF TAX.
(iv) *Capital payments made by an overseas resident settlement.* Broadly, trustees of overseas resident settlements must distribute capital gains no later than the end of the tax year following that in which the gains arose if a supplementary CGT charge under *TCGA 1992, s 91* on UK resident beneficiaries is to be avoided. See **42.21** OFFSHORE SETTLEMENTS for the detailed rules.

(f) **Twelve months from end of company accounting period.**
(i) *Chargeability to tax.* A company chargeable to corporation tax for an accounting period must, unless it has received notice to file a return for that period, notify HMRC, within twelve months after the end of that period, that it is so chargeable. (In limited circumstances for disposals on or after 1 April 2023, the time limit applies by reference to the accounting period in which conveyance or transfer takes place, rather than the period in which the disposal takes place for capital gains purposes, usually on exchange of contracts.) See **52.21** RETURNS.

(ii) *Corporation tax returns.* A company must generally comply with a notice to make a corporation tax return within twelve months of the end of the relevant accounting period or, if later, within three months of service of the notice. See **52.21** RETURNS.

One-year ten-month (approx.) time limits (and equivalent two-year time limits for companies)

[61.3] That is, for CGT, action in respect of **2022/23** must be taken on or before **31 January 2025** (and for the purposes of corporation tax on chargeable gains, where applicable, action must be taken within two years after the end of the accounting period in question).

(a) **Quoted shares and securities held on 6 April 1965: companies only.** Election for adoption of 6 April 1965 values for quoted securities (within either of the two categories) that were held on that date, where the first relevant disposal since 19 March 1968 took place during a particular company accounting period must be made within two years after the end of that accounting period. With respect to disposals after 31 March 1985 the foregoing is to be read as if '31 March 1985' were substituted for '19 March 1968'. See **8.12** ASSETS HELD ON 28 MARCH 1982. An election is only relevant if the rebasing rules for ASSETS HELD ON 28 MARCH 1982 (8) do not apply.

(b) **Miscellaneous disposals of assets held on 6 April 1965: companies only.** Election for adoption of 6 April 1965 value of miscellaneous assets (apart from quoted investments and UK land disposed of for a consideration including development value) disposed of must be made within two years after the end of the company accounting period in which the disposal was made. See **8.12** ASSETS HELD ON 28 MARCH 1982. An election is only relevant if the rebasing rules for ASSETS HELD ON 28 MARCH 1982 (8) do not apply.

(c) **Assets held on, and gains arising before, 31 March 1982: companies only.** The latest time for making an irrevocable election for universal re-basing at 31 March 1982 is two years after the end of the company accounting period in which 'the first relevant disposal' occurs. See **8.3** ASSETS HELD ON 31 MARCH 1982. A claim for 50% relief in taxing deferred charges on gains before 31 March 1982 must be made within two years after the end of the company accounting period in which the disposal or deferred gain in question occurs or accrues. See **8.11** ASSETS HELD ON 31 MARCH 1982.

(d) **Loss relief for subscribing individual shareholders.** A claim for a loss arising in a tax year on a disposal of qualifying unlisted shares by a subscriber to be set against his income of that year or the preceding year must be made on or before the first anniversary of 31 January following the year in which the loss is incurred. See **38.14** LOSSES.

(e) **Furnished holiday accommodation.** A claim for 'averaging' of let periods of holiday accommodation must be made on or before the first anniversary of 31 January following the relevant tax year (or within two years after the end of the relevant company accounting period). See **24.1** FURNISHED HOLIDAY ACCOMMODATION.

(f) **Loss on right to unascertainable consideration.** An election to treat a loss arising on disposal of a right to unascertainable consideration as accruing in an earlier year, enabling the loss to be set against the gain on the disposal in respect of which the right was acquired must be made on or before the first anniversary of 31 January following the actual tax year of the loss. See **38.18** LOSSES.

(g) **Relief for trading losses to be set against chargeable gains of a person other than a company.** A claim to set off a trading loss against chargeable gains of the same or the preceding tax year must be made on or before the first anniversary of 31 January following the tax year in which the loss is incurred. See **38.20** LOSSES.

(h) **Relief for post-cessation expenditure of a trade to be set against chargeable gains of a person other than a company.** A claim to set off excess post-cessation expenditure of a trade against chargeable gains, which can be made only in conjunction with a claim under *ITA 2007, s 96* against income, must be made on or before the first anniversary of 31 January following the tax year in which the expenditure is incurred. See **38.20** LOSSES.

(i) **Amendment of tax return.** A person other than a company has up to twelve months after the filing date (for this purpose normally treated as 31 January following the tax year) to notify an amendment to his tax return. See **52.9** RETURNS.

(j) **Appropriation of asset to trading stock.** An election may be made to treat the transfer as, effectively, taking place at cost instead of market value. See **16.9** COMPUTATION OF GAINS AND LOSSES.

(k) **Small part disposals of land (claim for disposal not to be treated as such).** See **35.7** and **35.9** LAND.

(l) **Earn-out rights.** An election for a right to receive securities of unascertainable value acquired in consideration for a transfer of securities not to be treated as a security itself for chargeable gains purposes must be made on or before the first anniversary of 31 January following the tax year in which the earn-out right is conferred (or within two years of the end of the accounting period in which it is conferred). See **57.6** SHARES AND SECURITIES.

(m) **Incorporation relief.** An election to disapply incorporation relief under *TCGA 1992, s 162* on a transfer of a business to a company must be made on or before the first anniversary of 31 January following the tax year in which the transfer takes place. This applies only if *all* the shares etc. received in exchange for the business transferred are disposed of by the end of the tax year following that in which the transfer takes place; in other cases, an extra one year is given to make the election (see **61.5** below). See **31.3** INCORPORATION AND DISINCORPORATION RELIEFS.

(n) **Same-day acquisitions of shares.** With regard to shares acquired by an individual on the same day, an election may be made to treat certain shares acquired under employee share options as acquired separately from other shares for the purpose of identifying the shares comprised in any subsequent part disposal. The election must be made on or before the first anniversary of 31 January following the tax year in which falls the first disposal falling to be matched with acquisitions on the day in question. See **58.2** SHARES AND SECURITIES — IDENTIFICATION RULES.

(o) **Trusts with vulnerable beneficiaries.** A vulnerable person election allowing claims to be made for special income tax and capital gains tax treatment must be made on or before the first anniversary of 31 January following the tax year in which the election is to take effect. See **56.13** SETTLEMENTS.

(p) **Sub-fund settlements.** An election by trustees of a settlement under which a specified part of the settled property is treated for capital gains tax purposes as a separate settlement must be made on or before the first anniversary of 31 January following the tax year in which the election is to take effect. See **56.12** SETTLEMENTS.

(q) **Business asset disposal relief.** Relief must be claimed on or before the first anniversary of 31 January following the tax year in which the qualifying business disposal is made. See **9.10** BUSINESS ASSET DISPOSAL RELIEF.

(r) **Investors' relief.** Relief must be claimed on or before the first anniversary of 31 January following the tax year in which the qualifying disposal is made. See **34.6** INVESTORS' RELIEF.

Fixed two-year time limits

[61.4] That is, for CGT, where applicable, action in respect of **2022/23** must be taken not later than **5 April 2025** (and for the purposes of corporation tax on chargeable gains, action must be taken within two years after the end of the accounting period in question).

(a) **Relief for assets of negligible value, loans to traders becoming irrecoverable and loans to traders evidenced by qualifying corporate bonds.** Broadly, a claim to this effect may be made within two years after the end of the tax year (or company accounting period) in which the relevant date falls. See **38.10, 38.11, 38.12** LOSSES. (The last-mentioned relief is abolished for loans made after 16 March 1998 — see **38.12** LOSSES.)

(b) **Loss relief for subscribing investment companies.** A claim for a loss arising on a disposal of qualifying unlisted shares by a subscribing investment company to be set against income must be made within two years after the end of the accounting period in which the loss is incurred. See **38.17** LOSSES.

(c) **Loss relief for companies which invested under the Corporate Venturing Scheme.** A claim for a loss arising on a disposal of shares to which corporate venturing scheme investment relief is attributable to be set against income must be made within two years after the end of the accounting period in which the loss is incurred. See **23.68** EXEMPTIONS AND RELIEFS.

(d) **Amendment of company tax return.** A company has up to twelve months after the filing date (which itself is normally twelve months after the end of the relevant accounting period) to notify an amendment to its tax return. [*FA 1998, Sch 18 para 15*].

Two-year ten-month (approx.) time limits

[61.5] Therefore, action in respect of **2021/22** must be taken on or before **31 January 2025**.

Incorporation relief

An election to disapply incorporation relief under *TCGA 1992, s 162* on a transfer of a business to a company must be made on or before the second anniversary of 31 January following the tax year in which the transfer takes place. If, however, *all* the shares etc. received in exchange for the business transferred are disposed of by the end of the tax year following that in which the transfer takes place, the deadline is brought forward by one year as in **61.3**(m) above. See **31.3** INCORPORATION AND DISINCORPORATION RELIEFS.

Fixed three-year time limits

[61.6] Therefore, action in respect of **2021/22** must be taken by **5 April 2025**.

Charities

Where property ceases to be held on charitable trusts in circumstances giving rise to a deemed disposal by the trustees, an assessment on the cumulative gains must be made within three years after the end of the tax year in which the cessation occurred. See **11.2** CHARITIES.

Three-year ten-month (approx.) time limits

[61.7] Therefore, action in respect of **2020/21** must be taken on or before **31 January 2025**.

Rollover relief — provisional claims

If not superseded by an actual claim or withdrawn, a provisional claim for rollover relief on replacement of business assets for capital gains tax (not corporation tax) purposes lapses on the third anniversary of 31 January following the tax year in which the disposal occurred. (This does not in itself prevent an actual claim being made at a later date.) See **53.11** ROLLOVER RELIEF.

Four-year time limits

[61.8] That is, for CGT, where applicable, action in respect of **2020/21** must be taken by **5 April 2025**.

The more important of these time limits are as follows.

(a) **Deceased persons.** Assessments on gains arising or accruing before death must be made on the deceased's personal representatives within four years following the tax year in which death occurred. See **6.12**.

(b) **Recovery of overpaid tax.** See **13.7** CLAIMS.

(c) **Raising assessments** other than where loss of tax brought about carelessly or deliberately or involving an offshore matter or offshore transfer. (In limited circumstances from April 2023, the time limit applies by reference to the tax year or accounting period in which conveyance or transfer takes place, rather than that in which the disposal takes place for capital gains purposes (usually on exchange of contracts).) See **6.12** ASSESSMENTS.

(d) **Claim against double assessment** where the same person has been assessed 'for the same cause' in the same year. See **6.4** ASSESSMENTS.

(e) **Relief against double taxation.** See **20** DOUBLE TAX RELIEF.

(f) **Relief for unremittable overseas gains.** See **43.6** OVERSEAS MATTERS.

(g) **Disposals by way of gift etc. (election for tax to be paid by instalments).** See **45.5** PAYMENT OF TAX.

(h) **Capital distributions in respect of shares etc.** Where allowable expenditure on shares etc. is less than the amount of a capital distribution, the taxpayer may make an election to set off all that expenditure against the distribution. See **57.11** SHARES AND SECURITIES.

(i) **Extension of private residence exemption to a residence occupied by a dependent relative on or before 5 April 1988.** See **47.13** PRIVATE RESIDENCES.

(j) **Hold-over relief** for gifts of business assets and assets on which inheritance tax is chargeable etc. See **30.2–30.11** HOLD-OVER RELIEFS.

(k) **Rollover relief.** See **53.11** ROLLOVER RELIEF and note that the period for claiming relief starts with the later of the end of the tax year or company accounting period in which the disposal takes place and the end of the tax year or company accounting period in which the new assets are acquired.

(l) **Relief on compulsory acquisition of land.** See **35.10** LAND and note also that proceeds must not be invested in land which would be exempt from CGT under the private residence rules on a disposal of it within six years of acquisition.

(m) **EIS deferral relief.** See **22.20** ENTERPRISE INVESTMENT SCHEME and note that the period for claiming relief starts with the later of the end of the tax year in which the gain accrues and the end of the tax year in which the qualifying investment (i.e. a subscription for EIS shares) is acquired.

(n) **Relief for post-employment deductions to be set against chargeable gains.** A claim can be made only in conjunction with a claim under *ITEPA 2003, ss 555–564* against income. See **38.20** LOSSES.

(o) **Notification of capital losses.** See **38.5** LOSSES.

Other action before 6 April 2025

Tax-loss selling

[61.9] Appropriate disposals should be made if it is desired to realise capital losses to set off against chargeable gains in 2024/25. See **38** LOSSES.

Use of annual exempt amount

Action should be taken so as to utilise the CGT annual exempt amount for 2024/25. See **2.5** ANNUAL RATES AND EXEMPTIONS.

Bed and breakfasting of shares and securities

'Bed and breakfasting' of shares and securities, i.e. the sale and subsequent repurchase of shares etc. where the seller and buyer are *not* the same person, e.g. disposal by one spouse or civil partner, repurchase by the other. See **58.2** SHARES AND SECURITIES — IDENTIFICATION RULES.

62

Time Limits — Miscellaneous

Cross-reference. See **61** TIME LIMITS — FIXED DATES (in particular, the section at **61.1** dealing with HMRC's practice regarding late claims and elections which apply equally here).

Introduction to time limits — miscellaneous

[62.1] Time limits which operate otherwise than by reference to the end of a tax year or company accounting period are set out in this chapter.

Time limits of one year or less

[62.2] Time limits of one year or less are as follows:

(a) **Thirty days:**

(i) For appeals against assessments, HMRC amendments to self-assessment tax returns and claims made outside returns, and HMRC conclusions on completion of enquiry, notice of appeal must be lodged within thirty days. See **5.3** APPEALS, **13.3** CLAIMS. For postponement of tax, see **36.2** LATE PAYMENT INTEREST AND PENALTIES, **45** PAYMENT OF TAX.

(ii) Rejections of HMRC corrections to self-assessment tax returns must be made within thirty days after the notice of correction. See **52.9** RETURNS.

(iii) A notice specifying the apportionment of a reduction in tax liability involving more than one period or person, in certain discovery cases, must be given within thirty days of HMRC issuing a notice apportioning it. See **13.5** CLAIMS.

(iv) Where HMRC offer to review a decision under appeal, the taxpayer has thirty days beginning with the date of the document notifying them of the offer to notify HMRC of acceptance of it. Alternatively, the appellant can, within the same thirty-day period, notify the appeal to the Tribunal for it to decide the matter in question. See **5.6** APPEALS.

(v) Following an HMRC review of a decision under appeal, the taxpayer can notify the appeal to the Tribunal. This must normally be done within the period of thirty days beginning with the date of the document notifying the conclusions of the review. Where, however, HMRC have failed to notify the conclusions within the required period, the time limit is extended to thirty days after the date of the document notifying the appellant that the review is to be treated as if concluded on the basis of HMRC's original opinion. See **5.6** APPEALS.

(b) **One month:**

(i) If the First-tier Tribunal gives permission to appeal to the Upper Tribunal (or the Upper Tribunal gives permission (see (ii) below) but directs that the application for permission should not be treated as a notice of appeal) an appellant can appeal to the Upper Tribunal by providing a notice of appeal, to be received by the Tribunal within one month after the notice giving permission to appeal was sent. See **5.27** APPEALS.

(ii) Applications to the Upper Tribunal for permission to appeal against a decision of the First-tier Tribunal must be received no later than one month after the date on which the First-tier Tribunal sent the notice refusing permission to appeal (see (d) below). See **5.27** APPEALS.

(iii) Applications to the Upper Tribunal for permission to appeal to the Court of Appeal etc. must be received by the Tribunal within one month after the date it sent written reasons for the decision. See **5.32** APPEALS.

(c) **Fifty six days:**

An application to the First-tier Tribunal for permission to appeal against its decision must be received by the Tribunal no later than fifty six days after the date it sent full reasons for the decision. See **5.22** APPEALS.

(d) **Sixty days:**

(i) Where a person makes a direct or indirect disposal of UK land to which the provisions at **35.23** or **35.24** LAND (disposals by non-residents or in the overseas part of a split tax year) apply and the completion date is on or after 27 October 2021, whether or not a gain is made, that person must make a return to HMRC in respect of the disposal on or before the 60th day following the day of the completion of the disposal. See **52.22** RETURNS.

(ii) Where a person makes a direct disposal of UK land not within (i) above and the completion date is on or after 27 October 2021, if a residential property gain (see **2.1** ANNUAL RATES AND EXEMPTIONS) arises, that person must make a return to HMRC in respect of the disposal on or before the 60th day following the day of the completion of the disposal. For earlier disposals, the return had to be made on or before the 30th day. See **52.22** RETURNS.

(e) **Ninety-two days:**

The grant of an option under the Enterprise Management Incentives scheme before 6 April 2024 must be notified to HMRC within 92 days after the option is granted. For options granted on or after 6 April 2024, HMRC must be notified on or before 6 July following the tax year in which the option is granted. See **21.21** EMPLOYEE SHARE SCHEMES.

(f) **Three months:**

(i) Applications for judicial review must be made within three months of the date when the grounds for application arose. See **5.35** APPEALS.

(ii) Certain particulars of a settlement with a foreign element etc. must be supplied within three months of the creation of it. See **42.22** OFFSHORE SETTLEMENTS.

(g) **Six months:**
In respect of the form of rollover relief available on a disposal of shares to a tax-advantaged share incentive plan, the disposal consideration must be used to acquire replacement assets within six months (or longer period in certain cases) of the disposal. See **21.17** EMPLOYEE SHARE SCHEMES.

(h) **Twelve months:**

(i) To qualify for rollover relief an acquisition must be made twelve months before the associated disposal (or three years after). See **53.2** ROLLOVER RELIEF. This applies also to the general relief for compulsory acquisition of land (see **35.10** LAND).

(ii) Where, within twelve months of receipt, a capital sum, received as compensation is applied in replacing an asset lost or destroyed, a claim may be made for the deemed disposal arising on the loss etc. to be treated as made for a 'no gain, no loss' consideration. See **10.4** CAPITAL SUMS DERIVED FROM ASSETS.

(iii) Certain particulars of a settlement with a foreign element etc. must be supplied within twelve months of certain events. See **42.22** OFFSHORE SETTLEMENTS.

(iv) Acquisition of EIS shares must, for the purpose of EIS capital gains deferral relief, take place within twelve months before the disposal or other chargeable event giving rise to the gain to be deferred (or three years after). See **22.17** ENTERPRISE INVESTMENT SCHEME.

Two-year time limits

[62.3] Two-year time limits are as follows:

(a) **Only or main residence.** The election by individuals with more than one private residence must normally be made within two years after the acquisition of the second residence. Subsequent notice of variation must normally be given within two years after the date from which it is to take effect. See **47.10** PRIVATE RESIDENCES.

(b) **Family arrangements and disclaimers after death** must be made within two years of the death. See **18.8** DEATH.

(c) **Unpaid corporation tax — certain capital distributions and reconstructions.** In a case where unpaid corporation tax falls to be recovered from a shareholder in receipt of a capital distribution, notice of liability must be served within two years after the later of the date on which the assessment was made on the company and the date on which the tax became due and payable. See **45.29** PAYMENT OF TAX. Similar rules apply in a case where unpaid corporation tax falls to be recovered from a third party following a scheme of reconstruction involving the transfer of a company's business to another company. See **14.12** COMPANIES.

(d) **Know-how.** A joint election for know-how not to be treated as goodwill must be made within two years of the disposal. See **7.4** ASSETS.

(e) **Share Incentive Plan: rollover relief.** In respect of the form of rollover relief available on a disposal of shares, other than by a company, to the trustees of a tax-advantaged share incentive plan, the relief must be claimed within the two years beginning with the acquisition of the replacement assets. See **21.18** EMPLOYEE SHARE SCHEMES.

Three-year time limits

[62.4] Three-year time limits are as follows:

(a) **Rollover relief** is only available if the acquisition is made within three years after the disposal (or twelve months before). See **53.2** ROLLOVER RELIEF. This applies also to the general relief for compulsory acquisition of land (see **35.10** LAND).

(b) **Acquisition of EIS shares** must, for the purpose of EIS capital gains deferral relief, take place within three years after the disposal or other chargeable event giving rise to the gain to be deferred (or twelve months before). See **22.17** ENTERPRISE INVESTMENT SCHEME.

(c) A gain deferred by means of **EIS capital gains deferral relief** becomes chargeable if the investor becomes neither resident nor ordinarily resident in the UK within the period ending immediately before the third anniversary of the issue date or, if later, the third anniversary of the date of commencement of the qualifying trade (except in certain cases of temporary working abroad). See **22.17** ENTERPRISE INVESTMENT SCHEME.

(d) **Unpaid corporation tax — groups and non-resident companies.** The principal company of the group (and other group members in certain circumstances) or a controlling director of a non-UK resident company trading in the UK through a permanent establishment (previously a branch or agency) can be held liable for unpaid corporation tax on a chargeable gain accruing to a group company or to the non-resident company in question. Notice of liability must be served within three years beginning with the date on which the liability of the defaulting company is finally determined. See **45.28** PAYMENT OF TAX and see also 62.3(e) above and (j) below.

(e) **Unpaid corporation tax — company ceasing to be UK-resident.** Any tax due by a company ceasing to be UK resident and not paid within six months of becoming payable can, within three years of the amount being finally determined, be recovered from a person who is, or was in the twelve months before residence ceased, a member of the same group or a controlling director. See **43.17** OVERSEAS MATTERS.

(f) **Distribution of gains by overseas companies.** Capital gains tax or corporation tax on chargeable gains paid by a participator on part of a gain which is apportioned to them can be used to offset income tax, capital gains tax or corporation tax in respect of the distribution if the gain is distributed within three years after the end of the period of account of the non-resident company in which it accrued or within four years beginning with the date it accrued, whichever gives the earlier date. See **43.7** OVERSEAS MATTERS.

Six-year time limits

[62.5] Six-year time limits are as follows:

(a) **Intra-group transfers: company ceasing to be a member of a group.** If a company leaves a group within six years of the transfer to it of a capital asset by another member of the group, it will be liable to a degrouping charge. See **26.7** GROUPS OF COMPANIES. Similar provisions apply where the company which acquired such an asset becomes an investment trust or venture capital trust. See **26.11**, **26.12** GROUPS OF COMPANIES.

(b) **Company ceasing to be UK resident etc. — postponement of charge on deemed disposal.** If within six years after the cessation of residence etc. the company disposes of assets held at that time, the whole or the appropriate part of the postponed gain (insofar as not already so treated) is deemed to accrue to the principal company. Only where a company ceases to be UK-resident before 1 January 2020. See **43.16** OVERSEAS MATTERS.

63

Unit Trusts and Other Investment Vehicles

Cross-references. See **8.2** ASSETS HELD ON 6 APRIL **1965** and **39.3** MARKET VALUE for valuation of units in unit trusts; **14.12** COMPANIES for transfers of businesses to authorised unit trusts and investment trusts; **26.3** GROUPS OF COMPANIES for intra-group disposals of assets by authorised unit trusts and investment trusts; **35.23** onwards LAND for offshore collective investment vehicles and disposals of UK land; **44.19** PARTNERSHIPS for carried interest arising to investment managers; **64.1** VENTURE CAPITAL TRUSTS.

Simon's Taxes. See **D7.339, D7.11, D8.1.**

Introduction to unit trusts and other investment vehicles

[63.1] This chapter describes capital gains provisions which are specific to various kinds of investment funds and vehicles. Where those provisions form part of a wider scheme for the taxation of a type of entity, that scheme is also summarised to give context to the capital gains provisions.

A '*collective investment scheme*' is an arrangement with respect to property of any description, including money, the purpose or effect of which is to enable persons taking part in the arrangements (whether by becoming owners of all or part of the property or otherwise) to participate in or receive profits or income arising from the acquisition, holding, management or disposal of the property or sums paid out of such profits or income. [*TCGA 1992, s 288(1); Financial*

Services and Markets Act 2000, s 235; SI 2006 No 964, Reg 109(2)]. The object of such a scheme is to enable a large number of investors to pool their money by investing in a professionally managed fund of investments, thus spreading risk. The most common forms of collective investment schemes are unit trusts (see **63.3** below), open-ended investment companies (see **63.7** below) and authorised contractual schemes (see **63.12** below).

Collective investment schemes — exchanges, mergers and schemes of reconstruction

[63.2] The following provisions apply to a collective investment scheme which is an authorised contractual scheme which is a co-ownership scheme (see **63.12** below), a unit trust scheme or an offshore fund. For the purposes of the provisions, 'unit' includes shares in a company.

For the purposes of the tax treatment of the participants, the reorganisation of share capital provisions of *TCGA 1992, ss 126–138A* (see **57.2–57.8** SHARES AND SECURITIES) are disapplied in general although the exchange of securities provisions of *TCGA 1992, ss 135–138A* (see **57.5** SHARES AND SECURITIES) may apply if Company A or Company B is not a collective investment scheme of a type listed above.

Notwithstanding the above, the share reorganisation provisions of *TCGA 1992, ss 127–131* apply with necessary adaptations as if the scheme were a company and the event in question were a reorganisation of its share capital where:

(1) there is an exchange of units for other units in the same scheme of substantially the same value where the property subject to the scheme and the participants' rights are substantially the same immediately before and after the event;
(2) there is a reorganisation in the units in a scheme in which all the participants, or all the participants holding a particular class of units, exchange all their units for other units in the same scheme;
(3) units in a scheme are issued in exchange for units in another scheme under a general offer made to participants in that other scheme (or a class of them) where the offer is made in the first instance on a condition that, if satisfied, would result in the property of the first scheme including units in the second scheme giving rights to more than 50% of its capital and income;
(4) under an arrangement, participants in a scheme exchange units for units of substantially the same value in another scheme and as a result 85% or more of the property in that other scheme is units in the first scheme;
(5) under a scheme of reconstruction (as defined) an arrangement is entered into by all the participants in a scheme (or all the participants holding any class of those units) under which units in a successor scheme or feeder fund (as defined) are issued to those participants in respect of and in proportion to their units in the original scheme and the units in the original scheme are either retained, cancelled or otherwise extinguished; or

(6) under a scheme of reconstruction units in a scheme are issued to participants in another scheme in exchange for and in proportion to their existing units in accordance with *SI 2011 No 1613, Reg 12(1)(b)*.

Events within (3)–(6) above must be effected for bona fide commercial reasons unless the participant in question holds no more than 5% of the units in the scheme following the event.

[*TCGA 1992, ss 103E–103K, Sch 5AZA*].

Authorised unit trusts

[63.3] These are 'unit trust schemes' in respect of which an order under *Financial Services and Markets Act 2000, s 243* is in force. A '*unit trust scheme*' is a collective investment scheme under which the property is held on trust for the participants, but the Treasury may by regulation provide for any scheme of a specified description not to be treated as a unit trust scheme for capital gains purposes. Certain limited partnership schemes and employee share schemes have been excepted from treatment as unit trust schemes for such purposes. [*CTA 2010, s 616; TCGA 1992, s 99(2)(3); Financial Services and Markets Act 2000, s 237(1), Sch 20 para 4(3); SI 1988 No 266*].

For capital gains purposes, any unit trust scheme is treated as if the scheme were a company and the rights of the unit holders were shares in the company, and in the case of an authorised unit trust as if the company were resident in the UK. This provision does not apply to offshore funds which are transparent funds. See **43.9** OVERSEAS MATTERS and **63.12** below. [*TCGA 1992, s 99(1)(1A)*]. For unit trust schemes other than authorised unit trusts, see **63.6** below.

Gains realised by authorised unit trusts (including umbrella schemes, see below) are not chargeable gains. [*TCGA 1992, s 100(1)*].

Accumulation units

No distributions are made to holders of accumulation units. Instead, the net amount that would normally be distributed is automatically reinvested in the fund. No new units are issued but the value of the existing holding of units is increased. Where the notional distribution is charged to income tax as income of the unit holder (or would be but for a relief) or is taken into account as a receipt in calculating the profits, gains or losses of the unit holder for income tax purposes, it is treated as allowable expenditure for CGT purposes. Where the trust is an authorised unit trust, the deemed expenditure is treated as having been incurred on the 'distribution date' for the 'distribution period' in respect of which the amount is reinvested. In the case of any other unit trust scheme, the expenditure is deemed to be incurred on the date on which the notional distribution is reinvested. For this purpose, a '*distribution period*' is a period by reference to which the total amount available for distribution to unit holders is ascertained, and the '*distribution date*' for a distribution period is the date specified under the terms of the trust for any distribution for that period or, if no such date is specified, the last day of the period. This provision does not apply to offshore funds which are transparent funds. See **43.9** OVERSEAS MATTERS and **63.12** below. [*TCGA 1992, s 99B; SI 2006 No 964, Regs 15(2)(4), 89*].

Umbrella schemes

An '*umbrella scheme*' is a collective investment scheme which is an authorised unit trust or an authorised contractual scheme which is a co-ownership scheme or an offshore fund which has arrangements for separate pooling of investors' contributions and the profits or income out of which payments are to be made to them, and under which investors can exchange rights in one pool for rights in another. [*TCGA 1992, s 99A(1); FA 2004, s 118(3)*].

Each sub-fund of the umbrella scheme is treated for capital gains purposes as being itself a collective investment scheme of the same type as the umbrella scheme as a whole. The umbrella scheme as a whole is treated as not being a collective investment scheme of that form or any other form (so that the provisions at **63.2** above do not apply to it). Any person who has rights in a particular sub-fund is treated as a unit holder in the deemed collective investment scheme consisting of that sub-fund. These provisions do not prevent gains or losses accruing to an umbrella scheme which is a unit trust scheme (but not an authorised unit trust) being regarded as gains or losses of the umbrella scheme as a whole. They also do not prevent gains of an umbrella scheme being regarded as the gains and losses of an authorised unit trust for the purposes of *TCGA 1992, s 100(1)* above and *TCGA 1992, s 139(4)* (reconstructions involving transfer of business — exclusion of transfers to authorised unit trusts etc. (see **14.12** COMPANIES)). [*TCGA 1992, s 99A(2)–(4)*].

Investment trusts

[63.4] See 63.5 below for real estate investment trusts.

Gains realised by investment trusts are not chargeable gains. [*TCGA 1992, s 100(1)*].

Definition of 'investment trust'

A company is an investment trust for an accounting period if it fulfils the following conditions.

(1) Throughout the period substantially all of its business consists of investing its funds in shares, land or other assets with the aim of spreading investment risk and giving its members the benefit of the results of the management of its funds.
(2) Throughout the period the shares making up the ordinary share capital or, if there are such shares of more than one class, those of each class, are admitted to trading on a regulated market (within the meaning of Directive 2014/65/EU).
(3) Throughout the period the company is neither a venture capital trust (see **64** VENTURE CAPITAL TRUSTS) nor a company UK real estate investment trust (see **63.5** below).
(4) The company is approved for the period by HMRC.

The Treasury has the power to make regulations amending condition (2) above or treating conditions (1) and (2) as satisfied in specified cases. Regulations may also be made specifying the circumstances in which a company can be approved and the process by which approval can be given, refused or withdrawn.

'*Shares*' includes stock.

'*Ordinary share capital*' means all the issued share capital (by whatever name called) of a company, other than that which produces a fixed rate of dividend and is non-participating. For HMRC's interpretation of 'ordinary share capital', see HMRC Brief 54/2007.

[*CTA 2010, ss 1119, 1158, 1159*].

Real estate investment trusts

[63.5] Companies meeting the necessary conditions (see below) can elect to become real estate investment trusts. The 'property rental business' (as defined, and including both UK and overseas property) of such a trust is ring-fenced and treated as if it were a separate business carried on by a separate company. Profits and gains arising in respect of the business (including dividends from other UK real estate investment trusts) are generally exempt from corporation tax (although a tax charge may arise in certain tax avoidance cases or where a company fails to meet certain debt funding requirements or where it pays a dividend to a person with a 10% or more interest in the company). Profits of the company which are not from the tax-exempt business are chargeable to corporation tax at the main rate (currently 25%). To the extent that dividends paid by the company derive from ring-fenced profits and gains they are taxed in the hands of the recipient as property income rather than as distributions. Companies may exit the regime at any time by notice, and may be required to do so by HMRC notice where they repeatedly fail to meet certain conditions. Exit from the regime is automatic where one or more of conditions (1), (2), (5) or (6) below cease to be met. The provisions apply in modified form to enable real estate investment trusts to participate in joint ventures and for groups of companies to become group real estate investment trusts. [*CTA 2010, ss 518–609; SI 2006 Nos 2864–2867; SI 2007 No 3425*]. For full coverage of the provisions see Tolley's Corporation Tax.

Conditions

A company may make an election to become a real estate investment trust only if it meets the following conditions.

(1) It is resident in the UK and not resident in another place for the tax purposes of that other place.

(2) It is not an open-ended investment company (see **63.7** below).

For the special tax regime to apply for an accounting period, the company must, subject to the exceptions noted below, meet the above conditions and the following conditions throughout the period.

(3) Either the shares forming its ordinary share capital are admitted to trading on a recognised stock exchange (see **57.27** SHARES AND SECURITIES) or, for accounting periods beginning on or after 1 April 2022, at least 70% of the ordinary share capital is owned by 'institutional investors' (as defined by *CTA 2010, s 528(4A)*).

(4) The company meets the 'non-close condition'. The 'non-close condition' is met in relation to a company if it is not a close company or is only a close company because it has an 'institutional investor' (as defined) as a

direct or indirect participator. The condition is met in relation to a person or scheme other than a company if the person's business or the scheme would meet the condition if it were a company. This version of the condition was introduced by *FA 2024, Sch 7* and is deemed to have always had effect.

(5) Each share issued by the company either forms part of the company's ordinary share capital or is a non-voting restricted preference share (as defined).

(6) The company is not a party to any loans under which the creditor is entitled to interest which varies according to the results of the company's business (except where the interest increases on the results deteriorating or decreases on their improving), which depends on the value of the company's assets or which exceeds a reasonable commercial return or under which the creditor is entitled on repayment to an amount greater than the amount lent or an amount reasonably comparable with the amount that would generally be repayable under the terms of securities listed on a recognised stock exchange.

(7) Either the shares forming its ordinary share capital are included in the official UK or qualifying overseas list or shares forming part of its ordinary share capital are traded on a recognised stock exchange.

The property rental business of the company must also meet the following conditions for the accounting period.

(i) Either:
  - (a) throughout the accounting period, the property rental business 'involves' at least three properties and no one property represents more than 40% of the total value (under international accounting standards) of the properties involved; or
  - (b) (with effect from 11 July 2023) throughout the accounting period, the property rental business involves at least one property which is designed, fitted or equipped for the purpose of being rented as a commercial unit and is either so rented or available for rent. That property must have had a value of at least £20 million at any time from the later of the date of entry to the REIT regime and the date the property was acquired. Before 22 February 2024, the property must have had a value of no less than £20 million, either on entry into the real estate investment trust regime or when either of the conditions in (a) above ceased to be met.

(ii) Subject to certain exceptions, at least 90% of the profits of the property rental business and all of those profits which are '*UK REIT investment profits*' (i.e. distributions from other UK real estate investment trusts) are distributed by way of dividend (either a cash dividend or a stock dividend), normally before the tax return filing date for the accounting period.

(iii) At least 75% of the company's total profits (as defined) for the accounting period arise from the property rental business.

(iv) At the beginning of the accounting period, at least 75% of the company's assets by value are involved in the property rental business or consist of cash or shares in the principal company of a group UK real estate investment trust or in another company UK real estate investment trust.

If condition (3) ceases to be met because less than 70% of the ordinary share capital comes to be owned by institutional investors, the condition is treated as continuing to be met for 12 months.

Condition (4) does not have to be met in the period of three years beginning with the specified date. Where the three-year period ends during an accounting period, condition (4) only has to be met throughout the part of the accounting period falling outside the three-year period. For such companies, condition (7) is treated as met in relation to the first three accounting periods if at the end of the third accounting period the shares forming its ordinary share capital are included in the official UK or qualifying overseas list or if, during the three accounting periods, shares forming part of its ordinary share capital are traded on a recognised stock exchange.

References above to property which is '*involved*' in a business are references to an estate, interest or right by the exploitation of which the business is conducted.

Minor or inadvertent breaches of conditions (3), (4), (7) and (i) to (v) above may be ignored or give rise to a charge to tax instead of requiring the company to leave the regime in certain circumstances. See *CTA 2010, ss 561–569*.

[*CTA 2010, ss 523–531, 549A, 561–569; FA 2022, Sch 3 paras 2, 6; F(No 2)A 2023, Sch 4 para 3; FA 2024, Sch 7 paras 2–5, 8; SI 2006 No 2864, Regs 2–9*].

Capital gains

On entry into the regime the company's accounting period is deemed to come to an end, and a new one begins. 'Assets' held by the company which immediately before entry into the regime are involved (as above) in the property rental business are treated for corporation tax purposes as sold immediately before, and reacquired immediately after, entry at market value. Any gain arising on the deemed sale is not a chargeable gain (and a loss is not an allowable loss). [*CTA 2010, s 536*].

A gain accruing to the company on the disposal of an asset which was used wholly and exclusively for the purposes of the property rental business is not a chargeable gain and a loss is not an allowable loss (but see below where the disposal is in the course of non-exempt trade). Likewise, a gain accruing on disposal of an asset, which was so used but for an aggregate period of less than one year in which it was partly used for the purposes of the property rental business and partly used for the purposes of '*residual business*' of the company (i.e. any business other than the property rental business), is not a chargeable gain (and a loss is not an allowable loss). Where the aggregate period of mixed use is one year or more, any gain or loss is apportioned and any part reasonably attributable to the property rental business, having regard to the extent of and the length of the periods of use for the different purposes, is not a chargeable gain or allowable loss.

Where the company (company A) disposes, on or after 6 April 2019, of an asset consisting of a right or interest in another company (company B) which is 'UK property rich', a proportion of the gain is not a chargeable gain and the asset is treated as having been used for the purposes of the property rental business to an extent equal to the same proportion. The proportion is that which, at the start of the accounting period of the disposal, the value of company B's 'PRB assets' bears to the total value of company B's assets. The value of company B's '*PRB assets*' is the value of those assets deriving (directly or indirectly) from assets used for the purposes of UK property rental business. Company B is '*UK property rich*' if the disposal would be of an asset deriving at least 75% of its value from UK land (under the provisions at **35.24** LAND).

This rule also applies to the disposal of a right or interest in an offshore collective investment scheme which is UK property rich and is transparent for income tax purposes (otherwise than as a result of being constituted by two or more persons carrying on a trade or business in partnership) if no election under *TCGA 1992, Sch 5AAA para 8* has been made (see **35.27** LAND). For disposals on or after 22 February 2024, the rule also applies to the disposal of a right or interest in a co-ownership authorised contractual scheme that is UK property rich. The rule does not apply to the extent that the gain is already exempt under the provisions at **60.6** SUBSTANTIAL SHAREHOLDINGS OF COMPANIES. In determining the amount of a gain which is not a chargeable gain under this rule, any unrelieved allowable losses on disposals made before 6 April 2019 and any other deficits or other losses for accounting periods ending before that date which would otherwise have been deducted from profits or gains or any kind of the residual business of the company may be deducted from the gain. In making the determination, *TCGA 1992, s 269ZBA* (restriction on deduction of carried forward capital losses – see **14.11** COMPANIES) is ignored. For this purpose, accounting periods straddling 6 April 2019 are treated as two separate periods, the first of which ends on 5 April 2019. Any necessary apportionments between the notional periods must be made on a time basis or, if a time basis would not be just and reasonable, on a just and reasonable basis.

If company B has acquired, directly or indirectly, one or more properties and has subsequently developed them, then if the development costs exceed 30% of the value of the property and company A's disposal of the right or interest in company B is made within the three-year period beginning with the completion of the development, the above rule does not apply to so much of any gain on the disposal as relates to the developed property. For disposals on or after 1 April 2023, the value of the property is taken to be whichever is the highest of its fair value (under international accounting standards) at the time of entry to the regime, at the time of its acquisition or at the beginning of the accounting period in which development commenced. Previously, the value was the fair value on acquisition of the property (or on entry to the regime if later).

Where an asset which has been used wholly and exclusively for the purposes of the property rental business begins to be used (otherwise than by being disposed of in the course of trade), wholly and exclusively for other purposes, it is treated as disposed of and immediately reacquired at that time at market value. Any gain is not a chargeable gain (and a loss is not an allowable loss).

Where an asset which has been used wholly and exclusively for the purposes of the property rental business is disposed of in the course of trade for the purposes of residual business of the company, the disposal is treated as made in the course of that business (so that the gain is brought into account as part of the business's trading profits) and any deemed disposal and reacquisition on entry into the regime is disregarded. Where the asset was held at the time of entry and the company had to pay the entry charge, the company may claim repayment of part of that charge. This provision applies in particular where a property has been developed since acquisition, the cost of that development exceeds 30% of the value of the property and the company disposes of the property within three years of completion of the development. For disposals on or after 1 April 2023, the value of the property is taken to be whichever is the highest of its fair value (under international accounting standards) at the time of entry to the regime, at the time of its acquisition or at the beginning of the accounting period in which development commenced. Previously, the value was the fair value on acquisition of the property (or on entry to the regime if later). This provision does not apply if the disposal is by a company which is a member of a group real estate investment trust to another member.

Where an asset which has been used wholly and exclusively for the purposes of residual business of the company begins to be used wholly and exclusively for the purposes of the rental property business, it is treated as disposed of by the residual business and immediately reacquired by the property rental business at market value. Any gain arising is a chargeable gain, and any loss an allowable loss.

There are special provisions to ensure continuity of treatment on the demerger of a tax-exempt business. The provisions apply where an asset is disposed of by a company's property rental business to a 75% subsidiary (S) of the company and the company disposes of its interest in S to another company (P). P must give notice to HMRC on the date it acquires the interest in S that the group of which S is now a member will enter the real estate investment trust regime from the start of a specified accounting period beginning within six months of the disposal and it must in fact so enter the regime. P may give such a notice even if it does not expect conditions (3) to (6) above to be met throughout the specified accounting period.

Where these conditions are met, the provisions above dealing with the transfer of assets out of the property rental business do not apply to the disposal of the asset and there is no deemed disposal and re-acquisition of the asset by S on entry of its group into the regime (and therefore no entry charge, where applicable, in respect of it). This does not apply, however, if conditions (3), (5) and (6) above (or, where the exception to condition (4) noted above does not apply, conditions (3) to (6) above) are not met by the end of the six-month period beginning with the disposal of the asset.

Similar provisions apply where a company leaves a group real estate investment trust.

[*CTA 2010, ss 535–535B, 555–560; FA 2020, Sch 4 paras 20, 22; F(No 2)A 2023, Sch 4 para 4; FA 2024, Sch 7 para 9*].

On exit from the regime, any assets involved in the property rental business immediately before exit are treated as being disposed of immediately before exit and reacquired immediately afterwards at market value. The above provisions then apply to determine whether, and to what extent, the gain is a chargeable gain or the loss is an allowable loss.

If a company which has chosen to leave the regime, having been within it for a continuous period of less than ten years, disposes of an asset which was involved in the property rental business within two years of exit, its liability to corporation tax is determined disregarding any deemed disposals of the asset on exit from the regime, on transfer out of the property rental business and, where a gain arose, on entry to the regime. Where a company is forced, by HMRC notice or automatically, to leave the regime within ten years of entry, HMRC may direct (subject to appeal) that the above provisions and corporation tax provisions generally will apply with specified modifications.

[*CTA 2010, ss 579–582*].

For the purposes of the above provisions, an '*asset*' includes part of an asset and an interest in, or right in relation to, an asset. References to assets used in a business include references to assets acquired for the purposes of the business and not in use in another business, assets available for use in the business and assets which are in any other way held in respect of, or associated or connected with, the business. Deemed disposals and reacquisitions of assets have effect for the purposes of all subsequent disposals, real or deemed, except where indicated above. [*CTA 2010, ss 602, 608*].

Unauthorised unit trusts

[63.6] An eligible unauthorised unit trust (UUT) may apply to HMRC for approval as an exempt UUT. A UUT is a unit trust scheme not within **63.3** above.

A UUT is an exempt UUT for a period of account if its trustees are UK resident, all of its unit holders are 'eligible investors', it is approved by HMRC and it is not treated by regulations as not being a unit trust scheme for the purposes of the definition of 'unauthorised unit trust' in *ITA 2001, s 989*. Otherwise a UUT is a non-exempt UUT. Once a UUT has been approved, the approval has effect for the period of account specified in the application and all subsequent periods, unless it is withdrawn by HMRC as a result of the failure of the UUT to satisfy the continuing requirements for approval.

A unit holder is an '*eligible investor*' if any gain on a disposal of its units would be wholly exempt from CGT or corporation tax (otherwise than by reason of residence) or if it holds all of its units pending disposal in the capacity of manager of the UUT.

Gains of an exempt UUT are not chargeable gains. The trustees of a non-exempt UUT are treated for tax purposes as if they were a UK resident company and the rights of the unit holders were shares in the company.

[*SI 2013 No 2819, Regs 1–10, 27, 28, 32*].

Open-ended investment companies

[63.7] An '*open-ended investment company*' (OEIC) is a collective investment scheme under which the investments belong beneficially to, and are managed on behalf of, a body corporate having as its purpose the spreading of investment risk and giving its members the benefit of the results of management of those funds which is incorporated in the United Kingdom. [*CTA 2010, s 613; TCGA 1992, s 99(2)(c) treated as inserted by SI 1997 No 1154, Reg 20; s 288(1); Financial Services and Markets Act 2000, s 236; SI 2006 No 964, Regs 4, 109(2)*]. It is a form of retail investment fund.

An OEIC is constituted as a company, with directors, and issues shares rather than units as with a unit trust. The tax regime is broadly equivalent to that which applies to authorised unit trusts and their investors. See Tolley's Corporation Tax for information concerning dividend and interest distributions.

OEICs are chargeable to corporation tax at a rate equal to the basic rate of income tax. [*CTA 2010, s 614*].

Gains accruing to an OEIC are not chargeable gains. [*TCGA 1992, s 100(1) as modified*].

Investors incur chargeable gains and allowable losses in the normal way on disposals of shares. Where shares of a given class consist of both smaller and larger denomination shares, and a person owns both, the shares are treated for CGT purposes as being securities of the same class. [*SI 2006 No 964, Reg 76*].

The provisions at **63.3** above, dealing with accumulation units of unit trusts, apply equally to accumulation shares in an OEIC (i.e. shares in respect of which income is credited periodically to the capital part of the scheme property of the OEIC). [*SI 2006 No 964, Reg 103*].

Authorised unit trusts are able to convert to, or merge with, OEICs without the incurring of any significant direct tax charges. [*SI 1997 No 1154, Regs 25–27; SI 2006 No 964, Regs 78–85*].

As far as investors are concerned, the exchange of units in an authorised unit trust for shares in an OEIC is subject to the normal rules for reconstructions (see **57.7** SHARES AND SECURITIES) so that the new shares will normally stand in the shoes of the old units and have the same acquisition date and cost for CGT purposes. (Revenue Press Release 7 April 1997, para 6).

Property AIFs

An OEIC meeting strict conditions can elect to become a property AIF. The regime is broadly similar to that for real estate investment trusts (see **63.5** above), but applies in relation to both property rental business and investments in real estate investment trusts and foreign equivalents. On entry or exit from the regime, the OEIC is deemed to dispose of and immediately re-acquire certain assets at market value, but any gains arising on such deemed sales are not chargeable gains (and losses are not allowable losses).

Where a fund which is not a property AIF converts, or intends to convert, to being a property AIF, *TCGA 192, ss 127–131* (reorganisation of share capital — see **57.7** SHARES AND SECURITIES) generally apply to the disposal and acquisition of units in the fund as part of the process of it becoming a property AIF. Also for disposals on or after that date, *TCGA 192, ss 127–131* generally apply to the exchange of units in a dedicated property AIF feeder fund (as defined) for units in the AIF (and vice versa). The application of *TCGA 192, ss 127–131* is in both cases subject to the anti-avoidance provision in *TCGA 1992, s 137* (see **4.16** ANTI-AVOIDANCE).

[*SI 2006 No 964, Regs 69A–69Z41*].

For full coverage of the provisions see Tolley's Corporation Tax.

Qualifying asset holding companies (QAHCs)

[63.8] *FA 2022* introduced a special tax regime for 'qualifying asset holding companies' or 'QAHCs'. The intention is to create an internationally competitive regime for companies used by investment funds to hold assets, which will limit the company's tax liabilities to an amount commensurate with its role, with investing funds and other investors being taxed as if they had invested in the underlying assets directly (see HM Treasury Explanatory Notes to the 2021/22 Finance Bill). The main features of the regime are as follows:

- The regime is elective: a company enters the QAHC tax regime by notifying HMRC that it intends to do so.
- It must meet stringent conditions, in particular relating to its ownership, activities and investment strategy.
- The QAHC must be at least 70% owned by 'category A investors' including collective investment schemes and alternative investment funds which meet a diversity of ownership condition, insurance companies, pension funds and REITs.
- The QAHC's main activity must be an investment business and any other activities must be ancillary to that business and not carried on to any substantial extent.
- The QAHC's investment strategy must not involve the acquisition of equity securities which are listed or traded on a recognised stock exchange or any other public market or exchange or other interests deriving their value from such securities. With effect from 11 July 2023, a QAHC can elect to treat all its equity securities as not so listed or traded for this purpose, but if it makes the election, distributions it receives in respect of those securities are not exempt from corporation tax.
- The investment business is ring fenced and treated as separate and distinct from all of the QAHC's other activities.
- The QAHC is generally exempt from corporation tax on profits of its overseas property business and on profits from loan relationships or derivative contracts to the extent that they relate to the ring fence business. Gains on the disposal of land outside the UK or 'qualifying shares' are also exempt.
- On entry to the regime, the QAHC is treated as disposing of and immediately reacquiring at market value any land outside the UK, loan relationships or derivative contracts to the extent that they relate to its overseas property business and qualifying shares it then holds. A similar rule applies on exit from the regime.

- Payments of interest by a QAHC are made without deduction of tax; see **35.2** INCOME TAX IN RELATION TO A COMPANY.
- A payment by a QAHC on the redemption, repayment or purchase of its own shares is, subject to some exceptions, not a distribution and will be treated as capital in the hands of the investor.
- Interest and distributions in respect of certain securities of a QAHC to which it is a party for the purposes of its ring fence business and which would otherwise be treated as distributions are treated as not being distributions. The effect is that a deduction in computing profits is not denied on the basis that the payments are distributions. This includes interest on profit participation loans.
- A transfer to a QAHC of its own shares or own loan capital is, subject to conditions, exempt from stamp duty and stamp duty reserve tax.
- A QAHC may leave the regime by notifying HMRC but must leave if it breaches any of the conditions for being a QAHC. Certain temporary non-deliberate breaches of the ownership or activity conditions are ignored, however, and the legislation allows for certain breaches of the ownership condition to be ignored if the QAHC winds down its investment business.

Notifications and information returns must be made electronically using the link provided at www.gov.uk/guidance/make-a-qualifying-asset-holding-company-qahc-notification-to-hmrc.

Capital gains

On becoming a QAHC

When a company becomes a QAHC the company's accounting period ends and a new one begins on the day it becomes a QAHC. The company is treated as selling and reacquiring the following assets at market value:

- land outside the UK; and
- qualifying shares (i.e. any shares other than shares whose disposal would be treated as a disposal of an asset deriving at least 75% of its value from UK land (see **35.24** LAND)).

'*Shares*' are widely defined for these purposes to include stock, any other interest of a member in a company, any interest as co-owner of shares, rights of unit holders in a unit trust, units in tax transparent funds and derivative contracts to the extent that the underlying subject matter is shares.

The sale is treated as occurring immediately before the end of the accounting period ending prior to joining the QAHC regime, and the reacquisition at the beginning of the first QAHC accounting period.

If the company has held qualifying shares in a company for less than 12 months at the time of the deemed sale and reacquisition, any gain on that deemed sale is not a chargeable gain if the company continues to hold the shares until it has held them for 12 months and any gain on a disposal immediately after the end of the 12-month period would be exempt under the substantial shareholding exemption (see **60** SUBSTANTIAL SHAREHOLDING EXEMPTION). In deciding whether the exemption would apply, the rule at **60.9** providing for aggregation of holdings of group companies is disapplied.

There is no deemed disposal and reacquistion of any assets held by a company which was previously non-UK resident and became UK resident within the 30 days before becoming a QAHC if the assets were held by the company immediately before it became UK-resident.

A gain arising on the deemed disposal of qualifying shares is reduced if the value of the shares reflects the value of another asset on which a chargeable gain is treated as arising to another company on its entry to the QAHC regime on or before the day on which the gain on the qualifying shares arose. This rule applies also if a gain on the other asset does not arise only because of the exemption for previously non-UK resident companies. The reduction is on a just and reasonable basis and cannot create a loss.

[*FA 2022, Sch 2 paras 17–19, 53(2)–(4); F(No 2)A 2023, Sch 4 para 14*].

Gains of a QAHC

Where an asset held outside the ring fence business enters that business, it is treated as sold by the QAHC immediately before entering the business and reacquired immediately afterwards at market value. This could happen, for example, on a change of use or of the status of the asset. Any resulting chargeable gain arises outside the ring fence business. This rule applies only where the asset is land outside the UK or qualifying shares (including anything which becomes a qualifying share on crossing the ring fence).

A similar rule applies when an asset within the above categories leaves the ring fence business. In this case, any chargeable gain or allowable loss arising on the deemed disposal will arise within the ring fence business.

A gain arising on a deemed disposal of shares entering the ring fence business is reduced, on a just and reasonable basis and not so as to create a loss, if it reflects the proceeds of a disposal of another asset in respect of which a chargeable gain has arisen to any person.

[*FA 2022, Sch 2 paras 22, 23*].

A gain arising to a QAHC on the disposal of land outside the UK or of qualifying shares is not a chargeable gain (and a loss is not an allowable loss). [*FA 2022, Sch 2 para 53(1)*].

The normal provisions which enable the transfer of assets between members of a group to be effectively tax neutral do not apply to a transfer between the ring fence business of a QAHC and another group member unless the transfer is between the ring fence businesses of two QAHCs.

If a chargeable gain or allowable loss is transferred to a QAHC from another company under *TCGA 1992, s 171A* (see **26.13** GROUPS OF COMPANIES), the gain or loss is treated as arising outside the ring fence business.

If a QAHC (Q) holds qualifying shares in a company as a result of a transfer from another group company (G) and G had held those shares for less than 12 months at the time of the transfer, any gain on that transfer is not a chargeable gain if Q continues to hold the shares until G and Q between them have held the shares for 12 months if any gain on a disposal immediately after the end of the 21-month period would be exempt under the substantial shareholding exemption (see **60** SUBSTANTIAL SHAREHOLDING EXEMPTION) on the assumption that Q had held the shares throughout. In deciding whether the exemption would apply, the rule at **60.9** providing for aggregation of holdings of group companies is disapplied. This rule applies even if Q has ceased to be a QAHC at the end of the 12 months.

Where a company (C) which has ceased to be a QAHC acquired shares (whether or not qualifying shares) from a group member (G) whilst it was a QAHC and G had held those shares for less than 12 months, then, if C continues to hold the shares until C and G between them have held the shares for 12 months, C is treated for the purposes of the substantial shareholding exemption as having held the shares throughout the 12-month period.

The following applies where a QAHC (B) disposes of qualifying shares in another group company (A) so that A ceases to be a member of the group at a time when it holds an asset transferred to it by B and the disposal of the shares is exempt because B is a QAHC. Any deemed gain accruing to A under the degrouping charge provisions at **26.7** GROUPS OF COMPANIES which would have resulted in an adjustment to B's gain or loss on the shares but for the exemption is instead treated as arising to B as a chargeable gain outside its ring fence business. A deemed loss is treated as an allowable loss of B outside its ring fence business. This rule does not apply if the asset held by A is land outside the UK or qualifying shares (so that a disposal by B would be exempt).

[*FA 2022, Sch 2 paras 20(9), 33–36*].

A payment by a QAHC on the redemption, repayment or purchase of its own shares is not a distribution and will be treated as capital in the hands of the investor. This rule does not, however, apply where the securities were obtained by reason of an employment by the QAHC (other than as a fund manager) or by a company in which the QAHC has at least a 25% interest. The rule also does not apply in certain circumstances where the payment is made during the period allowed for a QAHC to 'cure' a breach of the ownership condition. [*FA 2022, Sch 2 para 47*].

Ceasing to be a QAHC

The QAHC's accounting period ends at the end of the day on which it ceased to be a QAHC and the QAHC is treated as disposing of, and immediately reacquiring, land outside the UK and qualifying shares at market value. [*FA 2022, Sch 2 para 31*].

Qualified investor schemes

[63.9] A '*qualified investor scheme*' (QIS) is a fund (either an open-ended investment company or a unit trust), authorised by the Financial Conduct Authority, in which a statement that the fund is a qualified investor scheme is included in the instrument constituting the scheme. [*SI 2006 No 964, Reg 14B(4)*]. Only institutional and certain sophisticated investors are eligible to participate in such schemes.

A QIS is treated for tax purposes in the same way as any other open-ended investment company or authorised unit trust provided that it meets a 'genuine diversity of ownership condition'.

Where the genuine diversity of ownership condition is not satisfied for an accounting period of the scheme, the total amount available for income allocation to participants must only be allocated for distribution as a dividend and the small profits rate of corporation tax does not apply to the scheme.

[*SI 2006 No 964, Reg 14B; SI 2021 No 1270, Reg 4*].

A QIS meets the 'genuine diversity of ownership condition' for an accounting period if:

(a) the scheme documents contain a statement that units in the scheme will be widely available, specify the intended categories of investor and that the scheme manager must market and make available the units in accordance with (c) below;

(b) neither the specification of intended investor categories, nor any other terms or conditions of investing in the scheme have the effect of either limiting investors to a limited number of specified persons or specified groups of connected persons (within *ITA 2007, ss 993, 994*), or of deterring any reasonable investor within the intended categories from investing in the scheme; and

(c) units in the scheme are marketed and made available sufficiently widely to reach the intended categories of investors and in a way appropriate to attract those categories.

Condition (c) above is treated as met even where the scheme has no current capacity to receive additional investments, unless the capacity to receive investments is fixed and a pre-determined number of specified persons or groups of connected persons make investments which collectively exhaust all, or substantially all, of that capacity.

A QIS also meets the genuine diversity of ownership condition if an investor in the scheme is a unit trust and the conditions at (a)–(d) above are met after taking into account investors in the unit trust. Both the QIS and the unit trust must have the same manager (or proposed manager). This applies only if the scheme is a property AIF (see **63.7** above).

[*SI 2006 No 964, Reg 9A*].

There are procedures under which a QIS may obtain clearance from HMRC that it satisfies the genuine diversity of ownership condition. See *SI 2006 No 964, Reg 9B*.

Long-term asset funds

[63.10] A '*long-term asset fund*' is a fund (either an open-ended investment company or a unit trust), authorised by the Financial Conduct Authority, in which a statement that the fund is a long-term asset fund is included in the instrument constituting the scheme. [*SI 2006 No 964, Reg 14DA(4); SI 2021 No 1270, Reg 3*].

A long-term asset fund is treated for tax purposes in the same way as any other open-ended investment company or authorised unit trust provided that it meets a 'genuine diversity of ownership condition'.

Where the genuine diversity of ownership condition is not satisfied for an accounting period of the scheme, the total amount available for income allocation to participants must only be allocated for distribution as a dividend and the small profits rate of corporation tax does not apply to the scheme.

[*SI 2006 No 964, Reg 14DA; SI 2021 No 1270, Reg 3*].

A fund meets the 'genuine diversity of ownership condition' for an accounting period if:

(a) the fund's prospectus was published on or before 9 December 2021; or
(b) at least 70% of the shares or units in the fund are held by one or more 'relevant investors' (including collective investment schemes and alternative investment funds which meet the genuine diversity of ownership condition, insurance companies and pension funds) or by the fund's manager in its capacity as manager.

[*SI 2006 No 964, Reg 9A; SI 2021 No 1270, Reg 3*].

There are procedures under which a fund may obtain clearance from HMRC that it satisfies the genuine diversity of ownership condition. See *SI 2006 No 964, Reg 9B*.

Funds investing in non-reporting offshore funds

[63.11] Special rules apply to authorised investment funds (either unit trusts or open-ended investment companies) which invest in non-reporting offshore funds (see **43.12** OVERSEAS MATTERS). Such funds are known as 'FINROFs'. The detailed provisions are described in Tolley's Income Tax and Corporation Tax but a brief summary together with the chargeable gains effects are given below.

The rules apply automatically to a fund which meets the investment condition but can also apply by election. The '*investment condition*' is that the total amount invested by the fund in non-reporting offshore funds or in other FINROFs is more than 50% of the gross asset value of the fund. The rules apply from the date that the condition is first met or the date specified in the election. Where a fund ceases to meet the investment condition, the fund manager may, subject to certain conditions, elect for the fund to cease to be a FINROF. The rules nevertheless continue to apply to participants in the fund unless they elect to be treated as disposing of, and immediately reacquiring, their units at market value on the date the fund ceases to be a FINROF.

A gain on a disposal of a unit in a FINROF is charged to tax as income. This applies also where the fund has previously been a FINROF and the investor has not made the election for deemed disposal. Broadly, such gains are calculated using the rules for chargeable gains (but, for corporation tax purposes, without any deduction of indexation allowance).

[*SI 2006 No 964, Regs 85A, 85D, 85G, 85M, 85Z1, 85Z9, 85Z11*].

Capital gains

On entry into the FINROF regime, a participant in the fund may elect to be treated for chargeable gains purposes as disposing of all his units and immediately acquiring units in the FINROF for a consideration equal to their market value. An election must be made by inclusion in the tax return for the tax year or accounting period in which the fund enters the regime. [*SI 2006 No 964, Reg 85L*].

Where a disposal gives rise to an income gain under the above rules and is also a disposal for chargeable gains purposes, then, in computing the chargeable gain, the income gain is deducted from the disposal consideration (and *TCGA 1992, s 37(1)* (deduction of consideration chargeable to tax on income — see **33.1** INTERACTION WITH OTHER TAXES) does not apply). Where the disposal is a part disposal (see **16.5** COMPUTATION OF GAINS AND LOSSES), the deduction is not made in calculating the formula for apportioning the allowable expenditure. The deduction is, however, made in calculating the disposal consideration for the purposes of applying the fraction A/B where incorporation relief under *TCGA 1992, s 162* (see **31.2** INCORPORATION AND DISINCORPORATION RELIEFS) applies to the disposal. Where an income gain arises because *TCGA 1992, s 135* or *s 136* (exchange of securities and schemes of reconstruction — see **57.5**, **57.7** SHARES AND SECURITIES) are disapplied for the purposes of determining whether such gains arise, then, for chargeable gains purposes, the income gain is treated as if it were given by the person making the exchange as consideration for the new holding (within *TCGA 1992, s 128* — see **57.2** SHARES AND SECURITIES). [*SI 2006 No 964, Regs 85Z5–85Z8*].

Authorised contractual schemes

[63.12] An '*authorised contractual scheme*' is a type of collective investment scheme authorised by the Financial Conduct Authority. It may take the form of either a co-ownership scheme or a partnership scheme (as defined). [*Financial Services and Markets Act 2000, s 235A*]. Such schemes are broadly transparent for tax purposes, i.e. the scheme itself incurs no tax liability. This means that its investors are treated as if they had invested directly in the underlying assets of the scheme and are subject to personal taxation accordingly.

Participants in co-ownership schemes — disposals of units

A unit in an authorised contractual scheme which is a a co-ownership scheme is treated as an asset for capital gains purposes and, accordingly, a participant's interests in the scheme property is disregarded. In computing the gain on a disposal of units, any amount which represents income from the scheme property and is taken into account as a receipt or other credit of the participant in computing an amount chargeable to income tax is treated as enhancement expenditure within *TCGA 1992, s 38(1)(b)* (see **16.12**(b) COMPUTATION OF GAINS AND LOSSES). The deductions otherwise allowable from the consideration are reduced (but not below nil) by any amounts arising to the participant from the scheme property which is taken into account as an expense or debit of the participant in computing an amount chargeable to income tax or anything paid or transferred to, or anything else of value received by, the participant which is referable to the holding of the units. No reduction is made for CAPITAL SUMS DERIVED FROM ASSETS (**10**). If the amount of the reduction exceeds the otherwise allowable deductions, the excess is added to the consideration. Amounts which reduce the allowable deductions in this way are not also dealt with under the provisions at **33.1** INTERACTION WITH OTHER TAXES.

Any expenditure incurred by the participant in respect of which a capital allowance or renewals allowance has been, or may be, made is excluded from the allowable deductions in computing a loss on a disposal of units.

A participant's interest in scheme property is not disregarded under the above rules for the purposes of applying *TCGA 1992, s 37B* (consideration on disposal increased by reference to structures and buildings allowance — see **16.11** COMPUTATION OF GAINS AND LOSSES) where the participant has been entitled to a structures and buildings allowance by reference to expenditure in relation to any fund property.

Units in a scheme are treated as securities for the purposes of the rules in **58** SHARES AND SECURITIES — IDENTIFICATION RULES.

These provisions do not apply to expenditure incurred before 1 January 2018 nor to any amount arising, paid, transferred or received before that date which would otherwise be treated as enhancement expenditure or excluded from the allowable deductions.

[*TCGA 1992, ss 103D, 103DA; SI 2019 No 1087, Reg 4(9)*].

Note that these provisions apply also to interests in a transparent offshore fund (treating the participator's rights or interests in the fund, however described, as units) — see **43.9** OVERSEAS MATTERS.

See also **35.24** LAND for the treatment of units as shares in a company for the purposes of the charge on non-residents disposing of assets deriving 75% of their value from UK land.

See also **63.3** above as regards umbrella schemes.

Reserved investor funds

[63.13] A new type of investment fund, the 'reserved investor fund' (RIF), is to be introduced. *F(No 2A) 2024* enables the Treasury to introduce the tax rules for such funds by statutory instrument. [*F(No 2)A 2024, s 20*].

The RIF will be a UK-based unauthorised contractual scheme with 'lower costs and more flexibility' than the existing authorised contractual scheme. It will be open to professional and institutional investors and the government expects it to be particularly attractive for investment in commercial real estate. For capital gains purposes, the fund will be treated in broadly the same way as an authorised contractual scheme which is a co-ownership scheme.

Court investment funds

[63.14] These are common investment funds established under *Administration of Justice Act 1982, s 42*. The Accountant General is deemed to hold the funds (together with other funds in court) as nominee or bare trustee as in **56.3** SETTLEMENTS. [*TCGA 1992, ss 61, 100(3)*].

Gains realised by court investment funds are not chargeable gains. [*TCGA 1992, s 100(1)*].

Investment clubs

[63.15] An investment club is a group of people who join together to invest, primarily in the stock market. Each club will have its own rules, which will, *inter alia*, determine each member's proportionate entitlement to the club's investments, which will change frequently as capital is invested and withdrawn. Members share income, gains and losses according to their entitlement, are personally responsible for declaring the income etc. and are personally liable for tax. The club's treasurer or other officer is responsible for computing the capital gain and letting each member know their share. Form 185 (available from HMRC) can be used to show each proportionate share. Any reasonable method provided by the club's rules for dividing gains between members will be accepted by HMRC so long as it is based on the proportionate shares of the investments held by members and is consistently applied.

Treasurers should keep sufficient records as they may be required to make a return under *FA 2011, Sch 23*.

(HMRC Capital Gains Manual CG20600).

Venture capital trusts

[63.16] Chargeable gains of venture capital trusts are not chargeable gains. See **64.6** VENTURE CAPITAL TRUSTS below.

64

Venture Capital Trusts

Simon's Taxes. See E3.2.

Introduction to venture capital trusts

[64.1] The venture capital trust ('VCT') scheme described in this chapter is intended to encourage individuals to invest in unquoted trading companies through such trusts.

The scheme provides for a 30% income tax relief on investment in shares issued by an approved trust. The relief is withdrawn if the investor disposes of the shares within five years or the VCT loses its approval within that period. Dividends from a VCT are, subject to annual subscription limits, exempt from income tax. Gains made by a VCT are not chargeable gains and neither are gains made by investors in VCT shares (again subject to annual subscription limits). For shares issued before 6 April 2004 there was also a chargeable gains deferral relief for reinvestments in VCT shares; this is described at **64.8** below because deferred gains continue to be brought back into charge on the occurrence of certain chargeable events.

A VCT must meet strict conditions in order to receive approval, including conditions dealing with the nature and extent of its investments in unquoted trading companies. See Tolley's Corporation Tax.

The Treasury has wide powers to make regulations governing all aspects of the reliefs applicable to venture capital trust investments, and for the requirements as regards returns, records and provision of information by the trust. [*ITA 2007, ss 272, 284*]. See now *SI 1995 No 1979*.

VCT relief applies to shares issued before 6 April 2035, but this date may be amended by statutory instrument. [*ITA 2007, s 261(3); FA 2024, s 11*].

See generally HMRC Venture Capital Schemes Manual VCM2010–2070, 50000 onwards.

Income tax reliefs

[64.2] Relief from income tax is granted in respect of both investments in VCTs and dividends from such trusts.

Nominees

For the purposes of the income tax reliefs, shares subscribed for, issued to, held by or disposed of for an individual by a nominee are treated as subscribed for, issued to, held by or disposed of by the individual. [*ITA 2007, s 330A*].

Relief in respect of investments

[64.3] Subject to the conditions described below, an individual may claim relief for a tax year for the amount (or aggregate amounts) subscribed by him on his own behalf for 'eligible shares' issued to him in a year of assessment by a VCT (or VCTs) for raising money. There is a limit of **£200,000** on the relief which may be claimed for any year of assessment.

'*Eligible shares*' means new ordinary shares in a VCT which, throughout the five years following issue, carry no present or future preferential right to dividends or to assets on a winding up and no present or future right to redemption.

Relief is given by a reduction (a '*tax reduction*') in what would otherwise be the individual's income tax liability for the tax year by 30% of the amount eligible for relief.

Investors may restrict a claim to relief in respect of a tax year to only some of the shares issued to them. For the order in which tax reductions are given against an individual's tax liability, see Tolley's Income Tax under Allowances and Tax Rates. A tax reduction must be restricted to the extent (if any) that it would otherwise exceed the individual's remaining income tax liability after making all prior reductions.

An individual is **not** entitled to relief where:

(a) he was under 18 years of age at the time of issue of the shares;

(b) circumstances have arisen which, had the relief already been given, would have resulted in the withdrawal or reduction of the relief (see **64.4** below);

(c) the shares were issued or subscribed for other than for genuine commercial purposes or as part of a scheme or arrangement a main purpose of which was the avoidance of tax;

(d) a loan is made to the individual (or to an 'associate') by any person at any time in the period beginning with the incorporation of the VCT (or, if later, two years before the date of issue of the shares) and ending five years after the date of issue of the shares, and the loan would not have been made, or would not have been made on the same terms, if he had not subscribed, or had not been proposing to subscribe, for the shares. For HMRC's views on 'loan-linked' investments, see HMRC Statement of Practice SP 6/98. The granting of credit to, or the assignment of a debt due from, the individual or associate is counted as a loan for these purposes; or

(e) the shares were treated as issued by virtue of *FA 2003, s 195(8)* (company disposing of treasury shares — see **57.19** SHARES AND SECURITIES). Where a venture capital trust issues eligible shares to an individual in such circumstances it must give notice to the individual stating that he is not eligible for relief, and a copy of the notice must be sent to an HMRC officer within three months after the issue of the shares.

For the purposes of (d) above, an '*associate*' of any person is any 'relative' (i.e. spouse, civil partner, ancestor or linear descendant) of that person, the trustee(s) of any settlement in relation to which that person or any relative (living or dead) is or was a settler and, where that person has an interest in any shares of obligations of a company which are subject to any trust or are part of a deceased estate, the trustee(s) of the settlement or the personal representatives of the deceased. For this purpose, 'settlor' is defined as in *ITA 2007, ss 467–473.*

[*ITA 2007, ss 261–264, 265, 271(4), 273, 332*].

An individual or nominee subscribing for eligible shares may obtain from the VCT a certificate giving details of the subscription and certifying that certain conditions for relief are satisfied. [*SI 1995 No 1979, Reg 9*].

Linked sales

Relief is restricted if an individual subscribes for shares in a VCT and makes at least one 'linked' sale of other shares. The amount subscribed is treated as reduced by the total consideration given for the linked sales. If a sale is linked in relation to more than one subscription, the consideration for it is applied to reduce subscriptions in the order in which they are made. A sale of shares is '*linked*' if:

(i) the shares sold are in the VCT or (but only where Condition X below applies) in a company which is (or later becomes) a successor or predecessor of the VCT as a result of a merger or restructuring; and

(ii) either
  - the circumstances are such that the purchase of the shares from the individual is conditional upon his making the subscription or *vice versa*; or
  - the subscription and the sale are within six months of each other (irrespective of which is first).

The above does not apply if, or to the extent that, the subscription is the result of the individual's electing to reinvest dividends on his VCT shares in acquiring further shares in the VCT. Condition X in (i) above is that the date of the merger or restructuring is no later than two years after the individual subscribes for the VCT shares and either the individual could reasonably be expected to know when subscribing that the merger or restructuring would take place or a main purpose of the merger or restructuring is to enable individuals to obtain a tax advantage in connection with VCT relief. For this purpose, the date of the merger or restructuring is generally the date of the issue of shares by means of which it is effected.

[*ITA 2007, s 264A*].

Example

On 1 August 2024, A Ventura, who is UK resident but not a Scottish taxpayer and whose salary is £61,570 p.a. from UK employment, subscribes for 50,000 eligible £1 shares issued at par to raise money by VCT plc, an approved venture capital trust. On 1 March 2025, he purchases a further 190,000 £1 shares in VCT plc for £170,000 on the open market. The trust makes no distribution in 2024/25. Mr Ventura's other income for 2024/25 consists of dividends of £18,000.

Mr Ventura's income tax computation for 2024/25 is as follows.

	£
Earnings from UK employment	61,570.00
Dividends	18,000.00
Total income	79,570.00
Deduct personal allowance	12,570.00
Taxable income	£67,000.00
Tax payable:	£
37,700 @ 20%	7,540.00
11,300 @ 40%	4,520.00
500 @ 0%	0.00
17,500 @ 33.75%	5,906.00
	17,966.00
Deduct Relief in respect of investment in VCT plc:	
Lower of 30% of £50,000 subscribed and £17,966	15,000.00
Net tax payable (subject to PAYE deductions from salary)	£2,966.00

Withdrawal of relief on investment

Disposal of investment

[64.4] Where an individual disposes of eligible shares, in respect of which relief has been claimed as under **64.3** above, within five years of their issue and other than to a spouse or civil partner when they are living together (see below), then:

(a) if the disposal is otherwise than at arm's length, relief given by reference to those shares is withdrawn;

(b) if the disposal is at arm's length, the relief given by reference to those shares is reduced by an amount equivalent to 30% of the consideration received for the disposal or is withdrawn if the relief exceeds that amount.

For the above purposes, disposals of eligible shares in a VCT are identified with those acquired earlier rather than later. As between eligible shares acquired on the same day, shares by reference to which relief has been given are treated as disposed of after any other eligible shares.

Relief is **not** withdrawn where the disposal is by one spouse or civil partner to the other at a time when they are living together. However, on any subsequent disposal the spouse or partner to whom the shares were transferred is treated as if he or she were the person who subscribed for the shares, as if the shares had been issued to him or her at the time they were issued to the transferor spouse or partner, and as if his or her liability to income tax had been reduced by reference to those shares by the same amount, and for the same tax year, as applied on the subscription by the transferor spouse or partner. Any assessment for reducing or withdrawing relief is made on the transferee spouse or partner.

[*ITA 2007, ss 266, 267*].

Withdrawal of approval

Where approval of a company as a VCT is withdrawn (but not treated as never having been given), relief given by reference to eligible shares in the VCT is withdrawn as if on a non-arm's length disposal immediately before the withdrawal of approval. A VCT entering liquidation does not result in withdrawal of approval. [*ITA 2007, s 268*].

Relief subsequently found not to have been due

Relief which is subsequently found not to have been due is withdrawn. [*ITA 2007, s 269*].

Assessments withdrawing or reducing relief

Such assessments are made for the tax year for which the relief was given. No such assessment is, however, to be made by reason of an event occurring after the death of the person to whom the shares were issued. An assessment can be made at any time not more than six years after the tax year for which the relief was given. [*ITA 2007, s 270*].

Information

Particulars of all events leading to the reduction or withdrawal of relief must be notified to HMRC by the person to whom the relief was given within 60 days of his coming to know of the event.

The requirements of secrecy do not prevent HMRC disclosing to a VCT that relief has been given or claimed by reference to a particular number or proportion of its shares.

Penalties under *TMA 1970, s 98* apply for failure to comply with these requirements.

[*ITA 2007, s 271(1)–(3)(5)*].

Example

On 1 August 2025, A Ventura in the *Example* at **64.3** above, who since 2024/25 has neither acquired nor disposed of any shares in VCT plc, gives 30,000 shares to his son. On 1 March 2027, he disposes of the remaining 210,000 shares for £195,000. The relief given in **64.3** above is withdrawn as follows.

Disposal on 1 August 2025

The shares disposed of are identified with 30,000 of those subscribed for, and, since the disposal was not at arm's length, the relief given on those shares is fully withdrawn.

Relief withdrawn 30,000/50,000 × £15,000 =	£9,000

Disposal on 1 March 2027

The balance of £6,000 of the relief originally given was in respect of 20,000 of the shares disposed of. The disposal consideration for those 20,000 shares is

$$195{,}000 \times \frac{20{,}000}{210{,}000} = \quad £18{,}571$$

The relief withdrawn is the lesser of the relief originally given and 30% of the consideration received, i.e.

30% of £18,571 = £5,571.

Relief withdrawn is therefore	£5,571
The 2024/25 income tax assessment is therefore	£14,571

Relief on dividends

[64.5] A 'VCT dividend' to which a 'qualifying investor' is beneficially entitled is not treated as income for income tax purposes.

A '*qualifying investor*' is an individual aged 18 or over who is beneficially entitled to the dividend either as the holder of the shares or through a nominee (including the trustees of a bare trust).

A '*VCT dividend*' is a dividend (including a capital dividend) in respect of ordinary shares in a company which is a VCT which were acquired at a time when it was a VCT by the recipient of the dividend, and which were not shares acquired in excess of the 'permitted maximum' for the year of assessment. Shares must also have been acquired for *bona fide* commercial purposes and not as part of a tax avoidance scheme or arrangements. A VCT dividend does not include any dividend paid in respect of profits or gains of any accounting period ending when the company was not a VCT.

Shares are acquired in excess of the '*permitted maximum*' for a year where the aggregate of the market values of ordinary shares acquired in VCTs by the individual or his nominee(s) in that year exceeds £200,000, disregarding shares acquired other than for *bona fide* commercial reasons or as part of a scheme or arrangement a main purpose of which is the avoidance of tax. Shares acquired later in the year are identified as representing the excess before those acquired earlier, and in relation to same-day acquisition of different shares, a proportionate part of each description of share is treated as representing any excess arising on that day. Shares acquired at a time when a company was not a VCT are for these purposes treated as disposed of before other shares in the VCT. Otherwise, disposals are identified with earlier acquisitions before later ones, except that as between shares acquired on the same day, shares acquired in excess of the permitted maximum are treated as disposed of before any other shares. There are provisions for effectively disregarding acquisitions arising out of share exchanges where, for capital gains purposes, the new shares are treated as the same assets as the old.

[*ITTOIA 2005, ss 709–712; SI 1995 No 1979, Reg 10*].

Capital gains tax reliefs

[64.6] The capital gains of a VCT are not chargeable gains. [*TCGA 1992, s 100(1)*].

In addition, individual investors in VCTs are entitled to relief on disposal of VCT shares (see **64.7** below). An additional relief was previously available by deferral of chargeable gains on re-investment in VCT share issues before 6 April 2004 (see **64.8** below).

Various provisions of *TCGA 1992* which are superseded for these purposes by specific provisions (as below) are disapplied or applied separately to parts of holdings which do not fall within the reliefs.

Withdrawal of approval

Where approval of a company as a VCT is withdrawn (but not treated as never having been given), shares which (apart from the withdrawal) would be eligible for the relief on disposal (see **64.7** below) are treated as disposed of at their market value at the time of the withdrawal. For the purposes of the relief on disposal, the disposal is treated as taking place while the company is still a VCT, but the re-acquisition is treated as taking place immediately after it ceases to be so. [*TCGA 1992, s 151B(6)(7)*].

Relief on disposal

[64.7] A gain or loss accruing to an individual on a 'qualifying disposal' of ordinary shares in a company which was a VCT throughout his period of ownership is not a chargeable gain or an allowable loss.

A disposal is a '*qualifying disposal*' if:

(a) the individual is 18 years of age or more at the time of the disposal;
(b) the shares were not acquired in excess of the 'permitted maximum' for any year of assessment; and
(c) the shares were acquired for *bona fide* commercial purposes and not as part of a scheme or arrangement a main purpose of which was the avoidance of tax.

The identification of those shares which were acquired in excess of the '*permitted maximum*' is as under **64.5** above, i.e. where the aggregate of the market values of ordinary shares acquired in VCTs by the individual or his nominee(s) in that year exceeds £200,000, disregarding shares acquired other than for *bona fide* commercial reasons or as part of a scheme or arrangement a main purpose of which is the avoidance of tax. Shares acquired later in the year are identified as representing the excess before those acquired earlier, and in relation to same-day acquisition of different shares, a proportionate part of each description of share is treated as representing any excess arising on that day. Shares acquired at a time when a company was not a VCT are for these purposes treated as disposed of before other shares in the VCT. Otherwise, disposals are identified with earlier acquisitions before later ones, except that as between shares acquired on the same day, shares acquired in excess of the permitted maximum are treated as disposed of before any other shares. See the examples at HMRC Venture Capital Schemes Manual VCM52060, 52080, 52090.

The normal rules for the pooling of shares and identification of disposals in *TCGA 1992, ss 104, 105, 106A, 107* (see **58.2**, **58.3** SHARES AND SECURITIES — IDENTIFICATION RULES) are disapplied in respect of shares which are eligible for the above relief.

There are provisions (see below) for effectively disregarding acquisitions arising out of share exchanges where, for capital gains purposes, the new shares are treated as the same assets as the old.

Where an individual holds ordinary shares in a VCT which fall into more than one of the following groups:

(1) shares eligible for relief on disposal (as above) and by reference to which he has obtained or is entitled to claim relief under the provisions in **64.3** above (income tax relief on investments);
(2) shares eligible for relief on disposal but by reference to which he has not obtained or will be unable to claim relief under the provisions in **64.3** above;
(3) shares by reference to which he has obtained or is entitled to claim relief under the provisions in **64.3** above but which are not eligible for relief on disposal;
(4) shares not within (1)–(3) above,

then, if there is a reorganisation under *TCGA 1992, s 126*, the provisions in *TCGA 1992, s 127* (equation of original shares with new holding) (see **57.2** SHARES AND SECURITIES above) will apply separately to each group of shares (if any) in order that they continue to be kept within their respective groups.

Where an individual holds ordinary shares in a company ('the existing holding') and there is, by virtue of an allotment for payment within *TCGA 1992, s 126(2)(a)* (e.g. a rights issue), a reorganisation affecting the existing holding immediately following which the shares or allotted holding are shares falling within (1)–(3) above, the provisions in *TCGA 1992, ss 127–130* will not apply in relation to that existing holding. The effect is that the rights issue will be treated as an acquisition.

Where a holding consists of shares falling within (1) or (2) above and it is exchanged or is deemed to be exchanged for a second holding which does not consist of ordinary shares in a VCT, then the provisions in *TCGA 1992, ss 135, 136* will not apply (see **57.5** and **57.7** SHARES AND SECURITIES above). The effect is that there will be or deemed to be a disposal and acquisition.

[*TCGA 1992, ss 151A, 151B*].

See **64.6** above as regards relief on withdrawal of approval of the VCT.

Example

On the disposals in the *Example* at **64.4** above, a chargeable gain or allowable loss arises only on the disposal of the shares acquired in excess of the permitted maximum for 2024/25. The shares in VCT plc were acquired in 2024/25 for £220,000, so that there is a £20,000 excess over the permitted maximum. The 50,000 shares first acquired for £50,000 are first identified, so that shares representing the excess are two-seventeenths of the 190,000 shares subsequently acquired for £170,000 on 1 March 2025, i.e. 22,353 of those shares. The disposal identified with those shares is a corresponding proportion of the 210,000 shares disposed of for a consideration of £195,000 on 1 March 2027.

Mr Ventura's capital gains tax computation for 2026/27 is as follows.

Disposal consideration for 22,353 shares:

	$£195,000 \times \frac{22,353}{210,000} =$	£20,756
Deduct Cost:		
	$£170,000 \times \frac{22,353}{190,000} =$	£20,000
Chargeable gain		£756

Deferral relief on reinvestment

[64.8] Before 6 April 2004, deferral relief was available, subject to detailed conditions, where an individual subscribed for VCT shares a claim could be made to defer a chargeable gain on the disposal of other assets. Entitlement to relief has long been resolved and is no longer considered in this work. Gains previously deferred may, however, be brought back into charge on the happening of certain chargeable events, and the following coverage describes the CGT treatment.

Chargeable event

The original gain deferred through the making of the claim will subsequently crystallise if a chargeable event occurs. The only remaining possible chargeable events are:

(A) the investor disposes of the shares in his qualifying investment ('the relevant shares') otherwise than under *TCGA 1992, s 58* (a transfer between spouses or civil partners);

(B) the relevant shares are disposed of by the spouse or civil partner of the investor (otherwise than by a transfer back to him), the spouse or partner having first acquired them from the investor under *TCGA 1992, s 58*;

(C) where shares falling within **64.7**(3) above are exchanged or treated as exchanged for any non-VCT holdings and under *TCGA 1992, s 135* or *TCGA 1992, s 136* (see **57.5** and **57.7** SHARES AND SECURITIES above) there is a requirement (or, but for *TCGA 1992, s 116* (see **48** QUALIFYING CORPORATE BONDS above) there would be a requirement) for those holdings to be regarded as the same assets as those shares;

(D) the company in which the relevant shares are held has its approval as a VCT withdrawn (in a case in which approval is not treated as never having been given);

(E) the 'prescribed winding-up period' of a VCT-in-liquidation comes to an end, the VCT-in-liquidation then still being in existence.

There is no crystallisation of the original gain where a chargeable event occurs at or after the time of death of the investor or a person to whom the relevant shares were transferred under *TCGA 1992, s 58*.

Without prejudice to the following provisions in a case falling within (D) (or (E)) above, any reference above to a disposal excludes a reference to the disposal deemed to occur on the withdrawal of approval (or the deemed withdrawal at the end of the prescribed winding-up period within **64.6** above).

Crystallisation of original gain

Where a chargeable event mentioned in (A)–(E) above relating to relevant shares occurs for the first time in connection with those shares, a chargeable gain is deemed to accrue at that time equal to so much of the expenditure on those shares which was set against the original gain.

Identification of shares

In determining whether any shares to which a chargeable gain relates are shares the expenditure on which has been set against the whole or part of any gain, disposals of shares are identified with those subscribed for earlier rather than later, and as between shares in a company acquired on the same day, those the expenditure on which has been set against a gain are treated as disposed of after any other shares in that company. The normal rules at **58.2** SHARES AND SECURITIES — IDENTIFICATION RULES are disapplied (regardless of whether or not the shares are eligible for CGT relief under **64.7** above).

Assets

Where at the time of a chargeable event relevant shares are regarded as represented by assets which consist of or include assets other than relevant shares, the expenditure on those shares is apportioned between those assets on a just and reasonable basis. As between different assets regarded as representing the same relevant shares, the identification of those assets will be determined on a similar basis to the identification of shares.

Persons assessable

The chargeable gain is treated as accruing, as the case may be:

(i) to the individual who makes the disposal;
(ii) to the individual who holds the shares in question at the time of the exchange or deemed exchange;
(iii) to the individual who holds the shares in question when the withdrawal of the approval takes effect; or
(iv) to the individual who holds the shares in question immediately following the end of the VCT-in-liquidation's prescribed winding-up period.

A chargeable gain is computed separately for the investor without reference to any shares held at the time of the chargeable event by a recipient to the investor from a *TCGA 1992, s 58* transfer.

[*TCGA 1992, Sch 5C; SI 2004 No 2199, Reg 7; SI 2005 No 3229, Reg 128*].

Key points concerning venture capital trusts

[64.9] Points to consider are as follows.

- An investment in shares in a VCT provides for two types of tax relief:
  (a) income tax relief, including tax free dividends, and
  (b) exemption from capital gains tax.

  For shares issued before 6 April 2004 there was also the possibility of deferring some other capital gain. Where shares are disposed of any gain that had been deferred (before 6 April 2004) will be revived as though it was a gain arising at the date of disposal of the VCT shares.
- VCT income tax relief can be claimed via the self-assessment tax return or separately. If the VCT certificate is available early enough relief can be included in a PAYE code.
- The tax relief is only available in respect of VCT shares subscribed for within the annual limit which is currently £200,000.
- Where income tax relief is withdrawn or reduced it is done by means of an assessment issued by HMRC. It cannot be recovered through the self-assessment tax return although the liability will be added to the Statement of Account.

65
Wasting Assets

Cross-references. See **7.6** ASSETS for plant or machinery lease under a long finance lease; **23.4** EXEMPTIONS AND RELIEFS for tangible movable assets generally and **23.11** for private passenger motor vehicles; **35.12–35.21** LAND for leases of land which are wasting assets; and **53.9** ROLLOVER RELIEF for the relief available where assets are, or will within ten years, become wasting assets.

Simon's Taxes. See C2.9.

Introduction to wasting assets

[65.1] A wasting asset is, broadly, an asset with a predictable life of no more than 50 years. There are rules which apply to reduce the amount of the allowable expenditure on the disposal of such an asset. The original cost and any subsequent enhancement expenditure are, in most cases, treated as diminishing evenly day by day over the asset's life. Different rules apply to leases of land which are wasting assets, for which see **35.12–35.21** LAND, and there is an exclusion where the asset qualified for capital allowances. The detailed provisions are at **65.2** below. See also **23.4** EXEMPTIONS AND RELIEFS for the exemption for tangible movable assets (chattels) which are wasting assets.

This chapter also looks at three specific types of wasting assets: options and futures contracts, leases of property other than land and life interests.

Basic rule

[65.2] Subject to the following, where an asset disposed of is a 'wasting asset':

(a) the original cost, etc. (see **16.12** COMPUTATION OF GAINS AND LOSSES) less predictable residual value, is treated as diminishing evenly day by day over the asset's life, and

(b) additional expenditure (see **16.12** COMPUTATION OF GAINS AND LOSSES) is similarly treated as diminishing evenly over the remaining life of the asset as from the date the expenditure was first reflected in the state or nature of the asset and only so much of the original cost and additional expenditure as, on the above basis, remains at the date of disposal is then deductible. If additional expenditure under (b) above creates or increases a residual value, then the new residual value is taken into account in (a) above. [*TCGA 1992, s 46*].

A '*wasting asset*' is an asset with a predictable 'life' not exceeding 50 years and, in relation to tangible movable property, '*life*' means 'useful life', having regard to the purpose for which the tangible assets were acquired or provided by the person making the disposal. However, plant and machinery are always regarded as having a predictable life of less than 50 years and that life is to be based on normal usage. Freehold land is never a wasting asset, whatever its nature and whatever the nature of the building or works on it. The predictable life and predictable residual value, if not immediately ascertainable by the nature of the asset, are to be taken on a disposal as they were known or ascertainable at the time when the asset was acquired by the person making the disposal. [*TCGA 1992, s 44*].

A painting which was informally loaned to a company for display to the paying public as part of its trade was held to be plant and therefore a wasting asset in *Executors of Lord Howard of Henderskelfe v HMRC* CA, [2014] STC 1100. See now, however, **23.4** EXEMPTIONS AND RELIEFS for the denial of exemption under *TCGA 1992, s 45* for assets which are wasting assets only because of use in the trade etc. of a person other than the owner.

Assets qualifying for capital allowances

No restriction of allowable expenditure as above occurs where an asset, throughout the ownership, is used solely for the purposes of a trade, profession or vocation, and capital allowances have, or could have, been claimed in respect of its cost or any enhancement expenditure. This also applies where an asset has otherwise qualified in full for any capital allowances. Where, however, the asset disposed of has been used partly for non-business purposes or has only partly qualified for capital allowances, the expenditure and consideration are apportioned and the restrictions imposed above applied to that portion of expenditure which has not qualified for capital allowances or which relates to the period of non-business use. [*TCGA 1992, s 47*].

Chattels

Tangible movable assets (chattels) which are wasting assets are exempt subject to certain conditions. See **23.4** EXEMPTIONS AND RELIEFS. Chattels such as antique clocks and certain motor vehicles may be 'machinery' and so exempt subject to those conditions.

Example

V bought an aircraft on 31 May 2019 at a cost of £90,000 for use in his air charter business. It has been agreed that V's non-business use of the aircraft amounts to one-tenth, on a flying hours basis, and capital allowances and running costs have accordingly been restricted for income tax purposes. On 1 February 2025, V sells the aircraft for £185,000. The aircraft was agreed to have a useful life of 20 years at the date it was acquired.

	£	£
Amount qualifying for capital allowances		
Relevant portion of disposal consideration		
$^9/_{10}$ × £185,000		166,500
Relevant portion of acquisition cost $^9/_{10}$ × £90,000		81,000
Chargeable gain 2024/25		£85,500
Amount not qualifying for capital allowances		
Relevant portion of disposal consideration		
$^1/_{10}$ × £185,000		18,500
Relevant portion of acquisition cost		
$^1/_{10}$ × £90,000	9,000	
Deduct wasted $£9{,}000 \times \dfrac{5y8m}{20y}$	2,550	6,450
Gain		£12,050
The whole of the £12,050 is exempt.		
The total chargeable gain is therefore		£85,500

Options and futures contracts

[65.3] For CGT purposes, options are generally treated as wasting assets and are subject to the rules in **65.2** above. However, there are specific statutory exceptions to this which are covered in **7.7** ASSETS. For employee share options, see **21** EMPLOYEE SHARE SCHEMES. See **23.56** EXEMPTIONS AND RELIEFS for options held by pension schemes.

See **7.8** ASSETS for certain commodity and financial futures which are excepted from wasting asset treatment.

For corporation tax purposes, options and futures contracts fall within the derivatives contracts regime — see **15.8–15.12** COMPANIES — CORPORATE FINANCE AND INTANGIBLES.

Leases of property other than land

[65.4] In accordance with the definition of a wasting asset given in **65.2** above a 'lease of property other than land' may be or become a wasting asset. Such a lease which is a wasting asset is subject to the rules in **65.2** above, and in particular those regarding allowable expenditure. This treatment should be compared with leases of land which are wasting assets where, instead of allowable expenditure being written off at a uniform rate, a special basis is used (see **35.13** LAND). Despite this, the legislation regarding leases of property other than land is mainly by direct reference to that covering leases of land with 'necessary modifications'. [*TCGA 1992, ss 44, 46, 47, 240, Sch 8 para 9(1)*].

A '*lease of property other than land*' means any kind of agreement or arrangement under which payments are made for the use of, or otherwise in respect of, property and '*lessor*', '*lessee*' and '*rent*' are construed accordingly. [*TCGA 1992, Sch 8 para 10(1)(b)*].

Duration of a lease

The duration of a lease is to be decided by reference to the facts known or ascertainable at the time when the lease was acquired or created. In determining the duration, the following provisions apply.

(a) Where the terms of the lease include provision for the determination of the lease by notice given by the lessor, the lease is not to be treated as granted for a term longer than one ending at the earliest date on which it could be determined by notice given by the lessor.

(b) Where any of the terms of the lease or any other circumstances rendered it unlikely that the lease will continue beyond a date earlier than the expiration of the terms of the lease, the lease is not to be treated as having been granted for a longer term than one ending on that date. This applies in particular where the lease provides for rent to go up after a given date, or for the lessee's obligation to become more onerous after a given date, but includes provision for the determination of the lease on that date, by notice given by the lessee, and those provisions render it unlikely that the lease will continue beyond that date.

(c) Where the terms of the lease include provision for the extension of the lease beyond a given date by notice given by the lessee, the duration of the lease applies as if the term of the lease extended for as long as it could be extended by the lessee, but subject to any right of the lessor to determine the lease by notice.

(d) Where the leased asset is itself a wasting asset and also movable property, the lease is assumed to terminate not later than the end of the life of the asset.

[*TCGA 1992, Sch 8 paras 8, 9(3)*].

Premiums for leases of property other than land

[65.5] Where the payment of a 'premium' is required under a lease (or otherwise under the terms subject to which the lease is granted) there is a part disposal of the asset or other interest out of which that lease is granted.

In the part disposal computation (which follows the normal rules in *TCGA 1992, s 42*, see **16.5** COMPUTATION OF GAINS AND LOSSES) the property which remains undisposed of includes a right to any rent or other payments (other than a premium) payable under the lease, and that right is valued at the time of the part disposal. [*TCGA 1992, Sch 8 para 2*].

'*Premium*' includes any like sum, whether payable to the intermediate or superior lessor and includes any sum (other than rent) paid on or in connection with the granting of a lease except in so far as the other sufficient consideration for the payment is shown to have been given. Other capital sums payable by a tenant may fall to be treated as premiums (see **35.14** LAND).

Where by reference to any capital sum within the meaning of *ITA 2007, s 681DM* (assets leased to traders and others) any amount of that capital sum is charged to income tax then that amount is deducted from the consideration for capital gains tax purposes but not so as to convert a gain into a loss or increase a loss. [*TCGA 1992, Sch 8 para 9(2); TIOPA 2010, Sch 8 para 244*].

Sub-leases granted out of short leases of property other than land

[65.6] Where a sub-lease is granted out of a head-lease with less than 50 years to run, the normal part disposal rules do not apply. Instead, subject to below, a proportion of the cost and enhancement expenditure attributable to the lease is apportioned to the part disposed of as follows:

$$\frac{P(1)}{P(2)}$$

where:

P(1) = the duration of the sub-lease
P(2) = the duration of the lease at the date of acquisition (for apportionment of cost) or the duration of the lease at the date when expenditure is first reflected in the nature of the lease (for apportionment of enhancement expenditure).

If the amount of the premium is less than what would be obtainable by way of premium for the sub-lease if the rent payable under the sub-lease were the same as the rent payable under the lease, the percentage attributable to the sub-lease as calculated above must be multiplied by the premium received over the premium so obtainable before being applied to cost or enhancement expenditure. [*TCGA 1992, Sch 8 para 4(1)(2)*].

Example

P purchases a 40-year lease of a non-wasting asset (other than land) in 2019 for £15,000. In 2024, she grants a sub-lease of the asset to Q for 20 years for a premium of £8,000. Had the rent under head-lease and sub-lease been the same, the premium would have been £10,000. The expenditure attributable to the part disposal of the sub-lease is given by:

$$£15{,}000 \times \frac{20}{40} \times \frac{8{,}000}{10{,}000} = 0.4 \times £15{,}000 = £6{,}000$$

Where the sub-lease is a sub-lease of part only of the asset comprised in the lease, the cost and enhancement expenditure of the head-lease must be apportioned between the sub-lease and the remainder in proportion to their respective values. [*TCGA 1992, Sch 8 para 4(3)*].

Life interests

[65.7] Life interests in settled property are treated as wasting assets when the expectation of the life of tenant is 50 years or less. The predictable life of life tenants and annuities is ascertained from actuarial tables which have HMRC approval. [*TCGA 1992, s 44(1)(d)*]. See **56.15** SETTLEMENTS for the disposal of interests in settled property generally.

Example

N is a beneficiary under a settlement. On 30 June 2010, when her actuarially estimated life expectancy was 40 years, she sold her life interest to an unrelated individual, R, for £50,000. N dies on 31 December 2024, and the life interest is extinguished.

R will have an allowable loss for 2024/25 as follows:

	£	£
Disposal consideration on death of N		Nil
Allowable cost	50,000	
Deduct wasted $\frac{14y6m}{40y} \times £50,000$	18,125	
		31,875
Allowable loss		£31,875

Note to the example

(a) The amount of the cost wasted is computed by reference to the predictable life, not the actual life, of the wasting asset.

Key points concerning wasting assets

[65.8] Points to consider are as follows.

- Wasting assets are, broadly, assets with a predictable life of no more than 50 years.
- For most assets, the base cost, less predictable residual value, and additional expenditure, are treated as diminishing evenly over their life, except where they are used in a trade or profession and are eligible for capital allowances.
- There are special rules for chattels, options and futures contracts, leases of land and life interests.
- Care should be taken to identify where there is a wasting asset as the gain is impacted and the tax can be a surprise to the owner. This is particularly the case with lease transactions.

66

Finance Acts 2024 — Summary of CGT Provisions

[66.1] The following is a brief summary of the main provisions of the *Finance Act 2024* and *Finance (No 2) Act 2024* that are concerned with, or impinge upon, capital gains tax (CGT) and/or corporation tax on chargeable gains. For an exhaustive list of current *Finance Act* provisions covered in Tolley's Capital Gains Tax, see 75 TABLE OF STATUTES.

Finance Act 2024

(Royal Assent 22 February 2024)

s 8, Sch 7	**Real estate investment trusts.** A number of changes are made to the rules. These include a change to the non-close condition which is deemed always to have had effect. See **63.5** UNIT TRUSTS AND OTHER INVESTMENT VEHICLES.
s 9, Sch 8	**Tonnage tax.** Ship managers, who are not operators of ships, can elect to join the regime from 1 April 2024. See **23.17** EXEMPTIONS AND RELIEFS.
s 11	**Extension of EIS and VCT relief.** The sunset date for the enterprise investment scheme and venture capital trust scheme is extended from 5 April 2025 to 5 April 2035. See **22.3** ENTERPRISE INVESTMENT SCHEME and **64.1** VENTURE CAPITAL TRUSTS.
s 12	**Post Office Horizon compensation.** Compensation payments received by a company under certain Post Office Horizon schemes are exempt from corporation tax, whenever received. A capital gains tax exemption applies in respect of onward payments of the compensation to individual employees, directors or shareholders. See **23.18** EXEMPTIONS AND RELIEFS.
s 13	**Enterprise management incentives.** The time limit for notification of the granting of an option under the scheme is amended for options granted on or after 6 April 2024. The company must notify HMRC on or before 6 July following the tax year of grant. See **21.21** EMPLOYEE SHARE SCHEMES.
s 36	**Tax returns.** HMRC are given a power to make regulations requiring taxpayers to include in their tax returns additional information which is relevant to the general collection and management of tax (as opposed to establishing the amounts in which the taxpayer is chargeable to income tax and capital gains tax). Failure to comply with a requirement to include such information will result in a penalty of £60. HMRC have indicated that this power is to be used initially to obtain three types of information, none of which are relevant to capital gains tax. See **52.5** RETURNS.

s 37 **Making tax digital penalties.** The penalty regime for making tax digital late filing and late payment will apply to taxpayers who have elected to enter making tax digital voluntarily from 6 April 2024, subject to confirmation in Treasury regulations. See **46.7** PENALTIES.

Finance (No 2) Act 2024

(Royal Assent 24 May 2024)

s 6 **Rate of tax on residential property gains.** The higher rate of CGT for residential property gains is reduced from 28% to 24% for disposals on or after 6 April 2024. The lower rate remains at 18% for any gains that fall within an individual's basic rate band. The change does not apply to carried interest gains. See **2.1, 2.2** ANNUAL RATES AND EXEMPTIONS and **56.7** SETTLEMENTS.

s 20 **Reserved investor funds.** A new type of investment fund, the 'reserved investor fund' (RIF) is to be introduced. This section empowers the Treasury to introduce the tax rules for such funds by statutory instrument. For capital gains purposes, the funds will be treated in broadly the same way as an authorised contractual scheme which is a co-ownership scheme. See **63.13** UNIT TRUSTS AND OTHER INVESTMENT VEHICLES.

67 Table of Statutes

68 Table of Statutory Instruments

Note. Statutory Instruments (SIs) referred to at 21.3, 21.10 DOUBLE TAX RELIEF are not listed below. Also not listed are those SIs which do no more than confirm indexed rises in tax rates and allowances as announced in the Budget or which alter the rates of interest on overpaid and unpaid tax, though these are referred to in the text where appropriate.

The list below is in date order.

69 Table of Cases

A

B

C

D

E

F

G

H

I

J

K

N

O

P

Q

R

S

T

U

V

W

X

Y

Z

70 Index

This index is referenced to chapter and paragraph number.

B

C

E

F

G

J

K

L

M

P

S